C0-ARW-644

SOVIET FOREIGN RELATIONS
AND WORLD COMMUNISM

SOVIET FOREIGN RELATIONS AND WORLD COMMUNISM

A SELECTED, ANNOTATED BIBLIOGRAPHY OF 7,000 BOOKS IN 30 LANGUAGES

COMPILED AND EDITED BY

THOMAS T. HAMMOND

PRINCETON, NEW JERSEY
PRINCETON UNIVERSITY PRESS
1965

L.C. Card: 63-7069
Second Printing, with Revisions, 1966

THOMAS TAYLOR HAMMOND is Professor of History at the University of Virginia, and has also taught at Emory University, Louisiana State University, the University of Wisconsin, and Columbia University. He was graduated from the Russian Institute at Columbia, and received his Ph.D. degree in Russian history at that University. His field of interest is Soviet Russia and Eastern Europe and the world Communist movement. Among his publications are: *Lenin on Trade Unions and Revolution* (Columbia University Press, 1957), *Yugoslavia Between East and West* (Foreign Policy Association, 1954), and articles in *The American Slavic and East European Review*, *Foreign Affairs*, *Political Science Quarterly*, and *Virginia Quarterly Review*. He has held fellowships from the Social Science Research Council, the American Council of Learned Societies, the Ford Foundation, the Fulbright Fellowship Board, and the Inter-University Committee on Travel Grants. He has traveled extensively in Eastern Europe, most recently as a research scholar at Moscow University under the official American-Soviet exchange program.

Printed in the United States of America

To My Wife

Preface

THE last five decades have witnessed a great outpouring of books on almost all aspects of Russia, yet no major bibliography has appeared in any language on Soviet foreign relations and world Communism. Among bibliographies published in the United States, the most important in this area are the four volumes of *Foreign Affairs Bibliography*, but since these deal with all countries in the world their coverage of the Soviet Union is necessarily rather brief. The guide compiled by the American Universities Field Staff, *A Select Bibliography: Asia, Africa, Eastern Europe, Latin America*, is similarly so broad in scope that only four pages could be devoted to Soviet foreign relations. Philip Grierson's *Books on Soviet Russia* contains a short section on foreign affairs, but is limited to books in English published before July 1942. The small volume edited by Carew Hunt, *Books on Communism* (later revised by Walter Kolarz), is useful, but also is restricted to works in the English language. The most substantial Soviet bibliography in this field, *Mezhdunarodnye otnosheniia*, issued in 1961 under the editorship of V. N. Egorov, lists only Soviet books in the Russian language published from 1945 through 1960.

The present bibliography is designed to be more comprehensive than any of these works. It includes publications on four major subjects: Soviet diplomatic and economic relations with all major countries since 1917; Communist movements throughout the world since 1917; various aspects of Soviet foreign policy and Communist tactics (ideology, "front" organizations, espionage, international law, etc.); and major *internal* developments in all Communist countries except the USSR.

Originally the editor planned to limit the scope of the bibliography to the formal, official relations of the Soviet Union with other countries. However, in many cases the official diplomatic relations of the USSR have been less important than the unofficial ones conducted through the Comintern, the Cominform, "front" organizations, and the various Communist parties. Hence books on "World Communism" were added. Also, since the domestic policies inaugurated by the Communist regimes of Eastern Europe and Asia have been in part the result of Soviet influence, and thus are connected with Soviet foreign policy, we have added basic works on the Communist regimes that have appeared since 1917. As a result, this volume should be of use not only to specialists on the Soviet Union, but also to persons interested in almost all areas of the world.

Works on Soviet *internal* affairs have not been included because this would have made the bibliography twice as large and twice as expensive, and it would have taken twice as long to prepare. Whereas the number of significant works on Communism in other countries is still rather limited, the literature on developments inside the USSR is mountainous. A bibliography of scope similar to this one on Soviet domestic affairs would comprise several thousand entries; such a work would be tremendously valuable, and it is to be hoped that someone will undertake the formidable task of compiling it.

The bibliography is divided into three main parts. Part I, *Soviet Foreign Relations by Chronological Periods*, lists works that discuss Soviet dealings with more than one country. Part II, *Soviet Foreign Relations and Communism by Regions and Countries*, comprises the greater part of the volume. If a particular work deals only or primarily with one area or country, it has been put in this part, which is arranged geographically. Part III, *Special Topics*, deals with those aspects of Soviet foreign relations and world Communism which are not adapted to chronological or geographical classification—such topics as Communist ideology, strategy and tactics, propaganda, the Comintern, Soviet military power, and so on.

The bibliography includes books in 30 languages, doctoral dissertations, a few of the most significant journal articles and pamphlets, and the main newspapers and periodicals dealing with Communism in various foreign countries. It is hoped that it will be of assistance to professors and school teachers, to students preparing term papers and theses, to government officials who deal with Communism in various parts of the globe, to librarians wishing to order or identify books in this field, and to all others who desire to increase their knowledge of Soviet policy and Communism.

When this bibliography was first undertaken, the editor labored under the mistaken notion that, by utilizing the latest time-saving equipment, it would be possible to collect the titles quickly and easily. Using this approach, we obtained microfilms of pertinent sections of the subject catalogues of the Library of Congress and the New York Public Library; Xerox prints were then made from these films, thereby duplicating the original cards. Although several thousand titles were obtained rapidly in this manner, it soon became apparent that there was one fatal flaw in our method—namely, that the subject catalogues of even the best libraries are woefully incomplete. Thus our work had only begun. Years were spent in searching for additional titles from a great variety of sources (see the partial list on pages 1156-60). These included the following: (1) broad, national bibliographies such as *Knizhnaia letopis* and *Cumulative Book Index*; (2) more specialized bibliographies like *Foreign Affairs Bibliography* and Carew Hunt's *Books on Communism*; (3) book lists and reviews in scholarly journals; and (4) bibliographies in the monographs found in each section. This fourth type of source frequently proved to be disappointing, partly because of the fact that in recent years, with printing costs rising, many scholars have been forced to publish their works without bibliographies, or with only the briefest of lists.

After all of these sources had been canvassed, the titles were arranged by subjects. If a particular section was judged to be reasonably complete, it was sent to the section editor with the request that he add any important works that had been overlooked and omit those of little consequence.

Titles were collected in a systematic way during 1959-60-61. For publications since 1961, the bibliography does not claim to be as thorough, although the contributing editors were asked in 1963 to add any new books to their sections, while the general editor inserted those works that came to his attention, including a few published in 1964.

No bibliography on a subject as broad as the one treated here could possibly be exhaustive, and our intention from the first was to be selective. An attempt to make this work "complete" would have meant cluttering up the pages with many items of little or no value—ephemeral works, polemical tracts, and books which deal with the subject only tangentially. Establishing rigid criteria for the selection of titles was impossible: first of all because more than 100 editors participated in the selecting process, and secondly because more exacting standards had to be applied in fields where the literature is plentiful than in those where it is comparatively limited. The general editor asked the contributing editors to choose works which would be of greatest value to scholars—works that they would recommend to their students, judging by such qualities as the information the books contain, their comprehensiveness, reliability, and objectivity, while also representing a variety of viewpoints. Other things being equal, priority was given to works in English.

Another consideration which naturally influenced the selection was the availability of the books to the editors. Deciding whether or not to include a work which one has not been able to examine is a rather uncertain endeavor; nevertheless we have listed such works if the available information on the author, title, subject, and number of pages seemed to indicate that it might be a significant contribution. Wherever subsequent information or actual examination has revealed such a book to be of less consequence than was originally supposed, we have deleted the entry from our listing. Special efforts have been made to include Soviet works since they are less well known and have been insufficiently utilized in Western research. Unfortunately, many of the Soviet titles proved to be unavailable in this country, while many others were found to have only minimal scholarly value.

In some instances a fraudulent book has been listed and annotated for the purpose of warning prospective readers—for example, the so-called memoirs of Maxim Litvinov, "Colonel Kalinov," and "Captain Krylov."

In other cases an inferior work has been included so that readers could be informed of distortions, errors, bias, or other deficiencies.

Inevitably, some valuable works have been overlooked, or have been omitted because they could not be located. And, inevitably also, there will be differences of opinion regarding which books deserve to be included. Should the reader find an important work not listed, or listed without an annotation, let him bear in mind the difficulties of compiling and annotating a bibliography of this scope. Take, for example, the sections on Sino-Soviet relations. Here the editor needed an annotator who could read Chinese, Russian, Japanese, English, French, German, etc., who was also a specialist on both China and Russia, and who had the time and inclination to read and evaluate all the books in that section. Having found such a talented and accommodating person, the editor ideally should have sent him on a tour of the leading libraries of the U.S., Europe, the USSR, China, and Japan, where he might search for and examine the many books on this subject.

Such a procedure obviously was impossible. In many cases the annotator was forced to depend upon the resources of the library where he lived, plus those books he could manage to borrow through interlibrary loan. Even those annotators who were fortunate enough to live in a major research center such as Washington, New York, or Boston found that many of the titles were not available in the large libraries in those cities.

The editor of a section is not necessarily the author of all the annotations in his section. Sometimes titles had to be moved from one section to another. In other instances the editor of a section was unable to annotate all of his titles; then the general editor had to try to evaluate them himself or make the decision as to whether they should be listed without annotations. Since the contributing editors did not know what titles were included in other sections, or even what sections the bibliography would contain, the general editor had to make the final decision as to whether a title should be included and where it should be included. This applies particularly to items added at the last moment.

Since most of the contributing editors have written on the subjects covered in their sections, it often happened that they were called upon to rate their own works. If they declined to do so or evaluated them with excessive modesty, it became the task of the general editor to find someone else to annotate these entries. Thus if the reader finds that some of these works have high ratings, he should not jump to the conclusion that the author is responsible. The general editor felt that it would be foolish and misleading to give these works lower ratings than they deserved simply for the sake of presenting an appearance of modesty.

If a given title seemed to belong obviously in one and only one section, it was listed only there. However, if it appeared proper to include a title in two or more sections, this was done instead of burdening the reader with cross-references. Another argument against the use of cross-references was the fact that the annotation for one section often was not appropriate for the same title when it was listed in another section.

In the course of examining various bibliographies, the editor adopted certain features designed to make the present work more useful:

For example, we have tried to establish the correct Library of Congress author entry for every book, so that readers will not search in vain through card catalogues for a certain work, only to discover later that they were looking under the wrong heading. This problem is particularly vexing for books listed under a corporate entry, such as one of the branches of the Soviet Government or the U.S. Government. In some cases the Library of Congress system seemed illogical or inconsistent; however, most research libraries in this country follow its cataloging procedures, and consequently we have done the same.

It was also felt that the value of the bibliography would be greatly enhanced if each section were annotated by a scholar who had made a special study of that particular subject. Fortunately, we were able to obtain the assistance of many of the leading experts on Soviet foreign relations and world Communism in this country, as well as several from Europe and Asia. Aside from any value that the bibliography as a whole may have, the reader will find that many of the individual sections constitute the most comprehensive annotated bibliographies ever published on these specialized topics.

In order to supplement the annotations, we felt it would also be helpful to rate the titles in some simple and quickly discernible manner. Hence the annotators were asked to mark approximately 10 percent of the items in their sections with an "A" and the next 20 percent or so with a "B." A reader who has time to consult, say, 10 books or 30 books (but not 100) will thus know which ones deserve priority. These ratings may also be of guidance to library acquisitionists trying to build up collections of basic books in this field.

It is too much to expect that everyone will agree with all of the ratings and annotations given by over 100 editors to over 7,000 titles. The general editor does not agree with all of them himself. Such evaluations are necessarily subjective, reflecting personal opinions and tastes, but there seems to be no way of avoiding this difficulty. The only alternative would have been simply to list the titles, without any attempt to rate them at all, which surely would have made the bibliography much less useful. Even this would not have avoided the equally ripe field for disagreement over which titles should be included or excluded.

PREFACE

Some of the most significant research on Soviet foreign relations and world Communism is contained in unpublished dissertations. Consequently, doctoral dissertations accepted by American and British universities have been included. M.A. theses and other student essays generally have not been listed unless they were known to have special merit.

Originally it was our intention to list all editions of a book, in all languages, but in many instances the information could not be found, whereas in other cases the editions were too numerous (for example, Stalin's writings). Thus it was decided to give priority to editions in the original language and in English. Editions in other languages (especially Russian, French, German and Spanish) have been added if the information was readily available. Where a book was published in English in both the U.S. and Britain, but with different titles, we have listed both titles, lest unwary readers make the common mistake of assuming that they are two separate books.

A word about things that have been left out: There are many additional types of information which might conceivably have been included in this bibliography—magazine articles, newspaper articles, book reviews, book prices, Library of Congress card numbers, and so on *ad infinitum*. These items were omitted because of limited time, limited money, and limited personnel, as well as by a desire to produce a volume which individuals could afford to purchase. The addition of just one of the above—journal articles—would by itself have doubled the size of the present volume and delayed its publication for several years, while at the same time exhausting the patience of the editor and his collaborators. (During just the seven years, 1956-62, some 9,000 books and articles on Russia were published in the U.S.A. alone, not counting other countries.) What the editor attempted to do was to include the most essential information in a volume of convenient size and reasonable price. He was not willing to undertake a multi-volume, lifetime project, encompassing all information on all writings that could possibly be of interest to scholars and librarians in this field.

Words in the Cyrillic alphabet have been transliterated according to the Library of Congress system, except that diacritical marks, soft signs, and hard signs have been omitted. Titles have been capitalized according to the practice generally used in the language concerned. Cities of publication have been given in their English form, lest some readers be confused by such names as 's Gravenhage, Praha, or Wien.

Thomas Taylor Hammond

Charlottesville, Virginia
October 1965

Acknowledgments

THIS book, more than most, is the product of the ideas and cooperative endeavor of many scholars. In the planning stage I benefited especially from the advice of three people: Philip E. Mosely, Henry L. Roberts, and John Cook Wyllie. Professor Mosely, formerly Director of the Russian Institute and now Director of the European Institute at Columbia University, in his usual generous way took the time to discuss the scope and purpose of the bibliography with me and to suggest possible contributors. His support for the idea of such a bibliography—something he had once thought of compiling himself—was in part responsible for my decision to undertake the project.

I also profited greatly from the suggestions of Professor Roberts, formerly Director of the Russian Institute at Columbia University and editor of volumes III and IV of *Foreign Affairs Bibliography*. He shared with me his knowledge of the techniques of bibliographical compilation and assisted in enlisting the aid of several of the contributing editors. The *Foreign Affairs Bibliography* has in many respects served as a model for the present volume.

Mr. Wyllie, the Librarian of the University of Virginia, enthusiastically endorsed my initial impulse to compile the bibliography, made several time-saving suggestions regarding procedure, and placed the resources of Alderman Library at my beck and call.

I am of course greatly indebted to the contributing editors, whose specialized knowledge of the various countries and subjects, as well as their linguistic abilities, made the bibliography more authoritative and complete than would otherwise have been possible. That these scholars were willing to assume this obligation, and without financial compensation, is a tribute to the spirit of cooperation in the academic community. I would like to express special thanks to the Honorable George F. Kennan, who not only consented to serve as an editor but even took the time to annotate titles after he was named Ambassador to Yugoslavia.

Ideally a bibliography of this magnitude should have been backed by some scholarly organization and should have been financed from the start by a large grant, thus making possible the hiring of a permanent, full-time staff, as was done with the American Historical Association's *Guide to Historical Literature*. Attempts to obtain this type of support were unsuccessful, however, and the project was forced to subsist on a hand-to-mouth basis from a series of small grants. The initial funds came from the Research Council of the University Center in Virginia, Inc. The Wilson Gee Institute for Research in the Social Sciences of the University of Virginia made it possible for me to work full-time on the bibliography during the summers of 1959, 1961, and 1962. The Research Committee of the University of Virginia helped cover the costs of microfilming, travel, and clerical assistance. Finally, the Joint Slavic Committee of the American Council of Learned Societies and the Social Science Research Council kindly awarded two grants to permit the completion of the work. I am happy to be able to express appreciation to all these gentlemen for their kind support.

A number of libraries contributed significantly to the bibliography. First must be mentioned the Alderman Library of the University of Virginia, whose staff are the most courteous and cooperative of any I know. Although many helped in one way or another, I am especially grateful to Mr. John Cook Wyllie, Miss Louise Savage, Mr. Harvey Deal, Miss Helena Coiner, Miss Katherine Beville, and Mrs. Ethel Bloom.

The Library of Congress supplied microfilms of selected sections from its card catalogues, and several members of the staff took the time to answer my questions, including Messrs. Sergius Yakobson, Paul Horecky, Leon Herman, James B. Childs, and Miss Helen Conover. I am also indebted to the Library of Congress for the many bibliographies and bibliographical aids it has published.

The New York Public Library kindly microfilmed parts of its Slavonic collection for me. Mr. Howard P. Linton, Director of the East Asiatic Library of Columbia University, permitted me to microfilm a special card catalogue on Soviet relations with Asian countries. Madame Michaud, of the Bibliothèque de Documentation Internationale Contemporaine in Paris, arranged for the filming of parts of their catalogue.

Professor Jan F. Triska of Stanford University generously loaned me a card catalogue on Soviet foreign policy which he and Professor Robert M. Slusser of The Johns Hopkins University had compiled.

Among others who assisted in one way or another are: Mr. Hamilton Fish Armstrong, Editor of *Foreign Affairs*; Messrs. Phillips Talbot and Teg C. Grondahl of the American Universities Field Staff; Mr. Boyd C. Shafer, Executive Secretary of the American Historical Association; Professor Richard C. Pipes of Harvard University; Mr. C. E. Moran, Jr., of the University of Virginia Printing Office; Mr. Thompson Webb of the University of Wisconsin Press; Mr. Karol Maichel of the Hoover Institution at Stanford University; Messrs. William Turpin and Walter F. Cronin of the Department of State, Mr. Ellis Jaffe of Harvard University, and Dr. Fritz Epstein of Indiana University.

It was financially impossible to hire a permanent, full-time secretary or research assistant who could stay with the project from beginning to end. However, a succession of graduate students worked on a part-time basis for periods ranging from a few days to many months, and assisted in the enormous amount of tedious copying, checking, and searching for bibliographical data. The University of Virginia students were: Rayburn D. M. Hanzlik, Jr., W. Nathaniel Howell, Jr., Robert B. Janes,

Jr., Roland V. Layton, Jr., Donald R. Pascal, Hugh Ragsdale, Jr., and Benjamin W. Wright, Jr. Students at the University of Wisconsin who helped were: Elliot Benowitz, Duane Frankie, and James L. McKnight. Assisting in the typing at various stages of the project were: Mrs. Diana S. Campbell, Mrs. Naomi E. Hicks, and Mrs. Judith P. Matthias. Mrs. Olga Podtiaguine helped look through the many issues of *Knizhnaia letopis* for titles and also checked for errors in the Russian entries. Mrs. Kay Sargent and Miss Marilyn Hedges prepared form letters.

Mrs. Alena Hammond, Professor Walter Heilbronner, Professor Edoardo Lebano, and Mrs. Nicole Crosby assisted in checking some of the foreign languages, and Professor John J. Kennedy gave advice on Latin American titles. Professor Walter Hauser made some additions to the section on India.

Finally, I wish to express appreciation to the staff of Princeton University Press, who could not have been more pleasant and cooperative. I would like especially to thank Mr. Herbert S. Bailey, Jr., Director and Editor, Miss Miriam Brokaw, Managing Editor, Mr. Jay F. Wilson, Editor, and Mrs. Eve Hanle, Editor.

Contents

PART II

SOVIET FOREIGN RELATIONS AND WORLD COMMUNISM BY REGIONS AND COUNTRIES

CONTENTS

CONTENTS

CONTENTS

PART III

SPECIAL TOPICS

CONTENTS

CONTENTS

Part I

Soviet Foreign Relations by Chronological Periods

NOTE: If a work covers Soviet relations with only one country, it is not included in this section, but rather in Part II.

A. General Works on Soviet Foreign Relations Covering More than One Period and Country

EDITED BY ROBERT F. BYRNES AND PAUL K. COOK

A1 ADAMS, ARTHUR E., ed. *Readings in Soviet Foreign Policy; Theory and Practice.* Boston: Heath, 1961. 420 p. Selections from the works of Lenin, Stalin, E. H. Carr, Franz Borkenau, Winston Churchill, James F. Byrnes, etc. The readings are arranged chronologically and cover the high spots from 1917 to 1960. Edited by a professor at Michigan State University.

A2 AIRAPETIAN, M. E., and DEBORIN, G. A. *Etapy vneshnei politiki SSSR.* Moscow: Izd. sots.-ek. lit., 1961. 536 p. The authors divide the period 1917-58 into twelve "stages," and include a discussion justifying their delineations. Each "stage" was characterized by the desire of the USSR to obtain the international situation most favorable to the building of socialism at home. Twenty-page bibliography of Soviet and Western sources.

A3 AKADEMIIA NAUK SSSR, INSTITUT MIROVOGO KHOZIAISTVA I MIROVOI POLITIKI. *Polozhenie rabochego klassa v kapitalisticheskikh stranakh za 20 let (1917-1937).* Edited by L. Geller and B. Fogarash. Moscow: Gospolitizdat, 1938. 280 p.

A4 AMERICAN FOUNDATION FOR POLITICAL EDUCATION. *Readings in Russian Foreign Policy.* Ed. by Robert A. Goldwin and Marvin Zetterbaum. Chicago: 1953. 3 vols. and Supplement (51 p.). 2nd ed., 1953. 3 vols. and Supplement (44 p.). 3rd ed., 1958. 2 vols. and Supplement (48 p.). One volume paperback edition, ed. by Robert A. Goldwin, Marvin Zetterbaum, and Gerald Stourzh. N.Y.: Oxford, 1959. 775 p. An excellent selection from original documents and from secondary sources, arranged in a somewhat unorthodox grouping and with emphasis naturally on the 1950's. Designed for adult education and for political science courses. No bibliography or index. [B]

A5 ARMSTRONG, JOHN A. *The Politics of Totalitarianism; The Communist Party of the Soviet Union from 1934 to the Present.* N.Y.: Random House, 1961. 458 p. A detailed scholarly study by a University of Wisconsin political scientist, based on thorough analysis of available published information. Concentrates upon political issues and struggles at the highest levels of the Communist Party. The third part of a three-volume history of the Soviet Union's Communist Party. Excellent notes, but no bibliography. [A]

A6 ARMSTRONG, TERENCE. *The Russians in the Arctic; Aspects of Soviet Exploration and Exploitation of the Far North, 1937-57*. London: Methuen; N.Y.: Essential, 1958. 182 p. Generally a skillfully-created description of Soviet study of the Polar Sea, the opening of the Northeast Passage to merchant shipping, and the strategic development of Siberia, based on the random Soviet materials available. Probably exaggerates Soviet capability and experience in study of the Arctic and in logistics.

A7 BARMINE, ALEXANDRE. *Memoirs of a Soviet Diplomat; Twenty Years in the Service of the U.S.S.R.* London: L. Dickson, 1938. 360 p. Rev. ed., *One Who Survived; the Life Story of a Russian under the Soviets*. Intro. by Max Eastman. N.Y.: Putnam, 1945. 337 p. French ed., Paris: 1939. 382 p. Revealing memoirs of an old Bolshevik who turned against the regime during the Stalinist purges of the mid-thirties. He served in various capacities in Iran, France, Belgium, Poland, and, finally, Greece, where, when he severed his ties with Moscow, he was Chargé d'Affaires of the Soviet Legation. He also occupied posts in various Soviet bodies concerned with trade.

A8 BELOFF, MAX. *The Foreign Policy of Soviet Russia, 1929-1941*. London and N.Y.: Oxford, 1947-49. 2 vols. A dispassionate, painfully objective analysis by a distinguished British scholar for the Royal Institute of International Affairs, full of well-organized information. Concentrates on Soviet policy towards Europe, but also contains illuminating sections on the Far East in appendices. A standard work of outstanding importance, this is one of the best books ever written on Soviet foreign policy. [A]

A9 BESEDOVSKII, GRIGORII Z. *Na putiakh k termidoru; iz vospominanii sovetskogo diplomata*. Paris: "Mishen," 1930-31. 2 vols. German ed., *Im Dienste der Sowjets; den Klauen der Tscheka entronnen; Erinnerungen*. Leipzig: Grethlein, 1930. 2 vols. Abridged French ed., *Oui, j'accuse! Au service des Soviets*. Paris: A. Redier, 1930. 265 p. Abridged English ed., *Revelations of a Soviet Diplomat*. London: Williams & Norgate, 1931. 276 p. Slight memoirs of a Soviet diplomat who defected in 1929 after service in Warsaw, New York, various cities in Latin America, Tokyo, Harbin, and Paris.

A10 BISHOP, DONALD G., ed. *Soviet Foreign Relations; Documents and Readings*. Syracuse: Syracuse University Press, 1952. 223 p. An undistinguished selection of translated documents on various aspects of Soviet foreign policy.

A10A BOUSCAREN, ANTHONY T. *Soviet Foreign Policy; a Pattern of Persistence.* N.Y.: Fordham University Press, 1962.

A11 BROMAGE, BERNARD. *Molotov; The Story of an Era.* London: Owen, 1956. 256 p. A highly colored account of Soviet diplomacy by a British journalist as seen through the eyes of a eulogized Molotov. Selected bibliography.

A12 CARR, EDWARD H. *A History of Soviet Russia.* N.Y. and London: Macmillan, 1950—. A multi-volume history of the Soviet Union by a distinguished British scholar; seven volumes have appeared. Based almost entirely on official Soviet materials, even to the neglect of other sources and studies. The product of immense research, they reflect skilled mastery of details. The first three volumes are somewhat marred by uncritical admiration for Lenin and apparent acceptance of the official Bolshevik point of view. Vol. 3, entitled *The Bolshevik Revolution, 1917-1923*, is devoted entirely to Soviet foreign relations, and Vol. 4, *The Interregnum, 1923-1924*, has a section on this topic. Vol. 7, *Socialism in One Country, 1924-1926* (in two parts) deals with foreign relations for those years. Carr hopes to carry the story through 1929, with a total of 10 volumes. A work of great importance. [A]

A13 CARR, EDWARD H. *The Soviet Impact on the Western World.* N.Y.: Macmillan, 1946. 116 p. A series of lectures presented in Oxford in 1946, analyzing the effect upon the West of Soviet economic, political, social, and ideological practices and of Soviet foreign policy. A vastly exaggerated and flattering view of the impact of the Soviet Union upon the rest of the world, especially on Western Europe.

A14 CHAMBERLIN, WILLIAM H. *The Russian Enigma, an Interpretation.* N.Y.: Scribner's, 1943. 321 p. An honest effort by a highly informed and deeply critical observer of Soviet life and politics to view Soviet foreign policy in the perspective of Russian and Soviet history.

A15 CHICHERIN, GEORGII V. *Stati, rechi, doklady po mezhdunarodnym voprosam.* Moscow: Sotsekgiz, 1961. Articles and speeches by the man who was Commissar of Foreign Affairs from 1918 to 1930.

A16 COLE, GEORGE D. H. *A History of Socialist Thought.* Vol. 4, *Communism and Social Democracy, 1914-1931*, in 2 parts. Vol. 5, *Socialism and Fascism, 1931-1939.* London: Macmillan; N.Y.: St. Martin's, 1960. 350 p. Cole was a leading English socialist, a prolific author, and Professor of Social and Political Theory at Oxford. Vol. 4 describes the splits and schisms in the socialist movement from World War I to the crystallization of the socialist movement into two rival internationals, and the controversies between them. Vol. 5 is a chronicle of what happened to the Communist and non-Communist labor movements in the 1930's, with emphasis on Western Europe. Scholarly but not analytical.

A17 CRAIG, GORDON A., and GILBERT, FELIX, eds. *The Diplomats 1919-1939*. Princeton: Princeton University Press, 1953. 700 p. Seventeen scholarly, analytical essays, all of high quality, on important diplomats and statesmen who helped shape national foreign policies in the period between the two world wars. Includes a study of Chicherin (by Theodore H. von Laue) and of Litvinov (by Henry L. Roberts), both of which illuminate the spirit, goals, and methods of Soviet foreign policy.

A18 DALLIN, ALEXANDER, comp. *Soviet Conduct in World Affairs; a Selection of Readings*. N.Y.: Columbia, 1960. 318 p. A useful collection of articles by specialists on various aspects of Soviet foreign policy.

A19 DEBORIN, GRIGORII A. *Istoriia mezhdunarodnykh otnoshenii; istoriia zarubezhnykh stran*. Moscow: Izd. mezh. ot., 1957. 258 p. A collection of uneven monographs covering Soviet views on the colonial system, the liquidation of foreign military bases, the Spanish civil war, Korea after the Russo-Japanese War, post-World War II Czechoslovakia, and the diplomacy of the 1946 Paris Peace Conference.

A20 DENNIS, ALFRED L. P. *The Foreign Policies of Soviet Russia*. N.Y.: Dutton; London: Dent, 1924. 500 p. An early analysis of Soviet foreign policy in the first six years of the regime's history by an American professor. Scholarly for the time when written. Neglects policies of other countries toward the Soviet Union.

A21 DEUTSCHER, ISAAC. *Stalin; a Political Biography*. N.Y. and London: Oxford, 1949. 600 p. German ed., Stuttgart: W. Kohlhammer, 1951. 606 p. French ed., Paris: Gallimard, 1953. 446 p. The most important and widely read biography of Stalin; by a former Polish Communist, long resident in England. Actually a life and times of Stalin or a history of Russia from 1879 to 1949, with about one-third of the space devoted to foreign relations and their impact on domestic policies. Immensely readable, but fatalistic and partial to Stalin and the Soviet revolution. [B]

A22 *Diplomaticheskii slovar*. Ed. by A. Ia. Vyshinskii and S. A. Lozovskii. Moscow: Gosizdat, 1948-50. 2 vols. 2nd ed., ed. by A. A. Gromyko, and others. 1960—. (3 vols. planned) Soviet handbooks on modern diplomacy, especially since the Second World War, with especial emphasis on Soviet diplomacy. Provide basic information, from the

Soviet point of view, concerning international congresses and conferences, terms of treaties and other diplomatic acts, important diplomats and statesmen. Contain country and subject indices. [A]

A23 DRAKE, EDWARD S. "The Soviet Alliance System, 1917-1941." Ph.D. dissertation, New York University, 1957.

A24 FISCHER, LOUIS. *The Soviets in World Affairs; A History of the Relations Between the Soviet Union and the Rest of the World, 1917-1929.* London: J. Cape; N.Y.: J. Cape and H. Smith, 1930. 2 vols. 2nd ed., Princeton, N.J.: Princeton, 1951. 2 vols. Paperback ed., N.Y.: Vintage, 1961. French ed., Paris: Gallimard, 1933. 763 p. A remarkable, exciting description of the first twelve years of Soviet foreign policy, by an American journalist. Fischer was on friendly terms with Foreign Commissar Chicherin and other Soviet officials, and thus had a unique opportunity to get confidential information and see private and official documents. For many years a correspondent in Russia, Fischer was at that time highly sympathetic to the Soviet point of view. The second edition is unchanged except for an interesting introduction. An indispensable work, despite its bias. [A]

A25 FLEMING, DENNA F. *The Cold War and Its Origins, 1917-1960.* Garden City, N.Y.: Doubleday, 1961. 2 vols. A massive study by a professor of international relations at Vanderbilt University. Vol. I (540 p.) covers the period 1917-1950, while vol. II (619 p.) deals in more detail with the decade from 1950 to 1960. The author's main point is that the chief blame for the hostility between East and West lies with the latter. Interesting, but one-sided.

A25A FOREIGN AFFAIRS (New York). *The Soviet Union, 1922-1962: a Foreign Affairs Reader.* Ed. by Philip E. Mosely. Foreword by Hamilton Fish Armstrong. N.Y.: Pub. for the Council on Foreign Relations by Praeger, 1963. 497 p. A collection of articles on the USSR from Foreign Affairs, including excellent essays by Prof. Mosely, George F. Kennan, and others.

A26 GOODMAN, ELLIOT R. *The Soviet Design for a World State.* Foreword by Philip E. Mosely. N.Y.: Columbia, 1960. 512 p. A methodical, detailed, rather formless analysis of Communist views on the world state and on related strategic and tactical doctrines by a Brown University political scientist. Based largely on analysis of Communist doctrinal statements. Urges that the West must develop some kind of cooperative union and coordinated policy to survive.

A27 GRANSBERG, S., and ANBOR, G. *Kolonialnyi mir; spravochnik dlia propagandista.* Ed. by A. Lozovsky. Moscow-Leningrad: Gosizdat, 1929. 181 p. A general description of most of the world's colonies, with primary attention directed to British colonies.

A28 GURIAN, WALDEMAR and others. *Soviet Imperialism; Its Origins and Tactics; A Symposium.* Notre Dame, Ind.: Notre Dame University Press, 1953. 166 p. A collection of papers by seven American scholars originally presented at a symposium at Notre Dame in 1953. Designed to distinguish Russian from Soviet expansionism, with papers on this subject, the Ukraine, the Moslems, Tsarist and Soviet policy in Poland and in China, and Soviet propaganda. [B]

A29 HAINES, CHARLES GROVE, ed. *The Threat of Soviet Imperialism.* Baltimore: Johns Hopkins; London: Oxford, 1954. 402 p. A series of analytical articles by a group of specialists on various phases of Soviet and Communist policies. Now somewhat dated. [B]

A30 HARTLIEB, WILHELM W. *Das politische Vertragssystem der Sowjetunion, 1920-1935.* Leipzig: Noske, 1936. 267 p. A scholarly, detailed study of Soviet foreign policy of the period. Good bibliography and chronology of principal events.

A31 *History of the Communist Party of the Soviet Union.* By B. N. Ponomaryov and others. Ed. by Andrew Rothstein. Moscow: Foreign Languages Publishing House, 1960. 765 p. A thorough revision of the Stalinist *Short Course* (see below) to remove the former magnification of Stalin's role and increase the space devoted to Khrushchev. Presents the official view, as of the date of publication, of the main lines of Soviet foreign (and internal) policy. [A]

A32 HOETZSCH, OTTO. *Le Caractère et la situation internationale de l'Union des Soviets.* Geneva: Librairie Kundig, 1932. 104 p. A series of lectures, by a leading German expert before 1933 and editor of *Osteuropa*, presented at the Institute of International Studies.

A33 HUA, KANG. *Su lien wai chiao shih.* Shanghai: Petrels Bookstore, 1950. 465 p. A general survey of Soviet foreign relations by a former Nationalist Chinese professor. Published under the Communist regime. Written in Chungking around 1940-45 with limited sources. Bibliography.

A34 HUSZAR, GEORGE B. DE, ed. *Soviet Power and Policy.* N.Y.: Crowell, 1955. 598 p. A detailed analysis by fourteen scholars of factors which affect Soviet foreign policy, such as population, natural resources, economic growth, transportation, Party control, and the armed forces; the increase in Soviet power and Soviet expansion since 1945; and Soviet policy in the principal areas of the world. Useful but out of date. [B]

A35 ILIN, BORIS. *Borba za mir; fakty i dokumenty v illiustratsiiakh i vyderzhkakh iz istorii borby Sovetskogo Soiuza za mir.* Moscow-Leningrad: Izogiz, 1932. 255 p. A collection of documents and illustrations on the Soviet "fight for peace" from the Bolshevik Revolution to 1930. With many quotations from Lenin and Stalin. Highly propagandistic; intended for the masses.

A36 *Istoriia mezhdunarodnykh otnoshenii i vneshnei politiki SSSR.* Edited by V. G. Trukhanovskii. Moscow: Izd. IMO, 1961. Vol. I, 1917-33. 720 p. The first of a 3-volume series covering the period 1917-60. A good Soviet university textbook with chronology of principal events and name index. Source citations include English and American authors. Maps.

A37 IVASHIN, I. F. *Mezhdunarodnye otnosheniia i vneshniaia politika SSSR v 1919-1935 godakh; lektsii, prochitannye v Vysshei partiinoi shkole pri TSK KPSS.* Moscow: 1956. 190 p. A brief, propagandistic and heavily biased account of the coming of World War II, designed to show that the Soviet Union, of all powers, sought consistently to preserve peace and security and desperately tried to help the governments and peoples of Ethiopia, Germany, Spain, China, Austria, and Czechoslovakia.

A38 IVASHIN, I. F. *Ocherki istorii vneshnei politiki SSSR.* Moscow: Gospolitizdat, 1958. 560 p. A historical account of Soviet foreign policy based in part on USSR Communist Party and State archival materials, 1917-58. Designed for university students. Polemical in parts.

A39 IVASHIN, I. F. *Vsemirno-istoricheskoe znachenie Velikoi oktiabrskoi sotsialisticheskoi revoliutsii.* Moscow: Gospolitizdat, 1953. 143 p. A standard Soviet tract covering the period from 1917-53 and emphasizing the October Revolution and post-XIX Party Congress.

A40 *Iz istorii mezhdunarodnoi proletarskoi solidarnosti; dokumenty i materialy.* Ed. by G. A. Belov and others. Moscow: "Sovetskaia Rossiia," 1957-60. 4 vols. A collection of a large number of resolutions, letters, proclamations, etc., originating in labor groups, Communist Parties, and left-wing organizations all over the world. They are related to such topics as anniversaries of the Bolshevik revolution, the Sacco-Vanzetti case, Fascist "provocations," etc. The sources of the materials are Soviet archives and contemporary periodicals.

A41 JARAY, GABRIEL L. *Tableau de la Russie jusqu'à la mort de Staline.* Paris: Plon, 1954. 450 p. A well-documented survey of international and national affairs, 1917-54. Chapters cover relations between the Soviet Union and China, France, and Germany. Good bibliography.

A42 KENNAN, GEORGE F. *Russia and the West under Lenin and Stalin.* Boston: Little, Brown, 1961. 411 p. A gracefully written analysis of relations between Russia and the West, especially the U.S., since the 1917 Revolution, by a distinguished American diplomat-scholar. An unbalanced volume, with heavy emphasis on 1917-22 and the 1950's. Especially critical of Western statesmen and publics for continuing the First World War, for policies adopted towards the Soviet regime in the first critical years, and for the unconditional surrender policy in the Second World War. A highly moral review of American policy which is at the same time critical of the moralistic approach to world politics. A collection of brilliant, interpretive lectures rather than a detailed, factual history. [A]

A43 KENNAN, GEORGE F. *Soviet Foreign Policy, 1917-1941.* Princeton, N.J.: Van Nostrand, 1960. 192 p. (Anvil Paperbacks) A popular review supplemented by thirty-four documents. Too brief to be of much value.

A44 KHVOSTOV, V. M. *40 let borby za mir; kratkii ocherk.* Moscow: Gospolitizdat, 1958. 160 p. A short survey of the USSR's "fight for peace and disarmament" since 1917. A useful but militant summary by a Soviet propagandist.

A45 KIESER, GEORGES. *Why Is Russia So Strong? The Foundations of Russia's Strength.* Bienne, Switzerland: Chaseral, 1945. 264 p. Italian ed., Milan: Corticelli, 1945. A pro-Soviet account of the 1914-45 period. The first third deals with Soviet foreign policy; the last two-thirds with the economic, social and political foundations of Russian strength.

A46 KIM, MAKSIM P., ed. *Istoriia SSSR; epokha sotsializma, 1917-1957 gg.* Moscow: 1957. 772 p. German ed., *Geschichte der Sowjetunion, 1917-1957.* Berlin: Rütten & Loening, 1960. 791 p. A university textbook by noted Soviet experts. The first systematic Marxist treatise of 1917-57 domestic and foreign affairs, especially of Soviet-German-British-U.S. relations. Some problems of international politics at the end of World War II are much misinterpreted. Based partly on unpublished sources housed in the USSR archives.

A47 KLEIST, PETER. *Die völkerrechtliche Anerkennung Sowjetrusslands.* Berlin: Ost-Europa, 1934. 127 p. A scholarly, well-documented survey of West European and U.S. recognition of the Soviet regime. Translations of British, French, Italian, and U.S. notes in appendix. No Russian sources *per se.* [A]

A48 KOMMUNISTICHESKAIA AKADEMIIA, INSTITUT MIROVOGO KHOZIAISTVA I MIROVOI POLITIKI. *Desiat let kapitalisticheskogo okruzheniia SSSR.* Ed. by E. Pashukanis and M. Spektator. Moscow: Izd. Kom. Akad., 1928-29. Seven vols. in two. Treats Soviet relations with the Baltic States, Germany, the Entente, Poland, the East, the world proletariat, and the world economy. Interesting references to documents and periodical literature throughout the seven books.

A49 KOMMUNISTICHESKAIA PARTIIA SOVETSKOGO SOIUZA, TSENTRALNYI KOMITET. *History of the Communist Party of the Soviet Union (Bolsheviks); Short Course.* N.Y.: International Publishers, 1939. 364 p. (Many other editions in English and other languages.) For many years this was the official Stalinist version of the history of the CPSU and, incidentally, of the main lines of Soviet foreign policy. (For a revised version see above under *History.*) [A]

A50 KOMMUNISTICHESKAIA PARTIIA SOVETSKOGO SOIUZA, VYSSHAIA PARTIINAIA SHKOLA, KAFEDRA MEZHDUNARODNYKH OTNOSHENII. *Istoriia mezhdunarodnykh otnoshenii i vneshnei politiki SSSR, 1870-1957 gg.; kratkoe uchebnoe posobie.* Ed. by F. G. Zuev. Moscow: 1957. 579 p. A Soviet collection of monographs surveying Russian and Soviet foreign policy, 1870-1957. Written for secondary schools. No table of contents, no bibliography, no index. Short chronology of principal events.

A51 KYROU, ACHILEUS. *I Exoteriki Politiki tis Sovietikis Rossias.* Athens: Estia, 1950. Later ed., 1955. The author is a prominent Greek publisher who is the managing-editor of the daily *ESTIA.* He examines the foreign policy of the Soviet Union as the continuation of Russian expansionism since the days of the Tsars.

A52 LA PRADELLE, ALBERT G. DE. *Le Marxisme tentaculaire; la formation, la tactique et l'action de la diplomatie soviëtique, 1920-1940.* Issoudun, France: Les Éditions internationales, 1942. 314 p. A hostile study of Soviet policy towards and expansion into Poland, Finland, and the Baltic states by a distinguished French Catholic jurist and specialist in international law.

A53 LEDERER, IVO J., ed. *Russian Foreign Policy; Essays in Historical Perspective.* New Haven: Yale, 1962. 620 p. A collection of articles on Russian foreign policy since 1861 by 18 well-known American scholars, including C. E. Black, Robert F. Byrnes, Frederick Barghoorn, Gordon Craig, George Kennan, Henry L. Roberts, Robert Slusser, etc. Although few of the chapters represent original research or new facts, most of them contain thoughtful and original interpretations and analyses. A highly-stimulating book, which adds greatly to our understanding of both Tsarist and Soviet foreign policy and the similarities and differences between the two. [A]

A54 LINDH, NILS J. B. *Möten mellan Öst och Väst; studier i samtida rysk utrikespolitik.* Stockholm: Kooperativa förbundets bokförlag, 1949. 330 p. A series of unusually perceptive essays on Soviet foreign policy since the revolution by an able Swedish observer and writer and sometime Soviet expert in the Swedish Foreign Office. The author is sensitive to important traditions in Russian history.

A55 LITVINOV, MAKSIM M. *Notes for a Journal.* Introduction by E. H. Carr. N.Y.: Morrow, 1955. 347 p. London: Deutsch, 1955. 303 p. German ed., *Memoiren; Aufzeichnungen aus dem geheimen Tagebüchern.* Munich: Kindler, 1956. 292 p. According to Philip E. Mosely and Bertram Wolfe, these "memoirs" are a complete forgery, possibly the work of George Bessedovsky, a former Soviet diplomat living in Paris. Mr. Carr, however, seems to have been taken in, for he suggests in his introduction that at least part of the book is genuine.

A56 MARQUÈS-RIVIÈRE, JEAN. *L'URSS dans le monde; l'expansion soviétique de 1918 à 1935.* Preface by Georges Viance. Paris: Payot, 1935. 368 p. A popular French study of Soviet domestic and foreign policy from 1918 to 1935.

A57 MEZHDUNARODNAIA ZHIZN. *Voprosy vneshnei politiki SSSR i sovremennykh mezhdunarodnykh otnoshenii; sbornik statei.* Ed. by L. F. Ilichev and others. Moscow: Gospolitizdat, 1958. 349 p. Materials of an important Soviet conference in 1957 on the history of Soviet foreign policy, together with a series of articles by Soviet writers on aspects of the foreign policy of non-Communist states in the contemporary period.

A58 MILIUKOV, PAVEL N. *La Politique extérieure des Soviets.* Paris: Giard, 1934. 490 p. 2nd ed., Paris: Librairie Générale de Droit et de Jurisprudence, 1936. 530 p. A detailed, balanced, and judicious study by the exiled liberal Russian historian and statesman who served briefly as Foreign Minister in the Provisional Government in 1917. He divided Soviet foreign policy, hopefully, into three stages: the revolutionary offensive, 1917-21; the period of treaties and respectability, 1921-25; and the decline of and retreat from the revolutionary movement after 1925. Lists treaties in which the USSR participated. Brief bibliography. [B]

A59 MOORE, BARRINGTON. *Soviet Politics—the Dilemma of Power; the Role of Ideas in Social Change.* Cambridge: Harvard, 1950. 503 p. A valuable and stimulating study by a Harvard research sociologist of the Soviet governmental system, particularly of the interaction between Communist ideology and Soviet political practices, from the development of Lenin's ideas to the Stalinist bureaucratic state of the post-Second World War period. An important contribution for understanding Soviet domestic and foreign policy.

A59A MOSCOW, AKADEMIIA OBSHCHESTVENNYKH NAUK. *Nekotorye voprosy mezhdunarodnykh otnoshenii; sbornik statei.* Ed. by A. I. Shneerson and V. M. Kulakov. Moscow: VPSH, 1960. 273 p. Six articles on widely divergent topics: the financial dependence of pre-

1917 Russia on the West; the establishment of Soviet power in the Ukraine, 1917-20; Rumania's struggle for a "zone of peace" in the Balkans; U.S. foreign policy, 1953-56; and the German Social Democratic Party's position on foreign policy questions, 1955-59.

A60 MOSCOW, INSTITUT MEZHDUNARODNYKH OTNOSHENII. *Voprosy ekonomiki i mezhdunarodnykh otnoshenii; sbornik statei.* Moscow: 1957. 231 p. Some of the articles discuss various economic problems in China, Czechoslovakia, the U.S., West Germany, Spain, and Canada; others take up such diverse questions as the U.S. delegation at the Paris Peace Conference in 1919; Anglo-Soviet relations, 1929-32; the "depraved" concept of a capitalism without crises; French Social-Democracy; and England's reaction to West German rearmament.

A61 MOSELY, PHILIP E. *The Kremlin and World Politics; Studies in Soviet Policy and Action.* N.Y.: Vintage, 1960. 557 p. A collection of articles, covering a span of more than twenty years, by a foremost American specialist on Soviet affairs. From the research standpoint, Mosely's treatment of his experiences in negotiating with Soviet diplomats on the Berlin and Austrian issues (at the end of World War II) are especially valuable. [A]

A62 NOTOVICH, F. I. *Ot pervoi do vtoroi mirovoi voini; kratkii ocherk mezhdunarodnykh otnoshenii v 1919-1942 gg.* Tashkent: Gosizdat UzSSR, 1943. 211 p. An above average Soviet account of diplomacy of the inter-war period. Good coverage of the 1920's and early 1930's.

A63 OLBERG, PAUL. *Rysslands nya imperialism, de sma nationernas drama i diktaturstaten.* Stockholm: Bokförlaget Natur och kultur, 1940. 231 p. A careful study of Soviet imperialism, especially in Central Asia, the Caucasus, Poland, the Baltic states, and Finland, by a profoundly anti-Soviet Swedish journalist.

A64 PABÓN, JESÚS (JESÚS PABÓN Y SUÁREZ DE URBINA). *Zarismo y bolchevismo.* Madrid: Moneda y Crédito, 1948. 217 p. A critical review of Soviet domestic and foreign policy by an anti-democratic professor of history at the University of Madrid.

A65 PALENCIA, ISABEL DE. *Alexandra Kollontay.* N.Y.: Longmans, 1947. 309 p. A light and wholly admiring biography by a personal friend who was the Spanish representative to Sweden and Norway. Kollontay was an early Bolshevik, leading Russian feminist, Commissar for Social Welfare, Minister to Norway and Sweden, Ambassador to Mexico, and Ambassador to Sweden. Interesting information on Kollontay before 1917, but little on Soviet policy, politics, or politicians.

A66 POPE, ARTHUR U. *Maxim Litvinoff*. N.Y.: Fischer, 1943. 530 p. A highly sympathetic biography of the Soviet diplomat and foreign minister and a remarkably favorable survey of Soviet foreign policy from 1917 to World War II by a specialist on Persian art. Says that Litvinov "was always right," and describes him and his government as the strongest supporters of collective security.

A67 POTEMKIN, VLADIMIR P., ed. *Istoriia diplomatii.* Moscow: Ogiz, 1941-45. 3 vols. French ed., Paris: Librairie de Medicis, 1946-47. 3 vols. Yugoslav ed., Belgrade: Izd. Arkhiva za pravne i drushtvene nauke, 1946—. Spanish ed., Buenos Aires: Editorial Lautaro, 1943—. 2nd enlarged and revised ed., Moscow: Gospolitizdat, 1959—. Ed. by Valerian A. Zorin and others. (2nd ed. to be five vols.) An important Soviet interpretation of diplomatic history from antiquity to 1939. The first volume covers the period through 1871, the second 1872-1919, and the third 1919-1939. Reflects the Soviet view as of the first half of the 1940's. The ideological and propagandistic shortcomings and nationalistic point of view become increasingly significant as the study approaches the end. Extensive bibliographies. [A]

A68 PRINCE, CHARLES. "Economic, Legal and Political Factors Affecting Soviet Russia's Foreign Policy." Ph.D. dissertation, Georgetown, 1944.

A69 RADEK, KARL B. *Portrety i pamflety.* Moscow-Leningrad: Gosizdat, 1927. 286 p. Rev. ed., Moscow: Khudozhestvennaia Lit., 1934. 2 vols. English ed., *Portraits and Pamphlets.* London: McBride, 1935. A collection of Radek's articles, chiefly biographical sketches. Vol. II of the 1934 edition is largely extracted from *Izvestiia*, 1931-33. Some 1927 articles are conspicuously absent from the 1934 edition, particularly the article on Trotsky.

A70 RAYMOND, ELLSWORTH L. "Soviet Preparation for Total War, 1925-1951." Ph.D. dissertation, University of Michigan, 1952. A history of Soviet civilian and economic preparations for war by a professor of economics at N.Y.U. Based on Soviet sources, especially laws and statistics.

A71 RUBINSTEIN, ALVIN Z. ed. and comp. *The Foreign Policy of the Soviet Union.* N.Y.: Random House, 1960. 457 p. A useful collection of documents and analytical articles by a Soviet specialist at the U. of Pennsylvania. Particular emphasis on Soviet policies toward underdeveloped countries. Designed for use as a textbook. [B]

A72 RUSSIA (1923- USSR), NARODNYI KOMISSARIAT PO INOSTRANNYM DELAM. *Antisovetskie podlogi; istoriia falshivok, faksimile i kommentarii.* Moscow: Litizdat, NKID, 1926. 170 p. English ed., *Anti-Soviet Forgeries; A Record of Some of the Forged Documents Used at Various Times Against the Soviet Government.* London: Workers' Publishers, 1927. 141 p. French ed., Paris: 1926. German ed., Berlin: 1926. A collection of documents, pictures, and other materials, providing interesting information about certain professional forgers and their activities.

A73 RUSSIA (1923- USSR), NARODNYI KOMISSARIAT PO INOSTRANNYM DELAM. *Desiat let sovetskoi diplomatii; (akty i dokumenty).* Moscow: NKID, 1927. 124 p. Most of the book is devoted to three essays, one a historical sketch of Narkomindel, the second an account of the development of diplomatic relations with other countries, and the third a treatment of the contacts between the USSR and the League of Nations. About one-third of the book is excerpts from the more important treaties and diplomatic notes.

A74 SAYERS, MICHAEL, and KAHN, ALBERT E. *The Great Conspiracy; the Secret War against Soviet Russia.* Boston: Little, Brown, 1946. 433 p. Russian ed., Moscow: 1945. Spanish ed., Havana: Paginas, 1946. 130 p. German ed., 1949. Dutch ed., Republiek der Letteren, 1946. 480 p. Yiddish ed., N.Y.: 1946. 463 p. French ed., Paris: Ediciones Nuestro Pueblo, 1948. 383 p. A view of international relations since 1917 as a permanent dastardly plot versus the Soviet Union, with the melodramatic spies, saboteurs, and traitors familiar from the Soviet purge trials. All virtue is Soviet, all wickedness is anti-Soviet. The sensational and uncritical approach smothers the occasional grain of truth in the narrative.

A75 SCHAPIRO, LEONARD. *The Communist Party of the Soviet Union.* N.Y.: Random House, 1960. 648 p. An objective, detailed, and clear history based on thorough research in Soviet and other sources available in Western Europe and the U.S., by a member of the faculty of the London School of Economics. Emphasizes the roles played by Lenin and Stalin. The best history of Soviet Communist Party available and indispensable for an understanding of Soviet foreign policy. Valuable notes and bibliography; excellent index. [A]

A76 SCHUMAN, FREDERICK L. *Russia Since 1917; Four Decades of Soviet Politics.* N.Y.: Knopf, 1957. 508 p. A lively account of Soviet political history and policy by a Professor of Government at Williams College. Though somewhat more critical of Soviet domestic actions and foreign policy than his earlier volumes, it is still in some sections an apologia for the Soviet regime.

A77 SCHUMAN, FREDERICK L. *Soviet Politics, at Home and Abroad.* N.Y.: Knopf, 1946. 663 p. Japanese ed., Tokyo: Iwanami Shoten, 1956. A favorable appraisal of Soviet history and domestic and foreign policy "frankly designed to foster unity through a fuller understanding of the USSR." Emphasizes the relation between internal and external policy and the impact of world politics. Sees the Soviet government as a dictatorship but at the same time argues that it is a new and higher form of democratic government. Justifies Soviet policy in Eastern Europe at the end of the Second World War and generally gives the USSR the benefit of the doubt.

A78 SHUMELDA, IA. *Vid Marksa do Malenkova.* Paris: Éditions de la Première imprimerie Ukrainienne en France, 1955. 223 p. A cursory review of Communist history since Marx by an anti-Soviet Ukrainian resident in Paris.

A79 SLESSINGER, SEYMOUR. "The Idea of Nationalism in Soviet Foreign Policy." Ph.D. dissertation, Boston University, 1960. A study of Soviet use of nationalism at home and abroad for both defensive and offensive purposes, from 1917 to the present.

A80 SOCOLINE, VLADIMIR. *Ciel et terre soviëtiques.* Neuchâtel, Switz.: La Baconniere, 1949. 275 p. Memoirs of a former Soviet diplomat. Much of the book deals with the domestic scene, but there are accounts of his activities in various European countries in the 1920's and 1930's.

A81 SOLOVEYTCHIK, GEORGE. *Russia in Perspective.* N.Y.: Norton, 1947. 244 p. An attempt to explain the historical, geographic and economic elements in Soviet foreign policy.

A82 *Sovetskii soiuz v borbe za mir; sobranie dokumentov i vstupitelnaia statia.* Moscow-Leningrad: Gosizdat, 1929. 344 p. Includes a great variety of diplomatic notes, governmental decrees, Party resolutions, treaties, etc., from the period 1917-29, classified under these headings: (1) struggle for peace during the October Revolution, (2) Soviet Russia and international conferences, 1921-22, (3) disarmament, (4) nonaggression pacts, and (5) the Kellogg Pact.

A83 *Survey of International Affairs.* Ed. by Arnold J. Toynbee and others. Pub. under the auspices of the British Institute of International Affairs. London and N.Y.: Oxford Univ. Press, 1925—. These annual volumes, compiled with scholarly care, frequently have large sections on Soviet foreign relations. [A]

A84 TANIN, M. *Desiat let vneshnei politiki SSSR, 1917-1927.* Moscow: Gosizdat, 1927. 259 p. An interesting reflection of Soviet scholarship before the Stalinist dictatorship was firmly established. The author considers the English government the principal threat to Soviet security. Has a 23-page chronology of the period.

A85 TANIN, M. *Mezhdunarodnaia politika SSSR (1917-1924)*. Moscow: Izd. "Rabotnik Prosveshcheniia," 1925. 107 p. A survey organized on a country-by-country basis.

A86 TARACOUZIO, TIMOTHY A. *Soviets in the Arctic; An Historical, Economic and Political Study of the Soviet Advance into the Arctic*. N.Y.: Macmillan, 1938. 565 p. A scholarly, judicious, almost encyclopedic study of Soviet actions in the Arctic by a then member of the Harvard Bureau of International Research. Based on study of Soviet legislation and regulations, Russian and Soviet scholarship, and information from Soviet technical publications. In conclusion, urged an international conference and agreement concerning problems of sovereignty and jurisdiction in the Arctic. Excellent bibliography, six maps, fine index.

A87 TARACOUZIO, TIMOTHY A. *War and Peace in Soviet Diplomacy*. N.Y.: Macmillan, 1940. 354 p. A careful, well-documented study of Soviet foreign policy in the light of the fundamental principles of Marxism concerning war and peace. Based on a study of Soviet writings on theory and an analysis of Soviet practice. Neglects domestic policies and their effect. Good bibliography and an index of Soviet treaties, agreements, and conventions in force in 1940. [A]

A88 TIKHOMIROV, MIKHAIL N. *Vneshniaia politika Sovetskogo Soiuza*. Moscow: Gospolitizdat, 1940. 105 p. A popular survey of Soviet foreign policy by a distinguished Soviet medievalist.

A89 TROIANOVSKII, A. and SHTEIN, B. *Istoriia vneshnei politiki SSSR*. Moscow-Leningrad: Voenmorizdat, 1945. 288 p.

A90 TROTSKII, LEV. *My Life*. N.Y.: Scribner, 1930. 613 p. A full-length autobiography, over half devoted to the pre-1918 period. The rest is largely concerned with his struggles during the Soviet period and with bitter polemics against his opponents, but there is a chapter on the Brest-Litovsk negotiations and also a number of comments on the Communist International.

A91 U.S. INFORMATION AGENCY. *A Report on Communist Colonialism and International Communism*. Washington: U.S. Information Agency, Press Service, 1956. 2 vols. A collection of articles designed to aid U.S. Public Affairs Officers overseas. Surveys the historical growth and capabilities of Communism: Part I covers 40 countries and areas in the Far East, Middle East, and Africa; Part II covers Eastern and Western Europe and Latin America.

A92 U.S. LIBRARY OF CONGRESS, LEGISLATIVE REFERENCE SERVICE. *Trends in Russian Foreign Policy since World War I; A Chronology of Events from March 15, 1917 to January 1, 1947.*

Washington: G.P.O., 1947. 68 p. Divides 1917-46 into six periods, with each section preceded by a brief summary and with a sixteen page essay in conclusion.

A93 VINOGRADOV, BORIS M. *Mirovoi proletariat i SSSR.* Volume 5 of E. Pashukanis and M. Spektator, eds., *Desiat let kapitalisticheskogo okruzheniia SSSR.* Moscow: Izd. Kommunisticheskoi akademii, 1928. 227 p. A survey of the first decade of relations between the USSR and (a) the "capitalist" encirclement and (b) the proletarian movement in Europe and North America. Not Stalinist in character. (See entry A48 above.)

A94 WAGNER, WOLFGANG. *Die Teilung Europas; Geschichte der sowjetischen Expansion bis zur Spaltung Deutschlands, 1918-1945.* Stuttgart: Deutsche Verlagsanstalt, 1959. 242 p. English ed., *The Partitioning of Europe; a History of the Soviet Expansion up to the Cleavage of Germany, 1918-1945.* Stuttgart: 1959. Views the division of Germany as a function of the division of Europe. Based on extensive study of documentary sources.

A95 WOLFE, HENRY C. *The Imperial Soviets.* N.Y.: Doubleday, Doran, 1940. 294 p. An historical survey of Soviet foreign affairs, with emphasis on German-Soviet relations. Includes chapters on the Rapallo agreement, Russia and the League of Nations, disarmament, and the 1939 pact with Hitler. The author did not regard the pact with Nazi Germany as an indication of a basic shift in Communist ideology, but as proof that Stalin was a skilled *Realpolitiker*, who would shrink from no step that would advance the USSR along the path to world domination.

A96 YAKHONTOFF, VICTOR A. *USSR Foreign Policy.* N.Y.: Coward-McCann, 1945. 311 p. A popular, strongly pro-Soviet survey by a former Tsarist general who turned to support of the Stalinist system and goals. Based on lectures given at the New School for Social Research in 1945.

B. Soviet Foreign Relations, 1917-1921

1. GENERAL WORKS

(Edited by John M. Thompson)

B1 AKADEMIIA NAUK SSSR, INSTITUT ISTORII. *Sovetskaia Rossiia i kapitalisticheskii mir v 1917-23 gg.* Ed. by Isaak I. Mints. Moscow: Gos. izd-vo polit. lit-ry, 1957. 694 p. Examines the effect of the Great October Socialist Revolution on the capitalist world, 1917-23. Deals especially with events in Germany, Britain, Austria, Hungary, Italy, Bulgaria, and Czechoslovakia. The noted Soviet authors do not use primary sources when discussing non-Slavic countries. [A]

B2 *Boevoe sodruzhestvo trudiashchikhtsia zarubezhnikh stran s narodami sovetskoi Rossii (1917-1922).* Ed. by G. V. Shumeiko. Moscow: "Sovetskaia Rossiia," 1957. 574 p. 502 declarations by foreign Communist groups situated in Russia in support of the Bolsheviks during the Civil War. Casts some light on the role of various foreign prisoner-of-war units in the period of greatest confusion. Volume I of *Iz istorii mezhdunarodnoi proletarskoi solidarnosti.* (See A40.)

B3 CHICHERIN, GEORGII. *Two Years of Foreign Policy; The Relations of the R.S.F.S.R. with Foreign Nations, from November 7, 1917 to November 7, 1919.* N.Y.: Russian Soviet Government Bureau, 1920. 36 p. A collection of four articles by the Soviet Commissar for Foreign Affairs; originally appearing in *Izvestiia*, they review generally early Soviet policy. Though written to defend the Soviet position, they are franker and less distorted than subsequent Soviet accounts of this period. Included are several interesting personal observations by Chicherin. [A]

B4 DEBORIN, G. A. *Sovetskaia vneshniaia politika v pervye gody sushchestvovaniia Sovetskogo gosudarstva, 1917-1920 gg.* Moscow: Pravda, 1951. 31 p. German ed., Berlin, 1953. A popular lecture, distorted and shallow. Part of an anti-American campaign aimed at the Soviet public, it attempts to show the rapacity and villainy of American "imperialism" in the early years as a lesson for the 1950's. Especially vitriolic and fantastic, perhaps in part because historian Deborin was attacked in 1949 as insufficiently anti-American.

B5 DEUTSCHER, ISAAC. *The Prophet Armed; Trotsky, 1879-1921.* N.Y. and London: Oxford, 1954. 540 p. The last quarter of this brilliant and sympathetic study of Trotsky's early career, by a prominent British specialist on Russia, deals with Trotsky as Commissar of Foreign Affairs, then of War, during 1918-21. Includes a vivid account of

Trotsky's role at the Brest-Litovsk peace negotiations and the challenging conclusion that Trotsky finally accepted a separate peace to avoid an open split with Lenin. [B]

B6 DURDENEVSKII, VSEVOLOD, and BERTSINSKII, S., comps. *Opyt bibliografii obshchestvennykh nauk za revoliutsionnoe trekhletie (1918-1920).* Moscow-Leningrad: Gosizdat, 1925. 270 p. Lists thousands of books and pamphlets, unannotated, under such headings as trade, international law, foreign policy, the nationalities question, revolutionary Marxism, history of the Russian revolution, and many others.

B6A EPSTEIN, FRITZ T. "Studien zur Geschichte der 'Russischen Frage' auf der Pariser Friedenskonferenz von 1919," *Jahrbücher für Geschichte Osteuropas*, N.F., vol. 7, 1959, p. 431-78. Deals with the Russian Political Delegation, the nationalities of Russia at the Peace Conference, the attitude of the U.S. toward the aspirations for independence of the nationalities of Russia, and Russia and the League of Nations, 1919-21.

B6B EPSTEIN, FRITZ T. "Zur Interpretation des Versailler Vertrags. Der von Polen 1919-1922 erhobene Reparationsanspruch," *Jahrbücher für Geschichte Osteuropas*, N.F., vol. 5, 1957, p. 315-35. Discusses the origins and the significance of Section 14 (Russia and Russian states), Art. 116 and 117, of the Treaty of Versailles, the invalidation of Art. 116 by the Treaty of Rapallo, and the interpretation of the Article by the Reparations Commission (on the basis of its documentation).

B7 GOURE, LEON. "Soviet Foreign Policy and the March 1921 Crisis." Certificate essay, Russian Institute, Columbia, 1949. 125 p.

B8 GUKOVSKII, A. I. *Antanta i oktiabrskaia revoliutsiia (populiarnyi ocherk).* Moscow: Gos. sots.-ekon. izd., 1931. 157 p. A brief popular study of Western-Russian relations from the March Revolution to the summer of 1918, by an early Soviet historian of the Revolution and Intervention. Embodies a definite point of view, but is less biased than subsequent Soviet accounts. [B]

B9 HOHLFELD, ANDREAS. *Die besiegten Sieger; Marschall Foch und Winston Churchill im Kampf gegen den Bolschewismus 1918/1919.* Hamburg: Hanseatische Verlagsanstalt, 1943. 130 p. A Nazi-inspired work, whose thesis is that the "pro-Bolshevik Jews" behind President Wilson conspired to defeat the British-French intervention. "Our Leader Adolf Hitler" has been summoned by fate to finish the task of destroying Bolshevism, a task before which the Allies faltered, because they were unable "to overcome their hate for Germany and their fear for the German will-to-life."

B9A HÖLZLE, ERWIN. *Der Osten im ersten Weltkrieg.* Leipzig: Köhler and Amelang, 1944. A study of Eastern problems in diplomacy during and immediately after the First World War, by a German scholar. Stresses the Bolshevik threat to Europe. Some parts of the book are useful since the author uses unpublished French documents captured by the Germans during World War II.

B10 IVASHIN, I. F. *Mezhdunarodnye otnosheniia v period provedeniia Velikoi oktiabrskoi sotsialisticheskoi revoliutsii. Vneshniaia politika Sovetskogo gosudarstva v gody inostrannoi voennoi interventsii i grazhdanskoi voiny.* Moscow: Vysshaia partiinaia shkola pri TsK KPSS, 1955. 71 p. A brief outline of the international situation and Soviet policy in the early years by a Communist specialist in international relations. Strongly "anti-imperialist" and anti-American.

B11 MAIOROV, S. M. *Borba Sovetskoi Rossii za vykhod iz imperialisticheskoi voiny.* Moscow: Gospolitizdat, 1959. 295 p. A documented study, by a Soviet historian, of Bolshevik peace-making with the Central Powers during November, 1917-March, 1918. Dedicated to showing that Soviet foreign policy was "peace-loving" and in support of "proletarian internationalism" from earliest days. "Anti-imperialist" and anti-Trotsky, it contains a few interesting archival references.

B12 MAISKII, IVAN. *Vneshniaia politika RSFSR, 1917-1922.* Moscow: "Krasnaia Nov," 1922. 195 p. A brief review of Soviet policy, beginning with the Brest-Litovsk peace negotiations, by an early Soviet diplomat. Stresses Allied "imperialism" and claims the chief Entente objective was economic exploitation of Russia; nevertheless, less critical of the West, especially the U.S., than subsequent Soviet accounts. [A]

B13 MATHIS, WILLIE J. "The Problem of Russian Representation and Recognition at the Paris Peace Conference, 1919." Ph.D. dissertation, U. of North Carolina, 1947.

B14 MILIUKOV, PAVEL N. *Bolshevism; an International Danger.* London: Allen & Unwin, 1920. A polemic on the threat of Bolshevism in Russia and to Europe by a leading Russian liberal and Foreign Minister in the first cabinet of the Provisional Government. Emotional and propagandistic, but contains some interesting material gathered from sources in Russia.

B15 NANSEN, FRIDTJOF. *Russia and Peace.* N.Y.: Macmillan, 1924. 162 p. A general, popular account of economic conditions in Russia during the early NEP. Based on experiences of the author, a famous Norwegian explorer active in famine relief in Russia; pleads for restoration of economic and trade relations between Europe and Russia and for drawing Russia into European comity of nations.

B16 POKROVSKII, M. N. *Oktiabrskaia revoliutsiia i Antanta.* Moscow-Leningrad: Gosizdat, 1927. A popular outline by a leading Soviet historian of the 1920's, who was attacked and vilified in the 1930's. Claims Allied policy toward Russia up to the Armistice was determined by anti-German considerations and a desire to re-establish the Eastern Front with, or in spite of, the Bolsheviks. Discusses tentative and unofficial Allied offers of aid to Lenin prior to the Brest treaty. [B]

B17 PRIEST, LYMAN W. "The Cordon Sanitaire, 1918-1922." Ph.D. dissertation, Stanford Univ., 1954.

B18 *Proletarskaia solidarnost trudiashchikhtsia v borbe za mir (1917-1924).* Ed. by N. V. Matkovskii. Moscow: "Sovetskaia Rossiia," 1958. 560 p. Declarations by Communists outside Russia in support of the Bolshevik Revolution. Volume II of *Iz istorii mezhdunarodnoi proletarskoi solidarnosti.*

B19 RADEK, KARL. *Vneshniaia politika Sovetskoi Rossii.* Moscow: Gosizdat, 1923. 111 p. German ed., Hamburg, 1921. A collection of four popular articles by a prominent Bolshevik and leader in the international Communist movement. Written in 1918, 1919, 1921, and 1922, they present the Soviet point of view on, respectively, German intervention, Allied intervention, re-establishment of Soviet-Western relations, and the Genoa and Hague Conferences. Polemical but some interesting interpretations. [B]

B20 RUBINSTEIN, NIKOLAI L. *Sovetskaia Rossiia i kapitalisticheskie gosudarstva v gody perekhoda ot voiny k miru, 1921-1922 gg.* Moscow: Gos. izd. polit. lit., 1948. 461 p. Detailed treatment by a Soviet historian of Soviet-Western relations from early 1921 through the Hague Conference in 1922, with half the book devoted to the Genoa Conference. Stresses Soviet successes, recognition, and respectability, as well as early "peaceful coexistence." Based on Western and Soviet sources, including Soviet archives concerning famine relief operations.

B21 RUSSIA (1917-RSFSR), NARODNYI KOMISSARIAT PO INOSTRANNYM DELAM. *Correspondance diplomatique se rapportant aux relations entre la Rêpublique russe et les puissances de l'Entente, 1918.* Moscow: NKID, 1919. 51 p. A collection of notes exchanged between Soviet Russia and the Allies pertaining to war, Bolshevik repudiation of debts, nationals detained or imprisoned by both sides, position of Allied embassies, and Intervention. Designed to show Entente culpability in the Civil War and Intervention.

B22 RUSSIA (1917-RSFSR), NARODNYI KOMISSARIAT PO INOSTRANNYM DELAM. *Godovoi otchet NKID k VIII Sezdu sovetov; (1919-1920).* Moscow: NKID, 1921. 75 p. Annual report of the Commissariat for Foreign Affairs to the Congress of Soviets.

B23 RUSSIA (1917-RSFSR), NARODNYI KOMISSARIAT PO INOSTRANNYM DELAM. *Godovoi otchet Narodnogo komissariata inostrannykh del k IX Sezdu sovetov; (1920-1921).* Moscow: NKID, 1921. 74 p.

B24 RUSSIA (1917-RSFSR), NARODNYI KOMISSARIAT PO INOSTRANNYM DELAM. *Otchet Narodnogo komissariata po inostrannym delam sedmomu Sezdu sovetov; (noiabr 1918-dekabr 1919 g.).* Moscow: Gosizdat, 1919. 27 p. Annual report of the Commissariat for Foreign Affairs to the Congress of Soviets. A general survey and apologia.

B26 STEIN, BORIS E. *"Russkii vopros" na parizhskoi mirnoi konferentsii, 1919-1920 gg.* Moscow: Gospolitizdat, 1949. 462 p. German ed., Leipzig, 1953. A distorted, anti-American account of the handling of the Russian problem at the Paris Peace Conference in 1919. Though a former Soviet diplomat and specialist in modern diplomatic history, Stein wrote at the height of anti-Americanism in Soviet historiography, and argues unconvincingly that Intervention was a gigantic plot masterminded by American "imperialists."

B27 STEIN, BORIS E. *"Russkii vopros" v 1920-1921 gg.* Moscow: Gospolitizdat, 1958. Sequel to the work above. The first of two projected volumes analyzing Soviet-Western relations from January 1920, to the Genoa Conference, May 1922. Covers the period up to March 1921, from a strongly "anti-imperialist" point of view.

B28 SULTAN-ZADE, AVETIS S. *Krizis mirovogo khoziaistva i novaia voennaia groza.* Moscow: Gosizdat, 1921. 150 p. An Iranian Communist and prominent figure in the Comintern (who was also known as "Pishevari") takes a look at the world economic crisis and the threat of a new war.

B29 TANIN, M. *Mezhdunarodnaia politika SSSR, (1917-1924).* Moscow: Izd. "Rabotnik prosveshcheniia," 1924. 107 p. A popular outline of Soviet policy in the first years by an early Bolshevik historian of international relations.

B30 THOMPSON, JOHN M. "The Russian Problem at the Paris Peace Conference, 1919." Ph.D. dissertation, Columbia, 1960. A scholarly study of Western policy toward Russia from the Armistice to the Versailles Treaty. Focuses on relations among Allies, Bolsheviks, and Whites. Based in part on the archive of Maklakov, leader of the Russian Political Conference in Paris. Emphasizes the issue of Intervention; does not treat boundary and minority questions. To be published soon.

B30A TRUSH, M. I. *Vneshepoliticheskaia deiatelnost V.I. Lenina 1917-1920 den za dnem.* Moscow: 1963.

B31 VAKS, B. *Ot Oktiabria do Genui; mezhdunarodnye otnosheniia RSFSR; spravochnik.* Moscow: NKID, 1922. 130 p.

B32 VELTMAN, MIKHAIL (Mikhail Pavlovich, pseud.). *The Foundations of Imperialist Policy; A Course of Lectures Read to the Academy of the General Staff in 1918-1919 by Michael Pavlovitch.* London: Labour Pub. Co., 1922. 159 p. Russian ed.: Moscow: Gosizdat, 1923. 96 p. Lectures by a prominent Communist writer, propagandist, and specialist on Asian affairs during the early period of the Bolshevik regime.

B33 VYGODSKII, S. IU. *V. I. Lenin—rukovoditel vneshnei politiki sovetskogo gosudarstva 1917-1923.* Leningrad: 1960.

B34 WARTH, ROBERT D. *The Allies and the Russian Revolution; from the Fall of the Monarchy to the Peace of Brest-Litovsk.* Durham, N.C.: Duke Univ., 1954. 294 p. A scholarly, well-documented study of Western-Russian relations by an American historian. Covers the period from March 1917, to March 1918. Critical of Allied policy. Useful annotated bibliography. [A]

B35 ZITELMANN, FRANZ C. *Russland im Friedensvertrag von Versailles (Artikel 116, 117, 292, 293, 433 des Friedensvertrags).* Berlin: F. Vahlen, 1920. 125 p. The author, who in 1919 was advisor for Russian political affairs in the Berlin Foreign Office, comments extensively on selected articles of the Versailles Treaty. He does so in scholarly fashion, giving background, legislative intent, and implications of the articles, as well as discussing their internal inconsistency or incompatibility with existing international law. The appendix contains interesting documents pertaining to Allied demands for German evacuation of the Baltic States.

2. INTERVENTION AND CIVIL WAR IN RUSSIA

NOTE: The emphasis in this section is on Intervention, which may properly be considered *foreign* affairs, rather than on the Civil War, which was primarily domestic affairs. The two were intimately intermingled, however, and many books listed here deal with both topics.

For books about Intervention and Civil War in the Baltic area, see the sections on Finland and on the Baltic states.

a. GENERAL WORKS

(Edited by John M. Thompson and Leonid Strakhovsky)

B36 AKADEMIIA NAUK SSSR, FUNDAMENTALNAIA BIBLIOTEKA OBSHCHESTVENNYKH NAUK. *Velikaia oktiabrskaia sotsialisticheskaia revoliutsiia; borba za vlast sovetov v period inostran-*

noi voennoi interventsii i grazhdanskoi voiny; ukazatel literatury 1957-1958 gg. Ed. by A. E. Ioffe. Comp. by A. N. Baikova and others. Moscow: 1959. 4 vols. in 2.

B37 ALEKSEEV, S. A., comp. *Nachalo grazhdanskoi voiny.* Moscow: Gosizdat, 1926. 476 p. Excerpts from previously published memoirs of White leaders, including Denikin, Sakharov, Leit, Guins, and Budberg. Vol. III in the series, *Revoliutsiia i grazhdanskaia voina v opisaniiakh belogvardeitsev* (see below).

B38 ALEKSEEV, S. A., comp. *Revoliutsiia i grazhdanskaia voina v opisaniiakh belogvardeitsev.* Moscow: 1926-30. 5 vols. A compilation of the memoirs of leading military and political figures. Includes selections from accounts by Denikin, Wrangel, Lukomskii, and Krasnov among the Whites and materials on such anti-White movements as the "Greens" and Makhno, and events in the Ukraine.

B39 ANTONOV-OVSEENKO, V. A. *Zapiski o grazhdanskoi voine.* Moscow-Leningrad: Gos. voenn. izdat., 1924-33. 4 vols. A very valuable and fairly accurate account of the activities of the Red Army, principally in the South and on the Volga, by one of the outstanding Red commanders. Deals extensively with the organization, tactics and strategy of the Red forces. [B]

B40 *Bielyi arkhiv.* Ed. by Ia. M. Lisovoi. Paris: 1926-28. 3 vols. in 2. A compilation of articles and documents on the history of the White movement. The most valuable materials are transcripts of conferences, correspondence between major White leaders, participants' accounts, and reports from agents in major points such as Kiev. [B]

B41 BUNYAN, JAMES T., comp. *Intervention, Civil War, and Communism in Russia, April-December 1918; Documents and Materials.* Baltimore: Johns Hopkins, 1936. 594 p. A compilation of documents and texts, mostly from Soviet sources. Useful as a guide to further study of the subject. [A]

B42 CHAMBERLIN, WILLIAM HENRY. *The Russian Revolution, 1917-1921.* N.Y.: Macmillan, 1935. 2 vols. Republished in 1952. Based on extensive research in Soviet archives and libraries, this book remains a very useful study on the Russian Civil War. By an American who was a correspondent in Russia in the 1920's and 1930's. Highly readable and generally objective, this is Chamberlin's best book. [A]

B43 COATES, WILLIAM P. and ZELDA K. *Armed Intervention in Russia, 1918-1922.* London: Gollancz, 1935. 400 p. A historical monograph, openly pro-Soviet. Very critical of the policy of intervention and extremely unfair toward the anti-Bolshevik forces. However, it is useful because it contains documentation not available elsewhere, principally from British socialist sources. [B]

B44 DENIKIN, A. I. (GENERAL). *Ocherki russkoi smuty.* Paris: J. Povolozky; Berlin: Russkoe natsionalnoe knigoizdatelstvo, 1921-26. 5 vols. Abbreviated English eds., *The Russian Turmoil.* London: Hutchinson, 1922. *The White Army.* London: Cape, 1930. The most valuable and complete memoirs of any White leader, this is a detailed account and analysis from the beginning of World War I to April 1920, by the former Chief of Staff of the Imperial Russian Army and the successor to Kornilov as commander of the Volunteer Army in South Russia. As the leading figure in the anti-Bolshevik struggle in the South and the major recipient of Allied aid, Denikin was able to provide in his memoirs invaluable history and numerous documents. [A]

B45 DEUTSCHER, ISAAC. *The Prophet Armed; Trotsky, 1879-1921.* N.Y. and London: Oxford, 1954. 540 p. The first volume of a brilliant biography by a former Polish Communist. Deutscher is sympathetic toward his subject, but not uncritical. Based on extensive research, including use of the Trotsky archives at Harvard. Several chapters discuss Trotsky's role in the Civil War. [A]

B46 DIOGOT, VLADIMIR A. *Pod znamenem bolshevizma; zapiski podpolshchika.* 3rd ed. Moscow: Izd. Vsesoiuz. o-va. politkat. i ss.-pos., 1933. 416 p. Memoirs of a Bolshevik undercover agent in Siberia and in the South. Useful as a human document.

B47 DWINGER, EDWIN ERICH. *Zwischen Weiss und Rot; die russische Tragödie, 1919-1920.* Jena: Diederichs, 1930. 503 p. English ed., *Between Red and White.* N.Y.: Scribner, 1932. 492 p. A highly colored account of the experiences of a German war prisoner who took part in the fighting against the Bolsheviks in 1919 and in the retreat of the Kolchak army.

B48 GOLOVIN, NIKOLAI N. (GENERAL). *Rossiiskaia kontrrevoliutsiia v 1917-1918 gg.* Paris: Biblioteka "Illiustrirovannoi Rossii," 1937. Tallin: Libris, 1937. 5 vols. A detailed and critical review of events in the development of the anti-Bolshevik movement by a well-known military historian, formerly a professor at the Academy of the General Staff. Based on primary sources, printed materials, and the author's experiences in Russia and with a mission in Paris. Gives a general picture of the different attempts of the various groups to organize opposition to the Bolsheviks. Contains valuable information and documents on German intervention, the origins of Allied intervention, and the forces aided by the Allies.

B49 GOLUBEV, ALEKSANDR V. *Grazhdanskaia voina.* Moscow:

Molodaia Gvardiia, 1932. 221 p. A short history of the Russian Civil War and the counter-revolution of 1918-20.

B50 GORDON, ALBAN G. *Russian Civil War.* London: Cassell, 1937. 280 p. A general study, based on published material as well as on personal reminiscences, by a British journalist, dealing mainly with the Civil War in the South.

B51 GUKOVSKII, A. I. *Antanta i oktiabrskaia revoliutsiia (populiarnyi ocherk).* Moscow: Gos. sots.-ekon. izd., 1931. 157 p. A popular account of the Allied intervention in Russia within the context of the Civil War.

B52 GUSEV, S. I. (pseud. of Iakov D. Drabkin.) *Grazhdanskaia voina i krasnaia armiia (sbornik statei).* Moscow: Voennoe izd., 1958. 220 p. A posthumous collection of articles, written over a period of years and dealing mostly with the political organization of the Red Army. The author was a political commissar on the Eastern front against the armies of Kolchak and was eventually chief of the Political Administration of the Red Army.

B53 HILL, GEORGE A. *Dreaded Hour.* Toronto: McClelland, 1936. 280 p. An account of the experiences of an Allied agent during the Civil War; includes interesting sidelights on Allied and White Russian policies.

B54 IOFFE, IAKOV A. *Organizatsiia interventsii i blokady Sovetskoi respubliki, 1918-1920.* Moscow-Leningrad: Gosizdat, 1930. 166 p. A bold but disorganized and largely unsuccessful attempt by an early Soviet historian to show that the most important weapon of the Allied intervention was economic isolation and total blockade of Soviet Russia. An interesting though not wholly supportable thesis, with some useful interpretations.

B55 *Istoriia grazhdanskoi voiny v SSSR.* Ed. by Maksim Gorkii and others. Moscow: Gospolitizdat, 1938–. (5 vols. through 1960.) English ed., *The History of the Civil War in the USSR.* Moscow: Cooperative Publishing Society of Foreign Workers in the USSR, and Foreign Languages Publishing House; N.Y.: International Pub.; London: Lawrence and Wishart, 1938-47. Vols. I and II only. The official history of the Civil War from the Soviet point of view. Valuable not as a factual account, but as an expression of Soviet opinion. [A]

B56 *Iz istorii borby sovetskogo naroda protiv inostrannoi voennoi interventsii i vnutrennei kontrrevoliutsii v 1918 g.; sbornik statei.* Ed. by S. F. Naida and others. Moscow: Gospolitizdat, 1956. 573 p. A collection of twelve articles under the editorship of a prominent Soviet propagandist-historian of the Intervention and Civil War. Over half the articles deal with the Civil War, Bolshevik mobilization, and build-up of the Red Army. Articles on the Intervention are uneven and generally follow an "anti-imperialist," patriotic line.

B57 KAKURIN, N. *Kak srazhalas revoliutsiia?* Moscow: Gosizdat, 1925-26. 2 vols. A textbook on the Civil War for officers of the Red Army by a former Red commander. Valuable as a source of information on military events. [B]

B58 KERZHENTZEV, PLATON M. *Les Alliés et la Russie*. Moscow: Édition du Groupe communiste français, 1919. 154 p. Paris: Bibliothèque communiste, 1920. 127 p. A violent attack on the policy of Intervention by a prominent Bolshevik. Published as anti-interventionist propaganda in France and among French troops in Russia.

B59 KRASTIN, IA., and others. *Amerikano-angliiskaia interventsiia v Pribaltike v 1918-1920 godakh.* Talinn: Estgosizdat, 1954. 127 p.

B60 KUNINA, A. E. *Proval amerikanskikh planov zavoevaniia mirovogo gospodstva v 1917-1920 gg.* Moscow: Gospolitizdat, 1951. 235 p. 2nd ed., Moscow: Gospolitizdat, 1954. 318 p. German ed., Berlin: Dietz, 1953. 240 p. An openly anti-American tract, the premises of which are in direct contradiction with the documented monographs of Strakhovsky: *The Origins of American Intervention in North Russia, 1918; Intervention at Archangel; and American Opinion about Russia.* It is interesting as a manifestation of anti-American propaganda after the end of the last war.

B61 KUZMIN, G. V. *Grazhdanskaia voina i voennaia interventsiia v SSSR: voenno-politicheskii ocherk.* Moscow: Voennoe izd., 1958. 359 p. A popular Soviet account of events from the Austrian-German intervention in 1918 to the defeat of Wrangel and the Poles in 1920. Heavy emphasis on patriotic, "anti-imperialist," "anti-war" themes, and on collective leadership of Lenin's party in achieving victory. Maps included. A typical example of re-writing the history of Intervention according to the new policy of placing the major blame on the U.S., instead of on Britain, as previously.

B62 KUZMIN, NIKOLAI F. *Krushenie poslednego pokhoda Antanty.* Moscow: Gospolitizdat, 1958. 343 p.

B63 LAMPE, A. A. VON, ed. *Bieloe dielo; lietopis bieloi borby.* Berlin: Russkoe natsionalnoe knigoizdatelstvo "Miednyi vsadnik," 1926-1933. 7 vols. An extensive collection of articles by participants in the White movement and documents relating the character and organization of anti-Bolshevik forces from 1917 through 1920. The most notable contributions include memoir articles by Gen. P. Shatilov, Gen. P. N. Wrangel, the Kuban Ataman A. P. Filimonov, and the political leader V. V. Shulgin. [B]

B64 LENIN, VLADIMIR I. *Lenin ob interventsii (materialy dlia dokladchikov).* Moscow-Leningrad: Ogiz "Moskovskii rabochii," 1931. 230 p. Excerpts from Lenin's writings and speeches for use by lecturers and propagandists about Intervention. Omits, however, Lenin's famous article in *Pravda*, "About Itching," in which he advocated accepting help from the Allies to combat Germany.

B65 LENIN, VLADIMIR I. *V. I. Lenin ob inostrannoi voennoi interventsii i grazhdanskoi voine v SSSR (1918-1920 gg.).* Moscow: Gospolitizdat, 1956. 247 p. Similar to the previous title.

B66 LEVIDOV, MIKHAIL IU. *K istorii soiuznoi interventsii v Rossii.* Vol. I, *Diplomaticheskaia podgotovka.* Leningrad: "Priboi," 1925. 181 p. The first volume of a planned but uncompleted three-volume history of the Intervention by a Soviet writer. Covers the period from August 1917 to August 1918, emphasizing political-diplomatic aspects. Substantial though incomplete coverage of Western published sources—official documents, newspapers, and memoirs. The first Soviet historian to date Intervention from the Kornilov affair and to reject fully the Allied claim of desiring re-establishment of an Eastern Front.

B67 MARGULIES, MANUIL S. *God interventsii.* Berlin: Izd. Z. I. Grzhebina, 1923. 3 vols. The memoirs of a left-wing liberal, critical of the policy of the Allies. Vol. I covers the period from Sept. 1918 to April 1919; vol. II, April-Sept. 1919; vol. III, Sept. 1919 to Dec. 1920. First published in *Letopis Revoliutsii*, No. 11. [B]

B68 MARKOV, SERGI V. *Armee ohne Heimat.* Vienna: Höger, 1934. 344 p. An account of the Civil War campaigns of Denikin, Kolchak, Wrangel, and Yudenich.

B69 MILIUKOV, PAVEL N. *Rossiia na perelomie.* Paris: La Source, 1927. 2 vols. A study of the Russian Revolution, Civil War and Intervention by the well-known leader of the Constitutional-Democratic Party, based on published materials and on his reminiscences. Interesting and valuable as a personal expression of views. [B]

B69A MILIUKOV, PAVEL N. *Russia Today and Tomorrow.* N.Y.: Macmillan Co., 1922. 296 p. A very good analysis of the Revolution and the development of the anti-Bolshevik movement in Russia. The author, historian and former Minister of Foreign Affairs in the Provisional Government, participated in the organization of the Volunteer Army in South Russia and represented the White forces in Paris and London. One of the most objective first-hand accounts, it puts events in the perspective of critical review.

B69B MOSCOW, GOSUDARSTVENNAIA PUBLICHNAIA ISTORICHESKAIA BIBLIOTEKA. *Sovetskaia strana v period grazh-*

danskoi voiny, 1918-1920; bibliograficheskii ukazatel dokumentalnykh publikatsii. Moscow: Izd. Vsesoiuznoi knizhnoi palaty, 1961. 575 p. Lists approximately 3,500 titles on the Civil War period. Organized under various subject headings.

B70 MOULIS, E., and BERGONIER, E. *La Guerre entre les Alliés et la Russie (1918-1920).* Paris: Librairie générale de droit et de jurisprudence, 1937. 209 p. A documented monograph, extremely critical of the Allies, and particularly of France, for supporting the anti-Bolsheviks. Definitely pro-Soviet, but useful as it contains documents of French origin not available in other collections.

B71 NABOKOV, KONSTANTIN D. *The Ordeal of a Diplomat.* London: Duckworth, 1921. 320 p. Memoirs of a Russian diplomatic representative in London during the Civil War. Useful because of the author's close relations with top British spokesmen, and notable for his unusually critical attitude toward both the policies of the Russian Whites and the policies of the Allies on Intervention.

B72 NAIDA, S. F. *O nekotorykh voprosakh istorii grazhdanskoi voiny v SSSR.* Moscow: Voenizdat, 1958. 243 p. The principal general interpretive account of the Civil War from the official contemporary Soviet historical viewpoint. Completely unobjective. [B]

B73 NAIDA, S. F., and KOVALENKO, D. A., eds. *Reshaiushchie pobedy sovetskogo naroda nad interventami i belogvardeitsami v 1919 g.; sbornik statei.* Moscow: Gospolitizdat, 1960. 663 p. Companion volume to the 1956 collection of articles, *Iz istorii borby sovetskogo naroda . . . v 1918 g.* (see above). This compilation contains fifteen articles on the events of 1919; seven treat aspects of the military campaigns; the remainder deal with the work of the Communist Party and the "home front." Some are based on primary sources; all articles are from the Soviet point of view.

B74 OBSHCHESTVO SODEISTVIIA ZHERTVAM INTERVENTSII. *K desiatiletiiu interventsii; sbornik statei.* Moscow: Gosizdat, 1929. 245 p. A collection of articles designed both to support official Soviet claims against the West for Intervention damages and to arouse patriotic fervor against the alleged danger of renewed Intervention. Most articles are general or interpretive; those on Siberia, Crimea and Transcaspia are documentary and quite useful. [B]

B75 PAVLOVICH, MIKHAIL (pseud. of M. I. Veltman). *RSFSR v imperialisticheskom okruzhenii.* Moscow: 1922-23. 4 vols. The volumes deal with France, England, America, and Japan, respectively. Each gives a historical sketch of relations between Russia and the country under consideration, going into much detail for the post-revolutionary period, especially for the country's role in Intervention.

B76 PIONTKOVSKII, S. A., ed. *Grazhdanskaia voina v Rossii, 1918-1921 gg.; khrestomatiia.* Moscow: Izd. Kom. universiteta, 1925. 695 p. A valuable collection of documents, correspondence, excerpts from memoirs, and other materials pertaining to all major phases of the Civil War and Intervention. Compiled from Soviet archives for the use of students at the Communist University in Moscow. Pro-Soviet but useful.

B77 PRAGUE, RUSSKII ZAGRANICHNYI ISTORICHESKII ARKHIV. *Bibliografiia russkoi revoliutsii i grazhdanskoi voiny (1917-1921).* Ed. by Jan Slavik. Compiled by S. P. Postnikov. Prague: 1938. 448 p. The most complete and important bibliography up to the time of publication on the Russian Revolution and Civil War. Includes books, pamphlets and articles not only in Russian, but also in most of the European languages. Very useful. [A]

B78 SHLIAPNIKOV, ALEKSANDR G., and others, eds. *Les Alliés contre la Russie avant, pendant et apres la guerre mondiale (faits et documents).* Paris: Delpeuch, 1926. 392 p. Trans. from the Russian ed., *Kto dolzhnik? Sbornik dokumentirovannykh statei. . . .* Moscow: "Avioizdatelstvo," 1926. 587 p. A collection of 18 documentary articles designed generally to show Allied responsibility for Intervention and for Russia's losses in World War I, and specifically to support Soviet claims for damages against the French. The articles are biased, disorganized and poorly written, but some of the documents are useful.

B79 STEWART, GEORGE. *The White Armies of Russia; a Chronicle of Counter-Revolution and Allied Intervention.* N.Y.: Macmillan, 1933. 469 p. The only complete account, based on published sources, of the anti-Bolshevik movement and its military effort from the time of Brest-Litovsk to the end of 1922. Includes maps and a bibliography in many languages. Unfortunately it is full of factual mistakes, and must be used carefully. [B]

B80 STISHOV, M. I. *Razgrom trekh pokhodov Antanty; pobeda sovetskoi vlasti na natsionalnykh okrainakh i na Dalnem Vostoke.* Moscow: Izd. Moskovskogo universiteta, 1953. 178 p. In this account, Stalin played the major if not the only role in the defeat of all the Interventionists and Whites.

B81 SUBBOTOVSKY, I. *Soiuzniki, russkie reaktsionery i interventsiia; kratkii obzor. (Iskliuchitelno po ofitsialnym arkhivnym dokumentam kolchakovskogo pravitelstva).* Leningrad: Vestnik Leningradskogo soveta, 1926. 328 p. A Soviet monograph, based on the archival material seized after the fall of Kolchak's government; although dealing principally with events in Siberia, it covers the whole period of Intervention. An important source. [B]

B82 TROTSKII, LEV D. *Materialy i dokumenty po istorii krasnoi armii; kak vooruzhalas revoliutsiia.* Moscow: Vysshii voennyi redaktsionnyi sovet, 1923-1925. 3 vols. Trotsky here presents himself as the real builder of the Red Army and justifies his use of tsarist officers in the Red forces. Published at the time of the struggle for power in the Soviet Union just prior to and following the death of Lenin. An interesting source, later suppressed in the Soviet Union. [A]

B83 ULLMAN, RICHARD H. *Anglo-Soviet Relations, 1917-1921.* Vol. I: *Intervention and the War.* Princeton, N.J.: Princeton University Press, 1961. A study of this subject from the point of view of the making of British policy toward Russia. Vol. I is based almost entirely on unpublished materials, including papers of the British Foreign Office, War Office, Admiralty, and General Staff. An excellent account, by a Harvard professor. [A]

B84 U.S. DEPARTMENT OF STATE. Russian Series, no. 1 [-5]. No. 1: *Exchange of Notes with Admiral Kolchak*; No. 2: *Intercourse with Territory under Bolshevik Control*; No. 3: *Documents Relating to the Organization and Purposes of the Anti-Bolshevik Forces in Russia*; No. 4: *American Assistance in the Operation of the Trans-Siberian Railway*; No. 5: *Relations with Lithuania.* Washington: G.P.O., 1920.

B85 VLADIMIRTSEV, VASILII S. *Kommunisticheskaia partiia—organizator razgroma vtorogo pokhoda Antanty.* Moscow: Voen. Izdat., 1958. 164 p.

B86 VOLINE (pseud. of Vsevolod M. Eichenbaum). *La Révolution inconnue (1917-1921).* Paris: "Les Amis de Voline," 1947. 690 p. Condensed English ed., *Nineteen-Seventeen: the Russian Revolution Betrayed.* N.Y.: Libertarian Book Club, 1954. 269 p. A study of the Russian revolutionary movement from the Decembrists to the Bolsheviks by a prominent anarchist, in three parts. The English edition is a translation of the last part only, ending with the expulsion of Voline and his fellow anarchists from Soviet Russia in 1921. Deals mainly with the Third International, but covers also some phases of the Civil War and Intervention.

B87 VOLKOV, F. D. *Krakh angliiskoi politiki interventsii i diplomaticheskoi izoliatsii sovetskogo gosudarstva (1917-1924 gg.).* Moscow: Gospolitizdat, 1954. 399 p. An example of the worst sort of Stalinist scholarship: a free-swinging diatribe dressed up with copious references to published materials and some to Soviet archives.

B88 WELTER, GUSTAVE. *La Guerre civile en Russie, 1918-1920.* Paris: Payot, 1936. 200 p. A monograph based on published sources critical both of the Allies and of the Soviets. Interesting as the expression of a novel point of view, but not very valuable as a historical source.

B89 WRANGEL, PETER N. (BARON). *Always with Honour.* Foreword by Herbert Hoover. N.Y.: Speller, 1957. 356 p. Published previously as *The Memoirs of General Wrangel*, N.Y.: Duffield, 1930; and *Memoirs*, London: Williams & Norgate, 1929. Memoirs of the successor to Denikin as Commander of the South Russian armed forces, covering the entire period of 1917-20; most valuable for operations during 1920 in Crimea. Provides a critical review of Volunteer Army operations under Denikin and invaluable material, including documents, on Allied policy and aid during the final phase of the struggle. [A]

B90 ZAITSOV, ARSENII A. *1918 god; ocherki po istorii russkoi grazhdanskoi voiny.* Paris: N.P., 1934. 275 p. By a former colonel on the Russian Army's General Staff, who claims to be striving for a balanced account of the Civil War. Uses a rather wide variety of source material.

b. INTERVENTION IN THE SOUTH

(Edited by George Brinkley)

B91 ALEKSEEV, S. A., comp. *Denikin, Iudenich, Vrangel.* Moscow: Gosizdat, 1927. 2nd ed., Moscow-Leningrad: Gos. sots.-ekon. izd., 1931. 456 p. Also includes selections from the memoirs of Lukomskii, Rakovskii, Voronovich, Skobtsov, Obolenskii, Valentinov, Gori and others. One of the volumes in the series entitled *Revoliutsiia i grazhdanskaia voina v opisaniiakh belogvardeitsev.*

B92 *Antanta i Vrangel; sbornik statei.* Vol. I. Moscow-Petrograd: Gosizdat, 1923. 260 p. Ten articles on the period of Gen. Wrangel's command of Russian anti-Bolshevik forces in the Crimea, 1920, presenting Soviet views on relations with the Entente, economic policies, underground and workers' movements, the Tartar question, etc. Most useful is "Antanta i Vrangel," by I. Alf (pseud. of I. Seimovich), p. 5-39.

B93 ARSHINOV, PETR A. *Istoriia makhnovskogo dvizheniia, 1918-1921 gg.* Berlin: Gruppa russkikh anarkhistov v Germanii, 1923. 258 p. French ed., *L'Histoire du mouvement makhnoviste, 1918-1921.* Paris: Éditions anarchistes, Librairie internationale, 1924. An "official" history of the anarchist peasant movement in the Ukraine led by Nestor Makhno, written by one of his close associates. Relates policies, activities and relations of the movement, which clashed with both Bolsheviks and Whites and had a significant impact on the Civil War.

B94 AVALISHVILI (AVALOV), Z. D. *The Independence of Georgia in International Politics, 1918-1921.* London: Headley, 1940. Russian ed., *Nezavisimost Gruzii.* Paris: 1924. A documented history of the foreign relations of independent Georgia, by a leading Georgian diplomat who negotiated with the Germans and Turks and subsequently represented Georgia in London. Relations with foreign powers as viewed by a nationalist intimately acquainted with events but also critical of his government's policies. [B]

B95 BRINKLEY, GEORGE A. "Allied Intervention and the Volunteer Army in South Russia, 1917-1921." Ph.D. dissertation, Columbia University, 1964. 594 p. A case study of the policies of the White anti-Bolshevik forces in the Civil War and of the problems of Allied intervention on their behalf. Focuses on the Volunteer Army under Denikin and its relations with Allied representatives in the field and with the non-Russian nationalities. Based substantially upon archival sources. [A]

B96 CHAIKIN, VADIM A. *K istorii rossiiskoi revoliutsii.* Vol. I: *Kazn 26 bakinskikh komissarov.* Moscow: Grzhebin, 1922. A *cause célèbre* in the Soviet case against Allied intervention in South Russia, the shooting of 26 Bolshevik leaders in September 1918 was brought to public attention by the author, an S.R. journalist, in 1919. This book represents his personal findings and concludes that the British engineered the affair.

B97 DENIKIN, A. I. (GENERAL). *Ocherki russkoi smuty.* Paris: J. Povolozky, 1921-26. 5 vols. Berlin: Russkoe natsionalnoe knigoizdatelstvo, 1921-26. Abbreviated English eds., *The Russian Turmoil*, London: Hutchinson, 1922. *The White Army*, London: Cape, 1930. The most valuable and complete memoirs of any White leader, this is a detailed account and analysis from the beginning of World War I to April 1920, by the former Chief of Staff of the Russian Army and successor to Kornilov as commander of the Volunteer Army in South Russia. As the leading figure in the anti-Bolshevik struggle in the South and the major recipient of Allied aid, Denikin was able to provide invaluable history and numerous documents. [A]

B98 DENISOV, S. V. (GENERAL). *Zapiski; grazhdanskaia voina na iuge Rossii, 1918-1919 gg.* Constantinople: The Author, 1921. 120 p. The first volume of seven originally planned, it deals with the period of January to May 1918, relating the establishment of the autonomous government in the Don region, the beginning of the Civil War, and early relations with the Volunteer Army. The author became Commander of Don Cossack troops and writes from the point of view of the Don regime.

B99 DIOGOT, VLADIMIR A. *Pod znamenem bolshevizma; zapiski podpolshchika.* 3rd ed. Moscow: Izd. Vsesoiuz. o-va politkat. i ss.-pos., 1933. 416 p. Memoirs of a Bolshevik undercover agent in Siberia and in the South. Useful as a human document.

B100 DOBRYNIN, V. *Borba s bolshevizmom na iuge Rossii; uchastie v borbe donskogo kazachestva, fevral 1917–mart 1920.* Prague: Slavizdat, 1921. 123 p. French ed., *La Lutte contre le bolchévisme.* Prague: Melantrich, 1920. A history of the Civil War in South Russia, 1917-20, with particular reference to the role of the Don Cossacks, by the Chief of the Information Bureau of the Don General Staff. An unemotional first-hand account of the Don struggle and of the relations of the Don Cossacks with the Volunteer Army, Germans, and Allies.

B101 DONOHOE, MARTIN H. (MAJOR). *With the Persian Expedition.* London: Edward Arnold, 1919. 276 p. An account of the experiences of the British expedition under General Dunsterville which moved through Persia to Baku in 1918 to restore the Eastern Front against the Turks. The author was a journalist and intelligence officer attached to Dunsterforce.

B102 DUNSTERVILLE, LIONEL C. *The Adventures of Dunsterforce.* London: E. Arnold, 1920. 323 p. Exploits of the secret British expeditionary force which went through Persia to Baku and occupied the latter briefly in August 1918, related by its commander. Describes the origins of British intervention as an effort to restore the South-Eastern front against German-Turk invasion and to protect British interests in the area. Valuable information on British relations with both Bolsheviks and anti-Bolshevik elements during the first landing of troops. [B]

B103 ENUKIDZE, D. E. *Krakh imperialisticheskoi interventsii v Zakavkaze.* Tbilisi: Gosizdat Gruz. S.S.R., 1954. A Soviet version of British intervention in Transcaucasia, mainly Georgia, which revises some earlier accounts. Intervention is interpreted as pro-Denikin rather than pro-Georgia and not aimed at dismemberment. The fall of Transcaucasian governments to the Soviets is attributed more to Russian liberation than to internal revolution.

B104 GRUZINSKAIA DEMOKRATICHESKAIA RESPUBLIKA, PRAVITELSTVO. *Dokumenty i materialy po vneshnei politike Zakavkazia i Gruzii.* Tiflis: Respublika Gruzii, Ministerstvo vneshnikh del, 1919. 492 p. An official documentary record of the foreign policies of the Georgian Republic from November 1917 to early 1919, from the archives of the Ministry of Foreign Affairs. The largest part relates to events between the 1917 revolution and negotiation of peace with Turkey and Germany in June 1918; also provides invaluable material on relations with Russian Volunteer Army, British, and other Transcaucasian Republics (p. 375-492). [A]

B105 GUKOVSKII, A. I. *Frantsuzskaia interventsiia na iuge Rossii, 1918-1919.* Moscow: Gosizdat, 1928. 267 p. The best Soviet history of French intervention, far less distorted than most. Thorough and careful analysis as well as an account of events, by a prominent Soviet historian of the period. Based chiefly upon memoirs and documentary sources previously published, with a valuable chronology. [A]

B106 GURKO, V. I. "Iz Petrograda cherez Moskvu, Parizh, i London v Odessu," *Arkhiv russkoi revoliutsii*, Vol. xv, p. 5-84. A valuable first-hand account of the early formation of Russian anti-Bolshevik organizations, showing conflict between pro-German and pro-Allied orientations. Notable for its record of the Jassy conference which appealed for Allied aid, for subsequent work of the delegation sent to Paris and London, and for French intervention in Odessa.

B107 HODGSON, JOHN E. *With Denikin's Armies; Being a Description of the Cossack Counterrevolution in South Russia, 1918-1920.* London: Lincoln Williams, 1932. 195 p. Policies and operations of the Volunteer Army and Cossack forces under Denikin and their relations with the Allied Powers, as viewed by a perceptive and sympathetic British journalist and correspondent for the *Daily Express.*

B108 IAKUSHKIN, E. E. *Frantsuzskaia interventsiia na iuge, 1918-1919 gg.* Moscow: Gosizdat, 1929. A short history of French intervention in Ukraine, from the end of the Skoropadskii regime in 1918 to the recognition of Wrangel in 1920. Designed to discredit French aims and recipients of aid. The author's brief comments are supplemented by a limited but valuable selection of documents.

B109 IVANIS, VASIL. *Stezhkami zhittia: spogadi.* Neu-Ulm: "Ukrainski Visti," 1959. 4 vols. Valuable memoirs of civil war in South Russia, chiefly in the Kuban region, by a former member of the Kuban Rada (1918-20), Minister of Commerce and Industry (1919), and head of the government (1920). Written from the Kuban point of view, but retains balance and perspective, with new material on relations with the Volunteer Army.

B110 KALVARI, MIKHAIL A. *Interventsiia v Krymu.* Simferopol: Krymskoe gosudarstvennoe izdatelstvo, 1930. 180 p.

B111 KRASNOV, P. N. (GENERAL). "Vsevelikoe voisko Donskoe," *Arkhiv russkoi revoliutsii*, Vol. v, p. 190-321. Berlin: Izdat. "Slovo," 1922. Apologia of the Don Ataman who played a leading role in the Cossack independence movement and in efforts to obtain aid from Germany. Valuable for its description of relations with the Volunteer

Army and Allied representatives, leading to the author's resignation when Allied intervention forced a change in policy.

B112 LAMPE, ALEKSEI A. VON, ed. *Bieloe dielo; lietopis bieloi borby*. Berlin: Knigoizdat. "Miednyi vsadnik," 1926-33. 7 vols. A collection of documents and memoirs about the White movement. On the Civil War in the South includes accounts by V. V. Shulgin, A. P. Filimonov, P. Shatilov, and others. Vols. 5 and 6 contain memoirs of General P. N. Wrangel.

B113 LISHIN, N. N. *Na kaspiiskom more; god beloi borby*. Prague: Izdanie Morskogo zhurnala, 1938. 182 p. Memoirs of a Russian naval officer serving under British naval command on the Caspian Sea during Intervention, 1918-19. Contains descriptions of the establishment of British control and naval bases, of operations against the Bolshevik flotilla, and of aid to anti-Bolshevik forces in the area. Valuable as a critique of British policy from a Russian point of view.

B114 LORIS-MELIKOV, IVAN (MELIKOF, JEAN). *La Révolution russe et les nouvelles républiques transcaucasiennes; bolchévisme et antibolchévisme*. Paris: Alcan, 1920. 211 p. A brief history of Revolution and Civil War in South Russia with particular emphasis on Allied policy and conflicts between the Russian Volunteer Army and the Transcaucasian Republics. The author was given a personal and informal commission by Clemenceau to investigate conditions in Oct.-Dec. 1919. His account is followed by reports and letters of the author. A valuable critique of French policy and differences with the British.

B115 LUKOMSKII, A. S. *Vospominaniia*. Berlin: Otto Kirchner, 1922. 2 vols. English ed., *Memoirs of the Russian Revolution*. London: Unwin, 1922. 255 p. Memoirs of a leading Russian general, Head of the War Department, and President of the Special Council of the Volunteer Army under Denikin. Gives the history of the anti-Bolshevik movement in South Russia, relating both operations and policies of the Army and activities of political organizations, with valuable sections on Volunteer relations with the British and French during Intervention. [B]

B116 MARGOLIN, ARNOLD D. *Ukraina i politika Antanty*. Berlin: Efron, 1922. 397 p. One of the most valuable sources on Ukrainian relations with the Entente, 1918-1920, by a prominent Ukrainian jurist, member of the Socialist-Federalist Party, Jewish leader, and member of Ukrainian (Directorate) mission in Paris. The author played a major role in negotiations with the French in Odessa and in subsequent efforts to obtain aid and recognition. [A]

B117 MARGULIES, MANUIL S. *God interventsii*. Berlin: Izd. Z. I. Grzhebina, 1923. 3 vols. A detailed record, in diary form, of the efforts of anti-Bolshevik Russian groups to obtain Allied aid in 1918-20, as seen by the former President of the Central War Industries Committee and spokesman for the bourgeois element in the South. Includes an account of the Jassy Conference, a description of Russian organizations in Odessa, their relations with the French and with the Volunteer Army, and the author's subsequent work in Paris and London. [B]

B118 MARGULIES, VLADIMIR. *Ognennye gody; materialy i dokumenty po istorii voiny na iuge Rossii.* Berlin: "Manfred," 1923. 322 p.

B119 MARIN, DAVID P. "Failure in the South, An Account of André Marty, the French Mutiny and Withdrawal from Southern Russia, November 1918–April 1919." Certificate essay, Russian Institute, Columbia, 1950. 89 p. A scholarly history and analysis of the French intervention in Odessa and the Crimea. Events in South Russia, including the mutiny, are reviewed in the general context of French policy, and the problems of dealing with the situation in South Russia are analyzed.

B120 MARTY, ANDRÉ P. *La Révolte de la Mer Noire, 1918-1919.* 4th ed. Paris: Éditions sociales, 1949. 670 p. Italian ed., Rome: Edizioni Rinascita, 1951. 540 p. English ed., *The Epic of the Black Sea Revolt.* N.Y.: Workers' Library, 1941. A description of the author's participation in French naval operations in the Black Sea, especially of his role in organizing a mutiny of crews to protest Intervention. A valuable portrait of Leftist opposition and the sailors' and soldiers' reluctance to fight, but highly exaggerated by the author's egotism.

B122 OBSHCHESTVO SODEISTVIIA ZHERTVAM INTERVENTSII. *K desiatiletiiu interventsii; sbornik statei.* Moscow: Gosizdat, 1929. 245 p. Collection of articles commemorating the tenth anniversary of Intervention. Pro-Soviet in its interpretation and selection of information but also contains useful accounts based upon primary sources. See especially "Interventy v Krymu" by L. Poliarnyi, and "Interventsiia v Zakaspii" by Z. I. Mirkin, p. 126-200, relating French intervention and British support for anti-Bolshevik elements in Transcaspia, respectively. [B]

B123 "Ocherk vzaimootnoshenii vooruzhennykh sil Iuga Rossii i predstavitelei frantsuzskogo komandovaniia." *Arkhiv russkoi revoliutsii,* Vol. XVI, p. 233-262. Ed. by G. V. Gessen. Berlin: Izdat. "Slovo," 1925. An invaluable collection of reports, documents, correspondence, etc. compiled in May 1919 by the Volunteer Army Staff concerning its relations with the French during intervention in Odessa. Referred to as the "Orange Book," it sets forth the Volunteer position on differences with the French which led to a rupture of relations. [A]

B124 POKROVSKII, GEORGII. *Denikinshchina: god politiki i ekonomiki na Kubani, 1918-1919 gg.* Berlin: Z. Grschebin, 1923. 279 p. A history of relations between the Kuban Cossack government and the Volunteer Army from the latter's arrival in 1918 to its evacuation in 1920. Valuable for an account of conflicts between the two authorities and Denikin's efforts to effect Kuban subordination. Written from the Kuban point of view.

B125 RAEVSKII, A. *Angliiskaia interventsiia i musavatskoe pravitelstvo; iz istorii interventsii i kontr-revoliutsii v Zakavkaze.* Baku: Gostip. "Krasnyi Vostok," 1927. 190 p. A history of British intervention in Azerbaidzhan based upon primary materials including captured government archives. The author has a Soviet bias but also includes valuable documentation showing details on British economic policy, relations with neighboring territories and the Volunteer Army, and Bolshevik policies, 1918-20.

B126 RAKOVSKII, G. N. *V stane belykh; grazhdanskaia voina na iuge Rossii.* Constantinople: "Pressa," 1920. 340 p. *Konets belykh ot Dnepra do Bosfora.* Prague: Izdat. "Volia Rossii," 1921. 275 p. A two-volume history of the Civil War and White movement in South Russia by a Russian journalist associated with the information agency serving the Volunteer Army. His informed and critical analysis is designed to show why the Whites failed and the Bolsheviks succeeded. The first volume deals with the Denikin period, 1918-19, and the second with the final phase in the Crimea under Wrangel, 1920.

B127 RESHETAR, JOHN S., JR. *The Ukrainian Revolution, 1917-1920: a Study in Nationalism.* Princeton, N.J.: Princeton University Press, 1952. 363 p. A scholarly monograph giving an excellent history and analysis of events in the Ukraine during the Revolution and Civil War. Concerned largely with the Ukrainian independence movement but provides valuable information on relations with Germans, Allies, the Volunteer Army, and the impact of Ukrainian events in larger context. Good bibliography. [B]

B128 ROBERTS, CARL ERIC BECHHOFER. *In Denikin's Russia and the Caucasus, 1919-1920.* London: W. Collins, 1921. 324 p. A well informed and objective account of Civil War and Intervention in South Russia by a British journalist. The author travelled through Transcaucasia and South Russia, becoming closely acquainted with events and personalities. Good descriptions of conditions and problems, with a critical view of British policies. [B]

B129 SHAFIR, IAKOV M. *Secrets of Menshevik Georgia: the Plot Against Soviet Russia Unmasked.* London: Communist Party of Great Britain, 1922. 100 p. (Supplement to the author's *Grazhdanskaia voina v Rossii i menshevistskaia Gruziia.* Moscow: Tip. "Tsustran," 1921.) The Soviet author presents a distorted interpretation of Georgian policy, portraying it as a pawn of the British and ally of the Whites, but includes very useful information and documents from Georgian archives showing relations among Georgia, the British, and the Volunteer Army, 1919-20.

B130 SHCHEGOLEV, PAVEL E., ed. *Frantsuzy v Odesse; iz belykh memuarov Gen. A. I. Denikin, M. S. Margulies, M. V. Braikevich.* Leningrad: Krasnaia Gazeta, 1928. 262 p. A reprint of sections of the memoirs of Russian military and political leaders in the South relating to French intervention in Odessa. Especially valuable for the less accessible account by Braikevich, a leading liberal Russian figure in negotiations between Odessa organizations and the French command.

B131 SHLIAPNIKOV, ALEKSANDR G., and others, eds. *Les Alliés contre la Russie avant, pendant et après la guerre mondiale (faits et documents).* Paris: Delpeuch, 1926. 392 p. Trans. from the Russian ed., *Kto dolzhnik?* Moscow: "Avioizdatelstvo," 1926. 587 p. First-hand accounts and secondary articles providing a biased but useful history. See especially "Interventsiia na iuge Rossii, Kavkaze i v Turkestane, 1918-1920," by F. Kostiaev, p. 333-376.

B132 SHLIKHTER, A. G., ed. *Chernaia kniga; sbornik statei i materialov ob interventsii Antanty na Ukraine v 1918-1919 gg.* Ekaterinoslav: Gosizdat Ukrainy, 1925. 432 p. A useful collection of articles and documents based upon Bolshevik and Ukrainian eyewitness accounts and captured materials, compiled as a background and history of French intervention. See especially "Soiuznyi desant na Ukraine" by F. Anulov, p. 51-209, and "Direktoriia i Frantsuzskaia okkupatsiia," by S. Ostapenko, p. 260-271. [B]

B133 SOKOLOV, KONSTANTIN N. *Pravlenie Generala Denikina.* Sofia: Ross-Bolg. Izdat., 1921. 292 p. The internal history of the Volunteer Army, treating chiefly the critical problem of establishing political and administrative machinery in occupied territory during the Civil War. The author was legal adviser to the Special Council under Denikin and formulated the plan for cabinet government adopted shortly before the army's defeat.

B134 SUKHOV, A. A. *Inostrannaia interventsiia na Odeshchine v 1918-1919 gg.* Odessa: Izd. Istpart. Otdel Odesskogo Okrkoma KPBU, 1927. 104 p.

B135 VINAVER, M. *Nashe pravitelstvo (krymskie vospominaniia 1918-1919 gg.).* Paris: Voltaire, 1928. 240 p. A history of developments in the Crimea during German and French Intervention, by the

Foreign Minister of the Crimean government under S. S. Krym established after the fall of the Tatar regime. The author, a Kadet and member of the Constituent Assembly, provides a basic source on the erection of the moderate constitutional government and its relations with the Tatars, the Volunteer Army, and the Allies.

B136 WAHL, ERNEST G., VON. *K istorii belago dvizheniia: deiatelnost General-adiutanta Shcherbacheva.* Tallin: Izdanie avtora, 1935. (This book is also included along with: *Kak Pilsudskii pogubil Denikina* and *Znachenie i rol Ukrainy v voprose osvobozhdeniia Rossii ot bolshevikov* in a work entitled: *Prichiny raspadeniia Rossiiskoi Imperii i neudachi russkago natsionalnago dvizheniia.* Tallin: Izdanie avtora, 1938. 4 vols.) A detailed and documented history by an Estonian historian of the work of Gen. D. G. Shcherbachev, including his negotiation with the French for aid to the Volunteer Army in 1918 and his later representation of Denikin in Paris. Based upon memoirs and Shcherbachev's records on aid obtained. The larger work analyzes the Ukrainian movement and the relations of the Volunteer Army with Poland. [B]

B137 XYDIAS, JEAN. *L'Intervention française en Russie, 1918-1919; souvenirs d'un témoin.* Paris: Les Éditions de France, 1927. 382 p. An informed and critical review of French policies and actions during Intervention in Odessa, by a French resident of the city. Valuable insight into the difficulties of the French command, its mistakes, and its relations with local elements and with the Volunteer Army. [B]

c. INTERVENTION IN THE NORTH

(Edited by Leonid Strakhovsky)

B138 AKSENOV, ALEKSEI N. *Pobeda sovetskoi vlasti na severe, 1917-1920.* Archangel: Arkhangelskoe knizhnoe izd-vo, 1957. 138 p. A popular account of the Intervention and Civil War in North Russia, published to commemorate the fortieth anniversary of the Bolshevik Revolution. In addition to the usual quotations from the works of Lenin and Stalin, contains also some reference to archival material on the Bolshevik underground behind the lines.

B139 ALBERTSON, RALPH. *Fighting Without a War; An Account of Military Intervention in North Russia.* N.Y.: Harcourt & Brace, 1920. 138 p. A personal account by a former member of the YMCA who served in North Russia in 1918-19. Critical of the British in particular, of anti-Bolshevik Russian forces in general, and obviously representing the point of view of liberal Americans who opposed intervention against the Bolsheviks. Some interesting first-hand descriptions, but not a balanced historical work.

B140 ALEKSEEV, S. A., comp. *Grazhdanskaia voina v Sibiri i severnoi oblasti.* Ed. by N. L. Meshcheriakov. Moscow-Leningrad: Gosizdat, 1927. 480 p. Contains selections from the memoirs of Avksentev, Rakov, Zenzinov, Gopper, Sakharov, Budberg, Dobrovolskii, Sokolov, and Bullitt. Vol. IV of *Revoliutsiia i grazhdanskaia voina v opisaniiakh belogvardeitsev.* Offers a very useful chronology of events. [B]

B141 *Borba sovetskogo naroda s interventami i belogvardeitsami na sovetskom severe v 1918-1920 gg.* Moscow: Voenizdat, 1961.

B142 A CHRONICLER (pseud. of Cudahy, John). *Archangel; the American War with Russia.* Chicago: McClurg, 1924. 216 p. A description of American participation in the intervention in North Russia by a former member of the 339th U.S. Infantry regiment. Critical of the Allies and particularly the British. Interesting as an expression of American opinion at that time, but of little historical value.

B143 DRUJINA, GLEB. "The History of the North-West Army of General Yudenich." Ph.D. dissertation, Stanford Univ., 1950.

B144 GORN, V. *Grazhdanskaia voina na severo-zapade Rossii.* Berlin: Gamaiun, 1923. 416 p. Part memoir, part historical account of the anti-Bolshevik movement in northwest Russia by a former minister of the local White government. Emphasis is on politics and administration; little on military and foreign policy issues. Critical of Russian generals and "reactionaries" and of the Allies. Some documents.

B145 GREAT BRITAIN, WAR OFFICE. *The Evacuation of North Russia, 1919.* London: H. M. Stationery Office, 1920. 45 p. A very important and well documented British source, giving a brief description of the beginning of the Allied intervention in North Russia, a full enumeration of the armed units which participated in the British expedition, and a complete account of the evacuation of North Russia by the British in the autumn of 1919.

B146 HALLIDAY, E. M. *The Ignorant Armies.* Foreword by Brig. General S. L. A. Marshall. N.Y.: Harper, 1960. 232 p. The author is a member of the Department of Social Studies at North Carolina State College. Recounts the experiences and adventures of the 339th U.S. Infantry Regiment in North Russia, following closely stories of surviving members of this unit, who have an organization called "The Polar Bears" in Detroit. Critical of Intervention in general and of American participation in particular. Written for the general reader.

B147 IAKUSHKIN, E. E., and POLUNIN, S. *Angliiskaia interventsiia v 1918-1920 gg.* Moscow-Leningrad: Gospolitizdat, 1928. 76 p. A popular account which deals with English intervention in North

Russia as well as in Transcaucasia. Naturally very anti-British, but containing some information not available elsewhere.

B148 IRONSIDE, EDMUND (SIR). *Archangel, 1918-1919.* London: Constable, 1953. 219 p. The reminiscences of the late Field-Marshal Baron Ironside of Archangel about his experiences as commander-in-chief of the Allied forces in North Russia. Although based on some documentary evidence, it is essentially a personal narrative, written for the general reader. Nevertheless it has historical value. [B]

B149 KEDROV, MIKHAIL S. (Tsederbaum). *Bez bolshevistskogo rukovodstva (iz istorii interventsii na Murmane); ocherki.* Leningrad: Izd-vo "Krasnaia gazeta," 1930. 190 p. A documented study by a former Soviet commissar of the events in Murmansk in the spring and summer of 1918 which led to Allied intervention. One-sided, but valuable, although the interpretations of most of the events described are refuted in Strakhovsky: *The Origins of American Intervention in North Russia, 1918.* [B]

B150 KEDROV, MIKHAIL S. *Za sovetskii sever.* Leningrad: Gospolitizdat, 1927. 290 p. A documented monograph about the struggle for the establishment of Soviet power in Archangel from the Bolshevik Revolution of 1917 until the Allied intervention on Aug. 2, 1918 and the continuation of it underground, by the former extraordinary commissar for Archangel. Interesting sidelights on the relations with Allied and neutral consular representatives in Archangel during 1917-18. Very anti-Western. [B]

B151 MARUSHEVSKII, VLADIMIR V. *Belye v Arkhangelske.* Leningrad: Priboi, 1930. 279 p. Reminiscences of the major-general who was commander of anti-Bolshevik Russian troops in North Russia until the arrival of Lieutenant-General Eugene Miller. Originally published serially in three installments (*Bieloe delo*, vols. I, II, III, Berlin, 1926-27) under the title: "God na severe." Although personal and chatty in parts, it is still an important historical source of what was happening in North Russia in 1918-19. General Ironside, in his book, is rather critical of Marushevskii.

B152 MAYNARD, CHARLES CLARKSON MARTIN (SIR). *The Murmansk Venture.* London: Hodder, 1928. 334 p. A documented narrative of the events in North Russia during the period of Allied Intervention by Major-General Maynard, British commander in the Murmansk area. Valuable particularly from a military point of view. [B]

B153 MINTS, ISAAK I. *Angliiskaia interventsiia i severnaia kontrrevoliutsiia.* Moscow: Gos. sots.-ek. izd., 1931. 255 p. The most important monograph on the subject written by a prominent Soviet historian. Fully documented. Although it presents the Soviet point of view, it is a very valuable historical source. [A]

B154 MOORE, YOEL R., MEAD, HARRY H., and YAHNS, LEWIS E., eds. *The History of the American Expedition Fighting the Bolsheviki.* Detroit: The Polar Bear Assn., 1920. 320 p. A one-sided account of the activities of the 339th U.S. Infantry Regiment by three of its former officers. Very critical of Intervention, of American participation in it, and of the British and White Russians.

B155 MYMRIN, G. *V borbe za sovetskii sever; razgrom anglo-amerikanskikh i frantsuzskikh interventov i belogvardeitsev v 1918-1920 gg.* Archangel: Arkhangelskoe oblastnoe gosizdat, 1950. 154 p. A popular, though documented, account of the Intervention and Civil War in North Russia by one of the Bolshevik participants. Based largely on a book published in 1940 in collaboration with two other participants (see below).

B156 MYMRIN, G., PIROGOV, M., and KUZNETSOV, G. *Razgrom interventov i belogvardeitsev na severe.* Archangel: Arkhangelskoe oblastnoe izd., 1940. 100 p. A documented monograph by participants on the Bolshevik side in the Civil War in North Russia. Valuable particularly for underground activities and penetration behind the Allied lines.

B157 *Oktiabrskaia revoliutsiia i grazhdanskaia voina na severe.* Archangel: Partiinoe Izd., 1933. 2 vols.

B158 *Oktiabrskaia Revoliutsiia i interventsiia na severe, 1917-1920; sbornik.* Archangel: Gubkom. VKP(b), 1927. 320 p.

B159 OLSZEWSKI, GEORGE J. "Allied Intervention in North Russia, 1918-1919." Ph.D. dissertation, Georgetown, 1958.

B160 POPOV, ANDREI N. *Bibliografiia interventsii i grazhdanskoi voiny na severe.* Archangel: Istpart. arkhangelskogo gubkoma VKP (b), 1928. 51 p. A very valuable collection listing everything published in the Soviet Union on the subject up to 1928. [B]

B161 RUSSIA (1917– RSFSR), TSENTRALNOE ARKHIVNOE UPRAVLENIE. *Interventsiia na severe v dokumentakh.* Ed. by Isaak I. Mints. Moscow: Partizdat, 1933. 94 p. An important collection of annotated documents from both the Allied and Soviet sides. While reflecting the Soviet point of view, it is historically valuable. [B]

B162 SKVORTSOV, F. *Murman v borbe i stroike.* Leningrad: Izd. iubileinoi komissii pri murmanskom okrispolkome, 1930. 106 p. A popular yet documented account of the period of Intervention and Civil War as well as of that of reconstruction of the town of Murmansk, to commemorate the tenth anniversary of the "liberation" of the Murman area.

B163 SOUTAR, ANDREW. *With Ironside in North Russia.* London and Melbourne: Hutchinson, 1940. 250 p. Impressions by the correspondent of the *London Times* covering the period from April to October 1919. Strongly pro-interventionist and anti-Bolshevik. Not reliable as a historical source, but interesting as it reflects a certain trend in English thinking.

B164 STRAKHOVSKY, LEONID I. *Intervention at Archangel: The Story of Allied Intervention and Russian Counter-Revolution in North Russia, 1918-1920.* Princeton, N.J.: Princeton University Press, 1944. 336 p. British ed., London: Milford, Oxford, 1944. To date the most complete documented monograph on the subject by a Western historian, who maintains that the failure of the intervention was due to half-measures and difficulties encountered by foreign personnel (particularly military) in an occupied territory without proper knowledge of history, developments, and general conditions in a strife-torn country. [A]

B165 STRAKHOVSKY, LEONID I. *The Origins of American Intervention in North Russia (1918).* Princeton, N.J.: Princeton University Press, 1937. 140 p. British ed., London: Milford, Oxford, 1937. A documented study, supporting the thesis that there was legal ground for intervention in North Russia on the basis of an agreement signed on July 6, 1918 between representatives of the Murmansk Regional Soviet (which had broken relations with Moscow) and those of France, Great Britain and the United States. By a historian of Russian origin who was a participant in the events at Murmansk. [A]

B166 TARASOV, VASILII V. *Borba s interventami na Murmane v 1918-1920 gg.* Leningrad: Leningradskoe gazetno-zhurnalnoe i knizhnoe izd-vo, 1948. 305 p. A documented historical monograph to mark the thirtieth anniversary of the beginning of Intervention in Murmansk, using archival material particularly with reference to the Bolshevik underground movement behind the lines. [B]

B167 TARASOV, VASILII V. *Borba s interventami na Severe Rossii (1918-1920 gg.).* Moscow: Gospolitizdat, 1958. 311 p. Essentially a reprint of the preceding item.

B168 ZELENOV, N. P. *Tragedia severnoi oblasti.* Paris: Author's publication, 1922. 86 p. A personal account by a former colonel of artillery in the North Russian army, very critical of Allied policy and of the Russian commander-in-chief, General Miller, as well as of other Russian leaders, but interesting as an expression of the viewpoint of a considerable segment of the Russian officers of that time.

d. INTERVENTION IN SIBERIA AND THE FAR EAST

(1) General Works
(EDITED BY RICHARD H. ULLMAN)

B169 ACKERMAN, CARL W. *Trailing the Bolsheviki; Twelve Thousand Miles With the Allies in Siberia.* N.Y.: Scribner, 1919. 308 p. A good, journalistic account of Siberian conditions with much material on the action of U.S. forces. The author was a *New York Times* special correspondent.

B170 ALEKSEEV, S. A., comp. *Grazhdanskaia voina v Sibiri i severnoi oblasti.* Ed. by N. L. Meshcheriakov. Moscow-Leningrad: Gosizdat, 1927. 480 p. Contains selections by Avksentev, Rakov, Zenzinov, Gopper, Sakharov, Budberg, Dobrovolskii, Sokolov, and Bullitt. Volume IV of *Revoliutsiia i grazhdanskaia voina v opisaniiakh belogvardeitsev.*

B171 ARGUNOV, A. *Mezhdu dvumia bolshevizmami.* Paris: Imprimerie "Union," 1919. Interesting, valuable memoirs of political developments among anti-Bolshevik groupings in Siberia in 1918 by a right Socialist-Revolutionary who was one of the victims of the coup d'état carried out at Omsk in November 1918 by right-wing elements.

B172 BELIAEV, BORIS L. *Liudi i sobytiia Primoria; iz istorii borby za vlast Sovetov v Primore v 1917-1922 gg.* Moscow: Voennoe izd. Ministerstva Oborony Soiuza SSR, 1959. 228 p. A popular account of resistance to intervention in the Vladivostok region.

B173 BOCK, BENJAMIN. "The origins of the inter-Allied Intervention in Eastern Asia, 1918-1920." Ph.D. dissertation, Stanford, 1941.

B174 BOLDYREV, V. G. *Direktoriia, Kolchak, interventy.* Novonikolaevsk: Gosizdat, 1925. 565 p. Diary and notes of the commander-in-chief of the armed forces of the Omsk Directorate. Valuable for information concerning Allied-White relations both before and after the Kolchak coup d'état. [B]

B175 *Borba za Ural i Sibir; vospominaniia i stati uchastnikov borby s uchredilovskoi i kolchakovskoi kontr-revoliutsiei.* Moscow: Gosizdat, 1926. 390 p. Concentrates upon the period of Kolchak's activity and presents, through the eyes of Bolshevik writers and through documents, much useful material on the Czechs and their peace treaty with the Bolsheviks, the Red Army and partisan forces, and the execution of Kolchak. [B]

B176 CLEINOW, GEORG. *Neu-Sibirien (Sib-Krai); eine Studie zum Aufmarsch der Sowjetmacht in Asien.* Berlin: Hobbing, 1928. 426 p.

An excellent general work about Siberia and the establishment of Soviet power. Only about 60 pages, from published Russian sources, on Intervention and Civil War.

B177 DALNE-VOSTOCHNYI KRAY; KOMISSIIA PO PROVEDENIIU PRAZDNOVANIIA DESIATILETIIA OKTIABRSKOI REVOLIUTSII. *V ogne revoliutsii; sbornik statei i vospominanii o revoliutsionnykh sobytiiakh na Dalnem Vostoke.* Ed. by Ia. Ia. Grunt. Harbin: 1927. 291 p.

B178 GIRCHENKO, V. P. *Imperialisticheskaia interventsiia v Buriat-Mongolii, 1918-1920 gg.* Ulan-Ude: Buriat-Mongolskoe Gos. Izd., 1940. 108 p. An account of the Civil War and Intervention in this area, with some attempt at documentation, by a member of the Buriat-Mongolian State Scientific Institute for Languages, Literature, and History.

B179 GOLIONKO, V. P. *V ogne borby; iz istorii Grazhdanskoi voiny 1918-1922 gg. na Dalnem Vostoke.* Moscow: 1958. 295 p. A personal account by an old Bolshevik who fought as a partisan.

B180 GRIGORTSEVICH, STANISLAV S. *Amerikanskaia i iaponskaia interventsiia na Sovetskom Dalnem Vostoke i ee razgrom, 1918-1922 gg.* Moscow: Gospolitizdat, 1957. 200 p. Based on Russian archival and Western secondary sources. An account of the Siberian intervention, charging the Americans and Japanese with aiming first to overthrow the Soviet government and later to sever the Far Eastern areas from its control. Includes a description of the revolutionary movement in the Russian Far East. [A]

B181 GRONDIJS, LUDOVIC H. *La Guerre en Russie et en Sibérie.* Paris: Bossard, 1922. 574 p. A useful account by a Dutch war correspondent. [B]

B182 GUBELMAN, MOISEI I. *Borba za sovetskii Dalnii Vostok.* Moscow: Voennoe izd. Ministerstva Oborony Soiuza SSR, 1958. 273 p. A popular account based only on Russian materials and emphasizing the role played by individual Soviet heroes, especially V. K. Blukher, S. G. Lazo, and P. P. Postyshev. Maintains that the U.S.A. was the chief instigator and organizer of the Siberian intervention.

B183 GUINS, GEORGE C. *Sibir, soiuzniki i Kolchak; povorotnyi moment russkoi istorii, 1918-1920 gg.; vpechatlieniia i mysli chlena Omskago pravitelstva.* Peking: Tipo-lit. Russkoi dykhovnoi missii, 1921. 2 vols. An exceptionally thorough and objective account of Siberian politics and Allied Intervention from the Bolshevik seizure of power to early 1920, by an important official in the Kolchak government. [B]

B184 HODGES, PHELPS. *Britmis; a Great Adventure of the War; Being an Account of Allied Intervention in Siberia and of an Escape Across the Gobi to Peking*. London: Cape, 1931. 364 p. A personal account of a particular set of incidents; virtually useless for a larger picture.

B185 ILIUKHOV, N., and TITOV, M. *Partizanskoe dvizhenie v Primori 1918-1920 gg*. Leningrad: Priboi, 1928. 252 p. A detailed first-hand account by two partisan leaders concerned mainly with the internal politics and conflicts of the Civil War. Also contains some material and documents dealing with the relations of the partisans with American and Japanese forces in Siberia.

B186 JANIN, PIERRE T. C. M. (GENERAL). *Ma Mission en Sibérie, 1918-1920*. Paris: Payot, 1933. 307 p. Janin commanded the Czech Legion and the French Military Mission. His valuable account is generally anti-Kolchak, anti-British, and pro-Czech. [B]

B187 KHARTLING, K. N. *Na strazhie rodiny; sobytiia vo Vladivostokie, konets 1919 g.–nachalo 1920 g*. Shanghai: Izd. T. S. Filimonovoi, 1935. 168 p. The story of a colonel in the White Army, still unreconciled to the fall of Tsardom. Among other things he relates are some unfortunate incidents between the Whites and the American-Japanese interventionists, which exacerbated relations between them.

B187A KOMISSIIA PO ISTORII OKTIABRSKOI REVOLIUTSII I R.K.P. *Revoliutsiia na Dalnem Vostoke*. Vol. 1. Moscow: Gosizdat, 1923. 433 p. Contains a number of documents and also articles written, in part, by participants. Deals with the Russian Far East, Transbaikalia, Yakutia, and other areas.

B188 KONSTANTINOV, M. M., ed. *Poslednie dni kolchakovshchiny*. Moscow-Leningrad: Gosizdat, 1926. 231 p. A valuable collection of documents of White and Red origin for the period from September 1919 to mid-February 1920. More important as a source about the Civil War than about Intervention.

B189 LASIES, JOSEPH. *La Tragédie sibérienne*. Paris: Crès, 1920. 255 p. A journalistic account by a member of the French military mission in Siberia. Very anti-Omsk, anti-British, pro-Czech. Blames the British for the disaster of Kolchak.

B190 LENGYEL, EMIL. *Secret Siberia*. N.Y.: Random House, 1943; London: Hale, n.d. 277 p. The author was a prisoner of war in Siberia, but was repatriated in the autumn of 1917. His account of the civil war (40 p.) is derived largely from the book by General Graves. Of interest for its descriptions of the P.O.W. camps in Siberia immediately before the Bolshevik Revolution.

B191 MAKSAKOV, V. V., and TURUNOV, A., eds., *Khronika grazhdanskoi voiny v Sibiri, 1917-1918*. Moscow: Gosizdat, 1926. 299 p. A most useful collection of documents from local and central archives, together with published materials and a detailed chronology and bibliography. [A]

B192 MELGUNOV, SERGIEI P. *Tragediia Admirala Kolchaka.* Belgrade: Russkaia Biblioteka, 1930-31. 4 vols. Although an apology for Kolchak, this is probably the most detailed history of the Civil War in Siberia. Contains long quotations from and references to other Russian sources. [A]

B193 MONTANDON, GEORGE. *Deux ans chez Koltchak et chez les Bolchéviques pour la Croix-rouge de Génève, 1919-1921.* 3rd ed., Paris: Alcan, 1923. 319 p. The author was a Swiss physician who worked among prisoners of war in Siberia. Contains useful information on the Civil War.

B194 PARFENOV, PETR S. (Altaiskii, Petr, pseud.). *Borba za Dalnii Vostok, 1920-1922.* Leningrad: Priboi, 1928. 368 p. Moscow: Moskovskoe tovarishchestvo pisatelei, 1931. 358 p.

B195 PARFENOV, PETR S. *Uroki proshlogo: Grazhdanskaia voina v Sibiri 1918, 1919, 1920 gg.* Harbin: 1921. Revised ed., *Grazhdanskaia voina v Sibiri 1918-1920.* Moscow: Gosizdat, 1924. 168 p. A critical, fairly detailed account of Soviet and anti-Soviet activities by a participant. Written on the basis of his own knowledge and documents left by Rozanov in Vladivostok. The second edition is more clearly Marxist.

B196 PARFENOV, V. *The Intervention in Siberia in 1918-1922.* N.Y.: Workers Library, 1941. 64 p. Interesting as a short summary of the Soviet point of view at the time of publication. The villains of the piece are the Japanese, not the Americans.

B198 ROUQUEROL, JEAN J. *La Guerre des Rouges et des Blancs; l'aventure de l'Amiral Koltchak.* Paris: Payot, 1929. 187 p. The author was a member of the French military mission. His account covers the same ground as Janin's with much less thoroughness. Very anti-British.

B199 SAKHAROV, KONSTANTIN VON. *Das Weisse Sibirien.* Munich: Laubereau, 1925. 386 p. Memoirs of an extreme monarchist placed by the British in command of the Vladivostok officer training school on Russkii Ostrov, later briefly the commander of Kolchak's army. Interesting as an example of a mentality common among White officers.

B200 SEMENOV, GRIGORII M. *O sebe; vospominaniia, mysli i vyvody.* Harbin: Zaria, 1938. 228 p. This useful, but undocumented, autobiography of an important White Russian leader is sometimes vague about dates and needs to be checked against other sources. [B]

B201 SHISHKIN, S. N. *Grazhdanskaia voina na Dalnem Vostoke, 1918-1922 gg.* Moscow: Voennoe izd. Ministerstva oborony SSSR, 1957. 267 p.

B202 SPIRIN, LEONID M. *Razgrom armii Kolchaka.* Moscow: Gospolitizdat, 1957. 295 p. A scholarly account based on a wide range of published and archival materials. More balanced in tone and general approach than other similar Soviet works.

B203 TRETIAK, IVAN IA. *Partizanskoe dvizhenie v gornom altae 1919 g.* Novosibirsk: Zap.-Sib. kraeval izd., 1933. 168 p. A subsequent Bolshevik work written to supersede the original interpretations describing the non-Bolshevik nature of the anti-White revolts of the Altai peasants.

B204 TSYPKIN, S., comp. *Oktiabrskaia Revoliutsiia i Grazhdanskaia voina na Dalnem Vostoke; khronika sobytii, 1917-1922 gg.* Moscow: Dalgiz, 1933. 305 p.

B205 VARNECK, ELENA, and FISHER, HAROLD H., eds. *The Testimony of Kolchak and Other Siberian Materials.* Stanford, Cal.: Stanford University Press, 1935. 466 p. A translation of *Dopros Kolchaka* (Leningrad, 1925), Kolchak's frank and revealing testimony previous to his execution by partisans. The editors' exhaustive notes give much information on the Civil War in Siberia. Excellent 51-page annotated bibliography. [A]

B206 VILENSKII, VLADIMIR D. (SIBIRIAKOV). *Soiuznicheskaia interventsiia na Dalnem Vostoke i v Sibiri.* Moscow: 1925.

B207 WARD, JOHN. *With the "Die-Hards" in Siberia.* N.Y. and London: Cassell, 1920. 272 p. Russian ed., Moscow: 1923. 171 p. Ward was a Labour M.P. who commanded the 25th Middlesex Battalion in Siberia from August 1918 to mid-1919. Interesting on Allied relations with Kolchak, although his devotion to Kolchak should be discounted. Of limited value as an historical source, however, since it is neither precise nor complete. [B]

B208 WHITE, JOHN A. *The Siberian Intervention.* Princeton, N.J.: Princeton University Press, 1950. 471 p. A good, scholarly account, more concerned with the effects of Intervention on the Civil War in Siberia than with policy-making in Allied capitals. Based on an immense range of published materials in several languages. [A]

B209 *Za vlast Sovetov; vospominaniia uchastnikov partizanskogo dvizheniia v tylu u Kolchaka; dokumenty.* E. I. Pesikina, ed. Novosibirsk:

Novosibgiz, 1947. 344 p. Recollections of some 20 participants. The documents section contains government proclamations, army orders, etc. Maps, chronology.

(2) JAPANESE INTERVENTION
(EDITED BY JAMES H. MORLEY)

B210 ARAKI SADAO, comp. *Gensui Uehara Yūsaku Den.* Tokyo: Gensui Uehara Yūsaku Denki Hankō-kai, 1937. 2 vols. The standard biography of Field Marshal Uehara Yūsaku, a leading proponent of the Siberian expedition; includes brief extracts from his diary.

B211 CHANG, CHUNG-FU. *Chung-hua Min-kuo Wai-chiao Shih.* Vol. I, Chungking: Cheng chung shu-chu, 1936. This standard history of Chinese foreign relations by a distinguished political scientist and diplomat, based on western and Chinese sources, is useful for the Chinese component in Japanese policy concerning the Siberian expedition.

B212 CHINA, MINISTRY OF FOREIGN AFFAIRS. *Wai-chiao Wen-tu; Chung-Jih Chün-shin Hsieh-ting An.* Peking: 1921. 68 p. Chinese originals and English translations of official documents concerning the Sino-Japanese Military Agreement for Common Defense, May 1918, and its abrogation, January, 1921.

B213 COLEMAN, FREDERIC A. *Japan or Germany; the Inside Story of the Struggle in Siberia.* N.Y.: Doran, 1918. 232 p. British ed. *Japan Moves North.* London: Cassell, 1918. 177 p. A journalistic account by an on-the-spot observer, favorable to Japan.

B214 COMMUNIST INTERNATIONAL, FAR EASTERN SECTION. *Iaponiia na russkom Dalnem Vostoke; krovavaia epopeia iaponskoi interventsii.* Foreword by Karl Radek. Moscow: 1922. A Comminterm account, published in several languages, of the Japanese intervention in Siberia, stressing its aggressive and terroristic character.

B215 *Dai Nihon Teikoku Gikai-shi.* Shizuoka: Dai Nihon Teikoku Gikai-shi Hakko-kai. 17 vols. The standard selected record of the proceedings of the Japanese Diet. Interpellations and speeches relating to the Siberian expedition are in vols. 11-12.

B216 *Deistviia Iaponii v Priamurskom kraie; sbornik offitsialnykh dokumentov, otnosiashchikhsia k interventsii derzhav v predielakh Priamuria.* Vladivostok: T-vo izd. Svobodnaia Rossiia, 1921. 142 p.

B217 FAR EASTERN REPUBLIC. *Japanese Intervention in the Russian Far East.* Washington: The Special Delegation of the Far Eastern Republic to the United States of America, 1922. 165 p. An official attack on Japanese Intervention policy, combined with an official account of the origins of the Far Eastern Republic. Documents.

B217A GRIGORTSEVICH, STANISLAV S. *Amerikanskaia i iaponskaia interventsiia na Sovetskom Dalnem Vostoke i ee razgrom, 1918-1922 gg.* Moscow: Gospolitizdat, 1957. 200 p. Uses Russian archival and Western secondary sources to support the thesis that Japan and the United States sought first to overthrow the Soviet government, then to sever the Far Eastern area from its control.

B218 HARA, HEI'ICHIRO, ed. *Hara Kei Nikki.* Tokyo: Kengensha, 1950-51. 10 vols. The most valuable political diary of the period; volumes 7 to 9 cover Hara's membership in the Diplomatic Advisory Council and his premiership (1918-22). [B]

B219 HOSOYA, CHIHIRO. *Shiberia Shuppei ni Shiteki Kenkyu.* Tokyo: Yuhikaku, 1955. The best analytical study by an objective Japanese scholar of the origins of Japan's decision to send an expedition. This work is based primarily on cited diplomatic archives and published memoirs. An abridgement in English appears as "Origin of the Siberian Intervention," *The Annals of the Hitotsubashi Academy*, vol. IX, no. 1 (1958), p. 90-108. [A]

B219A HOSOYA, CHIHIRO. "Kaigun Rikusentai no Vladivostok Jōriku Mondai," *Rekishi Kyōiku*, 1960, no. 1. A scholarly study, based on official sources, of the Japanese naval landing at Vladivostok, January, 1918.

B219B HOSOYA, CHIHIRO. "Nihon to Kolchak Seiken Shōnin Mondai," *Hitotsubashi Daigaku Hōgaku Kenkyū*, 1961, no. 3, Japan's recognition of Kolchak explained as an effort to stem the spread of Bolshevism; based on primary sources.

B219C HOSOYA, CHIHIRO. "Shiberia Shuppei o meguru Nichi-Bei Kankei," *Kokusai Seiji*, 1961, no. 3. Interprets Japanese-American relations concerning the Expedition as influenced by common anti-Bolshevist views, but divergent attitudes toward Japanese expansion; based on primary sources.

B219D HOSOYA, CHIHIRO, comp., "Japanese Documents on the Siberian Intervention, 1917-1922, Part I, November 1917-January 1919," *The Hitotsubashi Journal of Law and Politics*, vol. I, no. 1 (1960). English translations of important materials from the Japanese diplomatic, naval, and other archives, by the leading Japanese authority on the Expedition.

B220 ISHIHARA, YUICHIRO. *Shiberia seikyoku no shinsō.* Tokyo: Tokyo dō, 1921. 169 p. A Japanese newspaperman's report of conditions in eastern Siberia and the Russian Far East, 1917-20, containing little on Japanese activity, but interesting for reports on Semenov, Kolchak, and Korean émigrés.

B221 ISTORIIA GRAZHDANSKOI VOINY V SSSR. *Sergei Lazo, vospominaniia i dokumenty.* Comp. by G. Reikhberg, A. Romanov, and P. Krol. Moscow: Gosizdat, 1938. 217 p. Letters, orders, notebook and diary extracts, together with explanatory articles, compiled to eulogize the Far Eastern partisan leader Sergei Lazo (1894-1920).

B222 JAPAN, ARMY GENERAL STAFF HEADQUARTERS. *Taishō Shichi-nen naishi Jūichi-nen Shiberia Shuppei-shi.* Tokyo: 1924. 7 vols. Formerly classified, this official, detailed history of the Japanese military operations in the Siberian Expedition is part of a series of official operational histories compiled for government use. [B]

B223 JAPAN, NAVY GENERAL STAFF. *Taishō Yon-nen naishi Kyū-nen Kaigun Senshi.* Tokyo: 1924. 4 vols. An official, formerly classified, detailed history of Japanese naval operations, 1915-20, including the Siberian Expedition; part of a series of official operational histories for government use. [B]

B224 *Japanese aggression in the Russian Far East. Extracts from the Congressional Record, March 2, 1922, in the Senate of the United States.* Washington: G.P.O., 1922. 111 p.

B224A KOBAYASHI, SACHIO. "Shiberia Kanshō to Nikolaevsk Jiken," *Kinki Daigaku Hōgaku*, vol. V, nos. 3-4; vol. VI, nos. 1-4; vol. VII, no. 1, 1956-58. Uses primary Japanese sources to emphasize the role of anti-Bolshevism in Japan's decision to continue the Expedition after 1920.

B225 KOMMISSIIA PO ISTORIIA OKTIABRSKOI REVOLIUTSII I R.K.P. *Revoliutsiia na Dalnem Vostoke.* Moscow: Gosizdat, 1923. 433 p. Deals with the Bolshevik struggle in the Soviet Far East, the fight against the Japanese in the Maritime Province, etc. Contains many documents and articles written, in part, by participants.

B226 LIU, YEN. *Ou-Chan Ch'i-Chien Chung-Jih Chiao-she Shih.* Shanghai: 1921. A detailed account, quoting Chinese newspaper and official sources, of the patriotic Chinese view of Sino-Japanese relations during World War I, including involvement in the Japanese expedition.

B227 MORLEY, JAMES W. *The Japanese Thrust into Siberia, 1918.* N.Y.: Columbia, 1957. 395 p. The standard work on the origins of the Japanese decision to intervene, based primarily on Japanese diplomatic and military archives, and published materials; contains a bibliography, chronology, and documentary appendix. [A]

B228 OTSU, JUN'ICHIRO. *Dai Nihon Kenseishi.* Tokyo: Hobunkan, 1927. 10 vols. A basic history of Japanese foreign and domestic politics, with voluminous quotations. Volume 8 includes the expedition. [B]

B229 REIKHBERG, G. E. *Iaponskaia interventsiia na Dalnem Vostoke, 1918-1922; kratkii ocherk.* Moscow: Gos. sots.-ekon. izd-vo., 1935. 114 p. The best scholarly summary of the Soviet indictment of Japanese "imperialism," based on Russian and Western materials, which are cited; no Japanese sources are used.

B230 REIKHBERG, G. E. *Razgrom iaponskoi interventsii na Dalnem Vostoke (1918-1922 gg.).* Moscow: Sotsekgiz, 1940. 212 p. A later account of Japanese Intervention by a Soviet scholar.

B231 RUSSIA (1917– RSFSR), TSENTRALNOE ARKHIVNOE UPRAVLENIE. *Iaponskaia interventsiia 1918-1922 gg. v dokumentakh.* Edited by Isaak I. Mints. Moscow: Tsentrarkhiv, 1934. 234 p. A collection of documents largely from the Central Archive of the October Revolution and that of the Red Army, plus newspaper clippings, etc.; a volume in the series *Massovaia istoricheskaia biblioteka.* [B]

B231A SEKI, HIROHARU. "1917-nen Harupin Kakumei," *Kokusaihō Gaikō Zasshi,* Vol. 57 (1958), No. 3 (August), p. 36-83; and No. 4 (September), p. 81-120. The revolution in Harbin in 1917 and the relation of Japan to Horvat's rise to power, based on primary sources.

B231B SEMENOV, GRIGORII M. *O sebe: vospominaniia, mysli i vyvody.* Harbin: Zaria: 1938. 228 p. This useful but undocumented autobiography of an important anti-Soviet leader who co-operated with the Japanese is sometimes vague about dates and needs to be checked against other sources. [B]

B232 SHINOBU, SEIZABURO. *Taishō Seiji-shi.* Tokyo: Kawade shobō, 1951-52. 4 vols. A standard political history of Japan during the 1905-27 period by a noted left-wing historian. Includes the Siberian expedition. Bibliography.

B233 TSURUMI, YUSUKE. *Gotō Shimpei.* Tokyo: Gotō Shimpei denki hensan-kai, 1938. 4 vols. A standard biography, based on the Gotō family and foreign Ministry archives, of a leading politician and Russian expert active in promoting the expedition and later in negotiating with Joffe for the establishment of Japanese-Soviet relations.

B234 VILENSKII, VLADIMIR D. ("SIBIRIAKOV"). *Chernaia godina sibirskoi reaktsii; interventsiia v Sibiri.* Moscow: VTSIK Sovetov R., S., K. i K. Deputatov, 1919. 56 p. German ed., Zurich: Internationaler Verlag, 1920. 72 p. A vigorously partisan account by a participant in the struggle of the Siberian "proletariat" against "White guards" and "interventionists" in 1918.

B235 VSESOIUZNAIA KOMMUNISTICHESKAIA PARTIIA (BOLSHEVIKOV), CHITA OKRUZHNYI KOMITET. *Partizany.* Chita: 1929. A collection of articles, memoirs, documents, and excerpts from letters and diaries, relating to "partisan" activities in the Chita area, 1917-20; includes a chronology.

B236 WHITE, JOHN A. *The Siberian Intervention.* Princeton, N.J.: Princeton University Press, 1950. 471 p. A good, scholarly account, emphasizing the effect on the Civil War in Siberia of the Intervention. Based on extensive study of published material in many languages. [A]

(3) The Far Eastern Republic (edited by James H. Morley)

B237 FAR EASTERN REPUBLIC. *Japanese Intervention in the Russian Far East.* Washington: The Special Delegation of the Far Eastern Republic to the U.S.A., 1922. 165 p. An official account, with documents, of the origins of the Far Eastern Republic according to its representatives, combined with an official attack on Japanese intervention policy.

B238 FAR EASTERN REPUBLIC. *A Short Outline History of the Far Eastern Republic.* Washington: The Special Delegation of the Far Eastern Republic to the U.S.A., 1922. 69 p. An official account by representatives of the Far Eastern Republic, stressing the theme of democratic self-determination of the peoples of the Russian Far East. Documentary appendix. [A]

B239 FLETCHER, FLORENCE A. "The Far Eastern Republic." M.A. thesis, Columbia, 1923. 121 p. An interesting contemporary estimate of the Kolchak movement and the FER, useful for biographical sketches of the FER leaders and analysis of the FER constitution.

B240 MARTEL, LEON C., JR. "Russian Foreign Policy and the Establishment of the Far Eastern Republic." Certificate essay, Russian Institute, Columbia, 1957. 121 p. A re-evaluation of Soviet and Japanese intentions concerning the FER, based on Russian and Western languages materials. Bibliography.

B241 NORTON, HENRY K. *The Far Eastern Republic of Siberia.* N.Y.: Holt, 1923. 316 p. A history of Eastern Siberia and the Russian Far East, and the Civil War there, attributing the formation of the FER to the rejection of Communism by the peasantry. Sympathetic analysis of the constitution, leadership, and policies of the new state. [B]

B242 PAPIN, LEONID M. *Krakh kolchakovshchiny i obrazovanie Dalnevostochnoi Respubliki.* Moscow: Moskovskii Universitet, 1957. 224 p. A detailed study of the downfall of the Kolchak government and the history of the Far Eastern Republic, attributing the failure of the Kolchak and interventionist movements to popular revulsion at their behavior, which the author charges was cruel and repressive. Based on Russian archives and documents as well as Western secondary sources. [B]

(4) American Intervention in the Far East (edited by Richard H. Ullman)

B243 BEREZKIN, ALEKSANDR V. *SShA—aktivnyi organizator i uchastnik voennoi interventsii protiv Sovetskoi Rossii 1918-1920 gg.* Moscow: Izd. politicheskoi lit., 1949. 183 p. 2nd ed., 1952. Essentially a Stalinist tract maintaining that the U.S. was the prime organizer and instigator of Intervention. Cites a wide range of published materials and a few Soviet archival references.

B244 BRANDENBURG, WILLIAM A., JR. "The Origins of American Military Intervention in Russia, 1918-1920." Ph.D. dissertation, U. of Colorado, 1947.

B245 CHANNING, C. G. FAIRFAX (pseud. of Christian C. Gross). *Siberia's Untouched Treasure: Its Future Role in the World.* N.Y. and London: Putnam, 1923. 475 p. A huge compendium of facts about Siberia and its resources combined with an account of the author's experiences as a lieutenant in the U.S. army expedition. Interesting for impressions; of little value for political information.

B246 DUPUY, RICHARD ERNEST. *Perish by the Sword; the Czechoslovakian Anabasis and our Supporting Campaigns in North Russia and Siberia 1918-1920.* Harrisburg, Pa.: Military Service, 1939. 302 p. A readable account based on published materials; this has been completely superseded by more recent literature, however.

B247 EITLER, WARREN J. "Diplomacy of the Graves Mission to Siberia." Ph.D. dissertation, Georgetown, 1953.

B248 FELCHLIN, HOWARD L. "United States Decision to Intervene in Russia, July 1918; Political and Military Factors." Certificate essay, Russian Institute, Columbia, 1948. 121 p.

B249 GRAVES, WILLIAM S. *America's Siberian Adventure, 1918-1920.* N.Y.: Cape and Smith, 1931. 363 p. N.Y.: Smith, 1941. Russian ed., Moscow: Gos. voen. izd., 1932. Lt.-Gen. Graves commanded the U.S. expedition to Siberia. The book is an apology; Graves holds that only he adhered to the intervention plan originally approved by President Wilson, while the British and Japanese deliberately subverted intervention for selfish national purposes. Some useful documentary material. [B]

B250 IVANOV, S. *Amerikanskaia agressiia na sovetskom Dalnem Vostoke.* Vladivostok: Primizdat, 1952. 247 p.

B251 KINDALL, SYLVIAN G. *American Soldiers in Siberia.* N.Y.: R. R. Smith, 1945. 251 p. A well-written, interesting, first-hand account by an American officer. Violently anti-Japanese: the theme of the book is how the Japanese used Americans for their own ends.

B252 MANNING, CLARENCE A. *The Siberian Fiasco.* N.Y.: Library Publishers, 1952. 210 p. A good, popular account of the U.S. Siberian expedition based on non-Russian materials. Written from the point of view of events in Siberia, not in Washington. Interesting concerning Semenov, Kolchak, and Japanese policy.

B253 PELZEL, SOPHIA R. *American Intervention in Siberia, 1918-1920.* Philadelphia: 1946. 98 p. Describes the evolution of American intervention from 1918 to 1920 and argues that this action was not a deviation from discernible trends in American Far Eastern policy. Treats the intervention within the context of unfolding events in Europe and Russia and as a part of the growing antagonism toward Japanese aims in that area. Based on a U. of Pennsylvania Ph.D. dissertation.

B254 UNTERBERGER, BETTY M. *America's Siberian Expedition, 1918-1920; A Study of National Policy.* Durham, N.C.: Duke, 1956. 271 p. An excellent scholarly account, primarily focussed on policy-making in Washington. The author thoroughly uses State, War, and Navy Department materials in the National Archives, plus a wide range of private manuscript collections. No Russian materials. [A]

(5) THE CZECHOSLOVAK LEGION IN RUSSIA (EDITED BY MIROSLAV FIC)

B255 BAERLEIN, HENRY P. B. *The March of the Seventy Thousand.* London: Parsons, 1926. 287 p. A popular and informative account of the Czechoslovak Legionaires' struggle in Russia, by a British publicist. [A]

B256 BEČVÁŘ, G. *The Lost Legion; a Czechoslovakian Epic.* London: Paul Stanley, 1939. 256 p. A member of the Czechoslovak Legion tells of the experiences that he and the members of his unit had in Russia. Recounts, among other things, the story of his contact with Admiral Kolchak.

B257 *Čechoslováci ve válce a v revoluci; Sbírka oficiálních dokumentů o hnutí imperialistickém a komunistickém mezi Čechy a Slováky v Rusku.* Kiev-Moscow: 1919. A collection of documents on the establishment of the Communist Party of Czechoslovakia, its functioning first as a section of the C.P. of Russia, then within Stalin's Ministry of Nationalities, and finally as a member of the Third International. A unique collection, made by the leadership of the Czechoslovak Communists in Russia in 1918.

B258 DUPUY, RICHARD ERNEST. *Perish by the Sword; the Czechoslovakian Anabasis and our Supporting Campaigns in North Russia and Siberia 1918-1920.* Harrisburg, Pa.: Military Service, 1939. 302 p. A readable account based on published materials. It has been completely superseded by more recent literature, however.

B259 FIC, MIROSLAV V. "The Origin of the Conflict of the Bolsheviks with the Czechoslovak Legion in 1918." Ph.D. dissertation, Columbia (in progress). Based on Czechoslovak and Soviet sources. Shows the conflicting attitudes of Lenin and Trotsky towards the Czechoslovaks, and attributes the origin of the Czechoslovak-Bolshevik conflict to the weak military position of the Bolshevik regime in January-April 1918 and to the subsequent drive of Trotsky to retain the Czechoslovaks in Russia. Its special contribution lies in its discussion of the number of prisoners of war of the Central Powers who joined the Red Army, of the role they played in the consolidation of Bolshevik power and in the origin of the Czechoslovak-Bolshevik fighting. The study gives all known interpretations of this struggle. The extensive bibliography is particularly useful.

B260 GAJDA, R. *Moje paměti; Československá anabase; zpět na Urál proti bolševikům.* 3rd ed. Prague: "Vesmír," 1924. 202 p. Personal memoirs written by one of the chief Czech commanders in Russia who later became a Fascist leader. Particularly valuable in explaining why Gajda joined Kolchak and subsequently broke with him. It is an account of the fundamental differences between Gajda and Kolchak with regard to the strategic direction of the anti-Bolshevik struggle, of the reasons for the Bolshevik break-through on the Samara Front, and of the subsequent collapse of the Russian Liberation Army. Throws light on the history of the Civil War in Russia and the failure of the democratic opposition. [B]

B261 JANIN, PIERRE T. C. MAURICE (GENERAL). *Ma Mission en Sibérie, 1918-1920.* Paris: Payot, 1933. 307 p. Czechoslovak ed., *Moje účast na československém boji za svobodu.* Prague: Otto, 1930. 384 p. French General Janin gives an account of the role the Czechoslovak Legion played in the development of French policy towards Russia. After the seizure of power by the Bolsheviks, Janin became the Supreme Commander of the Czechoslovak forces in Russia. Deals with the later phase of the Czechoslovak-Bolshevik conflict.

B262 KALINA, ANTONÍN S. *Krví a železem dobyto československé samostatnosti.* Prague: Nákladem vlastním, 1938. 333 p. Kalina collected every bit of information and every document known at the time that his book on the diplomatic background and implications of the Czechoslovak military operations in Russia was written. He severely criticised Masaryk for his war-time policies, particularly for his unwillingness to commit the Legion to the promotion of Wilson's plans for assistance to Russia. Had Masaryk agreed to these plans, the Czechoslovaks could have won recognition of their co-belligerent status much earlier than they actually did. The author coins the new thesis that it was the United States which was responsible for the outbreak of the Czechoslovak-Bolshevik conflict, because it denied the Czechoslovaks the ships needed to transport them to France. The author alleges that this denial was a part of a general policy aimed at the reopening of the Eastern Front in Russia. Subsequently published documents have made this thesis obsolete. The book is important, however, for its extensive collection of documents.

B263 KENNAN, GEORGE F. "The Czechoslovak Legion." Chap. VI in his: *The Decision to Intervene*. Princeton, N.J.: Princeton University Press, 1958. P. 136-165. The best brief account of the clash with the Bolsheviks and the influence this had on Allied—especially American—Intervention. [A]

B264 KLANTE, MARGARETE. *Von der Wolga zum Amur; Die Tschechische Legion und der Russische Burgerkrieg; dargestellt auf Grund authentischen Materials*. Berlin: Ost-Europa, 1931. 346 p. Written as a Ph.D. dissertation for a German University. Though the author did her research in Prague and had access to the original documents, the book fails to bring out the relevant documentary material. [B]

B265 KLECANDA, VLADIMÍR. *Operace československého vojska na Rusi v letech 1917-1920*. Prague: Československý vědecký ústav, 1921. 16 p. A brief outline of the military operations of the Czechoslovaks in Russia, by a competent military historian. Most valuable are the large and detailed maps showing not only the deployment of the Czechoslovak and Bolshevik forces on the Volga, the Urals, Lake Baikal, and the Far Eastern fronts, but also the relative strength of the two parties and their allies. Indispensable for a military historian.

B266 KRATOCHVÍL, JAROSLAV. *Cesta revoluce; (Československé Legie v Rusku)*. Prague: Čin, 1922. 674 p. An important source book on the origin of the Czech-Bolshevik conflict, written from the point of view of a radical Czech Socialist, who blames the Czechs, particularly General Gajda, for the outbreak of the fighting. Has a number of documents from private archives relating to the Czech as well as the Bolshevik side.

B267 KŘÍŽEK, JAROSLAV. *Penza; slavná bojová tradice československých rudoarmějců.* Prague: 1956. A study of the outbreak of the fighting between the Czechoslovaks and the Bolsheviks in Penza, written with a heavy bias in favor of the Bolsheviks. The book is useful, for it brings out a number of important documents throwing light upon the organization of the Czechoslovak Red Army. Written in Communist Czechoslovakia, the book places the blame for the outbreak of the conflict upon the shoulders of Trotsky and the Allies.

B268 KUDELA, JOSEF. *Profesor Masaryk a Československé vojsko na Rusi.* Prague: Památník Odboje, 1923. 234 p. Kudela deals with Masaryk's efforts at the stabilization of the Russian front following the Bolshevik-German armistice in December 1917, his negotiations with the Allies in Russia and Romania and with the Ukrainian Rada. He also describes Masaryk's efforts to organize other Slavic nationalities in Russia into a military group which could serve as a nucleus for the regeneration of the Russian army. Kudela also explains the reasons which prompted Masaryk to withdraw the Czechoslovaks from Russia and to transfer them to the French front. [B]

B269 KUDELA, JOSEF. *S naším vojskem na Rusi.* Vol. 1: *V době příprav.* Vol. 2: *Na druhou frontu.* Prague: Památník Odboje, 1922–. 2 vols. A collection of articles published in the *Československý Deník*, the official organ of the Czechoslovak National Council in Russia, on every aspect of the activities of the Legion in Russia. The book also gives the full text of a number of orders of the day of the command, of the decisions, decrees, and regulations of the National Council, and of the drafts of various proposals on the re-organization of the Legion. An important source.

B270 MASARYK, TOMÁŠ G. *Masarykovy projevy a řeči za války.* Vol. 2: *Dokumenty k Masarykovu pobytu v Rusku.* Prague: St. Minařík, 1920. 216 p. An important collection of documents relating to Masaryk's sojourn in 1917-18, to his efforts to fight the separate-peace trends evident in Russian political circles, his attempts at re-organizing a new Russian army, and his role in the attempts of the Allies to win the Ukraine to the Entente's side.

B271 MEDEK, R., VANĚČEK, O., and HOLEČEK, V. *Za svobodu.* Prague: Nákladem vlastním, 1925-1929. 4 vols. A comprehensive source book on the Czechoslovak Legion. Volume 1 deals with the participation of the Czechoslovaks in the military operations of the Tsarist army; Volume 2 deals with Masaryk's political and military efforts in Russia; Volume 3 documents the origin of the Czechoslovak-Bolshevik conflict; Volume 4 treats the military operations of the Czechoslovaks against the Bolsheviks, with the political efforts of the Czechoslovaks to establish an All-Russian Government on the liberated territories, and with the final withdrawal from Russia. Is extremely valuable, for it brings out the entire telegraphic exchange between Trotsky and the local commanders of the Red Army. [A]

B272 MUŠKA, J. and HOŘEC, J. *K úloze československých legií v Rusku.* Prague: Nakladatelství Mír, 1953. 200 p. Bratislava: SPB, 1954. 200 p. A study of the origin of the Czechoslovak-Bolshevik conflict, by two young Communist writers. Repeats the old and unfounded allegations of Soviet historians that the Czechoslovaks plunged into the conflict on the orders of the French and British, that the Czechoslovaks were a mere tool in the hands of the Allies, and that Masaryk and the Legion in Russia had nothing to do with the struggle of the Czechoslovaks to regain independence.

B273 PAPOUŠEK, JAROSLAV. *Chekhoslovaki i Sovety.* Prague: Slovanský ústav, 1928. An account of the origin of the Czechoslovak-Bolshevik conflict. Makes the Soviet Government responsible for the outbreak of the fighting, shows the duplicity of the Soviet Government, and attributes a large share of the responsibility for the militant attitude of the Bolsheviks to the Czechoslovak Bolsheviks and to the prisoners of war of the Central Powers serving in the ranks of the Red Army. [A]

B274 SKÁCEL, JINDŘICH. *Československá armáda v Rusku a Kolčak; (Protibolševický boj v roce 1918-1920).* Prague: Památník Odboje, 1926. 433 p. An important book on the efforts of the Czechoslovaks in Russia to organize the Russian Liberation Army, the participation of the Czechoslovaks in the political efforts of the Russian people to set up an All-Russian Government in Siberia, the split within the Czechoslovak camp, and on the work of the two groups, one urging the evacuation of Russia, the other assistance to the Russian people in their struggle with the Bolsheviks. The discussion of the relations between the Czechoslovaks and Kolchak is an important contribution to the history of the Civil War in Russia. [B]

B275 ŠTEIDLER, FRANTIŠEK V. *Československé hnutí na Rusi.* Prague: Památník Odboje, 1921. 113 p. A brief but important account of the Legion in Russia from 1914 to 1920. Written by the official military historian of the Legion. [B]

B276 ŠTEIDLER, FRANTIŠEK V. *Naše vystoupení v Rusku r. 1918.* Prague: Památník Odboje, 1923. 85 p. A brief but important account of the origin of the Czechoslovak-Bolshevik conflict. Refutes Kratochvil's charges that the Czechoslovaks were responsible for its outbreak, and in particular refutes the allegation that the collusion of the Czechoslovaks with the S.R.'s and other opponents of the Bolsheviks touched off the struggle. It gives Gajda's account of his interview with the Revolutionary Underground Organization of the S.R.'s in Novonikolaievsk on the day of the fight's beginning.

B277 ŠVEC, JOSEF J. *Denník Plukovníka Švece.* Prague: Památník Odboje, 1920. 2 vols. Diary of a brilliant Czech commander under whose direction the Czechoslovaks seized Penza. Švec later shot himself when Bolshevik propaganda began to affect his troops and they refused to fight the Bolsheviks.

B278 VERGE, ARSÈNE. *Avec les Tchécoslovaques; invraisemblable et véridique épopée.* Paris: Guillon, 1926. 201 p. Verge was a liaison officer from the French Military Mission in Russia to the Czechoslovaks. His book deals with the efforts of France to win the Ukrainian Government to the Allied side in December 1917-March 1918, and the role the Legion played in these efforts. Also gives an assessment of the military value of the Legion before its evacuation from the Ukraine in February 1918. Contains the text of an important memorandum drafted by Masaryk on March 3, 1918 which anticipated the military assistance of the Czechoslovaks to any Russian Government willing to resume war on the Central Powers.

B279 VESELÝ, JINDŘICH. *Češi a Slováci v revolučním Rusku, 1917-1920.* Prague: Státní nakl. politické literatury, 1954. 236 p. An account of the impact of the Bolshevik coup d'état upon the Czechs and Slovaks in Russia and the establishment of the Czechoslovak Communist Party in Russia. Discusses the fratricidal war between the Czechs and Slovaks following Masaryk and those following Lenin. Strongly biased.

B280 VESELÝ, JINDŘICH. *O vzniku a založení KSČ.* Prague: Státní nakl. politické lit., 1953. Deals with the impact of the Bolshevik seizure of power upon the Legion. Shows how the radical elements left the Legion, established themselves in Petrograd, Moscow and Kiev and laid the foundation for the Czechoslovak Communist Party. Throws light upon the military and political co-operation of the Czechoslovak Bolsheviks with the Soviet Government, and the efforts of the former to bring the Legion over to the Bolshevik side. The book and the documents in the appendix are an indispensable source on the origin of the Czechoslovak Communist Party.

B281 ZMRHAL, KAREL. *O samosprávu a demokracii v sibiřské armádě.* Prague: Knihovna Osvobození, 1923. 396 p. A detailed and well documented account of the reasons which prompted the Czechoslovaks to resort to arms in order to force their way into Vladivostok. Deals with the revolution that took place among the troops, the deposition of the leadership which had compromised with the Bolsheviks, the last attempt to negotiate the exit from Russia, and the final decision to mount military operations against the Bolsheviks. All these events took place at the Congress of the Legion in Cheliabinsk in May 1918. The author was Chairman of this Congress and draws upon its official minutes. The most important decisions of the Congress, and its telegraphic exchange with the Soviet Government and the Allies, are quoted in full. Absolutely indispensable for understanding the Czechoslovak side.

B282 ZMRHAL, KAREL. *Vláda sovětů a Čechoslováci; výklad konfliktu československého vojska na Rusi s bolševiky.* Prague: "Socialistické listy," 1919. 48 p. The first attempt to explain the reasons for the outbreak of the Czechoslovak-Bolshevik conflict. The book has a number of documents showing the duplicity of the Soviet Government in dealing with the Czechoslovaks, the operational orders of Trotsky to the local commanders to mount the attack upon the Czechoslovaks, and the role played by the prisoners of war of the Central Powers in this attack. [B]

C. Independence Movements by Minority Nationalities of Russia, 1917-1921

NOTE: This section covers only those countries that were unable to retain their independence beyond 1921. The independence movements of Finland and the Baltic States are covered in Part II.

1. GENERAL WORKS

(Edited by Serge A. Zenkovsky)

C1 AKADEMIIA NAUK SSSR, INSTITUT ISTORII. *Obrazovanie SSSR—sbornik dokumentov, 1917-1924.* Ed. by Esfir B. Genkina. Moscow: Izd. Akademii nauk SSSR, 1949. 469 p. A valuable collection of documents on the formation of the USSR and the problem of nationalism there. The documents have been arbitrarily selected and present primarily the Soviet interpretation of the historical process.

C1A ARSHARUNI, A. and GABIDULLIN, KH. *Ocherki panislamizma i pantiurkizma v Rossii.* Moscow: Bezbozhnik, 1931. 138 p. A good survey of relations between the Russian imperial and Soviet governments and Russia's Moslem minorities. Also partially treats the relations of Russia's Moslems with Turkey. Both authors are well-known experts in this field.

C2 BARGHOORN, FREDERICK C. *Soviet Russian Nationalism.* N.Y.: Oxford, 1956. 330 p. A detailed study of the evolution of Russian nationalism since the Revolution and the regime's attitude toward the nationalities of the USSR. Does not deal specifically with the independence movements of the Soviet minorities. The author is Professor of Political Science at Yale. [A]

C3 BOERSNER, DEMETRIO. *The Bolsheviks and the National and Colonial Question, 1917-1928.* N.Y.: Gregory Lounz; Geneva: Droz, 1957. 285 p. A detailed study of the policies of the Soviet State towards various national minorities of the USSR and toward the colonial policies of the Western European powers. Covers the first decade of Soviet rule in Russia. [B]

C4 BROIDO, GRIGORII I., ed. *Natsionalnyi i kolonialnyi vopros i R.K.P. (b); materialy i stati.* Moscow: Moskovskii rabochii, 1925. A study of the nationalities problems in Russia by a former Menshevik, later a Bolshevik leader in Central Asia, and one of the best Soviet specialists in the field.

C5 *Bütün Rusy a müsülmanlarinin 1917nci yilda 1-11 mayda Meskevde bulgan umumi isyezdinin protokollari.* Petrograd: 1917. A Tartar account of the proceedings of the All-Russian Moslem Congress in Moscow on May 1-11, 1917. One of the most important original sources on the feelings of Russian Moslems in 1917.

C6 BYSTRIANSKII, VADIM A. *Die nationale und koloniale Frage.* Moscow: Verlagsgenossenschaft ausländischer Arbeiter in der UdSSR, 1935. 178 p. A study of the nationalities problems in the USSR by an outstanding Ukrainian Communist.

C7 CARR, EDWARD H. *A History of Soviet Russia.* Vol. I, *The Bolshevik Revolution, 1917-1923.* London: Macmillan, 1950. N.Y.: 1951. 428 p. This first volume of the British historian's massive work contains a long section (p. 253-428) on the early theory and practice of Soviet nationality policy, particularly on the question of self-determination. Deals specifically with the western borderlands, the eastern borderlands, Central Asia, Transcaucasia, and Siberia. [A]

C8 CONGRESS OF DELEGATES OF INDEPENDENCE MOVEMENTS WITHIN THE U.S.S.R., EDINBURGH, SCOTLAND, 1950. *The Strength and Weakness of Red Russia; Congress held in Edinburgh 12th, 13th and 14th June 1950.* Intro. by John F. Stewart. Edinburgh: Scottish League for European Freedom, 1950. 143 p. Proceedings of the Congress of non-Russian émigrées from the Soviet Union and discussion of the situation of non-Russian nationalities in the USSR.

C9 CONQUEST, ROBERT. *The Soviet Deportation of Nationalities.* London: Macmillan; N.Y.: St. Martin's Press, 1960. 203 p. Describes the deportation in 1941-44 of the Volga Germans, Karachai, Kalmyks, Chechens, Ingushi, Balkars, and Crimean Tatars "as a test case of . . . Communist nationality policy." Based largely on Soviet sources, the book is all the more damning. Of interest for the light it casts on the amount of disaffection which persisted among minorities many years after the end of the Civil War.

C10 DIMANSHTEIN, SEMEN M., ed. *Natsionalnaia politika VKP(b) v tsifrakh.* Moscow: 1930. A statistical study of the national policies of the USSR by an outstanding Communist specialist in this field.

C11 HARDY, EUGENE N. "The Russian Soviet Federated Socialist Republic; The Role of Nationality in its Creation, 1917-1922." Ph.D. dissertation, U. of California (Berkeley), 1955.

C12 IAKUBOVSKAIA, S. I. *Obedinitelnoe dvizhenie za obrazovanie SSSR, 1917-1922.* Moscow: Ogiz, Gospolitizdat, 1947. 198 p. A study of the national movements in the USSR in the years 1917-22 and of the formation of the Soviet Union. By a Soviet scholar of the Stalinist era. Should be used with caution.

C13 KOHN, HANS. *Nationalism in the Soviet Union.* N.Y.: Columbia; London: Routledge, 1933. 164 p. German ed., Frankfurt am Main: Societäts-verlag, 1932. A short and slightly outdated survey of the national problem in the USSR by one of the leading authorities on nationalism. [B]

C14 KOLARZ, WALTER. *The Peoples of the Soviet Far East.* N.Y.: Praeger; London: Philip, 1954. 194 p. A continuation of *Russia and Her Colonies* (below). Describes the development of the many ethnic groups of Siberia up to 1954. [A]

C14A KOLARZ, WALTER. *Religion in the Soviet Union.* A most detailed and encyclopedic study of the numerous religious groups of the Soviet Union, many of which are associated with particular nationalities. Pays considerable attention to the Soviet government's attitude toward the religious organizations outside of the Soviet Union.

C15 KOLARZ, WALTER. *Russia and Her Colonies.* London: Philip, 1952; N.Y.: Praeger, 1953. 334 p. German ed., *Die Nationalitätenpolitik der Sowjetunion.* Frankfurt am Main: Europaische Verlagsanstalt, 1956. A survey of the national problem in the Soviet Union and the attitude of the Soviet Government toward the non-Russian nationalities of the USSR. Describes briefly the struggles for independence of many of the nationalities. By a leading British Sovietologist, formerly a resident of Czechoslovakia. [A]

C16 KOMMUNISTICHESKAIA AKADEMIIA, MOSCOW, KOMISSIIA PO IZUCHENIIU NATSIONALNOGO VOPROSA. *Revoliutsiia i natsionalnyi vopros; dokumenty i materialy po istorii natsionalnogo voprosa v Rossii i SSSR v XX veke.* Ed. by S. M. Dimanshtein. Comp. by I. Levin and E. Drabkin. Moscow: Izd. Kommunisticheskoi akademii, 1930. 467 p. The best collection of documents on the situation of the nationalities in Russia in 1917, compiled under the editorship of an outstanding Soviet specialist in the field. Only volume III of a projected series was published. [A]

C17 KOPREEVA, T. N. *Marksizm-leninizm o natsionalno-kolonialnom voprose; ukazatel literatury.* Leningrad: 1953. 47 p.

C18 LAZOVSKII, I. and BIBIN, I. A., comps. *Sovetskaia politika za 10 let po natsionalnomu voprosu v RSFSR; sistematicheskii sbornik deistvuiushchikh aktov pravitelstv Soiuza SSR i RSFSR po delam natsionalnostei RSFSR (oktiabr 1917-noiabr 1927).* Ed. by G. K. Klinger. Moscow: Gosizdat, 1928. 499 p. A collection of documents of the national policies of the Soviet Union, bearing the character of official propaganda. Contains many valuable documents, but some important ones for this period were not included.

C19 LENIN, VLADIMIR I. *Izbrannye stati po natsionalnomu voprosu.* Moscow: Gosizdat, 1925. 206 p. Lenin's essays on the national problem in Russia.

C20 LOW, ALFRED D. *Lenin on the Question of Nationality.* N.Y.: Bookman Associates, 1958. 193 p. An analysis of Lenin's writings on the nationality question, with emphasis placed upon his view of relations between the Great Russians and the other nationalities in the Soviet Union.

C21 McNEAL, ROBERT H. "Stalin on the Question of Nationality." Ph.D. dissertation, Columbia, 1958. 301 p.

C22 MAINARDI, LAURO. *USSR, prigione di popoli.* Rome: Cremonese, 1941. 290 p. A very general and rather one-sided review of the national problem in the Soviet Union, published in Italy under the auspices of Mussolini's government.

C23 MILIUKOV, PAVEL N. *Natsionalnyi vopros; proiskhozhdenie natsionalnosti i natsionalnye voprosy v Rossii.* Prague: Svobodnaia Rossiia, 1925. 192 p. One of the earliest studies of the national problem in Russia by an outstanding historian who was Minister of Foreign Affairs in the Provisional Government. Largely outdated; interesting primarily for the national philosophy of Miliukov himself. Deals mostly with the problem of Poland, the Baltic States and the Caucasus.

C24 PADMORE, GEORGE, and PIZER, DOROTHY. *How Russia Transformed Her Colonial Empire; A Challenge to the Imperialist Powers.* London: Dobson, 1946. 178 p. A study of the attitudes of the Soviet government and the Communist Party of the Soviet Union toward the nationality problem both inside and outside Russia. The author compares some achievements claimed by the leaders of the Soviet Union with the policies of Western European nations in their colonies. Padmore was a West Indian Negro, educated in the U.S. Although he broke with international Communism in the 1930's, he remained an admirer of Russian racial attitudes and Soviet nationalities policy.

C25 PESIKINA, E. I. *Narodnyi Komissariat po delam natsionalnostei i ego deiatelnost v 1917-1918 gg.* Ed. by D. I. Nadtocheev. Moscow: n.p., 1950. 154 p.

C26 PIPES, RICHARD E. *The Formation of the Soviet Union; Communism and Nationalism, 1917-1923.* Cambridge: Harvard, 1954. 355

p. An outstanding work by a Harvard professor on the national movement in Russia, as well as the participation of the national minorities in the Civil War and the Soviet rebuilding of the former Imperial Russia on new national and Marxist principles. Describes the Machiavellian tactics used by Stalin and others in trying to prevent the minorities from gaining independence. Contains a wealth of details. Long bibliography. [A]

C27 POPOV, NIKOLAI N., ed. *Lenin o natsionalnom voprose.* Moscow: Izd. "Krasnaia nov," 1924. 160 p. A very general study of Lenin's opinions on the national problems in Russia.

C28 RAVICH-CHERKASSKII, M., ed. *Marksizm i natsionalnyi vopros; sbornik statei i materialov.* Kharkov: Proletarii, 1923. 459 p.

C29 RUSSIA (1917– RSFSR), NARODNYI KOMISSARIAT PO DELAM NATSIONALNOSTEI. *Otchet narodnogo komissariata po delam natsionalnostei za 1921 god.* Moscow: 1921. A report of the People's Commissariat of National Affairs of the RSFSR regarding the achievements of the Soviet Government toward the various nationalities of the Soviet State. Propagandistic.

C30 RUSSIA (1917– RSFSR), NARODNYI KOMISSARIAT PO DELAM NATSIONALNOSTEI. *Politika sovetskoi vlasti po natsionalnym delam za tri goda, 1917-XI-1920.* Moscow: Gosizdat, 1920. 185 p. An interesting collection of documents and source material published by the Commissariat of National Affairs. The selection of documents sometimes follows a certain political bent.

C31 RUSSIA (1917– RSFSR), NARODNYI KOMISSARIAT PO DELAM NATSIONALNOSTEI, PETROGRADSKII OBLASTNOI OTDEL. *Izvestiia Peterburgskogo komissariata po delam natsionalnostei.* Petersburg: Tip. "Togblat," 1920. 191 p.

C31A SAFAROV, GEORGII I. *Kolonialnaia revoliutsia.* Moscow: Gosizdat, 1921. 147 p. A detailed treatment of the attitude of the Russian imperial and Soviet governments toward the minorities and specifically toward Moslem groups in Turkestan. The author is a well-known Soviet specialist on minority questions.

C32 SAFAROV, GEORGII I. *Natsionalnyi vopros i proletariat.* 2nd ed. Moscow: Krasnaia nov, 1925. 296 p. A study of the proletarian attitude toward the national problem by an outstanding early Communist expert on the nationalities of Russia in general and of Central Asia in particular.

C33 SMAL-STOCKI, ROMAN. *The Captive Nations; Nationalism of the Non-Russian Nations in the Soviet Union.* N.Y.: Bookman, 1960.

118 p. A one-sided study of the national question in the Soviet Union, bearing the character of political propaganda material. By a Polish-Ukrainian politician.

C34 SMAL-STOCKI, ROMAN. *The Nationality Problem of the Soviet Union and Russian Communist Imperialism.* Milwaukee: Bruce, 1952. 474 p. A biased analysis of the national relations in Russia and the Soviet Union, often containing incorrect information.

C35 *Sotsialnyi i natsionalnyi sostav VKP(b).* Moscow: Central Executive Committee of VKP(b), 1927. A statistical survey of the national and social structure of the Communist Party of the Soviet Union, based on material collected by the statistical office of the CPSU.

C36 STAHL, KATHLEEN MARY. *British and Soviet Colonial Systems.* N.Y.: Praeger, 1951. 114 p. A comparative study of the expansion and methods of administration of the former British Colonial Empire and the present system of control of non-Russian nationalities of the Soviet Union.

C37 STALIN, IOSIF V. *Marxism and the National and Colonial Question.* N.Y.: International Publishers, 1936. 304 p. The official, authoritative statement of the Soviet view of the national question. [A]

C38 STANKEVICH, VLADIMIR B. *Sudby narodov Rossii: Belorussiia, Ukraina, Litva, Latviia, Estoniia, Armeniia, Gruziia, Azerbaidzhan, Finliandiia, Polsha.* Berlin: Ladyzhnikov, 1921. 373 p. One of the pioneer works on the national problem in Imperial Russia and the early Soviet State. The study covers primarily the western border states and nationalities of the Soviet Union as well as some national groups of the Caucasus, written by a former Byelo-Russian liberal leader.

C39 STARUSHENKO, G. B. *Printsip samoopredeleniia narodov i natsii vo vneshnei politike sovetskogo gosudarstva.* Moscow: Izd. Instituta mezhdunarodnykh otnoshenii, 1960. 191 p. A politico-legal monograph on the slogan of self-determination and its uses in Soviet policy, by a Soviet writer.

C40 ULIANOV, GRIGORII K. *Obzor literatury po voprosam kultury i prosveshcheniia narodov SSSR.* Moscow: Narodnyi komissariat prosveshcheniia RSFSR, Gosizdat, 1930. 247 p. A very detailed bibliography of literature on the nationalities problem in Russia and the USSR. Pays particular attention to the question of the education of minorities of the Soviet Union.

C41 YARMOLINSKI, AVRAHM. *The Jews and Other Minor Nationalities under the Soviets.* N.Y.: Vanguard, 1928. 193 p. A short and comprehensive survey by an American scholar of Russian origin.

C42 ZENKOVSKY, SERGE A. *Pan-Turkism and Islam in Russia.* Cambridge: Harvard, 1960. 345 p. A historical study of the leading Turkic national groups of the Soviet Union (Tartars, Kazakhs, Uzbeks, Azerbaijanis, Bashkirs, etc.) and the growth of national consciousness among these and other Turkic peoples. Covers primarily the period from 1850 to 1922. Detailed bibliography. [A]

2. BELORUSSIA

C43 AGURSKII, SAMUEL. *Ocherki po istorii revoliutsionnogo dvizheniia v Belorussii (1863-1917).* Minsk: Belorusskoe gosizdat, 1928. 346 p. A Soviet account of the historical background of the revolutionary events of 1917 in Belorussia.

C44 AKADEMIIA NAVUK BSSR, MINSK, INSTYTUT FILASOFII. *Farmiravanne i razvitstse belaruskai satsyialistychnai natsyi.* Ed. by P. F. Glebka. Minsk: Vyd. Akademii navuk BSSR, 1958. 269 p.

C45 AKADEMIIA NAVUK BSSR, MINSK, INSTYTUT FILASOFII I PRAVA. *Revoliutsionnye komitety BSSR i ikh deiatelnost po uprochenniu sovetskoi vlasti i organizatsii sotsialisticheskogo stroitelstva (iiul-dekabr, 1920 g.); sbornik dokumentov i materialov.* Ed. by S. P. Margunskii and others. Minsk: Izd. Akademii nauk BSSR, 1957. 522 p.

C46 AKADEMIIA NAVUK BSSR, MINSK, INSTYTUT HISTORYI. *Historyia Belarusi u dakumentakh i materyialakh.* Vol. 4: *Iz istorii ustanovleniia sovetskoi vlasti v Belorussii i obrazovaniia BSSR, mart 1917 g.—fevral 1919 g.* 513 p. Ed. by A. I. Azarov and others. Minsk: Vyd. Akademii navuk BSSR, 1936. The establishment of Soviet authority in Belorussia and the formation of the Belorussian SSR in documents, records, and memoirs. [B]

C47 AKADEMIIA NAVUK BSSR, MINSK, INSTYTUT HISTORYI. *Istoriia Belorusskoi SSR.* Minsk: Izd. Akademii nauk BSSR, 1954-60.

C48 CHARVIAKOU, A. *Za savetskuiu Belarus.* Minsk: 1-aia dziarzh. druk., 1927. 135 p.

C49 *Droits de la Russie sur la Lithuanie et sur la Russie blanche.* Paris: 1919. A pamphlet summing up the facts of history justifying Russian claims on the territory of Lithuania and Belorussia.

C50 EZOVITOV, K. *Bielorussy i Poliaki; dokumenty i fakty iz istorii okkupatsii Bielorussii Poliakami v 1918 i 1919 godakh.* Kovna: Izd. im. F. Skoryny, 1919. 124 p. Selected documents and an eyewitness account of the Polish occupation of Belorussia by a Belorussian nationalist.

C51 ISACHENKO, S. *Praval amerykana-angliiskikh agresivnykh planau u Belarusi u 1917-1920 hh.* Minsk: Dziarzhaunae vydavetstva BSSR, 1954. 118 p. In this work, Poland is described as the Anglo-American stooge in fighting the Soviet power in Belorussia, 1917-20.

C52 KANCHER, IEVSEVII S. *Belorusski vopros.* Petrograd: Gosizdat, 1919. 132 p.

C53 KNORIN, V. G. *1917 god v Belorussii i na Zapadnom fronte.* Minsk: Gosizdat Belorussii, 1925. One of the best historical accounts of the Revolution in Belorussia.

C54 MARGUNSKII, S. P. *Sozdanie i uprochenie belorusskoi gosudarstvennosti, 1917-1922.* Minsk: Izd. Akademii nauk BSSR, 1958. 258 p. An official version of the history of the independent Belorussian SSR until the formation of the Soviet Union. [A]

C55 MINSK, UNIVERSITET, IURIDICHESKII FAKULTET. *Ocherki po istorii gosudarstva i prava Belorusskoi SSR.* Ed. by B. E. Babitskii and V. A. Dorogin. Minsk: 1958. A rewritten history of the Belorussian state and government, dealing with independence and federation.

C56 PARIS, PEACE CONFERENCE, WHITE RUTHENIAN REPUBLIC. *Petition of the White Ruthenian Republic.* Paris: 1919. [B]

C57 *Pravda.* Acts and Decrees pertaining to the incorporation of West Belorussia into the Belorussian SSR were originally published in *Pravda*: September 18, October 12, 30, 31, and November 4, 1939.

C58 SHCHERBAKOV, VASSILII K. *Kastrychnitskaia revoliutsyia na Belarusi i belapolskaia okupatsyia.* Minsk: Belaruskae dziarzhaunae vydavststva, 1930. 127 p.

C59 VAKAR, NICHOLAS P. *Belorussia; the Making of a Nation; a Case Study.* Cambridge: Harvard; London: Oxford, 1956. 297 p. Certainly the best book on Belorussia in English, and probably in any language. A thorough, dispassionate account by a former professor at Wheaton College, with emphasis on the years since 1917. [A]

C60 VAKAR, NICHOLAS P. *A Bibliographical Guide to Belorussia.* Cambridge: Harvard, 1956. 63 p. The most useful bibliography on Belorussia in any Western language. [A]

C61 VIKHAREV, SEMEN R. *Suverenitet Belorusskoi SSR v sostave SSSR.* Ed. by V. A. Dorogin. Minsk: Izd. Bolgosuniversiteta, 1958. 128 p. An authoritative interpretation of the USSR and the BSSR constitutions and of the subsequent amendments.

C62 WHITE RUSSIA, MINISTERSTVO INOSTRANNYKH DEL. *Belorusskaia SSR v mezhdunarodnykh otnosheniiakh; mezhdunarodnye dogovory, konventsii i soglasheniia Belorusskoi SSR s inostrannymi gosudarstvami, 1944-1959.* Comp. by S. P. Margunskii and A. S. Zaitsev. Minsk: Izd. Akad. nauk Belorusskoi SSR, 1960. 1049 p. A collection of documents giving treaties, conventions, and agreements with foreign states. [A]

C63 WHITE RUSSIA, TSENTRALNY VYKANAUCHY KOMITET. *Belarus.* Minsk: Tsentralny Vykanauchy Komitet, 1924. Contains important essays written by Communist participants in the revolutionary events in Belorussia.

C64 WYSLOUCH, S. *Rola Komunistycznej Partii Zachodniej Bialorusi w ruchu narodowym Bialorusinow w Polsce.* Vilna: 1933. Examines the part played by the Communist Party of West Belorussia (incorporated into Poland) in the Belorussian nationalist movement and its relation to Soviet foreign policy.

3. UKRAINE

(Edited by Basil Dmytryshyn and Robert S. Sullivant)

C64A ADAMS, ARTHUR E. *Bolsheviks in the Ukraine; the Second Campaign, 1918-1919.* New Haven: Yale, 1963. 440 p. The most detailed study of the Bolshevik military and political effort to regain control of the Ukraine after the 1918 German occupation. Gives greatest stress to the military campaign and the role of partisan units such as that headed by Grigorev. Evaluates the anti-Bolshevik movement as essentially rural and anarchistic rather than nationalist in its values. [A]

C65 AKADEMIIA NAUK URSR, KIEV, SEKTOR DERZHAVY I PRAVA. *Ukrainska RSR i mizhnarodnykh vidnosynakh; mizhnarodni dogovory, konventsii, ugody ta inshi dokumenty, iaki skladeni za uchastiu Ukrainskoi RSR abo do iakykh vona pryednalasia, 1945-1957.* Comp. by K. S. Zabigailo and M. K. Mikhailovskyi. Ed. by L. Kh. Palamarchuk. Kiev: Vyd. Akad. nauk Ukr. RSR, 1959. 750 p. [B]

C66 ALEKSEEV, S. A., comp. *Revoliutsiia na Ukraine po memuaram belykh.* Ed. by N. N. Popov. Moscow-Leningrad: Gosizdat, 1930. 435 p. Includes selections by Vinnichenko, Mogilianskii, Doroshenko, Denikin, Lukomskii, Gurko, Miakotin, Goldenveizer, Margolin, Cherikover, and others. One of the volumes of the series: *Revoliutsiia i grazhdanskaia voina v opisaniiakh belogvardeitsev.*

C67 ALEKSIEEV, I. *Iz vospominanii levogo esera.* Moscow: Gosizdat, 1922. Personal recollections of a Left Socialist Revolutionary about the underground movement in the Ukraine during 1917 and 1918. Sympathetic to the Bolsheviks.

C68 ANDRIEVSKYI, VIKTOR. *Z mynuloho*. Berlin: "Ukrainske Slovo," 1921. 2 vols. Recollections of an anti-Soviet Ukrainian nationalist about revolutionary events in the Poltava region, beginning with the calling of an All-Ukrainian Congress in Poltava May 21-22, 1917, and ending with the occupation of Poltava by the Germans in early 1918.

C69 ANTI-BOLSHEVIK BLOC OF NATIONS. *Zbirka dokumentiv, 1941-1956 pp*. n.p.: Vyd. Zakordonnykh chastyn orhanizatsii Ukrainskykh Natsionalistiv, 1956. 357 p. A collection of partisan but valuable and informative sources on some of the activities, hopes, and aspirations of Ukrainian nationalists. Contains appeals, programs, resolutions, and similar material. [B]

C70 ARMSTRONG, JOHN A. *Ukrainian Nationalism, 1939-1945*. N.Y.: Columbia, 1955. 322 p. A comprehensive, scholarly, carefully evaluated study of Ukrainian nationalism, based on widely scattered and little known sources, including interviews with major participants in the events. Shows that, in spite of many weaknesses, Ukrainian nationalism survived to World War II and was a relatively widespread movement. [A]

C71 ARSHINOV, PETR A. *Istoriia Makhnovskogo dvizheniia, 1918-1921 gg*. Berlin: Gruppa russkikh anarkhistov v Germanii, 1923. 258 p. French ed., *L'Histoire du mouvement makhnoviste, 1918-1921*. Paris: Éditions anarchistes, Librairie internationale, 1924. An "official" history of the anarchist peasant movement in the Ukraine led by Nestor Makhno, written by one of his close associates. Relates policies, activities, and relations of the movement which clashed with both Bolsheviks and Whites, with significant impact on the civil war.

C72 BABII, B. M. *Vozziednannia Zakhidnoi Ukrainy z Ukrainskoiu RSR*. Kiev: Akademiia nauk, 1954. 194 p. A brief résumé of events before 1939 in the Ukraine by a Soviet Ukrainian writer. Most attention is devoted to the preparation for the incorporation of Western Ukraine into the UkSSR, and subsequent achievements in economy, culture, etc. Appendix includes several key documents. [B]

C73 BELOUSOV, SEMEN N. *Vozziednannia ukrainskoho narodu v iedynii ukrainskii radianskii derzhavi*. Kiev: Akademiia nauk Ukrainskoi RSR, 1951. 165 p. A Ukrainian Soviet historian argues that only during the Soviet period was it possible for all Ukrainian territories to unite in one state and derive all benefits inherent therein. Stalin is credited with all achievements. Those who opposed Stalin are denounced.

C74 BILINSKY, YAROSLAV. "Ukrainian Nationalism and Soviet Nationality Policy after World War II." Ph.D. dissertation, Princeton, 1958. 650 p. A well-documented examination of Soviet nationality policy and Ukrainian political attitudes during the last years of Stalin's rule and Khrushchev's relaxation period. Feels that there is no radical hostility between Russians and Ukrainians, but at the same time all Soviet Ukrainians consider themselves Ukrainians and, given the chance, they would like to organize their life as they see fit.

C75 BORSCHAK, ELIE. *L'Ukraine à la conférence de la paix (1919-1923).* Dijon, France: Darantiere, 1938. 189 p. A study by a well-known Ukrainian émigré scholar of Ukrainian difficulties at the Versailles Peace Conference. Appeared first in the French monthly, *Le Monde Slave.* [B]

C76 BORYS, JURIJ. *The Russian Communist Party and the Sovietization of Ukraine; A Study in the Communist Doctrine of the Self-Determination of Nations.* Stockholm: The Author, 1960. 374 p. Bears the imprint of erudition and impressive integration of complex developments. Based on extensive use of source material scattered throughout various libraries. Argues that Lenin, not Marx, was the real architect of the Communist nationality policy. [A]

C77 BOSH, EVGENIIA. *God borby; borba za vlast na Ukraine s aprelia 1917 g. do nemetskoi okkupatsii.* Moscow-Leningrad: Gosizdat, 1925. 271 p. A fairly detailed and documented account by a Bolshevik of Bolshevik activity in the Ukraine prior to the German occupation. Shows the evolution of the struggle between Ukrainian elements in the RSDRP(b) who favored an independent Ukraine and Russian Bolsheviks who disapproved of the idea.

C78 *Die deutsche Okkupatsion der Ukraine; Geheimdokumente.* Strassbourg: Promethee, 1937. 246 p. A collection of official German documents published by the German Communist Party. Russian and Ukrainian editions appeared in 1936. The bulk of documents deal with German economic exploitation of the Ukraine in 1918, and the publication was evidently intended to warn the Ukrainians against collaboration with the Nazis.

C79 DMYTRYSHYN, BASIL. *Moscow and the Ukraine, 1918-1953; a Study of Russian Bolshevik Nationality Policy.* N.Y.: Bookman, 1956. 310 p. A documented, scholarly survey of Russian Bolshevik nationality policy (both theory and practice) in the Ukraine. Political, economic, cultural, legal, and Party relationships are examined at some length. The author argues that although Moscow produced vast changes in the Ukraine, some good and some bad, the Ukrainians have not been won over. [A]

C80 DOLENGA, SVIATOSLAV. *Skoropadshchyna.* Warsaw: Vyd. Modest Kunytskyi, 1934. 175 p. An indictment of the Hetman's regime, based largely on anti-Bolshevik Russian sources. The author argues that Skoropadsky came to power with the backing of Russian generals and German forces, as a first step in the restoration of pre-revolutionary conditions.

C81 DOROSHENKO, DMYTRO. *Istoriia Ukrainy, 1917-1923 gg.* Uzhgorod: Vyd. Dr. Osyp Tsiupka, 1930-1932. 2 vols. 2nd ed., N.Y.: Bulava, 1954. Abridged English ed., *History of the Ukraine.* Edmonton, Canada: Institute Press, 1939. 686 p. An authoritative treatment of events by a well-known Ukrainian historian and Foreign Minister of the Hetman government in 1918. Doroshenko's sympathies are with Skoropadsky. [A]

C82 DOTSENKO, OLEKSANDER. *Litopys ukrainskoi revolutsii.* Kiev-Lvov: 1923-24. 2 vols. A valuable collection of documents for the period of the Rada government, Hetmanate, and Directorate. Includes many letters, memoranda, and appeals to various layers of the Ukrainian population. [B]

C83 DOTSENKO, OLEKSANDER. *Zymovyi pokhid armii Ukrainskoi Narodnoi Respubliky (6 XII 1919—6 V 1920).* Warsaw: Vyd. Ukrainskyi naukovvi instytut, 1932. 240 p. Consists of two parts. The first is an account of the Ukrainian military campaign against the Bolsheviks in 1919-20; the second includes valuable documents, some of which provide interesting information on the activities of Ukrainian Communists and their Bolshevik allies. [B]

C84 ERDE, DAVID I. (pseud. of Raikhshtein). *Revoliutsiia na Ukraine; ot Kerenshchiny do nemetskoi okkupatsii.* Kharkov: Izd. Proletarii, 1927. 274 p. A Soviet writer traces the rise of Bolshevik influence in the Ukraine and argues that in 1917-18 the Donets Basin supported a Donets-Krivoi Rog Republic—a thesis that was later refuted by other writers.

C85 GERASIMENKO, M. P., and DUDYKEVICH, B. K. *Borba trudiashchikhsia Zapadnoi Ukrainy za vessoedinenie s Sovetskoi Ukrainoi, 1921-1939 gg.* Kiev: Gospolitizdat USSR, 1955. 246 p. An account by two respected Soviet scholars, only the first chapter of which relates to the pre-1923 period. Stress is placed on Polish activities in the West Ukraine and on the Soviet view of Allied activity in the region.

C86 HALAHAN, MYKOLA. *Z moikh spomyniv.* Lvov: Vyd. Chervona kalyna, 1930. 4 vols. Memoirs of a Ukrainian Social Democrat, abundant in material on political parties. Volume 4 has a first-hand account of negotiations between the Left Wing Ukrainian Social Democrats and Bela Kun's representatives on aid to the Hungarian revolution of 1919.

C87 HIRCHAK, EVHEN F. *Shumskizm i rozlam KPZU.* Kharkov: Derzhavne Vydavnytstvo Ukrainy, 1927. 247 p. A well-documented discussion by a highly placed member of the CP(b)U of the Shumsky "deviation" in the mid-1920's, and its impact on the split within the Communist Party in Western Ukraine (Galicia). Contains several resolutions of the Comintern dealing with this problem.

C88 KAMENETSKY, IHOR. *Hitler's Occupation of the Ukraine, 1941-1944.* Milwaukee: Marquette University Press, 1956. 112 p. A brief but correct treatment of German intentions in the Ukraine and a superficial and exaggerated exposition of Ukrainian nationalist activities. Contains many questionable generalizations and interpretations.

C89 KAPUSTIANSKYI, M. *Pokhid ukrainskykh armii na Kyiv-Odesu v 1919 rotsi.* 2nd ed. Munich: 1946. 2 vols. A history of a military expedition to Kiev and Odessa by a member of the General Staff of the Ukrainian Army. Contains, in addition, some information on the general mood of the Ukrainian people and on the activities of various revolutionary groups.

C90 KEDRYN, I., ed. *Beresteiskyi myr; z nahody 10-tykh rokovyn 9-11-1918—9-11-1928; spomuny ta materiialy.* Lvov: 1928. 320 p. A collection of various documents and memoirs written by Ukrainian participants in the Brest-Litovsk peace conference to commemorate the tenth anniversary of that event. [B]

C91 KHRISTIUK, PAVLO. *Zamitky i materiialy do istorii Ukrainskoi revoliutsii, 1917-1920 gg.* Vienna: Vyd. Ukr. Sotsiologich. Instytut, 1921-1922. 4 vols. A collection of sources by a member of the Ukrainian Socialist Revolutionary Party. Although political leanings influenced his selection, it contains vital information on social and national aspects of the Ukrainian Revolution. [B]

C92 KOMMUNISTICHESKAIA PARTIIA UKRAINY. *Desiatyi zizd Kommunistychnoi Partii (bilshovykiv) Ukrainy 20-29 lystopada 1927 r.; stenohrafichnyi zvit.* Kharkov: Derzhavne Vydavnytstvo, 1928. 620 p. An extremely valuable source of information on various national deviations in the Ukraine during the 1920's, as viewed by participants of the 10th Congress of the CP(b)U. Shortly thereafter, Moscow introduced a major purge in the Ukraine which affected many Party members, including some of the participants in the 10th Congress.

C93 KOMMUNISTICHESKAIA PARTIIA UKRAINY, INSTITUT ISTORII PARTII TSK KP UKRAINY. *Kommunisticheskaia Partiia Ukrainy v rezoliutsiiakh i resheniiakh sezdov i konferentsii, 1918-*

1956. Kiev: Gospolitizdat, 1958. 752 p. The first collection of its kind of resolutions and other key documents adopted by Congresses and Conferences of the CP(b)U. These documents deal with national, economic, cultural and educational matters, and give a clear picture of Moscow's intentions and policies in the Ukraine. [A]

C94 KOROLIVSKII, S. M., ed. *Podgotovka velikoi oktiabrskoi sotsialisticheskoi revoliutsii na Ukraine, fevral 1917-aprel 1918; sbornik dokumentov i materialov v trekh tomakh.* Kiev: Gospolitizdat USSR, 1957. 3 vols. The most comprehensive official collection of Soviet documents for the stormy first period of the Ukrainian revolution up to the German occupation. Especially valuable for its documentation on local revolutionary movements in areas such as Kiev, Kharkov, Odessa, etc. [B]

C95 KUBANIN, M. *Makhnovshchina; krestianskoe dvizhenie v stepnoi Ukraine v gody grazhdanskoi voiny.* Leningrad: 1927. 228 p. A well-documented work by a Soviet scholar on Soviet Russian agrarian and national policy in the Ukraine. Relations between Makhno and Ukrainian and Russian anarchists are examined at length, as is Makhno's struggle against Denikin.

C96 KUCHABSKII, VASIL. *Die Westukraine im Kampfe mit Polen und dem Bolschewismus in den Jahren 1918-1923.* Berlin: Junker und Dünnhaupt, 1934. 439 p. A detailed and abundantly documented treatment by a Ukrainian scholar of the West Ukrainian struggle for independence against Poland and Soviet Russia. Military campaigns and political problems are considered at length. [B]

C97 KURITSIN, V. M. *Gosudarstvennoe sotrudnichestvo mezhdu Ukrainskoi SSR i RSFSR v 1917-1922 gg.* Moscow: Gospolitizdat, 1957. 159 p. A Soviet historian argues that the Ukrainian economy was indispensable to Russia and to the success of the Revolution. Military and political cooperation is treated, as are events leading to the formation of the USSR. [B]

C99 KYRYCHENKO, MYKHAIL, ed. *Rezoliutsii vseukrainskykh zizdiv rada robitnychykh, selianskykh ta chervonoarmiiskykh deputativ.* Kharkov; Partvydov "Proletar," 1932. 412 p. The best collection of documents on the activities of the Ukrainian Congresses of Soviets from the First (December 11, 1917) to the Twelfth (March 4, 1931).

C100 LAWRYNENKO, JURIJ A. *Ukrainian Communism and Soviet Russian Policy Toward the Ukraine; an Annotated Bibliography, 1917-1953.* N.Y.: Research Program on the USSR, 1953. 454 p. Though it does not include the economic side of the national problem, this first attempt by a Ukrainian émigré scholar to compile scattered evidence is the most important and indispensable tool available for investigating the national problem in the Ukraine. Most of the items are annotated. [A]

C101 LENIN, VLADIMIR I. *Stati i rechi ob Ukraine.* Ed. by N. N. Popov. Kiev: Partizdat, 1936. 383 p. Selections from Lenin's *Works* of articles and speeches dealing with the Ukrainian problem. Though incomplete, this selection is valuable for its exposure of Lenin's views. The bulk of the material deals with Lenin's emphasis on the need for close cooperation between the Russian and Ukrainian peoples.

C102 LIKHOLAT, A. V. *Razgrom natsionalisticheskoi kontrrevoliutsii na Ukraine, 1917-1922 gg.* Moscow: Gospolitizdat, 1954. 665 p. This book, an enlargement of an earlier publication, appeared as part of the 300th anniversary celebration of the Ukrainian-Russian union. It argues that the defeat of Ukrainian nationalist forces was indispensable to the success of the Bolshevik revolution. Stalin is credited with various accomplishments; Trotskyites and bourgeois nationalists are blamed for various difficulties. [B]

C103 MAJSTRENKO, IWAN. *Borotbism; A Chapter in the History of Ukrainian Communism.* N.Y.: Research Program on the USSR, 1954. 325 p. A well-documented study, by a former member, of a Ukrainian leftist group later absorbed by the Bolsheviks. Valuable for its bibliography, biographical sketches of individuals, and appendixes. [A]

C104 MANILOV, V., ed. *Pid hnitom nimetskoho imperiializmu, (1918 g. na Kyivshchyni).* Kiev: Derzhavne vidavnitstvo Ukraini, 1927. 304 p. A valuable collection of articles, documents, and a chronology describing Bolshevik tactics in the Kiev region during the German occupation. [B]

C105 MANILOV, V., ed. *1917 god na Kievshchine.* Kiev: Gosizdat Ukrainy, 1928. 583 p. An official chronicle of revolutionary developments in Kiev in 1917, prepared by the Ukrainian Communist Party and based on archival materials. [B]

C106 MANNING, CLARENCE A. *Twentieth Century Ukraine.* N.Y.: Bookman Associates, 1951. 243 p. A concise survey of Ukrainian history in the 20th century by a Columbia University professor. Sympathetic to the Ukrainian struggle for independence. This is one of several works by Manning dealing with the Ukraine. [A]

C107 MARGOLIN, ARNOLD D. *From a Political Diary; Russia, the Ukraine, and America, 1905-1945.* N.Y.: Columbia, 1946. 250 p. Reminiscences of a Ukrainian Jew, onetime high official of the Ukrainian government, and sympathetic to the Ukrainian cause. Valuable for memoranda, letters, and other documents it contains, which were received or written by Margolin on behalf of the Ukrainians.

C108 MARGOLIN, ARNOLD D. *Ukraina i politika Antanty.* Berlin: Efron, 1922. 397 p. A criticism of Allied policy (or rather lack of policy) towards the Ukraine, by a man who was one of the chief Ukrainian delegates at the Versailles Peace Conference. [B]

C109 MARKUS, VASYL. *L'Ukraine sovietique dans les relations internationales et son statut en droit international, 1918-1923.* Paris: Les Éditions internationales, 1959. 326 p. A highly-placed Ukrainian nationalist spokesman argues in this critical and abundantly documented study that until it was absorbed into the USSR, the Soviet Ukraine was an independent state. Diplomatic relations with foreign countries and the conclusion of various international treaties are cited as evidence. [A]

C110 MAZEPA, ISAAK P. *Ukraina v ohni i buri revoliutsii 1917-1921 r.* Munich: Prometei, 1950-51. 3 vols. One of the best documented and most objective works on the Ukrainian revolution, by a Prime Minister during the reign of the Directorate. Valuable especially for its wealth of information on all political parties. The first two volumes were first published in 1942 in Prague.

C111 MINTS, ISAAK I., and GORODETSKII, E. N. *Dokumenty o razgrome germanskikh okkupantov na Ukraine v 1918 godu.* Moscow: OGIZ Gos. izd. polit. lit., 1942. 238 p.

C112 MIRCHUK, PETER. *Ukrainska povstanska armiia 1942-1952.* Munich: "Cicero" Druckerei, 1953. 319 p. A description by a participant of the activities of the Ukrainian Insurgent Army against the Nazis and the Soviets. Contains detailed accounts of various raids carried out by the partisans during and after World War II. Some photographs are included. [B]

C113 NAZARUK, OSYP. *Rik na velykii Ukraini.* Vienna: "Ukrainskii prapor," 1920. 344 p. Personal narratives by an anti-Soviet Ukrainian nationalist of incidents in the West Ukraine during the German occupation and the period of the Directory.

C114 *Oktiabrskaia revoliutsiia; pervoe piatiletie 1917-1922.* Kharkov: Gosizdat Ukrainy, 1922. 633 p. A rare and very informative collection of articles by major participants in the Ukraine. Contains material on military campaigns, Party, government, foreign trade, economy, etc.

C115 ORHANIZATSIIA UKRAINSKYKH NATSIONALISTIV. *V svitli postanov Velykykh Zboriv, konferentsii ta inshykh dokumentiv z borotby, 1929-1955; Zbirka dokumentiv.* n.p.: Vyd. Zakordonnykh chastyn orhanizatsii ukrainskykh natsionalistiv, 1955. 364 p. A collection of key documents, the first of its kind, on the aims and aspirations of Ukrainian nationalism, its struggle with Poland, Nazi Germany, and Soviet Russia. This biased but valuable source of information on Ukrainian nationalism was prepared by Ukrainian nationalist spokesmen abroad. [B]

C116 PARIS, PEACE CONFERENCE, 1919, UKRAINE. *Mémoire sur l'indépendence de l'Ukraine présenté à la conférence de la paix par la délégation de la République ukrainienne.* Paris: 1919. 125 p. An official Ukrainian justification for independent recognition, presented at Versailles. Historic, linguistic, religious, economic, and other factors are cited. [B]

C117 PARIS, PEACE CONFERENCE, 1919, UKRAINE. *Les Questions ukrainiennes.* 1919. No. 1.—*Les Ukrainiens et la guerre universelle.* 10 p. No. 2—*Pourquoi les Ukrainiens et les Polonais guerroient-ils uns contre les autres dans la Galicie orientale?* 13 p. No. 3—*La Guerre en Ukraine et le bolchévisme.* 10 p. No. 4—*La Galicie.* 19 p. No. 5.—*L'Ukraine et la conférence de la paix.* 124 p.

C118 PETLIURA, SYMON. *Statti, lysty, dokumenty.* N.Y.: Ukrainian Academy of Arts and Sciences, 1956. 479 p. A collection of articles, letters, and reviews written before, during, and after the Revolution by one of the most important Ukrainian leaders of the 20th century. Pre-World War I items reflect Petliura's socialist viewpoint; post-revolutionary items bear the imprint of statesmanship. [A]

C119 POPOV, NIKOLAI N. *Narys istorii Kommunistychnoi Partii (bilshovykiv) Ukrainy.* Kharkov: Derzhavne Vydavnytstvo Ukrainy, 1928. 300 p. Russian ed., 1929. By far the best Soviet work on the history of the CP(b)U up to 1928. Contains many references to, as well as excerpts from, documents which later became unorthodox.

C120 POPOV, NIKOLAI N. *Oktiabr na Ukraine.* Kiev: Partizdat TsK KP(b)U, 1934. 84 p. A brief account by an eminent Soviet historian of the revolutionary period in the Ukraine up to the Soviet occupation of Kiev in early 1918. Stress is placed on relations between the Central Rada and Bolshevik groups in Russia and the Ukraine. [B]

C121 RAFES, MOISSAIA G. *Dva goda revoliutsii na Ukraine.* Moscow: Gosizdat, 1920. 168 p. One of the best of the Bolshevik accounts of the Civil War in the Ukraine.

C122 RAVICH-CHERKASSKI, MOISEI. *Istoriia Kommunisticheskoi Partii (bolshevikov) Ukrainy.* Kharkov: Gosizdat Ukrainy, 1923. 248 p. An amply-documented history of the CP(b)U up to 1923, based on the theory that it was the outgrowth of both the Ukrainian and Russian Social Democratic movements—a theory that was later condemned.

C123 RESHETAR, JOHN S., JR. *The Ukrainian Revolution, 1917-1920; a Study in Nationalism.* Princeton, N.J.: Princeton University Press, 1952. 363 p. The most complete scholarly treatment in English. The development of the Ukrainian national movement, attitudes of different political parties to Ukrainian independence, and the attitude of the great powers are treated comprehensively. Contains 12 pages of annotated bibliography. [A]

C124 SADOVSKYI, VALENTYN. *Natsionalna polityka sovetiv na Ukraini.* Warsaw: Pratsi Ukrainskoho naukovoho instytutu, 1937. 173 p. One of the most-balanced and well-documented treatments by a Ukrainian émigré scholar. It is limited to the political side of the national problem.

C125 SALSKY, VOLODYMYR, ed. *Ukrainsko-Moskovska viyna 1920 Roku v dokumentakh.* Warsaw: Pratsi Ukrainskoho naukovoho instytutu, 1923. 401 p. A collection of operational documents of the General Staff of the Ukrainian Army, edited by Generals Salsky and Shandruk. [B]

C126 SCIBORSKII, MYKOLA. *Die Ukraine und die Nationalitätenpolitik Moskaus.* N.Y.: Ukrainian Press Service, 1938. 102 p. A documented treatment by a Ukrainian nationalist journalist who was later executed by the Germans. This book appeared first in an English-language monthly, *The Trident*, published in New York.

C127 SHAKHRAI, VASYL M. *Revolutsiia na Ukraini.* 2nd ed. Saratov: Borba, 1919. 150 p. A left-wing Ukrainian Social Democrat who joined the Bolsheviks and acted as one of their spokesmen at Brest-Litovsk reversed his position, and in this treatment bitterly assails Lenin's policy towards the Ukraine.

C128 SHANKOVSKYI, LEV. *Pokhidni hrupy OUN; prychynky do istorii pokhidnykh hrup OUN na tsentralnykh i skhidnykh zemliakh Ukrainy v 1941-1943 rr.* Munich: Ukrainskyi samostiinyk, 1958. 319 p. A documented but partisan account of the activities of various Ukrainian nationalist groups in the Ukraine during World War II, by one of their highly-placed members.

C129 SHAPOVAL, MYKYTA. *Velyka revolutsiia i ukrainska vyzvolna prohrama.* Prague: Vilna spilka, 1937. 324 p. Contains abundant data on the revolution of 1917-20, the Soviet Ukraine, and Moscow's Ukrainian policy, by a member of the Ukrainian Socialist Revolutionary Party, who was also quite active abroad.

C130 SHLIKHTER, A. G., ed. *Chernaia kniga; sbornik statei i materialov ob interventsii Antanty na Ukraine v 1918-1919 g.g.* Kharkov: Giz Ukrainy, 1925. 433 p. A collection of selected documents and articles on French intervention in the Ukraine. Some articles, while abundantly documented, contain factual errors. [B]

C131 SHULGIN, ALEKSANDR (SHULHYN, OLEKSANDR). *L'Ukraine contre Moscou, 1917*. Paris: Alcan, 1935, 222 p. The author was an anti-Soviet Ukrainian nationalist and a principal negotiator for the Central Rada in its efforts to gain recognition from the western Allies. Most valuable for its discussion of the government of the Central Rada and its relations with the Allies and Soviet Russia.

C132 SPILKA VYZVOLENNIA UKRAINY. *Stenografichnii zvit sudovoho protsesu.* Kharkov: Derzhavne vydavnytstvo Ukrainy, 1930. Verbatim reports of the 1929 trials of many leading Ukrainian intellectuals charged by the Bolsheviks with attempting to separate the Ukraine from the USSR. Informative and revealing. [B]

C133 STALIN, IOSIF V. *Stati i rechi ob Ukraine; sbornik.* Kiev: Partizdat, TsK, KP(b)U, 1936. 249 p. Selected references to the Ukraine from Stalin's speeches and articles. Appeared in the midst of the great purge in the Ukraine in order to emphasize the "correctness" of Stalin's national policies. A similar collection of Lenin's remarks on the Ukraine also appeared about the same time (see above).

C134 STERCHO, PETER. "The Carpatho-Ukraine in International Affairs, 1938-1939." Ph.D. dissertation, Notre Dame, 1959. 463 p. A carefully-documented and well-balanced study of the policies of the major powers and opinions of their spokesmen towards the Carpatho-Ukraine before and after the Munich crisis. Contains several appendices and a fifty-page bibliography.

C135 SULLIVANT, ROBERT S. *Soviet Politics and the Ukraine, 1917-1957*. N.Y.: Columbia, 1962. 438 p. A broad survey by an American scholar, based chiefly on Soviet sources, of Soviet policies and attitudes toward the Ukraine. In the pre-1923 period stress is placed on conflict among various Soviet factions. [A]

C136 SYMONENKO, R. H. *Imperialistichna politika SShA shchodo Ukraini v 1917-1918 r.r.* Kiev: Vid. Akademii nauk, Ukr. RSR, 1957. 302 p.

C137 *Ukraina proti Moskvy; zbirka stattei.* n.p.: Vyd. Zakordonnykh chastyn orhanizatsii ukrainskykh natsionalistiv, 1955. 388 p. A collection of 12 articles dealing with various aspects of the Ukrainian struggle with Moscow, by such Ukrainian nationalist spokesmen as Dontsov, Honcharuk, Bojko, Poltava, Bandera, and others. [B]

C138 UKRAINE. *L'Ukraine soviétiste; quatre années de guerre et de blocus; Recueil des documents officiels d'après les livres rouges Ukrainiens.* Berlin: Puttkammer und Mühlbrecht, 1922. 279 p.

C139 UKRAINE, ARKHIVNOE UPRAVLENIE. *Pid praporom Zhovtnia; vplyv Velykoi zhovtnevoi sotsialistychnoi revolutsii na pidnesennia revolutsiinoho rukhu v Zakhidnii Ukraini, 1917-1920; dokumenty i materialy*. Ed. by O. Iu. Karpenka. Lvov: Knyzhkovo-zhurnalne vyd., 1957. 690 p. Published to commemorate the 40th anniversary of the Bolshevik Revolution, this volume of selected items seeks to prove that only after the Bolshevik Revolution was there increased revolutionary activity in the Western Ukraine. Various resolutions and contemporary newspaper items are reproduced.

C140 UKRAINE, ARKHIVNOE UPRAVLENIE. *Radianskii Lviv, 1939-1955; dokumenty i materialy*. Ed. by M. K. Ivasiuta and others. Lvov: Knyzhkovo-zhurnalne vyd., 1956. 705 p. Issued on the 40th anniversary of the Bolshevik Revolution, this collection of decrees and resolutions is the first attempt to portray through documents the change that has taken place in the Western Ukraine. Abundant information is given on all aspects of life.

C141 UKRAINE, TSENTRALNYI GOSUDARSTVENNYI ARKHIV OKTIABRSKOI REVOLIUTSII I SOTSIALISTICHESKOGO STROITELSTVA. *Borba za vlast sovetov na Kievshchine (mart 1917 g.-fevral 1918 g.); sbornik dokumentov i materialov*. Kiev: Gospolitizdat, 1957. 659 p. Published on the 40th anniversary of the Bolshevik Revolution. Contains 672 documents from various government and Party archives in Moscow and Kiev. Some items are from periodical literature, and some non-Bolshevik documents are also included. [B]

C142 UKRAINE, TSENTRALNYI GOSUDARSTVENNYI ARKHIV OKTIABRSKOI REVOLIUTSII I SOTSIALISTICHESKOGO STROITELSTVA. *Kharkov i kharkovskaia guberniia v Velikoi oktiabrskoi sotsialisticheskoi revoliutsii; sbornik dokumentov i materialov, fevral 1917-aprel 1918 gg*. Kharkov: Kharkovskoe obl. izdat., 1957. 545 p. Commemorating the 40th anniversary of the Bolshevik Revolution, this is one of the largest collections of documents on the October Revolution in the Ukraine. It may be viewed as an enlarged edition of a 1947 publication which dealt only with Kharkov and included only 202 documents. [B]

C143 UKRAINE, TSENTRALNYI GOSUDARSTVENNYI ARKHIV OKTIABRSKOI REVOLIUTSII I SOTSIALISTICHESKOGO STROITELSTVA. *Velikaia oktiabrskaia sotsialisticheskaia revoliutsiia na Ukraine, fevral 1917-aprel 1918; sbornik dokumentov i materialov*. Ed. by S. M. Korolivskii. Kiev: Gospolitizdat, 1957. 3 vols. Vol. I: *Podgotovka Velikoi oktiabrskoi sotsialisticheskoi revoliutsii na Ukraine*. Vol. II: *Pobeda Velikoi oktiabrskoi revoliutsii i ustanovlenie sovetskoi vlasti na Ukraine*. Vol. III: *Borba za rasprostranenie i uprochenie sovet-*

skoi vlasti na Ukraine. This collection commemorating the 40th anniversary of the Bolshevik revolution attempts to show that the Soviet regime was accepted by the Ukraine voluntarily. [B]

C144 UKRAINSKA HOLOVNA VYZVOLNA RADA. *Zbirka dokumentiv za 1944-1950 rr.* n.p.: Vid. zakordonnikh chastyn orhanizatsii ukrainskikh natsionalistiv, 1956. 353 p. Presents, through documents, the activities and policies of the Ukrainian Chief Liberation Council. Contains platform, appeals, resolutions, etc. [B]

C145 *Ukrainska povstanska armiia; zbirka dokumentiv za 1942-1950 rr.* n.p.: Vyd. Zakordonnykh chastyn orhanizatsii ukrainskykh natsionalistiv, 1957. 380 p. The first major attempt to present, through documents, the activities of the Ukrainian Insurgent Army against the Germans and the Russians. Platforms, appeals, orders, and similar materials are included. Prepared by Ukrainian nationalist spokesmen abroad. [B]

C146 VYNNYCHENKO, VOLODYMYR K. *Vid rodzhennia natsii.* Kiev-Vienna: Dzvin, 1920. 3 vols. This memoir of a leftist Ukrainian Social Democrat and one-time Prime Minister of the Rada government contains authentic records as well as insinuations against his own government and his associates. Valuable, but must be used with caution.

C147 *Za derzhavnist; materialy do istorii Viiska Ukrainskoho.* Kalish: Vyd. Ukrainske voienno-istoriche tovarystvo, 1929-1936. 6 vols. A partisan but monumental source of information on the organization, operation, and activities of the Ukrainian army units during World War I and the revolutionary period. Contains many documents, pictures, maps, biographical sketches, and similar material.

4. CAUCASUS

(Edited by Firuz Kazemzadeh)

a. GENERAL WORKS

C148 ALLEN, WILLIAM E. D., and MURATOFF, PAUL. *Caucasian Battlefields; A History of the Wars on the Turco-Caucasian Border, 1828-1921.* Cambridge: Cambridge Univ. Press, 1953. 614 p. The best military history, with some attention paid to politics. Richly documented. Excellent maps. An indispensable work in its field. [A]

C149 ARKOMED, S. T. *Materialy po istorii otpadeniia Zakavkazia ot Rossii.* Tiflis: Krasnaia Kniga, 1923. 2nd ed., Tiflis: Gosizdat Gruzii, 1931. 112 p. Selected documents on the separation of Transcaucasia from Russia, intended to discredit anti-Bolshevik parties. Contains some materials unobtainable elsewhere. [A]

C150 BERIIA, LAVRENTI P. *K voprosu ob istorii bolshevistskikh organizatsii v Zakavkaze.* Moscow: Gospolitizdat, 1952. 287 p. Rewriting of history by Stalin's chief of the N.K.V.D. to demonstrate that Stalin was the only hero of the Bolshevik revolution and sovietization of Transcaucasia. Worthless for Transcaucasian history but significant for the study of Stalinist historiography.

C151 BUXTON, HAROLD J. *Transcaucasia.* London: Faith, 1926. 98 p. A very good outline of the history of the area, emphasizing World War I and the postwar period.

C152 DONOHOE, MARTIN H. *With the Persian Expedition.* London: Edward Arnold, 1919. 276 p. Reminiscences of a British officer, member of an expeditionary force in Persia and the Caucasus, who saw the surface of events and reported his impressions rather well.

C153 DUNSTERVILLE, LIONEL C. *The Adventures of Dunsterforce.* London: Edward Arnold, 1920. 323 p. 2nd ed., 1932. Memoirs of the commander of the British troops which participated in the defense of Baku in 1918. Although Dunsterville did not understand the intricacies of revolutionary politics and looked on events from a purely military point of view, this is a very important source and provides much factual information on the international intrigues in Transcaucasia. [A]

C154 ENUKIDZE, D. E. *Krakh imperialisticheskoi interventsii v Zakavkaze.* Tbilisi: Gosizdat Gruz. SSR, 1954. 294 p. A Soviet version of British intervention in Transcaucasia, mainly Georgia, which revises some earlier accounts. Intervention is interpreted as pro-Denikin rather than pro-Georgia and not aimed at dismemberment. The fall of the Transcaucasian governments to the Soviets is attributed more to Russian liberation than to internal revolution.

C155 FRENCH, J. F. *From Whitehall to the Caspian.* London: Odhams, 1920. Memoirs of a British officer attached to the intervention forces operating in Transcaucasia and Transcaspia from November 1918 to August 1919, the "Norperforce." Describes the establishment of control on the Caspian by British naval units and gives a perceptive account of British relations with local forces and governments, inadequacies of Allied policy, and contradictions in dealing with Russian and non-Russian elements.

C156 HIPPEAU, EDMOND. *Les Républiques du Caucase; Géorgie-Azerbaidjan.* Paris: Leroux, 1920. 72 p. A general survey of two Transcaucasian republics.

C156A IAKUSHKIN, E. E. and POLUNIN, S. *Angliiskaia interventsiia v 1918-1920 gg.* Moscow-Leningrad: Gospolitizdat, 1928. 76 p. A popular account of English intervention in North Russia and Transcaucasia. Naturally very anti-British, but containing some information not available elsewhere.

C157 KAZEMZADEH, FIRUZ. *The Struggle for Transcaucasia, (1917-1921).* N.Y.: Philosophical Library; Oxford: George Ronald, 1951. 356 p. Based on a Harvard Ph.D. thesis, this monograph provides one of the most complete accounts of events in Transcaucasia during the Revolution and Civil War. It is concerned chiefly with the development of state authorities in Georgia, Armenia, and Azerbaijan and their struggle for survival, but it is also a study of conditions and policies during the British intervention. The author is a professor of history at Yale. [A]

C158 LA CHESNAIS, P. G. *Les peuples de la Transcaucasie pendant la guerre et devant la paix.* Paris: Bossard, 1921. 218 p. A sympathetic and fairly well informed general account dealing with problems raised by war and revolution.

C159 LORIS-MELIKOV, IVAN. (MELIKOF, JEAN). *La Révolution russe et les nouvelles Républiques transcaucasiennes; Bolchévisme et antibolchévisme.* Paris: Alcan, 1920. 211 p. A contemporary account based on rather extensive personal knowledge, by a competent anti-Bolshevik observer.

C160 MAISKII, IVAN M. *Demokraticheskaia kontr-revoliutsiia.* Moscow-Leningrad: Gosizdat, 1923. 360 p. A Menshevik who joined the winners and became a high-ranking Soviet diplomat presents a polemical and pro-Soviet version of events.

C161 MAKHARADZE, FILIPP. *Ocherki revoliutsionnogo dvizheniia v Zakavkaze.* Tiflis: Gosizdat Gruzii, 1927. 416 p. Written by one of the founders of the Georgian Bolshevik movement, this work is unusually fair in its approach and quite reliable as a source. Based on extensive knowledge, it is indispensable for a serious study of the period. [A]

C162 ORAKHELASHVILI, M. D. *Zakavkazskie bolshevistskie organizatsii v 1917 godu.* Tiflis: 1927. Written by one of the leading Bolsheviks, who perished in Stalin's purges, this work is fairly reliable. It shows the weakness of the Bolsheviks in Tiflis and makes clear by implication that the sovietization of Georgia was carried out by Russians rather than by native Communists.

C163 PRICE, MORGAN PHILIPS. *War and Revolution in Asiatic Russia.* London: Allen & Unwin, 1918. 295 p. Impressions of a literate and observant journalist in sympathy with the revolution. Since it is a contemporary account, it is uncritical and must be used with caution. The author was correspondent for the Manchester *Guardian* in Russia during World War I and a member of Parliament for many years.

C164 RAWLINSON, ALFRED. *Adventures in the Near East, 1918-1922.* Introductions by L. C. Dunsterville and others. London: A. Melrose, 1923; N.Y.: Dodd, Mead, 1924. 353 p. Memoirs of a British intelligence officer who served with forces in Transcaucasia and later in neighboring countries. The author played a major role in North Caucasus establishing British contacts with native elements. Sketchy but valuable insight into conditions, with a critical view of British policy.

C165 ROBERTS, CARL ERIC BECHHOFER. *In Denikin's Russia and the Caucasus, 1919-1920.* London: W. Collins, 1921. 324 p. A well informed and objective account of civil war and intervention in South Russia by a British journalist. The author travelled through Transcaucasia and South Russia, becoming closely acquainted with events and personalities. Good descriptions of conditions and problems, with a critical view of British policies. [B]

C166 SEF, S. E. *Revoliutsiia 1917 goda v Zakavkaze.* Tiflis: 1927. Contains useful primary sources, including documents.

C167 STAVROVSKII, A. *Zakavkaze posle Oktiabria; vzaimootnosheniia s Turtsiei v pervoi polovine 1918 g.* Moscow-Leningrad: Gosizdat, 1925. 120 p.

C168 TODORSKII, A. *Krasnaia armiia v gorakh.* Moscow, 1924.

C169 VARANDIAN, MIKAEL. *Le Conflit Arméno-Géorgien et la guerre du Caucase.* Paris: Flinikowski, 1919. 152 p. A partisan attack on the government of Georgia and a defense of the position of Armenia in the territorial dispute between the two countries.

C170 VORONOVICH, N., ed. *Zelenaia kniga; sbornik materialov i dokumentov; istoriia krestianskogo dvizheniia v chernomorskoi gubernii.* Prague: Izdanie chernomorskoi krestianskoi delegatsii, 1921. A summary history of the neutralist "Green" movement on the eastern Black Sea coast by its military leader, with a collection of documents concerning its relations with the Whites, Bolsheviks, Transcaucasian Republics, and British. Contains valuable materials on the British efforts to mediate between the Greens and Volunteers.

b. ARMENIA

C171 BALDWIN, OLIVER. *Six Prisons and Two Revolutions; Adventures in Trans-Caucasia and Anatolia, 1920-1921.* London: Hodder & Stoughton; Garden City, N.Y.: Doubleday, Page, 1925. 271 p. Reminiscences of an adventurous Briton who was shocked by conditions in recently Sovietized Armenia. He was in Armenia in 1920-21 and worked for the Armenian government.

C172 BARRY, HENRY. *Les Extravagances Bolchéviques et l'épopée arménienne.* Paris: Michel, 1919. A description of the Armenian Problem during the period following the Bolshevik Revolution.

C173 BORIAN, BAGRAT A. *Armeniia, mezhdunarodnaia diplomatiia i SSSR.* Moscow-Leningrad: GIZ., 1928-1929. 2 vols. The most complete study of Armenia in international diplomacy available in any language, this work is richly documented and, on the whole, reliable. However, the writer has a strong Bolshevik bias and his interpretations are often far-fetched. [A]

C174 DÉLÉGATION DE LA RÉPUBLIQUE ARMÉNIENNE À LA CONFÉRENCE DE LA PAIX. *L'Arménie et la question arménienne avant, pendant et depuis la guerre.* Paris: Turabian, 1922. 143 p. A statement of Armenia's case after the fall of the independent Armenian Republic.

C175 HARBORD, J. G. "American Military Mission to Armenia," *International Conciliation*, No. 151 (June 1920), p. 275-312. Report by the head of the special American mission sent to Transcaucasia to investigate the situation and give advice on possible acceptance of a mandate by the U.S. Contains a good description of conditions during the British intervention and problems of policy formulation, as well as indications of American involvement. [B]

C176 LEPSIUS, JOHANNES, ed. *Deutschland und Armenien 1914-1918.* Potsdam: Temperverlag, 1919. 541 p. German reports on wartime massacres, issued by a confirmed pacifist and friend of the Armenians.

C177 POIDEBARD, A., ed. *Le Transcaucase et la République d'Arménie dans les textes diplomatiques du traité de Brest-Litovsk au traité de Kars, 1918-1921.* Paris: Imprimerie nationale, 1924. 85 p.

C178 RAPHAEL, JOAN R. "Russia, America and the Armenian Problem, 1918-1921." Certificate essay, Russian Institute, Columbia, 1948. 107 p.

C179 TORRY, GORDON H. "Armenia and the Great Powers, 1919-1921." Ph.D. dissertation, U. of Oregon, 1954.

C180 VARTANIAN, S. *Pobeda sovetskoi vlasti v Armenii.* Erevan: 1959. 223 p.

C181 VRATSIAN, S. *Hayastani Hanrapetouthiun.* Paris: 1928. Written by one of the leaders of the Dashnaktsutian, this is a clearly partisan view of Armenian history.

c. AZERBAIJAN

C182 BAGIROV, M. D. *Iz istorii bolshevistskoi organizatsii Baku i Azerbaidzhana.* 2nd ed., Moscow: Gospolitizdat, 1948. 242 p. Written by a high Party official with the purpose of glorifying Stalin, this work is dishonest and useless. Bagirov was purged after Stalin's death.

C183 BAGRII, A. V. *Materialy dlia bibliografii Azerbaidzhana.* Baku: n.p., 1924-1926. 3 vols.

C184 BAIKOV, B. "Vospominaniia o revoliutsii v Zakavkazii, 1917-1920 gg.," *Arkhiv Russkoi Revoliutsii*, vol. IX, p. 91-194. Ed. by G. V. Gessen. Berlin: Izdatelstvo "Slovo," 1923. Memoirs of a Russian resident of Baku, leader of the Russian National Council and its representative in contacts with the British Command during intervention. Valuable for the position of the Russian element in Azerbaijan in relations with the local government, the British, and other organizations. [B]

C185 CHAIKIN, VADIM A. *K istorii rossiiskoi revoliutsii.* Vol. I, *Kazn 26 bakinskikh komissarov.* Moscow: Grzhebin, 1922. A *cause célèbre* in the Soviet case against Allied intervention—the shooting of 26 Bolshevik leaders in September 1918. The case was brought to public attention by the author, an S.R. journalist, in 1919. This book represents his personal findings and concludes that the British engineered the affair.

C186 GUSEINOV, MIRZA-DAVUD. *Tiurkskaia demokraticheskaia partiia federalistov "Musavat" v proshlom i nastoiashchem.* Baku: Zakkniga, 1927. Written by a prominent Azerbaijani Bolshevik to discredit the Musavat Party, this book is biased and unreliable, but contains some interesting factual material.

C187 ISHKHANIAN, B. *Velikie uzhasy v gorode Baku; anketnoe issledovanie sentiabrskikh sobytii 1918 g.* Tiflis, 1920. A statistical study of the Armenian massacres carried out by the Azerbaijanis and the Turks in September 1918. Although partisan in intent, it is useful and apparently reliable.

C188 ISKENDEROV, M. S. *Iz istorii borby Kommunisticheskoi partii Azerbaidzhana za pobedu sovetskoi vlasti.* Baku: Azerbaidzhanskoe gosizdat, 1958. 537 p.

C189 KARAEV, A. G. *Iz nedavnego proshlogo; materialy k istorii Azerbaidzhanskoi kommunisticheskoi partii (b).* Baku: Bakinskii rabochii, 1926. A Baku Bolshevik who participated in the Sovietization of Azerbaijan gives a personal account of events as he saw them.

C190 MEHMET-ZADE, MIRZA BALA. *Milli Azerbaycan Hareketi.* Berlin: 1938. An anti-Soviet Azerbaijani émigré discusses the Azerbaijani national movement, throwing more light on the mentality of exiles than on the history of Azerbaijan.

C191 PARIS, PEACE CONFERENCE, AZERBAIJAN. *Claims of the Peace Delegation of the Republic of Caucasian Azerbaijan Presented to the Peace Conference in Paris.* Paris: 1919. Official statement of territorial and other claims made by the Azerbaijani delegation in Paris.

C192 POPOV, A. L. "Iz epokhi angliiskoi interventsii v Zakavkaze," *Proletarskaia Revoliutsiia,* No. 6-7 (18-19), p. 222-274; No. 8 (20), p. 95-132; No. 9 (21), p. 185-217. Moscow: Gosizdat, 1923. A documentary history of British intervention in Azerbaijan, compiled from records of the Aberbaijan Ministry of Foreign Affairs captured by the Bolsheviks in 1920. The author-editor's comments reflect Bolshevik bias, but the materials provide invaluable detail on British policy and relations with the Azerbaijan Republic, 1918-1919. [B]

C193 RAEVSKII, A. *Angliiskaia interventsiia i Musavatskoe pravitelstvo; iz istorii interventsii i kontr-revoliutsii v Zakavkaze.* Baku: Gostip. "Krasnyi Vostok," 1927. 194 p. Biased and tendentious but extremely valuable. The author, a Bolshevik, had access to a large number of documents which he cites and which are not otherwise available to Western scholars. [A]

C194 RAEVSKII, A. *Angliiskie druziia i musavatskie patrioty.* Baku: 1927. A competent Bolshevik historian attempts to discredit the Musavat Party and the government of independent Azerbaijan by picturing them as tools of British imperialism. Of no scholarly value.

C195 RAEVSKII, A. *Partiia Musavat i ee kontr-revoliutsionnaia rabota.* Baku: 1929. A Soviet attempt to discredit the Azerbaijani nationalist party, Musavat, whose government was overthrown by the Red Army in 1920.

C196 RASUL ZADE (RESUL ZADEH), MUHAMMAD E. *L'Azerbaidjan en lutte pour l'indépendence.* Paris: 1930. By the former head of the Azerbaijan Republic.

C197 RASUL ZADE (RESUL ZADEH), MUHAMMAD E. *O panturanizme v sviazi s kavkazskoi problemoi.* Paris: K.N.K., 1930. Thoughts on Pan-Turanism and the Caucasus by the leader of independent Azerbaijan and of the Musavat Party. Of minor importance.

C198 RATGAUZER, IA. *Borba za sovetskii Azerbaidzhan; k istorii aprelskogo perevorota.* Baku: 1928. Written by a Bolshevik defender of the Sovietization of Azerbaijan, this work is biased but instructive. [B]

C199 RATGAUZER, IA. *Revoliutsiia i grazhdanskaia voina v Baku.* Baku: 1927. Very valuable. Contains a considerable number of quotations from archival materials which are not available otherwise. Heavy Bolshevik bias. [A]

C200 SEF, S. E. *Kak Bolsheviki prishli k vlasti v 1917-1918 godakh v bakinskom raione.* Baku: 1927.

C201 TOKARZHEVSKII, E. A. *Iz istorii inostrannoi interventsii i grazhdanskoi voiny v Azerbaidzhane.* Baku: Izd. Akad. nauk AzSSR, 1957. 332 p.

d. GEORGIA

C202 ABRAMOWITZ, RAPHAEL; SUKHOMLIN, W.; and TSERETELLI, IRAKLII. *Der Terror gegen die sozialistischen parteien in Russland und Georgien.* Berlin: Dietz, 1925. 134 p. Leading Mensheviks in emigration denounce Soviet persecutions of the Mensheviks after the failure of the 1924 uprising.

C203 ADAMIIA, V. I. *Iz istorii angliiskoi interventsii v Gruzii, 1918-1921 gg.* Sukhumi: Abgiz, 1961. 258 p.

C204 AFRIC, LEO (pseud. of Louis Coquet). *Les Héritiers de la "Toison d'Or."* Paris: Maisonneuve, 1931. 256 p. A general history of Georgia, emphasizing the years during and after World War I.

C205 AMIA, M. *Put gruzinskoi zhirondy; fakty, dokumenty, materialy iz istorii reaktsionnogo pererozhdeniia menshevikov i izgnaniia ikh iz Gruzii.* Tiflis: Zakkniga, 1926. 151 p. Though written only to discredit the Georgian Mensheviks, the book contains a number of significant documents. Valuable. [B]

C206 AVALISHVILI, ZOURAB. *The Independence of Georgia in International Politics, 1918-1921.* London: Headley, 1940. 286 p. Russian ed., AVALOV, ZURAB. *Nezavisimost Gruzii v mezhdunarodnoi politike, 1918-1921 gg.* Paris: Navarre, 1924. 319 p. A conservative and learned Georgian patriot discusses the international position of Georgia. Personal observations and acquaintance with Georgian, Russian, and European leaders make this a valuable source. [A]

C207 DEVDERIANI, GAIOZ. *Dni gospodstva menshevikov v Gruzii; dokumenty i materialy.* Tiflis: Gos. Izd. Gruzii, 1931. 572 p. A large collection of documents carefully selected to discredit the Georgian Mensheviks and the government of independent Georgia. In spite of bias, this collection is very valuable. [B]

C208 DRABKINA, ELENA. *Gruzinskaia kontr-revoliutsiia.* Leningrad: Priboi, 1928. 177 p. A standard Soviet denunciation of Georgian nationalism and Menshevism by a competent Russian scholar who specialized in problems of Tsarist Russian imperialism and belonged to the Pokrovskii school.

C209 DUGUET, RAYMOND. *Moscou et la Géorgie martyre.* Paris: Tallandier, 1927. 217 p. An anti-Soviet, pro-Georgian work which adds very little to our knowledge.

C210 GENTIZON, PAUL. *La Résurrection géorgienne; en Mer Noire; un pays qui se réveille; La France et le Caucase; Tiflis et la société géorgienne; l'organisation de l'État; le complot turco-bolchéviste; une aventure de pirates.* Paris: Leroux, 1921. 320 p. A report by a contemporary observer very favorable toward independent Georgia, anti-Soviet and anti-Turkish. Interesting but not always factually reliable.

C211 GEORGIA (TRANSCAUCASIA). *Documents relatifs à la question de la Géorgie devant la Société des Nations.* Paris: 1925. A collection of documents and notes presented to the League of Nations by the Georgian Government-in-Exile.

C212 GEORGIA (TRANSCAUCASIA), ASSEMBLÉE CONSTITUANTE DE LA RÉPUBLIQUE GÉORGIENNE. *Le Peuple géorgien contre l'occupation bolchéviste russe.* Paris: 1922.

C213 GEORGIA (TRANSCAUCASIA), COMMITTÉE CENTRAL DU PARTI S-D DE GÉORGIE. *L'Internationale socialiste et la Géorgie.* Paris: n.p., 1921. 296 p.

C214 GEORGIA (TRANSCAUCASIA), TREATIES. *Traité conclu le 7 Mai 1920 entre la République démocratique de Géorgie et la République Socialiste Fédérative Soviétiste Russe et accord de transit et de commerce conclu le 14 Novembre 1920. . . .* Paris: Dupont, 1922. 19 p.

C215 GODWIN, ROBERT K. "Russian-Georgian Relations, 1917-1921." Certificate essay, Russian Institute, Columbia, 1951. 73 p.

C216 GRUZINSKAIA DEMOKRATICHESKAIA RESPUBLIKA, PRAVITELSTVO. *Dokumenty i materialy po vneshnei politike Zakavkazia i Gruzii.* Tiflis: Respublika Gruzii, Ministerstvo vneshnikh del, 1919. 492 p. An invaluable collection of official documents, diplomatic correspondence, etc., dealing with international affairs published by the government of independent Georgia. Perhaps the single most important source of documents on the period 1917-18. [A]

C217 KAUTSKY, KARL. *Georgia: A Social-Democratic Peasant Republic.* London: International Bookshop, 1921. 111 p. A famous German Marxist praises independent Georgia which, unlike Russia, did not give up democracy while establishing socialism. More important for a study of Kautsky's thought than for the history of Georgia.

C218 KHACHAPURIDZE, G. V. *Bolsheviki Gruzii v boiakh za pobedu sovetskoi vlasti.* Moscow: 1947. 2nd enlarged and revised ed., Moscow: Gospolitizdat, 1951. 340 p. Written at the height of the "Beria period" of Soviet historiography. A distorted and dishonest account.

C219 MAKHARADZE, FILIPP I. *Diktatura menshevistskoi partii v Gruzii.* Moscow: Gosizdat, 1921. 112 p. A strongly anti-Menshevik yet relatively fair treatment by a leading Georgian Bolshevik.

C220 MAKHARADZE, FILIPP I. *Sovety i borba za sovetskuiu vlast v Gruzii, 1917-1921.* Tiflis: 1928. A history of the Revolution and the sovietization of Georgia by one of the leading Georgian Bolsheviks. Propagandistic yet containing many important facts.

C221 RUSSIA (1917-RSFSR), NARODNYI KOMISSARIAT PO INOSTRANNYM DELAM. *Rossiiskaia Sotsialisticheskaia Federativnaia Sovetskaia Respublika i Gruzinskaia Demokraticheskaia Respublika; ikh vzaimootnosheniia; sostavleno po ofitsialnym materialam Narodnogo komissariata inostrannykh del Rossiiskoi Sotsialisticheskoi Federativnoi Sovetskoi Respubliki.* Moscow: Gosizdat, 1921. 101 p. A very valuable collection of diplomatic documents on Russo-Georgian relations, 1918-21. Most of the material is not available elsewhere. [A]

C222 SEF, S. E., ed. " 'Demokraticheskoe' pravitelstvo Gruzii i angliiskoe komandovanie," *Krasnyi Arkhiv*, Vol. 2 (XXI), p. 122-173 and Vol. 6 (XXV), p. 96-110. Moscow: Gosizdat, 1927. A very valuable documentary record of conferences between leaders of the Georgian Government and representatives of the British Command between February and September 1919. Contains transcripts from captured archives of the Georgian Ministries of War and Foreign Affairs. The Soviet editor's purpose is to discredit the Georgian Government and prove its collusion with the Whites through the British. [B]

C223 SHAFIR, IAKOV M. *Ocherki gruzinskoi zhirondy.* Moscow: Gosizdat, 1925. 207 p. Though partisan and biased, this work is valuable for its documentation. The author, a Bolshevik, had access to materials which are not generally available. [B]

C224 SHAFIR, IAKOV M. *Secrets of Menshevik Georgia; the Plot against Soviet Russia Unmasked, with Authentic Copies of Documents Taken from the Archives of the State Menshevik Governors of Georgia.* London: Communist Party of Great Britain, 1922. 100 p. A propaganda pamphlet to counteract the horrible impression produced on European democratic socialists by the Soviet conquest of Georgia in 1921.

C225 SURGULADZE, AKADII. *Ocherki iz istorii revoliutsionnogo dvizheniia v Gruzii, 1917-1921 gg.* Tbilisi: Izdat. Universiteta, 1954. 413 p.

C226 TROTSKII, LEV. *Mezhdu imperializmom i revoliutsiei; osnovnye voprosy revoliutsii na chastnom primere Gruzii.* Moscow: Gosizdat, 1922. 131 p. German ed., Hamburg, 1922. 153 p. English ed., *Between Red and White, with Particular Reference to Georgia.* London: Communist Party of Great Britain, 1922. 104 p. A wordy, angry attempt to justify through dialectical gymnastics the conquest of Georgia by Soviet Russia. Later in exile Trotsky blamed Stalin for actions which Trotsky defended so heatedly in 1922.

C227 TSERETELLI, IRAKLII G. *Séparation de la Transcaucasie de la Russie et l'indépendance de la Géorgie; discours prononcés à la Diète transcaucasienne.* Paris: Imprimerie Chaix, 1919. 55 p. Speech by a leading Georgia Menshevik, one-time member of Russia's Provisional Government, and a reluctant Georgian separatist.

C228 URTADZE, G. I. *Obrazovanie i konsolidatsiia Gruzinskoi Demokraticheskoi Respubliki.* Munich: 1956. A Georgian diplomat who participated in the conduct of Georgia's foreign policy attempts to reconstruct the past without contributing much that is new or significant.

C229 WOYTINSKY, WLADIMIR S. (VOITINSKII, VLADIMIR S.). *La Démocratie géorgienne.* Paris: Alcan Levy, 1921. 304 p. An able Russian scholar gives an excellent account of Georgia's Menshevik regime. Sympathetic to Georgia, but not violently anti-Soviet.

C230 WOYTINSKY, WLADIMIR S. (VOITINSKII, V. S.). *Stormy Passage.* N.Y.: Vanguard, 1961. 550 p. The autobiography of a Russian who was first a Bolshevik, then a Menshevik, who opposed Lenin's seizure of power, was arrested, released, and fled to the newly-independent Republic of Georgia. There he served as an adviser to the leaders of the Menshevik regime, and was sent abroad in 1920 to attempt to gain Allied recognition for the Georgian government.

e. DAGESTAN

C231 BAMMATE, HAÏDAR. *The Caucasus Problem; Questions Concerning Circassia and Daghestan.* Berne: Staempfli. 1919. 46 p. Special pleading by a leader of North Caucasian nationalists. Significant because of the insights it offers into the feelings of Daghestani Moslems.

C232 EMIROV, N. *Ustanovlenie sovetskoi vlasti v Dagestane i borba s german-turetskimi interventami, 1917-1919 gg.* Moscow: n.p., 1949.

186 p. A Soviet account of the Bolshevik struggle against German and Turkish interventionists in Dagestan.

C233 TAKHO-GODI, A. A. *Revoliutsiia i kontr-revoliutsiia v Dagestane*. Makhach-Kala: Dagestanskii nauch.-issl. institut, 1927. 244 p. Memoirs and history concerning events in the Northern Caucasus area from 1917 through 1920. An invaluable first-hand view of the struggle of the mountain peoples for self-determination, showing internal divisions and relations with the Volunteer Army, the British, the Transcaucasian Republics, and the Bolsheviks. Appendices with valuable documents.

f. NORTHERN CAUCASUS

C234 AVTORKHANOV, A. *Revoliutsiia i kontrrevoliutsiia v Chechne*. Groznyi, 1933.

C235 BORISENKO, I. *Sovetskie respubliki na Severnom Kavkaze v 1918 godu*. Rostov on Don: "Severnyi Kavkaz," 1930. 2 vols. An important work treating seven north Caucasian peoples in the Revolutionary and Civil War period. Describes how elements friendly to the Bolsheviks overcame the local "bourgeoisie," i.e., those who desired independence from Russia. Reprints numerous documents, mostly minutes of the local Soviets.

C236 IANCHEVSKII, N. L. *Grazhdanskaia borba na Severnom Kavkaze*. Rostov on Don: "Sevkavkniga," 1927. A valuable collection of documents.

C237 SVECHNIKOV, M. *Borba krasnoi armii na Severnom Kavkaze —sentiabr 1918-aprel 1919*. Moscow-Leningrad: 1926.

5. THE CRIMEAN TATARS

(Edited by Serge A. Zenkovsky)

C238 ATLAS, M. L. *Borba za sovety; ocherki po istorii sovetov v Krymu 1919 g*. Simferopol: Krymgosizdat, 1933. 144 p.

C239 BOCHAGOV, A. K. *Milli Firka; natsionalnaia kontrrevoliutsiia v Krymu*. Simferopol: Krymgosizdat, 1930. 117 p. A detailed study of the role of Milli Firka (Tatar Nationalist Party in the Crimea) and its role in the growth of Tatar national consciousness.

C240 BUNEGIN, MAKSIM F. *Revoliutsiia i grazhdanskaia voina v Krymu*. Simferopol: Krymgosizdat, 1927. 336 p. An important account of the Civil War period in the Crimean area. Treats the attitude of the

Tatar minority. One of the best books written from the Communist point of view.

C241 GUKOVSKII, A. I., ed. "Krymskoe kraevoe pravitelstvo v 1918-1919 g.," *Krasnyi Arkhiv*, Vol. XXII, p. 92-152. Moscow: Gosizdat, 1927. "Krym v 1918-1919 gg.," *Krasnyi Arkhiv*, Vol. XXVIII, p. 142-181 and Vol. XXIX, p. 55-85. Moscow: Gosizdat, 1928. A documentary account, edited and introduced by a Soviet historian, of the Crimean government's formation and activities, French intervention, and relations with the Russian Volunteer Army. Based largely upon reports made by participants and subsequently published by the RSFSR central archives. [B]

C242 KALVARI, M. *Interventsiia v Krymu*. Simferopol: Krymgosizdat, 1930. 183 p.

C243 KIRIMAL, EDIGE M. *Der Nationale Kampf der Krimtürken, mit besonderer Berücksichtigung der Jahre 1917-1918*. Emsdetten: Verlag Lechte, 1952. 374 p. A very detailed and well-documented study of the development of nationalism among the Crimean Tatars as well as the fate of the Crimea during the Civil War of 1918-20. Written from the point of view of Crimean Turkic nationalists.

C244 *Osvobozhdenie Kryma ot anglo-frantsuzskikh interventov, 1918-1919*. Simferopol: 1940. 176 p.

C245 PASMANIK, DANIIL S. *Revoliutsionnye gody v Krymu*. Paris: Imprimerie de Navarre, 1926. 212 p. A study of the Crimea during the years of the Civil War 1917-20, written by a liberal Russian-Jewish political leader.

C246 SEIDAMET, D. (DEISAMET, D.) *La Crimée*. Lausanne: 1921. A study of the Crimea, its history, geography and the Tatar national movement written by the most outstanding Crimean Tatar political leader. Presents a rather one-sided and exaggerated opinion on the importance of the Tatar minority in the Crimea. Interesting for the understanding of Crimean-Turkish relations.

C247 VINAVER, M. *Nashe pravitelstvo (Krymskie vospominaniia 1918-1919 gg.)* Paris: Voltaire, 1928. 240 p. A history of developments in the Crimea during German and French Intervention, by the Foreign Minister of the Crimean government under S. S. Krym established after the fall of the Tatar regime. The author, a Kadet and member of the Constituent Assembly, provides a basic source on the erection of the moderate constitutional government and its relations with the Tatars, Volunteer Army, and the Allies.

6. SOVIET CENTRAL ASIA

(Edited by Alexander G. Park)

C248 AKULININ, I. G. *Orenburgskoe kazachee voisko v borbe s Bolshevikami, 1917-1920*. Shanghai: Izd. "Slovo," 1937. Written by a Cossack general who participated in the *Dutovshchina*, this book gives an account of the struggle of the Orenburg Cossacks against the Soviet Government. An addendum reproduces several documents pertaining to the progress of the struggle.

C249 ANTROPOV, P. G. *Chto i kak chitat po istorii revoliutsionnogo dvizheniia i partii v Srednei Azii*. Samarkand-Tashkent: Uzbekskoe gosizdat, 1929. 98 p. A short, annotated bibliography of Soviet works.

C250 BABAKHODZHAEV, A. KH. *Proval agressionoi politiki angliiskogo imperializma (1917-1920)*. Tashkent: Izd. Akad. nauk SSSR, 1955. 159 p. *Proval angliiskoi antisovetskoi politiki v Srednei Azii i na Srednem Vostoke v period priznaniia sovetskogo gosudarstva de-fakto i de-iure (1921-1924)*. Tashkent: Izd. Akad. nauk SSSR, 1957. 216 p. A distorted account of British intervention in Soviet Central Asia during the Civil War period. The author tries to make a case for alleged efforts by the British to reassert their influence in the area after the collapse of Intervention. Useful bibliography.

C251 BAILEY, FREDERICK M. *Mission to Tashkent*. London: Cape, 1946. 312 p. Memoirs of the sole British agent to operate in Turkestan throughout the 1918-19 intervention period. The author had unusual contacts with Bolshevik authorities in Tashkent as well as with the anti-Bolshevik underground, but his perspective was limited because of the loss of outside contact during most of the period. Contains a vivid description of conditions in Tashkent after the Tashkent Soviet came to power. [B]

C252 BERLINER, JOSEPH S. *Soviet Central Asia; a Selected Bibliography*. Cambridge: Russian Research Center of Harvard University, 1948. 20 p. (duplicated). Based principally on the holdings of the various Harvard libraries, with some references to works in the Library of Congress. The emphasis is on geography, natural resources, and the economy. Most of the titles deal with the pre-1917 period.

C253 BOZHKO, F. *Grazhdanskaia voina v Srednei Azii*. Tashkent: 1930. An important early work on the Civil War in Central Asia. By a former Menshevik who became, as a Communist, one of the leading early Soviet specialists on Central Asia.

C254 BOZHKO, F. *Oktiabrskaia revoliutsiia v Srednei Azii.* Tashkent: 1932. An interesting work on the October events in Central Asia.

C255 BRUN, ALF H. (CAPTAIN) *Troublous Times; Experiences in Bolshevik Russia and Turkestan.* London: Constable, 1931. 243 p. The memoirs of a Danish Red Cross officer who was stationed in Tashkent during the period of Revolution and Civil War in Turkestan. Contains excellent descriptions of the atmosphere in Tashkent and the techniques of rule employed by the early Bolshevik rulers in Turkestan. [B]

C256 BUROV, N. A., and GARITSKII, A., comps. *Kratkii bibliograficheskii ukazatel literatury po Turkestanu.* Tashkent: Izd. Turkestanskogo ekonom. soveta, 1924. 111 p. A useful bibliography of Central Asia, containing many valuable entries on Russian and Soviet relations with England, China, Persia, and Afghanistan.

C257 CAROE, OLAF K. *Soviet Empire; the Turks of Central Asia and Stalinism.* N.Y.: Macmillan, 1953. 300 p. A study of Soviet policy in Central Asia, based largely on the work of A. Zeki Velidi Togan, a leading Turkic nationalist and one-time Basmachi leader. Discusses the workings of Soviet nationalities policy in terms of the desire of Turkic nationalist forces for self-determination. [A]

C258 CASTAGNÉ, JOSEPH. *Les Basmatchis; le mouvement national des indigènes d'Asie Centrale.* Paris: Leroux, 1925. 88 p. An examination of the resistance movement against Soviet rule in Central Asia by the editor of *Revue du Monde Mussulman.* The work is principally valuable for the documentary materials which it reproduces.

C259 CASTAGNÉ, JOSEPH. *Le Bolchévisme et l'Islam.* Paris: Leroux, 1922. 2 vols. An important work containing valuable source material, by the first French specialist in the field of Soviet-Moslem relations.

C260 CASTAGNÉ, JOSEPH. *Les Musulmans et la politique des Soviets en Asie Centrale. Les Indes et l'Egypte vues de Russie.* Paris: Leroux, 1925. 125 p. A study of the effect of the October Revolution on India and the Moslem Middle and Near East.

C261 CASTAGNÉ, JOSEPH. *Le Turkestan depuis la révolution russe, 1917-1921.* Paris: 1922. A treatise consisting mainly of documents and other translated materials relating to the Revolution and Civil War in Turkestan. A useful source of materials on the early period of Soviet rule. [B]

C262 CHOKAEV, MUSTAFA. *Turkestan pod vlastiu sovetov.* Paris: "Iash Turkestan," 1935. 127 p. A sharp attack on Soviet nationalities policies, using materials from Soviet sources to emphasize Soviet discrimination against the indigenous population of Turkestan. The author was head of the short-lived Kokand Autonomous Government and a leader of the Turkic nationalist emigration. [B]

C263 FILIPOV, S. T. *Boevye deistviia na Zakaspiiskom fronte.* Ashkhabad: 1928. A detailed description of military operations in Turkestan during the years 1918-20.

C264 GLOVATSKII, O. *Revoliutsiia pobezhdaet.* Tashkent: 1930. An historical study of the victory of the Communists in Turkestan in the 1917 Revolution and Civil War of 1917-20.

C265 GORKII, MAKSIM, and others. *Voina v peskakh; grazhdanskaia voina v Srednei Azii.* Moscow: Izd. "Istorii Grazhdanskoi voina," Ogiz, 1935. 541 p. Descriptions of the Bolshevik struggle for control of Turkestan by Soviet experts and participants. Particularly noteworthy is the account by Kolesov, Bolshevik commander of the Red Army forces involved, of the initial Soviet attempt to overthrow the Emir of Bokhara.

C266 HAYIT, BAYMIRZA. *Turkestan in XX Jahrhundert.* Darmstadt: C. W. Leske, 1956. 406 p. An examination of political and cultural developments in Soviet Central Asia, chiefly during the first decade of Soviet rule. The book is intensely nationalistic and anti-Soviet. [A]

C267 ILIUTKO, F. *Basmachestvo v Lokae.* Moscow-Leningrad: Gosizdat, 1929. A Soviet account of the rise of the Basmachi movement in Bokhara which recounts in detail the Soviet campaign against Ibrihaim Bek. Military engagements against the Basmachi are described in detail.

C268 ISHANOV, A. I. *Sozdanie Bukharskoi Narodnoi Sovetskoi Respubliki.* Tashkent: Izd. Akad. nauk Uzbek SSR, 1955. An orthodox Soviet history of the overthrow of the Emir of Bokhara, the organization of the Bokharan People's Republic, its transformation into a Soviet socialist republic, and its incorporation into the USSR. The author makes liberal use of documents from the State Archives of the Uzbek SSR.

C269 KHODZHAEV, FAIZULLA. *K istorii revoliutsii v Bukhare.* Tashkent: 1926. The story of the Soviet preparation for and execution of the seizure of power in Bokhara. The author, a leading Turkic Communist who participated in the events, describes the process by which the Bolsheviks took control of the Bokharan nationalist movement and turned it to their own ends. [B]

C270 KLEIN, DAVID. "The Basmachi; A Case Study in Soviet Policy toward National Minorities." M.A. thesis, Columbia, 1952. 113 p.

C271 KOESTENBERGER, R. *Mit der Roten Armee durch Russisch-Zentralasien.* Graz: 1925. 146 p.

C272 KOMUNISTICHESKAIA AKADEMIIA, MOSCOW, KOMISSIA PO IZUCHENIIU NATSIONALNOGO VOPROSA. *Revoliutsiia i natsionalnyi vopros.* Ed. by S. M. Dimanshtein. Moscow: Izd. Kom. akad., 1930. A collection of documents setting forth the policies of the Provisional Government and of the Soviets relating to the nationalities question in 1917. Part IV contains documents relating to the nationalist movement among the Turkic peoples of the Russian Empire.

C273 LUKNITSKII, PAVEL N. *Tadzhikistan.* Moscow: 1951. 366 p. Abridged English ed., *Soviet Tajikistan.* Moscow: Foreign Languages Publishing House, 1954. 254 p. German ed., Moscow: 1954. 243 p. A study of the geography, economics and, partially, the history of the Tajik SSR, written by an outstanding Soviet expert on Central Asian area problems.

C274 MAIER, ANATOLII. *Boevye epizody—Basmachestvo v Bukhare.* Moscow-Tashkent: 1934. An important work by a Communist historian on the genesis and development of the Moslem anti-Soviet guerrilla movement in Bukhara.

C275 MALLESON, W. "The British Military Mission to Turkestan, 1918-1920," *Journal of the Royal Central Asian Society*, IX (1922).

C276 MELNIKOV, G. N., comp. *Oktiabr v Kazakhstane; ocherki i rasskazy uchastnikov grazhdanskoi voiny.* Alma-Ata: 1930. Includes descriptions of the various military operations in Turkestan during the Civil War, by participants in the events. Despite its external fictionalized form, this work contains some important and rare detail on this period of Central Asian history.

C277 MENDE, GERHARD VON. *Der nationale Kampf der Russlandtürken; ein Beitrag zur nationalen Frage in der Sovetunion.* Berlin: Weidmann, 1936. 196 p. A history of the rise of nationalism among the Turkic peoples of Russia. Analyzes the response of both the Tsarist and Soviet regimes to these strivings.

C278 "M. V. Frunze na Turkestanskom fronte," *Krasnyi Arkhiv*, no. 3 (100) (1940), p. 36-78. A collection of documents, particularly useful for their revelation of the role played by Frunze in the preparation for and execution of the overthrow of the Emir of Bokhara.

C279 *Obrazovanie Kazakhskoi SSR.* Ed. by S. N. Pokrovskii. Alma-Ata: 1957. A collection of decrees, resolutions, appeals and other documentary materials drawn from the State Archives of the USSR, Kazakh

SSR, Uzbek SSR and from the oblast archives of the Central Asian republics. Despite obvious care taken in the selection of "appropriate" documents, this volume is a basic source of materials on the Revolution and Civil War in Kazakhstan.

C280 *Ocherki revoliutsionnogo dvizheniia v Srednei Azii.* Moscow: Nauchnaia assotsiatsiia vostokovedeniia, 1926. 152 p. A collection of articles by Soviet scholars on the revolutionary movement in Central Asia.

C281 OKAY, KURT (pseud.) *Enver Pascha, der grosse Freund Deutschlands.* Berlin: Verlag für Kulturpolitik, 1935. 506 p. The story of the Turkish military leader and former collaborator of Atatürk, who later went to Russia and there aspired to create a new Turkic state in Soviet Central Asia. Though this biography is in the form of fiction, it displays considerable knowledge of the subject.

C282 OLZSCHA, REINER, and CLEINOW, GEORG. *Turkestan, die politisch-historischen und wirtschaftlichen Probleme Zentralasiens.* Leipzig; Koehler und Amelang, 1942. 433 p. A detailed study of the events of the Revolution and Civil War of 1917-20 in Soviet Central Asia. [B]

C283 PARK, ALEXANDER G. *Bolshevism in Turkestan, 1917-1927.* N.Y.: Columbia, 1957. 428 p. An examination of the objectives and conduct of Soviet nationalities policies in Soviet Central Asia during the first decade of Bolshevik power. Chapters I and II deal with the establishment of Bolshevik rule in the region and the transformation of Turkestan and the neighboring areas into Soviet republics. Useful bibliography. [A]

C284 PIPES, RICHARD E. *The Formation of the Soviet Union; Communism and Nationalism, 1917-1923.* Cambridge: Harvard, 1954. 355 p. Russian Research Center Studies, 13. An examination of the disintegration of the Russian Empire after the October Revolution and its reintegration under the Bolshevik dispensation. Chapter IV sketches the course of the Revolution and Civil War in the Moslem Regions of the Empire. Excellent. [A]

C285 RAMZIN, K., comp. *Revoliutsiia v Srednei Azii v obrazakh i kartinakh.* Moscow: Izd. Saku, 1928. n.p. Interesting and informative pictures of the revolutionary movement in Central Asia.

C286 RUSSIA (1917–RSFSR), NARODNYI KOMISSARIAT PO DELAM NATSIONALNOSTEI. *Politika sovetskoi vlasti po natsionalnym delam za tri goda, 1917-1920.* Moscow: Gosizdat, 1920. 185 p. A compilation of decrees, resolutions and appeals issued mainly by the Commissariat of Nationalities and setting forth Communist nationalities policy during the early years of Soviet rule. The volume contains the principal documents outlining Soviet policy toward the peoples of Turkestan and defining the center's conception of Soviet administration in the Moslem borderlands. [B]

C287 RYSKULOV, TURAR R. *Kirgizstan.* Moscow: Sotsekonizdat, 1935. 188 p. A short historical and political survey of Kirghizia by a Turkic Communist.

C288 RYSKULOV, TURAR R. *Revoliutsiia i korennoe naselenie Srednei Azii.* Tashkent: 1925. The story of the plight of the indigenous peoples of Soviet Central Asia during the early period of Bolshevik rule. The book itself is an excellent delineation of the attitudes of left-wing native nationalists who accepted the Soviet system but deplored the excesses of the revolutionary period. [B]

C289 RYSKULOV, TURAR R. and others. *Ocherki revoliutsionnogo dvizheniia v Srednei Azii.* Moscow: 1936. The Revolution and Civil War in Turkestan as described by leading Communist participants.

C290 SAFAROV, GEORGII I. *Kolonialnaia revoliutsiia; opyt Turkestana.* Moscow: Gosizdat, 1921. 147 p. One of the best accounts of Soviet policies and practices in Turkestan during the Revolution and Civil War by a Communist Party official. Safarov, a member of the Turkestan Commission of the Party Central Committee, sets forth the Party view of conditions and their causes in the area at the time. [B]

C291 SAID, ALIM KHAN (EMIR OF BOKHARA). *La Voix de la Bukharie opprimée.* Paris: Maisonneuve frères, 1929. 71 p. The Emir of Bokhara sets forth his side of the dispute between Bokhara and the Soviet regime in a short account of the events leading to the Soviet seizure of power in Bokhara.

C292 SAMOILOVICH, A. N., ed. *Kazakhstan v izdaniiakh Akademii nauk SSSR 1734-1935.* Moscow: 1936. A bibliography.

C293 SAPARGALIEV, M. *Vozniknovenie kazakhskoi sovetskoi gosudarstvennosti.* Alma-Ata: 1948. A tendentious description of the first steps of Kazakh Soviet autonomy. A typical product of the late Stalin era.

C294 TAIMANOV, G. T. *Razvitie sovetskoi gosudarstvennosti v Kazakhstane.* Moscow: Gos. izd. iurid. lit., 1956. A short standardized summary of the events of the Revolution and Civil War in Kazakhstan, sprinkled liberally with quotations from Lenin and arguing the "progressive" nature of the incorporation of the territory into the Soviet state.

C295 TCHOKAIEFF, MARIIA (CHOKAI). *Iash Turkestan: Sbornik ko dniu 60-letiia so dnia rozhdeniia i 8-letiiu so dnia smerti glavy Kokandskoi Avtonomii i osnovateli Iash Turkestana, Mustafa Chokai.* Paris: 1949-50. A collection of articles by and on Mustafa Chokai, one of the outstanding leaders of Turkestan nationalism.

C296 TIMOSHKOV, S. P. *Borba s angliiskoi interventsiei v Turkestane.* Moscow: Voenizdat, 1941. 125 p. A short history of Soviet military campaigns in Turkestan during the Bolshevik Revolution and Civil War. Based largely on documents from the Central Archives of the Red Army.

C297 TOGAN, A. ZEKI VELIDI. *Bügünkü Türkili ve yakin tarihi.* Istanbul: I. Horoz ve Güven Basimevleri, 1942-1947. A detailed account of Turkic opposition to Bolshevik domination of Turkestan by a leader of the Turkic nationalist movement. The book is excellent for the insights it provides into the aims and mentality of the leaders of the Basmachi movement. [A]

C298 TURKMEN SSR, MINISTERSTVO VNUTRENNYKH DEL, ARKHIVNYI OTDEL. *Turkmenistan v period inostrannoi voennoi interventsii i grazhdanskoi voiny (1918-1920); sbornik dokumentov.* Ed. by Sh. Tashlieva. Comp. by A. V. Golovkin and others. Ashkhabad: Turk. gos. izd., 1957. 569 p. A collection of documents on the history of the Turkmen SSR during the Civil War of 1917-20. Contains interesting material on English military intervention in Russian Central Asia. [B]

C299 ULIANOV, I. I. *Kazaki i Sovetskaia Respublika.* Moscow: Gosizdat, 1919. 173 p. One of the earliest studies on the attitude of the Kazakhs toward the Soviet regime.

C300 *Velikaia oktiabrskaia revoliutsiia i Grazhdanskaia Voina v Kirgizii.* Frunze: 1957.

C301 VIATKIN, M. P., ed. *Istoriia Kirgizii.* Frunze: 1956. 2 vols. A rather dull and uninspiring history of Kirghizia, by a Soviet historian specializing in Central Asia.

C302 VITKIND, N. IA. *Bibliografiia po Srednei Azii.* Moscow: 1929.

C303 ZAREVAND. *Turtsiia i panturanizm.* Paris: 1930. 167 p. An examination of the rise of Pan-Turkism, its aims and its influence in Russia and Turkey before and after the Bolshevik Revolution, by a supporter of Pan-Turkism.

C304 ZENKOVSKY, SERGE A. *Pan-Turkism and Islam in Russia.* Cambridge: Harvard, 1960. 345 p. A scholarly study of the rise and development of the Pan-Turkic and national movement in the Soviet Middle East up to 1921. Several chapters deal specifically with the Revolution and Civil War in Turkestan. Excellent bibliography. [A]

C305 ZORIN, A. N. *Revoliutsionnoe dvizhenie v Kirgizii (severnaia chast).* Frunze, 1931. A study of the revolutionary events in the northern part of Kirghizia, which before the Revolution had become the main region of Russian agricultural settlement in Central Asia.

D. Soviet Foreign Relations, 1921-1928

EDITED BY ARTHUR E. ADAMS

1. GENERAL WORKS

D1 ARNOT, ROBERT PAGE. *Soviet Russia and Her Neighbors.* N.Y.: Vanguard Press, 1927. 168 p. A brief, general examination, with chapters on the Soviet Union's relations with the United States, Great Britain, France, Japan, Germany, the East European states, the colonial states, and China. Objective, simply written. A useful work for the beginning student.

D2 BRUKSON, IAKOV B. *Imperialisticheskie bloki.* Moscow-Leningrad: Gosizdat, 1929. 114 p.

D3 BUKHARIN, NIKOLAI I. *Kapitalisticheskaia stabilizatsiia i proletarskaia revoliutsiia.* Moscow-Leningrad: Giz, 1927. 347 p. Bukharin was one of the top theorists of the Russian Communist Party and a member of the Politburo during this period.

D4 BUKHARIN, NIKOLAI I. *O mezhdunarodnom i vnutrennem polozhenii SSSR; doklad, zakliuchitelnoe slovo na XV moskovskoi gubpartkonferentsii i rezoliutsiia po dokladu.* Moscow: Izd. "Pravda" i "Bednota," 1927. 107 p. Bukharin, an important Bolshevik theorist, argues the need to be prepared because of the threat of imminent imperialist invasion. The Moscow Gubernia Conference Resolution printed here agrees that international complications and the struggle for the world market threaten the USSR and call for preparedness. Useful for insight into the Communist mentality in 1927—a clear picture of the very real fear of intervention.

D5 CARR, EDWARD H. *A History of Soviet Russia.* Vol. III, *The Bolshevik Revolution, 1917-1923.* N.Y. and London: Macmillan, 1953. 614 p. Vol. IV, *The Interregnum, 1923-1924.* 1954. 392 p. A detailed and penetrating examination of the early years, coming down to the summer and fall of 1923. Carr's erudition is immense, and his understanding of the events described is most impressive. Extremely useful. Carr covers foreign relations for the following years in vol. VII, entitled *Socialism in One Country, 1924-1926.* [A]

D6 DEUTSCHER, ISAAC. *The Prophet Unarmed; Trotsky: 1921-1929.* London and N.Y.: Oxford, 1959. 490 p. The second volume of the masterful biography by a journalist-scholar who was active in the Polish Communist Party until his expulsion in 1932 for "Trotskyism." Deutscher believes that "Trotsky's heroic character" has "few equals in history," but the book is generally objective and Trotsky's weaknesses are not overlooked. Although concerned primarily with internal affairs in Russia, the book refers to Soviet foreign policy from time to time, especially in connection with the debate over "socialism in a single country."

D7 EUDIN, XENIA J., and FISHER, HAROLD H. *Soviet Russia and the West, 1920-1927; A Documentary Survey.* Stanford: Stanford University Press; London: Oxford, 1957. 450 p. Combines documents and extensive introductory narratives in the Hoover Institute tradition. Excellent scholarly analysis and collection of documents, though weak on materials of international Communism. [A]

D8 EUDIN, XENIA, and NORTH, ROBERT C. *Soviet Russia and the East, 1920-1927; A Documentary Survey.* Stanford: Stanford University Press, 1957. 478 p. An extremely valuable collection of documents, with long introductory essays for each section. Contains a chronology, biographical notes, and a fifty-page bibliography of books and articles. [A]

D9 FISCHER, LOUIS. *Oil Imperialism; the International Struggle for Petroleum.* N.Y.: International Publishers, 1926. 256 p. A well-documented account of the world competition for oil and the part played by the Soviet Republic and its oil resources in this struggle. Very sympathetic to the Soviet Union.

D10 FISCHER, LOUIS. *The Soviets in World Affairs; a History of the Relations between the Soviet Union and the Rest of the World, 1917-1929.* London: J. Cape; N.Y.: J. Cape and H. Smith, 1930. 2 vols. 2nd ed., Princeton, N.J.: Princeton University Press, 1951. 2 vols. French ed., Paris: Gallimard, 1933. Fischer, a journalist, profited immensely from personal friendship and extensive discussions with Litvinov, Chicherin, Rakovsky, Karakhan, Borodin, and other important participants in Soviet affairs. His work is one of the classics in this field, though it has a strong pro-Soviet bias. [A]

D11 GRAHAM, MALBONE W. *The Soviet Security System.* Worcester, Mass. and N.Y.: Carnegie Endowment for International Peace, 1929. 89 p. A brief scholarly analysis arguing that Soviet efforts to achieve security moved through four phases between 1920 and 1929. These were: sovietization, negotiation, conference and consolidation, and political agreement. Graham appends the documents he discusses, mainly peace treaties and non-aggression treaties or proposals. Useful.

D12 GURKO-KRIAZHIN, VLADIMIR A. *Poslevoennye mirovye konflikty.* Moscow: "Moskovskii Rabochii," 1924. 125 p. A scholarly Marxist examination of the world scene from 1921 to 1924. The emphasis is primarily on relations between European states from the point of view of one who deplored international imperialism and hoped to see Europe become a part of an anti-imperialist world.

D13 IVANOV, LEV N. *SSSR i imperialisticheskoe okruzhenie*. Moscow: Izd. Kommunisticheskoi akademii, 1928. 154 p. The first volume of the 7-volume series, *Desiat let kapitalisticheskogo okruzheniia SSSR*, sponsored by the Kommunisticheskaia Akademiia (see below). This one sets the stage for the series, dealing with various aspects of capitalist "encirclement" of Russia. Contains useful references to documents and periodical articles. Discusses Russia's attempt to gain recognition, with emphasis on relations with England.

D14 KOLODKIN, MILTON A. "Russian Interests at the Washington Conference on the Limitations of Armaments, 1921-22, with Special Reference to United States Policy." M.A. thesis, Columbia, 1955. 62 p. A brief but interesting study which deals with the problem of Russia's absence from the Washington Conference, where matters were discussed which very much concerned the Russians, i.e., the territorial integrity of Siberia and Sakhalin and the Chinese Eastern Railway. Russian resentments are fully explored.

D15 KOMMUNISTICHESKAIA AKADEMIIA, INSTITUT MIROVOGO KHOZIAISTVA I MIROVOI POLITIKI. *Desiat let kapitalisticheskogo okruzheniia SSSR*. Ed. by E. Pashukanis and M. Spektator. Moscow: Izd. Kom. akademii, 1928-29. 7 vols. in 2. A series of books treating Soviet relations with the Baltic States, Germany, the Entente, Poland, the East, the world proletariat, and the world economy.

D16 KOMMUNISTICHESKAIA AKADEMIIA, KABINET MEZHDUNARODNOI POLITIKI. *Mirovaia politika v 1924 g.; sbornik statei*. Ed. by F. A. Rotshtein. Moscow: Kom. akademiia, 1925. 333 p. A valuable collection of articles by Chicherin, Radek, Joffe, and other important Soviet diplomatic figures. Embraces a variety of problems including Lenin's influence on external politics, relations with the Near East, the Balkans, China, and the League of Nations, trade negotiations, and trade union movements. A useful bibliography of Soviet periodical literature on international life and politics for 1924 is appended. [B]

D17 KRETOV, FEDOR D. *O griadushchei voine imperialistov protiv SSSR*. Moscow: Moskovskii Rabochii, 1928. 127 p. A collection of Kretov's articles in *Izvestiia*. Considering attack by "imperialist" powers inevitable, he argued for systematic and planned defense preparations, without panic, at all levels of Soviet society. Universal mobilization, he believed, might become necessary; the Soviet Union would be transformed into an armed camp. The probable character of the next war was also considered. A valuable insight into the very genuine fear of intervention that influenced Soviet policy in the twenties.

D18 LAGARDE, ERNEST. *La Réconnaissance du gouvernement des Soviets.* Paris: Payot, 1924. 190 p. Russian ed., Moscow: 1925. A careful scholarly study covering the period from the end of World War I to the beginning of 1924. Competent but brief analyses of the Soviet Government's struggle for recognition.

D19 MAIZEL, B. *Sredizemnomorskaia problema i opasnosti voiny.* Moscow-Leningrad: Gosizdat, 1928. 134 p.

D20 *Mezhdunarodnaia solidarnost trudiashchikhsia v borbe s nastupleniem reaktsii i voennoi opasnostiu (1925-1927).* Ed. by P. B. Lebedev. Moscow: "Sovetskaia Rossiia," 1959. 544 p. 334 statements by foreign Communist groups in support of Russian foreign policy in the period indicated. Volume III of *Iz istorii mezhdunarodnoi proletarskoi solidarnosti.*

D21 NAKHIMSON, M. I. *K voprosu o stabilizatsii kapitalizma (kriticheskii etiud).* Moscow: Planovoe khoziaistvo, 1926. 184 p.

D22 PAVLOVICH, MIKHAIL (pseud. of Mikhail Veltman). *Borba za Aziiu i Afriku.* Moscow: Vserossiiskaia nauchnaia assots. vostokovedeniia pri Narodnom komissariate po delam natsionalnostei, 1923. 229 p. Although most of his work was theoretical, Pavlovich was one of the early Soviet writers on Africa and Asia.

D23 PAVLOVICH, MIKHAIL. *Imperializm (Kurs lektsii, chitannykh v Akademii Generalnogo shtaba v 1922-1923 gg.).* Moscow: "Krasnaia Nov," 1923. 236 p.

D24 PAVLOVICH, MIKHAIL. *RSFSR v imperialisticheskom okruzhenii.* Vol. I, *Sovetskaia Rossiia i kapitalisticheskaia Frantsiia.* Moscow: Gosizdat, 1922. 64 p. Vol. II, *Sovetskaia Rossiia i kapitalisticheskaia Angliia.* 2nd ed., Moscow: "Prometei," 1925. 203 p. Vol. III, *Sovetskaia Rossiia i kapitalisticheskaia Amerika.* Petrograd: Gosizdat, 1922. 101 p. Vol. IV, *Iaponskii imperializm na Dalnem Vostoke.* Moscow: Izd. "Krasnaia Nov," 1923. 145 p. Gives a historical sketch of relations between Russia and the country under consideration, going into much detail for the post-revolutionary period, especially for the country's role in the Intervention. Examines the domestic situation of the country, especially the possible effect of domestic factors, such as the agricultural situation, trade, and sympathetic elements in the social structure, on the fortunes of Soviet Russia.

D25 RADEK, KARL (pseud. of Karl Sobelsohn). *Genua, die Einheitsfront des Proletariats und die Kommunistische Internationale.* 2nd ed., Hamburg: Carl Hoym, 1922. 78 p. A prominent Bolshevik leader, known for his vitriolic pen, gives his interpretations of the international situation in 1922.

D26 RADEK, KARL. *Mezhdunarodnaia politika.* Vol. I, *Obozrenie za 1924 god.* Moscow-Leningrad: Gosizdat, 1925. 192 p. Radek here reviews the development of fascism, the Dawes Report, "democratic pacifism," and the Labour Government in Great Britain. He sees the year as one in which the United States and Great Britain managed to return to Europe, and he argues that new conflicts, possibly even armed conflicts, are being prepared for Asia and Eastern Europe. An authoritative Communist analysis.

D27 RADEK, KARL. *Vneshniaia politika Sovetskoi Rossii.* Moscow-Leningrad: Gosizdat, 1923. 112 p. A survey of policy from the Brest-Litovsk treaty to 1923. The last 20 pages are concerned with the Genoa and Hague Conferences. Provides little information, but gives a sharp and authoritative expression of the Soviet point of view.

D28 RAKOVSKII, KHRISTIAN G. *Liga Natsii i SSSR.* Preface by G. V. Chicherin. Moscow: Kommunisticheskaia akademiia, 1926. 81 p. A Soviet spokesman on international affairs portrays the League of Nations as an instrument of imperial aggression. Also discusses Locarno and the general international situation.

D29 REISNER, M. A. *Gosudarstvo burzhuazii i RSFSR.* Moscow: Gosizdat, 1923. 419 p.

D30 RUBINSTEIN, NIKOLAI L. *Mezhdunarodnye otnosheniia i vneshniaia politika SSSR v 1924-1929 gg.; Lektsiia.* Moscow: 1950. 39 p. Strongly biased. Discusses the Dawes Plan, Locarno, the War Scare of 1927, and the Soviet Union's efforts to achieve disarmament. [B]

D31 RUBINSTEIN, NIKOLAI L. *Sovetskaia Rossiia i kapitalisticheskie gosudarstva v gody perekhoda ot voiny k miru, 1921-1922 gg.* Moscow: Gospolitizdat, 1948. 461 p. A detailed and scholarly study of Soviet foreign relations by a Soviet scholar of considerable reputation in his own country. Includes chapters on the Genoa and Hague Conferences. Makes good use of U.S. Congressional sources as well as other Western materials in French, German and English. [B]

D32 RUBINSTEIN, NIKOLAI L. *Vneshniaia politika Sovetskogo gosudarstva v 1921-1925 godakh.* Ed. by E. M. Zhukov. Moscow: Gospolitizdat, 1953. 566 p. A full-scale scholarly history based upon extensive examination of documents and Western sources. Very strongly biased. [A]

D33 RUSSIA (1917– RSFSR), NARODNYI KOMISSARIAT PO INOSTRANNYM DELAM. *Godovoi otchet za 1923 g. Narodnogo komissariata po inostrannym delam k II sezdu sovetov.* Moscow: NKID, 1924. 160 p. A detailed summary of the year's developments, together with an evaluation of Soviet accomplishments, and an exposition of the objectives still to be reached. Clearly expresses policy objectives as envisioned by the Soviet Union, and the difficulties of achieving them.

D34 RUSSIA (1917– RSFSR), NARODNYI KOMISSARIAT PO INOSTRANNYM DELAM. *Mezhdunarodnaia politika RSFSR v 1922 g.; otchet Narodnogo komissariata po inostrannym delam.* Moscow: NKID, 1923. 82 p.

D35 RUSSIA (1917– RSFSR), NARODNYI KOMISSARIAT PO INOSTRANNYM DELAM. *Sbornik deistvuiushchikh dogovorov, soglashenii i konventsii, zakliuchennykh RSFSR s inostrannymi gosudarstvami.* Moscow: NKID, 1921-1923. 5 vols. in 2. The basic treaty series for the RSFSR period. Plagued by faulty editing, but more liberal in spirit and more inclusive in coverage than the later Soviet treaty series. [A]

D36 RUSSIA (1923– USSR), KOMISSIIA PO IZDANIIU DIPLOMATICHESKIKH DOKUMENTOV. *Dokumenty vneshnei politiki SSSR.* Vol. III, July 1, 1920–March 18, 1921; Vol. IV, March 19, 1921–December, 1921, Vol. V, Jan. 1, 1922–Nov. 19, 1922. Moscow: Gospolitizdat, 1957–. These are fully and carefully edited; valuable for their extensive treatment of policy during these years.

D37 RUSSIA (1923– USSR), KOMISSIIA PO IZDANIIU DIPLOMATICHESKIKH DOKUMENTOV. *Lokarnskaia konferentsiia, 1925 g., dokumenty.* Ed. by A. F. Dobrov and others. Moscow: Gospolitizdat, 1959. 511 p.

D38 RUSSIA (1923– USSR), NARODNYI KOMISSARIAT PO INOSTRANNYM DELAM. *Antisovetskie podlogi; istoriia falshivok, faksimile i kommentarii.* Moscow: Litizdat, NKID, 1926. 170 p. English ed., London: Workers' Publications, 1927. French ed., Paris: 1926. German ed., Berlin: 1926. An examination of a variety of "lies" and "slanders" made by non-Communist states against the Soviet Union. Includes an examination of the Curzon Note of 1921, and the "Red Letter," attributed by the British to Zinoviev. Photostatic copies of the "forgeries" are presented.

D39 RUSSIA (1923– USSR), NARODNYI KOMISSARIAT PO INOSTRANNYM DELAM. *Ezhegodnik Narodnogo komissariata po inostrannym delam na 19– g.* Moscow: NKID, 1925-1928. 4 annual vols. Each of these four annual "guides" of the Commissariat of Foreign Affairs contains much solid information: the Constitution of the USSR, organization of the central government, the diplomatic corps accredited to the Soviet Government, the official representatives of countries having relations with the USSR. Excellent reference material.

D40 RUSSIA (1923– USSR), NARODNYI KOMISSARIAT PO INOSTRANNYM DELAM. *Godovoi otchet za 1924 g. Narodnogo komissariata po inostrannym delam k III sezdu sovetov SSSR.* Moscow: NKID, 1925. 115 p. and appendices 36 p. Detailed and useful. Deals with re-establishment of diplomatic relations with other nations, relations during the year, and international economic and legal relations. The informative appendices provide charts on the organization, staffing and research resources of the NKID. [B]

D41 SABANIN, ANDREI V., comp. and ed. *Mezhdunarodnaia politika v 192– g.; dogovory, deklaratsii i diplomaticheskaia perepiska.* Moscow: Izd. Narkomindel, 192–. An excellent scholarly collection of documents arranged chronologically.

D42 *Sovetskii Soiuz v borbe za mir; sobranie dokumentov i vstupitelnaia statia.* Moscow: Gosizdat, 1929. 343 p. English ed., *The Soviet Union and Peace: The Most Important of the Documents Issued by the Government of the USSR Concerning Peace and Disarmament from 1917 to 1929.* Introduction by Henri Barbusse. London: Martin Lawrence; N.Y.: International, 1929. 292 p. A useful collection of documents organized under five headings: 1. The November Revolution and Peace; 2. Soviet Russia at Peace Conferences; 3. The USSR Disarmament Campaign; 4. The USSR and the Kellogg Pact; 5. The USSR and Pacts of Neutrality and Non-Aggression. Barbusse's strongly pro-Soviet introduction summarizes events from 1917 to 1928. [B]

D43 TILTON, R. F. "The Significance of the Locarno Treaties in the Foreign Policies of the Union of Soviet Socialist Republics." M.A. Thesis, U. of California, 1955.

D43A TROFIMOVA, L. I., comp. *G. V. Chicherin.* Moscow: Izd. sotsialno-ekonom. lit., 1961. A brief, official biography of the second Commissar of Foreign Affairs, followed by excerpts from his writings and official utterances.

D44 VARGA, EUGEN. *Krizis mirovogo kapitalisticheskogo khoziaistva.* Moscow: Gosizdat, 1923. 126 p. Varga was an official in the short-lived Hungarian Soviet government of 1919 and later moved to Russia, where he played a prominent role for several decades as one of the leading Soviet experts on the world economy.

D45 VARGA, EUGEN. *Mirovoe khoziaistvo i khoziaistvennaia politika v 1925 g.; obzor.* Edited by S. Sheverdin. Moscow-Leningrad: "Moskovskii rabochii," 1925-26. 4 vols.

D46 VARGA, EUGEN. *Mirovoe khoziaistvo i khoziaistvennaia politika v 1926 godu; obzor.* Trans. by M. Dikanskii and edited by S. Sheverdin. Moscow-Leningrad: "Moskovskii rabochii," 1926. 136 p.

D47 VARGA, EUGEN. *Mirovoe khoziaistvo i politika.* Ed. by S. Sheverdin. Moscow: "Moskovskii rabochii," 1925. 140 p.

D48 VARGA, EUGEN. *Plan Dauesa i mirovoi krizis 1924 goda (Obshchii obzor).* Trans. by Shul-Shental. Moscow: "Moskovskii rabochii," 1925. 127 p.

D49 VARGA, EUGEN. *Problemy mirovogo khoziaistva i mirovoi politiki.* Moscow: Izd. "Kom. akademii," 1929. 318 p. A selection of the famous Soviet economist's articles, divided into two sections. One embraces general themes—expanding the theoretical basis of the connection between capitalism and war, the influence on capitalism of the improvement of technology, etc. The other section treats special economic and other problems in particular countries—England, France, Italy, Rumania, India, and China, together with one article on the reparations problem and another on the U.S. as the "leading imperialist country."

D50 VINOGRADOV, B. *Mirovoi proletariat i SSSR.* Moscow: Izd. Kommunisticheskoi akademii, 1928. 227 p. This is vol. v in the series, *Desiat let kapitalisticheskogo okruzheniia SSSR*, issued by the Kommunisticheskaia Akademiia (see above). A scholarly study, about half of which deals with workers' movements in England, Germany and America, and their connotations for the Soviet Union and international Communism. Vinogradov argues that by putting its faith in the workers of the world the Soviet Union has chosen well.

D50A VOROVSKII, VATSLAV V. *Stati i materialy po voprosam vneshnei politiki, 1903-1923.* Moscow: Sotsekgiz, 1959. 254 p. Reprints of articles and other materials written by the first Soviet ambassador to Scandinavian countries and then to Italy, and a member of the Soviet delegations to the Genoa (1922) and Lausanne (1922) conferences. Includes a biographical sketch of Vorovskii (who was assassinated by an anti-Bolshevik in 1923), a bibliography, and a useful list of names of obscure diplomats and other figures connected with him.

D51 WOLFSON, MIRON B. *Soiuz Sovetskikh Sotsialisticheskikh Respublik i kapitalisticheskii mir; opyt politgramoty.* 3rd ed. Moscow: 1925. 480 p. Chapters x through xv deal with Soviet relations with other nations and with the Comintern. Wolfson, a Communist writer of popular books, gives his subject superficial treatment.

2. GENOA CONFERENCE

D52 *Der Kampf in Genua.* (Flugschriften der Kommunistischen Internationale, 13/14.) Hamburg: Carl Hoym, 1922. 39 p. Contains Chicherin's speech to the Genoa Conference on April 10, 1922. The major portion presents the various memoranda of the Russian Delegation at the conference. Useful.

D53 MILLS, JOHN S. *The Genoa Conference.* N.Y.: Dutton; London: Hutchinson, 1922. 436 p. A full treatment, from the preliminaries at Cannes to the speech of Lloyd George in the House of Commons on May 25, which summed up the British view of the conference. Mills defends the accuracy of the West's belief that Russia needed foreign capital for her development, and he clearly delineates the contradictory positions held by the Russians. A lengthy series of appendices include the Cannes Resolutions and the experts' Report on Russia and the Restoration of Europe. Useful, but very British. [A]

D54 RUSSIA, DELEGATSIIA NA GENUEZSKOI KONFERENTSII, 1922. *Matériaux et documents sur l'intervention, le blocus et les dommages causés par eux à la Russie.* Édition de la Délégation de Russie à la Conférence économique internationale de Gênes, 1922. Genoa: Topografia sociale, 1922. 4 vols. Materials prepared by the Soviets in support of their claims for damage done to Russia by Intervention and the blockade.

D55 RUSSIA (1917– RSFSR), NARODNYI KOMISSARIAT PO INOSTRANNYM DELAM. *Genuezskaia konferentsiia; materialy i dokumenty.* Moscow: NKID, 1922. Discusses at length the preliminaries to the Genoa Conference, the Conference at Cannes, the Assembly of Experts in London. Also presents a stenographic report of the first day of the Genoa Conference. Useful.

D56 RUSSIA (1917– RSFSR), NARODNYI KOMISSARIAT PO INOSTRANNYM DELAM. *Materialy Genuezskoi konferentsii; polnyi stenograficheskii otchet; podgotovka otchety zasedannii, raboty komissii, diplomaticheskaia perepiska i pr.* Moscow: Tipografiia t-va "Knigoizdatelstvo pisatelei v Moskve," 1922. 458 p. The basic documents of the Genoa Conference and the records of its meetings are presented in full. Very valuable. [B]

D57 SHTEIN, B. E. *Genuezskaia konferentsiia.* Moscow: Gosizdat, 1922. 126 p.

3. HAGUE CONFERENCE

D58 HAGUE, CONFERENCE ON RUSSIA, 1922. *Conference at The Hague; 1. Non-Russian Commission; 2. Russian Commission; June 26–July 20, 1922; Minutes and Documents.* The Hague: Department of Foreign Affairs, Government Printing Office, 1922. 235 p. French ed., The Hague: 1922. 243 p. Minutes of the meetings of both the Russian and the non-Russian Commissions, together with the documents presented at these meetings. Presented in an excellent format. Indispensable. [A]

D59 RUSSIA (1917– RSFSR), NARODNYI KOMISSARIAT PO INOSTRANNYM DELAM. *Gaagskaia konferentsiia; iiun-iiul 1922 g. (Sobraniie dokumentov).* Moscow: Tipografiia t-va "Knigoizdatelstvo pisatelei," 1922. 288 p. Includes the report of the Russian delegation to the Council of People's Commissars about the course of the work and the results of the Hague Conference. Presents the stenographic records of the sessions of the subcommissions and 88 pages of appended studies (largely economic) prepared for use at the Hague Conference. Valuable. [B]

D60 SHTEIN, B. E. *Gaagskaia konferentsiia.* Moscow: Giz, 1922.

E. Soviet Foreign Relations, 1929-1939

EDITED BY ROLAND V. LAYTON, JR.

E1 ALEKSANDROV, B. A. *Kolonialnye vladeniia imperialistiches-kikh gosudarstv.* Moscow: Sotsekizdat, 1937. 222 p. A factual survey whose "national-liberation" sections for each country indicate the official political estimation in 1937.

E2 ARMSTRONG, HAMILTON FISH. *When There Is No Peace.* N.Y.: Macmillan, 1939. 236 p. A study of the German-Czechoslovak crisis of 1938. The author holds that a major factor in the British appeasement of Hitler at Munich was the hatred of Soviet Russia felt by British conservative circles. They accepted Hitler's claim that Nazi Germany was a bulwark for Europe against Communism. Includes a very detailed chronology of the events of the crisis.

E3 BELOFF, MAX. *The Foreign Policy of Soviet Russia, 1929-1941.* London and N.Y.: Oxford, 1947-49. 2 vols. A dispassionate, painfully objective analysis by a distinguished British scholar for the Royal Institute of International Affairs, full of well-organized information. Concentrates on Soviet policy towards Europe, but also contains illuminating sections on the Far East in appendices. A standard work of outstanding importance, it is one of the best books ever written on Soviet foreign policy. [A]

E4 BORISOV, A. *Iapono-germanskoe soglashenie.* Moscow: Sotsekgiz, 1937. 101 p. A study of the anti-Comintern agreement of November, 1936, between Nazi Germany and Japan, depicting it as directed primarily against the Soviet Union and the Mongolian People's Republic, but also against the world in general.

E5 COATES, WILLIAM P. *World Affairs and the USSR.* London: Lawrence & Wishart, 1939. 251 p. A general account of Soviet foreign affairs, 1934-39, from a pro-Soviet point of view.

E6 COLE, GEORGE D. H. *Socialism and Fascism, 1931-1939.* Vol. v in his *A History of Socialist Thought.* London: Macmillan; N.Y.: St. Martin's, 1960. 350 p. The author was a leading English socialist and Professor of Social and Political Theory at Oxford, 1944-57. This volume is a chronicle of what happened to the Communist and non-Communist labor movements in the 1930's, with emphasis on Western Europe. Scholarly, but without much analysis. [B]

E7 DASHINSKII, S., and RADOPOLSKII, IAN. *Podgotovka voiny protiv SSSR.* Moscow-Leningrad: Giz otd. voen. lit., 1929. 223 p. German ed., Hamburg: C. Hoym, 1929. 240 p. French ed., Paris: Bureau d'Editions, 1929. 238 p.

E8 FISCHER, LOUIS. *Men and Politics; An Autobiography.* N.Y.: Duell, Sloan and Pearce, 1941. 672 p. London: Cape, 1941. 639 p. The famous American journalist ranges over all of Europe, where he lived for most of the inter-war period. He gives here some of his recollections of top Russian leaders whom he knew personally, but in a gossipy vein, with no attempt at a profound or extended analysis of Soviet foreign affairs in this period. Contains an interesting section on the Spanish Civil War.

E9 GRAHAM, GORE. *War and Peace and the Soviet Union.* London: Gollancz, 1934. 287 p. An effort by a British sympathizer with the Soviet Union to persuade Western states to recognize the threat posed to them as well as to the Soviet Union by the Nazi-Japanese combination.

E10 HARPER, SAMUEL N., ed. *The Soviet Union and World Problems.* Chicago: U. of Chicago, 1935. 253 p. The Harris Foundation lectures for 1935, delivered by Alexander A. Troyanovsky, then Soviet ambassador to the U.S., on "Basic Principles of Soviet Foreign Policy"; Ivan V. Boyeff, an Amtorg official, on "The Soviet State Monopoly of Foreign Trade"; Vladimir Romm, an *Izvestiia* correspondent on "Geographic Tendencies in the Soviet Union"; Prof. Hans Kohn on "The Nationality Policy of the Soviet Union"; and Prof. M. W. Graham on "The Peace Policy of the Soviet Union." Troyanovsky asserts that Soviet foreign policy rests on the creed of "fraternity of peoples."

E11 HOETZSCH, OTTO. *Le Caractère et la situation internationale de l'Union des soviets.* Geneva: Kundig, 1932. 104 p. A collection of lectures by a German expert on the Soviet Union, presented at the Institute of International Studies.

E12 IVASHIN, I. F. *Borba SSSR za mir i bezopasnost narodov nakanune Vtoroi mirovoi voini.* Moscow: Znanie, 1958. 40 p. A relatively factual account of Soviet foreign policy between 1933 and 1939. The Soviet Union is portrayed as the champion of the principle of collective security in the various crises. Munich and the unsuccessful Anglo-French-Soviet negotiations of the summer of 1939 are emphasized. Reactionary forces in England, France and U.S. are blamed for the failure of collective security. [B]

E13 IVASHIN, I. F. *Mezhdunarodnye otnosheniia i vneshniaia politika Sovetskogo Soiuza v 1935-1939 godakh.* Moscow: Vysshaia partiinaia shkola pri TsK KPSS, 1955. 66 p. Takes advantage of this dreary period in the history of Britain and France to portray the Soviet Union as the steadfast and noble supporter of Ethiopia, the Spanish Republic, Austria, Czechoslovakia, and collective security in general, not only against Fascist Italy and Germany, but against the schemings of the Western Powers as well. A short chapter on the Soviet-German Pact of 1939 describes the Pact as necessary because "ruling circles" in France and Britain—aided by American imperialists—had sabotaged the talks between the USSR and the West in the summer of 1939.

E14 IVASHIN, I. F. *Nachalo Vtoroi mirovoi voiny i vneshniaia politika SSSR.* Moscow: Pravda, 1951. 30 p. A model of Stalinist distortion, this pamphlet, with hardly a mention of the 1939 Pact between Germany and the USSR, ascribes World War II to two main factors: (1) the strengthening by the U.S.A. of the military-economic base of Hitler's Germany, and (2) the rejection by France and England of collective security. Underlying both factors was the desire for the destruction of the USSR. The "greatest genius of mankind, I. V. Stalin," created an "eastern front" against Germany in 1939-40 by "liberating" western White Russia and the western Ukraine, and by concluding pacts of "mutual assistance" with the Baltic states.

E15 KANNER, L. *Pakty i fakty; na putiakh vtoroi interventsii.* Leningrad: Ogiz-Priboi, 1931. 104 p. Part of the campaign waged by the regime at this time to make the masses "intervention conscious." The gloom in this book is relieved by its recognition of the existence of the pro-Soviet international proletariat.

E16 KOMMUNIST. *Mirovoi ekonomicheskii krizis i konets stabilizatsii kapitalizma; sbornik statei.* Moscow: Pravda, 1933. 440 p. A collection of articles on the world economy published in 1932 in *Bolshevik.*

E17 KOMMUNISTICHESKAIA AKADEMIIA, INSTITUT MIROVOGO KHOZIAISTVA I MIROVOI POLITIKI. *Obshchii krizis kapitalizma; sbornik statei.* Ed. by Evgenii Varga and L. Mendelson. Moscow: Kom. Akad., 1934. 174 p.

E18 KOMMUNISTICHESKAIA AKADEMIIA, INSTITUT MIROVOGO KHOZIAISTVA I MIROVOI POLITIKI. *Ot pervogo tura revoliutsii i voin ko vtoromu; stenogramma nauchnoi sessii IMKh 15 iiunia 1934 g.* Ed. by E. Khmelnitskaia, M. Zaretskii, and G. Voitinskii. Moscow: Sotsekgiz, 1934. 133 p.

E19 KOMMUNISTICHESKAIA AKADEMIIA, INSTITUT MIROVOGO KHOZIAISTVA I MIROVOI POLITIKI. *Plan Iunga i Gaagskaia konferentsiia 1929-1930 g.; dokumenty i materialy.* Ed. by L. Ivanov and A. Erusalimski. Moscow-Leningrad: Ogiz, 1931. 240 p.

E20 KOMMUNISTICHESKAIA AKADEMIIA, INSTITUT MIROVOGO KHOZIAISTVA I MIROVOI POLITIKI. *Podgotovka vtorogo tura imperialisticheskikh voin; sbornik*. Ed. by D. Bukhartsev and others. Moscow: Partizdat, 1934. 222 p. Articles on the military, naval, economic, and political preparations of the western countries for a resumption of war, collected for the edification of Party activists.

E21 KOMMUNISTICHESKAIA AKADEMIIA, MOSCOW, INSTITUT MIROVOGO KHOZIAISTVA I MIROVOI POLITIKI. *SSSR v borbe za mir; rechi i dokumenty*. Moscow: Tipo-litografiia im. Vorovskogo, 1935. 146 p. Speeches and documents on the "USSR in the struggle for peace," addresses by Stalin, Molotov, and Litvinov, and official Soviet pronouncements on the international situation, on non-aggression pacts, the "normalization" of Soviet relations with certain capitalist states, the League of Nations, the economic conferences, and disarmament, including correspondence between Roosevelt and Kalinin. Useful for studying Soviet policy in the 1930's.

E22 KORNEV, N. *Litvinov*. Moscow: Molodaia gvardiia, 1936. 110 p. A biography for popular consumption, written to commemorate Litvinov's sixtieth birthday.

E23 *Krizis kapitalizma, ugroza novykh voin i interventsii; stati, materialy*. Moscow: Partizdat, 1932. 167 p.

E24 LEMIN, IOSIF M. *Blok agressorov*. Moscow: Gospolitizdat, 1938. 96 p. Sees collective security as the best defense against Germany, Italy, and Japan. Harshly criticizes the "reactionary bourgeoisie" of England, France, and the U.S. for not accepting the fact that the Soviet Union must be a full partner if collective security is to work.

E25 LEMIN, IOSIF M. *Mezhdunarodnyi proletariat na zashchitu SSSR*. Moscow: Sotsekgiz, 1933. 106 p. Stalin told the 16th Party Congress that the support of the international proletariat for the Soviet Union was one of the main factors strengthening the world position of the USSR. This book adduces some specific examples to buttress the dictator's words—e.g., the mutiny of the British soldiers during Intervention, the refusal of stevedores around the world to load ships carrying arms to "White Poland" in 1920, and the sabotage by the Chinese Communists of the Kuomintang's efforts to take over the Chinese Eastern Railway.

E26 LEMIN, IOSIF M. *Propaganda voiny v Iaponii i Germanii*. Moscow: Gos. voennoe izdat., 1934. 171 p. Charges that the "imperialists" are leading the world to a new war, as in 1914. Public opinion is being ideologically prepared for war through chauvinist propaganda, especially by Germany, Japan, and "international Social-Democracy."

E27 LEMIN, IOSIF M. *Ugroza voiny i mirnaia politika SSSR*. Moscow-Leningrad: Sotsekgiz, 1935. 80 p. Written to instruct the Soviet public that the main threat of war comes from Germany and Japan. The USSR stands as a bulwark of peace by supporting the system of collective security and by strengthening its own defenses.

E28 LISOVSKII, PETR A. *SSSR i kapitalisticheskoe okruzhenie*. Leningrad: Gospolitizdat, 1939. 147 p. About one third of the book is devoted to the interventions of the various powers in the period 1918-1921—with Lenin's and Stalin's works providing the sole documentation. The author portrays fascist Germany—the "organizer of the bloc of aggressors"—as the leader of a new intervention, which will be defeated like the first one because of the great progress of the building of socialism led by Comrade Stalin.

E29 LITVINOV, MAKSIM M. *Protiv agressii*. Moscow: Ogiz, Gospolitizdat, 1938. 111 p. English ed., *Against Aggression*. N.Y.: 1939. 208 p. Spanish ed., Havana: 1942. French ed., Paris: 1939. A selection of Litvinov's speeches 1934-38 to the League of Nations, Congress of Soviets, and on other occasions. Almost half of the book contains texts of Soviet treaties of non-aggression with other states. [A]

E30 LITVINOV, MAKSIM M. *V borbe za mir; rechi*. Moscow: Partizdat, 1938. 192 p. Speeches of the Soviet Foreign Minister during the years 1933-37, delivered to the League of Nations, meetings of state and Party functionaries, receptions of foreign diplomats, etc.

E31 LOVENTHAL, MILTON, ed. "Documents on Soviet Foreign Policy, 1934-1936." San Jose: Author's typescript, 1959-1960. 547 p. An enigmatic group of documents, the status of which has not yet been determined. They purport to be summaries of decisions on foreign policy taken at meetings of the Politburo from Jan. 27, 1934 to March 14, 1936. The Russian language originals were acquired by German intelligence agencies at short intervals after the dates on which the reports were allegedly prepared. After the Second World War, the original Russian language texts and German translations came into the possession of the U.S. government.

E32 MARIEV, M. A. *Imperialisty gotoviat voinu i interventsiiu protiv SSSR*. Leningrad: Lenpartizdat, 1934. 134 p.

E33 *Mezhdunarodnaia proletarskaia solidarnost v borbe s nastupleniem fashizma (1928-1932)*. Compiled by A. I. Loginova and others. Moscow: "Sovetskaia Rossiia," 1960. 592 p. 344 resolutions, public statements, and editorials from Communist organizations, both within the Soviet Union and abroad, collected to show that the Communists were fighting fascism and the danger of a new war as early as the period indicated. Special emphasis is placed on the 1931 Manchurian conflict and on peace conferences. Volume IV of *Iz istorii mezhdunarodnoi proletarskoi solidarnosti.*

E34 NAMIER, LEWIS B. (Sir). *Diplomatic Prelude; 1938-1939.* N.Y.: Macmillan, 1948. 502 p. A distinguished British historian used newspaper materials and the few memoirs and published diplomatic papers which had appeared in the early post-war period to write an account of the frantic diplomatic moves which immediately preceded the outbreak of World War II. Includes a chapter on the abortive 1939 Anglo-Soviet negotiations, the failure of which was followed by the Hitler-Stalin pact.

E35 *O mezhdunarodnom polozhenii; sbornik.* Moscow: Partizdat, 1937. 221 p. A collection of about thirty articles, mostly from *Pravda* and *Kommunisticheskii Internatsional.* Over half deal with Germany and Japan; others treat the Spanish Civil War, Trotskyism as an instrument of "capitalist encirclement," Communist Party struggles in England and America, and other topics.

E36 POSPELOVA, N. *Mirovoi krizis i narastanie vooruzhennykh konfliktov.* Leningrad: Ogiz-Priboi, 1931. 112 p. The "contradictions" between the U.S. and Britain, and between France and Italy, aggravated by the newest crisis of capitalism—the world wide depression—are leading these countries to war with each other.

E37 RADEK, KARL (pseud. of Karl Sobelsohn). *Podgotovka borby za novyi peredel mira.* Moscow: Partizdat, 1934. 167 p. A statement of the official Soviet position on rearmament in Europe. Though critical of all European powers, it is particularly hostile towards Germany, perhaps foreboding the imminent Franco-Russian rapprochement.

E38 RUSSIA (1923– USSR), ARMIIA, GLAVNOE POLITICHESKOE UPRAVLENIE. *Mezhdunarodnoe polozhenie i vneshniaia politika SSSR; sbornik dokumentov i materialov.* Moscow: Gos. voen. izd., 1939. 205 p.

E38A RUSSIA (1923– USSR), NARODNYI KOMISSARIAT PO INOSTRANNYM DELAM. *Dogovory o neitralitete, nenapadenii i o soglasitelnoi protsedure, zakliuchennye mezhdu Soiuzom SSR i inostrannymi gosudarstvami.* Moscow: N.K.I.D., 1934. 196 p. A collection of Soviet treaties of neutrality, nonaggression, and procedures for conciliation of disputes.

E39 RYKOV, ALEKSEI I. *Ocherednye voprosy mezhdunarodnoi i vnutrennei politiki; doklad i zakliuchitelnoe slovo na V sezde sovetov*

SSSR. Moscow: Gosizdat, 1929. 141 p. A speech by the then Prime Minister of the USSR on its relations with the capitalist world, the movement for disarmament, and the Kellogg Pact to outlaw war. He finds that the capitalist states are following two different policies toward Soviet Russia: (a) aggressive attempts to overthrow the Communist regime, and (b) "peaceful coexistence."

E40 SABANIN, ANDREI V., ed. *Mezhdunarodnaia politika v 1929 godu; dogovory, deklaratsii i diplomaticheskaia perepiska.* Moscow: NKID, 1931. A similar volume was published in 1932 for 1930. [B]

E41 *The Soviet Union and the Cause of Peace*. By V. I. Lenin, J. Stalin, V. Molotov and others. N.Y.: International Publishers, 1936. 191 p. A collection of speeches, interviews with the press, and articles, all attempting to show that the USSR stands firmly for peace.

E42 VARGA, EUGEN and others, eds. *Sotsial-fashizm – organizator interventsii.* Moscow: Partizdat, 1932. 110 p. Various Communist authors charge that the socialists of the Second International are plotting armed intervention against the USSR. Chapters deal with the "social-fascists" of France, Germany, Britain, Czechoslovakia, and the Baltic States.

F. Soviet Foreign Relations, 1939-1945

EDITED BY ROLAND V. LAYTON, JR.

F1 ADAMHEIT, THEODORE. *Sowjetarmee und Weltrevolution; Moskaus Angriff gegen Europa und die Welt.* Berlin: Nibelungen, 1942. 295 p. An execrable Nazi propaganda tract.

F2 AKADEMIIA NAUK SSSR, INSTITUT ISTORII. *Ocherki istorii Velikoi otechestvennoi voiny, 1941-1945.* Ed. by B. S. Telpukhovskii and others. Moscow: Izd. Akademii nauk SSSR, 1955. 534 p. German ed., *Die sowjetische Geschichte des grossen vaterländischen Krieges, 1941-1945.* Ed. by Andreas Hillgruber and Hans-Adolf Jacobsen. Frankfurt am Main: Bernard & Graefe Verlag für Wehrwesen, 1961. 576 p. A detailed military history of the war, written for popular consumption, asserting that the USSR crushed both Germany and Japan almost single-handedly. Treats the wartime alliance with the West as simply a temporary stage in the long struggle with the imperialist powers. An introductory chapter by the German editors discusses the various Soviet interpretations of the war. Contains some previously unpublished materials.

F2A AKADEMIIA NAUK SSSR, INSTITUT ISTORII. *Velikaia otechestvennaia voina Sovetskogo Soiuza, 1941-1945; bibliografiia sovetskoi istoricheskoi literatury za 1946-1959 gody.* Comp. by G. A. Kumanev. Moscow: Izd. Akademii nauk SSSR, 1960. 137 p.

F3 ANISIMOV, I. V., and KUZMIN, G. V. *Velikaia otechestvennaia voina Sovetskogo Soiuza, 1941-1945 gg.* Moscow: Voenizdat, 1952. 190 p. Primarily a military account, but includes a short section on the forging of the "anti-Fascist coalition." The Red Army gets sole credit for the defeat of both Germany and Japan.

F4 ARMSTRONG, JOHN A. *Ukrainian Nationalism, 1939-1945.* N.Y.: Columbia, 1955. 322 p. An exhaustive study, based on archives, printed sources, and interviews, of all the manifestations of the Ukrainian independence movement during World War II. The movement, after the failure to establish rapport with the German invaders, was eventually directed against both the German and Russian regimes. An indispensable study, sponsored by the Russian Institute of Columbia University. [A]

F5 BRIDGES, WAYNE W. "An Interpretation and Application of the Yalta Agreements in Eastern Europe." Ph.D. dissertation, Chicago, 1951.

F6 CAMPBELL, JOHN R. *Soviet Policy and Its Critics.* London: Gollancz, 1939. 381 p. A pro-Soviet apology, linking the critics of the USSR to Trotsky and to Fascism.

F7 CARMAN, ERNEST DAY. *Soviet Imperialism; Russia's Drive toward World Domination.* Washington: Public Affairs Press, 1950. 175 p. (Also published under the title, *Soviet Territorial Aggrandizement, 1939-1948.*) A survey of Russian territorial expansion since 1939, country by country, with explanation in each case of the means by which the areas were acquired. A doctoral dissertation written for the Institute of International Studies, University of Geneva. [B]

F8 CHASSIN, L. M. *Histoire militaire de la Seconde Guerre Mondiale.* Paris: Payot, 1951. 536 p. The best general French military history of World War II, including extensive attention to the Soviet-German campaigns.

F9 CLAUSS, MAX W. *Der Weg nach Jalta.* Heidelberg: Vowinckel, 1952. 276 p. Blames the postwar situation on Roosevelt's diplomacy.

F10 DALLIN, DAVID J. *The Big Three; the United States, Britain, and Russia.* New Haven: Yale, 1945; London: Allen and Unwin, 1946. 232 p. An examination of the confrontation of the three powers throughout the world, with warnings of Soviet expansionism in the postwar period. The author was a Menshevik émigré journalist-scholar who wrote many books on Russia.

F11 DALLIN, DAVID J. *Russia and Post-war Europe.* New Haven: Yale, 1943. 230 p. Presents some prescient views of what paths Soviet policy was likely to follow in the postwar period, based on an astute analysis of past Soviet behavior in international affairs.

F12 DALLIN, DAVID J. *Soviet Russia's Foreign Policy, 1939-1942.* New Haven: Yale, 1942. 452 p. Although the bibliography lists only press accounts and diplomatic collections designed to justify national policies, this is a cogent book by an expert with long experience as an observer of the Soviet Union in the world arena. Now somewhat dated as a result of the availability of more documentation.

F13 DEBORIN, GRIGORII A. *Vtoraia mirovaia voina; voenno-politicheskii ocherk.* Ed. by I. I. Zubkov. Moscow: Voenizdat, 1958. 428 p. An important study of the war, based on Soviet and Western sources. It suffers from the usual distortions, for instance that Britain and the U.S. curtailed military operations in the early months of 1944 while they sought to make a deal with Germany through discussions between Bernadotte and a representative of Himmler. Includes sections on the Teheran, Yalta, San Francisco and Potsdam conferences.

F14 FEIS, HERBERT. *Between War and Peace; The Potsdam Conference.* Princeton, N.J.: Princeton University Press, 1960. 367 p. A work of great importance, based on American archives, personal papers of Secretary of State Byrnes and other figures, interviews with participants in the events, and secondary sources. Traces the growing discord among the wartime Big Three that followed the German collapse. The author is a former State Department official. [A]

F15 FEIS, HERBERT. *Churchill, Roosevelt, and Stalin; the War They Waged and the Peace They Sought.* Princeton, N.J.: Princeton University Press, 1957. 692 p. A massive study of the intricacies of relations among the wartime allies. Based on extensive study of American primary sources—State Department archives, private papers of President Truman and Ambassador Harriman, and other important figures—and a wide array of memoirs, biographies, and scholarly studies. Traces in great detail the forging of the coalition, the stresses to which it was subject, and its gradual deterioration as the end of the war approached. Of fundamental importance. [A]

F16 FEIS, HERBERT. *Japan Subdued: The Atomic Bomb and the End of the War in the Pacific.* Princeton, N.J.: Princeton University Press, 1961. 199 p. This well-documented study concentrates on the relation of the A-bomb to Japan's capitulation, but there is some discussion of the Soviet Union's entry into the Pacific War and of the negotiations with its allies which preceded it. The last in the series of books on the diplomacy of World War II by a veteran American scholar. [A]

F17 FENNO, RICHARD F., ed. *The Yalta Conference.* Vol. 23 of *Problems in American Civilization, Readings Selected by the Department of American Studies, Amherst College.* Boston: Heath, 1955. 112 p. Presents a variety of views on the Conference by people of such diverse outlooks as Charles E. Bohlen, Robert E. Sherwood, William Henry Chamberlin, and Patrick J. Hurley. Includes suggestions for further reading.

F18 FORESTIER, JACQUES. *Le Retour d'Attila.* Paris: Éditions Liberté, 1948. 311 p. An undocumented critique of Communism and Soviet foreign policy, with replies to attacks on the United States and suggestions as to how to defend the cause of freedom and prevent World War III.

F19 GAFENCU, GRIGORE. *Derniers jours de l'Europe; un voyage diplomatique en 1939.* Paris: L.U.F., 1946. 252 p. English ed., *The Last Days of Europe, A Diplomatic Journey in 1939.* New Haven: Yale, 1948. 239 p. The former Rumanian Minister of Foreign Affairs and Ambassador to the USSR travelled to most of the European capitals during the crisis-ridden spring and summer of 1939. Here he records his recollections of the situation in which the Soviet Union played a leading role. [B]

F20 GALLAGHER, MATTHEW P. *The Soviet History of World War II; Myths, Memories, and Realities.* N.Y. & London: Praeger, 1963. 205 p. Based on a doctoral dissertation at Harvard. "It is concerned primarily with the psychological and emotional conflicts generated within Soviet society by the mendacious account of the war given out in Soviet postwar propaganda. It is concerned secondarily with the official interpretations themselves, not for what they tell of the history of Soviet propaganda but for what they tell of the political and military history of the contemporary Soviet period." Based on Soviet accounts of the war by military men, historians, and professional writers.

F21 GOLLANCZ, VICTOR, ed. *The Betrayal of the Left; An Examination and Refutation of Communist Policy from October 1939 to January 1941.* Preface by H. J. Laski. London: Gollancz, 1941. 324 p. Essays by non-Communist English Leftists on a variety of topics.

F22 HOFER, WALTHER. *Die Entfesselung des Zweiten Weltkrieges; eine Studie über die internationalen Beziehungen im Sommer 1939.* Stuttgart: Deutsche, 1954. 221 p. A scholarly study, sponsored by the Institut für Zeitgeschichte in Munich. Begins with a survey of developments from the settlement of the Munich crisis in 1938 to the summer of 1939, devotes a chapter to the German-Soviet Pact, and uses the rest of the book to trace the repercussions of this Pact, which culminated in the outbreak of World War II.

F23 INTERNATIONAL CONFERENCE ON THE HISTORY OF THE RESISTANCE MOVEMENTS, 1st, LIEGE, ETC., 1958. *European Resistance Movements, 1939-45.* N.Y.: Pergamon, 1960. 410 p. An account of the papers delivered at the first conference, which was boycotted by the Soviet Union and her satellites because Polish Home Army General Bor-Komorowski delivered a paper on the Warsaw Uprising. It therefore concentrated on the resistance movements in Western Europe, including the role played by the Communists in it. The relations between the Jewish partisans and the Soviet partisans is covered, as is the Yugoslav Partisan movement. Eastern European Communists participated fully at the 2nd conference which was held in Milan in 1961.

F24 ISRAELIAN, VIKTOR L. *Diplomaticheskaia istoriia Velikoi otechestvennoi voiny, 1941-45 gg.* Moscow: Institut mezhdunarodnykh otnoshenii, 1959. 367 p. A serious study, based on numerous primary and secondary sources, both Soviet and Western, which gives the Soviet answer to such questions as the nature of the "Anti-Fascist Coalition," the degree to which the Western allies measured up to their obligations to the USSR, etc. Includes discussions of all the wartime conferences; accounts of the USSR's relations with Japan, China, the Polish government-in-exile, and the defeated German satellites; the Second Front question; and other related topics. [B]

F25 IVANOV, L. N. *Ocherki mezhdunarodnykh otnoshenii v period Vtoroi mirovoi voiny, 1939-1945 gg.* Moscow: Akad. nauk SSSR, 1958. 275 p. A major Soviet study of diplomatic relations in this period. In spite of a large bibliography, including the major Western memoirs and document collections, this book retains the interpretations current during the Stalinist period. France and Britain, supported by the U.S., sought to channel German aggression solely against the USSR. The Nazi-Soviet Pact gained time to strengthen the Soviet Union's defenses. The author discusses the destruction of Hitlerite Germany by the Soviet Union and the opening of the Second Front (in that order) and he sums up his study with the statement that "the war ended with the victory of the Soviet Union over the German-Japanese aggressors."

F26 IVASHIN, I. F. *Mezhdunarodnye otnosheniia i vneshniaia politika SSSR v period Vtoroi mirovoi voiny.* Moscow: Vysshaia partiinaia shkola, 1954. 127 p. Touches on all aspects of diplomacy during World War II, but maintains the single theme of the hostility of England and the United States to the Soviet Union. Thus these "imperialist powers" supported Hitler's absorption of Austria and Czechoslovakia, aided in the dissolution of the Spanish republic, sought to divert Germany against the USSR after September, 1939, and postponed the Second Front until it had become clear that the Red Army by itself would liberate Europe.

F27 JOESTEN, JOACHIM. *What Russia Wants.* N.Y.: Duell, 1944. 214 p. The author, an American journalist with a special interest in Soviet affairs, believed that the Soviet Union in the postwar period would be more interested in security than in Communizing the world. This desire for security would be satisfied by a line of satellites along her western frontier and by maintaining an important voice in general European affairs. He held that the U.S. and Russia were "predestined for solid friendship and mutually profitable intercourse"—if the U.S. followed his suggestions.

F28 KEETON, GEORGE W., and SCHLESINGER, RUDOLPH. *Russia and Her Western Neighbors.* London: Cape, 1942. 160 p. A discussion of Soviet relations with Finland, the Baltic states, Poland, and the Balkans, designed to educate the British public to accept enthusiastically the Anglo-Soviet Pact of 1941, including a recognition that the USSR has "legitimate" interests in east Europe.

F29 KRAMINOV, DANIIL F. *Pravda o vtorom fronte; zapiski voennogo korrespondenta.* Petrozavodsk: Gosizdat Karelskoi ASSR, 1960. 232 p. A propaganda piece on the Second Front.

F30 LASERSON, MAX M. *Russia and the Western World; the Place of the Soviet Union in the Comity of Nations.* N.Y., London: Macmillan, 1945. 275 p. The author, an American professor of Russian origin, believed that the Soviet Union, in the process of being "westernized," would cooperate with the Western powers in the postwar period for world peace.

F31 LIUSTERNIK, E. IA., and EPSHTEIN, E. G., comps. *Rost i ukreplenie mezhdunarodnikh sviazei nashei rodiny; materialy i dokumenty.* Ed. by A. N. Abramov. Leningrad: Gospolitizdat, 1942. 139 p.

F32 MARKS, STANLEY J. *The Bear that Walks like a Man; a Diplomatic and Military Analysis of Soviet Russia.* Philadelphia: Dorrance, 1943. 340 p. Justifies Soviet diplomacy in the immediate prewar period on the basis of the perfidy of Britain and France. Calls for making the USSR a full partner in the War and the peace that will follow.

F33 MOLOTOV, VIACHESLAV M. *Soviet Peace Policy; Four Speeches.* London: Lawrence and Wishart, 1941. 101 p. By the then Commissar of Foreign Affairs.

F34 MOSCOW, INSTITUT MARKSIZMA-LENINIZMA. *Istoriia Velikoi otechestvennoi voiny Sovetskogo Soiuza, 1941-1945.* Ed. by P. N. Pospelov and others. Moscow: Voenizdat, 1961—. 6 vols. planned. Prepared at the direction of the Presidium of the CPSU under a high-level editorial board, this series will be the definitive Soviet history of World War II. It is comprehensive, with much detailed information, and is a useful source of data, as well as being invaluable for understanding the current Soviet view of the period. [A]

F35 MURPHY, JOHN T. *Russia on the March.* London: Lane, 1941. 128 p. A popular account of Soviet foreign relations, by a former British Communist who left the Party over a doctrinal dispute. Argues that Britain and France should cooperate with Russia against Nazi Germany. Defends the "free elections" held in the Baltic states after their occupation by Soviet troops.

F36 NEUMANN, WILLIAM L. *Making the Peace, 1941-1945; The Diplomacy of the Wartime Conferences.* Washington: Foundation for Foreign Affairs, 1950. 101 p. A brief summary of the conferences of the Big Three.

F37 PARES, BERNARD (SIR). *Russia and the Peace.* Harmondsworth, England: Penguin; N.Y.: Macmillan, 1944. 293 p. The late

British expert on Russia examines the likely postwar role of the Soviet Union in terms of her history.

F38 PLATONOV, S. P., ed. *Vtoraia mirovaia voina, 1939-1945 gg.; voenno-istoricheskii ocherk.* Moscow: Voenizdat, 1958. 930 p. A Soviet study of the war, including sections on all theaters and fronts. Relatively balanced and moderate, it concedes to the U.S. and Britain major roles in the war, while retaining for the Soviet Union the chief role in the defeat of Germany. Utilizes a very large variety of Western and Soviet sources, including archives, enumerated by document file numbers, of the Ministry of Defense. Includes an interpretative essay on the development of military science in the USSR during the war.

F39 POTEMKIN, VLADIMIR P. *Politika umirotvoreniia agressorov i borba Sovetkogo Soiuza za mir.* Moscow: Gospolitizdat, 1946. 46 p. The official explanation of Soviet policy before the outbreak of war by the Deputy People's Commissar for Foreign Affairs.

F40 PRICE, MORGAN PHILLIPS. *Hitler's War and Eastern Europe.* London: Allen and Unwin, 1940. 160 p. A British journalist's view of events in Eastern Europe at the start of World War II. Price was correspondent for the Manchester *Guardian* in Russia during World War I.

F41 PRITT, DENIS N. *Light on Moscow; Soviet Policy Analysed.* Harmondsworth, England: Penguin, 1940. 223 p. French ed., Casablanca: Editions Liberation, 1945. 127 p. An ardently pro-Russian account by a British political maverick. Depth and documentation do not match his ardor, nor is the title's promise fulfilled.

F42 PRITT, DENIS N. *Must the War Spread?* Harmondsworth, England, and N.Y.: Penguin Books, 1940. 256 p. A Labor MP's apology for the Soviet Union's policy toward Finland and the Baltic States, 1939-40. Accuses "ruling circles" in Britain of wanting to make war on the USSR.

F43 RADOV, B. *Rol SShA i Iaponii v podgotovke i razviazyvanii voiny na Tikhom Okeane, 1938-1941 gg.* Moscow: Gospolitizdat, 1951. 198 p.

F44 ROGERS, VIVIAN A. "The Problem of Interpersonal Communication in Political Bargaining Conferences as Illustrated at the Yalta Conference." Ph.D. dissertation, Chicago, 1949.

F45 RUSSIA (1923- USSR), KOMISSIIA PO IZDANIIU DIPLOMATICHESKIKH DOKUMENTOV. *Correspondence between the Chairman of the Council of Ministers of the USSR and the Presidents of the USA and the Prime Ministers of Great Britain during the Great*

Patriotic War of 1941-1945. Vol. I, *Correspondence with Winston S. Churchill and Clement R. Attlee, July 1941-Nov. 1945*. Vol. II, *Correspondence with Franklin D. Roosevelt and Harry S. Truman, August 1941-December 1945*. Moscow: Foreign Languages Publishing House, 1957. Russian ed., Moscow: Gospolitizdat, 1957. Other English eds.; N.Y.: Dutton; London: Lawrence and Wishart, 1958. In the absence of full publication of the wartime correspondence of the Heads of State of Great Britain and the U.S., an indispensable source for study of wartime relations among the Big Three. [A]

F46 SCOTT, JOHN. *Europe in Revolution*. Boston: Houghton, 1945. 274 p. An analysis of the immediate post-World War II international situation as seen at the time by a U.S. correspondent stationed in Sweden. Argues that the U.S. must understand the fundamental revolutionary changes in Europe wrought by the War and must deal realistically with the Soviet Union. Feels that the only policy possible for U.S. toward Russia is one of coexistence. Interprets Soviet foreign policy in terms of traditional Russian interests. Believes post-war coexistence can be based on softening ideological positions of both Russia and the United States. [B]

F47 SNELL, JOHN L., ed. *The Meaning of Yalta; Big Three Diplomacy and the New Balance of Power*. Baton Rouge: Louisiana State U., 1956. 239 p. Six scholarly, balanced essays on the Yalta Conference and its repercussions for Germany, Eastern Europe, the Far East, and the U.N. Includes a useful critical bibliography essay and an analysis of the State Department's publication of the Yalta papers. Edited by a professor at Tulane University.

F48 SNOW, EDGAR. *The Pattern of Soviet Power*. N.Y.: Random House, 1945. 219 p. An American journalist, author of several books on Asia, records his impressions of the Soviet Union at war, and includes his opinions on what the USSR will want when the war is won. Rather sympathetic toward the Soviet Union.

F49 STALIN, IOSIF V. *The Great Patriotic War of the Soviet Union*. N.Y.: International, 1945. 167 p. Russian ed., *O Velikoi otechestvennoi voine Sovetskogo Soiuza*. Moscow: Gospolitizdat, 1942. 50 p. (Numerous other editions.) A collection of Stalin's speeches during the war, together with some statements to the American and British press.

F50 STALIN, IOSIF V. *War Speeches, Orders of the Day, and Answers to Foreign Press Correspondents during the Great Patriotic War*. London: Hutchinson, 1946. 140 p. Provides a great variety of Stalin's words, presented without introduction or editorial comment.

F51 STANIEWICZ, MARIAN. *Wrzesień 1939, polityka ZSRR w przededniu i w początkowej fazie drugiej wojny światowej.* Warsaw: Prasa Wojskowa, 1949. 144 p. An account of Soviet foreign policy on the eve of and in the initial stages of World War II.

F52 STETTINIUS, EDWARD R. *Roosevelt and the Russians; the Yalta Conference.* Ed. by Walter Johnson. Garden City, N.Y.: Doubleday, 1949. 367 p. French ed., 1951. The former Secretary of State's memoirs of the conference, an apologia for his and President Roosevelt's policy. His thesis is that the U.S. and Britain had no choice but to make an effort to attain postwar cooperation with the USSR. The schism between the wartime allies resulted from the Soviet failure to adhere to the agreements entered into by the West as a part of this effort. The book was written by Prof. Johnson, using the Stettinius papers at the University of Virginia. [A]

F53 SURVEY OF INTERNATIONAL AFFAIRS, 1920-1923—; THE WAR-TIME SERIES FOR 1939-1946. Vol. 1: *The World in March 1939.* Ed. by Arnold Toynbee and Frank T. Ashton-Gwatkins. London and N.Y.: Oxford, for the Royal Institute of International Affairs, 1952. 546 p. Contains a section on the USSR by Edward Crankshaw. Part II gives a comparison of the strength of the Great Powers, including Russia.

F54 SURVEY OF INTERNATIONAL AFFAIRS, 1920-1923—; THE WAR-TIME SERIES FOR 1939-1946. Vol. 2: *The Eve of War, 1939.* Ed. by Arnold and Veronica Toynbee. London and N.Y.: Oxford, for the Royal Institute of International Affairs, 1958. 744 p. A detailed narrative, based on published document collections and other sources, of the diplomatic events in Europe between Germany's absorption of Bohemia and Moravia and her attack on Poland. A separate section is devoted to the USSR; it includes the collapse of the Anglo-French-Soviet talks and the signing of the German-Soviet pact. [B]

F55 SURVEY OF INTERNATIONAL AFFAIRS, 1920-1923—; THE WAR-TIME SERIES FOR 1939-1946. Vol. 3: *The Initial Triumph of the Axis.* Ed. by Arnold and Veronica Toynbee. London and N.Y.: Oxford, for the Royal Institute of International Affairs, 1958. 742 p. Includes sections on the Soviet annexation of territories from Poland, Finland, and the Baltic States, as well as the breach between Russia and Germany, 1939-41.

F56 SURVEY OF INTERNATIONAL AFFAIRS, 1920-1923—; THE WAR-TIME SERIES FOR 1939-1946. Vol. 4: *Hitler's Europe.* Ed. by Arnold and Veronica Toynbee. London and N.Y.: Oxford, for the Royal Institute of International Affairs, 1954. 730 p. Though the bulk of the volume deals with Germany proper, there are sections on the Ukraine under German occupation and on the occupied and satellite countries of Eastern Europe.

F57 SURVEY OF INTERNATIONAL AFFAIRS, 1920-1923—; THE WAR-TIME SERIES FOR 1939-1946. Vol. 5: *America, Britain, and Russia; Their Co-operation and Conflict, 1941-1946.* By William H. McNeill. N.Y.: Oxford, for the Royal Institute of International Affairs, 1953. 819 p. An admirable scholarly study based on materials published in western languages. Has to a great extent been superseded, however, by Feis's three volumes, which are based upon archival materials. By a professor at the University of Chicago. [A]

F58 TIKHOMIROV, MIKHAIL N. *Vneshniaia politika Sovetskogo Soiuza.* Moscow: Gospolitizdat, 1940. 105 p. For popular consumption.

F59 TIPPELSKIRCH, KURT VON. *Geschichte des Zweiten Weltkriegs.* Bonn: Athenaum, 1951. 709 p. A good general history of the Second World War by a fairly objective former German general, with extensive and useful treatment of the Soviet-German campaigns.

F60 U.S. CONGRESS, HOUSE, COMMITTEE ON FOREIGN AFFAIRS. *World War II International Agreements and Understandings Entered into During Secret Conferences Concerning Other Peoples.* Washington: G.P.O., 1953. 138 p. A useful collection of documentary material—joint statements, declarations, and agreements, made by the Allied Powers during the war. A list of Soviet violations is appended to each document. Emphasis is on the Yalta and Potsdam conferences.

F61 U.S. DEPARTMENT OF STATE. *Foreign Relations of the United States; Diplomatic Papers. The Conference of Berlin (the Potsdam Conference) 1945.* Washington: G.P.O., 1960. 2 vols. A full documentary record of the conference in which the Big Three made an effort to reach agreement on the postwar world. [A]

F62 U.S. DEPARTMENT OF STATE. *Foreign Relations of the United States; Diplomatic Papers. The Conferences at Malta and Yalta, 1945.* Washington: G.P.O., 1955. 1032 p. German ed., Vienna: 1955. So far the fullest official account of the conferences published by any of the participating states. [A]

F63 *Vneshniaia politika Sovetskogo Soiuza v period Otechestvennoi voiny; dokumenty i materialy.* Moscow: Gospolitizdat, 1944-47. 3 vols. English trans. of vols. 1 and 2 by Andrew Rothstein, *Soviet Foreign Policy During the Patriotic War.* London: Hutchinson, 1944-45. A convenient but by no means complete record of Soviet diplomatic activity during World War II. [A]

F64 VSESOIUZNAIA KNIZHNAIA PALATA. *Ukazatel literatury po mezhdunarodnomu polozheniiu; 1940, ianvar-mai.* Moscow: 1940. 91 p. Enlarged edition, *Mezhdunarodnoe polozhenie; ukazatel literatury, 1939—sentiabr—1940.* Moscow: 1940. 140 p. These two small bibliographies, arranged by subject, list books, journal articles and newspaper analyses of the international situation published in the USSR from Aug. 1939 through Aug. 1940. Since this was the era of the Nazi-Soviet Pact, there are references to the "imperalist" war and the "striving of the masses for peace." Many of the articles listed deal with the annexation of the Baltic States, Western Ukraine, Western Belorussia, Bessarabia, and Northern Bukovina.

F65 WILMOT, CHESTER. *The Struggle for Europe.* N.Y.: Harper; London: Collins, 1952. 766 p. An account of World War II, primarily of its military aspects, but with some consideration of relations between the USSR and its western allies. Includes a chapter on the Yalta Conference, which the author terms "Stalin's greatest victory." By an Australian journalist.

F66 WOLFE, HENRY C. *The Imperial Soviets.* N.Y.: Doubleday, 1940. 294 p. Written soon after the Nazi-Soviet Pact of 1939, the book explains the curious alliance not as a reversal of Soviet policy, but as another step in Stalin's program of playing "his enemies against each other" to advance the cause of world revolution. Includes several chapters on earlier German-Soviet relations, on the USSR's policy toward disarmament and the League, on the Czech crisis of 1938, on relations with Poland and Finland, and on the Soviet domestic scene.

G. Soviet Foreign Relations, 1945-1963

1. GENERAL WORKS COVERING THE WHOLE PERIOD

(Edited by John A. Armstrong)

G1 BALINSKI, STANISLAW K. "The Pattern of Soviet Russian Maritime Expansion After the Second World War; European Captive Shipping 1945-1955." Ph.D. dissertation, Georgetown U., 1957.

G2 BRZEZINSKI, ZBIGNIEW K. *The Soviet Bloc; Unity and Conflict.* Cambridge: Harvard, 1960. 470 p. Rev. paperback ed., N.Y.: Praeger, 1961. 543 p. The most important and up-to-date of the surveys of relations within the Soviet bloc, by a professor at Columbia University. Contains a 15-page bibliography. [A]

G3 CURRENT DIGEST OF THE SOVIET PRESS. *Current Soviet Policies.* Ed. by Leo Gruliow. N.Y.: Praeger, 1953–. Vol. I: *The Documentary Record of the 19th Communist Party Congress and the Reorganization after Stalin's Death.* Vol. II: *The Documentary Record of the 20th Communist Party Congress and Its Aftermath.* Vol. III: *The Documentary Record of the Extraordinary 21st Congress of the Communist Party of the Soviet Union.* These collections of speeches and proceedings form indispensable source materials for the student of Soviet foreign policy since 1950, though only a small part of the material bears directly upon foreign policy. [B]

G4 FLEMING, DENNA F. *The Cold War and Its Origins: 1917-1960.* Garden City, N.Y.: Doubleday, 1961. 2 vols. A massive but unbalanced study contending that the Cold War originated with and has been maintained by the West. Churchill and Truman are criticized severely, but the Soviets are given the benefit of the doubt. By a professor at Vanderbilt University.

G5 GANIUSHKIN, B. V. *Sovremennyi neitralitet; politika neitraliteta i postoiannyi neitralitet v usloviiakh borby za mir.* Moscow: 1958. 162 p. A fairly systematic discussion of "neutrality" as a legal concept and in the practice of post-World War II international relations. Interestingly enough, the traditional neutrals receive more attention than the newer "neutralists." Useful as a presentation of the Soviet viewpoint.

G6 GORKIN, JULIÁN. *Destin du XXe siècle; de Lénine à Malenkov, coexistence ou guerre permanente?* Paris: Iles d'or, 1954. 301 p. A Western analysis of Kremlin policy, emphasizing the Malenkov era. Undocumented.

G7 HAINES, CHARLES GROVE, ed. *The Threat of Soviet Imperialism.* Baltimore: Johns Hopkins, 1954. 402 p. A useful collection, although somewhat vitiated by the crusading nature of some chapters. All, however, are well documented and offer good clues to further readings. [A]

G8 HINDUS, MAURICE G. *Crisis in the Kremlin.* Garden City, N.Y.: Doubleday, 1953. 319 p. An old-time Russian hand offers a well informed analysis of the post-war years in Russia and predicts a substantial change in Russian policy with the death of Stalin. Internal affairs are better presented than foreign affairs.

G9 KOMMUNISTICHESKAIA PARTIIA SOVETSKOGO SOIUZA,VYSSHAIA PARTIINAIA SHKOLA, KAFEDRA MEZHDUNARODNYKH OTNOSHENII. *Mezhdunarodnye otnosheniia i vneshniaia politika SSSR v period prevrashcheniia sotsializma v mirovuiu sistemu (1945-1949 gg.); lektsii, prochitannye v Vysshei Partiinoi Shkole pri TsK KPSS.* By F. G. Zuev and others. Moscow: Vysshaia Partiinaia Shkola, 1956. 134 p. Edited by a prominent Soviet historian of East Europe. Most of the articles are marked more by an attempt to create an Anglo-American villain than by any serious attempt at history. [A]

G10 KULSKI, WLADYSLAW W. *Peaceful Coexistence; An Analysis of Soviet Foreign Policy.* Chicago: Henry Regnery, 1959. 662 p. Extensive quotations from the writings of Lenin, Stalin and other Communist leaders, and excerpts from Soviet books, magazines and newspapers, together with critical commentary and analysis by a professor at Syracuse University. Designed to damn the Communists out of their own mouths, after the manner of the author's previous book, *The Soviet Regime.* Arranged under general headings such as "Russian Nationalism," "Soviet Colonial Possessions," "Soviet Policy Towards the Underdeveloped Countries," etc.

G10A LAVERGNE, BERNARD. *Pourquoi le conflit Occident-Union Soviétique?* Paris: Librarie Fischbacher, 1962. 359 p. A highly personal interpretation of the Cold War by a French Socialist which generally supports the Soviet position and strongly condemns the policies of the Western powers.

G11 LEONHARD, WOLFGANG. *Die Revolution entlässt ihre Kinder.* Cologne: Kiepenheuer & Witsch, 1955. 551 p. English ed., *Child of the Revolution.* Chicago: Regnery, 1958. 447 p. The personal and sensitive account of the defection of a major Soviet aide. Although centered on East Germany, the book is of much value in understanding Stalinist foreign policy in general. English edition is abridged, but not much is lost. [A]

G12 LUKACS, JOHN. *A History of the Cold War.* N.Y.: Doubleday, 1961. 288 p. Very one-sided treatment of recent Soviet foreign policy as a reflection of unchanging Russian national interest. Reflects the author's own adherence to theories (more common a generation ago in Central Europe than in the U.S. today) that racial and ethnic qualities heavily influence policies.

G12A MACKINTOSH, J. M. *Strategy and Tactics of Soviet Foreign Policy.* N.Y. and London: Oxford University Press, 1963. 353 p. An analytic-historical account of Soviet foreign policy from 1944 to 1963. Instead of giving a straight history of Soviet foreign relations in this period, the author has focused attention upon such key topics, historically distributed, as "Soviet Thinking on War," "The Role of Economic Power," and Sino-Soviet Relations. The book is especially useful and illuminating on the relations between foreign and military policy.

G13 MEIKSINS, GREGORY. "The Doctrine of Coexistence in Soviet Diplomacy." Ph.D. dissertation, The New School for Social Research, 1954.

G14 NIKHAMIN, V. P., ed. *Mezhdunarodnye otnosheniia i vneshniaia politika Sovetskogo Soiuza, 1950-1959.* Vol. I, Moscow: Izd. IMO, 1960. 224 p. This volume (1950-54) is practically valueless as a survey of the international relations of the period, since even Soviet positions are retrospectively distorted. It is interesting insofar as, in contrast to more recent Soviet statements, it does *not* indicate a break between the Stalin and post-Stalin periods. Three-fourths of the book deal with the Far East.

G15 OSIPOV, GEORGII. *Plamia gneva.* Moscow: Vsesoiuznoe uchebno-pedagogicheskoe izd. trudrezervizdat, 1953. 127 p. A propaganda work issued at an interesting time. Many quotations are from Stalin, with some from Malenkov added. Violently anti-American, the author swings around the colonial world, including Africa, Iran, Syria, Egypt, and Malaya.

G16 PERROUX, FRANÇOIS. *La Coexistence pacifique.* Paris: Presses Universitaires de France, 1958. 3 vols. A major effort by a French economist to analyze perspectives of economic competition between the Communist bloc and the non-Communist world. While the work is based for the most part on secondary sources, the scope and depth of the analysis are impressive.

G17 "Postwar Soviet Foreign Policy: A World Perspective," *Journal of International Affairs.* Vol. VIII, No. 1, 1954. A series of essays surveying the development of Soviet policy after World War II in all major areas of the world, and offering a general interpretation of the dynamics of Soviet policy in the period up to Stalin's death.

G18 RUSSIA (1923-USSR), TREATIES, ETC., 1958. *Soglasheniia o sotrudnichestve i pomoshchi v oblasti mirnogo ispolzovaniia atomnoi energii, zakliuchennye Sovetskim Soiuzom s drugimi stranami.* Moscow: Atomizdat, 1958. 26 p.

G19 SALISBURY, HARRISON E. *Moscow Journal; the End of Stalin.* Chicago: U. of Chicago Press, 1961. 450 p. Diary of the *New York Times* correspondent during the last years of Stalin. In parts frankly speculative, but with considerable insight. Though major stress is on internal affairs, much data can be gleaned on foreign policy.

G19A SCHUMAN, FREDERICK L. *The Cold War: Retrospect and Prospect.* Baton Rouge: Louisiana State University Press, 1962.

G20 SCHWARTZ, HARRY. *The Red Phoenix; Russia Since World War II.* N.Y.: Praeger, 1961. 427 p. This collection is especially valuable as a reflection of contemporary analyses of the shifting currents of Soviet foreign and domestic policy by the Soviet affairs editor of the *New York Times.*

G21 SETON-WATSON, HUGH. *Neither War Nor Peace; The Struggle for Power in the Postwar World.* N.Y.: Praeger; London: Methuen, 1960. 504 p. Brief coverage of the entire range of Soviet-Western disputes since World War II. The basically sound factual coverage and judgments are somewhat obscured by the attempt to provide a mass of detail.

G22 STRAUSZ-HUPE, ROBERT, and others. *Protracted Conflict.* N.Y.: Harper (for the Foreign Policy Research Institute), 1959. 203 p. Stimulating in its stress on the need for unceasing ingenuity in meeting Communist pressures, this book sometimes gives the jarring impression that it was written as an *apologia* for John Foster Dulles' policies. The authors are understandably concerned with U.S. policy failures, but present few concrete suggestions for improvement, and occasionally fall into actual error.

G23 TARASENKO, V. A. *Iadernoe oruzhie i vneshaia politika SShA.* Moscow: Sotsekgiz, 1961. A criticism of "the aggressive essence" of U.S. foreign policy.

G24 TUCKER, ROBERT C. *The Soviet Political Mind: Studies in Stalinism and Post-Stalin Change.* N.Y.: Praeger, 1963. 238 p. A collection of essays dealing in considerable part with Soviet foreign policy, with special reference to the meaning of Stalinism in the history of Soviet foreign policy and the changes after Stalin in the Soviet doctrine of international relations and conduct of world affairs.

G25 YEAGER, FREDERICK J. "Soviet Policy Toward NATO." Ph.D. dissertation, Princeton, 1959. 388 p. Studies Soviet tactics and strategy 1949-1959 and concludes that the Soviets considered themselves weaker than NATO until 1955, after which they felt at least as strong as NATO. Soviet troop withdrawals, the Rapacki Plan, and Soviet demands for an end to nuclear tests are regarded as tactics aimed at dividing the West, dissolving NATO and the Warsaw Pact in an All-European Collective Security Pact.

2. STALIN'S LAST YEARS, 1945-1953

(Edited by Warren Lerner)

G26 AKADEMIIA NAUK SSSR, INSTITUT EKONOMIKI. *Ekonomika kapitalisticheskikh stran posle Vtoroi mirovoi voiny; statisticheskii sbornik.* Ed. by A. M. Alekseev, V. D. Chermenskii, and V. P. Glushkov. Moscow: Izd. Akad. nauk SSSR, 1953. 292 p. German ed., Berlin: 1955.

G27 AKADEMIIA NAUK SSSR, INSTITUT EKONOMIKI. *Voprosy obshchego krizisa kapitalizma; sbornik statei.* Moscow: Izd. Akad. nauk SSSR, 1953. 237 p.

G28 AKADEMIIA NAUK SSSR, INSTITUT FILOSOFII. *Ideologi imperialisticheskoi burzhuazii-propovedniki agressii i voiny; sbornik statei.* Moscow: Gospolitizdat, 1952. 341 p.

G29 AMERICAN ACADEMY OF POLITICAL AND SOCIAL SCIENCE, PHILADELPHIA. *The Soviet Union Since World War II.* Ed. by Philip E. Mosely. Philadelphia: 1949. 278 p. (Its *Annals*, v. 263, May 1949). A valuable collection of articles by leading American scholars. A few are unavoidably dated, but all show thorough research. The documentation of individual articles adds to the general worth of the collection. [B]

G30 ARMSTRONG, HAMILTON FISH. *The Calculated Risk.* N.Y.: Macmillan, 1947. 68 p. A brief essay by the editor of *Foreign Affairs* on relations with the USSR. Although thoughtful, it is not focused primarily on Soviet foreign policy goals.

G31 BĄCZKOWSKI, WŁODZIMIERZ. *Towards an Understanding of Russia; A Study in Policy and Strategy.* Jerusalem: The Author, 1947. 215 p. An exposé of the Soviet Union's imperialist aspirations.

G32 BORKENAU, FRANZ. *European Communism.* London: Faber & Faber, 1953. 564 p. German ed., Berne: Francke, 1952. 540 p. An old Comintern hand offers a well-informed, if highly speculative, interpretation of Soviet policies, particularly since World War II. Of unusual interest is his thesis of the ephemeral supremacy of Zhdanov (even over

Stalin) in foreign affairs. Although many points are debatable, an exciting analysis. [A]

G33 BOUSCAREN, ANTHONY T. *Imperial Communism.* Washington: Public Affairs, 1953. 256 p. The author, who teaches at Le Moyne College, tries to present a country-by-country analysis of the Communist bloc, stressing Russian imperialism in creating this bloc.

G34 BOUSCAREN, ANTHONY T. *Soviet Expansion and the West.* San Francisco: Pacific States Printing Co., 1949. 199 p. Warns of an impending drive by the Soviet Union against the West. Most of the material was incorporated into his later book, *Imperial Communism.*

G35 BRILL, HERMANN L. *Das sowjetische Herrschaftssystem.* Cologne: Verlag rote Weissbücher, 1951. 181 p. A strongly anti-Soviet book largely concerned with internal policy, although it does have one section on foreign policy.

G36 BRIUKHANOV, A. *Vot kak eto bylo: o rabote missii po repatriatsii sovetskikh grazhdan; vospominaniia sovetskogo ofitsera.* Moscow: Gospolitizdat, 1958. 206 p. A useful and unusual account by a Soviet officer engaged in repatriation of Soviet citizens. Largely written as a personal journal, with an occasional attempt to exploit the readers' human sympathies. [B]

G37 BULLITT, WILLIAM C. *The Great Globe Itself; A Preface to World Affairs.* N.Y.: Scribner's, 1946. 310 p. London: Macmillan, 1947. 267 p. Norwegian ed., Oslo: 1947. Swedish ed., Stockholm: 1947. A former ambassador to the Soviet Union evaluates the post-war world and advocates a strong defense to forestall future crises. Does not have much perceptive analysis of the USSR.

G38 BURNHAM, JAMES. *The Coming Defeat of Communism.* N.Y.: Day; London: Cape, 1950. 286 p. An outspoken anti-Soviet writer sees strength as the key to stopping Bolshevism. Of limited scholarly value.

G39 BURNHAM, JAMES. *The Struggle for the World.* N.Y.: Day; London: Cape, 1947. 248 p. A polemical interpretation by a right-wing writer who argues that the U.S.A. does not have a proper appreciation of the Soviet threat.

G40 CARTON DE WIART, HENRY. *Chronique de la guerre froide, 1947-1949.* Brussels: Goemaere, 1950. 448 p. Utilizing a long career of public service, the author seeks to analyze the emergence of the Cold War, with better insights into the West's position than into Soviet foreign policy.

G41 CATHALA, JEAN. *L'U.R.S.S. contre la guerre, essai sur les principes de la politique étrangère soviétique depuis la victoire.* Paris: Éditions hier et aujourd'hui, 1948. 253 p. A French journalist maintains that the Soviet Union emerged stronger from the war because of its "loyalty to Leninist principles." Lacking in any depth as far as foreign policy goes.

G42 CHAMBERLIN, WILLIAM H. *Beyond Containment.* Chicago: Regnery, 1953. 406 p. A prominent and long-established American specialist on Soviet affairs argues that the Soviet danger is greater than realized. Much useful information is to be found, although this is not the center of the book. [B]

G43 CHAMBERLIN, WILLIAM H. *World Order or Chaos.* London: Duckworth, 1946. 292 p. American ed., *The European Cockpit.* N.Y.: Macmillan, 1947. 292 p. An analysis of Europe and of other critical areas at the end of the Second World War, and of the main goals of Soviet foreign policy.

G44 COURTADE, PIERRE. *Essai sur l'antisoviétisme.* Paris: Éditions Raisons d'être, 1946. 159 p. English ed., Paris: 1946. A polemical critique of Western opinion of the Soviet Union by a French Communist.

G45 CRANKSHAW, EDWARD. *Russia and the Russians.* N.Y.: Viking, 1948. 223 p. A specialist in Russian affairs for the *London Observer* offers a very speculative view of Russian intentions in 1948. Aside from being badly dated, the book could sorely use documentation.

G46 CRANKSHAW, EDWARD. *Russia By Daylight.* London: M. Joseph, 1951. 240 p. American ed., *Cracks in the Kremlin Wall.* N.Y.: Viking, 1951. 279 p. Tries to prove that Russia is not the powerful monolith it seems. Rather little on foreign policy.

G47 DALLIN, DAVID J. *The New Soviet Empire.* New Haven: Yale, 1951. 216 p. A prominent Menshevik émigré provides a thoughtful and informed, although openly hostile, view of Soviet conquests in the 1940's. [B]

G48 DEAN, VERA M. *Russia—Menace or Promise?* N.Y.: Foreign Policy Association, 1946. 96 p. 2nd ed., N.Y.: Holt, 1947. 158 p. A brief but thoughtful item in the *Headline* series by a well known analyst. The book is far too general to be of much value.

G49 DEBORIN, G. A. *Mezhdunarodnye otnoshenia i vneshniaia politika Sovetskogo Soiuza 1945-1949.* Moscow: Izd. IMO, 1958. 296 p. A standard attempt by a Soviet analyst to portray the U.S.A. as the cause of post-war tensions. Notable for its downplaying of Stalin's roles in these years. [B]

G50 DULLES, JOHN FOSTER. *War or Peace.* N.Y.: Macmillan, 1950. 274 p. A prominent American diplomat who later became Secretary of State argues that vigilance and righteousness will protect the free world. Little or no insight on Soviet foreign policy.

G51 ERENBURG, ILIA G. *Za mir!* Moscow: Sovetskii pisatel, 1950. 186 p. A mercurial Soviet writer issues a violent attack on the West, with the usual disclaimers of any hostile acts on the part of the Soviet Union. There is no real attempt to explain Soviet policy except to reiterate its peaceful intent.

G52 FISCHER, LOUIS. *The Great Challenge.* N.Y.: Duell, Sloan and Pearce, 1946. 346 p. Norwegian ed., Oslo: 1947. A well-known American journalist and former confidant of Soviet leaders tries to analyze the post-war world. Unlike his earlier works, this book does not have the advantage of "inside" information.

G53 FREDBORG, ARVID. *Tredje gången; öst mot väst efter det andra världskriget.* Stockholm: P. A. Norstedt, 1948. 463 p. A fairly thorough and exhaustive coverage of Soviet foreign policy in the years 1945-48. Documentation is badly needed, however.

G54 FREDERIX, PIERRE. *Washington ou Moscou.* Paris: Hachette, 1948. 311 p. A roving correspondent for *Le Monde* sees the world of 1948 as Armageddon of East and West. Though the analysis is interesting, the material is obviously very thin.

G55 GAUTHEROT, GUSTAVE. *Derrière le rideau de fer; la vague rouge déferle sur l'Europe.* Paris: L'auteur, Hachette, 1946. 200 p. 2nd ed., Paris: Éditions Hermes-France, 1947. A badly dated analysis of post-war Europe which sees the problem as one of Soviet vs. "Anglo-Saxon" camps. Very little supporting material is introduced.

G56 GURIAN, WALDEMAR, ed. *The Soviet Union; Background, Ideology, Reality.* Notre Dame, Ind.: University of Notre Dame Press, 1951. 216 p. Based on a symposium held at Notre Dame University, this volume offers a broad spectrum of views on the Soviet Union. Most of these are hostile, but the views of foreign policy are more balanced. [B]

G57 HARSCH, JOSEPH C. *The Curtain Isn't Iron.* Garden City, N.Y.: Doubleday; London: Putnam, 1950. 190 p. A former correspondent for the *Christian Science Monitor* offers an essay on the road to better understanding with Russia, but does not offer much detailed or unusual information on Soviet foreign policy or the East European satellites.

G58 HILTON, RICHARD. *Military Attaché in Moscow.* Boston: Beacon, 1951. 231 p. Despite a serious lack of documentation, this work of a former attaché has occasional insight into post-war Russian foreign policy. Of limited utility, however.

G59 INGRAM, KENNETH. *History of the Cold War, 1945-1953.* London: Darwen Finlayson; N.Y.: Philosophical Library, 1955. 239 p. Despite the title, this work is far too general and polemical to have serious scholarly value. Has very little outside of conventional information and that not too well presented. Tends to be favorable toward the Soviet Union.

G60 KELLY, DAVID V. (SIR). *Beyond the Iron Curtain.* London: Hollis and Carter, 1954. 83 p. A short essay devoid of new factual information about Soviet policy, but interesting as the considered view of a British Ambassador to Moscow who served his country ably between 1949 and 1951.

G61 KURELLA, ALFRED. *Ost und/oder West; Unsinn, Sinn und tiefere Bedeutung eines Schlagwortes.* Berlin: Volk und Welt, 1948. 236 p. A work which is stronger on polemic than documentation; verbose, but not much valuable material.

G62 LASERSON, MAX M. (Maksim Y. Lazerson). *Russia and the Western World; the Place of the Soviet Union in the Comity of Nations.* N.Y.: Macmillan, 1945. 275 p. A confident review of the evolution of Soviet political and legal institutions and thought. The author, who served briefly in the Kerensky regime before becoming an American political scientist, argues that the Soviet regime will develop a political system similar to that of its Western allies and that the growth of Soviet Russian nationalism will weaken the world revolutionary impulse.

G63 LUCAS, WILLIAM O. (Narvig, William van, pseud.) *East of the Iron Curtain.* Chicago: Ziff-Davis, 1946. 361 p. A general and rather unexciting view of the world of 1946. The material on the Soviet bloc, notwithstanding the title, is rather thin.

G64 MARTEL, GIFFARD LE QUESNE (SIR). *East versus West.* London: Museum Press, 1952. 220 p. A British general speculates on issues of the Cold War but fails to add anything to knowledge of Soviet foreign policy.

G65 MASLENNIKOV, VIACHESLAV A., ed. *Uglublenie krizisa kolonialnoi sistemy imperializma posle Vtoroi mirovoi voiny; sbornik statei.* Moscow: Gospolitizdat, 1953. 605 p. A variety of Soviet writers describe the progress of Communism in all the underdeveloped countries. A valuable view of the official outlook at the close of the Stalinist period. Gives sops to Stalin everywhere, even in Africa. [B]

G65A *Mezhdunarodnye otnosheniia posle vtoroi mirovoi voiny.* In 3 vols. Vol. 1, *1945-1949 gg.* Moscow: Gospolitizdat, 1962. 759 p.

G66 MIKSCHE, FERDINAND O., and COMBAUX, FRANÇOIS E. *War between Continents.* London: Faber, 1948. 211 p. A speculative account of a showdown between East and West which offers nothing new in understanding of Soviet foreign policy.

G67 MOLOTOV, VIACHESLAV M. *Rechi na parizhskoi mirnoi konferentsii, iiul-oktiabr, 1946 g.* Moscow: Gospolitizdat, 1946. 206 p. English ed., *USSR at the Paris Peace Conference.* London: "Soviet News," 1946. French ed., Paris: Éditions Mazarine, 1946. Although it attempts to present the Soviet Foreign Minister as the reasonable voice of the Conference, this selection does contain valuable documentary material. [A]

G68 MOLOTOV, VIACHESLAV M. *Speeches and Statements Made at the Moscow Session of the Council of Foreign Ministers, March 10-April 24, 1947.* London: Soviet News, 1947. 123 p. Spanish ed., Montevideo: Pueblos Unidos, 1947. An important collection of speeches by the former Soviet Foreign Minister. The Truman Doctrine is particularly attacked. As authoritative a Soviet viewpoint as exists on this one issue. [A]

G69 MOLOTOV, VIACHESLAV M. *Voprosy vneshnei politiki; rechi i zaiavleniia, aprel 1945 g.—iiun 1948 g.* Moscow: Gospolitizdat, 1948. 586 p. English ed., *Problems of Foreign Policy.* Moscow: Foreign Languages Publishing House, 1949. Also German and French eds., Moscow: 1949. A by-no-means comprehensive collection of important pronouncements by the former Soviet Foreign Minister. The general theme is that of the Soviet quest for peace treaties and settlements being frustrated by the West. [A]

G70 NATIONAL PEACE COUNCIL, COMMISSION ON EAST-WEST RELATIONS. *Two Worlds in Focus; Studies of the Cold War.* London: National Peace Council, 1950. 133 p. Except for some speculation on what are called "Soviet attitudes," the coverage of Soviet foreign policy is quite thin.

G71 NEARING, SCOTT. *The Soviet Union as a World Power.* N.Y.: Island Workshop Press, 1945. 105 p. An admittedly partisan discussion of Soviet policy at the close of the Second World War and an appeal for friendship toward Russia, by an American who was a Party member briefly in the 1920's and who believes in "the conscious improvement of society by society."

G72 NÉMANOFF, LÉON. *La Russie et les problèmes de la paix.* Genève: E.L.E.F., 1945. 455 p. A very thoughtful essay on the world situation at the end of the war, but offers little on Soviet foreign policy.

G73 NORBORG, CHRISTOPHER SVERRE. *Operation Moscow.* N.Y.: Dutton, 1947. 319 p. London: Latimer House, 1948, 285 p. A rambling review of Soviet policy after World War II by a Swedish-American philosopher-humanist and amateur political psychologist who was head of the Northern European section of UNRRA. He believed that Soviet policy deliberately threatened world peace, and urged a *cordon sanitaire* and religious revival in the West.

G74 OPIE, REDVERS, and others. *The Search for Peace Settlements.* Washington: Brookings Institution, 1951. 366 p. A general collection of essays on problems of international tensions which does not probe very deeply into Soviet policies, despite the good quality of the essays. [B]

G75 POLONIUS (pseud.). *Keine Angst vor Sowjet-Russland; eine realistische Betrachtung.* Heidelberg: K. Vowinckel, 1951. 127 p. The anonymous author is supposedly a former premier of an East European country. He offers no documentation in his analysis of Russian aims and of how Bolshevism can be defeated if war comes.

G76 PONOMAREV, B. N., ed. *Pravye sotsialisty na sluzhbe podzhigatelei novoi voiny; sbornik statei.* Moscow: Izd. inostrannoi lit., 1950. 176 p.

G77 PRITT, DENIS N. *The State Department and the Cold War.* N.Y.: International Publishers. 1948, 96 p. A pro-Russian British writer issues a violent attack on the State Department, accusing it of maintaining international tensions. Soviet policy is largely spared, both in attack and coverage.

G78 RAUSCHNING, HERMANN. *Ist Friede noch möglich? Die Verantwortung der Macht.* Heidelberg: Vowinckel, 1953. 331 p. Despite some very thoughtful analysis, the approach is basically from the problems of the West, with little consideration of the problems and goals of Soviet foreign policy.

G79 ROMASHKIN, P. S. *Voennye prestupleniia imperializma.* Moscow: Gospolitizdat, 1953. 438 p. A Soviet attempt to analyze Western foreign policy in terms of political science, introducing concepts of international law, the role of the military, etc. There is the usual homage to the doctrine of "Anglo-American imperialism." [B]

G80 ROYAL INSTITUTE OF INTERNATIONAL AFFAIRS. *Defence in the Cold War; the Task for the Free World.* London and N.Y.: 1950. 123 p. A useful essay by the Chatham House Study Group offering alternatives for the West. Despite the lack of documentation, some limited insights into Soviet foreign policy can be gained.

G81 RUSSIA (1923-USSR), MINISTERSTVO INOSTRANNYKH DEL. *Sovetskie delegatsii na parizhskoi konferentsii.* Moscow: Izd. Ministerstva inostrannykh del SSSR, 1947. 355 p. A useful if biased compilation of materials on the Paris Conference of 1946. The documents offer clues to the Soviet position on problems of post-war peace settlements and why no treaty emerged. [B]

G82 SHUB, BORIS. *The Choice.* N.Y.: Duell, 1950. 205 p. Evaluates the post-war world and advocates friendship toward the Russian people but not toward Stalin. Has occasional good insight into Russian activities. The problem of repatriation is well treated here.

G83 SHULMAN, MARSHALL D. *Stalin's Foreign Policy Reappraised.* Cambridge: Harvard U. Press, 1963. 320 p. A thoughtful analysis of the last years of Soviet foreign policy under Stalin. The author is Professor of International Affairs at the Fletcher School of Law and Diplomacy. [A]

G84 SNOW, EDGAR. *Stalin must have Peace.* N.Y.: Random House, 1947. 184 p. French ed., Paris: 1948. A leftist American journalist strives to find hope for an East-West rapprochement. Though willing to give Stalin some benefit of doubt, the author is not servile. Highly speculative, but with some insights even if debatable ones.

G85 *Soviet Views on the Post-War World Economy; an Official Critique of Eugene Varga's "Changes in the Economy of Capitalism Resulting from the Second World War."* Trans. by Leo Gruliow. Washington: Public Affairs Press, 1948. 125 p. A translation of the stenographic transcript of a discussion in Moscow in May 1947 for the purpose of correcting the purported errors contained in the book by Varga, *Izmeneniia v ekonomike kapitalizma* (see below). Varga made the mistake of predicting that the impending collapse of the capitalist world economy would not come for another 10 years, whereas Stalin apparently was convinced that it would come sooner. As a result of his book Varga was removed from some of his important posts in the Soviet academic world.

G86 SQUIRES, RICHARD. *Auf dem Kriegspfad.* Berlin: Rütten, 1951. 246 p. Memoirs of a British officer who deserted to the Soviets. Includes what are claimed to be excerpts from the diary of American General Grow, who was denounced by the Communists as typical of the "warmongers" among top American military leaders.

G87 STALIN, IOSIF V. *Après la victoire, pour une paix durable; discours, ordres du jour, déclarations et messages de Mai 1945 à Octobre 1949.* Paris: Éditions Sociales, 1949. 108 p. A standard collection of Stalin's speeches, most of which are available in English and other languages in other collections. Its unique value is that virtually all of these concern Soviet foreign policy. [B]

G88 STALIN, IOSIF V. *Economic Problems of Socialism in the USSR*. Moscow: Foreign Languages Publishing House; N.Y.: International Publishers, 1952. 103 p. (Various editions in other languages.) Stalin's last major writing. Implies a softening of Soviet views toward the outside world. Maintains that the Soviet Union will lead the struggle for peace as part of the struggle for socialism. An important statement of policy for the Soviet regime. [A]

G89 STERNBERG, FRITZ. *How to Stop the Russians without War*. N.Y.: J. Day, 1948. 146 p. London and N.Y.: T. V. Boardman, 1948. 159 p. German ed., Schwenningen/Neckar: H. Holtzhauer, 1950. 143 p. A prescription for Western action—defense through strength—which has little material of value to offer on Soviet foreign policy.

G90 SURVEY OF INTERNATIONAL AFFAIRS. *Survey of International Affairs, 1947-1948*. By Peter Calvocoressi. London and N.Y.: Oxford, for the Royal Institute of International Affairs, 1952. 581 p. Contains sections on, among other things, "The U.S.A. and the U.S.S.R.," "The Russian Riposts in Eastern Europe," and "The Clash over Germany." [A]

G91 SURVEY OF INTERNATIONAL AFFAIRS. *Survey of International Affairs, 1949-1950*. By Peter Calvocoressi. London and N.Y.: Oxford, for the Royal Institute of International Affairs, 1953. 590 p. The bulk of the volume is devoted to the conflict of the U.S. and its associates with the USSR and its associates. [A]

G92 SURVEY OF INTERNATIONAL AFFAIRS. *Survey of International Affairs, 1951*. By Peter Calvocoressi and Konstanze Isepp. London and N.Y.: Oxford, for the Royal Institute of International Affairs, 1954. 480 p. Deals in part with "The USSR and Central and Eastern Europe" (Part III) and Yugoslavia (Part IV).

G93 SURVEY OF INTERNATIONAL AFFAIRS. *Survey of International Affairs, 1952*. By Peter Calvocoressi and Konstanze Isepp. London and N.Y.: Oxford, for the Royal Institute of International Affairs, 1955. 449 p. Part III includes discussions of Soviet relations with the European satellites and the West and a note on the state of disarmament at the time of publication.

G94 TOKAEV, GRIGORI A. *Stalin Means War*. London: Weidenfeld & Nicholson, 1951. 214 p. A high-ranking defector from the Soviet Air Force describes his personal decision to go over to the West. Some of the personal memoirs are valuable for Soviet foreign policy, with the usual caveats applicable to all such memoirs.

G95 TRAKHTENBERG, IOSIF A., ed. *Voennoe khoziaistvo kapitalisticheskikh stran i perekhod k mirnoi ekonomike*. Moscow: Gosplanizdat, 1947. 438 p.

G96 TURCHINS, IA. B. *Obostrenie neravnomernosti razvitiia kapitalizma v itoge Vtoroi mirovoi voiny.* Leningrad: Gospolitizdat, 1953. 354 p.

G97 VARGA, EUGEN. *Izmeneniia v ekonomike kapitalizma v itoge Vtoroi mirovoi voiny.* Moscow: Gospolitizdat, 1946. 320 p. This book by a veteran Soviet economist of Hungarian origin created considerable public controversy in the USSR. While predicting a Western economic crisis in ten years, Varga declared that in the meantime capitalism would prosper. He was severely criticized at a conference in Moscow in May 1947 for what was considered to be an exaggerated view of the ability of capitalism to postpone its inevitable collapse. See above, *Soviet Views on the Post-War World Economy.*

G98 VARGA, EUGEN. *Marxism and the General Crisis of Capitalism.* Bombay: People's Pub. House, 1948. 68 p.

G99 VARGA, EUGEN. *Osnovnie voprosy ekonomiki i politiki imperializma posle vtoroi mirovoi voiny.* Moscow: Gospolitizdat, 1953. 575 p. 2nd ed., 1957. In this work the famous Soviet economist was forced to revise the ideas expressed in his controversial book, *Izmeneniia v ekonomike kapitalizma,* and to accept the Stalinist view that the forthcoming economic crisis of the capitalist world would be as severe as the Great Depression.

G100 VISKOV, S. I. *SSSR—v avangarde borby za mir.* Moscow: Gospolitizdat, 1952. 127 p. The standard line on the Soviet Union's attempt to hold off "Anglo-American imperialism." Offers very little.

G101 *Vneshniaia politika Sovetskogo Soiuza; dokumenty i materialy.* Moscow: Gospolitizdat, 1945-51. Annual, 1945-46; Semiannual, 1947-51. Continues the series initiated with *Vneshniaia politika Sovetskogo Soiuza v period Otechestvennoi voiny.* In effect, it replaced the *Sbornik deistvuiushchikh dogovorov . . . ,* but includes much documentation other than treaty texts. [A]

G102 VYSHINSKII, ANDREI IA. *The U.S.S.R. and World Peace.* Ed. by Jessica Smith. N.Y.: International, 1949. 128 p. An officially selected collection of speeches and writings at the third session of the U.N. by the late Soviet ambassador to that body. The Russian language collection of these anti-West speeches is far more complete. [B]

G103 VYSHINSKII, ANDREI IA. *Voprosy mezhdunarodnogo prava i mezhdunarodnoi politiki.* Moscow: Gosizdat iurid. lit., 1949-53. 5 vols. A collection of speeches delivered at the U.N. and at various conferences by the late Soviet diplomat. As convenient a collection as any of some of the more vituperative Soviet attacks on the West, although some are occasionally mild. The U.N. sessions of 1946-52 are covered. [A]

G104 WARBURG, JAMES P. *How to Co-Exist without Playing the Kremlin's Game.* Boston: Beacon, 1952. 228 p. A well known Western analyst offers a prescription for avoiding a showdown but has very little of value to say on Soviet foreign policy.

G105 WARD, BARBARA. *Policy for the West.* N.Y.: Norton, 1951. 317 p. Highly perceptive analysis by an outspoken British specialist in foreign affairs. Though the work is oriented toward an analysis of Western policies, Miss Ward evinces real understanding of Soviet policies.

G106 WARD, BARBARA. *The West at Bay.* London: Allen & Unwin, 1948. 234 p. N.Y.: Norton, 1948. 288 p. A well known British foreign affairs analyst examines the West's dilemma after World War II. Good comprehension of Soviet policies, but almost entirely focused on the West.

G107 WINTERTON, PAUL. *Inquest on an Ally.* London: Cresset; Toronto: Collins, 1948. 288 p. The author uses Soviet press and radio commentary—as well as his own war-time experiences—to form an analysis of Soviet policies. Despite heavy documentation, the book tends to become more of a crusade than scholarship.

G108 ZACHARIAS, ELLIS M., and FARAGO, LADISLAS. *Behind Closed Doors; The Secret History of the Cold War.* N.Y.: Putnam, 1950. 367 p. Naval officer and novelist combine to present a cloak-and-dagger approach to foreign policy. Despite dark hints, there is not much new here on Soviet foreign policy.

G109 ZIFF, WILLIAM B. *Two Worlds; a Realistic Approach to the Problem of Keeping the Peace.* N.Y. and London: Harper, 1946. 335 p. Sees the postwar world threatened by an expansionist Russia unchecked by an ineffectual U.N. Urges strong defensive measures by the U.S. and Britain to contain her.

3. SINCE STALIN, 1953-1963

(Edited by Robert C. Tucker and Roland V. Layton, Jr.)

G110 AIRAPETIAN, M. E., and KABANOV, P. *Leninskie printsipy vneshnei politiki sovetskogo gosudarstva.* Moscow: Gospolitizdat, 1957. 220 p. Discusses Marxism-Leninism as the theoretical foundation of Soviet foreign policy, including "peaceful co-existence," proletarian internationalism, and collective security.

G111 AKADEMIIA NAUK SSSR, INSTITUT MIROVOI EKONOMIKI I MEZHDUNARODNYKH OTNOSHENII. *Mezhdunarodnyi politiko-ekonomicheskii ezhegodnik, 1960.* Moscow: Gospolitizdat, 1960. 623 p. Annual handbook of developments throughout the world, including a statement of the main themes of Soviet foreign policy, and principal events in each country of the world. Contains a bibliography (p. 467-503) of Soviet books, statistical data, and chronology.

G112 BERLIN CONFERENCE, 1954. *Die Viererkonferenz in Berlin 1954; Reden und Dokumente.* Berlin: Presse- und Informationsamt der Bundesregierung, 1954. 314 p. Extensive documentary record of the Conference.

G113 BERLIN CONFERENCE, 1954. *Documents de la conférence des quatre ministres des affairs étrangères de France, des États-Unis d'Amérique, du Royaume-Uni et de l'Union des républiques soviétiques socialistes, tenue à Berlin du 25 janvier au 18 fèvrier 1954.* Paris: Documentation française, 1954. 99 p. The more important speeches, resolutions, propositions, etc., made at the conference.

G114 BERLIN CONFERENCE, 1954. *Foreign Ministers Meeting; Berlin Discussions, January 25-February 18, 1954.* Washington: G.P.O., 1954. 241 p. Wide selection of documents from the Conference.

G115 BOFFA, GIUSEPPE. *La grande svoltà.* Rome: Editori Ruiniti, 1959. 287 p. English ed., *Inside the Khrushchev Era.* N.Y.: Marzani, 1959. 226 p. Interesting confirmation, from an unimpeachable Communist source (Boffa was Moscow correspondent of the Italian Communist newspaper *Unità*) of secret Central Committee letters earlier reported by defectors. The English edition, a very free translation, is marred by a few significant omissions. [A]

G116 COLUMBIA UNIVERSITY, RUSSIAN INSTITUTE. *The Anti-Stalin Campaign and International Communism; A Selection of Documents.* N.Y.: Columbia, 1956. 338 p. The text of Khrushchev's secret speech at the 20th Party Congress in 1956 and a series of statements and articles reflecting the repercussions of this speech in the international Communist movement. Important for the student of international relations within the Communist bloc. [A]

G117 COLUMBIA-HARVARD RESEARCH GROUP. *United States Foreign Policy: U.S.S.R. and Eastern Europe; a study prepared at the request of the Committee on Foreign Affairs, United States Senate.* Washington: G.P.O., 1960. 80 p. Recommendations for U.S. foreign policy toward the USSR and Eastern Europe in the 1960's prefaced by an interpretation of the broad goals and assumptions of Soviet foreign policy during this period. [B]

G118 CONFERENCE OF FOREIGN MINISTERS, GENEVA, 1959. *Conference of Foreign Ministers at Geneva, May 11-June 20, 1959 and July 13-August 5, 1959.* London: H. M. Stationery Off., 1959. 357 p. Texts of the principal statements and proposals made at the 1959 Geneva Conference of Foreign Ministers, which failed to attain its aim of writing a peace treaty with Germany.

G119 CONFERENCE OF FOREIGN MINISTERS, GENEVA, 1959. *Die Aussenministerkonferenz in Genf, 1959.* Bonn: Presse- und Informationsamt der Bundesregierung, 1959—. Extensive documentary record of the Conference.

G120 CONFERENCE OF FOREIGN MINISTERS, GENEVA, 1959. *Foreign Ministers Meeting, May-August, 1959, Geneva.* Washington: Dept. of State, 1959. 603 p. A virtually complete documentary record of the Conference, together with some background materials.

G121 CORRY, JAMES A. *Soviet Russia and the Western Alliance.* Toronto: Canadian Institute of International Affairs, 1958. 102 p. A post-Sputnik evaluation of the kind of adversary faced by the West and the policies which might be adopted to cope with it.

G122 DALLIN, ALEXANDER, ed. *Soviet Conduct in World Affairs: A Selection of Readings.* N.Y.: Columbia U. Press, 1960. 318 p. A useful collection of various interpretations of Soviet foreign policy, chiefly of the postwar period, by Western scholars specializing in Soviet studies.

G123 DALLIN, DAVID J. *Soviet Foreign Policy After Stalin.* Philadelphia: Lippincott, 1961. 543 p. An excellent general survey using available materials and based on long acquaintance with Soviet affairs, yet inevitably bearing marks of having been written close to the events it describes. [A]

G124 DRAGILEV, M. S. *Protivorechiia mezhdy imperialisticheskimi derzhavami na sovremennom etape.* Moscow: Gospolitizdat, 1954. 149 p.

G125 DURDENEVSKII, V. N., and LAZAREV, M. I. *Piat printsipov mirnogo sosushchestvovaniia.* Moscow: Gosiurizdat, 1957. 119 p. A short but systematic reformulation of certain aspects of the Soviet ideology of coexistence, taking account of the Indian concept of *Pancha Shila.*

G126 *Efforts of the Soviet Union Towards Summit Talks; Documents, January-May, 1958.* London: Soviet News, 1958. 168 p. A variety of statements, press interviews, letters, excerpts from speeches, diplomatic notes, and the like, all selected to illustrate the Soviet Union's interest in peace.

G127 EMBREE, G. D. *The Soviet Union Between the 19th and 20th Party Congresses, 1952-1956*. The Hague: Nijhoff, 1959. 365 p. Contains a useful account, though without any significant interpretation and analysis, of Soviet diplomacy from 1954 to 1956.

G128 HALLE, UNIVERSITÄT, INSTITUT FÜR GESCHICHTE VÖLKER DER UDSSR. *Dokumente zur Aussenpolitik der UdSSR 1958*. Ed. by Günter Gorski. Berlin: Rütten & Loening, 1960. 770 p. [B]

G129 HILDEBRANDT, WALTER. *Die Sowjetunion; Macht und Krise*. 2nd ed. Darmstadt: C. W. Leske, 1956. 272 p. A journalistic study, concerned mostly with the domestic scene (industry, agriculture, nationalities problem, church, struggle for Stalin's throne), but with the final section devoted to Soviet foreign policy as it is conditioned by internal exigencies. The author concludes that the USSR is honestly interested in a relaxation of international tensions, but that the West must keep up its guard—without ceasing to strive for a genuine detente.

G130 HOFFMAN, GEORGE W., ed. *Recent Soviet Trends; Proceedings of the Conference Held at the University of Texas, October 11-12, 1956*. Austin: U. of Texas Press, 1956. 107 p. This collection contains a number of contributions on Soviet foreign policy, notably an analysis by John A. Morrison of hypotheses about the role of geographical factors in Russian and Soviet expansion.

G131 INSTITUT ZUR ERFORSCHUNG DER GESCHICHTE UND KULTUR DER UDSSR. *The USSR Today and Tomorrow; Proceedings of the Conference of the Institute for the Study of the History and Culture of the USSR, Munich, August 15 to 17, 1953*. Munich: 1953. 205 p. A series of papers and discussions, presented by scholars who are refugees from Communism. Most deal with domestic affairs, but one analyzes at some length the post-Stalin "soft line" in foreign policy, and others treat the Cominform, non-Soviet Communist Parties, and the Soviet military structure.

G132 INSTITUT ZUR ERFORSCHUNG DER UDSSR. *Report on the Soviet Union in 1956; A Symposium*. Ed. by Jaan Pennar. Munich: 1956. 218 p. Includes sections on Soviet policy in Asia and Mongolia, and on the USSR's trade and assistance programs, together with much material on domestic affairs. Experts on the panels include Philip E. Mosely, Soloman M. Schwarz, and Michael T. Florinsky.

G133 KARDELJ, EDVARD. *Socijalizam i rat*. Belgrade: Kultura, 1960. 231 p. English ed., *Socialism and War; a Survey of Chinese Criticism of the Policy of Coexistence*. London: Methuen, 1960. 238 p. In this major contribution from the Yugoslav side to the Communist foreign policy debate, a leading associate of Tito formulates the "revisionist" philosophy of international relations by way of a systematic critique of the "dogmatist" position of Peking. [A]

G134 KENNAN, GEORGE F. *Russia, the Atom, and the West.* London: Oxford, 1957. 120 p. N.Y.: Harper, 1958. 116 p. German ed., Berlin: 1958. The Reith Lectures given over B.B.C. in the autumn of 1957, when they had considerable impact on European opinion. Their most controversial theme was "disengagement" in Central Europe. [B]

G135 *Khronika mezhdunarodnykh sobytii.* Moscow: Izd. IMO, 1957—. Annual. Gives the principal events for each day of the year, usually in the form of quotes from *Izvestiia* and *Pravda.* Indexed by country.

G136 KHRUSHCHEV, NIKITA S. *Conquest without War; an Analytical Anthology of the Speeches, Interviews, and Remarks of Nikita S. Khrushchev.* Comp. and ed. by N. H. Mager and Jacques Katel. N.Y.: Simon and Schuster, 1961. 545 p. Numerous short selections from his speeches and articles, chosen to illustrate the USSR's drive toward world domination without war. Short commentaries elucidate the material. [A]

G137 KHRUSHCHEV, NIKITA S. *The Crimes of the Stalin Era; Special Report to the 20th Congress of the Communist Party of the Soviet Union.* Annotated by Boris I. Nicolaevsky. N.Y.: *The New Leader,* 1956. 67 p. Another edition: *The Anatomy of Terror; Khrushchev's Revelations about Stalin's Regime.* Washington: Public Affairs Press, 1956. 73 p. Although very little direct reference is made to Soviet foreign policy in the text of the Khrushchev secret speech as published in the West, the document is indispensable for the student of the external as well as internal policies of the USSR. [A]

G138 KHRUSHCHEV, NIKITA S. *Disarmament and Colonial Freedom.* London: Lawrence and Wishart, 1961. 299 p. Speeches, interviews, and statements made while the Soviet leader was attending the U.N. meeting in September-October, 1960.

G139 KHRUSHCHEV, NIKITA S. *Discours, entretiens, interviews sur les problémes de politique internationale.* Moscow: Éditions en langues Étrangères, 1957. 427 p.

G140 KHRUSHCHEV, NIKITA S. *K pobede v mirnom sorevnovanii s kapitalizmom.* Moscow: Gospolitizdat, 1959. 599 p. English ed., *For Victory in Peaceful Competition with Capitalism.* N.Y.: Dutton, 1960. 783 p. A collection of speeches, interviews, and statements, all from 1958, dealing mostly with foreign affairs.

G141 KHRUSHCHEV, NIKITA S. *Khrushchev in America; Full Texts of the Speeches Made by N. S. Khrushchev on his Tour of the United States, September 15-27, 1959*. N.Y.: Crosscurrents, 1960. 231 p. (Numerous editions in other languages.) Speeches, interviews, and many pictures, selected to portray a triumphant tour across America by the USSR's leading extrovert.

G142 KHRUSHCHEV, NIKITA S. *Mir bez oruzhiia—mir bez voin.* Moscow: Gospolitizdat, 1960. 2 vols. Press conferences, public statements, and speeches, either in full or excerpted, in 1959—including those given during his visit to the U.S.

G143 KHRUSHCHEV, NIKITA S. *O vneshnei politike Sovetskogo Soiuza, 1960 god*. Moscow: 1960. 2 vols. An extensive collection of Khrushchev's speeches, interviews, etc., on foreign affairs in 1960.

G144 KHRUSHCHEV, NIKITA S. *Za mir, za razoruzhenie, za svobodu narodov!* Moscow: Gospolitizdat, 1960. 336 p. Speeches, public statements, etc., most of them made while in New York at the U.N. meeting in 1960.

G145 KHRUSHCHEV, NIKITA S. *Za prochnyi mir i mirnoe sosushchestvovanie*. Moscow: Gospolitizdat, 1958. 368 p. English ed. *Speeches and Interviews on World Problems*. Moscow: Foreign Languages Pub. House, 1958. 386 p. Covers 1957.

G145A KINTNER, WILLIAM R., with KORNFEDER, JOSEPH Z. *The New Frontier of War*. Chicago: Regnery, 1962. 362 p. A description of the many-sided political warfare carried on by the Communist bloc against the free world, with proposals for a more positive and better managed American counteroffensive.

G146 KOROVIN, EVGENII A. *Osnovnye problemy sovremennykh mezhdunarodnykh otnoshenii*. Moscow: Sotsekgiz, 1959. 220 p. A restatement by a major Soviet scholar and ideologist of the general doctrine of Soviet foreign policy, covering such topics as coexistence, proletarian internationalism, colonialism, neutralism, and the international regime of cosmic space. [B]

G146A LENINGRAD, PUBLICHNAIA BIBLIOTEKA. *Vneshniaia politika SSSR—politika mira; rekomendatelnyi ukazatel literatury*. Comp. by Aleksandr A. Popov, ed. by A. N. Mylnikov. Leningrad: Izd. Publ. bib. imeni M. E. Saltykova-Shchedrina, 1956. 79 p. The introduction states that this is designed as a reading guide for Soviet propagandists and members of the toiling masses. Lists suggested readings on the Soviet foreign policy line adopted at the 20th Party Congress. Has sections on "Peaceful Coexistence," etc. Includes books, pamphlets, and articles from Soviet journals and newspapers.

G147 LEONTEV, BORIS L. *Pravda protiv lzhi; publitsistika.* Moscow: Molodaia gvardiia, 1957. 155 p. Numerous short articles, designed to instruct the Soviet masses in various foreign affairs topics, e.g., the Soviet position on disarmament and inspection, "the fifty men who rule America," peaceful coexistence, the U.S.A.'s neo-colonialism, socialism in France, and many others.

G148 LEONTEV, L. A. *Sotsialism v ekonomicheskom sorevnovanii s kapitalizmom.* Moscow: Gospolitizdat, 1958. 224 p. A comparison of the two economic systems, with the final chapter entitled, not surprisingly, "The Future Belongs to Communism." For popular consumption.

G149 LIDDELL HART, BASIL H. *Deterrent or Defense; A Fresh Look at the West's Military Position.* N.Y.: Praeger, 1960. 257 p. Speculation on military theories, Soviet and Western, by a British expert.

G150 LINDSAY, MICHAEL (Baron Lindsay of Birker). *Is Peaceful Coexistence Possible?* East Lansing: Michigan State U. Press, 1960. 252 p. An inquiry into the possibility of coexistence with the Communist world and a set of prescriptions for Western policy in the political and psychological competition with the Communist East.

G151 LIPPMANN, WALTER. *The Coming Tests with Russia.* Boston: Little, Brown, 1961. 37 p. A report on the 1961 meeting between Khrushchev and the dean of American commentators on world affairs. The Soviet leader spoke frankly about the international situation, especially about the Berlin crisis, then coming to a new boil. Lippmann found it "sobering," and felt that the Soviets were not bluffing, although they did not intend a full scale war.

G152 LIPPMANN, WALTER. *The Communist World and Ours.* Boston: Atlantic (Little, Brown), 1959. 56 p. Account of a lengthy interview with Premier Khrushchev in October, 1958, and an interpretation on this basis of the challenge of Soviet foreign policy from the standpoint of the West.

G153 MEETING OF FOREIGN MINISTERS OF FRANCE, UNITED KINGDOM, SOVIET UNION, AND UNITED STATES, GENEVA, 1955. *The Geneva Meeting of Foreign Ministers, Oct. 27-Nov. 16, 1955.* Washington: Dept. of State, 1955. 307 p. Record of speeches, proposals, and statements made at this conference, with a summary provided by Secretary Dulles.

G154 MEZHDUNARODNAIA NAUCHNAIA KONFERENTSIIA PO PROBLEMAM EKONOMICHESKIKH KRIZISOV I OBNISHCHANIIA RABOCHEGO KLASSA V USLOVIIAKH SOVREMENNOGO KAPITALIZMA, BERLIN, 1958. *Problemy krizisov i obnish-*

chaniia rabochego klassa posle vtoroi mirovoi voiny; materialy konferentsii. Edited by A. V. Kirsanov. Moscow: Izd. sotsialno-ekon. lit-ry, 1959. 630 p.

G155 *Mezhimperialisticheskie protivorechia na pervom etape obshchego krizisa kapitalizma; sbornik statei.* Moscow: Izd. sotsialno-ekon. lit-ry, 1959. 309 p.

G156 MOLOTOV, VIACHESLAV M. *Statements at Berlin Conference of Foreign Ministers of USSR, France, Great Britain, and USA ⟨Jan. 25-Feb. 18, 1954⟩.* Moscow: Foreign Languages Publishing House, 1954. 142 p. Russian ed., Moscow: Gospolitizdat, 1954. 154 p. German ed., Berlin: Dietz, 1954. 204 p. Molotov's contribution to the unsuccessful attempt to settle the problems of writing peace treaties with Germany and with Austria.

G157 MONTGOMERY, BERNARD L. (Field Marshal). *An Approach to Sanity; A Study of East-West Relations.* London: Collins, 1959. 94 p. Cleveland, Ohio: World, 1960. 94 p. A British hero of World War II expresses his controversial views on the Cold War.

G158 MOSCOW, NAUCHNO-ISSLEDOVATELSKII KONIUNKTURNYI INSTITUT. *Ekonomicheskoe polozhenie kapitalisticheskikh stran v 1954 g.* Edited by E. S. Shershnev and others. Moscow: Vneshtorgizdat, 1955. 420 p.

G159 NIKHAMIN, VLADIMIR P., ed. *Mezhdunarodnye otnosheniia i vneshniaia politika Sovetskogo Soiuza.* Moscow: Izd. IMO, 1960. 416 p.

G160 OVERSTREET, HARRY and BONARO. *The War Called Peace: Khrushchev's Communism.* N.Y.: Norton, 1961. 368 p. A popular analysis of the Communist threat.

G161 *Problemy sovremennogo kapitalizma; sbornik statei. K 80-letiiu E. S. Varga.* Moscow: Akad. nauk SSSR, 1959. 400 p. A collection of articles on the world economy, in honor of the prominent Soviet economist, Eugene Varga.

G162 RIMSCHA, HANS VON and others. *Das Sowjetsystem in der heutigen Welt.* Munich: Isar, 1956. 279 p. A collection of essays by West German scholars, including Georg von Rauch, who contributed a study on the fundamental lines of Soviet foreign policy. Other articles examine the satellites and Titoism, the USSR and Germany's reunification, and coexistence.

G163 ROTHSTEIN, ANDREW. *Peaceful Coexistence.* Harmondsworth, England: Penguin Books, 1955. 191 p. A Communist view of the idea and problems of coexistence, by a leading British Party member.

G164 RUSSIA (1923-USSR). *Deklaratsii, zaiavleniia i kommiunike Sovetskogo Pravitelstva s pravitelstvami inostrannykh gosudarstv, 1954-1957 g.g.* Moscow: Gospolitizdat, 1957. 328 p. Numerous documents, classified by country.

G165 RUSSIA (1923-USSR), TREATIES, ETC. *Dogovory ob okazanii pravovoi pomoshchi po grazhdanskim, semeinym i ugolovnym delam, zakliuchennye Sovetskim Soiuzom v 1957-1958 gg.* Ed. by M. D. Grishin. Moscow: Gosiurizdat, 1959. 285 p. [B]

G166 SCOTT, JOHN. *Political Warfare; a Guide to Competitive Coexistence.* N.Y.: Day, 1955. 256 p. A broad and wide-ranging study of "political warfare" as a form of activity in contemporary international relations, including two chapters on Soviet resources and experience in political warfare. Soviet political warfare strategy is touched upon. The author is with *Time* Magazine and has considerable experience in Russia.

G167 *Soviet Efforts for Peace in Europe and Against German Rearmament; Documents.* London: Soviet News, 1955. 160 p. A collection of Soviet diplomatic notes, speeches, statements to the press, etc., primarily concerned with Germany, although some deal with France and Britain.

G168 SULZBERGER, CYRUS L. *The Big Thaw; A Personal Exploration of the New Russia and the Orbit Countries.* N.Y.: Harper, 1956. 275 p. A report on and interpretation of the post-Stalinist scene in the Communist world, as well as post-Stalinist Soviet foreign policy, by the able and experienced foreign affairs observer of the *New York Times.*

G169 SURVEY OF INTERNATIONAL AFFAIRS. *Survey of International Affairs, 1953.* By Peter Calvocoressi and Coral Bell. London and N.Y.: Oxford, for the Royal Institute of International Affairs, 1956. 385 p. Treats the death of Stalin and its consequences for Soviet foreign policy, the situation on Russia's southern flank, Soviet trade with Red China, and the status of Communism in Latin America. [A]

G170 SURVEY OF INTERNATIONAL AFFAIRS. *Survey of International Affairs, 1954.* By Coral Bell. Ed. by F. C. Benham. London and N.Y.: Oxford, for the Royal Institute of International Affairs, 1957. 319 p. Contains material on the Geneva Conference on Indo-China, post-Stalin developments in the Soviet Union and Eastern Europe, and Soviet relations with Japan and Communist China. [A]

G171 SURVEY OF INTERNATIONAL AFFAIRS. *Survey of International Affairs, 1955-1956.* By Geoffrey Barraclough and Rachel

F. Wall. London and N.Y.: Oxford, for the Royal Institute of International Affairs, 1960. 327 p. The East-West conflict dominates the whole volume; in addition, there are separate chapters on "Soviet Foreign Policy," "Soviet Reappraisals," and "East-West Relations." [A]

G172 TIULPANOV, S. *Kolonialnaia sistema imperializma i ee raspad.* Moscow: Sotsekgiz, 1958. 258 p.

G173 TOMASIC, DINKO A., and STRMECKI, JOSEPH. *National Communism and Soviet Strategy.* Washington: Public Affairs Press, 1957. 222 p. An interpretation of Titoism as, since 1955-56, a conscious instrument of the "new Soviet plan for a global offensive," utilized by the USSR to woo undeveloped and neutral countries. According to the authors, the de-Stalinization campaign, the relaxation of controls over the satellites, and other measures instituted by the Soviet leaders since 1956 are all tactical devices of the same elaborate hoax.

G174 U.S. DEPARTMENT OF STATE. *The Quotable Khrushchev.* Washington: Department of State, 1957-61. 4 parts. (Nos. 215, 231, 241, and 252 of *Soviet Affairs Notes.*) Consists of selected quotations from speeches and other pronouncements, arranged by topics. Divided as follows: Part I, 1934-57; Part II, Oct. 1957-March 1959; Part III, April 1959-March 1960; Part IV, April 1960-March 1961. [A]

G175 U.S. DEPARTMENT OF STATE, HISTORICAL DIVISION. *Foreign Ministers Meeting, May-August, 1959, Geneva; Documentary Publication.* Washington: Dept. of State, 1959. 603 p. Includes all substantive statements made in the plenary sessions, important statements made outside the Conference by President Eisenhower and others, and related papers. [A]

G176 U.S. LIBRARY OF CONGRESS, LEGISLATIVE REFERENCE SERVICE. *Trends in Economic Growth; A Comparison of the Western Powers and the Soviet Bloc.* Washington: G.P.O., 1955. 339 p. A study prepared for the Joint Committee on the Economic Report by a number of American specialists on the Soviet economy. Emphasizes the role of Soviet economic growth in the East-West conflict. [A]

G177 VASILEVA, V. IA. *Raspad kolonialnoi sistemy imperializma.* Moscow: Akad. nauk SSSR, 1958. 610 p.

G178 VYGODSKII, S. IU. *Borba za mir i bezopasnost narodov—generalnaia liniia vneshnei politiki SSSR.* Leningrad: 1954. 221 p. Intended for "propagandists, agitators, and the wide circles of the public interested in questions of Soviet foreign policy," the book paints the standard picture of a USSR carrying on the good fight for the forces of decency—against exploiters, imperialists, and warmongers.

G179 VYGODSKII, S. IU. *Vneshniaia politika SSSR—politka mira i mezhdunarodnogo sotrudnichestva.* Moscow: Gospolitizdat, 1958. 334 p. Discusses the USSR's "struggle for peace" as manifested in its efforts to solve the German and Austrian problems, disarmament, peaceful competition with capitalism, support of the "national-liberation struggles" in the colonies, establishment of cultural relations with all countries, strengthening the U.N., etc. Not a major contribution to the study of Soviet foreign affairs.

G180 WERTH, ALEXANDER. *Russia Under Khrushchev.* N.Y.: Crest paperbacks, 1962. 352 p. British ed., *The Khrushchev Phase.* The author is a British citizen with considerable experience as a newspaper reporter in Russia and long a resident of France. Most of the book deals with internal affairs, but the last chapters give his interpretation of Soviet foreign policy under Khrushchev. Some of the material appeared originally in *The Nation* and *The New Statesman.*

G181 WOLFE, BERTRAM D. *Six Keys to the Soviet System.* Introd. by Leslie C. Stevens. Boston: Beacon, 1956. 258 p. A collection of essays, published in various periodicals, of a leading American specialist on Soviet affairs. Most deal with domestic matters, but three are concerned with Poland, China, and Yugoslavia. Concludes with a summary of the points he feels the U.S. should emphasize in its ideological struggle with Communism.

G182 WOLFERS, ARNOLD D., ed. *Alliance Policy in the Cold War.* Baltimore: Johns Hopkins Press, 1959. 314 p. Most of the book concerns the attempts of the West to attain security through collective action, but one chapter, by William Welch, Soviet expert at the Washington Center of Foreign Policy Research, discusses the Soviet moves along this line.

G183 ZHUKOV, IU. and others. *Tri mesiatsa v Zheneve.* Moscow: "Pravda," 1954. 228 p. *Pravda* correspondents tell the Soviet public about the struggle for peace waged by the USSR at the Geneva Foreign Ministers Conference in 1954, against the machinations of the USA. Of interest as a picture of the distortions presented to the Soviet masses.

Part II

Soviet Foreign Relations and World Communism by Regions and Countries

H. The Western Hemisphere

HA. THE UNITED STATES

1. GENERAL WORKS COVERING MORE THAN ONE PERIOD

(Edited by Robert P. Browder)

HA1 BAILEY, THOMAS A. *America Faces Russia; Russian-American Relations From Early Times to Our Day.* Ithaca, N.Y.: Cornell, 1950. 375 p. A lively account of diplomatic relations from the point of view of the United States and with emphasis upon American public opinion of Russia. [B]

HA1A BROWDER, ROBERT P. *The Origins of Soviet-American Diplomacy.* Princeton, N.J.: Princeton University Press, 1953. 256 p. Deals with the events leading up to the diplomatic recognition of the USSR by the United States, the recognition agreement, and the results to the summer of 1935. An objective, scholarly account, using both Soviet and American sources. The author is Professor of History at Kansas State University. [A]

HA2 COHEN, IRA S. "Congressional Attitudes Towards the Soviet Union, 1917-1941." Ph.D. dissertation, U. of Chicago, 1955. 98 p.

HA3 DULLES, FOSTER RHEA. *The Road to Teheran; The Story of Russia and America, 1781-1943.* Princeton, N.J.: Princeton University Press, 1944. 279 p. Italian ed., *Russia e Stati Uniti.* Rome: Editrice Faro, 1945. 323 p. French ed., N.Y.: 1945. 271 p. German ed., N.Y.: 1945. 278 p. An excellent summary based largely upon secondary sources. Reflects the optimism generally felt during the wartime alliance with Russia. [A]

HA4 FISHER, HAROLD H. *America and Russia in the World Community.* Claremont, Calif.: Claremont College, 1946. 175 p. A reasoned series of lectures on the factors affecting Soviet-American relations in the past and reflecting the hopes and desire for future cooperation at the end of World War II. [B]

HA5 FLEMING, DENNA F. *The Cold War and its Origins.* Garden City, N.Y.: Doubleday, 1961. 2 vols. A detailed history of Soviet-American relations and conflicting strategies since World War I. The author puts on the U.S. most of the responsibility for the origin and continuation of the Cold War and tends to give Russia the benefit of the doubt. By a professor at Vanderbilt University. [B]

HA6 HARPER, SAMUEL N. *The Russia I Believe In; The Memoirs of Samuel N. Harper, 1902-1941.* Ed. by Paul V. Harper. Chicago: U.

of Chicago, 1945. 278 p. Extremely interesting posthumously published memoirs and edited papers of one of the pioneers of Slavic studies in the United States. Covers the period 1900 to 1941.

HA7 KENNAN, GEORGE F. *Russia and the West Under Lenin and Stalin.* Boston: Little, Brown, 1961. 411 p. A brilliant presentation of Soviet-Western relations from 1917 to 1945. The early chapters cover some of the same ground as the author's detailed historical works on Russian-American relations. The whole book reflects both his own experience as a diplomat and his profound knowledge of Soviet reality. [A]

HA8 KRIESBERG, MARTIN. "Public Opinion on American-Soviet Relations." Ph.D. dissertation, Harvard, 1948.

HA9 MARGOLIN, ARNOLD D. *From a Political Diary; Russia, the Ukraine, and America, 1905-1945.* N.Y.: Columbia, 1946. 250 p. Some interesting sidelights on Russian-American relations in the thirties and forties by a former diplomat of the short-lived Democratic Ukrainian Republic, later an American citizen, who moved in official and unofficial circles attempting to promote understanding between the two countries.

HA10 MAZZA, R. P. (SISTER MARY A.). "A Survey of the Changing Attitudes Toward the Soviet Union as Reflected in American Periodicals, 1942-1949." Ph.D. dissertation, St. Johns, 1957.

HA11 RUSSIA (1923– USSR), NARODNYI KOMISSARIAT PO INOSTRANNYM DELAM. *Sovetsko-amerikanskie otnosheniia 1919-1933.* Vol. 9 of *Sbornik dokumentov po mezhdunarodnoi politike i mezhdunarodnomy pravu.* Ed. by K. V. Antonov and others. Moscow: NKID, 1934. 99 p. A collection of important documents.

HA12 SCHUMAN, FREDERICK L. *American Policy Toward Russia since 1917; a Study of Diplomatic History, International Law, and Public Opinion.* N.Y.: International, 1928. London: Lawrence, 1929. 412 p. Still a valuable study despite its limited use of Russian sources and the subsequent appearance of new material. Highly critical of American policies, including non-recognition. [A]

HA13 SMITH, GEORGE HORSLEY. "A Quantitative and Qualitative Study of American Attitudes Toward Russia (the Soviet Union)." Ph.D. dissertation, Cornell U., 1945.

HA14 SOLBERG, WINSTON U. "The Impact of Soviet Russia on American Life and Thought, 1917-1933." Ph.D. dissertation, Harvard, 1954.

HA15 TOMPKINS, PAULINE. *American-Russian Relations in the Far East.* N.Y.: Macmillan, 1949. 426 p. A carefully researched, scholarly account of the subject from the 1890's through the immediate post World War II years. Some Russian sources used. [B]

HA15A *The United States in World Affairs; An Account of American Foreign Relations.* 1931–. N.Y. and London: Harper, for the Council on Foreign Relations, 1932–. These annual volumes, prepared by various editors, frequently have sections on relations with Russia, especially the years since World War II.

HA16 U.S. LIBRARY OF CONGRESS, DIVISION OF BIBLIOGRAPHY. *A Selected List of References on the Diplomatic and Trade Relations of the United States with the Union of Soviet Socialist Republics, 1919-1935.* Compiled by Helen F. Conover. Washington, 1935. 29 p. (mimeographed). A very helpful listing of 332 books, pamphlets, articles, speeches, and government documents bearing on the subject, principally in English, but also in Russian and western European languages.

HA17 *Voprosy mezhdunarodnogo prava v teorii i praktike SShA.* Ed. by E. A. Korovin. Moscow: Izd. Instituta mezhdunarodnykh otnoshenii, 1957. 196 p. Critical appraisal of some American doctrines and practices by five Soviet jurists. Emphasizes the relation of law to politics.

HA18 WILLIAMS, WILLIAM A. *American-Russian Relations, 1781-1947.* N.Y.: Rinehart, 1952. 367 p. Despite the title, concentrates almost entirely on the period 1917 to 1939, making extensive use of the papers of Col. Raymond Robins, who is pictured most favorably. The author, a University of Wisconsin American diplomatic historian, is highly critical of United States' policies, which he sees as largely inspired by American "capitalists." The book suffers from an inadequate understanding of Russian developments.

HA19 WILLIAMS, WILLIAM A. "Raymond Robins and Russian-American Relations, 1917-1938." Ph.D. dissertation, U. of Wisconsin, 1951. Became the basis for the author's book, listed above.

2. 1917-1921

(Edited by George F. Kennan and Robert P. Browder)

HA20 ANDERSON, PAUL H. "The Attitude of the American Leftist Leaders Toward the Russian Revolution (1917-1923)." Ph.D. dissertation, Notre Dame, 1943. Contains useful material, though poorly organized.

HA21 BACON, EUGENE H. "Russian-American Relations, 1917-1921." Ph.D. dissertation, Georgetown, 1951. 354 p.

HA22 BRYANT, LOUISE. *Six Red Months in Russia; an Observer's Account of Russia Before and During the Proletarian Dictatorship*. N.Y.: George H. Doran, 1918. 299 p. Memoirs by John Reed's wife; interesting sidelights on the Russian scene at the time of the Revolution. Not of major importance.

HA23 BULLARD, ARTHUR. *The Russian Pendulum: Autocracy—Democracy—Bolshevism*. N.Y.: Macmillan, 1919. 256 p. A thoughtful, well-informed discussion of some of the issues and problems of the revolutionary period, by one of the most intelligent and qualified of America's official observers. [B]

HA24 BULLITT, WILLIAM C. *The Bullitt Mission to Russia; Testimony Before the Committee on Foreign Relations, United States Senate*. N.Y.: Huebsch, 1919. 151 p. Testimony by Mr. Bullitt concerning his mission to Russia in February-March 1919. Supplemented by reports of Lincoln Steffens and Captain W. W. Pettit who had accompanied him to Russia. [B]

HA25 DEYOUNG, CHARLES D. "David Rowland Francis; American in Russia." M.A. thesis, U. of Wisconsin, 1949. A useful thesis on Francis' career, including a number of personal data hard to find elsewhere. Not of major importance for Soviet-American relations.

HA26 FEDOTOFF WHITE, DMITRI. *Survival Through War and Revolution in Russia*. Philadelphia: U. of Pennsylvania; London: Milford, Oxford, 1939. 395 p. Engaging memoirs of a White naval officer attached to the Root Mission in 1917 and later with Kolchak in Siberia.

HA27 FINNEGAN, REVEREND EDWARD H., "The United States Policy Toward Russia, March, 1917–March, 1918." Ph.D. dissertation, Fordham, 1947. A detailed and objective account based upon English language sources and giving considerable attention to public opinion.

HA28 FISHER, HAROLD H. *The Famine in Soviet Russia, 1919-1923; The Operations of the American Relief Administration*. N.Y.: Macmillan, 1927. 609 p. 2nd ed., Stanford, Calif.: Stanford University Press; London: Oxford University Press, 1935. 609 p. Authoritative, reliable and restrained; a unique and revealing source of information on this subject. [A]

HA29 FOREIGN POLICY ASSOCIATION, NEW YORK. *Russian-American Relations, March, 1917–March, 1920; Documents and Papers Compiled and Edited by Caroline K. Cumming and Walter W.*

Pettit. N.Y.: Harcourt, Brace and Howe, 1920. 375 p. A collection of 158 documents, many drawn from the American and Soviet press. Also includes interesting material from the private papers of Raymond Robins and others. A primary source. [A]

HA30 FRANCIS, DAVID R. *Russia from the American Embassy, April, 1916–November, 1918*. N.Y.: Scribner, 1921. 361 p. Memoirs of the American Ambassador to Russia. While not very authoritative or well-informed with relation to the Russian scene, this is highly interesting from the standpoint of American policies and reactions. [B]

HA31 GOLDER, FRANK A. and HUTCHINSON, LINCOLN. *On the Trail of the Russian Famine*. Stanford: Stanford Univ., 1927. 331 p. Members of the American Relief Administration relate how they overcame the suspicions of Soviet officials (who feared that the A.R.A. was an instrument of American imperialism) to save Russian lives during the great famine in 1921.

HA32 GRAVES, WILLIAM S. *America's Siberian Adventure, 1918-1920*. N.Y.: Cape and Smith, 1931. 363 p. An important account of American intervention in Siberia by the commander of the expeditionary force, who became convinced that it was ill-advised, unjustified, and a debacle. [B]

HA33 HAGEDORN, HERMANN. *The Magnate; William Boyce Thompson and His Time*. N.Y.: John Day, 1935. 343 p. Contains interesting and revealing passages on Thompson's brief experience in Russia, 1917-18, as head of American Red Cross mission. The Thompson family is understood to consider it unjust to him.

HA34 HARD, WILLIAM. *Raymond Robins' Own Story*. N.Y.: Harper, 1920. 247 p. Summarizes what Robins had to say when he returned from Russia in 1918. Journalistic, vague, and unreliable in detail, it is interesting mostly as reflection of Robins' image of himself and his work.

HA35 HOLBROW, CHARLES H. "Lenin's Views of the United States." Certificate essay, Russian Institute, Columbia, 1957. 97 p.

HA36 IVANOV, S. *Amerikanskaia agressiia na sovetskom Dalnem Vostoke*. Vladivostok: Primizdat, 1952. 247 p.

HA37 JESSUP, PHILIP C. *Elihu Root*. N.Y.: Dodd, Mead, 1938. 2 vols. Passages dealing with Root's mission to Russia in 1917 are factually valuable and reliable. They do not, however, bring out clearly the grievous hiatus between concept and purposes behind the Root Mission and the objective situation it faced in Russia.

HA38 KALPASCHNIKOV, ANDREI. *A Prisoner of Trotsky's*. Garden City, N.Y.: Doubleday, Page, 1920. 287 p. A bitter book by a

Russian, formerly resident in the U.S., who served with the American Red Cross Commission in Rumania, was imprisoned several months in Petrograd for activity on behalf of that organization, and blamed Raymond Robins for his misfortunes.

HA39 KENNAN, GEORGE F. *Soviet-American Relations, 1917-1920.* Princeton, N.J.: Princeton University Press; London: Faber, 1956–. Vol. 1, *Russia Leaves the War.* 544 p. Vol. 2, *The Decision to Intervene.* 513 p. The first volume covers the period November 1917 to March 1918, and the second carries the story down to decisions which resulted in the dispatch of American forces to North Russia and Siberia. Detailed, authoritative, perceptive, and exceptionally well written. By a former American Ambassador to Russia. A third volume was originally planned, but has been postponed. [A]

HA40 KRASNOV, I. M. *Klassovaia borba v SShA i dvizhenie protiv antisovetskoi interventsii.* Moscow: Sotsekgiz, 1961.

HA41 KUNINA, A. E. *Proval amerikanskikh planov zavoevaniia mirovogo gospodstva v 1917-1920 gg.* Moscow: Gospolitizdat, 1951. 235 p. 2nd ed., 1954. 318 p. Stalinist, anti-American propaganda at its worst, masquerading under the guise of history. Tendentious, dishonest, and unreliable.

HA41A LASCH, CHRISTOPHER. *The American Liberals and the Russian Revolution.* N.Y. and London: Columbia Univ. Press, 1962. 290 p. A careful study by an American scholar of the attitudes of one group in the U.S. toward the momentous events in Russia.

HA42 McDUFFEE, RAY W. "The State Department and the Russian Revolutions, March–November, 1917." Ph.D. dissertation, Georgetown U., 1954.

HA43 PANOV, V. A. *Istoricheskaia poddelka; amerikanskie poddelnye dokumenty.* Vladivostok: 1920. Available in America only in the Library of Congress, this bibliographical oddity represents the defense of one of the persons discredited as evident German agents in the so-called Sisson documents. Panov names Ferdinand Ossendovsky as the likely fabricator of the documents, and cites abundant and interesting evidence in substantiation of this charge. (See HA53 below.)

HA44 PAVLOVICH, MIKHAIL I. (pseud. of M. L. Veltman). *Sovetskaia Rossiia i kapitalisticheskaia Amerika.* Moscow-Petrograd: Gosizdat, 1922. 101 p. A brief survey of relations from the beginnings to 1922. Although written by a prominent Bolshevik under the auspices of the Central Committee of the Party and adhering to the required doctrinal tenets, it is noteworthy for its moderate treatment of the American role in the Intervention and its expression of almost unqualified gratitude for the work of the American Relief Administration. Volume III of *RSFSR v imperialisticheskom okruzhenii.*

HA45 REITZER, LADISLAS F. "United States-Russian Economic Relations, 1917-1920." Ph.D. dissertation, U. of Chicago, 1950. A detailed study of a subject usually neglected in other accounts of the period.

HA46 ROOT, ELIHU. *The United States and the War; The Mission to Russia; Political Addresses.* Collected and ed. by Robert Bacon and James Brown Scott. Cambridge: Harvard, 1918. 362 p. Interesting reflections of a respectable Republican on the war in 1917. In view of Wilson's failure to consult Root subsequently, they have little value for the history of Soviet-American relations.

HA47 SISSON, EDGAR G. *One Hundred Red Days; A Personal Chronicle of the Bolshevik Revolution.* New Haven: Yale; London: Milford, Oxford, 1931. 502 p. Interesting, well-written memoirs of the head of the office of the Committee on Public Information in Petrograd (November 1917–February 1918) who was responsible for unearthing and bringing to Washington the so-called Sisson documents, purporting to prove that Lenin was a German agent.

HA48 STAMATOPULOS, STEPHEN. "Woodrow Wilson's Russian Policy; A Case Study of American-Russian Relations, 1913-1921." Ph.D. dissertation, Harvard, 1957.

HA49 STRAKHOVSKY, LEONID I. *American Opinion About Russia, 1917-1920.* Toronto: U. of Toronto, 1961. 135 p. Valuable for its many lengthy excerpts from the press, documenting contemporary confusion and misconceptions concerning Russian events. [B]

HA50 STRAKHOVSKY, LEONID I. *Intervention at Archangel: the Story of Allied Intervention and Russian Counter-Revolution in North Russia, 1918-1920.* Princeton, N.J.: Princeton, 1944. London: Milford, Oxford, 1944. A carefully prepared study of this episode with particular emphasis upon the administration of the Russian Provisional Government at Archangel and its relations with the Allied forces. [A]

HA51 STRAKHOVSKY, LEONID I. *The Origins of American Intervention in North Russia (1918).* Princeton, N.J.: Princeton, 1937. 140 p. A pioneer study, still valuable, by a Russian émigré historian who participated in the events recounted. [A]

HA52 UNTERBERGER, BETTY MILLER. *America's Siberian Expedition, 1918-1920; A Study of National Policy.* Durham, N.C.: Duke University Press, 1956. 271 p. A carefully documented and balanced study of the decision to intervene and its consequences. [A]

HA53 U.S. COMMITTEE ON PUBLIC INFORMATION. *The German-Bolshevik Conspiracy.* War Information Series, no. 20, October, 1918. The so-called Sisson documents. Appended is an inadequate appraisal of the authenticity of the documents by J. Franklin Jameson and Samuel M. Harper. See George Kennan's critique in *Journal of Mod. Hist.*, vol. 28, no. 2 (June 1956). (See also HA43).

HA54 U.S. CONGRESS, HOUSE, COMMITTEE ON EXPENDITURES IN STATE DEPARTMENT. *Russian Bonds; Hearings before the Committee on Expenditures in the State Department, House of Representatives, on H.R. 132, Resolution to Investigate in re Payment of Interest and Principal on Russian Bonds.* Washington: G.P.O., 1919. 3 vols. in 1.

HA55 U.S. CONGRESS, SENATE, COMMITTEE ON FOREIGN RELATIONS. *Relations with Russia; Hearing before the Committee on Foreign Relations, United States Senate, Sixty-Sixth Congress, Third Session on S. J. Res. 164; a Resolution Providing for the Reestablishment of Trade Relations with Russia, and so forth.* Washington: G.P.O., 1921. 112 p.

HA56 U.S. CONGRESS, SENATE, COMMITTEE ON FOREIGN RELATIONS. *Russian Propaganda; Hearing before a Subcommittee of the Committee on Foreign Relations, U.S. Senate, 66th Congress, 2nd Session, Pursuant to S. Res. 263, Directing the Foreign Relations Committee to Investigate Status and Activities of one Ludwig C. A. K. Martens, Claiming to be Representative of the Russian Socialist Soviet Republic.* Washington: G.P.O., 1920. 504 p.

HA57 U.S. CONGRESS, SENATE, COMMITTEE ON THE JUDICIARY. *Bolshevik Propaganda; Hearings before a Subcommittee of the Committee on the Judiciary, U.S. Senate, 65th Congress, Third Session.* Washington: G.P.O., 1919. Verbatim records of the 1919 investigation of the Russian situation. Includes testimony of a considerable number of Americans who had been in Russia in the preceding months. A major source on Soviet-American relations in this period. [A]

HA58 U.S. DEPARTMENT OF LABOR, BUREAU OF IMMIGRATION. *In the Matter of L.C.A.K. Martens, an Alleged Alien; Brief on Behalf of Mr. Martens, Charles Recht, Attorney for the Alleged Alien, Thomas F. (sic) Hardwick, of Georgia and Isaac A. Hourwich, of New York, of counsel.* Washington ? 1920 ? 104 p.

HA59 U.S. DEPARTMENT OF STATE. *Memorandum on Certain Aspects of Bolshevist Movement in Russia.* Washington: G.P.O., 1919. 55 p. Translations from Russian newspapers and reports from American representatives abroad transmitted to the Senate Foreign Relations

Committee by Secretary of State Lansing to illustrate the "ruthlessness" of the Bolsheviks and "the results of their exercise of power" in "demoralization, civil war, and economic collapse."

HA60 U.S. DEPARTMENT OF STATE. *Papers Relating to the Foreign Relations of the United States, 1918-1919; Russia.* Washington: G.P.O., 1931-37. 4 vols. The most important single source of information on official Russian- and Soviet-American relations from 1917 to 1919 inclusive. These 2,699 pages nevertheless are incomplete by virtue of omission of material which did not happen to be in State Department files; they represent only a selection from far larger documentation now available to scholars in the National Archives. [A]

HA61 U.S. LIBRARY OF CONGRESS, DIVISION OF BIBLIOGRAPHY. *List of References on the Russian Policy of the United States.* Washington, 1922. 13 p. (mimeographed) Supplement, 9 p. (mimeographed). The first lists 171 articles, pamphlets, and books. The supplement adds 110 more titles. Not annotated.

HA62 U.S. SPECIAL DIPLOMATIC MISSION TO RUSSIA. *America's Message to the Russian People; Addresses by the Members of the Special Diplomatic Mission of the United States to Russia in the Year 1917.* Boston: Marshall Jones, 1918. 154 p. Revealing on the Root Mission's moralistic and patronizing approach and general lack of understanding of contemporary Russian events.

HA63 WHITE, JOHN ALBERT. *The Siberian Intervention.* Princeton, N.J.: Princeton University Press, 1950. 471 p. An excellent, well documented account of the struggle for the Russian Far East from 1917 to 1921, based upon Russian, Japanese, and American sources. [A]

3. 1921-1933

(Edited by Robert P. Browder)

HA64 AMERICAN FOUNDATION, COMMITTEE ON RUSSIAN-AMERICAN RELATIONS. *The United States and the Soviet Union; A Report on the Controlling Factors in the Relation Between the United States and the Soviet Union.* Edited by E. E. Lape and E. A. Read. N.Y.: The American Foundation, 1933. 279 p. A valuable collection of documents and materials, obviously arranged and edited to promote recognition. [B]

HA65 BAUER, MANFRED. "Herbert Hoovers Verhältnis zu Sowjet-Russland von der Pariser Friedenskonferenz, 1919, bis zum Ende seiner Präsidentschaft, 1933." Dissertation, U. of Munich, 1954. 116 p.

HA66 BUEHLER, EZRA C., comp. *Selected Articles on Recognition of Soviet Russia.* N.Y.: Wilson, 1931. 387 p. A collection similar to but more extensive than Hodgson (see below), covering materials published and arguments advanced to the summer of 1931.

HA67 FISCHER, LOUIS. *Why Recognize Russia?; The Arguments For and Against the Recognition of the Soviet Government by the United States.* N.Y.: Cape & Smith, 1931. 298 p. Although delineating both sides of the question, the author, then an American correspondent in Moscow and sympathetic to the Soviets, strongly urges recognition. [B]

HA68 GALKOVICH, MOISEI G. *Soedinennye Shtaty i dalnevostochnaia problema.* Moscow: Gosizdat, 1928. 208 p. A historical survey of the United States in the Far East, which, among other things, depicts the "Open Door Policy" as an American stratagem for exploiting China. Sees a growing rivalry between Japan and the U.S., which may lead to war—a war which American bankers are trying to avert by gaining de facto control of the Japanese government, which will convert Japan into the "watchdog" of American interests in the Far East. Also considers the effect of the American position in the Far East on the Soviet Union.

HA69 GENKIN, I. I. *Soedinennye Shtaty Ameriki i SSSR, ikh politicheskie i ekonomicheskie vzaimootnosheniia.* Moscow-Leningrad: Sotsekgiz, 1934. 125 p. Appeared soon after the diplomatic recognition of the Soviet Union by the U.S., an act which the book ascribes to the realization on the part of "ruling circles" in the U.S. that the importance of the Soviet Union in the political and economic life of the world could no longer be denied. Touches on a variety of facets of relations between the two powers, ranging from the Tsarist debt problem to the effect on the USSR of the Japanese-American "conflict." Discusses the roles played by the various American political parties in the question of recognition of the USSR. Short bibliography of Soviet periodical material and American books; some statistical tables.

HA70 HODGSON, JAMES G., comp. *Recognition of Soviet Russia.* (The Reference Shelf, vol. II, no. 10.) N.Y.: Wilson, 1925. 111 p. A useful collection of excerpts from contemporary articles and speeches on the subject, with a helpful bibliography of books, pamphlets, and articles for and against recognition. Prepared for debaters.

HA71 IVANOV, V., and LEONIAN, V. *V interesakh narodov; k voprosu ob ustanovlenii diplomaticheskikh otnoshenii mezhdu SSSR i SShA v 1933 g.* Moscow: Gospolitizdat, 1957. 161 p. Concentrates on the establishment of diplomatic relations between the U.S. and the USSR and some of the results during the 1930's. Bibliography of English language and Russian sources. Documented. American need of Russia and the benefits of co-existence stressed.

HA72 LOVENSTEIN, MENO. *American Opinion of Soviet Russia.* Washington: American Council on Public Affairs, 1941. 210 p. An Ohio State professor analyzes the attitudes of American newspapers and magazines toward Russia, beginning in 1917. Particularly good on arguments voiced for and against diplomatic recognition. [A]

HA73 McCOY, PRESSLEY CRANE. "An Analysis of the Debates on Recognition of the Union of Soviet Socialist Republics in the United States Senate, 1917-1934." Ph.D. dissertation, Northwestern University, 1954. 899 p. Examines the Senate debates against the historical background of U.S.-Russian relations. The author sees the debates falling into three distinct periods, 1920-21, 1923-24, and 1931-34. The issues treated in the debates are classified in three categories: the legal-moral, the economic and the world-political. Includes a full discussion of the factors which finally brought the Senate to approve recognition.

HA74 MOYER, GEORGE S. *Attitude of the United States Towards the Recognition of Soviet Russia.* Philadelphia: U. of Pennsylvania, 1926. 293 p. A dissertation which considers diplomatic, commercial, ideological, and moral aspects of the problem and concludes that recognition at that time would be unwise, unrewarding, and unwarranted. [B]

HA75 ROOSEVELT, FRANKLIN D. *The Public Papers and Addresses of Franklin D. Roosevelt.* Intro. and Explanatory Notes by Pres. Roosevelt. Vol. II: *The Year of Crisis, 1933.* N.Y.: Random House, 1938. 622 p. Contains the Roosevelt-Litvinov communications on recognition.

HA76 RUSSIA (1923– USSR), NARODNYI KOMISSARIAT PO INOSTRANNYM DELAM. *Sovetsko-amerikanskii otnosheniia 1919-1933.* Moscow: Izd. NKID, 1934. 99 p. A collection of important documents on the relations between the two countries. Significantly omits the exchange of commitments in the Roosevelt-Litvinov recognition correspondence.

HA77 SEVOSTIANOV, G. N. *Aktivnaia rol SShA obrazovanii ochaga voiny na Dalnem Vostoke, 1931-1933.* Edited by A. F. Volchkov. Moscow: Izd. Akademii nauk SSSR, 1953. 245 p. In this work, the U.S. enjoys a monopoly of the role of villain in the chaotic events in the Far East in the first years of the 1930's. The U.S. managed secretly to encourage Japanese aggression in Asia, while at the same time using the Stimson doctrine of non-recognition of Japan's gains by conquest as a tool to secure American hegemony in China. The bibliography gives a wide range of sources, including some of the standard American studies of diplomacy in the Far East, but the inspiration for this history comes from the 34 works of Stalin cited.

HA78 U.S. CONGRESS, SENATE, COMMITTEE ON FOREIGN RELATIONS. *Recognition of Russia; Hearings before a Subcommittee, 68th Congress, 1st Session, pursuant to S. Res. 50 Declaring that the Senate of the United States Favors the Recognition of the Present Soviet Government in Russia.* Washington: G.P.O., 1924. 2 vols. in 1.

4. 1934-1945

(Edited by Henry J. Tobias)

HA79 BARGHOORN, FREDERICK C. *The Soviet Image of the United States; A Study in Distortion.* N.Y.: Harcourt, Brace, 1950. 297 p. By a Yale professor who was Press Attaché in the Moscow Embassy, 1942-1947. Based on personal observations and study of the press and literature. A description of how Soviet communication media pictured the U.S. over a long period, including pre-World War II and the war years. [A]

HA80 BATURIN, M. *SShA i Miunkhen; iz istorii amerikanskoi vneshnei politiki 1937-1938 gg.* Moscow: IMO, 1961. 208 p. A Soviet view of American policy and attitudes on the Munich crisis. Treats Munich as an anti-Soviet move in which the United States connived. Bibliography of English and Russian materials. Far from complete on use of published sources.

HA81 BROWDER, ROBERT P. *The Origins of Soviet-American Diplomacy.* Princeton, N.J.: Princeton University Press, 1953. 256 p. Contains chapters on the recognition of the USSR by the United States, as well as background and results until the summer of 1935. Uses both Soviet and American sources. Objective. Recognition seen as desirable. By a Kansas State University professor of history. [A]

HA82 CARROLL, WALLACE. *We're in This with Russia.* Boston: Houghton Mifflin, 1942, 264 p. Some personal accounts of life in Russia during the early part of World War II. A popular prognosis, by an American correspondent, of postwar possibilities in Russian-American relations.

HA83 CHERNIAVSKY, M. "The History of Soviet Opinion of the United States, 1936-1946, as Expressed in Russian Newspapers, Journals, Books and other Sources." M.A. thesis, U. of California (Berkeley), 1947.

HA84 CONGRESS OF AMERICAN-SOVIET FRIENDSHIP. *American Industry Commemorates the Tenth Anniversary of American-*

Soviet Diplomatic Relations, 1933-43. N.Y.: 1944. Contains testimonials from various industrial firms, illustrating the attitude of wartime friendship and respect held by some Americans toward the Soviet Union.

HA85 CONGRESS OF AMERICAN-SOVIET FRIENDSHIP. *Salute to Our Russian Ally; Report of the Congress of American-Soviet Friendship, New York City, November 7 & 8, 1942*. N.Y.: 1943. 131 p. Wartime statements by important Americans on America and the Soviet war effort. Includes senators, artists, ex-ambassadors. Highly sympathetic toward the Soviets. Valuable as sample of American attitudes during the war period.

HA86 DALLIN, DAVID J. *The Big Three; the United States, Britain, and Russia*. New Haven: Yale, 1945; London: Allen and Unwin, 1946. 232 p. Contains brief sections on U.S.-Soviet relations. Uses Russian materials which give the Soviet attitude toward U.S. policies. Hostile toward the Soviets.

HA87 DAVIES, JOSEPH E. *Mission to Moscow*. N.Y.: Simon and Schuster, 1941; London: Gollancz, 1942. 683 p. Italian ed., Milan: 1946. Spanish ed., Santiago, Chile: 1942. Swedish ed., Stockholm: 1942. French ed., Montreal: 1944. Diary of the U.S. ambassador, 1936-38, with some further notes extending to October, 1941. Also contains official reports and letters; discussion of Russian debt and trade matters; and talks with Litvinov and Stalin. Interesting material regarding the purge trials and relations with Germany. [B]

HA88 DAWSON, RAYMOND H. *The Decision to Aid Russia, 1941*. Chapel Hill: U. of North Carolina Press, 1959. 315 p. A detailed and objective study of the genesis of war aid to Russia in the context of U.S.-Soviet foreign relations and American public opinion. Based on American works and documents.

HA89 DEANE, JOHN R. (GENERAL). *The Strange Alliance; The Story of Our Efforts at Wartime Cooperation with Russia*. N.Y.: Viking, 1947. 344 p. Italian ed., Milan: Garzanti, 1947. German ed., Vienna: Verlag Neue Welt, 1946. The head of the American Military Mission to Russia during World War II describes the difficulties of dealing with the Russians during the heyday of Allied friendship.

HA90 DENNETT, RAYMOND, and JOHNSON, JOSEPH E., eds. *Negotiating with the Russians*. Boston: World Peace Foundation, 1951. 310 p. A collection of reminiscences by Americans who negotiated with the Russians from 1940-47. Explains the difficulties of dealing with Russia from the American point of view. Includes chapters by Philip Mosely, C. E. Black, John Hazard, Raymond Mikesell, and others.

HA91 FEIS, HERBERT. *Between War and Peace; the Potsdam Conference.* Princeton, N.J.: Princeton University Press, 1960. 367 p. Far the best work on the subject. Deals with the end of the war and the end of collaboration between the Russians and the Americans. Thorough and objective. One of a series of outstanding studies by a former American diplomat. This book won the Pulitzer Prize for history. [A]

HA92 FEIS, HERBERT. *Churchill, Roosevelt, and Stalin; the War They Waged and the Peace They Sought.* Princeton, N.J.: Princeton University Press, 1957. 692 p. The best overall account of wartime relations among the Big Three. Based on a wide range of sources, including some of Averell Harriman's papers. [A]

HA93 GERBERDING, WILLIAM P. "Franklin D. Roosevelt's Conception of the Soviet Union in World Politics." Ph.D. dissertation, U. of Chicago, 1959.

HA94 GUS, M. *Amerikanskie imperialisty—vdokhnoviteli miunkhenskoi politiki.* Moscow: Gospolitizdat, 1951. 245 p. German ed., *Die amerikanischen imperialisten als inspiratoren der Münchener politik.* Berlin: Dietz, 1954. 253 p. A Communist interpretation of the U.S. attitude toward Russia from the 1930's to 1945, with special emphasis on the Munich crisis. Attacks U.S. policy as hostile to Soviet Union.

HA95 HORGAN, ROBERT J. "Some American Opinion of the Soviet Union, 1933-1939." Ph.D. dissertation, Notre Dame, 1959.

HA96 HULL, CORDELL. *The Memoirs of Cordell Hull.* N.Y.: Macmillan, 1948. 2 vols. Extensive, detailed account of his tenure as American Secretary of State, 1933-44. Has chapters on his talks with Soviet leaders, including the Moscow Conference, and on the formulation of American policy toward Russia. [A]

HA97 JORDAN, GEORGE R., with STOKES, RICHARD L. *From Major Jordan's Diaries.* N.Y.: Harcourt, Brace, 1952. 284 p. Jordan was a Lend-Lease expediter, 1942-44. Relates evidence of shipments to Russians of materials (heavy water, uranium compounds) that went beyond the actual agreements, and which he considers to be part of a Communist conspiracy.

HA97A KUTER, LAURENCE S. *Airman at Yalta.* N.Y.: Duell, Sloan and Pearce, 1955. 180 p. General Kuter represented the U.S. Air Force at Yalta. His point here is that the U.S. did not make the sweeping concessions to the Russians claimed by later critics of American policy.

HA98 LANGER, WILLIAM L., and GLEASON, S. EVERETT. *The Challenge to Isolation, 1937-1940.* N.Y.: Harper, for the Council on Foreign Relations, 1952. 794 p. A semi-official account by two eminent historians of American foreign policy during the years leading to World War II. Fully documented.

HA99 LANGER, WILLIAM L., and GLEASON, S. EVERETT. *The Undeclared War, 1940-1941*. N.Y.: Harper, for the Council on Foreign Relations, 1953. 963 p. A continuation of *The Challenge to Isolation* and of equally high quality.

HA100 LAUTER, BEATRICE BRODSKY. "William C. Bullitt and the Soviet Union: The Education of a Diplomat." Ph.D. dissertation, Yale, 1959.

HA101 LEAHY, WILLIAM D. *I Was There*. N.Y.: Whittlesey House, 1950. 527 p. Admiral Leahy was Chief of Staff to Roosevelt 1941 to 1945. His war notes are the basis for the book. Important on military policy matters. He attended and comments on all the major wartime conferences with the Russians. Objective. [B]

HA102 McCLELLAND, ROBERT C. "The Soviet Union in American Opinion, 1933-1942." Ph.D. dissertation, U. of West Virginia, 1951.

HA103 MATLOFF, MAURICE, and SNELL, EDWIN M. *Strategic Planning for Coalition Warfare, 1941-42, 1943-44*. Washington: Office of the Chief of Military History, 1953-59. 2 vols. Deals with American military strategy regarding the Second Front and relating to the Tehran and Moscow Conferences. Objective, critical bibliography.

HA104 MELNIKOV, IURII M. *SShA i gitlerovskaia Germaniia, 1933-1939 gg*. Moscow: Gospolitizdat, 1959. 351 p.

HA105 MILLSPAUGH, ARTHUR C. *Americans in Persia*. Washington: The Brookings Institution, 1946. 293 p. First-hand experiences of the Administrator General of Finances in Persia, 1943-45. Describes Russo-American contacts there. An apologia, but a useful document.

HA106 MOTTER, T. H. VAIL. *The Persian Corridor and Aid to Russia*. Washington: Office of the Chief of Military History, Dept. of the Army, 1952. 545 p. Provides both large political and narrow army contexts of American activities in Iran, 1941-45, with emphasis on how supplies got to the Russians and U.S. relations with Russia. Indicates America's growing awareness of its Middle East position in relation to Russia. Heavily documented. Based on official sources.

HA107 RODOV, B. *Rol SShA i Iaponii v podgotovke i razviazyvanii voiny na Tikhom Okeane, 1938-1941 gg*. Moscow: Gospolitizdat, 1951. 198 p.

HA108 RUSSIA (1923– USSR), KOMISSIIA PO IZDANIIU DIPLOMATICHESKIKH DOKUMENTOV. *Correspondence between the Chairman of the Council of Ministers of the USSR and the Presidents of the USA and the Prime Ministers of Great Britain During the Great Patriotic War of 1941-1945.* Vol. II, *Correspondence with Franklin D. Roosevelt and Harry S. Truman, August 1941–December 1945.* Moscow: Foreign Languages Publishing House, 1957. 302 p. Russian ed., Moscow: Gospolitizdat, 1957. Other English eds., N.Y.: Dutton; London: Lawrence and Wishart, 1958. A significant volume which attempts to alter to some extent the impressions produced by American memoirs. Far from complete, but valuable. [B]

HA109 SCHWARTZ, ANDREW J. *America and the Russo-Finnish War.* Intro. by Quincy Wright. Washington: Public Affairs, 1960. 103 p. After examining the cautious attempts of the neutralist U.S. to aid Finland during the "Winter War," the author shows the strains placed upon the traditionally good American-Finnish relations when Finland reentered the war by joining Hitler in his attack on the USSR. When it was clear that Germany was heading toward defeat, the U.S. was able to use its good offices to bring Finland to switch sides and later to moderate the Soviet Union's demands on Finland. A well-documented study.

HA110 SHERWOOD, ROBERT E. *Roosevelt and Hopkins; An Intimate History.* N.Y.: Harper, 1948. 979 p. Rev. edition, N.Y.: 1950. 1002 p. By the famous playwright and speech writer for Roosevelt. Its value for Soviet-American relations is restricted largely to the war years. Extensive use of important papers belonging to Hopkins on Lend-Lease and wartime meetings with Stalin. Favorable to Roosevelt generally and skillfully done. [A]

HA111 SOBEL, ROBERT. *The Origins of Interventionism: The United States and the Russo-Finnish War.* N.Y.: Bookman Associates, 1960. 204 p. In this rather over-simplified study of the U.S. attitude toward the Winter War, the thesis is advanced that the small amount of aid from the U.S. to Finland set a precedent for more substantial grants to beleaguered states during and after World War II. Based on the Roosevelt Papers, the press, government publications, and secondary sources.

HA112 STANDLEY, WILLIAM H., and AGETON, ARTHUR A. *Admiral Ambassador to Russia.* Chicago: Regnery, 1955. 533 p. By the Admiral who was American ambassador to Russia from April, 1942 until October, 1943. Some interesting comments on wartime plans. Almost as hostile to Americans as to the Soviets.

HA113 STETTINIUS, EDWARD R., JR. *Lend-Lease; Weapon for Victory.* N.Y.: Macmillan, 1944. 358 p. German ed., Leipzig: List,

1946. By the former Lend-Lease administrator. Includes comments by Hull and Roosevelt. Reflects the spirit of wartime good will toward the Russians. Supplies to Russia are given considerable attention.

HA114 STETTINIUS, EDWARD R., JR. *Roosevelt and the Russians; the Yalta Conference*. Ed. by Walter Johnson. Garden City, N.Y.: Doubleday, 1949. 367 p. French ed., Paris; 1951. A University of Chicago professor's account of Yalta, based on the Stettinius papers at the University of Virginia and written from the former Secretary of State's point of view. Pro-Roosevelt. [A]

HA115 STIMSON, HENRY L., and BUNDY, McGEORGE. *On Active Service in Peace and War*. N.Y.: Harper, 1948. 698 p. By the American Secretary of War during World War II. Provides information on the beginnings of problems with Russia during the war and the atomic bomb.

HA116 SURVEY OF INTERNATIONAL AFFAIRS, 1920-1923—THE WAR-TIME SERIES FOR 1939-1946. Ed. by A. J. Toynbee. Vol. 3. McNEILL, WILLIAM H. *America, Britain, and Russia; Their Co-operation and Conflict, 1941-1946*. N.Y.: Oxford, for the Royal Institute of International Affairs, 1953. 819 p. A masterful, scholarly study of relations among the Big Three during World War II. Based on materials published in Western languages. Has to a great extent been superseded, however, by Feis's three volumes, based upon archival materials. [A]

HA117 TROIANOVSKII, A. *Pochemu SShA voiuiut protiv gitlerovskoi Germanii*. Moscow: Gospolitizdat, 1942. 112 p.

HA118 U.S. DEPARTMENT OF STATE. *The Conferences at Malta and Yalta, 1945*. Washington: G.P.O., 1955. 1032 p. German ed., Vienna: 1955. The fullest single-volume documentation on pre-conference and conference meetings. Relies on Bohlen, Hiss and Matthews notes and Moscow Embassy files. Important. [A]

HA119 U.S. DEPARTMENT OF STATE. *Foreign Relations of the United States; Diplomatic Papers; Europe, 1942*. Vol. III. Washington: G.P.O., 1961. 869 p. Negotiations between the United States and the Russians involving the prosecution of the war, supplies, trade relations, and treatment of U.S. citizens. [B]

HA119A U.S. DEPARTMENT OF STATE. *Foreign Relations of the United States; Diplomatic Papers; The British Commonwealth, The Soviet Union, The Near East and Africa, 1940*. Washington: G.P.O., 1958. American-Russian relations with respect to trade and the ill-feeling surrounding the war with Finland and the situation in the Baltic states.

HA120 U.S. DEPARTMENT OF STATE. *Foreign Relations of the United States; Diplomatic Papers, 1941; The Soviet Union.* Vol. I. Washington: G.P.O., 1958. 1948 p. A large collection of diplomatic dispatches to and from American embassies on Soviet activities in Eastern Europe and relations with belligerent powers. American responses to Soviet policy toward the Polish Government-in-Exile, American aid to the USSR, embassy problems, and the Russian attitude toward Japan. Important source. [A]

HA121 U.S. DEPARTMENT OF STATE. *Foreign Relations of the United States; Diplomatic Papers; The Conferences at Cairo and Tehran, 1943.* Washington: G.P.O., 1961. 932 p. State Department files plus materials drawn from private sources dealing with wartime meetings concerning the prosecution of the war. [A]

HA122 U.S. DEPARTMENT OF STATE. *Foreign Relations of the United States; Diplomatic Papers; The Conference of Berlin (The Potsdam Conference), 1945.* Washington: G.P.O., 1960. 2 vols. Volume I contains the background reports for the liquidation of war problems, Japan, the United States and Russia. Volume II concerns meetings, discussions of reparations, implementation of Yalta, the German and the Polish questions. Important. [A]

HA123 U.S. DEPARTMENT OF STATE. *Foreign Relations of the United States; Diplomatic Papers; The Soviet Union, 1933-1939.* Washington: G.P.O., 1952. 1034 p. American and some Russian documents relating to U.S. recognition of the USSR; questions of American claims; the Russian desire for credits; the Communist movement in the U.S. and Russian attitude toward it; trade discussion; 1935 trade agreement; and subsequent arrangements. An important source. [A]

HA124 U.S. DEPARTMENT OF STATE. *Foreign Relations of the United States; Papers Relating to Japan: 1931-1941.* Vol. II. Washington: G.P.O., 1943. 816 p. American-Japanese documents relating to the Russian entry into World War II and the problems of American aid to Russia and neutrality. [B]

HA125 U.S. DEPARTMENT OF STATE. *Foreign Relations of the United States; The Far East, 1941.* Vol. IV. Washington: G.P.O., 1956. 1044 p. The triangular relationship between the United States, Japan, and the Soviet Union with respect to the European War, the Russian entry into it and neutrality. [B]

HA126 WALLACE, HENRY A., and STEIGER, ANDREW J. *Soviet Asia Mission.* N.Y.: Reynal, 1946, 254 p. A popular account by Vice-President Wallace of his trip to Russia. Considers Russian conditions and post-war possibilities. An example of one American attitude toward the end of the war; sympathetic toward Russian accomplishments. Wallace's speeches included.

HA127 WELLES, SUMNER. *Seven Decisions That Shaped History.* N.Y.: Harper, 1951. 236 p. British ed., *Seven Major Decisions.* London: Hamilton, 1951. 224 p. By the Under Secretary of State under Hull. An analysis of policies, some of which he helped to shape. Includes conversations with Roosevelt respecting the position of Russia in the Far East during World War II. Defends Roosevelt. Comparatively little on Russia.

HA128 WOODBRIDGE, GEORGE, comp. *UNRRA.* N.Y.: Columbia, 1950. 3 vols. An official history. Volume I treats organization and administration; Volume II deals with field activities; and Volume III is devoted to documents.

5. 1945-1963

(Edited by John C. Campbell)

HA129 ABHAYAVARDHAN, HECTOR. *Russo-American rivalry in Asia.* Bombay: Vora, 1954. 182 p.

HA130 AKADEMIIA NAUK SSSR, INSTITUT EKONOMIKI. *Agressivnaia ideologiia i politika amerikanskogo imperializma.* Ed. by K. V. Ostrovitianov and others. Moscow: Gosplanizdat, 1950. 487 p. A collaborative work covering many aspects of American capitalism, militarism, and imperialism, with chapters on U.S. policy in Europe, the Middle East, the Pacific area, and Latin America. A final chapter deals with "progressive forces" in the U.S.A. [B]

HA131 AKADEMIIA NAUK SSSR, INSTITUT EKONOMIKI. *Militarizatsiia ekonomiki SShA i ukhudshenie polozheniia trudiashchikhsia.* Ed. by M. I. Rubinshtein. Moscow: Izd. Akad. nauk SSSR, 1953. 383 p. A collaborative work by eight authors consisting mainly of a Marxist analysis of the American economy since World War II. Includes long contributions on "aggressive" American policies in Europe and the colonial areas, and on "the struggle of the American people against militarism and for peace and democracy."

HA132 AKADEMIIA NAUK SSSR, INSTITUT MIROVOI EKONOMIKI I MEZHDUNARODNYKH OTNOSHENII. *Monopolisticheskii kapital SShA posle Vtoroi mirovoi voiny.* Edited by M. I. Rubinshtein and others. Moscow: Izd. Akad. nauk SSSR, 1958. 674 p. A Soviet interpretation of the American economy. A long final chapter by I. M. Lemin deals with "monopoly and foreign policy."

HA133 AKADEMIIA NAUK SSSR, INSTITUT MIROVOI EKONOMIKI I MEZHDUNARODNYKH OTNOSHENII. *Problemy sovremennogo kapitalizma.* Moscow: Izd. Akad. nauk SSSR, 1959. 400 p. A collection of essays dedicated to the economist Eugene Varga. The emphasis is on economic theory and analysis, but it is nevertheless a good example of Soviet thinking on the basic economic factors underlying U.S. foreign policy.

HA134 ALEKSEEV, ALEKSANDR M. *Atomnaia problema i politika SShA "s pozitsii sily."* Moscow: Gospolitizdat, 1955. 99 p.

HA135 AMERICAN ACADEMY OF POLITICAL AND SOCIAL SCIENCE, PHILADELPHIA. *Resolving the Russian-American Deadlock.* Ed. by James C. Charlesworth. Philadelphia, 1959. 210 p. (*Its Annals*, v. 324.) Short articles by a variety of authors including David J. Dallin, James P. Warburg, and Louis Fischer; more interesting in showing how the deadlock looked in 1959 than in proposals for resolving it.

HA136 ANDREEV, G. *Ekspansiia dollara.* Moscow: Sotsekgiz, 1961. 480 p.

HA137 BALDWIN, HANSON W. *The Great Arms Race; a Comparison of U.S. and Soviet Power Today.* N.Y.: Praeger, 1958. 116 p. An expert and sober presentation by the military analyst of *The New York Times.*

HA138 BARATASHVILI, D. I. *Amerikanskie teorii mezhdunarodnogo prava.* Moscow: Gosizdat iurid. lit., 1956. 113 p. A critical analysis of contemporary American doctrines of international law, by a Soviet jurist.

HA139 BOUSCAREN, ANTHONY T. *America Faces World Communism.* N.Y.: Vantage Press, 1954. 196 p. A plea for stronger policies against Communism both at home and abroad, based on an interpretation of the past that combines fact with oversimplified analysis.

HA140 BROWDER, EARL R. *War or Peace with Russia?* N.Y.: A. A. Wyn, 1947. 190 p. Writing after his removal from leadership and expulsion from the American Communist Party, Browder examines Soviet-American relations and the issues at stake, and denounces the "sharp change" in U.S. attitudes and the policies of Truman and Byrnes which refuse the USSR's "reasonable terms" for a lasting peace.

HA141 BUCAR, ANNABELLE. *The Truth About American Diplomats.* Moscow: Literaturnaia Gazeta, 1949. 197 p. (Editions in several other languages.) An exposé of U.S. diplomacy and diplomats, nominally written by a defector from the clerical staff of the American Embassy in Moscow; published for propaganda purposes.

HA142 BUKHAROV, BORIS I. *Voprosy dalnevostochnoi politiki SShA, 1953-1955 gg.* Moscow: Akad. nauk SSSR, 1959. 238 p. Although limited in time and area, this book is of some interest in its account of U.S. policy on two crucial questions, the Korean armistice and the Indochina crisis.

HA143 BURNHAM, JAMES. *The Struggle for the World.* N.Y.: John Day. 248 p. London: Jonathan Cape, 1947. 334 p. French ed., *Pour La Domination Mondiale.* Paris: Calmann-Levy, 1947. An exposition of Soviet aims and policies as seen by an American ex-Communist advocating strong anti-Communist policies for a democratic world order, as opposed to a policy of vacillation which can only end in war or surrender.

HA144 BYRNES, JAMES F. *Speaking Frankly.* N.Y.: Harper, 1947. 324 p. London: Heinemann, 336 p. Memoirs of the former U.S. Secretary of State dealing with the diplomacy of his period in office (1945-47). His story contains few revelations not in the public record, but is of interest in illustrating his own ideas on Soviet-American relations. [B]

HA145 CARR, ALBERT Z. *Truman, Stalin and Peace.* N.Y.: Doubleday, 1950. 256 p. A journalistic and spotty account of Truman and the Cold War.

HA146 CHAMBERLIN, WILLIAM H. *Beyond Containment.* Chicago: Regnery, 1953. 406 p. A review of basic Soviet aims and policies, together with a sharply critical analysis of American policy toward Russia under Roosevelt and Truman, by a well known journalist who favors a stronger American stand in the Cold War. [B]

HA147 DALIN, S. A. *Voenno-gosudarstvenyi monopolisticheskii kapitalizm v SShA.* Moscow: Izd. Akad. nauk SSSR, 1961. 352 p.

HA148 DEAN, VERA M. *The United States and Russia.* Cambridge: Harvard, 1947. 321 p. Rev. ed., 1948. 336 p. A popular survey which bears the imprint of the optimistic hopes for cooperation which marked the war period, and also of the Cold War just beginning. [B]

HA149 DENNY, BREWSTER C. "The Soviet Evaluation of the Instruments and Intentions of Postwar American Foreign Policy, 1952-1956." Ph.D. dissertation, Fletcher, 1959.

HA150 DMITRIEV, B. *Pentagon i vneshniaia politika SShA.* Moscow: Izd. IMO, 1961. 286 p.

HA151 DRUMMOND, ROSCOE, and COBLENTZ, GASTON. *Duel at the Brink; John Foster Dulles' Command of American Power.* Garden City, N.Y.: Doubleday, 1960. 240 p. Although concentrating almost entirely on Secretary of State Dulles and U.S. policy, this informed book by two journalists contains some useful material on Soviet-American relations seen from that angle.

HA152 DULLES, JOHN FOSTER. *War or Peace*. N.Y.: Macmillan, 1950. 274 p. 2nd ed., 1957. Interesting because the author states his views on Soviet-American relations before becoming Secretary of State; these can be compared with his statements and actions while in office.

HA153 DUNHAM, DONALD. *Kremlin Target: U.S.A., Conquest by Propaganda*. N.Y.: Ives Washburn, 1961. A former U.S. information officer in Europe gives his views on how Moscow is using propaganda to fight the U.S. and what we should do about it. Tends to exaggerate the effectiveness of Soviet propaganda.

HA154 FISCHER, JOHN. *Master Plan U.S.A., An Informal Report on America's Foreign Policy and the Men Who Make It*. N.Y.: Harper, 1951. 253 p. British ed., *America's Master Plan*. London: Hamilton, 1951. The Cold War seen from the American side, with a description of American grand strategy and some suggested changes, by the editor of *Harper's*.

HA155 FISCHER, JOHN. *Why They Behave Like Russians*. N.Y.: Harper, 1947. 262 p. The editor of *Harper's* had a brief tour of duty in the Ukraine with UNRRA after World War II and subsequently wrote down his feelings about the prospects for Soviet-American relations.

HA156 FISCHER, LOUIS. *Russia, America, and the World*. N.Y.: Harper, 1961. 244 p. A rather diffuse but generally sound essay on the state of the world at the end of the 1950's. Not comparable to the author's earlier work on Soviet foreign relations.

HA157 FISHER, HAROLD H. *America and Russia in the World Community*. Claremont, Calif.: Claremont College, 1946. 175 p. A series of lectures delivered near the close of World War II. Partly historical, they also include an informed and balanced presentation of the alternatives facing the two peoples and the two systems at that time.

HA158 FLEMING, DENNA F. *The Cold War and Its Origins*. Garden City, N.Y.: Doubleday, 1961. 2 vols. A detailed history of Soviet-American relations and conflicting strategies since World War I. The author has a strong thesis of his own which puts on the U.S. most of the responsibility for the origins and continuation of the Cold War.

HA159 FOREIGN POLICY CLEARING HOUSE, WASHINGTON, D.C. *Strategy for the 60's*. Ed. by Jay H. Cerf and Walter Pozen, with intro. by Senator J. W. Fulbright. N.Y.: Praeger, 1961. 155 p. Summary and analysis of thirteen studies on U.S. foreign policy, commissioned in 1959 by the Committee on Foreign Relations of the U.S.

Senate. The challenge of Communism and Soviet foreign policy is a main theme.

HA160 GRECHEV, M. A. *Kolonialnaia politika SShA posle Vtoroi mirovoi voiny.* Moscow: Izd. Akad. nauk SSSR, 1958. 383 p. Presents the history of U.S. policy in the postwar period as one of imperialism and colonialism, with particular emphasis given to Latin America and the Far East. The author cites many American sources but only to suit his own predetermined thesis. [B]

HA161 GUILHERME, OLYMPIO. *U.R.S.S. and U.S.A.* 2nd ed., Rio de Janeiro: Livraria Prado, 1955. 347 p. A well-presented survey of the Cold War and analvsis of its issues by a Brazilian economist and historian. No new material but an interesting interpretation.

HA162 HAHN, WALTER F., and NEFF, JOHN C., eds. *American Strategy for the Nuclear Age.* Garden City, N.Y.: Anchor, 1960. 455 p. A collection of papers and essays on various aspects of American strategy and policy, most of them bearing on Soviet-American relations. A number of the contributions were previously published elsewhere.

HA163 HALLE, LOUIS J. *Civilization and Foreign Policy; An Inquiry for Americans.* Introd. by Dean Acheson. N.Y.: Harper, 1955. 277 p. British ed., *The Nature of Power; Civilization and Foreign Policy.* London: R. Hart-Davis, 1955. A philosophical inquiry into various topics: the nature of political power, the American posture in the world arena, the essence of a foreign policy. A large part of the book is devoted to the challenges of the Soviet Union and Communism; it is based on a lucid account of the development of the Soviet system. The author, a former State Department official and University of Virginia professor, now teaches at the Graduate Institute of International Studies in Geneva.

HA164 HARRIMAN, AVERELL. *Peace With Russia?* N.Y.: Simon and Schuster, 1959. 174 p. An account of a visit to the USSR in 1959 by a former U.S. Ambassador to Moscow. The author gives his impressions of the temper of the people, the changes in the economy, and the political leadership.

HA165 HOWLEY, FRANK L. *Berlin Command.* N.Y.: Putnam, 1950. 276 p. A very personal and frequently belligerent account of experiences by the American garrison commander during the Berlin Blockade.

HA166 KENNAN, GEORGE F. *American Diplomacy, 1900-1950.* N.Y.: New American Library, 1952. 144 p. A series of lectures and articles, including two important articles originally in *Foreign Affairs,* "The Sources of Soviet Conduct" (July, 1947) and "America and the Russian Future" (April, 1951). [A]

HA167 KENNAN, GEORGE F. *Russia, the Atom, and the West.* London: Oxford, 1958. 120 p. N.Y.: Harper, 1958. 116 p. The Reith Lectures given over the B.B.C. in the autumn of 1957, when they had considerable impact on European opinion. Their most controversial theme was "disengagement" in Central Europe. [B]

HA168 KHRUSHCHEV, NIKITA S. *Khrushchev in America; Full Texts of the Speeches Made by N. S. Khrushchev on His Tour of the United States, September 15-27, 1959.* N.Y.: Crosscurrents, 1960. 231 p. Russian ed., *Zhit v mire i druzhbe.* Moscow: 1959. 444 p. The official version of Khrushchev's talks. The presentation (including pictures) is intended to give the impression of a triumphal tour.

HA169 KIEFFER, JOHN E. *Strategy for Survival.* N.Y.: McKay, 1953. 306 p. A brief survey of Soviet purposes and strategy, followed by a recommended positive strategy for the West, including plans for fighting the next war and de-communizing Russia after it is won.

HA170 KISSINGER, HENRY A. *The Necessity for Choice: Prospects of American Foreign Policy.* N.Y.: Harper, 1961. 370 p. The analysis is of American policy in the context of the Soviet threat. It represents hard and sometimes original thinking on political-military strategy. [B]

HA171 KORIONOV, V. G. *Amerikanskii imperializm—zleishii vrag narodov.* Moscow: Gospolitizdat, 1951. 182 p. 2nd ed., 1952. 338 p. Interesting only as a reflection of the "tough" Soviet line of the late Stalin years. The author exposes American "imperialism" in Eastern Europe, the "Marshallization" of Western Europe, and the "aggression" in Korea.

HA172 KUNINA, A. E. *Krovavyi amerikanskii imperializm.* Moscow: Gospolitizdat, 1952. 132 p. German ed., *Das wahre Gesicht des amerikanischen Imperialismus.* Berlin: Dietz, 1954. 140 p. A sketchy "history" of American imperialism, beginning before World War I. Reflects the spirit of the late Stalin period.

HA173 LEMIN, IOSIF M. *Anglo-amerikanskie protivorechiia posle Vtoroi mirovoi voiny.* Moscow: Izd. Akad. nauk SSSR, 1955. 485 p. More than a study of Anglo-American relations, this book dwells on the broader questions of the Cold War in Europe, as seen from Moscow, and on the "struggle for peace" by the "socialist camp."

HA174 LEONTEV, LEV A. *Imperializm dollara v zapadnoi Evrope.* Moscow: Gospolitizdat, 1949. 418 p. Covers both the inter-war years and the post-World War II period, concentrating on the theme of American domination of Europe through the Marshall Plan and preparations for a new war.

HA175 LIPPMANN, WALTER. *The Cold War; A Study in U.S. Foreign Policy.* N.Y.: Harper, 1947. 62 p. A collection of articles in which Mr. Lippmann gives his critique of the policy of "containment" of Russia set forth by George Kennan's "X" article in the July 1947 issue of *Foreign Affairs.*

HA176 LIPPMANN, WALTER. *The Communist World and Ours.* Boston: Atlantic (Little, Brown), 1959. 56 p. Report on a long talk with Khrushchev in 1958, plus Mr. Lippmann's own reflections on Soviet and American policy.

HA177 LUKACS, JOHN. *A History of the Cold War.* N.Y.: Doubleday, 1961, 288 p. A very personal approach to history, in which the author puts forward some theories of his own and speculates, often brilliantly, on what lies behind Soviet and American policies.

HA178 MARZANI, CARL. *We Can Be Friends.* Foreword by Dr. W. E. B. Dubois. N.Y.: Topical Books, 1952. 380 p. Interesting only as an attempt, using American sources almost exclusively, to defend Soviet policy and condemn U.S. policy over the years 1945-52.

HA179 MASLENNIKOV, VIACHESLAV A., ed. *Uglublenie krizisa kolonialnoi sistemy imperializma posle Vtoroi mirovoi voiny.* Moscow: Gospolitizdat, 1953. 605 p. A series of studies by Soviet authors on the struggle against colonialism and imperialism in the Far East, Middle East, Africa, and Latin America, with the United States cast in the role of principal imperialist power.

HA180 MASLENNIKOV, VIACHESLAV A., and others, eds. *Amerikanskii plan zakabaleniia Evropy; sbornik statei.* Moscow: Gospolitizdat, 1949. 598 p. A broadside against the Marshall Plan delivered shortly after its adoption. The authors take up in separate chapters American relations with individual Western European countries to illustrate the main theme of domination. Useful as a detailed statement of the Soviet position.

HA181 MASSACHUSETTS INSTITUTE OF TECHNOLOGY, CENTER FOR INTERNATIONAL STUDIES. *Some Aspects of United States Policy Towards the Soviet Union and its European Satellites.* Intro. by W. W. Rostow. Cambridge: 1953. 142 p. A venture in assessment and speculation concerning trends in the Soviet bloc and their significance for American policy. Dated but still useful.

HA182 MENSHIKOV, STANISLAV M. *Amerikanskie monopolii na mirovom kapitalisticheskom rynke.* Moscow: Sotsekgiz, 1958. 355 p. To illustrate his arguments on American monopolies and economic imperialism, the author makes heavy and tendentious use of Western sources. U.S. foreign trade policy is analyzed in the framework of the drives of American monopoly capital.

HA183 MICHIGAN, UNIVERSITY, SURVEY RESEARCH CENTER. *Attitudes toward United States-Russian Relations; October, 1948; A National Survey.* Ann Arbor: U. of Michigan, 1948. 94 p. The result of interviews with several hundred Americans, taken as a cross section of the population, in December 1946 and January 1947. A professional job, but obviously limited in its usefulness.

HA184 MOSELY, PHILIP E. *Face to Face With Russia.* N.Y.: Foreign Policy Assn., 1948. 63 p. A brief, but informative, account by an expert on Russian affairs who had recent experience in negotiations with Soviet representatives. It is published together with a short piece on "The Economics of Soviet Foreign Policy" by Harry Schwartz. The author was Director of the Russian Institute at Columbia University before becoming Director of Studies at the Council on Foreign Relations.

HA185 MOSELY, PHILIP E. *The Kremlin and World Politics.* N.Y.: Random House, Vintage Books, 1960. 557 p. A series of perceptive articles written over a period of years analyzing Soviet foreign policies and the issues they present for America. [A]

HA186 MOSTOVETS, N. *Progressivnye sily SShA v borbe za mir.* Moscow: Gospolitizdat, 1951. 111 p. A propaganda effort "exposing" American aggression in Korea and preparations for war in Europe, and calling for peace through the Stockholm Peace Appeal.

HA187 *O voennoi ideologii amerikanskogo imperializma; sbornik statei.* By V. Khlopov and others. Moscow: Voenizdat, 1951. 155 p. A series of articles by Soviet military writers on the strategic doctrines of the ruling group in the U.S. The writings of John Foster Dulles, Major General J.F.C. Fuller and Captain B. H. Liddell Hart, among others, are analyzed.

HA188 PERLA, LEO. *Can We End the Cold War? A Study in American Foreign Policy.* N.Y.: Macmillan, 1960. 251 p. Strongly critical of U.S. foreign policy, the author recommends a new approach based on true negotiation, reconciliation, and trust and faith in others.

HA189 POTAPOVA, A. A. *Eksport kapitala—orudie ekspansii SShA posle Vtoroi mirovoi voiny.* Moscow: Izd. Akad. nauk SSSR, 1958. 238 p. Primarily an economic study, but the detailed discussions on American private investment abroad and on U.S. governmental programs of foreign aid are useful in showing Soviet reasoning based on wide use of American sources.

HA190 POWERS, FRANCIS GARY, 1929–, DEFENDANT. *The Trial of the U2: Exclusive Authorized Account of the Court Proceedings of the Case of Francis Gary Powers Heard before the Military Division of the Supreme Court of the U.S.S.R., Moscow, August 17, 18, 19, 1960.* Intro. by Harold J. Berman. Chicago: Translation World Publishers, 1960. 158 p. British ed., London: Soviet Booklets, 1960. 92 p. French ed., N.P.: 1960. 126 p. Russian ed., Moscow: Gospolitizdat, 1960. 183 p. Essential to any study of the U-2 incident and the Soviet means of handling it. The introduction provides some of the background.

HA191 RAKOVE, MILTON L. "American Attitudes Towards Negotiations With the Soviet Union." Ph.D. dissertation, U. of Chicago, 1956. 263 p.

HA192 REITZEL, WILLIAM; KAPLAN, MORTON A., and COBLENZ, CONSTANCE G. *United States foreign policy, 1945-1955.* Washington: Brookings Institution, 1956. 535 p. A valuable survey, organized so as to present and analyze issues rather than merely to record events. American strategy in the face of the Communist threat is a main theme. [B]

HA193 ROBERTS, HENRY L. *Russia and America; Dangers and Prospects.* Foreword by John J. McCloy. N.Y.: Harper, for the Council of Foreign Relations, 1956. 251 p. Paperback ed., N.Y.: New American Library, 1956. Japanese ed., Tokyo: 1956. A penetrating study of Soviet-American relations in the mid 1950's, with recommendations for U.S. policy, prepared with the advice of an expert study group. The author was Director of the Russian Institute at Columbia University.

HA194 ROBERTS, LESLIE. *Home from the Cold Wars.* Boston: Beacon, 1948. 224 p. A rather superficial report of a Canadian journalist, whose main theme is "a plague on both your houses."

HA195 RYMALOV, V. V. *Kolonialnaia ekspansiia finansovogo kapitala SShA pod flagom "pomoshchi."* Moscow: Gospolitizdat, 1956. 200 p. A Party-line analysis of the U.S. foreign aid program, drawing on U.S. materials for statistics and on Khrushchev's pronouncements for interpretation.

HA196 SAINT-PHALLE, ALEXANDRE DE. *Pax Americana.* Paris: Julliard, 1948. 236 p. A Frenchman's reflections on America's world role and the Cold War. A stimulating, subjective book that has not been wholly outdated by the passage of time.

HA197 SALISBURY, HARRISON E. *American in Russia.* N.Y.: Harper, 1955. 328 p. The personal story of the Moscow correspondent of *The New York Times* covering the last years of Stalin's rule and the first of the new regime.

HA198 SALISBURY, HARRISON E. *To Moscow—And Beyond.* N.Y.: Harper, 1960. 301 p. A report on the USSR in 1959 based on two trips there and on the author's previous knowledge of Soviet affairs through service as resident correspondent of *The New York Times.* There is additional material on Outer Mongolia. The reflections on Soviet policy and the recommendations on American policy are very much the author's own.

HA199 SCHLESINGER, JAMES R. *The Political Economy of National Security.* N.Y.: Praeger, 1960. 292 p.

HA200 SELDES, GEORGE H. *The People Don't Know; the American Press and the Cold War.* N.Y.: Gaer, 1949. 342 p. Mr. Seldes has for several decades been conducting a crusade against the American press, accusing it of giving its readers a one-sided version of the news. This particular book is designed to prove that the American public does not get the truth about the Cold War. Though the author cites some striking examples of bias in U.S. newspapers, his own bias is at least as strong.

HA201 SELLEN, ALBERT R. "Congressional Opinion of Soviet-American Relations, 1945-50." Ph.D. dissertation, U. of Chicago, 1955.

HA202 SETON-WATSON, HUGH. *Neither War nor Peace: The Struggle for Power in the Postwar World.* N.Y.: Praeger; London: Methuen, 1960. 504 p. A general work covering a wide canvass of postwar developments, omitting some of the main issues in Soviet-American relationships and conflicts, but particularly good on Soviet strategy and techniques and on issues of relationship with the West. [A]

HA203 SMITH, WALTER BEDELL. *My Three Years in Moscow.* Philadelphia: Lippincott, 1950. 346 p. British ed., *Moscow Mission, 1946-1949.* London: Heinemann, 1950. Memoirs of the General who was American Ambassador to the USSR in the years which saw the Moscow Conference on Germany, the Berlin blockade, and Stalin's break with Tito. Informative but without notable revelations. [B]

HA204 *SShA proigryvaiut ekonomicheskoe sorevnovanie.* Moscow: Gospolitizdat, 1961.

HA205 *SSSR-SShA; tsifry i fakty.* Moscow: Gospolitizdat, 1961. 134 p.

HA206 STEVENS, LESLIE C. (VICE ADMIRAL). *Russian Assignment.* Boston: Little, Brown, 1953. 568 p. An eminently readable and generally sound estimate of the USSR by an experienced American observer who served as U.S. Naval Attaché in Moscow.

HA207 STRAUSZ-HUPE, ROBERT; KINTNER, WILLIAM, and POSSONY, STEFAN T. *A Forward Strategy for America.* N.Y.: Harper, 1961. 451 p. Adjures the U.S. to take a tougher line in the struggle with Communism and to back it up with a strengthening of its moral fiber.

HA208 TRUMAN, HARRY S. *Memoirs.* Garden City, N.Y.: Doubleday; London: Hodder and Stoughton, 1955-56. 2 vols. German ed., Bern: 1955-56. French ed., Paris: 1955-56. Italian ed., Verona: 1956. These memoirs contain considerable information on Mr. Truman's handling of relations with the USSR. Are of special interest in the absence of full documentary publications covering the period, against which many of his statements should eventually be checked. Especially valuable for the details on the year 1945, taking up the whole of volume I. [A]

HA209 TUGANOVA, OLGA E. *Politika SShA i Anglii na blizhnem i srednem vostoke.* Moscow: Izd. Inst. Mezh. Otn., 1960. 303 p. A study of "imperialist" policy in the Middle East which throws some light on Soviet attitudes and policies.

HA210 U.S. CONGRESS, HOUSE, COMMITTEE ON UNAMERICAN ACTIVITIES. *Report on the Communist Peace Offensive; A Campaign to Disarm and Defeat the United States.* Washington: G.P.O., 1951. 166 p. An exposé of Soviet tactics in propaganda and subversion aimed at the U.S., mainly concerned with the names and doings of Americans in various "front" activities.

HA211 U.S. DEPARTMENT OF STATE. *A Decade of American Foreign Policy; Basic Documents 1941-1949.* Washington: G.P.O., 1950. A useful collection containing, *inter alia*, the principal published documents of the war period, the establishment of the U.N., and the meetings of the Council of Foreign Ministers.

HA212 WHITE, WILLIAM L. *The Little Toy Dog: The Story of the Two RB-47 Flyers.* N.Y.: E. P. Dutton, 1962. 304 p. An account of the imprisonment and interrogations in the USSR of two survivors of a U.S. reconnaissance plane, shot down by the Soviets over the Bering Sea in 1960. Khrushchev released them soon after President Kennedy assumed office.

HA213 WISE, DAVID, and ROSS, THOMAS B. *The U-2 Affair.* N.Y.: Random House, 1962. 269 p. A judicious account by two American journalists, written from sources available to the public.

HA214 XYDIS, STEPHEN G. "The American Naval Visits to Greece and the Eastern Mediterranean in 1946; Their Impact on American-Soviet Relations; A Case Study of the Functions of Modern

Sea Power in Peacetime Foreign Policy." Ph.D. dissertation, Columbia University, 1956. 329 p.

6. U.S.-SOVIET ECONOMIC RELATIONS

(Edited by Mikhail V. Condoide)

HA215 BERMAN, HAROLD J. "The Legal Framework of Trade between Planned and Market Economies: Soviet-American Example," p. 483-528 in *Law and Contemporary Problems, State Trading*, Part II. Durham, N.C.: Duke U., School of Law, 1959. Condensed version in *Proceedings of the American Society of International Law.* Washington: 1959. An excellent discussion of legal problems encountered in trade relations between an open society with a private enterprise economy and a closed society with a planned economy, on the basis of Soviet-American trade relations. By a Professor of Law at Harvard University. [B]

HA216 BRON, SAUL G. *Soviet Economic Development and American Business.* N.Y.: Liveright, 1930. 160 p. The importance of Soviet industrialization under the Five Year Plans to American business in terms of expanded trade opportunities. By a Soviet official.

HA217 CAMPBELL, WILLIAM H. and others. *U.S.-Soviet Trade.* Cleveland: Trade Research Associates, 1960. 230 p. A historical review of the expansion and decline of trade between the two countries from 1920-59. It is descriptive and deals with the Soviet business structure, existing trade relations, procedures and practices, and recent experience. Addressed to the American businessman. [A]

HA218 CHAMBERLIN, WILLIAM H., and ROPES, ERNEST C. *Postwar Economic Relations with the USSR.* N.Y.: New York U., 1944.

HA219 CONDOIDE, MIKHAIL V. *Russian-American Trade.* N.Y.: Citizens Conference on International Economic Union, 1947. 25 p. A brief survey of Russian-American trade by an economics professor at Ohio State University.

HA220 CONDOIDE, MIKHAIL V., *Russian-American Trade; A Study of the Soviet Foreign-Trade Monopoly.* Columbus, Ohio: The Bureau of Business Research, College of Commerce and Administration, Ohio State University, 1946. 160 p. An economic analysis of Russian-American trade from 1920 to 1946 with special regard to the theory and practices of the Soviet monopoly of foreign trade. Contains a bibliography of Soviet and American sources. By an economics professor at Ohio State University. [A]

HA221 GERSCHENKRON, ALEXANDER P. *Economic Relations with the USSR.* N.Y.: The Committee on International Economic Policy in Co-operation with the Carnegie Endowment for International Peace, 1945. 73 p. A short study by a Harvard professor of economics, with emphasis on economic advantages which the Soviet Union would derive from a trade expansion between the two countries. [B]

HA222 HARDT, JOHN P., with STOLZENBACH, C. D. and KOHN, M. J. *The Cold War Economic Gap: The Increasing Threat to American Supremacy.* N.Y.: Praeger, 1961. 114 p. Drawing on material presented at Congressional hearings on trends in the economic growth of the USSR and the U.S., the authors warn that in the absence of new economic policies, the U.S. will fall behind in military power.

HA223 HEYMANN, HANS. *We Can do Business with Russia.* Chicago: Ziff-Davis, 1945. 268 p. A discussion of the economic advantages of increased trade relations between the two countries, by a professor at Rutgers University, with a historical survey of American participation in the industrialization of the Soviet Union in the thirties.

HA224 KNICKERBOCKER, HUBERT R. *Fighting the Red Trade Menace.* N.Y.: Dodd, Mead, 1931. 295 p. British ed., *Soviet Trade and World Depression.* London: Lane, 1931. 288 p. German ed., Berlin: Rowohlt, 1931. Soviet foreign trade expansion and trade practices discussed by an American journalist.

HA225 KNICKERBOCKER, HUBERT R. *The Red Trade Menace; Progress of the Soviet Five Year Plan.* N.Y.: Dodd, Mead, 1931. 277 p. Soviet industrialization and the expansion of Soviet foreign trade were a menace to the West in the 1930's, according to a well known American newspaper man.

HA226 LASSWELL, HAROLD D. *World Politics Faces Economics; with Special Reference to the Future Relations of the United States and Russia.* N.Y. and London: McGraw-Hill, 1945. 108 p. Relations between the United States and the Soviet Union, with emphasis on the economic differences between the two countries, by a well known political scientist and author.

HA227 MARGOLD, STELLA K. *Let's Do Business with Russia.* N.Y.: Harper, 1948. 244 p. A plea for expanded trade with the Soviet Union to improve American-Soviet relations.

HA228 REITZER, LADISLAS F. "United States-Russian Economic Relations, 1917-20." Ph.D. dissertation, U. of Chicago, 1950.

HA229 SHIPMAN, SAMUEL S. "The Outlook for Soviet-American Economic Relations." Ph.D. dissertation, New York Univ., 1946. 236 p.

HA230 TERESHTENKO, VALERY J. *American-Soviet Trade Relations: Past and Future.* N.Y.: Russian Economic Institute, Pamphlet Series no. 5, 1945. 26 p. A brief economic survey of American-Soviet trade and its future possibilities by an economics professor at Stanford University.

HA231 U.S. CONGRESS, HOUSE, COMMITTEE ON WAYS AND MEANS. *Embargo on Soviet Products; Hearings, 71st Congress, 3rd Session, on H.R. 16035, to Prohibit Importation of any Article of Merchandise from the Union of Soviet Socialist Republics.* Washington: G.P.O., 1931. 136 p. Congressional report of a hearing held to restrict imports from the Soviet Union.

HA232 U.S. CONGRESS, SENATE, COMMITTEE ON FOREIGN RELATIONS. *U.S.-U.S.S.R. Trade Relations.* Washington: G.P.O., 1959. 40 p. An important paper prepared by the U.S. State Department for the U.S. Senate Committee on Foreign Relations, stating the official position of the Department regarding American-Soviet economic relations. [B]

HA233 U.S. DEPARTMENT OF STATE. *Soviet Supply Protocols.* Washington: G.P.O., 1948. 156 p. (At head of title: *Wartime International Agreements*, publication 2759, European Series 22.) Texts of wartime protocols concluded between the U.S. and the USSR related to American economic and military aid to the USSR. [B]

HA234 YALEM, RONALD J. "The East-West Trade Control Program; A Defense of the Battle Act." Ph.D. dissertation, American Univ., 1956.

7. THE COMMUNIST PARTY OF THE U.S.A.

(Edited by George P. Rawick)

HA235 AARON, DANIEL. *Writers on the Left; Episodes in American Literary Communism.* N.Y.: Harcourt, Brace, 1961. 460 p. One of the volumes in the Fund for the Republic's "Communism and American Life" series, under the general editorship of Prof. Clinton Rossiter. The author, a literary critic and social historian, devotes much attention to the social context of radicalism among literary men in the 1930's. [B]

HA236 ALLEN, JAMES S. *The Negro Question in the United States.* N.Y.: International Publishers, 1936. 224 p. A classic Communist thesis that American Negroes constitute a national minority which should be granted the right to self-determination in the areas of the South where they are a majority of the population.

HA237 ALMOND, GABRIEL. *The Appeals of Communism.* Princeton, N.J.: Princeton University Press, 1954. 415 p. A study by a social psychologist of the reasons why individuals in various countries, including the U.S., join the Communist movement.

HA238 ALPERIN, ROBERT JAY. "Organization in the Communist Party, U.S.A., 1902-1919." Ph.D. dissertation, Northwestern U., 1959.

HA239 AMERICAN WRITERS CONGRESS, NEW YORK, 1935. *American Writers Congress, Proceedings.* Ed. by Henry Hart. N.Y.: International Publishers, 1935. 192 p. Includes the chief papers and discussion of the first American Writers Congress, a Communist-dominated organization for creative writers. Important for discussion of proletarian literature and for a view of the commitment of non-Communist intellectuals of the period to the leadership of the Communist movement.

HA240 AMERICAN WRITERS CONGRESS, 2nd, NEW YORK, 1937. *The Writer in a Changing World.* Ed. by Henry Hart. N.Y.: Equinox Cooperative Press, 1937. 256 p. Proceedings of the second American Writers Congress, with contributors from Ernest Hemingway to Earl Browder. Reflects the broadening out of Communist-dominated organizations in the period of the Popular Front.

HA241 BEAL, FRED E. *Proletarian Journey: New England, Gastonia, Moscow.* N.Y.: Hillman-Curl, 1937. 352 p. The autobiography of a working-class Communist who came from the I.W.W. Traces his career from the Lawrence strike of 1911 through his leadership of the Gastonia, N.C. textile strike of 1929, his subsequent exile in Moscow, and his disillusionment with Communism while maintaining a radical outlook. [B]

HA242 BELL, DANIEL. "Marxian Socialism in the United States." Chapter 6, Volume I of EGBERT, DONALD DREW, and PERSONS, STOW, eds., *Socialism and American Life.* Princeton, N.J.: Princeton University Press, 1952. 2 vols. The most knowledgeable history of American radicalism, with considerable emphasis on the history of the American Communist Party and those groups which separated from it in the 1930's. [A]

HA243 BENTLEY, ELIZABETH. *Out of Bondage.* N.Y.: Devin-Adair; London: Hart-Davis, 1951. 256 p. An autobiography of a former Communist who claims to have been an underground courier for the Soviet espionage system. Important in subsequent charges of Communist infiltration.

HA244 *Bibliography on the Communist Problem in the United States.* Compiled under the direction of Charles Corker. N.Y.: Fund for the Republic, 1955. 474 p. The most comprehensive, if much criticized, bibliography on the subject available; supervised by Professor Clinton Rossiter, Professor Joseph M. Snee, S.J., and Professor Arthur E. Sutherland. The Fund for the Republic is conducting a major revision of this work under the general editorship of Professor Joel Seidman. Government sources are covered in a separate volume, *Digest of the Public Record* (below).

HA245 BIMBA, ANTHONY. *History of the American Working Class.* N.Y.: International Publishers, 1927 and 1936. 360 p. A classic Communist history of the American working class movement with considerable emphasis on the role of Communists in the labor movement. There are certain substantive differences between the 1927 and 1936 editions.

HA246 BLOOR, ELLA REEVE. *We Are Many.* N.Y.: International Publishers, 1940. 319 p. Autobiography of "Mother" Bloor, labor leader, Socialist Party organizer, and charter member of the American Communist Party.

HA247 BLUMENSTOCK, DOROTHY, and LASSWELL, HAROLD D. *World Revolutionary Propaganda; a Chicago Study.* N.Y.: Knopf, 1939. 393 p. A comprehensive study of Communist propaganda and activity in Chicago in the 1930's, with considerable study of those who were attracted to the party. [B]

HA248 BROWDER, EARL. *Communism in the United States.* N.Y.: International Publishers, 1935. 352 p. A collection of articles by the then General Secretary of the Communist Party, U.S.A., reflects the transition from the revolutionary "line" of the so-called Third Period to the liberalistic stance of the Popular Front.

HA249 BROWDER, EARL. *The Communists in the People's Front.* N.Y.: Workers Library, 1937. 126 p. A report of the General Secretary of the CPUSA to the plenary meeting of the Central Committee of the Party in June 1937, fully reflecting the liberal line of the late 1930's in which the Communist stance merged softly into New Deal rhetoric.

HA250 BROWDER, EARL. *Fighting for Peace.* N.Y.: International Publishers, 1939. 256 p. Written during the halcyon days before the Hitler-Stalin pact. The most representative sample of the Communist position on foreign affairs by the General Secretary of the Party.

HA251 BROWDER, EARL. *Marx and America.* N.Y.: Duell, Sloan & Pearce, 1958. 146 p. By the former General Secretary of the CPUSA, expelled from the Party in the mid-1940's. A reflection upon both Marxism and American life, written from the perspective of an ex-Communist with considerable sympathy for his own past. Provides an ideological defense of Browder's claim to have attempted to Americanize Communism.

HA252 BROWDER, EARL. *Teheran and America; Perspective and Tasks.* N.Y.: International Publishers, 1944. 128 p. The leading figure of the wartime Communist Political Association analyzes the Teheran agreement as the beginning of a period of Big Three unity. Indicates the importance of this perspective for the development of wartime American Communism.

HA253 BUDENZ, LOUIS F. *The Cry Is Peace.* Chicago: Regnery, 1952. 242 p. An exposé of Communist activities, particularly within the area of foreign policy, in the United States. Budenz had been a leading member of the Communist Party from 1935 to 1945.

HA254 BUDENZ, LOUIS F. *Men Without Faces; the Communist Conspiracy in the USA.* N.Y.: Harper, 1950. 305 p. Argues that the CPUSA is a Russian-directed conspiracy which threatens the United States.

HA255 BUDENZ, LOUIS F. *This Is My Story.* N.Y., London: McGraw-Hill, 1947. 379 p. Budenz joined the Communist Party in 1935 and was Managing Editor of the *Daily Worker* from 1942 to 1945. This book is an autobiographical account of his experiences within the CP until he left it in 1945 to become a militant anti-Communist. [B]

HA256 BURNHAM, JAMES. *The Web of Subversion; Underground Networks in the U.S. Government.* N.Y.: Day, 1954. 248 p. Written by a former Trotskyist, who became an editor of the conservative *National Review*, this is an account of Communist penetration in the U.S. Government, based very largely on published hearings of Congressional Committees.

HA257 CANNON, JAMES P. *The First Ten Years of American Communism; Report by a Participant.* Intro. by Theodore Draper. N.Y.: Lyle Stuart, 1962. 352 p. Answers given by the American Trotskyist leader to the questions of Theodore Draper, the outstanding historian of the American Communist Party. [A]

HA258 CANNON, JAMES P. *The History of American Trotskyism.* N.Y.: Pioneer Publishers, 1944. 268 p. Written by the leading American Trotskyist, previously a leader of the Communist Party, this book is invaluable for an account of the factional situation in the American Communist Party in the 1920's. [A]

HA259 CHAMBERS, WHITTAKER. *Witness.* N.Y.: Random House, 1952. 808 p. An account of the life of the leading witness against Alger Hiss in the latter's trial for contempt of Congress. Chambers was a member of the CPUSA from 1925 to 1938, holding several important positions. [B]

HA260 CLEMENT, TRAVERS, and SYMES, LILLIAN. *Rebel America; the Story of Social Revolt in the United States.* N.Y.: Harper, 1934. 392 p. A history of American radicalism, including three chapters on the history of American Communism, written from the perspective of a left-wing, anti-Communist, democratic socialism.

HA261 COMMUNIST PARTY OF THE UNITED STATES OF AMERICA. *Report of the Central Committee to the Eighth Convention of the Communist Party of the U.S.A., Held in Cleveland, Ohio, April 2-8, 1934. Delivered by Earl Browder.* N.Y.: Workers Library, 1934. 128 p. An excellent statement of the CP line in the early days of the New Deal in which some of the revolutionary language of the early thirties has been toned down, and an appeal for the "united front from below" is made, but where the New Deal, the Socialist Party leaders and the leaders of the American Federation of Labor are reviled.

HA262 COMMUNIST PARTY OF THE UNITED STATES OF AMERICA. *Thesis and Resolutions for Seventh National Convention.* N.Y.: CPUSA, 1930. 94 p. Statement of the Communist position at the beginning of the depression, with emphasis upon revolutionary action. Attacks the former leadership of the Party around Jay Lovestone, by then out of the Party and considered its enemy.

HA263 COMMUNIST PARTY OF THE UNITED STATES OF AMERICA, 16th CONVENTION, NEW YORK, 1957. *Proceedings (abridged) of the 16th National Convention of the Communist Party, U.S.A., New York, Feb. 9-12, 1957.* N.Y.: New Century Publishers, 1957. 351 p. Russian ed., Moscow: 1958. The proceedings of the most interesting Communist convention, the special convention called during the internal crisis in the Party following the Russian Twentieth Party Congress revelations and the Hungarian Revolution. This convention provided an excellent opportunity to see the inside of the Party under stress.

HA264 COMMUNIST POLITICAL ASSOCIATION. *The Path to Peace, Progress and Prosperity; Proceedings of Constitutional Convention of the Communist Political Association.* N.Y.: 1944. 142 p. Record of the convention which unanimously dissolved the Communist Party, U.S.A., and formed the Communist Political Association. Based upon the slogans of "Win the War," "Open the Second Front," and "Build the Peoples' Anti-Monopoly Coalition," this convention was the highpoint of the liberalization of the rhetoric of the Communist Party.

HA265 CROSSMAN, RICHARD H. S., ed. *The God that Failed.* N.Y.: Harper; London: Hamilton, 1950. 272 p. Paperback ed., N.Y.: Bantam, 1952. 248 p. A collection of essays by ex-Communists and ex-fellow-traveller intellectuals telling of their experiences. Includes essays by two Americans: Richard Wright, the Negro author, and Louis Fischer, for many years a pro-Soviet newspaperman.

HA265A DELANEY, ROBERT FINLEY. *The Literature of American Communism; a Selected Reference Guide.* Washington: Catholic University of America Press, 1962. 433 p. Contains about 1,700 entries, with full comments, divided into such sections as "Pro-Communist Literature," "Anti-Communist Literature," and "Official Anti-Communist Publications." According to the preface, the book is designed: "1. To provide librarians with a well-rounded collection of books covering both international and American Communism, which . . . point out the basic dangers in both the philosophical and political sense of this totalitarian movement. 2. To provide an insight into the inherent evil of Communism. . . ."

HA266 DE TOLEDANO, RALPH, and LASKY, VICTOR. *Seeds of Treason: the True Story of the Hiss-Chambers Tragedy.* N.Y.: Funk and Wagnalls, 1950. 270 p. A popular account of the trial of Alger Hiss for contempt of Congress. Accepting Hiss' guilt as proven, the authors analyze the reasons why so many Americans cooperated with the Communists. They offer an account of the atmosphere of the New Deal which they believe permitted the growth of the seeds of treason.

HA267 DIES, MARTIN. *The Trojan Horse in America.* N.Y.: Dodd, Mead, 1940. 366 p. The chairman of the House Special Committee on Un-American Activities in the late 1930's and early 1940's details his view of Communist activities among such groups as youth, Negroes and labor.

HA268 *Digest of the Public Record of Communism in the United States.* Compiled and arranged by Charles Corker and staff. N.Y.: Fund for the Republic, 1955. 753 p. A collection of abstracts of decisions, laws, ordinances, hearings, reports, and other public documents relating to Communism in the United States. Done by a crew of legal scholars under the direction of Mr. Corker, formerly professor of Law at Stanford University. Other sources are covered in another volume, *Bibliography on the Communist Problem in the U.S.* (above).

HA269 DILLING, ELIZABETH. *The Red Network; a Who's Who and Handbook of Radicalism for Patriots.* Kenilworth, Illinois: the Author, 1938. 352 p. An attack on those the author considers to be the leading members of the "Communist conspiracy"; used as the basis for blacklisting by many groups afterwards, including those which did not agree with the author's far right-wing and anti-Semitic views.

HA270 DODD, BELLA V. *School of Darkness.* N.Y.: P. J. Kenedy, 1954. 264 p. An account of her career in the Communist Party by a former CP stalwart in the New York City Teachers' Union, who left the Party and rejoined the Catholic Church. [B]

HA271 DRAPER, THEODORE. *American Communism and Soviet Russia; the Formative Period.* N.Y.: Viking, 1960. 558 p. The second volume of the most important critical history of the American Communist Party. Based upon the most extensive research and expert knowledge. One of the "Communism and American Life" series. Deals with the second part of the 1920's. [A]

HA272 DRAPER, THEODORE. *The Roots of American Communism.* N.Y.: Viking; London: Macmillan, 1957. 498 p. The first volume of the most important critical history of the American Communist Party. Deals with the formation and early years of the Party. [A]

HA273 EGBERT, DONALD D., and PERSONS, STOW, eds. *Socialism and American Life.* Princeton, N.J.: Princeton University Press, 1952. 2 vols. While a general reference work and bibliography on American socialism, the volumes contain much valuable material on American Communism scattered through the various scholarly essays. Volume II is a selective and critical bibliography edited by T. D. Seymour Bassett. [A]

HA274 ERNST, MORRIS L., and LOTH, DAVID. *Report on the American Communist.* N.Y.: Holt, 1952. 240 p. Based on interviews with about 300 ex-Communists, this is a popular work which concludes that personal insecurity or psychological maladjustment had much to do with the reasons for Americans joining the Communist movement.

HA275 FAST, HOWARD. *The Naked God; the Writer and the Communist Party.* N.Y.: Praeger, 1957. 197 p. A memoir upon leaving the Communist Party by the leading American Communist novelist. A penetrating self-study of the intellectual and Communism. [B]

HA276 FINE, NATHAN. *Labor and Farmer Parties in the United States, 1828-1928.* N.Y.: Rand School of Social Science, 1928. 445 p. Along with studies of nineteenth century movements, this scholarly volume contains detailed discussions of the early Communist movement in the United States.

HA277 FLYNN, JOHN T. *While You Slept; Our Tragedy in Asia and Who Made It.* N.Y.: Devin-Adair, 1951. 187 p. Written by an old-time American radical turned right-winger, this popularly written account of the Communist victory in China lays the blame upon Communist propaganda, infiltration and underground activities in the United States.

HA278 FONER, PHILIP. *The Fur and Leather Workers Union, a Story of Dramatic Struggle and Achievements.* Newark, N.J.: Nordan Press, 1950. 708 p. A careful history of this Communist-led union by a leading American Communist historian.

HA279 FOSTER, WILLIAM Z. *American Trade Unionism; Principles and Organization, Strategy and Tactics; Selected Writings.* N.Y.: International Publishers, 1947. 383 p. A series of articles by the veteran Communist leader reflecting the development of the Communist position in respect to American trade unionism.

HA280 FOSTER, WILLIAM Z. *From Bryan to Stalin.* N.Y.: International, 1937. 352 p. A partial autobiography of a leading figure in the American Communist Party from the early 1920's to 1961. Reports his activities in the Socialist Party, the Industrial Workers of the World, and the Communist movement. (See below, *Pages from a Worker's Life.*)

HA281 FOSTER, WILLIAM Z. *History of the Communist Party of the United States.* N.Y.: International Publishers, 1952. 600 p. German ed., 1956. This is the definitive Communist Party treatment of its own history, written by its general chairman at the time of publication. [B]

HA282 FOSTER, WILLIAM Z. *Marxism-Leninism versus Revisionism.* N.Y.: New Century, 1946. 111 p. The new Communist orthodoxy as expressed by the then newly reascendent Foster. Directed against the policies of Earl Browder, the leading figure of the Communist movement from the mid-thirties through the end of World War II, it was a justification for the latter's expulsion from the CP.

HA283 FOSTER, WILLIAM Z. *Pages From a Worker's Life.* N.Y.: International Publishers, 1939. 314 p. The second volume of the autobiographical memoir of the veteran American Communist leader. (See above, *From Bryan to Stalin.*)

HA284 FOSTER, WILLIAM Z. *The Russian Revolution.* Chicago: Trade Union Educational League, 1921. 155 p. Report of a trip through Russia during the spring and summer of 1921. Attempts to link the Bolshevik Revolution to the aspirations of the American working-class. Written by the most important American trade union leader to become a Communist at that time.

HA285 FOSTER, WILLIAM Z. *Toward Soviet America.* N.Y.: Coward-McCann, 1932. 343 p. One of the most important and effective works of Communist propaganda in the United States in the early days of the Great Depression. Contrasts the failures of American capitalism with economic and cultural achievements in the Soviet Union. Written by the Communist presidential candidate of 1932.

HA286 FRAINA, LOUIS C. *Revolutionary Socialism; a Study in Socialist Reconstruction.* N.Y.: The Communist Press, 1918. 246 p. Written by one of the leading theoretical minds in the left-wing of the American Socialist Party, later a leader of the Communist movement, it contrasts the success of the proletarian revolution in Russia with the failures of the moderate Socialism which characterized the American movement prior to World War I. The leading manifesto around which the early American Communist movement was built.

HA287 FREEMAN, JOSEPH. *An American Testament; A Narrative of Rebels and Romantics.* N.Y.: Farrar & Rinehart, 1936. 678 p. Written by one of the most sensitive of the Communist intellectuals, this is an autobiography which is at the same time a history of the literary, cultural, and political avant-garde in America from the pre-World War *Masses* magazine through the mid-1930's. While written by a man then still a member of the Communist Party, this book was by no means a model of orthodoxy. [B]

HA288 GATES, JOHN. *The Story of an American Communist.* N.Y.: Nelson, 1958. 221 p. The autobiography of one of the leading figures of the Young Communist League of the 1930's, and then editor of the Communist *Daily Worker*, until he led what may have been a majority of its members out of the Communist Party after the emergency convention of 1957. [B]

HA289 GITLOW, BENJAMIN. *I Confess; the Truth About American Communism.* N.Y.: Dutton, 1940. 611 p. Benjamin Gitlow was an important Communist of the 1920's. He was ousted from the Party by Stalin as a follower of Jay Lovestone in 1929. Important for a view of the interior of the Communist movement in its formative days. [B]

HA290 GITLOW, BENJAMIN. *The Whole of Their Lives; Communism in America, a Personal History and Intimate Portrayal of Its Leaders.* N.Y.: Scribner, 1948. 387 p. A sequel to Gitlow's earlier memoir of his experiences in the Communist movement of the 1920's. This volume contains some revisions of incidents previously told, plus much material presented for the first time.

HA291 GLAZER, NATHAN. *The Social Basis of American Communism.* N.Y.: Harcourt, Brace, 1962. 244 p. A scholarly study, written by the co-author with David Riesman and Denny Reul of *The Lonely Crowd*, attempting to locate the Communist movement sociologically. Contains a theory of the origins of American Communism. One of the volumes in the "Communism and American Life" series. [B]

HA292 HAYWOOD, HARRY. *Negro Liberation.* N.Y.: International Publishers, 1948. 245 p. A restatement and revision of the Communist

Party position on the "Negro question" in which the slogan of self-determination for the Negro people in the Black Belt is no longer meant to be taken literally to imply the creation of a separate Negro state. Emphasis upon land redistribution and social and political liberation.

HA293 HICKS, GRANVILLE. *John Reed, the Making of a Revolutionary.* N.Y.: Macmillan, 1936. 445 p. Written by the leading Communist literary critic of the 1930's, now long since out of the Communist movement. A sympathetic biography of one of the founders of the American Communist movement and author of *Ten Days That Shook the World.*

HA294 HICKS, GRANVILLE. *Where We Came Out.* N.Y.: Viking, 1954. 250 p. After a four year involvement with Communism, ended by the Hitler-Stalin Pact, the author analyzes his motives and those of other intellectuals who became involved in the Communist movement in the 1930's.

HA295 HOOVER, JOHN EDGAR. *Masters of Deceit; the Story of Communism in America and How to Fight It.* N.Y.: Holt, 1958. 374 p. An analysis of the Communist Party and its influence by the head of the F.B.I.

HA296 HOWE, IRVING, and COSER, LEWIS. *The American Communist Party; a Critical History (1919-1957).* Boston: Beacon, 1957. 593 p. The most important single-volume history of the American Communist Party, written by a literary critic and a sociologist, both of whom have been long-time anti-Communist democratic socialists. [A]

HA297 HOWE, IRVING, and WIDICK, B. J. *The U.A.W. and Walter Reuther.* N.Y.: Random House, 1949. 309 p. Analysis of the U.A.W.-C.I.O. from an independent socialist point of view. The background and history of the union, the role of the Communists, the formation of an anti-Communist caucus under Walter Reuther and its triumph are dealt with at length.

HA298 IVERSEN, ROBERT. *The Communists and the Schools.* N.Y.: Harcourt, Brace, 1959. 423 p. A careful, scholarly account of Communist activities in American schools, universities, and teachers' unions. In the "Communism and American Life" series.

HA299 KAMPELMAN, MAX M. *The Communist Party vs. the C.I.O.; A Study in Power Politics.* N.Y.: Praeger, 1957. 299 p. An important study of the influence of the Communist Party in the American labor movement, written by a perceptive historian and sociologist. [A]

HA300 KEMPTON, MURRAY. *Part of Our Time; Some Ruins and Monuments of the Thirties.* N.Y.: Simon and Schuster, 1955. 334 p.

An important journalist's account of key events and individuals in American radicalism of the 1930's. Written from the perspective of support for democratic socialists and trade unionists and contempt for Communists. [B]

HA301 LENS, SIDNEY. *Left, Right and Center; Conflicting Forces in American Labor.* Hinsdale, Illinois: Regnery, 1949. 445 p. Written by a trade-union leader, journalist, and democratic socialist, this is an evaluation of the roles of various political tendencies, including the Communist, in the American labor movement.

HA302 LEVINSON, EDWARD P. *Labor on the March.* N.Y.: Harper, 1938. 325 p. A study of the labor movement during the depression years. The author discusses Communism in the C.I.O. from the standpoint of a moderate anti-Communist.

HA303 LYONS, EUGENE. *The Red Decade; the Stalinist Penetration of America.* N.Y.: Bobbs-Merrill, 1941. 423 p. A former radical who was disillusioned by his experiences in the Soviet Union as a journalist shows how Communist propaganda converted countless American liberals, humanitarians and intellectuals into fellow travellers. He provides much documentation, but occasionally allows his anti-Stalinist zeal to warp his critical judgment.

HA304 McCARTHY, JOSEPH. *McCarthyism, the Fight for America.* N.Y.: Devin-Adair, 1952. 101 p. The controversial Senator describes his activities in exposing alleged Communist activities in the U.S.

HA305 MARCANTONIO, VITO. *I Vote My Conscience; Debates, Speeches and Writings, 1935-1950.* Ed. by Annette Rubinstein and Associates. N.Y.: Vito Marcantonio Memorial, 1956. 494 p. A memorial volume of the speeches and writings of the left-wing City Councilman and then Congressman from New York City. Important for the history of the American Labor Party and for the distinctions between that organization and the Communist Party, about which it often revolved.

HA306 MASSING, HEDE. *This Deception.* N.Y.: Duell, Sloan & Pearce, 1951. 335 p. Autobiography of the first wife of Gerhart Eisler, Communist espionage agent, herself a former Soviet agent. Tells how she became involved in the Communist movement, with implications for the Hiss case.

HA307 MATTHEWS, J. B. *Odyssey of a Fellow Traveler.* N.Y.: Mount Vernon Publishers, 1938. 285 p. Story of the author's experiences as an active "fellow-traveler" of a variety of Communist front groups, including descriptions of the more important of these. The basis of the author's later activity as a leading identifier of people who had been associated with such front groups.

HA308 MEYER, FRANK S. *The Moulding of Communists; the Training of the Communist Cadre*. N.Y.: Harcourt, Brace, 1960. 214 p. Written by a former Communist leader, now turned conservative, this is a scholarly study of the process whereby members of the Communist cadre in the United States were trained. One of the volumes in the "Communism and American Life" series. [B]

HA309 MURRAY, ROBERT K. *The Great Red Scare of 1919-1920*. Minneapolis: U. of Minnesota, 1955. 337 p. A careful scholarly study of the Palmer Raids and anti-radical activities following World War I. Much discussion of the history of the early American Communist Party. [B]

HA310 NEW YORK (STATE), LEGISLATURE, JOINT COMMITTEE INVESTIGATING SEDITIOUS ACTIVITIES. *Revolutionary Radicalism, Its History, Purpose, and Tactics . . . Report of the Joint Legislative Committee Investigating Seditious Activities, Filed April 24, 1920, in the Senate of the State of New York*. Albany: J. B. Lyon, 1920. 4 vols. The report of the Committee headed by Senator Clayton Lusk investigating the early American Communist Party. Contains reprints of important Russian and American Communist writings as well as much other material on the origins of the American Communist movement. [B]

HA311 NOLAN, WILLIAM A. *Communism versus the Negro*. Chicago: Regnery, 1951. 276 p. A semi-popular book based on careful scholarship, written by a Jesuit scholar. Concludes that Communist propaganda among Negroes has been a failure.

HA312 NOMAD, MAX. *Rebels and Renegades*. N.Y.: Macmillan, 1932. 430 p. Written by an anti-Communist radical with a biting wit, it contains portraits of radical leaders, including a long study of William Z. Foster and the Communist movement.

HA313 O'NEAL, JAMES, and WERNER, G. A. *American Communism*. N.Y.: Dutton, 1947. 415 p. Until the late 1950's, this was the only non-Communist history of the CPUSA. The first thirteen chapters were originally published by O'Neal in 1927. Werner revised the early chapters slightly and added nine chapters of his own. While O'Neal was a veteran right-wing Socialist, his sections are more scholarly than those written by Werner, a professor of history. [A]

HA314 PERLO, VICTOR. *American Imperialism*. N.Y.: International Publishers, 1951. 256 p. A careful, Communist analysis of postwar developments in the political, military, and economic role of American capitalism in the world.

HA315 PHILBRICK, HERBERT. *I Led Three Lives; Citizen—"Communist"—Counterspy.* N.Y.: McGraw-Hill, 1952. 323 p. The author infiltrated the Communist Party for the F.B.I. and then became the leading government witness against the Communist leaders in the Smith Act trials. This is his account of his experiences.

HA316 RECORD, WILSON. *The Negro and the Communist Party.* Chapel Hill, N.C.: U. of North Carolina, 1951. 340 p. An exhaustive scholarly account of Communist activities among Negroes. An excellent source for much general history of the CPUSA. Concludes that the Party's Negro policy failed because it was tied to the needs of Soviet policy, not the needs of the American Negro. [B]

HA317 RIDEOUT, WALTER BATES. *The Radical Novel in the United States, 1900-1954; Some Interrelations of Literature and Society.* Cambridge: Harvard, 1956. 339 p. A scholarly account by a literary historian of the proletarian novel in the United States. Much material on the Communist literary movement.

HA318 ROSSITER, CLINTON. *Marxism: the View From America.* N.Y.: Harcourt, Brace, 1960. 338 p. The author, the general editor of the Fund for the Republic's "Communism and American Life" series, and an important American political scientist, offers his assessment of Marxism and American Communism.

HA319 ROY, RALPH L. *Communism and the Churches.* N.Y.: Harcourt, Brace, 1960. 495 p. Written by a Methodist minister and scholar, this is a study of Communist activities in American churches. One of the volumes in the "Communism and American Life" series.

HA320 SAPOSS, DAVID J. *Communism and the Unions.* N.Y.: McGraw-Hill, 1959. 279 p. A semi-popular general account of the role of Communists in American trade unions, written by a veteran labor journalist.

HA321 SAPOSS, DAVID J. *Communism in American Politics.* Washington, D.C.: Public Affairs Press, 1960. 259 p. A semi-popular general account of the role of Communists in American political life.

HA322 SAPOSS, DAVID J. *Left-Wing Unionism; a Study of Radical Policies and Tactics.* N.Y.: International Publishers, 1926. 192 p. A Communist analysis of left-wing activities in American labor movements from the Industrial Workers of the World to the Trade Union Educational League. Important for the Communist trade-union position of the early years of American Communism.

HA323 SCHMIDT, KARL M. *Henry A. Wallace: Quixotic Crusade, 1948.* Syracuse, N.Y.: Syracuse University Press, 1960. 362 p. An account of the Progressive Party of 1948, written by a careful historian. Much discussion of the role of the Communists in that movement.

HA324 SCHNEIDER, DAVID M. *The Workers' (Communist) Party and American Trade Unions.* Baltimore: Johns Hopkins, 1928. 117 p. An early history of Communist activity in the American trade union movement through the Trade Union Educational League. A scholarly and useful account.

HA325 SEIDMAN, JOEL. *American Labor from Defense to Reconversion.* Chicago: U. of Chicago, 1953. 307 p. A careful study of labor in America during World War II, including much discussion of the role of the Communists in this period. The author is a member of the faculty of the University of Chicago.

HA326 SELZNICK, PHILIP. *The Organizational Weapon; a Study of Bolshevik Strategy and Tactics.* N.Y.: McGraw-Hill, 1952. 350 p. While devoted to a study of Communist movements throughout the world, this volume written by an important academic sociologist, contains much theoretical discussion important for an understanding of the operations of the inner structure of the American Communist Party. [B]

HA327 SHANNON, DAVID A. *The Decline of American Communism; a History of the Communist Party of the United States since 1945.* N.Y.: Harcourt, Brace, 1959. 425 p. A major scholarly history of post World War II developments in the Communist Party. The author is Professor of History at the University of Wisconsin. One of the volumes in the Fund for the Republic sponsored series on "Communism and American Life." [A]

HA328 SHANNON, DAVID A. *The Socialist Party of America.* N.Y.: Macmillan, 1955. 320 p. An important scholarly history of the American Socialist Party, with much material bearing on the formation of the American Communist Party and its later activities.

HA329 SPOLANSKY, JACOB. *The Communist Trail in America.* N.Y.: Macmillan, 1951. 227 p. The story of the activities of a former special agent of the Department of Justice whose work was to combat radical activities. Has interesting material on the early history of the Communist movement. Written from the perspective of the professional anti-Communist agent.

HA330 STOLBERG, BENJAMIN. *The Story of the C.I.O.* N.Y.: Viking, 1938. 294 p. The history of the C.I.O. by a radical who supported the activities of anti-Stalinist radicals such as the Lovestonites against the influence of the Communists in the C.I.O.

HA331 STOLBERG, BENJAMIN. *Tailor's Progress.* N.Y.: Doubleday, Doran, 1942. 360 p. A history of the International Ladies Garment Workers Union. There is much detail on the Communist attempts to capture the union in the 1920's and on later Communist activities. Written from a perspective close to the leadership of the union.

HA332 UTLEY, FREDA. *The China Story.* Chicago: Regnery, 1951. 306 p. A former Communist attributes the failure to stop the growth of Communism in China to Communist subversion in the government, as well as to errors of judgment caused by the success of the Communists in confusing American liberals as to the true nature of Chinese Communism. Argues that Owen Lattimore played an important role in creating this atmosphere.

HA333 VORSE, MARY HEATON. *Footnote to Folly.* N.Y.: Farrar and Reinhart, 1935. 407 p. Autobiography of a labor writer and radical for the years 1912-22. Material on the Palmer Raids and the early history of American Communism.

HA334 WECHSLER, JAMES A. *The Age of Suspicion.* N.Y.: Random House, 1953. 333 p. Written by the editor of the liberal New York *Post*, it is an account of his earlier activities in the Communist youth movement, his break with the Communist Party, subsequent struggles between Communists and anti-Communists for control of the newspaper *PM*, and his interrogation by Senator McCarthy's Subcommittee in 1953.

HA335 WHEELER, ROBERT H. L. "American Communists; Their Ideology and Their Interpretation of American Life, 1919-1939." Ph. D. dissertation, Yale, 1953.

HA336 WORKERS PARTY OF AMERICA. *The Fourth National Convention.* Chicago: Daily Worker, 1925. 166 p. Reports and resolutions submitted to the 4th Convention of the Workers (Communist) Party in 1925. Contains a detailed account of the Party's activities in the preceding twenty months.

HA337 WORKERS PARTY OF AMERICA. *The Second Year.* Chicago: Workers Party, 1924. 127 p. Report of the Central Executive Committee of the Party to the Third National Convention summarizing the activities of the preceding year and outlining future policy.

HB. CANADA

EDITED BY WILLIAM RODNEY

1. BOOKS AND DISSERTATIONS

HB1 BARNES, SAMUEL. "The Ideology of Organized Labor in Canada." Ph.D. dissertation, Duke, 1957. 304 p. Touches very briefly upon the development and influence of the Communist movement in Canadian labor.

HB2 BUCK, TIM. *Canada; the Communist Viewpoint.* Toronto: Progress Books, 1948. 288 p. An undocumented attempt to formulate Communist Party proposals for a new Canada based on a calculated denigration of the nation's political, economic, and social development. By the former head of the Canadian C.P.

HB3 BUCK, TIM. *A Labor Policy for Victory; Submission presented by Tim Buck on behalf of the Dominion Communist Labor Total War Committee to the National War Labor Board Inquiry into Labor Relations.* Toronto: Eveready Printers, 1943. 90 p. A guarded Communist statement urging the Canadian government to adopt anti-inflationary measures, compulsory bargaining, and a national labor code.

HB4 BUCK, TIM. *Nasha borba za Kanady; izbranie proizvedeniia, 1923-1959.* Moscow: 1961. 432 p. An edited collection of writings by the Chairman of the Communist Party of Canada illuminating the Party's attitude on many issues from its earliest days. Highly selective, factually unreliable, but of some value in interpreting the Party's development. No index; no bibliography. [A]

HB5 BUCK, TIM. *Steps to Power.* Toronto: 1925. 62 p. A militant program of action and policy for left-wing trade union activity in Canada, written from the viewpoint of the Trade Union Educational League and the Communist Party. [A]

HB6 BUCK, TIM. *Thirty Years, 1922-1952; the Story of the Communist Movement in Canada.* Toronto: Progress Books, 1952. 224 p. An undocumented history of the Canadian Communist movement written by the National Chairman of the C.P. Slanted, inaccurate, unreliable in content and analyses, but revealing through its treatment of incidents and issues, and by its omissions. [A]

HB7 CANADA, ROYAL COMMISSION TO INVESTIGATE DISCLOSURES OF SECRET AND CONFIDENTIAL INFORMATION TO UNAUTHORIZED PERSONS. *The Report of the Royal Commission Appointed under Order in Council P.C. 411 of February*

5, 1946. . . . Ottawa: E. Cloutier, 1946. 733 p. Also issued in French. The findings of the Royal Commission following the disclosures of Soviet espionage activities in Canada by the Russian Embassy cipher clerk, Igor Gouzenko. A primary document revealing Soviet espionage organization and methods. [B]

HB8 COMMUNIST PARTY OF CANADA. *Documents of the 17th National Convention, January 19-21, 1962.* Toronto: 1962. 36 p. Contains the report of the National Executive Committee, policy resolutions, the Party's federal election platform, program amendments, and a partial list of the twelve-member Executive Committee. [B]

HB9 DAVIES, RAYMOND A. *Canada and Russia; Neighbors and Friends.* Foreword by Rt. Hon. W. L. Mackenzie King, Prime Minister of Canada. Introduction by L. Dana Wilgress, Canadian Ambassador to the USSR. Toronto: Progress Books, 1944. 111 p. A superficial account of Canadian-Soviet relations from the earliest times, drawn from secondary sources, written from the fellow-traveller viewpoint. [B]

HB10 JOYNT, CAREY B. "Canadian Foreign Policy Between the Wars." Ph.D. dissertation, Clark U., 1951. 313 p. Mentions Russia only in passing in connection with the post World War I Straits question and the Chanak incident in 1922.

HB11 LABOR-PROGRESSIVE PARTY OF CANADA. *Canadian Independence and a People's Parliament; Canada's Path to Socialism.* Toronto: 1954. 31 p. The Program of the Canadian Communist Party adopted at the Labor-Progressive Party's Fifth National Convention, March 1954. [B]

HB12 MILEIKOVSKII, A. G. *Kanada i anglo-amerikanskie protivorechiia.* Moscow: Gospolitizdat, 1958. 503 p. A Marxist analysis of Canadian history, contrasting American and Canadian development. Canada's retarded growth is attributed to the French colonists' feudal system which was replaced by British colonialism. Since Confederation (1867) Canadian history is a record of conflict between the U.S.A. and Britain for economic domination, with America victorious. Erroneously suggests that the Labour-Progressive (Communist) Party is important.

HB13 PIERCE, G. (pseud.). *Socialism and the C.C.F.* Montreal: Contemporary Publishing Assoc., 1934. 217 p. A bitter Communist attack upon the then newly-formed Cooperative Commonwealth Federation, a regional socialist party, which was labelled "social-reformist."

HB14 RODNEY, WILLIAM. "A History of the Communist Party of Canada 1919-1929." Ph.D. dissertation, London U., 1961. 412 p. Covers the background of pre-World War I socialist movements in Canada, and traces in detail the emergence and development of the Canadian

Communist Party, including the impact of Trotskyism and the theory of North American exceptionalism. Based on contemporary Party and Comintern documents and publications, and interviews. Full bibliography; no index. [A]

HB15 SMITH, A. E. *All My Life*. Toronto: Progress Books, 1949. 224 p. Autobiography of a Methodist clergyman who joined the Communist Party of Canada in 1925. Illuminates Party life with a Stalinist bias. [A]

HB16 SMITH, STEWART, ed. *Submission of the Central Committee of the Communist Party to the Royal Commission on Dominion-Provincial Relations*. Toronto: 1938. 124 p. The Communist Party of Canada's stand on the distribution of income, and its proposals for taxation, labor legislation, national health, education, and the necessity of unifying Canada through integrating Quebec into the national structure.

HB17 SUSHCHENKO, V. V. *Anglo-amerikanskie protivorechiia v Kanade posle Vtoroi mirovoi voiny*. Moscow: Gospolitizdat, 1956. 184 p. A Marxist interpretation of Canadian-American relations and Canadian development since 1945, in which Canada is portrayed as the exploited victim of American economic imperialism.

2. PERIODICALS

HB18 *Advance*. Toronto. Irregular. A Young Communist League publication.

HB19 *The Canadian Tribune*. Toronto, January 20, 1940–. Weekly. The principal Canadian Communist paper today.

HB20 *The Daily Clarion*. Toronto, May 1, 1936-1939. Daily.

HB21 *The Marxist Quarterly*. Toronto. The Party's literary, historical and philosophical journal. Replaced *Marxist Review* in the spring of 1962.

HB22 *Marxist Review*. Toronto. Published in alternate months by the National Executive Committee of the Canadian Communist Party.

HB23 *The Pacific Tribune*. Vancouver. Weekly. The Party's west coast publication.

HB24 *The Worker*. Toronto. 1922-1939 (15 March 1922–1 May 1936, weekly). The principal Canadian Communist Party newspaper until banned shortly after the outbreak of World War II.

HB25 *The Workers' Guard*. Toronto. October 1921 to March 1922. The earliest legal Party publication.

HC. LATIN AMERICA

EDITED BY ROBERT J. ALEXANDER

(Russian titles by J. Gregory Oswald)

1. GENERAL WORKS

HC1 AKADEMIIA NAUK SSSR, INSTITUT EKONOMIKI. *Narody Latinskoi Ameriki v borbe protiv amerikanskogo imperializma; sbornik statei.* Edited by M. I. Rubinshtein. Moscow: Izd-vo Akademii nauk SSSR, 1951. 462 p.

HC1A AKADEMIIA NAUK SSSR, INSTITUT MIROVOI EKONOMIKI I MEZHDUNARODNYKH OTNOSHENII. *Problemy sovremennoi Latinskoi Ameriki.* Ed. by M. V. Danilevich and A. F. Shulgovskii. Moscow: Akademiia nauk, 1959. 429 p. Eight scholarly essays on Latin America by distinguished Party-line Soviet historians, political scientists, and economists. Subjects: U.S.-Latin American relations since World War II, dictatorial regimes, middle-class politics and working class movements in Brazil, Catholicism in Latin America since 1945, problems of Latin American common market and agricultural economics since World War II. Well-documented.

HC2 ALBA, VICTOR. *Historia del comunismo en América latina.* Mexico City: Ediciones Occidentales, 1954. 150 p. A short survey of the history of the Communists in Latin America. Very sketchy, but of particular value for its discussions of the leadership problems of the Communist Parties in various Latin American countries. [B]

HC3 ALBA, VICTOR. *Le Mouvement ouvrier en Amérique Latine.* Paris: Editions ouvrières, 1953. 238 p. Discusses mainly the organized labor movement; deals with Communists only tangentially.

HC4 ALEXANDER, ROBERT J. *Communism in Latin America.* New Brunswick, N.J.: Rutgers, 1957. 449 p. The best general work on Communism in Latin America. Discusses history, activities in unions, leadership problems, and then surveys the history of the Communist Party in each country. The author is a professor of economics at Rutgers University. [A]

HC5 ALEXANDER, ROBERT J. *Prophets of the Revolution.* N.Y.: Macmillan, 1962. 322 p. The "revolution" in the title refers to the modernization of Latin America. Of the twelve "prophets" treated, only one, Castro, is now a Communist, but some of the others have been connected with the Communist movement in the past.

HC6 ALLEN, ROBERT L. *Soviet Influence in Latin America; the Role of Economic Relations.* Washington: Published for the Woodrow

Wilson Department of Foreign Affairs, University of Virginia, by the Public Affairs Press, 1959. 108 p. A study of the attempt of the Soviet Union to establish closer trade relations with Latin America. Takes the general point of view that these relations are not very extensive and are not likely to become so. Antedates the Castro regime's deals with the USSR. [B]

HC7 ANTIASOV, M. B. *Sovremennyi panamerikanizm; proiskhozhdenie i sushchnost doktrin panamerikanskoi "solidarnost."* Moscow: Izd. IMO, 1960. 328 p. A penetrating, scholarly, Soviet analysis of the nature of contemporary Pan-Americanism, its rationale and sources of strength; a cynical attack on the idea of "cultural community," its service to the Latin American bourgeoisie, and its harmfulness to the working class movement. Twelve-page bibliography of official documents, memoirs, letters, histories, and news reports. [B]

HC8 *Bajo la bandera de la CSLA, resoluciones y documentos varios del Congreso constituyente de la CSLA. . . . en Montevideo, en mayo de 1929.* Montevideo: Edíciones CSLA, 1929. Documents of the founding conference of the Communist continental trade union group. Gives a good idea of the Communist position at the beginning of the "Third Period." [A]

HC9 BLASIER, STEWART COLE. "Foundations of Comintern Policy toward Latin America, 1919-1924." Certificate essay, Russian Institute, Columbia, 1950. 71 p. Devotes special attention to the meager Soviet sources on this period. [B]

HC9A *Communism; Selected Books in Spanish and Portuguese.* No imprint; dated June 8, 1959. 27 p. (mimeographed). Includes 137 books in separate lists for Spanish and Portuguese. Also includes a "List of Sino-Soviet Bloc Periodicals Circulating in Latin America" and a list of "Communist Periodicals in Latin America" (by country). Probably compiled by some branch of the U.S. Government. Not annotated.

HC10 CONGRESO CONTRA LA INFILTRACIÓN SOVIÉTICA EN AMÉRICA LATINA, 1ST, MÉXICO, 1954. *Memoria.* Mexico: 1955. 312 p.

HC11 CONGRESO CONTRA LA INFILTRACIÓN SOVIÉTICA EN AMÉRICA LATINA, 2ND, RIO DE JANEIRO, 1955. *Memoria.* Mexico: 1956. 377 p.

HC12 CONGRESO CONTRA LA INFILTRACIÓN SOVIÉTICA EN AMÉRICA LATINA, 3RD, LIMA, 1957. *Resoluciones del Tercer Congreso contra la Infiltración soviética en América latina, celebrado en Lima, Peru, del 10 al 14 de abril de 1957, convocado por la Confederación interamericana de Defensa del Continente.* Lima: 1957. 80 p.

Three reports of an extreme right-wing, anti-Communist group. Not too reliable as a source of accurate information about Latin American Communists, but useful, however.

HC13 *C.T.A.L., 1938-1948, resoluciones de sus asambleas.* Mexico: 1948. A significant collection of resolutions of various conferences and executive meetings of the Communist-dominated trade union group of the hemisphere. Very useful in tracing the evolution of the political line during the decade covered.

HC14 DANILEVICH, M. V. *Polozhenie i borba rabochego klassa stran Latinskoi Ameriki.* Moscow: Izd. Akademii nauk SSSR, 1953. 380 p. This significant Stalin-era survey of Latin American working-class conditions and relations with other classes is a potential Soviet guide to political action for trade-unionists willing to accept Communist Party leadership and organizational techniques in the struggle against foreign and domestic politico-economic domination. [A]

HC15 DONSKII, GRIGORII M. *Borba za Latinskuiu Ameriku.* Moscow-Leningrad: Moskovskii Rabochii, 1928. 152 p. A popular, sympathetic Soviet account of the colonial and national periods in the historical development of Latin America, including criticism of Anglo-American imperialism and Pan-Americanism and a review of trade unionism. Based on U.S. monographs and periodicals.

HC16 *Ekonomicheskoe polozhenie stran Azii, Afriki, i Latinskoi Ameriki.* Moscow: Vneshtorgizdat, 1959. 446 p. Published by the USSR Ministry of Foreign Trade, this volume contains 125 pages of interpretive data on the major trading nations of Latin America. Concentrates on 1958: the rate of growth or decline of gross national product; comparative industrial and agricultural production; and trade relations of recent years. Based on Latin American sources.

HC17 *Ekonomicheskoe polozhenie stran Azii, Afriki, i Latinskoi Ameriki v 1956 g.* Moscow: Vneshtorgizdat, 1957. 379 p.

HC18 ERMOLAEV, V. I. *Natsionalno-osvoboditelnoe i rabochee dvizhenie v stranakh Latinskoi Ameriki posle vtoroi mirovoi voiny.* Moscow: Vysshaia partiinaia shkola, 1958. 98 p. A political tract by a Soviet Ph.D. candidate in history. A well-informed, but one-sided analysis of the "national-liberation movement" in Latin America since World War II.

HC19 ERNST, OTTO (pseud. of Otto E. Schmidt). *Internationales Arbeiterlesebuch; Kommunismus in Südamerika.* Hamburg: Verlag vom Stein, 1922. 96 p.

HC20 FOSTER, WILLIAM Z. *Outline Political History of the Americas.* N.Y.: International Publishers, 1951. 668 p. The development of inter-American relations from the viewpoint of the former leader of the U.S. Communist Party. Tends to greatly over-emphasize the importance of Latin American Communists, but has some valuable information about them. [B]

HC21 FRACARO, A. M. "The Role of the Third International (Comintern and Cominform) in Latin America, 1935-1951." M.A. thesis, U. of California (Berkeley), 1952.

HC22 GONIONSKII, S. A. *Latinskaia Amerika i SShA; ocherki istorii diplomaticheskykh otnoshenii, 1939-1959.* Moscow: Izd. IMO, 1960. 542 p. Highly-informed Soviet interpretive essays on U.S.-Latin American relations, 1939-59. Includes examination of: inter-American conferences and agreements of the epoch; revolutionary strife and the role of Communist Parties in Guatemala, Bolivia, Colombia, Venezuela and Cuba; and expansion of Latin American ties with USSR and Soviet-camp countries. Excellent 21-page bibliographical essay plus a bibliography of 50 pages. [A]

HC23 GOSUDARSTVENNYI INSTITUT "SOVETSKAIA ENTSIKLOPEDIIA," MOSCOW. *Strany Latinskoi Ameriki.* Ed. by F. N. Petrov. Moscow: 1949. 959 p. A one-volume encyclopedia on Latin America, which is spotty in coverage, popular in interpretation, highly prejudiced, and unbalanced in emphasis. Occasionally useful secondary bibliographic sources. Most interesting for gaining perspective on Soviet interpretations of Latin American affairs.

HC24 GRECHEV, M. *Imperialisticheskaia ekspansiia SShA v stranakh Latinskoi Ameriki posle vtoroi mirovoi voiny.* Moscow: Akademkniga, 1954. 262 p. A scathing attack on U.S. investments in Latin America since World War II, which underscores the military-political significance of U.S. ties, denounces Pan-Americanism and U.S. interpretations of Latin American history and defines the status of workers in the struggle to "liberate" their countries from U.S. imperialism. Important politico-economic criticism. [B]

HC25 HAYTON, ROBERT D. "Diplomatic Relations of Latin America with the Soviet Union." M.A. thesis, U. of California, 1950. A study of one of the important avenues through which Communist influence has been spread in Latin America.

HC26 KOMMUNISTICHESKAIA AKADEMIIA, INSTITUT MIROVOGO KHOZIAISTVA I MIROVOI POLITIKI. *Problemy revoliutsii v Iuzhnoi i Karaibskoi Amerike; sbornik statei.* Ed. by G. Sinani. Moscow: Kommunisticheskaia akademiia, 1934. 302 p. A collaborative work containing six of the earliest and most realistic Soviet essays on various Caribbean labor, agrarian, and social problems, written at the height of the depression and indicative of the exploitation of nationality and economic problems of the region; an implied call to revolutionary action. A serious Communist Party tract. [B]

HC26A LAUERHASS, LUDWIG, JR. *Communism in Latin America: a Bibliography; the Post-War Years (1945-1960).* Los Angeles: Center of Latin American Studies, University of California, 1962. 78 p.

HC27 LAVRETSKII, I. R. "A Survey of the Hispanic American Historical Review, 1956-1958," *Hispanic American Historical Review*, XL, no. 3 (August 1960), p. 340-360. Translated from the Soviet journal, *Voprosy istorii*, this article affords a good insight into the Soviet interpretation of the problems of Latin American history. Heavily documented from U.S. and Latin American sources. [A]

HC28 LOMBARDO TOLEDANO, VICENTE. *La C.T.A.L. ante la guerra y ante la postguerra.* Mexico: Universidad obrera de Mexico, 1945. 128 p. A statement of the position of the Communist-dominated trade unions of the hemisphere towards postwar problems. Writing before the outbreak of the Cold War, the author is chief of the Confederacion de Trabajadores de America Latina, the Communist-controlled trade union confederation.

HC29 LOZOVSKY, ALEXANDER (pseud. of Solomon Dridzo). *El Movímiento sindical latino americano—sus virtudes y sus defectos.* Montevideo: Ediciones C.S.L.A., 1928. An assessment of the trade union movement of Latin America, and the Communists' role in it by the head of the Red International of Labor Unions, delivered before a meeting of Latin American unionists in Moscow in November 1927.

HC30 MADARIAGA, SALVADOR DE. *Latin America between the Eagle and the Bear.* N.Y.: Praeger, 1961. A study of pro- and anti-Communist factors in Latin America by a leading democratic Spanish authority on Latin America.

HC31 *El movimiento revolucionario latino americano, versiones de la primera Conferencia Comunista Latino Americana, junio de 1929.* Buenos Aires: Editorial La Correspondencia Sudamericana, 1929. Selected excerpts from proceedings of the first hemispheric congress of Communist Parties. Especially interesting for the light it throws on the Comintern's attitude towards some of the national Communist Party leaders, particularly its condemnation of José Carlos Mariategui of Peru. [A]

HC31A *Natsionalno-osvoboditelnoe dvizhenie v Latinskoi Amerike na sovremennom etape.* Moscow: Sotsekgiz, 1961.

HC32 PENALOZA, JUAN RAMON. *Trotsky ante la revolucion nacional latinoamericana; una biografia politica.* Buenos Aires: Editorial

Indoamerica, 1953. 167 p. A collection of statements by Leon Trotsky concerning Latin American problems. It throws some side-lights on early Communist policy as well as indicating the position of Trotskyite deviators from official Communism. [B]

HC33 RAVINES, EUDOCIO. *América Latina; un continente en erupción*. Buenos Aires: Editorial claridad, 1956. 263 p. By a founder and ex-leader of the Peruvian Communist Party, an acute observer who knows a great deal, but who often writes to suit the particular political position he has at the moment.

HC34 RAVINES, EUDOCIO. *The Yenan Way; the Kremlin's Penetration of South America*. N.Y.: Scribner, 1951. 319 p. A study of the development of the Popular Front and allied techniques among Latin American Communists. Much interesting information but not entirely reliable on personal matters because of the strong prejudices of the author. 3rd Spanish ed., *La gran estafa*. Santiago de Chile: Editorial del Pacifico, 1954. 270 p. [A]

HC34A RED INTERNATIONAL OF LABOR UNIONS. *Ezhemesiachnyi informatsionyi biulleten latino-amerikanskoi sektsii Profinterna*. Moscow: 1929-33. This periodical published by the Profintern reported the state of the movement in Latin-American countries in the drive against the Pan-American Labor Federation. Contains reports on regional conferences.

HC35 *Resoluciones de la Conferencia Sindical Latino Americana*. Montevideo: Ediciones CSLA, 1928. The report of the founding congress of the Communist hemispheric labor group during the Third Period. Noteworthy for information on the efforts of the Communists to organize Party-controlled labor movements at the beginning of the Third Period.

HC36 REYTAN, JUAN. *Guerra a Stalin, estudio sobre la política del proletariado*. La Paz: Editorial universo, 1950. 143 p. Written by a Polish left-Socialist, anti-Communist exile; relevance to Latin America secondary.

HC37 RIENFFER, KARL, pseud. *Comunistas españoles en América*. Madrid: Editora nacional, 1953. 198 p.

HC38 SLEZKIN, L. IU. *Politika SShA v Iuzhnoi Amerike; 1929-1933*. Moscow: Izdatelstvo Akademii nauk SSSR, 1956. 304 p. A Soviet historical interpretation of the effects of the U.S. depression on Latin American politics. Latin American conflicts of the 1930's are explained as repercussions of contradictions and rivalries in the "imperialist West." Contains an 11-page bibliography.

HC39 SYMONENKO, R. H. *Vpliv velikoi zhovtnevoi sotsialistichnoi revoliutsii na rozvitok revoliutsiinogo rukhu v krainakh Ameriki.* Kiev: Vid. Akademii nauk Ukr. RSR, 1957. 86 p. Disappointing but enlightening insight into Ukrainian Communist thinking on the impact of the Bolshevik revolution of 1917 on socialist and working class aspirations in various states of Latin America. A popular interpretation.

HC39A TREVIÑO, RODRIGO GARCÍA. *La Ingerencia Rusa en Mexico y Sudamērica.* Mexico, D.F.: Editorial America, 1959. 256 p. Discussion of the links between Soviet-led international Communist activities and Communist parties of Latin America, especially Mexico.

HC40 U.S. LIBRARY OF CONGRESS, SLAVIC AND CENTRAL EUROPEAN DIVISION. *Latin America in Soviet Writings, 1945-1958; a Bibliography.* Compiled by Leo A. Okinshevich and Cecilia J. Gorokhoff. Edited by Nathan Haverstock. Washington: Library of Congress, 1959. 257 p. The most complete and useful bibliography extant on this subject. Efficiently organized, it contains 2,385 items treating each branch of knowledge delved into by Soviet writers between 1945 and 1958. Not annotated. [A]

HC41 ZUBOK, L. I. *Imperialisticheskaia politika SShA v stranakh Karaibskogo basseina; 1900-1939.* Moscow: Izd. Akademii nauk SSSR, 1948. 518 p. Extensive, but unoriginal, criticism of U.S. intervention policy in the Caribbean region and Mexico before World War II by a free-swinging Soviet political scientist.

2. ARGENTINA

HC42 BALDASSARRE, PEDRO B. *El justicialismo frente al comunismo.* Buenos Aires: El Ateneo, 1951. 559 p. A statement of the relationship of the Peronista movement to Communism. Written by a man then working with the Peron regime.

HC43 BUEZAS, ADOLFO. *Comunismo; oportunismo y liberación nacional.* Buenos Aires: Ediciones "Liberación nacional," 1956. 190 p.

HC44 CODOVILLA, VICTORIO. *Batir al Nazi-Peronismo para abrir una era de libertad y progreso.* Buenos Aires: Anteo, 1946. 48 p. A pamphlet by the Secretary General of the Argentine Communist Party, written during the period when the Party was strongly anti-Peron, and just before it veered around to critical support of him; interesting as an example of the extent of the violence of Communist vituperation of Peron in the 1943-46 period.

HC45 CODOVILLA, VICTORIO. *Defender la linea independiente del Partido, para construir el frente de la democracia, de la independencia nacional y la paz.* Buenos Aires: Anteo, 1953. Report by a founder and long-time boss of the Argentine Communist Party, putting the Party back on the "straight and narrow" after it wandered too close to support of Juan Peron's government.

HC46 CODOVILLA, VICTORIO. *¿Hacia dónde marcha el mundo? Análisis de los principales acontecimientos económicos, sociales y políticos de actualidad, nacionales o internacionales a través del método científico de la doctrina de Marx, Engels, Lenin y Stalin. Conferencias pronunciadas con motivo de la conmemoración del centenario del Manifesto comunista.* Buenos Aires: Anteo, 1948. 480 p. An interesting general statement of the philosophy of the chief leader of the Argentine Communist Party, and one of the most important Stalinist agents in Latin America.

HC47 CODOVILLA, VICTORIO. *La nueva relación de fuerzas en lo internacional y nacional y el camino argentino hacia la democracia, la independencia nacional y el socialismo.* Buenos Aires: Anteo, 1956. 110 p. A critique by the leader of the Argentine Communist Party of the situation of the country and Party in the wake of the fall of Peron.

HC48 CODOVILLA, VICTORIO. *Trayectoria histórica del Partido Communista.* Buenos Aires: Anteo, 1946. 104 p. A historical summary of the Argentine Communist Party, by the man who founded and led it from the beginning.

HC49 *Ezbozo de historia del Partido Comunista de la Argentina.* Buenos Aires: Anteo, 1947. An official history of the Argentine Communist Party. If one makes allowance for the fact that this is the Communists' own version, it provides information elsewhere unobtainable concerning the internal situation of the Argentine CP during its first twenty-nine years. [A]

HC50 FILIPPO, VIRGILIO. *El plan quinquenal de Perón y los comunistas.* 6th ed. Buenos Aires: Editorial lista blanca, 1948. 508 p. A critique of the role of the Communists under Peron, by a priest who was one of the most violent supporters of Juan and Evita.

HC51 *Resoluciones del Comite Central Ampleado del Partido Comunista, reunido en la Ciudad de Rosario durante los dias 28 y 29 de julio de 1951.* Buenos Aires: Editorial Anteo, 1951. The report of the meeting of the highest body of the Argentine Communist Party which passed a number of very pro-Peron resolutions.

HC52 SILVEYRA, CARLOS M. *El Communismo en la Argentina; origen, desarrollo, organización actual.* 2nd ed. Buenos Aires: La Editorial "Patria," 1937. 550 p. An interesting historical survey of Argentine Communists.

3. BOLIVIA

HC53 ALEXANDER, ROBERT J. *The Bolivian National Revolution.* New Brunswick, N.J.: Rutgers, 1958. 302 p. Though not primarily devoted to the Communists, it does discuss the role, a minor one, of both Stalinist and Trotskyite Communists in the Bolivian Revolution.

HC54 ANAYA, RICARDO. *Nacionalización de las minas de Bolivia.* Cochabamba, Bolivia: Imprenta Universitaria, 1952. 353 p. A study by a Bolivian Communist of the problem of nationalizing Bolivian mines. Discusses this as a first step towards establishing a Communist-style "socialist" regime.

HC55 CANDIA G., ALFREDO. *Bolivia; un experimento comunista en la América.* La Paz: Talleres gráficos Bolivianos, 1959? 241 p. A denunciation of the MNR government of Bolivia as Communist; of doubtful reliability.

HC56 COMMUNIST PARTY (BOLIVIA), COMISIÓN NACIONAL DE EDUCACIÓN. *El Partido comunista y sus principios marxistas leninistas stalinistas de organización.* Santa Cruz: Tipografia "Obrera," n.d. 180 p.

HC57 CONGRESO CONTRA LA INFILTRACIÓN SOVIÉTICA EN AMÉRICA LATINA, 3RD, LIMA, 1957. *El Marxismo en Bolivia; informe en mayoría de la comisión designada por el III Congreso de la Confederación Interamericana de Defensa del Continente, sobre la situación interna de Bolivia.* Santiago de Chile?: 1957. 284 p. The report of an extremely conservative group on the situation in Bolivia. Contains a number of interesting documents, but tends to see a great deal more Communist influence in the country, particularly in ruling MRR party, than other observers feel exists. [B]

HC58 CORNEJO S., ALBERTO. *Programas politicos de Bolivia.* Cochabamba, Bolivia: Imprenta Universitaria, 1949. 392 p. A compilation of the programs of all parties in Bolivia at the time of publication. Includes, among others, programs of the pro-Stalinist Partido de la Izquierda Revolucionaria and the Trotskyite Partido Obrero Revolucionario.

HC59 FERNÁNDEZ LARRAÍN, SERGIO. *El comunismo en Bolivia; versión taquigráfica de la conferencia ofrecida por el autor en el salón de actos del Partido conservador unido, el 3 de mayo de 1956.* Santiago de Chile: Publicaciones de Unión Democrática Boliviana,

1956. 71 p. A denunciation of the Bolivian MNR regime as Communist influenced or controlled; unreliable, but has some documents of interest.

HC60 MONTELLANO, JULIAN V. *Terror y angustia en el corazón de América.* Santiago de Chile: Impreso Gutenberg, 1954. 168 p. A Bolivian professor and former member of parliament describes the alleged Communist threat in Bolivia from the perspective of his personal experience. [A]

HC61 OSTRIA GUTIERREZ, ALBERTO. *A People Crucified; the Tragedy of Bolivia.* N.Y.: Prestige, 1958. 224 p. A study by a Bolivian newspaper editor of the revolution in progress since 1952. Alleges Communist influence in the MNR Party which has led the revolutionary regime.

HC62 PARTIDO DE LA IZQUIERDA REVOLUCIONARIA. *Programa de principios, estatutos y otros documentos.* La Paz, Bolivia: Editorial Trabajo, 1941. Documents concerning the establishment of PIR, an "independent Marxist" party, out of which the Communist Party of Bolivia developed a decade later.

HC63 VASQUEZ, EDMUNDO. *Bolivia en la encrucijada comunista.* Lima: Editorial Castrillón Silva, 1956. 230 p. Another denunciation of the MNR regime as Communist; unreliable.

4. BRAZIL

HC64 ALENKASTRE, A. *Braziliia i sotsialisticheskie strany.* Moscow: Izd. inostr. lit., 1961.

HC65 AMADO, JORGE. *Vida de Luiz Carlos Prestes; o cavalerio de esperanca.* 6th ed. Sao Paulo: Libraria Martins Editora, 1945. 366 p. Buenos Aires: Editorial Claridad, 1942. 395 p. Lyric and eulogistic biography of the head of the Brazilian Communist Party; written by one of the Brazilian CP's most important writers, a leading novelist.

HC66 BARBÊDO, ALCEU. *O fechamento do Partido comunista do Brasil.* Rio de Janeiro: Nacional, 1947. 114 p. Deals briefly with the outlawing of the Brazilian Communist Party.

HC67 BASTOS, ABGUAR. *Prestes e a revolução.* Rio de Janeiro: Editorial Calvino, 1946. Eulogistic and entirely favorable biography of the Brazilian Communist chief by a Communist writer who was once a comrade in arms of Prestes when a soldier. [B]

HC68 MACHADO, AUGUSTO (REIS MACHADO, AUGUSTO). *Cominho da revolucao operaria e Camponeza.* Rio de Janeiro: Calvino

Filho, 1934. A Communist estimate of the Brazilian situation during the "constitutional" phase of Getulio Vargas' long rule of Brazil.

HC68A PERALVA, OSVALDO. *O Retrato*. Rio de Janeiro: Editora Globo, 1962. The author is a former representative of the Brazilian CP in the Cominform. Very interesting and valuable for insights into the training in the Soviet Union of Brazilian Communists, the functioning of the Cominform, and the development of the split in the Brazilian CP in 1956-57, after the Khrushchev speech and Hungary.

HC68B PEREIRA, ASTROJILDO. *Formacao do PCB, 1922/28*. Rio de Janeiro: Editorial Vitoria, 1962. Reminiscences, by the first secretary of the Brazilian Communist Party, of its functioning during the 1920's. Quite objective, considering the source. First part of a larger study of Brazilian Communist history. Pereira is still an important figure in the PCB.

5. BRITISH GUIANA

HC69 JAGAN, CHEDDI. *Forbidden Freedom; the Story of British Guiana*. London: Lawrence and Wishart; N.Y.: International Pub., 1954. 96 p. Russian ed., Moscow: Izd. inostrannoi lit., 1955. 120 p. A study of the rise and first triumph of the pro-Communist Peoples Progressive Party, and its fall from power in 1953, told by the Party's chief leader, published in the U.S. by the Communist Party's publishing firm.

6. CHILE

(Edited by Cole Blasier and Robert J. Alexander)

HC70 ABARCA, HUMBERTO, and OCAMPO, SALVADOR. *La unidad del pueblo defendera las conquistas democraticas—discursos pronunciados en la camara por los diputados comunistas*. Santiago: Ediciones del Comite Central del Partido Comunista de Chile, 1941. A Chilean Communist Party pamphlet outlining that Party's position during the Stalin-Nazi Pact period. Written by two Communist deputies in Congress, one of them, Ocampo, being the principal Communist leader in the labor movement.

HC71 ALEGRIA, FERNANDO. *Recabarren*. Santiago: Editorial "Antares," 1938. 162 p. A short biography of the founder of the Chilean Communist Party, Luis Emilio Recabarren, written from the point of view of the Communists, at a period when they looked favorably on the biography of their founder—they did not always do so.

HC72 BLASIER, STEWART COLE. "The Cuban and Chilean Communist Parties; Instruments of Soviet Policy (1935-1948)." Ph.D.

dissertation, Columbia, 1954. 168 p. An interesting and well-informed discussion of the history of two of the most important Communist Parties in Latin America. Based almost exclusively on Latin American and primary Soviet sources. [A]

HC73 BOWERS, CLAUDE G. *Chile Through Embassy Windows, 1939-1953.* N.Y.: Simon and Schuster, 1958. 375 p. The memoirs of a very well-informed and liberal U.S. Ambassador to Chile. Contains a long discussion of the role of the Chilean Communist Party during the Second World War.

HC74 CONTRERAS LABARCA, CARLOS. *Adelante en la lucha por el programa del Frente Popular.* Santiago: Ediciones del Comite Central del Partido Comunista de Chile, 1940. A pamphlet by the then Secretary General of the Chilean Communist Party, concerning the position of that Party in the Popular Front, which was being imperiled by the pro-Axis position of the C.P.

HC75 ECHAIZ, RENE LEON. *Evolucion historica de los partidos politicos chilenos.* Santiago: Prensas de la Editorial Ercilla, 1939. 204 p. A study of the evolution of Chilean political parties. The history of the Chilean Communist Party is discussed at some length.

HC76 EDWARDS, ALBERTO, and FREI MONTALVA, EDUARDO. *Historia de los partidos politicos chilenos.* Santiago: Pacífico, 1949. 262 p. A standard sketch of Chilean political history to 1938. Includes a very brief treatment of the Communist Party.

HC77 *En defensa de la revolucion—informes, tesis y documentos presantados al Congreso Nacional del Partido Comunista a verificarse el 19 de marzo de 1933.* Santiago: Editorial Luis E. Recabarren, 1933. Report of the first congress of the Hidalgo (Trotskyite) faction of the Chilean Communists after the fall of the Ibanez dictatorship. Contains interesting information concerning the internal situation in the C.P. during the Ibanez regime, and causes for the split. [B]

HC78 FERNÁNDEZ LARRAÍN, SERGIO. *Traicion!!* Santiago: Talleres de El Imparcial, 1941. 218 p. A right-wing tract attacking the Communist Party for various policies, including its support of the Soviet-Nazi Pact. The author was at that time the member of Congress who sponsored legislation to outlaw the Communist Party.

HC79 GONZÁLEZ RODRÍGUEZ, ARMANDO. *Comunismo y democracia.* Santiago: Nascimento, 1951. 255 p. One man's opinion on how to stop Communism in Latin America.

HC80 *Hacia la formacion de un verdadero partido de clase—resoluciones de la Conferencia Nacional del Partido Comunista realizada en julio de 1933*. Santiago: Gutenberg, 1933. Report of the first congress of the Laferte (Stalinist) faction of the Chilean Communist Party after the fall of the Ibanez dictatorship. Gives the Stalinist version of the split in the Communists during the dictatorship. [B]

HC81 JOBET BURQUEZ, JULIO CESAR (JOBET, JULIO CESAR). *Luis Emilio Recabarren; los origenes del movimiento obrero y del socialismo chilenos*. Santiago: Prensa Latinoamericana, 1955. 180 p. The biography of the founder of the Chilean Communist Party, stressing in particular his earlier role as a Socialist and a trade union leader, and insisting on his belief in democracy. [B]

HC82 LAFERTE GAVINO, ELIAS (LAFERTE, ELIAS). *Vida de un comunista; páginas autobiográficas*. Santiago: Talleres Graficos Lautaro, 1957. The memoirs of the grand old man of Chilean Communism, now deceased.

HC83 MESA SECO, MANUEL F. *El comunismo ante la ley chilena*. Santiago: El Imparcial, 1947. 72 p. An anti-Communist pamphlet on the Communist Party's position before the law. In 1947 the Chilean Communist Party was outlawed following its break with the then President, Gabriel Gonzalez Videla. [B]

HC84 *Pacto de accion politica—Partido Socialista Autenico y Partido Comunista de Chile—documents*. Santiago: 1946. Documents concerning the united front of the Chilean Communists and one faction of the Socialists. Describes one of the many Communist attempts to infiltrate and destroy the Chilean Socialist movement.

HC85 PARTIDO COMUNISTA DE CHILE. *X sezd Kommunisticheskoi partii Chili (aprel 1956 g.)*. Moscow: Gospolitizdat, 1957. 247 p. A translation of materials published as a supplement to *Principios*, the Chilean Communist journal, during 1957. A most useful source, containing reports and speeches dealing with Chilean Communist activities and policies in 1956 and before. [A]

HC86 PARTIDO COMUNISTA DE CHILE. *Estatutos del Partido Comunista de Chile*. Antares: 1940. Chilean Communist Party statutes based on the Soviet model.

HC87 PARTIDO COMUNISTA DE CHILE. *Ricardo Fonseca, combatiente ejemplar*. Santiago: Lautaro, 1952. 184 p. Russian ed., Moscow: Izd. inostrannoi lit., 1955. 160 p. A Communist portrait of the deceased Secretary General. Fonseca took over the leadership of the Party in 1946 as Soviet policies towards the West and other leftist parties hardened. A tense and colorless personality, he was overshadowed by his predecessor, Carlos Contreras Labarca. His career was interrupted by illness and an early death. [B]

HC88 *Principios.* Santiago. Monthly. Theoretical journal and political magazine of the Chilean Communist Party. An almost indispensable source on Chilean Communism since 1941. [A]

HC89 *El Siglo.* Daily newspaper of the Chilean Communist Party. Preceded by *Frente Popular* and numerous other Communist papers. Publication suspended at various times. [A]

HC90 STEVENSON, JOHN R. *The Chilean Popular Front.* Philadelphia: U. of Pennsylvania; Oxford: H. Milford, 1942. 155 p. A skillful and informed treatment of an interesting period in Chilean politics. Contains a useful summary of Chilean history and a limited but adequate description of the Communist role in the Popular Front.

HC91 TEITELBOIM, VOLODIA. *Hijo del salitre.* 2nd ed. Santiago: Editora Austral, 1952. 460 p. A novel reportedly based on the life of Elías Lafertte, grand old man and sometime president of the Chilean Communist Party. Written by one of his Party comrades.

7. COLOMBIA

HC92 GOMEZ, EUGENIO J. *Problemas colombianos; comunismo, socialismo, liberalismo.* Bogota: Tipografia Colon-editorial, 1942. 460 p. A discussion of the relevance of Communism to other left-wing political trends, in a period when the Colombian Communist Party was at the apogee of its influence.

HC93 NIETO ROJAS, JOSÉ MARÍA. *La batalla contra el comunismo en Colombia; capítulos de historia patria, que deben ser faro y brujula para las futuras generaciones de Colombia.* Bogota: Empresa nacional de publicaciones, 1956. 390 p. A study of the problems of Communism in Colombia, published during the Rojas Pinilla dictatorship.

8. CUBA

(Edited by Rayburn D. M. Hanzlik)

HC94 ALEXANDER, ROBERT J. *Communism in Latin America.* New Brunswick, N.J.: Rutgers, 1957. 449 p. The chapter entitled "Stalinism in the Pearl of the Antilles" remains one of the most reliable sources on the history of Cuba's Communist Party. Despite the short length (25 pages), it covers the subject thoroughly and factually through 1956. [A]

HC95 BLASIER, STEWART COLE. "The Cuban and Chilean Communist Parties; Instruments of Soviet Policy (1935-1948)." Ph.D. dissertation, Columbia, 1954. 168 p. An interesting and well-informed discussion of the history of two of the most important Communist Parties in Latin America. Based almost exclusively on Latin American and primary Soviet sources. [A]

HC96 BRENNAN, RAY. *Castro, Cuba, and Justice.* Garden City, N.Y.: Doubleday, 1959. 282 p. A rather spectacular account of the Cuban rebellion, by an American journalist. Good for impressions of repressive conditions under the last years of Batista's rule, but of little scholarly value otherwise.

HC97 CASTRO, FIDEL. *History Will Absolve Me.* N.Y.: Stuart, 1961. 79 p. Translation of: *La historia me absolvera.* Castro's famous defense plea at his trial following the unsuccessful attack on the Moncada Barracks in 1953, which later provided the basis for the formation of the 26th of July Movement.

HC98 CASUSO, TERESA. *Cuba and Castro.* N.Y.: Random House, 1961. 249 p. The personal account of Castro's rise to power by an intimate compatriot who served as Castro's first delegate to the United Nations and who, disillusioned with Fidel's growing tyranny, defected to the U.S. Contains little on the influence of the Communists. Disputes the theory that Castro was ever a Communist.

HC99 DRAPER, THEODORE. *Castro's Revolution; Myths and Realities.* N.Y.: Praeger, 1962. 211 p. A valuable analysis of the relationship between Castro's revolution and Communism. Most of this material appeared in *The New Leader* in 1961 and 1962. Includes in an appendix an exchange of correspondence between the author and Herbert Matthews of *The New York Times* revealing fundamental differences in interpretation between two intensive students of the Castro revolution. Much of the book consists of devastating critiques of various writers who have looked upon Castro's regime through rose-colored glasses. [A]

HC100 DUBOIS, JULES. *Fidel Castro, Rebel, Liberator or Dictator?* Indianapolis: Bobbs-Merrill, 1959. 391 p. Written soon after Castro's victory, this is a fairly accurate account of the 26th of July Movement warfare against Batista. The author, who was with Castro during part of the revolution, speaks hopefully of Fidel, states he is not a Communist, but also warns that "the Communists would like to capture" him. Good for detailed information of the rebellion. The author is a correspondent for the Chicago *Tribune.*

HC101 *Fundamentos.* Havana. Monthly (Irregular). Theoretical journal and magazine of the Cuban Communist Party. Together with the Party's newspaper, the basic source on Communism in Cuba. Began publication in 1941. [A]

HC102 GUEVARA, ERNESTO (CHÉ). *Ché Guevara On Guerrilla Warfare*. Intro. by Maj. Harries-Clichy Peterson. N.Y.: Praeger, 1962. 85 p. A brief treatise on the essential factors for successful guerrilla warfare, by Fidel Castro's right-hand man in the conquest and Communization of Cuba.

HC103 *Hoy*. Newspaper of the Cuban Communist Party. First published in 1936. A day to day source of Party policies and activities. [A]

HC104 HUBERMAN, LEO, and SWEEZY, PAUL M. *Cuba; Anatomy of a Revolution*. 2nd ed. N.Y.: Monthly Review Press, 1961. 205 p. An account by two writers based on two three-week visits to Cuba in 1960. Sympathetic to the revolution; naïve to the potential of the Communists. Concludes that "if the United States would leave Cuba alone, the outlook would be excellent." Based on questionable sources. The authors are American leftists.

HC105 JAMES, DANIEL. *Cuba: The First Soviet Satellite in the Americas*. N.Y.: Avon, 1961. 320 p. A carefully-documented study of the origins and ends of the Cuban Revolution, based partly on interviews with some fifty Cuban exiles, formerly with Castro's movement. Lacks historic perspective and over-simplifies in places. By the author of *Red Design for the Americas—Guatemalan Prelude*.

HC106 KAYE, MARTIN, and PERRY, LOUISE. *Who Fights for a Free Cuba*? N.Y.: Workers Library Publishers, 1933. A pamphlet concerning Cuban conditions, written from the North American Communist Party's point of view.

HC107 LISTOV, B. B. *Po dorogam novoi Kuby*. Moscow: Profizdat, 1960. 154 p.

HC108 MARINELLO, JUAN. *Union revolucionaria comunista y la constitucion de 1940*. Havana: Ediciones Sociales, 1940. 64 p. A pamphlet on the Communist role in writing the constitution of 1940. Claims much credit for them in this effort. By the former head of the Cuban Communist Party. [B]

HC109 MATTHEWS, HERBERT L. *The Cuban Story*. N.Y.: Braziller, 1961. 318 p. An analysis of Castro's revolution by a prominent *New York Times* correspondent. Includes the story of the author's famous interview with Fidel in the Sierra Maestras in early 1957. Comments and reports on developments following Castro's victory, including the rise of the Communists. Not scholarly, but a useful account. Matthews was highly sympathetic toward Castro in the early years of the revolution. [B]

HC110 MILLER, WARREN. *90 Miles from Home.* Boston: Little, Brown, 1961. 279 p. A personal, pro-Castro account of the Cuban revolution, written as a novel. Includes little on Communism and is of limited scholarly value.

HC111 MILLS, C. WRIGHT. *Listen Yankee! The Revolution in Cuba.* N.Y.: McGraw, Hill, 1960. 192 p. British ed., *Castro's Cuba; the Revolution in Cuba.* London: Secker and Warburg, 1960. 191 p. A Professor of Sociology at Columbia University attempts to present the Cuban-United States crisis from the Cuban point of view. The result is a highly controversial book which has seldom been credited with objectivity.

HC112 NORTH, JOSEPH. *Cuba; Hope of a Hemisphere.* N.Y.: International Publishers, 1961. 95 p. A pro-Castro and pro-Communist diatribe by a long-time American Communist editor. The author, who was in Cuba and in contact with the rebels, castigates U.S. Cuban policy.

HC113 OBYDEN, K. M. *Kuba v borbe za svobodu i nezavisimost.* Moscow: Gospolitizdat, 1959. 95 p. A Soviet propaganda tract derogating the role of other than "peasant masses and Cuban Communists" in the Cuban revolution; emphasizes the need to extend the revolution to other Latin American countries.

HC114 PARTIDO COMUNISTA DE CUBA. *Estatutos del Partido comunista de Cuba.* Havana(?): Orientacion Social, 1939. Cuban Party statutes based on the Soviet model.

HC115 PARTIDO COMUNISTA DE CUBA, 3. ASAMBLEA NACIONAL, HAVANA, 1939. *Por la victoria popular; informes, conclusiones y discursos.* Havana: Imprenta "Alfa," 1939. 239 p. A detailed account in reports and speeches at the Third Party Congress of Communist policies during the period of rapprochement with Batista. [A]

HC116 PARTIDO SOCIALISTA POPULAR (CUBA), 2. ASAMBLEA NACIONAL, HAVANA, 1944. *Los socialistas y la realidad cubana; informes, resoluciones y discursos.* Havana: Ediciones del P.S.P., 1944. 309 p. A useful survey of Party policies and activities during the war as described in speeches and reports at the Second National Assembly of the Popular Socialist (Communist) Party. [A]

HC117 PFLAUM, IRVING P. *Tragic Island.* Englewood Cliffs, N.J.: Prentice-Hall, 1961. 196 p. A correspondent for the Chicago *Sun-Times*, formerly associated with the American Universities Field Staff, explains how U.S. policy helped lead to the present situation in Cuba.

HC118 PHILLIPS, RUBY HART. *Cuba: Island of Paradox.* N.Y.: McDowell, Obolensky, 1959. 434 p. The author, a veteran *New York Times* correspondent in Havana, gives her personal, day-by-day account of significant events in Cuba from the Machado regime to the overthrow of Batista. Written in a calm, objective manner, this work provides one of the better accounts of modern developments in Cuba. Little on Communism. [B]

HC119 RIVERO, NICOLAS. *Castro's Cuba; an American Dilemma.* N.Y.: Luce, 1962. 239 p. Among the best books written on the revolution. By a former Cuban diplomat under both Batista and Castro. Balanced, informative and candid. Author sees little hope for an indigenous uprising against Castro and suggests military intervention. [A]

HC120 ROCA, BLAS (pseud. of Francisco Calderio). *The Cuban Revolution; Report to the Eighth National Congress of the Popular Socialist Party of Cuba.* N.Y.: New Century, 1961. 127 p. A speech by the General-Secretary of the Cuban Communist Party to the Party Congress held in Havana during August, 1960. Praises the Castro revolution and sets forth the program of "unity" which eventually brought the Communists together with the 26th of July Movement. Invaluable for Communist attitudes toward Castro and the revolution during this period. [A]

HC121 ROCA, BLAS. *Siempre firmes.* Havana: Ediciones Sociales, 1940. A pamphlet on the Cuban Communists' position during the period when they were cementing their first alliance with General Fulgencio Batista. [B]

HC121A SMITH, EARL E. T. *The Fourth Floor; an Account of the Castro Communist Revolution.* N.Y.: Random House, 1962. 242 p. Mr. Smith was the American Ambassador to Cuba from June 1957 until shortly after Batista fell on January 1, 1959. In this book he blames the triumph of Castro and the Communists to the bureaucrats working on the fourth floor of the State Department.

HC122 SMITH, R. F. *The United States and Cuba; Business and Diplomacy, 1917-1960.* N.Y.: Bookman, 1961. 256 p. A diplomatic history with heavy emphasis on economic relations. The final chapter deals briefly with Castro's seizure of power.

HC123 SZULC, TAD, and MEYER, KARL E. *The Cuban Invasion.* N.Y.: Praeger, 1962. 156 p. Paperback ed., Ballantine. A careful examination of the 1961 American-backed attempt to overthrow the Castro regime.

HC124 TABER, ROBERT. *M-26; Biography of a Revolution.* N.Y.: Stuart, 1961. 348 p. A detailed, almost day-to-day, account of the revolution. Includes little on Communism; has limited scholarly value.

HC125 WEYL, NATHANIEL. *Red Star Over Cuba.* N.Y.: Hillman-Macfadden, 1961. 224 p. A polemical account of Castro's revolution and the rise of the Communists in Cuba. Claims that Castro was a "trusted Soviet agent" as early as 1949, and that the revolution was Communist-inspired. Of little scholarly value.

HC126 YOUNGBLOOD, JACK, and MOORE, ROBIN. *The Devil to Pay.* N.Y.: Coward, McCann, 1961. 320 p. A sensational account of Castro's revolution seen through the eyes of an adventurous American gunrunner who supplied the rebels with arms.

9. DOMINICAN REPUBLIC

HC127 DOMINICAN REPUBLIC, SECRETARIO DE ESTADO DE LO INTERIOR. *Libro blanco del comunismo en la República Dominicana.* Ciudad Trujillo: Editore del Caribe, 1956. 254 p. One of various tracts against enemies of the Trujillo dictatorship, published by that dictatorship; highly unreliable as to facts.

HC128 GALINDEZ SUAREZ, JESUS (Galindez, Jesus de). *La era de Trujillo; un estudio casuistico de dictadura hispanoamericana.* Santiago, Chile: Editorial del Pacifico, 1956. 452 p. A thorough study of the Trujillo regime, containing a sizable chapter on the evolution of the Dominican Communist Party, and Trujillo's role in making it an element of some importance in the Republic.

10. EL SALVADOR

HC129 SCHLESINGER, JORGE. *Revolución comunista—¿Guatemala en peligro?* Guatemala City: Union Tipográfica Castañeda, Avila y Cia, 1946. 284 p. A study, in spite of its title, of the attempted Communist Revolution in El Salvador in 1932. Contains photostats of many important documents. [B]

11. GUATEMALA

HC130 COMITÉ DE ESTUDIANTES UNIVERSITARIOS ANTICOMUNISTAS (GUATEMALA). *El calvario de Guatemala; publicación del Comité de Estudiantes Universitarios Anticomunistas en el primer aniversario del movimiento de liberación nacional, 3 de julio de 1954—3 de julio de 1955.* Guatemala: 1955. 397 p. A recounting of the Guatemalan experience under the pro-Communist regime of President Jacobo Arbenz, compiled by one of the principal organizations responsible for the downfall of that regime.

HC131 CONGRESO CONTRA LA INFILTRACIÓN SOVIÉTICA EN AMERICA LATINA, DELEGACIÓN DE GUATEMALA. 3RD, LIMA, 1957. *Informe al III Congreso contra la Internación Soviética en la América Latina que tendrá verificativo en la ciudad de Lima, Peru, durante los dias 10, 11, 12, 13 y 14 de abril de 1957.* Guatemala: 1957. 24 p. A report on the problem of Communism in Guatemala, given to an extreme right-wing congress. Accuracy questionable.

HC132 FORTUNY, JOSE MANUEL. *Informe sobre la actividad del Comite Central del Partido Comunista de Guatemala.* Guatemala City: Ediciones del Partido Guatemalteco del Trabajo, 1953. An important source of information on the activities of Guatemalan Communists during the Arbenz administration. Gives some indication of the degree to which Communists were coming to dominate that regime. [B]

HC133 GANDARIAS, LEON DE. *Democracia; la mejor arma contra el comunismo.* Guatemala: Secretaría de Divulgación, Cultura y Turismo de la Presidencia de la República, Sección de Impresos, 1957. 186 p. A defense of the anti-Communist regime which overthrew the Arbenz pro-Communist government, published by that regime.

HC134 GEIGER, THEODORE. *Communism versus Progress in Guatemala.* Washington: National Planning Association, 1953. 90 p. A more or less objective study of the role of the Communists in the Arevalo-Arbenz regimes.

HC135 GREAT BRITAIN, FOREIGN OFFICE. *Report on Events Leading up to and Arising out of the Change of Régime in Guatemala, 1954.* London: H. M. Stationery Office, 1954. An interesting report by a party without a direct interest in the Arbenz regime and its fall.

HC136 GUATEMALA, SECRETARÍA DE DIVULGACIÓN, CULTURA Y TURISMO. *Así se gestó la liberación.* L.A.H.A. Guatemala: 1956. 434 p. An official description of the movement which overthrew the pro-Communist Arbenz regime.

HC137 JAMES, DANIEL. *Red Design for the Americas; Guatemalan Prelude.* N.Y.: Day, 1954. 347 p. A study of the rise of the Communists in Guatemala between 1944 and 1954. Very good when discussing Guatemalan events, less reliable for information on other Latin American countries. Published only a few months after the fall of the Arbenz regime. [A]

HC138 JENSEN, AMY. *Guatemala; a Historical Survey.* N.Y.: Exposition Press, 1955. 263 p.

HC139 LOPEZ, VILLATORO M. *Por los fueros de la verdad historica, una voz de la patria escarnecida, Guatemala, ante la diatriba de uno de sus hijos renegados.* Guatemala?: 1956. 222 p.

HC140 MARTZ, JOHN D. *Communist Infiltration in Guatemala.* N.Y.: Vantage Press, 1956. 125 p. A study by one of the principal U.S. experts on Central America of Communist influence in Guatemala during the 1944-54 period.

HC141 NÁJERA FARFÁN, MARIO EFRAÍN. *Los estafadores de la democracia; hombres y hechos en Guatemala.* Buenos Aires: Glem, 1956. 301 p. An attack on the movement which overthrew the Arbenz regime.

HC142 OSEGUEDA, RAÚL. *Operación Guatemala $$OK$$.* México City: Editorial América nueva, 1955. 306 p. A study of the Arbenz regime and its overthrow, written by a former minister in the cabinets of both Arevalo and Arbenz.

HC143 SAMAYOA CHINCHILLA, CARLOS. *El quetzal no es rojo.* Guatemala City: Arana hermanos, 1956. 268 p. A defense of the movement against the Arbenz regime, written by a participant in the movement.

HC144 SCHATZSCHNEIDER, H. *Die neue Phase der Monroedoktrin angesichts der kommunistischen bedrohung Lateinamerikas unter besonderer berücksichtigung des falles Guatemala vor der Organisation Amerikanischer staaten und den Vereinten nationen.* Göttingen: Vandenhoeck and Ruprecht, 1957. 80 p.

HC145 SCHNEIDER, RONALD M. *Communism in Guatemala, 1944-1954.* N.Y.: Praeger, 1958. 350 p. A valuable study of Communist developments during the revolutionary period in Guatemala, based largely on Party documents which came to light after the fall of the Arbenz regime. [A]

HC146 U.S. DEPARTMENT OF STATE. *A Case History of Communist Penetration; Guatemala.* Department of State Publication 6465, Inter-American Series, April 1957. An official U.S. version of the rise of Communist influence in Guatemala during the 1944-54 period.

HC147 U.S. DEPARTMENT OF STATE. *Intervention of International Communism in Guatemala.* Washington: G.P.O., 1954. 96 p. The official United States indictment of Communist influence in the Arbenz regime. [A]

HC148 VALLE MATHEU, JORGE DEL. *La verdad sobre el "caso de Guatemala."* Guatemala?: 1956. 173 p. A defense of the overthrow of Arbenz, written by one of the chief participants in that overthrow.

12. MEXICO

HC149 BEALS, CARLETON. *Glass Houses; Ten Years of Free-Lancing.* Philadelphia: Lippincott, 1938. 413 p. Reminiscences of a famous American writer, of interest because of his account of the opera-boufé circumstances surrounding the founding of the Mexican Communist Party, in which he participated.

HC150 CLARAVAL, BERNARDO. *Cuando fuí communista.* Mexico: Polis, 1944. 232 p. An attack on Communists written by a former secondary leader of the Party.

HC151 GARCIA TREVINO, RODRIGO. *In ingerencia Rusa en Mexico y Sudamerica; pruebas y testimonios; documentos fehacientes de Lazaro Cardenas, Diego Rivera, Vicente Lombardo Toledano, David Alfaro Siqueiros, Emilio Portes Gil, Maxim Litvinov, etc.* Mexico: Editorial America, 1959. 253 p. A study by the leader of the Mexican Socialists of incidents in the history of the Mexican Communist Party, stressing particularly its subservience to the USSR.

HC152 LOMBARDO TOLEDANO, VICENTE. *La perspectiva de México, una democracia del pueblo; en torno al XX Congreso del Partido Comunista de la Unión soviética.* México: 1956. 253 p. An application of ideas of the CPSU's Twentieth Congress to Mexico, by the head of the Latin American trade union apparatus of the Communists. [B]

HC153 LOPEZ APARICIO, ALFONSO. *El movimiento obrero en México; antecedentes, desarrollo y tendencias.* 2nd ed. México: Editorial Jus, 1958. 280 p. Principally concerned with the labor movement; treats the Communists only tangentially.

HC154 PARTIDO COMUNISTA DE MEXICO. *Sobre la situacion politica actual y las tareas de los comunistas mexicanos; informe de la Comision politica al pleno del Comite central del Partido comunista mexicano celebrado el l. de diciembre de 1956, presentado por el camarada Dionisio Encina.* Mexico: Fondo de Cultura Popular, 1957. 116 p. An important survey of the Mexican situation and the role the Communists see themselves playing in it, in the mid-1950's. [B]

HC155 *Razon historica, principios, programa y estatutos del Partido Popular.* Mexico: 1948. Basic documents concerning the pro-Communist Popular Party of Mexico, led by Vicente Lombardo Toledano.

HC156 SALAZAR, ROSENDO. *Líderes y sindicatos.* México City: T. C. Modelo, 1953. 235 p. A study of leading individuals in the labor movement, by the principal historian of Mexican organized labor.

HC157 SHIFRIN, E. L. *Ekspansiia amerikanskogo imperializma v Meksike posle Vtoroi mirovoi voiny.* Moscow: Izd. Akademii nauk,

1952. 322 p. Shifrin, a Soviet political analyst, strains to support the thesis that a U.S. "imperialistic monopoly" grips Mexico in a stranglehold since World War II. Concludes that only "democratic forces" led by Mexican friends of Soviet-style socialism work toward achieving "national independence, progress and peace" for Mexico. Extensive use of U.S. and Mexican sources.

HC158 TREVIÑO, RICARDO. *El espionaje comunista y la evolucion doctrinaria del movimiento obrero en Mexico.* Mexico: 1952. 192 p. A study of various incidents in the history of the Communist Party in Mexico. The author was once a member of the I.W.W. and a leader of the Confederacion Regional Obrera Mexicana. [B]

13. PERU

HC159 BAZAN, ARMANDO. *Biografia de Jose Carlos Mariategui.* Santiago, Chile: Editorial Zig-Zag, 1939. 11 p. A short biography of the founder of the Peruvian Communist Party, who was one of the most original Peruvian thinkers of his time. Written from a very friendly point of view.

HC160 MARTINEZ DE LA TORRE, RICARDO. *Apuntes para una interpretación marxista de la historia social del Peru.* 2nd ed. Lima: Empresa Editora Peruana, 1947–. 4 vols. An invaluable collection of documents concerning the history of the Peruvian Communists and other radical groups as well as the trade union movement of the country. The author was one of the early associates of Mariategui, father of the Peruvian Communist Party. [A]

HC161 RAVINES, EUDOCIO. *La gran estafa.* 3rd ed. Santiago de Chile: Editorial del Pacifico, 1954. 270 p. English ed., *The Yenan Way; the Kremlin's Penetration of South America.* N.Y.: Scribner, 1951. 319 p. By a founder and one-time head of the Peruvian Communist Party.

HC161A SAN CRISTOBAL, A. *Economia, Educacion y Marxismo en Mariategui.* Lima: Ediciones Studium, SA., 1960. A study of the ideas and actions of Mariategui by a Catholic priest, designed to show that Mariategui was not really a Marxist and materialist, but rather an idealist and humanist. Very sympathetic to Mariategui the man.

HC162 TAVARA, SANTIAGO. *Historia de los partidos.* Lima: Editorial Huascarán, 1951. 264 p. Refers to Communists only in a minor way.

14. PUERTO RICO

HC163 ANDREU IGLESIAS, CESAR. *Independencia y socialismo.* San Juan, P.R.: Liberia Estrello Roja, 1951. 171 p. Written by the man who was at that time the Secretary General of the Communist Party of Puerto Rico. Later expelled, he became an Independence leader.

15. URUGUAY

HC164 ACUÑA, JUAN ANTONIO. *La maniobra y la calumnia política comunista; en torno a: la Confederación Sindical del Uruguay y al Sindicato Único de Obreros Arroceros y dentro del Partido Socialista. Defendamos el principio de un auténtico y libre gremialismo proletario.* Montevideo: 1957? 112 p. A denunciation of Communist infiltration of the Socialist Party of Uruguay by its former Labor Secretary, and Secretary General of the principal central labor body of the country. [B]

HC165 ARISMENDI, RODNEY. *El congreso de los constructores del comunismo; acerca de la obra de Stalin "Problemas económicos del socialismo en U.R.S.S."* Montevideo: Ediciones pueblos unidos, 1953. 166 p. A critique of the last important work of Stalin, with only incidental reference to Latin America, by the effective head of the Uruguayan Communists, one of the chief Latin American Communist "theorists."

HC166 CONFEDERACIÓN INTERAMERICANA DE DEFENSA DEL CONTINENTE. *Intrigas rojas en el Uruguay.* Montevideo: 1957. 99 p. A report on Communist influence in Uruguay by an extreme right-wing continental organization; of limited reliability. [B]

HC167 GOMEZ, EUGENIO. *Al servicio del pueblo.* Montevideo: 1943. A collection of pamphlets written by the leader of the Uruguayan Communist Party, between 1941 and 1943. Interesting because of the indications it gives of a shift in the Communist line during the Second World War.

HC168 GOMEZ, EUGENIO. *Europa, nuevo mundo.* Montevideo: Ediciones pueblos unidos, 1948. 256 p. One of many pamphlets by the man who was Secretary General of the Communist Party of Uruguay when this was written; only incidental reference to Latin America.

HC169 LITVINOV, MAKSIM M. *Relations Between the U.S.S.R. and Uruguay; Speeches Delivered Before the Council of the League of Nations.* London: Anglo-Russian Parliamentary Committee, 1936. 32 p. An account by the Soviet Commissar of Foreign Affairs of the rather turbulent history of diplomatic relations between the USSR and Uruguay.

HC170 MONTEVIDEO, JEFATURA DE POLICÍA. *Memorandum de actividades comunistas en el Uruguay.* Montevideo: 1951. 190 p. A police report on Communist activities; of limited reliability.

HC171 PINTOS, FRANCISCO R. *Batlle y el proceso historico del Uruguay*. Montevideo: La Bolsa de los Libros, 1938. 160 p. A study by a Uruguayan Communist leader of the work of Jose Batlle, father of the country's experiments in labor legislation and state socialism. Written while the Communists were in the Popular Front phase and therefore friendly to Batlle. Includes some discussion of the role of the Communist Party in carrying on the work Batlle started.

HC172 PINTOS, FRANCISCO R. *Historia del Uruguay (1851-1938); ensayo de interpretacion materialista*. Montevideo: Ediciones Pueblos Unidos, 1946. 204 p. A history of Uruguay written from the Communist point of view by one of the Party's leaders. Valuable discussion of the antecedents and history of Uruguayan Communists.

Addendum

HC173 POPPINO, ROLLIE E. *International Communism in Latin America; a History of the Movement, 1917-1963*. N.Y.: Free Press of Glencoe, 1964. 247 p. A handy and up-to-date précis of leading primary and secondary sources on the subject.

I. Europe

IA. GENERAL WORKS ON EUROPE

EDITED BY CURT F. BECK

IA1 AKADEMIIA NAUK SSSR, INSTITUT EKONOMIKI. *Polozhenie i borba rabochego klassa kapitalisticheskikh stran Evropy posle vtoroi mirovoi voiny*. Moscow: Akademiia nauk SSSR, 1952. 465 p. The theme of this collection of articles written shortly before Stalin's death is the increasing prosperity of the workers in the countries of the Socialist camp as against the pauperization of the working class in the capitalist countries of Europe. Articles on various countries are intended to document this myth.

IA2 AKADEMIIA NAUK SSSR, INSTITUT MIROVOI EKONOMIKI I MEZHDUNARODNYKH OTNOSHENII. *Polozhenie i borba rabochego klassa stran Zapadnoi Evropy*. Ed. by S. M. Ivanov. Moscow: Akademiia nauk SSSR, 1957. 420 p. Deals with the alleged difficult conditions and struggles of the working classes in France, Italy, England, and Western Germany. Statistics are used to prove the Marxist thesis that the conditions of workers in Western Europe deteriorate and that class divisions increase.

IA3 BOLDYREV, N. V., and GESSEN, S. N. *Sovremennaia Evropa; ekonomicheskii i politicheskii obzor vsekh gosudarstv Zapadnoi Evropy posle voiny*. Leningrad: "Seiatel," 1925. 252 p.

IA4 BORKENAU, FRANZ. *European Communism*. N.Y.: Harper; London: Faber & Faber, 1953. 564 p. German ed., Berne: Francke, 1952. 540 p. A detailed, factual account of Communism in Europe in the 1930's and 1940's by a German ex-Communist. Special emphasis on the French, Spanish, and Yugoslav Communist Parties and on Communist policy during the Popular Front era. In contrast to the author's earlier work, *World Communism* (British ed., *The Communist International*), published in 1938, this book is not based on personal experience. [A]

IA5 DALLIN, DAVID J. *Russia and Postwar Europe*. New Haven: Yale, 1943. 230 p. Written during the height of war-time friendship between the West and the Soviet Union, this was an appeal to the American public to be wary of Russian aims and not to be misled by talk that postwar Russia would be easy to get along with. Communist aims in Eastern Europe are spelled out.

IA6 EINAUDI, MARIO, GAROSCI, A., and DOMENACH, J. M. *Communism in Western Europe*. Ithaca, N.Y.: Cornell, 1951. 239 p.

An excellent brief survey of the French and Italian Communist Parties, edited by Mario Einaudi, a professor at Cornell University and the son of the former Italian president. Since it was written before 1951, it reflects the then current concern with the stagnant French and Italian economies and the unhealthy state of politics which were deemed largely responsible for the strength of the Italian and French Communist Parties. Contains a bibliographical article on French and Italian Communism. [B]

IA7 EINAUDI, MARIO. "Western European Communism; a Profile," *The American Political Science Review*, XLV, no. 1 (March 1951), p. 185-208. A bibliographical survey.

IA8 *Ekonomicheskoe polozhenie Zapadnoi Evropy; sbornik materialov.* Moscow: Izd. inostrannoi lit., 1958. 312 p. A collection of articles from Western European Communist sources evaluating economic conditions in Western Germany, Great Britain, France, Italy, and Belgium. The 1956-57 economic prosperity was not expected to last. Germany's faster pace of economic growth was attributed to her spending less on armaments than France or Great Britain.

IA9 EUDIN, XENIA J. and FISHER, HAROLD H. *Soviet Russia and the West, 1920-1927; a Documentary Survey.* Stanford: Stanford Univ. Press, 1957. 450 p. A valuable collection of official Soviet documents, statements by Russian leaders, and Comintern pronouncements made during a crucial but somewhat neglected period of Soviet foreign policy. With extensive commentary. A basic source. [A]

IA10 GRAHAM, MALBONE W. *The Soviet Security System.* (*International Conciliation*, no. 252.) Worcester: Carnegie Endowment for International Peace, 1929. 89 p. Traces Soviet foreign policy through several phases: security through sovietization, security through negotiation, security through conference, and consolidation and security through political agreements. Overemphasizes the treaty aspect of Soviet foreign policy. Contains a list of relevant treaties to which Russia was a signatory in the 1920's.

IA11 GRIGOREV, L., and OLENEV, S. *Borba SSSR za mir i bezopasnost v Evrope, 1925-1933 gg.* Moscow: Gospolitizdat, 1956. 158 p. A period in Soviet diplomacy somewhat neglected by historians under Stalin. Locarno is blamed for the division of Europe. Soviet policy is portrayed as furthering the cause of peace in disarmament conferences and the series of Soviet treaties implementing the Kellogg pact.

IA12 HÖPKER, WOLFGANG. *Europäisches Niemandsland; Moskaus Zwischeneuropa vom Nordkap bis Kreta.* Düsseldorf-Cologne: Eugen Diederich, 1956. 167 p. Rejects the Soviet policy of creating a neutrality zone between East and West, especially suggestions that West Germany be neutralized. Contends that the neutrality policy would not lead to peace but would bring war closer by weakening Western Europe.

IA13 JUST, ARTUR W. *Russland in Europa; Gedanken zum Ostproblem der abendlandischen Welt.* Stuttgart: Union Deutsche, 1949. 315 p. A German journalist who was in Moscow, 1926-38, pleads for a realistic assessment of Russia. Contains rambling observations on Russian history, the nature of Soviet politics, and the attitudes of others toward the Soviet Union, with special reference to German-Soviet relations.

IA14 KEETON, GEORGE W., and SCHLESINGER, RUDOLF. *Russia and Her Western Neighbours.* London: Cape, 1942. 160 p. A wartime plea for an understanding by the West of Russia's strategic interest in the areas bordering the Soviet Union in Europe. A case is also made for justifyiny the incorporation into the Soviet Union of the territories acquired during the 1939-40 period.

IA15 KHORVATSKII, VLADIMIR L. *Pan-Evropa i dunaiskaia federatsiia.* Ed. by Béla Kun. Moscow: Izdanie Mezhdunarodnogo agrarnogo instituta, 1933. 226 p. An attack on the 1929-33 plans for the Pan-European, as well as the Danubian Federations. Both are considered primarily the work of France and directed against the Soviet Union. They are also interpreted as capitalistic devices to divert attention from the agricultural problems facing agrarian Eastern Europe. [B]

IA16 KNIAZHINSKII, V. B. *Proval planov "obedineniia Evropy"; ocherk istorii imperialisticheskikh popytok antisovetskogo "obedineniia Evropy" mezhdu pervoi i vtoroi mirovymi voinami.* Moscow: Gospolitizdat, 1958. 212 p. An attempt to discredit the Pan-Europa movement by portraying it as a device to create an anti-Soviet front. Pan-Europe was allegedly organized by imperialistic monopolists and supported by reactionaries. Proposed by France and Western states, it led ultimately to Hitler's New Order.

IA17 *Kommunisten und Staatsmänner; im Kampf für den Sozialismus.* Vienna: Stern, 1947. 159 p. Published by the Austrian Communist Party. A collection of speeches by Communist leaders: Gottwald, Thorez, Tito, Dolores Ibarruri (Pasionaria), Togliatti, Rakosi, Gomulka, and Harry Pollitt. The introduction emphasizes that each country must find its own way to socialism.

IA18 LASERSON, MAX M. *Russia and the Western World; the Place of the Soviet Union in the Comity of Nations.* N.Y.: Macmillan,

1945. 275 p. Written at the close of World War II, the main theme is that social and political factors in the internal development of the Soviet Union will lead to coexistence with the West. Soviet policy toward Europe in the 1920's and 30's is portrayed as forming a basis for closer East-West relations after World War II.

IA19 LASERSON, MAX M., ed. *The Development of Soviet Foreign Policy in Europe, 1917-1942; a Selection of Documents.* N.Y.: Carnegie Endowment, 1943. 95 p. Largely superseded by later, more comprehensive collections, especially that of Jane Degras (see "Documents" section).

IA20 LAVRICHENKO, M. V. *"Plan Marshalla" i razorenie selskogo khoziaistva Zapadnoi Evropy.* Moscow: Gospolitizdat, 1950. 214 p. A Stalinist condemnation of the Marshall Plan as a plan for the enslavement of Western Europe by American imperialism. Its alleged failures are contrasted with the "great rise" of agriculture in the Soviet Union and Eastern Europe.

IA21 LAZIĆ, BRANKO. (Lazitch, Branko.) *Les Partis Communistes d'Europe, 1919-1955.* Paris: Les Iles d'Or, 1956. 255 p. A very useful reference for brief histories of individual European Communist parties, including membership figures and biographies of leading Communists as of 1955. Contains also a summary of Comintern and Cominform statistics and extracts of Comintern resolutions. The author, a Serbian anti-Communist, maintains illegality and low living standards do not necessarily help Communist strength. Such strength results from governmental instability, cleverness of Communist tactics, and help from the USSR. [A]

IA22 LEIBBRANDT, GOTTLIEB. *Bolschewismus und Abendland; Idee und Geschichte eines Kampfes gegen Europa.* Berlin: Junker und Dünnhaupt, 1939. 156 p. A Nazi interpretation of the nature of the Communist threat to Europe. Says the historical background of Russia provided fertile ground for "Jewish Marxism." Bolshevism is depicted as a Jewish device to undermine the West.

IA23 LISOVSKII, V. I. *Imperialisticheskie bloki.* Moscow: 1958. 119 p. Mostly devoted to the various West European plans for economic cooperation—Euratom, the Coal and Steel Authority, and the like, plans which forge the "West European Bloc" under America's baleful aegis.

IA24 MALYNSKI, EMMANUEL. *Pour sauver l'Europe.* Paris: Librairie Cervantes, 1922. 214 p. English ed., *How to Save Europe.* London: Palmer, 1925. 293 p. The author, who also wrote a 25 volume antisemitic study of the Jewish question, *La Mission du Peuple de Dieu,* condemns the application of democracy and nationalism to the post-

World War I settlement. He proposes the partition of Russia between Germany (northern Russia and northern Asia), England (southern Russia and Central Asia), Poland (Ukraine), with Austria getting the Balkans and France the Levant.

IA25 MARJAY, FRIEDRICH. *Europa oder Chaos? Ein Ungar über den Bolschewismus.* Nürnberg: Willmy, 1943. 287 p. A poorly-organized and disjointed account of the Soviet threat to Europe written by a Hungarian, a supporter of Admiral Horthy, based on the Nazi theme that the Jews were the main threat. Emphasizes the Béla Kun regime in Hungary. Interesting photographs.

IA26 MASLENNIKOV, VIACHESLAV A. and others, eds. *Amerikanskii plan zakabaleniia Evropy; sbornik statei.* Moscow: Gospolitizdat, 1949. 599 p. A broadside against the Marshall Plan, delivered shortly after its adoption. The authors take up in separate chapters American relations with individual Western European countries to illustrate the main theme of domination. Useful as a detailed statement of the Soviet position.

IA27 *Mezhdunarodnye problemy; stati o politike i ekonomike sovremennoi Evropy.* Moscow: "Bereg," 1922. 130 p. A collection of essays dealing primarily with the economic restoration of post-World War I Europe. Two articles deal with the problems faced by the 1922 Genoa Conference.

IA28 MINDEN, GERALD. *Europa zwischen USA und USSR; Grundlagen der Weltpolitik seit Ende des 2. Weltkrieges.* Bamberg: Bamberger, 1949. 334 p. A thorough and pessimistic view of the European scene in the immediate postwar years. The author ranges off into some speculation, which looks bad only in retrospect.

IA29 PECK, JOACHIM. *Was Wird aus Europa?* Berlin: Verlag der Nation, 1956. 2 vols. An East German Communist work accusing the U.S. of fostering aggression by dividing Europe into rival blocs and by hindering solution of the German question. Endorses Russian proposals on the German question.

IA30 SCHMIDT, ERIK I. *30 Aars Kommunistisk politik i Rusland og Vesteuropa; Gennemgang og Kritik.* Copenhagen: Munksgaards, 1948. 286 p. The author, who was personally acquainted with German, Danish, and Russian Communists, surveys Communism in Russia and Western Europe during the years 1917-47. He describes the Russian revolution, economic, political, and cultural developments in Russia, Comintern policy in Western Europe, and includes a special chapter on the Danish Communist Party. Good bibliography.

IA31 SOBAKIN, VADIM K. *Kollektivnaia bezopasnost v Evrope.* Moscow: Gos. izd. iurid. lit., 1956. 119 p. The Soviet Union is portrayed as the champion of collective security before and after World War II. NATO is a barrier to collective security. The U.S. is blamed for the split of Europe and the consequent sense of insecurity. Peace must be secured through negotiations.

IA32 *Soviet Efforts for Peace in Europe and against German Rearmament; Documents.* London: Soviet News, 1955. 160 p. A collection of documents to prove that Soviet policy is directed toward peace.

IA33 STARLINGER, WILHELM. *Russland und die Atlantische Gemeinschaft.* Würzburg: Marienburg, 1957. 163 p. A German professor, a former prisoner of the Russians, argues in a strongly nationalist vein for a Western policy of no concessions to the Russians. Such a policy must be based on Germany's reliance on NATO and especially the U.S.

IA34 STURM, ROBERT. *Europa Brennt; Moskau am Werk.* Bayreuth: Gauverlag Bayerische Ostmark, 1936. 184 p. A typical Nazi justification of their anti-Bolshevik policy. Soviet Russia is threatening capitalist Europe. Only Nazi Germany is aware of the threat; the rest of Europe is falling prey to Soviet schemes.

IA35 SUSLIN, P. N. *"Obshchii rynok" shesti evropeiskikh stran.* Moscow: Vneshtorgizdat, 1961. A Soviet view of the Common Market.

IA36 *Der unvermeidliche Kriege zwischen der Sowjet-Union und den Westmächten, die Vernichtung des Bolschewismus durch das geeinigte Europa; Betrachtungen eines europäischen Staatsmannes der Gegenwart.* Berlin: Verlag für Aktuelle Politik, 1930. 128 p. The anonymous author claims not to be a Nazi, but ties Bolshevism to Eastern European Jews who were neither acclimatized nor true to their racial-religious heritage. Advocates a combined European military intervention to oust Bolshevism, and claims such a campaign against Russia would take only three months.

IA37 VODOVOZOV, V. *Zapadnaia Evropa i Amerika posle voiny; fakty i tsifry.* Petrograd: Gosizdat, 1922. 208 p. A factual account of territorial and political changes which occurred in Europe between 1917 and 1921. An interesting commentary on how little Russia knew about what happened in the outside world while the Civil War was raging.

IB. EASTERN EUROPE

EDITED BY R. V. BURKS AND FRANCIS S. WAGNER

1. GENERAL WORKS

IB1 ASTERIOU, SOCRATES J. "The Third International and the Balkans, 1919-1945." Ph.D. dissertation, University of California, Berkeley, 1959.

IB2 BERRI, GINO. *Pace e guerra fra Danubio e Nilo*. Milan: Garzanti, 1949. 181 p. A popular account, but includes a careful analysis of the relative power positions of the Soviet Union and the West in the Balkans, the Straits, and the Middle East.

IB3 BLACK, CYRIL E., ed. *Challenge in Eastern Europe; 12 Essays*. New Brunswick, N.J.: Rutgers University Press, 1954. 276 p. Produced under the auspices of the Mid-European Studies Center of the National Committee for a Free Europe, Inc. The contributors are either East European exiles or American specialists on Eastern Europe. Organized topically, the work treats such developments as the liberal tradition, the peasant parties, and the prospects of federation.

IB4 BURKS, RICHARD V. *The Dynamics of Communism in Eastern Europe*. Princeton, N.J.: Princeton University Press, 1961. 244 p. An historical, geographic, and statistical analysis of the social and ethnic composition of eight East European Communist parties. The analysis covers the period 1917-1953, and is based on works in ten languages. Major emphasis is on the role of such ethnic factors as minority status in producing adherence to Communism. [A]

IB5 BYRNES, ROBERT F., ed. *Bibliography of American Publications on East Central Europe, 1945-1957*. Bloomington: Indiana University Publications (Slavic and East European Series), 1958. 213 p. The only bibliography of its kind. Contains a 15-page analysis of American writings on the area. Lists 2810 books and articles published in the U.S. The Baltic states are included, but Greece and Eastern Germany are not. Unannotated. [A]

IB6 BYRNES, ROBERT F., ed. *East Central Europe under the Communists*. N.Y.: Published for the Mid-European Studies Center of the Free Europe Committee by Praeger, 1956-57. 7 vols.

Albania (ed. by Stavro Skendi). 389 p.

Czechoslovakia (ed. by Vratislav Busek and Nicholas Spulber). 520 p.

Bulgaria (ed. by L. A. D. Dellin). 457 p.

Hungary (ed. by E. C. Helmreich). 466 p.

Romania (ed. by Stephen Fischer-Galati). 399 p.
Poland (ed. by Oscar Halecki). 601 p.
Yugoslavia (no editor given). 488 p.

An important series. Each volume consists of chapters by American-born and émigré specialists on such topics as geography, history, population, the arts, religion, labor, industry, agriculture, etc. Although the emphasis is on developments since 1945, most of the chapters also contain considerable background information. (For annotations on the individual volumes, see the appropriate country sections). [A]

IB7 BYSTŘINA, IVAN. *Lidová demokracie.* Prague: Nakl. Československá akademie věd, 1957. 240 p. A well-documented Marxist-Leninist survey of the 1917-47 developments in the Soviet Union, Bulgaria, Germany, Hungary, Poland, Rumania, and, above all, Czechoslovakia. The October Revolution of 1917 is treated as a model for all Marxist affairs. The concepts of bourgeois, people's, and socialist democracies, as well as of Communism, are elucidated by investigating factual situations. Important bibliographical notes. [A]

IB8 HALASZ, NICHOLAS. *In the Shadow of Russia; Eastern Europe in the Post-War World.* N.Y.: Ronald, 1959. 390 p. An historical narrative with major concentration on Eastern Europe since 1945, but with extensive material on earlier events. Halasz is a Hungarian born in Czechoslovakia and a writer and journalist of long experience. Little documentation.

IB9 HÖPKER, WOLFGANG. *Die Ostsee ein rotes Binnenmeer? Eine politisch-strategische Studie.* Berlin: Verlag E. S. Mittler and Sohn, 1958. 102 p. A study, sponsored by the Arbeitskreis für Wehrforschung in Frankfurt/M, of the Soviet effort to dominate the Baltic through "neutralization."

IB10 JAKSCH, WENZEL. *Europas Weg nach Potsdam; Schuld und Schicksal im Donauraum.* Stuttgart: Deutsche, 1958. 522 p. Jaksch was the leader of the Sudeten German Social Democrats at the time of the Munich crisis. His book, a compound of history, autobiography, and propaganda, is a passionate apologia for a lost cause.

IB11 KOLARZ, WALTER. *Myths and Realities in Eastern Europe.* London: L. Drummond, 1946. 274 p. An original and provocative study of the national myths of the East European peoples. While much of the material deals with pre-1917 history, and the author is inclined to see only the negative aspects of East European nationalism, the work is very useful as background to Soviet policy in the area. [B]

IB12 LUKACS, JOHN A. *The Great Powers and Eastern Europe.* N.Y.: American Book, 1953; Chicago: Regnery, 1954. 878 p. A detailed narrative account of the diplomatic history of Eastern Europe since the first World War, with emphasis on the period from 1934 to 1945. Finland and the Baltic countries are included. The author argues that the indifference and ignorance of the West were primarily responsible for the loss of Eastern Europe first to the Axis, then to Soviet Russia. Based on materials in many languages, but the documentation leaves something to be desired. [B]

IB13 PETROV, FEDOR N., ed. *Balkanskie strany.* Moscow: Gosudarstvennyi Institut "Sovetskaia Entsiklopediia," Moscow, 1946. 548 p. An encyclopedic compendium for general use, generally of high quality. The interpretation of the 19th century liberation movements in the Balkans is strongly pro-Russian, and the period of Nazi-Soviet collaboration is quietly passed over. But as a handbook the work is outstanding.

IB14 ROUCEK, JOSEPH S. *The Politics of the Balkans.* N.Y.: McGraw-Hill, 1939. 168 p. 2nd ed., *Balkan Politics; International Relations in No Man's Land.* Stanford, Cal.: Stanford Univ. Press, 1948. 298 p. A reference work based largely on secondary sources and marred by a multitude of errors. The treatment is objective and the facts are interestingly presented.

IB15 SCHLESINGER, RUDOLF. *Federalism in Central and Eastern Europe.* N.Y.: Oxford Univ. Press, 1945. 533 p. An analysis of the prerequisites of successful federalism, based on a survey of federalism in Germany, the Hapsburg empire, the Soviet Union, and two of the succession states. The author is an exile scholar of Marxian orientation.

IB16 STAVRIANOS, LEFTEN S. *Balkan Federation, a History of the Movement toward Balkan Unity in Modern Times.* Northampton, Mass.: Smith College, Department of History, 1944. 338 p. A work of original research dealing with both the efforts of Balkan diplomacy and of revolutionary Marxism to promote the unification of the Balkan peoples in a single state. Important background material for the study of the federation effort of the Yugoslav Communists.

IB17 STAVRIANOS, LEFTEN S. *The Balkans Since 1453.* N.Y.: Rinehart, 1958. 970 p. Written as a text but based on many sources not usually available to Western scholars, this work is in considerable part an original synthesis in English. The author argues that the oppressive character of the Ottoman empire, particularly in its hey-day, has been overplayed. A book of great value. [A]

IB18 SZTACHOVA, JIRINA, comp. *Mid-Europe, a Selective Bibliography.* N.Y.: National Committee for a Free Europe, Mid-European Studies Center, 1953. 197 p. Contains 1700 entries. Limited to works in Western languages, mainly those in English, French and German. Arranged by countries and topics. Unannotated.

IB19 U.S. LIBRARY OF CONGRESS, DIVISION OF BIBLIOGRAPHY. *The Balkans; a Selected List of References.* Comp. by Helen F. Conover under the direction of Florence S. Hellman. Washington: Library of Congress, 1945. 5 vols. in 1. This useful list is restricted in the main to works published since the Treaty of Versailles and, with few exceptions, to writings in the languages of Western Europe available in American libraries. Official works in the Balkan languages are included when they have summaries or captions in English, French or German. Consists of 5 parts: I. General, II. Albania, III. Bulgaria, IV. Rumania, and V. Yugoslavia. Indices.

IB20 WAGNER, WOLFGANG. *Die Teilung Europas, Geschichte der sowjetischen Expansion 1918-1945.* Stuttgart: Deutsche Verlags-Anstalt, 1959, 246 p. English ed., *The Partitioning of Europe.* Stuttgart: 1959. Views the division of Germany as a function of the division of Europe.

IB21 WOLFF, ROBERT LEE. *The Balkans in Our Time.* Cambridge: Harvard Univ. Press, 1956. 618 p. An able history of the Balkan countries (except Greece) from the earliest times, with emphasis on the period since 1939. The author is a professor of history at Harvard who has had considerable experience in the Balkans, partly as an expert on the Balkans for O.S.S. during World War II. [A]

2. 1917-1941

IB22 AKADEMIIA NAUK SSSR, FUNDAMENTALNAIA BIBLIOTEKA OBSHCHESTVENNYKH NAUK. *Literatura o mezhdunarodnom revoliutsionnom dvizhenii; Velikaia Oktiabrskaia sotsialisticheskaia revoliutsiia i podem revoliutsionnogo dvizheniia v Bolgarii, Vengrii, Polshe, Rumynii i Chekhoslovakii; ukazatel knig i statei vyshedshikh v svet v 1951-1958 gg.* Comp. by T. Ia. Eliseeva and others. Ed. by E. M. Kan. Moscow: Izd. Akademii nauk SSSR, 1959. 191 p. Deals only with the period 1917-23. Divided into 5 sections, by country. Each section is subdivided under such headings as "Statements of V. I. Lenin on the Revolutionary Movement in Bulgaria," "The Struggle for the Formation of a Communist Party," etc. Within each subdivision items in Russian are listed first, followed by works in the language of the particular country. Bibliographies are included at the end of each section.

IB23 BOSHKOVICH, B. *Malaia Antanta; sotsialno-ekonomichesko-politicheskii ocherk.* Moscow: Gos. sots.-ek. izd., 1934. 150 p. A Marxist recounting of economic history as well as a brief description of the Communist parties of the Little Entente states, and a review of the relationships between them and the USSR, focused on the years 1929-33. Poorly footnoted; with maps.

IB24 DUROSELLE, JEAN BAPTISTE, ed. *Les Frontières européennes de l'U.R.S.S., 1917-1941.* Paris: A. Colin, 1957. 354 p. (Cahiers de la Fondation Nationale des Sciences Politiques no. 85.) A very useful diplomatic historical study of the Soviet Union's European frontiers up to June 1941. The events leading to the incorporation of the Baltic States into the USSR cover half the volume. The rest deals with the Soviet Union's frontiers with Finland, Poland and Romania. Excellent bibliography. [A]

IB25 EGOROV, I. V. *Nashi sosedi; Finliandiia, Polsha, Rumyniia, Estoniia, Latviia, Litva.* Leningrad: Morskoe vedomstvo, 1925. 100 p. An introductory chapter on the Soviet Union's 1917-25 international relations precedes the interpretive description of the political, economic, military, and geographical conditions of its neighboring countries. Some statistics.

IB26 KABAKCHIEV, KHRISTO S., BOSHKOVICH, B., and VATIS, KH. *Kommunisticheskie partii Balkanskikh stran.* Moscow: Gosizdat, 1930. 240 p. A historical survey of the Communist movements in Bulgaria, Yugoslavia, and Greece by three Comintern officials. Introduction by Georgy Dimitrov. Unusually useful.

IB27 KOREK, VALERIE, and STARK, JOHANN. *Mitteleuropa-Bibliographie . . . eine Übersicht des Schriftums der Jahre 1919 bis 1934.* Berlin: C. Heymann, 1935. 265 p. An annotated bibliography of monographic and periodical literature. The entries on the agrarian question and socio-economic changes are very valuable. Consists of a general part and special sections on Germany, Austria, Hungary, Yugoslavia, Rumania, Czechoslovakia, and Poland.

IB27A MACARTNEY, CARLILE A., and PALMER, A. W. *Independent Eastern Europe; a History.* N.Y.: St. Martin's, 1962. 499 p. A political history with primary emphasis on international affairs and diplomacy, this very useful handbook concentrates its attention on the Danube valley. Well documented. Excellent critical bibliography. [A]

IB28 MALYNSKI, EMMANUEL. *Les Problèmes de l'Est et la Petite-Entente.* Paris: Librairie Cervantès, 1931. 560 p. Relates Communist as well as Soviet connections. Undocumented.

IB29 ROYAL INSTITUTE OF INTERNATIONAL AFFAIRS, INFORMATION DEPARTMENT. *Southeastern Europe; a Political and Economic Survey.* London: Royal Institute of International Affairs; N.Y.: Oxford Univ. Press, 1939. 203 p. A good survey of the politics and economies of the countries of southeastern Europe, with special emphasis on the rise of German and Italian influence. The most informative sections deal with foreign trade and related matters.

IB30 SAVADJIAN, LÉON, ed. *Bibliographie balkanique.* Paris: Société Générale d'Imprimerie 1931-37. 7 vols. Annotated. Indexed by authors. Lists articles published in key journals. Organized by country and to some extent by topic. Included in the 1937 volume is a *memento encyclopedique.* Includes books in French, English, Italian and German. Annual lists, except for Vol. 1 which covers the period 1920-30, and Vol. 2, which covers 1931-32. [A]

IB31 SETON-WATSON, HUGH. *Eastern Europe between the Wars; 1918-1941.* N.Y.: Cambridge University Press, 1945. 443 p. 2nd ed., N.Y.: 1946. A standard work by a leading English authority, who has long personal experience in the area and commands many of the languages. The author is Professor of History at the University of London. [A]

IB32 U.S. DEPARTMENT OF STATE. *Documents on German Foreign Policy, 1918-1945*; Series D (1937-45), Vol. v., *Poland; the Balkans; Latin America; the Smaller Powers, June, 1937-March, 1939.* Washington: G.P.O., 1953. 977 p. Though the documents deal overwhelmingly with Germany, many of them are useful on Soviet relations, especially in analyzing the international constellations of the Little Entente states, including Carpatho-Ruthenia, a part of Czechoslovakia. Well-edited, with an analytical list of documents and appendices.

IB33 WUEST, JOHN J. "Diplomatic Relations Between the Soviet Union and the Balkan States From the Bolshevik Revolution to the Outbreak of the Russo-German War, With Special Reference to Communist Activities in the Balkans." Ph.D. dissertation, U. of California, 1949.

3. 1941-1963

IB34 *The Absent Countries of Europe; Lectures held at the Collège de l'Europe libre, 6th Summer-Session (6 August-6 September, 1957) in Strasbourg-Robertsau.* Bern: Osteuropa-Bibliothek, 1958. 272 p. A collection of lectures given by various experts, most of them exiles. John Keep and Walter Kolarz deal directly with Soviet policy.

IB35 AKADEMIIA NAUK, INSTITUT FILOSOFII. *O narodnoi demokratii v stranakh Evropy; sbornik statei.* Ed. by Fedor T. Konstantinov. Moscow: Gospolitizdat, 1956. 375 p. Published in the shadow of the 20th Soviet Party Congress, this collective work emphasizes the divergencies among the Satellite paths to Socialism, the importance of the Soviet army in the establishment of the people's democracies, and the difficulties of exact periodization as between the years of democratic revolution and those of socialist construction.

IB36 AKADEMIIA NAUK, INSTITUT FILOSOFII. *Sodruzhestvo stran sotsializma.* Ed. by F. T. Konstantinov and A. I. Arnoldov. Moscow: Izd. Akad. nauk SSSR, 1958. 337 p. Six authors treat as many topics: the influence of the Bolshevik revolution on human history and on the structure of the "People's Democracies," socialist legality, socialism in China, the cultural revolution in the "People's Democracies," and "proletarian internationalism."

IB37 AMERICAN ACADEMY OF POLITICAL AND SOCIAL SCIENCE. *Moscow's European Satellites.* Ed. by Joseph S. Roucek. Philadelphia, 1950. 253 p. (Its *Annals*, Vol. 271, Sept. 1950). A summary of the then current situation, topically organized. On the whole a valuable addition, though assembled in haste and somewhat loosely edited. [B]

IB38 AMERICAN ACADEMY OF POLITICAL AND SOCIAL SCIENCE. *The Satellites of Eastern Europe.* Ed. by Henry L. Roberts. Philadelphia: 1958. 230 p. (Its *Annals*, Vol. 317, Sept. 1958). Devoted to the area's (including the Baltic states) 1945-57 social, economic, and cultural changes; the political and ideological crisis, East-West relations, as well as to the analysis of the Communist system in general by twenty distinguished authors, among them Hugh Seton-Watson, Robert F. Byrnes, and Ivo Ducháček. Useful statistics and bibliographical footnotes. [A]

IB39 ANTONOFF, NICOLAS. *The Soviet Block—Political, Economic and Cultural Organization.* Washington: National Committee for a Free Europe, 1953. 130 p. A general survey based extensively on secondary sources.

IB40 ASPATURIAN, VERNON V. "The Impact of Soviet Ideology and Institutions on Eastern Europe." Ph.D. dissertation, Univ. of California, Los Angeles, 1951.

IB41 BARKER, ELISABETH. *Truce in the Balkans.* London: Percival Marshall, 1948. 256 p. A survey of Bulgaria, Romania, Greece, Turkey and Trieste in 1945-46. Good analysis and well written.

IB42 BARTLETT, VERNON. *East of the Iron Curtain.* London: Latimer House, 1949; N.Y.: McBride, 1950. 212 p. A London newspaper correspondent and former League of Nations official writes about conditions in Eastern Europe after a three months' visit in the spring of 1949. Good reportage; the chapter on Finland is first class.

IB43 BARTON, PAUL. *Conventions collectives et réalités ouvrières en Europe de l'Est.* Paris: Les Editions Ouvrières, 1957. 287 p. A comparative analysis of collective labor contracts in the European Satellites and the Soviet Union. The author, formerly a member of the Czech Left, presents in evidence the first Soviet contracts to become available in the West.

IB44 BEAMISH, TUFTON V. H. *Must Night Fall?* London: Hollis & Carter, 1950. 292 p. A thorough investigation, based primarily on study of official Communist pronouncements, of conditions in Poland, Bulgaria, Hungary, and Romania, together with a final chapter stating the conservative position that Socialism is a half-way house to Communism.

IB45 BETTS, REGINALD R., ed. *Central and South Eastern Europe, 1945-48*. London: Royal Institute of International Affairs, 1950. 227 p. A useful political summary, but not free from error.

IB46 BIRKE, ERNST, and NEUMANN, RUDOLF, eds. *Die Sowjetisierung Ost-Mitteleuropas; Untersuchungen zu ihrem Ablauf in den einzelnen Ländern.* Frankfurt a/M.: Metzner, 1959. 398 p. A product of German expellee scholarship, this careful and detailed presentation covers the Baltic states and East Germany as well as Eastern Europe proper; it is marred by its failure to deal with the Nazi occupation of the area as a major factor in preparing the way for sovietization.

IB47 BLACK, CYRIL E., ed. *Readings on Contemporary Eastern Europe*. N.Y.: Mid-European Studies Center of the National Committee for a Free Europe, 1953. 346 p. Deals with such matters as economic nationalism, tactics of the People's Front, and the Yugoslav experiment in decentralization. A 30-page annotated bibliography is appended.

IB48 BORSODY, STEPHEN. *The Triumph of Tyranny; the Nazi and Soviet Conquest of Central Europe*. London: Cape, 1960; N.Y.: Macmillan, 1960. 285 p. A well-written treatise by a college teacher, formerly a diplomat and journalist, dealing exclusively with the political aspects of the changing situations, with heavy emphasis on Czechoslovakia and Hungary. Economic, cultural, and even Party connections are almost totally neglected. Too little space is devoted to Polish and Yugoslav events. Uses neither primary nor unpublished sources nor the author's personal experiences in post-1945 Hungary, but is based extensively on well-known English publications. Contains maps.

IB49 BRZEZINSKI, ZBIGNIEW K. *The Soviet Bloc; Unity and Conflict*. Cambridge: Harvard, 1960. 470 p. Rev. paperback ed., N.Y.: Praeger, 1961. 543 p. The first incisive and methodical treatment of intra-Bloc relations. Unusually rich in information and insights. Bulwarked by statistics, notes and a 15-page bibliography. [A]

IB50 CARLTON, RICHARD K., ed. *Forced Labor in the "People's Democracies."* N.Y.: Published for the Mid-European Studies Center of the Free Europe Committee by Praeger, 1955. 248 p. A collective work prepared by researchers at the Mid-European Studies Center. Covers the legal framework of forced labor in the Satellites, the operation of the forced labor system, the effect of the amnesties following Stalin's death and related matters.

IB51 CLARION, NICOLAS. *Le glacis soviëtique; théorie et pratique de la démocratie nouvelle.* Paris: A. Somogy, 1948. 283 p. Treats the establishment of Soviet domination in Eastern Europe from the legal, political, economic, and demographic points of view.

IB52 CLEMENTIS, VLADIMIR. *Slovanstvo kedysi a teraz.* Prague: Orbis, 1946. 141 p. Discusses the problems of synthesis between Slavdom and Communism and questions of national Communism, modified Pan-Slavism, etc. Russia, Yugoslavia, and Czechoslovakia are emphasized. A Slovak Communist, Clementis was for a while the Foreign Minister of Czechoslovakia, but was purged along with Slansky.

IB53 COMMUNIST INFORMATION BUREAU. *Rizoluzioni e documenti dell'Ufficio d'Informazione dei Partiti Comunisti e Operai, 1947-1951. A cura della redazione italiana di "Per una pace stabile, per una democrazia popolare."* Rome: VII congresso nazionale del Partito Comunista Italiano. Documenti per i delegati, 1951. 219 p. Various official documents concerning the foundation of the Cominform, the expulsion of the Yugoslav party, October anniversary speeches of Molotov, Malenkov, and Bulganin, etc.

IB53A COMMUNIST INFORMATION BUREAU, CONFERENCE, POLAND, 1947. *Informatsionnoe soveshchanie predstavitelei nekotorykh kompartii v Polshe v kontse sentiabria 1947 g.* Moscow: Gospolitizdat, 1948. 305 p. Key source material for the founding of the Cominform and the policy changes involved in its establishment.

IB54 *La Conferenza de Mosca. 29 novembre-2 decembre 1954.* Rome: Edizioni di Cultura Sociale, 1955. 235 p. Speeches of the Soviet Bloc foreign ministers at the conference preparatory to the meeting which created the Warsaw pact.

IB55 COUNCIL OF FOREIGN MINISTERS. *Treaty of Peace with Italy, Bulgaria, Hungary, Roumania, and Finland.* Washington: G.P.O., 1947. 5 vols. Contain the authentic texts of the Paris Peace Treaties of 1947 entered into by the "Allied and Associated Powers" with the respective governments. In Russian, English, French, and the language of the respective government.

IB56 DANIEL, HAWTHORNE. *The Ordeal of the Captive Nations.* Garden City, N.Y.: Doubleday, 1958. 316 p. A popular account, with major emphasis on Poland, Czechoslovakia and Hungary.

IB57 DANUBE CONFERENCE, BELGRADE, 1948. *Dunaiskaia konferentsiia, Belgrad 1948; sbornik dokumentov. Conference Danubienne, Beograd 1948; recueil des documents.* Belgrade: Izdanie Ministerstva inostrannykh del Federativnoi narodnoi respubliki Iugoslavii—Édition du Ministère des Affairs Etrangéres de la République Populaire Fédérative de Yougoslavie, 1949. 401 p. Contains the proceedings of the July 30-Aug. 18, 1948, Belgrade International Conference to Consider Free Navigation on the Danube, with the delegations of Austria, Bulgaria, Czechoslovakia, France, Britain, Hungary, Rumania, Ukraine, USA, USSR, and Yugoslavia participating. Parallel text in Russian and French.

IB58 DEUTSCHES INSTITUT FÜR RECHTSWISSENSCHAFT. *Die Verfassungen der europäischen Länder der Volksdemokratie. Mehrsprachige Ausgabe.* Berlin: VEB Deutscher Zentralverlag, 1954. 315 p. Constitutional texts, in the original tongue and in German translation.

IB59 DEUTSCHES INSTITUT FÜR RECHTSWISSENSCHAFT. *Das Wahlrecht der sozialistischen Staaten Europas.* Translated and edited by Heinz Engelbert. Berlin: VEB Deutscher Zentralverlag, 1958. 358 p. A collection of East European and Soviet electoral legislation, together with a brief introduction. Bibliographical footnotes.

IB60 *Dokumentation der Vertreibung der Deutschen aus Ost-Mitteleuropa.* 4 vols. in 6 parts.

Vol. I: *Die Vertreibung der deutschen Bevölkerung aus den gebieten östlich der Oder-Neisse.* Ed. by Theodor Schieder and others. 2 parts. 1954.

Vol. II: *Das Schicksal der Deutschen in Ungarn.* 1956.

Vol. III: *Das Schicksal der Deutschen in Rumänien.* Ed. by Eckhard G. Franz and Martin Broszat. 1957.

Vol. IV: *Die Vertreibung der deutschen Bevölkerung aus der Tschechoslowakei.* 2 parts. 1957.

Supplement I: *Ein Tagebuch aus Pommern, 1945-46.* By Käthe von Normann. 1955.

Supplement II: *Ein Tagebuch aus Prag, 1945-46.* By Margarete Schell. 1957.

Bonn: Bundesministerium für Vertriebene, Flüchtlinge und Kriegsgeschädigte. 1954-57.

These volumes present documentary material concerning the expulsion of the Germans from Hungary, Czechoslovakia, Romania, Poland, and the territories east of the Oder-Neisse line. They tend to emphasize the cruelty of the expulsion and the atrocities of the Soviet soldiery. Final evaluation must await completion of the series, particularly of the volume dealing with the historical, sociological, and legal significance of this mass population movement.

IB61 EHRENBURG, ILIA G. *Dorogi Evropy.* Moscow: Sovetskii pisatel, 1946. 145 p. English ed., *European Crossroad: A Soviet Journalist in the Balkans.* N.Y.: Knopf, 1947. 176 p. French ed., Paris: Éditions Hier et aujourdhui, 1946. 177 p. Reportage by a leading Soviet writer, who visited the Balkans from September 1945 to January 1946.

IB62 *Europe—Nine Panel Studies by Experts from Central and Eastern Europe.* N.Y.: Free Europe Committee, 1954. 146 p. A series of studies by prominent exiles of how a liberated Eastern Europe could be fitted into such emergent West European institutions as the Council of Europe and the Coal and Steel Community.

IB63 FABRE, MICHEL H. *Théorie des démocraties populaires; contribution à l'étude de l'état socialiste.* Paris: A. Pedone, 1950. 87 p. A constitutional study by a Marxist who was professor of law at the University of Algiers. Bibliographical footnotes.

IB64 FARBEROV, N. P. *Gosudarstvennoe pravo stran narodnoi demokratii.* Moscow: Politizdat, 1949. 326 p. An analysis of the constitutional structures of the People's Democracies. The author seeks to prove that the People's Democracies are truly socialist states in the process of transition from capitalism to communism. He condemns those Soviet writers who hold that the People's Democracies are neither capitalist nor socialist, but states of a third type. (For a revision, see below under: Moscow, Vsesoiuznyi iuridicheskii zaochnyi institut.)

IB65 FARBEROV, N. P. *Konstitutsii stran narodnoi demokratii; Stenogramna publichnoi lektsii, prochitannoi v Moskve.* Moscow: Pravda, 1949. 31 p. A short constitutional history of the Moscow-dominated European countries by a Russian jurist. Concludes that the presence of the Red Army made it possible to implement the Stalinist-Leninist model in their post-war constitutions.

IB66 FEJTÖ, FRANÇOIS. *Histoire des Démocraties Populaires.* Paris: Éditions du Seuil, 1952. 446 p. Possibly the most comprehensive, solidly-based, and perceptive study of postwar Eastern Europe in any language. Fejtö, an Hungarian exile with leftist sympathies, covers the political, the economic, and the diplomatic, but is at his even-handed best in his treatment of the East European intellectuals and their travail. [A]

IB67 FISCHER, LOUIS. *Russia Revisited; a New Look at Russia and Her Satellites.* Garden City, N.Y.: Doubleday, 1957. 288 p. German ed., Frankfurt a/M.: 1957. Fischer was a reporter in Russia from 1922 to 1938, and the first half of this book gives his impressions of Soviet Russia after an absence of eighteen years. In the second half, he deals with developments in the Satellites, particularly the emergence of the Gomulka regime in Poland.

IB67A FISCHER-GALATI, STEPHEN, ed. *Eastern Europe in the Sixties*. N.Y.: Praeger, 1963. 242 p. A symposium on political, economic, and cultural affairs, with emphasis on economic growth and political rifts in the Communist camp.

IB68 FORST-BATTAGLIA, OTTO. *Zwischeneuropa*. Vol. I: *Polen, Tschechoslowakei, Ungarn*. Frankfurt a/M: Verlag der Frankfurter Hefte, 1954. 438 p. Discusses domestic and foreign affairs from 1939 to 1952 from the point of view of old-type geopolitical considerations. Because of language barriers, no primary sources are used, and important turning points are quite misjudged by giving priority to secondary issues. The characterization of living personalities, including Communist ones, is in general incomplete. The forthcoming Volume II is to deal with Austria, the third with the Balkan states. No bibliography, no footnotes.

IB69 FREE EUROPE COMMITTEE. *Index to Unpublished Studies Prepared for Free Europe Committee, Inc. Studies 1-378*. N.Y.: 1958. 21 p. A list of 378 unpublished monographic studies on the economic and political problems of Central and Eastern Europe, with heavy emphasis on post-1945 conditions. Positive microfilm copies or enlargement prints of individual studies or of the entire series are available from the Library of Congress Photoduplication Service. [B]

IB70 FREE EUROPE COMMITTEE, MID-EUROPEAN STUDIES CENTER. *Index to Unpublished Studies Prepared for Mid-European Studies Center, National Committee for a Free Europe, Inc. Studies 1-164*. N.Y.: 1953. 13 p.

IB71 FREE EUROPE COMMITTEE, MID-EUROPEAN STUDIES CENTER. *Report of the Mid-European Studies Center; Publications and Projects*. N.Y.: 1955. 51 p. Records the achievements of the Studies Center, listing alphabetically by author the 91 monographs and 81 articles; describes its periodicals as well as 7 handbooks on East European countries; indicates studies in progress under the Center's sponsorship. Lists more than 300 manuscripts on Communism in Central and Eastern Europe. Contains indices by author and country (area), and to studies on international affairs.

IB72 FREE EUROPE PRESS RESEARCH STAFF. *Critical Bibliography of Communist Purges and Trials in the Soviet Union and in the "People's Democracies."* N.Y.: Free Europe Press, 1953.

IB73 GAUTHEROT, GUSTAVE. *Derrière le rideau de fer*. Paris: Hachette, 1946. 200 p. Rev. ed., Paris: Hermes-France, 1947. 257 p. An attempt to alert French public opinion to the dangers of Soviet imperialism. Has chapters on internal French affairs, the Baltic States, Austria and Germany.

IB74 GEORGE, PIERRE. *Les démocraties populaires. L'exemple des démocraties populaires européennes.* Paris: Ed. sociales, 1952. 157 p. A Marxist presentation, with lengthy quotations from regime sources.

IB75 GEORGE, PIERRE, and TRICART, JEAN. *L'Europe centrale.* Paris: Presses universitaires de France, 1954. 2 vols. The area is divided into capitalist central Europe (Germany, Switzerland, Austria), and the people's democratic republics (Poland, Czechoslovakia, Hungary, and Rumania). Reviews nationalization, planned economy and commerce, among other topics in the socialist countries. Based heavily on statistics. Each main chapter has an extensive bibliography with several annoying misspellings in non-Western language titles. [B]

IB76 GLUCKSTEIN, YGAEL. *Stalin's Satellites in Europe.* London: G. Allen & Unwin; Boston: Beacon Press, 1952. 333 p. Spanish ed., Madrid: 1955. Discusses the economics of East European industrialization, the totalitarian functioning of the people's democracies, and the spread of Titoism. The author questions the durability and prospects of Soviet imperial rule in Europe, since the mother country is more backward than the populations ruled or to be ruled.

IB77 GOROVE, STEPHEN. "Power Politics around the Iron Curtain; the Case of the Danube River." Ph.D. dissertation, Yale, 1955.

IB78 GSOVSKI, VLADIMIR, and GRZYBOWSKI, KAZIMIERZ, eds. *Government, Law, and Courts in the Soviet Union and Eastern Europe.* N.Y.: Praeger; London: Stevens, 1959. 2 vols. A comparative study of the legal systems of the Soviet Union and the European Satellites by a group of 28 exile lawyers. Major emphasis is placed on the effect on individual rights of the sovietization of East European law. The bibliography includes some 1100 items. [B]

IB79 GUNTHER, JOHN. *Behind the Curtain.* N.Y.: Harper, 1949. 363 p. British ed., *Behind Europe's Curtain.* London: Hamilton, 1949. French ed., Paris: Gallimard, 1951. Journalistic reporting in the Gunther tradition. Factually, there is not much new, and there are some errors; but the work is readable and the overview it presents is worth having.

IB80 GYORGY, ANDREW. *Governments of Danubian Europe.* N.Y.: Rinehart, 1949. 376 p. A survey which tends to disregard the proximity and power of Soviet Russia, but has value in explaining why the Soviet brand of socialism has difficulty in winning acceptance among the East European peoples.

IB81 HEALEY, DENIS, ed. *The Curtain Falls; The Story of the Socialists in Eastern Europe.* London: Lincolns-Prager, 1951. 99 p. An account of the destruction of the Social Democratic parties in Poland,

Czechoslovakia, and Hungary. The editor is active in the British Labor party.

IB82 HÖPKER, WOLFGANG. *Europäisches Niemandsland; Moskaus Zwischeneuropa vom Nordkap bis Kreta.* Düsseldorf: Diederichs, 1956. 164 p. A brief and well-written analysis of the role of the Satellites and Scandinavia in the strategic confrontation of East and West. The presentation is heavily military and is concerned to show that neutralization of large patches of European territory will not contribute to a relaxation of tensions.

IB83 HORNA, DAGMAR, ed. *Current Research on Central and Eastern Europe.* N.Y.: Free Europe Committee, 1956. 250 p. Includes projects dealing with the Baltic countries, Austria, and Yugoslavia, as well as the Satellites. Indexed.

IB84 *How Did the Satellites Happen? A Study of the Soviet Seizure of Eastern Europe, by a Student of Affairs.* Pref. by Hector McNeil. London: Batchworth Press, 1952. 304 p. Designed as a handbook, this work contains basic statistical information, chronological tables, and brief historical narratives for each country. Tends to be superficial.

IB85 INSTITUT FÜR OSTRECHT. *Das Eigentum im Ostblock.* Berlin: Verlag für Internationalen Kulturaustausch, 1958. 113 p.

IB86 INSTITUT FÜR OSTRECHT. *Fragen der Gerichtsverfassung im Ostblock.* Berlin: Verlag für Internationalen Kulturaustausch, 1958. 91 p. Western presentation of such matters as the independence of the judiciary in the USSR, Hungary, Poland, and East Germany.

IB87 INSTITUT FÜR OSTRECHT. *Fragen des Staatsrechts im Ostblock.* Berlin: Verlag für Internationalen Kulturaustausch, 1958. 95 p. A study that treats the real (as opposed to the formal) constitutional structure of the Soviet Bloc.

IB88 IZVESTIIA. *Pod znamenem sotsializma.* Moscow: 1959. 631 p. A collection of the Soviet newspaper's special issues on the construction of Communism in Europe and Asia, excluding the USSR and Yugoslavia. The articles, arranged by countries and written by well-known native authors and politicians, deal with political, cultural, economic and social aspects. [B]

IB89 KARSKI, JAN. "Material Towards a Documentary History of the Fall of Eastern Europe, 1938-1948." Ph.D. dissertation, Georgetown Univ., 1952.

IB90 KEETON, GEORGE W. and SCHLESINGER, RUDOLF. *Russia and Her Western Neighbours.* London: Jonathan Cape, 1942.

160 p. Two scholars discuss the prospects for Eastern Europe after Hitler's defeat. They foresee a continuation of the Anglo-American-Soviet alliance. They envision Finland, the Baltic states, and Poland as independent but closely associated with Soviet Russia. The formation of a Danubian federation composed of Austria, Czechoslovakia and Hungary is predicted, and, in addition, a Balkan League of peasant democracies. (See below: Pragier, Adam.)

IB91 KERNER, MIROSLAV. *Sovietization of the Military Law of the Soviet Satellite Countries in Central Europe.* Washington: Photoduplication Service, Library of Congress, 1955. 137 p. A comprehensive treatise of Eastern Europe's armed forces and military codes. No primary sources are used on non-Slavic countries. Useful bibliography. A Free Europe Committee study.

IB92 KERTESZ, STEPHEN D., ed. *East Central Europe and the World: Developments in the Post-Stalin Era.* Notre Dame, Ind.: Notre Dame, 1962. Deals with events from 1956 to 1962. Contains individual chapters on Poland, East Germany, Czechoslovakia, Hungary, Rumania, Bulgaria, Albania, Yugoslavia, Finland, Austria, and the Baltic states, as well as on economic developments in the area, the role of China in Eastern Europe, and Western policy. Kertesz is a former Hungarian diplomat who now heads the East European studies program at Notre Dame University. [A]

IB93 KERTESZ, STEPHEN D., ed. *The Fate of East Central Europe; Hopes and Failures of American Foreign Policy.* Notre Dame, Ind.: Notre Dame, 1956. 463 p. Sixteen experts deal with the creation of the Soviet empire in Eastern Europe and its bearing on American foreign policy. They are among other things concerned with the question of whether a different American military strategy during World War II would have saved Eastern Europe from occupation by the Soviet army. [A]

IB94 KLEIST, PETER. *Zwischen Hitler und Stalin, 1939-1945.* Bonn: Athenäum, 1950. 344 p. Memoirs of an Ostdeutscher who served on Ribbentrop's immediate staff and claims to have been involved in secret "peace" negotiations with the Soviets in the last two years of the war. Documentary appendix.

IB94A KLOKOV, V. I. *Borba narodov slavianskikh stran protiv fashistskikh porabotitelei (1939-1945 gg.).* Kiev: Izd. Akad. nauk Ukr. SSR, 1961. 430 p.

IB95 KOVAL, PANTELEI D. *Kommunisticheskie i rabochie partii evropeiskikh stran narodnoi demokratii—rukovodiashchaia i napravliaiushchaia sila v stroitelstve sotsializma.* Leningrad: 1957. 51 p. Describes the Communist and workers parties' role in the founding and furthering of the people's democratic system in Eastern Europe. Stresses the Soviet Union's influence on the transformation of political, socio-economic and cultural conditions from a bourgeois into a Marxist structure.

IB96 KRACAUER, SIEGFRIED, and BERKMAN, PAUL L. *Satellite Mentality; Political Attitudes and Propaganda Susceptibilities of Non-Communists in Hungary, Poland, and Czechoslovakia.* N.Y.: Praeger, 1956. 194 p. A study based on interviews conducted in 1951-52, among several hundred refugees from Poland, Hungary, and Czechoslovakia. Has been criticized for methodological weaknesses, such as perfunctory description of the respondents and failure to take into account the self-selected character of the sample.

IB97 LEHRMAN, HAROLD A. *Russia's Europe.* N.Y.: Appleton-Century, 1947. 341 p. Reminiscences by a U.S. correspondent of his experiences in the Balkans in the immediate post-World War II period. Countries covered: Yugoslavia and, more briefly, Hungary, Czechoslovakia, Rumania, Bulgaria, and Greece. His reactions are those of a liberal who had expected the Communists to carry out genuine reforms and who was disillusioned by the reality of the new Communist order.

IB98 MAKSAKOVSKII, V. *Stroiki sotsialisma v evropaiskikh stranakh.* Ed. by I. A. Vitver. Moscow: Gos. izd. geogr. lit., 1952. 197 p. Makes a brief, richly illustrated historical survey of the most significant newly built industrial centers of Poland, Czechoslovakia, Hungary, Rumania, Bulgaria, and Albania. Its data can also by used on social stratification and the Communist Party's leading role in building a new society. Several maps. [B]

IB99 MANKOVSKII, BORIS S. *Narodno-demokraticheskie respubliki Tsentralnoi i Iugo-Vostochnoi Evropy—gosudarstva sotsialisticheskogo tipa; stenogramma publichnoi lektsii, prochitannoi v Tsentralnom lektorii obshchestve v Moskve.* Moscow: Pravda, 1950. 28 p. Slovak ed., Bratislava: Tatran, 1951. A bird's eye view of the main characteristics and workings of the constitutions of the people's democratic regimes in Poland, Czechoslovakia, Bulgaria, Rumania, Hungary, and Albania by a noted Russian jurist. The role of the Red Army in the founding of the proletarian dictatorships, as well as the Soviet constitutional pattern, are accentuated.

IB100 MARTIC, MILOS. "The International Regime on the Danube River with Special Emphasis on the Postwar Period, 1945-1954." Ph.D. dissertation, U. of Colorado, 1958. Describes the process by which the 1948 Convention gave way to complete Soviet domination of the Danube waterway.

IB101 MASSACHUSETTS INSTITUTE OF TECHNOLOGY, CENTER FOR INTERNATIONAL STUDIES. *The Soviet Takeover of Eastern Europe.* Cambridge, Mass.: M.I.T., 1954. 1 vol. Demonstrates the Soviet influence in all domains, using chiefly secondary sources and in a few cases native language materials. The police-army section, arranged by countries, concludes that the bulwark of Communism is and will continue to be the Red Army. The economy part is arranged by subject headings and is focused on the nationalization of industry and collective farming, pointing out conflicting interests with the Soviet Union. Bibliographical footnotes and statistical tables. [B]

IB102 POLITICHESKII KONSULTATIVNYI KOMITET GOSUDARSV-UCHASTNIKOV VARSHAVSKOGO DOGOVORA O DRUZHBE, SOTRUDNICHESTVE I VZAIMNOI POMOSHCHI. *Materialy soveshchaniia, 24 maia 1958 goda.* Moscow: Gos. izd-vo polit. lit-ry, 1958. 143 p. A collection of documents about a meeting of the Warsaw Pact powers, including Khrushchev's speech and the proposed nonaggression pact with NATO.

IB103 MEISSNER, BORIS. *Der Warschauer Pakt.* Cologne: Verlag Wissenschaft und Politik, 1962. 203 p. By one of the leading West German specialists on Russia and Eastern Europe.

IB104 MEISSNER, BORIS, comp. *Das Ostpak-System; Dokumentensammlung.* Hamburg, 1951. 2 vols.

I. *Das sowjetische Paktsystem in Europe.* 153 p.

II. *Das sowjetische Paktsystem in Asien.* 72 p. Revised ed., Frankfurt a/M: A. Metzner, 1955. 208 p.

A collection of the documents which provide the legal framework of the Sino-Soviet Bloc. There are registers listing treaties chronologically and by nation.

IB105 MEYER, PETER, and others. *The Jews in the Soviet Satellites.* Syracuse, N.Y.: Syracuse Univ. Press, 1953. 637 p. Sponsored by the American Jewish Committee, this collective work analyzes the impact of Sovietization on the 700,000 Jews living in five Satellites. The work is the result of careful and scholarly examination of a mass of first-hand sources, primarily official documents, and the local press.

IB106 MID-EUROPEAN LAW PROJECT. *Church and State Behind the Iron Curtain; Czechoslovakia, Hungary, Poland, Romania, with an Introduction on the Soviet Union.* Ed. by Vladimir Gsovski. N.Y.: Publ. for the Mid-European Studies Center by Praeger, 1955. 311 p. Gsovski was chief of the Foreign Law Section of the Library of Congress. The studies were written by refugee lawyers. Useful as a reference work. Provides translations of basic legislation and other source materials.

IB107 MOSCOW, VSESOIUZNYI IURIDICHESKII ZAOCHNYI INSTITUT. *Gosudarstvennoe pravo stran narodnoi demokratii.* Odobreno Sovetom Vsesoiuznogo Iuridicheskogo zaochnogo instituta v kachestve uchebnogo posobiia dlia studentov VIUZI. Ed. by Aleksandr Kh. Makhnenko. Moscow: 1959. 418 p. Revision of an official text (see above N. P. Farberov). The revision deals with the constitutional law of the Asian people's democracies, as well as that of the European people's democracies, and takes the view that people's democracies constitute an alternative form of the dictatorship of the proletariat which is obedient to the general laws for the construction of socialism.

IB108 MOURIN, MAXIME. *Le Drame des états satellites.* Paris: Editions Berger-Levrault, 1957. 275 p. A study of Hungary, Romania, Bulgaria, and Finland in the transition from Nazi to Soviet domination. The author emphasizes the geographic vulnerability of the Satellite populations and the insistence of the Western Allies on the unconditional surrender of Nazi Germany.

IB109 NAMIER, LEWIS B. *Facing East.* London: Hamish Hamilton, 1947; N.Y.: Harper, 1948. 159 p. An undocumented study which devotes too much space to theorizing over the past and present of East Central Europe and Russia's relationships to it. Contains severe statistical mistakes and does not reflect an understanding of the essence of East Central Europe's economic development and its nationality problems. Also fails to comprehend the situations in which political parties developed there.

IB110 NATIONALE FRONT DES DEMOKRATISCHEN DEUTSCHLAND. *Von der Moskauer Konferenze Europäischer Länder bis zum Warschauer Vertrag; Dokumente von welthistorischer Bedeutung.* Berlin: Kongress-Verlag, 1955. 130 p. Speeches and communiqués dealing with the Warsaw Pact, selected for East German consumption.

IB111 ORMANDZHIEV, IVAN P. *Federatsiia na balkanskitě narodi; idei i prechki.* Sofia: Zaria, 1947. 191 p.

IB112 PALMER, G. *Partisanen, Christen und Bolschewiken; Erlebnisse in der östlichen Untergrundbewegung.* Luzem: Rex, 1950. 302 p.

IB113 PAPAKONSTANTINOU, TH. F. *Anatomia tis epanesteseos; theoritiki kai istonki analysis tis dynamikis tou kommounismou.* Athens: 1952. 267 p. A major work by a former Greek Communist and leading Greek newspaperman dealing with the Soviet theory and practice of revolution in the Balkans.

IB114 PFUHL, EBERHARDT. *Das Recht der Allgemeinen Lieferbedingungen im Zwischenstaatlichen Aussenhandel des Ostblocks.* Berlin: Dahlem, 1956. 169 p. Discusses the technicalities of intra-bloc trade: documentation, delivery periods, packing, liability, arbitration, etc.

IB115 POLITICHESKII KONSULTATIVNYI KOMITET GOSUDARSTV-UCHASTNIKOV VARSHAVSKOGO DOGOVORA O DRUZHBE, SOTRUDNICHESTVE I VZAIMNOI POMOSHCHI. *Materialy soveshchaniia 24 maia 1958 goda.* Moscow: Gospolitizdat, 1958. 143 p. Contains the communiqués, declarations, and proceedings of the May 24, 1958, Moscow session of the Warsaw pact countries with the government delegations of the Soviet Union (headed by Khrushchev).

IB116 POOL, ITHIEL DE SOLA, and others. *Satellite Generals; a Study of Military Elites in the Soviet Sphere.* Stanford, Cal.: Stanford Univ. Press, 1955. 165 p. A sociological analysis of the military commands developed by the Communist regimes in Czechoslovakia, Poland, Romania, Hungary and China. Deals particularly with the role of ethnic minority elements in these commands.

IB117 PRAGIER, ADAM. *How to Save Germany? (A Few Remarks in Connection with "Russia and her Western Neighbours," by Prof. George Keeton and Dr. Rudolph Schlesinger).* London: Barnard & Westwood, 1943. 56 p. An attack on Keeton and Schlesinger (see above) for advocating Soviet hegemony in Eastern Europe.

IB118 PRICE, MORGAN PHILIPS. *Through the Iron-laced Curtain; A Record of a Journey Through the Balkans in 1946.* London: Low, 1949. 133 p. Clearly reflects the preconceptions characteristic of Western travellers to Yugoslavia and Bulgaria in 1946. Offers little in the way of enlightenment on the major internal problems facing the two Slavic countries.

IB118A REALE, EUGENIO. *Nascita del Cominform.* Milano: A. Mondadori, 1958. 174 p. A memoir by one of the participants at the founding meeting. Reale had broken with the Italian Communist Party before publishing this work.

IB119 RIPKA, HUBERT. *Eastern Europe in the Postwar World.* Intro. by Hugh Seton-Watson. N.Y.: Praeger, 1961. Formerly an important official in the Czechoslovak government and a close associate of Eduard Beneš, Ripka was one of the many democratic statesmen who were forced to flee from Communism. This book presents his views on developments in Eastern Europe through 1956, with emphasis on Czechoslovakia.

IB120 ROUČEK, JOSEPH S. and others. *Central-Eastern Europe; Crucible of World Wars.* N.Y.: Prentice-Hall, 1946. 679 p. A reference work of uneven quality produced by eleven historians. Contains much useful information.

IB121 SANDERS, IRWIN T., ed. *Collectivization of Agriculture in Eastern Europe*. Lexington: Univ. of Kentucky, 1960.

IB122 SEMITJOV, WLADIMIR. *Jag fann ingen järnridå; en resa i Mellaneuropa*. Stockholm: Natur och kultur, 1947. 291 p. A Russian-born Swedish correspondent's travel notes from 1946 describing the political and economic situation in Poland, Czechoslovakia, Hungary, and Austria, with emphasis on Hungary. A fairly unbiased, journalistically written report with several illustrations.

IB123 SETON-WATSON, HUGH. *The East European Revolution*. London: Methuen, 1950. 406 p. N.Y.: Praeger, 1951. 3rd ed., 1956. 435 p. German ed., Munich: Isar, 1956. 400 p. A standard work by a leading British authority who teaches at the University of London. The presentation places the greatest emphasis on the Sovietization of Eastern Europe, but there are also chapters on the war and an introductory section which warns the reader that the interwar problems of the area were many and severe. The third edition covers developments down to the resignation of Malenkov as premier. [A]

IB124 SHARP, SAMUEL L. *New Constitutions in the Soviet Sphere*. Washington: Foundation for Foreign Affairs, 1950. 114 p. A pioneer effort in pointing out the origin and application of the concept of "People's Democracy," with special emphasis on Poland, Czechoslovakia, and Hungary. The texts of various constitutions are presented in appendices. Bibliographical footnotes.

IB125 SHEPHERD, GORDON. *Russia's Danubian Empire*. London: Heinemann, 1954; N.Y.: Praeger, 1954. 262 p. Concludes that the guiding hand in every Danubian state is Moscow's; that the most serious opposition has come from the clergy and the peasantry; that industrialization has been planned primarily for Soviet interests but nonetheless may have some permanent value for Eastern Europe. Austria is viewed as the possible nucleus of a future Danubian center. Shepherd was a correspondent for the London *Daily Telegraph* and a member of the Allied Control Commission for Austria.

IB126 SHUSTER, GEORGE N. *Religion Behind the Iron Curtain*. N.Y.: Macmillan, 1954. 281 p. A survey of religious conditions in the Satellite countries with emphasis on the state of the Catholic church. Special attention is given to the cases of Mindszenty and Stepinac.

IB127 SLOVENSKI KONGRES, 1st, BELGRAD, 1946. *Slovanský sjezd v Bělehradě r 1946*. Uspořádali V. Burian, A. Frinta, B. Havránek. Prague: Nákl. Slovanského výboru; v komisi Orbis, 1947. 157 p. Materials of the All-Slav Committee's Belgrade session in 1946. Among the speakers were Tito, Djilas, D. Grekov, Zdeněk Nejedlý, A. S. Gundorov. Its main topics: the Slavic contribution to world civilization and to the World War II triumph. Principal theme: Slavic solidarity under the Kremlin. Includes the All-Slav Committee's bylaws and its organizational setup.

IB128 SOVESHCHANIE EVROPEISKIKH GOSUDARSTV PO OBESPECHENIIU MIRA I BEZOPASNOSTI V EVROPE, MOSCOW, 1954. *Moskovskoe soveshchanie evropeiskikh stran po obespecheniiu mira i bezopasnosti v Evrope; Moskva, 29 noiabria—2 dekabria 1954 g; stenograficheskii otchet.* Moscow: Izd. "Pravda," 1954. 159 p. Stenographic records of the 1954 Moscow Conference of European Countries on Safeguarding European Peace and Security. Contains joint communiques, addresses, declarations by the government representatives of the USSR, Poland, Czechoslovakia, German Democratic Republic, Hungary, Rumania, Bulgaria, and Albania. Important documents on the "peace movement" and psychological warfare.

IB129 SOVESHCHANIE EVROPEISKIKH GOSUDARSTV PO OBESPECHENIIU MIRA I BEZOPASNOSTI V EVROPE, WARSAW, 1955. *Varshavskoe soveshchanie evropeiskikh gosudarstv po obespecheniiu mira i bezopasnosti v Evrope; Varshava, 11-15 maia 1955 g.* Moscow: Gospolitizdat, 1955. 142 p. Similar to the 1954 Moscow Conference of European Countries on Safeguarding European Peace and Security (see above). Includes the eleven point Warsaw Pact of military alliance concluded by Albania, Bulgaria, Hungary, the German Democratic Republic, Poland, Rumania, USSR, and Czechoslovakia.

IB130 *The Soviet Satellite Nations; a Study of the New Imperialism.* Ed. by John H. Hallowell. Gainesville, Florida: Kallman, 1958. 244 p. A symposium originally printed in the February 1958 issue of *The Journal of Politics.* Contains chapters by Hannah Arendt, Carl J. Friedrich, Richard Staar, Edward Taborsky, Alex Dragnich, Allen Whiting, George Lenczowski, Gene Overstreet, and Zbigniew Brzezinski. [A]

IB131 *Soviet Satellites; Studies of Politics in Eastern Europe*, by Andrew Gyorgy and others. Notre Dame, Ind.: Review of Politics, 1949. 64 p. A series of papers originally presented at the December, 1948, convention of the American Political Science Association, to which has been added an essay by Stephen Kerterz on the background of the Mindszenty trial.

IB132 STILLMAN, EDMUND O., ed. *Bitter Harvest; the Intellectual Revolt Behind the Iron Curtain.* N.Y.: Praeger, 1959. 313 p. A collection of essays, poems, and short stories translated from Eastern European (primarily Polish, Hungarian, and Russian) periodicals. There is also a Chinese, a Vietnamese, an East German, a Czech, a Balt, and a Yugoslav among the writers. Materials are arranged under such impressive headings as "National Communism—National Identity." Bondy's foreword does not adequately explain the efforts of the cultural elite to break out of its bonds. [B]

IB133 STOWE, LELAND. *Conquest by Terror; The Story of Satellite Europe*. New York: Random House, 1952. 300 p. The effort of an American newspaperman to make the West aware of the grim changes which seven years of Soviet domination had introduced in Eastern Europe. Based on interviews with exiles, and contacts with the "underground," the work verges on the sensational.

IB134 SULZBERGER, CYRUS L. *The Big Thaw; a Personal Exploration of the "New" Russia and the Orbit Countries*. N.Y.: Harper, 1956. 275 p. A blending of dispatches written by the foreign affairs columnist of the *New York Times* during visits to Soviet Russia and Eastern Europe. Sulzberger's principal conclusion is that Titoism should be encouraged wherever possible.

IB135 SURVEY OF INTERNATIONAL AFFAIRS, 1920-1923; THE WAR-TIME SERIES FOR 1939-1946. Vol. 6: Arnold and Veronica Toynbee, eds. *The Realignment of Europe*. London and N.Y.: Oxford, for the Royal Institute of International Affairs, 1955. 619 p. Sidney Lowery, Hugh Seton-Watson, Elizabeth Wiskemann, and William H. McNeill provide an authoritative and detailed account of Soviet policy toward the Eastern European countries during the last years of World War II and the immediate post-war period. [A]

IB136 TABORSKY, EDWARD. *Conformity under Communism*. Washington: Public Affairs Press, 1958. 38 p. A study of indoctrination techniques in the satellites, by a former aide to President Beneš of Czechoslovakia.

IB137 TOBIAS, ROBERT. *Communist-Christian Encounter in East Europe*. Indianapolis, Ind.: Butler School of Religion Press, 1956. 567 p. Examines thoroughly the tactics of the Communist assault on the churches, from the Russia of 1917 to the East European satellites of 1951. Provides summaries of church-state relations, and official documents pertaining thereto, in the satellites and the USSR. Anti-Catholic, anti-exile, and anti-liberation.

IB138 TOMAŠIĆ, DINKO A. *National Communism and Soviet Strategy*. Washington: Public Affairs Press, 1957. 222 p. In part an application of the Cvijec thesis concerning the interrelation of brigandage, patriotism, and guerrilla warfare to the Communist guerrilla movements of World War II in the Karst area of the Balkan peninsula.

IB139 U. S. JOINT PUBLICATIONS RESEARCH SERVICE. *Selected Translations from East European Political Journals and Newspapers.* Washington: February 28, 1958–. Irregular. Well-chosen articles in good translations. Mimeographed. [A]

IB140 U.S. LIBRARY OF CONGRESS, LEGISLATIVE REFERENCE SERVICE. *Tensions within the Soviet Captive Countries, Prepared at the Request of the Committee on Foreign Relations.* Washington: G.P.O., 1954. 7 pts. A series of pamphlets surveying the main aspects of Communist control of the individual countries of Eastern Europe.

IB141 U.S. DEPARTMENT OF STATE. *Moscow's European Satellites; A Handbook of Tables.* Washington: G.P.O., 1955. 52 p. Organizes basic facts and figures of the Kremlin's seven European satellites into charts under such headings as "History; Physical Survey; Government; Communist Party; Show Trials; Biographic Information; Religion; Diplomatic Relations; Sovietization (Political and Economic); International Front Organizations," etc. A useful compilation. [B]

IB142 USCATESCU, GEORGE. *Europa ausente.* 2nd ed., Madrid: Editora Nacional, 1957. 236 p. Hostile criticism of Communism with regard to Central and Eastern Europe. Examines its basic principles and workings especially in the fields of ethics, religion, and the nationality problem. No bibliography, no index.

IB143 VAN DYKE, VERNON. *Communism in Eastern and Southeastern Europe.* New Haven, Conn.: Institute of International Studies, 1947. 33 p. A keen-sighted news analysis using exclusively English language on-the-spot reports and essays. Its well-compiled bibliographical references reflect truly the public opinion of the English-speaking world.

IB144 VANHOPPLINUS, ROGER. *Sowjets "bevrijden" Oost-Europa; bloedige bladzijden uit de geschiedenis van landen in de communistische machtsgreep.* Almar: Wervik Druk, 1957. 288 p. Describes Communism in the Soviet Union, the Baltic States, and Eastern Europe, with special regard to state-church relations, focused on the persecutions suffered primarily by the Catholic Church. With illustrations, facsimiles, maps, and well-selected documents. [B]

IB145 VEDEL, GEORGES. *Les Démocraties marxistes.* Paris: Cours de droit, 1953. 3 vols. 448 p. A text in political science written by a member of the Faculté de Droit of Paris.

IB146 WANDYCZ, PIOTR S. *Czechoslovak-Polish Confederation and the Great Powers, 1940-1943*. Bloomington: Indiana Univ., 1956. 152 p. Deals with the abortive effort of the exile Czech and Polish governments to form a post-war federation. Essentially the effort failed because of the opposition of the USSR and the unwillingness of the Czech leaders to take any stand against the Russians.

IB147 WARRINER, DOREEN. *Revolution in Eastern Europe*. London: Turnstile Press, 1950. 188 p. A study of land reform, collectivization of agriculture, and industrial planning. The economic analysis is of considerable value, but the author leans over backwards to defend the new regimes against what she regards (often rightly) as the calumnies of Western propaganda.

IB148 WISKEMANN, ELIZABETH. *Germany's Eastern Neighbors; Problems Relating to the Oder-Neisse Line and the Czech Frontier Regions*. N.Y., and London: Oxford, 1956. 309 p. A major study by an English specialist of the expulsion of the Germans from Eastern Europe and Eastern Germany in 1944-45. Based on German, Czech, and Polish sources, the work has been severely criticized by West German scholars for its contention that both the integration of the expellees in the West German economy and the importance of the evacuated territories to Poland and Czechoslovakia make unwise any return to the pre-war situation.

IB149 ZILLIACUS, KONNI. *A New Birth of Freedom? World Communism after Stalin*. London: Secker and Warburg, 1957. 286 p. The author, formerly a British Labor M.P. who was expelled from the Party because of his left-wing position, favorably discusses the post-Stalin changes in and outside the USSR. Devotes chapters to each of the East European satellites.

IB150 ZINNER, PAUL E., ed. *National Communism and Popular Revolt in Eastern Europe; a Selection of Documents on Events in Poland and Hungary, February-November, 1956*. N.Y.: Columbia Univ. Press, 1956. 563 p. Party resolutions, speeches by leading Communists, and significant newspaper comment. Bibliographical footnotes. [A]

IB151 ZLATOPER, GRGA. *Survey of the Satellite Press Since 1945*. Washington: Photoduplication Service, Library of Congress, 1956. 147 p. Well-selected main topics of the East European Communist press are expertly analyzed. Useful bibliographical notes. A Free Europe Committee study.

4. ECONOMIC

IB152 AKADEMIIA NAUK SSSR, INSTITUT EKONOMIKI. *Ekonomicheskoe sotrudnichestvo i vzaimopomoshch mezhdu Sovetskim*

Soiuzom i evropeiskimi stranami narodnoi demokratii. Edited by A. K. Kozik. Moscow: Izdatelstvo Akademii nauk SSSR, 1958. 232 p. A Marxist analysis of the relationship between intra-bloc trade and aid and the process of industrialization.

IB153 AKADEMIIA NAUK SSSR, INSTITUT EKONOMIKI. *Evropeiskie strany narodnoi demokratii na puti k sotsialismu.* Ed. by F. P. Koshelev. Moscow: Gosplanizdat, 1951. 277 p. Essays on the dictatorship of the proletariat and socialist construction, the nationalization of industry, agrarian reform and collectivization, finance and currency, foreign trade, and living standards.

IB154 BALEK, A., HAVELKOVA, B., and TITERA, D. *Zeme socialisticke soustavy; statisticky prehled.* Prague: 1961. 229 p. A statistical survey of European and Asiatic Communist countries, including the USSR. Statistical data on post-1945 developments in industry, agriculture, construction, transportation, and the standard of living and costs. A comparative analysis of pre-1945 and post-1945 conditions in these fields.

IB155 BRIEFS, GODFREY E. "Shifting Patterns in Eastern Europe's Foreign Trade, 1928-1948." Ph.D. dissertation, Harvard University, 1952.

IB156 BUTAKOV, D., BOCHKOVA, V., and SHEVEL, I. *Finansy stran narodnoi demokratii.* Moscow: Gosfinizdat, 1959. 344 p. Soviet authors examine the national and local budgets of the countries of the Communist bloc, drawing on official statistics.

IB157 BYSTROV, F. P., and LOPATIN, G. S., eds. *Mezhdunarodnye raschety i valiutnye otnosheniia stran narodnoi demokratii.* Moscow: Vneshtorgizdat, 1956. 128 p. Discusses briefly and without reference to primary sources the budgetary, financial, and currency systems of the People's Democracies of Europe and Asia. Uses important statistical figures. Soviet connections are consistently discussed.

IB158 DEWAR, MARGARET. *Soviet Trade with Eastern Europe, 1945-1949.* London and N.Y.: Royal Institute of International Affairs, 1951. 123 p. Brings together publicly available data on the nature and extent of the trade of each of the satellite countries with the USSR, and concludes that the Soviet share of East European trade had not yet reached the volume achieved by Germany in the prewar period. [B]

IB159 DOUGLAS, DOROTHY W. *Transitional Economic Systems; The Polish-Czech Example.* London: Routledge, and Kegan Paul, 1953. 375 p. A factual analysis of postwar economic changes showing the sharp differences between the gradual socialization of the immediate postwar period and the radical changes after 1948, when the Communist parties took over the governments.

IB160 DUDINSKII, I. *Ekonomicheskoe sotrudnichestvo SSSR i stran narodnoi demokratii.* Moscow: Gos. izd-vo polit. lit-ry, 1954. 87 p. Deals with the emergence of a "democratic" world market, long- and short-term trade agreements, and technical assistance.

IB161 THE ECONOMIST (London). *The USSR and Eastern Europe.* Prepared by the Economist Intelligence Unit and the Cartographic Dept. of the Clarendon Press. London: Oxford Univ. Press, 1956. 134 p. (Oxford regional economic atlases). Maps and statistics showing economic and industrial conditions in the USSR and the European satellites.

IB162 FREE EUROPE COMMITTEE. *Satellite Agriculture in Crisis; a Study of Land Policy in the Soviet Sphere.* N.Y.: Praeger, 1954. 130 p. Traces the imposition in Eastern Europe of Soviet agricultural practices through the period of rapid collectivization and to the adoption of the New Course after Stalin's death. Omits East Germany and Albania. Written primarily by East European exiles.

IB163 GENKIN, DMITRII M., ed. *Pravovye voprosy vneshnei torgovli SSSR s evropeiskimi stranami narodnoi demokratii.* Moscow: Vneshtorg, 1955. 261 p. Deals with the legal aspects of Soviet-European Satellite trade, particularly as these concern or arise from the state of monopoly of foreign trade, the legal status of government trading organizations, international treaties and the terms of trade, credit and accounting, and arbitration of differences.

IB164 GEORGE, PIERRE. *L'économie de l'Europe centrale, slave et danubienne.* Paris: Presses Universitaires de France, 1949. 133 p. Reviews the economic development of Central European countries, 1919-47, with special regard to the post-1945 planned economies. Much space is devoted to agrarian reforms. Statistical tables.

IB165 GROSSMAN, GREGORY, ed. *Value and Plan: Economic Calculation and Organization in Eastern Europe.* Berkeley: Univ. of California, 1960. 370 p. A splendid and authoritative presentation of the problems and issues confronting Soviet and East European planners and economists prior to 1958.

IB166 HALÁSZ, ALBERT. *Das neue Mitteleuropa in wirtschaftlichen Karten. New Central Europe in Economical Maps.* Berlin: R. Hobbing, 1928. 149 p. Especially useful. In English and German, with overlay showing boundary changes.

IB167 HERMES, THEODOR. *Der Aussenhandel in den Ostblockstaaten.* Hamburg: Cram, 1958. 177 p. Discusses the Communist theory of two world markets, the role of foreign trade in economic planning, Bloc financing of foreign trade, the political aim of Bloc foreign trade, and the foreign trade apparatus. Has neither footnotes nor bibliography.

IB168 KIESEWETTER, BRUNO. *Der Ostblock; Aussenhandel des Ostlichen Wirtschaftsblockes Einschliesslich China.* Berlin: Safari-Verlag, 1960. 386 p. A substantial study describing and analyzing the pattern of foreign trade and economic aid within the Communist international system, including a discussion of the special position of China. Based largely on official Russian sources, this book gives detailed trade statistics, in both physical units and value, for selected years: 1938, and 1948-59. The author is Professor of Economics at the Free University of Berlin.

IB169 KOVRIZHNY, M. F., and others, eds. *Vneshniaia torgovlia stran narodnoi demokratii.* Moscow: Vneshtorgizdat, 1955. 320 p. A documented examination of principles guiding the foreign trade of Communist-bloc states, including a separate discussion of individual states' trading achievements.

IB170 KRÜGER, KARL. *Der Ostblock; die Produktion des Östlichen Wirtschaftsblockes Einschliesslich China, nach dem Schwerpunktprogramm.* Berlin: Safari-Verlag, 1960. 395 p. Analyzes the pattern of industrial production in the Communist bloc. Based largely on official Soviet sources. Summarizes the production situation in individual countries, as well as comparative advantage and bloc integration. Krüger is Professor of Economics at the (West) Berlin Polytechnical School.

IB171 McKITTERICK, THOMAS E. M. *Russian Economic Policy in Eastern Europe; Albania, Bulgaria, Czechoslovakia, Hungary, Jugoslavia, Poland, Roumania and Austria.* London: Fabian Publications, 1948. 41 p. The study is confined mainly to the trading policy of the USSR toward the countries of Eastern Europe.

IB172 MARCZEWSKI, JAN. *Planification et croissance économique des démocraties populaires.* 2 vols. I. *Analyse historique*; II. *Analyse économique.* Paris: Presses Universitaires, 1956. The first volume summarizes the economic history of the Satellites, country by country. The second volume is analytical and attempts to account for the high rates of growth achieved by the Communists. The author teaches at the Institut d'Études Politiques de Paris. Ten-page bibliography with works in various languages. [B]

IB173 MID-EUROPEAN STUDIES CENTER, MID-EUROPEAN LAW PROJECT. *Economic Treaties and Agreements of The Soviet Bloc in Eastern Europe, 1945-1951.* 2nd ed. N.Y.: Mid-European

Studies Center, 1952. 138 p. (mimeographed) A thorough job of research, useful particularly for its references to treaty sources of the partner states. Contains a summary of the general nature of intra-Bloc agreements, an inclusive list of such agreements, and the actual texts of typical treaties. [B]

IB174 MOORE, WILBUR E. *Economic Demography of Southern and Eastern Europe*. Geneva: League of Nations; N.Y.: Columbia, 1945. 299 p. A thoroughgoing statistical analysis of East European demographic and agricultural developments prepared by the Princeton Population Institute for the League of Nations. Indispensable. [A]

IB175 MOSCOW, NAUCHNO-ISSLEDOVATELSKII KONIUNKTURNYI INSTITUT. *Vneshnetorgovye organizatsii stran narodnoi demokratii; spravochik*. Ed. by V. G. Vaganov. Moscow: Vneshtorgizdat, 1954. 91 p. An official reference book on the foreign-trade organizations of the people's democracies.

IB176 *Plany razvitiia narodnogo khoziaistva stran narodnoi demokratii; sbornik materialov*. Introduction by I. V. Dudinskii. Moscow: Izd. inostrannoi lit., 1952. 469 p. Reproduces the laws and decrees providing for the economic plans of the European people's democracies.

IB177 POUNDS, NORMAN J. G., and SPULBER, NICHOLAS. *Resources and Planning in Eastern Europe*. Bloomington: Indiana Univ., 1957. 173 p. Presents the proceedings of a conference held at Indiana University in 1956.

IB178 *Problemy sotsialisticheskogo mezhdunarodnogo razdeleniia truda*. Comp. by I. I. Semenov. Ed. by Iu. Ia. Olsevich. Moscow: Izd. inostr. lit., 1960. 248 p. A collective work on different aspects of Communist-bloc trade and the central role of the USSR in it. Well documented.

IB179 *Razvitie ekonomiki stran narodnoi demokratii; obzor*. Moscow: Vneshtorgizdat, 1954—. (Annual) Includes material on the Communist countries of Europe and Asia. Organized country by country. Each national section deals with industry, agriculture, transport, foreign trade, the budget, and living standards. There is also a statistical appendix. Compiled by the Nauchno-Issledovatelskii Koniunkturnyi Institut in Moscow.

IB180 SERGEEV, SERGEI D. *Ekonomicheskoe sotrudnichestvo i vzaimopomoshch stran sotsialisticheskogo lageria*. Moscow: Vneshtorgizdat, 1956. 200 p. 2nd ed., 1959. 319 p. Deals with the origin and development of the Communist world market: trade, credit, and technical assistance; industrialization, the collectivization of agriculture, and living standards.

IB181 SHARP, SAMUEL L. *Nationalization of Key Industries in Eastern Europe.* Foundation for Foreign Affairs Pamphlet, No. 1. Washington: Foundation for Foreign Affairs, 1946. 80 p. Discusses the nationalization measures adopted in Czechoslovakia, Poland, and Yugoslavia and the trends in that direction in Hungary, Bulgaria, and Romania.

IB182 SPULBER, NICHOLAS. *The Economies of Communist Eastern Europe.* N.Y.: Wiley, jointly with the Technology Press of M.I.T.; London: Chapman & Hall, 1957. 525 p. Major emphasis is on the period of sovietization. The author concludes that the aim of Soviet policy was to forge out of the economies of Eastern Europe a "second world market" which would absorb the imbalances in the Soviet economy and supplement its deficiencies. 21-page bibliography. Based on Ph.D. dissertation, "The Economic Relations Between the USSR and the Eastern Countries After World War II," New School for Social Research, 1952. [B]

IB183 TRACHTENBERG, B., ed. *Osiagniecia gospodarcze krajów obozu pokoju.* Warsaw: Wydawn. Ministerstwa Oborony Narodowej, 1952. 189 p. A collection of articles by Polish, Russian, and German authors reviewing the policies and achievements of planned economy in the European and Asiatic countries of the socialist camp, including the USSR and China.

IB184 VAGANOV, B. S. *Voprosy organizatsii vneshnei torgovli stran narodnoi demokratii.* Moscow: Vneshtorgizdat, 1954. 106 p. A comprehensive survey of the foreign trade system of the people's democracies. Includes a list of government-controlled import-export firms.

IB185 WSZELAKI, JAN H. *Communist Economic Strategy; the Role of East-Central Europe.* Washington: National Planning Association, 1959. 132 p. One of a series of monographs on the "Economics of Competitive Coexistence." Assesses the economies of Eastern Europe and estimates the economic advantages and disadvantages of their relationship to the Soviet Union. By a Polish ex-diplomat and economist who now lives in the United States. [B]

IB186 ZALESKI, EUGENE. *Les Courants commerciaux de l'Europe danubienne au cours de la première moitié du XXme siècle.* Preface by Edouard Dolleans. Paris: Librairie Générale de Drost, 1952. 564 p. An economic history of the Danubian area. Special attention is given to the demographic problem and the economic ties of Danubia with the outside world. Eight-page bibliography. By an economist of Polish origin now a professor in Paris. [B]

5. PERIODICALS

IB187 COMMUNIST INTERNATIONAL. *La Fédération Balkanique; organe des peuples opprimés et minorités nationales des Balkans.* Semi-monthly (irregular). Vienna: 1923-31. Contains Marxist articles criticizing the political regimes of the Balkans. Issued in French or German, with translations (or additional articles) in various of the Balkan languages.

IB188 *East Europe.* Monthly. N.Y.: 1952—. Published by the Free Europe Committee, Inc., this periodical was titled *News From Behind the Iron Curtain* from 1952 to 1956. A very valuable source of information on current developments. In recent years it has also given some coverage to the USSR. Contains translations from the East European press, as well as analytical articles by Western specialists, including émigrés. [A]

IB189 LIBRARY OF CONGRESS. *East European Accessions Index.* Washington: 1951-61. 10 vols. (The years 1951-57 were issued under the title, *East European Accessions List.*) A monthly record of monographic publications issued after 1944 and periodical publications issued after 1950 which were received during the month by the Library of Congress and other American libraries. Imprints of the following countries as well as publications issued elsewhere in the languages of these countries are included: Albania, Bulgaria, Czechoslovakia, Estonia, Hungary, Latvia, Lithuania, Poland, Rumania, and Yugoslavia. Monographic and periodical publications are arranged by country and grouped under 17 general subjects. Publication ceased in 1961. Annotated.

IB190 *Journal of Central European Affairs.* 1941-64. Quarterly. Published at the Univ. of Colorado. Deals with current and historical topics on Central and Eastern Europe. Contains high-level book reviews and well-documented articles on Communism. [A]

IB191 MUNICH, SUEDOSTINSTITUT. *Wissenschaftlicher Dienst Suedosteuropa; Quellen ueber Staat Verwaltung, Recht, Bevoelkerung, Wirtschaft, Wissenschaft und Veroeffentlichungen in Suedosteuropa.* Monthly, 1951—. A reliable guide to developments in the countries of Southeast Europe.

IB192 *Osteuropa; Zeitschrift für gegenwartsfragen des Ostens.* Monthly. Stuttgart: 1951—. Issued by Deutsche Gesellschaft für Osteuropakunde, this periodical deals with Communism in Eastern Europe and the USSR. Its "Bücher und Zeitschriften" section is a well-compiled review and bibliography. [A]

IB192A *Studies for a New Central Europe.* N.Y.: 1963—. Quarterly. Published by the Mid-European Research Institute, New York City.

Contains articles on international relations of the past and present, with heavy emphasis on the Soviet Union and Germany.

IB193 *Survey; a Journal of Soviet and East European Studies.* Quarterly. London: 1956–. This publication, dealing primarily with the Soviet Union, is printed on behalf of the Congress for Cultural Freedom by the Eastern Press, London. The title varies; formerly *Soviet Survey*; also *Soviet Culture.*

IB194 U.S. LIBRARY OF CONGRESS, SLAVIC AND CENTRAL EUROPEAN DIVISION. *East and East Central Europe: Periodicals in English and Other West European Languages.* Compiled by Paul L. Horecky, with assistance of Janina Wojcicka. Washington: 1958. 126 p. A well-compiled annotated bibliography of current periodicals, primarily in English, French and German. Arranged by country, with titles concerning the area as a whole grouped separately. Title and entry index. [A]

Addenda

IB195 *The Central European Federalist.* Semiannual. N.Y.: 1953—. Issued by the Czechoslovak-Hungarian-Polish Research Committee. Contains studies on past and present-day political, cultural and socio-economic developments in Central and Eastern Europe and the USSR. Its "Short Notes" consist of commentaries on current topics. Has a well-written book review section.

IB196 GRZYBOWSKI, KAZIMIERZ. *The Socialist Commonwealth of Nations; Organizations and Institutions.* New Haven: Yale University Press, 1964. 300 p. A scholarly analysis by a well-known authority on the legal systems of Eastern Europe.

IB197 *Österreichische Ost-Hefte.* Six times a year. Vienna: 1959—. Issued by Arbeitsgemeinschaft Ost under the direct control of the Ministry of Education. Contains analyses and commentaries on present-day Eastern Europe and the USSR. Its book review section is very poor.

IB198 *Oriente Europeo.* Trimestral. Madrid: 1951—. Issued by the Centro de Estudios Orientales. Contains documented articles on all aspects of Eastern and Central Europe and the USSR. Its "Notes," "Documentation," "Chronicle," and "Bibliography" sections are well edited.

IC. ALBANIA

EDITED BY STAVRO SKENDI

1. BOOKS AND ARTICLES

IC1 AMERY, JULIAN. *Sons of the Eagle; A Study in Guerrilla War.* London: Macmillan, 1948. 354 p. Wartime resistance movements in Albania, particularly in the northern part and during the German occupation, as seen by a member of the British Military Mission attached to the Legality (Zogist) Movement. Intelligently written, but exaggerates the importance of the latter movement.

IC2 ARMSTRONG, HAMILTON FISH. *Tito and Goliath.* N.Y.: Macmillan, 1951. 312 p. One chapter, "From Sub-Satellite to Satellite" (p. 223-236), discusses objectively Albania's situation before and after the Tito-Cominform rupture, showing her strategic importance for the Soviet Union.

IC3 BROWN, J. F. "Albania, Mirror of Conflict," *Survey* (London), no. 40 (January 1962), p. 24-41. An outline of the course of the Albanian deviation, including the main charges and counter-charges during and after the 22nd Soviet Congress and an examination of the principal implications of the Albanian question.

IC4 DAVIES, EDMUND F. *Illyrian Venture; the Story of the British Military Mission to Enemy-Occupied Albania, 1943-1944.* London: Bodley Head, 1952. 246 p. Experiences of the chief of the British Mission in dealing with the various resistance groups, particularly the difficulties encountered with the Communists. Written simply and with humor.

IC5 DEDIJER, VLADIMIR, ed. *Jugoslavensko-albanski odnosi, 1939-1948; na osnovu službenih dokumenata, pisama i drugog materijala.* Zagreb: Borba, 1949. 225 p. Italian ed., Varese: Editoriale Periodici Italiana, 1949. 221 p. English translation (mimeographed) by U.S. Joint Publications Research Service, JPRS No. 13162. A Yugoslav account of Albanian-Yugoslav relations, mainly from the formation of the Albanian Communist Party in 1941 to the Tito-Cominform break, containing some important documents and letters of Albanian Communist leaders. There is also an Albanian edition, published in Belgrade in 1949. [A]

IC5A DILO, JANI I. *The Communist Party Leadership in Albania.* Washington: Institute of Ethnic Studies, Georgetown University, 1961. 20 p. Good in its factual part.

IC6 *Dokumenta mbi miqësinë shqiptaro-sovjetike.* Tirana: 1957. 551 p. A variety of documents, governmental and press, which aim to testify to the growth of friendship between Albania and the Soviet Union.

IC7 FREE EUROPE COMMITTEE. *Chronology of Major Events in Albania, 1944-1952.* Compiled by Shefki Miraku. N.Y.: Free Europe Comm., 1955. 150 p. Although rich in entries, the explanation of events is not always reliable.

IC8 FULTZ, JOAN. "The Origins and Nature of the People's Republic of Albania." M.A. thesis, U. of Chicago, 1948.

IC9 GRIFFITH, WILLIAM E. "An International Communism? Peiping, Tirana and Moscow: Polycentrism in Practice," *East Europe*, vol. x, no. 7 (July 1961), p. 3-9, 41-45. Treats the background of the Peiping-Tirana axis and examines possible consequences of the Sino-Soviet dispute in Eastern Europe. The footnotes contain a rich bibliography.

IC9A HAMM, HARRY. *Rebellen gegen Moskau.* Cologne: Verlag Wissenschaft und Politik, 1962. 191 p. After a survey of Albania's non-Communist and Communist past, one is introduced to the signs of a rebellion against Moscow, its motives, and the Soviet-Chinese conflict, including the 22nd Congress of the Soviet Communist Party. At the end, the author, one of the German journalists who visited Albania recently, asks whether the break threatens the West.

IC10 "History of the Albanian Communist Party," *News from Behind the Iron Curtain*, IV (November 1955), p. 3-10, and V (January 1956), p. 22-30. A rather good account.

IC11 HOXHA, ENVER. *Albanskii narod za mir i sotsializm.* Moscow: Gospolitizdat, 1956. 163 p. A collection of four speeches, delivered in 1954 and 1955, by the head of Albania's Communist Party, and two articles by him in 1955, dealing with domestic and international developments (Warsaw Pact, Bulganin-Tito Declaration).

IC12 KERTESZ, STEPHEN D., ed. *East Central Europe and the World; Developments in the Post-Stalin Era.* Notre Dame, Ind.: U. of Notre Dame Press, 1962. 386 p. The chapter on Albania (p. 197-228) by Stavro Skendi is a factual and interpretive essay, dealing with the various domestic aspects of Albanian life, Albania's relations with Yugoslavia and the rest of the world, her attitude toward the U.S., and her relations with the Soviet Union and China up to the summer of 1961.

IC13 KERTESZ, STEPHEN D., ed. *The Fate of East Central Europe: Hopes and Failures of American Foreign Policy.* Notre Dame, Ind.: U. of Notre Dame Press, 1956. 463 p. The chapter on Albania

(p. 297-318) by Stavro Skendi deals with the Albanian situation before, during, and after the Axis occupation, Soviet control, the Greek guerrilla war, and U.S. policy after 1948.

IC14 KREMNEN, P. "Podem prosveshcheniia i kultury v Narodnoi Respublike Albanii," *Sovetskaia Pedagogika*, VII (1952), p. 111-114. A Soviet educator describes how Albanian education and culture follow the Soviet pattern.

IC14A LAMBERG, ROBERT I. "Vorläufig Patt in Albanien," *Osteuropa,* vol. XII, no. 11/12 (Nov./Dec. 1962), p. 754-62. An interesting discussion of Albania's situation, economic and political, primarily from the international viewpoint, a year after the open rupture with the Soviet Union.

IC15 LOGORECI, ANTON. "Albania: A Chinese Satellite in the Making?" *The World Today*, XVII, no. 5 (May 1961), p. 197-205. Examines objectively—with an intimate knowledge of the country—the various developments which directed Albania toward China.

IC16 MANCHKHA, P. *Albaniia na puti k sotsializmu.* Moscow: Gospolitizdat, 1951. 134 p. A Soviet official gives a survey of various aspects of Albanian life—education, economy, culture, and party—showing the Soviet Union's role. Some statistics are included.

IC17 *Mbi influencëm e revolucionit të madh socialist të tetorit në Shqipëri (1917-1924)*. Tirana: 1957. 123 p. Documents from the Government Historical Archives and the press of the period, aimed at showing the influence of the Bolshevik Revolution in Albania.

IC18 MOISIU, VANGJEL. *Lëvizja puntore dhe komuniste në Shqipëri para krijimit të partisë komuniste shqiptare (1917-1939)*. Tirana: 1958. 79 p. The author, an Albanian Communist, shows how the political and economic conditions of the country during Zog's regime weighed heavily upon the workers, whose class consciousness began to grow through revolutionary programs for radical changes in living conditions. Dealing with the beginnings of the Communist movement, he points to the mistakes of the first Communists, most of whom later fell into disgrace.

IC19 MOURIN, MAXIM. "Le Satellite isolé—l'Albanie," *Revue de défense nationale* (Paris), XV (December 1959). A well-informed and thoughtful survey of various aspects of Albania under Communism, following Stalin's death, with stress on political and military developments.

IC20 PARTI E PUNËS SË SHQIPËRISË. *Materialy III sezda Albanskoi partii truda, 25 maia-3 iiunia 1956 goda.* Moscow: Gospolitizdat, 1957. 429 p. Includes: a long report by Hoxha on the Party, and on the domestic and international political situation; a speech by Premier Shehu on the completion of the First Five Year Plan and directives for the Second Five Year Plan (1956-60); changes in Party statutes; and a speech by the chief representative of the USSR delegation.

IC21 PARTI E PUNËS SË SHQIPËRISË, KOMITET QENDROR. *Tema mbi edukimin kommunist të rinisë*. Tirana: 1957. 180 p. Themes on the Communist education of Albanian youth.

IC22 PLASARI, NDREQI. *Krijimi i Partisë Komuniste të Shqipërisë (1939-1941)*. Tirana: 1959. 57 p. Primarily on the basis of Party documents, the Albanian Communist author deals with the Communist movement in the country before 1941, passing then to the Conference of Tirana (1941) and analyzing in detail its resolutions. His aim is to show that the formation of the Communist Party of Albania was historically prepared by the Albanian Communist movement, thus denying the role of the Yugoslavs, who were its real organizers.

IC23 SAIKOWSKI, CHARLOTTE. "Albania in Soviet Satellite Policy, 1945-1953." Certificate essay, Russian Institute, Columbia, 1954. 79 p. A short survey of Yugoslav domination, Albania's military importance, economic dependence, cultural Sovietization, and political instability since 1948, followed by a treatment of relations with neighboring countries. A good essay, partly based on Russian and Yugoslav sources.

IC24 SHMELEV, N. S. *Novaia Albania*. Moscow: Molodaia Gvardiia, 1951. A very superficial and propagandistic work.

IC25 SKENDI, STAVRO. "Albania and the Sino-Soviet Conflict," *Foreign Affairs*, vol. 40, no. 3 (April 1962), p. 471-478. After explaining the causes which lie at the root of the Albanian-Soviet conflict, the article proceeds to the events which made it obvious, placing Albania on the side of China. It then examines the reasons for Khrushchev's attack on the Albanian Communist leadership and the latter's capacity to resist, paying due attention to China's role.

IC26 SKENDI, STAVRO. "Albania, 1954-59," in *The Annual Register of World Events, 1959*. Ed. by Ivison Macadam. London: Longmans, 1960, p. 239-244. A mainly factual, but also partly interpretive, survey of Albanian developments in the post-Stalin era.

IC27 SKENDI, STAVRO. "Albania within the Slav Orbit: Advent to Power of the Communist Party," *Political Science Quarterly*, LXIII (June 1948), p. 257-274. Based partly on personal experiences and partly on other material, this essay deals with the formation of the Communist Party by Yugoslav emissaries, the resistance movements and their clashes, as well as with the Communist takeover and control, until the Tito-Cominform rupture.

IC28 SKENDI, STAVRO. *The Political Evolution of Albania, 1912-1944*. N.Y.: Mid-European Studies Center, 1954. 20 p. A concise survey, from the declaration of Albanian independence to the Communist seizure of power.

IC29 SKENDI, STAVRO, and others, eds. *Albania*. N.Y.: Publ. for the Mid-European Studies Center of the Free Europe Committee by Praeger, 1956. 389 p. A comprehensive and objective handbook on Albania since the Communist takeover, with a historical introduction in every chapter on developments prior to that date. Based mainly on first-hand Albanian materials, it contains an extensive bibliography. [A]

IC30 SMIRNOVA, N. D. *Obrazovanie Narodnoi Respubliki Albanii, 1939-1946*. Moscow: Izd. Akad. nauk SSSR, 1960. 195 p. A Soviet account of the developments leading to the formation of the Albanian Peoples Republic.

IC31 WOLFF, ROBERT L. *The Balkans in Our Time*. Cambridge: Harvard, 1956. 618 p. Dispersed through the book are several well-informed and useful sections on Albania under Communism.

IC32 ZAVALANI, TAJAR. "The Importance of Being Albania," *Problems of Communism*, vol. x, no. 7 (July-August 1961), p. 1-8. Based primarily on Albanian sources and an intimate knowledge of the country, it treats of the Soviet dispute with Albania and China and the reasons for Albanian dissatisfaction with Soviet policies.

2. PERIODICALS

IC33 *Bashkimi*. Tirana: Daily, 1944-. Organ of the Democratic Front (Government) of Albania.

IC34 *Rruga e Partisë*. Tirana: Monthly, 1954-. Theoretical journal of the Workers' (Communist) Party of Albania.

IC35 *Zëri i Popullit*. Tirana: Daily, 1944-. Organ of the Workers' (Communist) Party of Albania. [A]

Addendum

IC36 GRIFFITH, WILLIAM E. *Albania and the Sino-Soviet Rift*. Cambridge: M.I.T. Press, 1963. 423 p. Based primarily on an analysis of documentary material. Gives the background, causes, and significance of the events as related to Albania and the Sino-Soviet rift. There is some tendency to exaggerate the importance of Albanian nationalism. Major documents, particularly translations from *Zëri i Popullit*, follow the text (p. 183-409).

ID. AUSTRIA

EDITED BY THEODORE E. KYRIAK

ID1 *Allied Commission for Austria, September 1945–July 1955, Official Minutes and Stenographic Records of Meetings.* Comp. by Theodore E. Kyriak. Annapolis: Research Microfilms, 1960. (Microfilm, 23 reels, and index, 137 p.) The stenographic records of the 538 meetings represent an excellent source material on postwar Soviet behavior, techniques of negotiations, policies of Soviet occupation and their methods of intervention in local affairs. The original records were released without alteration or omission; the only complete documentary source material of high-level postwar negotiation with the USSR; detailed index. [A]

ID2 *Anschlag auf Österreich, ein Tatsachenbericht über den kommunistischen Putschversuch im September–Oktober 1950.* Published by the Central Secretariat of the Austrian Socialist Party, commissioned by the Party Chairman. Compiled by Alfred Migsch. Vienna: Vorwärts, 1950 (?). 63 p. Reports, photos, and day-to-day accounts of two Communist *coup d'état* attempts. Documented; notes Soviet support of the *Putsch* attempts. [B]

ID3 *Die Arbeit, Zeitschrift für Sozialpolitik, Wirtschaft und Betrieb.* Vienna, 1947–. Monthly, published by the C.P.

ID4 ARBEITSGEMEINSCHAFT FÜR OSTEUROPAFORSCHUNG. *Die Sowjetregierung und der österreichische Staatsvertrag; Bericht und Dokumente, 1943-1953.* 2nd enl. ed. Ed. by Dr. J. V. Hehn. Göttingen: 1953. 72 plus 58 p. A scholarly monograph on Soviet policy toward the Austrian State Treaty; the 58 page document section includes all major Soviet policy statements, declarations and agreements. [B]

ID5 BAUER, OTTO. *Die österreichische Revolution.* Vienna: Wiener Volksbuch; Berlin: Dietz, 1923. 294 p. English ed., *The Austrian Revolution.* Trans. and abridged by H. J. Stenning. London: L. Parsons. 288 p. Despite pressures from neighboring Soviet regimes after the War of 1914-1918, the Austrian Marxists renounced Bolshevism and chose the path of democratic socialism. The author was the Minister of Foreign Affairs in the first government of the Austrian Republic and one of the founders of Austro-Marxism. [B]

ID6 BUTTINGER, JOSEPH. *Am Beispiel Österreichs; ein geschichtlicher Beitrag zur Krise der sozialistischen Bewegung.* Cologne: Verlag für Politik und Wirtschaft, 1953. 668 p. English ed., *In the Twilight of Socialism, a History of the Revolutionary Socialists of Austria.* N.Y.:

Praeger, 1953. 577 p. French ed., Paris: Gallimard, 1956. An undocumented personal account by one of the leaders of the Revolutionary Socialists. While the focus is on the activities of the Socialists during 1934-38, it contains much valuable and objective information about the role of the Austrian Communists in the underground movement and workers organizations.

ID7 EFREMOV, A. *Sovetsko-avstriiskie otnosheniia posle Vtoroi mirovoi voiny.* Moscow: Gospolitizdat, 1958. 187 p.

ID8 GRATZ, GUSZTAV, and SCHÜLLER, RICHARD. *Die äussere Wirtschaftspolitik Österreich-Ungarns, mitteleuropäische Pläne.* Vienna: Hölder-Pichler-Tempsky, 1925. 334 p. English ed., *The Economic Policy of Austria-Hungary during the War in its External Relations.* New Haven: Yale, 1928. 286 p. Two high Austro-Hungarian officials discuss their country's Eastern policy during the war.

ID9 GRAYSON, CARY T., JR. *Austria's International Position, 1938-1953.* Geneva: Droz, 1953. 317 p. A well-documented scholarly study of the plans, policies and attitudes of the Allied powers toward Austria during 1943-53. The appendix includes tables, maps and over 100 pages of the English text of most important documents. Bibliography and index. [A]

ID10 GRUBER, KARL. *Zwischen Befreiung und Freiheit; der Sonderfall Österreich.* Vienna: Ullstein, 1953. 324 p. English ed., N.Y.: Praeger, 1955. 240 p. Dr. Gruber's personal account of the years 1945-53, during which period he was Austrian Minister of Foreign Affairs. Portrays the delicate problem of keeping a formal balance between East and West against Austria's traditionally Western-oriented background and sympathies. [B]

ID11 HARTEL, GUNTHER E. (COLONEL). *The Red Herring.* N.Y.: Ivan Obolensky, 1962. 177 p. The author was assigned as U.S. Liaison Officer with the Soviet Repatriation Mission in Salzburg, Austria after World War II. Here he tells, in fictionalized form, about the methods used by the Soviet Mission to force D.P.'s to return to Russia, as well as their various subversive activities. As a result of his reports on these activities, the Soviet Mission was expelled from Salzburg in 1961.

ID12 HELMER, OSKAR. *50 Jahre erlebte Geschichte.* Vienna: Volksbuchhandlung, 1957. 375 p. The author was the Minister of Interior during the postwar occupation of Austria, a lifelong Social Democrat who successfully resisted Communist manipulations and Soviet intimidation during 1945-55. Contains much information concerning Soviet and Communist policy during the occupation. [A]

ID13 IUDANOV, IU. I. *Avstriia; ekonomika i vneshniaia torgovlia.* Moscow: Vneshtorgizdat, 1958. 135 p.

ID14 *Die Kommunisten im Kampf für die Unabhängigkeit Österreichs; Sammelband.* Vienna: Stern, 1955. 294 p. This collection of articles, speeches, and declarations by the KPO and its functionaries reflects the views and policies of the Austrian Communists on national questions for the period of 1937-55. [B]

ID15 KOMMUNISTISCHE PARTEI ÖSTERREICHS, 15. PARTEITAG, VIENNA, 1951. *Der 15. Parteitag der Kommunistischen Partei Österreichs im Wiener Konzerthaus, 1. bis 4. November 1951; gekürztes Protokoll.* Vienna: Stern, 1951. 235 p.

ID16 KOMMUNISTISCHE PARTEI ÖSTERREICHS, 16. PARTEITAG, VIENNA, 1954. *Der 16. Parteitag der Kommunistischen Partei Österreichs, im Wiener Konzerthaus, 13. bis 16. Mai 1954; gekürztes Protokoll.* Vienna: Stern, 1954. 230 p.

ID17 KOMMUNISTISCHE PARTEI ÖSTERREICHS, 17. PARTEITAG, VIENNA, 1957. *Kommunisticheskaia partiia Avstrii; Sezd XVII, Vena 1957 i konferentsiia 1958 goda.* Moscow: Gospolitizdat, 1958. 183 p.

ID18 KOMMUNISTISCHE PARTEI ÖSTERREICHS, 17. PARTEITAG, VIENNA, 1957. *Der 17. Parteitag der Kommunistischen Partei Österreichs in den Wiener Sophiensaelen, 28. bis 31. Maerz 1957, gekürztes Protokoll.* Vienna: Stern, 1957. 350 p. The abridged records and summaries of the Communist Party have only limited usefulness as source information on *ad hoc* Party problems, aims and policy questions. The actual business is conducted in the various working subcommittees, mostly in advance; these records are not included, while discussions having potential propaganda value are disproportionately overemphasized. These publications tend to create a misleading picture of the state of C.P. affairs.

ID19 *Die Kommunistische Partei zur nationalen Fragen Österreichs 1937-1945.* Vienna: Stern, 1945. 24 p. An attempt to show a continuity of Communist policies toward national questions.

ID20 KOPLENIG, J. *Reden und Aufsätze, 1924-1950.* Vienna: Stern, 1951. 182 p. Articles and speeches by one of the leaders of the Austrian C.P.; the selection naturally reflects the prevailing Party line.

ID21 KUN, BELA. *The Revolutionary Struggle in Austria and Its Lessons.* London: Modern Books, 1934. 96 p. The author, a leading international Communist and former head of the Soviet Republic of Hungary in 1919, analyzes the background, strategy and tactics of the armed uprising by the workers of Austria. He blames the Social Democrats for the failure and regards February 1934 as the opportunity of a new beginning of Communist influence on the Austrian working class.

ID22 LEITNER, ALFRED. *Wenn die Russen kommen, ein Tatsachenbericht aus dem Nachbarland aus den Jahren 1945-1948.* Bern: H. R. Hugi, 1949. 80 p. A popular account about the behavior of Soviet occupation forces in Austria and its effect upon the Austrian population. Soviet declarations and policy statements toward liberated Austria are recalled.

ID23 LOW, ALFRED D. "Austria between Two Soviet Republics; In the Mirror of the Russian Press of 1919." Certificate essay, Russian Institute, Columbia, 1957. 130 p.

ID24 *Das neue Statut der Kommunistischen Partei Österreichs mit einleitendem Referat von Dr. Karl Altmann auf dem 13. Parteitag der KPO.* Vienna: Globus, 1946. 32 p. The first constitution and bylaws of the Austrian C.P. after the war; the guiding principle is "democratic centralism"—as stated in the introduction.

ID25 ÖSTERREICHISCHE FRIEDENSRAT. *Die Aufrüstung Österreichs, Dokumente und Tatsachen.* Vienna, Globus: 1952(?). 163 p. A report by the Soviet sponsored Austrian Peace Council accusing the Western Occupation powers with war preparations in Austria; describes the activities of the Peace Council; partially documented (photos, photocopies, and excerpts).

ID26 *Putschversuch—Oder Nicht? Ein Tatsachenbericht über das 4. Preis-und Lohnabkommen und die beiden gescheiterten kommunistischen Generalstreikversuche in September und Oktober 1950.* Comp. by Fritz Klenner. Vienna: Österreichischen Gewerkschaftbundes, 1950(?). 93 p. Reports, photos, and day-to-day accounts of two Communist *coup d'état* attempts. Documented; Soviet support noted; period covered: 25 September—6 October, 1950. [B]

ID27 SCHÄRF, ADOLF. *Österreichs Erneuerung 1945-1955, Das erste Jahrzehnt der Zweiten Republik.* Vienna: Volksbuchhandlung, 1955. 420 p. The author is a Socialist and served as a member of the cabinet during the occupation period. In 1957 he became president of Austria. His account of the first ten years of the second Austrian republic is not only an authoritative and detailed work, but is also most informative and scholarly. Contains much information concerning Soviet and Communist policy during the occupation. [A]

ID28 SCHÄRF, ADOLF. *Österreichs Wiederaufrichtung im Jahre 1945.* Vienna: Volksbuchhandlung, 1960. 228 p. Two earlier books by

Dr. Schärf, President of Austria, are in this edition: *April 1945* (Vienna, 1948) and *Zwischen Demokratie und Volksdemokratie* (Vienna, 1950). The best available account of the political developments in 1945 in Austria and on Soviet and Communist politics during that period. A well-documented, scholarly work which reflects the author's democratic socialist views. [B]

ID29 SCHONAU, ALEXANDER. *The February Insurrection of the Austrian Proletariat*. Moscow-Leningrad: Co-operative Publishing Society of Foreign Workers in the USSR. 75 p. The account credits the Communist Party for having started the workers' uprising (p. 57) and describes the role of the C.P. in the revolt. Partially documented; facsimiles; excerpts from newspaper reports.

ID30 SHEPHERD, GORDON. *The Austrian Odyssey*. N.Y.: St. Martin's; London: Macmillan, 1957. 302 p. The final part of this history of Austria deals with the East-West negotiations for a peace treaty.

ID31 *Sowjetpolitik gegenüber Österreich, April 1945–April 1947; Eine Dokumentensammlung*. Vienna: "Österreichische Zeitung," 1947. 120 p. Published by the official newspaper of the Soviet Occupation Forces of Austria (1945-55). There are 43 items in the collection. Documents of official Soviet policy toward liberated Austria and anti-Western propaganda statements are mixed together.

ID32 *Statut der Kommunistischen Partei Österreichs, beschlossen am 15. Parteitag 1951*. Vienna: Stern, 1951. 13 p. This new constitution, adopted at the 1951 Party congress, represents a major reorganization of the C.P.

ID33 TUROK, V. M. *Ocherki istorii Avstrii 1918-1929*. Moscow: Akad. nauk SSSR, 1955. 586 p.

ID34 *Volksstimme, Zentralorgan der Kommunistischen Partei Österreichs*. Vienna, 1918–. Title varies. The official newspaper of the C.P.

ID35 *Weg und Ziel, Monatschrift für Fragen der Demokratie und des wissenschaftlichen Socialismus*. Vienna, 1936-38, and 1946. The leading monthly on theoretical and practical problems of Austrian Communism; published by the C.P.

ID36 *Zwei Revolutionen, Kommunisten und Sozialdemokraten, 1918-1919*. Vienna: Volksbuchhandlung, 1932. 56 p. Social Democratic criticism of Austrian Communists, of their program and actions during 1918-1919. The Hungarian example is used as a parallel for potential developments in Austria under Communist rule.

IE. BALTIC STATES

EDITED BY ALFRED E. SENN AND STANLEY W. PAGE

1. GENERAL WORKS

IE1 AKADEMIIA NAUK SSSR, INSTITUT ISTORII. *Istoricheskie zapiski*, no. 45. Moscow: 1954. This issue is made up of reports by Soviet Baltic historians on the Baltic nations in the nineteenth and twentieth centuries.

IE2 BILMANIS, ALFREDS. *Baltic Essays*. Washington: Latvian Legation, 1945. 267 p. A Latvian statesman analyzes the historic role of the Baltic nationalities. Extensive consideration of Russian-Baltic relations. Strongest on the period since 1939 and weakest on the period 1917-20. Extremely hostile toward Russia.

IE3 MANNING, CLARENCE A. *The Forgotten Republics*. N.Y.: Philosophical Library, 1952. 264 p. A sympathetic but superficial and undocumented account of the history of the three Baltic states.

2. THE BALTIC STATES, 1917-1938

IE4 AVALOV, PAVEL M. (Bermondt-Avalov). *Im Kampf gegen den Bolschewismus; Erinnerungen von General Fürst Awaloff*. Glückstadt: J. J. Augustin, 1925. 563 p. Russian ed., Glückstadt: 1925. 540 p. The memoirs of the colorful Russian officer who led the German-Russian forces in the Baltic in 1919. A basic source on the build-up of the "West Russian" army. [B]

IE5 BAKH, M. G. (pseud. of M. I. Gertsbakh). *Politiko-ekonomicheskie otnosheniia mezhdu SSSR i pribaltikoi za desiat let, 1917-1927*. Moscow: Kommunisticheskaia akademiia, 1928. 166 p. A Soviet account reflecting Moscow's attitudes toward the Western world in 1927-28. Particularly useful for its discussion of events not generally mentioned in later Communist writings.

IE6 BALTISCHER LANDESWEHRVEREIN. *Die Baltische Landeswehr im Befreiungskampf gegen den Bolschewismus; ein Gedenkbuch herausgegeben vom Baltischen Landeswehrverein*. Riga: G. Löffler, 1929. 231 p. Short reminiscences by members of the Balt homeguard fighting by the side of the German Freikorps in Latvia during 1919. A useful military history that depicts the idealistic feelings of those fighting for their "homeland." Gives structure of *Landeswehr*, a casualty list by birthdate and company, and has a brief but good bibliography on the anti-Bolshevik struggle in the Baltic region.

IE7 BISCHOFF, JOSEPH. *Die Letzte Front; Geschichte der Eisernen Division im Baltikum 1919*. Berlin: Buch-und-Tiefd. Ges., 1934. 270 p. A memoir by the German patriot who was the creator and original commander of the Iron Brigade in 1919. Writing in Hitler's time, Bischoff had no need to conceal or rationalize any of his deceptions practiced in behalf of *Ostpolitik* in 1919. An important source with regard to the various military and displomatic forces competing in Latvia in that period. Excellent maps and photographs. [A]

IE8 BRAATZ, KURT VON. *Fürst Anatol Pawlowitsch Lieven*. Stuttgart: Chr. Belser, 1926. 165 p. A memoir by the personal adjutant of Prince Lieven, a Russian of Balt origin who organized a White Russian contingent to fight alongside the German Iron division and Latvian nationalist troops against the Reds in 1919. Sheds important light on White Russian-German-Balt-Latvian relations and military affairs in general in Latvia during that period. [B]

IE9 BRACKMANN, ALBERT; ENGEL, KARL; and WITTRAM, REINHARD, eds. *Der Bolschewismus und die Baltische Front*. Leipzig: Hirzel, 1939. 104 p. Six articles, some nationalist and some specifically Nazi in point of view, by academicians and military men. Dwells longingly on "what might have been" on Germany's eastern front in the final stages of World War I and the first half of 1919. Extremely valuable on Balt, Latvian, and Russian activities drawn from hard-to-find German and Latvian memoirs and official sources. Carefully documented. [A]

IE10 FOOTMAN, DAVID J. *The Civil War and the Baltic States*. (St. Anthony's Papers on Soviet Affairs.) Oxford: St. Anthony's College, 1959. 2 vols.

IE11 GOLTZ, RÜDIGER VON DER. *Meine Sendung in Finnland und im Baltikum*. Leipzig: Koehler, 1920. 312 p. 2nd ed., *Als politischer General im Osten, Finnland und Baltikum, 1918 und 1919*. 1936. 173 p. Memoirs of the Commander of the German forces in the Baltic, 1919, who hoped to re-conquer Latvia and Estonia as stepping-stones to a German conquest of Petrograd. A vital source of information for understanding the jigsaw puzzle of power politics involving the Baltic States and the Intervention. [A]

IE12 GRAHAM, MALBONE W. *The Diplomatic Recognition of the Border States*. Berkeley: U. of California, 1936-1941. 3 vols. A useful account, based on official publications, of the struggle for diplomatic recognition by the individual Baltic states. The three volumes are devoted to Finland, Latvia, and Estonia.

IE13 GRAVINA, MANFREDI. *Attualitá politiche; studi del dopoguerra*. Milan: Albrighi, Segati, 1926. 296 p. An Italian scholar's comment upon the post World War I situation, largely concerned with problems involving areas formerly part of the Russian empire. Three interesting but superficial chapters on the Baltic countries.

IE14 GRIMM, CLAUS. *Jahre Deutscher Entscheidung im Baltikum, 1918-1919*. Essen: Essener Verlagsanstalt, 1939. 514 p. This German scholar's nationalist bias detracts little from the value of his well-organized and thoroughly documented account. The best German study of the diplomatic-military and ideological turmoil in Latvia in 1919. Excellent bibliography. [A]

IE15 HALE, R. *Report of the Mission to Finland, Latvia, Lithuania and Esthonia on the Situation in the Baltic Provinces*. Washington: 1919. Marred by internal contradictions, apparently due to multiple authorship, this official U.S. Senate report is nevertheless useful in depicting conditions in 1919 in the Baltic area.

IE16 HEHN, JURGEN VON. "Die Entstehung der Staaten Lettland und Estland und der Bolschewismus und die Grossmächte," *Forschungen zur osteuropäischen Geschichte*, IV (1956), p. 103-218. A serious effort to put the emergence of Latvia and Estonia, 1917-20, into the proper international context. [A]

IE17 MEIKSINS, GREGORY. *The Baltic Riddle; Finland, Estonia, Latvia, Lithuania—Keypoints of European Peace*. N.Y.: L. B. Fischer, 1943. 271 p. Strongly denounces the "dictatorial regimes" in the Baltic states in the 1930's and generally supports the Soviet position.

IE18 NIESSEL, H. A. *L'Évacuation des Pays Baltiques par les Allemands*. 1935. 272 p. A memoir by the head of the Inter-Allied Commission charged with securing the evacuation of the German forces from the Baltic area in late 1919. Contains background and incidental information and some documents pertaining to German policy toward Lithuanian and Latvian struggles against the German and White Russian forces in 1919.

IE19 PAGE, STANLEY W. *The Formation of the Baltic States: A Study of the Effects of Great Power Politics upon the Emergence of Lithuania, Latvia, and Estonia*. Cambridge: Harvard, 1959. 193 p. A lucid, objective and well-documented account by an American professor analyzing the complex military, diplomatic, political and social struggles that marked the Civil War-Intervention period, 1917-20, in the Baltic countries. Some minor factual errors and some bibliographical omissions, but nonetheless one of the best books on the subject. [A]

IE20 PICK, FREDERICK W. *The Baltic Nations: Estonia, Latvia, and Lithuania*. London: Boreas, 1945. 172 p. An account, with footnotes, of the history of the three states between the wars. Emphasizes their role in international affairs, particularly Russo-British relations. Contains errors. [B]

IE21 POPOFF, GEORGES. *L'Invasion muscovite; cinq mois de domination bolchévique dans une ville balte.* Paris: Plon, 1929. 248 p. English ed., *The City of the Red Plague; Soviet Rule in a Baltic Town.* London: Allen & Unwin, 1932. 343 p. German ed., *Sowjetherrschaft in Europa.* Bern: Gotthelf, 1935. 280 p. A detailed, hostile account by a Balt native of Riga who experienced the occupation of that city by the Bolsheviks in 1919. Valuable if read with care. Contains important documentary material difficult to find elsewhere. [A]

IE22 ROYAL INSTITUTE OF INTERNATIONAL AFFAIRS. *The Baltic States; Estonia, Latvia, Lithuania.* London: Oxford, 1938. A general, objective account of the facts of life in the Baltic states in the 1920's and 1930's. [A]

IE23 RUTENBURG, GREGOR. *Die Baltischen Staaten und das Voelkerrecht.* Riga: Löffler, 1929. 156 p. A Lithuanian politician traces the development of the international identity of the Baltic states.

IE24 SCHABERT, OSKAR. *Baltisches Märtyrerbuch.* Berlin: Furche, 1926. 201 p. A Riga pastor's brief, sentimental biographies of pastors who were imprisoned or executed reveal something about Bolshevik anti-religious policies in Latvia and Estonia early in 1918 and again in 1919.

IE25 SCHRAM, STUART R. "L'Union soviétique et les États baltes." Chapter in: *Les Frontières européennes de l'URSS 1917-1941.* Ed. by Jean-Baptiste Duroselle. Paris: A. Colin, 1957. P. 25-168. An objective survey of relations through the 1920's and 1930's, with critical bibliographical comments in footnotes. [A]

IE26 SOBOLEVITCH, E. *Les États baltes et la Russie soviétique; relations internationales jusqu'en 1928.* Paris: Les Presses universitaires de France, 1930. 265 p. Stresses the right of the Baltic states to existence and recognizes the danger from Russia, but emphasizes the need for economic cooperation between the USSR and the Baltic states.

IE27 STENBOCK-FERMOR, ALEKSANDR. *Freiwilliger Stenbock; Bericht aus dem baltischen Befreiungskampf.* Stuttgart: J. Engelhorn, 1929. 236 p. The war reminiscences of a Latvian Balt. At age 16, in December 1918, he volunteered to join the Landeswehr (homeguard) of Balts and Russian Whites then being formed to try to drive back the invading Red Army, and participated in the reconquest of Mitau and Riga in 1919.

IE28 STUČKA, PETERIS. *Piat mesiatsev sotsialisticheskoi sovetskoi Latvii.* Moscow: 1919. 2 vols. Memoir by the President of Soviet Latvia recounting the five months of Soviet power in 1919. A valuable historical document. [A]

IE29 TARULIS, ALBERT N. *Soviet Policy Toward the Baltic States, 1918-1940.* Notre Dame, Ind.: U. of Notre Dame Press, 1959. 276 p. Concentrates on events of 1918-20 and 1939-40. Written by a Lithuanian émigré, who stresses the right of the Baltic states to independence. Contains useful references to periodical literature in Baltic languages. [A]

IE30 WAITE, ROBERT G. L. *Vanguard of Nazism; the Free Corps Movement in Postwar Germany, 1918-1923.* Cambridge: Harvard, 1952. 344 p. A competent treatise. Chapter V, "The Baltic Adventure," covers German intervention in the Baltic states. Contains an extensive and critical bibliography. [B]

IE31 WINNIG, AUGUST. *Am Ausgang der deutschen Ostpolitik.* Berlin: Staatspolitischer Verlag, 1921. 125 p. The detailed memoir of a Social-Democratic trade union leader who became "Plenipotentiary of the Reich for the Baltic Lands" prior to the armistice of 1918 and, somewhat later, German Ambassador to Latvia and Estonia. He tried by devious means to keep the Baltic countries out of nationalist and Bolshevik hands, hoping to snatch something for the Vaterland out of the flames of defeat. A valuable historical document. [A]

IE32 WINNIG, AUGUST. *Heimkehr.* Hamburg: Hanseatische Verlagsanstalt, 1935. 409 p. The Reichs commissioner, sent to German-held Latvia and Estonia just before the German West-front collapsed in 1918, here adds enlightening details to the story told in an earlier book of his attempts to keep Latvia in German hands in the face of Bolshevik, Allied, and Latvian nationalist opposition. A highly biased but useful narrative.

IE33 WRANGELL, WILHELM (BARON). *Geschichte des Baltenregiments; Das Deutschtum Estlands im Kampfe Gegen den Bolschewismus 1918-20.* Reval: F. Wassermann, 1928. 160 p. Largely an officer's chronicle; in fact, the official history of the activities of the Estonian-Balt homeguard of volunteers in its campaigns alongside the none-too-friendly Estonian nationalist forces against the Bolsheviks in the period December 1918 to November 1919. Important in a broader sense for its comments on relations between independence-seeking Estonians and Russians. [B]

3. THE BALTIC STATES, 1939-1963

IE34 ANDERSON, HERBERT F. *Borderline Russia.* London: Cresset, 1942. 238 p. An interesting account of the situation in the Baltic states at the beginning of World War II, by a British traveller.

IE35 BALTISKA KOMMITTÉN. *Ha de rätt att leva? Inför de baltiska folkens ödestimma, av Baltiska kommittén.* Stockholm: H. Geber, 1942. 351 p. A compilation of articles by members of the Stockholm Baltic Committee made up largely of émigré academicians and officials from Estonia, Latvia and Lithuania asking whether their countries have the right to exist. Some articles deal historically with events from 1917 to 1942. Others refer to culture, art, the people and relations with Sweden.

IE36 CHAMBON, HENRY DE. *La Tragédie des nations baltiques.* Paris: Revue Parlementaire, 1946. 226 p. A detailed account of events from 1939 to 1946, by a French journalist well known for his sympathies for the Baltic nations. He argues against recognition of the incorporation of the Baltic states in the USSR.

IE37 COATES, WILLIAM P. and ZELDA K. *Russia, Finland and the Baltic.* London: Lawrence and Wishart, 1940. 144 p. Seeks to justify Soviet policy vis-à-vis the Baltic states on the grounds of "sheer geographical and strategic necessity."

IE38 FARR, PHILIP. *Soviet Russia and the Baltic Republics.* London: Russia Today Society, 1944. 52 p. A pro-Bolshevik account by an astute Englishman. Worth reading for the Civil War-Intervention period, 1917-20. Despite his bias, the author calls many a spade a spade. Useful, if only in balancing the multitude of writings heavily weighted in one of the many other possible directions. The author's critical vision is badly blurred with respect to Estonian military forces in 1919. A brief but useful section of footnotes.

IE39 GERMANY, AUSWÄRTIGES AMT. *Nazi-Soviet Relations, 1939-1941; Documents from the Archives of the German Foreign Office.* Ed. by R. J. Sontag and J. S. Beddie. Washington: Dept. of State, 1948. 362 p. Contains documents pertaining to the agreements between Germany and the Soviet Union as to the disposition of the Baltic states.

IE40 KALME, ALBERT. *Total Terror; An Exposé of Genocide in the Baltics.* N.Y.: Appleton-Century-Crofts, 1951. 310 p. A Latvian émigré's account of the Sovietization of the Baltic states.

IE41 MEISSNER, BORIS. *Die Sowjetunion, die Baltischen Staaten und das Völkerrecht.* Cologne: Verlag für Politik und Wirtschaft, 1956. 377 p. Discussion of Soviet international law doctrines and practices, with special reference to the Soviet annexation of the Baltic states, by a leading West German authority on the Soviet Union. Valuable 26-page bibliography. [A]

IE42 OLBERG, PAUL. *Tragedin balticum, annektionen av de fria republikerna Estland, Lettland och Litauen.* Stockholm: Bokförlaget

Natur och Kultur, 1941. 102 p. A German Social-Democrat superficially traces the relations of the Baltic states with Soviet Russia and deplores their cloaked annexation by the USSR in 1940.

IE43 PUSTA, KAAREL R. *The Soviet Union and the Baltic States.* N.Y.: Felsberg, 1943. 79 p. A point by point rebuttal, by a leading Estonian politician, of the charges made in *Soviet Union, Finland, and the Baltic States* (see below). [B]

IE44 REPEČKA, JUOZAS. *Der gegenwärtige völkerrechtliche Status der Baltischen Staaten unter Besonderer Berücksichtigung der Diplomatischen Vorgeschichte der Eingliederung dieser Staaten in die Sowjetunion.* Göttingen: 1950. 392 p. A legal analysis of the independence of the Baltic states and their incorporation into the USSR in 1940.

IE45 ŠILDE, ĀDOLFS. *Pa Deportēto Pēdām.* N.Y.: Grāmatu Draugs, 1956. 304 p. English ed., *The Profits of Slavery.* Stockholm: Latvian National Foundation, 1958. 302 p. The Latvian author gives a seemingly fair description of Soviet forced labor camps with special emphasis on the fate of deported Lithuanians, Latvians and Estonians. He interviewed 2000 German and Austrian war prisoners and civilians released from the USSR since October 1955. The English edition has some omissions and some additions.

IE46 *Soviet Union, Finland and the Baltic States.* London: Soviet War News, 1941. 32 p. A syllabus of Soviet complaints against the Baltic states written with the aim of justifying the actions of the USSR in 1939-40. For a rebuttal, see above the work by K. R. Pusta. [B]

IE47 SWETTENHAM, JOHN A. *The Tragedy of the Baltic States; a Report Compiled from Official Documents and Eyewitness Stories.* London: Hollis & Carter, 1952. 216 p. By a former member of the DP Division of the Control Commission for Germany. Concentrates on events from 1940 on, with special emphasis on Estonia.

IE48 U.S. CONGRESS, HOUSE, SELECT COMMITTEE ON COMMUNIST AGGRESSION. *Baltic States Investigation.* Washington: G.P.O., 1954. 2 parts. 1448 p. Contains testimony by Baltic nationals on their experiences with the Russians, as well as a survey of the period of independence written by committee researchers. The testimony is particularly interesting for revelations on diplomatic and political affairs in 1939 and 1940. [B]

4. ESTONIA

IE49 DELLINGSHAUSEN, EDUARD VON. *Im Dienste der Heimat!* Stuttgart: Ausland und Heimat Verlags-Aktiengesselschaft,

1930. 352 p. Political autobiography of the leader of the Estonian Balt nobility. An indispensable source for Estonian and Latvian affairs in the period 1917-18, stressing the outlook of the Balt nobility. Replete with important data including appendices of documents. [A]

IE50 EESTI NSV TEADUSTE AKADEEMIA, AJALOO INSTITUT. *Velikaia Oktiabrskaia sotsialisticheskaia revoliutsiia v Estonii.* Ed. by I. M. Saat and others. Tallin: Estonskoe Gosizdat, 1958. 621 p. An extremely valuable chronicle by Soviet Estonian academicians describing events from March 1917 to March 1918 in terms of the activities of the Soviets in Estonia prior to the November *coup d'état* and of Soviet governmental, press, military, and other activities thereafter. Especially useful for a day to day calendar of events, a list of the names of Estonian Bolsheviks, and a toponymic index. [A]

IE51 *Eesti riik ja rahvas Teises maailmasôjas.* Stockholm: Kirjastus EMP, 1954-56. 3 vols. Volume III contains articles on various aspects of the Soviet occupation of Estonia, 1939-41, by prominent Estonian émigrés. [B]

IE52 *Eesti Vabadussôda 1918-1920.* Geislingen, Germany: Kultuuri Kirjastus, 1948-51. 2 vols. An Estonian research committee's account of Estonia's war of liberation. The best source on the subject. [A]

IE53 EFIMOV, M. *Sovetskaia Estoniia.* Moscow: Gospolitizdat, 1940. 57 p. A Soviet propaganda account of Estonia's domestic and foreign affairs, justifying the "liberation" of the Estonian people by the USSR in 1940. Useful for certain factual data regarding economic conditions prior to 1940 and for an understanding of the official Soviet view of Estonia's government and class structure.

IE54 ESTONIA (TERRITORY UNDER GERMAN OCCUPATION, 1941-44). *Eesti rahva kannatuste aasta; Eesti omavalitsuse väljaanne.* Tallin: Eesti Kirjastus, 1943. On the Russian occupation of Estonia, 1940-41. Documents included.

IE55 GORN, VASILII L. *Grazhdanskaia voina na severo-zapade Rossii.* Berlin: Gamayun, 1923. 416 p. A member of the White North-West government during the Civil War describes White Russian-Estonian relations in 1919 using his memory as well as many official documents. An excellent source. [A]

IE56 JACKSON, JOHN HAMPDEN. *Estonia.* London: Allen and Unwin, 1941. 248 p. 2nd ed. (with a postscript on the years 1940-47), London: Allen and Unwin, 1948; N.Y.: Macmillan, 1949. 272 p. An English view of Estonia's history, with special emphasis on the Sovietization in 1940 and after. It gives a distorted account of Estonia's war of liberation, but contains a good deal of useful information.

IE57 KAELAS, ALEKSANDR. *Das sowjetische besetzte Estland.* Stockholm: Estnischer Nationalfond, 1958. 136 p. An account by an Estonian émigré of Estonian conditions, mainly since 1944. His information is drawn from the Communist press and radio, the Soviet Estonian Academy of Science publications, and refugees. The tone is moderate and detached. A basic source. [A]

IE58 KAREDA, ENDEL. *Estonia in the Soviet Grip; Life and Conditions under Soviet Occupation, 1947-1949.* London: Boreas, 1949. 100 p. An anti-Soviet pamphlet published by the Estonian information center in London. Useful because of the author's information derived from Soviet Estonian newspapers and periodicals and from official sources. Described as a sequel to Survel's pamphlet of 1947, but more moderate in tone.

IE59 KAREDA, ENDEL. *Technique of Economic Sovietisation: A Baltic Experience.* London: Boreas, 1947. 127 p.

IE60 KAROTAMM, N. *Meie Järjekordsed Ülesanded; Kõnesid ja Kirjutusi 1946-1947, Aastal.* Tallin: Poliitiline Kirjandus, 1947. 410 p. Collected articles and speeches from December 1945 to March 1947 by Karotamm, First Secretary of the Estonian Communist Party. Stalin is lauded throughout.

IE61 KINGISSEPP, VIKTOR. *Kellele Iseseisvus, Kellele Ike.* Tallin: Poliitiline Kirjandus, 1946. 300 p. Writings of an Estonian Bolshevik leader.

IE62 LAAMAN, EDUARD. *Eesti iseseisvuse sünd.* Tartu: Loodus, 1936. 784 p. How Estonia got its independence from Russia.

IE63 LILL, VLADIMIR A., and MAAMIAGI, VIKTOR A. *Estonskaia SSR.* Moscow: Gospolitizdat, 1955. 167 p. Soviet Estonian academicians report on economic progress in Estonia, mainly since 1945. This is preceded by a Bolshevik-slanted history of Estonian-Russian relations and activities of Communists and workers in Estonia from 1917 to 1940. Useful for factual data and particularly for information on Communist Party policy since 1946.

IE64 MAIDE, JAAN. *Ülevaade Eesti Vabadussôjast 1918-20.* Tallin: Kaitseliidu Kirjastus, 1933. 448 p. An extremely detailed chronicle of the military operations of the Estonian and other forces involved in the Estonian war of liberation, by a Lt. Col. of the Estonian army. A basic source vastly implemented by nineteen military maps at the end of the book. [A]

IE65 MARTNA, MIHKEL. *L'Esthonie; les Esthoniens et la question esthonienne.* Paris: A. Colin, 1920, 268 p. Italian ed., Rome: 1919.

German ed., Olten: 1919. A plea by the leader of the Estonian Mensheviks and member of the Estonian Government in 1919 stressing Estonia's right to independence from Russia and Germany. Useful for material on political developments in 1917.

IE66 NAAN, G. I., ed. *Istoriia Estonskoi SSR; s drevneishikh vremen do nashikh dnei.* Tallin: Estonskoe gos. izd-vo, 1952. 552 p. A Soviet survey of Estonian history from ancient times, written during Stalin's later years.

IE67 ORAS, ANTS. *Baltic Eclipse.* London: Gollancz, 1948. 307 p. Memoirs of events in Estonia, 1939-46, by an émigré, formerly a professor at the University of Tartu. A story of terror and deportations by the NKVD in 1940-41, followed by the German invasion and Gestapo terror directed against Jews, Communists and others. A sensitive and honest account with much historically valuable eye-witness detail. [A]

IE68 *Pod znamenem oktiabria; trudiashchikhsia Estonii v borbe za sovetskuiu vlast, 1917-1940 gg.; sbornik statei.* Moscow: Gospolitizdat, 1959. 200 p. A recent Soviet collection of articles dedicated to depicting Soviet rule as the true expression of the desires of the Estonian people.

IE69 RAUD, VILLIBALD, comp. *Estonia; A Reference Book.* N.Y.: Nordic Press, 1953. 158 p. An attempt by an émigré to present a basic outline of life in independent Estonia between the wars. Contains a special section on life both in Estonia and among the émigrés after 1940.

IE70 *Situation in Soviet Occupied Estonia in 1955-1956.* N.Y.: Consulate General of Estonia, n.d. 62 p. (mimeographed). Statements by four eyewitnesses who escaped from Estonia in 1955 and 1956.

IE71 SURVEL, JAAK. *Estonia Today; Life in a Soviet-Occupied Country.* London: Boreas, 1947. 69 p. An anti-Soviet tract sponsored by Estonians in English exile, stressing the evils of the Soviet occupation of Estonia, 1940-41, and since 1944 when the Red Army drove out the Germans. Useful for information drawn from Soviet Estonian sources (press, radio, etc.).

IE72 TAIGRO, IU. *Borba trudiashchikhsia Estonii za sovetskuiu vlast i za mir v gody grazhdanskoi voiny, 1918-1919.* Tallin: 1959. 136 p. A Soviet account of the struggle for power in Estonia, 1918-19.

IE73 U.S., LIBRARY OF CONGRESS, SLAVIC AND CENTRAL EUROPEAN DIVISION. *Estonia: A Selected Bibliography.* Comp. by Salme Kuri. Washington: 1958. 74 p. Lists 491 titles, including periodicals, most of them without comment. Covers all aspects of Estonia, including history, religion, economics, intellectual life, etc. [B]

IE74 UUSTALU, EVALD. *The History of Estonian People.* London: Boreas, 1952. 261 p. A useful survey of Estonian history, quite fair despite the author's love for his country. Particularly good on the period of Estonia's liberation, 1917-20. Excellent bibliography.

IE75 "Voenno-revoliutsionnyi komitet estonskogo kraia 1917—nach. 1918 g. (Iz protokolov VRK)," *Krasnyi Arkhiv*, vol. 4, p. 3-63. Moscow: Gosizdat, 1940. The minutes of the sessions of the Military-Revolutionary Committee of Estonia in the period 1917-18. A basic source. [A]

IE76 WISELGREN, PER. *Från Hammaren till Hakkorset.* Stockholm: Idé och Form, 1942. 294 p. A quite detailed account of the Sovietization of Estonia from 1940 to the time of the Nazi occupation in 1941. Based on the personal experiences of the author, an Estonian scholar who escaped, and other generally reliable sources of information. Important material pertaining to political and economic affairs. [A]

5. LATVIA

IE77 BERZINSH, ALFREDS. *I Saw Vishinsky Bolshevize Latvia.* Washington: Latvian Legation, 1948. 55 p. The author, Latvian Minister of Public Affairs in 1940, gives an angry but generally true account of the Soviet annexation of Latvia in that year. Interesting factual details. Useful if the author's bias is kept in mind.

IE78 BĪLMANIS, ALFREDS. *Latvia in the Making.* Riga: B. Lamey, 1925. 40 p. German ed., 1925. French ed., 1925. 2nd ed., *Latvia in the Making, 1918-1928.* Riga: The Riga Times, 1928. 160 p. 3rd ed., *Latvia as an Independent State.* Washington: Latvian Legation, 1947. 405 p. An important survey of Latvia's twentieth century history, written by a leading Latvian historian.

IE79 CEICHNERS, ALFREDS. *Was Europa drohte; die Bolschewisierung Lettlands 1940-1941.* Riga: The Author, 1943. 751 p. A detailed examination of the Soviet takeover in Latvia in 1940. Published during the German occupation of Riga.

IE80 DINBERGS, ANATOL. "Incorporation of Latvia into the USSR, 1940-1941." Ph.D. dissertation, Georgetown, 1953.

IE81 DRĪZULIS, A. *Latviia pod igom Fashizma.* Riga: Latgosizdat, 1960. 385 p. A Soviet history of Latvia "under the yoke of fascism."

IE82 DRĪZULIS, A. *Ocherki istorii rabochego dvizheniia v Latvii, 1920-1940 gg.* Moscow: Gospolitizdat, 1959. 166 p. A completely Soviet-slanted history of Latvia, but useful for information on the activities of the Latvian Communist Party in that period.

IE83 DRĪZULIS, A. *Velikaia oktiabrskaia sotsialisticheskaia revoliutsiia v Latvii; kratkii istoricheskii ocherk.* Riga: Latgosizdat, 1957. 122 p. The Bolshevik Revolution in Latvia from the Communist point of view.

IE84 DRĪZULIS, A. and TIZENBERG, R. *Latviiskaia SSR v period Velikoi otechestvennoi voiny Sovetskogo Soiuza, 1941-1945.* Riga: Latgosizdat, 1954. 139 p. A Soviet account of Latvia during World War II.

IE85 ENGELHARDT, E. VON (BARON). *Der Ritt nach Riga; Aus den Kämpfen der Baltischen Landeswehr gegen die Rote Armee, 1918-1920.* Berlin: 1938. 152 p. One of the many accounts, so popular in Nazi Germany, of the Baltic Landeswehr that helped forestall the Red Army's invasion of East Prussia in 1919. Useful for military details. The author completes the writing of the memoirs of his father, a cavalry corps commander in the Landeswehr.

IE86 FREIVALDS, O. *Lielā Sāpju Draudze.* Copenhagen: Imanta, 1952. 335 p. A documentated study of Soviet rule in Latvia, 1940-41, with emphasis on Soviet deportations and terror.

IE87 GĒRMANIS, ULDIS, and VĀCIETIS, JUKUMS. *Pa Aizputinātām Pēdām.* Stockholm: Daugava, 1956. 360 p. The memoirs of Jukums Vācietis, introduced by Uldis Gērmanis. Vācietis, a Latvian colonel, was the first commander-in-chief of the Red Army. An important source on the Russian Revolution. A reproduction of a little-known two-volume edition, *Latviesu strelnieku vesturiska nozime*, published in Pskov in 1922-24.

IE88 KALNBĒRZINŠ, JĀNIS. *Ten Years of Soviet Latvia.* Moscow: Foreign Languages Publishing House, 1951. 271 p. The First Secretary of the Soviet Latvian Communist Party recounts the history of "bourgeois" Latvia, 1918-40, amid praise of Stalin, and then describes the industrial and agricultural progress made by Soviet Latvia mainly from 1946 to 1950. Not trustworthy, but useful for hard-to-locate crumbs of factual information.

IE89 LATVIA, SUTNIECIBA, U.S. *Latvia in 1939-1942; Background, Bolshevik and Nazi Occupation, Hopes for Future.* Washington: Press Bureau of the Latvian Legation, 1942. 137 p. A denunciation of the events of 1939 and 1940 and of the Soviet explanations of their actions.

IE90 LATVIA, SUTNIECIBA, U.S. *Latvian-Russian Relations; Documents, 1721-1944.* Comp. by Alfreds Bilmanis. Washington: Latvian Legation, 1944. 255 p. A collection of treaties, decrees, and protocols pertaining to Latvian-Russian relations since 1721. Three-fourths devoted to the period after 1917. The documents are selected mainly to emphasize Latvia's right to freedom from Russia in the period 1917-20 and from the USSR since Latvia's annexation.

IE91 LATVIJAS PADOMJU SOCIALISTISKAS REPUBLIKAS ZINATNU AKADEMIJA, VESTURES UN MATERIALAS KULTURAS INSTITUTS. *Latvijas PSR Vesture; saisinats kurss.* Ed. by K. Strazdina. Riga: Latvijas PSR Zinatnu akademijas izdevnieciba, 1956. 551 p. A recent Soviet history of Latvia. Includes a section on the period of independence.

IE92 "Meropriiatiia Sovetskogo pravitelstva Latvii, 1918-1919 gg.," *Krasnyi Arkhiv*, vol. 6, p. 45-84. Moscow: Gosizdat, 1940. Decrees and minutes of sessions of the Soviet Government of Latvia in 1918-19. A basic source. [A]

IE93 MOTT, HENRY W., III. "The Occupation and Incorporation of Latvia, June 17 to August 5, 1940." Certificate essay, Russian Institute, Columbia, 1957. 65 p.

IE94 *Oktiabrskaia revoliutsiia v Latvii, dokumenty i materialy; 40 let, 1917-1957.* Ed. by A. A. Drīzulis. Riga: Izd-vo Akademii nauk Latviiskoi SSR, 1957. 458 p. A highly selective but nevertheless important compilation of documentary materials by Soviet Latvian academicians about the Latvian revolutionary movement as it related to that of Russia proper from March 1917 to February 1918. The contents of the volume attest to the intensity of the soldier-peasant-proletarian ferment in unoccupied Latvia. [A]

IE95 OZOLS, KARL V. *Memuary poslannika.* Paris: Dom Knigi, 1938. 267 p. Memoirs of a Latvian diplomat.

IE96 RING, I. G. *Latviia.* Moscow: Sotsekgiz, 1936. 282 p. A Soviet view of the Baltic Republic.

IE97 SAVCHENKO, VASILII I. *Istoricheskie sviazi latyshskogo i russkogo narodov.* Riga: Izd. A.N. Latviiskoi SSR, 1959. 140 p. A Soviet version of the historic relations between the Latvian and Russian peoples.

IE98 SIPOLS, V. IA. *Za kulisami inostrannoi interventsii v Latvii, 1918-1920 gg.* Moscow: Gospolitizdat, 1959. 224 p. A Soviet account of events of 1918-20, picturing nationalist Latvia as part of a general Entente action to crush the Bolsheviks in Russia.

IE99 *Sotsialisticheskaia Sovetskaia Respublika Latvii v 1919 g. i inostrannaia interventsiia; dokumenty i materialy.* Moscow: 1959. 2 vols. A collection of documents chosen to illustrate the Soviet view that Communist rule was desired by the Latvian masses in 1919. Volume I is dedicated to the work of the Latvian Soviet government, while Volume II takes up the "struggle against the foreign intervention and the local counter-revolution."

IE100 SPEKKE, ARNOLDS. *History of Latvia; An Outline.* Stockholm: Goppers, 1951. 436 p. A survey by a leading Latvian historian.

IE101 *These Names Accuse; Nominal List of Latvians Deported to Soviet Russia in 1940-1941.* Stockholm: Latvian National Fund in the Scandinavian Countries, 1951. 547 p. A series of documents on the establishment of Soviet rule in Latvia, 1940-41; includes list of 30,000 Latvian deportees sent during this period to the Soviet Union.

IE102 UISKA, R. *Fashizm i sotsial-fashizm v sovremennoi Latvii.* Moscow-Leningrad: Partizdat, 1932. 134 p. "Fascism" and "social fascism" in Latvia as seen through Soviet eyes.

IE103 WALTERS, M. *Lettland, seine Entwicklung zum Staat und die Baltische Frage.* Rome: 1923. 509 p. Latvia's first Minister of the Interior describes Latvia's attainment of independence. Important, despite vagueness and bias, for information about events in unoccupied Latvia in 1917 prior to the November revolution and during the German occupation of 1918. [B]

6. LITHUANIA

IE104 ANDREEV, A. M. *Borba litovskogo naroda za sovetskuiu vlast, 1918-1919 gg.* Moscow: Gospolitizdat, 1954. 162 p. A Soviet account of the attempt to establish a Bolshevik government in Lithuania. Later criticized by other Soviet writers for having ignored the "positive" aspects of that government's work.

IE105 BALYS, JONAS, comp. *Lithuania and Lithuanians; a Selected Bibliography.* N.Y.: Praeger, 1961. 190 p. A comprehensive annotated bibliography of books and articles on all aspects of Lithuanian life—history, religion, government, people, etc., mainly in languages other than Lithuanian. Preference given to Western European languages, but important publications in Lithuanian are included. Contains 1182 entries. Sponsored by the Lithuanian Research Institute. [B]

IE106 CHASE, THOMAS J. *The story of Lithuania.* N.Y.: Stratford House, 1946. 392 p. A survey, by a Lithuanian priest, carrying the story up to the end of World War II.

IE107 HARRISON, E. J. *Lithuania Past and Present.* N.Y.: McBride, 1922. 230 p. A sympathetic effort to inform the British public of the background of the new Lithuanian state. Interesting personal notes on the author's work in Lithuania in 1919 and 1920. Marked by anti-Polish feeling.

IE108 HARRISON, E. J. *Lithuania's Fight for Freedom.* N.Y.: Lithuanian American Information Center, 1952. 95 p. A sketchy account by a former British Vice-Consul in Kaunas and Vilnius of Lithuania's ordeal since 1940. Basically an appeal for justice but contains some useful documents on Nazi and Soviet rule and the activities of Lithuanian émigrés.

IE109 "K istorii borby litovskogo naroda za sovetskuiu vlast v 1918-1919 gg," *Krasnyi Arkhiv*, vol. 5, p. 3-44. Moscow: Gosizdat, 1940. Decrees, manifestoes and minutes of the sessions of the Russian-made regime as it acted inside and outside of ethnographic Lithuania in late 1918 and early 1919. Useful information on official Communist policy. [B]

IE110 LIETUVOS TSR MOKSLU AKADEMIJA, VILNA, ISTORIJOS INSTITUTAS. *Lietuvos TSR istorija.* Ed. by K. Jablonskis and others. Vilna: Valstybine politines ir molslines literaturos leidykla, 1958. 519 p. A recent Soviet compendium on Lithuanian history, with an account of relations between the wars.

IE111 PALECKIS, JUSTAS. *Sovetskaia Litva.* Moscow: Gospolitizdat, 1949. 135 p. A survey of Lithuania's history in the nineteenth and twentieth century, by the Prime Minister of the Lithuanian SSR. Later criticized for accepting the "single-flow" idea of the national movement, i.e., that the movement was truly national and above class divisions.

IE112 POŽARSKAS, M. *Tarybų valdžios atkurimas Lietuvoje (1940-1941m.).* Vilna: 1955. An account, from the Soviet viewpoint, of the Sovietization of Lithuania.

IE113 RUSECKAS, PETRAS. *Savanoių Žygiai; Nepriklausomybēs Karų Atsiminimai*, vol. I. Kaunas: Lietuvos Kariuomenēs Kurējų Savanorių Sąjunga, 1937. 352 p. Recollections of military experiences in the Lithuanian war of independence.

IE114 ŠALKAUSKIS, STASYS. *Sur les confins de deux mondes.* Geneva: Atar, 1919. 271 p. A study of Eastern and Western influence on the formation of Lithuanian national character. One of the better books on the subject.

IE115 SENN, ALFRED E *The Emergence of Modern Lithuania.* N.Y.: Columbia, 1959. 272 p. On the formation of the independent Lithuanian state, 1918-20, with extensive coverage of Soviet-Lithuanian relations. Based on archives, newspapers, and public documents. By an American professor. [A]

IE116 SKORUPSKIS (COLONEL). *La Résurrection d'un peuple, 1918-1927.* Paris: Charles-Lavauzelle, 1931. 150 p. A behind-the-scenes account by one of the Lithuanian army officers who plotted and led the army-backed Nationalist Party coup of December 1926 in Kaunas, ousting the Socialist-dominated Sleževičius government because they considered it too permissive toward Moscow-guided Communists in Lithuania. [B]

IE117 SUDUVIS, N. E. *Ein kleines Volk wird ausgelöscht, braune und rote Staatspolizei am Werk; die Tragödie Litauens.* Zürich: Thomas Verlag, 1947. 99 p. An exiled Lithuanian's brief but remarkably calm and objective account of Lithuania thrice overrun between 1940 and 1944. Extremely useful because of the author's honesty and intelligent perceptiveness. [A]

IE117A TAURAS, K. V. *Guerrilla Warfare on the Amber Coast.* N.Y.: Voyages Press, 1963. 293 p. The story of the Lithuanian Freedom Army and its fight against the Soviet occupying forces.

IE118 VOLDEMAR, AUGUSTINAS. *Les Relations russo-polono-lithuaniennes.* Paris: Desmoineaux & Brisset, 1920. 32 p. An account by an erstwhile Lithuanian Foreign Minister. Especially important for his explanation of the Lithuanian attitude toward the Polish-Russian war of 1920.

IE119 ŽIUGŽDA, J. and others, eds. *Už socialistine Lietuva.* Vilna: Valstybine politinės ir mokslines literaturos leidykla, 1960. 295 p. A collection of articles describing various aspects of Communist activities in Lithuania from 1917 on. [B]

IE120 ŽIUGŽDA, ROBERTAS, and SMIRNOV, ANATOLII S. *Litovskaia SSR; Kratkii istoriko-ekonomicheskii ocherk.* Moscow: Gospolizdat, 1957. 182 p. Soviet Lithuanian academicians report on economic progress in Lithuania mainly since 1945. This is preceded by a Bolshevik-slanted history of "bourgeois" Lithuania until her liberation by the "democratic elements under leadership of the Communist Party," in 1940. Useful as a guide to Party policy from 1945 to about 1955.

IE121 VARDYS, V. STANLEY, ed. *Lithuania Under the Soviets.* N.Y.: Praeger, 1965. 299 p. An uneven collection, by emigré Lithuanian scholars, on Lithuanian history, with major emphasis on the period since 1939. Includes important accounts of Lithuanian resistance during and after World War II. [A]

IF. BULGARIA

EDITED BY MARIN PUNDEFF

IF1 AKADEMIIA NAUK SSSR, FUNDAMENTALNAIA BIBLIOTEKA OBSHCHESTVENNYKH NAUK. *Narodnaia Respublika Bolgariia; istoricheskaia bibliografiia.* Moscow: 1954, 1958. 2 vols. 675 p., 858 p. A comprehensive bibliography, compiled by Soviet and Bulgarian bibliographers, of the work done in or relating to Bulgarian history in the broadest sense of the word during the years 1944-47 (vol. I) and 1948-52 (vol. II). [B]

IF2 AKADEMIIA NAUK SSSR, INSTITUT SLAVIANOVEDENIIA. *Bolgarskii narod v borbe za sotsializm; sbornik statei.* Ed. by L. B. Valev and M. A. Birman. Moscow: Gospolitizdat, 1954. 228 p. A Soviet collaborative volume on the "building of socialism" in Bulgaria.

IF3 AKADEMIIA NAUK SSSR, INSTITUT SLAVIANOVEDENIIA. *Istoriia Bolgarii.* Ed. by Petr N. Tretiakov and others. Moscow: Izd. Akad. nauk SSSR, 1954-55. 2 vols. This Soviet official history of Bulgaria devotes its entire second volume to the period since 1917. [A]

IF4 ATANASOV, SHTERIU, and others. *Kratka istoriia na otechestvenata voina.* Sofia: 1958. 325 p. A substantial history of the part played by Bulgarian forces under Soviet command in the final operations against Germany in 1944-45. [B]

IF5 AVRAMOV, ASPARUKH G. "Za politicheskata strategiia i taktika na bulgarskata komunisticheska partiia v perioda na podgotovkata i po vreme na vtorata svetovna voina," *Trudove na Visshiia Ikonomicheski Institut.* Sofia, I (1958), p. 311-86. A study of Party policy and tactics in World War II.

IF6 BARKER, ELISABETH. *Macedonia: Its Place in Balkan Power Politics.* London: Royal Institute of International Affairs, 1950. 129 p. An outline by a British journalist, useful for its brevity and objectivity. Includes a discussion of Communist policies vis-à-vis the Macedonian problem. [B]

IF7 BIRMAN, MIKHAIL A. *Revoliutsionnaia situatsiia v Bolgarii v 1918-1919 gg.* Moscow: Akad. nauk SSSR, 1957. 389 p. A study, closely paralleling that of Khristo Khristov which appeared simultaneously, of the revolutionary conditions in Bulgaria at the end of World War I. [B]

IF8 BLAGOEV, DIMITUR. *Izbrani proizvedeniia v dva toma.* Sofia: BKP, 1950-51. 2 vols. The selected works of the founder of Bulgarian orthodox Marxism. [A]

IF9 BLAGOEV, DIMITUR. *Prinos kum istoriiata na sotsializma v Bulgariia.* Sofia: BKP, 1949. 606 p. A re-issue of the work first published in 1906. [A]

IF10 BLAGOEVA, STELLA D. *Georgi Dimitrov; biograficheski ocherk.* Sofia: BKP, 1953. 251 p. Russian ed., Moscow: Partizdat, 1937. A biography of Dimitrov, who became head of the Comintern in the 1930's and later was boss of Bulgaria after World War II, by the daughter of the founder of Bulgarian orthodox Marxism, with much attention to Dimitrov's part in the Reichstag Fire Trial. [B]

IF11 BOCHAROV, D. D. *Bolgarskii narod stroit sotsializm.* Moscow: Gospolitizdat, 1954. 110 p. A sketchy Soviet picture of the reorganization of the country since 1944.

IF12 BOZHINOV, VOIN. *Politicheskata kriza v Bulgariia prez 1943-1944.* Sofia: Bulgarska akademiia na naukite, 1957. 170 p. A study of the efforts of the last pre-communist Bulgarian governments to extricate the country from the war. The author has had access to the records of the Bulgarian foreign ministry. The study develops important documentary information concerning the armistice negotiations between the Bulgarians and the Allies at Istanbul, Ankara, and Cairo in 1944. [B]

IF13 BULGARIA, MINISTERSTVO NA VUNSHNITE RABOTI. *Documents on the Hostile and Aggressive Policy of the Government of the United States of America against the People's Republic of Bulgaria.* Sofia: Ministry of Foreign Affairs, 1952. 287 p. A highly tendentious collection of "documents" to support the thesis, discredited since Traicho Kostov's exoneration in 1956 and the resumption of diplomatic relations with the U.S., that U.S. diplomats in Bulgaria were subverting the Communist government. Review by Marin Pundeff in the *American Journal of International Law* (July 1954).

IF14 BULGARIA, MINISTRY OF INFORMATION AND ARTS. *The Trial of Nikola D. Petkov, before the Sofia Regional Court; Record of Judicial Proceedings, Aug. 5-15, 1947.* Sofia: 1947. The officially published record of the trial of the Agrarian leader who was executed in 1947.

IF15 BULGARSKA KOMUNISTICHESKA PARTIIA. *Bulgarskata Komunisticheska Partiia v resoliutsii i resheniia na kongresite, konferentsiite i plenumite na TsK.* Ed. by Khristo Kabakchiev. Sofia: 1947-57. 4 vols. Vol. I: 1891-1918. Vol. II: 1919-1923. Vol. III:

1924-1944. Vol. IV: 1944-1955. A very important collection of the resolutions and decisions adopted by Party conventions and meetings of the Central Committee. [A]

IF16 BULGARSKA KOMUNISTICHESKA PARTIIA. *Deset godini narodna vlast.* Sofia: 1954. 416 p. A propaganda volume issued for the tenth anniversary of the installation of the Soviet-sponsored regime.

IF17 BULGARSKA KOMUNISTICHESKA PARTIIA. *Dvadeset i pet godini "Rabotnichesko Delo"—Organ na Tsentralniia Komitet na Bulgarskata komunisticheska partiia, 1927-1952; sbornik.* Sofia: 1952. 520 p. A collection of materials reflecting the career of the principal periodical of the party. [A]

IF18 BULGARSKA KOMUNISTICHESKA PARTIIA. *Peti kongres 18-25 dekemvri 1948 g.; stenografski protokol.* Sofia: 1949. Stenographic record of the first and most important of the postwar congresses of the party. The main part was the Political Report read by the then secretary-general, Georgi Dimitrov (available in English). Important supplementary reports were read by Vulko Chervenkov on Marxist-Leninist education and the struggle on the ideological front (available in French) and by Dobri Terpeshev on the first Five-Year Plan (available in English). [A]

IF19 BULGARSKA KOMUNISTICHESKA PARTIIA. *Sto godini Dimitur Blagoev; sbornik statii.* Sofia: 1956. 380 p. A collaborative volume commemorating the centenary of Blagoev's birth. [B]

IF20 BULGARSKA KOMUNISTICHESKA PARTIIA, 3. KONFERENTSIIA, SOFIA, 1950. *Stenografski protokoli.* Sofia: BKP, 1950. 286 p. Important for reflecting the party purge and the hunting down of so-called Titoists. [A]

IF21 BULGARSKA KOMUNISTICHESKA PARTIIA, 6. KONGRES, SOFIA, 1954. *Stenografski protokoli.* Sofia: BKP, 1954. 670 p. Stenographic record of the 6th Congress, held in the intermediate period between Stalin's death and the emergence of Khrushchev and the new lines of Soviet policy, still reflecting the leadership of Vulko Chervenkov. [A]

IF22 BULGARSKA KOMUNISTICHESKA PARTIIA, 7. KONGRES, SOFIA, 1958. *VII sezd, Sofiia, 2-7 iiunia 1958 goda.* Moscow: Gospolitizdat, 1958. 318 p. Reports and resolutions (in Russian) of the 7th Congress, reflecting the leadership of the new secretary of the Party, Todor Zhivkov. Translated into Russian from the text published in *Rabotnichesko Delo*, June 1958. [A]

IF23 BULGARSKA KOMUNISTICHESKA PARTIIA, TSENTRALEN KOMITET, VISSHA PARTIINA SHKOLA. *Istoriia Bolgarskoi Kommunisticheskoi Partii; v pomoshch izuchaiushchim istoriiu BKP.* Moscow: Gos. izd. polit. lit., 1960. 392 p. Bulgarian ed., *Materiali po istoriia na Bulgarskata Komunisticheska Partiia.* Sofia: BKP, 1954. 394 p. Other eds., Sofia: 1956 and 1959. A tool issued as an aid in the study of Party history. The Russian translation is based on the 1959 Bulgarian edition.

IF24 BULGARSKI BIBLIOGRAFSKI INSTITUT. *Septemvriiskoto vustanie 1923; materiali za bibliografiia.* Comp. by Pavlina Kuncheva. Ed. by T. Borov, Sofia: 1948. 130 p. A useful preliminary bibliography on the 1923 uprising.

IF25 BULGARSKI BIBLIOGRAFSKI INSTITUT. *Vasil Kolarov; Bio-bibliografiia.* Elena Savova, ed. Sofia: 1947. 180 p. A valuable guide to the highlights of Kolarov's life and writings. [B]

IF26 BUSSE, N. V. and others, comps. *Istoriia Bolgarii do 9 sentiabria 1944; ukazatel literatury 1945-1958.* Moscow: Izd. Akad. nauk SSSR, 1962. 551 p. A valuable bibliography of primarily Communist studies on Bulgarian history to September 9, 1944. [B]

IF27 CHICHOVSKII, T. *The Socialist Movement in Bulgaria.* London: Lamley, 1931. 32 p. A brief survey.

IF28 *La Conspiration Bolchéviste contre la Bulgarie.* Sofia: Imprimerie de la Cour, 1925. 107 p. An official indictment of Comintern activities in Bulgaria in the early 1920's.

IF29 DIMITROV, GEORGI. *Dimitrov; Selected Speeches and Articles.* London: Lawrence, 1951. 275 p. A short English collection of the speeches, articles and reports of the late Bulgarian Communist leader.

IF30 DIMITROV, GEORGI. *Edinniiat front 1923 g.* Sofia: BKP, 1949. 115 p. Dimitrov's version of the efforts to establish a united front with left-wing Agrarians after the June 9, 1923 *coup d'état* which deposed the Agrarian regime. [A]

IF31 DIMITROV, GEORGI. *Suchineniia.* Sofia: Bulgarska Rabotnicheska Partiia, 1951-1955. 14 vols. A complete collection of the writings of the long-time boss of Bulgarian Communism and head of the Comintern during the Popular Front era. [A]

IF32 DIMITROV, GEORGI; KOLAROV, VASIL; and CHERVENKOV, VULKO. *Septemvriiskoto vustanie, 1923-1953.* Sofia: Nauka i izkustvo, 1953. 113 p. English ed., Sofia: 1953. A commemoration of the Communist uprising of September 1923, seen in retrospect by three leading Bulgarian Communists. [A]

IF33 DINEV, ANGEL. *Političkite ubistva vo Bugarija.* Skopje: Ilinden, 1951. 488 p. A monograph on the technique of political assassination which has found such wide use in Bulgarian politics before and under the Communists. The author is a Macedonian.

IF34 DRAMALIEV, KIRIL. *Istoriia na Otechestveniia front.* Sofia: 1947. 66 p. An early sketch of the Fatherland Front coalition by a Communist occupying a prominent place in its early phases. [B]

IF35 *Dvadeset i pet godishninata na Septemvriiskoto vustanie.* Sofia: 1948. 326 p. A volume commemorating the 25th anniversary of the 1923 uprising. [B]

IF36 EVANS, STANLEY G. *A Short History of Bulgaria.* London: Lawrence and Wishart, 1960. 254 p. A sketchy history, including a chapter on "The People's Republic," by a British clergyman sympathetic to the Communist regime.

IF36A GANEVICH, I. V., *Borba bolgarskogo naroda pod rukovodstvom Kommunisticheskoi partii za natsionalnoe i sotsialnoe osvobozhdenie (1941-1944 gg.).* Kiev: Izd. Kievskogo Universiteta, 1959. 321 p. Written to disprove the assertions of "international revisionism and above all of its Yugoslav representatives playing the tune of the American imperialists" that outside the Soviet Union, "socialist revolutions occurred only in Yugoslavia and China and that in Eastern Europe the socialist regimes were 'installed' from the outside."

IF37 GENOV, KRUSTO. *Nashata memoarna literatura za partizanskoto dvizhenie.* Sofia: Nauka i izkustvo, 1958. 177 p. A valuable bibliography of Communist memoir publications on the World War II resistance movement.

IF38 GINDEV, PANAYOT. *Kum vuprosa za kharaktera na narodnodemokraticheskata revoliutsiia v Bulgariia.* Sofia: Bulgarska akademiia na naukite, 1956. 294 p. An analysis of the establishment and development of the Communist regime in Bulgaria from a theoretical point of view. [B]

IF39 GORNENSKI, NIKIFOR. *Vuoruzhenata borba na bulgarskiia narod za osvobozhdenie ot hitleristkata okupatsiia i monarcho-fashistkata diktatura, 1941-1944 g.* Sofia: BKP, 1958. 336 p. A thoroughgoing study of the Communist efforts to mount and maintain a resistance movement during World War II. [B]

IF40 GORNENSKI, NIKIFOR, and others, eds. *Deveti Septemvri; spomeni.* Sofia: BKP, 1957. 568 p. A volume of memoirs relating to the events of the 1941-44 period. [B]

IF41 GOROV, M. P. *Borba krestian Bolgarii.* Moscow-Leningrad: Gosizdat, 1927. 160 p.

IF42 *Govori Radiostantsiia "Khristo Botev" 23 iuli 1941–22 septemvri 1944.* Sofia: 1948-52. 7 vols. A record of the broadcasts of the Soviet-based radio station of the Bulgarian Communists. Highly significant as a reflection of Soviet policy toward Bulgaria during the war years. [A]

IF43 GSOVSKI, VLADIMIR, and GRZYBOWSKI, KAZIMIERZ, eds. *Government, Law and Courts in the Soviet Union and Eastern Europe.* N.Y.: Praeger, 1959. 2 vols. 2067 p. The most comprehensive treatment available of the reception of Soviet law in Eastern Europe since 1944. The volumes are topically organized, with chapters for each country within each large topic of law. A law-focused 65-page bibliography contains a section on Bulgaria. [A]

IF44 IANEV, S., and DASKALOVA-RIBARSKA, L. *Deveti Septemvri 1944 godina—nachalo na sotsialisticheskata epokha v istoriiata na Bulgariia.* Sofia: Nauka i izkustvo, 1954. 142 p. Suggested readings issued on the occasion of the tenth anniversary of the Soviet-sponsored regime.

IF45 INSTITUT MEZHDUNARODNYKH OTNOSHENII. *Piatnadset let Narodnoi Respubliki Bolgarii.* Moscow: 1959. 196 p. A brief survey of various aspects of Bulgarian life by different authors, published under the auspices of the Institute of International Relations, Moscow.

IF46 IOTOV, IORDAN N. *Purviiat kongres na Bulgarskata komunisticheska partiia (tesni sotsialisti) 1919 g.* Sofia: BKP, 1959. 123 p. A study of the first congress of the Bulgarian Communist Party after severing ties with the parent Social Democratic Party.

IF47 KABAKCHIEV, KHRISTO. *Izbrani proizvedeniia.* Sofia: 1953. 856 p. The selected writings of a Communist intellectual of prominence in the interwar period. [B]

IF48 KABAKCHIEV, KHRISTO; BOSHKOVICH, B.; and VATIS, C. D. *Kommunisticheskie partii balkanskikh stran.* Moscow: Gosizdat, 1930. 239 p. A Soviet-sponsored outline of the history of the Communist parties in the Balkan countries. [B]

IF49 KAMENOV, EVGENII G. *Ekonomicheskata pomosht na Suvetskiia Sujuz—reshavasht faktor za izgrazhdaneto na sotsializma v Bulgariia.* Sofia: Izd. na Bulgarskata akademiia na naukite, 1955. 141 p.

IF50 KANAPA, JEAN. *Bulgarie d'hier et d'aujourd'hui.* Paris: Éditions Sociales, 1953. 236 p. A pro-Communist version of recent developments.

IF51 KAZASOV, DIMO. *Burni godini, 1918-1944.* Sofia: Naroden pechat, 1949. 784 p. Reminiscences of a Bulgarian politician, noted for a facile pen and protean political affiliations, who took part in nearly all important events of the 1918-44 period as an early socialist, member of the anti-Agrarian anti-Communist government of Alexander Tsankov, and collaborator with the Communists after 1944. [B]

IF52 KHADZHINIKOLOV, VESELIN. *Stopanski otnosheniia i vruzki mezhdu Bulgariia i Suvetskiia Suiuz do deveti septemvri, 1917-1944.* Sofia: BKP, 1956. 237 p. A valuable monograph by a professor of Bulgarian history at the University of Sofia, developing information concerning foreign trade relations between Bulgaria and the USSR prior to 1944. [B]

IF53 KHRISTOV, FILIU. *Voenno-revoliutsionnata deinost na Bulgarskata komunisticheska partiia, 1912-1944 g.* Sofia: 1959. 240 p. A party-line monograph on the revolutionary activities of the Party, particularly within the Bulgarian armed forces, prior to 1944.

IF54 KHRISTOV, KHRISTO. *Revoliutsionnata kriza v Bulgariia prez 1918-1919.* Sofia: BKP, 1957. 607 p. A large-scale study, written from the prevailing Communist point of view, of the revolutionary ferment in Bulgaria in 1918-19 and the repercussions of the Russian revolution. [B]

IF55 KHRISTOV, KHRISTO, ed. *Velikata Oktomvriiska sotsialisticheska revoliutsiia i revoliutsionnite borbi v Bulgariia prez 1918-1919; sbornik ot dokumenti i materiali.* Sofia: BKP, 1957. 867 p. An important source on the reflection of the Russian revolution in Bulgaria. [B]

IF56 KHRISTOV, KHRISTO, ed. *Vliianie na Velikata oktomvriiska sotsialisticheska revoliutsiia v Bulgariia; preporuchitelna bibliografiia.* Sofia: Nauka i izkustvo, 1957. 84 p. Suggested readings on the influence of the Bolshevik revolution in Bulgaria.

IF57 KIRCHEV, IVAN. *Otechestvenata voina, 1944-1945.* Sofia: 1946. 111 p. French ed., *La Guerre patriotique.* Important as one of the few studies on Bulgarian participation in World War II under Soviet direction and command.

IF58 KOLAROV, VASIL P. *Izbrani proizvedeniia.* Sofia: BKP, 1955. 3 vols. Selected works of Kolarov, a top Bulgarian Communist and Prime Minister from 1949 until his death in 1950. [A]

IF59 KOLAROV, VASIL P. *Protiv hitlerizma i negovite bulgarski slugi.* Sofia: BKP, 1947. 669 p. Kolarov's scripts written under Georgi Dimitrov's supervision and broadcast over Radio Moscow in 1941-44. [B]

IF60 KOLAROV, VASIL P. *Protiv liavoto sektantstvo i trotskizma v Bulgariia.* 2nd ed., Sofia: BKP, 1949. 202 p. Kolarov on problems of left deviationism and Trotskyism in the Bulgarian Communist Party. [B]

IF61 KOLAROV, VASIL P. *S pero i slovo za bulgaro-suvetskata druzhba.* Sofia: 1947. 264 p. A volume of propaganda reflecting basic Communist policies and objectives. [B]

IF62 KOLAROV, VASIL P. *Za oktomvriiskata revoliutsiia, Suvetskiia Suiuz i Bulgaro-Suvetskata druzhba; studii, statii, rechi, 1919-1948 g.* Sofia: BKP, 1949. 352 p. A collection of the writings of Kolarov on Bulgarian-Soviet relations. [B]

IF63 KONSTANTINOV, F. T. *Bolgariia na puti k sotsializmu.* 2nd ed., Moscow: Gospolitizdat, 1953. 382 p. A survey of the progress of the Communist government since 1944, by a Soviet specialist. [B]

IF64 KORENKOV, A. M. "Internatsionalistkaia pozitsiia bolgarskikh tesnykh sotsialistov v period pervoi mirovoi voiny, 1914-1918 gg.," *Uchenye zapiski instituta slavianovedeniia,* X (1954), p. 351-388. A study of the policies of Bulgarian Communists during World War I and their relation to Russian events.

IF65 KOSEV, DIMITUR. *Septemvriiskoto vustanie v 1923 godina.* Sofia: Bulgarska akademiia na naukite, 1954. 353 p. A substantial though slanted study of the Communist uprising of 1923 by the leading Communist historian in Bulgaria today. [B]

IF66 KOSEV, DIMITUR, and others, eds. *Istoriia na Bulgariia.* Sofia: Bulgarska akademiia na naukite, 1954-1955. 2 vols. The second volume of this large-scale Communist presentation of Bulgarian history covers the period since 1878, with some 700 pages devoted to the period from 1917 to 1954. Contains a 13-page bibliography of Communist-endorsed sources. 2nd rev. ed. in 3 vols., 1961-64. [A]

IF67 KOSEV, DINO G. *Istoriia na makedonskoto natsionalno revolutsionno dvizhenie.* Sofia: Izd. na natsionalniia suvet na otechestveniia front, 1954. 552 p. A history of the Macedonian revolutionary movement by a Macedonian Communist working in Bulgaria. [B]

IF68 KOSTOV, PAVEL. *Borbata na BKP za utvurzhdavane na narodnodemokratichnata vlast, za skliuchvane na miren dogovor i vuzstanoviavane na narodnoto stopanstvo.* Sofia: BKP, 1957. 95 p.

IF69 KOSTOV, PAVEL, and NEIKOV, PETUR. *Bulgarskata komunisticheska partiia v borba za utvurzhdavane na narodnodemokraticheskata vlast i za postroiavane osnovite na sotsializma, 9 sept.*

1944-1952. Sofia: BKP, 1957. 179 p. A survey of the policies and efforts of the Party to seize and retain power and effect the economic transformation of the country between 1944 and 1952.

IF70 KOZHUKHAROV, K., ed. *Aleksandur Stamboliiski; pulno subranie na suchineniiata mu.* Sofia: 1947. 322 p. A collection of the writings of the Agrarian leader, important for his policy and attitude toward the Communists. [B]

IF71 LEVI, RUBEN. *Partiiata na tesnite sotsialisti v perioda na balkanskata, mezhdusuiuznicheskata i purvata svetovna voina (1912-1918).* Sofia: BKP, 1950. 50 p. A Party view of the Party's behavior in the wars of 1912-18.

IF72 MID-EUROPEAN LAW PROJECT. *Legal Sources and Bibliography of Bulgaria.* By Ivan Sipkov. N.Y.: Publ. for the Free Europe Committee by Praeger, 1956. 199 p. Important as a guide to materials of a legal nature reflecting the changes since 1944.

IF73 MID-EUROPEAN STUDIES CENTER OF THE FREE EUROPE COMMITTEE. *Bulgaria.* Ed. by L. A. D. Dellin. N.Y.: Praeger, 1957. 457 p. One of a series of handbooks on Eastern European countries with emphasis on recent conditions. Contains chapters on various aspects of contemporary Bulgaria, biographical sketches of leading Communists, a list of treaties made since 1945, and a 24-page bibliography. [A]

IF74 MITEV, IONO. *Fashistkiiat prevrat na deveti iuni 1923 godina i iunskoto antifashistko vustanie.* Sofia: 1956. 336 p. A study of the *coup d'état* of June 9, 1923, which deposed the Agrarian government of Alexander Stamboliiski, by a former political commissar turned historian. [B]

IF75 MIZOV, NIKOLAI. *Vliianieto na velikata oktomvriiska sotsialisticheska revoliutsiia vurkhu Vladaiskoto vuoruzheno vustanie.* Sofia: 1957. 52 p. A pamphlet on the influence of the Russian revolution on the soldiers returning from the collapsing front in 1918 and mutinying against the government in the outskirts of Sofia.

IF76 MOJSOV, LAZO. *Bulgarskata rabotnichka partija (komunisti) i makedonskoto natsionalno prashanie.* Skopje: Zemskiot odbor na narodniot front na Makedonija, 1948. 275 p. Serbo-Croatian ed., Belgrade: Borba, 1948. 320 p. A propagandistic volume on the policies of the Bulgarian Communists toward Macedonia, by a Macedonian working in Yugoslavia. [B]

IF77 MOZOKHINA, A. G. *Organy gosudarstvennoi vlasti i gosudarstvennogo upravleniia narodnoi respubliki Bolgarii.* Moscow: Izd. Akad.

nauk SSSR, 1960. 167 p. A sketchy discussion of the principles, structure, and functioning of the central and local apparatus of government.

IF78 NARODNA REPUBLIKA BULGARIIA, TSENTRALNO STATISTICHESKO UPRAVLENIE. *Statisticheski godishnik na Narodna Republika Bulgariia 1960*. Sofia: Nauka i Izkustvo, 1960. 565 p. A detailed statistical abstract for all aspects of the country's life.

IF79 NATAN, ZHAK. *Istoriia ekonomicheskogo razvitiia Bolgarii*. Moscow: Izd. inostrannoi lit., 1961. 499 p. A Russian translation of the 1957 edition of a basic text by the leading Communist economic historian and editor of the history journal, *Istoricheski Pregled*. Discusses the economic development of Bulgaria through the Marxist periods of feudalism and capitalism, stopping short of the "socialist" period since 1944.

IF80 NEIKOV, STOIAN. *Bibliografiia na nelegalniia anti-fashistki periodichen pechat, 1923-1944*. Sofia: 1948. 127 p. A bibliography of Communist periodicals published underground between 1923 and 1944.

IF81 NEWMAN, BERNARD. *Bulgarian Background*. London: Robert Hall, 1961. 200 p. Impressions of a veteran British observer, based on his trip to Bulgaria in 1959.

IF82 OREN, NISSAN. "The Bulgarian Communist Party." Ph.D. dissertation, Columbia, 1960.

IF83 PADEV, MICHAEL. *Dimitrov Wastes No Bullets; Nikola Petkov, the Test Case*. London: Eyre and Spottiswoode, 1948. 160 p. An analysis of the political events leading to the trial of the Agrarian leader in 1947 and the trial itself, by a former Bulgarian journalist and press attaché in London.

IF84 PAVLOV, TODOR. *Za marksicheska istoriia na Bulgariia; statii, dokladi, izkazvaniia, retsenzii, 1938-1954*. Sofia: Bulg. akad. na naukite, 1954. 473 p. A collection of essays on problems of writing a Marxist history of Bulgaria, by the leading Communist philosopher and president of the Bulgarian Academy of Sciences.

IF85 PETKOV, NIKOLA D. *Aleksandur Stamboliiski; lichnost i idei*. Sofia: Zemledesko zname, 1930. 342 p. 2nd edition, Sofia: 1946. 380 p. Yugoslav ed., Belgrade: Štamparija "Radenković," 1933. 287 p. An analysis, with ample quotations, of the personality and ideas of Stamboliiski as a peasant leader and ideologist, by an adherent who was to become the leader of the Agrarian Union in 1945-47. Important as a reflection of Agrarian policy toward Communism. [A]

IF86 PETKOV, NIKOLA D. *Prez Bulgaria za Dardanelite pri Tsarska Russiia i Suvetite*. Sofia: 1943. 60 p. A brief pamphlet in a journalistic vein on Russian and Soviet efforts to arrive at the Straits by way of Bulgaria and their influence on Bulgarian affairs.

IF87 *Petnadeset godini narodna vlast; preporuchitelna bibliografiia.* Ed. by T. Topalova. Sofia: 1959. 171 p. What to read on the changes since 1944, compiled by a professional bibliographer.

IF88 PETROV, F. N., ed. *Balkanskie strany.* Moscow: Ogiz, 1946. 541 p. A handbook in a series issued by the Gosudarstvennyi Institut "Sovetskaia Entsiklopediia." The section on Bulgaria contains a survey of political developments and bibliography. [B]

IF89 PETROV, STOIAN. *Septemvriiskoto vustanie 1923 godina i bolshevizatsiiata na BKP.* Sofia: BKP, 1960. 179 p. A monograph on the effects of the abortive 1923 uprising on the party line in Bulgaria.

IF90 POPOV, PETUR. *Ustanovianane, razvitie i sistema na proletarskata diktatura u nas.* Sofia: Bulgarska akademiia na naukite, 1956. 268 p. Russian ed., *Ustanovlenie, razvitie, i sistema diktatury proletariata v Bolgarii.* Moscow: Gos. izd. iurid. lit., 1960. 325 p. An analytical effort to understand, from a Communist point of view, what happened politically since 1944.

IF91 POTSEV, SPIRIDON, and PETROV, DIMITUR. *Nelegalni pozivi na BKP; sbornik.* Sofia: 1954. 389 p. An important collection of Party leaflets and manifestoes issued during the underground period.

IF92 POZOLOTIN, M. *Borba bolgarskogo naroda za svobodu i nezavisimost v period vtoroi mirovoi voiny.* Moscow: Gospolitizdat, 1954. 152 p. A useful study of political developments in 1940-44, with emphasis on foreign policy.

IF93 *Predatelskata shpionska sabotiorska grupa na Traicho Kostov pred suda na naroda.* Sofia: 1949. 623 p. German ed., Berlin: Dietz, 1951. 667 p. Official record of the trial of a leading "native" Communist executed for Titoism in 1949 and exonerated in 1956. [B]

IF94 PUNDEFF, MARIN. "Bulgaria's Place in Axis Policy, 1936-1944." Ph.D. dissertation, U. of S. California, 1958. 537 p. Considerable attention is given to the Soviet interest in Bulgaria and the efforts of the Soviet government to obtain control of Bulgarian affairs, leading to the German-Soviet clash of late 1940.

IF95 PUNDEFF, MARIN. "Two Documents on Soviet-Bulgarian Relations in November, 1940." *Journal of Central European Affairs.* xv, no. 4 (January, 1956), p. 367-78. Makes public for the first time the extremely important Soviet proposals to Bulgaria of November 25, 1940, to effect a Soviet-Bulgarian alliance, and the Bulgarian reply to these proposals.

IF96 *Rabotnichesko Delo; izbrani statii i materiali, 1927-1944.* Comp. by Stefanov, Ts., Karutsin, K., and Georgiev, P. Sofia: BKP, 1954. 782 p. A collection of the significant materials which appeared in the principal Party newspaper before 1944. [A]

IF97 *Rabotnicheski Vestnik; izbrani statii i materiali.* Ed. by Khristov, I., Karutsin, K., and Tsanev, P. Sofia: BKP, 1953-55. 3 vols. A collection of the more significant materials which appeared in one of the Party newspapers of the underground period. [A]

IF98 *Razvitie ekonomiki evropeiskikh stran narodnoi demokratii; obzor.* Moscow: Vneshtorgizdat. Annual, 1954–. The chapter on Bulgaria in each volume provides official statistics and information on economic developments for that year.

IF99 ROTHSCHILD, JOSEPH. *The Communist Party of Bulgaria; Origins and Development, 1883-1936.* N.Y.: Columbia, 1959. 354 p. The first large-scale history of the Bulgarian Social Democratic movement and the Bulgarian Communist Party, from which it sprang, in any language. While the emphasis is on domestic developments in Bulgaria, Soviet-Bulgarian official relations and Soviet relations with Bulgarian Communists are adequately dealt with. A 20-page bibliography, particularly valuable for materials in periodicals, reflects the literature as of 1955. [A]

IF100 RUSSIA (1923– USSR), NARODNYI KOMISSARIAT PO INOSTRANNYM DELAM. *Suvetsko-bulgarskite otnosheniia; dokumenti.* Moscow: Kn-vo na chuzhdi ezitsi, 1944. 29 p. Soviet materials pertaining to the breaking of diplomatic relations and the Soviet declaration of war on September 5, 1944.

IF101 SAVOVA, ELENA. *Georgi Dimitrov; letopis na zhivota i revoliutsionnata mu deinost, 1882-1949.* Sofia: Bulgarska akademiia na naukite, 1952. 803 p. A thoroughgoing chronicle of the life and activity of Dimitrov, valuable for its data despite the adulatory tenor of presentation. [B]

IF102 SAXENA, HORI L. *Bulgaria under the Red Star.* Delhi, India: Chand, 1957. 622 p.

IF103 SHAROVA, KRUMKA. "Burzhoaznata istoriografiia i uchastieto na Bulgariia vuv voinite (1912-1918)." *Istoricheski Pregled* (Sofia), no. 2, 1950-51, p. 129-57. A useful bibliographic survey written to criticize old regime versions of Bulgaria's part in the wars of 1912-18.

IF104 SOFIA, INSTITUT PO ISTORIIA NA BULGARSKATA KOMUNISTICHESKA PARTIIA. *Dimitur Blagoev; sbornik ot doku-*

menti, 1875-1924. Sofia: BKP, 1956. 430 p. A collection of documents on the founder of the Party, published on the centenary of his birth.

IF105 SOFIA, INSTITUT PO ISTORIIA NA BULGARSKATA KOMUNISTICHESKA PARTIIA. *Iarki imena v nashata istoriia, kratki biografichni spravki; sbornik*. Sofia: BKP, 1955. 237 p. A brief biographical dictionary on personalities of importance, as judged by Party criteria.

IF106 *Statisticheski spravochnik na Narodna Republika Bulgariia, 1960*. Sofia: 1960. 255 p. Statistical abstract for 1960.

IF107 STOEV, GENCHO. *Voinishkoto vustanie 1918; spomeni*. Sofia: BKP, 1958. 263 p. Reminiscences of a participant in the soldiers' mutiny at the end of World War I.

IF108 TIKHOMIROV, P. *Uroki bolgarskogo vosstaniia; (sentiabr 1923 g.)*. Intro. by V. Kolarov. Moscow: Gosizdat, 1924. 88 p.

IF109 TODOROV, KOSTA. *Balkan Firebrand; the Autobiography of a Rebel, Soldier and Statesman*. Chicago: Ziff-Davis, 1943. 340 p. Memoirs of a close associate of Stamboliiski containing information on the abortive negotiations between Agrarian leaders and Moscow concerning united efforts against the Tsankov government after 1923. [B]

IF110 TROTSKII, LEV D., and KABAKCHIEV, KHRISTO. *Ocherki politicheskoi Bolgarii*. Moscow-Petrograd: Gosizdat, 1923. 204 p. An early view of Bulgarian political developments, now disowned by Soviet and Bulgarian Communist authorities. [B]

IF111 TSONEV, G., and VLADIMIROV, A. *Sentiabrskoe vosstanie v Bolgarii 1923 g*. Moscow: Sotsekgiz, 1934. 181 p. A Soviet-sponsored version by two Bulgarian exiles in the USSR of what happened in the 1923 uprising. G. Tsonev is the pseudonym of a leading party functionary, Gavril Genov. [B]

IF112 U.S. CONGRESS, HOUSE, SELECT COMMITTEE ON COMMUNIST AGGRESSION. *Communist Takeover and Occupation of Bulgaria; Special Report no. 7 of the Select Committee on Communist Aggression, House of Representatives, Eighty-third Congress, second session, under the authority of H. Res. 346 and H. Res. 438*. Washington: G.P.O., 1954. 18 p. A useful summary of the process of Communist destruction of the old order between 1944 and 1953. [B]

IF113 U.S. CONGRESS, SENATE, COMMITTEE ON FOREIGN RELATIONS. *Tensions within the Soviet Captive Countries; Bulgaria*. Document 70-1 (prepared by Marin Pundeff). Washington: G.P.O., 1954. 25 p. One of a series of reports prepared by the committee on conditions in the captive countries of Eastern Europe. [B]

IF114 VALEV, L. B. *Iz istorii Otechestvennogo fronta Bolgarii (iul 1942–sentiabr 1944 g.)*. Moscow: Akademiia nauk SSSR, 1950. 104 p. German ed., Berlin: Dietz, 1952. 132 p. A study by a Soviet specialist on Bulgarian affairs of the origin and activity of the Fatherland Front coalition of political forces operating during World War II and coming to power in September, 1944.

IF115 VASILEV, ORLIN. *Vuoruzhenata suprotiva sreshtu fashizma v Bulgariia, 1923-1944; ocherki i dokumenti.* Sofia: 1946. 672 p. A valuable source on Communist underground activities, especially those of the World War II period, by a Bulgarian Communist intellectual who has in recent years been in disfavor. [A]

IF116 VERGNET, PAUL and BERNARD-DEROSNE, JEAN. *L'Affaire Petkov.* Paris: Éditions Self, 1948. 344 p. An account of the trial of Nikola Petkov, the Agrarian leader who was killed by the Communists.

IF117 VULOV, VULO. *Rabotata na BKP v armiiata, 1941-1944.* Sofia: BKP, 1959. 616 p. A volume of documentary materials on the Party's work of subversion in the army before 1944.

Addenda

IF118 AVRAMOV, RUBEN and BOROV, TODOR, eds. *Istoriia na BKP, 1885-1944; Bibliografiia. Materiali publikuvani sled 9 septemvri 1944 g.* Sofia: BKP, 1965. 567 p. A comprehensive bibliography of over 3,200 items on Party history to 1944 published in Bulgaria. Lists, with some annotation, Party documents, works of Party leaders, histories of the Party, and biographical materials on Party personalities. An indispensable research tool.

IF119 PUNDEFF, MARIN V. *Bulgaria: a Bibliographic Guide.* Washington: Library of Congress, 1965. 98 p. A guide to the literature on various aspects of life in Bulgaria, in all relevant languages.

IF120 VALEV, L. B. *Bolgarskii narod v borbe protiv fashizma (Nakanune i v nachalnyi period vtoroi mirovoi voiny).* Moscow: "Nauka," 1964. 372 p. Mainly internal developments from the late 1930's to June, 1941, by a leading Soviet specialist in Bulgarian history.

IG. CZECHOSLOVAKIA

EDITED BY FRANCIS S. WAGNER AND JOSEF KORBEL

1. GENERAL WORKS

IG1 *Bojová cesta Pravdy.* Bratislava: S.V.P.L., 1960. 258 p. A collection of articles dealing with the history of the Czechoslovak Communist press, propaganda, and the progressive labor movement, with the accent on *Pravda*, the chief organ of the Communist Party of Slovakia, 1920-60. Contains rich material on Czechoslovak-Soviet connections. With 16 pages of photographs. [B]

IG2 CERNICEK, ALOIS D. "Czechoslovak-Russian Relations, 1914-1948, in the Foreign Policy of Dr. Eduard Beneš." Master's thesis, University of Chicago, 1952.

IG3 ČESKOSLOVENSKÁ AKADEMIE VĚD, SEKCE HISTORICKÁ. *25 ans d'historiographie tchécoslovaque, 1936-1960.* Ed. by Josef Macek. Prague: Nakladatelství Československé akademie věd, 1960. 493 p. An excellent bibliographic tool on the country's Marxist writings relating to the fundamental questions of Communist development and the country's foreign relations, chiefly with the USSR. Contains several studies in Czechoslovak-Marxist historiography and a list of historical and social periodicals. [B]

IG4 FIALOVÁ, BOŽENA. *Sjezdy Komunistické strany Československa - mezníky na cestě k socialismu; výběrová bibliografie.* Brno: Universitní knihovna, 1958. 31 p. A well-selected, indispensable bibliography on Communist Party congresses, beginning with the May 14-16, 1921, constituent meeting, as well as the Oct. 30-Nov. 4, 1921, merging session, and ending with the 10th Party congress held June 11-15, 1954.

IG5 GOTTWALD, KLEMENT. *Spisy, 1925-1938.* Prague: Svoboda, 1951-53. 8 vols. Supplementing the first volume is: *Za bolševickou orientaci KSČ.* Prague: SNPL, 1953. 304 p. (Contains documents from 1925 to 1929.) *Deset let; sborník statí a projevů, 1936-1946.* Prague: Svoboda, 1946. 373 p. *1946-1953.* Prague: Svoboda, 1949-54. 4 vols. (Contains his speeches from 1946 to his death.) The collected works of the man who was the leading Communist in Czechoslovakia until his death in 1953. [A]

IG6 GOTTWALD, KLEMENT. *Vybrané spisy.* Prague: S.N.P.L., 1954-1955. 2 vols. English ed., *Selected Speeches and Articles, 1929-1953.* Prague: Orbis, 1954. 248 p. German ed., Berlin: Dietz, 1955. [A]

IG7 HEGGIE, R. G. "The Development of Communist Influence in Czechoslovakia, 1918-1946." M.A. thesis, U. of California (Berkeley), 1949.

IG8 KOPECKÝ, VÁCLAV. *ČSR a KSČ: pamětní výpisy k historii Československé republiky a k boji KSČ za socialistické Československo.* Prague: S.N.P.L., 1960. 494 p. By a politician ranking high in the hierarchy since the founding of the Communist Party of Czechoslovakia. Gives a personal account of the 1918-60 history of the country with emphasis on Czechoslovak-Soviet links, furnishing previously unknown data on the December 1943 Czechoslovak-Soviet alliance, the 1944 Slovak National Uprising, and the Feb. 1948 Communist putsch. [A]

IG9 KOPECKÝ, VÁCLAV. *30 Let KSČ; vzpomínky na založeni KSČ a hlavní události jejího vývoje.* Prague: Svoboda, 1951. 195 p. A general, one-sided but documentary review of the history of the Communist Party of Czechoslovakia by an old-time leader, member of the Politburo and the Party's chief propagandist.

IG10 *O československé zahraniční politice v letech 1918-1939; sborník statí.* Prague: S.N.P.L., 1956. 444 p. The first Marxist reevaluation of Czechoslovakia's foreign policy, by Vladimír Soják, Pavel Auersperg, Zdeněk Tomeš and others, based partly on unpublished sources. Soviet connections, 1918-39, are also reexamined on the basis of "proletarian internationalism." [B]

IG11 PRAGUE, ÚSTAV DĚJIN KOMUNISTICKÉ STRANY ČESKOSLOVENSKA. *Dějiny Komunistické strany Československa.* By Pavel Reiman et al. Ed. by Bohuslav Graca et al. Prague: S.N.P.L., 1961. 710 p. The most complete and up-to-date review of the development of the Communist Party of Czechoslovakia since its founding. Its Soviet links are treated in some detail. Well-documented. Events, personalities, and institutions are viewed strictly in line with the present-day political pattern. Includes a well-selected bibliography. [A]

IG12 PRAGUE, ÚSTAV DĚJIN KOMUNISTICKÉ STRANY ČESKOSLOVENSKA. *Klement Gottwald, 1896-1953.* Prague: Artia, 1954. 311 p. (In German) Gottwald's life story in pictures, accompanied by lengthy commentaries. The introductory chapter under "Aus dem Leben und Wirken Klement Gottwalds" is by Václav Kopecký.

IG13 PRAGUE, ÚSTAV DĚJIN KOMUNISTICKÉ STRANY ČESKOSLOVENSKA. *Ze čtyřiceti let zápasů KSČ; historické studie.* Prague: S.N.P.L., 1961. 486 p. Eleven studies by Czech specialists on 40 years of activities of the Communist Party of Czechoslovakia, with emphasis on the post-1945 period and the assistance rendered by the Communist Party of the Soviet Union. František Horka has failed to furnish enough documents on the Party's mass contacts; M. Vartíková's study on the Slovak nationality problem is a typical Party-minded approach. [B]

2. 1917-1938

IG14 ARMSTRONG, HAMILTON FISH. *When There Is No Peace.* N.Y.: Macmillan, 1939. 236 p. A study of the German-Czechoslovak crisis of 1938. The author holds a major factor in the British appeasement of Hitler at Munich was the hatred of Soviet Russia felt by British conservative circles. They accepted Hitler's claim that Nazi Germany was a bulwark for Europe against Communism. Includes a very detailed chronology of the events of the crisis.

IG15 BATURIN, M. *SShA i Miunkhen; iz istorii amerikanskoi vneshnei politiki 1937-1938 gg.* Moscow: IMO, 1961. 208 p. A Soviet view of American policy and attitudes on the Munich crisis. Treats Munich as an anti-Soviet move in which the United States connived. Bibliography of English and Russian materials. Far from complete in the use of published sources.

IG16 BENEŠ, EDVARD. *Boj o mír a bezpečnost státu.* Prague: Orbis, 1934. 833 p. A collection of speeches and other statements by the then Czechoslovak Minister of Foreign Affairs.

IG17 BRATISLAVA, ÚSTAV DEJÍN KOMUNISTICKEJ STRANY SLOVENSKA. *Bojový odkaz roku 1919; spomienky bojovníkov za Slovenskú republiku rád a Maďarskú republiku rád.* 2nd ed. Bratislava: S.V.P.L., 1960. 212 p. Contains 20 reminiscences of the fighters for a Slovak Soviet Republic and a Hungarian Soviet Republic of 1919, elucidating military, social, and political conditions and the Soviet Union's influence. Includes Michal Dzvoník's documented study of the Slovak Soviet Republic. [A]

IG18 BRATISLAVA, ÚSTAV DEJÍN KOMUNISTICKEJ STRANY SLOVENSKA. *Bojová pieseň znela; spomienky slovenských červenoarmejcov, účastníkov Veľkej októbrovej socialistickej revolúcie a občianskej vojny v sovietskom Rusku 1917-1921.* Bratislava: S.V.P.L., 1958. 253 p. Reminiscences of 20 Slovaks who, as members of the Red Army, took part in the Great October Socialist Revolution and in the Civil War in Soviet Russia, 1917-21. The compiler Štefan Štvrtecký's treatise is a documented summary of the history of the Czechoslovaks in the Russian Civil War.

IG19 *Chekhoslovakiia pod ugrozoi fashistskoi agressii; sbornik statei i materialov.* Leningrad: Lenoblizdat, 1938. 92 p. A compilation of Soviet articles dealing with the partition of Czechoslovakia.

IG20 CZECHOSLOVAK REPUBLIC, MINISTERSTVO ZAHRANIČNÍCH VĚCÍ. *Nové dokumenty k historii Mnichova.* Ed. by V. F. Klochko and others. Prague: S.N.P.L., 1958. 128 p. English ed., Prague, 1958. German ed., Prague, 1959. French ed., Prague, 1958. Russian ed., Moscow: 1958. A collective work of the ministries of foreign affairs of Czechoslovakia and the Soviet Union. Contains 61 documents, most of them previously unpublished, relating to the diplomatic background of the Munich crisis, March 12-September 20, 1938. The Soviet Union's role is defended.

IG21 DZVONÍK, MICHAL. *Ohlas Veľkej októbrovej socialistickej revolúcie na Slovensku, 1918-1919.* Bratislava: S.V.P.L., 1957. 205 p. A general account of the influence of the Russian Revolution on Slovakia's labor movement in 1918-19, using published and archival sources. Fails to show how Bolshevik ideas spread to Slovakia. [B]

IG22 EDDY, R. T. "The Franco-Soviet and Czechoslovak-Soviet Pacts of Mutual Assistance, 1935." M.A. thesis, U. of California (Berkeley), 1941.

IG23 FIERLINGER, ZDENĚK. *Sovětské Rusko na nové dráze.* Prague: Ústřední dělnické nakladatelství, 1932. 195 p. An uncritical evaluation of Soviet economic policy in the early 1930's by a pro-Soviet Czechoslovak diplomat.

IG24 FILO, MILAN. *Boj KSČ na Slovensku za obranu republiky v rokoch 1937-1938.* Bratislava: S.V.P.L., 1960. 274 p. Reviews the role of the Communist Party of Czechoslovakia in its Moscow-directed anti-fascist struggles in Slovakia, 1937-38. Useful are sections dealing with the foreign aspects of the Spanish Civil War and the Soviet Union. The Party's mass support in Slovakia is exaggerated.

IG25 GUS, M. *Amerikanskie imperialisty—vdokhnoviteli miunkhenskoi politiki.* Moscow: Gospolitizdat, 1951. 245 p. German ed., *Die Amerikanischen Imperialisten als Inspiratoren der Münchener Politik.* Berlin: Dietz, 1954, 253 p. A Communist interpretation of the U.S. attitude toward Russia from the 1930's to 1945, with special emphasis on the Munich crisis. Attacks U.S. policy as hostile to Soviet Union.

IG26 HÁJEK, J. S. *Mnichov.* Prague: S.N.P.L., 1958. 162 p. Russian ed., Moscow: Sotsekizdat, 1960. 225 p. Reviews the international constellation, Czechoslovak domestic affairs, Lord Runciman's mission, and Soviet-Czechoslovak links just preceding the Munich Agreement. Decidedly pro-Soviet, it makes extensive use of unpublished documents. The chapter on "Literature and Sources" (p. 158-60) is noteworthy. **[B]**

IG27 HAPALA, MILAN E. "The Evolution of Czechoslovak Political Parties and the Russian Question, 1918-1921." Ph.D. dissertation, Duke University, 1956.

IG28 HOLOTÍK, L'UDOVÍT. *Októbrová revolúcia a národnooslobodzovacie hnutie na Slovensku v rokoch 1917-1918.* Bratislava: Vydavatel'stvo Slovenskej akademie vied, 1958. 165 p. Reviews in 12 chapters the socioeconomic conditions in the Austro-Hungarian Monarchy, 1917-1918, and the effect of the Bolshevik Revolution on the working classes, with emphasis on Slovakia and on the idea of Slavic solidarity. Though foreign, chiefly Hungarian, archival documents are also used, Bolshevik mass contact is not proved. [B]

IG29 HOLOTÍK, L'UDOVÍT. *Štefánikovská legenda a vznik ČSR.* Bratislava: Vydavatel'stvo Slovenskej akademie vied, 1960. 535 p. Uses much unpublished material to "prove" that Štefánik's role in the founding of Czechoslovakia was insignificant. Štefánik is depicted as an agent of French imperialism and an anti-Soviet reactionary in organizing Czech legions in Russia. Also sheds some light on post-1917 Soviet-Czechoslovak ties. The author's statements go much further than the documents warrant.

IG30 HOLOTÍKOVÁ, ZDENKA. *Klement Gottwald na Slovensku v rokoch 1921-1924.* Bratislava: SAV, 1953. 142 p. Describes the Czech Communist leader's Party work in Slovakia, 1921-24. Based partly on archival material.

IG31 INTERNATIONAL CONFERENCE ON THE OCCASION OF THE 20TH ANNIVERSARY OF MUNICH, PRAGUE, 1958. *Die Hintergründe des Münchner Abkommens von 1938; Auswahl von Referaten und Diskussionbeiträgen der Prager internationalen wissenschaftlichen Konferenz zum 20. Jahrestag der Münchner Ereignisse (25-27. September 1958).* Ed., by Prof. Dr. Karl Obermann and Prof. Dr. Josef Polišenský. Berlin: Rutten and Loening, 1959. 251 p. Contains the conference papers delivered by noted Czech, Slovak, East German, French and Russian historians, dealing with the Czechoslovak domestic and foreign constellations preceding the 1938 Munich agreement, and with the Communist-led anti-fascist mass movements. Documented.

IG32 KONEČNÝ, ZDENĚK. *Revoluční hnutí v Československu a jeho vztahy k SSSR. Morava a Slezsko; dokumenty 1879-1938.* Prague: Státní pedagogické nakl., 1960. 315 p. Czechoslovakia's revolutionary movements and their links to the USSR are reviewed with emphasis on Moravia and Silesia, 1879-1938. Cultural and economic relations are not dealt with. Based partly on previously unknown documents. With German and Russian summaries.

IG33 KOVÁŘ, LADISLAV. *KSČ v boji za jednotnou frontu proti fašismu (1933-1935).* Prague: S.N.P.L., 1958. 344 p. Records the history of the years 1933-1935, with emphasis on the anti-fascist activities of the Communist Party of Czechoslovakia and the role of international Communism in directing the Marxist labor movement. Czech-Soviet ties are also treated. Based partly on archival material, this is a typical Marxist-Leninist approach. Well-documented, with a useful bibliography.

IG34 LAZAREVSKII, VLADIMIR A. *Rossiia i chekhoslovatskoe vozrozhdenie; ocherk cheshsko-russkikh otnoshenii 1914-1918 g.g.* Paris: "Grad Kitezh," 1927. 175 p. Czech ed., Prague, 1927. Examines Russian-Czechoslovak relations during World War I, with emphasis on the revolutionary events of 1917-18 in Russia and the role of the Czechoslovak military units there. The activities of T. G. Masaryk in Russia are condemned. Poorly documented.

IG35 MABEY, M. P. "The Origins and Development of the Communist Party of Czechoslovakia (Until 1938)." Ph.D. dissertation, Oxford, 1955.

IG36 McMULLEN, AIDAN C. (REV.). "The Diplomatic Background of the Munich Agreement of 1938: a Re-examination." Ph.D. dissertation, Georgetown, 1952.

IG37 MATVEEV, V. A. *Proval miunkhenskoi politiki; 1938-1939 gg.* Moscow: Gospolitizdat, 1955. 264 p. Evaluates the chief events leading to the Munich Pact, with emphasis on the fate of Czechoslovakia and the goals of the Western Powers and the Soviet Union. The anti-Western attitude is based on one-sidedly selected documents and newspaper coverage. Accordingly the Western Powers appear to have the sole responsibility for the Munich crisis and its consequences.

IG38 MENCL, VOJTĚCH. *Politické boje KSČ a její vývoj v letech 1921-1924.* Prague: Naše vojsko, 1958. 173 p. A Marxist-Leninist documented review of the founding and the first political struggles of the Communist Party of Czechoslovakia, 1921-24. Its most valuable sections deal with the Party's international links, especially to the Comintern. Its main fault is that labor and Party developments are treated outside the framework of the country's domestic and foreign development. Uses unpublished documents.

IG39 NEČÁSEK, FRANTIŠEK, ed. *Dokumenty o protisovětských piklech československé reakce; z archivního materiálu o kontrarevoluční činnosti Masaryka a Beneše v letech 1917-1924.* Prague: S.N.P.L., 1954. 133 p. A Communist-selected collection of documents related to Czechoslovakia's purportedly anti-Soviet policy at the time of and after the October Revolution.

IG40 OLIVOVÁ, VĚRA. *Československo-sovětské vztahy v letech 1918-1922*. Prague: Naše vojsko, 1957. 641 p. (Živá minulost, sv. 31) Discusses Czechoslovak-Soviet relationships, 1918-22. The second part contains many relevant documents. Soviet institutions and personalities are idolized. With Russian summary. [A]

IG41 PAPOUŠEK, JAROSLAV. *Czechoslovakia, Soviet Russia and Germany*. Prague: Orbis, 1936. 65 p. German edition, Prague: 1936. 63 p. A Czechoslovak diplomat defends his country's foreign policy.

IG42 PEROUTKA, FERDINAND. *Budování státu*. Prague: Fr. Borový, 1933-36. 4 vols. A monumental work on the first decade of Czechoslovakia, including informative and objective chapters on the foundation, program, activities, and tribulations of the Communist Party of Czechoslovakia, by a prominent Czechoslovak journalist, now with Radio Free Europe.

IG43 PLEVZA, VILIAM. *Revolučné hnutie zemerobotníkov na Slovensku v rokoch 1929-1938; príspevok k dejinám Červených odborov.I. Triedne boje zemerobotníkov v rokoch svetovej hospodárskej krízy 1929-1933*. Bratislava: Práca, 1960. 220 p. Describes Slovakia's socioeconomic structure, and the class warfare of its agricultural proletariat, 1929-33, based heavily on archival sources, as well as newspaper coverage. Shows the role of the Communist Party and the Red labor unions in left wing demonstrations. Fails to point out the growing popularity of the bourgeois-led national minority parties.

IG44 PRAGUE, ÚSTAV DĚJIN KOMUNISTICKÉ STRANY ČESKOSLOVENSKA. *Na obranu republiky proti fašismu a válce; sborník dokumentů k dějinám KSČ v letech 1934-1938 a k VI., VII. a VIII. svazku Spisů Klementa Gottwalda*. Prague: S.N.P.L., 1955. 545 p. A collection of published addresses, resolutions, appeals, articles, etc., by noted Czech and foreign Communist leaders between 1934 and 1938, in order to create a united front of Marxists against the growing menace of Fascism in and outside of Czechoslovakia. Includes (p. 403-540) a comprehensive chapter on the economic development of Czechoslovakia, 1934-38, with a bibliography. [B]

IG45 PRAGUE, ÚSTAV DĚJIN KOMUNISTICKÉ STRANY ČESKOSLOVENSKA. *Ohlas Velké říjnové socialistické revoluce v Československu; sborník dokumentů z let 1917-1921*. Prague: S.N.P.L., 1957. 504 p. Contains 200 mostly unpublished archival documents relating to the influence of the Bolshevik Revolution on the country's left wing labor movement, up to the founding of the Communist Party of Czechoslovakia in 1921. Its lengthy preface overestimates the role of the Russian Revolution by neglecting the contact of the masses with their bourgeois leadership. [B]

IG46 PRAGUE, ÚSTAV DĚJIN KOMUNISTICKÉ STRANY ČESKOSLOVENSKA. *Sborník dokumentů k prosincové stávce 1920.* Prague: S.N.P.L., 1954. 225 p. A well-arranged collection of unpublished archival and published documents relating to the Communist-organized general strike of December 1920. With an introduction, explanatory notes, and a good map of the strike.

IG47 PRAGUE, ÚSTAV DĚJIN KOMUNISTICKÉ STRANY ČESKOSLOVENSKA. *Za bolševickou orientaci KSČ; sborník dokumentů k 1. svazku Spisů Klementa Gottwalda.* Prague: S.N.P.L., 1954. 301 p. Includes domestic as well as Comintern documents relating to the Bolshevization of the Communist Party of Czechoslovakia in 1925-29. Also contains a chapter on the economic situation in Czechoslovakia in 1924-29, with numerous statistics. Useful explanatory notes.

IG48 PRAGUE, ÚSTAV DĚJIN KOMUNISTICKÉ STRANY ČESKOSLOVENSKA. *Za chléb, práci, půdu a svobodu; sborník dokumentů k 2., 3., 4. a 5. svazku Spisů Klementa Gottwalda.* Prague: S.N.P.L., 1954. 512 p. Documents, addresses, articles, etc. by noted Czech and foreign (Comintern) Communists on the left-wing movements in and outside Czechoslovakia, 1929-33, and criticizing the bourgeois-democratic system and fascism. The last chapter gives a report on the Czechoslovak economic crisis of 1929-34.

IG49 PRAGUE, ÚSTAV DĚJIN KOMUNISTICKÉ STRANY ČESKOSLOVENSKA. *Založení Komunistické strany Československa; sborník dokumentů ke vzniku a založení KSČ, 1917-1924.* Prague: S.N.P.L., 1954. 201 p.

IG50 REIMANN, P. *Dějiny Komunistické Strany Československé.* Prague: Borecký, 1931. 280 p. An important work on the origin and policy of the Communist Party of Czechoslovakia in its first decade, written in the light of the interpretation demanded at the time of publication; by a theoretician of the Party of that period.

IG51 ŘÍHA, OLDŘICH. *Ohlas Říjnové revoluce v ČSR.* Prague: S.N.P.L., 1957. 308 p. By a noted Czech Marxist professor. Describes the influence of the Russian Revolution on Czechoslovakia's labor movement and Party conditions during the first years of the Republic's existence. His thirteen chapters deal almost exclusively with the Czech lands, so the title is misleading. The section on Slovakia contains many errors due to his ignorance of Hungarian.

IG52 RIPKA, HUBERT. *Munich; Before and After.* London: Gollancz, 1939. 523 p. A documented and highly informative study of Czechoslovakia's international position and England's and France's policy before and during Munich, by a then prominent and well informed Czechoslovak journalist.

IG53 RÖSSLER, FRITZ. *Das Gesicht der Tschechoslowakei; die Tschechoslowakei als Vorposten des Weltbolschevismus.* Fürstenwalde-Spree: Verlag für Militärgeschichte und Deutsches Schrifttum, 1938. 111 p. A characteristic product of the pre-1945 Drang nach Osten trend in German Ostforschung, centered on Czechoslovak-Soviet and Czech-German relations, as well as on the minorities of the country. Extremely hostile towards the Czechs. Undocumented.

IG54 ŠEBA, JAN. *Rusko a Malá Dohoda v politice světové.* Introd. by Kamil Krofta. 4th ed. Prague: Melantrich, 1936. 662 p. By Czechoslovakia's envoy to Bucharest. A well-footnoted treatise on European diplomacy from 1867 to 1936, focused on the role of Russia, but with special emphasis on the Little Entente states, particularly Czechoslovakia. The noted diplomat-author has decisively pro-French and pro-Soviet attitudes in the hope that his country's boundaries can be defended by these two great powers. Contains a French summary and a name index. Valuable on Czech-Soviet relations in the early period.

IG55 SEDLÁČEK, JIŘÍ, and VÁVRA, J. *Pro zemi milovanou; z bojů o československo-sovětské přátelství.* Prague: Svět Sovětů, 1960. 414 p. Gives a detailed analysis of Czechoslovak-Soviet friendship, 1917-39, based partly on archival sources. Relates extensively the history of Czechoslovakia's pro-Soviet institutions and societies, and Communist Party efforts during this period. [B]

IG56 SETON-WATSON, ROBERT W. *Munich and the Dictators.* London: Methuen, 1939. 188 p. Revised and enlarged edition, *From Munich to Danzig.* London: 1939. 287 p. The eminent British historian adds a great deal of confidential material about the Munich crisis to the tale begun in his *Britain and the Dictators.* Highly critical of the policies of the Chamberlain government.

IG57 STRAUSS, E. *Tschechoslowakische Aussenpolitik.* Prague: Orbis, 1936. 165 p. Traces the development of Czechoslovak foreign policy up to the time of writing.

IG58 SURVEY OF INTERNATIONAL AFFAIRS. *1938: The Crisis Over Czechoslovakia.* By R.G.D. Laffan. London and N.Y.: Oxford, for the Royal Institute of International Affairs, 1951. One of the volumes in the excellent series edited by Arnold J. Toynbee. [A]

IG59 VESELÝ, JINDŘICH. *Češi a Slováci v revolučním Rusku 1917-1920.* Prague: S.N.P.L., 1954. 235 p. Surveys the revolutionary activities of the Czechs and Slovaks in Russia, 1917-20. With maps.

IG60 VESELÝ, JINDŘICH. *Jak se zrodila naše strana.* Prague: S.N.P.L., 1961. 125 p. Examines the origins of the Communist Party of Czechoslovakia (1917-20) and the effect of the Great October Socialist Revolution on it, as well as the Party's struggles for the acceptance of Comintern policies. A Marxist-Leninist interpretation. [B]

IG61 VESELÝ, JINDŘICH. *O prvních bojích KSČ (1921-1924)*. Prague: S.N.P.L., 1958. 177 p. Relates the formation and the first struggles of the Communist Party of Czechoslovakia.

IG62 VESELÝ, JINDŘICH. *O vzniku a založení KSČ*. 2d ed. Prague: S.N.P.L., 1953. 172 p. (Za svobodu lidu, sv. 8) Russian ed., Moscow: 1956. German ed., Berlin: 1955. Relates events of 1917-21 with the accent on the founding and early activities of the Communist Party of Czechoslovakia; the Czechs and Slovaks in revolutionary Russia, and the influence of the Bolshevik Revolution on the left wing of Czechoslovakia's labor movement.

IG63 VIETOR, MARTIN. *Slovenská sovietská republika v r. 1919; príčiny jej vzniku a jej vplyv na další vývoj robotníckeho hnutia v ČSR.* Bratislava: SVPL, 1955, 391 p. Discusses the left-wing labor movement in Slovakia during the end of 1918 and the first half of 1919, with emphasis on the short-lived Slovak Soviet Republic, whose significance is much exaggerated, especially its effect upon the further development of Czechoslovakia's workers' movement. Based chiefly on archival sources and newspapers. With valuable illustrations and bibliography.

IG64 VONDRACEK, FELIX J. *The Foreign Policy of Czechoslovakia 1918-1935*. N.Y.: Columbia; London: P. S. King, 1937. 451 p. A sound treatment by an American university professor. [A]

IG65 WHEELER-BENNETT, JOHN W. *Munich; Prologue to Tragedy*. N.Y.: Duell, 1948. 507 p. A documented scholarly work on Big Power policy before and during the Munich crisis, by a prominent British historian. [A]

IG66 *Zoznam komunistických novin a časopisov marxistickej ľavice z rokov 1919-1938*. Turčanský Sv. Martin: 1961. 55 p. A bibliographic guide to 125 newspapers and periodicals published in Czechoslovakia (primarily in Slovakia), 1919-38. The language breakdown of the 125 Communist and other Marxist left-wing papers shows: 71 Slovak, 50 Hungarian, 3 German, and 1 Ukrainian. Of utmost importance for students of Czechoslovakia, Communism, and Soviet foreign relations. [B]

3. 1939-1963

IG67 *Ako sa rodilo priatelstvo na večné časy; sborník spomienok sovietských a československých partizánov.* Bratislava: S.V.P.L., 1959. 372 p. Comprises 41 reminiscences by Soviet and Czechoslovak Communists participating in the 1944 anti-German Slovak National Uprising. In addition, Karol Bacílek's introduction shows the Communist Party's role, and Jaroslav Šolc's documented study investigates Czechoslovak-Soviet links.

IG68 BARTON, PAUL. *Prague à l'heure de Moscou; analyse d'une Democratie Populaire.* Paris: P. Horay, 1954. 355 p. A former Czech trade unionist, now living in Paris, writes with personal knowledge and unusual insight about Communist Czechoslovakia. [A]

IG69 BARTOŠEK-HEJDA. *Československo-sovětské vztahy.* Prague: S.N.P.L., 1955. 144 p.

IG70 BENEŠ, EDVARD. *Czechoslovak Policy for Victory and Peace.* London: Lincolns-Prager, 1944. Speeches and other statements by the Czechoslovak President during World War II.

IG71 BENEŠ, EDVARD. *Paměti; od Mnichova k nové válce a k novému vítězství.* Prague: Orbis, 1947. 518 p. English ed., *Memoirs of Dr. Eduard Beneš; from Munich to New War and New Victory.* London: Allen and Unwin, 1954. A documentary and authoritative account of Czechoslovak foreign policy during World War II by the key statesman. [A]

IG72 BEUER, GUSTAV. *New Czechoslovakia and Her Historical Background.* London: Lawrence, 1947. 275 p. A Communist view of developments in Czechoslovakia immediately after World War II.

IG73 BLANCHARD, H. SABIN. *Good Neighbors in Europe; Czechoslovak-Soviet Relations.* N.Y.: Inter-Allied Publ., 1944. 95 p.

IG74 BOLTON, GLORNEY. *Czech Tragedy.* London: Watts; Toronto: Saunders, 1955. 240 p. A former associate of Beneš and Jan Masaryk writes about them and about Thomas Masaryk.

IG75 BRATISLAVA, ÚSTAV DEJÍN KOMUNISTICKEJ STRANY SLOVENSKA. *Príspevok k dejinám ľudovej demokrácie v ČSR; Košický vládný program na Slovensku.* Bratislava: S.N.P.L., 1955. 279 p. Well-documented studies by M. Šurín, Michal Falťan, F. Vartík, Štefan Rais and others, on the genesis, significance and implementation of the Moscow-inspired Košice Government Program (April 1945) aiming at the gradual Bolshevization of Czechoslovakia.

IG76 BROWN, JOHN (pseud.). *Who's Next? The Lesson of Czechoslovakia.* Introduction by Lord Vansittart. London: Hutchinson, 1951. 220 p. A Czech author describes the Communist *coup* in his country.

IG77 BUREŠ, JAN, comp. *Na památku osvobození Československa sovětskou armádou; vzpomínky na květen 1945.* Prague: Svět

Sovětů, 1951. 237 p. Includes 81 reminiscences by Czechoslovak and Russian officers of the Red Army's activities and its reception in Czechoslovakia in 1945. Valuable illustrations.

IG78 BUŠEK, VRATISLAV. *Poučení z únorového převratu.* N.Y.: C. S. Publishing Company, 1954. 123 p. By a noted university professor of church law. Describes and draws lessons from the February 1948, Communist takeover.

IG79 BUŠEK, VRATISLAV, and SPULBER, NICOLAS, eds. *Czechoslovakia.* N.Y.: Published for the Mid-European Studies Center of the Free Europe Committee by Praeger, 1957. 520 p. (In the series, *East-Central Europe under the Communists.*) An informative symposium of political, economic, and cultural developments in Communist Czechoslovakia by a group of competent scholars. [A]

IG80 CHALUPA, VLASTISLAV. *Rise and Development of a Totalitarian State.* Leiden: H. E. Stenfert-Kroese, 1959. 294 p. Deals with Communist parties, the seizure of power, etc., in general and the case of Czechoslovakia in particular. The author has a doctorate from Masaryk University.

IG81 CHICAGO, UNIVERSITY, DIVISION OF THE SOCIAL SCIENCES. *A Study of Contemporary Czechoslovakia.* Edited by Jan Hajda. Chicago: University of Chicago, for the Human Relations Area Files, 1955. 637 p. (Preliminary edition.) A general reference book, from the point of view of anthropologists. Its chapters on sociological and political aspects are useful, as is its 11-page bibliography.

IG82 CLEMENTIS, VLADIMÍR. *Odkazy z Londýna.* Bratislava: Obroda, 1947. 520 p. Clementis was a high ranking Slovak Communist in exile (1939-45). He became State Secretary in the Prague Foreign Ministry, 1945-48, and after Jan Masaryk's death Foreign Minister. This volume contains his radio speeches and messages over BBC during World War II. Interestingly discusses the future reconstruction of Czechoslovakia and Europe in harmony with Communist patterns, national Communism, the synthesis between Slavism and Communism, internal affairs, problems of the future, postwar Czechoslovakia, and Eastern Europe. [A]

IG83 CZECHOSLOVAK REPUBLIC, MINISTERTVO ZAHRANIČNÍCH VĚCÍ. *Four Fighting Years.* London and N.Y.: Hutchinson, 1943. 202 p. Documents and official information on political and military activities of the Czechoslovak Government in exile during the first part of World War II.

IG84 DAXNER, I. *L'udáctvo pred Národným súdom 1945-1947.* Bratislava: 1961. 299 p. By the president of the People's Court of

Slovakia. Describes political and legal aspects of trials, Communist Party influence, etc., in his analysis and recollections. An important Marxist work. It reveals, in essence, the inner nature of Communist trials. [B]

IG85 DIAMOND, WILLIAM. *Czechoslovakia between East and West.* London: Stevens (for the London Institute of World Affairs), 1947. 258 p. A narrative of developments, economic and political, in Czechoslovakia from 1945 to early 1947. The author optimistically espoused the notion that Czechoslovakia could serve as a "bridge" between East and West, without belonging to either camp.

IG86 DOLEŽAL, JIŘÍ, and HROZIENČIK, JOZEF. *Medzinárodná solidarita v slovenskom národnom povstaní.* Bratislava: Osveta, 1959. 278 p. By a Czech and a Slovak historian who chiefly through unpublished sources describe the activity of 27 nationality groups in the 1944 anti-German, Communist-led Slovak National Uprising, with heavy emphasis on the Czechs and the Russians. The idea of Slavic solidarity is also stressed, as well as proletarian internationalism with non-Slavic peoples. The significance of the then disorganized Communist Party of Slovakia is overrated.

IG87 DUCHACEK, IVO. *The Strategy of Communist Infiltration; The Case of Czechoslovakia.* New Haven: Yale Institute of International Studies, 1949. An informative and revealing study of the Communist technique of seizure of power by the former Chairman of the Foreign Relations Committee of the Czechoslovak Parliament, now teaching at New York City College.

IG88 EVSEEV, I. F. *Narodnye komitety Zakarpatskoi Ukrainy; organy gosudarstvennoi vlasti (1944-1945).* Moscow: Gos.izd-vo iuridicheskoi lit-ry, 1954. 146 p. A poorly documented history of the Communist movement, Red Army operations, and Soviet administration in the Carpathian Ukraine, 1944-1945.

IG89 FALŤAN, SAMUEL. *Partizánska vojna na Slovensku.* Bratislava: Osveta, 1959. 283 p. By a high-ranking Slovak leader in partisan organizations. His account, although methodologically primitive, of the partisan warfare in Slovakia, 1941-45, is realistic when it reduces the role of the Moscow leadership of the Communist Party of Czechoslovakia, and focuses investigation on the significance of the rebellious Slovak army officers in organizing the anti-German Slovak National Uprising in August, 1944.

IG90 FALŤAN, SAMUEL. *Slováci v partizánských bojoch v Sovietskom Sväze.* Bratislava: S.V.P.L., 1957. 208 p. The life and struggles of anti-German Slovak partisans in the Soviet Union during

World War II are recorded by one of them. The Slovak soldiers' attitude toward the Soviet Union and its system is characterized as reflected in the idea of Slavic solidarity. The Moscow leadership of the Communist Party of Czechoslovakia is also dealt with. Uses many unpublished sources. Methodologically weak.

IG91 FEIERABEND, I. K. "The Communist Infiltration of Czechoslovakia, 1945-1948." M.A. thesis, U. of California (Berkeley), 1953.

IG92 FIERLINGER, ZDENĚK. *Od Mnichova po Košice; Svědectví a dokumenty 1939-1945.* Prague: Práce, 1946. 2nd. rev. ed., *Ve službách ČSR.* Prague: Svoboda, 1947-48. 2 vols. A documentary work on Czechoslovak-Soviet relations during World War II by the Czechoslovak Ambassador in Moscow in the period, who turned Communist. Biased, highly personal, but indispensable for publication of important official messages. The second edition was revised according to political needs. [A]

IG93 FRIEDMAN, OTTO. *The Breakup of Czech Democracy.* London: Gollancz; Toronto: Longmans, Green, 1950. 176 p. An analytical account of Communist policy leading to the overthrow of Czechoslovak democracy, by a British scholar of Czechoslovak origin.

IG94 GADOUREK, IVAN. *The Political Control of Czechoslovakia; A Study in Social Control of a Soviet Satellite State.* Leyden: Stenfert Kroese, 1953. N.Y.: Praeger, 1955. 285 p. The first part of this scholarly study is a description of Communist rule in Czechoslovakia; the second part is an analysis of the forces working for and against that rule in the present and in the future.

IG95 GRACHEV, SERGEI I. *Pomoshch SSSR narodam Chekhoslovakii v ikh borbe za svobodu i nezavisimost, 1941-1945 gg.* Moscow: Gos.izd. polit.lit., 1953. 237 p. Relates Soviet-Czechoslovak ties, 1941-45, focused on the December 12, 1943, pact and the Red Army's assistance in liberating the country. Completely neglects Western efforts. Uses Russian and Czech published material.

IG96 HÁJEK, MILOŠ. *Od Mnichova k 15. březnu; příspěvek k politickému vývoji českých zemí za pomnichovské republiky.* Prague: S.N.P.L., 1959. 179 p. Describes Czechoslovakia's domestic as well as foreign situation between the Munich Agreement and March 15, 1939, focused on the foreign policy of the Communist Party of Czechoslovakia with its Moscow-oriented efforts. Based partly on archival documents. The alleged pro-German attitude of the ruling Czech bourgeoisie is highly exaggerated, to say the least.

IG97 HORNA, DAGMAR. "The Military and Diplomatic Struggle for the Boundaries of Czechoslovakia." Ph.D. dissertation, University of California (Los Angeles), 1954.

IG98 HULICKA, KAREL. "The Politics of Czechoslovakia, 1938-1951." Ph.D. dissertation, University of California (Berkeley), 1952.

IG99 JOSTEN, JOSEF. *Oh, My Country.* London: Latimer House; N.Y.: Macdonald, 1949. 256 p. A sentimental and at times informative account of the Communization of Czechoslovakia, by a Czechoslovak journalist in exile.

IG100 KARCH, JOHN J. "Czech-Soviet Relations; 1938-1948." Ph.D. dissertation, American University, 1951.

IG101 KOKAVEC, D., KOŠŤA, L., and ŠOLTÉS, J. "Významné etapy socialistickej prestavby pol'nohospodárstva v ČSR," *Právnické Štúdie*, vol. 8, no. 3, 1960. Describes political, social and legal aspects of the socialist transformation of Czechoslovakia's agriculture under Party leadership, 1945-60. Has a useful chronological list of statutory provisions, decrees, and laws on collective farming.

IG102 *KSČ v boji za svobodu.* Prague: Svoboda, 1949. 280 p. A Communist-selected collection of documents, meant to prove that the Communist Party of Czechoslovakia was the sole active fighter in the country against Germany during World War II.

IG103 KOMUNISTICKÁ STRANA ČESKOSLOVENSKA, CELOSTÁTNÍ NÁRODOHOSPODÁŘSKÁ KONFERENCE, 1st, PRAGUE, 1946. *Hospodářství ČSR na jaře 1946; sborník národohospodářských statí.* Prague: Svoboda, 1946. 191 p. An important survey by 24 Czech Communist economists and engineers of the situation of the country's economy in the spring of 1946 and its immediate tasks regarding nationalization. The correlation between the resettlement of the population and the confiscation of property is also dealt with in line with the Soviet pattern.

IG104 KOMUNISTICKÁ STRANA ČESKOSLOVENSKA, ÚSTŘEDNÍ VÝBOR. *Od. X. do XI.* sjezdu *KSČ; usnesení a dokumenty ÚV KSČ.* Prague: S.N.P.L., 1958. 799 p. Records all important stages of Party history from the 10th Congress in June 11-15, 1954. Includes resolutions and other documents issued by the Party's Central Committee.

IG105 KORBEL, JOSEF. *The Communist Subversion of Czechoslovakia; The Failure of Co-existence, 1938-48.* Princeton, N.J.: Princeton University Press, 1959. 258 p. An informative history of the Communist Party's policy which led to its seizure of power, by an American scholar and former Czechoslovak Ambassador to Yugoslavia. Based on Communist and other documentary sources, and personal unpublished notes of democratic leaders. [A]

IG106 KOSIK, FRANK P. "From Masaryk to Gottwald: Reflections on the Czechoslovak Experience." Ph.D. dissertation, Northwestern, 1959.

IG107 KRÁL, VÁCLAV. *O Masarykově a Benešově kontrarevoluční a protisovětské politice.* Prague: S.N.P.L., 1953. 234 p. Russian ed., Moscow: Izd. inostrannoi lit., 1955. 277 p. Based on unpublished archival sources, this example of politically-oriented scholarship claims that Thomas Masaryk and Edvard Beneš were anti-Soviet and counter-revolutionary in conducting the country's foreign policy from 1917 to 1938.

IG108 KRYCHTÁLEK, VLADIMÍR. *Bolševici, Beneš a My.* Prague: Orbis, 1941. 157 p. German ed., Prague: 1942. A propaganda piece against Beneš by a Czechoslovak traitor in the service of Germany during World War II.

IG109 LANSING, AUGUSTA E. "Czechoslovakia's Foreign Policy, 1939-45; A Study in Futility." Ph.D. dissertation, University of Chicago, 1951.

IG110 LAUŠMAN, BOHUMIL. *Kdo byl vinen?* Vienna: Vorwärts, 1953. 238 p. An informative but personally biased account of political developments leading to the communization of Czechoslovakia, by a leading member of the Czechoslovak Social Democratic Party.

IG111 LAUŠMAN, BOHUMIL. *Pravda a lož o slovenskom národnom povstaní.* Petrovec, Yugoslavia: Bratrstvo-Jednota, 1951. An informative narrative on Slovak politics during, and Soviet attitudes towards, the Slovak national uprising of August 1944 by an eyewitness, one of the leaders of the Czechoslovak Social Democratic Party. [A]

IG112 LETTRICH, JOZEF. *History of Modern Slovakia.* N.Y.: Praeger; London: Thames and Hudson, 1955. 329 p. Parts of the book contain important information on political developments in Slovakia during and after World War II, and on events leading to the Communist seizure of power. By a prominent leader of the Slovak Democratic Party.

IG113 LOCKHART, ROBERT H. BRUCE. *Jan Masaryk.* N.Y.: Philosophical Library, 1951. 80 p. A moving account of the personality and convictions of the former Czechoslovak Minister of Foreign Affairs by his intimate friend, a prominent British diplomat and writer.

IG114 MACHONIN, P. *Cesty k beztřídní společnosti.* Prague: SNPL, 1961. 169 p. Analyzes Soviet methods leading through the liquidation of capitalism to a classless society. Its final chapter reviews the socio-economic composition of the Peoples Democracies, pointing out certain differences in their transition period. In several instances neglects historical causality in order to prove utopian theses.

IG115 MARKUS, VASYL. *L'Incorporation de l'Ukraine subcarpathique à l'Ukraine soviëtique 1944-1945.* Louvain: Centre Ukrainien d'Etudes en Belgique, 1956. 144 p. Relates the main events of 1944-45 leading to the incorporation of Carpatho-Ruthenia into the USSR. President Beneš' and Zdeněk Fierlinger's roles are widely discussed. A Ukrainian approach. Documented, with a three-page bibliography and index.

IG116 MAUROY, R. *Comment on Bolchevise un Pays.* Ninove, Belgium: Imprimerie Anneessens, 1951. 147 p. Comments and background analysis by a well-informed Major General of developments in 1945-50, with heavy emphasis on the preparation and course of the February 1948 putsch and its aftermath. Bolshevization of the economy is also dealt with.

IG117 MICHAL, JAN M. *Central Planning in Czechoslovakia; Organization for Growth in a Mature Economy.* Stanford: Stanford Univ. Press, 1960. 274 p. A detailed, matter-of-fact description of economic development. In comparing the country's production volume with those of the other People's Democracies, the author relies too heavily upon second-hand materials, which is partly responsible for his incapacity to depict realistically the standard of living. Contains a 4-page bibliography, indices, and several bibliographical footnotes.

IG118 MID-EUROPEAN LAW PROJECT. *Legal Sources and Bibliography of Czechoslovakia.* By Alois Bohmer et al. N.Y.: Publ. for the Free Europe Committee by Praeger, 1959. 180 p.

IG119 NEJEDLÝ, ZDENĚK. *Klement Gottwald v boji za osvobození ČSR.* Prague: Československý spisovatel, 1949. 86 p. A survey of Gottwald's activities, 1932-45, by an historian ranking high in the Party and government hierarchy. Through Gottwald's career the important questions of Czechoslovak-Soviet ties are also reviewed.

IG120 NEJEDLÝ, ZDENĚK. *Moskevské stati v "Československých Listech," 1943-1945.* Prague: Svoboda, 1946. 215 p. A collection of war-time articles by a Communist leader in a Czechoslovak periodical published in Moscow during World War II.

IG121 NĚMEC, FRANTIŠEK, and MOUDRÝ, VLADIMÍR. *The Soviet Seizure of Subcarpathian Ruthenia.* Toronto: W. B. Anderson, 1955. 375 p. An important, documented account of Soviet policy in eastern Czechoslovakia toward the end of World War II, by an official delegate of the Czechoslovak government in exile. [A]

IG122 POLLAK, STEPHEN. *Strange Land behind Me.* London: Falcon, 1951. 337 p. The author was a member of the Czechoslovak Communist Party for a decade, but became disillusioned after the seizure of power in 1948.

IG123 PRAGUE, ÚSTAV DĚJIN KOMUNISTICKÉ STRANY ČESKOSLOVENSKA. *Klement Gottwald, 14.III.1953; dokumenty o nemoci a úmrtí Klementa Gottwalda.* Prague: S.N.P.L., 1953. 132 p. Includes documents on the illness and death of President Gottwald in order to refute rumors about his alleged unnatural death. Richly illustrated.

IG124 PRAGUE, ÚSTAV DĚJIN KOMUNISTICKÉ STRANY ČESKOSLOVENSKA. *Prehľad dejin Komunistickej strany Československa; tézy.* Bratislava: S.V.P.L., 1958. 230 p. A collective work of Czech and Slovak historians under the editorship of Jindřich Veselý, on the development of the left wing labor movement in Czechoslovakia (1868-1917), the effect of the Russian Revolution on it, and on the history of the Communist Party of Czechoslovakia up to 1948, with Soviet influence accentuated.

IG125 PRAGUE, ÚSTAV DĚJIN KOMUNISTICKÉ STRANY ČESKOSLOVENSKA. *Únor 1948; sborník dokumentů.* Ed. by Miroslav Bouček. Prague: S.N.P.L., 1958. 243 p. A collection of one-sidedly selected documents relating to the course of the February 1948 Communist coup d'état. The documents cover the period of February 10-29, 1948, and a few deal with postrevolutionary events up to December, 1948. Has a good chronology of events. [B]

IG126 PRAGUE, ÚSTAV DĚJIN KOMUNISTICKÉ STRANY ČESKOSLOVENSKA. *V bojích se zocelila KSČ.* Prague: S.N.P.L., 1956. 557 p. A documented, up-to-date summary of the struggles of the Communist Party of Czechoslovakia. Party-minded and full of exaggerations.

IG127 PRAGUE, ÚSTAV DĚJIN KOMUNISTICKÉ STRANY ČESKOSLOVENSKA. *Za svobodu českého a slovenského národa; sborník dokumentů k dějinám KSČ v letech 1938-1945 a k IX., X., a XI. svazku Spisů Klementa Gottwalda.* Prague: S.N.P.L., 1956. 394 p. An important collection of Communist documents related to the wartime period, some of them considered secret at the time, designed primarily to demonstrate the uncompromising revolutionary and class-conscious attitude of the Communist Party of Czechoslovakia towards the problems of liberation of the country.

IG128 PROCHAZKA, ZORA B. "Foreign Trade and Economic Development of Czechoslovakia." Ph.D. dissertation, Harvard, 1960.

IG129 REISKY DE DUBNIC, VLADIMIR. *Communist Propaganda Methods; A case study on Czechoslovakia.* N.Y.: Praeger, 1961. 287 p. Employing the Czech experience as a vehicle, the author examines indoctrination within the Party, themes and techniques of mass agitation, and the campaign for the intelligentsia. Concludes that dogmatism is the cause of the propaganda failure in Czechoslovakia.

IG130 RIPKA, HUBERT. *Czechoslovakia Enslaved; The Story of the Communist Coup d'État.* N.Y.: Macmillan, 1950. 339 p. French ed., *Le Coup de Prague; une révolution préfabriquée.* Paris: Plon, 1949. A personal, informative account of the struggle between Czechoslovak democrats and Communists, leading to the latter's seizure of power. A documented study of Soviet intervention in Czechoslovak national affairs, by a late member of the Czechoslovak democratic government and expert on international affairs. [A]

IG131 RIPKA, HUBERT. *East and West.* London: Lincolns-Prager, 1944. 151 p. Czech ed., London: 1944. A series of political essays on problems between the East and West and Czechoslovakia's attitude toward them, written in the light of wartime experiences and expectations by a member of the Czechoslovak government in exile.

IG132 RUSSIA (1923-USSR), MINISTERSTVO INOSTRANNYKH DEL. *Sovetsko-chekhoslovatskie otnosheniia vo vremia Velikoi otechestvennoi voiny 1941-1945 gg; dokumenty i materialy.* Ed. by Ia. Vlchek and others. Moscow: Gos. izd. polit. lit., 1960. 290 p. A selection of mostly unpublished documents on Soviet-Czechoslovak party, diplomatic, and other relations, 1941-45. Issued jointly by the foreign ministries of the USSR and Czechoslovakia. [B]

IG133 SCHMIDT, DANA ADAMS. *Anatomy of a Satellite.* Boston: Little, Brown, 1952. 512 p. A highly informative report on the first years of the Communist regime, by a *New York Times* correspondent stationed in Prague during this period. [A]

IG134 SHEDIVYI, Ia., and KORZHALKOVA, K. *Vneshniaia politika Chekhoslovatskoi Sotsialisticheskoi Respubliki v 1945-1960 gg.* Moscow: Sotsekgiz, 1960. 171 p. Czech ed., *Zahraniční politika ČSR v letech 1945-1960*, Prague: S.N.P.L., 1960. 161 p. A brief survey of the country's 1945-1960 foreign relations by the members of Ústav pro mezinárodní politiku a ekonomii in Prague. Soviet foreign links are reviewed broadly since the December 12, 1943 Moscow pact and the April 1945 Košice Government Program. Undocumented.

IG135 SLIMÁK, C., comp. *Pod vedením strany; sborník spomienok ilegálnych a protifašistických bojovníkov z rokov 1938-1945.* Bratislava: S.V.P.L., 1959. 351 p. A collection of reminiscences of over 30

Communists who took part in the anti-German Slovak National Uprising in 1944 and who fought German occupation forces prior to that in collaboration with Soviet Communists and Red Army units. Useful for describing Communist Party leadership in partisan warfare.

IG136 SMUTNÝ, JAROMÍR. *Únorový převrat 1948*. London: Ústav dr. Edvarda Beneše, 1953-57. 5 vols. (mimeographed). An important documentary review of Czechoslovak politics, including the Communist Party of Czechoslovakia, prior to and during the Communist putsch; by the chief officer of President Edvard Beneš' office.

IG137 STRANSKY, JAN. *East Wind Over Prague*. London: Hollis & Carter, 1950. 244 p. A report on the political scene in Czechoslovakia in the period of, and shortly after, the liberation of Czechoslovakia, by a former Czechoslovak politician and journalist.

IG138 SVEJDA, GEORGE J. "The Political and Diplomatic Preparations for the Communist Conquest of Czechoslovakia in February of 1948." Ph.D. dissertation, Georgetown, 1959.

IG139 SVOBODA, ALOIS, TUČKOVÁ, ANNA and SVOBODOVÁ, VĚRA. *Jak to bylo v únoru*. Prague: Ústřední výbor Národní fronty, 1949. 176 p. Russian edition, Moscow: 1950. A routine Communist treatment of the events in Czechoslovakia during February 1948. Texts of important statements and a day-by-day chronology of developments are included.

IG140 SZÁMUEL-SZABÓ, J. *V znamení proletárského internacionalizmu (Interhelpo)*. Bratislava: S.V.P.L., 1958. 145 p. By a former local Party secretary and high-ranking regional economic organizer in the Soviet Union, with assistance of some former members of *Interhelpo*, a Czechoslovak skilled workers' cooperative to help build Communism in the USSR between the two world wars. It does not utilize important Soviet archival material published in *Istoricheskii arkhiv* (1958).

IG141 TABORSKY, EDWARD. *Communism in Czechoslovakia, 1948-1960*. Princeton, N.J.: Princeton University Press, 1961. 628 p. By a former diplomat and secretary to President Beneš. Deals with general political developments, 1945-1948. Documented. Excellent bibliography. [A]

IG142 VESELÝ, JINDŘICH. *Kronika únorových dnů 1948*. Prague: S.N.P.L., 1958. 240 p. French ed., Paris: 1958. A documentary narrative by a Czechoslovak Communist of events leading up to Communist seizure of power, pointing to a well-conceived plan.

IG143 VYTISKA, JOSEF. "Přehled literatury k dějinám dělnického hnutí a KSČ v českých zemích za posledních deset let, 1948-1958."

Sborník Matice Moravské, vol. 78 (1959), p. 307-368. A well-arranged bibliographical survey of Czechoslovakia's monographic and periodical literature published in 1948-58, on the labor movement in the Czech lands (Slovakia not included) and the Communist Party of Czechoslovakia, as well as on the country's Soviet relations. Contains 1300 entries.

IG144 WESTIN, AVRAM R. "Soviet Interference in the Affairs of Czechoslovakia, 1941-1947." M.A. thesis, Columbia, 1958. 174 p.

IG145 ZÁPOTOCKÝ, ANTONÍN. *Nová odborová politika.* Prague: Práce, 1948. 517 p. A top Czech Communist, later to become President, expresses his views on various trade union questions in 1945 and 1946.

IG146 ZINNER, PAUL E. "The Strategy and Tactics of the Czechoslovak Communist Party, 1945-1952." Ph.D. dissertation, Harvard University, 1953.

IG146A ZINNER, PAUL E. *Communist Strategy and Tactics in Czechoslovakia, 1918-48.* N.Y.: Praeger, 1963. 288 p. A full-length history of the Communist Party of Czechoslovakia and of the various steps leading to its seizure of power. The author formerly was a professor at Columbia University and is now at the University of California at Davis. [A]

a. NEWSPAPERS AND PERIODICALS

IG147 *Mladá Fronta.* Prague. A daily published by the Czechoslovak Union of Youth.

IG148 *Nová Mysl.* Prague. A theoretical and political monthly issued by the Central Committee, Communist Party of Czechoslovakia. [A]

IG149 *Praha-Moskva.* Prague. A monthly on Czechoslovak-Soviet cultural, scientific and technical collaboration issued by the Czechoslovak-Soviet Friendship Society.

IG150 *Pravda.* Bratislava. A daily published by the Central Committee, Communist Party of Slovakia. [A]

IG151 *Příspěvky k dějinám KSČ.* Prague. Studies on the history of the Communist Party of Czechoslovakia. Issued irregularly by Ústav dějin Komunistické strany Československa. First appeared in 1957. [A]

IG152 *Rudé Právo.* Prague. A daily issued by the Central Committee of the Communist Party of Czechoslovakia. Absorbed *Právo lidu.* The most important newspaper published in Communist Czechoslovakia. [A]

IG153 *Slovanský Přehled.* A magazine on relations among the Slavic nations, with emphasis on the USSR's achievements, issued by the Slavic Institute of the Czechoslovak Academy of Sciences. Six issues a year.

IG154 *Život Strany*. Prague. A semimonthly on Party work, including comments on World Communism, issued by the Central Committee, Communist Party of Czechoslovakia. Supersedes *Funkcionář*, *Propagandista*, and the old *Život Strany*, which was issued previously by Komunistická strana Slovenska. [A]

IG155 *Zprávy Kateder Dějin KSČ a Dějin SSSR a KSSS*. Prague. Reports of the Chairs of the History of the Communist Party of Czechoslovakia and of the History of the USSR and the Communist Party of the USSR at the faculty of Philosophy, Charles University. The first issue of this semiannual publication appeared in 1958.

IH. FINLAND

EDITED BY C. LEONARD LUNDIN

NOTE: The capital of Finland is cited as "Helsinki" for books in Finnish and as "Helsingfors" for books in Swedish.

There are two large publishing firms named Söderström in Finland. One, which publishes books in Swedish, Söderström & C:o Förlagsaktiebolag, is indicated here by "Söderström." The other, which publishes books in Finnish, is called Werner Söderström Osakeyhtiö and is indicated here by the common abbreviation, "WSOY."

1. GENERAL WORKS

IH1 BLÜCHER, WIPERT VON. *Gesandter zwischen Diktatur und Demokratie.* Wiesbaden: Limes Verlag, 1951. 414 p. Memoirs of the German Ambassador in Finland from 1935 to 1944. Detailed and interesting with respect to Finnish foreign and domestic policies. [A]

IH2 BORENIUS, TANCRED. *Field-Marshal Mannerheim.* London: Hutchinson, 1940. 288 p. Uncritical in admiration of Mannerheim and Finland. There is no good biography of Mannerheim in any major language, and only one really good one, that by Heinrichs, in Finnish and Swedish. [B]

IH3 HEINRICHS, ERIK. *Mannerheim-gestalten.* Helsingfors: Schildt, 1957-59. 2 vols. Finnish ed., *Mannerheim Suomen kohtaloissa.* Helsinki: Otava, 1957-60. 2 vols. The chief of Staff of the Finnish Army during the Second World War writes by far the best biography of Mannerheim, based on personal acquaintance, wide reading, and access to many commonly unavailable sources. More unbiased than most Finnish books dealing with the Civil War of 1918 and the Second World War. Perhaps too discreet in sparing the feelings of persons still living. [A]

IH4 JACKSON, J. HAMPDEN. *Finland.* N.Y.: Macmillan, 1940. 243 p. Still the best general book in English about Finland and its background. The treatment of relations with Russia through the centuries is, like everything else in the book, good but very generalized.

IH4A JUTIKKALA, EINO. *A History of Finland.* New York: Praeger, 1962. 291 p. This, the fullest English-language history of Finland, devotes a relatively short space to the Civil War of 1918, its international context, and the Karelian question. It mentions in passing the Academic Karelian Society between the wars, without bringing out the essentially warlike program of the organization. The discussion of the period 1939-44 inevitably centers on Soviet-Finnish relations, but offers nothing new in facts or interpretation. The author ignores the historical controversies which have taken place over Finland's foreign policy in this period, and in this respect the work might almost be called official Finnish history.

IH4B JUVA, EINAR W. *P. E. Svinhufvud.* Helsinki: WSOY, 1957-61. 2 vols. An excellent biography, based in part upon public archives, private papers, and conversations. Vol. II deals with the period 1917-44. Svinhufvud, as head of the White government in the civil war of 1918 and in the months thereafter, played an important role in foreign relations, including relations with Russia. He was one of the principal negotiators for German intervention in 1918. His views on foreign policy also have some importance in his term as President of Finland, 1931-37. The author brings to light some interesting material on Svinhufvud's activity in the last months of his life, as one of the authors of a "national program" which aimed at the retention of Eastern Karelia.

IH5 JUVA, EINAR W. *Rudolf Walden, 1878-1946.* Helsinki: WSOY, 1957. 640 p. A good biography of Finland's War Minister before and during the Second World War. Does not throw much light on Finnish-Russian relations.

IH6 KORHONEN, ARVI H., ed. *Suomen Historian Käsikirja.* Helsinki: WSOY, 1948. 2 vols. The best cooperative history of Finland. The contributors include some of the most distinguished twentieth-century Finnish historians. The treatment of relations with Russia over the centuries is fairly full. Bibliographies.

IH7 LEKHEN, T., LEKHTINEN, EIKIIA A. and others. *Iz istorii Kommunisticheskoi partii Finliandii.* Moscow: Gospolitizdat, 1960. 207 p.

IH8 MANNERHEIM, CARL GUSTAF EMIL (Friherre). *The Memoirs of Marshal Mannerheim.* N.Y.: Dutton; London: Cassell, 1954. 540 p. Original Swedish ed., Helsingfors: Schildts; Stockholm: Norstedt, 1952. 2 vols. Finnish ed., Helsinki: 1952. German ed., Zurich: Atlantis, 1952. French ed., Paris: 1952. The most important figure in Finland's military history, an officer in the Tsar's army until the collapse of the Romanov dynasty, the leader of Finland's resistance to the USSR in the Winter War and of Finland's offensive and defensive struggle of 1941-44, has left a fascinating account of his life which is more valuable as a sort of political testament than as a well-rounded or consistently reliable presentation of events. [A]

IH9 MAZOUR, ANATOLE. *Finland Between East and West.* Princeton, N.J.: Van Nostrand, 1956. 298 p. The author is a professor of History at Stanford University. His book is a history of Finland, more than half of it devoted to the period since 1939. Twelve appendices include some of Finland's most important treaties, from the treaty of Tartu (Dorpat) in 1920 to the Soviet-Finnish Treaty of Friendship and Mutual Assistance of 1948. A 9-page bibliography includes numerous important titles in Russian.

IH10 RANTANEN, S. HJ. *Kuljin SKP:n tietä.* Helsinki: Otava, 1958. 200 p. Swedish ed., *Som politruk i Finland.* Stockholm: Natur och kultur, 1958. 165 p. The history of a prominent Communist during the period between the two World Wars and, to some extent, after World War II. (Rantanen eventually broke with the Communists.) Little of value about relations with Russia, except the well-known fact that the Finnish Communists had close relations with it, and sometimes their headquarters were there.

IH12 ROUSSILLON, DIDIER DE. *Vérités sur la Finlande.* Paris: Raisons d'Être, 1947. 223 p. Surveys the internal and foreign problems of Finland during the period 1918-45.

IH13 SALOMAA, E. *Kratkii ocherk istorii profsoiuznogo dvizheniia v Finliandii.* Moscow: Profizdat, 1960. 103 p.

IH14 SUOMEN KOMMUNISTINEN PUOLUE. *Kipinästä tuli syttyi; muistiinpanoja Suomen Kommunistisen Puolueen 40-vuotistaipaleelta.* Helsinki: Kustannusosakeyhtiö yhteistyö, 1958. 263 p. Mostly about the internal problems of the Communist Party and its relations with the rest of Finland from the founding of the Finnish Communist Party in Moscow in 1918 to 1958. One very short chapter is devoted to the Winter War, adding nothing to our knowledge. Almost nothing on the rest of the Second World War or on relations with the Soviet Union since 1944.

2. 1917-1938

IH15 DELAVOIX, R. *Essai historique sur la séparation de la Finlande et de la Russie.* Paris: Loviton, 1932. 125 p. A doctoral dissertation.

IH16 ENCKELL, CARL. *Politiska Minnen.* Helsingfors: Söderström, 1956. 2 vols. Memoirs of the first Finnish diplomatic representative to Bolshevik Russia (Jan.-Feb. 1918), Foreign Minister, 1918-19, and later one of the negotiators of the Peace of Tartu, 1920. Contains much material, including some reproduced documentation, on Finland's relations with both Bolshevik and White Russians, and also on the Eastern Karelian question after the Peace of Tartu. Dispassionate. [A]

IH17 *Finliandskaia revoliutsiia; sbornik statei.* Moscow: Gosizdat, 1920. 116 p.

IH18 GOLTZ, RÜDIGER VON DER (GENERAL, GRAF). *Meine Sendung in Finnland und im Baltikum.* Leipzig: Koehler, 1920. 312 p. Swedish ed., Helsingfors: Söderström, 1920. Memoirs of the general who headed the German expeditionary force which intervened in the Finnish civil war in 1918 and the German force fighting Reds and others in Latvia in 1919. Not much about Finnish-Russian relations. A revised edition, bringing it completely into conformity with the Nazi line, was published as: *Als politischer General im Osten (Finnland und Baltikum) 1918 und 1919.* Leipzig: Koehler, 1936. 173 p.

IH19 HÄMÄLÄINEN, KALLE. *Sosialistinen ulkopolitiikka; Piirteitä Suomen ja Neuvostoliiton välisistä suhteista historian valotuksessa.* Helsinki: Tammi, 1946. 105 p. A Socialist criticism of Finland's foreign policy, 1917-19. The author alleges that the Finnish bourgeoisie started off on a bad footing with Bolshevik Russia, precipitated civil war, and established a disastrous tradition of Soviet-Finnish relations.

IH20 HANNULA, JOOSE O. *Suomen Vapaussodan historia.* 1st ed., Porvoo: 1930. 5th ed., Porvoo: 1956. English ed., *Finland's War of Independence.* London: Faber, 1939. 229 p. French ed., Paris: Payot, 1938. 206. A highly-colored, pro-White account of the civil war of 1918 by a military man who was active in the struggle. Valuable for detailed and clear studies of military operations by an expert.

IH21 HJELT, EDVARD. *Från händelserika år.* Stockholm: Norstedt, 1919. 252 p. Does not concern Finnish-Russian relations directly, but deals with the closely connected German-Finnish relations, 1917-19. Hjelt was the principal Finnish negotiator in Berlin for German aid. A strong, conservative, pro-German bias.

IH22 IDMAN, KARL GUSTAF. *Diplomatminnen; Hågkomster från vår självständighets begynnelseskede 1919-1927.* Helsingfors: Söderström, 1954. 240 p. The author was a Finnish diplomat. His book includes brief discussions, based on personal experiences, of Finland's relations with Russian émigrés in 1919, the question of neutralizing the Baltic, the negotiations for the Peace of Tartu in 1920, the Genoa Conference of 1922, and the problems of a *cordon sanitaire.*

IH23 ITKONEN, O. V. *Muurmannin suomalainen legioona.* Helsinki: Kustannusosakeyhtiö Kansanvalta, 1927. 158 p. A friendly account of the "Murmansk Legion" of defeated Finnish Reds who operated for a while under the protection of the British expeditionary authorities.

IH24 KILPI, SYLVI-KYLLIKKI. *Lenin ja suomalaiset.* Helsinki: Tammi, 1957. 141 p. The author was active in the Social Democratic

Party. In form, this is not a scholarly work; the numerous quotations are without source references. Nevertheless, the book is based on extensive reading and on conversations with Finns who remembered Lenin. It traces Lenin's contacts with Finns from the time of his exile in Siberia to his death.

IH25 KUUSINEN, OTTO V. *Suomen tie rauhaan ja demokratiaan.* Helsinki: 1947. Finland's prominent Communist-in-exile, who had been made head of the short-lived puppet government of Finland during the Soviet invasion of 1939-1940, discusses after the war "Finland's road to peace and democracy." This would certainly represent the official view of the Soviet government. [A]

IH26 KUUSINEN, OTTO V. *Suomen vallankumouksesta.* Leningrad: 1918. German ed., *Die Revolution in Finnland*, Hamburg: Verlag der Kommunistischen Internationale, 1921. 41 p. One of the members of Finland's revolutionary Socialist government of 1917-18, who later became a Communist and a prominent figure in the politics of the Soviet Union, discusses Finland's unsuccessful socialist revolution in retrospect. [A]

IH27 LA CHESNAIS, P. G. *La Guerre civile en Finlande (janvier-avril 1918).* Paris: Bossard, 1919. 198 p. The principal purpose of the author is to prove that the Finnish civil war of 1918 was the work of the Russian Bolsheviks. He presents 121 documents to substantiate this thesis.

IH28 LANDTMANN, GUNNAR. *Finlands väg till oavhängighet.* Helsingfors: Söderström, 1919. 309 p. Covers the Finnish independence movement from the outbreak of the First World War to 1919. The author was a sociologist in Helsinki, not an historical scholar or an important actor in the events he describes. Anti-Russian, anti-Bolshevik, and pro-German. [B]

IH29 LAPORTE, HENRY. *La Guerre des rouges et des blancs; le premier échec des rouges; Russie, Finlande (janvier-mai 1918).* Paris: Payot, 1929. 192 p.

IH30 *Offener Brief an den Genossen Lenin von finnischen Kommunisten in Russland.* Petrograd: 1919. 16 p.

IH31 ÖHQVIST, JOHANNES. *Lejonfanan; Finlands folks väg till friheten.* Helsingfors: Schildt, 1923. 304 p. The author was a teacher of German at the University of Helsinki and was active during World War I in Central Europe seeking German aid for Finnish independence. His book is popular, not scholarly, and strongly prejudiced against Russia and the Bolsheviks.

IH32 PAASIVIRTA, JUHANI. *Ensimmaisen maailmansodan voittajat ja Suomi.* Porvoo-Helsinki: WSOY, 1961. 267 p. Finland's most competent scholar in the field of twentieth-century history writes on a subject never before covered adequately: Finland and the victors of the First World War. Valuable chapters on the "Murmansk Legion" of Finnish Reds, the Eastern Karelian question, and Finland's relationship to Allied intervention in Russia. Bibliography of archival and printed materials, and a brief critical essay on sources. [A]

IH33 PAASIVIRTA, JUHANI. *Suomen itsenäiskysymys 1917.* Porvoo-Helsinki: WSOY, 1947-49. 2 vols. The fullest, best-documented study of the steps leading to Finnish independence in 1917. Objective. Bibliography includes many unpublished sources. [A]

IH34 PAASIVIRTA, JUHANI. *Suomi vuonna 1918.* Porvoo-Helsinki: WSOY, 1957. 383 p. The best book on the Finnish civil war of 1918 and what followed. Paasivirta is accused by some Rightist historians of having a left-wing bias; to an outsider he seems remarkably objective. The bibliography includes unpublished archival material from Finland, Sweden, and Denmark. Not much on Finnish-Russian relations, but something about the East Karelian question. [A]

IH35 RÄIKKÖNEN, ERKKI. *Svinhufvud, the Builder of Finland; an Adventure in Statecraft.* London: Alan Wilmer, 1938. 252 p. German ed., *Svinhufvud baut Finnland; Abenteuer einer Staatsgründung.* Munich: Albert Langen, 1936. 222 p. An uncritically admiring, completely undocumented study of Finland's most powerful White politician in the period of the civil war of 1918.

IH36 RÄIKKÖNEN, ERKKI. *When Finland Blocked the March Route of Red Russia into Western Europe.* Helsinki: 1936. By an intemperate White writer.

IH36A RINTALA, MARVIN. *Three Generations: the Extreme Right Wing in Finnish Politics.* Bloomington: Indiana University, 1962. 281 p. By far the best study in any language (not excepting Finnish) of the extreme nationalist-conservative aspect of Finnish politics between the two World Wars. One chapter on the civil war of 1918 as a war of independence against Russia; one on the development of the "Greater Finland" program for making Finland the great power of Northern Europe; one on the Academic Karelian Society. Heavily documented with bibliographical footnotes, primarily to sources in Finnish.

IH37 SIHVO, JUSSI. *Etappijääkärinä meren hengessä.* Porvoo: 1935. German ed., *Sturmfahrten für Finnlands Freiheit.* Essen: Essener Verlagsanstalt, 1939. 312 p. Experiences of one of the military men engaged in bringing supplies and reinforcements to the White Army in the civil war of 1918.

IH38 SMITH, CLARENCE JAY. *Finland and the Russian Revolution, 1917-1922.* Athens, Ga.: U. of Georgia Press, 1958. 251 p. The author is a professor of history at the University of Georgia. His bibliography includes works in Russian, but no Finnish works unless they have been translated into a major language. Shows careful scholarship and a serious attempt to be objective, but contains a slight, probably unconscious, pro-White bias. Inadequate understanding of the underlying causes of the Finnish civil war. The work is in general very valuable. [A]

IH39 SÖDERHJELM, HENNING. *Det röde upproret i Finland år 1918; en karakteristik med stöd av officiella dokument.* Helsingfors: 1918. French ed., Geneva: Payot, 1920. 151 p. English ed., *The Red Insurrection in Finland in 1918; a Study Based on Documentary Evidence.* London: Harrison, 1919. 159 p. An account of the Finnish Civil War, based on "Bolshevik documents" found by the Whites.

IH40 STENBERG, H. *The Greater Finland.* Helsinki: 1919.

IH41 STENROTH, OTTO. *Puoli vuotta Suomen ensimmäisenä ulkoministerinä; Tapahtumia ja muistelmia.* Helsinki: Otava, 1931. 253 p. Stenroth was the Finnish Foreign Minister in 1918 immediately after the civil war. Since Finland had no normal relations with Russia at this time, there is little directly concerning Russia in the book, but there is material on Finland's ambitions with respect to Eastern Karelia, the Kola Peninsula, and the Murmansk-Petsamo area.

IH42 SVECHNIKOV, M. S. *Revoliutsiia i grazhdanskaia voina v Finliandii 1917-1918 gg. (vospominnaniia i materialy.)* Moscow-Petrograd: Gosizdat, 1923. 112 p. Finnish ed., Helsinki: Otava, 1925. The author was a former Tsarist officer who continued in the service of the Bolshevik regime. During the Finnish civil war of 1918, he served as commander of the Russian forces remaining in south-western Finland and of the Finnish Red Guard, then as deputy supreme commander of the Finnish Red Army. He describes the course of the civil war and evaluates it by the standards of Bolshevist ideology. [A]

IH43 TALAS, ONNI. *Ei se niin tapahtunut.* Hämeenlinna: Karisto, 1949. 210 p. A reply to Väinö Tanner's *Kuinka se oikein tapahtui* on the civil war of 1918, by a politician prominent on the White side. Not much on relations with Russia.

IH44 TALAS, ONNI. *Finlands kamp för sin självständighet enligt Mannerheims minnen.* Helsingfors: Söderström, 1953. 110 p. A biting commentary on Mannerheim's memoirs, insofar as they touch on the civil war and Finnish independence, by a man who was a prominent White politician at the time.

IH45 TANNER, VÄINÖ A. *Kuinka se oikein tapahtui; vuosi 1918 esivaiheineen ja jälkiselvittelyineen.* Helsinki: Tammi, 194–. 499 p. A narrative and analysis of the Socialist revolution in Finland and the civil war of 1918, by a prominent Socialist leader who was not an active participant in the events. Not much about Russia.

IH46 TANNER, VÄINÖ A. *Tarton rauha; sen syntyvaiheet ja- vaikeudet.* Helsinki: Tammi, 1949. 259 p. The author was a Social Democratic leader, one of the negotiators of the Peace of Tartu (Dorpat) between Finland and Russia in 1920. Gives the text of the treaty and some background on domestic politics and general international relations. The best book on the subject. [A]

IH47 *Texts of the Finland "Peace."* Washington: G.P.O., 1918. 55 p. Includes the treaty between the Finnish Socialist Republic and the Russian Soviet Republic, and the treaty between Finland and Germany, March 1918, with other documents. [B]

IH48 TOKOI, OSKARI S. *"Even Through a Stone Wall"; the Autobiography of Oskari Tokoi.* N.Y.: Speller, 1957. 252 p. A greatly abridged translation of the author's *Maanpakolaisen muistelmia* (Helsinki: Tammi, 1948). Tokoi was a Social Democrat, Speaker of the Finnish Diet in 1913, President of the Senate (i.e., Prime Minister) in 1917, and Minister of Food in the Red revolutionary government in 1917-18. After the civil war, he fled to Russia and joined the Finnish Legion in Eastern Karelia. Eventually, he escaped to England, Canada, and the United States. [A]

IH49 TUOMINEN, ARVO. *Kremlin kellot; Muistelmia vuosilta 1933-1939.* Helsinki: Tammi, 1956. 393 p. Swedish ed., *Kremls klockor.* Helsingfors: Söderström, 1958. The author was a leader of the Finnish Communists in the 1920's and spent some time in the Soviet Union. This volume of his memoirs is useful for discussions of Soviet conditions and politics in the 1930's and of the Finnish Communists, especially those in exile. Written from the point of view of a man who broke with the Communists in 1939 and became a Social Democrat. [A]

IH50 TUOMINEN, ARVO. *Maan alla ja päällä; muistelmia vuosilta 1921-1931.* Helsinki: Tammi, 1958. 357 p. This volume of Tuominen's memoirs deals with his adventures "above ground and underground" as a Communist in Finland in the 1920's. Discusses mostly Finnish politics, but also mentions the Karelian question and relations with Russia. [A]

IH51 TUOMINEN, ARVO. *Sirpin ja vasaran tie; muistelmia.* Helsinki: Tammi, 1956. 315 p. Swedish ed., *Skärans och hammarens väg.* Helsingfors: 1957. This volume of Tuominen's memoirs discusses various parts of his life but is especially useful for accounts of the activities and problems of exiled Finnish Communists in Russia between the two world wars. [A]

3. 1939-1963

IH52 AMBURTSUMOV, E. A. *Sovetsko-finliandskie otnosheniia.* Moscow: Gospolitizdat, 1956. 104 p. A review of Finnish-Soviet relations from the Soviet point of view by one of the younger Soviet historians, perhaps the leading Soviet authority on the subject. [A]

IH53 AUER, JAAKKO. *Suomen sotakorvaustoimitukset Neuvostoliitolle; Tutkimus tavaroiden luovutusohjelmista, niiden toteuttamisesta ja hyvityshinnoista.* Porvoo-Helsinki: WSOY, 1956. 339 p. A factual study of Finnish war reparations to the Soviet Union, the plans, deliveries, and prices credited. Contains an English-language summary, p. 311-39. [A]

IH54 *Boi v Finlandii; vospominaniia uchastnikov.* Moscow: Voenizdat, 1941. 2 vols.

IH55 BORGMAN, FRIEDRICH W. *Der Überfall der Sowjetunion auf Finnland 1939-1940.* Berlin: Stalling, 1943. 311 p. Some anti-Soviet comment, but on the whole a factual account of military operations in the Winter War. Useful maps.

IH56 BRODY, ALTER and others, eds. *War and Peace in Finland.* N.Y.: "Soviet Russia Today," 1940. 128 p. Strongly pro-Soviet and anti-Finnish. Includes some Soviet documents.

IH57 CHEW, ALLEN F. "The Russo-Finnish War, 1939-1940; the Facts and the Communists' Versions of Soviet Military Operations in Finland." Ph.D. dissertation, Georgetown, 1960.

IH58 COATES, WILLIAM P. *The Soviet-Finnish Campaign, Military and Political, 1939-1940.* London: Eldon, 1942. 172 p. A Soviet apologist seeks to counteract the plethora of pro-Finnish books and to discredit the press and government of Great Britain for their partiality during the Winter War.

IH59 COATES, WILLIAM P. and ZELDA K. *Russia, Finland, and the Baltic.* London: Lawrence & Wishart, 1940. 144 p. An extremely one-sided, pro-Soviet presentation of the relations between the USSR, Finland, and the Baltic republics.

IH60 COX, GEOFFREY. *The Red Army Moves.* London: Gollancz, 1941. 279 p. The author was a British journalist who arrived in Finland on the day the Winter War broke out and stayed until after it was over. Good, lively, conscientious reporting and intelligent interpretation.

IH61 ELLISTON, HERBERT B. *Finland Fights.* Boston: Little, Brown, 1940. 443 p. By an American radio correspondent who was in

Finland at the outbreak of the Winter War, but soon left Finland and wrote this book while the war was still under way. Reasonably accurate.

IH62 ERFURTH, WALDEMAR. *Der finnische Krieg 1941-1944.* Wiesbaden: Limes Verlag, 1950. 324 p. A clear, factual account of the war between Finland and the USSR from 1941 to 1944, by the general who was the German liaison officer at Finnish Army Headquarters during the entire period. The author seems completely honest and accurate. [A]

IH63 ERFURTH, WALDEMAR. *Krigsdagbok November 1943-September 1944.* Helsingfors: Söderström, 1951. 307 p. Finnish ed., Porvoo-Helsinki: WSOY, 1954. A translation, for the critical year 1944, from the manuscript diary of the German liaison officer at Finnish Army Headquarters.

IH64 ERFURTH, WALDEMAR. *Problemet Murmanbanan.* Helsingfors: Söderström, 1952. 61 p. Finnish ed., Porvoo-Helsinki: WSOY, 1952. Discusses in detail and convincingly the various plans of Germans and Finns for severing the Murmansk Railway during the Second World War. Though he does not expressly contradict Mannerheim's memoirs on this subject, his testimony is completely irreconcilable with that of the Finnish Marshal.

IH65 FINLAND, MINISTERIET FÖR UTRIKESÄRENDENA. *The Development of Finnish-Soviet Relations during the Autumn of 1939 in the Light of the Official Documents.* London: Harrap, 1940. 114 p. An official documentary publication. The purpose was to prove the soundness of Finland's juridical position, which was not hard to do.

IH66 FINLAND, MINISTERIET FÖR UTRIKESÄRENDENA. *Finland Reveals Her Secret Documents on Soviet Policy, March 1940-June 1941; The Attitude of the USSR to Finland after the Peace of Moscow.* Helsinki: Oy. Suomen Kirja, 1941. 109 p. N.Y.: Funk, 1941. German ed., Helsinki: Oy. Suomen Kirja, 1941. French ed., Lausanne: Imprimeries réunies, 1941. Swedish ed., Helsingfors: Oy. Suomen Kirja, 1941.

IH67 FINLAND, MINISTERIET FÖR UTRIKESÄRENDENA. *The Finnish Blue Book; The Development of Finnish-Soviet Relations during the Autumn of 1939, Including the Official Documents and the Peace Treaty of March 12, 1940.* Helsinki: Oy. Suomen Kirja, 1940; Philadelphia: Lippincott; London: Harrap, 1940. 120 p. French ed., Paris: Flammarion, 1940. Danish ed., Copenhagen: Hagerup, 1940. German ed., Basel: Birkhäuser, 1940. Swedish ed., Stockholm: Kooperativa förbundets bokforlag, 1940. [A]

IH68 FRIETSCH, CARL O. *Finlands Ödesår, 1939-1943*. Helsingfors: Söderström, 1945. 536 p. By an economist, a former banker, and a member of the Finnish Parliament 1936-45. His book, published in the period of disillusionment after Finland's defeat, is highly critical of the government's undemocratic practices during the war and unrealistic policies before the war. Describes the growth of the "Peace Opposition" during the war. [A]

IH69 HALSTI, WOLF H. *Suomen sota 1939-1945*. Vol. I, *Talvisota 1939-40*. Helsinki: WSOY, 1955. 458 p. Vol. II, *Kesäsota 1941*. Helsinki: Otava, 1956. 627 p. Vol. III, *Ratkaisu 1944*. Helsinki: Otava, 1957. 530 p. A three-volume history of the Russo-Finnish wars of 1939-45. By a noted historian who is chief of training in the Finnish Army, this study presents a useful survey of the often confusing events. Many maps. [A]

IH70 HANNULA, JOOSE O. *Neuvostoliitto hyökkää pohjolaan; Suomen-Venäjän Talvisota 1939-1940*. Helsinki: Suomen Kirja, 1944. 174 p. German ed., Berlin: Wiking, 1941. The author was a colonel in the Finnish Army, who had already published several books on military history. This is primarily a military study, competent and informed, on the Finno-Soviet War of 1939-40. The political interpretations are what might be expected in wartime.

IH71 HANNULA, JOOSE O., ed. *Suomi taistelee, kodin, uskonnon ja isänmaan puolesta, 1939-1940*. Helsinki: Oy. Suomen Kirja, 1940. 143 p. German ed., *So kämpfte Finnland; Der finnisch-sowjetische Krieg 1939-1940*. Berlin: Wiking, 1941. Popular; many maps; more illustrations than text. No footnotes or bibliography.

IH72 HARPE, WERNER VON. *Die Sowjetunion, Finnland, und Skandinavien, 1945-1955; zwei Berichte zu den internationalen Beziehungen der Nachkriegszeit*. Cologne: Böhlau, 1956. 66 p. An incisive and objective analysis of the impact of Soviet foreign policy in the North after World War II. [A]

IH73 HEIDEMAN, BERT M. "A Study of the Causes of Finland's Involvement in World War II at Three Separate Times: November 1939; June 1941; September 1944." Ph.D. dissertation, U. of Michigan, 1952.

IH74 HYVÄMÄKI, LAURI. *Vaaran vuodet 1944-48*. Helsinki: Otava, 1954. 191 p. Describes the "years of danger" after the Second World War under pressure from the Soviet Union and Finnish Communists. [A]

IH75 ILINSKII, IA. *Finliandiia*. Moscow: Sotsekgiz, 1940. 212 p.

IH75A JAHVETTI (pseud.). *Suomi Neuvostoliiton radiossa.* Helsinki: Oy. Suomen Kirja, 1942. 200 p. Swedish edition: *Finland i Rådsförbundets radio.* Helsinki: Oy. Suomen Kirja, 1942. 197 p. A wartime publication to demonstrate the hostility of the Soviet radio broadcasts against Finland, as a propaganda weapon, from November, 1939, through December, 1941. Extensive comments and extensive excerpts from broadcasts from Moscow, Leningrad, and Petrozavodsk.

IH76 JAKOBSON, MAX. *Diplomaattien Talvisota; Suomi maailmanpolitiikassa 1938-1940.* Porvoo-Helsinki: WSOY, 1956. 399 p. English ed., *The Diplomacy of the Winter War; an Account of the Russo-Finnish Conflict, 1939-1940.* Cambridge: Harvard, 1961. 281 p. A lively, well-informed, and intelligent study of Finland in the general context of European international politics from 1938 to the conclusion of the Peace of Moscow in March 1940. [A]

IH77 JÄRVINEN, ERKKI (pseud.). *Vi vill inte kvävas.* Stockholm: Bonniers, 1942. 110 p. Writing under a pseudonym, a Finnish liberal analyzes acutely some of the political attitudes in his country. Though patriotically determined to have Finland preserve its independence against Russia, he is critical of the pro-Nazi elements who he says have profited by the war to exercise a disproportionate influence on Finland's policies. He describes vividly the "nightmare" state of mind into which the Finns were driven after the Winter War by Soviet bluster. The author's real name is Laurin Zilliacus.

IH78 JÄRVINEN, Y. A. *Jatkosodan taistelut; Jatkosodan taktiikkaa ja tapahtumia.* Porvoo-Helsinki: WSOY, 1950. 395 p. A study of Finnish and Soviet tactics in the war of 1941-44.

IH79 JÄRVINEN, Y. A. *Suomalainen ja Venäläinen taktiikkaa Talvisodassa.* Helsinki: WSOY, 1948. 268 p. A technical study of Finnish and Soviet tactics in the Winter War.

IH80 KAARET, RAYMOND H. "The Government of Finland since 1947." Ph.D. dissertation, American U., 1958.

IH81 KAILA, TOIVO T. *Sotaansyyllisemme säätytalossa.* Porvoo-Helsinki: WSOY, 1946. 234 p. A distinguished economist and man of public affairs evaluates the war-responsibilities trial of Finnish political leaders which took place after the Second World War. [A]

IH81A KORHONEN, ARVI. *Barbarossa-Suunnitelma ja Suomi.* Porvoo-Helsinki: WSOY, 1961. 340 p. One of Finland's leading contemporary historians deals with the involvement of Finland in the plans for Operation Barbarossa, the German military campaign against Russia. Based on thorough study of German archival material, but not of Finnish. Leaves unanswered most of the questions about the attitudes of Finland's leaders and the public.

IH82 KORHONEN, ARVI. *Viisi sodan vuotta; Suomi toisen maailmansodan myrskyissä.* Porvoo-Helsinki: WSOY, 1961. 662 p. By a Professor Emeritus of History at the University of Helsinki, noted for scholarship and strength of opinions. Includes 85 p. of text, a 2-page bibliography, 572 p. of excellent photographs of Finland's wars with Russia, 1939-44. The text is a convenient factual summary, but is completely uncritical of anything done by a Finnish government. [B]

IH83 KUUSINEN, OTTO V. *Finland Unmasked.* London: Caledonian, 1944. 31 p. This wartime publication of the leading Moscow Finn represents the official Soviet view of Finland at the time. [A]

IH84 KUUSSAARI, EERO, and NIITEMAA, VILHO. *Suomen Sota vv. 1941-1945; Maavoimien sotatoimet.* Helsinki: Mantere, 1948. 265 p. An official study of the activities of Finland's land forces, 1941-45, published by the Historical Section of the General Staff.

IH85 LANGDON-DAVIES, JOHN. *Invasion in the Snow; a Study of Mechanized War.* Boston: Houghton Mifflin, 1941. 202 p. British ed., *Finland; The First Total War.* London: G. Routledge, 1941. An interesting account of the first part of the Winter War by a British correspondent who was there part of the time. Rather uncritically pro-Finnish; more factual than much of the writing produced by foreign correspondents.

IH86 LUNDIN, CHARLES LEONARD. *Finland in the Second World War.* Bloomington: Indiana U., 1957. 303 p. Finnish ed., Jyvaskyla: Gummerus, 1960. Swedish ed., Ekenas, Finland: Ekenas Tryckeri Ab:s Forlag, 1958. The author is Professor of History at Indiana University. His book is primarily a critical comparison of memoirs of Finns and Germans connected in a political or military way with Finland's part in the Second World War. The Swedish-language edition and even more the Finnish edition are greatly expanded on the basis of archival and other material, but do not differ significantly in their conclusions from the English original. [A]

IH87 MEISTER, JÜRG. *Der Seekrieg in den osteuropäischen Gewässern 1941-1945.* Munich: Lehmann, 1958. 392 p. The author is Swiss and his book is based on published and unpublished materials including oral interviews. A discussion, among other things, of naval warfare in Finnish coastal and inland waters and on Lake Ladoga. The author acknowledges "unconcealed sympathy" for his Finnish friends and says: "All Soviet sources are of extremely meager value."

IH88 NIUKKANEN, JUHO. *Talvisodan puolustusministeri kertoo.* Helsinki: WSOY, 1951. 286 p. Swedish ed., Stockholm: Fritzes, 1951. Niukkanen was Minister of Defense during the Winter War; favored requesting British and French help and opposed accepting Russian peace terms. Believes the Winter War need not have been lost by Finland; bitter against Tanner and other ministers. [A]

IH89 OESCH, KARL L. *Suomen kohtalon ratkaisu Kannaksella v. 1944.* Helsinki: Otava, 1957. 216 p. Swedish ed., Helsingfors: Söderström, 1957. 228 p. The author was a lieutenant-general in the Finnish Army, commanding in 1944 the Finnish force on the Karelian Isthmus where the decisive Soviet breakthrough took place, leading to Finland's exit from the war. He describes the military operations and discusses, sometimes critically, the decisions and measures of Finland's high command.

IH90 ÖHQUIST, HAROLD. *Talvisota minun näkökulmastani.* Helsinki. WSOY, 1949. 404 p. Swedish ed., *Vinterkriget 1939-40 ur min synvinkel.* Helsingfors: Söderström, 1949. 391 p. The Winter War described by a lieutenant-general who was in command of a Finnish army corps on the Karelian Isthmus.

IH92 PAASIKIVI, JUHO KUSTI. *Toimintani Moskovassa ja Suomessa 1939-1941.* Porvoo-Helsinki: WSOY, 1958. 2 vols. Memoirs of Finland's principal negotiator with the USSR in 1939 and Finnish Ambassador to Moscow, 1940-41. The fullest account of the abortive negotiations of 1939; numerous documents incorporated into the text. Strongly opinionated; critical of both Soviet and Finnish governments, but not embittered. [A]

IH93 PERRET, JEAN LOUIS. *La Finlande en guerre.* Paris: Payot, 1940. 211 p. The author was a professor at the University of Helsinki. He was in Helsinki at the outbreak of the Winter War, but left the country within a few days. He wrote this book while the Winter War was still in progress, and in it appealed to the world for help for the Finns.

IH94 PRITT, DENIS N. *Must the War Spread?* Harmondsworth: Penguin Books, 1940. 256 p. The author was a Labour Member of the British Parliament, strongly Left-wing and pro-Russian. Contains two chapters on Finland, extremely critical of Finnish conservatives and especially of Mannerheim. Written during the Winter War; opposes British involvement.

IH95 PROCOPÉ, HJALMAR J. H., ed. *Fällande dom som friar; dokument ur Finlands krigsansvarighetsprocess.* Stockholm: Fahlcrantz & Gumaelius, 1946. 289 p. A selection of materials from the war-responsibility trial of Finnish political leaders after World War II. Selection and commentary favor the defendants. Procopé was the Finnish Minister to Washington until 1944, but appears to have been pro-German.

IH 96 RENDULIC, LOTHAR. *Gekämpft, gesiegt, geschlagen.* Heidelberg: Welsermühl, 1952. 306 p. An opinionated, self-satisfied, Nazi-minded general, imprisoned for war crimes, reports on his career in World War II without showing any regret for anything either he or Hitler did. Inaccurate. Rendulic commanded German troops in Finland, but never understood Finland's problems or its withdrawal from the war.

IH97 RUUTU, YRJÖ O. *Suomen politiikka 1939-1944.* Helsinki: Yhteiskuntatieteellisen Kirjallisuuden Kustannusosakeyhtiö Tiede, 1945. 48 p. The author was a professor of political science at the University of Helsinki and had leaned in various political directions during his career. This pamphlet criticizes Finnish foreign policy and thinks the country's involvement in World War II might have been averted. [B]

IH98 RYSAKOV, P. *Sovetsko-finliandskie otnosheniia; stenogramma publichnoi lektsii, prochitalnoi v Tsentralnoi lektornoi obshchestve v Moskve.* Moscow: Pravda, 1948. 23 p. Brief and superficial, revealing nothing but the fact that at the time of the signing of the Finnish-Soviet Treaty of Friendship and Mutual Assistance in 1948 the official Soviet position towards Finland was very friendly.

IH99 RYTI, RISTO HEIKKI. *Stunden der Entscheidung; Reden des Finnischen Staatspräsidenten Risto Ryti.* Leipzig: Lühe, 1944. 132 p. Wartime speeches of the President of Finland.

IH100 SCHWARTZ, ANDREW J. *America and the Russo-Finnish War.* Washington: Public Affairs Press, 1960. 103 p. After examining the cautious attempts of the neutralist U.S. to aid Finland during the "Winter War," the author shows the strains placed upon the traditionally good American-Finnish relations when Finland reentered the war by joining Hitler in his attack on the USSR. When it was clear that Germany was heading toward defeat, the U.S. was able to use its good offices to bring Finland to switch sides and later to moderate the Soviet Union's demands on Finland. A well-documented study.

IH101 SIILASVUO, HJALMAR F. *Suomussalmen taistelut.* Helsinki: Kustannusosakeyhtiö Otava, 1940. 180 p. German ed., Potsdam: Ruetten & Loening, 1943. Swedish ed., Stockholm: Meden, 1940. Norwegian ed., Oslo: Aschehoug, 1941. A description of the fighting at Suomussalmi, where the Soviet forces suffered one of their principal defeats in the Winter War. The author was in command of the Finnish troops there.

IH102 SOBEL, ROBERT. *The Origins of Interventionism: The United States and the Russo-Finnish War.* N.Y.: Bookman Associates, 1960. 204 p. In this rather over-simplified study of the U.S. attitude toward the Winter War, the thesis is advanced that the small amount of aid from the U.S. to Finland set a precedent for more substantial grants to beleaguered states during and after World War II. Based upon the Roosevelt Papers, the press, government publications, and secondary sources.

IH103 *Sotasyyllisyysoikeudenkäynnin asiakirjoja.* Helsinki: 1945-46. 3 vols. Official but highly incomplete protocols of the trials of Finnish political leaders after World War II for involving Finland in war on the side of Germany.

IH104 *Suomen ulkopolitiikka toisen maailmansodan aikana; Erikoiskomitean toimittama.* Fitchburg, Mass.: 1946. A strongly pro-Finnish survey of Finland's foreign policy in the Second World War. [A]

IH105 SUVIRANTA, BRUNO. *Suomen sotakorvaus ja maksukyky.* Helsinki: Otava, 1948. 160 p. The author was a professor of economics at the University of Helsinki. This is a factual study of Finland's reparations to the Soviet Union and its ability to pay. [A]

IH106 TANNER, VÄINÖ A. *Suomen tie rauhaan 1943-44.* Helsinki: Tammi, 1952. 414 p. Swedish ed., *Vägen till fred 1943-1944.* Helsingfors: Schildt, 1952. 295 p. Finland's leading Social Democrat describes his country's problems in extricating itself from the Second World War. Perhaps biased in favor of the government, though he was not in it at the time. Reproduces considerable original source material. [A]

IH107 TANNER, VÄINÖ A. *The Winter War; Finland Against Russia, 1939-1940.* Stanford, Cal.: Stanford University Press, 1957. 274 p. Finnish ed., *Olin ulkoministerina Talvisodan aikana*, Helsinki: Tammi, 1950. Swedish ed., *Finlands väg 1939-1940*, Helsingfors: Schildts; Stockholm: Bonniers, 1950. The author was a leader of the Social Democratic Party and Foreign Minister during the Winter War. An important book, including many quotations from contemporary documents. Remarkably free of bias. [A]

IH108 TIGERSTEDT, ÖRNULF, comp. *Finnland von Krieg zu Krieg.* Dresden: Müller, 1943. 112 p. By a professional author, who held strongly pro-Nazi views before World War II. Deals with the period from the Peace of Moscow, March 1940, to the outbreak of war on June 22, 1941. Advocates annexation of Eastern Karelia. Popular; no pretence of scholarliness.

IH109 TÖRNUDD, KLAUS. *Soviet Attitudes Towards Non-Military Regional Cooperation.* Helsinki: 1961.

IH110 WARD, EDWARD. *Despatches From Finland, January-April 1940.* London: Lane, 1940. 160 p.

IH111 WUORINEN, JOHN H., ed. *Finland and World War II, 1939-1944.* N.Y.: Ronald, 1948. 228 p. A translation of a work by an able and anonymous author, generally rumored in knowledgeable circles in Finland to be a well-known and strongly opinionated historian. A careful account, factual and solid, never critical of anything done by a Finnish government. Includes texts of the armistice agreement of September 1944 and of the Treaty of Paris, February 1947. [A]

IH112 ZIEMKE, EARL F. *The German Northern Theater of Operations, 1940-1945.* Department of the Army Pamphlet no. 20-271. Office of the Chief of Military History, Washington, 1959. 342 p. Nine of the sixteen chapters deal with German military operations in Finland from 1941 to 1944. Some account is given of the political relations of Germany and Finland as they related to military affairs. Based solidly on the records of the German armies and higher headquarters.

IH113 ZILLIACUS, LAURIN. *Ett Folk en Front.* Helsingfors: Söderström, 1941. 331 p. Swedish ed., Stockholm: Kooperativa Förbundets Bokförlag, 1941. Finnish ed., *Yksi kansa - yksi rintama.* Porvoo-Helsinki: WSOY, 1941. The author is an engineer, educator, and a well-known patriotic liberal among the Swedish-speaking Finns.

4. KARELIA

IH114 AKATEEMINEN KARJALA-SEURA. *A.K.S:n tie.* Helsinki: Akateeminen Karjala-Seura, 1937. 294 p. The Academic Karelian Society, which had become the most powerful organization among university students, published this work by 16 authors on its history, its goals, and the problems of Finland. Extremely anti-Russian, contemptuous of the League of Nations, cool to Scandinavian countries, favorable to the creation of a (geographically) "Great Finland." [B]

IH115 AKATEEMINEN KARJALA-SEURA. *A.K.S:n tie, 1938,* (*1939* and *1940*). Helsinki: Akateeminen Karjala-Seura, 1938, 1939, and 1940. The yearbooks of the Academic Karelian Society, continuing the general tone of the first issue of *A.K.S:n tie* published in 1937 (above).

IH116 AKATEEMINEN KARJALA-SEURA. *East Carelia, a Survey of the Country and its Population, and a Review of the Carelian Question.* Helsinki: Suomalainen Kirjakauppa, 1934. 216 p. A very biased survey of East Karelia by the powerful Finnish organization of university students which was dedicated to the conquest of Eastern Karelia and became increasingly favorable to the totalitarian governments of Italy and Germany and hostile to democracy. [B]

IH117 ANTIKAINEN, TOIVO, ed. *Neuvosto-Karjalan puolesta; Taistelukuvauksia pohjoiselta rintamalta.* Leningrad: 1927. A pro-Soviet account of the struggle for Eastern Karelia, edited by a prominent Finnish Communist whose political trial later attracted world interest.

IH118 AUER, VÄINÖ; JUTIKKALA, EINO; and VILKUNA, KUSTAA. *Finnlands Lebensraum; das geographische und geschichtliche Finnland.* Berlin: Metzer, 1941. 154 p. A distinguished geographer, a distinguished historian, and a distinguished ethnographer, all professors at the University of Helsinki, are carried away by wartime enthusiasm and write a book to justify Finland's annexation of Eastern Karelia and the Kola Peninsula.

IH119 *Aunuksen ääni; Karjalan vapausliikkeiden 15-vuotismuistojulkaisu. 1919-1934.* Joensuu: Julk. M. Liete, 1934. A publication memorializing the Finnish invasion and the Karelian insurrection in 1919, published by Karelian refugees in Finland.

IH120 BALAGUROV, IA. A. *Borba za sovety v karelskom pomore.* Petrozavodsk: Gosizdat Karelskoi ASSR, 1958. 128 p. Deals with events in Karelia from 1917 through the failure of Allied intervention. The many footnotes include references to archival material. [A]

IH121 BORISOV, A. D. *Osvobozhdenie sovetskoi Karelii, 1944 g.* Moscow: Voenizdat, 1956. 99 p.

IH122 FINLAND, MINISTERIET FÖR UTRIKESÄRENDENA. *La Question de la Carélie orientale.* Helsinki: Imprimerie du gouvernement, 1922-24. 3 vols.

IH123 FORTUIN, HUGO. *La Question carélienne; un différend moderne de droit international.* The Hague: M. Nijhoff, 1925. 138 p.

IH124 GADOLIN, AXEL VON. *Ostkarelien—das finnische Grenzland.* Munich: Röhrig, 1943. 119 p. Dr. Gadolin, a trade expert, assumed the German prefix of "von" only during the Second World War. He was strongly pro-Nazi and his book advocated Finland's annexation of Eastern Karelia and the Kola Peninsula, and Russia's reduction to "Europe's greatest colony."

IH125 *God tvorcheskogo sozdaniia; k pervoi godovshchine obrazovanii Karelo-finskoi sovetskoi sotsialisticheskoi respubliki 31. III. 1940—31. III. 1941; sbornik statei.* Petrozavodsk: 1941.

IH126 GOUVERNEMENT CENTRAL DE LA CARÉLIE. *Le Droit de la Carélie.* Helsinki: 1922. 109 p. A propaganda work by a group styling itself the government of Karelia, most of which was in the Soviet Union. Includes seven documents and an ethnographic statistical map.

IH127 HÄRKÖNEN, I. *Karjala Suomen kirjallisuudessa; Pääpiirteellinen esitys Suomen julkaistusta Karjalaa kirjallisuudesta.* Helsinki: 1935. An essay on Finnish writings on Karelia.

IH128 HELIN, RONALD A. "Economic-Geographic Reorientation in Western Finnish Karelia; a Result of the Finno-Soviet Boundary Demarcations of 1940 and 1944." Ph.D. dissertation, UCLA, 1961. A study of changes in the Etelä-Saimaa district of pre-World War II Finland, caused by the boundary put through the area in 1940 and 1944.

IH129 ITÄ-KARJALAN KOMITEA. *Die Ostgrenzfrage Finnlands; Veröffentlichungen der ostkarelischen Kommission N:o 3.* Helsinki: 1918.

IH130 ITKONEN, O. V. *Maapakolaisen muistelmia.* Porvoo: 1928. Memoirs of a Karelian refugee.

IH131 JAAKKOLA, JALMARI. *The Finnish Eastern question.* Helsinki: WSOY, 1942. 90 p. German ed., *Die Ostfrage Finnlands*, Berlin: Metzner, 1942. By one of the outstanding Finnish historians, long an authority on Finland's eastern boundary. He advocates the annexation of Eastern Karelia and the Kola Peninsula to Finland. [A]

IH132 JÄÄSKELÄINEN, M. *Itä-Karjalan kysymys; Kansallisen laajennusohjelman synty ja sen toteuttamisyritykset Suomen ulkopolitiikassa vuosina 1918-1920.* Porvoo: 1961. 356 p. A doctoral dissertation on the rise of the Karelian question and the policy of the Finnish government in 1918-20.

IH133 JUVA, EINAR W., MERIKOSKI, K., and SALMELA, ALFRED. *Itä-Karjalan vaiheista.* Helsinki: 1942. A wartime study of Finland's eastern question. Juva is one of Finland's most distinguished historians.

IH134 *Kaksikymmen-vuotismuistojulkaisu Aunuksen vapaustaistelun, 1919-1939.* Joensuu: 1939. A twenty-year anniversary publication on the invasion of Eastern Karelia from Finland in 1919, written from the point of view of those who considered it a war of liberation.

IH135 *Kampen om Östkarelen.* Stockholm: Fahlcreutz & Gumaelius, 1941. Contains contributions by several distinguished Finnish historians and scholars, as well as by some well-known nationalist politicians. Purpose: to justify by historical exposition the severance of East Karelia from Russia. [A]

IH136 KARELISCH-INGERMANLÄNDISCHE DELEGATION. *Der nationale Kampf der Karelier, Denkschrift.* Helsinki: 1937.

IH137 KAUKORANTA, T. *Itä-Karjalan kysymyksen kehitys kansainväliseksi asiaksi.* Helsinki: 1941. A study of the development of the Eastern Karelian question into an international matter.

IH138 KAUKORANTA, T. *Itä-Karjalan kysymyksen vaiheista vv. 1917-1925; Katsaus ilmeistyneeseen kirjallisuuteen.* Helsinki: 1926. A survey of the literature on Eastern Karelian conditions, 1917-25.

IH139 KEMPPAINEN, E. *Vienan kävijöitä; Muistelmia Vienan sodasta 1918.* Oulu: 1919. Memoirs of the border fighting in Eastern Karelia in 1918.

IH140 KEYNÄS, W. *Itä-Karjalan olojen kehitys; millainen se on kymmenen viime vuoden aikana ja millainen se olisi voinut olla; Esitelmä.* Oulu: 1930. A lecture on the development of conditions in Eastern Karelia for the previous decade by a man who regarded that development as regrettable.

IH141 KIANTO, ILMARI. *Suomi suureksi, Viena vapaaksi; Sotakesän näkemyksiä.* Hämeenlinna: 1918. Propaganda for the annexation of Eastern Karelia, by one of Finland's leading literary figures.

IH142 KIVINEN, LAURI. *Karjalan puolesta; Muistelmia Vienan Karjalan toisen retkikunnan vaihesta.* Helsinki: 1919. Memoirs of a participant in the Finnish invasion of Eastern Karelia, 1919.

IH143 KUUSSAARI, E. *Vapaustaistelujen teillä; Sotahistoriallinen katsaus Suomen rajantakaisilla 1900-luvun heimoalueilla 1900-luvun alkupuoliskolla käytyihin sotatoimiin.* Loviisa: 1957. 222 p. Unusual among books published in Finland since the Second World War, in that it treats Finnish military operations in Eastern Karelia in the first half of the twentieth century as aspects of a process of liberation. Of little scholarly value.

IH144 *Livre vert; actes et documents concernant la question carélienne.* Helsinki: 1922. 231 p. Documents attacking Russian rule in Eastern Karelia. [A]

IH145 MAYNARD, CHARLES C. M. (SIR). *The Murmansk Venture.* London: Hodder & Stoughton, 1928. 332 p. Maynard commanded the British expedition to Murmansk in 1918. His knowledge of Finnish and Karelian history was not very good, and he harbored probably unjustified suspicions of German aims; but his work is a useful contribution to an understanding of the tangled Karelian question.

IH146 MAZHERSKII, V. *Ustanovlenie sovetskoi vlasti v Karelii (1917-1918).* Petrozavodsk: 1957. 207 p. Some scholarliness; considerable use of archival materials; frequently footnoted. No bibliography. [A]

IH147 MAZHERSKII, V., and TROFIMOV, F. *Karelo-finskaia SSR.* 1940. 67 p. A popular, pro-Soviet account. Deals principally with the events of 1917-20 and the subsequent upbuilding of the Karelian Republic. Only 3 pages are about the Winter War, which had just been concluded at the time of publication.

IH148 MERIKOSKI, V. *Suomalainen sotilashallinto Itä-Karjalassa 1941-1944.* Helsinki: 1944. A study of Finnish military government in Eastern Karelia, 1941-44.

IH149 *Ocherki istorii Karelii.* Petrozavodsk: 1957. 431 p.

IH150 OSBORN, ROBERT J. "Soviet Karelia; a Case History in Soviet Nationality Policy and the Pattern of Russian Expansion." Certificate essay, Russian Institute, Columbia, 1953. 119 p.

IH151 *An Outline of the East Carelian Question.* Helsinki: The Carelian Delegation, 1935.

IH152 RÄIKKÖNEN, ERKKI. *Valkoinen upseeripartio Karjalan sodassa.* Helsinki: 1935. Memoirs of a White officer in the Karelian war, 1922.

IH153 *Rapports des jurisconsultes sur la question carélienne (1922).* Helsinki: 1922. 51 p. *Avis des jurisconsultes étrangers sur la question de la Carélie orientale (1922-1923).* Helsinki: 1923. 239 p. A number of prominent Finnish jurists and other Finnish scholars wrote in 1922 to various European experts on international law for their opinions on certain international-law aspects of the East Karelian question. The *Rapports* contain the question and some of the answers; the *Avis*, more of the answers. A number of the replies from foreign experts were also published separately.

IH154 RUSSIA (1917– RSFSR), NARODNYI KOMISSARIAT PO INOSTRANNYM DELAM. *Livre rouge; documents et correspondance diplomatique russo-finlandaise concernant la Carélie orientale.* Moscow: Narkomindel, 1922. 131 p.

IH155 RUUTU, YRJÖ O. *Karjalan kysymys vuosina 1917-1920 eli katsaus Karjalan-kysymyksen poliittiseen luonteeseen.* Jyväskylä: 1921. A discussion of the East Karelian question by a Finnish publicist who was at this time still a strong nationalist and later moved to the Left.

IH156 SALMINEN, VÄINÖ. *Viena-Aunus; Itä-Karjala sanoin ja kuvin.* Helsinki: Otava, 1941. A distinguished professor of Finnish language and folklore issues a book on Eastern Karelia, with many pictures. The tendency is to celebrate the conquest of this region by Finland and to regard it as permanent. [B]

IH157 SIHVO, A., TALVELA, P., PAJULA, P., and NORDSTRÖM, R., eds. *Muistojulkaisu Aunuksen retken.* Helsinki: 1930. Memorial publication about the Finnish invasion of Eastern Karelia in 1919. The editorial committee included the names of very distinguished Finnish military men.

IH158 SIUKIIAINEN, I. *Karelskii vopros v sovetsko-finliandskikh otnosheniiakh v 1918-1920 godakh.* Petrozavodsk: Gos. izd. Karelo-Finskoi SSR, 1948. 168 p. A semi-scholarly, pro-Soviet account. Contains a three-page bibliography. The numerous footnotes include references to books and newspapers published in Finland. [A]

IH159 STENBERG, H. *Kaukokarjala suhteissaan Suomeen ja Venäjään.* Helsinki: 1918. 4th rev. and enl. ed., Helsinki: 1919. German ed., *Ostkarelien im Verhältnis zu Russland und zu Finnland.* Stockholm: 1917.

IH160 STENBERG, H. *Østkarelen; Landet, Befolkingen, dets Frihedskamp.* Helsingfors: 1922. A study of the East Karelian question by a man actively engaged in propaganda for the separation of the region from Russia.

IH161 STRUPP, K. *La Question carélienne.* Helsinki: 1924.

IH162 *Suomalaiset kommunistit Itä-Karjalassa.* Tampere: 1958. 136 p. On Finnish Communists in Eastern Karelia.

IH163 TAKALA, ROOPE, and IEVALA, IIVARI, eds. *Karjala; Karjalan vapaussodan 10-vuotismuistojulkaisu, 1922-1932.* Helsinki: 1932. A memorial volume on the Karelian insurrection in 1922, written from the point of view of the defeated insurgents.

II. FRANCE

EDITED BY ALFRED J. RIEBER

1. GENERAL WORKS

II1 BAINVILLE, JACQUES. *La Russie et la barrière de l'Est.* Paris: Plon, 1937. 294 p. Essays by a learned, conservative French royalist, published between 1908 and 1936, largely in the *Action Française.* Mostly on Franco-Russian relations, but includes some articles on Turkey and Eastern Europe. Bainville opposed the Franco-Russian alliance and foresaw the 1939 pact.

II2 *Frantsuzskii ezhegodnik; stati i materialy po istorii Frantsii.* Moscow: Izd. Akademii nauk SSSR, 1958–. A collection of scholarly articles on French history, including several dealing with Franco-Soviet relations. Especially important is S. S. Bantke's "Massovoe rabochee dvizhenie vo Frantsii v 1920 g.," an unpublished chapter from the book of an eminent Soviet expert on French Communism. It is a documented study of the struggle between revolutionary syndicalists and reformists over strike tactics and intervention in Russia.

II3 HERRIOT, ÉDOUARD. *Jadis.* Vol. II, *D'une Guerre à l'autre, 1914-1936.* Paris: Flammarion, 1952. 647 p. Memoirs of a Radical Party leader. Valuable, first-hand information on negotiations preceding the entry of the Soviet Union into the League of Nations, on the recognition of the Soviet Union by France, and on early contacts with the Soviet government leading to the Franco-Soviet treaty of alliance. [B]

II4 MOSCOW, INSTITUT MEZHDUNARODNYKH OTNOSHENII. *SSSR-Frantsiia, iz istorii politicheskikh, ekonomicheskikh i kulturnykh otnoshenii.* Moscow: 1960. 92 p.

II5 PETROV, F. N., ed. *Frantsiia i ee vladeniia.* Moscow: Gosudarstvennyi nauchnyi institut "Sovetskaia Entsiklopedia," 1948. 800 p. A complete survey of France, with a history from the Soviet point of view as of 1948.

2. 1917-1934

II6 BRINKLEY, GEORGE A. "The Volunteer Army and General Denikin's Relations with the French, 1918-1920." Certificate essay, Russian Institute, Columbia, 1955. 174 p. A history and analysis of the major anti-Bolshevik force in South Russia and its relations with France, chiefly during the French occupation of Odessa. [A]

II7 CHAMPCOMMUNAL, J. *La Condition des Russes à l'étranger, spécialement en France.* Paris: Sirey, 1925. 70 p. A scholarly, well-documented study of legal questions involved in the recognition and non-recognition of the Soviet Union, with emphasis on the rights of Russian emigrants and Soviet citizens in France, by a professor at the Law Faculty of Limoges. Critical of official governmental policy based on a "legal fiction."

II8 DELBOS, YVON. *L'Expérience rouge*. Paris: Au Sans Pareil, 1933. 246 p. A balanced, popular account of an unofficial trip to the Soviet Union in 1932, by a Radical leader. Deplores the decline in French economic and cultural influence and recommends political cooperation with the Soviet Union to restrain Germany and insure European peace.

II9 GEDAR, L. *Antisovetskaia politika frantsuzskogo imperializma*. Preface by Karl Radek. Moscow-Leningrad: Ogiz, 1931. 182 p. A detailed survey of the main incidents in Franco-Soviet relations, 1917-31. Accuses France of being the main organizer of intervention and of planning a new attack on the USSR with the help of White émigrés, Poland and Rumania. Scanty documentation.

II10 GOLDFARB, A. *Frantsiia i SSSR*. Moscow-Leningrad: Molodaia Gvardiia, 1925. 157 p. A popular Bolshevik survey of "French imperialism," with emphasis on French Intervention. Useful on the recognition of the Soviet Union by France and includes some material on White emigration. Primary sources used with but a few references in this often superficial study. Short, annotated bibliography on the Communist press and a sympathetic introduction by Pierre Pascal.

II11 GUINET, ALPHONSE. *En Mission à travers la Russie de Lénine*. Paris: Fournier, 1921. 322 p. Anti-Soviet reminiscences of a member of the French military mission to Rumania, the Ukraine, and Siberia. A largely impressionistic, popular account since the author considered the mission "too confidential" to reveal.

II12 GUKOVSKII, A. I. *Frantsuzskaia interventsiia na iuge Rossii, 1918-1919 gg*. Moscow: Gosizdat, 1928. 268 p. A well-documented study based on a mass of primary sources, including local newspapers and archival material. Originally a report to a seminar on the Civil War at the Institute of Red Professors, by a collaborator of M. N. Pokrovskii's, this biased but thoughtful analysis discusses contacts of the French with anti-Bolshevik groups and the activity of the Bolshevik underground in Odessa. Useful documents and a detailed chronology of events in the appendices. The outstanding Soviet work on the subject. [A]

II13 HERBETTE, JEAN. *Un Diplomate français parle du péril bolchéviste; rapports de Jean Herbette, Ambassadeur de France à Moscou (1927-1931)*. Paris: Les Documents Contemporains, 1943. 205

p. German ed., Berlin: Deutscher, 1943. Spanish ed., Madrid: Autores Literarios Asociados, 1944. Carefully selected excerpts of reports from the files of the French Ambassador to Moscow, published by the Nazis as anti-Soviet propaganda. Comments mainly on internal developments and the author's disillusionment with Soviet policies. Facsimile of August 19, 1927 report. Selections appear to be authentic.

II14 HERRIOT, ÉDOUARD. *La Russie nouvelle.* Paris: Ferenczi, 1922. The Radical leader's popular account of his first Soviet trip, including views on ideology, government, state institutions, commerce, and industrial resources. He records his brief talks with Kamenev, Trotskii, and Krassin and pleads for the re-establishment of diplomatic relations between Paris and Moscow in the mutual interest.

II15 HOROWITZ, SIDNEY. "The Soviet Union and the French Left Bloc, 1924-1925." Certificate essay, Russian Institute, Columbia, 1953. 140 p. An objective study based on French and Russian primary sources. Analyzes Soviet fears of a united "capitalist" attack against the Soviet Union and the consequent preference of Moscow for temporary cooperation with Germany instead of with France.

II16 "Iz istorii frantsuzskoi interventsii v Odesse," *Krasnyi Arkhiv*, vol. 45. Moscow-Leningrad: Gos. sots-ekon. izd., 1931, p. 53-80. Reports of Colonel Novikov of the General Staff in the Volunteer Army. Covers French relations with Denikin and Petliura and outlines the aims of the French intervention. Includes complete documents from the archives of the French army and an introduction by Professor A. I. Gukovskii, who considers the material an important primary source.

II17 JANIN, MAURICE (GÉNÉRAL). *Ma Mission en Sibérie, 1918-1920.* Paris: Payot, 1933. 307 p. Reminiscences of the chief of the French military mission in Siberia, appointed commander of Allied and Russian forces by the Supreme Council. He was hostile to the Bolsheviks and Kolchak, but many excerpts from his journal concern relations with the Czech Legion, Allied forces, revolutionary groups, and Allied leaders in Paris. [B]

II18 "K istorii frantsuzskoi interventsii na iuge Rossii, dekabr 1918-aprel 1919," *Krasnyi Arkhiv*, vol. 19. Moscow: Gosizdat, 1926, p. 3-38. Reports to Admiral Kolchak by his agent on the situation in South Russia, primarily about French relations with Denikin and Petliura. Contains a commentary by Professor D. Kin that gives the Soviet version of the reasons for the French evacuation. Favorable to V. V. Shulgin.

II19 LABRY, RAOUL. *Autour du Bolchévisme, dans les coulisses du gouvernement bolchéviste; la France face à la Russie bolchéviste en 1918, 1919, et 1920.* La Roche-sur-Yon: Author, 1921. 270 p. A scholarly, perceptive review of French policy toward Soviet Russia, 1918-20 by a former member of the French Institute in Petrograd and agrégé. He is critical of the Russian Bureau in the French Foreign Ministry, of Allied intervention which led to "polarization of Russian society," and of official opinion that Bolshevism was transitory and rootless in Russia. The author suggests a wait-and-see policy. Short bibliography of French books with useful, lengthy annotations. [B]

II20 LAGARDE, ERNEST. *La Reconnaissance du gouvernement des Soviets*. Paris: Payot, 1924. 190 p. Russian ed., Moscow: 1925. 153 p. A scholarly, dispassionate discussion of the legal, political and economic problems of co-existence with Soviet Russia. An optimistic interpretation of the development of Soviet foreign policy toward peaceful ends. No Russian language sources, yet still the most useful study of Franco-Soviet relations, 1921-24. A doctoral dissertation for the Law Faculty, Paris, but the original citations are omitted. [A]

II21 LIUBIMOV, N. N. *SSSR i Frantsiia; Franko-Russkaia finansovaia problema v sviazi s mezhdunarodnoi zadolzhennostiu*. Leningrad: Priboi, 1926. 162 p. A scholarly analysis of Franco-Russian financial problems and the general problem of indebtedness, by a leading Soviet economist. Biased, but well-documented with primary sources, and cogently argued on legal, economic, and political grounds. Useful annotated bibliography of Russian, French, German, and English sources.

II22 LORIS-MELIKOV, IVAN (MELIKOF, JEAN). *La Révolution russe et les nouvelles républiques transcaucasiennes; Bolchévisme et antibolchévisme*. Paris: Alcan, 1920. 211 p. A brief history of the Civil War in South Russia, with emphasis on Allied policy. The author was given a personal and informal commission by Clémenceau to investigate conditions in Oct.-Dec. 1919. His account is followed by reports and letters of the author. A valuable critique of French policy.

II23 MARIN, DAVID P. "Failure in the South; an Account of André Marty, the French Mutiny and Withdrawal from Southern Russia, November 1918-April 1919." Certificate essay, Russian Institute, Columbia, 1950. 89 p. A scholarly history and analysis of the French intervention in Odessa and the Crimea. Events are reviewed in the general context of French policy.

II24 MARTY, ANDRÉ P. *La Révolte de la Mer Noire*. Paris: Bureau d'Éditions, 1927. English ed., *The Epic of the Black Sea Revolt*. N.Y.: Workers' Library, 1941. (Many other editions.) A highly colored treatment by a participant in the uprising of French sailors during the Intervention in South Russia, with emphasis on the White Terror. Includes selected documents on subversive activities in the French forces and broadsides issued by French sympathizers with the Bolsheviks in Odessa. The author later became a top French Communist.

II25 MONZIE, ANATOLE P. A. DE. *Du Kremlin au Luxembourg.* Paris: Delpeuch, 1924. 267 p. A general account of an unofficial trip to Moscow by an independent socialist French senator to observe Soviet society first-hand. Brief conversations with Chicherin, Krassin, Kamenev and comments on Soviet law, press, and industrialization. Monzie favored a rapprochement with Moscow in the name of political realism and commercial advantage.

II26 NOULENS, JOSEPH. *Mon Ambassade en Russie soviétique, 1917-19.* Paris: Plon, 1933. 2 vols. The Ambassador to Russia from June 1917 to January 1919, Noulens never quite understood the significance of the momentous events of the period.

II27 PAUL-BONCOUR, J. *Entre deux guerres; souvenirs sur la IIIe République.* Vol. 2, *Les Lendemains de la victoire, 1919-1934.* N.Y.: Brentano, 1946. 431 p. Chapter eight of the memoirs of an independent socialist and Foreign Minister (1932-34) is valuable for the origins of the Franco-Soviet pact.

II28 PAVLOVICH, MIKHAIL I. (pseud. of Mikhail L. Veltman). *Frantsuzskii imperializm.* Moscow-Leningrad: Gosizdat, 1926. The first part is the author's diary in Paris in 1914. The second part consists of enlarged versions of articles published in Moscow in 1917 on Soviet and French Communist views of French colonial policy, especially in Morocco. A popular treatment, with little documentation, by a prolific Soviet publicist who died in 1927.

II29 PAVLOVICH, MIKHAIL I. *Sovetskaia Rossiia i Frantsiia.* Moscow: Vysshii voennyi redaktsionnyi sovet, 1924. 103 p. Volume I of his *Sovetskaia Rossiia i kapitalisticheskie derzhavy.*

II30 PAVLOVICH, MIKHAIL I. *Sovetskaia Rossiia i kapitalisticheskaia Frantsiia.* Moscow: Gosizdat, 1922. 64 p. Volume I of *RSFSR v imperialisticheskom okruzhenii.*

II31 SEMENOFF, MARC, ed. *Les Relations de la France avec les Soviets russes.* Paris: Delpeuch, 1923. 80 p. A collection of short essays for and against the recognition of the Soviet Union by economist F. Lop, Radical leader É. Herriot, Communist Paul-Lois, Senator A. de Monzie, and Russian expatriates B. Mirsky and E. Semenoff. Popular, with no documentation. Economic articles are informative.

II32 SHLIAPNIKOV, ALEKSANDR G. and others, eds. *Kto dolzhnik; sbornik dokumentirovannykh statei po voprosu ob otnosheniakh mezhdu Rossiei, Frantsiei i drugimi derzhavami Antanty do voiny 1914 g., vo vremia voiny i v period interventsii.* Moscow: "Avioizdatelstvo," 1926. 587 p. French ed., Paris: 1926. A tract designed to present counter-claims to offset the repudiation by the Bolsheviks of the debts which earlier Russian governments owed to France and other countries. The Soviets demanded compensation for the damage done in Russia by the intervention of French and other foreign troops during the Russian Civil War.

II33 SLOVÈS, CH. H. *La France et l'Union Soviétique*. Paris: Rieder, 1935. 409 p. A scholarly survey of Franco-Soviet relations up to 1935. Extensive research in primary sources, but no citations. Contains excellent chapters on commerce, debts, and diplomatic recognition. Sympathetic to the early Soviet regime and optimistic about the future course of Soviet foreign policy which is viewed as "exclusively defensive." Good bibliography with Russian titles included. [A]

II34 SLOVÈS, CH. H. *Les Relations commerciales entre la France et l'Union des Républiques Soviétiques Socialistes*. Paris: Rodstein, 1935. 126 p. A separate publication of chapter six, "Le Commerce," of *La France et l'Union Soviétique* with an additional section on the commercial agreement of January 1934. Russian sources are included.

II35 XYDIAS, JEAN. *L'Intervention française en Russie, 1918-1919*. Paris: Éditions de France, 1927. 382 p. Reminiscences of a journalist, a member of the French colony in Odessa. Anti-Bolshevik, suspicious of the British, critical of Denikin, sympathetic to Petliura, and favorable to French intervention, this work is an eye-witness account of the French occupation. Useful on relations with Ukrainian nationalists, White armies, the activities of Henno and the Jassy Conference. A serious work. [B]

3. 1934-1939

II36 ABÈLES, CONSTANT. "Le Pacte franco-soviétique de 1935; un aspect du problème de la sécurité collective." Doct. en droit dissertation, U. of Paris, 1945. 106 p.

II37 ALLEN, LUTHER A. "The French Left and Soviet Russia to 1936; Interaction between French Party Alliances and Franco-Soviet Diplomacy." Ph.D. dissertation, U. of Chicago, 1955. 486 p. Based on French primary sources, but relies mainly upon secondary sources for Soviet policy. This study traces the parallel policies of Soviet and French Communists toward the French Left in an effort to align French foreign policy with Soviet. Most useful for the period 1933-36. Contains a twelve-page bibliography.

II38 COULONDRE, ROBERT. *De Staline à Hitler; souvenirs de deux ambassades, 1936-1939*. Paris: Hachette, 1950. 334 p. German ed., Bonn: Athenäum, 1950. The first part is the reminiscences of the

French Ambassador to Moscow (October 1936-October 1938), who was a hopeful proponent of French military conversations with Moscow. Gives the views of Bonnet, Daladier, Polish and other East European diplomats on the acceptance of Soviet military aid against Germany. Several excerpts quoted from his reports warn of an approaching Nazi-Soviet alliance.

II39 DUPEUX, GEORGES. *Le Front Populaire et les élections de 1936*. Paris: Colin, 1959. 183 p. Includes a scholarly analysis of Communist election themes, candidates, and relations with Moscow. No Russian sources. Useful 6-page bibliography. Two excellent maps of Communist electoral strength. Footnoted with primary sources. Published under the auspices of the Fondation Nationale des Sciences Politiques.

II40 GELBRAS, P. *Vneshniaia i vnutrenniaia politika Frantsii*. Moscow: Izd. polit. lit., 1939. 175 p. A scholarly, documented, hostile analysis of French foreign policy, 1934-39, based on French primary sources. This work accuses France of deserting collective security at the height of the Spanish Civil War and carefully examines the attitude of each French political party toward the international crisis from the Soviet point of view.

II41 SCOTT, WILLIAM E. *Alliance against Hitler; The Origins of the Franco-Soviet Pact*. Durham: Duke University Press, 1962. 296 p. Partially devoted to Franco-Soviet relations, 1931-1935, mainly from the French side. For Soviet policy, the author relies on secondary sources and translations of the Soviet press, but no Russian sources. Good information on French public opinion toward Russia, some from unpublished diplomatic reports of the United States Embassy in Paris.

II42 VARFOLOMEEVA R. *Reaktsionnaia vneshniaia politika frantsuzskikh pravykh sotsialistov (1936-1939)*. Moscow: Gosizdat, 1949, 147 p. Severe condemnation of the French Socialists and their role in the Spanish Civil War and of Anglo-French-Soviet military conversations in 1939. Based on primary sources with no extensive documentation. Strongly biased.

4. 1939-1963

II43 BORISOV, IU. V. *Sovetsko-frantsuzskie otnosheniia i bezopasnost Evropy*. Moscow. Izd. IMO, 1960. 199 p. A political tract which stresses the long tradition of Franco-Soviet cooperation and includes a short analysis of diplomatic relations.

II44 CATROUX, GEORGES (GÉNÉRAL). *J'ai vu tomber le rideau de fer; 1945-1948.* Paris: Hachette, 1952. 317 p. Informative reminiscences of the French Ambassador to Moscow, 1944-46. Covers his discussions with Soviet leaders on Poland, the founding of the United Nations, reparations, the "Western bloc," trade relations, and the peace conferences of 1946. Hostile to the Soviet Union, this work offers insights into Soviet policy toward France. [A]

II45 CHARLES-ROUX, F. *Cinq Mois tragiques aux affaires étrangères (21 mai-1 novembre 1940).* Paris: Plon, 1949, 404 p. Chapter VI deals with an attempted rapprochement between Vichy France and the Soviet Union and gives details of mutual German-Soviet suspicions based on reports of the French Ambassador in Moscow. By a distinguished diplomat and historian, who during this period was Secretary-General of Foreign Affairs. Objective.

II46 "La Deuxième Guerre mondiale," *Recherches Internationales*, nos. 9-10. Paris: Éditions Sociales, 1959. 320 p. A French Communist analysis of the character of World War II, the role of the Soviet Union in the war and the Warsaw insurrection of 1944. Documents from the archives of the Gestapo on the early days of the French Resistance and the activities of the Party are included. The acquisition of the documents is unexplained.

II47 EFREMOV, A. *Frantsuzskii narod v borbe za mir i demokratiiu.* Moscow: Gospolitizdat, 1954. 112 p. A polemic against the United States, the militarization of West Germany, the war in Viet Nam, and U.S. bases in France, with quotes from Malenkov.

II48 EVNINA, E. M. *Literatura frantsuzskogo soprotivleniia; period fashistskoi okkupattsii 1940-1944 godov.* Moscow: Akademii nauk SSSR, 1951. 169 p. By a leading literary critic, this source is primarily useful for the excellent four-page Russian language bibliography on the French Communist Party and Soviet policy toward France.

II49 GAULLE, CHARLES DE. *Mémoires de guerre.* Paris: Plon. Vol. 1, *L'Appel.* 1954. 680 p. Vol. 2, *L'Unité.* 1956. 653 p. Vol. 3, *Le Salut.* 1959. 712 p. English ed., N.Y.: Viking, 1955, 1959 and 1961. Each volume contains complete texts of important documents and the author's reminiscences of his relations with the Soviet Union and the French Communist Party. He discusses conversations with Soviet diplomats on postwar territorial changes in Europe, the Franco-Soviet treaty of alliance, wartime diplomatic and military co-operation, the French Communist Party, relations between the Big Four, and the future of Germany. Compare with *Sovetsko-Frantsuzskie otnosheniia vo vremiia velikoi otechestvennoi voiny, 1941-1945 gg.* (II56 below). [A]

II50 GUITON, RAYMOND J. *Paris-Moskau; Die Sowjetunion in der Auswertigen Politik Frankreichs seit dem zweiten Weltkrieg*. Stuttgart: Vorwerk, 1956. 336 p. A scholarly, heavily-footnoted work based on primary and reliable secondary sources. Includes a good bibliography of German, French, and English titles, but no Russian sources. Critical of Soviet policy, it is mainly diplomatic with emphasis on the German problem. [A]

II51 GUTERMUTH, ROLF. *Die Krise des französischen Imperialismus nach dem zweiten Weltkrieg*. Berlin: Verlag die Wirtschaft, 1953. 359 p. Russian ed., Moscow: Gos. inostr. lit., 1955. 360 p. Concentrates on France proper, with the colonies receiving very brief attention.

II52 HALEY, HAROLD D. "Germany, Russia and France, 1950-1952." Certificate essay, Russian Institute, Columbia, 1959. 186 p. Too sketchy and cursory an analysis of French Communist and Soviet attitudes toward the German question. Critical of United States and Soviet policy in Germany. German, French and Soviet newspapers form the bulk of the documentation.

II53 LIUBIMOVA, V. V. *Ekonomika Frantsii i polozhenie trudiashchikhsia mass posle Vtoroi mirovoi voiny*. Moscow: Izd. Akad. nauk SSSR, 1952. 346 p. German ed., *Die Wirtschaft Frankreichs und die Lage der Werktätigen nach dem zweiten Weltkrieg*. Berlin: Verlag Tribune, 1955. 196 p. A survey from the Soviet view of the French labor movement from 1941 to 1952, with emphasis on the postwar period. Based on some French documentary sources.

II54 MOLCHANOV, N. N. *Vneshniaia politika Frantsii, 1944-1954*. Moscow: Gosizdat, 1959. 404 p. A post-Stalinist revision of earlier Soviet works. Uses recently-published Soviet documents on relations with France and presents Soviet views on the domestic activities of the French Communist Party, on the Indo-Chinese and Algerian conflicts. Documented but shows shoddy scholarship.

II54A OUZEGANE, AMAR. *Le Meilleur Combat*. Paris: Julliard, 1962. 307 p. A disillusioned former Communist deputy, now a member of the FLN, shrewdly analyzes the failure of Soviet and French Communists to develop an indigenous Algerian Party.

II55 "Les Rélations franco-soviétiques, 1939-1945," *Recherches Internationales*, no. 12. Paris: Éditions Sociales, 1959. 224 p. A complete French translation of Soviet texts of the De Gaulle-Stalin talks, December 1944. Also contains a translation of the Soviet version of the Anglo-French-Soviet military conversations of August 1939. Published by the French Communist Party. [B]

II56 RUSSIA (1923– USSR), KOMISSIIA PO IZDANIIU DIPLOMATICHESKIKH DOKUMENTOV. *Sovetsko-frantsuzskie otnosheniia vo vremia Velikoi otechestvennoi voiny, 1941-1945 gg; dokumenty i materialy.* Moscow: Gospolitizdat, 1959. 551 p. Consists of 288 selected documents, mostly heretofore unpublished, from the archives of the Soviet Foreign Ministry on official relations between the Free French and Moscow. Heavily footnoted with useful bibliographical references. Covers negotiations on the mutual assistance treaty of 1944, conversations with De Gaulle and other French leaders on Poland, recognition of the Free French, and French pleas for Soviet diplomatic support against Britain and the United States as well as reports of Soviet Ambassadors in London, Washington and Algiers, and memoranda of officials in the Foreign Ministry. Introduction to documents is by K. Tsybina. Documents should be compared with French version in the De Gaulle memoirs listed above. [A]

II57 WILLARD, GERMAINE. *La Drôle de Guerre et la trahison de Vichy.* Paris: Éditions Sociales, 1960. 176 p. The first monograph in an official Party history reinterprets the Communist position during the phony war. Maintains the Party was never defeatist, strove for peace until the fall of 1939, then sought to turn the imperialist war into an anti-fascist war. Stresses the resistance of the Party to the Nazis from 1940. Discusses the Party's underground organization. Some primary sources are falsified.

5. FRENCH COMMUNIST PARTY

II58 ARAGON, LOUIS. *L'Homme communiste.* Paris: Gallimard (NRF), 1946. 246 p. A series of sharply-etched vignettes of French Communist heroes, distilling the essence of the new Communist man—a fusion of proletarian empiricism and Marxist ideology. Portraits of Vaillant-Couturier, Éluard, Duclos, Thorez, and J. R. Bloch, brilliantly drawn by the most famous French Communist author.

II59 BABY, JEAN. *Critique de base; le Parti communiste français entre le passé et l'avenir.* Paris: Maspero, 1960. 256 p. Sharp criticism of Party leaders including Thorez and Billoux for ideological dogmatism and tactical rigidity since 1956 by a member of the Central Committee. Condemns the Party's "neo-colonialist policy" in Algeria, its opposition to birth control, and the lack of intra-Party democracy. Rejects revisionism, extols Soviet leadership, and calls for a united front with socialists and left intellectuals against Gaullism.

II60 BANTKE, S. *Borba za sozdanie Kommunisticheskoi Partii Frantsii.* Moscow: Partizdat, 1936. 252 p. Intended as the first part of a study of the formation of the French Communist Party, this volume covers in detail the Zimmerwald movement in France, 1914-18. Heavily footnoted, it contains a very useful nine-page bibliography of French and Russian titles. Written by a Soviet specialist on the founding of the Party, this book is very hostile toward the Second International.

II61 BARANÈS, ANDRÉ. *Jacques Duclos m'a dit.* Paris: Dervy, 1956. 224 p. Purports to be a record of conversations with Duclos on a variety of political topics, 1952-1954, by a former Communist journalist tried in "l'affaire des fuites." The authenticity of these records is open to question. They are edited to leave the impression of a Communist threat to France.

II62 BRAYANCE, ALAIN. *Anatomie du Parti communiste français.* Paris: Denoël, 1952. 288 p. This handbook about the French Communist Party seeks to prove that the Party "has not lost its revolutionary ardor" but needs Soviet aid to triumph in France. A scholarly, dispassionate analysis of recruiting, leaders, press, trade union activities, membership statistics, and front organizations. Annexes reproduce Party statutes, questionnaires and many other documents of internal Party life. Compare with Ferlé (below) for the earlier period. [A]

II63 CAHIERS DU BOLCHÉVISME. *Les Documents de l'opposition française et réponse du Parti.* Paris: Bureau d'Éditions, 1927. 163 p. This important documentary source includes the platform of the Trotskyite opposition in the French Central Committee, the declaration of A. Treint to the Central Executive Committee of the Comintern, July 22, 1927 on the Chinese question, and the reply of the French Stalinists and resolutions of the Central Committee, November 9, 1927 against the opposition. Complete texts published by the official organ of the Party. [B]

II64 CASANOVA, LAURENT. *Le Parti communiste, les intellectuels et la nation.* 2nd. enlarged ed., Paris: Éditions Sociales, 1951. 197 p. A collection of previously published articles urging French intellectuals to accept socialist realism in the arts and the superiority of the "proletarian science" of the USSR. Raises more questions than it settles, especially concerning the dilemma of French Communist artists and scientists. By a former member of the Central Committee, purged in 1961. Bears Thorez' personal approval.

II65 CEYRAT, MAURICE. *La Politique russe et le Parti communiste français, 1920-1945.* Paris: Paix et Liberté, 1946. 112 p. An extremely hostile work, heavily-documented from primary sources. It was written for popular consumption but the long citations and notes are useful in leading scholars to further valuable material. [B]

II66 CEYRAT, MAURICE. *La Trahison permanente; Parti communiste et politique russe.* Paris: Spartacus, 1948. 164 p. A revised edition of *La Politique russe et le Parti communiste français, 1920-1945* (above).

II67 COMMUNIST INTERNATIONAL, EXECUTIVE COMMITTEE. *Klass protiv klassa; "natsionalnoe edinenie" i Kompartiia Frantsii.* Moscow: Gosizdat, 1928. 132 p. A stenographic report of the speeches of Semard, Ercoli, Thorez, Kolarov, Doriot, and others at the Ninth Plenum of the Executive Committee held in February 1928 to outline the new hard line of the French Communists preparing for the elections of 1928. Includes resolutions of the Executive Committee, of the French Party, and an open letter of the Central Committee of the French Party to its members.

II68 COTY, FRANÇOIS. *Contre le communisme.* Paris: Grasset, 1928. 359 p. This strongly anti-Communist, popular exposé of French Communist espionage, by the Right-wing editor of *Le Figaro*, is critical of de Monzie, Herriot, and Blum for their attitude toward the Soviet Union. Much undocumented but detailed information on the Communist influence in the regular army, reserve and Fédération de la Marine is included. Sketches of K. Rakovskii and V. Dovgalevskii are also presented.

II69 DALE, LEON A. *Marxism and French Labor.* N.Y.: Vantage, 1957. 273 p. A biased, uncritical survey of the French labor movement from 1789 to the present, by a former assistant to the A.F. of L. representative in Paris. It is based on extensive research, but makes no original contribution. Deals mainly with the period after 1917.

II70 DORIOT, JACQUES. *Les Colonies et le communisme.* Paris: Montaigne, 1929. 160 p. A Stalinist analysis of socialist and Communist policy toward the colonial areas, by a member of the Central Committee and deputy. Useful for comparing French Communist and Soviet views on the French Empire.

II71 DORIOT, JACQUES. *Toutes les preuves; c'est Moscou qui paie.* Paris: Flammarion, 1937. 102 p. A denunciation of French Communist ties to Moscow, by a former member of the Central Committee, Secretary-General of the Communist Youth, and deputy. Important for Soviet financing of *L'Humanité*, though it is vague about other means of Soviet influence in France. Includes a sketchy outline of Party organization as well as a list of Communist front organizations, newspapers, and organizations for foreigners in France, including the names and addresses of Party officials. [B]

II72 DUCLOS, JACQUES. *Batailles pour la république.* Paris: Éditions Sociales, 1947. 479 p. A collection of all major speeches by the

French Communist leader in the French Assemblée, November 1944-January 1947. [B]

II73 DUCLOS, JACQUES. *Izbrannye proizvedeniia.* Moscow: Gospolitizdat, 1959. 2 vols. Selected essays, speeches, and lectures by the French Communist leader.

II74 DUCLOS, JACQUES. *La Signification politique du cahier de Jacques Duclos.* Paris: Anonymous, 1952. 119 p. Photographic reproduction of thirty pages of hand-written notes purported to be from an eighty-six-page notebook taken from Duclos in May 1952 after his arrest. Includes minutes of Politburo and Secretariat meetings from April to the end of May 1952, notes on Billoux's report of his trip to Moscow, Duclos' comments on political problems and a list of important active Communists in the Provinces. Accompanied by extremely hostile commentary, this volume makes no spectacular revelations.

II75 EHRMANN, HENRY W. *French Labor from Popular Front to Liberation.* N.Y.: Oxford, 1947. 329 p. A scholarly, objective, well-documented section on the reaction of French Communists to the Nazi-Soviet Pact, by a professor of political science at the university of Colorado. Throughout the book, citations suggest further research on Communist labor's attitude toward international problems.

II76 EINAUDI, MARIO and others. *Communism in Western Europe.* Ithaca: Cornell, 1951. 239 p. Einaudi wrote a sketchy, introductory survey of Western European Communism, the reasons for its growth and the changes needed to bring about its decline. J. M. Domenach, editor of *Esprit*, contributed a superficial twelve-page history of the Party and a valuable outline of Party organization. Based on primary and secondary sources, this study is footnoted and includes a short bibliography with important articles from periodicals.

II77 FELDMAN, LLOYD. "The Soviet Impact on the French Communist Party, 1927-1931." Certificate essay, Russian Institute, Columbia, 1958. 119 p. A scholarly study of Soviet influence on the organization and discipline of the French Communist Party during its real formative years. This work is based on Russian and French primary sources and contains a four-page bibliography that includes a useful list of articles in periodicals.

II78 FERLÉ, T. *Le Communisme en France; organisation.* Paris: Bonne Presse, 1937. 346 p. (Collection "Documentation catholique.") This well-documented, thorough outline of the structure and functioning of the French Communist Party provides a good introductory sketch of the origins of the Party and reproduces in full the 1921 and 1926 Party statutes. Also includes the names and addresses of regional secretaries, membership of the Politburo, the Secretariat and Financial Control Commission, and identifies the leading victims of purges. It is a mine of information on the formation of cadres, the structure of cells and municipal elections of 1935. By a Catholic scholar, the book carries the nihil obstat and imprimatur. Compare with Brayance (above) for later period. [B]

II79 FERRAT, ANDRÉ. *Histoire du Parti communiste français.* Paris: Bureau d'Éditions, 1931. 259 p. A detailed, "official" history of the Party from its origins in 1914 to the beginning of 1930, by a former member of the Central Committee who was purged in the 1930's. The author concentrates on the period 1917-27 with the express purpose of pointing out errors of the past to young Party militants. Based on primary sources but not documented. [B]

II79A FREVIL, ZHAN (Fréville, Jean). *Rozhdenie Frantsuzskoi kommunisticheskoi partii.* Moscow: Izd. Inostrannoi lit., 1951. An important, well-documented study of the early contacts between the French Communists and Moscow, by a member of the French Party.

II80 FROSSARD, LUDOVIC O. (FROSSARD, LOUIS-OSCAR). *De Jaurès à Lénine; notes et souvenirs d'un militant.* Paris: Bibliothèque de Documentation Sociale, 1930. 303 p. Written by one of the founders of the PCF. The two annexes have valuable documentary material on the process by which the French Party joined the Comintern.

II81 FROSSARD, LUDOVIC O. *De Jaurès à Léon Blum; souvenirs d'un militant.* Paris: Flammarion, 1943. 208 p. Memoirs of a former secretary-general of the French Communist Party who resigned in 1923 after his attempts to harmonize the teachings of Lenin and Jaurès failed. Useful for French Communist ties with the Comintern before 1923. Published after the author had become a supporter of Vichy.

II82 GODUNOV, N. I. *Borba frantsuzskogo naroda protiv gitlerovskikh okkupantov i ikh soobshchnikov (1940-1944 gg.).* Moscow: Gosizdat, 1953. 168 p. An important documented study by a former Soviet secretary for cultural affairs in Paris. Contains information on the clandestine organization of the French Party unavailable elsewhere. Provides valuable insights into French Communist foreign policy. The author, who is sharply critical of De Gaulle, was disavowed in *Pravda*, January 3, 1955. [B]

II83 GOGUEL-NYEGAARD, FRANÇOIS. *La Politique des partis sous la IIIe République.* Paris: Seuil, 1946. 2 vols. Very brief, objective treatment of French Communist activity and relations with the Soviet Union. Scholarly, but lacks substantial documentation. Vol. 1 covers 1877-1932, vol. 2, 1933-39.

II84 HERVÉ, PIERRE. *Lettre à Sartre et quelques autres par la même occasion.* Paris: La Table Ronde, 1956. 252 p. A polemic denouncing left sectarianism in the French Communist Party, 1952-56; casts light on the internal struggle between Stalinists and revisionists. Includes an unpublished article attacking R. Garaudy and documents on Hervé's exclusion from the Party.

II85 HERVÉ, PIERRE. *La Révolution et les fétiches.* Paris: La Table Ronde, 1956. 204 p. A searching essay by the former *enfant terrible* of the Party, stressing the need for creative development of Marxism. A subtle, indirect attack on Stalinist dogmatism in the French Party. Led to the purge of the author.

II86 KOZHEVNIKOVA, L. P. *Rabochee i sotsialisticheskoe dvizhenie vo Frantsii v 1917-1920 gg.* Moscow: Sots.-ekon. lit., 1959. 288 p. A Soviet historian claims the split in the French workers' movement leading to the formation of the Communist Party was a result of internal class conflict influenced by the Russian Revolution. Emphasizes Lenin's role. Scholarly, useful references; primary sources.

II87 KRIEGEL, ANNIE. *Aux Origines du communisme français, 1914-1920.* Paris: Mouton, 1964. 2 vols. [A]

II88 LECOEUR, AUGUSTE. *L'Autocritique attendue.* Paris: Girault, 1955. 78 p. Apologia of a former member of the French Communist Politburo excluded from the Party in October 1954. The author is very critical of Soviet foreign policy and of the leadership of Thorez and Duclos. He reveals intra-Party strife and the Tillon affair. Unsympathetic to Marty, Lecoeur is now an independent socialist.

II89 LEFRANC, GEORGES. *Les Expériences syndicales en France de 1939 à 1950.* Paris: Aubier, 1950. 381 p. The most complete scholarly study of the Communist seizure of power in the CGT, of Communist activity in the ministries of nationalized industries, and of political strikes 1945-47. By the former secretary of l'Institut supérieur ouvrier, this work, hostile to the Communists, is based on primary sources and personal experiences. Good five-page bibliography. [B]

II90 LEFRANC, GEORGES (Jean Montreuil, pseud.). *Histoire du mouvement ouvrier en France; des origines à nos jours.* Paris: Aubier, 1946. 603 p. A scholarly history of the French labor movement, which deals briefly with Communist activities in the CGT.

II91 LORWIN, VAL R. *The French Labor Movement.* Cambridge: Harvard; London: Oxford, 1955. 346 p. This scholarly, well-written and thoughtful book includes (chapters 4-7) a survey of Communist activities in the labor movement, 1918-47. Chapter 15 gives a penetrating analysis of Soviet-inspired Communist strategy and tactics in trade unions since 1947. By a professor of economics at the University of Oregon. Excellent eleven-page annotated bibliography. [A]

II92 MANUSEVICH, A. *Borba za demokratiiu vo Frantsii.* Moscow: Gospolitizdat, 1947. 194 p. The most important secondary study from the Soviet viewpoint of Moscow's attitude toward France during World War II. Widely researched, occasionally documented, it covers the period 1941-46 and contains much information on the activities of French Communists not available elsewhere. [B]

II93 MARTY, ANDRÉ. *L'Affaire Marty.* Paris: Deux Rives, 1955. 290 p. This apologia of a former member of the French Communist Politburo excluded from the Party in December 1952 is critical of Party leadership for its passivity in 1944, tactical errors in 1952-53, and Thorez' cult of personality. An important source for understanding Marty's views, but reveals little on direct relations between the Party and the Soviet Union. Contains documents on Marty's exclusion from the Party.

II94 MARTY, ANDRÉ. *Contre la guerre impérialiste; pour la défense de l'U.R.S.S.; rapport du Comité central présenté au VIIe Congrès du Parti communiste.* Paris: Bureau d'Éditions, 1932. 158 p. This report on the nature of wars advocates turning the "imminent war" of France against the Soviet Union from an imperialist into a civil war. Reflects Stalinist views on the Sino-Japanese war and analyzes French military strength, denounces bourgeois pacifism, and demands Party mobilization for war.

II94A MICAUD, CHARLES A. *Communism and the French Left.* N.Y.: Praeger, 1962. By a professor of French origin, now teaching political science at the University of Denver. Based on extensive research and interviews in France since World War II. [A]

II94B MOSCOW, AKADEMIIA OBSHCHESTVENNYKH NAUK. *Sorok let Frantsuzskoi kommunisticheskoi partii.* Moscow: VPSh i AON pri TsK KPSS, 1961. 152 p. Five Soviet scholars and a member of the Central Committee of the French Party contribute articles on the Party's origins, the Popular Front, and the *Résistance.* Though only briefly documented from secondary sources, it does suggest new interpretations.

II95 NEUBERG, A. *Le Plan communiste d'insurrection armée; documents originaux résumés et commentés par Léon de Poncins.* Paris: Les Libertés Françaises, 1939. 120 p.

II95A REALE, EUGENIO. *Nascita del Cominform.* Milan: Mondadori, 1958. 174 p. French ed., *Avec Jacques Duclos au banc des accusés à la réunion constitutive du Kominform à Szklarska Poreba*

(*22-27 septembre 1947*). Paris: Plon, 1958. 203 p. A former prominent Italian Communist's fascinating behind-the-scenes account of the meeting of European Communist leaders at which the Cominform was founded. Critique of issues at the meeting and of personalities, views, and speeches of participants. Appended are short biographies of European Communist leaders at the meeting. [A]

II95B RED INTERNATIONAL OF LABOR UNIONS. *Petite bibliothèque de l'Internationale syndicale rouge*. Paris: 1921-30. A collection of the Profintern's most important published documents, and articles and speeches by Profintern leaders, including much material on Communist activities in the French trade union movement.

II96 RIEBER, ALFRED J. *Stalin and the French Communist Party, 1941-1947*. N.Y.: Columbia, 1962. 416 p. Based on interviews as well as French and Russian primary sources. A study of the attempt to create "popular democracy" in France through the joint efforts of Soviet leaders and French Communists, it traces shifts in Stalinist views on world revolution, the activities of French Communists in the Resistance and Soviet policy toward the United States and Great Britain. Contains a twenty-page bibliography. [A]

II97 ROSSI, ANGELO (pseud. of Angelo Tasca). *La Guerre des papillons; quatre ans de politique communiste, 1940-1944*. Paris: Les Iles d'Or, 1954. 332 p. This analysis of French Communism from 1940 to 1944 concentrates on ideology and tactical shifts in the Party line to demonstrate Party subservience to Soviet goals. There is little mention of Communist action in the Resistance organizations. The documentary evidence is almost exclusively French. Forty-eight valuable plates reproducing rare items of clandestine Communist propaganda are included. [B]

II98 ROSSI, ANGELO. *Physiologie du Parti communiste français*. Paris: Éditions Self, 1948. 465 p. Abridged English ed. *A Communist Party in Action*. New Haven: Yale, 1949. 301 p. A scholarly but very hostile treatment of the French Communist Party, June 1940–June 1941. Rossi concentrates on the organizational and propaganda activities in the army, among intellectuals, workers and peasants. A vast number of primary sources are presented, including rare clandestine Communist literature, brochures, throw-aways and wall-posters. The author, a founding member of the Italian Communist Party, later an independent French socialist, maintains that the French Communists are completely subservient to Moscow but opposes their suppression by force. [A]

II99 ROSSI, ANGELO, ed. *Les Cahiers du Bolchévisme pendant la campagne 1939-1940*. Paris: Wapler, 1952. 160 p. Photographic reproduction of rare, complete text of *Cahiers du Bolchévisme*, from the second half of 1939 to January 1940, with articles by Thorez, Marty, Dmitrov, and Molotov. This important primary source is supplemented by the author's skillful, detailed, but very hostile analysis of each article. Extensive footnotes based on primary sources correct later Communist editing of the originals.

II100 ROSSI, ANGELO, ed. *Les Communistes français pendant la Drôle de Guerre*. Paris: Les Iles d'Or, 1951. 365 p. This volume, covering French Communist policy from August 1939 to July 1940, is heavily documented with many useful bibliographical comments in citations. Lengthy quotations from primary sources are included with fifty-six valuable photo-reproductions of clandestine Communist literature in the possession of the author. French, Italian, and a few Russian sources are used in this work which repeats some of the material found in Rossi (ed.), *Cahiers du Bolchévisme, 1939-1940*, above. [B]

II101 SHULMAN, MARSHALL D. *Stalin's Foreign Policy Reappraised*. Cambridge: Harvard University Press, 1963. 320 p. A scholarly study of the origins of the Soviet policy of "peaceful coexistence" in the period 1949-52, with particular attention to the activities of the French Communist Party. Shulman, a professor at the Fletcher School of Law and Diplomacy, views France as a testing ground for Soviet tactical shifts. A useful eight-page bibliography is included. Utilizes Russian and French primary sources. Interviews with French Communists and non-Communists provided some material for this study.

II102 THOREZ, MAURICE. *Au Service du peuple de France*. Paris: Éditions du Parti communiste français, 1947. 89 p. This report to the Eleventh Party Congress summarizes Communist policy since the liberation. An important statement on the Party's dilemma between its exclusion from the government and the founding of the Cominform is included. The author supports the tactic of unity among the Big Three and unity of action with the French Left.

II103 THOREZ, MAURICE. *Fils du peuple*. Paris: Éditions Sociales Internationales, 1937. 219 p. Rev. ed., 1949. 253 p. English ed., N.Y.: 1938. Apologia in the form of an autobiography of the long-time Secretary-General of the French Communist Party. Mainly Party history with few references to personal life before 1933 and none thereafter. First revised edition adds new material up to 1949. Second revised edition alters some key facts of period 1939-45. It is most informative on pre-1933 period.

II104 THOREZ, MAURICE. *France Today and the People's Front*. N.Y.: International, 1936. 255 p. This political tract explaining the

Popular Front to non-Communists contains a general outline of the economic crisis with an interesting Communist analysis of the banking oligarchy in France.

II105 THOREZ, MAURICE. *La Lutte pour l'indépendance nationale et pour la paix; XIIe congrès national du Parti communiste français, Gennevilliers, 2-6 avril 1950.* Paris: Éditions Sociales, 1950. 95 p. A report to the Twelfth party congress on the themes of the Communist peace movement, United States responsibility for the Cold War, and the Party's program for France.

II106 THOREZ, MAURICE. *La Mission de la France dans le monde.* Paris: Éditions Sociales Internationales, 1938. 152 p. Report to the Ninth Party Congress summarizing the achievements of the Popular Front after two years and portraying this new tactic as an original French Communist contribution to World Communism.

II107 THOREZ, MAURICE. *Notre Lutte pour la paix.* Paris: Éditions Sociales Internationales, 1938. 199 p. This volume includes a preface by J. Duclos and excerpts from Thorez' speeches, January 1936-October 1938, emphasizing opposition to fascism and criticism of Nazi and Western diplomacy.

II108 THOREZ, MAURICE. *Oeuvres de Maurice Thorez.* Paris: Éditions Sociales, 1950–. Book One (in preparation); Book Two (January 1930-December 1935), 10 vols.; Book Three (January 1936-September 1938), 5 vols.; Book Four (October 1938-August 1939), 3 vols.; Book Five (October 1939-July 1944), 1 vol. This is the official Party edition of Thorez' writings, including some originally unsigned articles in clandestine *Résistance* presses. The documents have been carefully edited and occasionally cut. Compare with originals and later versions in Party publications for changes indicative of the shifting Party line. For example, compare the "Appeal of July 10, 1940" in *L'Humanité* for that date (clandestine issue), *L'Humanité*, December 12, 1947 and *Oeuvres*, vol. 5, p. 54. [A]

II109 THOREZ, MAURICE. *Une Politique de grandeur française.* Paris: Éditions Sociales, 1945. 384 p. Prefaced by J. Duclos, this volume contains extracts from the reports of Thorez to the Eighth (1936), Ninth (1937), and Tenth (1945) Congresses and to the Central Committee (1939) on the theme of reconstructing French society under Communist leadership.

II110 THOREZ, MAURICE. *Pour l'Union; Communistes et Catholiques.* Paris: Éditions Sociales, 1949. 47 p. Excerpts from the speeches of Thorez, 1936-49, advocating unity of action with Catholic republicans against Fascists, Nazi occupation forces, and "American imperialists."

II111 THOREZ, MAURICE. *Pour l'Union; le front français.* Paris: Éditions Sociales, 1949. 93 p. Prefaced by J. Duclos, this work contains excerpts from the speeches of Thorez purporting to show how "the policy of the French Communist Party reflects the interests of France."

II112 THOREZ, MAURICE, and DUCLOS, JACQUES. *Pour l'Union; Communistes et Socialistes.* Paris: Éditions Sociales, 1949. 63 p. Contains excerpts from the speeches of Thorez 1932-49, advocating fusion and/or unity of action with the Socialist Party (S.F.I.O.).

II112A TILLON, CHARLES. *Les F. T. P.* Paris: Julliard, 1962. 688 p. Memoirs of the former chief of the French Communist paramilitary forces in the *Résistance.*

II113 TROTSKII, LEV. *Kommunisticheskoe dvizhenie vo Frantsii.* Moscow: "Moskovskii rabochii," 1923. 454 p. A collection of letters from Trotskii to French Communists and Comintern documents on the French Communist Party covering the years 1919-22. An important source for the founding of the French Party. Contains a useful list of short biographies of French Communists.

II114 TSEBENKO, M., ed. *Frantsuzskie kommunisty v borbe za progressivnuiu ideologiu.* Moscow: Inostrannaia literatura, 1953. 478 p. An important collection of articles attacking revisionism, by leading French Communists, introduced and analyzed by a Soviet political specialist. Includes translated condensations of books by G. Politzer, Georges Cogniot, and J. Canapa as well as articles from *La Pensée*, *La Nouvelle Critique* and *Cahiers du Communisme*, 1945-49.

II115 WALTER, GERARD. *Histoire du Parti communiste français.* Paris: Somogy, 1948. 390 p. This scholarly study, covering the period 1917-39, is often sympathetic with French Communist views. Footnotes, chapter bibliographies, and a good seven-page general bibliography organized by subjects are included. Russian sources are used by the author, who presents detailed lists of French Communist newspapers, articles in *Cahiers du Bolchévisme* and *Bulletin Communiste.* Though outdated, this remains the best general history in print. [A]

II116 WOHL, ROBERT A. "The Soviet Union and the Formation of the French Communist Party, 1914-1925." Ph.D. dissertation, Princeton, 1961. Based on interviews with former leaders of the French Communist Party and the Third International, as well as on extensive library research. Emphasizes the growth of the relationship between the Moscow International and the French C.P.

II117 WRIGHT, GORDON. *The Reshaping of French Democracy.* N.Y.: Reynal & Hitchcock, 1948. 277 p. The most complete treatment of the Communist role in writing the constitution of the Fourth Republic, by a former American Embassy official, later professor of history at Stanford University. This perceptive, well-written study is based on primary materials including interviews and personal observations. A good bibliography is included. [B]

II118 ZÉVAÈS, ALEXANDRE B. *Histoire du socialisme et du communisme en France de 1871 à 1947.* Paris: Éditions France-Empire, 1947. 439 p. Covers the period from 1914 to 1947 in one hundred pages—very sketchily after 1939. The author drifted from Guesdism to Communism to Vichy and back to Communism after 1945. A very biased work based on primary sources, with spotty references.

a. PERIODICALS AND NEWSPAPERS ON THE FRENCH C.P.

II119 *Bulletin Communiste.* Paris: 1920-24. Official organ of the Central Committee, replaced in November 1924 by *Cahiers du Communisme.*

II120 *Cahiers du Communisme* (*Cahiers du Bolchévisme*). Paris: 1924–. The official organ of the Central Committee. Issued monthly or every two months with the exception of the period 1939-44. Includes translations of important articles from Soviet periodicals.

II121 *Cahiers du Monde Russe et Soviétique.* Paris: 1960–. Published by the École pratique des hautes études. Includes documents and scholarly articles on Franco-Soviet relations and Soviet foreign policy in general.

II122 *Est et Ouest.* Paris: 1949–. Bimonthly anti-Communist publication. Combines popular and scholarly articles, documents, bibliographies and reviews. It is an important source for French Communism, but includes material on all Communist Parties. Formerly called *B.E.I.P.I.*

II123 *L'Humanité.* Paris: 1921–. The daily organ of the French C.P. Has been under Communist control since 1921, though it was published earlier by the Socialists. Continued clandestine publication from 1939 to 1944.

Addenda

II124 CAUTE, DAVID. *Communism and the French Intellectuals.* N.Y.: Macmillan, 1964. 413 p. [A]

II125 LECOEUR, AUGUSTE. *Le Partisan.* Paris: Flammarion, 1963. 313 p.

IJ. GERMANY

1. GENERAL WORKS

(Edited by Arnold H. Price)

IJ1 BARANCA, MARIO DA. *Germania e Russia, 1921-1941; Venti Anni di Storia Diplomatica.* Milan: Istituto per gli Studi di Politica Internazionale, 1942. 141 p.

IJ2 CARR, EDWARD H. *German-Soviet Relations between the Two World Wars, 1919-1939.* Baltimore: Johns Hopkins, 1951. 146 p. German ed., 1955. Six lectures delivered at Johns Hopkins by the well-known British historian. [B]

IJ3 GERMANY, AUSWÄRTIGES AMT. *Documents on German Foreign Policy, 1918-1945; From the Archives of the German Foreign Ministry.* Ed. by R. J. Sontag and others. Washington: G.P.O.; London: H. M. Stationery Office, 1949–. German ed., Baden-Baden: Impr. nationale, 1950–. French ed., Paris: Plon, 1950–. A multi-volume work divided chronologically into series. Series C, of which three volumes have appeared (1957–), covers 1933-37. Eleven volumes of series D (1937-45) have been published. This is the basic publication of German Foreign Office records, undertaken by a group of experts for the British, French, and American governments. The documents for the Weimar period are being edited under the auspices of the government of the Federal Republic of Germany. [A]

IJ4 HALLE, UNIVERSITÄT, INSTITUT FÜR GESCHICHTE DER VÖLKER DER UdSSR. *Proletarischer Internationalismus.* Berlin: 1961. 235 p. Materials of a symposium arranged by the University's Institut für Geschichte der Völker der UdSSR, in Halle, November 6-7, 1959. Lectures deal with the multinational character of the USSR, the relevant role of proletarian internationalism, and with the relations between the German nation and the nations of the USSR between 1917 and now.

IJ5 HILGER, GUSTAV, and MEYER, ALFRED G. *The Incompatible Allies; A Memoir-History of German-Soviet Relations, 1918-1941.* N.Y.: Macmillan, 1953. 350 p. German ed., *Wir und der Kreml.* Frankfurt am Main: A. Metzner, 1956. Informative memoirs of a German diplomat who spent many years in the German embassy in Moscow. In writing the book he was assisted by Prof. Meyer of Michigan State University. [A]

IJ6 *Jahrbuch für Geschichte der UdSSR und der volksdemokratischen Länder Europas.* Berlin: Rütten & Loening, 1956–. Title varies: 1956-

58: *Jahrbuch für Geschichte der deutsch-slawischen Beziehungen und Geschichte Ost- und Mitteleuropas.* Studies in the *Jahrbuch* are focused on Russian-German relations based on revolutionary events and wars for freedom.

IJ7 LENIN, VLADIMIR I. *Über Deutschland und die deutsche Arbeiterbewegung; aus Schriften, Reden, Briefen.* Berlin: Dietz, 1957. 695 p. An East German selection from Lenin's works, including official papers.

IJ8 ROSENFELD, GÜNTER. *Sowjetrussland und Deutschland, 1917-1922.* Berlin: Akademie-Verlag, 1960. 423 p. A serious contribution, though presented within the framework of Communist ideological restrictions. It relies on both German and Russian publications, and also on Soviet and particularly East German archival records. Has an extensive bibliography and contributes some new information to our knowledge of this period.

IJ9 RÜHLE, JÜRGEN. *Literatur und Revolution; die Schriftsteller und der Kommunismus.* Cologne: Kiepenheuer & Witsch, 1960. 611 p. This work by its organization in three parts (USSR, Germany, and other) stresses Soviet-German affinities. It provides a panorama of Communist and other dissident writers. [B]

IJ10 STECHERT, KURT. *Tyskland och Sovjetunionen.* Stockholm: Kooperativa Förbundets Bokförlag, 1940. 124 p. A very general survey of German-Soviet relations in the inter-war period.

IJ11 TRÖMEL, C. *Die Entwicklung der deutsch-sowjetrussischen Handelsbeziehungen seit 1928 unter besonderer Berücksichtigung ihrer handelsvertraglichen Grundlagen.* Leipzig: 1939. 118 p.

IJ12 WÜST, EDUARD. *Die Finanzierung der deutschen Lieferungen nach Sowjet-Russland in den Jahren 1925 bis 1936.* Speyer a. Rh.: Pilger, 1938. 106 p. An analysis relying mostly on newspaper and periodical articles, based on a Heidelberg dissertation.

2. IMPERIAL GERMANY, 1917-1918

(Edited by Arnold H. Price)

IJ13 BOTHMER, KARL B. L. F. *Mit Graf Mirbach in Moskau; Tagebuchaufzeichnungen und Aktenstücke vom 19. April bis 24. August 1918.* Tübingen: Osiander'sche Buchhandlung, 1922. 157 p. Memoirs of and documents relating to the first German diplomatic representative accredited to the Soviet government, Mirbach, who was murdered on July 8, 1918.

IJ14 BRÄNDSTRÖM, ELSA. *Unter Kriegsgefangenen in Russland und Sibirien, 1914-1920.* Berlin: Deutsche Verlagsgesellschaft für Politik und Geschichte, 1922. 134 p. 2nd ed., Leipzig: Koehler & Amelang, 1931. 241 p. English ed., *Among Prisoners of War in Russia and Siberia.* London: Hutchinson, 1929. 284 p. Translations from the Swedish of the account of the Swedish Red Cross delegate for prisoners of war in Russia during World War I. This is one of the great humanitarian epics.

IJ15 BRIUNIN, V. G. *Der erste Wiederhall in der deutschen Arbeiterklasse auf die grosse sozialistische Oktoberrevolution und den Friedensvorschlag der Sowjetregierung.* Berlin: Akademie-Verlag, 1957. 44 p. A short study by a Soviet author, who also wrote "Die deutsche Regierung und der Friedensvorschlag der Sowjetregierung (November-Dezember 1917)," *Zeitschrift für Geschichtswissenschaft,* v (1957), 964-1010. Both are based on German archival material.

IJ16 FISCHER, FRITZ. "Deutsche Kriegsziele, Revolutionierung und Separatfrieden im Osten 1914-1918." *Historische Zeitschrift*, Vol. 188, no. 2 (October, 1959), pp. 249-310. A critical discussion of the problem of German war aims in the East, based largely on unpublished German Foreign Office material. [A]

IJ17 GERMANY, AUSWÄRTIGES AMT. *Germany and the Revolution in Russia, 1915-1918; Documents from the Archives of the German Foreign Ministry.* Ed. by Z. A. B. Zeman. London and N.Y.: Oxford, 1958. 157 p. A critical and important edition of German Foreign Office records pertaining to Germany's Eastern wartime policy, excluding the Brest-Litovsk negotiations. Of special interest are the references to financial aid given by the German government to the Bolsheviks to facilitate their rise to power. [A]

IJ18 GERMANY, AUSWÄRTIGES AMT. *Lenins Rückkehr nach Russland, 1917: die deutschen Akten.* Ed. by Werner Hahlweg. Leiden: Brill, 1957. 139 p. A basic collection of German documents essential for the understanding of Soviet relations with the German Imperial Government. Critically edited by a well-known German historian. [A]

IJ19 KOMMISSION DER HISTORIKER DER DDR UND DER UDSSR. *Protokoll der wissenschaftlichen Tagung in Leipzig vom 25. bis 30. November 1957. Die Oktoberrevolution und Deutschland; Referate und Diskussion zum Thema: Der Einfluss der Grossen Sozialistischen Oktoberrevolution auf Deutschland.* Ed. by Albert Schreiner. Berlin: Akademie-Verlag, 1958. 494 p. A collection of papers presented by East German and some Soviet historians (many of them young staff members) on various aspects of Soviet-German relationships during World War I. Based on published and unpublished (mostly East German) material.

IJ20 *Krakh germanskoi okkupatsii na Ukraine (po dokumentam okkupantov).* Ed. by M. Gorkii and others. Moscow: Ogiz, 1936. 205 p. German ed., *Die deutsche Okkupation der Ukraine.* Strasbourg: Promethée, 1937. 246 p. Soviet publication of secret German documents relating to German and Austro-Hungarian relations with the Ukraine in 1918. While the documents are believed to be genuine, their selection may have been slanted so as to identify Ukrainian independence as being closely linked with German oppression. See H. C. Meyer's "Germans in the Ukraine," *The American Slavic and East European Review*, IX, 105.

IJ21 MINTZ, ISAAK, and GORODETSKII, E. N., eds. *Dokumenty o razgrome germanskikh okkupatov na Ukraine v 1918 godu.* Moscow: 1942. 239 p. Publication of Soviet records pertaining to German military operations in the Ukraine in 1918.

IJ22 MOSCOW, INSTITUT MARKSA-LENINA-ENGELSA. *Razgrom nemetskikh zakhvatchikov v 1918 godu; sbornik materialov i dokumentov.* Moscow: Gospolitizdat, 1943. 335 p. A wartime Soviet publication of documents relating to 1918 German military operations in the East.

IJ23 VOLKMANN, ERICH O. *Der Marxismus und das deutsche Heer im Weltkriege.* Berlin: Hobbing, 1925. 319 p. The value of this work lies in the fact that the author had access to German central archives and used and reprinted a number of documents.

a. *TREATY OF BREST-LITOVSK*

IJ24 BEACH, PETER K. "Lenin's Defense of a Separate Peace with the Central Powers." Certificate essay, Russian Institute, Columbia, 1954. 73 p.

IJ25 CZERNIN VON UND ZU CHUDENITZ, OTTOKAR. *Im Weltkriege.* Berlin-Vienna: Ullstein, 1919. 428 p. English ed., *In the World War.* London: Cassell, 1919. 382 p. Memoirs of the Austro-Hungarian Minister for Foreign Affairs and chief delegate to Brest-Litovsk. Contains partial reprints of his diary and correspondence.

IJ26 DRAHN, ERNST, ed. *Brest-Litowsk; Reden, Aufrufe und Manifeste der russischen Volkskommissare Trotzki, Lenin, Joffe, Radek u. a. m. anlässlich der russisch-deutschen Friedensverhandlungen im Winter 1917-18.* Berlin: Malik, 1920. 72 p.

IJ27 HAHLWEG, WERNER. *Der Diktatfriede von Brest-Litowsk 1918 und die bolschewistische Weltrevolution.* Münster: Aschendorff, 1960. 87 p. A reworked paper by a German historian who has made himself thoroughly familiar with the subject matter. This study reviews the present status of research on the Brest-Litovsk treaty and summarizes also the author's own findings. Relies heavily on unpublished German Foreign Office archives. [A]

IJ28 HOFFMANN, MAX (GENERAL). *Aufzeichnungen.* Berlin: Verlag für Kulturpolitik, 1928. 2 vols. English ed., *War Diaries and Other Papers.* London: Secker, 1929. 2 vols. Hoffmann was chief of staff of German forces in the East and the official delegate of the German High Command at Brest-Litovsk. This is a collection of memoirs, diaries, and other writings.

IJ29 HORAK, S. "Der Brest-Litowsker Friede zwischen der Ukraine und den Mittelmächten vom 9. Februar 1918 in seinen Auswirkungen auf die politische Entwicklung der Ukraine." Dissertation, Erlangen, 1949.

IJ30 JOHN, VOLKWART. *Brest-Litowsk; Verhandlungen und Friedensverträge im Osten 1917 bis 1918.* Stuttgart: Kohlhammer, 1937. 149 p. An attempt by a young German scholar to provide a basic study of the Brest-Litovsk treaty. Relies on published material, unpublished archives (from the Austrian state archives), and personal interviews. Has a solid bibliography and reprints some of the original material. Written with technical competence, but lacks depth of interpretation. [B]

IJ31 KAMENEV, LEV B. (pseud. of Lev Rosenfeld). *Borba za mir. Otchet o mirnykh peregovorakh v Breste. S prilozheniem dogovora o peremirii, germanskikh i russkikh uslovii mira i deklaratsii i etnograficheskoi politicheskoi i voennoi karty predlozhennoi germantsami granits.* Petrograd: Izd. Zhizn i znanie, 1918. 82 p.

IJ32 KÜHLMANN, RICHARD VON. *Erinnerungen.* Heidelberg: Schneider, 1948. 590 p. Memoirs of the German Secretary of State for Foreign Affairs (1917-18) and head of the German peace delegation at Brest-Litovsk. The memoirs appear to have been written many years after the events they describe, probably during the last years of the Nazi period. The author's memory is not entirely at its best and the book should be used with caution. Reveals little that is new on German-Soviet relations.

IJ33 LENIN, VLADIMIR I. *Lenin i Brestskii mir; Stati i rechi N. Lenina v 1918 godu o Brestskom mire.* Moscow: Gosizdat, 1924. 117 p. A collection of articles and speeches by Lenin on the Treaty of Brest-Litovsk.

IJ34 LEVIN, DAVID B. *Oktiabrskaia revoliutsia i Brestskii mir.* Moscow: 1930. 95 p. A monograph on the effects of the October Revolution on Germany.

IJ35 MAIOROV, SEMEN M. *Borba Sovetskoi Rossii za ukhod iz imperialisticheskoi voiny.* Moscow: Gospolitizdat, 1959. 294 p. Discusses Soviet peace policies in 1917-18 in a wide framework. Has notes and bibliography, but relies mostly on Soviet publications.

IJ36 MASLOVSKII-MSTISLAVSKII, SERGEI D. (S. Mstislavskii, pseud.). *Brestskie peregovory; iz dnevnika.* 2nd ed. Petrograd: 1918. Excerpts from the memoirs of a Soviet participant in the Brest-Litovsk negotiations. Includes documents.

IJ37 NIESSEL, HENRI A. *Le Triomphe des Bolcheviks et la paix de Brest-Litovsk.* Paris: Plon, 1940. 381 p. Memoirs of the chief of the French mission in Russia.

IJ38 RUSSIA (1917– RSFSR), NARODNYI KOMISSARIAT PO INOSTRANNYM DELAM. *Brest-Litovskaia konferentsiia; zasedaniia Ekonomicheskoi i pravovoi komissii (protokoly).* Edited by B. E. Shtein. Moscow: NKID, 1923. 154 p. Protocols of the legal and economic negotiations of the peace conference at Brest-Litovsk. [B]

IJ39 RUSSIA (1917– RSFSR), NARODNYI KOMISSARIAT PO INOSTRANNYM DELAM. *Mirnye peregovory v Brest-Litovske s 22/9 dekabria 1917 g. po 3 marta (18 fevralia) 1918 g.* Vol. I. *Plenarnye zasedaniia; zasedaniia politicheskoi komissii; polnyi tekst stenogramm.* Ed. by A. A. Joffe and preface by Leon D. Trotskii. Moscow: NKID, 1920. 268 p. Protocols of the negotiations between the Soviets and Germans at Brest-Litovsk; stenographic text with notes. [A]

IJ40 *Texts of the Russian "Peace."* Washington: G.P.O., 1918. 233 p. The Russian peace treaty and other documents in English translation.

IJ41 *Texts of the Ukraine "Peace."* Washington: G.P.O., 1918. 160 p. English text of the treaty and other documents.

IJ42 U.S. DEPARTMENT OF STATE. *Proceedings of the Brest-Litovsk Peace Conference; the Peace Negotiations Between Russia and the Central Powers, 21 November 1917-3 March 1918.* Washington: G.P.O., 1918. 187 p. Texts of official releases (mostly Russian and German) on negotiations. Sources are indicated. Taken largely from British *Daily Review of the Foreign Press.*

IJ43 VELTMAN, MIKHAIL (Mikhail P. Pavlovich, pseud.). *Brestskii mir i usloviia ekonomicheskogo vozrozhdeniia Rossii.* Moscow: 1918. 87 p.

IJ44 WHEELER-BENNETT, JOHN W. *Brest-Litovsk; the Forgotten Peace.* London: Macmillan, 1938; N.Y.: Morrow, 1939. 478 p. The best all around study of the treaty of Brest-Litovsk. Based on published material and on personal interviews, it carries the narrative to November 1918. Written for the 20th anniversary of the treaty, its evaluations are mostly presented within a framework of subsequent Nazi and Soviet developments. Factual in detail, sound in opinion. It is not conceived primarily as a contribution to W.W.I diplomatic history. [A]

3. GERMAN REVOLUTIONARY MOVEMENT, 1917-1923

(Edited by Eric Waldman and Arnold H. Price)

IJ45 AKADEMIE DER WISSENSCHAFTEN, BERLIN, INSTITUT FÜR GESCHICHTE. *Revolutionäre Ereignisse und Probleme in Deutschland während der Periode der Grossen Sozialistischen Oktoberrevolution, 1917-1918; Beiträge zum 40. Jahrestag der Grossen Sozialistischen Oktoberrevolution.* Ed. by Albert Schreiner. Berlin: Akademie, 1957. 353 p. An East German work emphasizing internal German developments in 1917-18. Based on published material and unpublished East German archives.

IJ46 ANGRESS, WERNER T. *Stillborn Revolution: The Communist Bid for Power in Germany, 1921-1923.* Princeton, N. J.: Princeton Univ. Press, 1964. A scholarly account, based on a Ph.D. dissertation at the University of California (Berkeley).

IJ47 BERLIN, INSTITUT FÜR MARXISMUS-LENINISMUS. *Dokumente und Materialien zur Geschichte der deutschen Arbeiterbewegung.* East Berlin: Dietz, 1957–. 3 vols. to date. A highly selective collection of documents compiled by the Marxist-Leninist Institute in the DDR on orders from the Central Committee of the Socialist Unity Party. Documents include letters, newspaper extracts, proclamations, "secret" police reports, etc. The two main themes to be "proven" by this collection are: the "criminal nature" of the war, and the "treason" committed by the Social Democrats. Volume I covers the period 1914 to 1917; Volume II, 1917 to 1918; and Volume III, January to May, 1919.

IJ48 BERLIN, INSTITUT FÜR MARXISMUS-LENINISMUS. *Die Märzkämpfe 1921; mit Dokumentenanhang.* East Berlin: Dietz, 1956. 188 p. The book contains the leading lecture of a Communist sponsored conference (28 February 1956) on "The Revolutionary Struggle in March of 1921 in Central Germany—Significance and Lessons to Be Learned" by Fritz Knittel. It further contains the most important contributions made during the ensuing discussion. 31 carefully selected documents support the thesis proposed by the conference: the betrayal of the working class by the Social Democrats and right wing provocation.

IJ49 BERLIN, INSTITUT FÜR MARXISMUS-LENINISMUS. *Vorwärts und nicht vergessen; Erlebnisberichte aktiver Teilnehmer der Novemberrevolution 1918-1919*. East Berlin: Dietz, 1958. 584 p. A Communist propaganda item, this volume was published on the occasion of the 40th anniversary of the German November Revolution. The leading account is by Walter Ulbricht entitled "About the Nature of the November Revolution." The rest of the book is comprised of reports of 35 revolutionary leaders who participated in the November upheaval.

IJ50 BLUMBERG, N. B. "The German Communist Movement, 1918-1923." D.Phil. thesis, Oxford, 1950.

IJ51 BUCHNER, EBERHARD, comp. *Revolutionsdokumente; die Deutsche Revolution in der Darstellung der zeitgenössischen Presse*. Berlin: Deutsche Verlagsgesellschaft für Politik und Geschichte, 1921. Vol. I: *Im Zeichen der roten Fahne*. 400 p. A very useful collection of brief newspaper accounts covering the period October 31, 1918 to November 30, 1918. The compiler utilized a great number of newspapers. Included are also a few foreign newspaper accounts which deal with the revolutionary events of this period. Though six volumes were planned, only one was published.

IJ52 CLEMENS, WALTER C., JR. "Bolshevik Expectations of a German Revolution During War Communism." Certificate essay, Russian Institute, Columbia, 1957. 201 p.

IJ53 COPER, RUDOLF. *Failure of a Revolution, Germany in 1918-1919*. London: Cambridge University Press, 1955. 294 p. A usable presentation of the history of the German Revolution of 1918-19 by a former German journalist who presently teaches economics in the U.S. Emphasis on discussion of events and on some of the personalities involved in the revolutionary actions. No footnotes, but a short bibliography.

IJ54 DRABKIN, IA. S. *Revoliutsiia 1918-1919 gg. v Germanii*. Moscow: Izd. sots.-ek. lit., 1958. 443 p. A detailed history of the German revolution from November 1918 to the Weimar constitution, by a Soviet specialist. Does not deal with German-Soviet relations. Interesting and extensive bibliography includes a great deal of non-Communist literature, but omits all items about, or by, dissident Communists.

IJ55 FLECHTHEIM, OSSIP K. *Die Kommunistische Partei Deutschlands in der Weimarer Republik*. Offenbach a. M.: Bollwerk-Verlag

K. Drott, 1948. 294 p. Chapters I and II of this work deal with the revolutionary events in 1918-19 and their relation to Communist activities. Flechtheim is the recognized authority in this field. [A]

IJ56 GERMANY, NATIONALVERSAMMLUNG, UNTERSUCHUNGSAUSSCHUSS, 1919-20, ÜBER WELTKRIEGSVERANTWORTLICHKEIT. *Die Ursachen des deutschen Zusammenbruchs im Jahre 1918.* Berlin: 1925-27. 12 vols. (Series 4 of *Das Werk des Untersuchungsausschusses, 1919-1930.*) Condensed English ed., *The Causes of the German Collapse in 1918; Sections of the Officially Authorized Report of the Commission of the German Constituent Assembly and of the German Reichstag, 1919-1928. The Selection and the Translation Officially Approved by the Commission Selected by Ralph H. Lutz.* Stanford, Cal.: Stanford U.; London: H. Mitford, Oxford, 1934. 309 p. The publication of the German parliamentary committee charged with uncovering the causes of the German collapse in 1918. Contains testimony and documents. [B]

IJ57 HABEDANK, HEINZ. *Zur Geschichte des Hamburger Aufstandes 1923.* Berlin: Dietz, 1958. 215 p. A doctoral dissertation written in the German Democratic Republic under the guidance of well-known Communist historians. It attempts to prove that the Hamburg uprising was not an irresponsible revolutionary action but a mass-supported venture to establish a German Workers' and Peasants' State. Six page bibliography.

IJ58 HERBST, WOLFGANG; MATERNA, INGO; and TROPITZ, HEINZ. *Die Novemberrevolution in Deutschland; Dokumente und Materialien.* Berlin: Volk und Wissen, 1958. 200 p. An East German compilation on the German Revolution of 1918. Selected for teachers and student teachers, but includes material from East German archives.

IJ59 *Illustrierte Geschichte der Deutschen Revolution.* Berlin: Internationaler Arbeiter-Verlag, 1929. 528 p. An official Communist account of the 1918-20 revolutionary events in Germany, based on KPD records and on contributions by leading Communists. Designed to be placed in the hands of the worker as propaganda. Objectivity is not its avowed purpose, but it does have historical merit because of its valuable source materials and photographic reproduction of rare documents.

IJ60 LINDAU, RUDOLF. *Revolutionäre Kämpfe 1918-1919; Aufsätze und Chronik.* Berlin: Dietz, 1960. 268 p. A collection of essays written at various times in the past by a KPD official who is now a professor in the Institut für Marxismus-Leninismus. The value of the book to the historian has been greatly lessened because the articles have been altered, with no indication given of the extent of the changes, and neither the time nor the place of the original publication of the article is noted. The appendix contains among other things statistical material and a chronicle of the revolutionary years, 1917-19.

IJ61 MÜLLER, HERMANN. *Die November-Revolution; Erinnerungen.* Berlin: Bücherkreis, 1928. 285 p. A general account of the revolutionary events by a sympathetic observer. He regards the Revolution as the introductory stage in the task of the liberation of the working class. The Revolution's lesson: socialist society can be built only if the working class remains united.

IJ62 MÜLLER, RICHARD. *Vom Kaiserreich zur Republik.* Berlin: Malik, 1924-25. 2 vols. Vol. I: *Ein Beitrag zur Geschichte der revolutionären Arbeiterbewegung während des Weltkrieges.* Vol. II: *Die Novemberrevolution.* A study of the origins, events, and outcome of the Revolution in Germany, by the former chairman of the Executive Council of the German Workers' and Soldiers' Councils. He defends the Revolution against those who characterize it as the "stab in the back." A large part of the work is given over to a selection of important documents, including proceedings of the Councils, Socialist proclamations, excerpts from the press, correspondence of leading government and military figures, etc.

IJ63 NOSKE, GUSTAV. *Von Kiel bis Kapp; zur Geschichte der deutschen Revolution.* Berlin: Verlag für Politik und Wirtschaft, 1920. 210 p. An important memoir by a leading government figure during the Revolution. Noske was a moderate Social-Democrat who entered the cabinet as Reichswehrminister after the military collapse of Imperial Germany. In this post he played a major role in the suppression of the Spartacist uprising; this book records his experiences and impressions.

IJ64 RADEK, KARL. *Germanskaia revoliutsiia; sbornik statei.* Moscow-Leningrad: Gosizdat, 1925. 2 vols. Volume I is exclusively concerned with German socialism prior to 1917. Volume II, *Imperializm; voina i vozniknovenie germanskoi kompartii*, is a collection of writings dealing with revolutionary prospects in Germany. It is of particular value in its treatment of the Spartacist revolt. Many of the documents are not available elsewhere.

IJ65 RADEK, KARL. *Na strazhe germanskoi revoliutsii.* Moscow: Gosizdat, 1921. 269 p. A collection of Radek speeches and articles on the German Communist movement in the years right after World War I. Virtually all of this material is available in his *Germanskaia Revoliutsiia.*

IJ66 ROSENBERG, ARTHUR. *Die Entstehung der Deutschen Republik, 1871-1918.* Berlin: E. Rowohlt, 1928. 283 p. English ed., *The*

Birth of the German Republic, 1871-1918. N.Y. and London: Oxford, 1931. 286 p. The first scholarly analysis of the 1918 Revolution and a classic in its field. While more material has been published since this work was completed, its evaluations have remained the basis for all later discussions. [A]

IJ67 SHELAVIN, KONSTANTIN I. *Avangardnye boi zapadno-evropeiskogo proletariata; ocherki germanskoi revoliutsii, 1918-1919 gg*. Leningrad: Izd. "Krasnaia gazeta," 1930. Part 2: 270 p. A narrative account of the Revolution, which adopts Karl Radek's explanation of the failure to communize Germany: the Social-Democrats succeeded in carrying a majority of the German workers to the side of the bourgeoisie. Footnotes cite Russian and German sources.

IJ68 SHERMAN, GEORGE F., JR. "Bolshevik Internationalism and the German Revolution, 1917-1918." Certificate essay, Russian Institute, Columbia, 1954. 104 p.

IJ69 SPETHMANN, HANS. *Die rote Armee an Ruhr und Rhein, aus den Kapptagen, 1920*. Berlin: R. Hobbing, 1932. 250 p. An interesting account of the impact made by the right-wing extremists' attempt to overthrow the legal government in Berlin in March 1920 (Kapp Putsch) upon the highly revolutionary situation in the industrialized region of the Ruhr and Rhine. One of the most significant events was the emergence of a fairly well-organized Red Army which tried to establish a dictatorship by the German Communists. The author relies on 22 key sources which he enumerates.

IJ70 STADTLER, E. *Die Weltkriegsrevolution*. Leipzig: Koehler, 1920. 255 p. An examination of the impact of the Bolshevik Revolution and the Spartakusbund on German politics.

IJ71 STERN, LEO, ed. *Die Auswirkungen der grossen sozialistischen Oktoberrevolution auf Deutschland*. Berlin: Rütten & Loening, 1959. 4 vols. This East German collection of mostly hitherto unpublished documents presents some 800 items covering the period from February 1917 to November 9, 1918. The material has been taken mostly from local and state archives and reflects domestic German developments. However, the records of the former royal Saxon government have been singled out for selection in depth. Volume I contains an introduction by Stern and a useful bibliography, particularly on other recent East German publications. [B]

IJ72 TIEDEMANN, HELMUT. *Sowjetrussland und die Revolutionierung Deutschlands 1917-1919*. Berlin: Verlag Dr. Emil Ebering, 1936. 154 p. Written with a pro-Nazi bias, this work tries to assign a decisive influence to Soviet propaganda in the German collapse of 1918.

For that purpose, the author has diligently collected evidence of such propaganda, but has nevertheless failed to describe and measure its impact.

IJ73 TORMIN, WALTER. *Zwischen Rätediktatur und sozialer Demokratie; die Geschichte der Rätebewegung in der deutschen Revolution 1918-1919.* Published by the Kommission für Geschichte des Parlamentarismus und der politischen Parteien in Bonn. Düsseldorf: Droste, 1954. 148 p.

IJ74 WALDMAN, ERIC. *The Spartacist Uprising of 1919 and the Crisis of the German Socialist Movement; a Study of the Relation of Political Theory and Party Practice.* Milwaukee: Marquette University Press, 1958. 248 p. An analysis of the German Communists during their period of political infancy and an examination of the impact of the Communists on the German Revolution, by a political science professor. A critical evaluation of the revolutionary events which climaxed in the abortive uprising of January 1919. 15-page bibliography. [A]

IJ75 YOUNG COMMUNIST INTERNATIONAL. *Germanskaia revoliutsiia; sbornik.* Edited by Vl. Miroshevskii. Moscow-Petrograd: "Molodaia gvardiia," 1924. 282 p.

IJ76 ZEITSCHRIFT FÜR GESCHICHTSWISSENSCHAFT. *Zum 40. Jahrestag der deutschen Novemberrevolution 1918.* Berlin: Rütten & Loening, 1958. 300 p. A series of articles on various aspects of the history of German Communism. Includes the official East German Communist position on the 1918 revolution, a historiography of non-Communist works on the November Revolution (from a Communist point of view), and a chronology for the period from October 1918 to May 1919.

IJ77 ZINOVEV, GRIGORII. *Dvenadtsat dnei v Germanii.* Petersburg: Gosizdat, 1920. 119 p. By the Bolshevik leader who was at that time the chief of the Communist International and who was very much concerned with the possibilities of revolution in Germany.

IJ78 ZINOVEV, GRIGORII. *Probleme der deutschen Revolution.* Hamburg: C. Hoym, 1923. 109 p. French ed., Paris: L'Humanité, 1923. 72 p. A relatively optimistic statement written in the fall of 1923 by the then head of the Comintern. Concerns itself with the consequences of the KPD defeat.

a. *THE BAVARIAN REVOLUTION*

(Edited by Sterling Fishman)

IJ79 BEYER, HANS. *Von der Novemberrevolution zur Räterepublik in München.* Berlin: Rütten & Loening, 1957. 184 p. A recent Communist interpretation published in East Germany. Excellent source study. Very didactic in presentation, with oversimplified Communist phraseology in places. Excellent collection of documents in the appendix.

IJ80 CATTELL, NANCY G. "Soviet Attitude toward the Bavarian Revolution of April 1919." Certificate essay, Russian Institute, Columbia, 1949. 79 p.

IJ81 FISHMAN, STERLING. "Prophets, Poets and Priests; A Study of the Men and Ideas that Made the Bavarian Revolution of 1918-1919." Ph.D. dissertation, U. of Wisconsin, 1960. An examination of the intellectual milieu of the principal revolutionists and the search for a new society after the war. Largely based on memoir and diary accounts. Extensive bibliography. [A]

IJ82 HOFMILLER, JOSEF. *Revolutionstagebuch 1918-19; Aus den Tagen der Münchner Revolution.* Leipzig: Rauch, 1938. 307 p. Invaluable anti-revolutionary diary account by a school teacher and co-editor of the *Süddeutsche Monatshefte*. Contains some excellent social analysis.

IJ83 HURWITZ, HAROLD J. "The Bavarian Revolution and Its Meaning to the Sociology of Revolution and National Development." Baccalaureate honors thesis, Bates College, 1945. Especially valuable for personal interviews which the author conducted with many important figures of the Bavarian Revolution. Purpose is to evaluate the importance of the abortive revolution in the sociology of revolution.

IJ84 KANZLER, RUD. *Bayerns Kampf gegen den Bolschewismus; Geschichte der bayerischen Einwohnerwehren.* Munich: Vark-Verlag, 1931. 295 p. More a defense of the *Einwohnerwehren* than a serious study of the Revolution. Written from the reactionary point of view.

IJ85 MÜHSAM, ERICH. *Von Eisner bis Leviné; Die Entstehung der bayerischen Räterepublik; persönlicher Rechenschaftsbericht über die Revolutionsereignisse in München vom 7. Nov. 1918 bis zum 13. April 1919.* Berlin: Fanal, 1929. Written in September, 1920, to enlighten Lenin as to the events of the Bavarian Revolution, by one of the chief participants. One of the best contemporary accounts of events. Written as a defense by the author and to correct commonly held "misconceptions" among Communists.

IJ86 NEUBAUER, HELMUT. *München und Moskau 1918-1919; zur Geschichte der Rätebewegung in Bayern.* (In the series, *Jahrbücher für Geschichte Osteuropas, Beiheft 4.*) Munich: Isar, 1958. 100 p. Deals primarily with: 1) how far the Russian Revolution provided a model for the revolutionary governments in Bavaria, and 2) relations between the Bavarian and Russian governments during the revolution. Especially valuable for extensive use of Russian sources. [A]

IJ87 RAATJES, JOHN. "The Role of Communism during the Munich Revolutionary Period, November, 1918-May, 1919." Ph.D. dissertation, U. of Illinois, 1958. 277 p. Very thorough use of official Bavarian documents. Examines the endemic nature of the Communist movement in Munich. Contains various documents and excellent bibliography. No use of Russian sources. [A]

IJ87A SCHADE, FRANZ. *Kurt Eisner und die bayerische Sozialdemokratie*. In the series, *Schriftenreihe der Forschungsstelle der Friedrich-Ebert-Stiftung*. Hanover: Verlag für Literatur und Zeitgeschehen, 1961. 200 p. The most thorough discussion of Eisner's role in the Bavarian SPD, USPD, and Revolution. Contains photographs and excellent bibliography.

IJ88 SIEGERT, MAX. *Aus Muenchens schwerster Zeit; Erinnerungen aus dem Muenchener Hauptbahnhof waehrend der Revolutions-und Raetezeit*. Regensburg: Verlagsanstalt G. J. Manz, 1928. 147 p. A memoir by the head of the guards in the Munich railroad station during the Revolution. Of minor importance.

IJ89 SLONIMSKI, M. *Eugen Leviné; Erzählung*. Translated from the Russian by Erich Salewski. Berlin: Dietz, 1949. 103 p. A literary account of the last days of the Communist leader, Eugen Leviné, in Munich. Generally reliable. A Communist justification for Leviné's actions.

IJ90 TOLLER, ERNST. *Eine Jugend in Deutschland*. Amsterdam: Querido, 1933. 287 p. English edition, *I Was a German; The Autobiography of Ernst Toller*. N.Y.: Morrow, 1934. A most literate account by the leader of the first Bavarian Council Republic, from a radical, humanitarian point of view. A frank recognition of many tactical errors.

IJ91 WERNER, PAUL (pseud. of Paul Frölich). *Die bayerische Räterepublik; Tatsachen und Kritik*. Leipzig: Franke, 1919; Petrograd, 1920. 195 p. A highly critical study. The accepted Communist interpretation until recently. The First Council Republic is condemned as a plot by Social Democrats. Frölich was later eliminated from the Party in 1929 for Bukharinist deviations.

IJ92 WOLLENBERG, ERICH. *Als Rotarmist vor München; Reportage aus der Münchener Räterepublik*. Berlin: Internationaler Arbeiterverlag, 1929. 160 p. An account of the military campaign by a man who led part of the Munich Red Army against the Whites at Dachau.

4. WEIMAR GERMANY, 1918-1933
(Edited by Alfred G. Meyer and Arnold H. Price)

IJ93 ANDERLE, ALFRED. "Die deutsch-sowjetischen Verträge von 1925/26." *Zeitschrift für Geschichtswissenschaft*, v (1957), p. 470-501. An East German study, using unpublished German archives.

IJ94 ANDERS, RUDOLF. *Der Handelsverkehr der UdSSR mit Deutschland.* Berlin: 1928. 108 p. Relies mostly on statistical material.

IJ95 BERNDORFF, HANS R. *General zwischen Ost und West; aus den Geheimnissen der Deutschen Republik.* Hamburg: Hoffmann und Campe, 1951. 320 p. A sketchy, undocumented, popular biography of General Kurt von Schleicher. Unreliable to the point of uselessness, but contains interesting tidbits about German-Soviet military relations.

IJ96 BLÜCHER, WIPERT VON. *Deutschlands Weg nach Rapallo; Erinnerungen eines Mannes aus dem zweiten Gliede.* Wiesbaden: Limes, 1951. 180 p. The author, a conservative aristocrat, was a minor foreign office official in the Ostabteilung. His book deals with German policies, views, and personalities from the summer of 1918 to 1922. Somewhat sketchy and superficial, but a useful complement to the memoirs of Dirksen and Hilger. Revealing no special knowledge of the USSR, the author in general disapproves of the so-called Rapallo spirit.

IJ97 BURCKHARDT, JULIUS. *Der deutsch-russische Rechts- und Wirtschaftsvertrag vom 12. Oktober 1925 nebst Wirtschaftsprotokoll vom 21. Dezember 1928.* Würzburg: Selbstverlag, 1930. 139 p. A printed dissertation.

IJ98 CLEINOW, GEORGE, ed. *Die deutsch-russischen Rechts- und Wirtschaftsverträge nebst Konsularvertrag vom 12. Oktober 1925.* Berlin: R. Hobbing, 1926. 358 p. Contains texts of treaties and other agreements, diplomatic notes, and also commentary and bibliogaphy. [B]

IJ99 CURTIUS, JULIUS. *Sechs Jahre Minister der Deutschen Republik.* Heidelberg: Winter, 1948. 274 p. Memoirs of the German statesman who was Minister of Foreign Affairs, 1929-31. The parts on foreign affairs were written after 1945. A brief section is devoted to his trip to the USSR in 1932.

IJ100 DEUTSCH, OTTO. *Die Technik des Russlandsgeschäftes.* Berlin; Vienna: Springer, 1928. 132 p. A technical presentation; also contains statistical material.

IJ101 DEUTSCH-RUSSISCHER VEREIN ZUR PFLEGE UND FOERDERUNG DER GEGENSEITIGEN HANDELSBEZIEHUN-

GEN, BERLIN. *Deutsch-Russisches Vertragswerk vom 12. Oktober 1925*. Ed. by Rafael Glanz. Berlin: R. von Decker, 1926. 300 p. A detailed commentary, in the style of German legal commentaries, on the commercial and consular treaty system of 1925, edited by the legal counsel of the German-Russian Association for the Furtherance of Mutual Trade Relations. Meant as a handbook for people interested in trade relations with the USSR, it is still a valuable summary of the background and implications of each article contained in the treaties. [B]

IJ102 DIRKSEN, HERBERT VON. *Moskau-Tokio-London*. Stuttgart: Kohlhammer, 1949. 279 p. English ed., Norman: U. of Oklahoma Press, 1952. Autobiography of the man who served as a consular official in Kiev, 1918-19, as chief of the Eastern Department of the German Foreign Office, 1925-28, and as Ambassador in Moscow from 1928 to 1933. An important source about German policies in the 1920s, even though there are matters, such as military collaboration, about which he has said less than he knows. Unassuming but informative. [B]

IJ103 EICHHORN, LOUIS. *Die Handelsbeziehungen Deutschlands zu Sowjetrussland; ein Beitrag zum Problem des deutsch-sowjetrussischen Handelsverkehrs*. Rostock: C. Hinstorffs, 1930. 94 p. A University of Rostock dissertation.

IJ104 ERUSALIMSKII, ARKADII S. *Germaniia, antanta i SSSR*. Moscow: Izd. Kommunisticheskoi akad., 1928. 187 p. An outstanding specialist on Germany within the Soviet Foreign Office attempts to analyze, from a fairly narrow diplomatic point of view, the motives and aims of German foreign policy, especially in relation to England, France, and the USSR. His main theme: Germany's successful attempt to remain neutral between East and West. An optimistic and sober book, on the whole, it is valuable because it probably reflects views prevailing in the Soviet Foreign Office at the time. This is vol. 3 in the series: *Desiat let kapitalisticheskogo okruzheniia SSSR*, issued by the Kommunisticheskaia Akademiia. [B]

IJ105 EULER, HEINRICH. *Die Aussenpolitik der Weimarer Republik 1918-1923*. Aschaffenburg: Pattloch, 1957. 471 p. A detailed treatment of German foreign policy from November 1918 to the occupation of the Ruhr in 1923.

IJ106 FISHER, ERNEST F., JR. "Road to Rapallo, A Study of Walter Rathenau and German Foreign Policy, 1919-1922." Ph.D. dissertation, U. of Wisconsin, 1952.

IJ107 FREUND, GERALD. *Unholy Alliance; Russian-German Relations from the Treaty of Brest-Litovsk to the Treaty of Berlin*. N.Y.: Harcourt, Brace; London: Chatto and Windus, 1957. 283 p. An important work, based on German military and diplomatic archives, by an author who does not seem to know Russian. Treats German relations with the USSR (diplomatic as well as military) and Germany's place in the plans of the Communist International, from 1918 to 1926. Contains the most complete and valuable bibliography of Western literature regarding this period. [A]

IJ108 GASIOROWSKI, ZYGMUNT J. "The Russian Overture to Germany of December 1924." *Journal of Modern History*, xxx (1958), p. 99-117. A solid study, relying on unpublished material. [A]

IJ109 GATZKE, HANS W. *Stresemann and the Rearmament of Germany.* Baltimore: Johns Hopkins Univ. Press, 1954. 132 p. By an American scholar, using Stresemann's archives. Diplomatic relations with the USSR are mentioned only occasionally, but one entire chapter deals with military relations. Valuable bibliography and notes. See also his "Russo-German Military Collaboration during the Weimar Republic," *Amer. Hist. Review*, vol. 63, no. 3 (April 1958).

IJ110 GOLTZ, RÜDIGER, GRAF VON DER. *Meine Sendung in Finnland und im Baltikum.* Leipzig: 1920. Memoirs of the German commander in Finland and the Baltic states, 1918-19.

IJ111 HELBIG, HERBERT. *Die Träger der Rapallo-Politik.* Göttingen: Vandenhoeck & Ruprecht, 1958. 214 p. Three scholarly essays, based on important unpublished documents as well as published sources, dealing with (a) the preparations for the Rapallo Treaty after the November 1918 armistice; (b) the personality and policies of Count Brockdorff-Rantzau, and his relations with Seeckt, Stresemann, Hindenburg, Chicherin, and others; and (c) German-Soviet military relations. [B]

IJ112 HILGER, GUSTAV, and MEYER, ALFRED G. *The Incompatible Allies; a Memoir-History of German-Soviet Relations, 1918-1941.* N.Y.: Macmillan, 1953. 350 p. Memoirs of a German diplomat who served about 20 years in the Moscow Embassy, and whose memory (or that of his collaborator) seems to have been refreshed by access to the captured German archives. Thorough coverage of diplomatic, military, and economic relations, with attempts to see at least Soviet policies within the framework of broader problems. Contains little information about politics within the German Foreign Office. [A]

IJ113 HILLMEISTER, LEO. *Russischer Aussenhandel in der Nachkriegszeit unter besonderer Berücksichtigung zu Deutschland.* München-Gladbach: Volksverein, 1928. 122 p. A University of Cologne dissertation.

IJ114 IAKOVIN, GRIGORII IA. *Politicheskoe razvitie sovremennoi Germanii.* Leningrad: "Priboi," 1927. 294 p.

IJ115 KLEIN, FRITZ. *Die diplomatischen Beziehungen Deutschlands zur Sowjetunion, 1917-1932.* Berlin: Rütten & Loening, 1952. 190 p. A monograph treating only diplomatic relations by an East German author who did not have access to the archives. Western sources are used, but only the most carefully selected Soviet sources—a great limitation. Leaving out much that is known in the West, this work is no more than an interesting statement of the Soviet line on German-Soviet relations.

IJ116 KOBLIAKOV, I. K. *Ot Bresta do Rapallo; ocherki istorii sovetsko-germanskikh otnoshenii s 1918 po 1922 g.* Moscow: Gos. izd. polit. lit., 1954. 249 p. German ed., Berlin: 1956. 302 p. Distorting all facts in order to prove an eternal conspiracy of Wall Street, Junkers, Social-Democrats, Trotskyites, and Bukharinites against the USSR, this work is without scholarly value.

IJ117 KOCHAN, LIONEL E. *Russia and the Weimar Republic.* Cambridge, England: Bowes and Bowes, 1954. 190 p. German ed., 1955. A British scholar's learned monograph dealing with diplomatic and military relations, as well as with the relations between the Communist International and the KPD. Based on extensive reading of Western and Soviet sources. Excellent bibliography. [A]

IJ118 KOLSHORN, JOHANN. *Russland und Deutschland durch Not zur Einigung.* Leipzig: Hammer-Verlag, 1922. 202 p. An anti-semitic, Fascist pamphlet about Bolshevism, admonishing Aryans and Slavs to assume cultural hegemony in Europe in order to destroy "Jewish domination."

IJ119 LASSNER, FRANZ GEORG. "Germany, the German Army, and Greater Russia, 1871-1933." M.A. thesis, Georgetown U., 1951. 318 p. A thesis based on materials found in the archives of Generals Seeckt and Groener about the influence of the German army as the shaper of German-Russian and German-Soviet relations. Maintains that the army determined relations between the Weimar Republic and the USSR. Onesided and outdated, overestimating grossly the influence of Seeckt and other military leaders.

IJ120 LORENZ, HERBERT. *Handbuch des Aussenhandels und Verkehrs mit der UdSSR und der staats-und wirtschaftspolitischen Verhältnisse der Sowjetunion.* Berlin-Grunewald: Kurt Vowinckel, 1930. 438 p.

IJ121 MAINZ, KARL. *Die Auswirkungen des Aussenhandelsmonopols der UdSSR auf die deutsch-sowjetrussischen Wirtschaftsbezie-*

hungen; eine Untersuchung unter dem Gesichtspunkt handelspolitischer Gegenseitigkeit. Berlin: G. Stilke, 1930. 211 p. A well-documented analysis of Soviet-German trade relations with particular emphasis on economic factors. [B]

IJ122 MAISKII, I. *Sovremennaia Germaniia. (Ekonomika, politika, rabochee dvizhenie).* Moscow-Leningrad: "Krasnaia nov," 1924. 167 p.

IJ123 MELVILLE, CECIL F. *The Russian Face of Germany; an Account of the Secret Military Relations between the German and Soviet-Russian Governments.* London: Wishart, 1932. 230 p. An exposé by a Liberal, anti-German journalist of the secret dealings between the Reichswehr and Red Army in the 1920's. Based principally on the materials furnished by the German Social-Democratic Party and publicized in 1926 by the *Manchester Guardian.* Hysterical in tone, a "scoop" in its day, the book has been made obsolete, since much of the story has more recently been told in memoirs and captured documents.

IJ124 POHLE, RICHARD. *Russland und das Deutsche Reich.* Bonn: Schroeder, 1922. 142 p. A political tract written by a Baltic German, directed against Pan-Slavism and Bolshevism, and favoring a vigorous expansionist policy in the East. Deals at length with Germans in the USSR.

IJ125 RABENAU, FRIEDRICH VON. *Seeckt; Aus seinem Leben, 1918-1936.* Leipzig: 1940. 2 vols. An authorized biography by the Chief of the German Army Archives, based on unpublished private and public documents. The reader must dig painstakingly to extract tidbits of information about German policy toward the USSR, though an entire chapter deals with Seeckt's ideas on this score. The book makes no substantial revelations about German-Soviet military collaboration. To what extent the National-Socialist take-over led to distortions in this work is difficult to say.

IJ126 ROSENBAUM, KURT. "The Brockdorff-Rantzau Period: German-Russian Diplomatic Relations, 1922-1928." Ph.D. dissertation, Syracuse U., 1961. Deals primarily with Brockdorff-Rantzau's literary legacy, based on German Foreign Office records.

IJ127 ROTTER, SEYMOUR. "Soviet and Comintern Policy Toward Germany, 1919-1923; A Case Study of Strategy and Tactics." Ph.D. dissertation, Columbia U., 1954. 585 p. A study of Soviet pursuance of mutually contradictory objectives: a German proletarian revolution, and good relations with a "bourgeois" Germany. Traces Soviet and Comintern tactics in this dualism and the resultant effects. [B]

IJ128 RUGE, WOLFGANG. "Zur Problematik und Entstehungsgeschichte des Berliner Vertrages von 1926." *Zeitschrift für Ge-*

schichtswissenschaft, IX (1961), 4, p. 809-848. Written from an East German point of view, this article relies on unpublished archival material and provides an extensive discussion of recent publications.

IJ129 RUSSIA (1923- USSR), TREATIES, ETC. *Sovetsko-germanskii torgovyi dogovor 12 oktiabria 1925 g.* By B. E. Stein (Shtein) and A. Iu. Rapoport. Moscow: Ekonomicheskaia Zhizn, 1927. 278 p. German ed., *Handels- und Wirtschaftsvertrag zwischen der UdSSR und dem Deutschen Reich, vom 12. Oktober 1925 nebst Konsularvertrag.* Explained by A. Rapoport and B. Shtein. Berlin: Handelsvertretung der UdSSR in Deutschland Informationsabteilung, 1926. 217 p. A detailed commentary on the commercial and consular treaties of 1925 by Soviet foreign office members who helped draft it. Should be read as a companion piece to *Deutsch-russisches Vertragswerk vom 12. Oktober 1925*, ed. by Rafael Glanz.

IJ130 SCHEFFER, PAUL. *Sieben Jahre Sowjetunion.* Leipzig: Bibliographisches Institut, 1930. 451 p. English ed., *Seven Years in Soviet Russia.* London: Putnam, 1931. Reports and wires of the Moscow correspondent of the *Berliner Tageblatt*, 1921-29. Scheffer's intimate contacts within the Kremlin and the Soviet Foreign Commissariat rendered him knowledgeable and sensitive. Moreover, he belonged to the inner circle of the German Embassy in Moscow. His reports are balanced, and his evaluations of German policy toward the USSR were read with attention by policy-makers. His description of the conflict between Stalin and his rivals, though vivid and interesting, is colored by his preference for Trotsky. [B]

IJ131 SCHIEDER, THEODOR. *Die Probleme des Rapallo-Vertrags; eine Studie über die deutsch-russischen Beziehungen 1922-26; Abhandlung.* Cologne: Westdeutscher Verlag, 1956. 98 p. An important essay on German-Soviet relations, by a German historian, which tries to analyze the conflict of motives and aims determining German and Soviet policies. Makes extensive use of unpublished documents. An indispensable brief work. [A]

IJ132 SOLONEVICH, TAMARA V. *Drei Jahre bei der Berliner Sowjethandelsvertretung.* Essen: Essener Verlag-Anstalt, 1939. 227 p. Memoirs of a Russian employee of the Soviet Trade Delegation in Berlin, covering 1928-31.

IJ133 STANKA, VLADAS. *Rossiia i Germaniia; proshloe, nastoiashchee, budushchee.* Berlin: Russkoe universalnoe izd., 1922. 120 p. A work by a Russian emigré, probably a narodnik, who believed that Weimar Germany and Soviet Russia might, if led by wise leaders, pioneer an international policy of world solidarity on the ruins wrought by World War I.

IJ134 STERN-RUBARTH, EDGAR (Peter Laukhard, pseud.). *Graf Brockdorff-Rantzau, Wanderer zwischen zwei Welten; ein Lebensbild.* Berlin: Reimar Hobbing, 1929. 171 p. A sympathetic biography of the German Ambassador with all the one-sidedness of a hagiography. Gives a good summary of Rantzau's views toward the USSR, his methods of work in Moscow, and his personal life.

IJ135 TRACHTENBERG, JAKOW. *Vierjahresplan der deutsch-russischen Handelsbeziehungen.* Translated from the Russian. Berlin: J. Trachtenberg, 1933. 118 p.

IJ136 WILISCH, ERHART. *Die Bedeutung der Konzessionen der Union der Sozialistischen Sowjetrepubliken für die deutsch-russischen Wirtschaftsbeziehungen.* Breslau: Priebatsch, 1932. 108 p. Discussion of the background and institutional aspects of economic concessions in Russia until 1931. Bibliography.

5. NAZI GERMANY, 1933-1945

(Edited by Gerhard L. Weinberg)

IJ137 ARMSTRONG, JOHN A. *Ukrainian Nationalism, 1939-1945.* N.Y.: Columbia Univ. Press, 1955. 322 p. A thoughtful, reliable, and well-researched work, by an American professor. Based on interviews as well as documentary sources, the book offers both a clear exposition of the complex Ukrainian nationalist movement and a picture of its position between the Germans and the Soviet authorities. A revised edition was published in 1963. [A]

IJ138 BENNETT, THOMAS H. *The Soviets and Europe, 1938-1941.* Geneva: Université de Genève, Institut universitaire de hautes études internationales, 1951. 112 p. A Ph.D. thesis by a Canadian scholar on Soviet-German relations, 1938-41, with special emphasis on factors responsible for the 1939 Nazi-Soviet Pact and on the consequences of this pact for Eastern Europe. Based on secondary and some primary sources which in 1951 were not yet fully explored.

IJ139 BLAU, GEORGE E. *The German Campaign in Russia; Planning and Operation, 1940-1942.* Washington: Dept. of the Army, 1955. 187 p. A very helpful account based on German military records; contains 17 maps.

IJ140 BREGMAN, ALEKSANDER. *Najlepszy Sojusznik Hitlera; Studium o Współpracy Niemiecko-Sowieckiej, 1939-1941.* London: Orbis, 1958. 160 p. A superficial survey based on secondary sources.

IJ141 COMMUNIST INTERNATIONAL EXECUTIVE COMMITTEE. *Der Faschismus in Deutschland.* Moscow: Verlagsgenossenschaft Ausländischer Arbeiter in der UdSSR, 1934. 282 p. A collection of speeches and reports dealing with Germany at the XIII Plenum of the Executive Committee of the Communist International in December 1933.

IJ142 DALLIN, ALEXANDER. *German Rule in Russia, 1941-1945; A Study of Occupation Policies*. N.Y.: St. Martin's Press, 1957; London: Macmillan, 1957. 695 p. German ed., Düsseldorf, 1958. A thorough, comprehensive, and reliable study; unlikely to be replaced as definitive study for many years. The author is a professor at Columbia University. [A]

IJ143 DALLIN, ALEXANDER. *Odessa, 1941-1944; A Case Study of Soviet Territory Under Foreign Rule*. Santa Monica, Calif.: RAND Corporation, 1957. 466 p. Detailed study of Soviet citizens under Rumanian rule, with comparisons of German occupation policy and practice. Includes a bibliography.

IJ144 DALLIN, ALEXANDER. *Reactions to the German Occupation of Soviet Russia*. Maxwell Air Force Base, Ala.: Air University, Human Resources Research Institute, 1952. 51 p. A survey based largely on refugee interviews, and dealing primarily with the civilian population in the German-occupied areas.

IJ145 DALLIN, ALEXANDER, comp. *The German Occupation of the USSR in World War II; A Bibliography*. Washington: External Research Staff, Office of Intelligence Research, Department of State, 1955. 76 p. A valuable aid to research, indicating location of scarce items and serials. It constitutes the bibliography for the author's *German Rule in Russia*.

IJ146 DIRKSEN, HERBERT VON. *Moscow, Tokyo, London; Twenty Years of German Foreign Policy*. London: Hutchinson, 1951; Norman, Oklahoma: University of Oklahoma Press, 1952. 288 p. German ed., Stuttgart: Kohlhammer, 1949. Includes memoirs of author as German ambassador to Russia, 1928-33 and as Ambassador to England in 1939. Illuminates the background of the Nazi-Soviet Pact, as viewed from London. The German and English editions differ. Dirksen's papers were captured by the Russians and published in: GERMANY, AUSWÄRTIGES AMT, *Documents and Materials Relating to the Eve of the Second World War*, vol. 2 (see IJ157).

IJ147 DODD, WILLIAM E. *Ambassador Dodd's Diary*, 1933-1938. N.Y.: Harcourt, 1941. 464 p. Observations in Berlin by the American ambassador, with only incidental references to German-Soviet relations.

IJ148 *Dokumenty obviniaiut; sbornik dokumentov o chudovishchnykh zverstvakh germanskikh vlastei na vremenno zakhvachennykh imi sovetskikh territoriiakh.* Moscow: Ogiz, 1943-45. 2 vols. Two volumes of German and Russian documents on German atrocities in the occupied USSR.

IJ149 DUROSELLE, JEAN BAPTISTE, and others. *Les Relations Germano-Soviétiques de 1933 á 1939.* Paris: Colin, 1954. 279 p. Surveys of German-Soviet relations 1933-36, 1936-39, Litvinov's career, and German-Soviet military relations 1920-39. Dated in part, but still extremely useful. [A]

IJ150 EINSIEDEL, HEINRICH VON. *Tagebuch der Versuchung.* Berlin: Pontes, 1950. 239 p. English ed., *I Joined the Russians.* New Haven: Yale Univ. Press, 1953. 306 p. British ed., *The Shadow of Stalingrad.* London: A. Wingate, 1953. 254 p. Memoirs of a founder of the Nationalkomitee "Freies Deutschland," an organization of anti-Nazis recruited from German prisoners of war captured by the Russians, especially at and after Stalingrad. He later renounced Communism.

IJ151 ELLIS, EVI. "Russo-German Relations in 1939: The Territorial Aspects of the Pact and Their Significance." Ph.D. dissertation, U. of Chicago, 1952.

IJ151A FABRY, PHILIPP W. *Der Hitler-Stalin-Pakt, 1939-1941.* Darmstadt: Fundus: 1962. 535 p. Very detailed but quite unreliable. Apologetic in tone.

IJ152 FISCHER, GEORGE. *Soviet Opposition to Stalin.* Cambridge: Harvard Univ. Press, 1952. 230 p. Material on the German occupation and Soviet nationals collaborating with the Germans, including General Vlasov and his army of former Soviet citizens. The author is a professor at Cornell University. Much of the information was based on interviews with Soviet refugees who participated in the various anti-Communist movements during World War II. [B]

IJ153 FISCHER, LOUIS. *Stalin and Hitler; The Reasons for and the Results of the Nazi-Bolshevik Pact.* N.Y.: The Nation, 1940; London: Penguin Books, 1941. 95 p. A very thoughtful analysis, by the former Moscow correspondent of *The Nation*, written during the Russo-Finnish War, 1939-40.

IJ154 FREYTAGH-LORIGHOVEN, AXEL VON. *Deutschlands Aussenpolitik 1933-1941.* 9th ed. Berlin: O. Stollberg, 1941. 345 p. French ed., Paris, 1942. A survey from a semi-official National Socialist point of view. Many editions in various languages.

IJ155 GAFENCU, GRIGORE. *Préliminaries de la guerre à l'est de l'accord de Moscou, 21 août 1939, aux hostilités en Russie, 22 juin,*

1941. Paris: Egloff, 1945. 406 p. English ed., *Prelude to the Russian Campaign*. London: 1945. German ed., Zurich: 1944. Italian ed., Milan: 1946. Spanish ed., Madrid: 1945. A combination memoir and study by the former Rumanian Foreign Minister (1938-40) and Ambassador to Moscow (1940-41). Though seen from the perspective of a participant in the events and written before the opening of any documents, this book is both suggestive and informative. [B]

IJ156 GERMANY, AUSWÄRTIGES AMT. *Die Beziehungen zwischen Deutschland und der Sowjetunion 1939-1941; Dokumente des Auswärtigen Amtes aus den Archiven des Auswärtigen Amtes und der Deutschen Botschaft in Moskau*. Ed. by Alfred Seidl. Tübingen: H. Laupp, 1949. 414 p. A collection including a few items not in the State Department edition (IJ159), but omitting others. [B]

IJ157 GERMANY, AUSWÄRTIGES AMT. *Documents and Materials Relating to the Eve of the Second World War*. Moscow: Foreign Languages Publishing House; N. Y.: International Pub., 1948. 2 vols. French ed., Moscow: 1948. German ed., Moscow: 1948-49. Russian ed., Moscow: Gospolitizdat, 1948. Published by the Ministry of Foreign Affairs of the USSR in response to the publication by the State Department of *Nazi-Soviet Relations, 1939-1941*, (see below) these documents were selected to prove the guilt of the West in its dealings with Hitler, and thus to justify the Nazi-Soviet Pact. Volume I, dealing with 1937-38, consists of records of conversations of Hitler, Ribbentrop and others with various foreign statesmen, etc. Volume II consists of the private papers of Herbert von Dirksen, German Ambassador to Moscow, Tokyo, and London in the period between the two World Wars. These papers, found by the Soviet army, are particularly interesting for events leading up to the Nazi-Soviet Pact, as viewed from England. [A]

IJ158 GERMANY, AUSWÄRTIGES AMT. *Documents on German Foreign Policy, 1918-1945; From the Archives of the German Foreign Ministry*. Ed. by R. J. Sontag and others. Washington: G.P.O.; London: H. M. Stationery Office, 1949–. German ed., Baden-Baden: Impr. nationale, 1950-56; Keppler, 1961–. French ed., Paris: Plon, 1950–. Series C, 1933-36, and Series D, 1937-45 contain basic materials for German relations with the Soviet Union. [A]

IJ159 GERMANY, AUSWÄRTIGES AMT. *Nazi-Soviet Relations, 1939-41: Documents from the Archives of the German Foreign Office*. Ed. by Raymond J. Sontag and James S. Beddie. Washington: Department of State, 1948; N.Y.: Didier, 1948. 363 p. French ed., Paris, 1948. German ed., Berlin: 1948. Japanese ed., 1948. A basic documentary collection on the background of the Nazi-Soviet Pact of August

1939, and on Soviet-German relations up to the German attack on the Soviet Union. The German edition is the most reliable. Superseded by volumes VI ff. of Series D of *Documents on German Foreign Policy, 1918-1945*. In response to this volume the Soviets issued their own collection. (See above: *Documents and Materials Relating to the Eve of the Second World War*, IJ157). [A]

IJ160 GERMANY (TERRITORY UNDER ALLIED OCCUPATION, 1945- U.S. ZONE), MILITARY TRIBUNALS. *Trials of War Criminals before the Nuremberg Military Tribunals*. Vols. X-XIV. Washington: G.P.O., 1951-52. Selections from the testimony and evidence in the "High Command" and "Weizsaecker" cases of the Nuremberg subsequent proceedings. Extensive material on German policy toward the USSR and policy and practice in war and occupation.

IJ161 GERMANY, WEHRMACHT, OBERKOMMANDO. *Hitler Directs His War; The Secret Records of His Daily Military Conferences, Selected and Annotated by Felix Gilbert from the Manuscript in the University of Pennsylvania Library*. N.Y.: Oxford, 1950. 187 p. Complete German ed., Stuttgart: Deutsche Verlagsanstalt, 1962. 971 p. Excerpts from surviving fragments of stenographic notes of Hitler's situation conferences. Many relate to Eastern Front problems.

IJ162 GOERING, HERMANN, DEFENDANT. *Trial of the Major War Criminals before the International Military Tribunal, Nuremberg. 14 November 1945-1 October 1946*. Nuremberg: International Military Tribunal, 1947-49. 42 vols. Full transcript and large selection of documents from the main trial at Nuremberg. Much on German military, foreign, and occupation policy. [B]

IJ163 GREINER, G. K. E. HELMUTH. *Die Oberste Wehrmachtführung, 1939-1943*. Wiesbaden: Limes, 1951. 444 p. The author kept the war diary of the High Command of the German armed forces. The last chapter covers preparations for the attack on Russia; pp. 393-441 contain excerpts from the war diary (mainly Eastern Front) for August 1942-March 1943.

IJ164 GUDERIAN, HEINZ. *Erinnerungen eines Soldaten*. Heidelberg: Vowinckel, 1951. 462 p. Memoirs of the German Panzer Army commander on the Eastern Front in 1941 and army Chief of Staff 1944-45. Important for military history of the war.

IJ165 HALDER, FRANZ. *Diary, Covering the Period August 14, 1939 to September 24, 1942*. Nuremberg: Office of Chief Counsel for War Crimes, Office of Military Government for Germany (U.S.), 1946. 4 vols. Diary of the German army Chief of Staff, August 1939-September 1942. Basic for German-Soviet relations and war. German ed., Stuttgart: Hans-Adolf Jacobsen, 1962-64. 3 vols. [B]

IJ166 HASSELL, ULRICH VON. *Vom anderen Deutschland; aus den nachgelassenen Tagebüchern 1938-1944.* Zurich: Atlantis, 1946. 416 p. English ed., Garden City, N. Y.: Doubleday, 1947. French ed., Neuchâtel: Baconnière, 1948. Diary entries, 1938-44, by the former German ambassador to Italy, later executed by the Nazis. Touches on all aspects of German internal and foreign policy. The English edition is incomplete.

IJ166A HILGER, GUSTAV, and MEYER, ALFRED G. *The Incompatible Allies; A Memoir-History of German-Soviet Relations, 1918-1941.* N.Y.: Macmillan, 1953. 350 p. German ed. Frankfurt-am-Main, 1956. 322 p. Memoirs of a German diplomat intimately involved in German-Soviet relations. [B]

IJ167 HITLER, ADOLF. *Hitlers Zweites Buch.* Ed. by Gerhard L. Weinberg. Stuttgart: Deutsche Verlagsanstalt, 1961. English ed., *Hitler's Secret Book.* N.Y.: Grove, 1962. 230 p. Though originally written in 1928, it contains materials for understanding German policy toward Russia, 1933-45. The manuscript was discovered by Professor Weinberg among documents seized in Germany at the end of World War II. The English translation is not dependable.

IJ168 HITLER, ADOLF. *Mein Kampf.* Munich: Eher, many editions. English ed., N.Y.: Reynal and Hitchcock, 1939. 1003 p. Though written in 1924-25, this work is basic for an understanding of German policy in 1933-45. [A]

IJ169 ILNYTZKYI, ROMAN. *Deutschland und die Ukraine, 1934-1945; Tatsachen europäischer Ostpolitik.* Munich: Osteuropa Institut, 1955. 2 vols. 2nd ed.: 1958. Useful, especially for its long quotations from documents not otherwise available. Interpretation is rather one-sided.

IJ170 KAZANTSEV, ALEKSANDR S. *Tretia sila; istoriia odnoi popytki.* Frankfurt-am-Main: Posev, 1952. 372 p. An account of General Vlasov's anti-Communist Russian army, formed from Russian prisoners of war in German hands, which fought under the German flag in World War II. Nazi ideologues were never able to reconcile themselves to its existence, and consequently it never played a major role.

IJ171 KLEIST, PETER. *Zwischen Hitler und Stalin, 1939-1945; Aufzeichnungen von Dr. Peter Kleist.* Bonn: Athenäum, 1950. 344 p. Memoirs of a former official of the German Ministry for the Occupied Eastern Territories and associate of Ribbentrop, who played a major role in German-Soviet peace feelers, 1943-44. Important, but to be used with great caution. [B]

IJ172 KORDT, ERICH. *Wahn und Wirklichkeit; die Aussenpolitik des Dritten Reiches, Versuch einer Darstellung.* Stuttgart: Union Deutsche Verlagsgesellschaft, 1948. 430 p. A useful survey of all aspects of German foreign policy, by a former German diplomat.

IJ172A KRUPINSKI, KURT. *Die Komintern seit Kriegsausbruch.* Berlin: O. Stollberg, 1941. 105 p. A biased but useful survey, with special emphasis on the Comintern and Soviet attitudes toward Germany.

IJ172B LEONHARD, WOLFGANG. *Die Revolution entlässt ihre Kinder.* Cologne: Kiepenheuer & Witsch, 1956. 558 p. English ed., Chicago: Regnery, 562 p. Memoirs of a German communist who was in the Soviet Union 1935-45 and subsequently became a high functionary in Soviet-occupied Germany. An important source on Soviet attitudes toward Germany. [B]

IJ173 MEISSNER, BORIS. *Russland, die Westmächte und Deutschland; die sowjetische Deutschlandpolitik, 1943-1953.* Hamburg: Nölke, 1953. 372 p. The first part of this excellent work reviews Soviet policy toward Germany, 1943-45. [B]

IJ174 NADOLNY, RUDOLF. *Mein Beitrag.* Wiesbaden: Limes, 1955. 188 p. Memoirs of a German diplomat containing an important chapter on his ambassadorship to Russia, 1933-34.

IJ175 PRITT, DENIS NOWELL. *The State Department and the Cold War; A Commentary on its Publication, "Nazi-Soviet Relations, 1939-1941."* N.Y.: International Publishers, 1948. 96 p. A Party-line view of the 1938-45 period by a former British M.P.

IJ176 REITLINGER, GERALD. *The House Built on Sand; the Conflicts of German Policy in Russia, 1939-1945.* London: Weidenfels and Nicolson, 1960; N.Y.: Viking, 1961. 459 p. A general survey of considerable interest, but not as important as Dallin's book (IJ142). subject.

IJ177 RHODE, GOTTHOLD and WAGNER, WOLFGANG, eds. *Quellen zur Entstehung der Oder-Neisse Linie in den diplomatischen Verhandlungen während des Zweiten Weltkrieges.* Stuttgart: Brentano, 1956. 291 p. 2nd ed., 1959. English ed., *The Genesis of the Oder-Neisse Line . . . Sources and Documents.* Stuttgart: 1959. A collection of documents including many dealing with Soviet policy toward the German borders during World War II. See also: WAGNER, WOLFGANG. *Die Entstehung der Oder-Neisse-Linie. . . .*

IJ178 RIBBENTROP, JOACHIM VON. *Zwischen London und Moskau; Erinnerungen und Letzte Aufzeichnungen.* Leoni am Starnberger See: Druffel, 1953. 336 p. A wholly unreliable apologia.

IJ179 ROSSI, AMILCARE (pseud. of Angelo Tasca). *Deux Ans d'alliance Germano-Soviétique, août 1939-juin 1941.* Paris: A. Fayard, 1949. 225 p. English ed., *The Russo-German Alliance, August 1939-June 1941.* London: Chapman, 1950; Boston: Beacon, 1951. German ed., Cologne, 1954. Italian ed., Florence, 1951. A valuable study by a resourceful student of fascism and communism. Based on extensive documentary research, but not always dependable in its interpretations. [B]

IJ180 ROSSI, AMILCARE (pseud. of Angelo Tasca). *Le Pacte Germano-Soviétique, l'histoire et le mythe.* Paris: Preuves, 1954. 114 p. Refutation of pro-Soviet apologies for the Russo-German Non-Aggression Pact of 1939.

IJ181 SCHELLENBERG, WALTER. *The Labyrinth; Memoirs.* N.Y.: Harper, 1956. 423 p. British ed., *The Schellenberg Memoirs.* London: 1956. Apologia of a German intelligence officer with scattered material of dubious veracity on the Soviet Union.

IJ182 SCHEURIG, BODO. *Freies Deutschland: Das Nationalkomitee und der Bund Deutscher Offiziere.* Munich: Nymphenburg, 1960. 269 p. The best and most comprehensive work on the anti-Nazi organizations established among German prisoners of war in Russia. Includes sophisticated analysis of the interaction of Soviet policy during the war years with the military situation and Soviet postwar plans for Germany. [A]

IJ183 SCOTT, JOHN. *Duel For Europe; Stalin Versus Hitler.* Boston: Houghton Mifflin, 1942. 381 p. Discussion of the 1938-42 period by a newspaper correspondent who spent much of the time in Moscow. Some interesting details, but also much misinformation.

IJ183A SCOTT, WILLIAM EVANS. *Alliance against Hitler; the Origins of the Franco-Soviet Pact.* Durham: Duke Univ. Press, 1962. 296 p. Somewhat superficial, but containing some material on Soviet policy toward Germany in the first years of National Socialism.

IJ184 SERAPHIM, HANS G. *Die deutsch-russischen Beziehungen, 1939-1941.* Hamburg: Nölke, 1949. 94 p. A superficial apologia for Hitler's foreign policy and the German attack on Russia.

IJ185 SNELL, JOHN L. *Wartime Origins of the East-West Dilemma Over Germany.* New Orleans: Hauser Press, 1959. 268 p. Useful for the background of Allied discussions during World War II. By a professor of history at Tulane. [A]

IJ186 STRONG, ANNA LOUISE. *The Soviets Expected It.* N.Y.: Dial Press, 1941. 279 p. Spanish ed., Mexico City: Editorial Seneca,

1942. A propagandistic presentation of the German invasion of Russia from the pro-Soviet point of view.

IJ187 TIPPELSKIRCH, KURT VON. *Geschichte des Zweiten Weltkriegs.* Bonn: Athenäum, 1956. 731 p. A useful military history of the Eastern Front by a German general who held high staff and field command positions.

IJ188 TOSCANO, MARIO. *L'Italia e gli accordi tedesco-sovietici dell'agosto 1939.* Florence: Sansoni, 1952. 96 p. Important material from Italian archives on German-Soviet relations by one of the editors of the Italian Foreign Ministry documents. [B]

IJ189 U.S. CHIEF OF COUNSEL FOR THE PROSECUTION OF AXIS CRIMINALITY. *Nazi Conspiracy and Aggression.* Washington: G.P.O., 1947. 8 vols. A collection of documents and interrogations from the Nuremberg trial in (not always accurate) English translation. There is much material on German policy and practice in occupied Russia, treatment of POW's and slave laborers, and German military and foreign policy.

IJ189A U.S. DEPARTMENT OF STATE. *Foreign Relations of the United States; Diplomatic Papers, 1933—.* Washington: GPO, 1950—. These volumes, especially those for 1939-41, contain extremely valuable reports on relations between the Soviet Union and Germany. [B]

IJ190 VILENCHUK, A., ed. *Fashistskaia Germaniia gotovitsia k voine; sbornik statei.* Moscow-Leningrad: Sotsekgiz, 1935. 188 p.

IJ191 WEINBERG, GERHARD L. *Germany and the Soviet Union, 1939-1941.* Leiden: Brill, 1954. 218 p. A basic work drawn largely from unpublished sources and covering economic and military as well as diplomatic subjects, with an extensive bibliography. Based largely on captured German documents. The author is a professor of history at the University of Michigan. [A]

IJ192 WEINERT, ERICH. *Das Nationalkomitee "Freies Deutschland" 1943-1945; Bericht über seine Tätigkeit und seine Auswirkung.* Berlin: Rütten und Loening, 1957. 165 p. Report by a German Communist who was president of the Nationalkomitee. Slanted but useful.

IJ193 WIRSING, GISELHER (Vindex, pseud.). *Stalinism; Soviet Policy in the Second World War.* Prague: Graphis-Verlag, 1944. 144 p. German ed., Berlin: Deutscher, 1944. An apology for Nazi Germany. World War II began when the Powers sought to stop Germany from securing the living space to which it was "historically entitled." The war became, however, a crusade led by Germany to protect Europe against Soviet barbarism. Presents a Nazi view of Soviet diplomacy in the pre-war and wartime period.

IJ194 ZIEMKE, EARL F. *The German Northern Theater of Operations, 1940-1945.* Washington: G.P.O., 1960. 342 p. The best single work in a Western language on the Russian-Finnish-German triangle and the fighting on the northern part of the Eastern Front. Based largely on unpublished sources. Maps. [B]

6. POSTWAR GERMANY, 1945-1963

a. GERMANY AS A WHOLE

(Edited by Gerald Freund)

IJ195 ABUSCH, ALEXANDER. *Stalin und die Schicksalsfragen der deutschen Nation.* Berlin: Aufbau-Verlag, 1949. 159 p. Soviet policy towards Germany seen as the expression of Stalin's personal motives, interpreted as benevolent and altruistic. The author is State Secretary in the East German Ministry of Culture.

IJ196 AKADEMIIA NAUK SSSR, INSTITUT EKONOMIKI. *Voprosy stroitelstva edinogo demokraticheskogo miroliubovogo germanskogo gosudarstva.* Ed. by A. M. Alekseev and others. Moscow: Izd. Akad. nauk SSSR, 1951. 340 p.

IJ197 BENNETT, LOWELL. *Berlin Bastion.* Frankfurt a M.: Rudl, 1951. 263 p. A descriptive account of the Berlin airlift.

IJ198 *Berlin—Pivot of German Destiny.* Ed. and trans. by Charles B. Robson. Intro. by Willy Brandt. Chapel Hill: U. of North Carolina Press, 1960. 233 p.

IJ199 BITTEL, KARL. *Vom Potsdamer Abkommen zur Viermächte-Konferenz; der Weg zur friedlichen Lösung der deutschen Frage.* With Documents. Berlin: Kongress, 1953. 189 p. An East German Communist interpretation of the Potsdam Conference and succeeding events in East and West Germany. Its only value lies in its collection of Communist speeches, protocols, and notes regarding Germany's future.

IJ200 BOURTHOUMIEUX, C. *La Politique et le régime interallié d'occupation de l'Allemagne de 1945-1949.* Paris: 1950.

IJ201 BRANDT, WILLY. *My Road to Berlin.* Garden City, N. Y.: Doubleday, 1960. 287 p.

IJ202 BURCHETT, WILFRED G. *Cold War in Germany.* N.p.: World Unity Publications, 1950. 258 p. A vitriolic account of postwar Germany which follows the Communist Party line in most particulars.

IJ203 BUTLER, EWAN. *City Divided; Berlin, 1955.* N.Y.: Praeger; London: Sidgwick & Jackson, 1955. 187 p. Report on life in postwar

Berlin, including a brief chapter on relations between East and West sectors.

IJ204 CLAY, LUCIUS D. *Decision in Germany*. N.Y.: Doubleday, 1950. 522 p. German ed., Frankfurt a/M.: 1950. A revealing basic source work on the early history of the East-West split over Germany, by the chief of the U.S. Military Government for four years. [A]

IJ205 CLAY, LUCIUS D. *Germany and the Fight for Freedom*. Cambridge: Harvard University Press; Oxford: S. J. R. Saunders, 1950. 83 p. General Clay made use of the Godkin Lectures for reminiscence and interpretations of his four years' experience as the senior U.S. representative in Occupied Germany. Revealing about Soviet tactics in the Allied Control Council.

IJ206 COLBY, REGINALD E. *De Wonde van Europa*. Amsterdam: Holdert, 1950. 307 p. An average descriptive account of postwar Germany in the early Cold War years. Revealing about popular German attitudes towards Russia. Excellent photographs.

IJ207 CONFERENCE OF FOREIGN MINISTERS, GENEVA, 1959. *Dokumentation der Genfer Aussenministerkonferenz*. Comp. by Heinrich von Siegler. Bonn: Köllen, 1959. 2 vols. Collection of all official and unofficial statements of conferees including press conferences during the Geneva Conference of 1959; very valuable, because the Conference dealt with the German peace treaty and the Berlin question.

IJ208 CORNIDES, WILHELM. *Die Weltmächte und Deutschland; Geschichte der jüngsten Vergangenheit, 1945-1955*. Tübingen: Wunderlich; Stuttgart: Metzler, 1957. 322 p. A balanced summary history to 1955 of Soviet and Western policies towards East and West Germany, by the editor of *Europa-Archiv*. [B]

IJ209 CORNIDES, WILHELM, and VOLLE, HERMANN. *Um den Frieden mit Deutschland; Dokumente zum Problem der deutschen Friedensordnung 1941 bis 1948 mit einem Bericht über die Londoner Aussenministerkonferenz 1947*. Oberursel [Taunus]: Europa-Archiv, 1948. 122 p. Key documents of Allied wartime and early postwar policies towards Germany.

IJ210 DAVISON, W. PHILLIPS. *The Berlin Blockade*. Princeton, N.J.: Princeton Univ. Press, 1958. 423 p. The definitive study of the Berlin Blockade, analyzing its impact on the policies of the major powers. [B]

IJ211 DEUERLEIN, ERNST. *Die Einheit Deutschlands; ihre Erörterung und Behandlung auf den Kriegs- und Nachkriegskonferenzen, 1941-1949; Darstellung und Dokumentation*. Frankfurt a/M.: Metzner, 1957. 349 p. 2nd, enlarged ed., 1961. Annotated documents and maps concerning agreements and negotiations on German reunification. Discussion chapters are conscientious renderings of official West German policies. Extensive bibliography. [B]

IJ212 DEUTSCHES INSTITUT FÜR ZEITGESCHICHTE. *Dokumente zur Deutschlandpolitik der Sowjetunion.* Comp. by Gerhard Arnold; ed. by Hansjürgen Krüger. Berlin: Rütten and Loening, 1957-. Soviet policy towards Germany as revealed in excerpts from speeches, articles and documents published under the auspices of the East German regime. Includes some materials not easily found elsewhere. [B]

IJ213 DONNER, JÖRN. *Report from Berlin.* Bloomington: Indiana Univ. Press, 1961. 284 p. Finnish ed., Helsinki: Söderström, 1958. 236 p.

IJ214 ERFURT, WERNER (pseud.). *Die sowjetrussische Deutschlandpolitik, 1945-1955; eine Studie zur Zeitgeschichte.* 4th rev. ed. Esslingen: Bechtle, 1959. 202 p. English ed., *Moscow's Policy in Germany; a Study in Contemporary History.* Esslingen: 1959. 138 p. A popular account, with limited documentation, using some primary sources. A sound analysis of Soviet policy toward Germany, reflecting the West German government's concept of this policy at that time. The author is possibly an official of the West German government. [B]

IJ215 FIEDLER, RUDOLF. *Würfelspiel um Deutschland, 1944-1956; eine kritische Untersuchung der Zerstückelungs- und Wiedervereinigungspolitik.* Düsseldorf: Kämmerer, 1957. 351 p. An episodic account presenting neither new facts nor original analysis.

IJ216 FREUND, GERALD. *Germany Between Two Worlds.* N.Y.: Harcourt, Brace, 1961. 296 p. Includes analyses and discussion of West Germany's relations with East Germany, Soviet Russia and other Communist bloc countries. The author, of German origin, also wrote *Unholy Alliance*; he is now an official of the Rockefeller Foundation. [A]

IJ217 FRIEDMANN, WOLFGANG. *The Allied Military Government of Germany.* London: Stevens, 1947. 362 p. Expert examination of administrative and legal problems of the Occupation to 1947 by a prominent international law scholar. Appendix includes all key official documents.

IJ218 GERMANY (FEDERAL REPUBLIC, 1949-), BUNDESMINISTERIUM FÜR GESAMTDEUTSCHE FRAGEN. *Literatur zur deutschen Frage.* Ed. by Günter Fischbach. Bonn: 1958. 210 p. A fairly comprehensive official West German bibliography.

IJ219 GERMANY (FEDERAL REPUBLIC, 1949-), BUNDESMINISTERIUM FÜR GESAMTDEUTSCHE FRAGEN. *Sow-*

jetische Auffassungen zur Deutschlandfrage, 1945-1953; Dargestellt nach amtlichen Dokumenten. Bonn: Deutscher Bundes-Verlag, 1954. 35 p. A useful brief compilation of Soviet statements on Germany.

IJ220 GOTTLIEB, MANUEL. *The German Peace Settlement and the Berlin Crisis.* N.Y.: Paine-Whitman, 1960. 275 p. Suggests that the history of the German issue be re-examined in the light of the failure of both East and West to grasp the opportunities for a compromise solution which would have permitted a unified but neutral Germany, capable of serving as a buffer state.

IJ221 HARCOURT, ROBERT D. *Visage de l'Allemagne actuelle.* Paris: Flammarion, 1950. 250 p. One of three sections of this book is devoted to an urbane discussion of relations between Soviet Russia and the East Germans and with West Germany. Full of sharp insights.

IJ222 HILL, RUSSELL. *Struggle for Germany.* N.Y.: Harper, 1947. 260 p. London: Gollancz, 1947. 191 p. A journalist's rambling account of inter-allied relations and developments in Germany during the early Occupation period.

IJ223 HORNE, ALISTAIR. *Return to Power: A Report on the New Germany.* N.Y.: Praeger, 1956. 415 p. A journalist's history of West Germany to the London and Paris Agreements. Gives interesting sidelights on the role of the Soviet Union in the Berlin Blockade and East German Revolt.

IJ224 HOWLEY, FRANK L. *Berlin Command.* N.Y.: Putnam, 1950. 276 p. A very personal and frequently belligerent account of experiences by the American garrison commander during the Berlin Blockade.

IJ225 JAECKEL, EBERHARD, ed. *Die deutsche Frage, 1952-1956; Notenwechsel und Konferenz-dokumente der vier Mächte.* Frankfurt a/M.: Metzner, 1957. 168 p. A basic reference work. Excellent selection and annotations of key documents. Good index and short selective bibliography. [A]

IJ226 JOESTEN, JOACHIM. *Germany, What Now?* Chicago: Ziff-Davis, 1948. 331 p. A superficial and outdated account of the early Occupation years.

IJ227 MCINNIS, EDGAR; HISCOCKS, RICHARD; and SPENCER, ROBERT. *The Shaping of Postwar Germany.* N.Y.: Praeger, 1960. 195 p. A well-organized and thorough study. Spencer's chapter gives an excellent précis of the origins and development of the Berlin problem. [A]

IJ228 MEISSNER, BORIS. *Russland, die Westmächte und Deutschland; die sowjetische Deutschlandpolitik, 1943-1953.* Hamburg: H. H. Nölke, 1954. 372 p. A major scholarly study, with an unbiased and detailed examination of all facets of West German-Soviet relations, completely documented. The author is an expert on East Europe and a member of the West German Diplomatic Corps. [A]

IJ229 MELNIKOV, D. *Borba za edinuiu, nezavisimuiu, demokraticheskuiu, miroliubivuiu Germaniiu.* Moscow: Gospolitizdat, 1951. 294 p.

IJ230 MERKUROV, G. *Borba nemetskogo naroda za mir i edinstvo Germanii.* Moscow: Gospolitizdat, 1958. 151 p.

IJ231 MIDDLETON, DREW. *The Struggle for Germany.* N.Y.: Bobbs-Merrill, 1949; London: Wingate, 1950. 304 p. Perceptive and readable analysis of the East-West struggle over Germany to 1949 by the former Chief Correspondent in Germany of the *New York Times.* Includes reports of the Council of Foreign Ministers meetings, 1947-49.

IJ232 MOLOTOV, VIACHESLAV M. *For a Democratic Peace with Germany; Speeches and Statements made at the London Session of the Council of Foreign Ministers, November 25-December 15, 1947.* London: Soviet News, 1948. 99 p. An authoritative statement which offers good clues to later developments in Germany. The work is without commentary or annotation.

IJ233 MOLOTOV, VIACHESLAV M. *L'Union soviétique et le problème de l'Allemagne.* Paris: Édition France-U.R.S.S., 1947. 207 p.

IJ234 MUHLEN, NORBERT. *The Return of Germany; a Tale of Two Countries.* Chicago: Regnery, 1953. 310 p. This history of postwar Germany to 1952 analyzes the events leading to partition and includes informative chapters on the Soviet Zone. The author is staunchly pro-Adenauer.

IJ235 NATIONALE FRONT DES DEMOKRATISCHEN DEUTSCHLAND. *Die Genfer Konferenz der Aussenminister, 11. Mai bis 20. Juni und 13. Juli bis 5. August 1959.* Berlin: Kongress, 1959. 133 p.

IJ236 NEAL, FRED WARNER. *War and Peace and Germany.* N.Y.: Norton, 1962. 166 p. A professor at Claremont College argues that: (1) "Our position in Berlin is untenable . . . it is one to be gotten out of, not to stand firm in." (2) The goal of German reunification is not a vital matter to the U.S., and we are foolish to refuse under any conditions to reach an agreement with Russia recognizing the division of Germany.

IJ237 NISBET, ANDREW. "The Berlin Blockade; A Study of Errors." Certificate essay, Russian Institute, Columbia, 1958. 60 p.

IJ238 PLISCHKE, ELMER. *The Allied High Commission for Germany*. N.P.: Historical Division, Office of the Executive Secretary, Office of the U. S. High Commissioner for Germany, 1953. 215 p. A basic work. A documented history of the Allied High Commission, also describing its organization and functions. [A]

IJ239 PLISCHKE, ELMER. *Berlin: Development of its Government and Administration*. N.P.: Historical Division, Office of the U.S. High Commissioner for Germany, 1952. 257 p. A good historical account.

IJ240 POLLOCK, JAMES K., MEISEL, JAMES H., and BRETTON, HENRY L. *Germany under Occupation; Illustrative Materials and Documents*. Rev. ed. Ann Arbor, Mich.: G. Wahr, 1949. 305 p. A valuable compilation of major documents concerning the Occupation of Germany, including the Soviet Zone, from the Yalta Conference to the proclamation of the Basic Law for the Federal Republic, May 1949. [A]

IJ241 RAUSCHNING, HERMANN. *Die deutsche Einheit und der Weltfriede*. Hamburg: Holstein, 1955. 98 p. A polemic asserting that German unity and neutrality is a *sine qua non* of an East-West reconciliation.

IJ242 RUHM VON OPPEN, BEATE. *Documents on Germany under Occupation, 1945-1954*. London: Oxford University Press, 1955. 660 p. An indispensable documentary collection, intelligently selected and meticulously edited. [A]

IJ243 RUSSIA (1923- USSR), MINISTERSTVO INOSTRANNYKH DEL. *Sovetskii Soiuz i berlinskii vopros; dokumenty*. Moscow: Gospolitizdat, 1948-49. 2 vols. English ed., *The Soviet Union and the Berlin question; documents*. Moscow: Gospolitizdat, 1948-49. 2 vols. A selection of material on the Berlin question, consisting of diplomatic exchanges, statements to the press, etc.

IJ244 RUSSIA (1923- USSR) MINISTERSTVO INOSTRANNYKH DEL. *Sovetskii Soiuz i vopros o edinstve Germanii i mirnom dogovore s Germaniei*. Moscow: Gospolitizdat, 1952. 93 p. English ed., *The Soviet Union and the Question of the Unity of Germany and of the German Peace Treaty*. Moscow: 1952. 85 p.

IJ245 SCHOLZ, ARNO. *Berlin im Würgegriff; eine politische Chronik der Zeit*. Berlin-Grunewald: Arani, 1953. 559 p. Very detailed and often sentimental social and political history of the city. Includes a useful chronology of events to 1952.

IJ246 SIEGLER, HEINRICH VON. *Deutschlands Weg 1945-1955; von der Kapitulation bis zur Moskau-Reise Adenauers.* Cologne: König, 1955. 215 p. A comprehensive chronology of events. Comments represent the official West German Government point of view. [B]

IJ247 *Soviet Efforts for Peace in Europe and against German Rearmament; Documents.* London: Soviet News, 1955. 160 p.

IJ248 *Die Sowjet-Union und das Deutschlandproblem der Sowjet-Delegation auf der Moskauer Konferenz.* Halle: Mitteldeutsche Verlags-Gesellschaft, 1948. 140 p. A Communist publication of excerpts from Molotov and Vyshinsky and a highly interpretive diary of conference proceedings. Useful for the official Soviet line.

IJ249 SPEIER, HANS. *Divided Berlin: The Anatomy of Soviet Political Blackmail.* N.Y.: Praeger, 1961. 201 p. Discusses Communist moves and Western countermoves to the end of July, 1961. A revision and expansion of a study prepared for the RAND Corporation, with which the author is connected. Based in part on two trips to Berlin and conversations with Germans in both Berlin and Bonn.

IJ250 STRAUSS, HAROLD. *The Division and Dismemberment of Germany; From the Casablanca Conference (January 1943) to the Establishment of the East German Republic (October 1949).* Ambilly, Switzerland: Les Presses de Savoie, 1952. 240 p. An angry but interesting critique of Allied wartime policies and their bearing on the extension of Soviet influence into Central Europe.

IJ251 SURVEY OF INTERNATIONAL AFFAIRS, 1920-1923—; THE WAR-TIME SERIES FOR 1939-1946. *Four-Power Control in Germany and Austria, 1945-1946.* By Michael Balfour and John Mair. London and N.Y.: Oxford, for the Royal Institute of International Affairs, 1956. 390 p. An indispensable factual account, though somewhat limited in analysis. [B]

IJ252 SZAZ, ZOLTAN M. *Germany's Eastern Frontiers; The Problems of the Oder-Neisse Line.* Chicago: Regnery, 1960. 256 p. A strongly pro-German and anti-Polish study by an American professor of Hungarian origin. About one-third of the work is devoted to West German-Soviet relations. Insists that Germany must be reunited and most of the Oder-Neisse territories returned to Germany, but does not explain how these objectives are to be accomplished without war. Good 14-page bibliography.

IJ253 THILENIUS, RICHARD. *Die Teilung Deutschlands; eine zeitgeschichtliche Analyse.* Hamburg: Rowohlt, 1957. 195 p. Good discussion and analysis of events leading to partition, by a West German journalist.

IJ254 U.S. DEPARTMENT OF STATE. *Germany, 1947-1949; The Story in Documents.* Prepared by Velma H. Cassidy. Washington: G.P.O., 1950. 631 p. Highly detailed and indispensable collection of documents on the evolution of the German policy of the major powers in the crucial period just before the formal establishment of the two German states. [B]

IJ255 U.S. DEPARTMENT OF STATE, HISTORICAL DIVISION. *Documents on Germany, 1944-1959. Background Documents on Germany, 1944-1959, and a Chronology of Political Developments Affecting Berlin, 1945-1956.* Washington: G.P.O., 1959. 491 p. A very helpful compilation, although not primarily concerned with Soviet policy; useful for supplying some of the elements needed to put Soviet policy in a larger framework. [B]

IJ256 VIRALLY, MICHEL. *L'Administration internationale de l'Allemagne, du 8 mai 1945 au 24 avril 1947.* Paris: Pedone, 1948. 180 p. Well-organized and documented account of the organization of the Occupation, including the Soviet Zone. Appendix lists Control Council decisions and proclamations to 1946. [A]

b. EAST GERMANY

(Edited by Robert M. Slusser)

(1) Bibliographies

IJ257 BOENINGER, HILDEGARD R. *The Hoover Library Collection on Germany;* Pt. IV: *Germany since 1945.* Stanford, Cal.: Stanford University Press, 1955. 56 p. Lists holdings of the Hoover Institution on the Soviet Zone of Occupation of Germany for the first postwar decade.

IJ258 MASON, JOHN BROWN. "Government, Administration, and Politics in East Germany: A Selected Bibliography," *The American Political Science Review.* Vol. LIII, June 1959, pp. 507-523. Valuable particularly on internal developments.

IJ259 MATTHIAS, ERICH. "Zur Bibliographie des 17. Juni." *Ost-Probleme.* 6th year, no. 35, Sept. 4, 1954. Helpful in locating contemporary accounts and evaluations of the June Uprising of 1953.

IJ260 MOSCOW, VSESOIUZNAIA GOSUDARSTVENNAIA BIBLIOTEKA INOSTRANNOI LITERATURY. *Germanskaia Demokraticheskaia Respublika, bibliograficheskii ukazatel.* Moscow: 1958. 179 p. A standard Soviet bibliography.

IJ261 RICHERT, ERNST. "Grundsätzliche Bemerkungen zur Literatur über die Sowjetzone." *Politische Literatur.* Vol. III, 1954, col. 457-467. Limited in scope but useful.

IJ262 RICHERT, ERNST. "Die Sowjetzone in der westlichen Literatur (1953-1956)." *Neue politische Literatur.* Vol. II, 1957, col. 665-684. A good survey of the literature for the period.

IJ263 U.S. LIBRARY OF CONGRESS, REFERENCE DEPARTMENT, SLAVIC AND CENTRAL EUROPEAN DIVISION. *East Germany, a Selected Bibliography.* Comp. by Fritz T. Epstein. Washington: 1959. 55 p. An excellent basic bibliography. Arranged by subject and with an author index. Contains both books and articles. A few of the titles are annotated. [A]

IJ264 U.S. LIBRARY OF CONGRESS, SERIAL DIVISION. *German Federal Republic Official Publications, 1949-1957, with Inclusion of Preceding Zonal Official Publications; a Survey.* Prepared by James B. Childs. Washington: 1958. 2 vols. A handy check list of publications of the Bonn Government, including those dealing with East Germany. Vol. I, p. 211-239 lists serial publications dealing with East Germany which have been published or distributed by the Bundesministerium für Gesamtdeutsche Fragen.

(2) General Works

IJ265 ABBES, GERHARD. *Die Planwirtschaft der "Deutschen Demokratischen Republik" und der "Union der Sozialistischen Sowjet Republik"; ein Vergleich.* Heidelberg: 1951. 2 vols.

IJ266 *Bericht über die Verhandlungen des 15. Parteitages der Kommunistischen Partei Deutschlands, 19. und 20. April 1946 in Berlin.* Berlin: 1946. An official publication of the KPD, covering the party congress immediately preceding the absorption of the Socialist Party.

IJ267 BERLIN, INSTITUT FÜR GESELLSCHAFTSWISSENSCHAFTEN. *Der dialektische Materialismus und der Aufbau des Sozialismus; Konferenz des Instituts für Gesellschaftswissenschaften beim ZK der SED über den dialektischen Materialismus, die theoretische Grundlage der Politik der Partei der Arbeiterklasse und seine erfolgreiche Anwendung durch die SED, 5. und 6. Mai 1958 in Berlin; Diskussionsbeiträge.* Berlin: Dietz, 1958. 190 p. The German Communists in the German Democratic Republic have shown a marked aptitude for elaborating the theoretical superstructure of Communist doctrine. This record of a major conference on the subject may serve as a typical specimen.

IJ268 BOHN, HELMUT. *Die Aufrüstung in der sowjetischen Besatzungszone Deutschlands.* Bonn: Bundesministerium für Gesamtdeutsche Fragen, 1958. 174 p. Based on materials available to the Federal Republic of Germany. Factual and well-balanced.

IJ269 BOHN, HELMUT. *Ideologie und Aufrüstung in der Sowjetzone; Dokumente und Materialien.* Cologne: Markus, 1956. 241 p.

IJ270 BOLZ, LOTHAR. *Es Geht um Deutschland; Reden.* 2nd ed. Berlin: Verlag der Nation, 1955. 773 p. Speeches by the leader of the stooge National Democratic Party, useful as an epitome of Soviet policy towards former Nazis.

IJ271 BOUTARD, R. J. *L'Armée en Allemagne orientale; de la "police populaire" à l'armée nationale, 1945-1955.* Paris: Nouvelles éditions latines, 1955. 208 p. A good account of the evolution of the Volkspolizei.

IJ272 BRANT, STEFAN (pseud. of Klaus Harpprecht). *Der Aufstand; Vorgeschichte, Geschichte und Deutung des 17. Juni 1953.* Stuttgart: Steingrueben, 1954. 324 p. English ed., *The East German Rising, 17th June 1953.* London: Thames and Hudson, 1955; N.Y.: Praeger, 1957. 202 p. An admirable monograph on the June uprising.

IJ273 BRUNN, WALTER. *Die rechtliche, politische und wirtschaftliche Lage des Berliner Sowjetsektors.* Berlin: Kulturbuch-Verlag, 1954. 144 p.

IJ273A CASTELLAN, GEORGES. *La République Démocratique Allemande (R.D.A.)* Paris: Presses Universitaires Françaises (Collection "Que Sais-je?"), 1961. 126 p. A compact account, favorable to the East German regime.

IJ274 CASTELLAN, GEORGES, and others. *D.D.R.: Allemagne de l'Est.* Paris: Édition du seuil, 1955. 411 p. Probably the best scholarly study of Soviet policy in the German Democratic Republic. [A]

IJ275 CROAN, MELVIN. "Dependent Totalitarianism: The Political Process in East Germany." Ph.D. dissertation, Harvard, 1960.

IJ276 *Deutsche Aussenpolitik.* Berlin: Rütten and Loening. Bimonthly, 1956; Monthly, 1957—. The official East German foreign policy journal.

IJ277 DEUTSCHES INSTITUT FÜR ZEITGESCHICHTE. *Dokumente zur Aussenpolitik der Regierung der Deutschen Demokratischen Republik.* Berlin: Rütten & Loening, 1954-59. 6 vols. Russian ed., Moscow: Izd. inostrannoi lit., 1955—. The standard foreign policy publication of the East German government, including much material not easily available elsewhere. [A]

IJ278 DORMONT, ALEXIS. *La Nouvelle Armée allemande est là.* Paris: Amiot-Dumont, 1954. 220 p. Development of the Volkspolizei, based mainly on published sources.

IJ279 DUHNKE, HORST. *Stalinismus in Deutschland, Die Geschichte der sowjetischen Besatzungszone.* Cologne: Verlag für Politik und Wirtschaft, 1955. 375 p. Short English version: "The Sovietization of Eastern Germany, 1945-1951." M.A. thesis, U. of California (Berkeley), 1952. Admirably combines the scholarly detachment of academic history with the moral earnestness of a man deeply concerned with the future of Germany. Based on extensive research and firsthand information. [B]

IJ280 EINSIEDEL, HEINRICH VON. *Tagebuch der Versuchung.* Berlin: Pontes, 1950. 239 p. English ed., *I Joined the Russians: a Captured German Flier's Diary of Communist Temptation.* New Haven: Yale University Press, 1953. 306 p. British ed., *Shadow of Stalingrad.* London: Wingate, 1953. 254 p. A firsthand account of Soviet indoctrination and propaganda work among German prisoners during the Second World War. The author was vice-president of the Nationalkomitee Freies Deutschland from 1942 to 1947, but left the Communist movement in 1949.

IJ281 FINN, GERHARD. *Die politischen Häftlinge der Sowjetzone 1945-1958.* Berlin: Kampfgruppe gegen Unmenschlichkeit, 1958. 231 p. Extensive and generally reliable information on persons arrested and imprisoned in East Germany for opposition to Soviet policies or for other reasons.

IJ282 FOERSTER, WOLFGANG. *Das Aussenhandelssystem der Sowjetischen Besatzungszone Deutschlands; die Entwicklung der Organisation und Technik des sowjetzonalen Aussenhandels.* Bonn: Bundesministerium für Gesamtdeutsche Fragen, 1955. 130 p.

IJ283 FRIEDRICH, CARL J. *The Soviet Zone of Germany.* New Haven: Human Relations Area Files, 1956. 646 p. Thorough treatment of the major aspects of life under the German Democratic Republic. [B]

IJ284 FRIEDRICH, GERD. *Die Freie Deutsche Jugend; Auftrag und Entwicklung.* Cologne: Verlag Rote Weissbücher, 1953. 201 p.

IJ285 FRIEDRICH, GERD, and ZUR MÜHLEN, HEINRICH VON. *Die Pankower Sowjetrepublik und der deutsche Westen.* Cologne: Verlag Rote Weissbücher, 1953. 153 p. Concentrates mainly on East German policy with regard to the question of German reunification.

IJ286 *Germanskaia Demokraticheskaia Respublika; sbornik dokumentov.* Moscow: 1958. 130 p. A Soviet collection which is valuable chiefly as evidence of what the Soviet policy-makers considered significant at the time of publication.

IJ287 GERMANY (DEMOCRATIC REPUBLIC, 1949-) AMT FÜR INFORMATION. *Freundschaft der Tat; wie die Sowjetunion hilft.*

Berlin: Verlag Kultur und Fortschritt, 1952. 333 p. Painstaking assembly of available evidence to bolster the thesis that the Soviet Union is a friend and helper of the East German regime.

IJ288 GERMANY (DEMOCRATIC REPUBLIC, 1949-), CONSTITUTION. *Soviet Zone Constitution and Electoral Law; Prepared by Policy Reports Secretary, Office of Executive Secretary.* Washington: G.P.O., 1951. 107 p.

IJ289 GERMANY (DEMOCRATIC REPUBLIC, 1949-), STAATLICHE ZENTRALVERWALTUNG FÜR STATISTIK. *Statistisches Jahrbuch der Deutschen Demokratischen Republik.* Berlin: Deutscher Zentralverlag, 1955- . Official statistical annual for the German Democratic Republic.

IJ290 GERMANY (DEMOCRATIC REPUBLIC, 1949-), VOLKSKAMMER. *Handbuch der Volkskammer der Deutschen Demokratischen Republik.* Berlin: Kongress-Verlag, 1957. 536 p. The official reference work on the East German legislature.

IJ291 GERMANY (FEDERAL REPUBLIC, 1949-), BUNDESMINISTERIUM FÜR GESAMTDEUTSCHE FRAGEN. *SBZ von A bis Z; ein Taschen- und Nachschlagebuch über die Sowjetische Besatzungszone Deutschlands.* Ed. by E. Stamm. 3rd Ed., Bonn: Deutscher Bundes-Verlag, 1956. 319 p. A handy reference work, edited for its propaganda impact in the East-West struggle for German unification.

IJ292 GERMANY (FEDERAL REPUBLIC, 1949-), BUNDESMINISTERIUM FÜR GESAMTDEUTSCHE FRAGEN. *SBZ von 1945 bis 1954; die Sowjetische Besatzungszone Deutschlands in den Jahren 1945-1954.* Ed. by Fritz Kopp. Bonn: Deutscher Bundes-Verlag, 1956. 361 p. Continued with: *SBZ von 1955 bis 1956; die sowjetische Besatzungszone Deutschlands in Jahren 1955-56.* Ed. by Fritz Kopp and Günter Fischbach. Bonn, 1958. 255 p. Useful summaries of developments in the German Democratic Republic from the official West German standpoint.

IJ293 GERMANY (FEDERAL REPUBLIC, 1949-), BUNDESMINISTERIUM FÜR GESAMTDEUTSCHE FRAGEN. *Die sowjetische Hand in der deutschen Wirtschaft. Organisation und Geschäftsgebaren der sowjetischen Unternehmen.* Bonn: Dt. Bundes-Vlg., 1952. 100 p.

IJ294 GERMANY (TERRITORY UNDER ALLIED OCCUPATION, 1945—, RUSSIAN ZONE), OBERSTER CHEF. *Befehle. Aus dem Stab der Sowjetischen Militärverwaltung in Deutschland.* Sammelheft 1—. Berlin: n.p., 1945—. An indispensable collection of decrees and edicts issued by the Soviet Military Administration in Germany. [B]

IJ295 GESELLSCHAFT FÜR DEUTSCH-SOWJETISCHE FREUNDSCHAFT. *Dokumente des 4. Kongresses.* Berlin: Verlag Kultur und Fortschritt, 1953. 136 p. Official record of the 4th Congress of the German-Soviet Friendship Society, valuable for its documentary materials illustrating this facet of the Soviet Union's German policy.

IJ296 GÖTTINGER ARBEITSKREIS. *Das östliche Deutschland; ein Handbuch.* Würzburg: Holzner, 1959. 1013 p. English ed., *Eastern Germany, A Handbook.* Würzburg: Holzner, 1961. 3 vols. Volume I deals with law, volume II with history, volume III with economy.

IJ297 GROTEWOHL, OTTO. *Im Kampf um die einige Deutsche Demokratische Republik.* Berlin: Dietz, 1954. 3 vols. Official papers and speeches by the most important non-Communist political figure in the German Democratic Republic, of particular value for the light it casts on the process whereby the German Socialists were absorbed into the Communist-directed Socialist Unity Party (SED). [B]

IJ298 GROTHE, PETER. *To Win the Minds of Men: The Story of the Communist Propaganda War in East Germany.* Palo Alto, Cal.: Pacific Books, 1958. 241 p. A useful analysis of Communist propaganda techniques in East Germany, based on personal observation as well as documentary material.

IJ299 HAGERTY, JAMES J. "Soviet Consolidation of Political Power in East Germany, 1945-1948." Certificate essay, Russian Institute, Columbia, 1958. 93 p. An excellent survey of available evidence on a crucial period in the evolution of Soviet policy towards Germany. [B]

IJ300 HERZ, HANNS PETER. *Freie Deutsche Jugend; Berichte und Dokumente zur Entwicklung und Tätigkeit der Kommunistischen Jugendorganisation.* Munich: Juventa-Verlag, 1957. 124 p.

IJ301 HILDEBRANDT, RAINER. *The Explosion; The Uprising behind the Iron Curtain.* N.Y.: Duell, Sloan and Pearce, 1955. 198 p. German ed., Berlin: 1956. Emphasis on the dramatic aspects of unrest and uprising; in the light of subsequent events, it is somewhat too sanguine in its prognostications.

IJ302 INFORMATIONSBÜRO WEST. *Chronologische Materialien zur Geschichte der SED.* Berlin-Schlachtensee: 1956. 637 p.

IJ303 JOESTEN, JOACHIM F. *Soviet Rule in Eastern Germany.* Hartsville, Great Barrington, Mass.: 1948-1949. 2 vols. Uneven treatment of the subject, but valuable for the extensive detail from contemporary sources.

IJ304 KLIMOV, GREGORY P. *Berliner Kreml.* Cologne: Kiepenheuer, 1951. 446 p. English ed., *The Terror Machine; the Inside Story of the Soviet Administration in Germany.* N.Y.: Praeger, 1953. 400 p. French ed., *Les Russes à Berlin.* Paris: A. Bonne, 1953. The best account of Soviet administration in postwar Germany from the inside. The author is intelligent and makes good use of his extensive experience as a Soviet officer in Germany. The original version, in Russian, appeared in the émigré publication *Posev*; the translation is condensed. [B]

IJ305 KNOP, WERNER. *Prowling Russia's Forbidden Zone; A Secret Journey into Soviet Germany.* N.Y.: Knopf, 1949. 200 p. A disorganized but useful account of firsthand observations in the Soviet Zone of Occupation.

IJ306 KOHLER, HEINZ. "East Germany's Economic Integration into the Communist Bloc." Ph.D. dissertation, U. of Michigan, 1961.

IJ306A KOMISSAROV, V., and POPOV, A. *Mezhdunarodnye ekonomicheskie otnosheniia Germanskoi Demokraticheskoi Respubliki.* Moscow: Institut Mezhdunarodnykh Otnosheniia, 1963. 190 p.

IJ307 KOPP, FRITZ. *Chronik der Wiederbewaffnung in Deutschland; Daten über Polizei und Bewaffnung 1945-1958; Rüstung der Sowjetzone—Abwehr des Westens.* Cologne: Markus, 1958. 160 p. A well-informed but not entirely reliable account of East German rearmament.

IJ308 KRAUSE, HEINZ. *Economic Structure of East Germany and its Position within the Soviet Bloc.* Washington: Council for Economic and Industrial Research, 1955. 2 vols.

IJ309 KRISCH, HENRY. "The East Berlin Riots of June 17, 1953; Their Interpretations in the Soviet Press." Certificate essay, Russian Institute, Columbia, 1954. 90 p. Useful for the light it throws on Soviet reactions to a crucial event in the history of Soviet-German postwar relations.

IJ310 LEONHARD, WOLFGANG. *Die Revolution entlässt ihre Kinder.* Cologne: Kiepenheuer & Witsch, 1955. 551 p. English ed., *Child of the Revolution.* Chicago: Regnery, 1958. 447 p. An autobiographical account of a German who went to the Soviet Union as a youth in the early 1930's and was later trained in a Comintern school. He helped to establish the Soviet regime in East Germany in 1945, but broke with the Party in 1948. One of the best books available on the psychology and policies of East European Communism. [B]

IJ311 LÖWENTHAL, FRITZ. *News from Soviet Germany.* London: Gollancz, 1950. 343 p. Somewhat journalistic in tone, and disorganized in presentation, but valuable for evidence on conditions in the German Democratic Republic.

IJ312 MÜLLER, HANS. *Die Entwicklung der SED und ihr Kampf für ein neues Deutschland (1945-1949).* Berlin: 1961. 258 p. History of the Soviet occupation zone and the merger of the Communist and Socialist parties. Marxist-minded.

IJ313 NETTL, J. P. *The Eastern Zone and Soviet Policy in Germany, 1945-1950.* London: Oxford, 1951. 324 p. German ed., *Die deutsche Sowjetzone bis heute; Politik, Wirtschaft, Gesellschaft.* Frankfurt am Main: 1953. 376 p. A detached, at times somewhat dry account of the postwar years, but reliable and eminently useful. [A]

IJ314 NUSCHKE, OTTO. *Reden und Aufsätze, 1919-1950.* Berlin: Union, 1957-. A carefully selected documentary compilation designed to illustrate and make attractive the career of a turncoat whom the Soviets found useful at a stage of their policy in Germany. Author was one of the founders and a leader in the Christian Democratic Union.

IJ315 PIECK, WILHELM. *Gesammelte Reden und Schriften.* Foreword by Walter Ulbricht. Berlin: Dietz, 1959-. The history of the Stalinization of the German Communist movement, as reflected in the collected writings of a man who played a cardinal role in the process and who was President of the GDR until his death. Planned to consist of 15 volumes.

IJ316 *Prebyvanie N.S. Khrushcheva v Germanskoi Demokraticheskoi Respublike 4-12 marta 1959.* Moscow: Gospolitizdat, 1959. 158 p. Official documents on Khrushchev's visit to the German Democratic Republic in March 1959, during which the demands for signature of a peace treaty with Germany and the expulsion of the Western Allies from Berlin were first made.

IJ317 PUTTKAMER, JESKO H. VON. *Irrtum und Schuld: Geschichte des Nationalkomitees "Freies Deutschland."* Neuwied: Michael-Verlag, 1948. 130 p. New ed., *Von Stalingrad zur Volkspolizei; Geschichte des Nationalkomitees "Freies Deutschland."* Wiesbaden: Michael, 1951. 120 p. A brief history of the Communist group formed during World War II by Soviet authorities from German prisoners of war and German Communists already in Russia. It played a role in the founding of the East German state.

IJ318 RICHERT, ERNST. *Macht ohne Mandat, Der Staatsapparat in der Sowjetischen Besatzungszone Deutschlands.* Cologne: Westdeutschen Verlag, 1958. 181 p.

IJ319 SAREL, BENNO. *La Classe ouvrière d'Allemagne Orientale, essai de chronique (1945-1958).* Paris: Éditions ouvrieres, 1958. 268 p.

IJ320 SCHAFFER, GORDON. *Russian Zone; A Record of the Conditions found in the Soviet-Occupied Zone of Germany during a Stay of Ten Weeks.* London: Allen & Unwin, 1947. 192 p. Well-informed journalism, with details on living conditions, occupation policies, etc.

IJ321 SCHEURIG, BODO. *Freies Deutschland; das Nationalkomitee und der Bund Deutscher Offiziere.* Munich: Nymphenburg, 1960. 269 p. A valuable account of the origins of Soviet policy towards postwar Germany in the form of the Free Germany movement among German prisoners of war, 1943-45. [A]

IJ322 SCHOLZ, ARNO, and NIEKE, WERNER. *Der 17. Juni; Der Tag der Volkserhebung. Dokumente, Berichte, Fotos.* Berlin-Grunewald: Arani, 1953. 96 p. Deals with the East German uprising in June 1953.

IJ323 SCHULTZ, JOACHIM. *Der Funktionär in der Einheitspartei —Kaderpolitik und Bürokratisierung.* Stuttgart: Ring-Verlag, 1956. 285 p.

IJ324 SHERMAN, GEORGE F., Jr. "Soviet Policy and Eastern Germany, July 1952-April 1954." B.Litt. thesis, Oxford, 1956. A valuable survey of a crucial turning-point in Soviet policy towards Germany.

IJ325 SLUSSER, ROBERT, ed. *Soviet Economic Policy in Postwar Germany; A Collection of Papers by Former Soviet Officials.* N.Y.: Research Program on the USSR, 1953. 184 p. Papers of varying merit on the Soviet Zone of Occupation in the first postwar years. Covers the formation of Soviet economic policy towards Germany, agriculture, and the exploitation of uranium deposits. Bibliography. [B]

IJ326 SOLBERG, RICHARD W. *God and Caesar in East Germany.* N.Y.: Macmillan, 1962. 294 p. An authoritative account of the struggle between the Communist regime and the Lutheran Church.

IJ327 SOZIALISTISCHE EINHEITSPARTEI DEUTSCHLANDS. *Dokumente.* Berlin: Dietz, 1951-. 6 vols. Official documents of the Socialist Unity Party, chief political organ for the execution of Communist policies in Eastern Germany. Indispensable. [A]

IJ328 SOZIALISTISCHE EINHEITSPARTEI DEUTSCHLANDS. *Zur ökonomischen Politik der SED und der Regierung der DDR; Zusammenstellung von Beschlüssen der SED sowie Gesetzen und Verordnungen der DDR, 11. Juni 1945 bis 21. Juli 1955.* Berlin: Dietz, 1955. 828 p.

IJ329 SOZIALISTISCHE EINHEITSPARTEI DEUTSCHLANDS, PARTEIKONFERENZ, 1st, BERLIN, 1949. *Protokoll der ersten*

Parteikonferenz, 25. bis 28. Januar 1949 im Hause der Deutschen Wirtschaftskommission zu Berlin. Berlin: Dietz, 1950. 556 p. (Also other volumes for later party conferences.) Although the published documentary records of the SED conferences and congresses omit much of what took place, they provide essential firsthand evidence on the overall framework of Communist policy in East Germany. [B]

IJ330 STERN, CAROLA (pseud.). *Porträt einer bolschewistischen Partei; Entwicklung, Funktion und Situation der SED.* Cologne: Verlag für Politik und Wirtschaft, 1957. 367 p. A well-informed study of the development and organization of the Communist-dominated Socialist Unity Party.

IJ331 STERN, CAROLA (pseud.). *Die SED, ein Handbuch über Aufbau, Organisation und Funktion des Parteiapparates.* Cologne: Rote Weissbücher, 1954. 256 p.

IJ332 STOLPER, WOLFGANG F., and ROSKAMP, KARL W. *The Structure of the East German Economy.* Cambridge: Harvard, 1961. A searching study of economic policy in the Communist East German regime, based on meticulous evaluation of a great mass of factual data. Of general significance for the study of Soviet-satellite economic relations, as well as for the study of Soviet economic policy in general.

IJ333 STRASSNER, PETER. *Verräter; das Nationalkomitee Freies Deutschland—Keimzelle der sogenannten DDR.* Munich: Schild, 1960. 452 p. Not written by a historian and conceived as a "political book" to point up the dangers of Communism. Relies mostly on German language publications. Has footnotes, bibliography, and documentation. Covers not only the National Committee, but also preceding and subsequent role of Germans in Soviet employ. A critical compilation of available information and an attempt to arrive at valid value judgments, although the author has more than average bias (as the title alone indicates) against Germans working for the Soviets.

IJ334 ULBRICHT, WALTER. *Lehrbuch für den demokratischen Staats- und Wirtschaftsaufbau.* Berlin: Dietz, 1950. 350 p. An authoritative blueprint for Communist policy in the German Democratic Republic.

IJ335 ULBRICHT, WALTER. *Zur Geschichte der deutschen Arbeiterbewegung; aus Reden und Aufsätzen.* Berlin: Dietz, 1953—. A Stalinist version of the history of the working-class movement. Valuable for the light it throws on the scale of values of the author. Must be used with caution, because important material is missing; for example, articles written from the fall of 1939 to the spring of 1941.

IJ336 ULBRICHT, WALTER. *Zur Geschichte der neuesten Zeit; die Niederlage Hitler-deutschlands und die Schaffung der antifaschistisch-demokratischen Ordnung.* 2nd ed. Berlin: Dietz, 1955. 452 p. German history of the wartime and postwar periods as seen and shaped by the most important political figure in the German Democratic Republic, a satellite leader of remarkable ability, great ambition, and no scruples.

IJ337 U.S., DEPARTMENT OF STATE. *East Germany under Soviet Control.* Washington: G.P.O., 1952. 94 p. Despite its avowedly propagandist purpose, a sound factual presentation within its limits.

IJ338 VEREINIGUNGSPARTEITAG DER SOZIAL-DEMOKRATISCHEN PARTEI DEUTSCHLANDS UND DER KOMMUNISTISCHEN PARTEI DEUTSCHLANDS, BERLIN, 1946. *Protokoll des Vereinigungsparteitages der Sozialdemokratischen Partei Deutschlands (SPD) und der Kommunistischen Partei Deutschlands (KPD) am 21. und 22. April 1946 in Berlin.* Berlin: Dietz, 1946. 215 p. Records of the congress which saw the absorption of the Socialist Party in the Soviet Zone of Occupation by the smaller but more aggressive Communist Party, with Soviet support. An indispensable, although far from complete, source of information on a crucial turning-point in Soviet policy towards Germany in the postwar years. [B]

IJ339 WEGENER, HERTHA C. "Economic Relations between Soviet Russia and Eastern Germany, 1945-1950." Certificate essay, Russian Institute, Columbia, 1951. 93 p. A valuable academic treatment of a major but often neglected aspect of Soviet policy towards Eastern Germany, the economic exploitation of German resources and labor power.

IJ340 WEINERT, ERICH. *Das Nationalkomitee "Freies Deutschland" 1943-1945; Bericht über seine Tätigkeit und seine Auswirkung.* Berlin: Rütten und Loening, 1957. 165 p. Report by a German Communist who was president of the Nationalkomitee. Slanted but useful.

IJ341 *Wer ist Wer in der SBZ? Ein biographisches Handbuch.* Berlin-Zehlendorf: Verlag für Internationalen Kulturaustausch, 1958. 307 p. A handy and remarkably inclusive reference work on leading figures in the German Democratic Republic.

c. WEST GERMANY

(Edited by Werner Feld)

IJ342 ALEXANDER, EDGAR. *Adenauer und das neue Deutschland; Einführung in das Wesen und Wirken des Staatsmannes; mit einem Anhang Bonn und Moskau, Dokumente der Moskauer Konferenz und zur Wiedervereinigung Deutschlands.* Recklinghausen: Paulus, 1956. 284 p. English ed., N.Y.: 1957. An authorized biography of Adenauer, the man and his achievements as Chancellor, as he sees them. Well documented, mostly with primary sources. About one-third of the book is devoted to West German-Soviet relations, with a stout defense of Adenauer's policies. (In the English edition, footnotes and references are omitted.)

IJ343 BACKHAUS, WILHELM. *Begegnung im Kreml; so wurden die Gefangenen befreit.* Berlin: Ullstein, 1955. 93 p. A popular account emphasizing the human interest side of the Moscow negotiations in 1955, with no documentation, by a journalist. Supports the West German government point of view.

IJ344 BESPALOV, G. M. *Vozrozhdenie germanskogo militarizma—ugroza miru.* Moscow: Gospolitizdat, 1953. 238 p. Sees the U.S. utilizing West German militarism to accomplish its plans for world hegemony. Makes accusations in the worst style of the Stalinist period—e.g., that Wall Street and the Nazi government conspired during World War II to prevent the victory of progressive forces.

IJ345 BOHN, HELMUT. *Die Letzten; Was wurde und was wird aus den deutschen Gefangenen in Sowjetrussland und den anderen Ostblockstaaten?* Cologne: Markus, 1954. 108 p. A popular account with very limited documentation, reflecting the view prevailing generally in Germany on the fate and number of German prisoners of war in the Soviet Union in the years after World War II. By a journalist.

IJ346 FELD, WERNER. *Reunification and West German-Soviet Relations.* The Hague: Nijhoff, 1963. 204 p. A scholarly study, completely documented, mainly on the basis of primary German sources, by an American college professor. Devoted to a critical appraisal of West German foreign policy in respect to major West German-Soviet issues, with an analysis of the decision making process and emphasis on the value orientation of the policy makers. [A]

IJ347 FLECHTHEIM, OSSIP K. *Die deutschen Parteien seit 1945, Quellen und Auszüge.* Berlin: C. Heymann, 1955. 158 p. Selections from leading German experts writing on the legal status, social composition, organization and finance of the West German parties. The role of German partition as a factor in the party system is more implicit than explicit in these excerpts.

IJ348 GREWE, WILHELM G. *Deutsche Aussenpolitik der Nachkriegszeit.* Stuttgart: Deutsche Verlags-Anstalt, 1960. 539 p. A scholarly approach, mostly on the basis of primary sources, but not completely documented. About half of the book is devoted to West German-

Soviet relations and supports official West German government policies. Written by an international law expert and West German ambassador to the United States, the book contains a number of the author's previous articles and speeches.

IJ349 HINTERHOFF, EUGENE. *Disengagement.* London: Stevens, 1959. 782 p. A critical appraisal of West German foreign policy emphasizing relations with Eastern Europe. The author, a former officer, uses mainly secondary sources to support proposals for military disengagement in Europe. Contains a table analyzing plans for European disengagement, 1946-59. [B]

IJ350 KLUTH, HANS. *Die KPD in der Bundesrepublik, ihre politische Tätigkeit und Organisation, 1946-1956.* Cologne: Westdeutscher, 1959. 154 p. A serious scholarly study, completely documented, mainly from primary sources, based on the author's doctoral dissertation. An objective investigation of all facets of KPD activities from 1945 to 1956 and certain illegal activities during 1957. [A]

IJ351 KOMMUNISTISCHE PARTEI DEUTSCHLANDS. *Weissbuch der KPD ueber die muendliche Verhandlung im Verbotsprozess vor dem Bundesverfassungsgericht in Karlsruhe; zusammengestellt nach dem amtlichen Verhandlungsprotokoll des Gerichts.* Berlin: Dietz, 1955. 311 p. Eng. ed., *The Karlsruhe Trial for Banning the Communist Party of Germany.* London: Lawrence & Wishart, 1956. 127 p. A Communist commentary on the trial to ban the KPD in West Germany, with extensive selections from the trial record. The trial is viewed as analogous to the Nazi-organized trial of the German Communist Party following the Reichstag fire in 1933. The new trial was arranged by "monopolists, big property owners, revanchist politicians and militarists," all directed by American reaction, and all viewing the trial as the first step in the forcible reunification of Germany.

IJ352 KOMMUNISTISCHE PARTEI DEUTSCHLANDS, DEFENDANT. *Weissbuch der KPD ueber die ersten 6 Monate des Verbotsprozesses vor dem Bundesverfassungsgericht in Karlsruhe; zusammengestellt nach dem amtlichen Verhandlungsprotokoll des Gerichts.* Düsseldorf, 1955. 176 p. An interim "White Book" issued while the trial to determine the legality of the German Communist Party in West Germany was in progress. The *Weissbuch der KPD ueber die muendlich Verhandlung* . . . is more complete, since it was published after the conclusion of the trial.

IJ353 KOMMUNISTISCHE PARTEI DEUTSCHLANDS, RESPONDENT. *KPD-Prozess; Dokumentarwerk zu dem Verfahren über den Antrag der Bundesregierung auf Feststellung der Verfassungswid-*

rigkeit der KPD vor dem Ersten Senat des Bundesverfassungsgerichts. Pub. by Gerd Pfeiffer and Hans-Georg Strickert. Karlsruhe: C. F. Mueller, 1955-56. 3 vols. Condensed English version, GERMANY (FEDERAL REPUBLIC, 1949-), BUNDESVERFASSUNGSGERICHT. *Action Against the Communist Party of Germany.* Washington: 1957. 372 p. Also published under the title *Outlawing the Communist Party, A Case History.* N.Y.: Bookmailer, 1957. 227 p. A complete record of the trial, including oral testimony, statements and documents submitted by the Federal Republic and the Communist Party for the trial record, and the text of the court decision. Very detailed indexes and registers facilitate use of the volumes. The text of the court decision has been excerpted and published separately by the Mueller Verlag.

IJ354 KUCZYNSKI, JURGEN. *Polozhenie rabochego klassa v Zapadnoi Germanii, 1945-1956 gg.* Moscow: Izd. Inostr. lit., 1957. 408 p. Translation of Volume II of the author's *Die Geschichte der Lage der Arbeiter unter dem Kapitalismus.* Berlin: Tribune, 1954-56, 8 vols. in 13. A Communist view which sees the postwar developments in West Germany divided into three phases: "Colonization, 1945-1947," "Transformation, 1948-1950," and "Return of German Imperialism, 1951-1954."

IJ354A MASON, JOHN BROWN. "Government, Administration, and Politics in West Germany: a Selected Bibliography," *The American Political Science Review*, vol. LII, no. 2 (June 1958), pp. 513-530.

IJ355 MUNKE, STEPHANIE. *Wahlkampf und Machtverschiebung; Geschichte und Analyse der Berliner Wahlen vom 3. Dezember 1950.* Berlin: Duncker and Humblot, 1952. 282 p. An exhaustive but wordy study of the West Berlin elections of December 1950. Includes sections on the role of the Communist Party and influence exercised from the East Sector. Useful tables and charts, but no bibliography.

IJ356 REIMANN, M. *Die nationale Bedeutung der Volksbewegung in Westdeutschland und die Aufgaben der KPD.* Berlin: Dietz, 1954. 91 p. A report to the Executive Committee of the KPD, surveying the international and domestic situation in typical Communist fashion. Among the more blatant distortions is one describing West Germany as a place where four-fifths of the people make less than the minimum income for existence, while in the DDR wages are rising as prices drop because "industry belongs to the people."

IJ357 RICHTER, KARL. *Die trojanische Herde, ein dokumentarischer Bericht.* Cologne: Verlag für Politik und Wirtschaft, 1959. 314 p. By a journalist. A political study not entirely objective and with limited documentation, perhaps due to the subject matter. Discusses Communist underground activities and alleged pro-Communist fronts in West Germany.

IJ358 SCHÜTZ, WILHELM W. *Deutschland am Rande zweier Welten; Voraussetzungen und Aufgabe unserer Aussenpolitik.* Stuttgart: Deutsche Verlag-Anstalt, 1952. 117 p. A keen observer discusses debatable proposals for a new and active West German policy in Eastern Europe.

IJ359 SCHÜTZ, WILHELM W. *Die Stunde Deutschlands; Möglichkeiten einer Politik der Wiedervereinigung.* Stuttgart: Deutsche, 1954. 139 p. A provocative polemic proposing an active West German eastern policy and other measures to achieve reunification, by a brilliant independent commentator who also heads the organization "Unteilbares Deutschland."

IJ360 SETHE, PAUL. *Zwischen Bonn und Moskau.* Frankfurt/Main: Scheffler, 1957. 179 p. A popular account of West German-Soviet relations 1945-56, with limited documentation, mostly secondary sources. Highly critical of official policy of Federal government, recommending direct negotiations with the Soviet Union, but also continued, yet more flexible, cooperation with the West. By a journalist. [B]

IJ361 SIEGLER, HEINRICH VON, comp. *Dokumentation zur Deutschlandfrage, von der Atlantik Charta 1941 bis zur Genfer Aussenministerkonferenz 1959.* Bonn: Bundesdruckerei, 1959. 2 vols. A very valuable collection containing official and unofficial documents, declarations, and statements either in full or pertinent parts thereof, pertaining to West German-Soviet relations. [A]

IJ362 SIEGLER, HEINRICH VON, comp. *Wiedervereinigung und Sicherheit Deutschlands; eine dokumentarische Diskussionsgrundlage.* 3rd enlarged and revised ed. Bonn: Siegler, 1958. 305 p. English ed., Bonn: Siegler, 1957. 184 p. A useful volume containing major official and unofficial documents, declarations, and statements in full, in part, or summarized, pertaining to West German-Soviet relations. [B]

IJ363 STARLINGER, WILHELM. *Grenzen der Sowjetmacht im Spiegel einer West-Ostbegegnung hinter Palisaden von 1945-1954; Mit einem Bericht der deutschen Seuchenkrankenhäuser Yorck und St. Elisabeth über das Leben und Sterben in Königsberg von 1945-1947; zugleich ein Beitrag zur Kenntnis des Ablaufes gekoppelter Grosseuchen unter elementaren Bedingungen.* Würzburg: Holzner-Verlag, 1955. 131 p. Composed of 3 unrelated parts: the author's experiences as director of a hospital in Königsberg after its fall to the Russians, his life in a Soviet prison camp, and his reflections on the future of Soviet policy. This third part is said to have influenced Adenauer's foreign policy. Starlinger sees future Soviet policy determined by a break with Communist China, which will force the USSR to turn to its western neighbors. This will restore Germany to a primary position in world affairs, as a link between the two giants, the U.S. and the USSR. This requires that the Bundesrepublik remain true to its American ties—which sums up Adenauer's policy.

IJ364 TETENS, TETE H. *Germany Plots with the Kremlin.* N.Y.: Schuman, 1953. 294 p. A highly biased popular account by a journalist-political analyst of German secret plans for future close cooperation with the Soviet Union alleged to be designed by Adenauer and former Ribbentrop diplomats. Documented, but the genuineness of many primary sources is doubtful, excerpts are often incomplete, and the evidence is frequently inconclusive.

IJ365 U.S. LIBRARY OF CONGRESS, SERIAL DIVISION. *German Federal Republic Official Publications, 1949-1957; A Survey.* Prepared by James B. Childs. Washington: 1958. 2 vols. A handy check list of publications of the Bonn Government.

IJ366 *Verschwörung gegen die Freiheit, die kommunistische Untergrundarbeit in der Bundesrepublik.* Munich: Münchener Arbeitsgruppe "Kommunistische Infiltration und Machtkampftechnik" im Komitee "Rettet die Freiheit," 1960. 175 p. A comprehensive study of Communist underground activities in West German news media, trade unions, armed forces, political parties, youth organizations, intellectual circles, and "peace campaigns." Very limited documentation, perhaps due to subject matter; possibly not entirely objective.

IJ367 VOSLENSKII, M. S. *Vneshniaia politika i partii FRG.* Moscow: Izd. IMO, 1960. 310 p.

IJ368 WORLICZEK, ADALBERT. *Bonn-Moskau; die Ostpolitik Adenauers.* Munich: Isar, 1957. 160 p. A serious study by a former journalist, but with very limited documentation and some primary sources. Attempts to refute the arguments of critics of official West German policy toward the Soviet Union and stoutly defends this policy.

IJ369 ZALETNYI, A. *Bundesver; zapadno-germanskie vooruzhennye sily—orudie agressii.* Moscow: 1958. 142 p. In this Soviet view, German militarists have returned to the saddle under the aegis of the "North Atlantic Bloc."

IJ370 *Zapadnyi Berlin.* Ed. by P. A. Shteiniger. Moscow: Izd. inostr. lit., 1961. 349 p.

7. GERMAN COMMUNIST PARTY, 1917-1945

(Edited by Siegfried Bahne)

a. INTRODUCTORY NOTE

The following selective bibliography is intended for both the student and those with more advanced interests in the history of the KPD; it endeavors to give in limited space a comprehensive survey of the most important printed sources and literature. For additional bibliographical aid, consult the following: Enzo Colotti, ed., *Die Kommunistische Partei Deutschlands, 1918-1933* (Milan: Istituto G. Feltrinelli, 1961. 217 p.) This is the most complete (though selective) bibliography yet published on the history of the KPD, and is useful, despite the editor's preference for the Communist line in the selection of books, and above all, in his introductory passages. It is valuable also for listing articles from *Die Internationale* and *Die Rote Fahne*.

Relatively unimportant for serious studies are the partial bibliographies published in East Germany, such as: *Bibliographie zur Geschichte der kommunistischen und Arbeiterparteien (Literatur aus den Jahren 1945-1958)*, Bd. 2, Teil 1 (KPD and SED), edited by the Institut für Gesellschaftswissenschaften beim ZK der SED, Berlin: printed as MS., 1959, IV, 531 p. See also the bibliographies concerning Rosa Luxemburg and Karl Liebknecht, Clara Zetkin, and Ernst Thälmann published in the *Schriftenreihe der Gesellschaftswissenschaftlichen Beratungsstellen* and the *Bibliografia Pierwodruków Rózy Luksemburg* in the Polish periodical, *Z Pola Walki*, 1962, p. 161-226.

For unprinted dissertations in the German Democratic Republic see the special publication of the *Zeitschrift für Geschichtswissenschaft: Historische Forschungen in der DDR* (Berlin: 1960, p. 300-402).

Only a limited number of periodical articles could be cited. For leads to periodical literature see: *R. Dietrichs deutsche Bibliographie der Zeitschriftenliteratur* (Osnabrück); *Internationale Bibliographie der marxistischen Zeitschriftenliteratur* (Berlin: since 1950); and the bibliographies in the *Vierteljahrshefte für Zeitgeschichte*, the *Zeitschrift für Geschichtswissenschaft*, and the *Beiträge zur Geschichte der deutschen Arbeiterbewegung*.

For the difficulties and ambiguities of Communist historical literature, the reader should refer to an article by Jane Degras, "Sur l'histoire du Comintern" in *Le Contrat Social*, v (1961), no. 1, p. 5-12. The following should also be kept in mind: general works on the history of the Communist International (Franz Borkenau, Jane Degras, C.L.R. James, Christo Kabaktschieff, Günther Nollau, William Z. Foster), and on the history of the German parties (Ludwig Bergsträsser), the protocols of the proceedings of the German Reichstag and the Prussian Landtag, and, finally, the speeches and writings—after 1924—of Stalin. The student should also note the protocols of the congresses of the Communist International and of the Red International of Labor Unions, as well as the protocols of the sessions of the presidium of the Executive Committee of the Communist International and of the Central Council of the Red International of Labor Unions (for bibliographical aid, see: Giuliano Procacci, "L'Internazionale Comunista dal I al VII Congresso, 1919-1935," in: Istituto Giangiacomo Feltrinelli, *Annali*, I, Milan: Feltrinelli Editore, 1958, p. 283-315).

b. LITERATURE ABOUT THE KPD

IJ371 AKADEMIE DER WISSENSCHAFTEN, BERLIN, INSTITUT FÜR GESCHICHTE. *Revolutionäre Ereignisse und Probleme in Deutschland während der Periode der Grossen Sozialistischen Oktoberrevolution, 1917-1918; Beiträge zum 40. Jahrestag der Grossen Sozialistischen Oktoberrevolution.* Ed. by Albert Schreiner. Berlin: Akademie, 1957. 353 p. A Communist collective work with contributions on the Berlin strike of 1917-18 (H. Scheel and W. Bartel), the revolutionary movement in the navy (H. J. Bernhard and K. Zeisler), the council (soviet) movement (A. Schreiner and G. Schmidt) and the position of the German worker parties toward the October revolution (R. Leibbrand and K. Mammach).

IJ372 ANDERSON, EVELYN. *Hammer or Anvil; the Story of the German Working-Class Movement.* London: Gollancz, 1945. 207 p. A concise survey of German history from 1918 to 1945 from the Social-Democratic standpoint, written by a longtime member of the German workingclass movement (who later lived as a journalist in England) from "critical distance" with relatively thorough consideration of the KPD. (See also R. T. Clark, *The Fall of the German Republic*, London: 1935; and A. Rosenberg, *Geschichte der Weimarer Republik*, Karlsbad: 1935; English ed., London: 1936.)

IJ372A ANGRESS, WERNER T. *Stillborn Revolution: The Communist Bid for Power in Germany, 1921-1923.* Princeton, N.J.: Princeton Univ. Press, 1964.

IJ373 BAHNE, SIEGFRIED. "Die Kommunistische Partei Deutschlands," p. 655-739 in *Das Ende der Parteien: 1933.* Ed. by E. Matthias and R. Morsey. Düsseldorf: Droste, 1960. A narrative of the policies of the KPD in the last years of the "ultra-left" tactics (1932-35), its reaction to Hitler's assumption of power, and its gradual shift to the policies of "unity" and "People's Front" in 1934-35. Includes an introductory survey of the organizational and sociological membership of the KPD before 1932. Based chiefly on printed primary sources, it includes a selection of documents. (See also *Zeitschrift für Politik*, 1960, pp. 168-178.)

IJ374 BAHNE, SIEGFRIED. "Der Trotzkismus in Deutschland, 1931-1933; ein Beitrag zur Geschichte der KPD und der Komintern." Dissertation, University of Heidelberg, 1958. 359 p. After a survey of Trotsky's career and the content and the development of his theories, which have come to be known as "Trotskyism," the "Trotskyite" judgment of the political situation in Germany and the policies of the KPD before 1933 are described. The conclusion is devoted to a survey of the period 1933-40. The bibliography contains a list of Trotsky's books, pamphlets, and articles published in German.

IJ375 BAHNE, SIEGFRIED. "Zwischen 'Luxemburgismus' und 'Stalinismus'; die 'ultralinke' Opposition in der KPD." *Vierteljahrshefte für Zeitgeschichte*, VIII (1961), 359-383. Treats the oppositional Communist groups around the left leaders I. Katz, Karl Korsch, and E. Schwarz, with a short discussion of Korsch's theories.

IJ376 BARTEL, WALTER. *Deutschland in der Zeit der faschistischen Diktatur, 1933-1945*. Berlin: Volk und Wissen, 1956. 270 p. Originally composed as a letter of instruction for correspondence studies of teachers of the intermediate level, this is a popular narrative of the history of the "Third Reich," in which the KPD appears as the single serious and consequential domestic opponent of National Socialism ("Fascism"). Bartel is a professor in the University of East Berlin and Director of the Institut für Zeitgeschichte in the DDR.

IJ377 BARTEL, WALTER. *Die Linken in der deutschen Sozialdemokratie im Kampf gegen Militarismus und Krieg*. Berlin: Dietz, 1958. 640 p. Bartel investigates the policies of the Liebknecht-Luxemburg group and the Bremer "Arbeiterpolitik." The Bremer group is rather neglected and Radek is not mentioned (see K. Radek, *In den Reihen der deutschen Revolution, 1909-1919*, Munich: Wolff, 1921, 464 p.). In spite of its deficiencies (see *Zeitschrift für Geschichtswissenschaft*, VI, p. 1153ff), this is an important contribution to the early history of the KPD from the contemporary Communist point of view (with an unhistorical emphasis on the national components!), utilizing archival material. [A]

IJ378 BARTEL, WALTER. "Probleme des antifaschistischen Widerstandskampfes in Deutschland." *Zeitschrift für Geschichtswissenschaft*. VI (1958), p. 999-1016. Brings together the provisional results of Communist historiography of the KPD's resistance in the Third Reich. (Cf. F. Knittel, in *Zeitschrift für Geschichtswissenschaft*, VI, Sonderheft, p.

190-201, and in *Der 2. Weltkrieg, 1939-1945*, Berlin: 1959, p. 63ff., and *Der deutsche Imperialismus und der zweite Weltkrieg*, Berlin: 1961, vol. II, p. 711-765.)

IJ379 BECHER, JOHANNES R. *Walter Ulbricht: ein deutscher Arbeitersohn.* Berlin: Dietz, 1958. 227 p. 2nd ed.: 1960. A popular biography by the prominent Communist poet and first Minister of Culture of the DDR. A new biography of Ulbricht by Carola Stern was published in Cologne in 1964.

IJ380 BERLIN, INSTITUT FÜR GESELLSCHAFTSWISSENSCHAFTEN. *Die Gründung der Kommunistischen Partei Deutschlands; Protokoll der wissenschaftlichen Tagung des Instituts für Gesellschaftswissenschaften der Parteihochschule "Karl Marx" und des Instituts für Marxismus-Leninismus beim Zentralkomitee der SED am 22./23. Jan. 1959 in Berlin anlässlich des 40. Jahrestages der Gründung der KPD.* Berlin: Dietz, 1959. 243 p. A collective work with contributions of 16 Communist historians and Party officials (among others H. Matern, R. Lindau, W. Raase) dealing with the organizational construction of the KPD in 1919, the relation of the Bremer left-radicals to the Spartacus group, Liebknecht's role, the character of the councils (soviets) in the November revolution, and so forth.

IJ381 BERLIN, INSTITUT FÜR MARXISMUS-LENINISMUS. *Die Märzkämpfe 1921; überarbeitetes Protokoll einer wissenschaftlichen Beratung am 28. Februar 1956.* Berlin: Dietz, 1956. 188 p. A Communist collective work with contributions by F. Knittel, B. Koenen, S. Ittershagen (about Max Hoelz), R. Lindau, and others.

IJ382 BERTHOLD, LOTHAR. *Das Programm der KPD zur nationalen und sozialen Befreiung des deutschen Volkes vom August 1930.* Berlin: Dietz, 1956. 308 p. This work was accepted as a dissertation by the "Karl Marx" Party school in 1955. The author is now Director of the Institut für Marxismus-Leninismus. The work treats from the Communist point of view the program declaration of August 24, 1930, which had as an important aim the combatting of the growing Nazi influence, and its implementation through a peasants aid program and a plan for the lessening of unemployment (May 1931), in order to draw useful applications for the present.

IJ383 BERTHOLD, LOTHAR. "Der Kampf der KPD gegen den drohenden Krieg; Die Berner Konferenz." *Zeitschrift für Geschichtswissenschaft.* VIII (1960), p. 583-598. Also in: *Der deutsche Imperialismus und der 2. Weltkrieg.* Berlin: 1960. Originally presented as a contribution to the discussion at a conference of Communist historians, this essay examines the significance for Party tactics of the so-called "Bern Conference" of the KPD in January 1939.

IJ384 BLUMBERG, N. B. "The German Communist Movement, 1918-1923." D. Phil. dissertation, Oxford, 1950.

IJ385 BORKENAU, FRANZ. *The Communist International.* London: Faber and Faber, 1938. 442 p. American ed., *World Communism.* N.Y.: Norton, 1939. A standard history of the Comintern. Since the author was a former member of the KPD, there is much information about the Communist movement in Germany. [A]

IJ385A BRAUN, WILHELM. "Sowjetrussland zwischen SPD und KPD. Eine Untersuchung zum Problem des gegenseitigen Verhältnisses von SPD und KPD in den Jahren des Zerfalls der Weimarer Republik (1930-1933)." Dissertation, Univ. of Tübingen, 1959. 122 p.

IJ386 BREDEL, WILLI. *Ernst Thälmann; Beitrag zu einem politischen Lebensbild.* Berlin: Dietz, 1948. 199 p. 7th ed.: 1953. Russian ed., Moscow: 1952. A popular biography by a prominent Communist publicist. Contains a memorial address by W. Ulbricht delivered in 1949. For a supplementary work, see I. Thälmann, *Erinnerungen an meinen Vater*, Berlin: 1960.

IJ387 BRY, GERHARD. "Ein Beitrag zur Geschichte der KPD." Unpublished manuscript, Institute of Social Research, Columbia University.

IJ388 BUBER, MARGARETE. *Von Potsdam nach Moskau; Stationen eines Irrweges.* Stuttgart: Deutsche Verlags-Anstalt, 1957. 477 p. Recollections of the former comrade of the KPD leader Heinz Neumann, who died in 1937 in the USSR, and the sister-in-law of W. Münzenberg. An important, but often rather subjective, report on the atmosphere and directional struggles within the KPD leadership, especially in the years from 1929 to 1932. [B]

IJ389 COLM, GERHARD. *Beitrag zur Geschichte und Soziologie des Ruhraufstandes vom März-April, 1920.* Essen: Baedeker, 1921. 142 p. A narrative of the construction and organization of the "Red Army" in the Ruhr and its struggle with the Reichswehr after the Kapp Putsch. The study, which originated at the suggestion of Max Weber, utilizes testimony of witnesses and some documents.

IJ389A COLOTTI, ENZO, ed. *Die Kommunistische Partei Deutschlands, 1918-1933.* Milan: Istituto G. Feltrinelli, 1961. 217 p. In spite of the obvious pro-Communist orientation of the editor, this remains the most comprehensive of the bibliographies on the KPD that have appeared to date. [A]

IJ390 *Deutschlands unsterblicher Sohn; Erinnerungen an Ernst Thälmann.* Berlin: Dietz, 1961. 476 p. A collective work for popular consumption with contributions from prominent Communists (Pieck, Ulbricht, Lindau, Abusch, Selbmann, Weinert, Rau, Einicke, Reimann, Dahlem, Rosa Thälmann, Walter Bartel). The dates when the various contributions were written are not given.

IJ391 DIAKIN, V. S. *Kommunisticheskaia Partiia Germanii i problema edinogo fronta v gody otnositelnoi stabilizatsii 1924-1929 gg.* Moscow-Leningrad: Izd. Akad. nauk SSSR, 1961. 139 p. Relies mainly on the contemporary press and on documents from the Museum of the Revolution in the USSR.

IJ392 DORNEMANN, LUISE. *Clara Zetkin; ein Lebensbild.* Berlin: Dietz, 1957. 439 p. A Communist biography written in a popular vein.

IJ393 EHRT, ADOLF. *Bewaffneter Aufstand.* Berlin: Eckart, 1933. 183 p. A Nazi compilation of statistics and other information about Communist treason and terrorism.

IJ394 EHRT, ADOLF, and SCHWEICKERT, JULIUS. *Entfesselung der Unterwelt.* Berlin: Eckart, 1932. 320 p. An extensive and hostile survey of Communist activity and organization in the Weimar Republic. The same account is available in Ehrt's *Communism in Germany* (Berlin: Eckart, 1933, 179 p.), published under the auspices of the General League of German Anti-Communist Associations.

IJ395 ERPENBECK, FRITZ. *Wilhelm Pieck; ein Lebensbild.* Berlin: Dietz, 1951. 172 p. 2nd ed., 1952. A Communist biography written for popular consumption.

IJ395A ERSIL, WILHELM. *Aktionseinheit stürzt Cuno; zur Geschichte des Massenkampfes gegen die Cuno-Regierung 1923 in Mitteldeutschland.* Berlin: Dietz, 1963. 440 p. A Communist exploration of the strikes and the actions of the KPD in the Prussian governmental districts of Magdeburg and Merseburg (province of Saxony) and the state of Anhalt during the spring and the summer of 1923, without regard to the fights in the fall. The author relies on documents and on accounts of former combatants.

IJ396 FISCHER, RUTH. *Stalin and German Communism; a Study in the Origins of the State Party.* Cambridge: Harvard; London: Oxford, 1948. 687 p. German ed., Frankfurt a/M: 1950. 831 p. The author, who—with Maslow—was a leader of the "left" wing and, in 1924-25, of the KPD, was expelled from the Party in 1926 as a "Leftist-deviator." Her account, which extends to 1927, is not free from subjective evaluations and apologetic tendencies, and her facts are not always trustworthy. It is, nevertheless, one of the most important descriptions of the first years of the KPD, concluding with the subordination of the Party to Stalin's will. [A]

IJ397 FLECHTHEIM, OSSIP K. *Die Kommunistische Partei Deutschlands in der Weimarer Republik.* Offenbach a/M: Bollwerk-Verlag K. Drott, 1948. 294 p. The first comprehensive history of the Party for the Weimar period. It is based on a Heidelberg dissertation, but rests on a rather limited selection of sources and literature. It is indispensable as an introduction for anyone interested in the history of the KPD. Contains a chapter on the ideology and sociology of the KPD and a documentary appendix. The author, who was closely connected with Social Democracy, had to leave Germany after 1933; he was active for several years in the U.S. and today is a Professor at the West Berlin University. [A]

IJ398 FRÖLICH, PAUL. *Rosa Luxemburg; Gedanke und Tat.* Paris: Nouvelles Internationales, 1939. 302 p. New ed., Hamburg: Oetinger, 1949. English ed., *Rosa Luxemburg, Her Life and Work.* London: Gollancz, 1940. 336 p. A biography of the leader of the left-wing of the SPD and the co-founder of the KPD, murdered in 1919. Her activity in the Polish and German workers' movement and her political and economic ideas are presented in detail. The author was an official of the KPD until 1928, when he was expelled as a "rightist" follower of Brandler. [B]

IJ399 FRÖLICH, PAUL. *Zehn Jahre Krieg und Bürgerkrieg.* Vol. I, *Der Krieg.* Berlin: Vereinigung Internationaler Verlags-Anstalten, 1924. 256 p. A Communist narrative of the political course of World War I, and of the attitude of German Social-Democracy and the left-Socialist opponents of the "imperialist war." The author himself was a leader of the "Bremer Linke." Vol. II has never been published.

IJ400 GEYER, CURT. *Der Radikalismus in der deutschen Arbeiterbewegung; ein soziologischer Versuch.* Jena: Thüringer Verlagsanstalt, 1923. 111 p. By a former leader of the USPD (Independent Social-Democratic Party of Germany) and the VKPD (United Communist Party of Germany) who returned to the SPD in 1921. He seeks to explain the social-psychological background of Communistic radicalism in Germany after the first World War, portraying this type of radicalism as un-Marxist and as "political romanticism." He relies to a considerable extent on Scipio Sighele, *Psychologie des sectes*, Paris: 1898.

IJ401 GIRARDET, HERBERT. *Der wirtschaftliche Aufbau der kommunistischen Tagespresse in Deutschland von 1918-1933, unter besonderer Berücksichtigung der Verhältnisse im Regierungsbezirk Düsseldorf.* Essen: Girardet, 1938. 124 p. The value of this published University of Leipzig dissertation by a professor of journalism lies in the information it passes on of studies of deeds and interrogations of imprisoned Communists. It throws some light on the KPD's property holdings (publishing houses, presses, real estate). The reader should take into account that the book was written during the Nazi era.

IJ402 GLONDAJEWSKI, GERTRUD, and SCHUMANN, HEINZ. *Die Neubauer-Poser-Gruppe; Dokumente und Materialien des illegalen antifaschistischen Kampfes (Thüringen, 1939-1945).* Berlin: Dietz, 1957. 128 p. A Communist narrative of the KP-resistance in a section of Middle-Germany, with short biographies of, among others, M. Poser and T. Neubauer, who in 1943-44, together with G. Schumann, A. Saefkow, B. Bästlein and F. Jacob, belonged to the so-called "central operative command of the KPD" in Germany. The authors are members of the Institut für Marxismus-Leninismus.

IJ403 GROSS, GÜNTHER. *Der gewerkschaftliche Widerstandskampf der deutschen Arbeiterklasse während der faschistischen Vertrauensräte-Wahlen 1934.* Berlin: Tribüne, 1961. 88 p. An account of Communist tactics in the election of the "Vertrauensräte" (the Nazi term for shop committees—"Betriebsräte"), which were substituted for the Betriebsräte in the spring of 1934. The author is a member of the Institut für Gesellschaftswissenschaften beim ZK der SED. For a description of the shop committee elections in 1935, see W. Wehling, *Beiträge zur Geschichte der deutschen Arbeiterbewegung*, 1960, II, p. 488-507.

IJ403A *Grundriss der Geschichte der deutschen Arbeiterbewegung.* Berlin: Dietz, 1963. 304 p. The official history of the German workers' movement, as laid down by the Central Committee of the SED. Begins with the commencement of the political activities of Marx and Engels in the years about 1848, and is divided in five main periods. Those chapters of the book which treat of the time after the foundation of the KPD at the end of 1918 are essentially a short survey on the history of the KPD, cut up according to the present necessities of the SED, with an over-estimation of the role of the Party. See the critiques in *Jahrbuch für die Geschichte Mittel- und Ostdeutschlands*, Bd. XIII, and Hermann Weber's book on the *Grundriss* (Köln: 1964). [A]

IJ404 HABEDANK, HEINZ. *Zur Geschichte des Hamburger Aufstandes 1923.* Berlin: Dietz, 1958. 216 p. A Communist narrative of the struggle in Hamburg in October 1923, developed from an East-Berlin dissertation. Uses archival material and oral statements. Seeks to prove that the uprising was not a Putsch "carried out by adventurers," but that real foundations existed for a Communist revolution in the autumn of 1923. About half the book is devoted to the events leading up to the uprising.

IJ405 HAMMER, FRANZ. *Theodor Neubauer; ein Kämpfer gegen den Faschismus.* Berlin: Dietz, 1956. 104 p. A Communist biography of the long-time foreign affairs expert of the delegation of the KPD in the Reichstag before 1933, who was executed in February 1945.

IJ406 HEYE, HAROLD E. "The Communist Party of Germany, 1928-1930." Ph.D. dissertation, Yale, 1954.

IJ407 IMIG, WERNER. *Der Streik der Mansfelder Arbeiter im Jahre 1930*. Berlin: Dietz, 1957. 104 p. Enlarged ed., *Streik bei Mansfeld, 1930; Der Streik der Mansfeld-Arbeiter im Jahre 1930 und seine Unterdrückung mit Hilfe des Staatsapparates der Weimarer Republik*. Berlin: Tribüne, 1958. 264 p. Deals with one of the most important German strikes of the Depression period, which occurred in June and July of 1930 and in which about 13,000 persons took part. Based on archives of the State and of the Mansfeld joint-stock company record office and on the accounts of KPD officials who participated. Investigates the application of tactics developed after 1928 by the KPD and RGO (Revolutionäre Gewerkschaftsopposition) from the present-day Communist point of view.

IJ407A INSTITUT FÜR GESELLSCHAFTSWISSENSCHAFTEN BEIM ZK DER SED. *Bibliographie zur Geschichte der kommunistischen und Arbeiterparteien (Literatur aus den Jahren 1945-1958)*. Berlin: 1959. 531 p. An incomplete East German bibliography, of little use to serious students of the KPD and SED.

IJ408 KARL, HEINZ. *Die deutsche Arbeiterklasse im Kampf um die Enteignung der Fürsten, 1925-1926*. Berlin: Dietz, 1957. 108 p. A Communist account of the referendum concerning uncompensated appropriation of the property of the German princely families which ruled before 1918. Includes a rather large documentary appendix, mostly KPD texts.

IJ409 KIESSLING, WOLFGANG. *Ernst Schneller; Lebensbild eines Revolutionärs*. Berlin: Dietz, 1960. 243 p. A popular Communist biography of a leading KPD official, an expert on military affairs and "Agitprop" activities, who was shot in a concentration camp in 1944. Utilizes archive material and eye witness accounts.

IJ410 KISLJAKOW, W. S. "Der Kampf der KPD für die Schaffung der antifaschistischen Einheitsfront in den ersten Jahren der faschistischen Diktatur." p. 396-418 in: *Sowjetwissenschaft; Gesellschaftswissenschaftliche Beiträge*. East Berlin: 1960. An essay of a Soviet historian which first appeared in *Voprosy Istorii* (No. 12, 1959). It examines KPD policies from 1933 to 1936, and attempts to demonstrate that the German Communists, in spite of some errors in 1933-34, were willing, after the establishment of Nazi rule, to set up a true unity front with the SPD.

IJ411 KÖLLER, HEINZ. *Kampfbündnis an der Seine, Ruhr und Spree; der gemeinsame Kampf der KPF und KPD gegen die Ruhrbesetzung 1923.* Berlin: Rütten & Loening, 1963. 348 p. A Communist account of the common fight of the German and French Communist Parties against the governments of Cuno and Poincaré. Uses documents of the German government from the Deutsches Zentral-Archiv, Potsdam. Calls special attention to the national politics of the KPD.

IJ412 KRAUSE, ILSE. *Die Schumann-Engert-Kresse-Gruppe; Dokumente und Materialien des illegalen antifaschistischen Kampfes (Leipzig 1943-45).* Berlin: Dietz, 1960. 152 p. A Communist account of the KPD resistance in Saxony in the last years of the war.

IJ412A LABOOR, ERNST. *Der Kampf der deutschen Arbeiterklasse gegen Militarismus und Kriegsgefahr 1927 bis 1929.* Berlin: Dietz, 1961. 363 p. A Communist account of the activities of the German Communist Party in the years mentioned. Originally a dissertation, accepted by the Institut für Gesellschaftswissenschaften beim ZK der SED.

IJ413 LANGE, KARLHEINZ. "Die Stellung der kommunistischen Presse zum Nationalgedanken in Deutschland, untersucht an Hand der Jahrgänge der 'Roten Fahne' 1918-1933." Dissertation, U. of Munich, 1946. 437 p. An essay limited by insufficient knowledge of Communist ideology and the history of the KPD. Elucidates the methods of work of Communist journalists in Germany, using as an example their treatment of the concept of the nation. Appendix includes statistics of the KPD daily press.

IJ414 LEONTEV, A. *Kommunisticheskaia partiia Germanii; ocherk razvitiia.* Moscow: "Krasnaia nov," 1924. 127 p.

IJ415 LOWENTHAL, RICHARD. "The Bolshevisation of the Spartacus League." In: *International Communism.* St. Antony's Papers, no. 9, ed. by David Footman. London: Chatto & Windus, 1960. pp. 23-71. A serious scholarly study describing the beginning phase of the KPD's assimilation process, with its Bolshevik methods and leadership. The author begins with a description of the Party at the time of its founding, and follows this up with a sketch of the gradual growth of Moscow's influence (Zinoviev, Radek, Lenin) with the "mechanical" splitting of the USPD (Independent Social-Democratic Party of Germany), together with Levis' resistance to this process. Lowenthal (alias Paul Sering) is a former German left-socialist who for years lived in England, where he was a prominent member of the *Observer's* staff; he is now a professor at the West Berlin University. [A]

IJ416 MASLOWSKI, PETER. *Thälmann.* Leipzig: Kittler, 1932. 94 p. The first detailed Communist biography of the KPD chairman, written before the "Thälmann-cult" came into being. Thälmann is portrayed as "a product and a result of the revolutionary workers' movement with all its greatness, but with all its defects and weaknesses."

IJ417 MATERN, HERMANN. *Aus dem Leben und Kampf der deutschen Arbeiterbewegung*. Berlin: Dietz, 1958. 368 p. A selection of speeches and essays from the years 1946 to 1958 of a member of the SED's Political Bureau, including his memorial address on Liebknecht and his lectures at the Parteihochschule on KPD policies in the period from 1924 to 1933.

IJ418 MEYER, KARL W. *Karl Liebknecht, Man without a Country*. Washington: Public Affairs Press, 1957. 180 p. By a young American historian, a professor at Wisconsin State. The emphasis is on an account of the suppression of Liebknecht after the outbreak of war in 1914; his "political immaturity and emotional idealism" are given prominence.

IJ419 MIERENDORFF, CARL. "Die Wirtschaftspolitik der KPD." Dissertation, U. of Heidelberg, 1923. 158 p. Concerns itself with the economic policies of the KPD in the first years of the Weimar Republic. Organized by sections: "Die Phase der Intransigenz" (problem of syndicalism, etc.), "Praktische Politik" (KPD economic program), and "Versuche einer eigenständigen Wirtschaftspolitik" (position on the tax and trade union questions, etc.). The author was later a prominent Social Democrat.

IJ420 MSTISLAVSKII, S. *Klassovaia voina v Germanii*. Moscow: Gosizdat, 1924. 220 p.

IJ421 NITZSCHE, GERHARD. *Die Saefkow-Jacob-Bästlein-Gruppe; Dokumente und Materialien des illegalen antifaschistischen Kampfes, 1942-1945*. Berlin: Dietz, 1957. 211 p. A Communist account of the Berlin resistance group of the KPD. The author is an assistant in the Institut für Marxismus-Leninismus.

IJ422 OELSSNER, FRED. *Rosa Luxemburg; eine kritische biographische Skizze*. Berlin: Dietz, 1952. 218 p. New ed., 1956. A former chief theoretician of the SED—demoted since this book was written—gives the best present-day German Communist evaluation of Luxemburg.

IJ422A POLZIN, HANS. "Der Kampf der KPD für eine marxistisch-leninistische Gewerkschaftspolitik von Mitte 1928 bis zum XII. (Weddinger) Parteitag." Dissertation, Institut für Gesellschaftswissenschaften beim ZK der SED, Berlin, 1962.

IJ423 PULS, URSULA. *Die Bästlein-Jacob-Abshagen-Gruppe; Bericht über den antifaschistischen Widerstandskampf in Hamburg und an der Wasserkante während des 2. Weltkrieges.* Berlin: Dietz, 1959. 227 p. A Communist narrative of the KP resistance in north Germany, chiefly according to reports of participants, since only a few documents were found. The appendix includes among other things reports of Polish and French resistance fighters.

IJ424 RAASE, WERNER. *Ernst Thälmanns revolutionäre Gewerkschaftspolitik.* Berlin: Tribüne, 1953. 114 p. 2nd ed., 1954. 109 p. A Communist account of the KPD's trade union policies during the Weimar Republic, based on a lecture delivered at the FDGB school "Fritz Heckert" in 1952. It shows how the SED views these policies, especially for the years 1924-33, and at the same time it constitutes an example of the Thälmann-cult.

IJ425 REMMELE, GERMAN. *Germanskaia kommunisticheskaia partiia.* In the series *Kompartii vsekh stran.* Ed. by Bela Kun and I. Komora. Moscow-Leningrad: Moskovskii rabochii, 1928. 157 p. The author was a prominent leader of the KPD before 1933.

IJ426 RETTIG, RUDOLF. "Die Gewerkschaftsarbeit der KPD von 1918 bis 1925; unter besonderer Berücksichtigung der Auseinandersetzungen mit den freien Arbeitergewerkschaften." Dissertation, U. of Hamburg, 1954. 268 p. An account of the fluctuations of Communist trade union policy between the founding of a special "revolutionary trade union" and the establishment of oppositional "fractions" within the so-called free (socialist) trade unions in the first years of the KPD until the inauguration of Thälmann's leadership.

IJ427 RIST, WALTER (pseud.). "Der Weg der KPD" (and other articles). *Neue Blätter für den Sozialismus.* Potsdam. II (1931), p. 434-445; III (1932), p. 79-91, 134-149, 207-211. This sequence of articles under various titles ("Die KPD in der Krise," "Der Weg der KPD," etc.) by a former long-time KPD official rests in part on unpublished official Party material. The articles treat concisely, from the critical point of view of a disillusioned comrade, the political and organizational development of the KPD as well as of splinter groups. With diagrams.

IJ427A ROGGENBUCK, HELENE. "Der Widerstandskampf der illegalen KPD während des 2. Weltkrieges in den wichtigsten Zügen und an den Schwerpunkten der inneren Front." Dissertation, U. of East Berlin, 1961.

IJ427B ROSSMANN, GERHARD. *Der Kampf der KPD um die Einheit aller Hitlergegner.* Berlin: Dietz, 1963. 300 p. A Communist story of the Communist resistance during the last years of the war, and of the organization of the illegal KPD, especially in the Berlin-Brandenburg district. Was accepted as a dissertation by the Institut für Gesellschaftswissenschaften beim ZK der KPD. Relies on archival material from the Institut für Marxismus-Leninismus, and on Communist literature, almost without regard to non-Communist literature.

IJ428 ROTTER, SEYMOUR. "Soviet and Comintern Policy Toward Germany, 1919-1923; a Case Study of Strategy and Tactics." Ph.D. dissertation, Columbia, 1954. 574 p. A study of Soviet pursuance of mutually contradictory objectives: a German proletarian revolution, and good relations with a "bourgeois" Germany. Traces Soviet and Comintern tactics in pursuing these dual policies and the results thereof.

IJ429 SCHEURIG, BODO. *Freies Deutschland; das Nationalkomitee und der Bund Deutscher Offiziere in der Sowjetunion, 1943-1945.* Munich: Nymphenburg, 1960. 269 p. An account of the goals and structure of the "Bund" and of the "Nationalkomitee" which was led by emigré German Communists. The two organizations combined in 1943 to form the NKFD (Nationalkomitee freies Deutschland). Soviet sources could not be used, but the author has tried to compensate for this lack through oral testimony of participants.

IJ429A SCHUMANN, WOLFGANG. *Oberschlesien 1918-19; Vom gemeinsamen Kampf deutscher und polnischer Arbeiter.* Berlin: Rütten & Loening, 1961. 314 p. This book, originally a dissertation at the U. of Jena, deals with the situation of labor in Upper Silesia during World War I, with the organization of councils during the revolution, the founding of the KPD there (the "KP Oberschlesiens" only came into being in 1920), and the strikes and fights in that district in 1919. A supplement contains documents. As well as published literature, documents from Polish and German archives are utilized. The author is a deputy director of the Institut für Gesellschaftswissenschaften beim ZK der SED.

IJ429B TJADEN, KARL HERMANN. "Struktur und Funktion der 'KPD-Opposition' (KPO); eine organisationssoziologische Untersuchung zur 'Rechts'-Opposition im deutschen Kommunismus zur Zeit der Weimarer Republik." Dissertation, U. of Marburg, 1963. 580 p.

IJ429C VIETZKE, SIEGFRIED. *Deutschland und die deutsche Arbeiterbewegung 1933-1939.* Berlin: Dietz, 1962. 214 p. A history, originally intended for students at the academy of the SED "Karl Marx," which lays stress upon the activities of the KPD after 1933. Almost half of the book contains statistics on German production and, above all, appeals of the KPD, and some documents of the SPD.

IJ430 WAGNER, RAIMUND. "Zur Frage der Massenkämpfe in Sachsen vom Frühjahr bis zum Sommer 1923." *Zeitschrift für*

Geschichtswissenschaft IV (1956), p. 246-264. A Communist description of the political situation in Saxony before the formation of the Social-Democratic-Communist coalition government in the fall of 1923 and the suppression of this government with military force by the central government. The author is a member of the Institut für Gesellschaftswissenschaften beim ZK der SED. (See Wagner's article in *Beiträge zur Geschichte der deutschen Arbeiterbewegung*, III, 1961, p. 188-208; and H. Gast in *Zeitschrift für Geschichtswissenschaft*, IV, p. 439-465.)

IJ431 WALDMAN, ERIC. *The Spartacist Uprising of 1919 and the Crisis of the German Socialist Movement: A Study of the Relation of Political Theory and Party Practice*. Milwaukee: Marquette, 1958. 248 p. The first section concerns itself with the development of the Left Socialists and the Spartacus Group before the November Revolution in 1918, the second with the influence of this Revolution on the various groupings of German socialism, and the third with the Spartacist Uprising in January 1919, its origin and its consequences.

IJ431A WEBER, HERMANN, ed. *Der deutsche Kommunismus; Dokumente*. Köln, Berlin: Kiepenheuer & Witsch, 1963. 679 p. Important documents on the history of German Communism, beginning with the "Leitsätze" of the Spartacus group from January 1916, and the platform of this group, which was accepted by the founding congress of the KPD, up to the documents of the SED from 1960. As a supplement the volume contains surveys on the congresses and conferences of the KPD and the SED, and on the leaderships of these parties. About two-thirds of the volume is devoted to the KPD before 1945. [A]

IJ432 WEBER, HERMANN. *Von Rosa Luxemburg zu Walter Ulbricht; Wandlungen des deutschen Kommunismus*. Hanover: Verlag für Literatur und Zeitgeschehen, 1961. 112 p. A short survey of the history of the KPD, beginning with the left opposition groups in the SPD in the first World War up to the present policy of the SED. The author—a former student of the "SED-Parteihochschule Karl Marx," who now lives in West Germany—particularly tries to show the political decline of German Communism. Suitable as an introductory account. Short chronological table. [A]

IJ433 WEINERT, ERICH. *Das Nationalkomitee "Freies Deutschland," 1943-45; Bericht über seine Tätigkeit und seine Auswirkung*. Berlin: Rütten & Loening, 1956. 200 p. An account by the well-known Communist author, who was a co-founder and president of the "The National Committee 'Free Germany,'" which was formed in the Soviet Union during World War II from German prisoners of war and émigré German Communists.

IJ434 WENZEL, OTTO. "Die KPD im Jahre 1923." Dissertation, Freie Universität Berlin, 1955. 314 p. Utilizes oral communications of KPD leaders of that year, such as Brandler, Frölich, Enderle and Wollenberg. Deals with the "proletarian" and "national" unity-front tactics, the struggle of the KPD in 1923 in occupied and unoccupied areas, the planned German "October Revolution," and the consequences of the Communist defeat. The author considers the year 1923 as the high point of the KPD's influence in the Weimar Republic, which was dangerously threatened by the greatest Communist uprising in Europe after 1917, although no "objective revolutionary situation" existed.

IJ435 WERNER, KARL and BIERNAT, KARL H. *Die Köpenicker Blutwoche 1933.* 2nd ed. Berlin: Dietz, 1960. 104 p. A Communist narrative of the Nazi terror directed against political opponents in the Berlin districts in the first months after Hitler's assumption of power in January 1933. Includes documents.

IJ436 WINZER, OTTO. *Zwölf Jahre Kampf gegen Faschismus und Krieg; ein Beitrag zur Geschichte der KPD, 1933-1945.* Berlin: Dietz, 1955. 276 p. 5th ed., 1960. A weakly documented account of the struggle of the KPD against National Socialism after 1933, based on KPD literature and material from Gestapo and court archives. The author is deputy Foreign Minister of the DDR and the long-time chief of the Präsidialkanzlei of W. Pieck. Official and "populärwissenschaftlich." [B]

IJ437 WONNEBERGER, GÜNTHER. *Deutsche Arbeitersportler gegen Faschisten und Militaristen 1929-1933; zur historischen Bedeutung des revolutionären Arbeitersports.* Berlin: Sportverlag, 1959. 225 p. Originally a dissertation for the U. of Leipzig (1956); uses archive material. Concerned most of all with the relation of the KPD to the "Interessengemeinschaft zur Wiederherstellung der Einheit im Arbeitersport," a society founded in May 1929.

IJ438 YPSILON (pseud. of Karl Volk). *Pattern for World Revolution.* Chicago-N.Y.: Ziff-Davis, 1947. 479 p. French ed., Paris: Table Ronde, 1948. 446 p. Background information on the Comintern according to the recollections and notes of a former German Communist, with rather strong consideration of the KPD and separate chapters on Thälmann, Hölz, H. Neumann, and Münzenberg. Since many of the assertions cannot be checked, the book must be used with great caution. The French edition is rather defective.

IJ439 ZEITSCHRIFT FÜR GESCHICHTSWISSENSCHAFT. *Zum 40. Jahrestag der deutschen Novemberrevolution 1918.* Berlin: Rütten & Loening, 1958. 300 p. A series of articles on various aspects of the history of German Communism. Includes a historiography of non-Communist works on the November Revolution (from a Communist point of view), and a chronology for the period from October 1918 to May 1919, as well as the official thesis of the Central Committee of the SED on the November Revolution and Ulbricht's arguments for it.

IJ440 ZEUTSCHEL, WALTER. *Im Dienst der kommunistischen Terror-Organisation (Tscheka-Arbeit in Deutschland).* Berlin: Dietz, 1931. 159 p. A report of experiences of a Communist (A. Burmeister) who participated in the Hamburg Uprising of 1923 and who then worked in the KPD's underground in north and central Germany. Written from Communist point of view, but critical of KPD leadership.

c. LITERATURE OF THE KPD

IJ441 BERLIN, INSTITUT FÜR MARXISMUS-LENINISMUS. *Dokumente und Materialien zur Geschichte der deutschen Arbeiterbewegung; Reihe II: 1914-1945.* Berlin: Dietz, 1957—. Three volumes have so far appeared: vol. I covers the period July 1914 to October 1917; vol. II, October 1917 to December 1918; and vol. III, January 1919 to May 1919. The volumes contain among other things documents having to do with the history of the Spartacus group, the Bremer Left-Radicals (IKD), and the KPD. This very important collection is, according to the *Zeitschrift für Geschichtswissenschaft* (VI, p. 1344), "not simply a collection of materials . . ., but, in the selection, the proportions, the commentaries, and so forth, a work that rests on Marxist-Leninist values." It is arranged chronologically and contains detailed chronological indexes. [A]

IJ442 BERLIN, INSTITUT FÜR MARXISMUS-LENINISMUS. *Erkämpft das Menschenrecht; Lebensbilder und letzte Briefe antifaschistischer Widerstandskämpfer.* Ed. by Heinz Schumann and Gerda Werner. Berlin: Dietz, 1958. 694 p. Contains about 500 short biographies and excerpts from the last letters of resistance fighters (predominantly Communists) in the "Third Reich."

IJ443 BERLIN, INSTITUT FÜR MARXISMUS-LENINISMUS. *Unter der roten Fahne; Erinnerungen alter Genossen.* Berlin: Dietz, 1958. 331 p. Recollections of old KPD members such as G. Sobottka, P. Schwenk, M. Arendsee, H. Marchwitza, K. Grünberg, E. Weinert, and others, from the beginning of the century to the end of the "Third Reich." Emphasis is on the decade from 1914 to 1924. Written in popular style. (Compare the Institute's publication, *Vorwärts und nicht vergessen; Erlebnisberichte aktiver Teilnehmer der Novemberrevolution, 1918-19.* Berlin: Dietz, 1958, 584 p.)

IJ444 BERLIN, INSTITUT FÜR MARXISMUS-LENINISMUS. *Zur Geschichte der KPD; eine Auswahl von Materialien und Dokumenten aus den Jahren 1914-1946*. 2nd ed. Berlin: Dietz, 1955. 473 p. A richly illustrated collection of resolutions, newspaper articles, pamphlets, etc., many of which are abstracted; included are condensations from the writings of Pieck and Ulbricht. Contains the "Program-Declaration" of August 24, 1930 as well as facsimiles of the first pages of the first and last issues of the *Rote Fahne*. Meant for popular consumption.

IJ446 COMMUNIST INTERNATIONAL, EXECUTIVE COMMITTEE. *Die Lehren der deutschen Ereignisse; das Präsidium des Exekutivkomitees der Kommunistischen Internationale zur deutschen Frage, Januar 1924*. Hamburg: Verlag der Kommunistischen Internationale, 1924. 120 p. Contains the reports of K. Radek, H. Brandler, H. Remmele, Ruth Fischer, and G. Zinoviev to the session of the Communist International's Executive Committee on January 11, 1924 concerning the collapse of the Communist uprising in October 1923. Appendix includes resolutions and proclamations, both of the "right" group of Zetkin, Brandler, and Pieck and of the Executive Committee of the Communist International. [B]

IJ447 CREUTZBURG, AUGUST. *Die Organisationsarbeit der KPD*. Hamburg-Berlin: Hoym, 1931. 124 p. A high KPD official's report of the meeting of the Executive Committee of the Communist International (ECCI) in the beginning of 1931, with an explanation of the organizations of the KPD and of the RGO (Revolutionäre Gewerkschaftsopposition) and their weaknesses. An appendix includes contributions to the discussions by participants, including among others Piatnitskii (see his pamphlets on this theme), Pieck, Knorin, and Lozovskii. [B]

IJ448 DIMITROV, GEORGI. *Reichstagsbrandprozess; Dokumente, Briefe und Aufzeichnungen*. Moscow: Verlag für fremdsprachige Literatur, 1942; Berlin: Verlag Neuer Weg, 1946. 198 p. Other German eds., Berlin: Dietz. Italian eds., Moscow: Edizioni in lingue estere, 1944; Rome: Rinascita, 1949. 181 p. English ed., WORLD COMMITTEE FOR THE VICTIMS OF GERMAN FASCISM. *The Reichstag Fire Trial*. London: John Lane, 1934. 362 p. Contains Dimitrov's speeches before the court in Leipzig in 1933, letters written while under arrest, abstracts from the stenograph of the court proceedings, and articles and interviews after his release. (See also Dimitrov, G., *Letters from Prison*, N.Y.: International Publishers, 1935; London: Gollancz, 1936, 156 p.; German ed., Paris: Carrefour, 1935. 175 p.)

IJ449 DRAHN, ERNST, and LEONHARD, SUSANNE, eds. *Unterirdische Literatur im revolutionären Deutschland während des*

Weltkrieges. Berlin-Fichtenau: Gesellschaft und Erziehung, 1920. 200 p. A selection from illegal socialist literature (pamphlets, booklets) of 1914-18 written by, among others, Luxemburg, Liebknecht, Mehring, and Radek.

IJ450 FLORIN, WILHELM. *Wie stürzen wir Hitler? Der Weg zur Einheitsfront und zur antifaschistischen Volksfront in Deutschland; Rede und Schlusswort auf der Brüsseler Konferenz der KPD (Oktober 1935)*. Strasbourg: Prométhée, no date. 80 p. An important speech by a member of the Political Bureau of the KPD, who died in 1936. Shows the Communist judgment of National Socialism and the self-criticism of its political tactics in the preceding years at the moment of change to the Popular Front tactics.

IJ451 GERMANY (DEMOCRATIC REPUBLIC, 1949- , MINISTERIUM FÜR NATIONALE VERTEIDIGUNG. *Zur Geschichte der deutschen antifaschistischen Widerstandsbewegung 1933-1945; eine Auswahl von Materialien, Berichten und Dokumenten*. Ed. by Käthe Haferkorn and Hans Otto. Berlin: Verlag des Ministeriums für nationale Verteidigung, 1957. 432 p. 2nd ed., 1958. A popular, richly illustrated, official collection of KPD proclamations and abstracts of articles and speeches of Communist and Social-Democratic leaders (among others, Pieck, Ulbricht, Breitscheid). Its purpose is to portray the KPD as "the fighter for the interests of the whole German people" during the National-Socialist regime. Stresses the necessity for unity of the working class.

IJ452 HOELZ, MAX. *Vom "weissen Kreuz" zur Roten Fahne; Jugend-, Kampf- und Zuchthauserlebnisse*. Berlin: Malik, 1929. 393 p. The popularly written autobiography of the famous Communist volunteer, covering the years until his dismissal from prison in 1928. Hoelz was the leader of the uprising in central Germany in March 1921.

IJ453 HOERNLE, EDWIN. *Grundfragen der proletarischen Erziehung*. Berlin: Jugendinternationale, 1929. 212 p. A high KPD official writes on the relation between social class and family and education, as well as on the fundamentals of Communist education. Important for a knowledge of the pedagogical standpoint of the German Communists in the Weimar Republic (see also Clara Zetkin's speeches).

IJ454 *Illustrierte Geschichte der Deutschen Revolution*. Berlin: Internationaler Arbeiter-Verlag, 1929. 528 p. A Communist account of the events before the Kapp-Putsch in 1920, intended as a "weapon in the struggle for liberation of the German workingclass." Many KPD leaders who in the meantime had been proscribed participated in the editing of the book. Chief significance is that it enables one easily to determine the shift in the Communist view of the German Revolution of 1918-19. [B]

IJ456 INTERNATIONALER ANTIFASCHISTEN-KONGRESS, BERLIN, 1929. *Faschismus; Bericht vom Internationalen Antifaschisten-Kongress Berlin 9.-10.3.1929*. Berlin: Neuer Deutscher Verlag, 1930. 94 p. Contains contributions by the German participants Ledebour, Hornik and F. Heckert (KPD), whose report is important for an evaluation of the development of the Communist theory of "Social Fascism" in Germany.

IJ457 *Jahrbuch für Wirtschaft, Politik und Arbeiterbewegung*. Hamburg: Hoym, 1922-23, 1108 p. 1923-24, 926 p. 1925-26, 1051 p. A Communist reference book dealing with political and trade union workers' organizations, the situation of the working class, world economy, developments in the Soviet Union, and containing short descriptions of all countries for the years under consideration. Many statistics. German contributors include Brandler, Dietrich, Münzenberg, Pieck, and Thalheimer. [B]

IJ458 *Kapitalismus-Imperialismus; Einführung in die marxistisch-leninistische Oekonomie*. Vol. II of *Lehrbücher für den proletarischen Klassenkampf*. Berlin: Internationaler Arbeiter-Verlag, 1931. 205 p. An introduction to political economy, characterized as a "weapon of the proletariat," for Communist officials and supporters. Contains, among other things, a polemic against Rosa Luxemburg and N. Bukharin. Important for an evaluation of the economic theories spread in the KPD before 1933.

IJ459 KOMMUNISTISCHE PARTEI DEUTSCHLANDS. The following are reports of the congresses of the German Communist Party held before Hitler's assumption of power.

1. *Bericht über den Gründungsparteitag der KPD (Spartakusbund) vom 30.12.1918-1.1.1919*. [Berlin]: [1919]. 56 p.

2. *Bericht über den 2. Parteitag der KPD (Spartakusbund) vom 20.-24. 10. 1919*. [Berlin]: [1919]. 68 p.

3. *Bericht über den 3. Parteitag der KPD (Spartakusbund) am 25. und 26.2.1920*. [Berlin]: [1920]. 90 p.

4. *Bericht über den 4. Parteitag der KPD (Spartakusbund) am 14. und 15.4.1920*. [Berlin]: [1920]. 110 p.

5. *Bericht über den 5. Parteitag der KPD (Sektion der Kommunistischen Internationale) vom 1. - 3. 11.1920 in Berlin*. Leipzig-Berlin: Franke, 1921. 196 p.

6. *Bericht über die Verhandlungen des Vereinigungs-parteitages der USPD (Linke) und KPD (Spartakusbund), abgehalten in Berlin vom 4. - 7. 12.1920*. Appendix: *Bericht über die 1. Frauen-Reichskonferenz vom 8.12.1920 in Berlin*. Leipzig-Berlin: Franke, 1921. 334 p.

7. *Bericht über die Verhandlungen des 2.* [that is, 7] *Parteitages der KPD (Sektion der Kommunistischen Internationale), abgehalten in Jena vom 22. - 26. 8. 1921.* Berlin: Vereinigung Internationaler Verlagsanstalten [VIVA], 1922. 454 p.

8. *Bericht über die Verhandlungen des 3.* [that is, 8] *Parteitages der KPD (Sektion der Kommunistischen Internationale), abgehalten in Leipzig vom 28.1. - 1.2.1923.* Berlin: VIVA, [1923]. 454 p.

9. *Bericht über die Verhandlungen des 9. Parteitages der KPD (Sektion der Kommunistischen Internationale), abgehalten in Frankfurt a/M. vom 7. - 10.4.1924.* Berlin: VIVA, 1924. 404 p.

10. *Bericht über die Verhandlungen des 10. Parteitages der KPD (Sektion der Kommunistischen Internationale), Berlin vom 12. - 17.7. 1925.* Berlin: VIVA, 1926. 776 p.

11. *Bericht über die Verhandlungen des 11. Parteitages der KPD (Sektion der Kommunistischen Internationale), Essen vom 2. - 7.3. 1927.* Berlin: VIVA, 1927. 423 p.

12. *Protokoll der Verhandlungen des 12. Parteitages der KPD (Sektion der Kommunistischen Internationale), Berlin-Wedding vom 9. - 16. 6.1929.* Berlin: Internationaler-Arbeiter Verlag, [1930]. 535 p. [A]

IJ460 KOMMUNISTISCHE PARTEI DEUTSCHLANDS. *21 Monate sozialdemokratische Koalitionspolitik 1928-1930; Handbuch der kommunistischen Reichstagsfraktion.* Berlin: IAV, 1930. 479 p. Supplement: *Vier Monate Brüning-Regierung; auf dem Wege zur faschistischen Diktatur.* Berlin: IAV, 1930. 126 p. A collection of materials for the struggle against the SPD, excluded from the government after the fall of Hermann Müller's cabinet on March 27, 1930. Contributions by E. Hörnle, H. Kippenberger, P. Maslowski, T. Neubauer, G. Schumann, E. Torgler, and others. The supplement for the period leading up to the dissolution of the Reichstag in July 1930 (new elections held on September 14) seeks to show that the policy of Brüning's cabinet was only a continuation of the course adopted by Müller's government. [B]

IJ461 KOMMUNISTISCHE PARTEI DEUTSCHLANDS. *Spartakus-Briefe.* Berlin: Franke, 1920-21. 2 vols. 2nd ed., 1926. New ed., INSTITUT FÜR MARXISMUS-LENINISMUS. *Spartakusbriefe.* Berlin: Dietz, 1958. 476 p. A very important source for the background of the KPD. These informational and political "letters" were distributed illegally throughout the first World War; after September 1916 they were printed under the title "Spartakus." The chief writers were R. Luxemburg, Liebknecht, Mehring, J. Marchlewski, H. Duncker, E. Meyer, L. Jogiches, and P. Levi. The 1958 edition is based on the edition of 1926 and includes a foreword by H. Kolbe as well as the foreword of E. Meyer to the 1926 edition. It contains also all Spartacist material besides the illegal pamphlets of the left, and a facsimile of the Spartacus letter no. 12. No index. [A]

IJ462 KOMMUNISTISCHE PARTEI DEUTSCHLANDS. *Vier Jahre Weimarer Koalition in Preussen; Handbuch der kommunistischen Fraktion des preussischen Landtags.* Ed. by R. Schnetter and P. Schwenk. Berlin: VIVA, 1928. 474 p. Intended chiefly as a source of material for Communist speakers and editors for the Prussian Landtag electoral campaign in 1928. Its most important aim was to "unmask" SPD policies. [B]

IJ463 KOMMUNISTISCHE PARTEI DEUTSCHLANDS. *Die Wahrheit über Preussen; Material der kommunistischen Landtagsfraktion zum Preussenwahlkampf 1932.* Berlin: Internationaler Arbeiter-Verlag, 1932. 128 p. A handbook for Party speakers and editors, containing violent attacks on the SPD. [B]

IJ464 KOMMUNISTISCHE PARTEI DEUTSCHLANDS, ZENTRAL-KOMITEE. *Richtlinien für die Parlamentspolitik der KPD in den Ländern und Gemeinden.* Berlin: IAV, 1928. 66 p. An official handbook for Communist delegates to local legislative assemblies. Contains essays by W. Koenen, T. Neubauer, and P. Schwenk, and directions for positions to take on special questions.

IJ465 *Die KPD im eigenen Spiegel; aus der Geschichte der KPD und der 3. Internationale.* Published by the Kommunistische Arbeiter-Partei Deutschlands. Berlin: Arbeiter-Literatur, 1926. 172 p. A collection of quotations, mostly from KPD newspapers and periodicals, organized according to subjects, which seeks to show the treason of the KPD and the Comintern to revolutionary Communism.

IJ466 LENZ, JOSEF. *Proletarische Politik im Zeitalter des Imperialismus und der sozialistischen Revolution.* Part I: *Grundbegriffe der marxistisch-leninistischen Strategie und Taktik.* Vol. III of *Lehrbücher für den proletarischen Klassenkampf.* Berlin: IAV, 1931. 186 p. Treats Leninism as the only correct development of Marxism, the role of the Communist Party as the representative of all the interests of the working class, the relation of strategy and tactics, the policies of preparing the mass strike movement and the "unity front from below," policies which were regarded as necessary for the given situation in Germany. Lenz (alias Kraus alias Winternitz) has been a high KPD-official for Agitprop affairs.

IJ467 LEVI, PAUL. *Unser Weg wider den Putschismus.* Appendix: *Die Lehren eines Putschversuchs*, by Karl Radek. Berlin: Seehof, 1921. 55 p. 2nd ed., 1921. 64 p. The former (1919-21) KPD chairman's famous critique of the March uprising of the KPD in 1921, characterized by him as the "greatest Bakunin-Putsch of history." Also contains Levi's "Exposé über die Lage der Partei" of March 10, 1921 and Radek's article from the *Communist International* concerning the crisis in the Austrian Communist Party. Cf. the continuation of Levi's critique in *Was ist das Verbrechen? Die Märzaktion oder die Kritik daran?* Berlin: Seehof, 1921. 45 p. [B]

IJ468 LIEBKNECHT, KARL. *Gesammelte Reden und Schriften.* Published under the auspices of the Institut für Marxismus-Leninismus. Berlin: Dietz, 1958—. Volume I, published in 1958, covers the period 1900-07; volume II (1960) covers 1907-10; volume III (1960) February to December, 1910; volume IV (1961) January 1911 to February 1912. The first volume includes, besides a foreword by W. Pieck, Liebknecht's "Militarismus und Antimilitarismus." The entire work is expected to run to six or seven volumes; it will be devoted to Liebknecht's political writings, with an occasional introduction by the Institut für Marxismus-Leninismus. The collection is not complete; for example, volume IV lacks Liebknecht's "Ordensrede" of March 20, 1911.

IJ469 LIEBKNECHT, KARL. *Reden und Aufsätze.* Published by J. Gumperz for the Communist International, Commission for Germany. Hamburg: Hoym, 1921. 374 p. New, rev. ed., *Ausgewählte Reden, Briefe und Aufsätze.* Published under the auspices of the Marx-Engels-Lenin Institut. Berlin: Dietz, 1952. 551 p. The first edition intended to draw "a complete picture of Liebknecht's political personality," and, although it presents mostly abstracts, its theme is more encompassing than the new Dietz edition, which emphasizes Liebknecht's struggle against "militarism" and "reformism." Both editions contain some Spartacus Letters, and the new edition also contains condensations of articles and other writings about Liebknecht. [B]

IJ470 LINDAU, RUDOLF. *Revolutionäre Kämpfe 1918-1919; Aufsätze und Chronik.* Berlin: Dietz, 1960. 268 p. A collection of essays written at various times in the past by a KPD official who is now a Professor in the Institut für Marxismus-Leninismus. The value of the book to the historian has been greatly lessened because the articles have been altered, with no indication given of the extent of the changes, and neither the time nor the place of the original publication of the articles is noted. The appendix contains among other things statistical material and a chronicle of the revolutionary years, 1917-19.

IJ471 LUXEMBURG, ROSA. *Ausgewählte Reden und Schriften.* Berlin: Dietz, 1951-52. 2 vols. Volume I contains "Massenstreik, Partei und Gewerkschaften" (1906), "Die Krise der Sozialdemokratie (Junius-Broschüre)" (1915) and "Einführung in die Nationalökonomie" (lectures given in the SPD's party-school before 1914). Volume II contains a selection of speeches and essays from the years 1893-1919. The following writings are missing: "Akkumulation des Kapitals"; her critique on Bolshevism, "Organisationsfragen der russischen Sozialdemokratie" (which appeared in *Die Neue Zeit*, 22/II, 1903-04); and "Die russische Revolution" (first printed in Berlin, 1922; complete edition: Paris, 1939; reprinted: Hameln, 1957, and Frankfurt/M., 1963). However, Lenin's answer to her article "Organisationsfragen der russischen Sozialdemokratie" is included. [B]

IJ472 LUXEMBURG, ROSA. *Gesammelte Schriften.* Vols. III and IV edited by C. Zetkin and A. Warski. Berlin: Vereinigung Internationaler Verlagsanstalten [VIVA], 1923-28. Only volumes III, IV, and VI were published. Volume III, published in 1925, bears the title *Gegen den Reformismus* (540 p.); volume IV (1928) *Gewerkschaftskampf und Massenstreik* (702 p.); volume VI (1923) *Die Akkumulation des Kapitals; ein Beitrag zur ökonomischen Erklärung des Imperialismus* (493 p.). Volume III includes among other things her "Sozialreform oder Revolution?" according to the first edition of 1900; speeches and essays on party tactics, on French ministerialism, and on the Social-Democratic position toward budget proceedings in parliament. Volume IV contains essays on Party problems—trade unions, debates on the mass strike, and the question of electoral law. Volume VI contains the controversial essay of 1912 which treated the "accumulation problem" described by Marx in the second volume of *Kapital.* The appendix to this volume contains G. Eckstein's Critique and Luxemburg's "Anti-Kritik." These volumes represent the beginning of the collected edition of Luxemburg's writings called for by Lenin in 1922 (*Kommunistische Internationale*, 1924, No. 33, p. 5). According to the editor of this edition, P. Frölich, "the publication of this literary legacy proceeded in the face of many hindrances and a determined resistance, which, however, was never conceded." (See Paul Frölich, *Rosa Luxemburg, Gedanke und Tat*, Hamburg: Oetinger, 1949, p. 5.) [A]

IJ472A MATERN, HERMANN. *Im Kampf für Frieden, Demokratie und Sozialismus; ausgewählte Reden und Schriften. Band I, 1926-1956.* Berlin: Dietz, 1963. 582 p. A selective collection of speeches and writings of an important Communist functionary. Only about a fifth of this volume deals with the years 1926-45; vol. II covers the years 1956-63.

IJ473 MÜNZENBERG, WILLI. *Die Entwicklung und der Stand der faschistischen Bewegung Frühjahr 1924.* Appendix: *Der Bauer und der Faschismus.* I. Steinborn, *Die Völkischen und die Gewerkschaften.* Berlin: Neuer Deutscher Verlag, 1924. 95 p. This booklet is an example of the Communist judgment—and illusions—of so-called German "Fascism" after the unsuccessful "Hitler-Putsch" of November 9, 1923.

IJ474 NEUBAUER, THEODOR. *Deutsche Aussenpolitik heute und morgen.* Berlin-Vienna-Zurich: IAV, 1932. 142 p. An analysis of factors which were decisive for German foreign policy in the concluding phase of the Weimar Republic. The foreign affairs expert of the KPD faction in the Reichstag before 1933 also presents a concise outline of the foreign policy program of a Communist "Soviet-Germany."

IJ475 NEUMANN, HEINZ. *Maslows Offensive gegen den Leninismus; kritische Bemerkungen zur Parteidiskussion.* Hamburg: Hoym, 1925. 80 p. A pamphlet directed against the "left" leadership of R. Fischer and A. Maslow. Ostensibly written on Stalin's suggestion. (See also: A. Maslow, *Die zwei russischen Revolutionen des Jahres 1917.* Berlin: 1924. Vol. I.)

IJ476 NEUMANN, HEINZ. *Was ist Bolschewisierung*? Hamburg: Hoym, 1925. 156 p. An important booklet on this main internal policy theme of non-Russian Communist parties after the 5th Congress of the Communist International in 1924. The author was then one of the most active partisans of Stalin in the KPD, then from 1929 to 1932 one of the most important leaders of the Party. He was purged in the USSR in 1937. [B]

IJ477 PIECK, WILHELM. *Gesammelte Reden und Schriften.* Published under the auspices of the Institut für Marxismus-Leninismus. Berlin: Dietz, 1959—. The complete edition will encompass 15 volumes (including an index volume). Three volumes have so far appeared: volume I, published in 1959, covers the period 1904 to 1919; volume II (1959) covers 1920 to 1925; volume III (1961), 1925 to 1927. Volume I contains among other things a foreword by W. Ulbricht; volume III is introduced with an abstract from a lecture given by Pieck in December 1943. The work is constructed chronologically—"in principle," that is, there are exceptions. There are omissions; for example, there is no mention of Pieck's participation in the session of the Presidium of the Executive Committee of the Communist International of January 1924, or of the role of Pieck in the "Brandler-course" of 1923. The volumes contain notes, biographical data, and formerly unpublished material from the Pieck archive. [B]

IJ478 PIECK, WILHELM. *Der neue Weg zum gemeinsamen Kampf für den Sturz der Hitlerdiktatur; Referat und Schlusswort auf der Brüsseler Parteikonferenz der KPD Oktober 1935.* Berlin: Dietz, 1948. 184 p. 6th ed., 1960. Pieck's two important speeches to the so-called "Brussels" KPD conference after the VII Congress of the Comintern, in which the new "People's Front" tactics were defined for the KPD, the situation in Germany analysed, and the general line of the Party for the next period laid down. Also contains the KPD's detailed self-criticism because of the "under-estimation of the Fascist danger" and the too long maintained tactics of directing the main attack against the SPD. The appendix contains the resolution of the conference and the manifesto of October 1935 to the German working class to form a "People's Front" against Hitler. [A]

IJ479 PIECK, WILHELM. *Reden und Aufsätze*. Published under the auspices of the Marx-Engels-Lenin Institut. Berlin: Dietz, 1950-55. 4 vols. Volume I, published in 1950, is entitled *Auswahl aus den Jahren 1908-1950*; volume IV, 1955, bears the title *Parlamentsreden; Auswahl aus den Jahren 1906-1933*. Volumes II and III contain later writings. A selection from the speeches and publications of the former chairman of the KPD faction in the Prussian Landtag, successor to Thälmann (after 1935), and the first president of the DDR.

IJ480 PIECK, WILHELM. *Wir kämpfen für ein Rätedeutschland; der revolutionäre Kampf der deutschen Arbeiterklasse unter Führung der KPD gegen die faschistische Diktatur*. Moscow-Leningrad: Verlagsgenossenschaft ausländischer Arbeiter, 1934. 76 p. Pieck's report on the activity of the KPD in 1932-33 to the 13th plenary session of the Executive Committee of the Communist International in Moscow in December 1933. Contains an important speech on the judgment of the final phase of the KPD's "ultra-left" tactics. The speech retains the thesis that Social-Democracy, which has led the masses to Fascism, must be annihilated. [B]

IJ481 *Protokoll des ersten Reichskongresses der revolutionären Gewerkschaftsopposition Deutschlands. Abgehalten am 30.11. und 1.12.1929 in Berlin*. Berlin: Betrieb und Gewerkschaft, 1930. 143 p. This congress was originally planned by A. Lozovsky and P. Merker to found a Communist Labor Union in Germany. Contains speeches by Thälmann and Merker.

IJ482 RADEK, KARL. *Soll die VKPD eine Massenpartei der revolutionären Aktion oder eine zentristische Partei des Wartens sein?* Hamburg: Hoym, 1921. 119 p. Radek's attack on Levi, Däumig, Zetkin and others because of their "centralist" position in the questions of the KAPD and the exclusion of the Italian section from the Communist International, as well as against Levi's pamphlet *Unser Weg*. [B]

IJ483 SCHMIDT, WALTER A., ed. *Damit Deutschland lebe; ein Quellenwerk über den deutschen antifaschistischen Widerstandskampf 1933-1945*. Berlin: Kongress, 1958. 759 p. 2nd enlarged, ed., 1959. A selective collection of pamphlets, newspaper articles, brochures, and reports, with emphasis on the Communist resistance. No index. The individual sections treat the resistance in the factories (workers and employees), other occupations (relating to women and youth), the concentration camps and prisons, the general struggle of the resistance groups, and the resistance in the Wehrmacht.

IJ483A SCHNELLER, ERNST. *Arbeiterklasse und Wehrpolitik; eine Sammlung von Reden und Schriften aus den Jahren 1925-1929.* Berlin: Verlag des Ministeriums für Nationale Verteidigung, 1960. 392 p. A selection of speeches and articles of one of the most important military experts of the KPD and head of one military "apparatus" of the Party before 1933. The author died in a Nazi concentration camp.

IJ484 SCHULZE, FIETE. *Briefe und Aufzeichnungen aus dem Gestapo-Gefängnis in Hamburg.* Published under the auspices of the Institut für Marxismus-Leninismus. Berlin: Dietz, 1959. 143 p. A selection from the writings of a Communist executed in 1935, including condensations from letters written to his family and notes for his defense before the court. The appendix contains a memorial essay and a protest against his execution. Schulze was a leading KPD official in Hamburg who lived in the USSR for several years after the unsuccessful uprising in 1923.

IJ485 SCHUMANN, HEINZ, and NITZSCHE, GERHARD. "Gestapoberichte über den antifaschistischen Kampf der KPD im früheren Regierungsbezirk Aachen 1934-1936." *Zeitschrift für Geschichtswissenschaft.* VII (1958), p. 118-130. Intended as a critical supplement to B. Vollmer's *Volksopposition im Polizeistaat* (Stuttgart: 1957). It reprints and comments upon Gestapo reports from Aachen and Düsseldorf in 1934-37 concerning Communist underground activity in the Rhine province.

IJ486 SONTER, R. *Der neue deutsche Imperialismus.* Vol. II of *Probleme der Weltpolitik und der Arbeiterbewegung.* Hamburg-Berlin: Hoym, 1928. 192 p. Communist criticism of Germany's international role and internal affairs during the Anglo-Russian conflict after the English general strike and before the inauguration of the Comintern's left tactics. Contains a rather detailed description of German Social Democracy.

IJ487 THÄLMANN, ERNST. *Kampfreden und Aufsätze.* [Berlin: 1932.] 96 p. Published on the occasion of the election campaign of 1932. All but one selection date from the years 1928-31.

IJ488 THÄLMANN, ERNST. *Reden und Aufsätze zur Geschichte der deutschen Arbeiterbewegung.* Berlin: Dietz, 1955—. Volume I, published in 1955, deals with the years 1919-28; volume II, 1956, with the period 1928-30. This collection of speeches and writings published under Thälmann's name (he was leader of the KPD after 1925) is useful. However, for detailed studies, one must still turn to the original publications, because the texts in this edition have occasionally been shortened without a notice to that effect. (For supplementary material of diary notes and letters, see E. Thälmann, *Bilder und Dokumente aus seinem Leben*, Berlin: 1955, 254 p.) [B]

IJ489 THÄLMANN, ERNST. *Der revolutionäre Ausweg und die KPD; Rede auf der Plenartagung des ZK der KPD am 19.2.1932 in Berlin.* [Moscow: 1932.] 96 p. Thälmann's important speech against war, Fascism, and especially against the SPD ("the main impulse towards Social-Democracy"), as well as against the remnants of Luxemburgism and "individual terror." [A]

IJ490 TROTSKII, LEO. *Was nun? Schicksalsfragen des deutschen Proletariats.* Berlin: Grylewicz, 1932. 116 p. Trotskii's most detailed critique of the policies of the "Stalinist" KPD leadership before 1933, the theory of "Social-Fascism," etc. For his smaller pamphlets see the forthcoming bibliography of Trotskii's publications which will be edited by Louis Sinclair. [B]

IJ491 ULBRICHT, WALTER. *Zur Geschichte der deutschen Arbeiterbewegung; aus Reden und Aufsätzen.* Berlin: Dietz, 1953—. A selective collection of the writings of the First Secretary of the SED and the Chairman of the Council of State of the DDR, of which two volumes deal with our period. The first volume, published in 1953, encompasses the period 1918 to 1933; the second, also published in 1953, embraces the years from 1933 to 1946. The work must be used with caution because important material is missing; for example, articles written from the fall of 1939 to the spring of 1941. For supplementary material see: W. Ulbricht, *Über Gewerkschaften; aus Reden und Aufsätzen, 1922-1945*, Berlin: Tribüne, 1953, 438 p. and his *Zur Geschichte der neuesten Zeit*, Berlin: Dietz, 1955—. [B]

IJ492 ZETKIN, CLARA. *Ausgewählte Reden und Schriften.* Berlin: Dietz, 1957-1960. 3 vols. Volume I covers the period 1889 to 1917; volume II 1918 to 1923; and volume III 1924 to 1933, when Zetkin died. A collection of important articles of Rosa Luxemburg's friend. There are some omissions, for example, her critique of the "March Action" of 1921, in which she supported Levi, with whom she left the KPD Central Committee in February, 1921. Volume III contains her recollections of Lenin, her speech as president of the Reichstag delivered on August 30, 1932, and several previously unpublished letters.

IJ493 ZINOVEV, GRIGORII. *Probleme der deutschen Revolution.* Hamburg: C. Hoym, 1923. 109 p. French ed., Paris: L'Humanité, 1923. 72 p. A relatively optimistic statement written in the fall of 1923 by the then head of the Comintern. Concerns itself with the consequences of the KPD defeat. [B]

d. KPD PERIODICALS AND NEWSPAPERS

IJ494 *Betrieb und Gewerkschaft; Organ für marxistische Strategie und Taktik.* Berlin: 1929-1933. Periodical of the Red International of Labor Unions, successor of *Die Einheit* (1926-29), which described itself as "a periodical for questions of socialism and trade union unity." *Betrieb und Gewerkschaft* was the parent periodical of *Der rote Betriebsrat* (1931-32) and *Erwerbslosenführer* (1931-32). [B]

IJ495 *Die Internationale; Zeitschrift für Praxis und Theorie des Marxismus.* Berlin (until 1933): 1915 and 1919-37. The theoretical journal of the KPD, founded by Rosa Luxemburg and Franz Mehring. [A]

IJ496 *Die Kommune; Zeitschrift für kommunistische Kommunalpolitik.* Published by the KPD. Berlin: 1921-1933.

IJ497 *Der Parteiarbeiter; Monatsschrift für die Praxis revolutionärer Organisationsarbeit.* Published by the Central Committee of the KPD. Berlin: 1922-1933. The practical-organizational journal for KPD officials.

IJ498 *Proletarische Sozialpolitik.* Organ der Arbeitsgemeinschaft sozialpolitischer Organisationen (ARSO). Published by S. Rädel. Berlin: 1928-1932.

IJ499 *Der Propagandist; Monatsschrift für die Propaganda des Marxismus-Leninismus.* Published by the Central Committee of the KPD. Berlin: 1930-1932. Periodical for "Agitprop" officials of the KPD (cf. *Der Agitator*).

IJ500 *Der rote Aufbau; Monatsschrift für die Propaganda des Marxismus-Leninismus.* Organ of the Central Committee of International Red Aid. Published by W. Münzenberg. Berlin (until 1933): 1922 and 1929-35. An important periodical of the Communist "unpartisan" International Red Aid and of the so-called "Münzenberg-Concern." Appeared after January 1933 as *Unsere Zeit.* [B]

IJ501 *Die rote Fahne.* Central Organ of the KPD. Berlin: 1918-1933. The most important daily newspaper of the KPD; occasionally appeared illegally after 1933. [A]

Also see the following German editions of Communist publications:

Internationale Presse-Korrespondenz (Inprekorr). Berlin: 1921-33. (After 1933 it was published in a small format for illegal distribution.)

Die Kommunistische Internationale. Petrograd-Moscow; Hamburg-Berlin: From 1919. From 1933: Basel, Strasbourg.

Die Rote Gewerkschaftsinternationale. Moscow-Berlin: From 1921.

Rotes Gewerkschaftsbulletin. Moscow-Berlin: 1921-1930. After 1931: *Internationale Gewerkschaftspressekorrespondenz.*

Rundschau über Politik, Wirtschaft und Arbeiterbewegung. Basel: 1932-1939. [Substitute for *Inprekorr.*] After 1939 see *Die Welt*, Stockholm.

Sozial-Oekonomische Arbeiter-Rundschau. Moscow-Berlin: 1926—. [Information sheet of the Social-Economic Division of the Red International of Labor Unions.]

Unter dem Banner des Marxismus. Vienna-Berlin: 1925-1936.

Addenda

IJ502 FISCHER, FRITZ. *Griff nach der Weltmacht; die Kriegzielpolitik der kaiserlichen Deutschland, 1914-1918.* Düsseldorf: Droste, 1961. 896 p. An important work on German war aims in the east during World War I.

IJ503 ZIMMERMANN, LUDWIG. *Deutsche Aussenpolitik in der Aera der Weimarer Republik.* Göttingen: Musterschmidt, 1958. 486 p. A basic work on the foreign policy of the Weimar government.

IK. GREAT BRITAIN

1. GENERAL WORKS

(Edited by Richard H. Ullman)

IK1 ALTMAN, V. V., ed. *Imperializm i borba rabochego klassa (Anglii i Germanii, XIX-XX vv.); sbornik statei pamiati akademika Fedora A. Rotshteina.* Moscow: Akad. nauk SSSR, 1960. 507 p. Commemorates the noted Soviet authority on international affairs who devoted part of his life to the British workers' movement before World War I and who, after 1920, divided his time between active diplomacy (in Iran, 1921-22) and extensive publications. Includes a ten-page list of Rotshtein's works. The bulk of the book is devoted to articles on those phases of Soviet foreign policy with which he was especially concerned. Those dealing with Britain in the post-revolutionary period are: M. M. Karlinger, "The October Revolution and the English Bourgeois Press"; C. V. Nikonova, "England and the Balkan Bloc (1924-27)"; J. N. Undasinov, "The Position of the Laboring Class of Great Britain during the Economic Crisis of 1930-32"; and N. N. Yakovlev, "The Politics of the Anglo-German Agreement of March 1939."

IK2 BOLTE, C. G. "The Soviet Question in British Politics." B.Litt. thesis, Oxford, 1949.

IK3 COATES, WILLIAM P., and ZELDA K. *A History of Anglo-Soviet Relations.* London: Lawrence & Wishart, 1943-58. 2 vols. Very useful, despite the authors' Communist bias, for the great volume of quotations from and references to newspaper articles and editorials, Parliamentary debates and papers, texts of treaties and agreements, and other such materials. Excellent detailed index. The first volume ends in early 1943, the second in 1958. [B]

IK4 DVORKIN, I. *Ideologiia i politika pravykh leiboristov na sluzhbe monopolii.* Moscow: Gospolitizdat, 1953. 471 p. Accuses the British Labour Party of every political, social, and economic crime known to man. A final chapter on the British Communist Party sees this Moscow-directed group as the sole hope of the suppressed British proletariat.

IK5 GREAT BRITAIN, FOREIGN OFFICE. *Documents on British Foreign Policy, 1919-1939.* Edited by E. L. Woodward, Rohan Butler, and J. P. T. Bury. London: H. M. Stationery Office, 1946–. This well-edited, still-continuing series of many volumes is divided into three series, the first covering the period from the signature of the Treaty of Versailles to 1930, the second the period from 1930 to the outbreak of World War II, and the third the events in 1938 and 1939 specifically leading to the outbreak of hostilities. While no volume yet published is entirely devoted to the Soviet Union, the collection will fully document Anglo-Soviet relations during the period. Documents are arranged by chapters, chronologically according to subject. Each volume contains an analytical table of contents. [A]

IK6 KRÖNINGER, HORST. *Die britische Russlandpolitik seit 1917; eine Übersicht mit Dokumenten.* Göttingen: Arbeitsgemeinschaft für Osteuropaforschung, 1952-53. 2 vols.

IK7 MARRIOTT, JOHN A. R. (SIR). *Anglo-Russian Relations, 1689-1943.* London: Methuen, 1944. 227 p. A low-level survey. Includes 52 pages on events since the Bolshevik Revolution.

IK8 MIDDLETON, K. W. B. *Britain and Russia; An Historical Essay.* London and N.Y.: Hutchinson, 1947. 238 p. An interesting survey covering the period from 1553 to the end of World War II. Slightly more than half of the book is devoted to the Soviet era. The author emphasizes the continuity of Russian policy, holding that Soviet policy is influenced primarily by territorial, rather than ideological, considerations.

IK9 SAMRA, CHATTAR S. *India and Anglo-Soviet Relations, 1919-47.* Bombay, London: Asia Publishing House, 1959. 186 p. A very competent, scholarly account written at the Center for South Asian Studies of the University of California. Based upon published non-Russian materials. Emphasizes relations between Moscow and Indian Communists. [B]

IK10 SETON-WATSON, ROBERT W. *Britain and the Dictators.* N.Y.: Macmillan, 1938. 460 p. By the eminent English historian of Eastern Europe, now deceased. Contains one forty-page chapter on Anglo-Soviet relations between the end of World War I and the German-Austrian Anschluss.

IK11 SLOAN, PAT. *Russia—Friend or Foe?* London: Muller, 1939. 200 p. Written before the Nazi-Soviet pact by a pro-Communist journalist, this work contains a brief survey of Anglo-Soviet relations from the Bolshevik Revolution to the time of writing, with a plea for Anglo-Soviet union against fascism. Not of great value.

2. 1917-1927

(Edited by Richard H. Ullman)

IK12 ADLER, F. *The Anglo-Russian Report; a Criticism of the Report of the B.T.U. Delegation from the Point of View of International Socialism.* London: King, 1925. 52 p. A criticism of the report of the

British trade union delegation that visited Russia in 1924 and wrote a rather pro-Soviet report. (See below, *Russia; The Official Report. . . .*)

IK13 *Angliia i SSSR; sbornik statei, materialov i dokumentov.* Moscow-Leningrad: "Moskovskii rabochii," 1927. 164 p.

IK14 *Angliiskaia stachka i rabochie SSSR.* Moscow: Vsesoiuznyi tsentralnyi sovet professionalnykh soiuzov, 1926. 103 p.

IK15 BUCHANAN, GEORGE W. (SIR). *My Mission to Russia and Other Diplomatic Memories.* London: Cassell; Boston: Little, Brown, 1923. 2 vols. Russian ed., Berlin: Izd. "Obelisk," 1924. 2 vols. in 1. Buchanan was Ambassador to Russia from 1910 until early January 1918. Only the latter half of his second volume deals with the events following the Bolshevik seizure of power. Nevertheless, the account (consisting of excerpts from Buchanan's diary) is invaluable. [B]

IK16 BULLOCK, ALAN. *The Life and Times of Ernest Bevin.* Vol. 1: *Trade Union Leader 1881-1940.* London: Heinemann, 1960. 672 p. A definitive biography based almost entirely upon original sources. The first volume contains a brief (27 p.) but important account of the Labour movement's Councils of Action during the Polish-Soviet war in 1920.

IK17 CHURCHILL, WINSTON S. *The Aftermath; Being a Sequel to the World Crisis.* London: Thornton Butterworth, 1929. 474 p. Churchill was Secretary of State for War during the period between the Armistice of November 1918 and the end of British intervention in Russia. His memoirs add much to our knowledge of British policy, but should be read in conjunction with the works of Lloyd George and others.

IK18 COATES, WILLIAM P., and ZELDA K. *Armed Intervention in Russia, 1918-1922.* London: Gollancz, 1935. 400 p. Very useful, despite the authors' Communist sympathies, because of the copious quotations from press articles and editorials and Parliamentary debates and papers. [B]

IK19 COWDEN, MORTON H. "The Soviet Union, International Communism, and the British General Strike of May, 1926." M.A. thesis, Columbia, 1951.

IK20 *Delegatsiia Britanskogo generalnogo soveta professionalnykh soiuzov v SSSR.* Moscow: Vsesoiuznyi tsentralnyi sovet professionalnykh soiuzov, 1925. 227 p.

IK 21 FREDBORG, ARVID. *Storbritannien och den Ryska Frågan, 1918-1920; Studier i de Anglo-Ryska Relationerna Från Vapenstilleståndet den 11. November 1918 till den Begynnande Avspänningen i*

Januari och Februari 1920. Stockholm: Norstedt, 1951. 327 p. A doctoral dissertation based upon somewhat incomplete coverage of available published material.

IK22 GLASGOW, GEORGE. *MacDonald as Diplomatist; The Foreign Policy of the First Labour Government in Great Britain*. London: Cape, 1924. 232 p. A compilation of the author's articles in the Foreign Affairs section of the *Contemporary Review*, issued just after the fall of MacDonald's first Government in October 1924. Good interpretive journalism. Much on the Anglo-Soviet conference and treaty of 1924.

IK23 GRAUBARD, STEPHEN R. *British Labour and the Russian Revolution, 1917-1924*. Cambridge: Harvard; London: Oxford, 1957. 305 p. A good, scholarly account covering not only the Labour Party, but such other left-wing groups as the I.L.P. and the infant British Communist Party. Based upon a wide range of published (and some unpublished) English-language sources. [A]

IK24 GREAT BRITAIN, FOREIGN OFFICE. Cmd. 8. *A Collection of Reports on Bolshevism in Russia, Russia no. 1 (1919)*. London: H. M. Stationery Office, 1919. 109 p. A collection of dispatches made by Foreign Office and military officials to their superiors in London. They record various aspects of the domestic scene, including clashes between British civilians and officials and the Bolshevik authorities. Many of them simply report wild and unconfirmed rumors.

IK25 GREAT BRITAIN, FOREIGN OFFICE. *A Collection of Reports on Bolshevism in Russia; Abridged Edition of Parliamentary Paper, Russia no. 1 (1919)*. London: H. M. Stationery Office, 1919. 88 p.

IK26 GREAT BRITAIN, FOREIGN OFFICE. Cmd. 2895. *Russia no. 3 (1927). A Selection of Papers Dealing with the Relations Between His Majesty's Government and the Soviet Government, 1921-1927*. London: H. M. Stationery Office, 1927. 72 p. A white paper showing how the Soviet Government (through the Comintern) refused to curtail its propaganda activities in Britain and the Empire, despite repeated British protests. Covers the period between the Anglo-Soviet Trade Agreement of March 1921 and the rupture of relations in February 1927. Also deals with Soviet actions in China and Persia. See also Cmds. 2822 and 2874, Russia nos. 1 and 2 (1927), *Note from His Majesty's Government to the Government of the Union of Soviet Socialist Republics Respecting the Relations between the Two Countries and Note in Reply, February 23/26, 1927*, and *Documents illustrating the Hostile Activities of the Soviet Government and Third International against Great Britain*, 25 p. and 31 p. [B]

IK27 GREAT BRITAIN, FOREIGN OFFICE. *Documents on British Foreign Policy 1919-1939*. First Series, Vol. III, *1919*. Ed. by E. L. Woodward and Rohan Butler. London: H. M. Stationery Office, 1949. 909 p. Contains a well edited selection of Foreign Office papers on Russia, both intra-departmental and to and from the field, for the period May 26, 1919 to March 12, 1920. An invaluable source. [A]

IK28 GREAT BRITAIN, FOREIGN OFFICE. *Sbornik donesenii o bolshevizm v Rossii (Angliiskaia "Belaia Kniga") predstavlen Parlamentu po ukazu Ego Velichestva, aprel 1919; opublikovan sobstvennoi Ego Velichestva kantseliariei, London.* Novocherkassk: Izd. Upr. general-kvartirmeistera shtaba Donskoi Armii, 1919. 158 p.

IK29 GUROVICH, P. V. *Vseobshchaia stachka v Anglii 1926 g.* Moscow: Izd. Akad. nauk SSSR, 1959. 222 p. Surveys a wide range of published material, as well as archives. Emphasizes Russian aid to the strikers.

IK30 HORNING, ROSS C., JR. "Winston Churchill and British Policy Towards Russia, 1918-1919." Ph.D. dissertation, George Washington Univ., 1958.

IK30A IAKUSHKIN, E. E., and POLUNIN, S. *Angliiskaia interventsia v 1918-1920 gg.* Moscow-Leningrad: Gospolitizdat, 1928. 76 p. A popular account of English intervention in North Russia and Transcaucasia. Naturally very anti-British, but containing some information not available elsewhere.

IK31 IAROTSKII, V. *Sovremenaia rabochaia Angliia; ocherki.* Moscow: VTsSPS, 1925. 245 p.

IK32 IOFFE, IAKOV A. *Angliia v nashi dni.* Moscow: Gosizdat, 1925. Comments by a prominent Soviet diplomat.

IK33 IVANOV, LEV N. *Anglo-Frantsuzskoe sopernichestvo 1919-1927 gg.* Moscow-Leningrad: Gosizdat, 1928. 164 p. A fairly straightforward Marxist analysis purporting to show (among other things) that the divergence between British and French policy toward Russia during the period under discussion stemmed from differing economic conditions in the two western countries.

IK34 IVANOVICH, V. *Pochemu Angliia boretsia s Sovetskim Soiuzom?* Moscow-Leningrad: "Moskovskii rabochii," 1927. 112 p.

IK35 KHINCHUK, L. M. *K istorii Anglo-Sovetskikh otnoshenii.* Moscow-Leningrad: Gosizdat, 1928. 68 p. Perceptive, factual, rather non-doctrinaire observations on various aspects of Anglo-Soviet Relations.

IK36 KOMMUNISTICHESKAIA AKADEMIIA, KABINET MEZHDUNARODNOI POLITIKI. *Londonskaia konferentsiia edinstva, 6-9 apr. 1925 g.; sbornik materialov.* Moscow: VTsSPS, 1925. 103 p.

IK37 KRASINA, LIUBOV (KRASSIN, LUBOV). *Leonid Krassin: His Life and Work.* London: Skeffington, [1929]. 284 p. Krassin led the Soviet mission to London which negotiated the Anglo-Soviet trade agreement of March 1921, and was later Chargé d'Affaires in London. This study, by his widow who remained in London, consists primarily of excerpts from Krassin's letters to her. Unfortunately, he did not often discuss policy in the letters.

IK38 LABOUR PARTY (GREAT BRITAIN). *British Labour Delegation to Russia, 1920; Report.* London: Trades Union Congress and Labour Party, 1921. 151 p. An impressive, discerning report dealing largely with Soviet internal conditions, attributing, in part, restrictions of personal freedom and other of the harsher measures of the Bolshevik regime to necessities created by Allied intervention and the Civil War.

IK39 LEMIN, IOSIF M. *Vneshniaia politika Velikobritanii ot Versalia do Lokarno, 1919-1925.* Moscow: Gospolitizdat, 1947. 487 p. Some 80 pages devoted to Anglo-Soviet relations. Based only on published materials. A fairly straightforward Soviet treatment with a few Stalinist flourishes (Zinoviev Letter called Comintern Letter, etc.).

IK40 LENIN, VLADIMIR I. *Lenin on Britain.* Comp. by C. Leiteizer. Translation edited by T. Dexter and I. Lasker. Moscow: Foreign Languages Publishing House, 1960. 624 p. Chronologically arranged excerpts from Lenin's speeches and writings. On British working-class movements, capitalism, colonial policy, role in World War I and Intervention, etc.

IK41 LLOYD GEORGE, DAVID. *The Truth about the Peace Treaties.* London: Gollancz, 1938. 2 vols. New Haven: Yale, 1938. 1470 p. An important source on British policy towards Russia at the Peace Conferences. [B]

IK42 LLOYD GEORGE, DAVID. *War Memoirs.* London: 1933-36. 6 vols. 2nd ed., unabridged, London: Odhams, 1938. 2 vols. Contains important material on the British reaction to the Bolshevik seizure of power and on the beginnings of intervention. [B]

IK43 LOCKHART, ROBERT H. BRUCE. *British Agent.* N.Y.: Putnam, 1932. 354 p. British ed., *Memoirs of a British Agent.* London: Putnam, 1932. German ed., Stuttgart: Deutsche Verlags-Anstalt, n.d. 335 p. Reprinted American ed., Garden City, N.Y.: Doubleday, 1936. A superbly written account of the author's experiences as a British agent unofficially in contact with the Bolshevik regime, January to September 1918. Based not upon documents, but upon Lockhart's very accurate recollections. An invaluable source for the period. [B]

IK44 LOZOVSKII, A. (pseud. of Solomon Dridzo). *Anglo-sovetskaia konferentsiia professionalnykh soiuzov.* Moscow-Leningrad: Gosizdat, 1925. 112 p. German ed., *Die Englisch-Russische Gewerkschaftskonferenz.* Berlin: 1925. French ed., Paris: 1925. An account of the Anglo-Soviet trade-union conference, by the head of the Red International of Labor Unions.

IK45 LYMAN, RICHARD W. *The First Labour Government, 1924.* London: Chapman and Hall, 1957. 302 p. A scholarly work based on published materials only. The best existing account of MacDonald's handling of Russia in 1924 and the Zinoviev letter. [B]

IK46 MC MANUS, ARTHUR. *History of the Zinoviev Letter.* London: Communist Party of Great Britain, 1925. 47 p. The author was one of the alleged signers of the letter. His pamphlet contains the letter, the debate upon it in Parliament, and the British Communist Party's denials of its authenticity.

IK47 MADDOX, WILLIAM P. *Foreign Relations in British Labour Politics.* Cambridge: Harvard, 1934. 253 p. Contains a good brief account of labour's Councils of Action during the Polish-Soviet war in 1920, but virtually nothing about the treatment of Russia by the Labour governments.

IK48 MSTISLAVSKII, S. D. *Rabochaia Angliia; (Ot O'Braiena k Makdonaldu).* Moscow: Gosizdat, 1924. 134 p.

IK49 NABOKOV, KONSTANTIN D. *The Ordeal of a Diplomat.* London: Duckworth, 1921. 320 p. Russian ed., Stockholm: Severnye Ogni, 1921. 282 p. The author was Chargé d'Affaires of the Russian Embassy in London during the rule of the Provisional Government and Bolshevik seizure of power. Especially interesting concerning Russian émigré politics in London during 1917; also for his treatment by British authorities during 1918.

IK50 NICOLSON, HAROLD G. *Curzon, the Last Phase, 1919-1925; a Study in Post-War Diplomacy.* London: Constable, 1934. 416 p. An admirable study of Curzon's years as Foreign Secretary, based in part upon Curzon's private papers. Curzon was not much interested in Russia and, especially when Lloyd George was Prime Minister, left the handling of that problem to others; consequently relatively little of Nicolson's book deals with Anglo-Soviet relations.

IK51 *Otvet moskovskikh rabochikh i krestian na notu Kerzona (Resoliutsii, nakazy, rechi na plenume Mossoveta); sbornik.* Moscow: MK

RKP, 1922. 177 p. Expressions of indignation by "the people of Moscow" in response to the Curzon Ultimatum.

IK52 *Parizh-Berlin; stenograficheskii otchet; kratkaia zapis zasedanii Anglo-Russkogo komiteta 30-31 iiulia i 23-25 avgusta 1926 g.* Moscow: VTsSPS, 1926. 177 p.

IK53 PAVLOVICH, MIKHAIL I. (pseud. of M. L. Veltman). *Russkii vopros v angliiskoi vneshnei politike, 1922-24.* Moscow: Vsesoiuznaia nauchnaia assotsiatsiia vostokovedeniia, 1924. 54 p. A discussion of British policy towards Russia as seen in the general context of British eastern policy.

IK54 PAVLOVICH, MIKHAIL I. *Sovetskaia Rossiia i kapitalisticheskaia Angliia.* 2nd ed. Moscow: "Prometei," 1925. 203 p. Volume II of *RSFSR v imperialisticheskom okruzhenii.*

IK55 PIERSON, JOHN C. "Great Britain and Russia, 1918-1920: a Study in Policy and Public Opinion." Ph.D. dissertation, Indiana Univ., 1952.

IK56 POPOV, VIKTOR I. *Anglo-sovetskie otnosheniia (1927-1929).* Moscow: Institut mezhdunarodnikh otnoshenii, 1958. 193 p. A scholarly study of the period from the breaking off to the re-establishment of diplomatic relations. Covers all published materials and some from Soviet archives. Popov spent six months at St. Antony's College, Oxford, doing research; the same book could, however, have been written entirely from Moscow libraries. [B]

IK57 *Possibilities of British-Russian Trade.* London: Anglo-Russian Parliamentary Committee, 1926. 115 p. Some leftist members of Parliament present a sober, non-emotional plea for expansion of trade and renewal of normal relations between Britain and the USSR. Numerous tables and trade statistics.

IK58 RADEK, KARL. *Vseobshchaia zabastovka i sotsialnyi krizis v Anglii.* Moscow-Leningrad: Gosizdat, 1926. 48 p.

IK59 RUSSIA (1923– USSR), NARODNYI KOMISSARIAT PO INOSTRANNYM DELAM. *Anglo-sovetskie otnosheniia so dnia podpisaniia torgovogo soglasheniia do razryva (1921-1927 gg.); noty i dokumenty.* Moscow: NKID, 1927. 172 p. A good selection of notes between the two governments covering the trade agreement of March 1921, the propaganda question, the Curzon ultimatum of 1923, recognition by Britain in 1924, the Zinoviev letter, Russian support of the general strike, the Arcos raid, and the breaking off of relations in 1927. [A]

IK60 RUSSIA (1923– USSR), NARODNYI KOMISSARIAT PO INOSTRANNYM DELAM. *Antisovetskie podlogi; istoriia falshivok, faksimile i kommentarii.* Moscow: Litizdat NKID, 1926. 170 p. English ed., London: Workers' Publications, 1927. French ed., Paris: 1926. German ed., Berlin: 1926. A selection of forged documents which, according to the Soviet compilers, purported to prove "first, that the Soviet Government is intimately connected with the Comintern; and, secondly, that the Soviet Government makes a practice of interfering in the internal affairs of other countries."

IK60A *Russia; The Official Report of the British Trades Union Delegation to Russia in November and December, 1924.* London: T.U.C. General Council, 1925. 250 p. A controversial book, containing separate reports on life and conditions of labor in Soviet Russia and Transcaucasia. Since the delegates were given an official tour under close supervision, they got a somewhat one-sided view. Important for the influence that the book had on British opinion and the controversy that it created.

IK61 SACKS, BENJAMIN. *J. Ramsay MacDonald in Thought and Action.* Albuquerque: U. of New Mexico, 1952. 591 p. Excerpts from and summaries of MacDonald's speeches and journalistic writings. Some 20 pages devoted specifically to MacDonald's thought on Russia and Soviet policy; some 50 others contain discussion of Russia in the context of wider world problems.

IK62 SHANE, THEODORE K. "British Reaction to the Soviet Union, 1924-1929; A Study of Policy and Public Opinion." Ph.D. dissertation, U. of Indiana, 1953. Deals with the abortive negotiations of 1924, the Zinoviev letter, and the Arcos raid. Discusses the relationship between the domestic political climate in Britain and the convolutions of official policy.

IK63 TALLENTS, STEPHEN (SIR). *Man and Boy.* London: Faber, 1943. 431 p. Tallents was British High Commissioner in the Baltic Provinces, February 1919-October 1920. His memoirs contain a detailed account of his mission.

IK64 TOMSKII, MIKHAIL P. *Getting Together; Speeches Delivered in Russia and England, 1924-1925.* London: Labour Research Department, 1925. 111 p. The usual stuff—urging working-class solidarity, condemning reformism, etc. The Labour Research Dept. was (and is) an organ of the Communist Party, not the Labour Party. Tomskii was for many years the leader of the Soviet trade unions.

IK65 ULLMAN, RICHARD H. *Anglo-Soviet Relations, 1917-1921.* Vol. 1: *Intervention and the War.* Princeton, N.J.: Princeton Univ.

Press; London: Oxford, 1961. 360 p. An exhaustive study, based largely upon unpublished British sources, of the making of British policy towards Russia during the period between the Bolshevik seizure of power and the Armistice in November 1918. A second volume will carry the narrative forward to de facto recognition of the Soviet government by Britain in March 1921. [A]

IK66 VALERIN, R. *Ot razryva do vosstanovleniia anglo-sovetskikh otnoshenii.* Moscow: Gosizdat RSFSR, 1930. 108 p. A Soviet survey of Anglo-Russian relations, 1924-29.

IK67 VOLKOV, F. D. *Anglo-sovetskie otnosheniia, 1924-1929 gg.* Moscow: Gospolitizdat, 1958. 464 p. Based on a wide range of published materials and some from Soviet archives. Scarcely more balanced in tone than the author's volume below, however. [B]

IK68 VOLKOV, F. D. *Krakh angliiskoi politiki interventsii i diplomaticheskoi izolatsii sovetskogo gosudarstva, 1917-1924 gg.* Moscow: Gospolitizdat, 1954. 399 p. An example of the worst sort of Stalinist scholarship: a free-swinging diatribe dressed up with copious references to published materials and some to Soviet archives. [B]

3. 1928-1963

(Edited by Richard H. Ullman)

IK69 AKADEMIIA NAUK SSSR, INSTITUT MIROVOI EKONOMIKI I MEZHDUNARODNYKH OTNOSHENII. *Ekonomika i politika Anglii posle vtoroi mirovoi voiny.* Edited by I. M. Lemin. Moscow: Izd-vo Akademii nauk SSSR, 1958. 663 p. An ambitious study with numerous graphs and charts and a large bibliography, but marred by rigid adherence to a Marxist framework.

IK70 BARNES, LEONARD. *Soviet Light on the Colonies.* Hammondsworth, Middlesex: Penguin, 1944. 286 p. An Englishman wants to remake the British Empire along the lines of the system of "self governing" minorities in the USSR.

IK71 BILAINKIN, GEORGE. *Diary of a Diplomatic Correspondent.* London: Allen & Unwin, 1942. 272 p. Excerpts from the diary for 1940 of the author, diplomatic correspondent for the Allied Newspaper chain. Bilainkin was a friend of Soviet Ambassador Maisky and had many other similarly interesting connections. Contains much material on Anglo-Soviet relations, but little of great importance.

IK72 BILAINKIN, GEORGE. *Maisky, Ten Years Ambassador.* London: Allen & Unwin, 1944. 400 p. An interesting journalistic account, rather lacking in depth. Maisky, Counsellor of the Soviet Embassy in London 1925-27 and Ambassador 1932-43, is presented as an unflagging advocate of Anglo-Soviet co-operation. Especially interesting for the period between the Nazi-Soviet pact and the German attack in June 1941.

IK73 BILAINKIN, GEORGE. *Second Diary of a Diplomatic Correspondent.* London: Low, 1947. 423 p. Excerpts from the author's diary for 1945. Bilainkin was in Berlin for the Potsdam Conference, also in Yugoslavia.

IK74 BONCH-OSMOLOVSKII, A. *Angliia i Soedinennye Shtaty v borbe za mirovuiu gegemoniiu.* Moscow-Leningrad: Gosizdat, 1930. 148 p.

IK75 BRYANT, ARTHUR. *The Turn of the Tide, 1939-1943.* London: Collins; Garden City, N.Y.: Doubleday, 1957. 766 p. and 624 p. Excerpts from the diaries of Field Marshal Sir Alan Brooke (later Lord Alanbrooke), Chief of the Imperial General Staff, strung together with background material by Bryant. Many details concerning Allied-Soviet military co-operation.

IK76 BRYANT, ARTHUR. *Triumph in the West.* Garden City, N.Y.: Doubleday, 1959. 438 p. Lord Alanbrooke's diaries from September 1943 through June 1946. Alanbrooke accompanied Churchill to Moscow and then to Yalta; there are interesting chapters on each of these conferences. Like the preceding volume, this one contains much on Allied-Soviet military co-operation, but relatively little on political relations.

IK77 BULGANIN, NIKOLAI A. *Visit to Britain of the Soviet Leaders, N. A. Bulganin and N. S. Khrushchev, April 18th-27th, 1956: Speeches, Statements, Press Conference, Trade Programme.* London: Soviet News, 1956. 54 p.

IK78 BUSH, HENRY C. "British Press and Parliamentary Opinion About the Soviet Union, 1946-1950." Ph.D. dissertation, Chicago, 1954.

IK79 CHURCHILL, WINSTON S. *The Second World War.* Boston: Houghton Mifflin; London: Cassell, 1948-53. 6 vols. The British Prime Minister's brilliantly written memoirs with many direct quotations from key documents. The most important work published on Anglo-Soviet relations in World War II. [A]

IK80 CHURCHILL, WINSTON S. *The War Speeches of the Rt. Hon. Winston S. Churchill.* Comp. by Charles Eade. London: Cassell; Boston: Houghton Mifflin. Vol. 1 (*9 May 1938-22 June 1941*), 1951. 483 p. Vol. 2 (*25 June 1941-6 September 1943*), 1952. 560 p. Vol. 3 (*11 September 1943-16 August 1945*), 1952. 578 p. Many references to Soviet policy and to Anglo-Soviet relations.

IK81 COATES, WILLIAM P. *Why Anglo-Russian Diplomatic Relations Should be Restored.* London: The Anglo-Russian Parliamentary Committee, 1928. 77 p. A plea by a prolific propagandist for the USSR.

IK82 CONGRESS OF PEACE AND FRIENDSHIP WITH THE U.S.S.R. *Britain and the Soviets; Verbatim Report.* London: Lawrence, 1936. 197 p. A special congress held in London December 7 and 8, 1935. Consists of praise heaped upon the Soviet Union by various worthies of the British Left and semi-Left. Relatively little discussion of Soviet foreign policy.

IK83 CONGRESS OF PEACE AND FRIENDSHIP WITH THE U.S.S.R. *For Peace and Friendship; Proceedings of the Second National Congress of Peace and Friendship with the U.S.S.R., London, March 13 and 14, 1937.* London: Gollancz, 1937. 202 p.

IK84 CRANKSHAW, EDWARD. *Russia and Britain.* London: Collins, 1944. 126 p. Three-quarters of the book deals with pre-Revolutionary Anglo-Russian relations. The remainder is an invocation for a better (but realistic) understanding of the wartime and postwar Anglo-Soviet partnership.

IK85 DASHINSKII, S. *Britanskii imperializm i antisovetskii front.* Moscow: Gosizdat, 1929. 111 p. Written during the intervention hysteria of the late twenties and early thirties, this book reviews British-Soviet relations and analyzes the contemporary situation to show that Britain is preparing an attempt to overthrow the workers' and peasants' regime of the USSR.

IK86 DUKES, PAUL. *Come Hammer, Come Sickle!* London: Cassell, 1947. 187 p. Written in the form of conversations with workers about Soviet behavior. Contains little of interest to the serious student.

IK87 EDEN, ROBERT ANTHONY (SIR). *Days for Decision.* London: Faber, 1949; Boston: Houghton, 1950. 239 p. Eden's speeches in opposition during the period 1946-49. Those dealing with foreign policy, including considerable commentary on relations with the Soviet Union, are on p. 161-234.

IK88 EDEN, ROBERT ANTHONY (SIR). *Freedom and Order.* London: Faber, 1947; Boston: Houghton, 1948. 436 p. Eden's speeches during the period 1939-46 in the House of Commons and at political and ceremonial occasions, some on Anglo-Soviet relations.

IK88A EDEN, ROBERT ANTHONY (SIR). *Facing the Dictators; the Memoirs of Anthony Eden, Earl of Avon.* London: Cassell; Boston: Houghton, 1962. 746 p. Covers the period from 1931, when Eden became Parliamentary Under-Secretary at the Foreign Office, until his resignation as Foreign Secretary in February 1938. Written from the author's privileged access to official documents, it is the most authoritative account of British foreign policy during these years yet available. Russia did not loom large in this policy, but Eden's contemporary views of Soviet actions and responses receive ample attention in his book. Of particular interest is his account of his visit to Stalin in 1935. The period between this and the following work (IK89) will be covered in a forthcoming volume. [A]

IK89 EDEN, ROBERT ANTHONY (SIR). *Full Circle; the Memoirs of the Rt. Hon. Sir Anthony Eden.* London: Cassell, 1960. 619 p. Although primarily an apology for the author's Suez policy as Prime Minister in 1956, the volume contains much valuable material on Eden's preceding five-year term as Foreign Secretary. Naturally, relations with the Soviet Union occupy a major part of the whole. [B]

IK90 EGOROV, V. N. *Politika Anglii na Dalnem Vostoke; sent. 1939-dek. 1941 gg.* Moscow: Izd. IMO, 1960. 222 p.

IK91 ESTORICK, ERIC. *Stafford Cripps; A Biography.* London: Heinemann, 1949. 378 p. American ed., *Stafford Cripps; Master Statesman.* N.Y.: Day, 1949. 245 p. Cripps was Ambassador in Moscow from May 1940 to January 1942. This book contains interesting descriptions of embassy life, and of Cripps' relations with Soviet leaders, but very little on Soviet or British policy.

IK92 EVANS, TREVOR. *Bevin of Britain.* N.Y.: Norton, 1946. 282 p. Written in 1946, this volume nevertheless contains about 30 informative pages on Bevin's first year as Foreign Secretary, particularly concerning his views of Soviet policy.

IK93 FEIS, HERBERT. *Churchill, Roosevelt, Stalin; the War They Waged and the Peace They Sought.* Princeton, N.J.: Princeton Univ. Press, 1957. 692 p. Probably as definitive an account as will ever be drawn—from American archives at least—of the workings of the Grand Alliance. Much material on U.S. and British interpretations of Soviet policy. [A]

IK93A GERMANY, AUSWÄRTIGES AMT. *Documents and Materials Relating to the Eve of the Second World War.* Moscow: Foreign Languages Publishing House; N.Y.: International Pub., 1948. 2 vols. French ed., Moscow: 1948. German ed., Moscow: 1948-49. Russian ed., Moscow: Gospolitizdat, 1948. Published by the Ministry of Foreign Affairs of the USSR in response to the publication by the State Department of *Nazi-Soviet Relations, 1939-1941*, these documents were selected to prove the guilt of the West in its dealings with Hitler, and thus to justify the Nazi-Soviet Pact. Volume I, dealing with 1937-38, consists of records of conversations of Hitler, Ribbentrop and others with various foreign statesmen, etc. Volume II consists of the private papers of Herbert Von Dirksen, German ambassador to Moscow, Tokyo, and London in the period between the two World Wars. These papers, found by the Soviet army, are particularly interesting for events leading up to the Nazi-Soviet Pact, as viewed from England. [A]

IK94 GOLLANCZ, VICTOR. *Russia and Ourselves*. London: Gollancz, 1941. 131 p. Written during the month following Germany's attack on Russia. Combines a condemnation both of Soviet policy and of the policies of Western European Communist parties during the period between the Nazi-Soviet pact and the German attack with a plea for all-out support of Russia. 40-page appendix summarizes the arguments of the author and other members of the British non-Communist Left against the policies of the Communist Party of Great Britain.

IK95 GOSUDARSTVENNYI INSTITUT "SOVETSKAIA ENTSIKLOPEDIIA," MOSCOW. *Britanskiia imperiia*. Moscow: Ogiz, 1943. 463 p. A very detailed political, social, and economic survey of Britain and her Empire. The history sections reflect the desire of the regime to inculcate pro-British feelings in the Soviet population during the critical period of the war when the book was published.

IK96 GREAT BRITAIN, FOREIGN OFFICE. *Documents Relating to the Meeting of Foreign Ministers of France, the United Kingdom, the Soviet Union and the United States of America, Geneva, October 27-November 16, 1955*. London: H.M.S.O., 1955. 186 p. This meeting was devoted largely to discussion of the problem of German reunification. The White Paper contains the various proposals and arguments presented by the four powers, including the so-called "Eden plan."

IK96A GREAT BRITAIN, FOREIGN OFFICE. *History of the Second World War; British Foreign Policy in the Second World War*. By Sir Llewellyn Woodward. London: H.M. Stationery Office, 1962. 592 p. An abridged version of a longer unpublished work, written for official reference. Woodward had access to all Foreign Office papers, although apparently not to Cabinet papers or to those from other Departments. Relations with the USSR are naturally a dominant theme of the work; of particular interest is the way in which the Foreign Office's appraisal of Soviet actions and policies sometimes varied from that of the Prime Minister. The book necessarily should be read in conjunction with Churchill's history (IK79); it is second in importance only to that work as source material for the study of Anglo-Soviet relations during World War II. [A]

IK97 GREAT BRITAIN, UNITED KINGDOM MILITARY SERIES. *History of the Second World War; Grand Strategy*. Ed. by J.

R. M. Butler. London: H. M. Stationery Office. Vol. I, *1933 to September 1939*, by N. H. Gibbs (to be published). Vol. II, *September 1939-June 1941*, by J. R. M. Butler, 1957. 603 p. Vol. III, *June 1941-October 1942*, by J. M. A. Gwyer & J. R. M. Butler (to be published). Vol. IV, *October 1942-August 1943*, by Michael Howard (to be published). Vol. V, *August 1943-September 1944*, by John Ehrman, 1956. 634 p. Vol. VI, *October 1944-August 1945*, by John Ehrman, 1956. 422 p. All of these volumes contain information on how British (and American) strategy was affected by Soviet actions and policies.

IK98 HOWE, JACK H. "Britain and the U.S.S.R., March-September 1939; Emergence and Dissolution of Entente Hopes." Ph.D. dissertation, U. of Nebraska, 1954. Utilizes published Foreign Office documents to present an account of the 1939 negotiations largely from the British point of view. Argues that the ultimate responsibility for the failure to form a common front against Hitler must be shared by both Britain and the Soviet Union.

IK99 IVANOV, LEV N., and SMIRNOV, P. *Anglo-amerikanskoe morskoe sopernichestvo*. Moscow: Institut mirovogo khoziaistva i mirovoi politiki, 1933. 319 p. A detailed account of the Anglo-American-Japanese rivalry in the decade following the Washington Naval Conference. Although scholarly, it is of little interest except as a reflection of the Soviet view of the inevitability of conflict among capitalist powers. Particular attention is given to colonial questions.

IK100 KALININ, N. N. *Anglo-amerikanskie protivorechiia na sovremennom etape*. Moscow: Gospolitizdat, 1958. 163 p. A serious attempt, complete with graphs and bibliography to define in Marxist terms the conflicts of interest between Britain and the U.S. These conflicts manifest themselves in the competition for markets, raw materials, and investment opportunities, as well as in the struggle to alter power relationships all over the world. The U.S. is the villain—extending her power in Europe and Asia at the expense of a Britain weakened by World War II.

IK101 KEETON, GEORGE W. *The Problem of the Moscow Trial*. London: Black, 1933. 143 p. A very interesting and scholarly technical examination of the trial in Moscow of the Metro-Vickers engineers, and the reaction of the British Foreign Office to it, examined first from the standpoint of Soviet legal procedure and then from that of international law. The author concludes that the trial was un-British, but not unfair.

IK102 KELLY, DAVID V. (SIR). *The Ruling Few*. London: Hollis & Carter, 1953. 449 p. The author was British Ambassador to Moscow 1949-1951. Some 90 pages devoted to this period. Many interesting observations on diplomatic life in Moscow, although relatively little on Soviet policy.

IK103 KRASILNIKOV, ALEKSEI N. *Politika Anglii v otnoshenii SSSR, 1929-1932 gg.* Moscow: Gospolitizdat, 1959. 306 p. A competent, rather scholarly work based solely on published materials—but an immense range of these. More restrained than most recent similar works, but its period (the years of the Depression) affords the author much expostulation on "English aggressive policy" due to "contradictions in capitalism." [B]

IK104 LAMMERS, DONALD N. "Russia in British policy, 1929-1934." Ph.D. dissertation, Stanford, 1960.

IK105 MARSHALL, JOYCE D. "Soviet Attitude toward the Foreign Policies of the Left Wing of the British Labour Party since 1948." Certificate essay, Russian Institute, Columbia, 1951. 54 p.

IK106 MEEHAN, EUGENE J. *The British Left Wing and Foreign Policy: A Study of the Influence of Ideology.* New Brunswick, N.J.: Rutgers, 1960. 201 p. A theoretical study of how an ideology makes the thinking of persons adhering to it rigid and dogmatic. The author uses the left wing (formally non-Communist but often fellow-travelling) of the British Labour Party from 1945 to 1951. This group was highly suspicious of the U.S. and inclined to give the USSR a second chance—again and again; these attitudes led it to revolt against the Labour Party leadership as early as 1946.

IK107 MONTGOMERY OF ALAMEIN, FIELD-MARSHAL THE VISCOUNT. *Memoirs.* Cleveland: World, 1958. 508 p. Some information on difficulties of working with the Russians and the coordination of Allied policy, particularly concerning the German Control Commission.

IK108 NEKRICH, A. M. *Politika angliiskogo imperializma v Evrope, oktiabr 1938-sentiabr 1939.* Moscow: Izd-vo Akad. nauk SSSR, 1955. 476 p. Sponsored by the Institute of History of the Soviet Academy of Sciences, but inspired by the numerous works of Stalin cited in the long bibliography, this study sees British policy as motivated by one single aim: war between Germany and the USSR.

IK109 PETERSON, MAURICE D. (SIR). *Both Sides of the Curtain.* London: Constable, 1950; N.Y.: Macmillan, 1951. 314 p. The author was British Ambassador in Moscow from January 1946 until 1949. The 45 pages devoted to his ambassadorship are typical of Foreign Office memoirs: lots of interesting details concerning embassy life, Soviet suspiciousness, and the like, but virtually nothing about policy.

IK110 POZDEEVA, L. V. *Angliiskaia politika remilitarizatsii Germanii, 1933-36 gg.* Moscow: Izd. Akad. nauk SSSR, 1956. 268 p. Illustrates the ability of a Marxist scholar to select bits of truth from a wide variety of sources in order to create a wholly distorted picture. In this view, the "ruling circles" of England singlemindedly pursued the goal of arming Germany, with the aim of unloosing her on the USSR.

IK111 QUISLING, VIDKUN. *Russia and Ourselves.* London: Hodder and Stoughton, 1931. 284 p. Norwegian ed., Oslo: Blix, 1941. 201 p. German ed., Oslo: Blix, 1942. 227 p. Urges an alliance between Britain and Scandinavia directed against Bolshevism. By the Norwegian traitor who personified and thereby originated the term "quisling."

IK112 RUSSIA (1923– USSR), MINISTERSTVO INNOSTRANNYKH DEL. *Correspondence Between the Chairman of the Council of Ministers of the U.S.S.R. and the Presidents of the U.S.A. and the Prime Ministers of Great Britain During the Great Patriotic War of 1941-1945.* Vol. I, *Correspondence with Winston S. Churchill and Clement R. Attlee (July 1941-November 1945).* Moscow: Foreign Languages Publishing House, 1957. 401 p. A very valuable collection, selected, however, with a view towards presenting Russian policy in the best possible light. [B]

IK113 SIMON, JOHN A. S., 1st VISCOUNT. *Retrospect.* London: Hutchinson, 1952, 327 p. Relatively little on Russia. Useful, however, for information on the Metropolitan-Vickers Trial, which took place when Simon was Foreign Secretary.

IK114 SLOAN, PAT. *Russia—Friend or Foe?* London: F. Muller, 1939. 200 p. By a pro-Soviet graduate of Cambridge, who lived in the USSR in the thirties.

IK115 STRANG, WILLIAM, LORD STRANG. *Home and Abroad.* London: Deutsch, 1956. 320 p. An important book. Strang dealt with Russia during almost all of the 34 years he spent in the Foreign Service. Much useful information on the Metropolitan-Vickers Trial (when Strang was Chargé d'Affaires of the Moscow Embassy) and the abortive British mission (which Strang led) to negotiate an agreement with the USSR in August 1939. Of equal interest is Strang's account of his stint as Permanent Under Secretary in the Foreign Office from 1949 until his retirement in 1953. [A]

IK116 STRAUSS, PATRICIA (O'FLYNN). *Cripps; Advocate Extraordinary.* N.Y.: Duell, 1942. 423 p. British ed., 1943. An interesting chapter on Cripps' eighteen months as Ambassador in Moscow, during which the German attack occurred. A nice vignette of life at the Moscow Embassy and at the temporary embassy at Kuibyshev.

IK117 SURVEY OF INTERNATIONAL AFFAIRS, 1920-1923; THE WAR-TIME SERIES FOR 1939-1946. Ed. by A. J. Toynbee.

Vol. 3. McNEILL, WILLIAM H. *America, Britain, and Russia; Their Co-operation and Conflict, 1941-1946.* London: Oxford, for the Royal Institute of International Affairs, 1953. 819 p. An admirable, scholarly study based on materials published in western languages. Has to a great extent been superseded, however, by Feis's three volumes, which are based upon archival materials. By a professor of history at the University of Chicago. [B]

IK118 UMIASTOWSKI, ROMAN. *Poland, Russia and Great Britain, 1941-45: A Study of Evidence.* London: Hollis and Carter, 1946. 544 p. A Polish patriot ascribes the disappearance of Poland behind the Iron Curtain to the incompetence and perfidy of the Western leaders in their dealings with the diabolically clever Stalin. In spite of exaggerations, this may be considered an honest exposition of a sincerely held point of view, one which a Pole might naturally maintain.

IK119 UNDASYNOV, I. N. *Rabochee dvizhenie i leiboristskaia partiia Velikobritanii, 1929-1932 gg.* Moscow: Izd. IMO, 1961.

IK120 WOOD, EDWARD F. L., 1ST EARL OF HALIFAX. *Fullness of Days.* London: Collins; N.Y.: Dodd, Mead, 1957. 319 p. Although Halifax's memoirs contain much on his tenure as Foreign Secretary (February 1938 to January 1941), they contain virtually nothing concerning Soviet policy or Anglo-Soviet relations—a fact that more than speaks for itself!

4. BRITISH COMMUNIST PARTY

(Edited by Stephen R. Graubard)

IK121 ARNOT, ROBERT PAGE. *The General Strike, May, 1926; Its Origin and History.* London: Labour Research Department, 1926. 245 p. An account of the General Strike written by a British Communist. Important as a document illustrating the position taken by British Communists on the issue. [B]

IK122 BEER, MAX. *A History of British Socialism.* Intro. by R. H. Tawney. London: G. Allen and Unwin, 1940. 361 p. Communism is treated only briefly in what remains one of the classic texts on British Socialism.

IK123 BELL, THOMAS. *The British Communist Party; A Short History.* London: Lawrence and Wishart, 1937. 201 p. The only history of the Party by one of its members; disavowed, however, by the Party leadership. [A]

IK124 BELL, THOMAS. *John Maclean, a Fighter for Freedom.* Glasgow: Communist Party, Scottish Committee, 1944. 173 p. The biography of a Scottish "radical" who agitated for the creation of a Scottish Communist Party.

IK125 BELL, THOMAS. *Pioneering Days*. London: Lawrence and Wishart, 1941. 316 p. The autobiography of a Communist, active in the formation of the Communist Party in Great Britain. The author is particularly proud of his work for the Third International and his encounters with Lenin. [B]

IK126 BROCKWAY, ARCHIBALD FENNER. *Inside the Left; Thirty Years of Platform, Press, Prison, and Parliament*. London: Allen and Unwin, 1942. 352 p. Written by a Labour "radical" and M.P., this is one of the most important works documenting the relations between the "radicals" in the Labour Party and the Communists. Important for its chapters on British participation in the Spanish Civil War. [A]

IK127 BROCKWAY, ARCHIBALD FENNER. *Workers' Front*. London: Secker and Warburg, 1938. 254 p. A tract directed against the United Front proponents. The author, against relations with bourgeois parties, insisted on a Workers' Front. A useful document for the mood of the 1930's among British Left doctrinaires.

IK128 COCKBURN, CLAUD. *Crossing the Line*. London: MacGibbon & Kee, 1958. 214 p. Continuing the autobiography of a *Daily Worker* journalist, until, and beyond, his retirement to Ireland. (See next title.)

IK129 COCKBURN, CLAUD. *In Time of Trouble*. London: Hart Davis, 1956. 264 p. The amusing autobiography of a journalist who worked first for the *Times* of London and then for the *Daily Worker*. Ends in 1938.

IK130 COMMUNIST PAPERS. *Documents Selected from those Obtained on the Arrest of the Communist Leaders on the 14th and 21st October, 1925*. Cmd. 2682. London: H. M. Stationery Office, 1926. 135 p. Invaluable for the relationship of the British Party with the Comintern, and for its special responsibilities in the colonial territories. [A]

IK131 COMMUNIST PARTY OF GREAT BRITAIN. *Communist Policy in Great Britain; The Report of the British Commission of the 9th Plenum of the Comintern*. London: Communist Party of Great Britain, 1928. 195 p.

IK132 COMMUNIST PARTY OF GREAT BRITAIN. *Report of the Commission on Inner Party Democracy to the Executive Committee*. London: The Communist Party, 1957. 59 p.

IK133 COMMUNIST UNITY CONVENTION, LONDON, 1920. *Communist Unity Convention, London, July 31 and August 1, 1920, Official Report.* London: Communist Party of Great Britain, 1920. 72 p.

IK134 COPEMAN, FRED. *Reason in Revolt.* London: Blandford Press, 1948. 235 p. The political biography of a British Communist of the 1930's, with especial value for the Spanish Civil War, in which he played an important role.

IK135 CROOK, WILFRID H. *The General Strike, a Study of Labor's Tragic Weapon in Theory and Practice.* Chapel Hill, N.C.: U. of North Carolina, 1931. 649 p. Still the best work on the subject. Although written almost too soon after the event, it does not suffer from that fact. The interpretations are modest but judicious. [A]

IK136 DARKE, CHARLES H. *The Communist Technique in Britain.* London: Penguin, 1952. 159 p. American ed., *Cockney Communist.* N.Y.: Day, 1952. 190 p. A London bus conductor writes of his experiences and disillusionments with the British Communist Party and how and why he came to leave the Party. An adequate work by the sort of man who does not generally choose to write about such things. [B]

IK137 DONOGHUE, AUGUSTINE P. "History of the Communist Party of Great Britain, 1939-1946." Ph.D. dissertation, Stanford, 1953.

IK138 DRIDZO, SOLOMON A. (A. Lozovskii, pseud.). *Angliiskii proletariat na rasputi; sbornik statei.* Moscow: Profintern, 1926. 312 p. An account by an important and widely travelled official of the Profintern. Confined to questions of British internal politics, particularly the relations between the Labour and Communist parties. Naturally, strongly anti-reformist.

IK139 GALLACHER, WILLIAM G. *The Case for Communism.* Harmondsworth, Middlesex: Penguin Books, 1949. 208 p. A leading Communist explains his Party to those who seek instruction about its principles. Companion volumes were written about the major British political parties by their adherents. [B]

IK140 GALLACHER, WILLIAM G. *Revolt on the Clyde.* London: Lawrence and Wishart, 1936. 301 p. The conventional British Communist autobiography; important because of the author's position as one of the leaders of the Party. [A]

IK141 GALLACHER, WILLIAM G. *Rise like Lions.* London: Lawrence and Wishart, 1951. 253 p. An expression of the classic British Communist arguments about the Soviet Union, the United States, and other subjects which seemed important to British Communists after the end of World War II.

IK142 GALLACHER, WILLIAM G. *Rolling of the Thunder.* London: Lawrence and Wishart, 1947. 229 p. Reminiscences of a prominent Communist M.P., covering the years 1920-41. [B]

IK143 GODDEN, GERTRUDE M. *The Communist Attack on Great Britain.* London: Burns, Oates, 1935. 87 p. A well-documented tract by a Roman Catholic journalist on the activities of the British Communist Party and its direction from Moscow. No Russian materials are used.

IK144 GOLDSTEIN, JOSEPH. *The Government of British Trade Unions; A Study of Apathy and the Democratic Process in the Transport and General Workers Union.* Foreword by Arthur Deakin. London: Allen and Unwin, 1952. 300 p. An extraordinary study of how a small group of men may come to control the branch of a major trade union. Written by an American, now a professor of law, it is most useful for any scholar who wishes to understand how British unions have come, in some instances, to be controlled by Communists. [B]

IK145 GOLLANCZ, VICTOR, ed. *The Betrayal of the Left; An Examination and Refutation of Communist Policy from October 1939 to January 1941.* London: V. Gollancz, 1941. 324 p. A collection of articles by Gollancz, Laski, Orwell and Strachey explaining the dishonesty of Communist Party policy in Great Britain after the signing of the Soviet-German Pact and before the Nazi invasion of the Soviet Union. [B]

IK146 GRAUBARD, STEPHEN R. *British Labour and the Russian Revolution, 1917-1924.* Cambridge: Harvard; London: Oxford, 1957. 305 p. An account of the origins of the British Communist Party and of the early conflicts between that party and the Labour Party. Relations between the Second and Third Internationals are studied. [A]

IK147 GREAT BRITAIN, HOME DEPARTMENT. *Russian Banks and Communist Funds, Report of an Enquiry into Certain Transactions of the Bank for Russian Trade, and the Moscow Narodny Bank.* London: H. M. Stationery Office, 1928. 58 p. Of interest because of its revelation of political purposes behind various Russian economic transactions in Britain. (Cmd. 3125)

IK148 GREENWALD, NORMAN D. "Communism and British Labour; A Study of British Labour Party Politics, 1933-1939." Ph.D. dissertation, Columbia, 1958.

IK149 GUEST, CARMEL H. *David Guest, A Scientist Fights for Freedom (1911-1938).* London: Lawrence and Wishart, 1939. 256 p. A memoir of a British Communist killed in Spain; of some interest because of his role as a "Cambridge intellectual."

IK150 HALDANE, CHARLOTTE. *Truth Will Out.* London: Weidenfeld and Nicolson, 1949. 339 p. Mrs. Haldane, the wife of the scientist, J. B. S. Haldane, here describes her work for the Party, including that of forwarding British recruits for the International Brigade in the Spanish Civil War. [B]

IK151 HANNINGTON, WALTER H. *Unemployed Struggles, 1919-36.* London: Lawrence and Wishart, 1936. 328 p. A useful account by one of the Communist organizers in the unemployed movement of the 1920's and 1930's in which the Communists were conspicuous members. [B]

IK152 HARDY, GEORGE. *Those Stormy Years; Memories of the Fight for Freedom on Five Continents.* London: Lawrence and Wishart, 1956. 256 p. Russian ed., Moscow: Inlitizdat, 1957. 318 p. The author joined the Communist Party from the I.W.W. and worked for the Comintern and the British Communist Party in various attempts to form Communist unions on the waterfront.

IK153 HORNER, ARTHUR. *Incorrigible Rebel.* London: Macgibbon & Kee, 1960. 235 p. Autobiography of the British miners' union leader, a faithful Party member throughout his life.

IK154 HUTT, GEORGE ALLEN. *The Condition of the Working Class in Britain.* Intro. by Harry Pollitt. London: Lawrence, 1933. 272 p. A classic Communist history of the British working-class movement. Useful as a document illustrating the argument commonly given in Communist literature. [B]

IK155 HUTT, GEORGE ALLEN. *The Post-War History of the British Working Class.* London: Gollancz, 1937. 320 p. N.Y.: Coward, McCann, 1938. 274 p. A brief history. 1918. The parts on Labour and Communist party rivalry are quite good.

IK156 HYDE, DOUGLAS. *I Believed; the Autobiography of a Former British Communist.* London: Heinemann, 1951; N.Y.: Putnam, 1950. 303 p. German ed., Freiburg: 1952. The autobiography of a Communist, who wrote for the *Daily Worker*, and who eventually abandoned Communism to become a convert to Roman Catholicism. [B]

IK157 JACKSON, THOMAS A. *Solo Trumpet; Some Memories of Socialist Agitation and Propaganda.* London: Lawrence & Wishart, 1953. 166 p. Reminiscences of a London Marxist who became a Communist, covering the period 1900-20 only.

IK158 JONES, JACK. *Unfinished Journey.* Preface by David Lloyd George. London: H. Hamilton, 1937. 318 p. This work is of interest only for the foundation of the British Party and its first few years, when he was a member.

IK159 LERNER, SHIRLEY. *Breakaway Unions and the Small Trade Union.* London: Allen & Unwin, 1961. 210 p. Contains an interesting account of the United Clothing Workers, a Communist union.

IK160 McCARTHY, MARGARET. *Generation in Revolt.* London: Heinemann, 1953. 276 p. A revealing biography of a girl who worked as a Communist in the 1920's, first as a Lancashire textile operative and then as a member of the Comintern bureaucracy in Moscow. [A]

IK161 MURPHY, JOHN T. *New Horizons.* London: John Lane, 1941. 352 p. The autobiography of one of Britain's more engaging Communists, who left the Party in 1932. Written with wit and verve; in this respect, very different from most other such works. [A]

IK162 PAUL, LESLIE A. *Angry Young Man.* London: Faber and Faber, 1951. 302 p. Of some interest for the atmosphere of British working-class politics at the local level in the 1920's and 1930's.

IK163 PELLING, HENRY. *America and the British Left: From Bright to Bevan.* London: A. and C. Black, 1956; N.Y.: New York University Press, 1957. 174 p. A brief study by an Oxford don; the material on the British Communist Party's attitudes towards the U.S. is rather brief.

IK164 PELLING, HENRY. *The British Communist Party; A Historical Profile.* London: Black, 1958; N.Y.: Macmillan, 1959. 204 p. The best single volume on the British Communist Party. Written by a historian who is viewing the Party from the outside, it necessarily depends primarily on printed sources. [A]

IK165 PIRATIN, PHILIP. *Our Flag Stays Red.* London: Thames Publications, 1948. 91 p. A brief self-justification by a Communist M.P., with some account of struggles against Fascism in the East End of London in the 1930's.

IK166 POLLITT, HARRY. *How to Win the Peace.* London: The Communist Party, 1944. 96 p.

IK167 POLLITT, HARRY. *How to Win the War.* London: 1939.

IK168 POLLITT, HARRY. *Serving My Time; An Apprenticeship to Politics.* London: Lawrence and Wishart, 1940. 292 p. A classic British Communist autobiography, which holds no surprises but needs to be read as a document. [A]

IK169 *Radcliffe Report. Report of the Committee on Security Procedures in the Public Service. (Chairman: Rt. Hon. Lord Radcliffe) Nov. 21, 1961.* H. M. Stationery Office, 1962. 42 p. Cmd. 1681. The committee was "disturbed at the number of Communists and Communist sympathizers" holding positions as paid officials or unpaid officers in Civil Service staff associations and trade unions.

IK170 REDMAN, JOSEPH (pseud. of Brian Pearce). *The Communist Party and the Labour Left, 1925-1929*. Hull, England: 1957. 31 p. A scholarly account of the Comintern's intervention in British Communist politics at a crucial juncture. [A]

IK171 ROLPH, C. H., ed. *All Those in Favor? The E. T. U. Trial*. London: André Deutsch, 1962. 247 p. A condensation of some 1,365,-000 words of official court transcript of a case where four Communist officials were found guilty of rigging union elections.

IK172 RUST, WILLIAM. *Britons in Spain: the History of the British Battalion of the XV International Brigade*. London: Lawrence & Wishart, 1939. N.Y.: International Publishers, 1939. 212 p. The official Party memoir, containing useful information. [B]

IK173 RUST, WILLIAM. *The Story of the "Daily Worker."* London: People's Press Printing Society; N.Y.: Universal Distributors, 1949. 128 p. The brief history of the official Party paper from its foundation in 1930, told by its editor. [B]

IK174 SPENDER, STEPHEN. *World within World*. N.Y.: Harcourt Brace, 1951. 312 p. The autobiography of the British poet who found the Communist Party a temporary home in the 1930's. The association was very brief.

IK175 THOMAS, JAMES H. *My Story*. London: Hutchinson, 1937. 311 p. The autobiography of a British trade union leader, who never enjoyed good relations with the British Communists. A libel suit which Thomas instituted against *The Communist* created something of a stir in the early 1920's.

IK176 TOYNBEE, PHILIP. *Friends Apart; A Memoir of Esmond Romilly and Jasper Redley in the Thirties*. London: MacGibbon and Kee, 1954. 189 p. A touching tale of two young men who lost their lives in the war. A brilliant exposition of the mood of the 1930's in Britain among young people of good birth and education who found in Communism a seeming solution to the iniquities of the day. [B]

IK177 UTLEY, FREDA. *Lost Illusion*. Intro. by Bertrand Russell. London: Allen and Unwin, 1949. 237 p. The experiences of a Party member first in Britain and then in Russia.

IK178 WOOD, NEAL. *Communism and British Intellectuals*. N.Y.: Columbia, 1959. 256 p. A perceptive and useful study by an American political scientist who seeks to explain the appeal of Communism to certain British intellectuals. The attraction of Communism for scientists is one of the most important themes treated. Excellent bibliography. [A]

II. GREECE

EDITED BY CHARILAOS G. LAGOUDAKIS

INTRODUCTORY NOTE

Greece and the USSR established diplomatic relations in March 1924. Soviet policy toward Greece, however, is chiefly reflected in the history and activities of the Communist Party of Greece (*Kommunistikon Komma Ellados,* or KKE). Although almost nothing has been published on Greek-Soviet relations, the scholar will find a plethora of sources on Communism in Greece. The records of the KKE and its affiliates contain evidence of the USSR's attitude toward the Greek Communists and of Soviet aspirations in the Balkans. There is also a wealth of anti-Communist materials.

With the exception of Th. Papakonstantinou's writings, Greek Sovietologists have largely confined themselves to editorials and articles in the Greek press. It is expected that Papakonstantinou, a journalist and the author of the valuable study, *I Anatomia tis Epanastaseos* (below), will produce the definitive history of the KKE in relation to Soviet policy in Greece. No study by foreigners, including those by the Russians, discusses Greece within the framework of Soviet foreign relations.

The first part of this section (General Works) contains studies on three subjects: (a) The history of the KKE from the time it was known as the Socialist Party of Greece (*Socialistikon Komma Ellados*, or SEK, which gained Comintern recognition in 1920) to the present. (b) The Communist-controlled resistance movement during World War II, *i.e.*, the National Liberation Front (*Ethnikon Apeleftherotikon Metopon*, or EAM), and its military arm, the National Popular Liberation Army (*Ethnikos Laikos Apeleftherotikos Stratos*, or ELAS). (c) The postwar period from December 1944 to the end of 1950, during which the Communist guerrilla movement reflected the Cominform's effort to bring Greece within the Soviet orbit. There is a wealth of materials on this Communist insurgency, headed by the "mountain government" under Markos Vafiades, who was also the Commander of the so-called Democratic Army of Greece (*Dimokratikos Stratos Ellados*, or DSE). Several of the sources discuss the role of Yugoslavia, Bulgaria and Albania in providing logistic support to the Communist guerrillas in Greece. They also include materials showing Soviet action in the United Nations in support of the KKE.

The fundamental problem between Greece and the Soviet bloc following World War II was the Macedonian question, which has a long history in the relationship between Greece and her Slavic neighbors. Bulgarian and Yugoslav designs on Greek Macedonia and Thrace motivated these two states to exert military pressure on Greece with the political support, at least, of Moscow. The sources listed under the

Macedonian question consist largely of works by Greek authors, pointing up the issue as it pertains to Greek-Soviet relations.

Part 3 lists those periodicals and newspapers which reveal the motivation and aims of the Greek Communists. No reference is made to the national Greek press, but the scholar will find in it a strong reaction against the Communist effort to subvert Greece.

1. GENERAL WORKS

IL1 *Ai Archai kai to Programma tou Sosialistikou Ergatikou Kommatos.* Athens: Central Committee of the SEK, 1919. The SEK changed its name to the KKE in 1924, although on September 21, 1920, it had been recognized by the Comintern as the Communist Party of Greece. It called at the time for a Balkan Federation without distinction of race or religion, which implied the eventual release of some Greek territory to Bulgaria.

IL2 *Ai Machai to Grammou kai tou Vitsi.* Athens: Greek General Staff, 1949. 248 p. An official military account of the battles in which the Communist guerrillas were defeated and forced out of Greece. It discusses the tactics of the guerrilla warfare which the Soviet Union and its bloc sponsored in Greece during 1946-49.

IL3 ALBANIA. *Actes agressifs du gouvernement monarcho-fasciste grec contre l'Albanie.* Tirana: Albanian Govt., 1947.

IL4 *Antartopolemos.* Athens: Greek General Army Staff, Office A2. An official military account of the Communist guerrilla war in Greece, covering the period 1946-49. It describes how guerrilla tactics and regular military methods were used to combat this type of Communist warfare sponsored by the USSR. An indispensable source in the study of Soviet bloc military pressure on Greece. [A]

IL5 BARTSOTAS, VASSILIS. *I Politiki ton Stelechon tou KKE sta Teleutea Deka Chronia.* No place: Central Committee of the KKE, 1950. An official account of Greek Communist policy during the years 1940 to 1950. Bartsotas was at the time among the chief members of the Party's Central Committee, but in 1957 he was expelled from the Party. During World War II he was political commissar of the Communist guerrillas ELAS.

IL6 BURKS, R. V. *The Dynamics of Communism in Eastern Europe.* Princeton, N.J.: Princeton University Press, 1961. 256 p. Contains considerable data on Greek Communism. Based on a year's research and observations on the basis of interrogations in Greek reform prisons for Communist detainees. The author is an American professor, currently with Radio Free Europe. [A]

IL7 CAPELL, RICHARD. *Simiomata; A Greek Note Book, 1944-1945.* London: Macdonald, 1946. 224 p. The author was a British correspondent of the *Daily Telegraph*, and the book records his travels in Greece during the first Communist effort after liberation to dominate Greece by force. Presents a picture of EAM/ELAS from first-hand observations, but nonetheless seems to be unaware of the power and support behind the Greek Communists in the EAM.

IL7A CHAMBERLIN, W. C., and IAMS, J. D. "Rebellion: The Rise and Fall of the Greek Communist Party." Washington: Foreign Service Institute, Department of State, June 2, 1963. 487 p. (mimeographed). The best discussion of the Greek Communist Party available in English. It is modestly described as a "term paper" for the Fifth Senior Seminar in Foreign Policy of the Foreign Service Institute. As senior officers in the Defense and State Departments, the authors had personal experience in Greece, and they have made good use of Greek sources, which are listed in an impressive bibliography. Explains the failure of the KKE in Greece as a result of wrong political decisions. [A]

IL8 CHARALAMBIDIS, N., HADJIANASTASIOU, A., and PARASCHOS, A. "To 'Mystikon Archeion'." *Ethnikos Kyrix*, beginning October 9, 1949. Articles in an Athens newspaper containing the "revelations" of Metaxas' Minister of Public Order, who suppressed the KKE from 1936 to 1940. Konstantinos Maniadakis presents documentary materials which are interesting and useful.

IL8A CONDIT, D. M. *Case Study in Guerrilla War: Greece During World War II*. Washington: Special Operations Research Office, American University, 1961. 338 p. Examines the guerrilla war in Greece against the Axis as an instrument of Soviet foreign policy and analyzes the Communist-controlled National Liberation Front (EAM) in its political implications and long-term effects. A useful aid to the scholar and the policy maker. Presents a clear account of the tactics and strategy employed by EAM's military arm, ELAS, which became the dominant resistance movement during the war.

IL9 DENNET, RAYMOND, and JOHNSON, JOSEPH E., eds. *Negotiating with the Russians*. Boston: World Peace Foundation, 1951. 310 p. Contains an account on "Negotiating in the Balkans, 1945-1947" by Mark Ethridge, publisher of the *Louisville Times and Courier Journal*, and C. E. Black, professor at Princeton University and advisor to the State Department, 1943-46. The authors relate their first-hand experiences with the Soviet effort to capture Greece by Trojan Horse tactics. They point out the failure of the U.S. to appreciate Soviet intentions, which were to Communize Eastern Europe under the guise of "popular democracy." Communist confidence in surmounting the obstacles was illustrated in the vigorous assistance given by Albania, Yugoslavia, and Bulgaria to the Communist guerrillas in Greece. [A]

IL10 DESPOTOPOULOS, K. *In Kosmoistoriki Simasia tis E. S. S. D.* Athens: Greek-Soviet Union Society, 1946. 40 p. A lecture by one of the leading Greek Communists. Illustrative of the Greek Communist effort to indoctrinate the youth of Greece on the importance of the Soviet Union.

IL11 DORANTHES, N. *Ellas kai Rosia, 860-1941.* Athens: 1948. Develops the thesis that Russia has never been a friend of Greece, despite the notion that imperial Russia went all out to protect the Christian Greeks of the Ottoman Empire from oppression.

IL12 DRAGOUMIS, PHILIPOS. *Prosochi sti Voreio Ellada.* Thessalonika: 1947. The author, an old conservative politician from Macedonia, demands a strong policy for the defense of Northern Greece, because it is vulnerable to Soviet-Slavic pressure. Once Minister of Foreign Affairs and Governor of Northern Greece, Dragoumis' views on Balkan affairs give weight to this discussion.

IL13 ETHNIKON APELEUTHERŌTIKON METŌPON. *White Book, May 1944-March 1945.* N.Y.: Greek-American Council, 1945. 137 p. Greek ed., Athens: 1945. A collection of documents aiming to incriminate the British for the EAM troubles in Athens during the period December 1944 to January 1945. The Greek-American Council supported the Communist-led National Liberation Movement (EAM).

IL14 GLYNOS, DIMITRIOS. *Ta Simerina Provlimata tou Ellinismou.* Athens: Ta Nea Vivlia, 1945. A collection of the writings of a Greek intellectual in the service of Communism. Ta Nea Vivlia (New Books) was the publishing firm of the Greek Communist Party.

IL15 GREECE, HYPHYPOURGEION TYPOU KAI PLEROPHORION. *The Conspiracy against Greece.* Athens: 1947. 166 p. Greek ed., Athens: 1947. An official account of the Communist conspiracy to subvert Greece after World War II. Contains evidence compiled by the Ministry of Press and Information. Its thesis is that the Greek Communists are agents of the Cominform plot to subvert Greece.

IL16 GYALISTRAS, SERGE A. *Hellenism and Its Balkan Neighbors during Recent Years.* Athens: HESTIA, 1945. 197 p. Examines primarily Greek-Bulgarian relations as the principal concern of Greece in the Balkans. The author views the creation of Bulgaria in 1878 as the pivot of Russia's Balkan policy. Although the author refrains from treating Greek-Soviet relations directly, his discussion illustrates the Greek viewpoint of the situation in the Balkans as it had developed by 1944-45 under Soviet influence and pressure.

IL17 HADJIVASSILIOU, CHRYSSA. *To Kommunistiko Komma tis Ellados kai to Gynaikeio Zitima.* Athens: Central Committee of the KKE, 1945. Discusses the Greek Communist position on women.

IL17A HOUTAS, STYLIANOS T. *I Ethniki Antistasis ton Ellinon, 1941-1945*. Athens: 1961. 634 p. The most recent Greek study on the resistance movement during World War II. The author, now Minister of Public Welfare, was a guerrilla leader in EDES.

IL18 HOWARD, HARRY N. *Greece and the United Nations, 1946-1949; A Summary Record. Report of the UN Special Committee on the Balkans; A Chronology*. U.S. Dept. of State, pub. 3645, Int. Org. and Conf. Series III, 40. Washington: 1949. 31 p. A careful summary by a historian and State Department official of the UN discussions on Greece during the period of the Communist guerrilla war. The author followed closely these debates and served on the American contingent of UNSCOB in Greece.

IL19 HOWARD, HARRY N. *The Greek Question; Developments in the 6th Session of the General Assembly, 1951-52*. Washington: G.P.O., 1952. As a State Department official, the author was a member of the American delegation on the U.N. Commission to investigate the violation of Greek territorial integrity by the Communist guerrillas supported from the Soviet bloc during the years 1946 to 1949. This is a reprint from Department of State Bulletins of Feb. 25 and March 3, 1952. It gives a review of the Greek case in the U.N. and the position taken by the USSR.

IL20 HOWARD, HARRY N. *The Greek Question in the 4th General Assembly of the United Nations*. U.S. Dept. of State, pub. 3785, Int. Org. and Conf. Series III, 47. Washington: 1950. 36 p.

IL21 HOWARD, HARRY N. *The United Nations and the Problems of Greece*. Washington: G.P.O., 1947. 97 p. A useful summary of the U.N. debates over Greece up to 1947.

IL21A KABAKCHIEV, KHRISTO S., BOSHKOVICH, B., and VATIS, KH. *Kommunisticheskie partii Balkanskikh stran*. Moscow: Moskovskii rabochii, 1930. 239 p. This Soviet publication contains a history of the Greek Communist Party and a discussion of the conference for the Communist Balkan Federation. It reflects the Soviet viewpoint on Greece as well as on the Balkans, and indicates the role each Communist Party is to play.

IL22 KANELLOPOULOS, P. *Ellinikos Marxismos*. Athens. The author is a Greek scholar and politician, who examines Greek Communism as a special case in Marxist philosophy. He held the chair of sociology at the U. of Athens, and later became Deputy Prime Minister.

IL23 KOMMOUNISTIKON KOMMA TĒS HELLADOS. *Deuzième Livre Bleu sur l'intervention Americano-Anglaise, sur le régime monarcho-fasciste, sur la lutte libératrice du peuple*. Athens: KKE, 1949. A Communist account.

IL24 KOMMOUNISTIKON KOMMA TĒS HELLADOS. *Pente chronia agones, 1931-1936*. Athens: 1946. 452 p. Covers the period during which the KKE became increasingly active, culminating in the general strike of 1936, which provoked the dictatorship of the Fourth of August under General Ioannis Metaxas. Contains basic documents of the policy and structure of the Party. [A]

IL25 KOMMOUNISTIKON KOMMA TĒS HELLADOS. *To Eudomo Synedrio tou KKE*. Athens: Central Committee of the KKE, 1945. Deals with the procedures and resolutions of the 7th Congress of the Greek Communist Party, and contains speeches of the leaders, G. Siantos, N. Zachariades, and A. Stringos.

IL26 KOMMOUNISTIKON KOMMA TĒS HELLADOS. *To KKE apo to 1918 eos to 1926*. Athens: 1937. *To KKE apo to 1926 eos to 1931*. Athens: 1947. 484 p. These two volumes contains official records of the KKE, a basic source for the philosophy and activities of the Greek Communist Party. [A]

IL27 KOMMOUNISTIKON KOMMA TĒS HELLADOS. *To KKE apo to 1935 eos to 1945 - deka chronia agones*. Athens: Central Committee of the KKE, 1946. Covers the period during which the KKE was underground, suppressed by dictator Metaxas in 1936. Having developed an underground structure, the Greek Communists were prepared to take over and direct the major resistance movement, EAM. [A]

IL28 KOMMOUNISTIKON KOMMA TĒS HELLADOS. *To KKE - yia Sena Ellada*. Athens: KKE, 1946. A publication of the Greek Communist Party presenting what it has done for Greece. An effort to show the patriotism of the Greek Communists as a departure from the usual Marxist emphasis on internationalism.

IL29 KOUFOUDAKES, G. *O.E.N.O., e satanike organsosi tou K.K.E. sten emporike naftilia*. Athens: 1949. By a Communist Party member who held high office in the marine union known as OENO, which is under Communist influence. His discussion of OENO contains revealing observations of a Communist instrument which maintains world-wide connections through the Greek merchant marine.

IL30 KOUSOULAS, DIMITRIOS G. "The Communist Party of Greece since 1918; A Case Study of Communist Strategy and Tactics in Underdeveloped Countries." Ph.D. dissertation, Syracuse U., 1956. More a history of the KKE than a case study of Communism in an underdeveloped country. A valuable survey of the Party's chronological development, orientation, and activities from 1918 to February 1945. [A]

IL31 KOUSOULAS, DIMITRIOS G. *The Price of Freedom; Greece in World Affairs, 1939-1953*. Syracuse: Syracuse University Press,

1953. 210 p. Over half is devoted to the Italian and German attacks on Greece, but there are several sections on the Communist attempt to take over Greece and the attitude of the USSR and its satellites. Bibliography.

IL32 KYRKOS, MICHAEL. *O "Kindynos" tou Kommounismou.* Athens: Ta Nea Vivlia, 1946. 37 p. A lecture delivered on July 5, 1946, in Athens, under the patronage of Rizospastikon Dimokratikon Komma (Radical Democratic Party) "to enlighten public opinion against the right-wing campaign opposing any collaboration with the democratic parties." This lecture illustrates the effort of the Left with the support of Moscow to allay Greek fears of Communism and Panslavism. The author was the editor of the Communist front newspaper *Eleftheri Ellada* (Free Greece).

IL33 KYROU, ALEXIS AD. *Elliniki Exoteriki Politiki.* Athens: No Pub., 1955. 459 p. The author presents this book as a declaration of faith in the historic mission of Greece in international affairs. Greek-Russian relations are treated briefly in pages 194-216, with emphasis on Greece's policy toward the Soviet bloc. The scope of the study is limited, but as one of the few books on Greek foreign policy, it provides a framework for the student of Greek-Russian relations since 1821.

IL34 LEEPER, REGINALD W. A. *When Greek Meets Greek.* London: Chatto and Windus, 1950. 243 p. An official account by the British Ambassador to Greece, dealing with the period 1943-46.

IL35 *Lefki Vivlos.* Trikkala, Thessaly: Ethnikon Apeleftherotikon Metopon, 1945. An apológia of the National Liberation Front (EAM) which describes its policy as a resistance movement for the internal and external freedom of Greece. Throws light on how the Greek Communists developed their underground as an instrument of Soviet policy in Greece and the Balkans.

IL36 MC NEILL, WILLIAM H. *Greece; American Aid in Action, 1947-56.* N.Y.: Twentieth Century Fund, 1957. 240 p. Covering the period of the Communist guerrilla war, the author points out the meaning of American assistance to Greece in defeating the Communists and in building internal strength to stabilize the country within the framework of the Western Alliance. By a professor of history at the University of Chicago.

IL37 MC NEILL, WILLIAM H. *The Greek Dilemma: War and Aftermath.* London: Gollancz; Philadelphia: Lippincott, 1947. 291 p. McNeill was Assistant U.S. Military Attaché to Greece. His account is partly based on first-hand observations and mainly on intelligence materials to which he had access during his duty tour. He covers the period from 1941 to 1947, during which the Greek Communists led the principal resistance activity in Greece (EAM) with an eye to dominating the country upon liberation. [A]

IL38 MANUELIDES, DIMITRI S. "Communist Tactics in Greece." M.A. thesis, U. of Virginia, 1952. 219 p.

IL39 MARC, LEON. *Les Heures douloureuses de la Grèce libérée.* Paris: Librairie le François, 1947. 254 p. The author was in Greece from October 1944 to January 1945 and describes here his first-hand observations of the stormy events during the first days after liberation.

IL40 *Mavri Vivlos; To Eklogiko Praxikopima Tis 31 Marti, 1946.* Athens: Ethnikon Apeleftherotikon Metopon, 1946. 62 p. The "Black Book" of the Communist front, EAM, which seeks to discredit the first post-war elections in Greece, which were observed by the Allied Mission to Observe the Greek Elections (AFOGE) on the basis of the Yalta commitment. The Soviet Union declined the invitation to join the U.S., U.K. and France in helping to restore political order in Greece.

IL41 METAXAS, IOANNIS. *O Kommunismos Stin Ellada.* Athens: 1936? The views of Greece's dictator in the mid-thirties, who came to power in 1936 in the wake of a general strike staged by the Communists. Contains interesting documentary material on the KKE and its activities in the Greek armed forces.

IL41A MURRAY, J. C. "The Anti-Bandit War," *Marine Corps Gazette* (January-May, 1954). A Marine colonel with field experience in Greece discusses the Communist guerrilla war as a case study in developing effective counter-measures for the containment of covert Soviet aggression.

IL42 MYERS, EDMUND C. W. *Greek Entanglement.* London: Hart-Davis, 1955. 289 p. The chief of the British Mission to Greece, 1942-43, tells of his experiences in Axis-occupied Greece. He maintains that it was not until January 1943 that British intelligence ascertained the "inseparableness of EAM and ELAS and the full character of their direction." He testifies that "a third of the arms of ELAS' permanently embodied force of fifty thousand men had been supplied by the Middle East Command," and concludes that "our short-term military policy supporting EAM/ELAS turned out to be in direct contradiction to our long-term political policies." [A]

IL43 NISSYRIOU, K. *Oi Protes Gnoseis tou Komounismou.* Athens: Central Committee of the Greek Communist Party, 1946. 52 p. Gives an answer to why the Communist Party fights, outlines the duties of the Communist, and describes the organization of his Party.

IL44 NOEL-BAKER, FRANCIS G. *Greece, the Whole Story.* London: Hutchinson, 1946. 64 p. An excellent brief survey of Greece from 1935 to 1946. While the booklet is designed as an apology for British policy, it serves as a frame of reference for the impact of international Communism in Greece. The author was not able to detect any Soviet support for the Communist-led EAM, observing that "at no time during the occupation was there evidence that EAM was being run from Moscow (though various interested parties would have liked to have proved otherwise) and pro-EAM propaganda in Soviet broadcasts was spasmodic and comparatively mild." He concludes that the struggle of EAM was hopeless, little realizing that within a year after the truce signed on February 2, 1946, international Communism would make a second venture to dominate Greece. The author is among those who treat the EAM/KKE revolt as a "civil war," free from Soviet support and manipulation.

IL45 *O Kommounismos Stin Ellada.* Athens: Ethniki Etairia. Ethniki Etairia is a national anti-Communist society with the aim of enlightening the public at home and abroad about Greece's national interests. In this publication, it describes the presence of Communism in Greece as an alien influence which seeks to enslave the country.

IL46 PANAYOTOPOULOS, H. *To aishos tes Symphonias tes Varkizas: prodosia kata tou Ethnous.* Athens: 1949. A Greek nationalist view on the Varkiza agreement of February 1945 between the Greek government and the Greek Communist Party, terminating the EAM uprising. It reflects that Greek opinion which opposed any compromise brought about by the British. The second round of the struggle with the Communists in 1947-49 vindicates the author's view that the war against the Reds should have been prosecuted to the end.

IL47 PAPAKONSTANTINOU, TH. *I Anatomia tis Epanastaseos.* Athens: 1952. 267 p. The author is Greece's foremost student of Soviet affairs and an expert on Greek Communism. Once a Marxist himself in the early thirties, he broke with the Greek Communists and became the most perceptive Greek critic of Communism and Marxism. In the third part of this book, Papakonstantinou, who is now the editorial writer of the daily *Eleftheria*, analyses the war and postwar armed effort of the Greek Communists to dominate Greece.

IL48 PAPANDREOU, GEORGE E. *E Apeleftherosis tes Ellados.* 2nd ed., Athens: Skazikes, 1945. 252 p. The author was Prime Minister of Greece at the end of the war. Here he gives his version of the Communist rebellion of 1944-45, as well as other events of that period. In November 1963 he again became Prime Minister. His writings and speeches in Parliament constitute a rich anti-Communist literature.

IL49 PETSOPOULOS, GIANNES. *Ta Ethnika Zitimata kai oi Ellines Kommounistes.* Athens: No Pub., 1946. 41 p. A former Communist (see his long exposition below), the author examines the origin of Greece's national policies in contrast to Communist aims. Worth noting is the introduction of B. Panos, who discusses the "democratic" solution of Greece's national questions.

IL50 PETSOPOULOS, GIANNES. *Ta pragmatika aitia tes diagraphes mou apo to KKE.* Athens: no pub., 1946. 476 p. An account of the author's conflict with the leadership of the Greek Communist Party, arising from his disagreement with its policies during World War II and up to the national elections of 1946. The points of his dissent on the Caserta agreement, the December revolt, and the abstention from the 1946 elections throw some light on Soviet direction of KKE.

IL51 PURYEAR, EDGAR F. "Communist Negotiating Techniques; A Case Study of the United Nations Security Council Commission Concerning the Greek Frontier Incidents." Ph.D. dissertation, Princeton, 1959.

IL52 PYROMAGLOU, KOMNENOS. *E Ethnike Antistasis.* Athens: 1947. 265 p. A prominent leader of the EDES resistance organization gives an account of the years 1941-44 and his struggle against both the Nazis and the Communists of EAM-ELAS.

IL53 SARAPHES, STEPHANOS. *O Ellas.* Athens: Ta Nea Vivlia, 1946. 479 p. Abridged English ed., *Greek Resistance Army; the Story of ELAS.* London: Birch Books, 1951. 324 p. The Commander of ELAS tells in a very direct style the story of the Communist-led resistance to the Axis during World War II. Begins with a long survey of prewar Greek affairs from 1922 to 1941 before concentrating on the internal and external affairs of ELAS from 1943 to its dissolution in February 1945. Many details about ELAS' classic guerrilla operations. Before the war the author was a liberal and anti-royalist rather than an avowed Communist. His irreconcilable feelings toward the Right led him into ELAS; after the war he was elected to Parliament as a Communist. [A]

IL54 STAVRIANOS, LEFTEN S. *Greece; American Dilemma and Opportunity.* Chicago: Regnery, 1952. 246 p. A defender of the EAM, the author disregards Soviet aims in Greece while being highly critical of the British and American efforts. Stavrianos was in the OSS during the war; he now teaches history at Northwestern University.

IL55 STRINGOS, LEONIDAS. "E Syskepsi tis Moschas kai e Simasia tis gia to Dimokratiko Kinima tis Ellados," *Neos Kosmos*, XII, no. 12 (Dec., 1960), p. 51-66. An article in the Greek Communist Party's theoretical journal analyzing the declaration of the Moscow Conference as a guide for the Communists in Greece, stressing the idea that the Communist Party in the USSR has the necessary experience to continue leading the international Communist movement. The author is a leading member of the KKE Politburo.

IL56 SWEET-ESCOTT, BICKHAM. *Greece; a Political and Economic Survey, 1939-53.* N.Y. and London: Royal Institute of International Affairs, 1954. 207 p. A brief summary.

IL57 *To Megalo Psemma—O Kommounismos stin Rossia, ston Kosmo Kai stin Ellada.* Athens: Ekdoseis Ethnikis Diaphotiseos, 1948. 158 p. The chapter on the "Patriotic KKE" deals exclusively with the Greek Communists as Soviet agents. The anonymous author stresses the thesis that Moscow is using Bulgaria to dominate Greece and the other Balkan countries.

IL58 TOLKUNOV, L. M. *Balkany dolzhny byt zonoi mira.* Moscow: Znamia, 1959. 31 p. A pamphlet, typical of the series, which is designed to popularize the idea of a "peace zone" in the Balkans, a theme stressed in Soviet bloc propaganda beamed to Greece.

IL59 UNITED NATIONS, SECURITY COUNCIL, BALKAN COMMISSION. *Report of the Commission of Investigation Concerning Greek Frontier Incidents.* (UN Document S/360, May 27, 1947) Lake Success, N.Y.: 1947. 3 vols. [A]

IL60 U.S. LIBRARY OF CONGRESS, EUROPEAN AFFAIRS DIVISION. *War and Postwar Greece; An Analysis Based on Greek Writings.* Compiled by Floyd Spencer. Washington: 1952. 175 p. Primarily a bibliography, interspersed with a chronological account of the main developments in Greece from 1940 to 1952. Chapters III, IV, V, and VI contain much on Communist activities, especially their attempt to seize power. The author was able to observe many of the events since he was in Greece at the time on assignment by the U.S. Army. Concerned mainly with writings in the Greek language. Very useful. [A]

IL61 VOIGT, FRITZ A. *The Greek Sedition.* London: Hollis, 1949. 258 p. An anti-Communist British journalist examines the Red effort to subvert Greece following World War II.

IL62 VUKMANOVIĆ, SVETOZAR. *Le Parti communiste de Grèce dans la lutte de libération nationale.* Paris: Le Livre yougoslave, 1949. 62 p. English ed., *How and Why the People's Liberation Struggle of Greece Met with Defeat.* London: 1950. 101 p. Yugoslav ed., Zagreb: Kultura, 1950. 131 p. Italian ed., Milan: Prospective-Progressive, 1951.

171 p. A leading Yugoslav Communist gives a critical account of the Greek Communist Party's conduct of the EAM resistance and the guerrilla war from 1945 to 1949. He condemns its strategy of seeking aid from "outside" rather than relying on mass support of the Greek people.

IL63 VUKMANOVIĆ, SVETOZAR ("Tempo," pseud.). "The Unknown History of EAM, the ELAS and the Guerrilla War," (in Greek) *Ethnos*. Athens: 1952. An exposé by a top Yugoslav Communist of KKE republished in serial form. Appeared originally in *Borba* (Belgrade), August 29 to September 1, 1949. The author blames KKE's failure on Moscow's interference. The articles contain much circumstantial evidence of Yugoslav aid to the Greek guerrillas. The exposition is significant in its uncovering of the ramifications of Communist international Party relations.

IL64 WOODHOUSE, CHRISTOPHER M. *Apple of Discord—A Survey of Recent Greek Politics in Their International Setting*. London; N.Y.: Hutchinson, 1948. 320 p. The author, former Chief of the Allied Mission to the Greek guerrillas, was a part of the Greek scene for five years during World War II; his knowledge of the Greek language, history, and politics makes him the foremost English authority on modern Greece. The section on the USSR (p. 106-116) asserts that Soviet policy toward Greece was obscure and under cover so long as Moscow recognized the anti-Communist government of Greece. References to the USSR in Greek affairs and to the Communist groups, EAM and ELAS, cover the years from 1942 to 1946. Sources are almost entirely British, consisting of unpublished reports. The author avoided Greek sources because they are "contaminated by exaggeration and the Greek desire to please the inquirer" and "lack critical spirit." [A]

IL65 YIANNOPOULOS, PYRROS (EPIROT). *Oi Sklavoi kata ton Ellinon—I Sovietiki Enosis katergazetai tin ypodoulosin kai Ekmidenisin tou Ellinikou Ethnous*. Athens: No Pub., 1949. 32 p. Reviews Greek-Russian relations from 576 to 1918 in a brief exposition to document Shelley's conviction that "Russia intends to destroy, not liberate, Greece." His thesis is that the Slavs are a deadly threat to the national existence of Greece. The author is a former journalist and one time governor of a Greek province.

IL66 ZACHARIADES, NIKOS. *O Kommunistis Laikos Agonistis, Melos tou K.K.E.* Athens: Central Committee of the Communist Party of Greece, 1946. 29 p. The Secretary-General of the KKE instructs the hard core Communists in how to conspire and fight. He demonstrates how a Communist carries out his responsibility as an agent of international Communism. This pamphlet was indicative of the KKE's preparation for the Communist guerrilla war in the following three years. Zachariades was demoted after the military defeat of the KKE armed forces.

IL67 ZACHARIADES, NIKOS. *Thesis gia tin Istoria tou KKE.* Athens: Central Committee of the KKE, 1945. As Secretary-General of the KKE, the author discusses the origin of the Party from the Socialist Labor Party (SEK) organized in 1918. He develops his view of "liquidationism" and defines the "ultimate aim" of the KKE as leading the masses "on the broad path of open political conflict toward the basic goal: power." This thesis was indicative of what developed in Greece following World War II, when the KKE, with Moscow's support, initiated an armed struggle for power. Zachariades wrote these essays in prison before World War II.

IL68 ZAPHEIROPOULOS, DIMITRIOS G. *O Antisymoriakos Agon, 1945-1949.* Athens: No Pub., 1956. 686 p. The best public account of the Communist war in Greece. The author is a Greek Army officer who took part in the operations against the armed Communists. He bases his account on (a) official reports and personal experience, and (b) captured Communist documents and articles published in the guerrilla periodical *Dimokratikos Stratos.* An excellent presentation of the military operations and guerrilla tactics in relation to climate, geography, political objectives and the structure of a guerrilla force. Demonstrates how the Communist forces were defeated in their first postwar effort to use the guerrilla weapon. An abridged English edition would fill a serious gap in our understanding of militant international Communism. [A]

IL69 ZVIAGIN, IU. *Pravda o Gretsii.* Ed. by L. Teleshov. Moscow: Izd. inos. lit., 1949. 208 p. A translation from a work in French sponsored by the Greek Communist rebel so-called "Provisional Democratic Government of Greece." The contents of the book indicate its thesis: the "Anglo-American occupation" of Greece; the "monarcho-fascist" regime in Athens, and the "struggle" of the Greek people. Covers the period 1944 to 1948.

2. MACEDONIAN QUESTION

IL70 BARKER, ELIZABETH. *Macedonia; Its Place in Balkan Power Politics.* London: Royal Institute of International Affairs, 1950. 129 p. A history of the Macedonian question from 1870 to 1950 by a British journalist probably writing from British secret reports. The Macedonian question has created difficulties for the Balkan Communists for decades. In the 1930's, the Comintern was subject to internal strain as the Greek, Bulgarian, and Yugoslav parties split over the problem of Macedonia's fate. The USSR forced an autonomous Macedonia policy—which split the Greek CP and lost its support at home in the critical period during and after World War II. Since 1950, when the Greek Communist guerrillas were defeated, the Soviet Union's Macedonian policy has been obscure. [A]

IL71 MIKHAILOV, IVAN. *Stalin and the Macedonian Question*, by Macedonicus, pseud. Ed. by Christ Anastasoff. St. Louis: Pearlstone, 1948. 92 p. A nationalist Bulgarian exposition based on Stalin's *Marxism and the National Question.* Seeks to prove that the Communists are denationalizing the Macedonians by stressing the existence of a Macedonian ethnic entity and rejecting the Bulgarian character of Macedonia in Greece and Yugoslavia. Argues that Russian imperialism keeps the Macedonian question unresolved. Published under auspices of the Central Committee of the Macedonia Political Organization of the United States and Canada (Indianapolis, Indiana).

IL72 NALTSAS, CRYSTOPHOROS A. *To Makedoniko zitima kai i Sovietiki politiki.* Thessalonika: Society of Macedonian Studies, 1954. 544 p. A well documented study of the Macedonian question from 1828 to 1954. Develops the thesis that Russia, and not Bulgaria and Yugoslavia (Serbia before 1918), has been the directing and manipulating power of the Macedonian question. Author is a Greek specialist on Balkan and Slavic affairs. He maintains that ethnological changes in Macedonia have removed the demographic basis for a Greater Macedonia, but that the question has taken a new aspect under the Communist scheme for an autonomous Macedonia within a Soviet Balkan Confederacy, to which the Greek Communists have been committed since World War II. Bibliography, including Bulgarian, Yugoslav, and Greek sources.

IL73 *To Makedonikon Zitima kai o Kommunismos.* Thessalonika: Third Army Corps, Press Office, 1949. An official Greek army publication showing how the Cominform exploited the Macedonian question to undermine Greece. Exposes the Greek Communist Party as a part of the conspiracy.

IL74 YIALISTRAS, SERGIOS A. "Oi Slavoi, O Kommunismos kai I Makedonia tou Aegaiou," *Parnassos*, III, no. 1 (Jan.-March, 1961), p. 31-62. A documented article by a retired General and former Cabinet member of the Greek government, whose thesis is that Russian policy toward Greece prior to 1918 and Soviet aims since World War II coincide in the aim of keeping an open Macedonian question in favor of Bulgaria. Yialistras reviews the whole Macedonian question in the light of Panslavism. He notes the Slav aim of exterminating the Greek factor in the Balkans—a process that has been going on since the Panslav Congress in Moscow in 1867.

IL75 ZAPHEIROPOULOS, DIMITRIOS. *To K.K.E. kai i Makedonia.* Athens: no pub., 1948. 179 p. By a Greek army officer, written with the approval of the Greek General Staff. He exposes the KKE as part of the Slav conspiracy to create a Macedonian state under Slav control, backed and manipulated by the Soviet Union.

IL75A ZEVGOS, GIANNIS. *O Slavikos Kindinos.* Athens: Central Committee of the KKE, 1947. A reply to the charge that the KKE had yielded to Slav pressure on Macedonia. It is a compilation of ten articles written by a top Greek Communist for the Party newspaper, *Agonistis*, a daily paper of the KKE regional committee of Macedonia and Thrace. The articles reveal how sensitive the Greek Communists are about their official position on Macedonia and its effects on relations with Yugoslavia, Bulgaria, and the USSR.

IL76 ZOTIADES, G. B. *The Macedonian Controversy.* Thessalonika: Society of Macedonian Studies, 1954. 92 p. A general survey which concludes that the "Slav-Soviet conspiracy" used the Greek CP as an instrument to secure its own ends.

3. PERIODICALS AND NEWSPAPERS

IL77 *Archeia Ethnikis Antistasis.* Athens: 1946-1947. A periodical publication of the Communist-oriented Society of Ta Nea Vivlia (The New Books). Includes studies and documents of the Communist resistance movement in Greece during World War II, known as the National Liberation Front (EAM) and the National Popular Liberation Army (ELAS). It reflects the structure of the movement which aimed at bringing Greece within the Soviet bloc. Publication ceased with the outlawing of the KKE.

IL78 *Bulletin analytique de bibliographie hellenique.* Athens: Institut Français d'Athenes, 1947—. Quarterly. The most useful publication of its kind, covering all aspects of Greek affairs, with particularly helpful sections on politics, history, and international law, which list books and articles on Greece's foreign relations. Most of the books are annotated. [A]

IL79 *Eleftheri Ellada.* Athens. The newspaper of the National Liberation Front (EAM), Communist controlled; began during the Axis occupation of Greece as an underground paper. After liberation it became a regular daily. It was suppressed in 1947 along with all other Communist publications. Thereafter it appeared for a while as an irregular underground paper. [A]

IL80 *Kommounistiki Epitheorisis.* Athens. The monthly theoretical organ of the Communist Party of Greece, founded in 1921. Suppressed by the Metaxas Dictatorship in 1936, it resumed publication in 1944, but was proscribed in 1947 with the banning of the Party. Indispensable for the Greek Communist line and Greek-Soviet relations. Succeeded by *Neos Kosmos* in 1948. [A]

IL81 *Neos Kosmos.* 1948—. Monthly political-theoretical periodical of the Greek Communist Party. Gives no place of publication, but Prague is probably its headquarters.

IL82 *Rizospastes.* Athens. The official daily organ of the Greek Communist Party. Existed as an underground periodical during the Axis occupation and was suppressed in 1947 when the KKE was proscribed. It continues to appear clandestinely from time to time in Greece and in the Soviet bloc. [A]

IL83 *Sosialistiki Epitheorisis.* Athens. Organ of the Socialist Party of Greece, ELD (Greek Popular Democracy). First appeared in July 1945, but has ceased publication. Its articles reflected the views of the Greek socialists, who have cooperated with the Communist Party of Greece on domestic and foreign issues.

IM. HUNGARY

EDITED BY C. A. MACARTNEY AND FRANCIS S. WAGNER

1. GENERAL WORKS

IM1 COMIN COLOMER, EDUARDO. *El Comunismo en Hungria, 1919-1946.* Madrid: Nos Graficas Valera, 1946. 240 p. A bird's-eye view of the 1919 and the post-1945 situations by an anti-Marxist. The role of Béla Kun and the Kremlin is accentuated.

IM2 KÁROLYI, MIHÁLY, COUNT. *Memoirs; Faith without Illusion.* London: Cape; Toronto: Clarke, Irwin, 1956. 392 p. By an aristocrat who from 1919 to 1946 lived in exile. Though an autobiography written in self-defense, it contains much of historical value, excepting those parts which record the author's well-known experience with Communism in 1919 and 1946-49. These parts show his naïveté in handing over power to the Communists in 1919 and his lack of knowledge of the post-1945 period. Includes interesting notes, illustrations, index. Undocumented. [A]

IM3 STANFORD RESEARCH INSTITUTE, STANFORD UNIVERSITY. *The Tactics and Strategy of Communism in Hungary; 1919-1949.* Stanford, Cal.: Stanford University Press, n.d. 324 p.

IM4 SULYOK, DEZSÖ. *A magyar tragédia. 1. rész. A trianoni béke és következményei.* New Brunswick, N.J.: Szerzö kiadása, 1954. 624 p. By a former member of the Hungarian parliament and leader of the Liberty Party who played a distinguished role up to the summer of 1947, when he emigrated to the West. His vast experience is excellently utilized in describing the theory and workings of the Hungarian Soviet Republic of 1919 and the Soviet tactics applied in 1945-47. A very important work though partly not objective. Six-page bibliography. [A]

IM5 SULYOK, DEZSÖ. *Zwei Nächte ohne Tag.* Zurich: Thomas, 1948. 464 p. A long book which, after several chapters highly critical of the Horthy regime, goes on to give the author's experiences during the opening months of the Soviet occupation, of which he is no less critical. The author finds very few people indeed to praise in either Hungary, and despite its wealth of material, his book has been ill-received. [B]

IM6 SZTÁRAY, ZOLTÁN. *Bibliography on Hungary.* N.Y.: Kossuth Foundation, 1960. 101 p. Especially useful for its section on modern Hungary.

2. 1917-1945

IM7 ASHMEAD-BARTLETT, ELLIS. *The Tragedy of Central Europe*. London: Butterworth, 1923. 320 p. Vivid and entertaining reminiscences of the author's experiences as *Daily Telegraph* correspondent in Central Europe in 1919. He saw the Béla Kun regime at close quarters (although his background knowledge is exceedingly superficial) and also knew the Hungarian counter-revolutionary émigrés in Vienna, whom he helped to achieve their famous burglary of the (Bolshevik) Hungarian Legation. Most frankly anti-Bolshevik in outlook.

IM8 BANDHOLTZ, HARRY H. *An Undiplomatic Diary, by the American Member of the Inter-allied Military Mission to Hungary, 1919-1920*. N.Y.: Columbia University Press, 1933. 394 p. The author represented the U.S.A. on the Inter-Allied Commission in Hungary in 1919-20. He was very strongly sympathetic to the Hungarian "restoration," by whom he was held in great affection for his pertinacity in fighting their battles against the Rumanian occupying army. A personal narrative. [A]

IM9 BERLIN, INSTITUT FÜR MARXISMUS-LENINISMUS. *Die ungarische Räterepublik im Jahre 1919 und ihr Widerhall in Deutschland; eine Sammlung von Aufsätzen und Dokumenten*. Berlin: Dietz, 1959. 152 p. The articles, especially László Réti's, are superficial. Selected documents do not show considerable German mass reaction to the Hungarian Soviet Republic. Published material is used. The latest document is dated March 21, 1929.

IM10 BIRO, KARL. *Sotsial-demokraticheskaia partiia i kontrrevoliutsiia v Vengrii*. Ed. by S. S. Dikanskii. Moscow: "Moskovskii rabochii," 1925. 108 p. A Marxist-Leninist interpretation of the failures of the 1919 Hungarian Soviet Republic. Right wing Socialist leaders are attacked for their anti-Communist attitude. Counterrevolutionary activities are exaggerated. Undocumented. [B]

IM11 BIZONY, LÁSZLÓ. *133 Tage ungarischer Bolschewismus; die Herrschaft Béla Kuns und Tibor Szamuellys; die blutigen Ereignisse in Ungarn*. Leipzig-Vienna: Waldheim-Eberle, 1920. 111 p. Italian ed., Bologna: Capelli, 1920. A journalistic report. The Russian background of Béla Kun and Tibor Szamuelly as well as Red atrocities are described in some detail. [B]

IM12 BÖHN, WILHELM. *Im Kreuzfeuer zweier Revolutionen*. Munich: Verlag für Kulturpolitik, 1924. 552 p. The author was Minister of War in the short-lived Communist government in Hungary and also Supreme Commander of the Hungarian Red Army. He discusses the background and events of the Hungarian Bolshevik Revolution and of the following Counter Revolution. A highly subjective and partisan account which the author intended to be a mixture of a historical treatment and of his personal memoirs. Very few source references; no index; no bibliography. [B]

IM13 CATTELL, DAVID T. "Soviet Russia and the Hungarian Revolution of 1919." M.A. thesis, Columbia, 1949. 122 p. A very good summary, with an excellent bibliography. [B]

IM14 COMNEN, N. P. *O prima experienta comunista in Ungria.* Madrid: Colección Destin, 1957. 133 p. A critical survey of the Béla Kun 1919 proletarian dictatorship with special regard to the Rumanian Army's part in its defeat. Offers neither a new approach, nor new source material. French summary.

IM15 EISELE, HANS. *Bilder aus dem kommunistischen Ungarn.* Innsbruck, Austria: 1920. 131 p.

IM16 ESZTERHÁZY, NIKOLAUS, GRÓF. *Meine Erlebnisse und Eindrücke aus der Zeit vom 1 November 1918 bis 2 August 1919.* Budapest: St. Stephan, 1921. 126 p.

IM17 GAIDU, PAVEL. *Kak borolas i pala sovetskaia Vengriia.* Foreword by Béla Kun. Moscow-Leningrad: Ogiz, 1931. 80 p.

IM18 GARAMI, ERNÖ. *Forrongó Magyarország; emlékezések és tanulságok.* Leipzig-Vienna: Pegazus kiadás, 1922. 243 p. By a Socialist leader in exile. Personal reminiscences of the October, 1918 revolution and the 133-day Hungarian Soviet Republic of 1919. Proves that the Entente note delivered by Col. Vyx was directly responsible for proclaiming the Soviet system on March 21, 1919. A strong criticism of the Communist and counterrevolutionary regimes alike. [B]

IM19 GRATZ, GUSZTÁV. *A forradalmak kora; Magyarország története 1918-1920.* Budapest: Magyar Szemle Társaság, 1935. 354 p. By a middle-of-the road liberal-minded statesman. A serious historian's objective approach to the October, 1918 Revolution and the 1919 proletarian dictatorship, as well as the counterrevolutionary "white terror." All sorts of extreme actions are revealed and condemned. Based heavily on unpublished documents and the best literature. Its annotated bibliography and detailed chronology of events are outstanding. [A]

IM20 GRÁTZ, GUSZTÁV, ed. *A bolsevizmus Magyarországon.* Budapest: Franklin, 1921. 861 p. A detailed, documentary analysis of the politics, economy, public administration, culture, and the Bolshevik terror in the 1919 Hungarian Soviet Republic, with a description of the Soviet Union's influence. Contains 24 pages of very valuable bibliographical notes and 6 maps. [A]

IM21 HAJDU, TIBOR. *A tanácsok Magyarországon 1918-1919-ben.* Budapest: Kossuth Könyvkiadó, 1958. The effect of World War I and of the 1917 Bolshevik revolution in Russia on Hungary's labor movement and the founding of the system of the Soviet-type local councils are related by using unpublished archival material, press accounts, and memoirs. Deals also with the initial phase of the Communist Party of Hungary.

IM22 HERCZEG, GÉZA. *Béla Kun; Eine historische Grimasse.* Berlin: Verlag für Kulturpolitik, 1928. 188 p. A fairly full and well-documented account of the Kun regime by a newspaper correspondent of Hungarian origin. Strongly hostile to Kun. [B]

IM23 HETÉS, TIBOR, comp. *A Magyar Vörös Hadsereg 1919; válogatott dokumentumok.* A bevezetö tanulmányt írta Liptai Ervin. Budapest: Kossuth Könyvkiadó, 1959. 530 p. A collection of 274 important documents on the military operations of the Hungarian Red Army in 1919, and the diplomatic relations of the Hungarian Soviet Republic, focused on the USSR. Ervin Liptai's Marxist-minded introduction, in many instances, is not in line with the documents. [B]

IM24 *La Hongrie dans les relations internationales.* Budapest: Magyar Külügyi Társaság, 1935. 383 p. An official collection of diplomatic documents dealing with the period 1919-20.

IM25 HUNGARY, KÜLÜGYMINISZTÉRIUM. *Papers and Documents Relating to the Foreign Relations of Hungary*, Vol. 1: *1919-1920.* Budapest: Royal Hungarian University, 1939. An official collection of diplomatic documents, dealing chiefly with the negotiations between Hungary and the Powers before the signature of the Treaty of Trianon. The most interesting documents relate to certain underground and abortive negotiations with a group at the Quai d'Orsay. [B]

IM26 HUSZÁR, KARL, ed. *Die Proletarier-Diktatur in Ungarn.* Regensburg: Kösel & Pustet, 1920. 212 p. The author was Minister-President of one of the first governments after the fall of Kun. This was written after that event. Chiefly personal experiences. [B]

IM27 KÁLLAI, GYULA. *A magyar függetlenségi mozgalom, 1939-1945.* 4th ed. Budapest: Szikra, 1955. 283 p. By an old-line Communist, ranking high in the Party and state hierarchy. Summarizes the anti-Nazi activities of the Communist Party, with some emphasis on the work of its Muscovite leadership. Relates also the Russian-led partisan warfare and the birth of postwar Hungary. Poorly documented. [B]

IM28 KÁLLAY, MIKLÓS. *Hungarian Premier; A Personal Account of a Nation's Struggle in the Second World War.* N.Y.: Columbia, 1954. 518 p. Indispensable memoirs on foreign relations between Hungary and the Soviet Union, from June 1941, when war was declared on the USSR, to March 1944, when the Germans occupied Hungary. Reveals also the main causes for the Hungarians' antipathy toward the Soviet system. [A]

IM29 JÁSZI, OSZKÁR. *Revolution and Counterrevolution in Hungary.* Intro. by R. W. Seton-Watson. London: King & Son, 1924. 239 p. German ed., Verlag für Kulturpolitik, 1923. By the veteran Hungarian radical. More of an essay than a history. A strong partisan of Count Károlyi, the author is hostile to Kun and the revolution as well as to Horthy and the counterrevolution.

IM30 KAAS, ALBERT, BARON VON, and LAZAROVICS, FEDOR. *Der Bolschewismus in Ungarn.* Munich: Südost-Vlg. Dresler, 1930. 318 p. English ed., London: Richards, 1931. A hostile, but on the whole solid and well-documented account, by two Conservative Hungarians, of the Bolshevist regime of 1919. One of the best books on the subject. [A]

IM31 LEBOV, MARTIN F. *Vengerskaia sovetskaia respublika 1919 goda.* Moscow: Izd. sots.-ek. lit-ry, 1959. 274 p. A Marxist-Leninist interpretation of the history of the 1919 proletarian dictatorship with emphasis on the work of Béla Kun, Tibor Szamuelly, and Lenin. Soviet Russian influences are related by using unpublished materials housed in the USSR archives. Well-footnoted and illustrated; contains maps, facsimiles. [B]

IM32 MACARTNEY, CARLILE A. *Hungary and Her Successors; The Treaty of Trianon and Its Consequences 1919-1937.* London: Oxford, 1937. 504 p. The author, a Fellow of All Souls College, Oxford, has for many years specialized on the history and conditions of Central Europe, particularly Hungary, about which he has written many books. This is a study for the Royal Institute of International Affairs, which commissioned the author to make a detailed and impartial study of the arguments for and against revision of the Treaty of Trianon. Contains much statistical and other detail, and a bibliography. [A]

IM33 MACARTNEY, CARLILE A. *October Fifteenth; A History of Modern Hungary, 1929-1945.* Edinburgh: Edinburgh U., 1956-57. 2 vols. American ed., *A History of Hungary, 1929-1945.* N.Y.: Praeger, 1957. 2 vols. A massive work of some 1,000 pages which, after a short introduction and relatively brief treatment of the years 1921-29, then tells in increasing detail the story of Hungary's fortunes, internal and international, up to April 4, 1945. The author studied all sources available to him when he wrote, *inter alia* collecting much information from Hungarian émigrés and other persons concerned in the events described. The book thus contains much information not to be found elsewhere. [A]

IM34 MACARTNEY, CARLILE A. *Problems of the Danube Basin.* Cambridge: Cambridge U., 1942. 160 p. The title explains the character of this book, which is a short one, written for the non-specialist, but not for the non-intelligent public. Except for the last chapter, it is cast mainly in historic form.

IM35 *A Magyar munkásmozgalom történetének válogatott dokumentumai.* Budapest: Szikra (Kossuth Könyvkiadó), 1956-1959. Vols. v and vi. The most significant source publication issued by the Institute of Party History of the Central Committee, Hungarian Socialist Workers Party. These volumes deal with the workers' movement in the period of the Bolshevik Revolution in Russia and the Hungarian Soviet Republic of 1919. Richly illustrated, valuable bibliography, facsimiles, index. [A]

IM36 MAGYAR SZOCIALISTA MUNKÁSPÁRT, KÖZPONTI BIZOTTSÁG, PÁRTTÖRTÉNETI INTÉZET. *A Magyar Tanácsköztársaság történelmi jelentösége és nemzetközi hatása; Elöadásgyüjtemény.* Budapest: Kossuth Könyvkiadó, 1960. 387 p. By one Hungarian (Dezsö Nemes) and 17 foreign Party historians discussing Soviet influence on the founding of the Hungarian proletarian dictatorship in 1919 and its international effects. Partly documented with unpublished sources selected to present one side of the story.

IM37 MAGYAR SZOCIALISTA MUNKÁSPÁRT, KÖZPONTI BIZOTTSÁG, PÁRTTÖRTÉNETI INTÉZET. *Nagy idök tanúi emlékeznek, 1918-1919.* Budapest: Kossuth Könyvkiadó, 1958. 194 p. Eyewitness accounts of the Soviet-Russian origins of the Communist Party of Hungary, the Bolshevik Revolution in Russia and its product, the Hungarian Soviet Republic of 1919, prepared by 25 Hungarian and foreign Communists, with a preface by József Révai. A thoroughly Party-minded, carefully edited approach.

IM38 MAGYAR TUDOMÁNYOS AKADÉMIA, TÖRTÉNETTUDOMÁNYI INTÉZETE. *Magyarország és a második világháború: titkos diplomáciai okmányok a háború elözményeihez és történetéhez.* Ed. by Ádám Magda, Juhász Gyula, Kerekes Lajos. Budapest: Kossuth Könyvkiadó, 1959. 550 p. Contains 178 heretofore largely unpublished documents, dated between February 1, 1933 and October 16, 1944, primarily diplomatic reports and minutes of cabinet meetings, all dealing with Hungarian-Soviet relations. Each chapter has a documented Marxist treatise. Includes chronology of events and index.

IM39 MÁLYUSZ, ELEMÉR. *Sturm auf Ungarn.* Munich: Dresler, 1931. 295 p. English ed., *The Fugitive Bolsheviks.* London: Richards, 1931. 441 p. A well-documented but very hostile account of the Károlyi and Kun regimes by a serious historian. Much detail and solid fact, but also much invective. Deals in detail with what is seldom heeded elsewhere: Communist propaganda against Hungary after the fall of Kun.

IM39A NEMES, DEZSÖ. *K istorii krovavoi kontrrevoliutsii v Vengrii 1919-1921 gg.* Budapest: Academia Scientiarum Hungarica, 1954. 124 p. A Communist account of the counter-revolution in Hungary after the fall of the Béla Kun regime.

IM40 POGANI, I. *Belyi terror v Vengrii.* Moscow: Kom. intern., 1921. 149 p.

IM41 RÁKOSI, MÁTYÁS. *A Rákosi-per.* 4th ed. Budapest: Szikra, 1950. 593 p. French ed., *Face au tribunal fasciste.* Paris: Éditions Sociales, 1952. 222 p. A record (somewhat touched up for the benefit of admirers) of the Communist leader's self-defence, which he conducted, with a courage and eloquence which should not be denied, before the courts which tried him in 1926 and 1935.

IM42 SZAMUELLY, G. *Matias Rakoshi; zhizn i borba geroia mezhdunarodnoi proletarskoi revoliutsii.* Moscow: 1935. 171 p. A laudatory account of the long-time leader of Hungarian Communism by one of his comrades.

IM43 SZÁNTÓ, BÉLA. *Klassenkämpfe und Diktatur des Proletariats in Ungarn.* Intro. by Karl Radek. Berlin: Schwarz, 1920. 115 p. A serious study of the Béla Kun regime by a well-known Communist, who wished to discover the reasons for its failure. Of considerable interest, although many of the real reasons for the failure do not occur to the author.

IM44 SZEKFÜ, GYULA. *Három nemzedék és ami utána következik.* 5th ed. Budapest: Királyi Magyar Egyetemi Nyomda, 1938. 514 p. An intelligent evaluation using primary sources of the country's modern development, including the 1917-19 revolutionary period and the problem of Communism, by Hungary's most outstanding historian. Bibliographical footnotes. [B]

IM45 THARAUD, JÉRÔME and JEAN. *When Israel is King.* N.Y.: McBride, 1924. 248 p. A brilliantly written account of the Béla Kun regime, by two Jewish journalists. No very great historical detail, but much psychological insight. Especially concerned with harm done to Jewry by the disreputable actions of Jews such as Kun.

IM46 TORMAY, CÉCILE. *Le Livre proscrit; scènes de la révolution communiste en Hongrie.* Paris: Plon, 1925. 226 p. English ed., *An Outlaw's Diary.* N.Y.: 1924. Mme. Tormay was a practical authoress, but no great politician. This work, in diary form, describes her painful experiences under Béla Kun. It gives a good picture of the life of the bourgeoisie during those months, but the entries relating to wider affairs seldom rise above the level of scrappy gossip. [B]

IM47 ULLEIN-REVICZKY, ANTAL. *Guerre allemande, paix russe; le drame hongrois.* Neuchâtel: La Baconnière, 1947. 235 p. Personal reminiscences of the man who was head of the press under Kállay and afterwards Minister in Stockholm, being privy to the secret negotiations proceeding at that time between Hungary and the West. The tendency is to show Hungary's resistance to Germany. Of very considerable historical interest, but not always entirely reliable on points of detail. [B]

IM48 VARJASSY, LOUIS. *Révolution, Bolchévisme, Réaction.* Paris: Jouve, 1934. 154 p. By a Jewish Radical of the Jászi group, who for a time held office in the Szeged "Government" of 1919. This small book is essentially a polemic in favor of the ideas of the author and his friends, but would be of considerable value as a source for the history of the Szeged Government, were the doings of that body worthy of detailed narration.

IM49 WELTNER, JAKAB. *Forradalom, Bolsevizmus, Emigráció.* Budapest: 1929. 317 p. Mainly personal reminiscences. The author was editor of the Social Democratic daily, *Népszava*, at the time of the 1919 revolution. [B]

3. 1945-1963

IM50 ACZÉL, TAMÁS, and MÉRAY, TIBOR. *The Revolt of the Mind; A Case History of Intellectual Resistance Behind the Iron Curtain.* N.Y.: Praeger, 1959. 449 p. Well-written memoirs of a writer and a journalist who once belonged to the Communist élite of the Stalinist Rákosi regime. Well describes the changes which took place in certain Muscovites and their writer-followers as a result of the de-Stalinization process launched by the Moscow Party Congress, February 1956. The part of the Hungarian Writers Association in preparing the 1956 anti-Communist revolt is related chiefly on the ground of their personal experience. Undocumented, poorly footnoted. [B]

IM51 APTHEKER, HERBERT. *The Truth about Hungary.* N.Y.: Mainstream, 1957. 256 p. Thoroughly Communist interpretation of the country's postwar political evolution and the 1956 revolt. His data and statements are overwhelmingly erroneous, reflecting the views of the

János Kádár government. Poorly documented, even its footnotes are unreliable. By an official of the American C.P.

IM52 ARON, RAYMOND. *La Révolution hongroise; histoire du soulèvement d'octobre, précédée de "Une révolution antitotalitaire."* Paris: Plon, 1957. 334 p. By a prominent French professor and political analyst.

IM53 AUSCH, SÁNDOR, *Az 1945-1946. évi infláció és stabilizáció.* Budapest: Kossuth Kiadó, 1958. 189 p. A Marxist survey of postwar economic and financial conditions, including Hungarian-Soviet trade relations. The Moscow-dictated role of the country's Supreme Economic Council and of the Hungarian Communist Party are also related.

IM54 BALASSA, BÉLA A. *The Hungarian Experience in Economic Planning; A Theoretical and Empirical Study.* New Haven: Yale, 1959. 285 p. A many-sided study of a Soviet-type planned economy based essentially on the situation prevailing between the end of World War II and the 1956 revolt. Illustrative statistics and select bibliography. [B]

IM55 BALÁZS, BÉLA. *Népmozgalom és nemzeti bizottságok 1945-1946.* Budapest: Kossuth Könyvkiadó, 1961. 231 p. A posthumous volume by a member and Party commissar of the Historical Institute, Hungarian Academy of Sciences. Discusses the organizational activity of the Moscow Committee of the Hungarian Communist Party and the Hungarian National Independence Front. Proves that the Moscow-directed Communist Party alone laid down the country's foundations. An invaluable work based heavily on unpublished material and participants' recollections. Stylistically very poor. [A]

IM56 BAUDY, NICOLAS. *Jeunesse d'Octobre; témoins et combattants de la révolution hongroise.* Paris: Le Table Ronde, 1957. 443 p. A description and sympathetic appraisal of the 1956 anti-Marxist revolt based exclusively on interviews with émigré university students. Contains several facsimiles, one of which proves that the Szeged university youth exerted great influence, prior to October 23, 1956, on the revolutionary efforts of the Budapest youth. [B]

IM57 BIBÓ, ISTVÁN. *Harmadik út; politikai és történeti tanulmányok; sajtó alá rendezte és a bevezetöt irta: Szabó Zoltán.* London: Magyar Könyves Céh, 1960. 380 p. The most complete edition of a jurist-statesman's works discussing the country's postwar political and socio-economic evolution, focused on the presence of the Moscow-directed Communist Party and the Soviet Army. Includes his November 9, 1956 compromise for solving the Hungarian question and the 1957 memorandum on Hungary's position in East-West relations. Very poorly edited. [A]

IM58 CSICSERY-RÓNAY, ISTVÁN. *Russian Cultural Penetration in Hungary*. 3rd rev. ed. N.Y.: National Committee for a Free Europe, 1952. 42 p. Embraces all fields of culture subject to Russification. Offers no basic research; based only on Hungarian newspaper items.

IM59 DELANEY, ROBERT F., ed. *This is Communist Hungary*. Chicago: Regnery, 1958. 260 p. A symposium dealing with postwar socio-economic and political developments including family life, with emphasis on the coming uprising of 1956. The introductory analysis by John MacCormack, Vienna correspondent for the *New York Times*, is worth mentioning.

IM60 DEWAR, HUGO, and NORMAN, DANIEL. *Revolution and Counter-Revolution in Hungary*. London: Socialist Union of Central-Eastern Europe, 1957. 96 p. Interesting scrutiny of the causes and character of the 1956 events. A strongly anti-Communist approach. Useful, detailed chronology. [B]

IM61 FARKAS, MIHÁLY. *A béke arcvonalán*. Budapest: Szikra, 1949. 408 p. By Mátyás Rákosi's closest collaborator. Its data on the Bolshevization of the armed forces are of importance. [B]

IM62 FEJTÖ, FRANÇOIS. *La Tragédie hongroise; ou, une révolution socialiste anti-soviétique*. Paris: Horay, 1956. 314 p. English ed., N.Y.: McKay, 1957. By an émigré in Paris. Before leaving Hungary, the author moved in fellow-travelling circles, and his thesis, which is expounded at some length and with considerable ability, is essentially that what Hungary really wanted was the rule of the little group of men who were just one hair's breadth to the right of Rákosi.

IM63 FREE EUROPE COMMITTEE. *The Revolt in Hungary; A Documentary Chronology of Events Based Exclusively on Internal Broadcasts by Central and Provincial Radios, October 23, 1956-November 4, 1956*. N.Y.: Free Europe Comm., 1956. 112 p. [A]

IM64 GERÖ, ERNÖ. *Harcban a szocialista népgazdaságért; válogatott beszédek és cikkek, 1944-1950*. Budapest: Szikra, 1950. 638 p. By the former economic dictator of Communist Hungary. [A]

IM65 HELMREICH, ERNST C., ed. *Hungary*. N.Y.: Published for the Mid-European Studies Center of the Free Europe Committee by Praeger, 1957. 466 p. A detailed study by various hands of almost all aspects of Hungarian life under the Communist regime since World War II. Some of the chapters are very able. An important work. [A]

IM66 HONTI, FERENC. *Le Drame hongrois; une grande bataille de la civilisation chrétienne*. Paris: Triolet, 1949. 318 p. The end of Horthy Hungary and the beginnings of Bolshevism. The author was a "Westerner." Rather slight, and makes only a few original contributions, either of fact or of comment.

IM67 HORVÁTH, PÉTER. "Communist Tactics in Hungary Between June 1944 and June 1947 (An Analysis and Appraisal)." Ph.D. dissertation, New York Univ., 1956. By a Smallholders' Party organizer and secretary to Béla Varga, Speaker of the Parliament, up to their defection to Austria, June 1947. The most reliable scholarly treatise on the subject. Very useful bibliography. [A]

IM68 HUNGARIAN NATIONAL COUNCIL. *Genocide by Deportation: An Appeal to the United Nations to Enforce the Law.* N.Y.: 1951. 131 p. A documentary treatise on the concentration camps of Hungary and the Soviet Union, with emphasis on political and legal aspects in connection with persons deported by the Communist regime from Hungary.

IM69 *Hungarians in Czechoslovakia.* N.Y.: Research Institute for Minority Studies, Inc., 1959. 166 p. The only monograph on the topic, by Francis S. Wagner, Stephen Révay and others. A factual description of the theory and workings of the Stalinist-Leninist nationality policy as applied by the Czechoslovak and Hungarian Communist Parties, with Moscow behind the scenes, 1945-49. Based on published and unpublished sources. With maps, bibliographical notes, and index. [A]

IM70 HUNGARY, KÜLÜGYMINISZTÉRIUM. *La Hongrie et la Conférence de Paris.* Budapest: Magyar Külügyminisztérium, 1947. 4 vols. An official collection of papers and documents relating to the 1945-47 preparatory work before the signature of the Treaty of Paris. A basic source book on the Soviet-Hungarian-Czechoslovak disputes. [A]

IM71 HUNGARY, LAWS, STATUTES, ETC. *Hatályos jogszabályok gyüjteménye, 1945-1958. Készült a Magyar Forradalmi Munkás-Paraszt Kormány 2011/1959 (III.18) sz. határozata alapján.* Összeállította: Nezval Ferenc, Szénási Géza és Gál Tivadar. Budapest: Közgazdasági és Jogi Könyvkiadó, 1960. 4 vols. Contains laws, National Assembly decisions, edicts, decisions by the Presidium (vol. I); government decrees and decisions (vol. II); ministerial orders (vol. III); international agreements; cumulative, number and subject indexes (vol. IV). [B]

IM72 HUNGARY, LAWS, STATUTES, ETC. *Törvények és rendeletek hivatalos gyüjteménye. Közzéteszi az Igazságügyminisztérium közremüködéséval a Magyar Forradalmi Munkás-Paraszt Kormány Titkársága.* Budapest: Közgazdasági és Jogi Könyvkiadó. Issued yearly beginning with 1949 (vol. 1 published 1950).

IM73 HUNGARY, MINISZTERTANÁCS. *The Counter-Revolutionary Forces in the October Events in Hungary.* Budapest: Information Bureau of the Council of Ministers of the Hungarian People's Republic, 1957. 4 vols. German ed., Budapest: 1957. Hungarian ed., Budapest: 1957. A one-sided selection of unpublished sources to stress the "inhuman and reactionary character of the 1956 revolt." Richly illustrated.

IM74 HUNGARY, MINISZTERTANÁCS. *Nagy Imre és bűntársai ellenforradalmi összeesküvése.* Budapest: Magyar Népköztársaság Minisztertanácsa Tájékoztatási Hivatala, 1958. 159 p. English ed., Budapest: 1958. Excerpts from the records of the trial in 1958 against Imre Nagy and his "accomplices" (Dr. Ferenc Donáth, Miklós Gímes, Zoltán Tildy, Pál Maléter, etc.) for their alleged anti-state activities and high treason committed prior, during, and after the 1956 anti-Communist revolt. Unnamed compilers comment at length in a violently anti-Western manner on the defendants' statements. Includes also documents drawing a parallel between the 1919 and the 1956 "white terror." Richly illustrated, facsimiles. [B]

IM75 IGNOTUS, PAUL. *Political Prisoner.* N.Y.: Macmillan, 1960. 201 p. A Social Democrat who thought that he could work with the Communists in building a democratic Hungary, Ignotus became disillusioned, was arrested, and sentenced to 15 years at hard labor. Now living in London as head of the Hungarian Writers' Association Abroad, he tells in this book of his experiences in prison from 1949 to 1956.

IM76 INTERNATIONAL COMMISSION OF JURISTS. *The Hungarian Situation and the Rule of Law.* The Hague: 1957. 144 p. The findings of the Commission on the "legality" of the Soviet action in 1956. Dispassionate but annihilating. [A]

IM77 JUHÁSZ, VILMOS. *Blueprint for a Red Generation; the Philosophy, Methods, and Practices of Communist Education as Imposed on Captive Hungary.* N.Y.: Mid-European Studies Center, 1952. 101 p. By a National Peasant Party member, journalist, and, until 1948, assistant professor of cultural history at the University of Szeged. Superficial, full of generalizations; criticizes the educational system without making reference to curricula, educational laws and statutes. Good bibliography.

IM78 KÁLLAI, GYULA. *A szocialista kultúráért.* Budapest: Gondolat Kiadó, 1958. 237 p. Concludes, through a false interpretation of the nation's modern history, including the 1956 revolution, that there has been and will be full equality in Hungarian-Soviet relationships. The collection of the author's studies and addresses treats all fields of cultural and political Russification. An important work to show the interaction between socialist patriotism and proletarian (Soviet) internationalism.

IM79 KARTUN, DEREK. *Tito's Plot Against Europe. The Story of the Rajk Conspiracy.* London: Lawrence and Wishart, 1949. 124 p. A Communist account of the trial of László Rajk in Hungary and Tito's alleged relation to it. Fits into the general pattern of the propaganda war against Tito after his split with Stalin.

IM80 KECSKEMETI, PAUL. *The Unexpected Revolution; Social Forces in the Hungarian Uprising.* Stanford, Cal.: Stanford University Press, 1961. 178 p. A scholarly analysis of the 1956 revolt, using published as well as unpublished sources. Prepared for The RAND Corporation. [B]

IM81 KEMÉNY, GYÖRGY. *Economic Planning in Hungary 1947-49.* London: Royal Institute of International Affairs, 1952. 146 p. By a Marxist who was Secretary of Finance until the summer of 1948. Important for its firsthand information. [B]

IM82 KERTESZ, STEPHEN D. *Diplomacy in a Whirlpool: Hungary Between Nazi Germany and Soviet Russia.* Notre Dame, Ind.: University of Notre Dame Press, 1953. 273 p. A diplomatic history of Hungary during the last years of the Horthy regime and the first years after World War II, up to and including the Peace Conference. The author, a trained diplomat, served in the Foreign Ministry before 1945, but for those years he has had to write with incomplete documentation. For the later period, he had been able to draw on personal knowledge. Very valuable work. [A]

IM83 KIRÁLY, ERNÖ. *Die Arbeiterselbstverwaltung in Ungarn; Aufsteig und Niedergang, 1956-1958; Ein Dokumentarbericht.* Munich: R. Oldenbourg, 1961. 111 p. Gives a well-founded account of the aims and activities of the revolutionary labor organizations. With a well-compiled chronology of events and a selected bibliography. [B]

IM84 KOVÁCS, ENDRE, ed. *Magyar-orosz történelmi kapcsolatok.* Budapest: "Müvelt Nép" Tudományos és Ismeretterjesztö Kiadó, 1956. 455 p. A Marxist-Leninist reevaluation of Hungarian-Russian relations through history, edited by a section chief of the Historical Institute, Hungarian Academy of Sciences. Based partly on unpublished sources. The author's guided enthusiasm toward the Soviet Union precludes objectivity. Bibliographical notes. [A]

IM85 KOVÁCS, IMRE. *Im Schatten der Sowjets.* Zürich: Thomas, 1948. 298 p. French ed., *D'Une Occupation à l'autre; la tragédie hongroise.* Paris: Calmann-Lévy, 1949. 297 p. By a man who before 1944 belonged to the very radical group of "Village Explorers," who made it their chief task to expose the lamentable conditions prevailing among Hungary's rural poor. Took an active part in underground politics, standing very close to the Communists, with whom he subsequently broke. Mainly a personal narrative, but the author knew a good deal, and tells it well. Not, however, entirely free from mistakes. [A]

IM86 KOVÁCS, IMRE, ed. *Facts about Hungary.* N.Y.: Hungarian Committee, 1958. 280 p. A many-sided description and objective analysis of what happened in Hungary from 1945 to 1957 in politics, the Party, economic, and cultural life. Its statistical figures are reliable. Most studies furnish historical background. George Torzsay-Biber's essay on the legal aspects of the Imre Nagy trial is brilliant. [A]

IM87 KRUSHINSKII, SERGEI, and others. *Chto proizoshlo v Vengrii; reportazh.* Moscow: "Pravda," 1956. 157 p. Distorted, on-the-spot situation reports by well-trained Soviet journalists on the 1956 revolt in Budapest. Illustrations.

IM88 LASKY, MELVIN J., ed. *The Hungarian Revolution; the Story of the October Uprising as Recorded in Documents, Dispatches, Eye-Witness Accounts, and World-Wide Reactions.* N.Y.: Praeger; London: Secker & Warburg, 1957. 318 p. Contains a chapter on the historical background by Hugh Seton-Watson and an epilogue by François Bondy. A valuable collection, with striking photographs. [B]

IM89 LUKÁCS, GYÖRGY. *Irodalom és demokrácis.* Budapest: Szikra, 1947. 190 p. A collection of a Muscovite theoretician's 1945-46 lectures and articles on the post-1945 development of the country's cultural life, with emphasis on literature. Anti-Communist phenomena and writers, as well as any symptom of a Western orientation, are sharply criticized. Laid down the foundation for Communist literary and cultural policies in Hungary. [B]

IM90 LUKÁCS, GYÖRGY. *Új magyar kultúráért.* Budapest: Szikra, 1948. 234 p. A compilation of a leading Communist theoretician's criticisms of the non-Marxist state of cultural movements. Gives a detailed program of how the Marxist-Leninist-Stalinist transformation should be performed under Hungarian conditions but in line with the Soviet pattern. Formulates official Communist cultural policy. [A]

IM91 LUKÁCS, JÁNOS. *Magyar-orosz kapcsolatok 1914 óta.* Budapest: Officina, 1945. 28 p. An early work showing the influence of the presence of the Red Army occupation forces. Admittedly advocates the Stalinist concept of history in re-evaluating Hungarian-Soviet relationships. Attacks the nation as a whole for its negative attitude toward the Soviet Union. [A]

IM92 MAGYAR DOLGOZÓK PÁRTJA, 1. KONGRESSZUS, BUDAPEST, 1948. *A Magyar Kommunista Párt IV. kongresszusa (1948 június 12); A Szociáldemokrata Párt XXXVII. kongresszusa*

(1948 június 12). A Magyar Kommunista Párt és a Szociáldemokrata Párt Egyesülési Kongresszusa jegyzökönyve (1948 június 12-13-14). Budapest: Szikra, 1948. 372 p. Documents relating to the merger of the two Marxist parties under the name Magyar Dolgozók Pártja (Hungarian Working People's Party), the most significant landmark in the country's postwar politics. Contains also the united Party bylaws and directives. [A]

IM93 MAGYAR SZOCIALISTA MUNKÁSPÁRT, KÖZPONTI BIZOTTSÁG, PÁRTTÖRTÉNETI INTÉZET. *A munkásosztály az újjáépítésért 1945-1946; dokumentumok.* Budapest: Kossuth Könyvkiadó, 1960. 224 p. Contains 95 unpublished archival and press materials dealing with the country's postwar economic recovery up to August, 1946. Stresses the rebuilding of industry, agriculture, and transportation by means of the local Communist Party and the Soviet Union. Some documents reveal organized resistance to the economic policy of the Party. Valuable illustrations, facsimiles, bibliographical footnotes, and statistical tables. [A]

IM94 MAGYAR SZOCIALISTA MUNKÁSPÁRT, 7. KONGRESSZUS, 1959. *A Magyar Szocialista Munkáspárt VII. Kongresszusának jegyzökönyve, 1959. november 30-december 5.* Budapest: Kossuth Könyvkiadó, 1960. 640 p. Important source material dealing with Party history, Soviet-Hungarian relations, and domestic affairs after the 1956 uprising. [A]

IM95 MÉRAY, TIBOR. *Thirteen Days That Shook the Kremlin.* N.Y.: Praeger, 1959. 290 p. A scholarly account of the 1956 revolution; not produced, as most books were, in over-haste. [A]

IM96 MÉSZÁROS, ISTVÁN. *La Rivolta degli intellettuali in Ungheria.* Turin: Einaudi, 1958. 213 p. Intelligent analysis by a young man formerly a Communist.

IM97 MICHENER, JAMES A. *The Bridge at Andau.* N.Y.: Random House; London: Secker & Warburg, 1957. 270 p. Well prepared by a keen-sighted observer, versed in social and political sciences. In the fall of 1956 he interviewed hundreds of Hungarian refugees in Austria to get the necessary background material to depict the essence of Russian Communism as displayed during and after the revolt. [A]

IM98 MID-EUROPEAN LAW PROJECT. *Legal Sources and Bibliography of Hungary.* By Alexander K. Bedo and George Torzsay-Biber. N.Y.: Publ. for the Free Europe Committee by Praeger, 1956. 157 p. Up-to-date lists of the more important laws and statutory provisions with excellent comments. Based chiefly on Library of Congress holdings. [B]

IM99 MIKES, GEORGE. *The Hungarian Revolution.* London: Deutsch, 1957. 192 p. A journalistic account of the events leading to the October 1956 Revolution, with some analysis of its origins. During the Revolution the author spent a few days as BBC TV reporter in Hungary, then in Vienna, where he interviewed scores of refugees. Some illustrations.

IM99A MIKES, GEORGE. *A Study in Infamy; the Operations of the Hungarian Secret Police (AVO) Based on Secret Documents Issued by the Hungarian Ministry of the Interior.* London: André Deutsch, 1959. 175 p.

IM100 MINDSZENTY, JÓZSEF, CARDINAL. *Cardinal Mindszenty Speaks; Authorized White Book Published By Order of Joseph Cardinal Mindszenty, Prince-Primate of Hungary.* N.Y. and London: Longmans, Green, 1949. 234 p. German ed., Zürich: Thomas, 1949. French ed., Paris: Amiot-Dumont, 1949. A collection of 105, some previously unpublished, documents relating to the Cardinal's fight against the Communists, up to his arrest, December 1948. Some of the sources deal with the condemnation of the Marxist-Leninist nationality policy as applied in post-1945 Hungary and Czechoslovakia. [B]

IM101 MINDSZENTY, JÓZSEF, CARDINAL. *Mindszenty-Dokumentation.* Vol. I: *Kardinal Mindszenty warnt; Reden, Hirtenbriefe, Presseerklärungen, Regierungsverhandlungen, 1944-1946.* Vol. II: *Kardinal Mindszenty kämpft; Dokumente zum Kirchenkampf, 1946-1947.* Vol. III: *Kardinal Mindszenty geht in den Kerker; Das Jahr 1948, der Process und die Gefangenschaft.* Ed. and trans. by Dr. Josef Vecsey and Johann Schwendemann. St. Polten: Verlag der Pressvereins-Druckerei, 1957. The most authentic critical edition of the writings of the famous Cardinal, with workmanlike comments in an accurate translation. [B]

IM102 MINDSZENTY, JÓZSEF, CARDINAL, DEFENDANT. *The Trial of József Mindszenty.* Budapest: Hungarian State Publishing House, 1949. 191 p. Hungarian ed., Budapest: Állami Lapkiadó, 1949. French ed., Budapest: Éditions d'État, 1949. Slovak ed., Bratislava: 1949. Stenographic materials of the trial for conspiracy to overthrow the Hungarian People's Republic held in February 1949, in the People's Court of Budapest, against the Cardinal and his "accomplices." Contains pictures and facsimiles. [B]

IM103 MÓD, ALADÁR. *Marxizmus és hazafiság.* Budapest: "Müvelt Nép" Tudományos és Ismeretterjesztö Kiadó, 1956. 313 p. The last scholarly effort, on the threshold of the 1956 Revolution, to synthesize Moscow-interpreted Marxism-Leninism and Hungarian patriotism. The collection of the author's articles analyzes public thought and tries to harmonize Soviet ideology and the country's progressive traditions. Love of and loyalty to the Soviet Union is the chief criterion of the new Hungarian ideal in the mind of the noted ideologist-professor. [B]

IM104 MOLDEN, FRITZ, and POGÁNY, EUGEN. *Ungarns Freiheitskampf.* Vienna: Libertas, 1956. 127 p. A matter-of-fact description of the 1956 events and their aftermath by the publisher and the Southeast European correspondent of the Vienna *Die Presse.* Sympathetic to the revolt, accentuating its spontaneity and international significance.

IM105 MOLNÁR, MIKLÓS, and NAGY, LÁSZLÓ. *Imre Nagy, réformateur ou révolutionnaire?* Geneva: Droz; Paris: Minard, 1959. 260 p. An appreciative examination of Nagy's political guiding principles within the framework of his biography. Investigation is focused on the Communist reformer's literary activity, premiership, and his role in the 1956 Hungarian revolt. 14-page, partly annotated bibliography.

IM106 MONTGOMERY, JOHN F. *Hungary; the Unwilling Satellite.* N.Y.: Devin-Adair, 1947. 281 p. Reminiscences of the U.S. Minister to Budapest, 1938-41. Exceedingly sympathetic to the Hungary of that day, and to its rulers. Rather naïve. Contains a few documents on Hungaro-Yugoslav relations.

IM107 NAGY, FERENC. *The Struggle Behind the Iron Curtain.* N.Y.: Macmillan, 1948. 471 p. The personal account of his Premiership by the Minister President of Hungary, 1946-47. Nagy was a Smallholder, of peasant origin, and tells the story of his efforts to give Hungarian policy a Western orientation, against overwhelming pressure from the Communists. Many intimate details of the struggle, but somewhat lacking in background; one feels that the author had no long experience in high politics. [A]

IM108 NAGY, IMRE. *Egy évtized; válogatott beszédek és írások.* Budapest: Szikra, 1954. 2 vols. The most complete edition of his publications and addresses. [A]

IM109 NAGY, IMRE. *On Communism; In Defence of the New Course.* N.Y.: Praeger; London: Thames & Hudson, 1957. 306 p. German ed., Munich: Kindler, 1959. 376 p. Contains among other things Nagy's "Dissertation" written in the summer of 1955 for submission to the Central Committee of the Hungarian Workers' Party. Nagy defends his short-lived regime and sharply criticizes the agrarian and industrial policies of the Rákosi clique as well as Western economic systems. The authenticity of this manuscript has not yet been sufficiently proven for the scholarly world. [A]

IM110 NEMES, DEZSÖ. *Osvobozhdenie Vengrii.* Moscow: Izd. inos. lit., 1957. 278 p. Hungarian ed., Budapest: 1955. Reviews three significant phases: Hungary's position in World War II with emphasis on Red Army achievements; the first period of liberation, including Regent Horthy's unsuccessful October 15, 1944 putsch; and the beginnings of the postwar regime up to April 4, 1945, when the Red Army fully occupied the country. Based partly on unpublished documents. The 1960 Hungarian edition includes a chapter on developments from 1945 to 1956, including the revolt. [B]

IM111 NYÁRÁDI, NICHOLAS. *My Ringside Seat in Moscow.* N.Y.: Crowell, 1952. 320 p. The author was Minister of Finance in the Ferenc Nagy government after World War II and an early refugee from Communism. Interesting personal information on the refusal of the Marshall Plan in East Europe. [A]

IM112 ORME, ALEXANDRA. *Comes the Comrade!* N.Y.: Morrow, 1950. 376 p. British ed., *From Christmas to Easter; A Guide to a Russian Occupation.* London: Hodge, 1949. 343 p. French eds., Neuchâtel: Baconnière; Paris: Presse française et étrangère, 1948; Paris: Éditions du Seuil, 1950. Italian ed., Milan: Longanesi, 1948. A realistic diary kept by a Polish writer in a village near Budapest, recounting her experiences with the Red Army occupation forces from December 1944 to March 1945.

IM113 PAÁL, JÓB, and RADÓ, ANTAL, eds. *A debreceni feltámadás.* Debrecen: 1947. 384 p. A collection of indispensable on-the-spot reports by 16 well-informed authors on 1944-46 Hungarian-Soviet relations, including the Moscow intergovernmental negotiations and the very beginnings of the Communist-dominated postwar administration. Its data are of utmost importance; comments are overwhelmingly naïve. [A]

IM114 PETROVICS, BÉLA. *J'ai echappé aux Rouges.* Paris: Paix et Liberté, 1951. 444 p. A one-time card-bearing Communist newspaperman's personal account of 1945-51 domestic affairs in Hungary, with special regard to the technique of the secret police (AVO), Bolshevization of the press, and the workings of the Party machinery. Some facsimiles. [B]

IM115 PRIESTER, EVA. *Was war in Ungarn wirklich los? Bericht einer Augenzeugin.* Berlin: Dietz, 1957. 123 p. By a Marxian Viennese newspaperwoman, editor of the *Volksstimme.* Her colorful but tendentious eyewitness accounts are full of erroneous data on the political happenings of the last quarter of 1956. Undocumented.

IM116 RAJK, LÁSZLÓ, DEFENDANT. *László Rajk and his Accomplices before the People's Court.* Budapest: 1949. 319 p. French ed., Paris: 1949. Russian ed., Sofia: 1949. Hungarian ed., Budapest: 1949. German ed., Berlin: 1950. Italian ed., Milan: 1949. Bulgarian ed., Sofia: 1949. Serbo-Croatian ed., Budapest: 1950. Stenographic records with some illustrations of the trial of László Rajk, formerly one of the top Communists of Hungary, but later accused (probably falsely) of Titoism.

IM117 RÁKOSI, MÁTYÁS. *A békéért és a szocializmus építéséért.* 2nd ed. Budapest: Szikra, 1955. 436 p. Contains the speeches and articles, May 1949-February 1951 of the long-time Communist dictator of Hungary.

IM118 RÁKOSI, MÁTYÁS. *A magyar jövöért.* 4th ed. Budapest: Szikra, 1950. 563 p. A collection of his selected articles, radio addresses, and lectures. [B]

IM119 RÁKOSI, MÁTYÁS. *Válogatott beszédek és cikkek.* 4th enlarged ed. Budapest: Szikra, 1955. 639 p. The most complete collection of his addresses and articles. [A]

IM120 RÁKOSI, MÁTYÁS. *Wir Bauen ein Neues Land.* Berlin: Dietz, 1952. 244 p. Hungarian ed., Budapest: Szikra, 1955. 440 p. Speeches and articles, delivered or written between 1945 and 1951, by the well-known Communist boss.

IM121 RÉVAI, JÓZSEF. *Élni tudtunk a szabadsággal; válogatott cikkek és beszédek, 1945-1949.* Budapest: Szikra, 1949. 687 p. Révai's selected articles and addresses (1945-49) are official interpretations of (and primary sources on) the people's democratic regime in the making; the ill-famed "salami tactics"; state-church and East-West relations; Party life and directives, as well as the cultural revolution. [A]

IM122 RÉVAI, JÓZSEF. *Kulturális forradalmunk kérdései.* Budapest: Szikra, 1952. 215 p. Contains 7 articles and lectures, all pertaining to the most important documents on the forceful Bolshevization of Hungary's cultural life during the Stalinist Rákosi period. [A]

IM123 RÉVAI, JÓZSEF. *Marxizmus, népiesség, magyarság.* Budapest: Szikra, 1948. 373 p. An unsuccessful effort to make a synthesis between the so-called progressive traditions of Hungary's culture and Marxist-Leninist-Stalinist principles by a leading Communist theoretician and politician. Criticizes extensively the sociographic literature on the peasantry in order to promote the worker-peasant alliance. With bibliographical footnotes. [B]

IM124 RÉVAI, JÓZSEF. *Válogatott irodalmi tanulmányok.* Budapest: Kossuth Könyvkiadó, 1960. 447 p. A posthumous collection of studies on the Marxist revaluation of the main trends and personages of

Hungarian literature and intellectual life up to the mid-thirties, focused on Endre Ady, Zsigmond Móricz, and Attila József.

IM125 *La Révolte de la Hongrie d'après les émissions des radios hongroises, octobre-novembre, 1956. Preface by François Fejtö.* Paris: P. Horay, 1957. 242 p.

IM125A *La Révolution hongroise vue par les parties communistes de l'Europe de l'Est; présentation quotidienne par les organes officiels* (*23 octobre-15 novembre 1956*). Paris: Centre d'Études Avancées du Collège de l'Europe Libre, 1957. 316 p.

IM126 SHUSTER, GEORGE N. *In Silence I Speak; The Story of Cardinal Mindszenty Today and of Hungary's "New Order."* With the assistance of Dr. Tibor Horanyi. N.Y.: Farrar, Straus & Cudahy, 1956. 296 p. A documentary treatise of 1945-55 state-church relations, with emphasis on the Cardinal's struggle for his nation's freedom. Also a biography of the Cardinal. A masterful revaluation of the Communist leadership's tactics against the Christian churches. Illustrations. [B]

IM127 SZEKFŰ, GYULA. *Forradalom után.* Budapest: Cserépfalvi, 1947. 207 p. A series of essays by the most famous of modern Hungarian historians. The first part describes (with an eye to the date—1944—when it was written) the ideas and work of the group of the 1840's known as the "Centralists" or "Doctrinaires." The latter essays, written when the author was Hungarian Minister in Moscow, brought him many reproaches from his former friends for his relatively favorable comments on the regime. Main conclusions: Western disinterestedness in the area and peoples; therefore, internal revolutions and Soviet-Hungarian alliance are lasting necessities. [A]

IM128 UNITED NATIONS, GENERAL ASSEMBLY, SPECIAL COMMITTEE ON THE PROBLEM OF HUNGARY. *Report.* N.Y.: 1957. 148 p. Well-edited eyewitness reports on the 1956 uprising and its aftermath.

IM129 URBAN, GEORGE. *The Nineteen Days; A Broadcaster's Account of the Hungarian Revolution.* London: Heinemann; N.Y.: British Book Service, 1957. 361 p. Relates chronologically the most significant occurrences of the October-November 1956 period, based on invaluable eyewitness' accounts. His main theses on the Hungarian Workers Party's continuing blindness, and on the failure of Soviet methods to capture the nation's mind, are well-founded. Several striking photographs. [B]

IM130 VÁLI, FERENC A. *Rift and Revolt in Hungary; Nationalism vs. Communism.* Cambridge: Harvard, 1961. 590 p. A most scholarly analysis of political and, to a certain extent, of economic developments from the 1947 Communist takeover through 1957, including the 1956 Revolution. Based partly on unpublished sources. Statistical figures as well as interpretations are convincing. Masterful depiction of contemporary political correlations between Hungary and the other East European nations. Bibliography. [A]

IM131 *La Vérité sur l'affaire Nagy, les faits, les documents, les témoignages internationaux.* Preface by Albert Camus; postface by François Fejtö. Paris: Plon, 1958. 256 p. English ed., *The Truth about the Nagy Affair; Facts, Documents, Comments.* N.Y.: Praeger; London: Secker & Warburg, 1959. 215 p. To some extent a tendentious compilation in order to paint a Titoist image of Imre Nagy and the uprising. The report-like investigation of the character of the revolt by F. Fejtö, a Marxist, is wholly arbitrary; his postface is omitted from the English edition. Contains some facsimiles.

IM132 WAGNER, FRANCIS S. *Cultural Revolution in East Europe.* N.Y.: Danubian Research Service, 1955. 16 p. Examines the Bolshevization process affecting all domains of cultural life as directed by Party and government organs, with special regard to Hungary and Czechoslovakia. Based heavily on published sources. Statistical tables and a rich multilingual bibliography. [A]

IM133 WAGNER, FRANCIS S. *A magyar történetíras új útjai, 1945-1955.* Washington: A szerzö kiadása, 1956. 28 p. The only existing non-Marxist survey of developments in the historical and social sciences within the framework of the country's political transformation. Special attention is devoted to the Bolshevization of the Academy of Sciences and other top organs. Based on Czech, Slovak, and Russian published and unpublished sources. 101 bibliographical notes. [B]

IM133A ZINNER, PAUL E. *Revolution in Hungary.* N.Y. and London: Columbia University Press, 1962. 380 p. An intelligent, penetrating analysis by a professor who formerly taught at Columbia University and who is now at the University of California (Davis). Based in part on Columbia's Hungarian refugee interview project material. The first half of the volume surveys developments to 1956, while the second half is a detailed dissection of the revolution. [A]

IM134 ZINNER, PAUL E., ed. *National Communism and Popular Revolt in Eastern Europe; a Selection of Documents on Events in Poland and Hungary, February-November, 1956.* N.Y.: Columbia, 1956. 563 p. The too early publication of these documents explains several shortcomings of the selection. The sources on Hungary do not illustrate sufficiently the true character of this violently anti-Communist period. Documents on Poland are much better selected and arranged. Such an important documentary enterprise should have been equipped with workmanlike explanatory notes and index.

IM135 ZSOLDOS, LÁSZLÓ. "Hungary's Economic Integration with the Soviet Bloc: Foreign Trade Developments, 1950-1959." Ph.D. dissertation, Ohio State, 1961.

a. PERIODICALS AND NEWSPAPERS

IM136 *Magyar Nemzet.* Budapest. Daily, 1945–. Central organ of the Patriotic People's Front for convincing the non-Communist masses.

IM137 *Népszabadság.* Budapest. Daily, 1943–. Central newspaper of the Hungarian Socialist Workers Party. Prior to November 1956 it was called *Szabad Nep.* [A]

IM138 *Népszava.* Budapest. Daily. Central organ of the National Council of Trade Unions. Appeared as *Népakarat*, Nov. 1956-Jan. 1958. [B]

IM139 *Ország-Világ.* Budapest. Weekly, 1957–. Illustrated magazine issued by the Hungarian-Soviet Friendship Society.

IM140 *Pártélet.* Budapest. Monthly, 1956–. Journal for Party work, organizational life, and Party directives issued by the Central Committee, Hungarian Socialist Workers Party. [A]

IM141 *Párttörténeti Közlemények.* Budapest. Quarterly, 1956–. On the history of Hungarian and world Communism, issued by the Institute of Party History of the Central Committee. [B]

IM142 *Társadalmi Szemle.* Budapest. Monthly, 1946–. Official theoretical and political organ of the Socialist Workers Party. [A]

IM143 *Történelmi Szemle.* Budapest. Quarterly, 1958—. The journal of the Institute of History of the Academy of Sciences. French, German, and Russian summaries. Superseded *A Magyar Tudományos Akadémia Történettudományi Intézetének Értesitöje.*

Addendum

IM144 HALASZ DE BEKY, I. L. *A Bibliography of the Hungarian Revolution 1956.* Toronto: Univ. of Toronto Press, 1963. 179 p. Contains 2,136 entries. [A]

IN. ITALY

EDITED BY JOHN MC KAY CAMMETT

1. ITALIAN-SOVIET RELATIONS

IN1 BAZZANI, GAETANO. *Soldati italiani nella Russia in fiamme 1915-1920*. Trent: Legione Trentina dell'Associazione nazionale volontari di guerra, 1933. 431 p. A history of Italian soldiers in Russia during World War I and the Civil War by a strongly anti-Bolshevik participant. Considerable detail on the Siberian campaigns of the Allies (including 3,000 Italians) and Admiral Kolchak.

IN2 DUCOLI, J. A. "Conventional and Subversive Italian-Soviet Relations, 1943-52." M.A. thesis, U. of California (Berkeley), 1955.

IN3 LISOVSKII, PETR A. *Abissinskaia avantiura italianskogo fashizma*. Moscow: Sotsekgiz, 1936. 223 p. A Soviet view of the Italo-Ethiopian War, sponsored by the Soviet Academy of Sciences.

IN4 MESSE, GIOVANNI. *La guerra al fronte russo; il corpo di spedizione italiano (CISR)*. 3rd ed. Milan: Rizzoli, 1954. 311 p. By the commander of the Corps. Although this is almost strictly a military history, there are many reflections on the contacts of the Corps with the civilian population. The author's thesis is that his troops were always humane and just and also fought well, considering their inferiority in arms and equipment. This edition includes an inquiry about the Italian prisoners still in the USSR.

IN5 PETRANOVICH, I. I. *Bezrabotitsa i polozhenie rabochikh v Italii*. Moscow: Sotsekgiz, 1961.

IN6 TOSCANO, MARIO. *L'Italia e gli Accordi Tedesco-Sovietici dell' agosto 1939*. Florence: Sansoni, 1952. 96 p. The first use of Italian diplomatic documents for this problem. Shows the intense suspicion of Stalin toward English intentions. Although in the earlier months Mussolini was strongly in favor of a German-Soviet rapprochement, an attitude which no doubt had some influence on Hitler, he was astonished at the successful conclusion of the Pact.

IN7 TOSCANO, MARIO. *Una mancata intesa italo-sovietica nel 1940 e 1941*. Florence: Sansoni, 1953. 144 p. A detailed examination of the fruitless attempts to negotiate an Italo-Soviet Pact, based on extensive use of unpublished diplomatic papers. The importance of the role of Germany and the subservience of Italy to her is clearly shown.

2. ITALIAN COMMUNIST PARTY

IN8 AMENDOLA, GIORGIO. *La democrazia nel mezzogiorno.* Rome: Ed. Riuniti, 1957. 448 p. Articles and speeches from 1946 to 1957 of a leading Party specialist on the "question of the South." Important for the PCI attitude toward land reform and for understanding the reasons for Communist advances in the area.

IN9 ARFÈ, GAETANO. *Storia dell'Avanti!, 1896-1940.* Milan: Edizioni Avanti!, 1956-58. 2 vols. A history of the official daily of the Italian Socialist Party which epitomizes the history of the Party itself, by one of the best Socialist historians. For Communism, the chapters on the polemic between Serrati and the "Ordine Nuovo" group (vol. I), and the beginning and development of the policy of united action with the Communists (vol. II), are especially important.

IN10 BASSO, LELIO. *Il Partito Socialista Italiano.* Milan: Nuova Accademia Editrice, 1958. 174 p. A history of the PSI by one of its left-of-center leaders, mostly devoted to the post World War II period and especially to the problem of the relationships of the PSI to the PCI and to the Christian Democrats.

IN11 BATTAGLIA, ROBERTO. *Storia della Resistenza italiana (8 settembre 1943-25 aprile 1945).* 2nd rev. and enl. ed., Turin: Einaudi, 1954. 623 p. Communist. Perhaps the standard history of the Resistance, which is presented as a vast popular movement aiming at the renewal of Italian life in addition to the defeat of the Nazis and Fascists. The author asserts that the movement was led by the working class of the northern cities, which was in turn led by the Communist Party. Battaglia and Giuseppe Garritano have also published *Breve storia della Resistenza italiana* (Milan: Einaudi, 1955. 337 p.), which is a skillfully abridged version of the above. For a Communist evaluation of the literature on the Resistance, see Battaglia, "La Storiografia della Resistenza; dalla memorialistica al saggio storico," *Il movimento di liberazione in Italia*, vol. 57 (Oct.-Dec., 1959), p. 80-131. [A]

IN12 BRAGA, GIORGIO. *Il comunismo fra gli Italiani; saggio di sociologia.* Milan: Edizioni di Comunità, 1956. 190 p. A sociological and statistical study which links the growth of Italian Communism to "social rigidities." Demonstrates the importance of the working class and petty bourgeois elites to the movement, and attempts by this method to explain the propinquity of Italian Socialism and Communism. Contains many extremely detailed maps showing the distribution of Communist votes. [B]

IN13 CAMMETT, JOHN McKAY. "Antonio Gramsci and the 'Ordine Nuovo' Movement; a Study in the Rise of Italian Communism." Ph.D. dissertation, Columbia, 1959. Main thesis: the work of the mature Gramsci as seen in the *Prison Notebooks* can be understood only with knowledge of his struggles and writings at Turin through 1920. Deals with his years at the University of Turin, his journal *Ordine Nuovo* and the movement for Italian Soviets led by him, the special characteristics of the Turin labor movement which was so important to early Italian Communism, the occupation of the factories, and the struggle leading to the foundation of the PCI.

IN14 CANDELORO, GIORGIO. *Il movimento sindacale in Italia.* Rome: Ed. di Cultura Sociale, 1950. 214 p. Communist. An outline of the development of trade union organizations and their struggles from the early nineteenth century to 1950. The principle of trade union unity is regarded as the logical result of these struggles, despite "renewed attempts at schism." Emphasizes the CGIL (Confederazione Generale Italiana del Lavoro).

IN15 CARACCIOLO, ALBERTO, and SCALIA, GIANNI, eds. *La città futura: saggi sulla figura e il pensiero di Antonio Gramsci.* Milan: Feltrinelli, 1959. 391 p. An important group of essays of various political persuasions, unified in the attempt to rediscover an "historical" Gramsci, rather than the "abstract" or "mythical" Gramsci of most recent literature. The initial part of the book deals with his early life and work. Most of the book is concerned with the mature Gramsci's relationship to Labriola and Croce and his views on scientific thought, linguistics, sociology, and esthetics. [B]

IN16 CARLI-BALLOLA, RENATO. *Storia della Resistenza.* Milan: Avanti!, 1957. 369 p. A compact and well-written survey, though with a strong Socialist bias. Admits the tremendous importance militarily of the Communists in the Resistance, but claims that the Socialists were more correct in always emphasizing the "political" (rather than generically "patriotic") aims of the liberation movement.

IN17 CATALANO, FRANCO. *Storia del C.L.N.A.I.* Bari: Laterza, 1956. 458 p. An objective work based on a complete study of the C.L.N.A.I. and the Corpo Volontario della Libertà. A political history of the National Committee of Liberation for Upper Italy, the controlling body of the Resistance movement on which were represented the Communists and all the other anti-Fascist parties.

IN18 COMMUNIST INTERNATIONAL. *Italianskaia sotsialisticheskaia partiia i Kommunisticheskii international; sbornik materialov.* Petrograd: Kom. intern., 1921. 192 p. Documents from September 1920 to May 1921. Letters, resolutions, and articles by the various factional leaders of the I.S.P. and by the leaders of the Comintern giving the background to and results of the Congress of Livorno. The purpose was to justify the imposition of the "Twenty-one Points" on the Italian party. See also Partito Socialista Italiano, *Lettere e polemiche* (below).

IN19 CONFEDERAZIONE GENERALE ITALIANA DEL LAVORO. *La CGIL dal Patto di Roma al Congresso di Genova.* Intro. by Giuseppe di Vittorio. Rome: A cura dell' Ufficio stampa e propaganda della C.G.I.L., 1949–. Purpose is to provide documentary materials for a history of the CGIL from September 1944 to October 1949. The introduction gives a brief history of pre-Fascist trade-unions. Included are accounts of all congresses held in this period.

IN20 CONVEGNO DI STUDI GRAMSCIANI, 1st, ROME, 1958. *Studi Gramsciani; atti del Convegno tenuto a Roma nei giorni 11-12 gennaio 1958.* Rome: Ed. Riuniti, 1958. 592 p. A collection of essays, reports, and comments from many political positions dealing with all aspects of Gramsci's life and thought. This work, with that of Caracciolo and Scalia, began a new and more profound approach to Gramscian studies. The Istituto Antonio Gramsci promises other meetings and publications dealing with more restricted themes of Gramsciana. [B]

IN21 DELZELL, CHARLES F. *Mussolini's Enemies; the Italian Anti-Fascist Resistance.* Princeton, N.J.: Princeton University Press, 1961. 620 p. A detailed and well-documented study, including much information on the Italian Communists. The first 200 pages deal with 1924-43. Especially good on relations between the Allies and the Resistance, which Delzell asserts "proved itself to be one of the most effective clandestine movements in Nazi-dominated Europe."

IN22 DI VITTORIO, GIUSEPPE. *L'unità dei lavoratori.* Ed. by Gianluigi Bragantin and Antonio Tatò. Rome: Ed. Riuniti, 1957. 228 p. Communist. A collection of articles and speeches (1945-57) by a leader of the CGIL, emphasizing the need for trade-union unity as well as for solidarity with the World Federation of Trade Unions.

IN23 DI VITTORIO, GIUSEPPE and others. *I sindacati in Italia.* Bari: Laterza, 1955. 420 p. Essays by leading figures in the Italian labor movement representing all positions except the Fascist. Originated in response to a questionnaire asking opinions on the functions of trade-unions, the labor problem in the South, the possibility of reuniting the labor movement, etc. Though the "philosophy" of trade-unionism is emphasized, the work as a whole is a good survey of post-war Italian labor.

IN24 EINAUDI, MARIO and others. *Communism in Western Europe.* Ithaca: Cornell, 1951. 239 p. The second essay is by the liberal-radical Aldo Garosci on "The Italian Communist Party." A pioneering work, it is now very much out of date, but is still useful as a brief introduction for those who do not read Italian.

IN25 EMILIANI, PAOLO. *Dieci anni perduti; cronache del Partito Socialista Italiano dal 1943 ad oggi.* Pisa: Nistri-Lischi, 1953. 153 p. By an independent socialist. A history of relations between the PSI and the PCI, deploring the "subjugation" of the former to the latter by such leaders as Nenni and Morandi.

IN26 ENTE PER LA STORIA DEL SOCIALISMO E DEL MOVIMENTO OPERAIO ITALIANO. *Bibliografia del socialismo e del movimento operaio italiano.* Vol. I: *Periodici, tratti dalle raccolte della Biblioteca Nazionale di Firenze.* Vol. II: *Libri, opuscoli, articoli, almanacchi, numeri unici.* Tome I (A-DU). Rome-Turin: Edizioni ESMOI, 1956-62. 1427, 561 p. Indispensable. A detailed description of nearly all Italian newspapers, magazines, and other periodicals published from 1848 to 1950 dealing with the labor movement, anarchism, socialism, communism, and other left ideologies. Each entry contains full bibliographical information. There are a number of very useful indexes: a list of trade union periodicals according to the type of work; lists of political periodicals according to 1) political position 2) chronology 3) place published; and an alphabetical list of the names of every person cited in the descriptions. Volume III will be even more useful when completed. It lists and describes books and articles drawn from ninety Italian libraries.

IN27 FERRARA, MARCELLA and MAURIZIO. *Conversando con Togliatti.* Rome: Edizioni di Cultura Sociale, 1954. 391 p. French ed., *Palmiro Togliatti; essai biographique.* Paris: Éd. Sociales, 1955. 420 p. Communist. Based on Party archives as well as on printed matter, this is the most successful Party history written from the official point of view. Despite the title, Togliatti might almost be considered a co-author. The chapters on the early years of the PCI (up to 1930) are especially important. Ends at 1948. [A]

IN28 FERRARA, MARCELLA and MAURIZIO. *Cronache di vita italiana, 1944-1958.* Rome: Ed. Riuniti, 1960. 505 p. Communist. A journalistic account of post-Fascist Italy. The most significant development for the authors is the birth of new political forces, i.e., mass Communist and Socialist Parties; hence, much attention is given to the role of the PCI and the PSI.

IN29 FORLANI, A. *Il P.S.I. di fronte al comunismo dal 1945 al 1956.* Rome: Cinque Lune, 1956. 143 p.

IN30 GALLI, GIORGIO. *La sinistra italiana nel dopoguerra.* Bologna: Mulino, 1958. 287 p. A general attack on the leaders of the

Italian Left (PCI and PSI) for their alleged inability either to work out a program of reforms or to create a revolution. Much of the analysis is devoted to the year 1948, regarded as decisive in the formation of the "conservative" character of the Italian Left.

IN31 GALLI, GIORGIO. *Storia del Partito Comunista Italiano*. Milan: Schwarz, 1958. 374 p. Argues that from 1924 the PCI has been completely subservient to Moscow and that the leadership of the Party is actually an opportunistic ruling group whose only care is to maintain the status quo. [A]

IN32 GALLI, GIORGIO, and BELLINI, FULVIO. *Storia del Partito Comunista Italiano*. Milan: Schwarz, 1953. 433 p. More oriented toward Trotskyism than Galli's 1958 work of the same title. Asserts that the PCI missed an opportunity for revolution in 1945.

IN33 GAROSCI, ALDO. *Storia dei fuorusciti*. Bari: Laterza, 1953. 309 p. A history of all the anti-Fascist exiles, perhaps giving too much space to members of the "Giustizia e Libertà" group of which the author was a member. Chapter IV on the unity of action of the PSI and the PCI is informative. Contains an extensive bibliography as well as documents in the "Notes." [B]

IN34 GERMANETTO, GIOVANNI. *Memorie di un barbiere*. Rome: Ed. Riuniti, 1962. 321 p. Other Italian eds., Paris: 1930; Moscow: Edizioni in Lingue Estere, 1943. 187 p.; Rome: Edizioni Rinascita, 1949. 307 p. Russian ed., Moscow: Khudozhestvennaia literatura, 1935. 188 p. German eds., Moscow: Verlags-genossenschaft Ausländischer Arbeiter in der UdSSR, 1933. 297 p.; Berlin: Dietz, 1957, 362 p. English ed., N.Y.: International Publishers, 1935. 360 p. Communist. Memoirs covering the period from about 1900 to 1926. Over one million copies in 23 languages have been sold. Togliatti calls this the first really "popular" work of Italian proletarian literature. Important for the history of Piedmontese socialism and Communism. Use either the Paris edition in Italian or the English edition, because Germanetto's remarks on such figures as Bordiga and Tasca were deleted in later editions. [B]

IN35 GIOLITTI, ANTONIO. *Riforme e rivoluzione*. Turin: Einaudi, 1957. 73 p. A Communist who switched to the Socialist Party raises questions regarding the nature of contemporary capitalism and the road to socialism, questions typical of those involved in the crisis of 1956-57 in the Italian Communist Party. The CP's answer was given in Longo's *Revisionismo nuovo e antico* (below).

IN36 GRADILONE, ALFREDO. *Storia del sindacalismo*. III: *Italia*. Milan: dott. A. Giuffrè editore, 1959. 448 p. Scholarly. This massive work unfortunately gives little space to post-World War II developments in Italian trade unions. The appendix contains labor legislation, trade union organization, the statutes of the CGIL, CISL, UIL, CISNAL.

IN37 GRAMSCI, ANTONIO. *Opere*. Turin: Einaudi, 1947-60. 10 vols. English ed., *The Modern Prince and other Writings*. London: Lawrence and Wishart, 1957. 192 p. French ed., *Oeuvres choisies*. Paris: Éd. sociales, 1959. 560 p. The leader of the PCI in the years before his arrest in 1926, Gramsci was one of the outstanding creative thinkers of the world Communist movement. He died in 1937 after more than ten years of imprisonment. His work abounds in observations of great insight and originality. Volume I, the *Lettere dal carcere*, consists of letters written mainly to his family in the USSR. Its publication was a great literary event, regarded as a milestone in Italian humanism. Volumes II-VII are his *Quaderni del carcere*, or notebooks written while in prison. They are essays and notes on Marxist and other philosophies, Italian history, political science, literature, etc. Volumes VIII-X are his journalistic writings from 1914 to 1920, including his striking editorials on the factory councils in volume IX. His work from 1921 to 1926 is to be published. Though the editing of this work leaves much to be desired, it is nevertheless a very important contribution to Marxist literature. The English translation is poor. [A]

IN38 HILTON-YOUNG, WAYLAND. *The Italian Left; a Short History of Political Socialism in Italy*. N.Y.: Longmans, 1949. 219 p. An occasionally useful outline from the 19th century to the present. Although marred by the author's inability to take socialism seriously and by many errors of fact and emphasis, this was the first book in English to impart more than a vague idea of such figures as Gramsci and Gobetti.

IN39 ISTITUTO GIANGIACOMO FELTRINELLI. *Annali, 1958–*. Milan: Feltrinelli, 1959–. The Istituto is now one of the most important centers in Europe for the study of the labor movement and its ideologies. These *Annuals* contain articles and documents on all phases of the movement, Italian and foreign, as well as extensive bibliographies arranged by country in many languages of relevant books and periodical literature. In volume III there is an excellent bibliography of the PCI from 1921 to 1926 by Stefano Merli and a very important article by Togliatti on the formation of the leadership of the PCI in the crucial years 1923-24. (Compare IN82A.) [A]

IN40 KABAKCHIEV, KHRISTO S. *Die Gründung der Kommunistischen Partei Italiens*. Hamburg: Verlag der Kommunistischen Internationale, 1921. 56 p. Kabakchiev was a representative of the Third International at the last united Socialist Congress and at the founding

Congress of the PCI. Contains his speeches to the two congresses and an explanation to justify the schism.

IN41 KOVALSKII, N. *Italianskii narod—protiv fashizma; iz istorii osvoboditelnoi borby v gody vtoroi mirovoi voiny.* Moscow: Gospolitizdat, 1957. 184 p. A Soviet work dealing with the Italian Resistance movement during World War II.

IN42 LENIN, VLADIMIR I. *Sul movimento operaio italiano.* Ed. by Felice Platone. Rome: Rinascita, 1947. 218 p. New ed., Rome: Ed. Riuniti, 1962. 341 p. A collection of all his articles and speeches on the topic. Illuminates the Bolshevik role in the schism of the Italian Socialist Party at Livorno in 1921 and documents the importance of the Communist International in the development of the PCI. The new edition contains an appendix (p. 249-330) of relevant speeches and documents, mostly from 1920-21, by Zinoviev, Serrati, Terracini, and others. [B]

IN43 LEONETTI, ALFONSO. *Mouvements ouvriers et socialistes (chronologie et bibliographie); l'Italie (des origines à 1922).* Paris: Éditions ouvrières, 1952. 198 p. By an ex-Communist and former associate of Gramsci at Turin. A useful chronology of the main facts of Italian labor and socialist history up to the March on Rome. The bibliography is arranged by chronology and topic. [B]

IN44 LOMBARDO-RADICE, LUCIO, and CARBONE, GIUSEPPE. *Vita di Antonio Gramsci.* 3rd ed. Rome: Edizioni di Cultura Sociale, 1952. 262 p. Communist. Though extremely propagandistic, this is still the only complete biography. Valuable for information on his family and his sojourn in the USSR.

IN45 LONGO, LUIGI. *Le Brigate Internazionali in Spagna.* Rome: Ed. Riuniti, 1956. 409 p. Longo was the "Commissario Ispettore Generale" of the International Brigade, the historical archives of which were consulted for this book. Emphasizes the value of the training received in Spain for the future Resistance movement in Italy. Contains important documents and much information on activities of Italian Communists in the late 1930's.

IN46 LONGO, LUIGI. *Un popolo alla macchia.* Milan: Mondadori, 1947. 501 p. Communist. A classic narrative of the Resistance by the General Commander of the "Garibaldi" Brigades. [B]

IN47 LONGO, LUIGI. *Revisionismo nuovo e antico.* Turin: Einaudi, 1957. 87 p. A reply of the second most authoritative Italian Communist to Giolitti's *Riforme e rivoluzione.* The two books are excellent examples of the kind of debate which raged around the Party in 1956-57.

IN48 LONGO, LUIGI. *Sulla via dell'Insurrezione Nazionale.* Rome: Edizioni di Cultura Sociale, 1954. 486 p. A collection of articles and documents, many of which were previously published, from the period of the Resistance in World War II. Attributes an extremely important role in the Resistance to the Communists. Contains documents on the industrial strikes of early 1944 which were led by the Communists. [B]

IN49 LOVECCHIO, ANTONINO. *Il Marxismo in Italia.* Milan: Bocca, 1952. 206 p. A useful but overly ambitious survey. Regards Labriola and Mondolfo as the most important Italian Marxists. Stresses the anti-positivist and anti-determinist elements in Marx and Marxism, a stress which makes inexplicable his neglect of Gramsci. For Lovecchio, Marxism as socialism lies between Communism and social democracy.

IN50 LUERS, WILLIAM. "De-Stalinization and the Italian Left." M.A. thesis, Columbia, 1958. 97 p. Mainly devoted to an analysis of Togliatti's articles and speeches during this crisis, but a brief study is also made of the reactions of Nenni, Longo, Secchia, Giolitti, and Reale. Avoids arriving at definitive conclusions because the crisis was still in existence in 1958.

IN51 LURAGHI, RAIMONDO. *Il movimento operaio torinese durante la Resistenza.* Turin: Einaudi, 1958. 372 p. Scholarly. The Resistance in Turin was the best organized in all Italy and the Communists were particularly important in it; much space is given to their activities. Also contains a detailed account of the dissident Communist movement, "Stella Rossa," and material on the Turin working class and the strikes of 1943. [B]

IN52 MAGNANI, VALDO, and CUCCHI, ALDO. *Crisi di una generazione.* Florence: Nuova Italia, 1952. 94 p. By ex-Communists, whose clamorous resignation from the PCI in 1951 was an important event. Asserts that the Party was betraying socialist ideals and was too dependent upon "Russian bayonets," rather than exerting itself to find "national" solutions to Italian problems. Magnani returned to the PCI in 1962.

IN53 MAITAN, LIVIO. *Teoria e politica comunista del dopoguerra.* Milan: Schwarz, 1959. 287 p. Trotskyite. An impassioned, though well informed, attack on the politics of the PCI since 1945. Some of the main issues dealt with are the question of the South, the agrarian problem, the "Italian road to socialism," and Togliatti and the 20th Congress of the CPSU. Bibliography. [B]

IN54 MONTAGNANA, MARIO. *Ricordi di un operaio torinese.* 3rd ed. Rome: Rinascita, 1952. 437 p. Communist. Written during World War II, these memoirs, widely read by Italian Communists, are important for the early struggles of the Turin Socialist and Communist movements, from which much of the present leadership of the PCI is drawn. [B]

IN54A NENNI, PIETRO. *Le prospettive del socialismo dopo la destalinizzazione*. Turin: Einaudi, 1962. 162 p. His collected articles and speeches on the meaning of the 20th and 22nd Congresses of the CPSU, in addition to some articles from 1938 on the Moscow trials.

IN55 NENNI, PIETRO. *Storia di quattro anni, 1919-1922*. 2nd ed. Rome: Einaudi, 1946. 223 p. Socialist. First published in 1926, this work is a very informative account of the "Red Years" and the rise of Fascism. Based on an extensive use of newspapers and Party and trade-union documents as well as the author's personal experiences. Considerable material on the origin and role of the PCI. [B]

IN56 NEUFELD, MAURICE F. *Italy: School for Awakening Countries; the Italian Labor Movement in its Political, Social, and Economic Setting from 1800 to 1960*. Ithaca, N.Y.: Cornell, 1961. 589 p. A definitive work on the Italian labor movement. Unlike most Italian books, it separates the history of labor from the history of the Marxist movement as much as possible. Charts comparing the structures of principal labor organizations and an "English-Italian guide to labor relations terminology" are helpful. Also contains an excellent bibliography and valuable tables on industry, working conditions, and standards of living. [A]

IN57 ONOFRI, FABRIZIO. *Classe operaia e partito*. Bari: Laterza, 1957. 300 p. An ex-Communist (a member of the PCI from 1940 to 1957) tells the story of his experiences on p. 9-197. Fundamentally a critique of the various conceptions of the Party and its relationship to the working class which have prevailed in the PCI since 1945. In the appendix see especially the article "La via sovietica (Leninista) alla conquista del potere e la via italiana, aperta da Gramsci."

IN58 OTTINO, CARLO L. *Concetti fondamentali della teoria politica di Antonio Gramsci*. Milan: Feltrinelli, 1956. 156 p. A thorough, if somewhat scholastic and abstract, treatment of Gramsci's thought. The most important topics are Gramsci's idea of the State, his concept of "hegemony," and his thoughts on the role of the political party.

IN59 PARTITO COMUNISTA ITALIANO. *Atti del IX Congresso del Partito Comunista Italiano*. Rome: Ed. Riuniti, 1960. 2 vols. Russian ed., Moscow: Gospolitizdat, 1960. 307 p. This congress attempted to give more specific meaning to the slogan, "The Italian road to socialism," first advanced at the Eighth Congress. The most important development was a more positive appreciation of reforms, hitherto considered as misleading and inadequate for the working class. Togliatti's report has also been published separately as *Per avanzare verso il socialismo*, Rome: Ed. Riuniti, 1960, 120 p. [A]

IN60 PARTITO COMUNISTA ITALIANO. *Breve corso Togliatti sul Partito Comunista Italiano*. Rome: La Sfera, 1953. 155 p. A collection of articles by various Party leaders for the use of Party cadres. The work forms the basis for the study *Trenta anni di vita e di lotte del PCI*. It is interspersed with many quotations from the Marxist classics and from the Party leaders.

IN61 PARTITO COMUNISTA ITALIANO. *Documenti politici del Comitato centrale, della Direzione e della Segreteria, a cura dell'Ufficio di segreteria del Partito*. Rome: 1951. 478 p. An important collection of resolutions, reports, and statements issued by the Central Committee and other Party organizations between 1948 and 1950. Especially interesting are those dealing with the condemnation of Yugoslavia, the attempt on Togliatti's life, the elections of April 18, 1948, and the lengthy reports of Party commissions on the youth and women's movements, the trade unions, and the press.

IN62 PARTITO COMUNISTA ITALIANO. *Due anni di lotta dei comunisti italiani; relazione sull'attività del P.C.I. dal V al VI Congresso*. Rome: 1948. 284 p.

IN63 PARTITO COMUNISTA ITALIANO. *Il Partito Comunista Italiano contro la guerra, contro il fascismo, per la libertà, per la democrazia, per l'indipendenza d'Italia; relazione della direzione del Partito al V. Congresso, Roma, 29 dicembre 1945*. Rome: L'Unità, 1946. 302 p. Includes a history of the party from 1934 to 1945 (p. 5-119). Also contains a collection of documents covering the same period and illustrating the role of the Party in the underground and liberation and its relationship to Italian governments in the more recent of those years. [B]

IN64 PARTITO COMUNISTA ITALIANO. *Per la costituzione democratica e per una libera cultura; rapporti alla sessione del C.C. del PCI del 10-12 novembre 1952 di Togliatti, Longo, Salinari*. Rome: Ufficio stampa del Partito Comunista Italiano, 1953. 165 p. A good source for Party attitudes at the height of the Cold War. Togliatti's speech is a defense of the Italian Constitution and an attack on its alleged violators. Longo reports on the 19th Congress of the CPSU, and Salinari states the position of the Party on questions of culture.

IN65 PARTITO COMUNISTA ITALIANO. *La politica dei comunisti dal Quinto al Sesto Congresso; risoluzioni e documenti raccolti a cura dell'Ufficio di segreteria del P.C.I.* Rome: La Stampa Moderna, 1948. 406 p. Covers the period from January 1946 to December 1947. Important for understanding the role of the Communists in the government and in the nation during the time of their greatest prestige. The documents also show the transition from postwar unity to the Cold War. [B]

IN66 PARTITO COMUNISTA ITALIANO. *IV Conferenza nazionale del Partito Comunista Italiano; resoconto.* Rome: Ed. di Cultura Sociale, 1955. 432 p. Held January 9-14, 1955 at Rome. Important subjects of the many speeches and reports are the death of Stalin, the elections of June 7, 1953, and the struggle against monopolies and for peace. Includes Togliatti's report "La Lotta dei comunisti per la libertà, la pace, il socialismo."

IN67 PARTITO COMUNISTA ITALIANO. *Il IV Congresso del Partito Comunista d'Italia (Aprile, 1931); tesi e risoluzioni.* Paris: Ed. di Cultura Sociale, 1931. 197 p. Important for material on Party dissensions and expulsions from 1926 to 1931, on the Party attitudes toward Social Democracy and Fascism, and on its clandestine activities. [B]

IN67A PARTITO COMUNISTA ITALIANO. *La seconda conferenza del Partito comunista d'Italia (Resoconto stenografico).* Paris: Edizioni del Partito Comunista d'Italia, 1928. 314 p. The verbatim record of the Conference. Includes Grieco's speech on "La situazione italiana e i compiti del Partito," two reports by Togliatti (one on Italian affairs and one on the international situation), the theses of the Central Committee on the Italian situation, and a great deal of debate on the nature of Fascism.

IN68 PARTITO COMUNISTA ITALIANO. *Unione del popolo italiano per il pane, la pace e la libertà; documenti e direttive del P.C.I.* Paris: Edizioni di Cultura Sociale, 1939. 166 p.

IN69 PARTITO COMUNISTA ITALIANO. *Verso il VII Congresso del Partito Comunista Italiano; rapporto di Palmiro Togliatti, interventi di Longo, et al., Comitato centrale del PCI, 10-12 ottobre 1950.* Rome: 1950. 156 p. Served as a framework for discussion preceding the 7th Congress. Togliatti indicates peace, economic well-being, and democratic liberties as the main problems of the day. Longo elaborates on the economic problems; Secchia points out ways in which the Party organization can be improved; Scoccimarro emphasizes the connection between war and economic crises; D'Onofrio speaks on the training of cadres; and Sereni explains the program of the "Partigiani della pace."

IN70 PARTITO COMUNISTA ITALIANO, 7. CONGRESSO NAZIONALE, ROME, 1951. *VII Congresso del Partito Comunista Italiano, 3-8 aprile 1951; resoconto.* Rome: Edizioni di Cultura Sociale, 1954. 364 p. An extensive collection of speeches given at the 7th Congress. Principal themes are the Cold War and its causes, current attempts increasingly to isolate the Communist Party, and how to achieve more effective organization of the Party and closer unity of action with the Socialists in order to combat this isolation. [B]

IN71 PARTITO COMUNISTA ITALIANO, 8. CONGRESSO NAZIONALE, ROME, 1956. *Atti e risoluzioni*. Rome: Riuniti, 1957. 1017 p. English ed., *The Eighth Congress of the Italian Communist Party, Rome 8-14 December, 1956*. Rome: Italian Communist Party, Foreign Section, 1957. 256 p. Russian ed., Moscow: Gospolitizdat, 1957. 343 p. Contains Togliatti's important report dealing with the 20th Congress of the CPSU, the events in Hungary, and the problem of an "Italian road to socialism." The revised constitution of the Party is presented with a commentary by Longo. [A]

IN72 PARTITO SOCIALISTA ITALIANO. *Lettere e polemiche fra l'Internazionale Comunista, il Partito Socialista e la Confederazione Generale del Lavoro d'Italia;* ("*Atti della Terza Internazionale*," 4). Milan: Società editrice Avanti!, 1921. 94 p. Covers the period from August 1920 to January 1921. This collection of letters and documents represents the first quarrel between the Comintern and the left minority of Italian socialists on the one hand and the majority of the PSI and the CGL on the other. The main issue was the insistence of the former on expulsion of the reformists from the Party, the name of which was to be changed to PCI. This book is essential for understanding the schism at Livorno in January 1921. [B]

IN73 PEREGO, ANGELO. *Idee crisi finanze delle Botteghe Oscure*. Rome: Ed. Paoline, 1956. 319 p. Catholic. A kind of popular handbook of Italian Communism. After a discussion and rejection of Marxist principles, the author devotes a chapter to the dangers of Communism for the peasantry. A brief history of the Party follows. The most informative section deals with the structure, organization, and financing of the Party (p. 204-292).

IN74 PUGLIESE, GUIDO. *Il bolscevismo in Italia*. Florence: Bemporad, 1920. 110 p. Sympathetic to Reformist Socialists. An early attempt, based on newspapers and Party documents, to trace the influence of Russian Bolshevism on the Italian Socialist movement. Considerable material on the Italian Soviet movement.

IN74A REALE, EUGENIO. *Nascita del Cominform*. Milan: Mondadori, 1958. 174 p. French ed., *Avec Jacques Duclos au banc des accusés à la réunion constitutive du Kominform à Szklarska Poreba (22-27 septembre 1947)*. Paris: Plon, 1958. 203 p. A former prominent Italian Communist's fascinating behind-the-scenes account of the meeting of European Communist leaders at which the Cominform was founded. Critique of issues at the meeting and of personalities, views, and speeches of participants. Appended are short biographies of European Communist leaders at the meeting. [A]

IN75 ROBOTTI, PAOLI, and GERMANETTO, GIOVANNI. *Trent'anni di lotte dei comunisti italiani, 1921-1951*. Rome: Edizioni di Cultura Sociale, 1952. 273 p. German edition, 1955. A popular history by two older Communist militants, both of whom spent many years in the USSR. Especially important for the years of exile. Contains a succinct chronology of the PCI (p. 263-273).

IN76 SCOCCIMARRO, MAURO. *Nuova democrazia*. Preface by Enrico Molé. Ed. by Bruzio Manzocchi. Rome: Ed. Riuniti, 1958. 263 p. A collection of articles and speeches written or delivered from 1943 to 1957. The basic theme attempts to demonstrate the democratic and Italian character of the PCI in theory and in practice.

IN77 SCOCCIMARRO, MAURO. *Il secondo dopoguerra*. Ed. by Bruzio Manzocchi. Rome: Ed. Riuniti, 1956. 2 vols. Communist. The author was Minister of Finance in the postwar Italian government. Volume I deals mainly with that experience and the Communist position toward problems of budgeting and finance. Volume II emphasizes the financial effects of the Marshall Plan, rearmament, and the Vanoni Plan. [B]

IN78 SECCHIA, PIETRO. *I Comunisti e l'Insurrezione*. Rome: Ed. di Cultura Sociale, 1954. 513 p. Communist. A collection, arranged chronologically, of previously published articles, speeches, and documents by the General Commissar of the "Garibaldi" Brigades during the Resistance. Emphasizes political rather than military problems. [B]

IN79 SECCHIA, PIETRO, and MOSCATELLI, GINO. *Il Monte Rosa è sceso a Milano; la Resistenza nel Biellese, nella Valsesia e nella Valdossola*. Torino: Einaudi, 1958. 656 p. Moscatelli was the Communist leader of the Resistance in the northern areas of Piedmont. This is one of the few detailed works on the operations of the Communist Brigades in a specific and very important area.

IN79A *Sorok let Italianskoi Kommunisticheskoi Partii*. Moscow: Izd. VPSh i AON, 1961.

IN80 SPRIANO, PAOLO. *Torino operaia nella grande guerra (1914-1918)*. Turin: Einaudi, 1960. 347 p. Communist. The first thoroughly-documented work on the Turin labor movement, the source of many present leaders of the PCI. It is based on the files of the Ministry of the Interior, especially the reports of the prefects of Turin, and on the memoirs, published and unpublished, of many participants. Principal problems are: the increasingly "political" character of the Turin labor movement, especially its resolute opposition to the war; study of the extreme left of the PSI in Turin and its effect on the national leadership; the rise of a new generation of Socialist leaders in the city. Antonio Gramsci's career in this period is examined in detail.

IN81 TASCA, ANGELO. "I primi dieci anni del Partito Comunista Italiano," *Il Mondo*, V, nos. 33-38 (August 18-September 22, 1953). A series of six articles. Tasca was an important leader of the PCI in the 1920s and a collaborator of Gramsci and Togliatti in the "Ordine Nuovo" movement; he was expelled from the Party in 1929. Of great help in understanding the politics of various factions in early Piedmontese and Italian Communism. [B]

IN82 TOGLIATTI, PALMIRO. *Discorsi alla Costituente*. Rome: Ed. Riuniti, 1958. 341 p. A collection of all his speeches and comments made in the Constituent Assembly from June 1946 to January 1948. Especially important for the Communist position on constitutional questions, relations between Church and State, and democracy and antifascism. It is claimed that the work is also important for understanding the "Italian way to socialism," which was first expressly proclaimed by Togliatti in 1956. [A]

IN82A TOGLIATTI, PALMIRO. *La formazione del gruppo dirigente del Partito comunista italiano*. Rome: Ed. Riuniti, 1962. 380 p. A series of letters and documents illustrating the process of development of the Turin group from a subordinate to a leading position within the PCI. The material has been drawn from the archives of Angelo Tasca (an important ex-Communist) and the Italian Communist Party. The foreword to the work and the introduction to each document were written by Togliatti. In its scope and character, this work is almost certainly unique in the history of the world Communist movement.

IN83 TOGLIATTI, PALMIRO. *Gramsci*. Florence: Parenti, 1955. 140 p. A series of articles written from 1937 to 1954 almost in the spirit of a disciple. Presents Gramsci as the "Italian Lenin," and deals with his role as leader of the PCI, his relationship to Sardinia and the University of Turin, his anti-fascist activities, and his contributions to Italian culture.

IN84 TOGLIATTI, PALMIRO. *Linea d'una politica*. Milan: Milano-Sera, 1948. 170 p. A collection of Togliatti's speeches and writings from April 1944, to April 1948. The main theme is the insistence on a "united and democratic" policy of all anti-fascist parties.

IN85 TOGLIATTI, PALMIRO. *Pace o guerra*. Milan: Milano-Sera, 1949. 144 p. Continues his *Linea d'una politica*. Contains speeches and writings, mainly from *Rinascita* and *L'Unità*, from October 1948 to the signing of the Atlantic Pact (April 4, 1949). The main theme is an attack on the Truman Doctrine, the Marshall Plan, the political role of the Papacy, and other aspects of the Cold War. [B]

IN86 TOGLIATTI, PALMIRO. *Il Partito Comunista Italiano.* Milan: Nuova Accademia Editrice, 1958. 149 p. Written for the general public, this work points out the principal characteristics and phases of development of the PCI. To provide a framework of understanding, the author frequently analyzes Italian and European historical problems in general. His observations are highly interesting and stimulating, if sometimes debatable. A brilliant little book. [B]

IN87 TOGLIATTI, PALMIRO. *Per la salvezza del nostro paese.* Turin: Einaudi, 1946. 423 p. Speeches and articles from 1941 to 1945. Contains his Radio Moscow broadcasts to Italy. Important for Togliatti's attitude, after his return in April 1944, toward the Italian government, the other political parties, and Italian foreign policy. [A]

IN87A TOGLIATTI, PALMIRO. *Problemi del movimento operaio internazionale.* Rome: Ed. Riuniti, 1962. 410 p. His articles and speeches from 1956 to 1962. Fundamental to an understanding of the recent policy of the PCI. Should be read in conjunction with IN54A.

IN88 TOGLIATTI, PALMIRO. *Rinnovare l'Italia.* Rome: L'Unità, 1946. 119 p. His report to the 5th Congress of the PCI. The main stress is put on the causes of Fascism in the past and how to avoid it in the future. Presents ideas of the Party on the drafting of the new Constitution.

IN89 TOGLIATTI, PALMIRO. *Tre minacce alla democrazia italiana.* Rome: Edizioni Rinascita, 1948. 242 p. His report to the 6th Congress of the PCI. The "threats" are: 1) to peace (the developing Cold War); 2) to national independence (subservience to the U.S.); 3) to freedom (failure to implement the new Constitution). [B]

IN90 TOGLIATTI, PALMIRO. *La via italiana al socialismo.* Rome: Ed. Riuniti, 1956. 145 p. His report to the Central Committee of the PCI on June 24, 1956. Contains important judgments on the 20th Congress of the CPSU, and reflections on the "Italian road to socialism." Also included is Togliatti's contribution to the debate on the 20th Congress held by the journal *Nuovi Argomenti.* Both of these writings have been translated in COLUMBIA UNIVERSITY, RUSSIAN INSTITUTE, *The Anti-Stalin Campaign and International Communism,* p. 97-139, 193-267. [A]

IN91 TOGLIATTI, PALMIRO and others. *Gramsci.* Rome: Ed. Rinascita, 1948. 211 p. A collection of memorial writings by leaders of the PCI recalling the several stages of Gramsci's political life and the contributions which he made to the future of the Party. [B]

IN92 TOGLIATTI, PALMIRO, ed. *Trenta anni di vita e di lotte del PCI*. ("*Quaderni di Rinascita*," 2). Rome: Ed. Rinascita, 1952. 260 p. The most extensive history of the PCI. Dozens of articles by nearly all the important leaders and scholars of the movement as well as many articles and documents from the earlier literature of the Party. Includes two detailed chronologies: the Italian labor movement 1853-1920 and the Italian Communist Party, 1921-51. [A]

IN93 TREVISANI, GIULIO, ed. *Piccola Enciclopedia del socialismo e del comunismo*. 4th ed. Milan: Soc. ed. de "Il Calendario del Popolo," 1958. 742 p. Communist. A very useful reference work, though it is often highly dogmatic. Includes entries for persons, Marxist terms, movements, institutions, parties, and articles devoted to the labor and socialist movements in specific important countries. Italy and Italian developments are of course emphasized. See also: *Appendice alla IV edizione della Piccola Enciclopedeia del socialismo e del comunismo*. Milan: 1962. 278 p. [B]

IN94 VALIANI, LEO. *Questioni di storia del socialismo*. Turin: Einaudi, 1958. 451 p. Contains an enormous bibliography at the end of the first essay: "Il movimento socialista in Italia dalle origini al 1921; studi e ricerche nel ventennio 1937-1957." Despite the chronological limitation, many of the books referred to also deal with more contemporary developments. Most of the other articles are perceptive reviews of books on the labor and socialist movements, whether in Italy or elsewhere. [A]

a. PERIODICALS AND NEWSPAPERS

IN95 *Avanti!* Milan: 1896–. Official daily of the Italian Socialist Party. Published sporadically abroad from 1926 to 1945. A Piedmontese edition was published at Turin from December 5, 1918 to December 31, 1920. This was the organ of the Communist faction of the PSI led by Antonio Gramsci.

IN96 *Il Comunista*. Rome: October 1921-October 1922. An official daily of the PCI edited by Togliatti.

IN97 *Foreign Bulletin of the Italian Communist Party*. Rome: 1959–. Published periodically (usually monthly) by the Foreign Section of the Central Committee of the PCI. Includes translations of documents and reports as well as major articles by Party leaders in the Italian Communist press.

IN98 *Movimento Operaio*. Milan: 1949-56. Monthly or bimonthly. The first serious periodical devoted to study of the Italian labor movement. Often accused of antiquarianism, but indispensable for its previously unpublished documents and pioneering studies. The index, in volume VIII, no. 6, because of its analytical tables and general completeness, makes the periodical even more useful.

IN99 *L'Ordine Nuovo.* Turin: 1919-20 (weekly), 1921-22 (daily), 1924-25 (weekly). Under the editorship of Antonio Gramsci, this paper led the drive for Italian Soviets in 1919-20. After the foundation of the PCI, it became an official organ of the new Party.

IN100 *Politica ed Economia.* Rome: 1957-62. Monthly. Communist. Formed by the merging of *Critica Economica* (1946-56), *Riforma Agraria* (1953-56), and *Notizie Economiche* (1949-56). Articles and documents are mainly devoted to economic theory and developments.

IN101 *Problemi del Socialismo.* Milan: 1958–. Monthly. Represents the point of view of one of the more left factions of the Italian Socialist Party.

IN102 *Rassegna Sindacale.* Rome: 1955–. Monthly. Published by the CGIL (Confederazione Generale Italiana del Lavoro), the Communist-dominated trade union movement. Was preceded by *Notiziario CGIL.* News, articles, and documents on problems of labor and trade unions.

IN103 *Rassegna Sovietica.* Rome: 1950–. Monthly. Published by the Associazione Italia-USSR. Preceded by *Rassegna della Stampa Sovietica* (1946-49). Articles on Soviet social and cultural developments and on Italo-Soviet relations.

IN104 *Rinascita.* Rome: 1944–. The official monthly (weekly since January 1962) of the Italian Communist Party. Togliatti is the editor.

IN105 *Rivista Storica del Socialismo.* Milan: 1958—. Quarterly. Well edited, scholarly journal containing articles, documents, and reviews on all aspects of the labor and socialist movements, Italian and foreign. Its contributors are of various political persuasions.

IN106 *Società.* Florence: 1945-61. Bimonthly. The outstanding philosophical and cultural journal of the Italian Communist Party. Index for volumes I-X in volume X.

IN107 *Lo Stato Operaio.* Milan and Rome: 1923-25; Paris: 1927-39; N.Y.: 1940-43. Weekly or monthly. A Communist theoretical journal. A prime source of Party history in the years of Fascism.

IN108 *Studi Storici.* Rome: 1959–. Quarterly. High quality historical journal published by the Istituto Gramsci, an historical institution operated by the Italian Communist Party. Emphasis is on modern and contemporary history.

IN109 *L'Unità*. Rome. 1924–. The official daily of the Italian Communist Party. Suppressed in 1926 but issued clandestinely from time to time. Publication was resumed in 1944 at Rome. From 1945 to 1957, separate editions were published at Milan, Genoa, and Turin. Since 1957 only the Milanese edition has appeared in the North.

3. THE VATICAN

IN110 BORREGALES, GERMAN. *"Izvestia" Ante la Historia*. Caracas: Editorial Venezuela, 1944. 147 p. Catholic. A defense of the Church against *Izvestia's* accusation that the Vatican was the "direct accomplice" of Nazi-Fascism, and that it kept silent during the Italian aggression against France in 1940. An analysis of papal pronouncements made before and during World War II which indicate hostility to Fascism or political neutrality.

IN111 CIANFARRA, CAMILLE M. *The Vatican and the Kremlin*. N.Y.: Dutton, 1950. 285 p. A journalistic work on the struggle between Communism and religion, with emphasis on Roman Catholicism. Concentrates on Poland, Hungary, and Yugoslavia.

IN112 RIBARD, ANDRÉ. *1960 et le Secret du Vatican*. Paris: Robin, 1954. 222 p. An attack on Vatican policy toward the Soviet Union. Until 1927, the Vatican was allegedly not strongly anti-Soviet because of its hope of converting Russia. Thereafter, its policy was guided by anti-Communism. The conversion of Russia was first suggested with the miracle of Fatima in 1917; the year 1960 would see the revelation of the "third secret of Fatima."

IN113 SHEINMAN, MIKHAIL M. *Ideologiia i politika Vatikana na sluzhbe imperializma*. Moscow: Gospolitizdat, 1950. 222 p.

IN114 SHEINMAN, MIKHAIL M. *Sovremennyi Vatikan*. Moscow: Izd. Akademii nauk SSSR, 1955. 180 p.

IN115 SHEINMAN, MIKHAIL M. *Vatikan mezhdu dvumia mirovymi voinami*. Moscow: Akademiia nauk SSSR, 1948. 236 p. The struggle against Communism and the USSR as the main theme of Vatican diplomacy. The author asserts that the Vatican attitude toward Fascism and Nazism was sympathetic, though he does not deny that conflicts existed. Conflict between liberal Catholicism and the "reactionary" politics of the Vatican receives some attention.

IN116 TOGLIATTI, PALMIRO. *L'Opera di De Gasperi ("Testimonianze del tempo," 45)*. Florence: Parenti, 1958. 238 p. A series of essays written from 1929 to 1958 on problems of relations between Church and State. More than half is devoted to an examination of De

Gasperi's work, the aim being to judge not by what he wanted to do, but by what he actually did. Much space is also given to Communist support of Lateran Pacts, thought necessary in order not to alienate the Catholic workers.

IN117 TREVISANI, GIULIO, and CANZIO, STEFANO. *Il papato contro l'Italia.* Milan: Cultura Nuova, 1950. 151 p. Communist. A history of "the inauspicious work of the Papacy in every period, and especially in the first Risorgimento, against the freedom, independence, and unity of Italy."

IN118 VOLGIN, V. I. *Vatikan-tsentr reaktsii i mrakobesiia.* Leningrad: Lenizdat, 1960. 136 p. A typical Soviet attack on the Vatican as a bastion of reaction.

IO. THE NETHERLANDS

EDITED BY FRITS KOOL

IO1 *Het A.B.C. van het communisme.* Amsterdam: Pegasus, 1934-35. 7 vols. The "A.B.C.," in seven small volumes totaling 256 pages, is a full orthodox course in Communism; the last volume by the then Party leader L. L. H. de Visser, contains a Communist interpretation of the Dutch labor movement.

IO2 BAKKER, MARCUS. "Some Notes on the Dutch Party Congress," *World Marxist Review*, vol. 2, no. 3 (March 1959); and "Bourgeois Democracy in Holland," *Ibid.*, vol. 2, no. 7 (July 1959). These articles present the official Communist Party line on the issues involved in the crisis and split of 1958.

IO3 *XIX sezd Kommunisticheskoi partii Niderlandov, 1958 g.* Transl. from Dutch. Moscow: Gospolitizdat, 1959. 127 p.

IO4 GORTER, HERMAN. *Offener Brief an den Genossen Lenin.* Berlin: Verlag der Kommunistischen Arbeiter-Partei Deutschlands, 1920. 88 p.

IO5 GORTER, HERMAN. *De wereldrevolutie* (*het communisme, VIII*). 3rd ed. Amsterdam: J. J. Bos, 1920. 102 p. Two early publications by a "left-wing" Communist theoretician reflecting his increasing uneasiness over the dictatorship of the Party in Russia. His criticisms and those of Pannekoek (see below) form the basis of "council Communism," which found adherents in the Netherlands, where its theoretical significance far surpassed its numerical strength.

IO6 HOLST, ROLAND, and VAN DER SCHALK, HENRIETTE. *Kapitaal en arbeid in Nederland.* 4th rev. ed. Rotterdam: W. L. and J. Brusse, 1932. 2 vols. The second volume treats, among other things. various currents in post-war Dutch Socialism and Communism. It is a popular account based on broad personal experience and a knowledge of contemporary sources.

IO7 KOOL, FRITS. "Communism in Holland: A Study in Futility." *Problems of Communism*, vol. IX, no. 5 (Sept.-Oct., 1960). A concise discussion especially on the post-war history of the Communist Party and the intra-Party conflicts. The documentation includes printed sources.

IO8 PANNEKOEK, ANTON. *Weltrevolution und kommunistische Taktik* (*Probleme der proletarischen Revolution, Nr. 2*). Vienna: Verlag der Arbeiterbuchhandlung, 1920. 50 p. A pamphlet by an important figure in the European socialist movement, who became increasingly disillusioned over the trend of events in Soviet Russia. (See above pamphlets by Gorter.)

IO9 PERTHUS, M., ed. *Voor vrijheid en socialisme; gedenkboek van het Sneevleit Herdenkingscomité*. Rotterdam: Gramo, 1953. 195 p. An undocumented, unscholarly work of interest because of the light it throws on Sneevliet's activities after he left the Communist Party and tried, with some success, to build up a Revolutionary Socialist Party. It is important for its treatment of his leadership of the leftist "National Labor Secretariat."

IO10 *De politieke achtergrond van de crisis in de C.P.N.* Amsterdam: "De Brug" Pamphlet No. 7, n.d. This pamphlet unveils some controversies on Soviet and international Communist policies, on the trade union issue and on Party discipline, which led to the expulsion of formerly top-ranking members and the eventual founding of a dissident party in 1958.

IO11 RAVESTEYN, W. VAN. *De wording van het communisme in Nederland, 1907-1925*. Amsterdam: P. N. van Kampen, 1948. 240 p. The only important monograph on the history of the Dutch Communist Party and its curious predecessor, a "Marxist" party split-off from the Social Democratic mother party in 1909. Based on personal recollections of the author, who was one of its leaders, and on archival materials in his possession, this intelligently written, but sparsely documented, work contains too much retrospective self-justification to meet high scholarly standards.

IO12 RUETER, A. J. C. "De illegale actie voor de eenheidsvakbeweging in historisch perspectief." *Varia Historica*. Assen: Van Gorcum, 1954. A short survey, by the professor of Netherlands history at Leiden University, of the politically different roots of what was to become the Unified Trade Union Organization (E.V.C.); a case study on Communist tactics which eventually resulted in the conquest of the movement.

IO13 SIJES, B. A. *De Februari-staking 25-26 Februari 1941*. The Hague: M. Nijhoff, 1954. 237 p. The authoritative monograph on the strike against the Nazi deportation of the Amsterdam Jews, with a careful analysis of the role played by the illegal Communist Party. An English summary is included.

IO14 VALKOV, V. A. *Ekonomika i politika Gollandii posle vtoroi mirovoi voiny*. Moscow: Izd. IMO, 1961. 222 p.

IO15 VISSER, L. L. H. DE. *Herinneringen uit mijn leven*. Amsterdam: Pegasus, 1939. 184 p. The "Recollections" of a former Party leader, written in a somewhat less rigid spirit than his earlier works.

IP. POLAND

1. GENERAL WORKS

(Edited by Zygmunt Gasiorowski)

IP1 ALIUS (pseud. of Alexandre Abramson). *La Ligne Curzon.* Neuchâtel: La Baconnière, 1944. 77 p. German ed., *Die Curzon-Linie; Das Grenzproblem Sowjetunion-Polen.* Zurich and N.Y.: Europa-Verlag, 1945. 100 p. Appeared first in the May 1944 issue of the *Suisse Contemporaine.* A popular account based on secondary sources, and *Izvestiia* and *The Times* for the period, 1939-44. Reflects the author's Soviet sympathies.

IP2 COATES, WILLIAM P., and ZELDA K. *Six Centuries of Russo-Polish Relations.* London: Lawrence & Wishart, 1948. 235 p. A popular survey based on secondary sources and the Soviet and English press. Pages 91-215 deal with the period from World War I to Yalta. Written from the Soviet point of view.

IP2A DĘBICKI, ROMAN. *Foreign Policy of Poland, 1919-39, from the Rebirth of the Polish Republic to World War II.* With a foreword by Oscar Halecki. New York: Praeger, 1962. 192 p. A dispassionate and, despite its pro-Polish slant, reliable discussion of Poland's role in world affairs, by a former Polish diplomat. The treatment of Polish-Soviet relations is somewhat fragmentary.

IP3 DRUNIN, V. P. *Polsha, Rossiia i SSSR; istoricheskie ocherki.* Moscow: Gosizdat, 1928. 219 p. A short survey based on the *Krasnaia Kniga* and Soviet secondary sources. Pages 180-219 deal with Polish-Soviet relations to 1927. A Soviet propaganda work.

IP4 KIRKIEN, LESZEK. *Russia, Poland and the Curzon Line.* London: Caldra House, 1944. 62 p. 2nd ed., 1945. A short, popular account based on secondary sources. Written from the Polish point of view by a Polish journalist. Studded with statistics from the Polish census of 1931.

IP5 KONOVALOV, SERGE, ed. *Russo-Polish Relations; An Historical Survey.* Princeton, N.J.: Princeton University Press, 1945. 102 p. London: Cresset, 1945. 90 p. A short, popular account based on Sir John Maynard's report, edited and supplemented by Konovalov (Oxford professor of Russian). Much material is taken from B. H. Sumner's *Survey of Russian History.* The book consists half of text and half of appendices. Objective.

IP6 LASERSON, MAX M. *The Curzon Line.* N.Y.: Carnegie Endowment for International Peace, 1944. 102 p. Published for private circulation for the Division of Economics and History, Carnegie Endowment for International Peace.

IP7 PIŁSUDSKI, JÓZEF. *Pisma Zbiorowe*. Ed. by L. Wasilewski and others. Warsaw: Instytut Józefa Piłsudskiego, 1937-38. 10 vols. Volumes V-IX of the collected works of Piłsudski contain some material on Polish-Soviet relations. [B]

IP8 POLAND, AMBASADA, U. S. *Polish-Soviet Relations, 1918-1943; Official Documents*. Washington: Polish Embassy, 1943. 251 p. Part I consists of six short chapters on some aspects of Soviet-Polish relations from 1939-43 (mass deportations, release of Polish Delegates, Polish Army in the USSR, the relief and citizenship questions). Part II consists of 90 documents (11 for the period 1918-39, and 79 for the period September 1939-April 1943). [B]

IP9 POLISH INFORMATION CENTER. *Polish-Soviet Relations, 1918-1943; Documents*. N.Y.: Polish Information Center, 1943. 62 p. A shortened version of the collection of documents published by the Polish Embassy in the U.S. with several unimportant documents added. For the most part only excerpts from documents are included.

IP9A POLSKA AKADEMIA NAUK, INSTYTUT HISTORII. *Materiały archiwalne do historii stosunków polsko-radzieckich*. Ed. by Natali Gasiorowską. Warsaw: Książka i Wiedza, 1957—. An extremely valuable, competently edited collection of documents; when completed, it is likely to become the most important single source for the study of Polish-Soviet relations. To date two volumes, covering the period from March 1917 to April 1920, have been released. [A]

IP10 SHOTWELL, JAMES T., and LASERSON, MAX M. *Poland and Russia, 1919-1945*. N.Y.: Publ. for the Carnegie Endowment for International Peace by King's Crown Press, 1945. 114 p. Discusses the question of the Polish-Russian frontier in 1919-21 and during World War II, and Soviet-Polish relations in 1944-45. The latter part is largely based on press reports, particularly the *New York Times*. Contains a 3-page bibliography. [B]

IP11 SUPER, MARGARET L. (Ann Su Cardwell, pseud.). *Poland and Russia; The Last Quarter Century*. N.Y.: Sheed & Ward, 1944. 251 p. A sketchy, superficial survey of Polish-Soviet relations uneven in style and value. In addition to containing many inaccuracies, it has the drawback of being documented almost exclusively from the Polish side.

IP12 UMIASTOWSKI, ROMAN. *Russia and the Polish Republic, 1918-1941*. London: "Aquafondata," 1945. 319 p. A highly emotional indictment of Russia and a glorification of Poland by a colonel of the Polish army, based mainly on secondary sources. [B]

IP13 WALTERSON, JOHN. *Öster om Bug; Fakta kring de östpolska problemen.* Stockholm: A. Bonnier, 1944. 159 p. "East of the Bug" describes the territory between the Curzon Line and the Riga frontier. A popular account based on secondary, mostly Polish, sources. Provides a brief historical survey but devotes closest attention to the economic potentialities of the area.

2. 1917-1921

(Edited by Bohdan B. Budurowycz)

IP14 ARENZ, WILHELM. *Polen und Russland, 1918-1920.* Leipzig: Hirzel, 1939. 112 p. A concise and readable popular review of a crucial period in the history of Polish-Soviet relations. Though based for the greatest part on secondary sources, it is, on the whole, well abreast of the scholarly literature on the subject. [B]

IP15 BAUERMEISTER, ALEXANDER. *Das Wunder an der Weichsel, Polens schwerste Stunde.* Berlin: Stalling, 1937. 159 p. A colorful narrative of the Polish-Soviet War, allegedly based on the diary of an officer of the Russian General Staff. The main stress is on the military operations, with the diplomatic and political aspects of the campaign somewhat neglected. [B]

IP16 COFFEY, JOSEPH I. "The Pattern of Soviet Imperialism; A Case History, Poland, 1919-1921." Ph.D. dissertation, Georgetown U., 1954. A competent account of the Polish-Soviet War and its aftermath, going deeply into the ideological and political background of the conflict. The problem of the eastern borderlands is treated from the Polish point of view.

IP17 COMITÉ EXÉCUTIF DE LA CONFÉRENCE DES MEMBRES DE LA CONSTITUANTE DE RUSSIE. *Mémoire sur le traité de Riga conclu entre la Pologne d'une part, le gouvernment des Soviets d'autre part, le 18 mars 1921.* Paris: Imprimerie Presse Franco-Russe, 1921. 99 p. Some of the leading members of the Constituent Assembly of 1918, meeting in French exile, but purporting to act as the legitimate representatives of the Russian people, protest against the territorial settlement of Riga, which they regard as illegal and injurious to the national interests of Russia.

IP18 D'ABERNON, EDGAR V., 1ST VISCOUNT. *The Eighteenth Decisive Battle of the World; Warsaw, 1920.* London: Hodder & Stoughton, 1931. 178 p. A British member of the Allied mission dispatched to advise Poland on the eve of the "Miracle of the Vistula" discusses his personal experiences and gives a colorful, but not always accurate, picture of the decisive phase of the Polish-Soviet War and of General Weygand's controversial role in its planning. [B]

IP19 DĄBSKI, JAN. *Pokój ryski; wspomnienia, pertraktacje, tajne układy z Joffem, listy*. Warsaw: 1931. 224 p. A factual and well-documented account of the Polish-Soviet peace negotiations in 1920-21, written by the leader of the Polish delegation. Impersonal and dispassionate in tone, it sheds much light on the forces and motives behind the policies of Warsaw and Moscow. [A]

IP20 ENGEL, DAVID H. "Soviet-Polish Relations, November 1918 to April 1920." M.A. thesis, Columbia, 1949. 85 p. An objective and fairly detailed outline of the period of diplomatic wrangling preceding Piłsudski's ill-fated Kievan expedition, based on secondary sources and on the official collections of Russian documents.

IP21 KAKURIN, N. E., and MELIKOV, V. A. *Voina s belopoliakami 1920 g*. Moscow: Voenizdat, 1925. 520 p. A detailed, comprehensive study of the Polish-Soviet campaign, from Piłsudski's April offensive to the armistice, based on archival and other unpublished materials. A pro-Soviet bias is apparent in the discussion of political issues.

IP22 KOMARNICKI, TITUS. *Rebirth of the Polish Republic; A Study in the Diplomatic History of Europe, 1914-1920*. London and Toronto: Heinemann, 1957. 776 p. A former Polish diplomat devotes a substantial part of his well-documented but somewhat biased work to a detailed account of Polish-Soviet relations from the October Revolution to the Treaty of Riga. [A]

IP23 KOWALSKI, JÓZEF. *Wielka Październikowa Rewolucja Socjalistyczna a wyzwolenie Polski*. Warsaw: Książka i Wiedza, 1952. 274 p. A Communist historian stresses in this popular account the alleged influence of the Russian Revolution and of Russian revolutionary ideology in general on Poland's struggle for liberation during World War I.

IP24 KUNTZ, CHARLES A. H. *L'Offensive militaire de l'Étoile Rouge contre la Pologne; la bataille pour Varsovie et la manoeuvre librératrice*. Paris: Charles-Lavauzelle, 1922. 123 p. A brief, popular account of the campaign of 1920, bent on sensationalism, containing many inaccuracies, and marred by the author's tendency toward sweeping statements. The documentation is scanty and not always reliable.

IP25 KUTRZEBA, TADEUSZ. *Wyprawa kijowska 1920 roku*. Warsaw: Gebethner i Wolff, 1937. 358 p. One of the best monographs on the Polish-Soviet War of 1920, dealing chiefly with the military aspect of the campaign, but also discussing its diplomatic and political background. Based on primary sources, it is the most complete and scholarly treatment of the subject in the Polish language. [B]

IP26 LAPINSKII, N. M., ed. *Russko-polskie otnosheniia v period mirovoi voiny.* Moscow: Moskovskii Rabochii, 1926. 162 p. A valuable collection of materials illustrating Russia's attitude toward Poland and the Polish problem during World War I, especially comprehensive for the years 1917-18 but less satisfactory for the earlier period.

IP27 LERNER, WARREN. "The Russian Plan to Sovietize Poland in 1920." Certificate essay, Russian Institute, Columbia, 1954. 96 p. A competent and objective analysis of Soviet policy toward Poland and of the relationship between Moscow and the nascent Communist Party of Poland, based on a close study of contemporary Russian sources.

IP28 LIBERT, FELIKS. *Materiały do bibljografji wojny polsko-sowieckiej.* Warsaw: Wojskowe Biuro Historyczne, 1935. 162 p. This basic bibliographical guide to the voluminous literature in various European languages on the Polish-Soviet campaign gives a wide, though not complete, survey of the mass of printed material in the field.

IP29 PIŁSUDSKI, JÓZEF. *Rok 1920. Z powodu pracy M. Tuchaczewskiego "Pochód za Wisłę."* Warsaw: "Ignis," 1924. 224 p. 2nd ed., Warsaw: Instytut Badań Najnowszej Historji Polskiej, 1927. 378 p. French ed., Paris: 1929. Russian ed., Moscow: 1926. A sober personal account of the Polish-Soviet campaign, by the Commander-in-Chief of the Polish Army and the future dictator of Poland. Marked by bluntness and dramatic power, it provides an incisive and revealing commentary on Poland's internal situation during the critical phase of the war. [A]

IP30 RUSSIA (1917– RSFSR), NARODNYI KOMISSARIAT PO INOSTRANNYM DELAM. *"Krasnaia Kniga"; sbornik diplomaticheskikh dokumentov o russko-polskikh otnosheniiakh 1918-1920 g.* Moscow: Gosizdat, 1920. 112 p. French ed., Moscow: 1920. A fairly complete collection of diplomatic correspondence and some of the more important unilateral pronouncements of the Soviet and Polish governments. In spite of its obvious propaganda purpose, it throws valuable light on the negotiations preceding the outbreak of hostilities between the two countries. [A]

IP31 RUSSIA (1917– RSFSR), NARODNYI KOMISSARIAT PO INOSTRANNYM DELAM. *Sovetskaia Rossiia i Polsha.* Moscow: NKID, 1921. 118 p. French ed., Moscow: 1921. Polish ed., Moscow: 1921. A documentary record, based for the most part on the "Krasnaia Kniga" of 1920, bringing the story of the Polish-Soviet conflict and peace negotiations up to the Treaty of Riga and its aftermath. [B]

IP32 SAINT DIZIER, GÉRALD V. *L'Aigle Blanc contre l'Étoile Rouge; guerre polono-bolchévique en 1920.* Paris: Berger-Levrault,

1930. 144 p. A readable review of the Polish-Soviet War, based almost exclusively on secondary sources, dealing primarily with the military side of the campaign but also giving a fairly satisfactory account of its political and ideological aspects.

IP33 SIERADZKI, JÓZEF. *Białowieża i Mikaszewicze: Mity i prawdy*. Warsaw: Wyd. Min. Obrony Narodowej, 1959. 115 p. A concise, well-documented study of the origins of the Polish-Soviet War of 1920. Partially based on some hitherto inaccessible materials, it throws light on the unsuccessful secret negotiations between the two countries which preceded Piłsudski's Ukrainian expedition. [B]

IP34 SUSLOV, P. V. *Politicheskoe obespechenie sovetsko-polskoi kampanii 1920 goda*. Moscow: Gosizdat, 1930. 174 p. A substantially documented study of the ideological background of the Polish-Soviet War, discussing primarily the role of the political commissars in the campaign and their contribution to the victories of the Red Army.

IP35 TESLAR, TADEUSZ. *Polityka Rosji Sowieckiej podczas wojny z Polską*. Warsaw: Gebethner i Wolff, 1937. 265 p. A compact, well-documented study of Moscow's political and diplomatic maneuvers during the Polish-Soviet War, with special emphasis on the activities of the Comintern and its preparations for a revolution in Poland. [B]

IP36 TESLAR, TADEUSZ. *Propaganda bolszewicka podczas wojny polsko-rosyjskiej 1920 g*. Warsaw: 1938. A scholarly analysis of the anti-Polish campaign waged by the Soviet propaganda machine during the War of 1920, based on a close scrutiny of unpublished documents and other archival materials.

IP37 UKRAINIAN S.S.R., NARODNYI KOMISSARIAT PO INOSTRANNYM DELAM. *Sovetskaia Ukraina i Polsha; sbornik diplomaticheskikh dokumentov i istoricheskikh materialov*. Kharkov: Vseukr. gosizdat, 1921. 144 p. A compilation of official documents and other materials referring to the occupation of Western Ukraine by Polish troops and to Poland's military and diplomatic support of the Petliura government in 1920.

IP38 ZUEV, F. *Mezhdunarodnyi imperializm—organizator napadeniia panskoi Polshi na Sovetskuiu Rossiiu 1919-1920 gg*. Moscow: Gospolitizdat, 1954. 231 p. A typical Soviet propaganda treatise, attempting to burden the Western Powers with the responsibility for Piłsudski's abortive attack against Russia. Documentary evidence presented by the author is of questionable value, and his narrative abounds in inaccuracies and factual errors.

3. 1921-1939
(Edited by Bohdan B. Budurowycz)

IP39 ARSENEV, E. *Podzhigateli voiny; 4 pokusheniia na polpredstvo SSSR v Varshave*. Moscow: Moskovskii Rabochii, 1931. 95 p. The Polish Government is charged, in this semi-official publication, with direct or indirect responsibility for several assassination attempts against Soviet diplomatic representatives in Warsaw and with preparing a military intervention against the USSR.

IP40 BECK, JÓZEF. *Dernier rapport; politique polonaise 1926-1939*. Neuchâtel: La Baconnière, 1951. 361 p. Polish ed., Warsaw: 1955. English ed., *Final Report*. N.Y.: Speller, 1957. The Polish Foreign Minister from 1932 to 1939 makes an unsuccessful attempt to defend himself from a wide variety of attacks and accusations by telling his side of the story. There is little of interest in his cursory and not always frank treatment of Poland's relations with the Soviet Union. [B]

IP41 BECK, JÓZEF. *Przemówienia, deklaracje, wywiady, 1931-1939*. Warsaw: Gebethner i Wolff, 1939. 446 p. German ed., *Beiträge zur europäischen Politik*. Essen: Essener Verlagsanstalt, 1939. In spite of Beck's deliberate vagueness, this collection of his speeches, official statements and interviews contains many revealing references to Poland's relations with the Soviet Union and her "policy of balance" between Germany and the USSR. [B]

IP42 BRATKOVSKII, IURII V. *Polskii fashizm - forpost interventsii*. Moscow-Leningrad: Partizdat, 1932. 110 p. A sharply critical appraisal of Polish foreign policy, accusing Marshal Piłsudski and his government of pursuing an openly anti-Soviet course and of acting as the tool and vanguard of Western imperialism in its alleged plans for a new intervention against the USSR.

IP43 BUDUROWYCZ, BOHDAN B. *Polish-Soviet Relations 1932-39*. N.Y.: Columbia, 1963. 299 p. Based chiefly on primary sources, this study traces the course of Polish-Soviet relations from the conclusion of the non-aggression pact of July 1932 to the fourth partition of Poland in September 1939, and interprets the policies of Warsaw and Moscow against the background of contemporary diplomatic developments in Europe. Twenty-page bibliography. [A]

IP44 DRUNIN, V. P. *Polsha, Rossiia i SSSR*. Moscow: Gosizdat, 1928. 219 p. A comprehensive, conspicuously pro-Russian survey of the age-old struggle between Warsaw and Moscow for political and cultural hegemony in Eastern Europe, followed by a brief discussion of the prospects for Polish-Soviet reconciliation

IP45 GROWSKI, JÓZEF. (Pseud. of Wacław Grzybowski). *Z.S.S.R.; Notatki ze wspomnień.* Paris: "Kohorta," 1940. 88 p. The Polish Ambassador to Moscow in 1936-1939 combines the melancholy story of his country's relations with the USSR with a caustic commentary on Stalin's Russia during the years of the Great Purge.

IP46 IPOHORSKI-LENKIEWICZ, WITOLD. *Minister z Pałacu Brühla; U źródeł drugiej wojny światowej.* Buenos Aires: "Codzienny Niezależny Kurjer Polski w Argentynie," 1943. 217 p. A former official of the Polish Foreign Ministry gives a pathetic and disjointed account of his country's policy on the eve of the Second World War. The author's personal reminiscences, interspersed with violent diatribes against Beck, contain little of value and interest.

IP47 KON, FELIKS IA. *Sovremennaia Polsha.* Moscow: "Krasnaia nov," 1924. 115 p. A concise, skilfully-argued survey of Poland's internal situation and foreign policy by a prominent Polish-born Communist leader, former member of the so-called "Provisional Revolutionary Committee for Poland," and onetime secretary of the Executive Committee of the Comintern.

IP48 MACKIEWICZ, STANISŁAW. *O jedenastej—powiada aktor—sztuka jest skończona; Polityka Józefa Becka.* London: Kolin, 1942. 172 p. English ed., *Colonel Beck and His Policy.* London: Eyre, 1944. An interesting but strongly opinionated reappraisal of Polish foreign policy during the 1930's, by one of Poland's leading publicists. The author is especially outspoken in his criticism of Beck, whom he portrays as the principal villain of the story.

IP49 POLAND, MINISTERSTWO SPRAW ZAGRANICZNYCH. *Official Documents Concerning Polish-German and Polish-Soviet Relations, 1933-1939; Published by Authority of the Polish Government.* N.Y.: Roy; London: Hutchinson, 1940. 222 p. French ed., Paris: Flammarion, 1940. A handy compilation of the most important documents illustrating Poland's relations with her two dangerous neighbors. Unfortunately, the diplomatic correspondence relating to the period of the Polish-Soviet "cold war" in 1937-38 has been almost entirely omitted. [A]

IP50 POLISH RESEARCH CENTER, LONDON. *Poland and the U.S.S.R., 1921-1941.* With an introductory note by W. F. Reddaway. London: n.d. 156 p. A well-documented, fact-crammed review of the diplomatic, political and economic aspects of Polish-Soviet relations, setting forth the traditional Polish views and claims but containing much information not available elsewhere. [B]

IP51 *Politicheskie partii v Polshe, Zapadnoi Belorussii i Zapadnoi Ukraine.* Minsk: Izd. Belorusskoi Akademii nauk, 1935. 335 p. A strongly biased and not always accurate survey of the political groupings of the national minorities and of the activities and role of the Communist Party of Poland and its autonomous sections in Western Ukraine and Western Belorussia.

IP52 PUSHAS, I. O. *Sovremennaia Polsha i SSSR (ekonomicheskii ocherk)*. Moscow: Kommunisticheskaia akademiia, 1928. 104 p. A critical analysis of Poland's economic policy, with special reference to her trade with the Soviet Union and with emphasis on the interdependence of economic interests of the two countries.

IP54 ROMANSKII, ANATOLII I. *Ocherki sovremennoi Polshi*. Moscow: "Prometei," 1926. 256 p. A clear and balanced survey, dealing primarily with Poland's internal situation at the time of Piłsudski's *coup d'état*. Comparatively sound and well-informed on economic matters, but less reliable in its treatment of the country's domestic and foreign policies.

IP55 ROOS, HANS. *Polen und Europa; Studien zur polnischen Aussen-politik, 1931-1939*. Tübingen: Mohr, 1957. 421 p. The best available account of Polish foreign policy in the 1930's, backed with painstaking research into every conceivable source of information. Some of the author's theses are debatable, but his concise analysis of Polish-Soviet relations shows sound judgment and objectivity. 12-page bibliography. [A]

IP56 ROSE, ADAM. *La Politique polonaise entre les deux guerres*. Neuchâtel: La Baconnière, 1944. 207 p. A lucid though somewhat superficial account by a Polish economist and former diplomat. In the main the facts are accurate and interpretations plausible, but the survey is too short to discuss all the nuances in Polish-Soviet relations.

IP57 SHOTWELL, JAMES T., and LASERSON, MAX M. *Poland and Russia, 1919-1945*. N.Y.: King's Crown, 1945. 114 p. A concise, scholarly analysis and interpretation of the general principles underlying Polish and Soviet foreign policies, followed by an impartial and competent survey of the relations between the two nations during the most crucial period of their history. [B]

IP58 SIKORSKI, WŁADYSŁAW. *Le Problème de la paix; le jeu des forces politiques en Europe orientale et l'alliance franco-polonaise*. Paris: Éditions de la Vie Latine, 1931. 268 p. A well-known Polish statesman and military leader discusses the dangers and advantages of his country's geographical position between Germany and Russia and the importance of the Franco-Polish alliance of 1921 as a stabilizing factor in the general European situation.

IP59 STUTTGART, WELTKRIEGSBÜCHEREI. *Bibliographie zur Aussenpolitik der Republik Polen, 1919-1939, und zum Feldzug in Polen, 1939.* Stuttgart: Weltkriegsbücherei, Institut für Weltpolitik, 1943. 100 p. A fairly comprehensive list of monographs and articles in various languages relating to Poland's foreign policy, with two sections devoted to Polish-Soviet relations. The most satisfactory coverage is provided for publications in German and Polish; comparatively few Russian sources are listed.

IP60 SZEMBEK, JAN, HRABIA. *Journal 1933-1939.* Paris: Plon, 1952. 504 p. An abbreviated French version of the unpublished diplomatic diary left by the Polish Under-Secretary of State for Foreign Affairs, 1932-39. In spite of some gaps, it remains the basic and indispensable source for any serious student of Poland's foreign policy during that period. [A]

IP61 UMIASTOWSKI, ROMAN. *Russia and the Polish Republic, 1918-1941.* London: "Aquafondata," 1945. 319 p. A strongly emotional indictment of Soviet Russia for her relentless hostility toward Poland, presented with much documentary evidence, but impaired by the author's lack of skill and his tendency to see only the Polish side of the case. [B]

IP62 WAHL, ERNEST G. VON. *Zwei Gegner im Osten; Polen als Widersacher Russlands.* Dortmund: Volkschaft-Verlag, 1939. 98 p. An interesting but not always accurate analysis of the ideological, political, military and economic factors governing Polish-Soviet relations on the eve of the approaching world crisis, by the author of several controversial books on the Russian Civil War.

IP63 ZALESKI, AUGUST. *Przemowy i deklaracje.* Warsaw: Drukarnia W. Łazarskiego, 1929. 249 p. A selection of speeches and declarations by the Polish Foreign Minister in 1926-32, shedding light on Poland's attitude toward the Soviet Union during the years immediately following Piłsudski's *coup d'état.* [B]

4. 1939-1963

(Edited by Kazimierz Grzybowski and Edward J. Rozek)

IP64 ALTON, THAD P. *Polish Postwar Economy.* N.Y.: Columbia; London: Oxford, 1955. 330 p. Deals with the economic changes and transformations in Poland following World War II, including territorial changes, the reconstruction phase, and Sovietization policies, with emphasis on the structural and institutional changes in the Polish economy due to the planned industrialization and collectivization policy. [A]

IP65 ANDERS, WŁADYSŁAW. *An Army in Exile; The Story of the Second Polish Corps.* N.Y.: Macmillan, 1949. 319 p. After organizing several divisions of the Polish Army in Russia, the author (Gen. of the Army) led them through the Middle East and North Africa to Italy where they fought for the liberation of Europe. An informative account of one of the contributions which Poland made to the Allied cause. [B]

IP66 ANDERS, WŁADYSŁAW. *Katyn.* Paris: Edition France-Empire, 1949. 345 p. The author was deported by the Russians to Lubianka Prison in Moscow. After his release in the fall of 1941, he became the Commander-in-Chief of the Polish Army in Russia, formed out of those who had survived the deportation. In this book, he gives a factual explanation of what happened to the 14,000 Polish officers, professors, and doctors whose bodies were discovered in Katyn forest in 1943. [B]

IP67 ANDERSON, HERBERT F. *What I Saw in Poland—1946.* Stough, England: Windsor, 1946. 194 p. Impressions of a traveller who visited Poland after the War. Describes the economic and social conditions of a country which went through a period of enemy occupation and then found itself under an imposed regime.

IP68 ANONYMOUS. *The Dark Side of the Moon.* London: Faber & Faber, 1946. 232 p. N.Y.: Scribner, 1947. 299 p. "Written by one of a people who have suffered so deeply as the Poles have suffered," this story of what happened to Poland between 1939 and 1945 is based on personal experience with NKVD terror, life in Soviet prisons and in concentration camps. A moderate narrative.

IP69 BARANSKI, JAN. *Mon Pays perdu, 1939-1951.* Paris: Les Iles d'Or, 1956. 188 p. Describes his war experiences, including capture by the Germans. Discusses the impact of the war and of Soviet domination on Poland. Also includes an account of the refugee problem.

IP70 BEDNARCZYK, CHESTER P. "Soviet Technique of Domination in Poland, 1943-1947." Ph.D. dissertation, U. of California (Berkeley), 1956.

IP71 BOR-KOMOROWSKI, TADEUSZ. *The Secret Army.* N.Y.: Macmillan, 1951. 407 p. Polish ed., *Armia Podziemna.* London: Veritas, 1951. The last Commander-in-Chief of the Polish underground Army which fought against the Nazis describes the organization and accomplishments of that army as well as its liquidation by the Communists. [A]

IP72 BRANT, IRVING. *The New Poland.* N.Y.: International Universities Press, 1946. 116 p. Republished articles sent to the *Chicago Sun* and the *New Republic* during the author's trip to Poland in the fall of 1945 as a correspondent. Presents a pro-Soviet, distorted picture of the situation at that time.

IP73 BREGMAN, A. *Dzieje Pustego Fotela; Konferencja w San Francisco i Sprawa Polska.* London: Światpol, 1948. 220 p. The author of a book about the League of Nations, Bregman was close to the Polish government-in-exile. Contains a penetrating analysis of the San Francisco Conference, which the author observed, and presents a dim view of the future of the UN as well as apprehension about the Soviet danger. A very good study. [A]

IP74 BRONSKA-PAMPUCH, WANDA. *Polen zwischen Hoffnung und Verzweiflung.* Cologne: Verlag für Politik und Wirtschaft, 1958. 375 p. A historical study of Polish political and social development after World War II, including the events leading to the liberalization of the Polish regime after the revolt of 1956. [B]

IP75 BRUNOT, LOUIS. *Pologne d'hier et d'aujourd'hui.* Paris: Raisons d'Être, 1947. 270 p. An account of the social, economic and political changes in Poland drawn against the background of Polish history and against the general international situation resulting from World War II.

IP76 BUDZ, ANDREW I., JR. "The Oder-Neisse Border, Weapon in Communist Domination Over Poland." M.A. thesis, Columbia, 1954. 86 p. Budz tries to show that the issue of the Oder-Neisse line is being exploited by the present Warsaw government and its Soviet masters with the ultimate purpose of gaining complete domination of Poland. Based primarily on Polish and Russian sources from behind the Iron Curtain, this is a well-documented study.

IP77 CARY, WILLIAM H. *Poland Struggles Forward.* N.Y.: Greenberg, 1949. 192 p. A rather factual description of the economic and social changes in Poland after World War II, written on the eve of the switch to the Sovietization policies by the Communist-dominated regime.

IP78 CIECHANOWSKI, JAN. *Defeat in Victory.* Garden City, N.Y.: Doubleday, 1947. 397 p. The war-time Ambassador of Poland to the United States describes from his point of observation the diplomatic events which led to the loss of freedom in Poland. A well-written, informative book. [A]

IP79 CO-ORDINATING COMMITTEE OF AMERICAN-POLISH ASSOCIATIONS IN THE EAST. *Polish-Russian Problem.* N.Y.: Coordinating Committee of American-Polish Associations in the East, 1945. 67 p. This well-documented volume throws light on the methods used by the Russians in their work of Sovietizing Poland. Many first-hand documents illustrate Soviet activities in Poland in the years 1945-47. See Council of Polish Political Parties (below). [B]

IP80 COUNCIL OF POLISH POLITICAL PARTIES. *For the Freedom of Poland and Central-Eastern Europe; Documents, 1946-1947.* London: Council of Polish Political Parties, 1948. 62 p. Distributed by the Polish government-in-exile information center, this book treats the defense of the Polish-Russian frontier of 1939. 13 appendices deal with many aspects of Polish-Russian relations. See Co-ordinating Committee of American-Polish Associations in the East (above).

IP81 CZAPSKI, JOSEPH. *The Inhuman Land.* Introd. by Edward Crankshaw. N.Y.: Sheed and Ward, 1952. 301 p. The personal experiences of the author in Russia, to which he was deported at the beginning of the Second World War. A very interesting account of many tragic events. The author is a good writer and lives presently in Paris. [A]

IP82 DAVIES, RAYMOND A. *The Truth About Poland.* Toronto: World News, 1946. 91 p. Davies, Eastern European correspondent of Saturday Night, the Canadian Broadcasting Corporation, and the Mutual Broadcasting System, reads and speaks Polish, Russian, and Ukrainian. This leftist, pro-Soviet book is an enthusiastic description of his personal observations in Poland just after World War II.

IP83 DE LAVAL, ERIK. *Det Polska Dramat.* Stockholm: Fahlcrantz & Gumaelius, 1948. 189 p. A history of World War II in Poland, with emphasis on the regime instituted on Polish territory during the War, especially its treatment of the Polish population and institutions.

IP84 GIBNEY, FRANK B. *The Frozen Revolution; Poland: A Study in Communist Decay.* N.Y.: Farrar, Straus & Cudahy, 1959. 269 p. An interesting and rather optimistic analysis of the bloodless October Revolution in Poland. The author implies that the events of 1956 indicate the beginnings of the disintegration of Communism. [B]

IP85 GOMUŁKA, WŁADYSŁAW. *Przemowienia (pazdziernik 1956-wrzesien 1957).* Warsaw: Książka i Wiedza, 1957. 481 p. Gomulka at that time was the standard-bearer of the Polish struggle for greater freedom from Soviet control of Polish public life, and for the liberalization of the Communist regime in Poland. His speeches are important for an understanding of Polish sentiments and desires, and for the plans of the regime for the future. [A]

IP86 GRABSKI, STANISŁAW. *Myšli o dziejowej drodze Polski.* Glasgow: Książnica Polska, 1944. 187 p. By a Polish political leader, a member of the Polish wartime government in London, a scholar of note, and a partisan of Polish-Russian collaboration to stem the tide of the German *Drang nach Osten.* He reviews the chances for the cooperation of the two Slavic nations in the future.

IP87 GRABSKI, STANISŁAW. *Na Nowej Drodze Dziejowej*. Warsaw: Państwowy Instytut Wydawniczy, 1946. 98 p. One of the Rightist leaders of the pre-war Polish party of National Democrats presents a political treatise, with historical and philosophical digressions, about the future of Poland after World War II. He argues that Poland must direct her natural expansion to the Baltic Sea and have the powerful Soviet ally as a counterbalance against Germany.

IP88 GRIFFIS, STANTON. *Lying in State*. Garden City, N.Y.: Doubleday, 1952. 315 p. A rather light account of the author's experiences in Warsaw, where he was the second postwar U.S. Ambassador to Poland. Interesting narrative. [B]

IP89 GROSZ, VICTOR. *La Vérité sur le drame polonais de Septembre 1939*. Paris: Éditions du Pavillon, 1951. 135 p. A very interesting political explanation of the Polish tragedy in September 1939 by the former ambassador of Poland to Prague. Reveals French and English diplomacy toward Germany and Poland.

IP90 HALECKI, OSKAR, ed. *Poland*. N.Y.: Published for the Mid-European Studies Center of the Free Europe Committee by Praeger, 1957. 601 p. (In the series, *East-Central Europe under the Communists*). A very large and informative work written by many specialists, American and Polish, and edited by an outstanding historian. An excellent handbook, indispensable as a reference work. [A]

IP91 HERLING, GUSTAV. *A World Apart*. N.Y.: New American Library, 1952. 256 p. A simple, vivid, sincere description of life in Soviet prisons and concentration camps, based on personal experience. An impressive indictment of Soviet tyranny, by a Polish writer.

IP92 HUMAN RELATIONS AREA FILES. *Contemporary Poland; Society, Politics, Economy*. Ed. by Alicja Iwanska. Chicago: U. of Chicago Press, 1955. 578 p. An important collection of monographic articles dealing with various aspects of life in Poland in the period after World War II. Polish institutions, politics, government, and economic problems are described, with particular attention to the impact of the Sovietization policies adopted by the regime. [A]

IP93 JANTA, ALEKSANDER. *Bound With Two Chains*. N.Y.: Roy, 1945. 234 p. An account of wartime experiences. Important for characterizing the changes produced in the life of members of the Polish intellectual classes by the war and the occupation of the country by Germany and Russia.

IP94 JARS, ROBERT. *La Campagne de Pologne (septembre 1939)*. Paris: Payot, 1949. 222 p. A former officer of the reserve in pre-war Poland recounts the German-Polish campaign in September 1939 from the Polish military point of view. Well-documented, this work contains 11 appendices with documents and a two-page bibliography.

IP95 JĘDRZEJEWICZ, WACŁAW, ed. *Poland in the British Parliament 1939-1945*. Vol. 1, *British Guarantees to Poland to the Atlantic Charter (March 1939-August 1941)*. N.Y.: Józef Piłsudski Institute of America, 1946. 493 p. The Polish war effort was to a great degree linked to the British guarantees for Poland. Polish questions were discussed in the British Parliament, and this work is a collection of such discussions in view of the British commitments.

IP96 KARSKI, JAN. *Story of a Secret State*. Boston: Houghton Mifflin, 1944; London: Hodder and Stoughton, 1945. 318 p. French ed., *Mon Temoignage devant le monde*. Paris: 1948. An excellent, first-hand account of the underground organization (political and military) which was formed in Poland to fight the Nazi occupants, by a Georgetown University professor. [A]

IP97 KERSTEIN, EDWARD S. *Red Star Over Poland; A Report From Behind the Iron Curtain*. Appleton, Wisconsin: Nelson, 1947. 174 p. An American of Polish extraction vividly sketches the Polish situation and life in 1945 in his reports to the Milwaukee *Journal*. He is sympathetic to the Polish government-in-exile.

IP98 KOMARNICKI, TITUS. *Piłsudski a polityka wielkich mocarstw zachodnich*. London: Instytut Jósefa Piłsudskiego, 1952. 82 p. A historical account of Poland's international relations in the inter-war period, particularly the foreign policy of Jozef Piłsudski.

IP99 KORBOŃSKI, STEFAN. *Fighting Warsaw; The Story of the Polish Underground State, 1939-1945*. N.Y.: Macmillan; London: Allen & Unwin, 1956. 495 p. A political diary written around the author's and his wife's experiences in Warsaw during and immediately after the Second World War.

IP100 KORBOŃSKI, STEFAN. *Warsaw in Chains*. N.Y.: Macmillan; London: Allen & Unwin, 1959. 319 p. The diary from 1945 to 1948 of one of the leaders of the Polish underground during World War II. Briefly discusses the Poznań uprising and the Gomułka October Revolution of 1956. A severe indictment of Soviet policy in postwar Poland. A sequel to his *Fighting Warsaw*.

IP101 KORBOŃSKI, STEFAN. *W imieniu Kremla*. Paris: Instytut Literacki, 1956. 381 p. An account of Poland's regime after World War II, established under Soviet influence, and to serve the policies of the Soviet Union. Includes an analysis of political, economic and social conditions in the period of Stalinization.

IP102 KOROWICZ, MAREK S. *W Polsce pod Sowieckim Jarzmem.* London: Veritas, 1955. 360 p. The author was formerly a Professor of International Law at the Yagiellonian University in Krakow who emigrated, returned to Poland in 1945, became a member of the Polish delegation to the U.N., and then, in 1954, asked for asylum in the U.S. This book is not scholarly, but is an extensive presentation by an intelligent observer of the situation in Poland before 1956, especially of the feelings, aspirations and actions of the Polish intelligentsia living under Soviet domination.

IP103 KOT, STANISŁAW. *Listy z rosji do Gen. Sikorskiego.* London: Jutro Polski, 1955. 576 p. The author, a Polish historian and scholar of note, was made Ambassador to the Soviet Union after the German attack on Russia, in 1941. His letters to General Sikorski, Polish Prime Minister and Commander-in-Chief, deal with various aspects of Russo-Polish relations and émigré policies. [A]

IP104 KOT, STANISŁAW. *Rozmowy z Kremlem.* London: Jutro Polski, 1959. Documentation relative to conversations of the Polish Ambassador in Moscow with Soviet leaders, including Stalin, in the period of World War II. [B]

IP105 KRZESIŃSKI, ANDRZEJ J. *Poland's Rights to Justice.* N.Y.: Devin-Adair, 1946. 120 p. An indictment of the Yalta decision concerning Poland by the author of other books, among them: *Nazi Germany's Foreign Policy* (1945). Discusses the defense of the Polish-Russian frontier of 1939.

IP106 KUŚNIERZ, BRONISŁAW. *Stalin and the Poles; An Indictment of the Soviet Leaders.* London: Hollis & Carter, 1949. 317 p. By the Minister of Justice in the Government of General Bor-Komorowski, this is the story of Polish-Soviet relations from 1939 to 1948.

IP107 KWAPIŃSKI, JAN. *1939-1945; Kartki z pamietnika.* London: Światpol, 1947. 187 p. Personal impressions of a Polish political leader, a member of the Polish Peasant Party, during World War II.

IP108 LANE, ARTHUR B. *I Saw Poland Betrayed; an American Ambassador Reports to the American People.* Indianapolis: Bobbs-Merrill, 1948. 344 p. British ed., *I Saw Freedom Betrayed.* London: Regency, 1949. Memoirs of the former Ambassador of the United States to Poland; covers the period 1944-47, till after the elections of January 1947. Contains interesting observations on Polish Communist leaders and their attitude toward the Soviet Union. [B]

IP109 LEWIS, FLORA. *A Case History of Hope; The Story of Poland's Peaceful Revolutions.* Garden City, N.Y.: Doubleday, 1958. 267 p. London: Secker & Warburg, 1959. An interesting story of Poland after October 1956 presented by a talented American woman correspondent stationed in Poland at the time. Very perceptive and informative. [B]

IP110 LONDON, INSTYTUT HISTORYCZNY IMIENIA GENERAŁA SIKORSKIEGO. *Documents on Polish-Soviet Relations, 1939-1945.* London: Heinemann, 1961–. This important compilation of documents from the archives of the Polish government-in-exile and many other sources brings together much material not otherwise accessible. Volume I ends with the severance of diplomatic relations between Poland and the USSR in April 1943. [A]

IP111 LONDON, INSTYTUT HISTORYCZNY IMIENIA GENERAŁA SIKORSKIEGO. *Polskie Sily Zbrojne w II-iej Wojnie Swiatowej.* London: Instytut Historyczny Imienia Sikorskiego, 1950. 3 vols. A history of the Polish war effort from the September 1939 campaign till the end of the War. [B]

IP112 MACKIEWICZ, JOSEPH. *The Katyn Wood Murders.* London: Hollis, 1951. 252 p. German ed., Zurich: 1949. 224 p. A well-known Polish writer presents a precise, well-documented account of the Katyn tragedy, based on personal observation of the forest graves.

IP113 MACKIEWICZ, STANISŁAW. *Colonel Beck and His Policy.* London: Eyre and Spottiswoode, 1944. 139 p. A study of the foreign policy of Colonel Beck, who was Foreign Minister of Poland through most of Piłsudski's regime and during the initial months of World War II.

IP114 MACKIEWICZ, STANISŁAW. *Lata Nadziei.* London: The Author, 1946. 216 p. A history of the Polish war effort against the background of the establishment of Soviet control in Poland.

IP115 MAKS, LEON. *Russia by the Back Door.* London; N.Y.: Sheed & Ward, 1954. 264 p. The personal notes of a soldier of the Polish Home Army, a doctor by profession, who experienced his adventures during World War II. Very vivid and intelligent presentation of the life in the Soviet hinterland (the Ukraine, Don Region, Siberia) during the war.

IP116 MALARA, JEAN, and REY, LUCIENNE. *La Pologne d'une occupation à l'autre, 1944-1952.* Paris: Éditions du Fuseau, 1952. 371 p. A factual, well-written and documented account of the Communist takeover and consolidation of power in Poland. [B]

IP117 MEISSNER, BORIS. *Das Ostpakt-System.* Hamburg: 1951. 2 vols. 2nd ed., Frankfurt/Main: Metzner, 1955. 208 p. An important collection of documents concerning treaty relations of the Soviet Union with the satellite countries of Eastern Europe, including Poland. [A]

IP118 MID-EUROPEAN RESEARCH AND PLANNING CENTRE, PARIS. *The Sovietization of Culture in Poland.* Paris: Mid-European Research and Planning Centre, 1953. 207 p. Describes cultural and educational policies of the Communist regime in Poland during the period of forced Stalinization. [B]

IP119 MIKOŁAJCZYK, STANISŁAW. *The Rape of Poland; Pattern of Soviet Aggression.* N.Y.: Whittlesey House, 1948. 309 p. British ed., *The Pattern of Soviet Domination.* London: Low, Marston, 1948. French ed., Paris: 1949. Italian ed., Milan: 1950. Memoirs of the leader of the Polish Peasant Party, Minister of Interior and Premier of the Polish Government in London, and later Vice-Premier of the Provisional Government of National Unity (June 1945-February 1947). Contains valuable material on Polish Communist leaders and their attitude toward the Soviet Union [A]

IP120 MILOSZ, CZESŁAW. *The Captive Mind.* N.Y.: Knopf; London: Secker and Warburg, 1953. 251 p. Paperback ed., N.Y.: Vintage, 1955. French ed., Paris: 1953. Polish ed., Paris: 1953. An important analysis of the Sovietization of Polish cultural life, including writers and creative artists. Discusses the psychology of political involvement, and its effect upon creative ability. By a prominent Polish author who lived for several years in Communist Poland. [A]

IP121 MONTANUS, B. *Polish-Soviet Relations in the Light of International Law.* N.Y.: University Publication, 1944. 54 p. A scholarly, well-documented, instructive presentation of the problem of Polish-Soviet relations solely from the legal point of view. Includes legal interpretations of various Polish-Soviet international treaties, with an appendix containing the text of the Treaty of Riga and others.

IP121A MONTIAS, JOHN MICHAEL. *Central Planning in Poland.* New Haven: Yale University Press, 1962. 410 p. A scholarly analysis of the Communist direction of the Polish postwar economy, by an American economist. [A]

IP122 *Moscow Trial of the Sixteen Polish Diversionists, June 18-21, 1945.* London: Soviet News, 1945. 69 p. An official Soviet account of the trial of sixteen Poles, members of the Polish underground government, lured out of hiding by an offer of cooperation and later tried for alleged collaboration with the Nazis.

IP123 MULAK, JAN. *Wojsko Podziemne, 1939-1945.* Warsaw: Spoldzielnia Wydawnicza "Wiedza," 1946. 77 p. A presentation of the Polish underground movement against the Nazi occupation in the years 1939-45 from a Leftist, pro-Soviet point of view. Also an indictment of the Warsaw Insurrection of 1944 as being made without proper coordination and cooperation.

IP124 NATIONAL COUNCIL OF AMERICAN-SOVIET FRIENDSHIP, NATIONALITIES DIVISION. "*We Will Join Hands with Russia*" *on Polish-Soviet Relations*. By Oscar Lange and others. N.Y.: 1944. 38 p. A collection of speeches made by O. Lange, S. Orlemański, L. Krzycki, and others at a meeting organized in 1943 by the Council. Illustrates the wartime tactics of the Soviet Union toward Poland.

IP125 NEWMAN, BERNARD. *Russia's Neighbour—The New Poland*. London: Gollancz, 1946. 256 p. A well-known English writer, the author of: *The Story of Poland* (1940) and a pro-Polish specialist on Middle Europe, presents an extensive discussion of Polish eastern and western frontiers, with historical digressions. He also discusses the future of Poland and his personal observations during his stay in Poland in 1945.

IP126 NOARO, JEAN. *La Pologne*. Paris: Éditions Sociales, 1951. 309 p. A personal impression of Poland by a visitor during the height of the forced collectivization and industrialization according to the Soviet-inspired plan. Economic and social conditions are described.

IP127 ONACEWICZ, WLODZIMIERZ. "The Diplomatic and Military Preparation of the Aggression Against Poland in 1939." Ph.D. dissertation, Georgetown, 1954. A conventional but competent and creditable study, based largely on published collections of documents and secondary sources. While giving evidence of a pro-Polish bias, it presents a fairly complete and reliable picture of the political and military situation in Eastern Europe on the eve of the Polish-German war.

IP128 ORSKA, IRENA. *Silent Is the Vistula*. N.Y.: Longmans, 1946. 275 p. Personal experiences of a member of the Warsaw population, including the Warsaw uprising during World War II. [B]

IP129 OSTASZEWSKI, JAN. *Powstanie Warszawskie*. Rome: 1945. 184 p. Discusses the Warsaw uprising in 1944, including an analysis of Soviet attitudes. [B]

IP130 PAWŁOWICZ, JERZY. *Z dziejów konspiracyjnej KRN, 1943-1944*. Warsaw: Książka i Wiedza, 1961. 256 p. Discusses underground activities of the Polish National Council as the top organization of leftwing organizations, 1943-44. Uses archival sources, recollections, and news items from the Polish underground press, etc. According to its Communist-oriented author, this is a great contribution to the history of the Polish national liberation war.

IP131 PENZIK, IRENA. *Ashes to the Taste*. N.Y.: University Publishers, 1961. 378 p. An important account of the realities of life in a country governed by a Communist regime.

IP132 *Piat let narodnoi Polshi, 1944-1949.* Moscow: Izd. Inostrannoi lit., 1951. 365 p. Contains factual material concerning the development of the Polish Republic for the years 1944-49. There is no indication as to who is the author in the original Polish and no Polish editor mentioned. Strongly pro-Soviet, it is sheer and clever Soviet propaganda, probably written by a Polish Stalinist.

IP133 PISARETS, I. G., KOZIK, A. K., and MISHINA, V. V. *Polsha; ekonomika i vneshniaia torgovlia.* Moscow: Vneshtorgizdat, 1954. 132 p. A collective work of Soviet economists dealing with the Polish economy and foreign trade, including official statistics and an account of the policies of industrialization in Poland.

IP135 PRAGIER, ADAM. *Polish Peace Aims.* London: Max Love, 1944. 127 p. Polish ed. Glasgow: 1944. A professor at the Universal College in Warsaw and at the Polish Faculty of Law in Oxford presents Polish peace aims from circles close to the Polish Government-in-exile. The Polish attitude toward Germany, the USSR, and the U.N. and the concept of the establishment of the Central-East European zone are also discussed.

IP136 RACZYŃSKI, EDWARD H. *W sojuszniczym Londynie.* London: Polish Research Center, 1960. 450 p. The diplomatic memoirs of the Polish Ambassador in London from 1934 to 1945 contain no startling revelations, but provide a detailed and intelligent account of Poland's precarious wartime relations with Russia and the Western Powers. [B]

IP137 ROZEK, EDWARD J. *Allied Wartime Diplomacy; A Pattern in Poland.* N.Y.: Wiley, 1958. 481 p. Prefaced by W. Y. Elliott, this is a thoroughly documented analysis of the policies of Stalin, Churchill, and Roosevelt toward Poland at the time of the Second World War. Based on many original, top-secret documents and private files of former Prime Minister Mikolajczyk, which have never before been published. The author is a professor of history at the University of Colorado. [A]

IP138 ROZMARYN, STEFAN. *The Seym and People's Councils in Poland.* Warsaw: Polonia, 1958. 153 p. A study of Polish constitutional law and government with emphasis on the role of representative institutions in a regime of the Soviet type.

IP139 RUBINSTEIN, NIKOLAI L., ed. *Proval imperialisticheskikh planov v otnoshenii Polshi v gody vtoroi mirovoi voiny.* Moscow: Gospolitizdat, 1952. 205 p. A dialetical interpretation of political events leading to World War II, and of Allied policies towards Poland, aiming to demonstrate that the Western Powers sought to enslave Poland.

IP140 RUDZKA, MARTHA (pseud. of Beata Obertynska). *Workuta; Weg zur Knechtschaft.* Zurich: Thomas, 1948. 268 p. Personal experiences with Soviet prisons and labor camps (1939-1942), N.K.-V.D. terror, and human suffering. A touching narrative with keen observations.

IP141 SCHNEIDERMAN, SAMUEL L. *The Warsaw Heresy.* N.Y.: Horizon, 1959. 253 p. A very intelligent and informative description of what happened in Poland after Władysław Gomułka came to power in October 1956. The story of Polish revisionism and ideological ferment, based on personal observation during the author's stay in Poland. At the end, there are some notes on the key figures of present-day Poland. [B]

IP142 SHARP, SAMUEL L. *Poland; White Eagle on a Red Field.* Cambridge: Harvard, 1953. 326 p. A presentation of the Polish problem in its historical and contemporary setting. One chapter is devoted to American-Polish relations and in the text many primary sources are mentioned. An intelligent, instructive work.

IP143 SKRZYPEK, STANISLAUS T. "The Soviet Elections in Eastern Poland, October 1939." Ph.D. dissertation, Fordham, 1955. An extensive and carefully documented treatment of Moscow's elaborate attempts to legalize the incorporation of Eastern Poland into the USSR by means of elections to the Soviet-sponsored "National Assemblies" of Western Belorussia and Western Ukraine.

IP144 SKRZYPEK, STANISŁAW. *The Problem of Eastern Galicia.* London: Polish Association for the South-Eastern Provinces, 1948. 94 p. Political, economic and demographic problems in Eastern Galicia, which was part of inter-war Poland and at present is part of the Soviet Ukraine. A contribution to the study of Polish-Ukrainian relations.

IP144A STAAR, RICHARD F. *Poland 1944-1962; the Sovietization of a Captive People.* Baton Rouge: Louisiana State University Press, 1962. 300 p. A study of postwar Poland by a professor of political science at Emory University.

IP145 STAAR, RICHARD F. "The Political Framework of Communist Poland." Ph.D. dissertation, University of Michigan, 1954. An analysis of the government and politics of Poland under Soviet domination, including various aspects of Soviet control.

IP146 STAHL, ZDZISŁAW, ed. *Zbrodnia Katyńska w Świetle Dokumentów.* London: Gryf, 1948. 384 p. 2nd ed., London: 1950. 455 p. A collection of documents relative to the murder of Polish officers and civilians in Katyn forest.

IP147 STANIEWICZ, MARIAN. *Klęska wrześniowa na tle stosunków międzynarodowych.* Warsaw: Ministerstwo Obrony Narodowej, 1952. 233 p. An analysis of the Polish defeat in September 1939, from the point of view of the political situation in Europe at that time. An *apologia* for Soviet policies of collaboration with Germany.

IP148 STANKIEWICZ, WŁADYSŁAW J., and MONTIAS, JOHN M. *Institutional Changes in the Postwar Economy of Poland.* N.Y.: Mid-European Studies Center, Free Europe Committee, 1955. 125 p. The authors trace the policies of socialist construction in Poland, including industrial expansion in the light of institutional changes in the Polish economy.

IP149 STRONG, ANNA LOUISE. *I Saw the New Poland.* Boston: Little, Brown, 1946. 280 p. The author of numerous books, many about the Soviet Union, presents her leftist, pro-Soviet, firsthand observations on what happened in Poland just after liberation toward the end of 1944 and at the beginning of 1945; contains information about the Lublin government.

IP150 STYPUŁKOWSKI, ZBIGNIEW. *W Zawierusze Dziejowej; Wspomnienia 1939-1945.* London: Gryf, 1951. 496 p. French ed., Paris: 1952. American eds., *Invitation to Moscow.* N.Y.: Thames, 1951; N.Y.: McKay, 1951. 359 p. An ex-member of the Polish Sejm and practicing lawyer in Warsaw, the author was one of the leaders of the Polish resistance movement against Nazi Germany and one of the 16 leaders of the Polish underground who were invited to Moscow for open negotiations and immediately arrested and then tried. A very intelligent presentation of his personal experiences and adventures during the Polish struggle against the Germans and Russians during World War II. An indictment of Soviet perfidy and brutality. [B]

IP151 SUPER, MARGARET L. (Ann Su Cardwell, pseud.). *The Case for Poland.* Ann Arbor, Mich.: 1945. 92 p. An American living in Poland 1922-39, who speaks and writes Polish, gives a pro-Polish general discussion of Polish problems during World War II, especially arising out of the Yalta decision. Based on secondary sources, the book has little value.

IP152 SYROP, KONRAD. *Spring in October; The Story of the Polish Revolution, 1956.* London: Weidenfeld & Nicolson, 1957. 207 p. N.Y.: Praeger, 1958. This very instructive story of the Gomulka October Revolution in 1956 includes many quotations from Polish newspapers, articles and speeches as well as a very full account of the VIII Plenum of the Central Committee of the Polish Communist Party. At the end there is a chronology of events. [A]

IP153 TAYLOR, JACK. *The Economic Development of Poland, 1939-1950.* Ithaca: Cornell; London: Oxford, 1952. 222 p. A study of economic planning, social reconstruction, and industrial development in Poland in the first years of the Communist regime. [B]

IP154 ULAM, ADAM B. *Titoism and the Cominform.* Cambridge: Harvard, 1952. 243 p. Includes a penetrating account of the fall of Gomulka and relations between the Soviet Union and Poland, although most of the book deals with Yugoslavia. [A]

IP155 UMIASTOWSKI, ROMAN. *Poland, Russia, and Great Britain, 1941-45; A Study of Evidence.* London: Hollis and Carter, 1946. 544 p. An analysis of British and Russian policies toward Poland during World War II, with emphasis on the diplomatic aspects.

IP156 WAGNER, STANLEY P. "The Diplomacy of the Polish Government in Exile, September 1939 to June 1945." Ph.D. dissertation, U. of Pittsburgh, 1953.

IP157 WÓJCICKI, B. *Prawda o Katyńiu.* Warsaw: Czytelnik, 1953. 218 p. An account and analysis of the evidence connected with the murder of Polish officers and civilians in Katyn forest, seeking to demonstrate German responsibility.

IP158 YAKEMTCHOUK, ROMAIN. *La Ligne Curzon et la IIe Guerre Mondiale.* Louvain: Éditions Nauwelaerts, 1957. 135 p. A thorough and well-documented discussion of the Curzon line, its defense and justification, by a professor of international law in Belgium. Told from the Ukrainian point of view, this work is based on primary sources and includes a bibliography.

IP158A ZAWODNY, J. K. *Death in the Forest; the Story of the Katyn Forest Massacre.* Notre Dame, Ind.: University of Notre Dame Press, 1962. 235 p.

IP159 ZINNER, PAUL E., ed. *National Communism and Popular Revolt in Eastern Europe; a Selection of Documents on Events in Poland and Hungary, February-November, 1956.* N.Y.: Columbia, 1956. 563 p. A collection of press articles, speeches, declarations, appeals, etc., concerning political events in Poland and Hungary in 1956. [B]

5. POLISH COMMUNIST PARTY

(Edited by M. K. Dziewanowski)

IP160 BRUN, JULIAN (BRUNOWICZ, JULIAN, pseud.). *Stefana Żeromskiego Tragedia Pomyłek.* Warsaw: 1924, and Warsaw: Książka i Wiedza, 1958. 131 p. A series of brilliant essays by a leading Polish Communist theoretician with unorthodox views of the "National Bolshevist" variety; the main thesis is that the relationship between the Polish and Soviet Communist Parties should be an alliance between the two national revolutions.

IP161 DZIEWANOWSKI, M. K. *The Communist Party of Poland; an Outline of History.* Cambridge: Harvard, 1959. 369 p. The first scholarly attempt to deal with the subject from the origins of the Communist Party of Poland through its transformations up to the middle of 1958. Based on both extensive research and personal observation. Contains a selected bibliography of twenty pages. [A]

IP162 GOMUŁKA, WŁADYSŁAW. *Statii i rechi.* Moscow: 1959. 375 p. Selected speeches and articles of the Polish Communist leader made after his return to power in 1956. [B]

IP163 GOMUŁKA, WŁADYSŁAW. *W Walce o Demokrację Ludową (artykuły i przemowienia).* Warsaw: "Książka," 1947. 2 vols. Collected speeches and articles of the Polish Communist leader made during the period of the German occupation and the Communist take-over. [B]

IP164 KOMUNISTYCZNA PARTIA POLSKI. *KPP w Obronie Niepodległosci Polski; Materiały i Dokumenty.* Warsaw: Książka i Wiedza, 1953. 419 p. Russian ed., Moscow: 1955. A careful selection of documents and press excerpts prepared and published by the Historical Section of the United Polish Workers' Party to prove that the Communist Party of Poland was a patriotic group defending Poland's independence against attempts of foreign capitalists. Some falsifications; see *Nowe drogi*, May 1956. [B]

IP165 KOMUNISTYCZNA PARTIA POLSKI. *Materiały do programu KPP.* Moscow: Wydawnictwo partyjne, 1933. 185 p. The minutes of the discussion held during the Sixth Congress of the Communist Party of Poland and the resulting project of the Party's program, with addition of amendments introduced by the Program Section of the Central Committee.

IP166 KOMUNISTYCZNA PARTIA POLSKI. *Sprawozdanie z III Konferencji KPRP.* Warsaw: 1922. Minutes of the Third Conference of the Communist Workers' Party of Poland of 1922, a steppingstone toward acceptance by the Party of the right of self-determination for all national groups.

IP167 KOMUNISTYCZNA PARTIA POLSKI. *Uchwaly i Rezolucje.* Warsaw: Książka i Wiedza, 1954-1956. 3 vols. A careful selection of statements and resolutions of the Communist Party of Poland, prepared by the Historical Section of the United Polish Workers' Party.

There are numerous omissions and falsifications; see J. Kowalski's article in *Nowe drogi*, May 1956; also *Trybuna ludu*, December 13, 1956, and February 15, 1957, and *Nowe drogi*, June 1956.

IP168 KOMUNISTYCZNA PARTIA POLSKI. *Uchwały II Zjazdu KPRP*. Warsaw: 1923. Minutes of the Second Congress of the Communist Workers' Party of Poland of 1923, momentous because of its acceptance of Polish statehood by the Party and on account of the final formulation of the slogan of "the national unification of the Ukrainians and Byelorussians with the Soviet Ukrainian and Byelorussian Republics."

IP169 KOMUNISTYCZNA PARTIA POLSKI. *Uchwały III Zjazdu KPP*. Warsaw: 1925. Resolutions of the Third Congress of the Communist Workers' Party of Poland of 1925, emphasizing Bolshevization of the Party, the right of national self-determination, including separation, and the necessity of preparing for an armed uprising.

IP170 KWIATKOWSKI, J. K. (REN, pseud.). *Komuniści w Polsce; Rodowód, Taktyka, Ludzie*. Brussels: Polski Instytut Wydawniczy, 1946. 123 p. A collection of essays, written under a pseudonym by a former leading member of the Polish anti-Communist underground, to prove the dependence of the Communist movement of Poland on the Soviet Union.

IP171 LEŃSKI, JULIAN. *O Front Ludowy w Polsce, 1934-1937; Publicystyka*. Warsaw: Książka i Wiedza, 1956. 308 p. A selection of articles and statements, made by a former leader of the Communist Party of Poland, advocating setting up a "Popular Front" in Poland; carefully edited by the Historical Section of the United Polish Workers' Party. Included is a biographical introduction.

IP172 POLSKA PARTIA ROBOTNICZA. *O co Walczymy? Deklaracja Programowa Polskiej Partii Robotniczej*. Warsaw: 1943. The ideological platform of the Polish Workers' Party issued during the German occupation of Poland; altered in 1945 and replaced in 1948 after the merger with the Polish Socialist Party and the setting up of the United Polish Workers' Party.

IP173 POLSKA PARTIA RABOTNICZA. *W Dziesiątą Rocznicę Powstania Polskiej Partii Robotniczej; Materiały i Dokumenty, Styczeń 1942 r.-Grudzień 1948 r*. Warsaw: Książka i Wiedza, 1952. 644 p. A selection of documents published by the United Polish Workers' Party on the tenth anniversary of the foundation of its predecessor, the Polish Workers' Party. Carefully edited by the Historical Section of the Party.

IP174 POLSKA ZJEDNOCZONA PARTIA ROBOTNICZA. *Deklaracja Ideowa PZPR; Statut PZPR*. Warsaw: Książka i Wiedza, 1949.

76 p. The platform and the rules of the United Polish Workers' Party as voted at its first Party Congress. Amended at the second and third Congresses in 1954 and 1959.

IP175 POLSKA ZJEDNOCZONA PARTIA ROBOTNICZA. *Statut, uchwalony przez II zjazd PZPR.* Warsaw: Książka i Wiedza, 1955. 122 p. The rules and regulations of the United Polish Workers' Party as recommended by the Second Party Congress of March 1954.

IP176 REGUŁA, JAN A. *Historia Komunistycznej Partii Polski w Świetle faktów i dokumentów.* Warsaw: Zakł. graf. Drukprasa, 1934. 343 p. An attempt to write a history of the Communist Party of Poland on the part of an investigating judge for political cases. Despite its obvious bias, the book is valuable because it contains a wealth of material in the form of long quotations from underground Communist publications and from minutes of Central Committee's meetings, some of them not published in the official selections issued by the Historical Section of the United Polish Workers' Party. [B]

IP177 SCAEVOLA (pseud.). *A Study in Forgery.* London: Rolls, 1945. 123 p. A story of the transformation of the Union of Polish Patriots in Moscow into the Polish Committee of National Liberation and, later on, into the Provisional Government of Poland; written on the basis of material collected by the Polish Government in London.

IP178 ŚWIATŁO, JÓZEF. *Za Kulisami Bezpieki i Partii.* N.Y.: 1955. An important pamphlet containing the revelations of a former high official of the Polish Secret Police ("Bezpieka"); solid and substantiated by facts, despite its sensational form. Also published in English in *News From Behind the Iron Curtain.* These revelations, when broadcast to Poland, helped further to discredit the Stalinist regime on the eve of Gomulka's return to power.

IP179 ZAMBROWSKI, ROMAN, and SWIĄTKOWSKI, HENRYK. *O Statucie i Zagadnieniach Organizacyjnych PZPR.* Warsaw: Książka i Wiedza, 1949. 94 p. An official commentary on the statute of the United Polish Workers' Party by two leading theoreticians of the Party.

a. PERIODICALS AND NEWSPAPERS ON POLISH COMMUNISM

IP180 *Czerwony Sztandar.* 1902-18, 1918-35. *The Red Banner*; the official press organ of the Central Committee of the Social Democratic Party of the Kingdom of Poland and Lithuania. Irregular, published at various places; legal in 1918, then published underground.

IP181 *Głos Ludu.* 1944-48. The main daily press organ of the Polish Workers' Party up to its merger with the Polish Socialist Party in December 1948. [B]

IP182 *Kultura.* Paris: 1948-60. A monthly review published by the Polish Literary Institute in Paris. Contains numerous articles and documents concerning Polish Communism and Russo-Polish relations. Five special issues, published in 1952 and 1953, are devoted entirely to these subjects; the issues were translated into English in a series of pamphlets. [A]

IP183 *Nowe Drogi.* Monthly, Warsaw: 1947-60. The main theoretical organ of the Central Committee of the Polish Workers' Party and the United Polish Workers' Party. Bi-monthly 1947-51, monthly since 1952. [A]

IP184 *Nowy Przeglad.* 1922-38. This was the main theoretical organ of the Communist Workers' Party of Poland and the Communist Party of Poland; disappeared with the Party's liquidation by Stalin during the Great Purge.

IP185 *Trybuna Ludu.* Warsaw: 1948–. The main daily press organ of the United Polish Workers' Party. [B]

Addenda

IP186 GOMULKA WLADYSLAW. *Przemowienia 1956-1959.* Warsaw: Ksiazka i Wiedza, 1964. 3 vols. A selection of the official pronouncements of the Polish Party boss.

IP187 HISCOCKS, RICHARD. *Poland, Bridge for the Abyss? An Interpretation of Developments in Post-War Poland.* London, New York: Oxford Univ. Press, 1963. 359 p. The author believes that Poland, a Communist country with a Western culture, may provide a point of contact, perhaps a bridge, between the two worlds.

IP188 KORBEL, JOSEPH. *Poland between East and West; Soviet and German Diplomacy toward Poland, 1919-1933.* Princeton, N.J.: Princeton University Press, 1963. 321 p. An important study by the Director of the Graduate School of International Studies at the University of Denver. [A]

IP189 U.S. CONGRESS, SENATE, COMMITTEE ON THE JUDICIARY. *Soviet Espionage through Poland. Hearing before the Subcommittee to Investigate the Administration of the Internal Security Act. . ., U.S. Senate, Eighty-Sixth Congress, Second Session. Testimony of Pawel Monat, June 13, 1960.* Washington: G.P.O., 1960. 41 p.

IQ. RUMANIA

EDITED BY STEPHEN FISCHER-GALATI

IQ1 ARNAUTU, NICOLAE I. *Douze invasions russes en Roumanie.* Buenos Aires: Éditions Cuget Romanesc, 1956. 190 p. A standard polemical account of Russian imperialism in the Rumanian provinces. Representative of the views of Rumanian exiles with strong anti-Russian and anti-Communist feelings.

IQ2 BISHOP, ROBERT, and CRAYFIELD, E. S. *Russia Astride the Balkans.* N.Y.: McBride, 1948. 287 p. A popular account of the Russian seizure of power in Rumania and the early Communization of the country. The authors, former U.S. intelligence agents, base their work largely on first-hand experiences. Certain sections are penetrating but, in general, the book lacks depth.

IQ3 BLAIRY, JEAN. *Crépuscule danubien.* Paris: Plon, 1946. 253 p. An uninspired popular account of conditions in Rumania and Yugoslavia at the end of World War II.

IQ4 BRAHAM, RANDOLPH (Abraham, Adolf). "The People's Republic of Rumania; A Study of its Genesis, Politics, and Government." Ph.D. dissertation, The New School for Social Research, 1952. A basic but rather shallow study by one of the able students of contemporary Rumanian problems. Based primarily on Rumanian sources. Excellent bibliography.

IQ5 CIUREA, ÉMILE C. *Le Traité de paix avec la Roumanie du 10 février 1947.* Paris: Pedone, 1954. 284 p. An excellent, fundamental study of the peace negotiations and of the peace treaty itself by one of the foremost students of Rumanian affairs. Based on extensive collections of primary sources and personal recollections. [B]

IQ6 CRETZIANU, ALEXANDRE. *The Lost Opportunity.* London: Cape; Toronto: Clarke, Irwin, 1957. 188 p. A critical account of the shortcomings of western policies in Eastern Europe in general and Rumania in particular, by an outstanding former Rumanian diplomat and political writer. Nationalistic plus anti-Russian and anti-Communist undertones detract from basically sound argumentation.

IQ7 CRETZIANU, ALEXANDRE, ed. *Captive Rumania; a Decade of Soviet Rule.* N.Y.: Praeger, 1956. 424 p. A lengthy symposium on the Sovietization of Rumania after World War II. The editor, vastly experienced in the conduct of Rumanian foreign affairs, does not hide his bias nor do the collaborators. Hence, the entire work has a strong émigré flavor. [B]

IQ8 FISCHER-GALATI, STEPHEN A., ed. *Romania.* N.Y.: Published for the Mid-European Studies Center of the Free Europe Committee by Praeger, 1957. 399 p. The most comprehensive symposium on the Sovietization of Rumania, by a group of American-trained students of Rumanian affairs. A long, annotated bibliography is included. [A]

IQ9 GAFENCU, GRIGORE. *Derniers Jours de l'Europe; un voyage diplomatique en 1939.* Paris: L.U.F., 1946. 252 p. English ed., *Last Days of Europe, a Diplomatic Journey in 1939.* New Haven: Yale, 1948. A profound analysis of European conditions on the eve of World War II by an outstanding Rumanian diplomat. The incidental pages devoted to Russo-Rumanian relations are excellent.

IQ10 GAFENCU, GRIGORE. *Prelude to the Russian Campaign, from the Moscow Pact (August 21, 1939) to the Opening of Hostilities in Russia (June 22, 1941).* London: F. Muller, 1945. 348 p. French ed., Paris: Egloff, 1945. German ed., Zurich: Amstutz, Herdeg, 1944. Italian ed., Milan: A. Mondadori, 1946. Spanish ed., Madrid: Morata, 1945. An outstanding contribution on the immediate origins of World War II by a former Rumanian Minister of Foreign Affairs and Ambassador to the USSR. The chapters devoted to Russo-Rumanian relations are exceptionally valuable, being based on personal experiences and judiciously set forth. [B]

IQ11 GEORGESCU-COSMOVICI, ADRIANA. *Au Commencement était la fin; la dictature rouge à Bucarest.* Paris: Hachette, 1951. 300 p. An indictment of Russian policies in Rumania after World War II by an unsympathetic observer. Based on author's personal experiences. Dramatic and moving, but of little scholarly value.

IQ12 GHEORGHE, ION. *Rumäniens Weg zum Satellitenstaat.* Wels, Austria: Welsermuhl, 1952. 444 p. A scholarly, objective study of the Sovietization of Rumania by an able student of Rumanian affairs. Inadequate documentation and bibliographical references detract from its overall quality.

IQ13 GRAUR, STEFAN ST. *Les Relations entre la Roumanie et l'URSS depuis le traité de Versailles.* Paris: A. Pedone, 1936. 164 p. A rather mediocre dissertation containing, however, valuable information on Russo-Rumanian relations in the inter-war years. This single, essentially comprehensive, monograph on the subject is based primarily on newspaper materials, despite the rather copious notes and bibliographical references.

IQ14 GURIAN, SORANA. *Les Mailles du filet; mon journal de Roumanie.* Paris: Calmann-Lévy, 1950. 376 p. Italian ed., *Per Aver*

Scelto il Silenzio. Florence: Sansoni, 1950. 421 p. An interesting personal account of the closing of the Soviet web around Rumania.

IQ15 HANGA, V. *Istoria statului si dreptului R.P.R.* Cluj: Universitatea "Victor Babes," 1954. 478 p. An attempt by a leading contemporary student of Rumanian law to legitimize the Communist regimé on the basis of legal and constitutional continuity. Valuable for students of recent Communist legislation and constitutionalism; otherwise, worthless in view of grave distortions of pre-Communist materials.

IQ16 KARRA, V. A. *Stroitelstvo sotsialisticheskoi ekonomiki v Rumynskoi Narodnoi Respublike.* Moscow: Izd. Akademii nauk SSSR, 1953. 216 p. An adequate survey of Rumanian economic development under Communism, based on Russian and Rumanian statistics. Tendentious interpretation of Rumanian economic policies and Russian assistance to Rumania detracts from its value.

IQ17 KING, WILLIAM B., and O'BRIEN, FRANK. *The Balkans; Frontier of Two Worlds.* N.Y.: Knopf, 1947. 278 p. An amateurish account of Rumanian conditions since World War II by two popularizers of Russo-Rumanian relations. No footnotes or bibliographic references.

IQ18 LEE, ARTHUR S. G. *Crown Against Sickle; The Story of King Michael of Rumania.* London: Hutchinson, 1950. 199 p. A sympathetic, pro-royalist account of ex-King Michael's struggle against Communism in Rumania by a retired British air vice-marshal. Of very limited scholarly value.

IQ19 LINDSAY, JACK, and CORNFORTH, MAURICE. *Rumanian Summer; a View of the Rumanian People's Republic.* London: Lawrence & Wishart, 1953. 152 p. A pro-Communist description of Rumanian conditions in the early fifties by two British sympathizers. No footnotes or bibliography but numerous photographs.

IQ20 MARKHAM, REUBEN H. *Rumania under the Soviet Yoke.* Boston: Meador, 1949. 601 p. A lengthy, polemical, strongly anti-Communist account of the seizure and early consolidation of Communist power in Rumania by an American newspaperman. Based on first hand experiences and observations. [B]

IQ21 MITRANY, DAVID. *The Land and the Peasant in Rumania; The War and Agrarian Reform (1917-21).* London: Carnegie Endowment for International Peace, 1930. 627 p. A scholarly account of Rumanian problems after World War I by an eminent authority. Problems of Russo-Rumanian relations are discussed in an incisive manner in conjunction with agrarian change. Excellent bibliographic references.

IQ22 MITRANY, DAVID. *Marx Against the Peasant; A Study in Social Dogmatism.* Chapel Hill, N.C.: U. of North Carolina Press; London: Weidenfeld & Nicolson, 1951. 301 p. Essentially peripheral in respect to Russo-Rumanian relations, this excellent study nevertheless includes valuable references to Communist influences in Rumania. Good bibliography. [B]

IQ23 MOT, GHEORGHE. *Contributii la istoria organizatiei marxist-leniniste de tineret din Romania.* Bucharest: Editura Tineretului, 1959–. An extensive selection of documents related to the rise and consolidation of the Union of Working Youth. Essential for the study of the subject despite the inane and biased introductory statements of the author. [B]

IQ24 PARTIDUL COMUNIST DIN ROMÎNIA. *Documente din istoria Partidului Comunist din Romînia.* Bucharest: Editura Partidului Muncitoresc Romîn, 1951. 375 p. 2nd ed., 1953. 404 p. Selected documents of Party history, stressing internal developments. Of limited value because of the exclusion of materials on important problems in the thirties and early forties.

IQ25 PARTIDUL COMUNIST DIN ROMÎNIA. *Documente din istoria Partidului Comunist din Romînia, 1923-1928.* Bucharest: 1953. 677 p. Essential for the student of Rumania, this limited collection emphasizes the internal affairs of the Rumanian Communist Party. An official compilation. [B]

IQ26 PARTIDUL MUNCITORESC ROMÎN. *Rezolutii si hotariri ale Comitetului Central al Partidului Muncitoresc Romîn.* Bucharest: Editura pentru Literatură Politică, 1952—. An essential collection of resolutions and decisions of the Party's Central Committee. The coverage, limited to principal documents, is incomplete. Students of Rumanian Communism must consult the press for a complete record of pronunciamentos.

IQ27 PARTIDUL MUNCITORESC ROMÎN. *30 let borby partii za sotsializm, za mir, za schaste rodiny, 1921-1951; k tridtsatiletiiu Kommunisticheskoi partii Rumynii.* Moscow: Izd. inostrannoi lit., 1951. 118 p. A propagandistic publication of very limited value. Representative of the meaningless routine statements issued periodically by the Rumanian Workers' Party propaganda machine, in this instance on Party activities between 1921 and 1951.

IQ28 PARTIDUL MUNCITORESC ROMÎN, COMITETUL CENTRAL, INSTITUTUL DE ISTORIE A PARTIDULUI. *Din istoricul formarii şi dezvoltarii clasei muncitoare din Romînia pina la Primul Razboi Mondial.* Ed. by N. N. Constantinescu. Bucharest: Editura Politică, 1959. 539 p. An invaluable documentary account. Explanatory statements, though biased, are also indispensable. The coverage is naturally selective, emphasizing anti-labor attitude of the government and collaboration between the working class and "progressive" peasantry. [B]

IQ29 PARTIDUL MUNCITORESC ROMÎN, COMITETUL CENTRAL, INSTITUTUL DE ISTORIE A PARTIDULUI. *Documente din istoria Partidului Comunist din Romînia.* Bucharest: Editura pentru Literatură Politică, 1953—. A compilation of selected documents dealing with the internal affairs of the Party. Limited coverage, yet invaluable for inter-war years. [B]

IQ30 PARTIDUL MUNCITORESC ROMÎN, COMITETUL CENTRAL, INSTITUTUL DE ISTORIE A PARTIDULUI. *Erinnerungen ehemaliger rumänischer Freiwilliger in der Roten Armee an die grosse sozialistische Oktoberrevolution und den Bürgerkrieg, 1917-1922.* Ed. by R. Deutsch. Bucharest: Staatsverlag für Politische Literatur, 1957. 320 p. Rumanian ed., Bucharest: Editura de Stat pentru Literatură Politică, 1957. 273 p. These "reminiscences," written by contemporary Party propagandists, are most entertaining because of their obvious naïveté and fraudulence. Interesting in terms of propaganda techniques but worthless otherwise.

IQ31 PARTIDUL MUNCITORESC ROMÎN, 2. CONGRESUL, BUCHAREST, 1955. *Congresul al II—lea al Partidului muncitoresc romîn, 23-28 decembrie, 1955.* Bucharest: Editura pentru Literatură Politică, 1956. 906 p. An exhaustive compilation of all documents presented and speeches made at the Second Congress of the Rumanian Workers' Party. Indispensable to the specialist. [A]

IQ32 PARTIDUL MUNCITORESC ROMÎN, 3. CONGRESUL, BUCHAREST, 1961. *III sezd Rumynskoi rabochei partii.* Moscow: Gospolitizdat, 1961. 240 p. A summary of activities of the Third Congress of the Rumanian Workers' Party, including leading speeches. Not nearly as valuable as the equivalent publication on the Second Party Congress. [B]

IQ33 PARTIDUL MUNCITORESC ROMÎN, INSTITUTUL DE ISTORIE A PARTIDULUI. *Din istoria luptelor greviste ale proletariatului din Romînia in ajutorul celor ce studiaza istoria P.M.R.* Bucharest: Editura consiliului Central al Sindicatelor, 1957. 306 p. A distorted, biased, scientifically unreliable history of Rumanian workers' strikes under "bourgeois" rule. Interesting only for students of propaganda techniques.

IQ34 PARTIDUL MUNCITORESC ROMÎN, INSTITUTUL DE ISTORIE A PARTIDULUI. *Documente din istoria Uniunii Tineretului*

Comunist din Romînia, 1917-1944. Bucharest: Editura Tineretului, 1958. 494 p. A valuable compilation despite its limited coverage. Reveals the great weakness of the Communist youth movement in the period covered. [B]

IQ35 PARTIDUL MUNCITORESC ROMÎN, INSTITUTUL DE ISTORIE A PARTIDULUI. *Zece ani de la conferința naționale a P.C.R., 1945-1955.* Bucharest: Ed. de stat pentru Literatură Politică, 1956. 278 p. A biased summary of achievements of the Rumanian Workers' Party in the decade 1945-55. Of no value to the student of Rumanian affairs, who must rely instead on the press.

IQ36 PATRASCANU, LUCRETIU D. *Sub trei dictaturi.* Bucharest: Forum, 1945. 256 p. French ed., *Sous trois dictatures.* Paris: J. Vitiano, 1946. 326 p. A masterful, powerful but tendentious analysis of Rumanian politics in the inter-war years and part of World War II. Patrascanu, the leading Communist theoretician of that period, was executed for anti-Party activities in the fifties. The book is therefore all the more valuable as an expression of the "liberal" Communist view. [A]

IQ37 PAVLOVICH, M., and RAFAIL, M. *Ocherki sovremennoi Rumynii.* Odessa: Gosizdat Ukrainy, 1925. 162 p. An unusually violent indictment of Rumanian politics by obviously biased and incompetent authors. Interesting for students of Russian Communism.

IQ38 PERSKII, K. K. *Nashi sosedi: Rumyniia.* Petrograd: "Mysl," 1923. 176 p. A popular diatribe against Rumania by an unfriendly Communist writer. Worthless except as a statement of the early Russian Communist position vis-à-vis a "hostile" neighbor.

IQ39 PETRESCU, C. TITEL. *Socialismul in Romînia.* Bucharest: 1945. 497 p. A penetrating, indispensable study of the rise and contemporary role of Rumanian socialism by the late leader of the Rumanian Socialist Party. Contains useful bibliographical notes, but is particularly valuable as the only authoritative source on the subject. [A]

IQ40 PROST, HENRI. *Destin de la Roumanie, 1918-1954.* Paris: Berger-Levrault, 1954. 279 p. An interesting interpretation of the factors leading to Rumania's downfall by a leading French observer of the Rumanian scene. Superficial in detail and, because of an essentially personal approach, of limited scholarly value.

IQ41 REESE, HOWARD C. "Russian-Rumanian Relations, 1944-1947." Ph.D. dissertation, New York University, 1961.

IQ42 RING, CAMIL. *Stalin m'a dit.* Paris: Creator, 1952. 236 p. Italian ed., *Stalin le Aveva Detto, Ma . . . ; Il Dramma di Anna Pauker.* Milan: Mondadori, 1953. Hearsay evidence of Stalin's plans for Rumania through the mouth of Anna Pauker and the pen of an ingenious Rumanian writer.

IQ43 ROBERTS, HENRY L. *Rumania; Political Problems of an Agrarian State.* New Haven: Yale, 1951. 414 p. An outstanding contribution to the study of Rumanian affairs by a leading authority. The scope of the work is broader than the title implies. Relations between Rumania and Russia, particularly problems of Communist influences in Rumania, are discussed with admirable insight. Excellent bibliography and highly informative footnotes add to the value of the work. [A]

IQ44 ROUMANIAN NATIONAL COMMITTEE. *Suppression of Human Rights in Roumania.* Washington: Roumanian National Committee, 1949. 163 p. A heavily documented indictment of Communist policies in postwar Rumania. An excellent compilation by the leading anti-Communist group in exile.

IQ45 SEICARU, PAMFIL. *Rien que des Cendres (Dotla).* Paris: Bonne, 1949. 313 p. Strongly anti-Communist analysis of the destruction of Rumania by well-known right-wing Rumanian journalist.

IQ46 SERBANESCO, DEMETER G. R. *Ciel rouge sur la Roumanie.* Paris: Sipuco, 1952. 309 p. 2nd ed., *Sous la botte soviëtique.* Paris: Éditions Internationales, 1957. A strongly anti-Communist account of the fall of Rumania and of Communist rule in that country by a Rumanian in France. The second edition emphasizes the author's lack of objectivity.

IQ47 SOCOR, MATEI. *Cintece muncitoresti revolutionare.* Bucharest: Editura Tineretului, 1957. 150 p. A collection of songs, many ludicrously artificial and propagandistic, compiled and edited by a leading composer and conductor. Essential for students of the Rumanian labor movement, revolutionary tradition and contemporary propaganda.

IQ48 SOFRONIE, GHEORGHE. *La Position internationale de la Roumanie.* Bucharest: Centre de Hautes Études Internationales, 1938. 162 p. An interesting discussion of Rumania's international position during the inter-war period by a professor of law at the University of Cluj. Russo-Rumanian relations are, however, peripheral to the author's main arguments.

IQ48A SPECTOR, SHERMAN DAVID. *Rumania at the Paris Peace Conference; a Study of the Diplomacy of Ioan I. C. Bratianu.* New York: Bookman Associates, 1962. 368 p. Includes a careful analysis of Russo-Rumanian relations between 1914 and 1920.

IQ49 SPIRU, BASIL. *Freiheit, die sie Meinen . . . Rumänien unter der eisernen Ferse der City und der Wallstreet (1918-1938).* Berlin:

Dietz, 1957. 294 p. A biased but valuable survey of Rumania's economic development in the inter-war years. Excellent statistical information. Published in East Berlin.

IQ50 TROTSKII, LEV, and RAKOVSKII, KHRISTIAN. *Ocherki politicheskoi Rumynii.* Moscow: Gosizdat, 1923. 169 p. A strong Communist statement, this interesting monograph is valuable not for its objectivity or historic merits, but as a sample of the views of its celebrated authors.

IQ51 *Y Existimos! Tres siglos de lucha del pueblo rumano contra el imperialismo moscovita.* Madrid: Comunidat de los Rumanos en España, 1953. 77 p. A polemical account of several aspects of the Rumanian struggle against Soviet imperialism. Of interest as an extreme statement by the strongest right-wing element of the Rumanian emigration groups in Europe.

1. COMMUNIST PARTY PERIODICALS AND NEWSPAPERS

IQ52 *Analele.* Bimonthly. 1956–. Indispensable for the study of Rumanian Communism. Articles, documents, and notes all emphasize internal Party history. Russian influence in Rumania, particularly the ideological contribution of Russian Communism to Rumanian Communists, is also included with amazing frequency. [B]

IQ53 *Lupta De Clasa.* Monthly theoretical organ of the Central Committee of the Rumanian Workers' Party. Bucharest, 19–. The main political periodical publication containing both theoretical articles and practical discourses on Communist matters, Rumanian and foreign. Indispensable for the serious student of Rumanian Communism. Original date of publication is unknown.

IQ54 *Scînteia.* Daily organ of the Central Committee of the Rumanian Workers' Party. Bucharest, 19–. The principal newspaper in Rumania. Essential for any systematic investigation of Party and government policies since World War II. Not available for prewar years. The exact date when it began publication is a debated point.

IQ55 *Scînteia Tineretului.* Daily organ of the Central Committee of the Union of Working Youth. Bucharest, 19–. A particularly significant newspaper as the principal publication of the Union of Working Youth. Most valuable for students of propaganda dissemination among Rumania's youth. Not available for prewar years. First date of publication uncertain.

2. BESSARABIAN QUESTION

IQ56 ALEKSANDRI, LEV N. *Bessarabiia i bessarabskii vopros.* Moscow: Gosizdat, 1924. 104 p. A brief historical account which lays the foundations for Russia's claims to repossession in terms of reason and tradition. Biased documentation and no bibliography.

IQ57 BABEL, ANTONY. *La Bessarabie: étude historique, ethnographique et économique.* Paris: Alcan, 1926. 360 p. A good survey, but contains little relevant material on Russo-Rumanian relations.

IQ58 BAERLEIN, H. *Bessarabia and Beyond.* London: Methuen, 1935. 278 p. A popular account of the Bessarabian question by an amateur historian. Of little value.

IQ59 BOLDUR, ALEXANDRU V. *La Bessarabie et les relations russo-roumaines; la question bessarabienne et le droit international.* Paris: J. Gamber, 1927. 410 p. A scholarly discussion of the legal and historic aspects of the Bessarabian question. The author, a Rumanian law professor, uses excellent legal documentation to present the Rumanian and Russian cases as impartially as possible. [A]

IQ60 CLARK, CHARLES U. *Bessarabia, Russia and Roumania on the Black Sea.* N.Y.: Dodd, 1927. 333 p. A justification through the use of the history of Rumanian rights to Bessarabia. A strong pro-Rumanian bias is augmented by the utilization of statements of Rumanian politicians as the documentary basis of the argument. A lengthy annotated bibliography includes mostly pro-Rumanian sources.

IQ61 GIURGEA, EUGENIU N. *Din Trecutul si Prezentul Basarabiei.* Bucharest: Bucovina, 1928. 176 p. A pro-Rumanian monograph emphasizing the righteousness of Rumanian possession of Bessarabia by a geologist with political interests. The chapters on Russo-Rumanian relations are interesting if not impartial.

IQ62 MILIUKOV, PAVEL N., ed. *The Case for Bessarabia; A Collection of Documents on the Rumanian Occupation.* 2nd ed., London: Russian Liberation Committee, 1919. 70 p. Interesting as a non-Communist statement of Russia's claims to Bessarabia. Although Miliukov's comments and editorship are valuable in themselves, the documents have no particular merit.

IQ63 NISTOR, ION. *Bessarabia and Bukovina.* Bucharest: Rumanian Academy, 1939. 56 p. A strong justification of Rumanian rights to Bessarabia and Bukovina as opposed to the claims of the USSR, by a former professor at the University of Cernauti.

IQ64 POPOVICI, ANDREI. *The Political Status of Bessarabia.* Washington: Ramsdell, 1931. 288 p. A rather lengthy doctoral dissertation by a Georgetown University Ph.D. of Rumanian origin. Of doubtful scholarly value because of its pronounced Rumanian bias, the work nevertheless contains several valuable chapters on post-World War I Russo-Rumanian relations. A valuable bibliography is appended. [B]

IQ65 RAKOVSKII, KHRISTIAN G. *Roumanie et Bessarabie.* Paris: Librairie du Travail, 1925. 75 p. English ed., London: 1925. Russian ed., Moscow: 1925. A polemical and strongly biased study by a leading Balkan Communist and official in Soviet Russia. The justification of Russia's claims to Bessarabia is weak and unsubstantiated by sources, footnotes, or bibliographic references. Of interest only to students of Rakovskii.

IQ66 *The Rumanian Occupation in Bessarabia: Documents.* Paris: Lahure, 1920. 211 p. Favorable to the Rumanian cause, this collection of documents is too selective to be used by the impartial scholar.

IQ67 SLUTSKAIA, K. *Pobeda Oktiabrskoi revoliutsii i ustanovlenie sovetskoi vlasti v Moldavii.* Kishinev: Kartia Moldoveniaske, 1962. 300 p. An exceptionally valuable study on Bolshevik policies in Bessarabia between March 1917 and March 1918. Based on generally inaccessible Russian and Bessarabian sources.

IQ68 UHLIG, CARL L. G. *Die bessarabische Frage; eine geopolitische Betrachtung.* Breslau: F. Hirt, 1926. 107 p. A valuable geopolitical analysis of Bessarabian problems by a professor of geography at the University of Tübingen. Written in the best tradition of German scholarship. [B]

IR. SCANDINAVIA

EDITED BY ALBIN T. ANDERSON

IR1 ANDERSSON, GUSTAV. *Från bondetåget till Samlingsregeringen; Politiska minnen.* Stockholm: Tidens, 1955. 331 p. Memoirs of a Liberal cabinet minister in the Swedish wartime coalition government, 1939-44. An important supplement to the memoirs of Wigforss. [B]

IR2 BEKSTREM, K. *Rabochee dvizhenie v Shvetsii.* Moscow: Izd. inostr. lit., 1961.

IR3 COMMUNIST INTERNATIONAL. *Die Kommunistischen Parteien Skandinaviens und die Kommunistische Internationale; die Aussprache mit den Skandinavischen Genossen über die Grenzen des Zentralismus in der Konferenz der Erweiterten Exekutive der Kommunistischen Internationale Moskau, 12-23 Juni 1923.* Hamburg: C. Hoym Nachf., 1923. 193 p.

IR4 GIHL, TORSTEN. *Den svenska Utrikespolitikens Historia.* Stockholm: Norstedt, 1951. Vol. IV, 1914-1919. The fourth of a 5-volume series on Swedish foreign relations written by scholars. Covers wartime difficulties and evaluates briefly the imbalance of power in the North brought on by the Russian Revolution, Finnish independence, and German defeat. The author utilized Foreign Ministry archives. [A]

IR5 HARPE, WERNER VON. *Die Sowjetunion, Finnland, und Skandinavien, 1945-1955; zwei Berichte zu den Internationalen Beziehungen der Nachkriegszeit.* Cologne: Böhlau, 1956. 66 p. An incisive and objective analysis of the impact of Soviet foreign policy in the North after World War II. [B]

IR6 HORNBORG, EIRIK. *Sverige och Ryssland genom tiderna; Politiska relationer och krigiska konflikter.* 1st ed., Stockholm: Natur och Kultur, 1941. 2nd ed., Helsinki: H. Schildt, 1942. 144 p. Primarily pre-1917, but also a competent summary of Russo-Swedish relations by a long-time Finno-Swede observer, statesman, and scholar.

IR7 KILBOM, KARL. *Ur mitt Livs Aventyr.* Stockholm: Tidens, 1953-1955. 3 vols. Memoirs by a Swedish journalist who left the Party in the 1930's. Contains items of personal and political importance on Communism in the North—especially in Sweden—until after World War II. Stockholm is portrayed as a Bolshevik contact point, both before and after the Revolution.

IR8 KOHT, HALVDAN. *Norsk Utanrikspolitik fram til 9 april 1940.* Oslo: Tidens, 1947. 82 p. One of Norway's most prolific scholars, who was foreign minister in 1939, summarizes Norway's pre-war efforts to remain neutral in the diplomatic struggle of the Big Powers.

IR9 LINDH, NILS J. B. *Möten mellan Öst och Väst; studier i samtida rysk utrikes-politik.* Stockholm: Kooperativa förbundets bokförlag, 1949. 330 p.

IR10 LÖNNROTH, ERIK. *Den svenska Utrikespolitikens Historia.* Vol. v, 1919-1939. Stockholm: Norstedt, 1959. The final volume in this important series, it is most important for Soviet relations with the North during the period of the Aaland Islands dispute in the early 1920's. [A]

IR11 MEURLING, PER. *Kommunismen i Sverige.* Stockholm: Wahlström and Widstrand, 1950. 229 p. An insight into 30 years of Communist Party activity in Sweden by one who hopped off the bandwagon in the late 1940's. Important for his personality sketches of the leading Swedish Communists. [A]

IR12 MONTGOMERY, ARTHUR. *Ryssland och vår Utrikespolitik.* Stockholm: Skoglund, 1949. 210 p. A reprint of newspaper articles written by an economist who is a Swedish specialist on Soviet affairs. Examines the impact of Soviet policies upon Swedish political and economic policy in an objective, analytical manner.

IR13 NERMAN, TURE. *Kommunisterna från Komintern till Kominform.* Stockholm: Tidens, 1949. 280 p. Half of the book is devoted to the Comintern; the remainder to the Cominform and to a short history of the Swedish Communist Party.

IR14 NERMAN, TURE. *Svensk och Ryss, ett Umgänge i krig och handel.* Stockholm: Saxon & Lindström, 1946. 367 p. A Swedish writer, literary critic, and political liberal examines Swedish relations with tsarist and Soviet Russia, emphasizing the economic ties that have bound, and the ideological issues that have separated, the two countries.

IR15 PALMSTIERNA, ERIK. *Dagjämningen 1920-1921; Politiska Dagboksanteckningar.* Stockholm: Tidens, 1954. 248 p. A continuation of his two volumes of memoirs entitled *Orostid* (see below). Important. [B]

IR16 PALMSTIERNA, ERIK. *Orostid: Politiska Dagboksanteckningar.* Stockholm: Tidens, 1952-1953. 2 vols. Important memoirs by the foreign minister in Branting's first Social Democratic government in Sweden, who served later as a Swedish diplomat. Covers the period of the First World War with frequent references to problems posed by an emergent, dynamic Soviet state, including its effect upon Finno-Swedish relations. [B]

IR17 PANTENBURG, VITALIS. *Russlands Griff um Nordeuropa.* Leipzig: Schwarzhaupter, 1938. 171 p. A German geopolitician's view of the strategic dangers posed for the Northern countries by the size, resources and dynamic policy of the Soviet Union. The facts are sometimes impressive even when used for frequent far-fetched conclusions. Significant as a summary of what German geopoliticians and a few pro-Nazi Scandinavians believed, or professed to believe in the 1930's.

IR18 QUISLING, VIDKUN. *Russia and Ourselves.* London: Hodder and Stoughton, 1931. 284 p. Norwegian ed., Oslo: Blix, 1941. 201 p. German ed., Oslo: Blix, 1942. 227 p. Urges an alliance between Britain and Scandinavia directed against Bolshevism. Written by the Norwegian Nazi who later betrayed his country and thereby coined the word "quisling."

IR19 LA RUCHE, FRANCIS. *La Neutralité de la Suède; dix années d'une politique, 1939-1949.* Paris: Nouvelles éditions latines, 1953. 223 p. The position and policy of Sweden during World War II, particularly in respect to Finland, Norway, and Germany.

IR20 RYSAKOV, P. *Monopolii SShA i strany Severnoi Evropy.* Moscow: Gospolitizdat, 1956. 296 p. A polemic against U.S. intervention in northern Europe through the Marshall Plan and NATO, and an indictment of monopolistic "lackeys" in Scandinavia, with bouquets for the peace-loving Scandinavians who have protested against the action of their governments. Important as a revelation of the official Soviet position vis-à-vis Scandinavia (and Finland).

IR21 SCHMIDT, ERIK I. *30 Aars Kommunistisk Politik i Rusland og Vesteuropa; Gennemgang og Kritik.* Copenhagen: Munksgaard, 1948. 286 p. This survey of European Communism includes a special chapter on the Danish Communist Party.

IR22 SEGALL, IA. *Rabochee dvizhenie v skandinavskikh stranakh; (Shvetsiia, Daniia, Norvegiia).* Moscow: Profintern, 1927. 299 p. A Communist view of the labor movement in Sweden, Denmark and Norway.

IR23 SJOEBERG, VALENTIN. *Der Angriff auf die Flanke der Welt.* Foreword by J. F. C. Fuller. Berlin: Nibelungen, 1942. 236 p. Swedish ed., Stockholm: Fahlcrantz and Gumaelius, 1942. 274 p. A long-time political and military commentator for the Swedish right-wing newspaper *Aftonbladet* evaluates Soviet policy in the Northland and concludes that only Germany can provide the necessary countervailing force against Communist expansion, at the same time providing a bastion for Western civilization. Cf. Pantenburg's *Russlands Griff um Nordeuropa* (above).

IR24 SVERGES KOMMUNISTISKA PARTI. *Nutid, framtid; arbetarrörelsens programdebatt.* Stockholm: Arbetarkultur, 1957. 164 p. Seven Marxist essays on Swedish economics, politics, and social questions. That by Per-Olov Zennström, "Rīksdag och folkmakt," gives an indication of the political techniques and goals of the Swedish Communist Party.

IR25 SVERGES KOMMUNISTISKA PARTI, KONGRESS, 18TH, STOCKHOLM, 1957. *XVIII sezd Kommunisticheskoi partii Shvetsii, Stokgolm, 28-31 dekabria, 1952 g.; vazhneishie materialy.* Moscow: Gospolitizdat, 1959. 142 p. Official speeches and resolutions of the Swedish C.P. Congress in 1957 conveniently summarizing the party's internal and external policies, especially important being Hilding Hagberg's, "New Times—New Tasks." Includes a list of members and candidates of the Central Committee.

IR26 SWEDEN, UTRIKESDEPARTEMENTET. *Documents on Swedish Foreign Policy.* Stockholm: Norstedt, 1957-1959. 7 vols. A convenient collection of official statements and various communications which the Swedish government has had with other powers, including the USSR, in the period from 1950-57.

IR27 TINGSTEN, HERBERT L. G. *The Debate on the Foreign Policy of Sweden, 1918-1939.* London: Oxford, 1949. 324 p. Swedish ed., Stockholm: 1944. A valuable compilation of speeches by Swedish statesmen, parliamentary debates on foreign policy, and other public (including newspaper) discussion which has been skillfully woven together by Professor Tingsten's connective commentary. The author was the editor-in-chief of *Dagens Nyheter*, Sweden's largest liberal newspaper.
[B]

IR28 UTRIKESPOLITISKA INSTITUTET, STOCKHOLM. *Svensk Utrikespolitik under andra Världskriget; Statsrådstal, Riksdagsdebatter och Kommunikér.* Stockholm: Kooperativa förbundets bokförlag, 1946. 652 p. A collection of documents, statements, and debates which reflect Swedish foreign policy during World War II.

IR29 WIGFORSS, ERNST J. *Minnen.* Stockholm: Tidens, 1954. 3 vols. These memoirs antedate World War I and go beyond World War II. Volumes II and III provide rare insights, on occasion, into Swedish policy vis-à-vis the Soviet Union. By an outstanding Social Democrat and member of the government who was privy to all major decisions.
[A]

IS. SPAIN AND THE SPANISH CIVIL WAR

EDITED BY DAVID T. CATTELL AND STANLEY G. PAYNE

IS1 AKSANOV, EVGENII A. *Portugaliia i ee rol v fashistskoi interventsii v Ispanii.* Moscow: Sotsekgiz, 1937. 118 p. The Soviet Union considered Portugal to be the primary agent and channel of German and Italian aid to the Nationalist rebels. This volume allegedly proves the complete complicity of the Salazar regime.

IS2 ALLEN, DAVID E., JR. "The Soviet Union and the Spanish Civil War, 1936-1939." Ph.D. dissertation, Stanford, 1952. An unbiased analysis of the role of the Soviet Union in the Spanish Civil War, making use of the sources of the Hoover Library.

IS3 ÁLVAREZ DEL VAYO, JULIO. *Freedom's Battle.* London: Heinemann, 1940. 367 p. N.Y.: Knopf, 1940. 389 p. By a prominent figure in the Spanish Republic who became Foreign Minister during the Civil War, and was active in trying to get the Western democracies to aid the Loyalist cause. [B]

IS4 ALVAREZ DEL VAYO, JULIO. *The Last Optimist.* N.Y.: Viking, 1950. 405 p. Memoirs of the Foreign Minister of the Spanish Republic during the Civil War.

IS5 ARAQUISTÁIN, LUIS. *El comunismo y la guerra en España.* Carmaux: 1939. A discussion of the role of Communism in the Spanish Civil War, by one of the principal leaders of the Spanish Left Socialists. [B]

IS6 ARAQUISTÁIN, LUIS. *Mis tratos con los comunistas.* Toulouse: 1939. The author here gives his version of his personal dealings with the Communists while a Left Socialist leader during the Spanish Civil War. This volume and the book above are to some extent repetitious; each provides useful information.

IS7 BARDOUX, JACQUES. *Chaos in Spain.* London: Burns, Oates, and Washbourne, 1937. 56 p. This pamphlet represents the French right-wing view of events in Spain. The author claims to have discovered various Communist plots throughout Western Europe during the 1930's.

IS8 BELFORTE, FRANCESCO. *La Guerra Civile in Spagna; gli interventi stranieri nella Spagna rossa.* Rome: Istituto per gli Studi di Politica Internazionale, 1938-39. 4 vols. This semi-official account of the Fascist Government of Italy alleges that the Spanish Civil War was caused by a Communist plot to set up a Soviet satellite in Spain.

IS9 BERLIN, INSTITUT FÜR MARXISMUS-LENINISMUS. *Der Freiheitskampf des spanischen Volkes und die internationale Solidäritat; Dokumente und Bilder zum nationalrevolutionären Krieg des spanischen Volkes 1936-1939.* Berlin: Dietz, 1956. 481 p. A collection of interviews, documents and official declarations of various sections of the Third International during the Spanish war, drawn mainly from the Spanish and German Communist parties. Valuable chiefly as a propaganda sampling.

IS10 BILAINKIN, GEORGE. *Maisky, Ten Years Ambassador.* London: Allen and Unwin, 1944. 400 p. Maisky was the Soviet representative on the Non-Intervention Committee in London. This is a sympathetic biography of his attempts to cooperate with the British and French governments against the Nazis and Fascists.

IS11 BLUM, LEON. *L'Histoire jugera.* Montreal: Editions de l'arbre, 1943. 335 p. In this volume Blum tried to explain and justify why he took such a neutral attitude toward the Spanish Civil War in spite of his overwhelming sympathy for the Loyalists. [B]

IS12 BOLLOTEN, BURNETT. *The Grand Camouflage; the Communist Conspiracy in the Spanish Civil War.* N.Y.: Praeger, 1961. 350 p. A heavily documented account of Communist and Anarchist politics in Republican Spain, 1936-37. Poorly organized and unbalanced, it nonetheless provides valuable detail. The author is a former Welsh journalist, who spent years collecting original material. [A]

IS13 BORKENAU, FRANZ. *The Spanish Cockpit.* London: Faber, 1937. 303 p. Borkenau, a recognized authority on International Communism, went to Loyalist Spain in 1937, and this is a report of his travels. It must be ranked as one of the three or four best contemporary studies of the Civil War. [B]

IS14 BOWERS, CLAUDE G. *My Mission to Spain; Watching the Rehearsal for World War II.* N.Y.: Simon and Schuster, 1954. 437 p. Mr. Bowers, U.S. Ambassador to Republican Spain from 1933 to the end of the Civil War, was a passionate supporter of the Loyalists and tended to discount the role played by Moscow in influencing the policies of the Loyalist Government. The book is not well documented.

IS15 BREEN, JOHN M. "The Russian Attempt to Control Spain, 1946." Ph.D. dissertation, Georgetown, 1953. 277 p. There is useful material in this dissertation on Soviet-Spanish relations, 1945-46, yet the work, on the whole, is strongly slanted and misleading because of the author's almost total inability to distinguish between Communists and Anarchists.

IS16 BRENAN, GERALD. *The Spanish Labyrinth; an Account of the Social and Political Background of the Civil War.* London: Cambridge; N.Y.: Macmillan, 1943. 584 p. 2nd ed., London: Cambridge, 1950. An excellent analysis of the social and political issues and groups leading up to the Civil War. It is particularly good on the laboring class groups which participated in the struggle, including the Communists.

IS17 BROUÉ, PIERRE, and TÉMIME, EMILE. *La Révolution et la Guerre d'Espagne.* Paris: Éditions de Minuit, 1961. 542 p. A good general account of the Spanish Civil War by two French historians. Describes the origins of Spanish Communism and also of Anarchist-Communist relations. [B]

IS18 CANOVAS CERVANTES, S. *De Franco a Negrin pasando por el Partido Comunista; historia de la Revolución Espanola.* Toulouse: "Paginas Libres," n.d. Written after the end of the Civil War in Spain, this work presents the Anarchist view of the betrayal of the Spanish revolution and civil war by the USSR and the Communists. [A]

IS19 CASADO, SEGISMUNDO. *The Last Days of Madrid.* London: Davies, 1939. 302 p. Colonel Casado headed the Central Army of the Republic during the last days of the Civil War and led the coup against the Negrin Government which was seeking to fight on. He describes in detail the end of the regime and the attempts by Negrin and the Communists to keep the war going. [B]

IS20 CASTRO DELGADO, ENRIQUE (Delgardo, Enrique Castro). *La vida secreta de la Komintern.* Madrid: E.P.E.S.A., 1950. 419 p. French ed., *J'ai perdu la foi à Moscou.* Paris: Gallimard, 1950. The most authoritative edition is *Mi fe se perdió en Moscú.* Mexico: Editorial Horizontes, 1951. 351 p. A disillusioned Spanish Communist leader's account of the life of the Spanish Communist Party in exile in the Soviet Union through the mid-1940's. Contains some valuable information and is fairly objective. [B]

IS21 CATTELL, DAVID T. *Communism and the Spanish Civil War.* Berkeley: U. of California, 1955. 290 p. This study, based on a wide range of source materials, is an analysis of the amount of Soviet contributions to the Loyalist cause and the influence of the Spanish Communists and Soviet agents on the Republican Government. [A]

IS22 CATTELL, DAVID T. *Soviet Diplomacy and the Spanish Civil War.* Berkeley: U. of California, 1957. 204 p. The thesis of this study is that the frustrations of the Soviet Union in its diplomatic attempts during the Spanish Civil War was an important factor in turning Stalin toward an alliance with Hitler. The study is based on the documents of the Non-Intervention Committee and of the Italian, German, British, and United States Governments. [A]

IS23 CHURCHILL, WINSTON S. *Step by Step, 1936-1939.* London: Butterworth, 1939. 365 p. N.Y.: Putnam, 1939. 324 p. A collection of letters and statements criticizing the foreign policy being pursued by the British Government. In respect to Spain he is critical of the policies of both the Communists and the democracies.

IS24 COLODNY, ROBERT G. *The Struggle for Madrid; the Central Epic of the Spanish Conflict, 1936-1937.* N.Y.: Paine-Whitman, 1958. 256 p. A detailed account of the fighting around Madrid in 1936-37, which spotlights the role of the Communists and the International Brigades. The author is a Brigade veteran. [A]

IS25 DASHEVSKII, G. *Fashistskaia piataia kolonna v Ispanii.* Moscow: Voenizdat, 1938. 112 p. A Soviet analysis of the Nazi infiltration and control of Spain, beginning even before the Civil War. [A]

IS26 DÍAZ, JOSÉ. *Lessons of the Spanish War, 1936-1939.* London: Modern Books, 1940. This volume of speeches of José Díaz, head of the Spanish Communist Party, was translated into several languages, including Russian, and represents the official Communist interpretation of the Civil War at this time. [A]

IS27 ERENBURG, ILIA G. *Estampas de España.* Madrid: Ediciones S.R.I., 1937. A leading Soviet writer's account of his visit to the fronts during the Civil War. Editions appeared in several languages.

IS28 ESCH, PATRICIA A. M., VAN DER. *Prelude to War; The International Repercussions of the Spanish Civil War, 1936-1939.* The Hague: Martinus Nijhoff, 1951. 190 p. One of the first postwar studies of the diplomatic crisis created by the Spanish Civil War, based on the newly released German Foreign Office archives and a scattering of documentation from Italy and Great Britain. Highly critical of the French and British governments. [B]

IS29 FABIÁN, E. *Sprísahanie proti Španielskej republike, 1936-1939.* Bratislava: S.V.P.L., 1961. 192 p. An account, based partly on unpublished documents, of the Spanish Civil War, with emphasis on the relevant activities of the Comintern and the Soviet Union on the one hand, and the capitalist world on the other hand. Glorifies Communist policy.

IS30 FISCHER, LOUIS. *Men and Politics; an Autobiography.* N.Y.: Duell, Sloan and Pearce, 1941. 672 p. Fischer had close personal contact during the Spanish Civil War with both the Loyalist and Russian leaders. His sympathies were pro-Loyalist, and his insights into the events at the time are useful in understanding Communist politics in Spain. [B]

IS31 FOSS, WILLIAM, and GERAHTY, CECIL. *The Spanish Arena.* London: Gifford, 1938? 515 p. The introduction to this work is by the Duke of Alba, which makes it more or less the official version of the conservative groups supporting Franco during the Civil War.

IS32 GANNES, HARRY, and REPARD, THEODORE. *Spain in Revolt.* London and N.Y.: Knopf, 1936. 235 p. A discussion of the formation of the Popular Front in Spain from the Communist point of view, by a leader of the British Communist Party.

IS33 GARCÍA, JOSÉ. *Ispaniia Narodnogo Fronta.* Moscow: Izd. Akademii nauk SSSR, 1957. 246 p. The current official Communist view of the Spanish Civil War.

IS34 GARCÍA, JOSÉ. *Ispanskii narod v borbe za svobodu i demokratiiu protiv fashizma, 1931-1939.* Moscow: Gospolitizdat, 1956. 200 p.

IS35 GARCÍA PRADAS, J. *Cómo terminó la guerra de España.* Buenos Aires: Ediciones Imán, 1940. 156 p. An anarchist's criticism of the role played by Soviet agents and Communists in the Civil War.

IS36 GARCÍA VENERO, MAXIMIANO. *Historia de las Internacionales en España.* Madrid: Ediciones del Movimiento, 1956-57. 3 vols. An informative but very unfriendly general account of the working class movement in modern Spain, written by a leading Spanish journalist and historian. Sheds some light on the origins of Spanish Communism. [B]

IS37 GELBRAS, P. *Vneshniaia i vnutrenniaia politika Frantsii.* Moscow: Gospolitizdat, 1939. 175 p. This volume on French foreign policy in the 1930's has a large section on the Spanish Civil War and is critical of the indecisive and weak policies of the French Government toward Spain. [B]

IS38 GEORGIEVSKII, GEORGII K. "Zolotoi zapas Ispanii v SSSR v obmen na oruzhii, boepripaci, stratecheskie materiali i prodovolstvie." N.Y.: Research Program on the USSR, 1953. (Manuscript.) A former Soviet citizen reports from his own experience on the fate of the Spanish gold which the Nationalists alleged had been sent to Russia for safekeeping and never returned.

IS39 GERMANY, AUSWÄRTIGES AMT. *Documents on German Foreign Policy, 1918-1945*, Ser. D., vol. III, *Germany and the Spanish Civil War, 1936-1939.* Ed. by R. J. Sontag and others. Washington: G.P.O., 1950. A comprehensive collection of documents from the German Foreign Office in relation to its participation in and negotiations concerning the Spanish Civil War.

IS40 GERMANY, AUSWÄRTIGES AMT. *Dokumenti.* Vol. III: *Germanskaia politika i Ispania (1936-1943 gg.)*. Moscow: Gospolitizdat, 1946. These documents were published by the Soviet Union from the archives of the German Foreign Office captured by the Soviet Army. The contents differ little from those published by the United States.

IS41 GODDEN, GERTRUDE M. *Conflict in Spain, 1920-1937.* London: Burns, Oates and Washbourne, 1937. 112 p. Of all the works published by conservative groups during the Spanish Civil War on Communist Activities in Spain, this is one of the best documented and argued.

IS42 GÓMEZ GORKIN, JULIÁN. *Canibales políticos, Hitler y Stalin en España.* México City: Ediciones "Guetsal," 1941. 351 p. A description of the role of the Gestapo and the GPU in Spain as seen by the Secretary-General of the POUM, a dissident Communist group. He alleges complicity between Hitler and Stalin in Spain before 1939. [A]

IS43 GONZALEZ, VALENTIN R. ("El Campesino," pseud.). *Comunista en España y antistalinista en la U.R.S.S.* México City: Editorial Guarania, 1952. 137 p. Valentin Gonzalez was a general in the Communist brigades of the Loyalist army. At the end of the Civil War he went to Russia and later defected. He gives the appearance of being a colorful adventurer, but his stories are difficult to verify.

IS44 GONZALEZ, VALENTIN R. *La Vida y la muerte en la URSS.* Ed. by Julian Gorkin. Mexico City: Ediciones Avante, 1951. 216 p. French ed., Paris: Plon, 1950. 220 p. English ed., *El Campesino: Life and Death in Soviet Russia.* N.Y.: Putnam, 1952. 218 p. Highly colored memoirs of the years spent in the Soviet Union by a Spanish Communist general.

IS45 GOROZHANKINA, NADEZHDA. *Rabochii klass Ispanii v gody revoliutsii.* Ed. by L. Geller. Moscow: Sotsekgiz, 1936. 117 p.

IS46 HÉRICOURT, PIERRE. *Arms for Red Spain.* London: Burns, Oates, and Washbourne, 1938. 64 p. A leading spokesman of the French right "proves" the source of the large amount of aid received by the Spanish Loyalists from abroad.

IS47 HERNÁNDEZ, JESÚS. *Yo, Ministro de Stalin en España.* Madrid: NOS, 1954. 447 p. Mexico City: Editorial America, 1953. 365 p. French ed., *La Grande Trahison.* Paris: Fasquelle, 1953. 254 p. Jesús Hernández was a Minister in the Loyalist Government and a leader of the Spanish Communist Party who went to Russia at the end of the Civil War but later defected. His memoirs provide an interesting insight into Communist and Soviet operations in Spain. [A]

IS48 IBARRURI, DOLORES. *Informe del Comité Central al V Congreso del P. C. de España.* Nice: 1954. 125 p. Official report of the Spanish Communist Party's Central Committee, 1954. [A]

IS49 IBARRURI, DOLORES. *Speeches and Articles, 1936-1938.* London: Lawrence and Wishart, 1938. 263 p. Dolores Ibarruri was one of the leaders of the Spanish Communist Party, particularly known for her impassioned speeches. At the end of the Civil War she escaped to Russia where she has continued to work on behalf of the Spanish Communist Party.

IS50 *Ispanskaia kompartiia boretsia za pobedu; sbornik materialov.* Moscow: Sotsekgiz, 1938. 179 p. A comprehensive collection of materials on the Spanish Communist Party, brought together from various sources.

IS51 IVASHIN, I. F. *Mezhdunarodnye otnosheniia i vneshniaia politika Sovetskogo Soiuza v 1935-1939 gg.* Moscow: Vysshaia partiinaia shkola pri TsK KPSS, 1955. 66 p. This postwar study of Soviet international relations was one of the first works to report that "the Soviet Union rendered to Republican Spain not only moral and diplomatic aid but also material and military support." [B]

IS52 JELLINEK, FRANK. *The Civil War in Spain.* London: Gollancz, 1938. 637 p. The most comprehensive account of the Civil War from the pro-Communist point of view.

IS53 KRIVITSKY, WALTER. *In Stalin's Secret Service.* N.Y.: Harper, 1939. 273 p. A former high-ranking officer in the GPU describes the methods used by the Soviet Union to collect and smuggle arms into Spain and the role of the GPU in Spain. [B]

IS54 LANDAU, KATIA. *Le Stalinisme en Espagne.* Paris: 1938. An indictment of the Communist terror against the POUM and the Anarchists which cites specific cases.

IS55 LITVINOV, MAKSIM M. *Protiv aggressii.* Moscow: Gospolitizdat, 1938. 111 p. English eds., *Against Aggression.* N.Y.: International Publishers, 1939; London: Lawrence and Wishart, 1939. Spanish ed., Havana: Editorial "Paginas," 1942. Contains Litvinov's speeches before the League of Nations in which he staunchly defends the Loyalist Government.

IS56 LONGO, LUIGI. *Le Brigate internazionali in Spagna.* Rome: Editori riunita, 1956. Russian ed., Moscow: 1960. 383 p. An extremely biased but sometimes informative account, by a man who served in an important post in the International Brigades, and later became one of the principal leaders of the Italian Communist Party during the 1940's and 50's, before becoming chief of the Party in 1964.

IS57 LOW, MARY, and BREA, JUAN. *Red Spanish Notebook.* London: Secker and Warburg, 1937. 256 p. The first six months of the revolution and Civil War in Spain as viewed by Trotskyites.

IS58 MAIDANIK, K. L. *Ispanskii proletariat v natsionalno-revoliutsionnoi voine, 1936-1937 gg.* Moscow: Akad. nauk SSSR, 1960. 383 p.

IS59 MATORRAS, ENRIQUE. *El Comunismo en España; Sus orientaciones—su organizacion—sus procedimientos.* Madrid: No publisher, 1935. 187 p. An excellent analysis and record of Spanish Communism, 1931-34, by the former Secretary of the Central Committee of the Spanish Communist Youth. A fundamental source for the history of Spanish Communism in this period. [A]

IS60 MC GOVERN, JOHN. *Terror in Spain; How the Communist International has Destroyed Working Class Unity, Undermined the Fight Against Franco, and Suppressed the Socialist Revolution.* London: Independent Labour Party, 1938? 14 p.

IS61 MINLOS, B. *Ispanskaia revoliutsiia.* Moscow: Izd. Mezhdunarodnogo agrarnogo instituta, 1931. 108 p.

IS62 MIRALLES, RAFAEL. *Españoles en Rusia.* Madrid: Ediciones y Publicaciones Hispañolas, 1947. 241 p. A bitterly disenchanted account of life in the USSR by an ex-Spanish Communist, based on his personal experience as a Cuban diplomat in Moscow, 1945-46. Contains some additional information on the Spanish Communists during World War II.

IS63 MORENO HERNANDEZ, RAMÓN. *Rusia al Desnudo: Revalaciones del Comisario Comunista Español Rafael Pelayo de Hungria, Comandante del Ejército Ruso.* Madrid: Mundial, 1956. 406 p. Memoirs of a disillusioned ex-Communist leader. Highly subjective, but sheds some light on Spanish Communist Party relations inside the Soviet Union.

IS64 MORROW, FELIX (pseud.). *Revolution and Counter-Revolution in Spain.* N.Y.: Pioneer, 1938. 202 p. A Trotskyite attack on all the parties in Spain, including the POUM. The author is especially critical of the Communists, not because they dominated the government, but because they were allied with the bourgeoisie in betraying the revolution.

IE65 MUGGERIDGE, MALCOLM, ed. *Ciano's Diplomatic Papers.* London: Odhams, 1948. 490 p. Ciano was Italian Minister for Foreign Affairs, 1936-39. This collection includes his conversations and negotiations with France and England on the Spanish question.

IS66 *The Nazi Conspiracy in Spain.* By the editor of *The Brown Book of the Hitler Terror.* Trans. from the German manuscript by Emile Burns (pseud.). London: Gollancz, 1937. 256 p. A collection of materials on Nazi intervention in Spain from newspapers, speeches and allegedly diplomatic archives. It was compiled by the Communists, originally in German. [A]

IS67 NELSON, STEVE. *Die Freiwilligen; Erlebnisbericht vom Kampf gegen den Faschismus in Spanien.* Berlin: Dietz, 1955. 220 p. A highly colored account of the International Brigades by an American Communist volunteer, who later worked for the Soviet espionage network in the United States and eventually fled to the Communist bloc.

IS68 NIKOLAEV, N. N. *Vneshniaia politika pravykh leiboristov Anglii v periode podgotovki i nachala vtoroi mirovoi voiny, 1935-1940 gg.* Moscow: Gospolitizdat, 1953. 251 p. The aim of this Soviet work was to denounce the English Socialists for Soviet purposes in 1953. One of its methods was to stress the weak and ineffective support which British Labour gave the Spanish Republicans, thereby betraying the anti-Fascist cause.

IS69 ORWELL, GEORGE. *Homage to Catalonia.* London: Secker and Warburg, 1938. 313 p. A personal account of the British author's visit to Spain in 1937.

IS70 OVINNIKOV, R. S. *Za kulisami politiki "nevmeshatelstva"; ispanskii vopros v politike imperialistov Anglii, Frantsii i SSHA nakanune vtoroi mirovoi voiny.* Moscow: Izd. IMO, 1959. 326 p. A typical example of a contemporary Soviet study on the Spanish Civil War, whose purpose is to support a current Communist line. It allegedly describes how monopoly capitalists of England, France and the U.S. dominated Spain and were forced to come to terms with the German monopolists during the Civil War. [A]

IS71 PADELFORD, NORMAN. *International Law and Diplomacy in the Spanish Civil Strife.* N.Y.: Macmillan, 1939. 710 p. A discussion of the legal implications of the Civil War and the international legal status of the two warring factions, by a leading American professor of international law.

IS72 PARTIDO COMUNISTA DE ESPAÑA. *El Partido comunista por la libertad y la independencia de España (Llamamientos y discursos).* Valencia: P.C. de E. (S.E. de I.C.), 1937. 190 p. A collection of Communist speeches and propaganda from the first part of the Civil War. [B]

IS73 PARTIDO COMUNISTA DE ESPAÑA. *Plenum TSK Kommunisticheskoi partii Ispanii, avgust 1956 god.* Moscow: Gospolitizdat, 1957. 268 p.

IS74 PATTEE, RICHARD. *This Is Spain.* Milwaukee: Bruce, 1951. 541 p. The author gives the conservative Church view of the Spanish Civil War and is bitterly anti-Loyalist in his sympathies.

IS75 PLUMB, ROBERT L. "Soviet Participation in the Spanish Civil War." Ph.D. dissertation, Georgetown, 1956. This study lacks insight and discrimination, and parts of it are misleading or simply mistaken. Nonetheless, though it can only be used with care, it does collect some important material on Russian activity in Spain during the Civil War. [B]

IS76 PRIETO, INDALECIO. *Como y por que sali del Ministerio de Defensa Nacional; intrigas de los rusos en España.* Mexico City: Impresos y Popeles, 1940. 123 p. French and Spanish eds., Paris: 1939. Prieto held the important position of Minister of Defense in the Loyalist Government. In the spring of 1938 the Communists had him removed because he felt the war was lost and wanted to negotiate a peace. This is the text of the speech he gave to the Socialist Party explaining his position.

IS77 PRIETO, INDALECIO. *Yo y Moscú.* Madrid: 1955. A collection of writings that touch on Communism by the leader of the Spanish Right Socialists. They are helpful on a number of points and supplement Prieto's report to the Socialist Party (above). [B]

IS77A *Problemy rabochego i antifashistkogo dvizheniia v Ispanii.* Moscow: Izd. Akad. nauk SSSR, 1960. 260 p.

IS77B PUZZO, DANTE A. *Spain and the Great Powers, 1936-1941.* N.Y.: Columbia University Press, 1962. 296 p.

IS77C RED INTERNATIONAL OF LABOR UNIONS. *Boletín de la Internacional sindical roja.* Paris: Secretariado Internacional de la C.G.T.U., 1927-32. A multigraphed weekly. An important source on Communist trade unionism in Spain and Portugal.

IS78 RIEGER, MAX. *Espionnage en Espagne; fait et documents recueillis par un officier de l'Armee Espagnole.* Paris: Les Editions Denoël, 1938. 235 p. Contains in detail the Communist case against the dissident Communist organization, POUM, accusing it of treason against the Loyalist Government.

IS79 RUSSIA (1923– USSR), ARMIIA, GENERALNYI SHTAB. *Upravlenie voiskami i rabota shtabov v ispanskoi respublikanskoi armii.*

Moscow: Voenizdat, 1939. 157 p. One of three or four volumes published in the Soviet Union on the military aspects of the Spanish Civil War.

IS80 *Soviet Shipping in the Spanish Civil War.* East European Fund, Mimeographed Series, No. 59. N.Y.: Research Program on the USSR, 1954. 22 p. A former Soviet citizen and participant in the Soviet project to ship arms to the Loyalists in the Spanish Civil War describes how the smuggling was carried out. [B]

IS81 SPAIN, TRIBUNAL SUPREMO, MINISTERIO FISCAL. *La Dominación roja en España, avance de la información instruída por el Ministerio Público.* Madrid: Ministerio de justicia, 1944. 264 p. The Franco regime labeled the entire Loyalist movement as "Red" or "Communist." This is Franco's white paper describing the extent of the "Red terror" under the Republican regime.

IS82 *SSSR i fashistskaia agressiia v Ispanii; sbornik dokumentov.* Moscow: Sotsekgiz, 1937. 72 p. This collection of documents contains the Soviet case against Italy and Germany for illegally arming the Spanish rebels, although the actual documentation is sparse. It is difficult to understand why the Communists did not choose to put forward more convincing evidence.

IS83 SURVEY OF INTERNATIONAL AFFAIRS. *The International Repercussions of the War in Spain, 1936-1937.* Ed. by Arnold J. Toynbee, assisted by V. M. Baulter. London: Oxford, for the Royal Institute of International Affairs, 1938. A detailed, well-documented survey of the diplomacy surrounding the first two years of the Civil War.

IS84 THOMAS, HUGH. *The Spanish Civil War.* N.Y.: Harper, 1961. 720 p. This history of the Spanish Civil War is based on the mass of documentation now available and is one of the most detached and comprehensive analyses of the struggle. [B]

IS85 VARFOLOMEEVA, R. *Reaktsionnaia vneshniaia politika frantsuzskikh pravykh sotsialistov, 1936-1939 gg.* Moscow: Gospolitizdat, 1949. 146 p. This post-war study deals extensively with the role of the French socialists in betraying the cause of the Loyalist Government through inactivity and selling out to the Right. [B]

IS86 VARGA, EUGEN. *Ispaniia i revoliutsia.* Moscow: Sotsekgiz, 1937. 119 p. A pamphlet analyzing the social and economic forces operating in the Spanish Civil War from the Soviet point of view.

IS87 VOROS, SANDOR. *American Commissar.* Philadelphia: Chilton, 1961. 477 p. Acerbic memoirs of an Hungarian-American officer in the International Brigades. A useful source, though the author's bitterness detracts from his objectivity.

IS88 ZUGAZAGOITIA, JULIAN. *Historia de la guerra en España.* Buenos Aires: Editorial La Vanguardia, 1940. 590 p. One of the better histories of the Spanish Civil War. Provides good insight into the inner politics of the Loyalist Government. [B]

IT. SWITZERLAND

EDITED BY KURT MÜLLER

IT1 AUBERT, THÉODORE. *L'Affaire Conradi; plaidoirie prononcée pour Arcadius Polounine devant le Tribunal Criminel de Lausanne les 14 et 15 novembre 1923.* Geneva: SA Editions Sonor, 1924. 132 p. An apology for the Russian-Swiss Maurice Conradi who on May 10, 1923, murdered Vatzlav Vorovsky, member of the Soviet delegation at the peace conference at Lausanne.

IT2 BALABANOFF, ANGELICA. *Erinnerungen und Erlebnisse.* Berlin: E. Laubsche Verlagsbuchhandlung, 1927. 300 p. The first secretary of the Comintern devotes 15 pages on her stay in and her expulsion from Switzerland in 1918, due to her revolutionary machinations. Violently criticizes the Swiss authorities and the Swiss petty bourgeoisie.

IT3 BODENMANN, MARINO. *Zum 40. Jahrestag der Gründung der Kommunistischen Partei der Schweiz.* Zurich: Verlag der Partei der Arbeit der Schweiz, 1961. 104 p. A one-sided presentation of the history of the Communist Party by a member of the Politburo. Informative on the tactics of Communism in Switzerland. Some periods falsified. [B]

IT4 BONJOUR, E. *Geschichte der schweizerischen Neutralität; drei Jahrhunderte eidgenössischer Aussenpolitik.* Basel: Helbing & Lichtenhahn, 1946. 434 p. English ed., *Swiss Neutrality, its History and Meaning.* London: G. Allen & Unwin, 1946. 135 p. By a professor of history of the University of Basel. A standard work on Swiss neutrality and foreign policy since the French revolution. The last chapters are on relations with the USSR among others. [A]

IT5 BRETSCHER, WILLY. *Geteilte Welt im Zwielicht der "Entspannung"; Unsere schweizerische Haltung; Wiedergabe eines am 18. Oktober 1955 gehaltenen Referats.* Zurich: Buchdruckerei "Neue Zürcher Zeitung." 38 p. Defines the Swiss position toward the new Soviet tactics, especially "peaceful coexistence." The author is chief editor of the *Neue Zürcher Zeitung*, a member of the Swiss parliament, and President of the Committee for Foreign Affairs of the Nationalrat.

IT6 BRETSCHER, WILLY. *"Neue Zürcher Zeitung" 1933-1944; Siebzig Leitartikel.* Zurich: Buchdruckerei der "Neuen Zürcher Zeitung," 1945. 204 p. Contains a series of editorials, commenting on Swiss policy toward the USSR from the vote against its admission to the League of Nations up to the Soviet decision against diplomatic relations with Switzerland in 1944. Reflects the standpoint of the majority of the Swiss people.

IT7 BRETSCHER, WILLY. *Die politische Lage der Schweiz am Kriegsende; Referat gehalten am 28. Okt. 1945 an der ausserordentlichen Delegiertenversammlung der Freisinnig-demokratischen Partei der Schweiz in Basel.* Zurich: Buchdruckerei der "Neuen Zürcher Zeitung," 1945. 32 p. A justification of Swiss foreign policy before and during World War II.

IT8 BRETSCHER, WILLY. *Schweizerische Aussenpolitik in der Nachkriegszeit.* Zurich: Buchdruckerei der "Neuen Zürcher Zeitung," 1951. 27 p. A presentation of the standpoint held by the majority of Swiss people in the East-West conflict.

IT9 BRETSCHER, WILLY, and STEINMANN, E. *Die sozialistische Bewegung in der Schweiz 1848-1920.* Bern: Buchdruckerei Gottfried Iseli, 1923. 160 p. An excellent presentation of Communism and Socialism in Switzerland until 1920. Liberal-conservative standpoint on Communist influences during and after World War I and during the general strike in 1918. E. Steinmann was Central Secretary of the Freisinnig-demokratische Partei der Schweiz (liberal-conservative party), 1919-46. [B]

IT10 BRINGOLF, WALTHER. *Die Schweiz und die Sowjetunion; zur Krise unserer Aussenpolitik.* Schaffhausen: Unionsdruckerei AG, 1944. 23 p. By the president of the Social Democratic Party of Switzerland; the book was published under the auspices of this party. A good survey of diplomatic and commercial relations with the USSR since 1917.

IT11 BRUNNER, A. *Bericht des Ersten Staatsanwalts A. Brunner an den Regierungsrat des Kantons Zürich über die Strafuntersuchung wegen des Aufruhrs in Zürich im November 1917. (vom 9. November 1918).* Zurich: Buchdruckerei zur Alten Universität, 1919. 157 p. Liberal-conservative standpoint. Valuable documents on the increasing Communist influence on the left wing of the workers movement during World War I.

IT12 BRUPBACHER, FRITZ. *Selbstbiographie; 60 Jahre Ketzer.* Zurich-Leimbach: B. Rupli, 1935. 381 p. Subjective recollections, with some value as a source, by an important Communist in the early days of the Swiss Communist Party.

IT13 DUERRENMATT, PETER. *Die Welt zwischen Krieg und Frieden.* Bern: Hallway AG, 1959. 246 p. By a member of Parliament and chief editor of the liberal-conservative newspaper, *Basler Nachrichten*, this is an analysis of the balance of power in the East-West conflict and the task of the free world as seen from the Swiss point of view.

IT14 EGGER, HEINZ. *Die Entstehung der Kommunistischen Partei und des Kommunistischen Jugendverbandes der Schweiz.* Zurich: Genossenschaft Literaturvertrieb, 1952. 294 p. A onesided and historically unreliable presentation by a Communist. In the appendix are 3 well-known papers of Lenin and 12 pages of a useful but incomplete bibliography. [B]

IT15 FELDMANN, MARKUS. *Die Schweiz und Sowjetland.* Bern: Verbandsdruckerei, 1944. 35 p. A good survey of relations with the USSR since its foundation and on the various attempts to restore diplomatic and commercial relations after the rupture in 1918. Favors relations without making concessions in domestic policy. By a member of the government from 1951-58, representing the Bauern-, Gewerbe- and Bürgerpartei (farmers' party). [B]

IT16 FREYMOND, JACQUES. *La Suisse devant la lutte des grandes puissances.* Lausanne: Rencontres Suisses, Imprimerie Centrale, 1955. 43 p. A critical presentation of Soviet developments and aims, especially of peaceful coexistence. Gives the position of Switzerland in the East-West conflict. By a professor of modern history at the University of Geneva and Director of the Graduate Institute of International Studies at Geneva.

IT17 GAUTSCHI, WILLI. *Das Oltener Aktionskomitee und der Landes-Generalstreik von 1918.* Affoltern am Albis: 1955. 269 p. A valuable work, attempting to put to good account various standpoints on the question of the national strike. Based too much on late oral sources. 36 pages of important documents and a good bibliography.

IT18 GERMANY, AUSWÄRTIGES AMT. *Lenins Rückkehr nach Russland, 1917; die deutschen Akten.* Ed. by Werner Hahlweg. Leiden: Brill, 1957. 139 p. Documents and comments on the preparations for Lenin's departure from Switzerland, the assistance of Swiss socialists, and position of the Swiss authorities.

IT19 GRIMM, ROBERT. *Geschichte der sozialistischen Ideen in der Schweiz.* Zurich: Verlag Dr. Oprecht and Helbling, 1931. 231 p. The most important leader of the Swiss socialists from World War I until the middle of the thirties discusses Communism. The one-sided standpoint of a class fighter.

IT20 HARDMEIER, BENNO. *Geschichte der sozialdemokratischen Ideen in der Schweiz (1920-1945).* Winterthur: P. G. Keller, 1957. 196 p. The Secretary of the Schweizerische Gewerkschaftsbund gives a good, solid, documented socialist presentation, on the relations between the Socialists and the Communists. [B]

IT21 HEEB, FRIEDRICH. *Der schweizerische Gewerkschaftsbund 1880-1930; Denkschrift zum fünfzigjährigen Jubiläum.* Bern: Verlag des schweizerischen Gewerkschaftsbundes, 1930. 572 p. By the editor of the socialist newspaper, *Volksrecht.* A judgment of the national strike of 1918 by trade-unionists. Contains 10 interesting pages on the conflicts between Socialists and Communists after their separation in 1920 over the balance of power in the trade unions. [B]

IT22 HEEB, FRIEDRICH, ed. *Aus der Geschichte der Zürcher Arbeiterbewegung; Denkschrift zum 50 jährigen Jubiläum des "Volksrechts" 1898-1948; mit Beiträgen zahlreicher Mitarbeiter.* Published by the Sozialdemokratischen Presseunion des Kantons Zürich. Zurich: Genossenschaftsdruckerei, 1948. 399 p. A socialist interpretation of the general strike of 1918, the fight over the newspaper *Volksrecht* and over power in the Zurich trade unions between the Communists and Socialists after 1920.

IT23 HOFMAIER, KARL. *Schweiz-Sowjetunion; Der Kampf um die Neuorientierung der schweizerischen Innen- und Aussenpolitik; Rede gehalten am 5. Dez. 1944 im Volkshaus, Zürich.* Zurich: Verlag der Partei der Arbeit, 1945. 63 p. By the General Secretary of the Swiss Communist Party, 1944-46, who in 1947 was expelled from the Party. Demands an accommodation of Swiss policy with the increase of Communist power in the world.

IT24 *Kommunismus in der Schweiz; Skizze über seine Anfänge, Geschichte und Gegenwart.* Lausanne: Aktion Freier Staatsbürger, 1955. 174 p. French ed., 158 p. Published without the name of the author: Karl Stark, a Jesuit father. The best brief, critical study of the history of Swiss Communism and its exponents in Switzerland, by an anti-Communist. [A]

IT25 *Die Kommunistische Partei der Schweiz, 1922-24.* Basel: Genossenschaftsbuchdruckerei, 1924. 123 p. Issued by the Central Office of the Communist Party. An official statement on organization, agitation, and national and international questions.

IT26 LA HARPE, JEAN DE. *Considérations sur la Russie et sur nos rapports avec elle.* Glarus, Switzerland: Tschudi, 1944. 126 p. German ed., 140 p. By the central president of the Swiss Association for the League of Nations and professor of philosophy at the University of Neuchâtel. A not uncritical, almost popular, account of the Russian revolution and its development, written in part from personal experiences. Typical for the illusions held by intellectuals of the left wing of the non-socialist parties at the end of World War II.

IT27 *Der Landesstreik-Prozess gegen die Mitglieder des Oltener Aktionskomitees vor dem Militärgericht III vom 12. März bis 9. April*

1919; Stenogramm der Verhandlungen mit einem Vorwort von Robert Grimm und Bildern der Prozessbeteiligten von Hanni Bay. Bern: Unionsdruckerei, 1919. 2 vols. An interesting collection of sources by the socialist accusers.

IT28 MARBACH, FRITZ. *Les Relations commerciales entre la Suisse et la Russie.* Berne: Imprimerie de l'Union, 1939. 68 p. German ed., 64 p. By a Professor at the University of Bern and a Social Democrat. Demands diplomatic relations before building up commercial relations with the USSR.

IT29 MESTRAL DE, A. *Bundesrat Motta; die Schweiz zwischen zwei Weltkriegen.* Bern: A. Scherz, 1941. 306 p. French ed., Lausanne: Payot, 1941. 320 p. The first major biography of the Swiss Minister for Foreign Affairs, 1920-40, written by a personal acquaintance of his. Motta's policy toward the USSR is well summarized in 10 pages. An uncritical, almost popular account, with abundant use of oral sources, by a publicist of conservative outlook. [B]

IT30 MOREL, GEORGES. *Les Rapports économiques de la Suisse avec la Russie.* Geneva: Imprimeries Réunies de Chambéry, 1934. 198 p. A thesis written at the University of Geneva.

IT31 MOTTA, GIUSEPPE. *Testimonia temporum; discorsi e scritti scelti.* Bellinzona: Istituto editoriale ticinese, 1931-41. 3 vols. Text in Italian, French, and German. An extremely valuable source of writings and speeches of the Swiss Minister of Foreign Affairs, 1920-40, in which can be found numerous important remarks on relations with the USSR, especially speeches in the national parliament and the League of Nations. Among others in vol. II is the speech of Sept. 17, 1934 in the League of Nations against the admission of the USSR. [A]

IT32 MÜLLER, KURT. *Schicksal einer Klassenpartei; Abriss der Geschichte der schweizerischen Sozialdemokratie.* Zurich: Buchverlag der "Neuen Zürcher Zeitung," 1955. 228 p. By the editor of the *Neue Zürcher Zeitung*, a liberal-conservative. A critical survey of the history of the Socialist Party, taking into consideration the development of Communism in Switzerland and its influence on the Socialist Party. [B]

IT33 MÜNZENBERG, WILLI. *Die dritte Front; Aufzeichnungen aus 15 Jahren proletarischer Jugendbewegung.* Berlin: Neuer deutscher Verlag, 1929. 389 p. By an official of the Communist international youth movement. About 200 pages of personally tinted recollections of his infiltration of the Swiss socialist youth organization with Communist ideas and of his attempt to infiltrate even the Socialist Party.

IT34 NICOLE, LÉON. *Die Wideraufnahme der Beziehungen zwischen der Schweiz und der UdSSR.* Geneva: Coopérative d'imprimerie, n.d.

IT35 PARTEI DER ARBEIT. *Was will die Partei der Arbeit der Schweiz? Politische Berichte erstattet am ersten Parteitag am 14. Okt. 1944 in Zürich von Karl Hofmaier und Léon Nicole.* Zurich: Verlag der Partei der Arbeit. 95 p. Illustrates Communist aims for the establishment of a mass party at the end of World War II. Annex: Program of action for 1944 of the Swiss Communist Party.

IT36 PIANZOLA, MAURICE. *Lénine en Suisse.* Ambilly-Annemasse, France: La Librairie nouvelle, 1952. 227 p. A one-sided Communist version. Interesting references to the relations between Lenin and the Swiss socialists and the events in Zimmerwald and Kienthal. Includes "La tâche des représentants de la gauche de Zimmerwald dans le parti socialiste suisse," for the first time in the French version, edited by Lenin.

IT37 RAGAZ, JAKOB. *Die Arbeiterbewegung in der Westschweiz.* Vol. III of *Die Schweizerischen Beiträge zur Wirtschafts- und Sozialwissenschaft.* Aarau: Sauerländer, 1938. 260 p. Useful hints in the discussion with the Communists in the workers' movement of the French part of Switzerland, from a socialist point of view. 14-page bibliography. [B]

IT38 SAGER, PETER, and DAETWILER, RICHARD. *Osthandel.* Wabern-Bern: Büchler, 1960/62. 67 p. Consists of two parts: (1) "Die Rolle der Wirtschaftspolitik and insbesondere der Aussenhandelsbeziehungen in der Sowjetrussischen Weltpolitik," by Dr. Sager, who is Director of the Swiss East Institute in Bern; and (2) "Warum ich gegen den Osthandel bin," by Dr. Daetwiler, who is secretary of Redressement National. Both authors examine the question of trade with the Communist East and advocate for Switzerland as little trade as possible with these countries.

IT39 SALIS, J. R. VON. *Giuseppe Motta; dreissig Jahre eidgenössische Politik.* Zurich: Orell Füssli, 1941. 472 p. A standard biography of the Swiss Minister for Foreign Affairs, 1920-40. A solid presentation by a professor of history at the Swiss Federal Institute of Technology. Based on primary sources. [A]

IT40 SAMSONOW, MICHAEL S., *Swiss Neutrality and the U.S.S.R.* San Francisco: H. Nadai, 1953. 45 p. A good summary of the problem.

IT41 SCHENKER, ERNST. *Die sozialdemokratische Bewegung in der Schweiz von ihren Anfängen bis zur Gegenwart.* Appenzell: Anzeiger, 1926. 224 p. A valuable historical survey, especially on the events that led to the separation from the Communists. Reserved in his judgments. [B]

IT42 SCHNEIDER, FRIEDRICH. *Hieronymus Roggenbachs Erlebnisse.* Basel: Volksdruckerei, 1959. 392 p. Recollections of an important socialist leader and participant in the national strike of 1918. Presentation of the events from a later point of view.

IT43 *Die Schweiz und die Sowjetunion.* N.P.: Kommunistischen Partei der Schweiz, n.d. 34 p. An interesting document on the opinions of the Swiss Communists before the German attack on the USSR. Justification of the German-Soviet non-aggression pact of 1939 as a "glamour piece of Leninist policy." Pleads for restoration of diplomatic relations and negotiations on a commercial treaty.

IT44 *Sowjetfeindlich? Dokumente und Tatsachen.* Zurich: Verlag der Partei der Arbeit, 1945. 104 p. A polemical pamphlet of the Communist Party against Swiss policy toward the USSR and the standpoint of the liberal, conservative and socialist parties.

IT45 SOZIALDEMOKRATISCHE PARTEI DER SCHWEIZ. *Protokolle über die Verhandlungen der Parteitage & der Schweizerischen Arbeiterkongresse.* (Various dates and places of publication.) Extremely interesting sources on the discussions of Communist ideas and Communists in the Socialist Party of Switzerland. [B]

IT46 SWITZERLAND, BUNDESRAT. *Bericht des Bundesrates an die Bundesversammlung über die antidemokratische Tätigkeit von Schweizern und Ausländern im Zusammenhang mit dem Kriegsgeschehen, 1939-1945.* Bern: 1945. 60 p. The sole official document on Communist activity in Switzerland. Of great historical value. Interesting citations from Communist remarks. [A]

IT47 VALLOTTON, HENRY. *Suisse et Soviets; deux interpellations, 1926-1936.* Lausanne: Imprimerie vaudoise, 1936. 38 p. By a former president of the liberal-conservative faction (1935-38) of the Federal Assembly, which represented the majority of the Government until 1943. Two interpellations: 1926, after the failure of the Bern-Moscow discussions, and 1936, against recognition of the Soviet Government.

IT48 VERIDICUS (pseud.). *Suisse et Soviets, histoire d'un conflit; l'expulsion de la mission soviétique, l'assassinat impuni de Vorovsky, pourquoi l'URSS n'assistait pas à la conférence du désarmement.* Paris: A. Delpeuch, 1926. 127 p. A one-sided critique of the stand of the Swiss Government on the rupture of diplomatic relations with the USSR in 1918 and on the murder of Vorovsky in 1923. Documents interspersed in the text.

1. COMMUNIST NEWSPAPERS

IT49 *Basler Vorwärts*. Basel, 1936-39.

IT50 *Der Kämpfer*. Basel, Zurich, 1921-36.

IT51 *Schweiz-USSR*. Newspaper of the association Switzerland-USSR. Quarterly since 1954.

IT52 *La Voix ouvrière*. Geneva, 1944–. Daily since 1945. [A]

IT53 *Vorwärts*. Geneva/Basel, 1945-57, daily, 1957–, weekly.

IU. YUGOSLAVIA

EDITED BY WAYNE S. VUCINICH

INTRODUCTORY NOTE

One can find a voluminous amount of fragmentary materials (speeches, declarations, notes, articles, etc.) on specific aspects of Yugoslav-Soviet relations, especially since 1944, but not a single systematic study of that subject.

Serious students of Yugoslav-Soviet relations should consult, in addition to the works listed below: (1) the pre-War and post-War parliamentary debates and papers (*Narodna Skupština. Stenografske beleške*, 1919—; *Savezna Narodna Skupština. Stenografske beleške*, 1945—); (2) the official gazettes (*Službene novine Kraljevine Jugoslavije*, Belgrade, 1918—; *Službeni list FNRJ*, Belgrade, 1944—); (3) the proceedings and papers of the congresses of the Alliance of Communists of Yugoslavia (Communist Party of Yugoslavia); (4) speeches, resolutions, and activities of the Yugoslav delegates at the United Nations, strewn throughout various U.N. publications; (5) speeches of prominent Yugoslav Communist leaders (especially those by Tito, Kardelj, Pijade); and, (6) the organs of the Alliance of Communists of Yugoslavia—*Komunist*, a monthly treating of problems in Marxian theory and practice; *Komunist*, a weekly newspaper; *Socijalizam*, organ of the Central Committee of the Alliance of Communists); and, *Naša stvarnost*.

Three additional periodicals are also useful to anyone interested in Yugoslavia's foreign relations: *Medjunarodni problemi*, a quarterly, and *Spoljnopolitička dokumentacija*, which appears in twelve numbers annually. Especially useful for those who cannot read Serbo-Croatian is the bi-weekly journal, *Review of International Affairs*.

Two daily newspapers are of particular importance: *Politika*, prior to the Second World War was one of the best and most informative newspapers in the Balkans. Since the end of the War it has become, like all other journals, an official organ. *Borba*, organ of the Communist Party, is unquestionably the principal mouthpiece of the Government and the Party.

1. 1917-1939

IU1 *Četrdeset godina; zbornik sećanja aktivista jugoslovenskog revolucionarnog radničkog pokreta.* Belgrade: Kultura, 1960—. Three volumes have appeared: I, 1917-1929; II, 1929-1935; III, Part 1, 1935-1941; and, III, Part 2, 1935-1941. A collection of reminiscences of individual Communists, written in popular language.

IU2 CILIGA, ANTON. "Jugoslavischer Komunismus und der russische Bolshevismus." Photostatic copy of a typewritten report written in 1948, Hoover Institution, Stanford, Cal. A discussion of the Russian revolutionary movement and the Balkan Slavs in the nineteenth century and Bolshevik influence and activities (1919-41), Moscow's role in building the Yugoslav Communist Party, and the conflict between Belgrade and Moscow in 1948.

IU3 ČULINOVIĆ, FERDO. *Jugoslavija izmedju dva rata.* Zagreb: Jugoslavenska Akademija Znanosti i Umjetnosti, 1961. 2 vols. The most complete history of interwar Yugoslavia from a Marxian point of view. It treats *inter alia* the founding of the Yugoslav Communist Party, its political and other activities. [A]

IU4 HASANAGIĆ, EDIB. *Komunistička partija Jugoslavije 1919-1941; izabrani dokumenti.* Zagreb: Školska knjiga, 1959. 316 p.

IU5 HOPTNER, JACOB B. *Yugoslavia in Crisis 1934-1941.* N.Y.: Columbia, 1962. 328 p. The best work on the subject. Adequately documented, scholarly and well-written. [A]

IU6 JOVANOVIĆ, JOVAN M. *Diplomatska istorija Nove Evrope, 1918-1938.* Belgrade: 1938-1939. 2 vols. A diplomatic history of interwar Europe in which numerous topics involving Yugoslavia are discussed. The work is carelessly done and inadequately documented, but is valuable for its presentation of Yugoslav foreign affairs by an erstwhile Yugoslav diplomat.

IU7 KERNER, ROBERT J., ed. *Yugoslavia.* Berkeley: U. of California, 1949. 558 p. A symposium of articles on various topics from contemporary Yugoslav history. The stress is on the pre-World War II period. Also included are superior chapters on post-war political and economic developments. [A]

IU8 KERNER, ROBERT J., and HOWARD, HARRY N. *The Balkan Conferences and the Balkan Entente 1930-1935.* Berkeley: U. of California, 1936. 271 p. A discussion of various conferences that led to the conclusion of the Balkan Entente. The work is important for its many references to Soviet policy regarding the Balkans.

IU8A KRLEŽA, MIROSLAV. *Deset krvavih godina i drugi politički eseji.* Zagreb: Zora, 1957. This makes up volumes 14 and 15 of his collected works. Especially important is the essay "Teze za jednu diskusiju iz godine 1935," which analyzes the socialist movement in Yugoslavia, and the role of the Communists in the Popular Front.

IU9 MAUR, GILBERT IN DER. *Die Jugoslawen einst und jetzt.* Vienna: Gunther, for vols. I and II; Berlin: Payer, for vol. III; 1935-38.

A survey of Yugoslav internal and foreign policies in the interwar period. A factual work and, considering the absence of comparable studies, a useful one. Volume II deals with foreign affairs, 1919-35.

IU9A TOMASEVICH, JOZO. *Peasants, Politics, and Economic Change in Yugoslavia.* Stanford: Stanford University Press, 1955. 743 p. A large, scholarly tome on the economic history of the Yugoslav peoples until the Second World War. Useful as background material.

IU10 WILLIAMS, SUZANNE S. "The Communist Party of Yugoslavia and the Nationality Problem, 1922-1925." Certificate essay, Russian Institute, Columbia, 1955. 95 p.

2. 1939-1963

IU11 ADAMIC, LOUIS. *The Eagle and the Roots.* Garden City, N.Y.: Doubleday, 1952. 531 p. A popular account of Tito's life and Communist activities, the Yugoslav-Soviet dispute, and Titoism. By an American author strongly in favor of Tito.

IU12 ARMSTRONG, HAMILTON FISH. *Tito and Goliath.* N.Y.: Macmillan, 1951. 312 p. A balanced account of the Tito-Stalin controversy and of Yugoslav internal developments and foreign relations. The author finds it "easier to live alongside" Yugoslavia than "the absolutist, monolithic, imperialist and reactionary government of Soviet Russia." The author is the distinguished editor of *Foreign Affairs* and has long been interested in Yugoslavia. [A]

IU13 AURORA, ELIO D'. *Fascino slavo, inchiesta sulla Jugoslavia di Tito; carteggio segreto Tito-Stalin.* Torino: Società editrice internazionale, 1956. 263 p.

IU14 AVAKUMOVIĆ, IVAN. "History of the Communist Party of Yugoslavia—an Interim Study." Ph.D. dissertation, Oxford, 1958.

IU15 AVAKUMOVIĆ, IVAN. "Literature on the Marxist Movement in Yugoslavia." *Journal of Central European Affairs*, xv, p. 66-70.

IU16 BASS, ROBERT, and MARBURY, ELIZABETH, eds. *The Soviet-Yugoslav Controversy, 1948-58; A Documentary Record*, N.Y.: Prospect Books, for the East Europe Institute, 1959. 229 p. A useful collection of letters and other official documents concerning the Yugoslav-Soviet controversy. Material is organized by chapters corresponding to the evolution of the controversy: Yugoslavia and the Cominform, 1948; The Road to Brioni; The Yugoslav Road to Socialism and the Hungarian Revolt; The Schism Revived. [A]

IU17 BASSI, MAURIZIO. *Due Anni fra le Bande di Tito.* Bologna: Cappelli, 1950. 320 p. A participant in Italian military action and administration of occupied Yugoslavia discusses Partisan warfare and cooperation between Italians and Chetniks. Sheds light on Communist organizational and tactical methods.

IU18 BELGRADE, VOJNI ISTORISKI INSTITUT. *Oslobodilački rat naroda Jugoslavije, 1941-1945*. Vol. I, *Od raspada stare Jugoslavije do Drugog zasedanja AVNOJ-a*. Vol. II, *Od Drugog zasedanja AVNOJ-a do konačne pobede*. Belgrade: 1957-58. An official history of the Partisan struggle during World War II.

IU19 BELGRADE, VOJNI ISTORISKI INSTITUT. *Završne operacije za oslobodjenje Jugoslavije 1944-1945*. Belgrade: 1957. 731 p. Deals with the final stages of the Partisan struggle.

IU20 BELGRADE, VOJNI ISTORISKI INSTITUT. *Zbornik dokumenata i podataka o narodno-oslobodilačkom ratu jugoslovenskih naroda*. Belgrade: 1949—. A multi-volume collection of documents on the War of National Liberation. Omits some material on delicate Party questions. Otherwise valuable for understanding the organization of Communist resistance forces and military and political tactics employed.

IU21 BENEŠ, VÁCLAV, BYRNES, ROBERT F., and SPULBER, NICHOLAS, eds. *The Second Soviet-Yugoslav Dispute; Full Text of Main Documents, April-June, 1958, with an Introductory Analysis*. Bloomington: Indiana Univ., 1959. 272 p. A collection of documents that contain the essence of the Soviet-Yugoslav dispute of April-June, 1958, with an introductory analysis by the editors covering the historical background. [A]

IU23 BILAINKIN, GEORGE. *Tito*. N.Y.: Philosophical Library, 1950. 287 p. A sympathetic account of Tito's early experiences and activities and his negotiations with and struggle against Mihailovich. Includes an inadequate discussion of Soviet-Yugoslav relations.

IU24 BLAIRY, JEAN. *Crépuscule danubien*. Paris: Plon, 1946. 253 p. An uninspired popular account of conditions in Rumania and Yugoslavia at the end of World War II.

IU25 BOBROWSKI, CZESLAW. *La Yougoslavie socialiste*. Paris: Colin, 1956. 237 p. A sympathetic study of the Yugoslav revolution, with special reference to problems of economic reconstruction, socialist planning, and the "new system." Of some value in understanding Titoism.

IU26 BOURDET, CLAUDE. *Le Schisme Yougoslave*. Paris: Éditions de Minuit, 1950. 124 p. A brief, popular discussion of the Tito-Stalin schism and the general economic and political situation in Yugoslavia in the years immediately after the country's expulsion from the Cominform in 1948.

IU27 BULGARSKA KOMUNISTICHESKA PARTIIA. *Krizata v Iugoslavskata komunisticheska partiia.* Sofia: Izd. na BRP(k), 1948. 28 p. Contains the communique and resolution of the Communist Information Bureau on the June 1948 split between the Yugoslav Communist Party and the Kremlin, as well as some subsequent documents on the split issued by the Bulgarian Communist Party strongly condemning Tito.

IU28 BULGARSKA KOMUNISTICHESKA PARTIIA. *Titovata banda—orudie na imperialistite.* Ed. by Dino Kosev. Sofia: 1951. 663 p. A criticism of Tito's policies by Bulgarian Communists. Propagandistic.

IU29 CARNETT, GEORGE S. "Communist Exploitation of the Yugoslav Nationality Problem with Specific Reference to the Serbo-Croat Antagonism and the Second World War." Ph.D. dissertation, Yale, 1955.

IU30 *Catalogue of Foreign Language Publications and Articles about Yugoslavia.* Belgrade: "Jugoslavija," 1960. 142 p.

IU31 *Četrdeset godina revolucionarne borbe Komunističke partije Jugoslavije; govori rukovodilaca o proslavi 40-godišnjice KPJ.* Belgrade: Kultura, 1959. 194 p. A volume commemorating the 40th anniversary of the Yugoslav Communist Party.

IU32 CHILATY-FARD, AMIR. "La Frontière italo-yougoslave et la problème de Trieste en fonction de la politique des grandes puissances." Doct. en droit dissertation, U. of Paris, 1949. 322 p.

IU33 CILIGA, ANTON. *La Yougoslavie sous la menace intérieure et extérieure.* Paris: Les Iles d'Or, 1951. 132 p. An analysis of the conflict between Stalin and Tito, Tito's wartime achievements, and Yugoslavia's internal divisiveness (ethnic and regional conflicts). The author is a one-time Communist who has become an ardent Croat nationalist.

IU34 CLISSOLD, STEPHEN. *Whirlwind; an Account of Marshal Tito's Rise to Power.* N.Y.: Philosophical Library; London: Cresset, 1949. 245 p. Italian ed., Milan: 1950. An assessment of the wartime activities of the Yugoslav Communist Party, the policies of great powers regarding Tito and his followers, and the problems concerning the founding of the Communist state. Written by a member of the British mission to Tito's Partisans. The work is marred by an absence of source references. [A]

IU35 ČOLAKOVIĆ, RADOLJUB. *Zapisi iz Oslobodilačkog Rata.* Sarajevo: Oslobodjenje, 1948-51. 4 vols. Notes from the "War of Liberation" (1941-45) by a prominent Yugoslav Communist. Replete with valuable factual material which can be taken as official by virtue of the author's position. Background material helps to explain why the Yugoslav-Soviet conflict was inevitable.

IU36 CONRAD, G. J. *Die Wirtschaft Jugoslawiens*. Berlin: Duncker and Humbolt, 1952. 176 p.

IU37 ČUBELIĆ, TOMO, and MILOSTIĆ, MILOVAN. *Pregled historije Narodnooslobodilačkog rata i revolucije naroda Jugoslavije*. 8th ed., Zagreb: Matica hrvatska, 1959. 255 p. A history of the Partisan struggle and the Communist rise to power.

IU38 DALMAS, LOUIS. *Le Communisme yougoslave depuis la rupture avec Moscou*. Paris: Terre des hommes, 1950. 220 p. German ed., *Quo Vadis, Tito? Das jugoslawische Experiment*. Frankfurt a/M: 1952. An analysis of the dispute between the USSR and Yugoslavia. The author sees a profound rupture and lasting after-effects in the world Communist movement.

IU39 DAVIDSON, BASIL. *Partisan Picture*. N.Y.: Universal Distributors, 1945. 351 p. Bedford, England: Bedford Books, 1946. The author, a British journalist, was sent to Yugoslavia in 1943 as a member of the British Mission to Tito's Partisans. This is his sympathetic account of what he saw and did in Yugoslavia in 1943-44.

IU40 DEDIJER, VLADIMIR. *The Beloved Land*. N.Y.: Simon & Schuster, 1961. 382 p. An autobiography carrying his story to 1945. Contains recollections of his work in the underground Yugoslav Communist Party in the 1930's and as a Partisan fighter in World War II. Also describes his relationship with Milovan Djilas, who was instrumental in bringing Dedijer into the Party.

IU41 DEDIJER, VLADIMIR. *Dnevnik*. Belgrade: Jugoslovenska Knjiga, 1945-50. 3 vols. Abridged ed., 1951. 871 p. English ed., *With Tito through the War; Partisan Diary, 1941-44*. London: 1951. 403 p. A well-written account of the day-by-day activities of the Yugoslav Communist Party during World War II by an able analyst and dedicated Communist, who later championed heretical ideas along with his friend Djilas. [A]

IU42 DEDIJER, VLADIMIR. *Jugoslovensko-Albanski odnosi, 1939-1948*. Belgrade: Borba, 1949. 243 p. A detailed description of the relations between Yugoslav and Albanian Communist groups. Significant references to wartime contacts and postwar relations between the Soviet and Yugoslav and Albanian Parties. An English translation was prepared by the Joint Publications Research Service. [A]

IU43 DEDIJER, VLADIMIR. *Tito*. N.Y.: Simon & Schuster, 1953. 443 p. British ed., *Tito Speaks*. London: Weidenfeld & Nicolson, 1953.

Original Serbo-Croatian ed., *Josip Broz Tito; Prilozi za biografiju.* Belgrade: Kultura, 1953. 518 p. A semi-official biography by a one-time trusted friend of Tito, who fought with the Partisans, became an important Communist editor, but who later left Yugoslavia because of his agreement with Milovan Djilas. An extremely interesting and informative book, based on personal knowledge and extensive conversations with Tito and other Communist leaders. Much on World War II and the Tito-Stalin break. The Serbo-Croatian edition is much more detailed and includes important material not in the foreign editions. [A]

IU44 DIMITRIJEVIĆ, SERGIJE. *Bibliografija socijalističkog i radničkog pokreta u Srbiji, s osvrtom na okolne krajeve naše zemlje.* Belgrade: Rad, 1953. 213 p.

IU45 DJILAS, MILOVAN. *Anatomy of a Moral; the Political Essays of Milovan Djilas.* Ed. by Abraham Rothberg. N.Y.: Praeger, 1959. 181 p. Translations of 18 articles which appeared in 1953-54 in *Borba*, official organ of the Yugoslav Communist Party, plus a sensational attack on Communist snobbery published in *Nova Misao.* The articles record, step by step, the intellectual process by which the author separated himself from the Communist Party and broke with Tito. For an analysis of the articles and the background of the dispute, see: "The Djilas Affair and Jugoslav Communism," by Thomas T. Hammond in *Foreign Affairs* (January 1955). It was these articles that led to the removal of Djilas from his former positions of power and prestige in the Yugoslav Communist hierarchy. [A]

IU46 DJILAS, MILOVAN. *Članci, 1941-1946.* Zagreb: Kultura, 1947. 333 p. A collection of articles on diverse subjects in politics and literature, published during World War II. Chapters on "Red Army" (p. 129-152) and "The Twenty Sixth Anniversary of the Bolshevik Revolution" (p. 157-163) shed light on Yugoslav-Soviet relations in the war.

IU47 DJILAS, MILOVAN. *Conversations with Stalin.* Trans. by Michael B. Petrovich. N.Y.: Harcourt, Brace & World, 1962. 214 p. Consists of reminiscences of official trips that Djilas made to Russia in 1944, 1945, and 1948, where he had extensive talks with Stalin, Molotov, and Khrushchev, as well as other Soviet dignitaries. Also describes briefly the founding of the Cominform and other details of relations among Communist states in the post-war period. Though valuable as an unusual peek behind the scenes of the Communist world, the book is tantalizingly brief and stingy on details. For writing this account Djilas was again arrested by the Yugoslav authorities. [A]

IU48 DJILAS, MILOVAN. *Lénine et les rapports entre états socialistes.* Paris: Livre Yougoslave, 1949. 125 p. English ed., N.Y.: Yugoslav Information Center, 1950. 56 p. States that one of the most essential tasks for "strengthening the unity of socialist lands and for the successful and correct development of the revolutionary and democratic struggle of the working class and people" is to revive, develop, and defend Lenin's theses on the subject. (Translation of an article in *Komunist*, September 1949.) [B]

IU49 DJILAS, MILOVAN. *The New Class; an Analysis of the Communist System.* N.Y.: Praeger, 1957. 214 p. A prominent Yugoslav, who defected from the Communist movement, accuses the Communist leaders of not understanding social democracy. When Communists rate the modern Western countries as "blind instruments of the monopolies," they are just as wrong as they are in interpreting their own system as a "classless society." When one class, party, or leader "stifles criticism completely, or holds absolute power, it or he inevitably falls into an unrealistic, egotistical, and pretentious judgment of reality." [A]

IU50 DJILAS, MILOVAN. *O agresivnom pritisku vlada sovjetskog bloka.* Belgrade: Borba, 1951. 68 p. Various speeches presenting the Yugoslav official line on the controversy between the USSR and Yugoslavia and on pressures exerted by Soviet satellites on Yugoslavia. [B]

IU51 DJILAS, MILOVAN. *On New Roads of Socialism.* Belgrade: Jugoslovenska Knjiga, 1950. 36 p. A critical analysis of the Soviet system by a Yugoslav Communist with special reference to economic "antagonisms" inside the USSR, the emergence of a privileged "bureaucratic stratum" in the USSR, and the subjugation and exploitation of other socialist countries. [B]

IU52 DJORDJEVIĆ, JOVAN. *Društveno-političko i državno uredjenje Jugoslavije.* Belgrade: Savez udruženja pravnika Jugoslavije, 1959. 350 p. An analysis by one of the leading legal experts of the Communist regime.

IU53 DJORDJEVIĆ, JOVAN. *Sistem lokalne samouprave u Jugoslaviji.* Belgrade: Savremena administracija, 1957. 250 p.

IU53A DRACHKOVICH, MILORAD M. *United States Aid to Yugoslavia and Poland; Analysis of a Controversy.* Washington: American Enterprise Institute for Public Policy Research, 1963. 124 p. The author holds that American aid to the two countries did not induce hoped-for internal democratization and a pro-Western orientation in foreign policy.

IU54 DRAGNICH, ALEX N. *Tito's Promised Land.* New Brunswick, N.J.: Rutgers U. Press, 1954. 337 p. A criticism of Yugoslavia's Communist government and its domestic and foreign policies by a former American government official, now a university professor. Questions the motives and integrity of the Yugoslav government and discourages American aid to it.

IU55 DRASKOVICH, SLOBODAN M. *Tito: Moscow's Trojan Horse.* Chicago: Regnery, 1957. 357 p. A Serbian nationalist view of the Yugoslav Communist regime. His thesis is that there is no difference between Yugoslav and Soviet Communism, and that the two belong to a single world-wide conspiracy.

IU56 ERIĆ, MILIVOJE. *Agrarna reforma u Jugoslaviji, 1918-1951 god.* Sarajevo: Veselin Masleša, 1958. 547 p.

IU57 FARRELL, ROBERT B. *Jugoslavia and the Soviet Union, 1948-1956; an Analysis with Documents.* Hamden, Conn.: Shoe String Press, 1956. 220 p. A useful handbook on the principal issues in the controversy between Yugoslavia and the Soviet Union. [B]

IU58 FOTICH, CONSTANTINE C. *The War We Lost; Yugoslavia's Tragedy and the Failure of the West.* N.Y.: Viking, 1948. 344 p. A nationalist Serbian view of Communist Yugoslavia and of Mihailovich's Chetniks by the wartime Yugoslav Ambassador in Washington. A powerful critique of Tito's government and those who helped bring it to power.

IU59 FREE EUROPE COMMITTEE, FREE EUROPE PRESS, RESEARCH AND ANALYSIS DEPARTMENT. *The Case of Milovan Djilas; the "New Course" on Trial.* (Research Report 4). N.Y.: 1954. 94 p.

IU60 FREE EUROPE COMMITTEE, FREE EUROPE PRESS, RESEARCH AND ANALYSIS DEPARTMENT. *A Chronology of Post-War Events in Yugoslavia; Consolidation and Concession, 1951-1953.* N.Y.: 1954. 3 vols.

IU61 GASTEYGER, CURT. *Die feindlichen Brüder. Jugoslawiens neuer Konflikt mit dem Ostblock 1958.* Bern: Sager, 1960. 314 p. A collection of documents concerning the 1958 conflict between Yugoslavia and the Eastern Bloc. Includes speeches of Tito, Kardelj, Rankovich, and Khrushchev, plus newspaper articles and certain other materials.

IU62 GRIBANOV, B. *Banda Tito—orudie amerikano-angliiskikh podzhigatelei voiny.* Moscow: Gospolitizdat, 1951. 150 p. An unfavorable statement on the activities of Tito's Partisans in World War II, and a development of the thesis that the USSR won the war and that the Red Army liberated Yugoslavia. A tirade against Tito and his followers.

IU63 HALPERIN, ERNST. *Der siegreiche Ketzer; Titos Kampf gegen Stalin.* Cologne: Verlag für Politik und Wirtschaft, 1957. 390 p. English ed., *The Triumphant Heretic; Tito's Struggle against Stalin.* London: Heinemann, 1958. 324 p. A superior analysis of the Soviet-

Yugoslav controversy and the Yugoslav type of socialism. The author concludes that the Hungarian Revolution "has affected not only the Soviet leaders but also the Yugoslav Communists." This he attributes to "two mistakes committed" by Tito: (1) He took the side of the "Party apparatus against the innovator Djilas"—an act which has doomed the Titoist ideology to "stagnation"; and (2) Tito's abandonment of "his Hungarian friends" and his coming to "terms with the Stalinist Gerö."
[A]

IU64 HALPERN, JOEL M. *A Serbian Village.* N.Y.: Columbia, 1958. 325 p. An anthropological study, by a professor at Brandeis, of the village of Orašac. Although not dealing directly with the Communist regime in Yugoslavia, it describes the changes occurring in village life as a result of policies instituted since the Communists rose to power. Excellent for a background understanding of Yugoslavia today.

IU65 HAMMOND, THOMAS T. *Yugoslavia Between East and West.* N.Y.: Foreign Policy Association, 1954. 61 p. An analysis of Yugoslavia's international position and internal developments from 1948 through 1953. Based on research and observation in Yugoslavia in 1953.

IU66 HODGKINSON, HARRY. *West and East of Tito.* London: Victor Gollancz, 1952. 190 p. American ed., *Challenge to the Kremlin.* N.Y.: Praeger, 1952. 190 p. Thesis: The Soviet-Yugoslav dispute is no surprise, because three "vital features" of Stalin's make-up explain it. These features: his views on the spread of revolution; the primacy of "military and strategic factors" in his thoughts on foreign affairs; and, his habit of repeating "previous patterns of action."

IU67 HOFFMAN, GEORGE W., and NEAL, FRED WARNER. *Yugoslavia and the New Communism.* N.Y.: Twentieth Century Fund, 1962. 546 p. A useful reference work, covering many aspects of contemporary Yugoslav civilization.
[A]

IU68 HOFFMANN, WALTER. *Marxismus oder Titoismus? Titos Versuch zur Neuordnung gesellschaftlicher Beziehungen im Staate.* Munich: Isar, 1953. 116 p. A short statement on the development of Yugoslavia's Communist society, economic problems and internal transformation, expulsion from the Cominform and relations with the Soviet Union.

IU69 HUOT, LOUIS (Major). *Guns for Tito.* N.Y.: L. B. Fischer, 1945. 273 p. An American officer describes his visit to Yugoslavia in 1943 and the methods by which arms were shipped from Italy to the Partisans.

IU70 HUSSARD, J. *Vu en Yougoslavie, 1939-1944.* Lausanne: Éd. du Haut-Pays, 1945. 267 p. A popular description of times and events concerning Yugoslavia from the outbreak of the war until its end. The author sympathizes with the plight of the Serbs and their cause.

IU71 *Istorijski arhiv Komunističke partije Jugoslavije.* Belgrade: Istorijsko odeljenje centralnog komiteta KPJ, 1949-51. 8 vols. Primarily documents and files from the Central Committee's archives. Various materials, including announcements, letters, newspaper articles. Useful chiefly for a study of Yugoslav Communist activities before and during World War II. [B]

IU72 JACKSON, GEORGE D., JR. "Soviet-Yugoslav-Bulgarian Relations since World War II." Certificate essay, Russian Institute, Columbia, 1956. 95 p.

IU73 JONES, WILLIAM. *Twelve Months with Tito's Partisans.* Bedford, Eng.: Bedford Books, 1946. 128 p. A description of the activities of the Partisans in Croatia, by a member of the R.A.F. who was there in 1943-44.

IU74 JOVANOVIĆ, BATRIĆ. *Komunistička partija Jugoslavije u Crnoj Gori 1919-1940.* Belgrade: Vojno delo, 1959. 341 p. An official history of the Communist movement in Montenegro.

IU75 *Jugosloveni u Španiji.* Sarajevo: Svjetlost, 1959. 272 p. On the role of Yugoslavs on the Loyalist side in the Spanish Civil War, where a number of the Partisans received their first military experience.

IU76 JUKIĆ, ILIJA. *Tito between East and West.* London: Demos, 1961. 99 p. A former official of the Yugoslav government-in-exile analyzes the origins and causes of Stalin's break with Tito, the Western "rescue" of Tito, the reconciliation between Khrushchev and Tito, and the "new rift" and "ideological difference" between Khrushchev and Tito. In view of Tito's role in preparation of the Summit Conference of non-aligned nations in Belgrade in 1961 and Tito's declarations on that occasion, the author urges "the earliest possible re-examination by the West of its present policy toward the Tito regime."

IU77 KALVODA, JOSEP. *Titoism and Masters of Imposture.* N.Y.: Vintage, 1958. 327 p. An attempt to show that the U.S. policy of aiding Tito is wrong and that Tito "works for the same world-wide conspiracy as Khrushchev, Mao, or Gomulka." Of some value is the author's treatment of Yugoslav-Soviet relations, although he adds nothing new.

IU78 KARDELJ, EDVARD. *After Five Years; Socialist Movements and the USSR Five Years after the Yugoslav-Cominform Split.* N.Y.: Yugoslav Information Center, 1953. 24 p. A criticism of Stalinism by the prominent Yugoslav political leader and theorist. Comments also on the future of the "Soviet system." [B]

IU79 KARDELJ, EDVARD. *The Communist Party of Yugoslavia in the Struggle for New Yugoslavia, for People's Authority and for Socialism*. Belgrade: 1948. 96 p. German ed., Belgrade: 1948. 128 p. An important statement on Yugoslavia's internal and foreign policies prior to the expulsion from the Cominform. Criticises American policies and praises the Soviet Union and the "anti-imperialist front." Valuable also for an understanding of Party tactics prior to 1948.

IU80 KARDELJ, EDVARD. *Deset godina Narodne Revolucije, 1941-1951*. Belgrade: Kultura, 1951. 106 p. A discussion of miscellaneous topics pertaining to Yugoslavia's internal and foreign policies by a leading Communist and government official.

IU81 KARDELJ, EDVARD. *Ekspoze o vanjskoj politici FNRJ*. Zagreb: "Naprijed," 1951. 88 p. A foreign policy statement, including a discussion of relations with the USSR.

IU82 KARDELJ, EDVARD. *On People's Democracy in Yugoslavia*. N.Y.: Yugoslav Information Center, 1949. 97 p. A justification of the Yugoslav political and doctrinal position *vis à vis* the Soviet model.

IU83 KARDELJ, EDVARD. *Problemi naše socijalističke izgradnje*. Belgrade: Kultura, 1954-60. 3 vols. A collection of articles, reports and speeches covering a wide range of topics on internal and external affairs of Yugoslavia. A valuable source by virtue of the official position held by the author. Discusses relations between Yugoslavia and Soviet Union and the errors of Stalinism in several items, especially in Volume III. [A]

IU84 KARDELJ, EDVARD. *Put nove Jugoslavije (1941-1945)*. Belgrade: Kultura, 1949. 580 p. A collection of articles and speeches on wartime Communist activities and on problems in foreign relations.

IU84A KARDELJ, EDVARD. *Razvoj slovenačkog nacionalnog pitanja*. Belgrade: Kultura, 1958. 452 p. A new edition of Kardelj's prewar work on the nationalities question. A new introduction attacks the Stalinist view of the nationalities question and defines the Yugoslav position on this issue.

IU85 KARDELJ, EDVARD. *Socijalizam i rat*. Belgrade: Kultura, 1960. 231 p. English ed., *Socialism and War; a Survey of Chinese Criticism of the Policy of Coexistence*. London: Methuen, 1960. 238 p. In this major contribution from the Yugoslav side to the Communist foreign policy debate, a leading associate of Tito's formulates the "revisionist" philosophy of international relations by way of a systematic critique of the "dogmatist" position of Peking. The author holds firmly to the concept of peaceful coexistence between states with differing social systems. [A]

IU86 KARDELJ, EDVARD. *Trieste and Yugoslav-Italian Relations.* N.Y.: Yugoslav Information Center, 1953. 60 p. An official statement on policy regarding Trieste and Italy.

IU87 KARDELJ, EDVARD. *Yugoslavia's Foreign Policy; Address Delivered during the Debate on the Budget in the Federal Assembly on December 29, 1948.* Belgrade: 1949. 61 p. A special address by the Vice-President and Foreign Minister of Yugoslavia, delivered when there was still hope that the schism between the USSR and Yugoslavia would be mended. The speaker drew a distinction between the USSR and the capitalist states and expressed hope that the USSR and Yugoslavia would resolve their differences "socialistically."

IU88 KARDELJ, EDVARD, and DJILAS, MILOVAN. *Nova Jugoslavija u savremenom svetu.* Belgrade: Kultura, 1951. 110 p. An official statement on Yugoslavia's relations with the USSR, and on foreign policy in general.

IU89 KARDELJ, EDVARD, and DJILAS, MILOVAN. *O agresivnom pritisku vlada Sovjetskog bloka na Jugoslaviju.* Zagreb: "Naprijed," 1951. 96 p. Speeches by leading Yugoslav Communist spokesmen denouncing the tactics of the Soviet bloc and explaining the kind of pressures and provocations that were used to try to force Yugoslavia's submission.

IU90 KARDELJ, EDVARD, and PIJADE, MOŠA. *Ekspozeji.* Belgrade: 1949. 35 p. Yugoslav official spokesmen defend their country's foreign policy despite Soviet attacks. A discussion of Yugoslavia's position as regards the projected Balkan Federation, which was opposed by the USSR.

IU91 KARTUN, DEREK. *Tito's Plot against Europe; the Story of the Rajk Conspiracy.* London: 1949; N.Y.: International, 1950. 127 p. A propaganda tirade by the editor of the London *Daily Worker* against Tito and his supporters. Cites crimes allegedly committed by Tito against those loyal to the Cominform. Most of the book is based on the Hungarian Blue Book, *Laszlo Rajk and His Accomplices.*

IU92 KLEIN, GEORGE. "Yugoslavia in World Affairs." Ph.D. dissertation, Illinois, 1960.

IU93 KLUGMANN, JAMES. *From Trotsky to Tito.* London: Lawrence & Wishart, 1951. 204 p. A one-time English official and UNRRA employee in Yugoslavia writes critically of those who deviated from Stalinism. A propaganda piece.

IU94 KNEŽEVIĆ, RADOJE, ed. *Knjiga o Draži*. Vol. I, *1941-1943*. Windsor, Canada: Srpska Narodna Odbrana, 1956. 412 p. An emigré account of the Mihailovich case.

IU94A KOLIŠEVSKI, LAZAR. *Macedonian National Question*. Belgrade: "Jugoslavija," 1959. 50 p. A re-examination of the Macedonian national question by a leading Yugoslav Communist. First published as *Istorija stvarnost aspiracii*. Skoplje: Kultura, 1958.

IU95 KORBEL, JOSEF. *Tito's Communism*. Denver: U. of Denver, 1951. 368 p. A criticism of Yugoslavia's Communist government and its domestic and foreign policies. The author was the Minister in Belgrade of the democratic government of Czechoslovakia after World War II and thus had personal contact with Tito and other Yugoslav leaders. He sees Yugoslav Communism basically unchanged during the period 1948-50. [A]

IU96 KUIĆ, VUKAN. "The Titoist Deviations from the Orthodox Bolshevist Doctrine." Ph.D. dissertation, U. of Chicago, 1959.

IU97 LAZIĆ, BRANKO M. *Tito et la révolution yougoslave, 1937-1956*. Paris: Fasquelle, 1957. 279 p. An analysis of the reorganization of the Yugoslav Communist Party under Tito's leadership, the Party's tactics and successes during World War II, and the post-war developments and conflict with the USSR. An informed author re-states familiar issues.

IU98 LAZIĆ, BRANKO M. *Titov pokret i režim u Jugoslaviji, 1941-1946*. Munich: The Author, 1946. 219 p. A Serbian nationalist writes of the beginnings of the Yugoslav Communist movement, interwar changes in Party tactics and personnel, the Chetniks and Partisans, and the peculiarities and shortcomings of the Yugoslav Communist system.

IU99 LENOV, IU. *Borba iugoslavskogo naroda za nezavisimost i svobodu svoei rodiny*. Moscow: Gospolitizdat, 1944. 135 p. A propagandistic brochure on Yugoslav Communist resistance during World War II. The work reflects Soviet policy toward Yugoslavia in the summer of 1944. The author exalts the achievements of Yugoslav Partisan troops. Of some interest are references to Soviet negotiations with the Yugoslav government-in-exile.

IU100 LEONHARD, WOLFGANG. *Die Wahrheit über das sozialistische Jugoslawien; eine Antwort auf die Kominform-Verleumdungen*. Belgrade: Jugoslovenska Knjiga, 1949. 70 p.

IU101 MAČEK, VLADKO. *In the Struggle for Freedom*. N.Y.: Robert Speller, 1957. 280 p. Memoirs of the head of the Croatian Peasant Party. Argues that Communism is "one and indivisible regardless of form" and that there is no such thing as "national Communism."

IU102 MACLEAN, FITZROY. *Eastern Approaches.* London: J. Cape, 1949. 543 p. American ed., *Escape to Adventure.* Boston: Little, Brown, 1950. Deals in part with the author's experiences as British liaison officer with Tito's Partisans during the Second World War. A British Conservative writing sympathetically of the Communist resistance movement. Valuable also for first-hand accounts of Churchill's policies regarding Tito. [A]

IU103 MACLEAN, FITZROY. *The Heretic; the Life and Times of Josip Broz-Tito.* N.Y.: Harpers, 1957. 436 p. British ed., *Disputed Barricade.* London: J. Cape, 1957. A biography replete with facts, carefully and well presented. The author was a wartime British liaison officer with the Partisans of Tito. He treats Yugoslav political affairs with sympathy. His conclusion: "For his leadership in the War of National Liberation, and . . . his resolute rejection of Stalin's overlordship, Tito . . . will always be remembered in the history and legend of his own people." [A]

IU104 MCVICKER, CHARLES P. *Titoism; Pattern for International Communism.* N.Y.: St. Martin's, 1957. 332 p. A solid study of Yugoslavia's government, its structure, and domestic and foreign policies. The author sees in Yugoslavia's form of Communism a new way to Communism which is different from the Soviet model. But unless Tito grants "increasingly full political democracy," in the long run "it is doomed to fail, even as benevolent totalitarianism." [A]

IU105 MARJANOVIĆ, JOVAN. *Narodnooslobodilački rat; Narodna revolucija u Jugoslaviji 1941-1945; kratak pregled.* 3rd ed. Belgrade: Kultura, 1959. 144 p. Relates Yugoslavia's Communist-led liberation war against the Germans, 1941-45, including the wartime reorganization of its Communist Party, and Yugoslav-Soviet links. The international character of the country's partisan warfare is also discussed, while the significance of the other resistance groups is neglected.

IU106 MARKERT, WERNER. *Jugoslawien.* Cologne: Böhlau, 1954. 400 p. Useful as a reference book. Contains an excellent bibliography and a good index. One section of the book treats Yugoslav foreign relations, including the conflict with the USSR.

IU107 MARKHAM, REUBEN H. *Tito's Imperial Communism.* Chapel Hill: U. of North Carolina Press, 1947. 292 p. An indictment of Tito and his Communist movement. The author sees in it a powerful conspiratorial and undemocratic movement which relies on terror and police for its survival.

IU108 MARKOVIĆ, DRAGAN, and RISTOVIĆ, LJUBIŠA. *Pred nepriznatim sudom.* Vol. I., *Veliki sudski procesi komunistima u predratnoj Jugoslaviji.* Belgrade: Kultura, 1959. 428 p.

IU109 MARKOVIĆ, MOMA, and LAĆA, IVAN. *Organizacioni razvitak Komunističke partije Jugoslavije (SKJ)*. Belgrade: Kultura, 1960. 114 p.

IU110 MARTIN, DAVID. *Ally Betrayed; the Uncensored Story of Tito and Mihailovich*. Foreword by Rebecca West. N.Y.: Prentice-Hall, 1946. 372 p. Strongly critical of Yugoslavia's Communist regime and favorable to the cause of Mihailovich and his Chetniks. Condemns what the author calls the "Allied betrayal" of the Serb leader and attributes this to nefarious influences in the U.S. government.

IU111 MEIER, VIKTOR. *Das neue jugoslawische Wirtschaftssystem*. Zürich: Polygraphischer, 1956. 216 p.

IU112 MIHAILOVIĆ, DRAŽA, defendant. *The Trial of Dragoljub-Draža Mihailović, Stenographic Record and Documents from the Trial of Dragoljub-Draža Mihailović*. Belgrade: Union of the Journalists' Associations of the Federative People's Republic of Yugoslavia, 1946. 552 p. A collection of the portions of the 1946 treason trials which relate to Mihailovic. This partial stenographic record, interspersed with photographs and facsimiles, contains his indictment, examination, and condemnation.

IU113 MIOKOVATS, SRBISLAV M. *La Yougoslavie sous le knout*. Paris: Nouvelles Éditions Latines, 1948. 255 p. A sketchy history of the Yugoslav Communist Party from 1919 to 1948. Pleads with the Western democracies "to aid morally and materially the Yugoslav people that they may liberate themselves from the Communist dictatorship." Critical of Soviet designs on Yugoslavia.

IU114 MIR, LJUBO. *Das neue Jugoslawien*. Zürich: Europa, 1945. 140 p. A discussion of the Communist resistance movement in wartime Yugoslavia and the founding of the Communist state, by a political sympathizer.

IU115 MOCH, JULES. *Yougoslavie, terre d'experience*. Monaco: Éditions du rocher, 1953. 340 p.

IU116 MOJSOV, LAZO. *Bulgarskata rabotnička partija (komunisti) i makedonskoto nacionalno prašanje*. Skopje: Zemskiot odbor na Narodniot front na Makedonija, 1948. 273 p.

IU117 NATIONAL PEACE COUNCIL, LONDON. *Yugoslavia and Peace, a Study of Cominform Accusations; Report of the National Peace Council Delegation to Yugoslavia, September, 1950*. London: 1950. 27 p. Describes as "untrue" several important Cominform accusations leveled at Yugoslavia.

IU118 NEAL, FRED WARNER. *Titoism in Action; the Reforms in Yugoslavia after 1948*. Berkeley: U. of California Press, 1958. 331 p. A good treatment of Yugoslavia's domestic and foreign relations, government reforms, administrative reorganization, and the nature of the Soviet-Yugoslav controversy. The author is an American professor who has had considerable experience in Yugoslavia. [A]

IU119 NEILL, ROY S. *Once Only*. London: Cape, 1947. 285 p. The personal story of a British prisoner of war who escaped from a camp in Graz, Austria, in August 1944, and succeeded in joining Tito's Partisans in Slovenia. Relates the events of seven weeks of guerrilla warfare before reaching Bari by plane.

IU120 NEWMAN, BERNARD. *Tito's Yugoslavia*. London: Robert Hale, 1952. 269 p. A popular account of Yugoslav history and ethnography, including developments under Communism.

IU121 NEWMAN, BERNARD. *Unknown Yugoslavia*. London: Herbert Jenkins, 1960. 221 p. A journalistic work by a prolific British writer.

IU122 *O Kontrarevolucionarnoj i klevetničkoj kampanji protiv Socijalističke Jugoslavije*. Book I. Belgrade: Borba, 1949. 559 p. An official publication on the "counter-revolutionary" and other anti-Yugoslav activities by the Soviet Union and its satellites.

IU123 OSTOVIĆ, PAVLE D. *The Truth about Yugoslavia*. N.Y.: Roy, 1952. 300 p. By a patriotic Croat who believes in the necessity of a unified Yugoslav state and who is a critic of Serbian nationalists and the Chetniks. Sees no alternative for the time being to the existing Yugoslav Communist government.

IU124 PADEV, MICHAEL. *Marshal Tito*. London: F. Muller, 1944. 126 p. A superficial, uncritical and totally panegyrical work, based largely on material furnished to the author by the Slovene-American writer Louis Adamic and the Partisan Republican Association in Great Britain.

IU125 PATTEE, RICHARD F. *The Case of Cardinal Aloysius Stepinac*. Milwaukee: Bruce, 1953. 499 p. A defense of the Catholic primate of Croatia, who was accused by the Communists of collaborating with the Pavelich regime.

IU126 PETER II, KING OF YUGOSLAVIA. *A King's Heritage*. N.Y.: Putnam, 1954. 304 p. A sketchy account of the King's experiences and observations from his youth through the Second World War. Of some interest are his comments on the Soviet attitude to the Chetnik-Partisan civil war in Yugoslavia. Shows a lack of first-hand knowledge of many issues.

IU127 PETKOVIĆ, RADIVOJE. *Local Self-Government in Yugoslavia; the Commune.* Belgrade: "Jugoslavija," 1955. 114 p.

IU128 PIJADE, MOŠA S. *Izabrani govori i članci.* Zagreb: Kultura, 1948-50. 2 vols. A selection of speeches and articles on Yugoslavia's domestic and foreign affairs. Important statements on Yugoslavia's policy regarding Albania, Trieste, Bulgaria, and Greece. Vol. I covers 1941-47 and vol. II covers 1948-49. Pijade was an old pre-war Communist and friend of Tito's who played an important role in the Communist regime until his death.

IU129 PIJADE, MOŠA S. *O tridesetogodišnjici Komunističke partije Jugoslavije; referat održan u Beogradu 30 apr., 1949 g.* Belgrade: Kultura, 1949. 36 p. A history of the Yugoslav Communist Party from 1919 to 1949. Condemns the Cominform campaign against Yugoslavia. See also his "Trideset godina KPJ," *Komunist*, No. 2 (1949), p. 17-25. [B]

IU130 PIJADE, MOŠA S. *Priča o sovjetskoj pomoći za dizanje ustanka u Jugoslaviji.* Belgrade: Glavna polit. uprava Jugoslovenske armije, 1950. 38 p. English ed., *About the Legend that the Yugoslav Uprising Owed its Existence to Soviet Assistance.* London: 1950. 24 p. A refutation of the Soviet claim that the liberation of Yugoslavia was "the work of the Red Army." Gives a series of notes exchanged between Tito and Soviet Communist leaders during the Second World War which prove that the USSR gave little assistance to the Yugoslav Communists.

IU131 PIRADOV, A. *Titovtsy.* Moscow: Znanie, 1952. 48 p. An indictment of Tito, who is accused of being a capitalist stooge. Includes a description of alleged Tito-Rankovich terror in Yugoslavia. Although propagandistic in form, the brochure is helpful for understanding Soviet tactics employed in fighting Tito.

IU132 POPOVIĆ, MILENTIJE. *On Economic Relations Among Socialist States.* London: Yugoslav Press, 1950. 72 p. French ed., *Des rapports économiques entre états socialistes.* Paris: Livre yougoslave, 1949. 140 p. A leading Yugoslav economist tells what economic relations between socialist states should be. The economy should be developed according to local conditions and needs. Condemns Soviet economic practices and interference in the affairs of other socialist countries.

IU132A *Pregled Istorije Saveza Komunista Jugoslavije.* Belgrade: Institut za izučavanje radničkog pokreta, 1963. 570 p. A survey of the history of the Yugoslav Communist party and its relations with Moscow before and after 1948. Official but not documented. Lacks both index and bibliography.

IU133 PRIDONOFF, ERIC L. *Tito's Yugoslavia.* Washington: Public Affairs Press, 1955. 243 p. An account highly critical of both the Tito government and U.S. policy toward it. Focuses on the first several years of Tito's rule.

IU134 *Priručnik za istoriju Saveza komunista Jugoslavije.* Belgrade: "Rad," 1958. 268 p.

IU135 RADULOVIĆ, MONTY. *Tito's Republic.* London: Coldharbour, 1948. 241 p. A native of Yugoslavia who became a British correspondent, Radulović returned at the end of World War II, but quickly became disillusioned with the Communist regime.

IU136 RANKOVIĆ, ALEKSANDAR. *Izabrani govori i članci, 1941-1951.* Zagreb: Kultura, 1951. 430 p. A collection of speeches and articles on a variety of subjects, but primarily on internal Yugoslav problems and the Communist Party's activities and policies. The author has been one of the top leaders in Yugoslavia ever since the Communist rise to power and is considered one of those most likely to succeed Tito.

IU137 REALE, EUGENIO. *Avec Jacques Duclos au banc des accusés à la réunion constitutive du Kominform à Szklarska Poreba (22-27 Septembre 1947).* Paris: Plon, 1958. 203 p. The importance of this volume, which contains notes taken by one of two delegates of the Italian Communist Party at the founding meeting of the Cominform, is that it reproduces "ultra leftist" speeches made by Edvard Kardelj and Milovan Djilas, who attended the gathering in the name of the Communist Party of Yugoslavia.

IU137A RIBAR, IVAN. *Politički zapisi.* Belgrade: Prosveta, 1948-1952. 4 vols. A valuable work by a prominent and active political figure, President of the Constituent Assembly at the end of the First World War. Discusses the author's experiences and political philosophy. In the Second World War he joined Tito's Partisans.

IU138 RISTIĆ, DRAGOLJUB. *Moskovske satelitske trupe.* Belgrade: Narodna kniga, 1952. 38 p. Discusses military conditions in the people's democratic countries, including their defense budgets, with heavy emphasis on Yugoslavia's neighboring states. Reveals also the numerical strength of the satellite armies, as well as that of the Soviet occupation forces. Concludes that the satellite armies are aggressive tools under the command of the USSR.

IU139 ROOTHAM, JASPER. *Miss Fire; the Chronicle of a British Mission to Mihailovich, 1943-1944.* London: Chatto & Windus, 1946. A British colonel who was sent on an official mission to Mihailovich describes his attempts to keep the Chetniks fighting against the Germans, and the various difficulties that he encountered.

IU140 RUSSIA (1923-USSR), MINISTERSTVO INOSTRANNYKH DEL. *Noty sovetskogo pravitelstva iugoslavskomu pravitelstvu, 11, 18, 29 avgusta, 28 sentiabria 1949 goda.* Moscow: Gospolitizdat, 1949. 46 p. Two of the notes pertain to the Yugoslav territorial claims against Austria. A third note protests Yugoslav "illegal arrests" of Soviet citizens, and the final note has to do with the Soviet renunciation of the agreement of friendship and mutual aid with Yugoslavia.

IU141 ST. JOHN, ROBERT. *The Silent People Speak.* Garden City, N.Y.: Doubleday, 1948. 397 p. The author, an American journalist, published a highly popular book about Yugoslavia before the Communists, entitled *The Land of the Silent People.* After a return journey to post-war Yugoslavia, he wrote this rather pro-Tito account.

IU142 SAVEZ KOMUNISTA HRVATSKE, CENTRALNI KOMITET. *Dokumenti historije KPH.* Zagreb: Izd. Historijskog odjeljenja CK KPH, 1951-53. 3 vols. Volume I reprints articles from *Srp i čekić* from the period 1940-41; volume II does the same from *Vjesnik* (1941-43); and volume III from *Naprijed* (1943). Articles treat many subjects, including the Soviet Union, which is praised for its accomplishments and for the success of the Red Army.

IU143 SAVEZ KOMUNISTA HRVATSKE, 2 KONGRES, ZAGREB, 1948. *Drugi kongres Komunističke partije Hrvatske, 21-25 XI, 1948.* Zagreb: Ognjen Prica, 1949. 284 p. Many topics, including Yugoslav-Soviet relations, are discussed in this report of a Croatian Communist Party congress.

IU144 SAVEZ KOMUNISTA JUGOSLAVIJE. *Political Report of the Central Committee of the Communist Party of Yugoslavia.* Belgrade: 1948. 136 p. French ed., Paris: 1948. 156 p. A report delivered by Tito at the 5th Congress of the CPY. The most essential official interpretation of the history of Yugoslav Communism, concerning the inter-war period, the Partisan struggle, and the "Stalinistic" period of Yugoslav Communism. [A]

IU145 SAVEZ KOMUNISTA JUGOSLAVIJE. *Program of the Communist Party of Yugoslavia.* Belgrade: 1948. 38 p. The program adopted by the 5th Congress.

IU146 SAVEZ KOMUNISTA JUGOSLAVIJE. *The Program of the League of Yugoslav Communists; Adopted by the VII Congress of the League of Yugoslav Communists Held from 22-26 April, 1958 in Ljubljana.* Belgrade: "Jugoslavija," 1958. 271 p. Other English editions: Belgrade: Kultura, 1958. 258 p. *Yugoslavia's Way; the Program of the League of Communists of Yugoslavia*, transl. by S. Pribichevich. N.Y.: All Nations Press, 1958. 263 p. French ed., Paris: R. Julliard,

1958. 300 p. The most complete statement of "Titoism." The program was subjected to severe criticism by the Soviets and the Chinese Communists, who denounced it as "revisionism." The key document of the second Soviet-Yugoslav controversy. This is the final version, as adopted, after some changes had been made in response to criticisms by other Communist parties. [A]

IU147 SAVEZ KOMUNISTA JUGOSLAVIJE. *Šesti kongres KPJ (Zagreb 2-7 novembra 1952).* Belgrade: Kultura, 1952. 274 p. Abridged English ed., *Sixth Congress, November 3-7, 1952.* Belgrade: 1953. 128 p.

IU148 SAVEZ KOMUNISTA JUGOSLAVIJE. *Statut Komunističke partije Jugoslavije; usvojen na V kongresu KPJ, 28 jula 1948.* Belgrade: 1951. 30 p. English ed., Belgrade: 1948. 19 p.

IU149 SAVEZ KOMUNISTA JUGOSLAVIJE. *Statut Saveza komunista Jugoslavije (usvojen na VI kongresu KPJ).* Belgrade: Kultura, 1952. 32 p.

IU150 SAVEZ KOMUNISTA JUGOSLAVIJE. *Statut Saveza komunista Jugoslavije; usvojen na VII kongresu Saveza komunista Jugoslavije.* Belgrade: Kultura, 1958. 35 p.

IU151 SAVEZ KOMUNISTA JUGOSLAVIJE, CENTRALNI KOMITET, KOMISIJA ZA PROGRAM. *Nacrt programa Saveza Komunista Jugoslavije.* Belgrade: Kultura, 1958. 230 p. The original *draft* of the program of the Communist Party which was adopted, after changes had been made, at the 7th Party Congress in 1958. Compare with the final version, listed above. Chapter III of the draft appeared in English in *Yugoslav Facts and Views*, no. 48 (April 22, 1958), p. 1-10. This is the Chapter which underwent the major changes, while revisions elsewhere were nominal. [A]

IU152 SAVEZ KOMUNISTA JUGOSLAVIJE, 5 KONGRES, BELGRAD, 1948. *V Kongres, 21-28 Jula, 1948; stenografske bilješke.* Zagreb: Kultura, 1949. 858 p. French ed., Paris: 1949. Covers a wide range of subjects on the internal and foreign affairs of Yugoslavia, including Yugoslav-Soviet relations. [A]

IU153 SAVEZ KOMUNISTA JUGOSLAVIJE, 5 KONGRES, BELGRAD, 1948. *V Kongres Komunističke partije Jugoslavije; izvještaji i referati.* Belgrade: Kultura, 1949. 575 p. Includes a long statement on the history of Yugoslav socialism and the Yugoslav Communist Party. Also refutations of Cominform charges and some comments on Soviet-Yugoslav relations. [B]

IU154 SAVEZ KOMUNISTA JUGOSLAVIJE, 6 KONGRES, ZAGREB, 1952. *Borba komunistov Jugoslavije za socialistično demokratiju (Sveze Komunistov Jugoslavije).* Ljubljana: Cankarjeva založba, 1952. 324 p. Contains many references to Yugoslav-Soviet relations. Of special importance are speeches by Tito (p. 3-104) and Edvard Kardelj (p. 142-166), which strongly criticize Soviet foreign policy and Stalin. Individual international problems are cited and Soviet policy regarding them analyzed. [A]

IU155 SAVEZ KOMUNISTA JUGOSLAVIJE, 6 KONGRES, ZAGREB, 1952. *VI Kongres Komunističke partije Jugoslavije, 2-7 novembra 1952; stenografske beleške.* Belgrade: Kultura, 1953. 442 p. The unequivocal condemnation of Stalinism by Yugoslav Communists. An essential document for understanding this specific stage in the development of Yugoslav Communism. [A]

IU156 SAVEZ KOMUNISTA JUGOSLAVIJE, 7 KONGRES, LJUBLJANA, 1958. *Stenografske beleške Sedmi Kongres SKJ, 22-26 aprila, 1958, Ljubljana.* Belgrade: Kultura, 1958. 1156 p. As indispensable as the reports of the 5th and 6th congresses for information on the evolution of the internal and foreign policies of the Tito regime. [A]

IU157 SAVEZ KOMUNISTA JUGOSLAVIJE, CENTRALNI KOMITET. *Statement of the Central Committee of the Communist Party of Yugoslavia.* Belgrade: 1948. 36 p. Contains various official statements of the Yugoslav Communist Party: (1) Statement on the Cominform Resolution to close ranks; (2) Statement of June 20, 1948, sent to the Cominform; (3) Decision to expel Andrija Hebrang and Sreten Žujović from the Yugoslav Communist Party; (4) Reply to the Bulgarian Communist leaders. [A]

IU158 SAVEZ KOMUNISTA SRBIJE. *II Kongres komunističke partije Srbije.* Belgrade: Prosveta, 1949. 310 p. Speeches and resolutions. References to Soviet-Yugoslav relations interspersed throughout the pages. Especially useful on this subject is Pijade's speech.

IU159 SCHNEIDERMAN, JEREMIAH. "Russo-Yugoslav Relations: 1941-1948." Ph.D. dissertation, Chicago, 1953.

IU160 SHOUP, PAUL. "The Solution of the National Problem in Yugoslavia after World War II." Ph.D. dissertation, Columbia, 1961. An excellent analysis of the Communist regime's treatment of the non-Slavic minorities. Based on extensive research and field work in Yugoslavia. The author is a professor of foreign affairs at the University of Virginia.

IU160A SLIJEPČEVIĆ, DJOKO. *The Macedonian Question.* Chicago: Balkanski Institut, 1958. 267 p. A discussion of the Macedonian problem, the Yugoslav Communist policy for Macedonia and the Soviet objectives before, during and since the end of the Second World War.

IU161 SMOLE, JOŽE, and ŠTAJDUHAR, RUDI. *Pretsednik Tito u zemljama Azije i Afrike*. Belgrade: Kultura, 1959. 200 p.

IU162 SOTIROVITCH, DRAGAN M. *L'Europe aux enchères*. Paris: Téqui, 1952. 346 p. The story of a Yugoslav officer who fought both in the ranks of Mihailovich and in the Polish underground. The author's purpose is to show that Roosevelt and Churchill are responsible for the emergence of Communist tyranny in Eastern Europe.

IU163 *The Soviet-Yugoslav Dispute; Text of the Published Correspondence*. London & N.Y.: Royal Institute of International Affairs, 1948. 79 p. Serbo-Croat edition, *Pisma CK KPJ i pisma CK SKP (b)*. Belgrade: "Borba," 1948. Full texts of letters exchanged between the Yugoslav and Soviet Communist parties on the points of dispute between Tito and Stalin, March 20 to June 29, 1948. A rare and fascinating look into the hidden world of relations among Communist parties. Documents of fundamental importance. [A]

IU164 STOJKOVIĆ, LJUBIŠA, and MILOŠ, MARTIĆ. *National Minorities in Yugoslavia*. Belgrade: "Jugoslavija," 1952. 226 p. An official view of the nationality policy of the Communist regime, under which, it is claimed, there is "complete equality, freedom and cooperation between the Yugoslav peoples." Has separate sections on the Albanians, Hungarians, Italians, Slovaks, Czechs, Rumanians, Ruthenians, Bulgarians, and Turks.

IU165 TADIĆ, JORJO, ed. *Ten Years of Yugoslav Historiography, 1945-1955*. Belgrade: National Committee for Historical Sciences, 1955. 685 p.

IU166 TENNYSON, HALLAM. *Tito Lifts the Curtain; the Story of Yugoslavia Today*. London: Rider & Co., 1955. 240 p. An impressionistic and narrative, sympathetic but not uncritical account of the writer's travels throughout Yugoslavia, with the emphasis on Tito's regime "experimenting with antidotes to totalitarianism." Parts of the book were published in the *New Statesman and Nation*.

IU167 THOMPSON, ELIZABETH M. "Yugoslavia and the Soviet Union, 1941-1948." Certificate essay, Russian Institute, Columbia, 1950. 350 p.

IU168 TITO, JOSIP BROZ. *Borba za oslobodjenje Jugoslavije, 1941-1945*. Belgrade: Kultura, 1947. 298 p.

IU169 TITO, JOSIP BROZ. *Deset godina narodne revolucije; govori*. Belgrade: Kultura, 1951. 213 p.

IU170 TITO, JOSIP BROZ. *Govori i članci.* Zagreb: Naprijed, 1959. 12 vols. Speeches and articles by Tito during the period 1941-57. Included are numerous statements on Soviet-Yugoslav relations and Tito's views on many foreign problems. [A]

IU171 TITO, JOSIP BROZ. *President Tito on the International Situation; Excerpts from President Tito's Report, Delivered before the National Assembly in March, 1955.* N.Y.: The Yugoslav Information Center, 1955. 25 p. A short statement on the "Normalization of Relations with the Soviet Union" and Tito's comments on several other problems in his country's foreign relations.

IU172 TITO, JOSIP BROZ. *Real Reasons behind the Slanders against Yugoslavia.* Belgrade: Jugoslovenska knjiga, 1949. 56 p. Discusses relations with the USSR and its satellites, accusing them of violating trade agreements and other commitments. Says that Soviet slanders are intended "to delude the world" that Yugoslavia cannot build socialism. Criticizes the Soviet "capitalist mode" of trading with Yugoslavia and alleges an attempt to make Yugoslavia a raw materials producing country.

IU173 TITO, JOSIP BROZ. *Spisi.* Vols. 1-4, *Izgradnja nove Jugoslavije.* Vols. 5-7, *Borba za socijalističku demokratiju.* Vols. 8 and 9, *Borba za mir i medjunarodnu saradnju.* Belgrade: Kultura, 1947-57. 9 vols. Articles, speeches, interviews, and declarations on a variety of subjects, including many references to relations with the USSR. [A]

IU174 TITO, JOSIP BROZ. *Workers Manage Factories in Yugoslavia.* Belgrade: Jugoslovenska knjiga, 1950. 54 p. An official pronouncement about the introduction of the well-known system of workers' councils, by which the employees of an enterprise were given a voice in management.

IU175 TOMAŠIĆ, DINKO A. *National Communism and Soviet Strategy.* With the assistance of Joseph Strmecki. Washington: Public Affairs Press, 1957. 222 p. The conclusion is that Titoism is not "a recent phenomenon" and that the USSR had similar experience with Outer Mongolia. Titoism could become "an instrument of Communist world strategy, its asset, not its liability" but it could also indicate "a basic weakness of Communism and signal the beginning of its disintegration as a unified world movement." Finally, "if Communist rulers fail to satisfy the basic human needs and longings of the people . . . disintegration of monolithic Party rule and the end of national as well as of international Communism" will follow.

IU176 TOMAŠIĆ, DINKO A. *Personality and Culture in Eastern European Politics.* N.Y.: G. W. Stewart, 1948. 249 p. The author, a professor at Indiana University, analyzes the politics of Yugoslavia within the context of the social and cultural traditions of the various peoples.

IU177 TOPALOVIĆ, ŽIVKO. *Pokreti narodnog otpora u Jugoslaviji 1941-1945*. Paris: Izd. Jugoslovenskih sindikalista, 1958. 216 p. Topalović was head of the Socialist Party in Yugoslavia before World War II. He now writes as an exile, hostile to the Tito regime.

IU178 ULAM, ADAM B. *Titoism and the Cominform*. Cambridge: Harvard, 1952. 243 p. The best statement on the crux of the political and ideological controversy between the Yugoslav and Soviet leaders. Also contains much material on real or alleged "Titoism" in other countries of Eastern Europe, especially Poland. By a Harvard professor. [A]

IU179 UNITED NATIONS, GENERAL ASSEMBLY, AD HOC POLITICAL COMMITTEE. *The Threat to Yugoslavia; Discussion in the Ad Hoc Political Committee of the United Nations Organization, 6th Session*. Belgrade: "Yugoslavia," 1952. 161 p. A dispute between Yugoslav and Soviet bloc delegations over a request for a mixed commission for settlement of border disputes.

IU180 U.S. CONGRESS, SENATE, COMMITTEE ON THE JUDICIARY. *Yugoslav Communism, a Critical Study*. By Charles Zalar. Washington: G.P.O., 1961. 387 p. Written for the Subcommittee to Investigate the Administration of the Internal Security Act and Other Internal Security Laws, by a former Yugoslav career diplomat who has worked for the Library of Congress since 1952. Argues against U.S. aid to Tito on the grounds that, as a national Communist, he has been a far more successful missionary of Communism than he could have been as a Moscow Communist. The work exhibits anti-Serbian sentiments. Excellent bibliography.

IU181 *Unprincipled Accusations Against the Communist Party of Yugoslavia*. Belgrade: 1948. 44 p. A refutation of Soviet charges against the Yugoslav Communist Party and Tito. Reprinted from *Borba*, October 2-3-4, 1948. [A]

IU182 WHITE, LEIGH. *Balkan Caesar*. N.Y.: Scribner, 1951. 245 p. An American journalist with considerable experience in the Balkans presents a very hostile account of Tito and his regime and argues against the possibility that Tito will ever be a dependable friend of the West.

IU183 WOLFF, ROBERT L. *The Balkans in Our Time*. Cambridge: Harvard, 1956. 618 p. A history of the Balkans, with emphasis on the 20th century, and containing several excellent sections on Yugoslavia. The author is a professor of history at Harvard and dealt with Yugoslav affairs during World War II for the O.S.S. [A]

IU184 WOLFE, THOMAS W. "The Role of the Armed Forces in the Soviet-Yugoslav Dispute." M.A. thesis, Columbia, 1950. 182 p.

IU185 YINDRICH, JAN H. *Tito v. Stalin; The Battle of the Marshals.* London: E. Benn, 1950. 215 p. A discussion of Yugoslavia in the United Nations, Tito's challenges to Stalin, and the persecution of Titoists by the Soviet satellite states. A brief biography of Tito is also included. The author urges support for Tito for his resistance to Stalin. Somewhat outdated.

IU186 YOURICHITCH, EVGUÉNIYÉ. *Le Procès Tito-Mihailovitch.* Paris: Société d'éditions françaises et internationales, 1950. 188 p. A critique of the trial by a former member of Mihailovich's army.

IU187 *Yugoslavia.* Intro. by Robert F. Byrnes. N.Y.: Praeger, for the Mid-European Studies Center of the Free Europe Committee, 1957. 488 p. A valuable handbook covering all major aspects of Yugoslavia, with emphasis on conditions under the Communist regime. One chapter covers Yugoslav relations with Russia since 1945. The contributors are American scholars. One of the volumes in the series, *East-Central Europe under the Communists*, edited by Robert F. Byrnes. Good bibliography. [A]

IU188 YUGOSLAVIA, AMBASADA, GREAT BRITAIN. *The Treason of Mihailovitch; 81 military documents, Chetnik, German, Italian, and Quisling; with Plates Showing Mihailovitch's Handwriting and an Editorial Commentary by Alec Brown.* London: Yugoslav Embassy Information Office, 1945. 71 p.

IU189 YUGOSLAVIA, DIREKCIJA ZA INFORMACIJE. *Informativni priručnik o Jugoslaviji; opšti podaci o političkom, privrednom kulturnom i prosvetnom životu u FNRJ.* Belgrade: 1948-51.

IU190 YUGOSLAVIA, DIREKCIJA ZA INFORMACIJE. *Jugoslovenska bibliografija, 1945-1949.* Belgrade: 1950. 5 vols.

IU191 YUGOSLAVIA, KOMISIJA ZA RATNU ŠTETU. *Human and Material Sacrifices of Yugoslavia in Her War Efforts 1941-1945.* Belgrade: 1945. 53 p.

IU192 YUGOSLAVIA, MINISTARSTVO INOSTRANIH POSLOVA. *White Book on Aggressive Activities by the Governments of the USSR, Poland, Czechoslovakia, Hungary, Rumania, Bulgaria, and Albania towards Yugoslavia.* Belgrade: 1951. 481 p. Also in French. A collection of miscellaneous documents, including newspaper articles and radio broadcasts, pertaining to Soviet and satellite propaganda and other forms of anti-Yugoslav activities.

IU193 YUGOSLAVIA, SAVEZNI ZAVOD ZA STATISTIKU. *Statistical Yearbook of the Federal People's Republic of Yugoslavia; English Text*. Belgrade: 1954.

IU194 ZAGORIA, DONALD S. "The Origins and Background of Tito's Split with the Cominform." M. A. thesis, Columbia, 1950.

IU195 ZILLIACUS, KONNI. *Tito of Yugoslavia*. London: Joseph, 1952. 303 p. A biography of Tito by an author who claims to know Tito "better than anyone else in the West except Brigadier Fitzroy Maclean." Includes a treatment of the Tito-Stalin break and its consequences. Conclusion: By including "democracy, humanism and the freedom and rights of the individual in the Socialism" the Yugoslav Communists made "negotiation and compromise" possible and "common interests can be discovered between Communist and non-Communist states on which we can make a peace that will endure."

3. PERIODICALS AND NEWSPAPERS

IU196 *Borba*. Began appearing as a Communist organ in 1922 in Zagreb, and was outlawed by the government on January 13, 1929. It reappeared for a time during the Second World War in Užice (October 19 to November 27) and then in Drinić (October 8, 1942 to February 27, 1943). Since November 15, 1944, it has been published in Belgrade and has appeared regularly there. Although officially described as the organ of the Socialist Alliance of the Working People of Yugoslavia, it is in fact the chief organ of the Yugoslav Government and Communist party. [A]

IU196A *Glasnik srpskog istorisko-kulturnog društva "Njegoš" u Americi*. Chicago, 1958—. Semi-annual, edited by Jovan M. Kontić. Published by Serbian émigrés and dedicated to the cause of Draža Mihailović and Serbian nationalism. Publishes reminiscences from the war and the struggle with Tito's Partisans.

IU197 *Hrvatska Revija*. Buenos Aires, 1951—. Tri-monthly. Published by Croatian émigrés and dedicated to the cause of Croatian nationalism. Publishes articles on the Croatian past and present.

IU198 *Komunist*. Belgrade, 1946-58. Monthly. Official mouthpiece of the Communist Party of Yugoslavia for Marxian theory and practice. A very valuable periodical which carries important articles by leading Yugoslav Communists on domestic and foreign affairs. [A]

IU199 *Komunist*. Belgrade, 1958—. Weekly. Articles on Party work, issued by the Communist Party. Published in Serbian, Croatian, Macedonian, and Slovenian. The title has varied from time to time. Not to be confused with the monthly publication of the same name.

IU200 *Medjunarodni Problemi.* Belgrade, 1948—. Published by the Institute for International Politics and Economics. A periodical carrying articles on a wide range of topics including the USSR and its domestic and foreign affairs.

IU201 *Naša Stvarnost.* Belgrade, 1948—. A periodical for social questions. Has articles on domestic as well as foreign affairs. Published by the Central Committee of the Communist Party.

IU202 *Politika.* Belgrade, 1904-15; 1919-41; 1945—. In theory an independent journal, but in reality government controlled. The second most important newspaper in the country. [A]

IU202A *Poruka.* London,1950—. Published by Jugoslovenski Narodni Odbor. Contains statements by Yugoslav émigrés on recent Yugoslav foreign relations, Communism and the Soviet Union.

IU202B *Review.* London, 1960—. Published by the Study Centre for Yugoslav Affairs. Carries serious, scholarly articles on Yugoslavia's internal and foreign affairs.

IU203 *Review of International Affairs.* Belgrade, 1949—. Published by the Federation of Yugoslav Journalists. A bi-weekly periodical which carries many articles on Yugoslavia's foreign affairs. Important for the Yugoslav view of the USSR, the U.S., Western Europe, and the underdeveloped countries. Also useful for the study of Titoism.

IU204 *Socijalizam.* Belgrade, 1958—. Bi-monthly. Official mouthpiece of the Central Committee of the Communist Party. Includes articles on Yugoslav internal and foreign problems. [A]

IU205 *Spoljnopolitička Dokumentacija.* Belgrade, 1948—. Monthly. Published by the Institute for International Politics and Economics. Publishes documents, reports and articles on a variety of topics concerning international relations.

IU206 *Yugoslav Survey.* Belgrade, 1960—. Quarterly. Published by the Yugoslav Publishing House. An informational and documentary periodical on domestic and foreign affairs.

J. Asia and the Pacific Area

JA. ASIA, GENERAL

EDITED BY PAUL F. LANGER

1. BIBLIOGRAPHIES

JA1 AKADEMIIA NAUK SSSR, INSTITUT VOSTOKOVEDENIIA. *Bibliografiia Vostoka.* Leningrad: Izd. Akademii nauk SSSR, 1932-37. 10 vols. An annotated bibliography, published irregularly, and containing many references and reviews.

JA2 EGOROV, DMITRII N., ed. *Bibliografiia Vostoka.* Moscow: 1928. 299 p. Close to two thousand annotated entries concerning Russian language books and periodical articles (taken from 150 journals) published between 1917 and October 1925. Includes the Near East, Asia, and Africa. Author and subject index facilitates its use. An appendix contains a preliminary list of Soviet works published during 1926 and the first half of 1927. [A]

JA3 EUDIN, XENIA J., and NORTH, ROBERT C. *Soviet Russia and the East, 1920-1927; a Documentary Survey.* Stanford, Cal.: Stanford University Press, 1957. 478 p. Contains an extensive, 50-page bibliography of works on Soviet policy and Communism in Asia, particularly Soviet publications. Not annotated.

JA4 THE JOURNAL OF ASIAN STUDIES. *Bibliography of Asian Studies.* Published annually by the Association for Asian Studies, Ann Arbor, Mich., 1957–. Prior to 1957 it was called *Far Eastern Bibliography*, issued each year (1941-56) by the *Far Eastern Quarterly*, which was published from Nov. 1941 to May 1956 by what was then called the Far Eastern Association, Ithaca, N.Y. Recent volumes list many articles and books in Russian and non-European, as well as Western, languages. For materials on Soviet-Asian relations and Asian Communism, see the subject index under "Asia," "Far East," and under the individual country sections.

JA5 KERNER, ROBERT J. *Northeastern Asia; a Selected Bibliography.* Berkeley: U. of California, 1939. 2 vols. Compiled by a pioneer of American academic work in the Russian field. The bibliography ends with 1938 and lacks annotations, but remains an indispensable reference work. Entries cover contributions in most European languages, including Russian as well as some Oriental sources. Titles in Slavic languages are also translated; in non-European languages, transcribed and translated. Includes reference, general, specialized works, and periodical literature listing important articles. The bulk of the entries on Soviet policy in Asia and world Communism are in vol. II, part 4 "The Russian Empire and the Soviet Union in Asia and on the Pacific," containing close to 4,000 items. Particularly valuable within this chapter are Sections XVII "The Communist Party and the Third International" and XXIII "Russia in the Far East." The detailed table of contents and subject index enhance its usefulness. [A]

JA6 LOEWENTHAL, RUDOLF. *Bibliography of Russian Literature on China and Adjacent Countries, 1931-1936*. Cambridge: Harvard Russian Research Center, 1949. 93 p. (mimeographed). Comprehensive and useful.

JA7 LOEWENTHAL, RUDOLF. "Works on the Far East and Central Asia Published in the USSR, 1937-47," *Far Eastern Quarterly*, vol. 8 (Feb. 1949).

JA8 U.S. DEPARTMENT OF STATE, BUREAU OF INTELLIGENCE AND RESEARCH, EXTERNAL RESEARCH DIVISION. *External Research; a List of Recently Completed Studies. USSR and Eastern Europe* (List 1.17). *East Asia* (2.17). *Southeast Asia and Southwest Pacific* (3.17). *South Asia* (4.17). *Middle East* (6.17). *Africa* (7.17). Washington, D.C. Non-cumulative, annual lists reporting under subject and geographic sub-headings on research completed. Gives pertinent data (author, subject, type of study, place of publication) and often also annotations prepared by the authors. (Research in progress is reported in separate annual lists.) [A]

JA9 VOIAKINA, S. M. *Strany Azii; rekomendatelnyi ukazatel literatury*. Moscow: Gos. Ordena Lenina Biblioteka SSSR, 1960. 136 p. An annotated listing of recommended books, pamphlets, and major periodical articles on the political, economic, and cultural life of Afghanistan, Burma, North Borneo, Vietnam (North and South), Israel, Yemen, India, Indonesia, Jordan, Iraq, Iran, Cambodia, Cyprus, China, Korea, (North and South), Laos, Lebanon, Malaya, Mongolia, Nepal, Pakistan, Singapore, Thailand, Turkey, Philippines, Ceylon, and Japan. Aimed at the educated, non-specialist Soviet reader. A section on "Struggle of the Peoples of Asia for National Independence" includes references to pertinent statements by Lenin, Khrushchev, Mukhitdinov, Ho Chi-minh, Mao Tse-tung, and Sukarno. Author index. [A]

2. GENERAL WORKS

JA10 AFRO-ASIAN PEOPLES' SOLIDARITY CONFERENCE, CAIRO, 1957-58. *Afro-Asian Peoples' Solidarity Conference, Cairo, December 26, 1957-January 1, 1958*. Moscow: Foreign Languages

Publishing House, 1958. 265 p. French ed., Moscow: Éditions en langues étrangères, 1958. 226 p. Russian ed., Moscow: Gospolitizdat, 1958. 223 p. Official conference documents and speeches including reports and resolutions. The Soviet Union was one of the 45 nations represented. For the Soviet role, see specifically: text of message from Voroshilov and speech by A. A. Azumanian on economic cooperation.

JA11 AFRO-ASIAN PEOPLES' SOLIDARITY CONFERENCE, CAIRO, 1957-58. *Principal Reports Submitted to the Conference: Political Reports, Economic Reports, Social Reports, Cultural Reports.* Cairo: Permanent Secretariat, 1958. 382 p.

JA12 AKADEMIIA NAUK SSSR, INSTITUT EKONOMIKI. *Uglublenie krizisa kolonialnoi sistemy imperializma posle Vtoroi mirovoi voiny.* Ed. by V. A. Maslennikov. Moscow: Gospolitizdat, 1953. 605 p. A symposium on "national independence movements" in China, Korea, Vietnam, India, Southeast Asia, the Near East, Latin America, and Africa, written by nine Soviet area specialists. Little documentation.

JA13 AKADEMIIA NAUK SSSR, INSTITUT ISTORII ESTESTVOZNANIIA I TEKHNIKI. *Iz istorii nauki i tekhniki v stranakh vostoka; sbornik statei.* Moscow: Izd. vostoch. literatury. Vol. 1, 1960. Vol. 2, 1961. Contains some useful essays, based on materials in the archives of the Soviet Academy of Sciences, on scientific relations between the USSR and certain Asian countries: China (vol. 1, p. 7-33), India (vol. 1, p. 155-72), Japan (vol. 2, p. 135-66), UAR (vol. 2, p. 159-73).

JA14 AKADEMIIA NAUK SSSR, INSTITUT MIROVOI EKONOMIKI I MEZHDUNARODNYKH OTNOSHENII. *Agrarno-krestianskii vopros v suverennykh slaborazvitykh stranakh Azii. (India, Birma, Indoneziia).* Moscow: Izd. Akademii nauk, 1961. 353 p. A discussion of land tenure and utilization, agrarian reform and class structure, agricultural cooperatives, "capitalist influences" and other aspects of the agrarian problem in the three underdeveloped Asian countries. Some documentation. [B]

JA15 AKADEMIIA NAUK SSSR, INSTITUT MIROVOI EKONOMIKI I MEZHDUNARODNYKH OTNOSHENII. *Mezhdunarodnyi politiko-ekonomicheskii ezhegodnik.* Moscow: Gospolitizdat, 1958–. (Yearly.) This handbook frequently carries brief articles on Asian countries and Asian problems, as well as on Communist front organizations active in Asia. (See the 1958 volume, on the Asian Solidarity Council.) Volumes for 1959 and 1960 contain a bibliographic section listing writings relevant to Asia, complete with annotations and references to pertinent Soviet book reviews. See also Section III of the bibliography in the 1960 volume regarding reference works in Russian and local languages on Asian Communist countries.

JA16 AKADEMIIA NAUK SSSR, INSTITUT NARODOV AZII. *Agrarnye reformy v stranakh vostoka.* Moscow: Izd. vost. lit., 1961. 234 p. A symposium by a group of experts from the Institute of the Peoples of Asia and the Institute of World Economics and International Relations. The authors examine the cases of India, Burma, South Vietnam, Japan, South Korea, UAR, Iraq, Turkey, and Iran.

JA16A AKADEMIIA NAUK SSSR, INSTITUT NARODOV AZII, INSTITUT AFRIKI. *Ekonomicheskoe polozhenie stran Azii i Afriki v 1960 g.* Moscow: Izd. vost. lit., 1962. 597 p.

JA17 AKADEMIIA NAUK SSSR, INSTITUT NARODOV AZII. *Gosudarstvennyi kapitalizm v stranakh Vostoka.* Moscow: Izd. vost. lit., 1960. 291 p. Probably the first Soviet symposium on state capitalism in Asia. Eight Soviet specialists discuss the cases of India (most substantial contribution), Afghanistan, Burma, Ceylon, Turkey, Iran, Thailand and the Philippines utilizing Soviet, Western and local Asian documentary materials. [B]

JA17A AKADEMIIA NAUK SSSR, INSTITUT NARODOV AZII. *Polozhenie rabochego klassa i rabochee dvizhenie v stranakh Azii i Afriki, 1959-1961.* Moscow: Izd. vost. lit., 1962. 243 p. A symposium by Soviet area specialists, including essays on India, South Vietnam, South Korea, Japan, the Arab countries, Turkey, Iran, and Africa. A 20-page chronology covers the strike movement in these areas.

JA18 AKADEMIIA NAUK SSSR, INSTITUT NARODOV AZII. *SSSR i strany vostoka; ekonomicheskoe i kulturnoe sotrudnichestvo.* Moscow: Izd. vost. lit., 1961. 139 p. A survey authored by several Soviet specialists. Covers the Communist nations of Asia and those non-Communist nations which were receiving Soviet aid in 1961. Some useful though undocumented statistical data. Good bibliography of Soviet books and periodical articles on the subject (p. 131-39).

JA19 AKADEMIIA NAUK SSSR, INSTITUT VOSTOKOVEDENIIA. *Ekonomicheskoe polozhenie stran Azii i Afriki v 1957 g. i v pervoi polovine 1958 g.* Ed. by B. M. Dantsig and B. I. Potapovskii. Moscow: Izd. vost. lit., 1959. 294 p. A heavily-footnoted statistical survey covering Morocco, Tunisia, Turkey, UAR, Lebanon, Jordan, Israel, Iran, Afghanistan, India, Pakistan, Burma, Indonesia, and Japan. Supplemented by chapters on the oil industry in the Middle East and on West German economic expansion in the Middle East and South Asia. The bulk of sources are of local origin or from the UN. [B]

JA20 AKADEMIIA NAUK SSSR, INSTITUT VOSTOKOVEDENIIA. *Ekonomicheskoe polozhenie stran Azii i Afriki v 1958 godu.* Ed. by N. A. Vaganov, B. M. Dantsig, and I. P. Iastrebova. Moscow: Izd. vost. lit., 1960. 459 p. Similar in approach to the preceding work, but covering a wider range of countries: Afghanistan, Burma, Cambodia, Ceylon, India, Indonesia, Iraq, Iran, Israel, Japan, Kuwait, Laos, Lebanon, Pakistan, Thailand, Turkey, Congo, Kenya, Libya, Malagasy Republic, Morocco, Rhodesia, Nyasaland, Tanganyika, Tunisia, Uganda, UAR, and the Union of South Africa. A useful chronology follows each country section. Has a 10-page chapter on Soviet economic relations with underdeveloped countries. [B]

JA21 AKADEMIIA NAUK SSSR, INSTITUT VOSTOKOVEDENIIA. *Ekonomicheskoe polozhenie stran Azii i Afriki v 1959 g.* Ed. by B. M. Dantsig and others. Moscow: Izd. vost. lit., 1961. 511 p. Similar to the preceding items.

JA22 AKADEMIIA NAUK SSSR, INSTITUT VOSTOKOVEDENIIA. *Mezhdunarodnye otnosheniia na Dalnem Vostoke, 1870-1945 gg.* Moscow: Gospolitizdat, 1951. 790 p. 2nd ed., *Mezhdunarodnye otnosheniia na Dalnem Vostoke, 1840-1949.* Moscow: Gospolitizdat, 1956. 783 p. By G. N. Voitinskii and others. Ed. by E. M. Zhukov. German ed., Shukow, J. M., ed. *Die Internationalen Beziehungen im Fernen Osten (1870-1945).* Berlin: Akademie-Verlag, 1955. 647 p. Several noted Soviet scholars are responsible for this propagandistic work which draws on Soviet and Western literature and makes occasional use of Soviet archival materials. The villain is "American imperialism" and its allies; the hero is Russia, the Soviet Union, and especially Stalin. The emphasis is on China. Somewhat less attention is given to Japan and practically none to Korea. Chronology. A lengthy but not very useful bibliography, dominated by Stalin's writings. The 2nd edition has a chapter covering the 1840-70 period, more extensive treatment of postwar developments, a revised bibliography and chronology, and much less talk about the role of Stalin.

JA23 AKADEMIIA NAUK SSSR, INSTITUT VOSTOKOVEDENIIA. *Poslednie kolonii v Azii.* Ed. by G. L. Bondarevskii. Moscow: Izd. vost. lit., 1958. 171 p. Several Soviet specialists briefly discuss the background and present status of the British protectorates in the Near East, the Portuguese colonies in India, Dutch New Guinea, Macao, Hong Kong, Singapore, and British Borneo. Some documentation. [B]

JA24 AKADEMIIA NAUK SSSR, INSTITUT VOSTOKOVEDENIIA, INSTITUT KITAEVEDENIIA. *Lenin i Vostok; sbornik statei.* Moscow: Izd. vost. lit., 1960. 304 p. Ten essays concerned with Lenin's thoughts on the Eastern countries and the role of Leninism in their development. All but two of these essays are devoted to specific countries (China, Mongolian People's Republic, Korea, Turkey, Iran, Afghanistan, India, Indonesia).

JA25 AKADEMIIA NAUK SSSR, TIKHOOKEANSKII INSTITUT. *Krizis kolonialnoi sistemy; natsionalno-osvoboditelnaia borba narodov Vostochnoi Azii.* Ed. by Evgenii M. Zhukov. Moscow: Akad. nauk, 1949. 289 p. English ed., *Crisis of the Colonial System; National Liberation Struggle of the People of East Asia.* Bombay: People's Publishing House, 1951. 268 p. Nine Soviet academic area specialists analyze the postwar independence movements in India, Ceylon, Indonesia, Vietnam, Malaysia, the Philippines, and Korea. [A]

JA26 ALIMOV, A., and GODES, M., eds. *Ocherki po istorii vostoka v epokhu imperializma.* Moscow: Sotsekgiz, 1934. 431 p. Scholarly, documented essays on the political and economic history of modern Turkey (A. Alimov), India (D. Smirnov and A. Suleiman), China (M. Kokin and P. Kh. Sergienko) and Japan (E. Zhukov). The focus is on revolutionary movements. [B]

JA27 AVARIN, VLADIMIR I. *Borba za Tikhii Okean; agressia SShA i Anglii, ikh protivorechiia i osvoboditelnaia borba narodov.* Moscow: Gospolitizdat, 1952. 670 p. An orthodox Stalinist view, couched in vehement language, of the historical role of the U.S. and Britain in the Pacific area. Emphasis is on the period after World War II. The author, a noted Soviet specialist on Far Eastern affairs, concentrates on the role of "U.S. imperialism" in China, but touches also on Japan, Korea, Southeast Asia, Australia, New Zealand, and Canada, as well as on Soviet policy in the Far East. Although the bulk of the documentation consists of Stalin and *Pravda*, a few standard American, British, and French sources have been consulted. [A]

JA28 AVARIN, VLADIMIR I. *Borba za Tikhii Okean; iapono-amerikanskie protivorechiia.* Moscow: Gospolitizdat, 1947. 466 p. Contemporary international relations in the Far East as seen by a Soviet specialist. The emphasis is on Japanese imperialism, but it is not lacking in bitter attacks against the U.S. Meager documentation in Russian and English. [B]

JA29 BALL, WILLIAM M. *Nationalism and Communism in East Asia.* Carlton, Australia: Melbourne University; London and N.Y.: Cambridge, 1952. 210 p. 2nd, rev. ed., 1956. 220 p. An Australian political scientist's country-by-country assessment providing background, but little specific information on Communism in the area. Does not concern itself with Soviet policies. Covers Japan, China, Korea, Indochina, Philippines, Thailand, Burma, Malaya, Indonesia, and India to the end of 1954 (revised edition). [B]

JA30 BARGHOORN, FREDERICK C. *The Soviet Cultural Offensive; the Role of Cultural Diplomacy in Soviet Foreign Policy.* Princeton, N.J.: Princeton University Press, 1960. 353 p. Much of the survey is relevant to Asia, and portions of chapter VII deal specifically with the area. Especially good on India.

JA31 BELOFF, MAX. *Soviet Policy in the Far East, 1944-1951.* London and N.Y.: Oxford, 1953. 278 p. A scholarly account of Soviet policy in China, Japan, Korea, and Southeast Asia. Heavy emphasis on thorough chronological reporting of events but little analysis. Based mainly on the Soviet and Western press. The appendix contains the text of Soviet treaties with Mongolia (1946), Korea (1949), Communist China (1950). Detailed index. The author is an Oxford professor and authority on Soviet and U.S. foreign policies. The Southeast Asia chapter is by Joseph Frankel. [A]

JA32 BIENSTOCK, GREGORY. *The Struggle for the Pacific.* N.Y.: Macmillan, 1937. 299 p. French ed., Paris: 1938. 275 p. The struggle for hegemony in the Far East viewed in terms of power politics and military strategy. While the Pacific War proved the author wrong on some points, his work contains valuable insights into the factors at play. Substantial documentation in Russian and European languages. Bibliography and strategic maps. [B]

JA33 BRUTENTS, KAREN N. *Protiv ideologii sovremennogo kolonializma.* Moscow: Izd. sots.-ek. lit., 1961. 359 p. The theory and practice of Western (especially American) policy toward the underdeveloped nations of Asia and Africa analyzed by a Soviet specialist who sees in this policy a new form of colonialism. The author draws on recent Western works in support of these views. [B]

JA34 BUKHAROV, BORIS I. *Voprosy dalnevostochnoi politiki SShA (1953-1955 gg.).* Moscow: Izd. Akad. nauk SSSR, 1959. 238 p. A sharp attack against alleged U.S. imperialist policy in the Far East. The focus is on U.S.-Chinese relations. The last chapter deals with the Bandung Conference. Based largely on Western Communist and non-Communist periodical literature.

JA35 BULGANIN, NIKOLAI A., and KHRUSHCHEV, NIKITA S. *Visit of Friendship to India, Burma, and Afghanistan; Speeches and Official Documents (November-December 1955).* Moscow: Foreign Languages Publishing House, 1956. 327 p. Russian ed., *Missiia druzhba.* Moscow: Pravda, 1956. 2 vols. (Several other editions.) Speeches of the two Soviet leaders during their extended and highly-publicized tour in 1955.

JA36 BURSKII, PAVEL D. *Dalnevostochnye teatry voennykh deistvii; voenno-geograficheskii ocherk.* Ed. by I. A. Troitskii. Moscow:

Gosizdat, otdel. voennoi lit-ry, 1928. 200 p. Written for Red Army staff officers and concerned with the two potential Far Eastern war theaters where Soviet interests were involved: the Maritime Province and the Manchurian area, the latter including North Manchuria, North Korea and East Mongolia. Dwells heavily on physical geography, economic factors and communications.

JA37 BUTAKOV, D., BOCHKOVA, V., and SHEVEL, I. *Finansy stran narodnoi demokratii.* Moscow: Gosfinizdat, 1959. 344 p. Chapters 8, 9, and 10 (p. 196-343) examine the national and local budgets of China, North Korea, and Outer Mongolia. (North Vietnam is omitted for lack of statistical data.) The author of these chapters, I. Shevel, draws heavily on the official documentation of the three governments.

JA38 CLARIDGE, DUANE R. "The World Federation of Trade Unions in Asia." Certificate essay, Russian Institute, Columbia, 1955. 112 p. The background, policies, and organization of the Asian sector of the WFTU studied in a not entirely successful attempt to define that organization's relationship to and role in the international Communist movement. Based largely on Western language sources and WFTU publications.

JA39 CONOLLY, VIOLET. *Soviet Economic Policy in the East; Turkey, Persia, Afghanistan, Mongolia, Tana Tuva, and Sin Kiang.* London: Oxford, H. Milford, 1933. 168 p. The first competent work in English on early Soviet economic policy in the area. Still valuable today. The author went on to become a key figure in British Foreign Office Soviet research. Discusses the evolution of Soviet economic policy in the Orient and then each area separately. Used a wide range of materials, including Russian and Near Eastern, as well as consular reports. Heavily documented. Good but unannotated bibliography. [A]

JA40 CONOLLY, VIOLET. *Soviet Trade from the Pacific to the Levant, with an Economic Study of the Soviet Far Eastern Region.* London: Oxford, H. Milford, 1935. 238 p. A sequel to the previously mentioned work. Economic relations with Japan, China (including a useful chapter on the Chinese Eastern Railway from 1917 to 1934), India, Egypt, and Iraq. The author used a wide range of sources as well as Russian archives of the Ost-Europa Institut (Breslau) and the Deutsche Hochschule für Politik (Berlin), making good use of their Russian periodical clipping files. Full but unannotated bibliography. Useful maps. Has 12 appendices with documentary materials and statistics. [A]

JA41 DALLIN, DAVID J. (pseud. of David Iu. Levin). *The Rise of Russia in Asia.* New Haven, Conn.: Yale, 1949; London: Hollis and

Carter, 1950. 293 p. Tsarist and Soviet expansion in the Far East to 1931. A factual presentation by a well-known writer on Soviet foreign policy. Based largely on Russian sources. Although more recent, detailed monographs, utilizing also Asian documentary materials, have superseded portions of this study (especially where Communism in China is concerned), it remains a useful overall treatment of the subject. Maps and bibliography. A companion volume to his *Soviet Russia and the Far East.* [B]

JA42 DALLIN, DAVID J. *Soviet Russia and the Far East.* New Haven, Conn.: Yale, 1948; London: Hollis and Carter, 1949. 398 p. A sequel to *The Rise of Russia in Asia*, and similar in approach and documentation. New materials on Asian Communism and on diplomatic relations in the pre- and post-World War II era have sharply reduced the value of this once useful survey. Maps and bibliography. The author was a well-known Menshevik émigré, journalist, and author of many books.

JA43 *Dalnii Vostok; sbornik dokumentov i materialov*, no. 1. Leningrad: Kabinet po izucheniiu Dalnego Vostoka VPAT, 1932. 148 p.

JA44 DEGRAS, JANE, ed. *The Communist International 1919-1943; Documents.* London and N.Y.: Oxford, for the Royal Institute of International Affairs. Vol. I, 1919-22 (1956); vol. II, 1923-28 (1960). (To be continued.) The most comprehensive, detailed and reliable collection of documents on the Communist International and Communist Parties throughout the world, based on a wide range of sources, presented chronologically and provided with perceptive explanatory notes by an outstanding British authority on the international Communist movement. Contains many rare but basic theses, manifestos, resolutions, letters, etc. illuminating the development of Communism in Asia. Strong on the "China Question." (See vol. II). [A]

JA45 DEGRAS, JANE, ed. *Soviet Documents on Foreign Policy.* London and N.Y.: Oxford, for the Royal Institute of International Affairs. Vol. I, 1917-24 (1951); vol. II, 1925-32 (1952); vol. III, 1933-41 (1953). This massive collection of diplomatic documents includes many translations from Soviet sources indispensable to the student of Soviet policy in the Far East. The documents include official Soviet statements, communiques, reports, interviews, and speeches. Comprehensive tables of contents and detailed indices facilitate the use of this invaluable reference work. [A]

JA46 DEGRAS, JANE, comp. *Calendar of Soviet Documents on Foreign Policy, 1917-1941.* London and N.Y.: Royal Institute of International Affairs, 1948. A very useful reference work that lists chronologically and by country many Russian and other sources for treaties and agreements as well as important Soviet speeches, interviews and newspaper articles. Much material on Asia. [A]

JA47 DOLIVO-DOBROVOLSKII, B. I. *Tikhookeanskaia problema.* Intro. by M. Pavlovich. Moscow: Vysshii voen. redaktsionnyi sovet, 1924. 234 p. A military geography and analysis of the military situation in the Pacific region.

JA48 EELLS, WALTER C. *Communism in Education in Asia, Africa, and the Far Pacific.* Washington: American Council on Education, 1954. 246 p. A country-by-country collection of data, based largely on personal visits, interviews and the local English-language press. Rather superficial and undiscriminating. Ignores the Soviet role. The author served as educational adviser to the Supreme Commander of the Allied Powers, Tokyo.

JA49 EIDUS, KHAIM T. *Ocherki rabochego dvizheniia v stranakh Vostoka.* Moscow-Leningrad: Giz, 1922. 96 p. Brief, factual sketches dealing with Japan, China, Korea, India, the Dutch East Indies, and the Near East (Turkey, Syria, Mesopotamia, Palestine, Egypt, Persia). The author, a Soviet expert on Japan, devotes the most substantial section to that country.

JA50 *Ekonomicheskoe polozhenie stran Azii, Afriki i Latinskoi Ameriki. v 1958 g.* Moscow: Vneshtorgizdat, 1959. 444 p. Documented, statistical surveys covering the industry, agriculture and foreign trade of South and Southeast Asia (India, Indonesia, Pakistan, Ceylon, Burma, Malaya, Philippines), the Near and Middle East (Afghanistan, UAR, Iraq, Iran, Turkey), and Latin America (Argentina, Bolivia, Brazil, Venezuela, Mexico, Paraguay, Uruguay, Chile). Africa is not included.

JA51 EUDIN, XENIA J., and NORTH, ROBERT C. *Soviet Russia and the East, 1920-1927; a Documentary Survey.* Stanford, Cal.: Stanford University Press, 1957. 478 p. Translations of Russian documents, grouped chronologically and preceded by analytical essays. Focuses on the Communist movement rather than on official contacts with Asia. Much of the material (from the collections of the Hoover Library) is rare. Mrs. Eudin is a noted expert on the international Communist movement and Professor North is known for his studies of Chinese Communism. A chronology (p. 397-403), the best bibliography in the field (p. 405-55), and biographic notes on major international Communist figures (p. 457-64) complete this indispensable work. [A]

JA52 FISCHER, LOUIS. *The Soviets in World Affairs.* 2nd ed., Princeton, N.J.: Princeton University Press, 1951. 2 vols. The standard work on Soviet foreign policy to 1929. Valuable for the study of Soviet-Asian relations because the author had access to the persons, files and memoirs of Karakhan, Rothstein, Joffe and other Soviet policy-makers concerned with the East.

JA53 FISCHER, RUTH. *Von Lenin zu Mao; Kommunismus in der Bandung-Aera.* Düsseldorf: E. Diederichs, 1956. 240 p. Despite its sub-title, less than half of this book is concerned with Asian Communism. The emphasis is on China, India and Vietnam. The author, a German ex-Communist of considerable reputation and experience, knows more about the past history of the Communist movement than about the present, and more about Europe than Asia.

JA54 FUSE, KATSUJI. *Sovueto toho-saku.* Tokyo: 1926. 479 p. English ed., *Soviet Policy in the Orient.* East Peking: Enjinsha, 1927. 409 p. A perceptive interpretation by a widely traveled Japanese newsman who had important interviews with most Soviet leaders, including Lenin, Stalin, and Trotsky. Covers the area from Afghanistan to China, with emphasis on the latter. The English translation is occasionally inaccurate. [B]

JA55 GALKOVICH, MOISEI G. *Vostok i SSSR; ekonomicheskii ocherk.* Moscow: Izd. Komm. akad., 1928. 122 p. The sixth volume in the series, *Desiat let kapitalisticheskogo okruzheniia SSSR*, issued by the Kommunisticheskaia Akademiia, under the editorship of E. Pashukanis and M. Spektator. A short but useful documented account of the "national liberation movements," their struggle against "Western imperialism," and Soviet relations with the Middle and Far East. [B]

JA56 GOSUDARSTVENNYI INSTITUT "SOVETSKAIA ENTSIKLOPEDIIA," MOSCOW. *Strany Tikhogo Okeana.* Moscow: Ogiz RSFSR, 1942. 563 p. A handbook dealing with historical, political, economic, cultural and military developments of the Pacific area up to the beginning of World War II. Includes Japan, China, Thailand, British, Dutch, French, Portuguese and U.S. possessions, British dominions, and the Pacific countries of the American continent. Contains a chronology and bibliography.

JA57 GRIMM, ERVIN D., ed. *Sbornik dogovorov i drugikh dokumentov po istorii mezhdunarodnykh otnoshenii na Dalnem Vostoke, 1844-1925.* Moscow: Izd. Instituta vostokovedeniia, 1927. 218 p.

JA58 HARRISON, MARGUERITE E. (BAKER). *Red Bear or Yellow Dragon.* N.Y.: Doran, 1924. 296 p. Curiously little information emerges from this travelogue of a journalist whose adventurous trip, in 1922, took her through Sakhalin, the Far Eastern Republic, Korea, Manchuria, Mongolia, and the Soviet Union. Some interesting sidelights on the Soviets at the Changchun Conference and on their relationship to the Far Eastern Republic.

JA59 KENNEDY, MALCOLM D. *A History of Communism in East Asia.* N.Y.: Praeger, 1957. 556 p. British ed., *A Short History of Communism in Asia.* London: Weidenfeld and Nicolson, 1957. A valuable work by a British specialist on Japan. A massive, well-documented narrative which examines in much detail the rise of Communist movements in China, Japan, Korea, and South and Southeast Asia. Some attention is given to the role played by the Soviets. Good bibliography and index. [A]

JA60 KHEIFETS, A. N. *Lenin; velikii drug narodov Vostoka.* Moscow: Izd. vost. lit., 1960. (Issued under the auspices of the Oriental Institute of the Academy of Sciences.) 247 p. An enthusiastic presentation of Lenin's thoughts and policies with regard to the East.

JA61 KITAIGORODSKII, PAVEL V. *Ot kolonialnogo rabstva k natsionalnoi nezavisimosti; revoliutsionnoe dvizhenie v perednei Azii i Severnoi Afrike.* Intro. by Mikhail Pavlovich. Moscow: "Moskovskii rabochii," 1925. 114 p. A discussion of the revolutionary movement in the Near East and in North Africa.

JA62 KOMMUNISTICHESKAIA AKADEMIIA, INSTITUT MIROVOGO KHOZIAISTVA I MIROVOI POLITIKI. *Kolonialnye problemy.* Ed. by E. Varga, A. Veltner and L. Madiar. Moscow: Partizdat, 1933. 258 p. A Marxist view of the colonial problem, edited by a leading Soviet economist and associates. Varga was for many years the head of the Institute of World Economy and World Politics.

JA63 *Kommunisticheskii Internatsional i osvobozhdenie Vostoka; pervyi sezd narodov Vostoka, Baku, 1-8 sent., 1920; stenograficheskie otchety.* Petrograd: Izd. Komm. internatsionala, 1920. 232 p. The Baku Congress, organized by the Communist International, was an early and historically important Communist attempt to mobilize the peoples of Asia (and especially those of the Near East) in support of the Soviet struggle against "Western imperialism." Among the participants were such noted figures as Zinoviev, Radek, Pavlovich (Veltman), Bela Kun, and John Reed. [B]

JA64 LATTIMORE, OWEN. *The Situation in Asia.* Boston: Little, Brown, 1949. 244 p. A popular, somewhat polemical analysis focused on Soviet and U.S. policies in the area, by a somewhat controversial specialist on Inner Asia and China.

JA65 LAVRICHENKO, MIKHAIL V. *Ekonomicheskoe sotrudnichestvo SSSR so stranami Azii, Afriki i Latinskoi Ameriki.* Moscow: Gospolitizdat, 1961. 144 p. Written for the general reader.

JA66 LEMIN, I. M. *Obostrenie krizisa Britanskoi imperii posle Vtoroi mirovoi voiny.* Moscow: Izd. Akad. nauk SSSR, 1951. 567 p. A substantial Soviet study, sponsored by the Institut Ekonomiki, of Great Britain's postwar political and economic position in relation to her dominions and possessions.

JA67 LENIN, VLADIMIR I. *O natsionalno-osvoboditelnom dvizhenii narodov Vostoka.* Moscow: 1957. English ed., *The National-Liberation Movement in the East.* Moscow: Foreign Languages Publ. House, 1957. 348 p. Articles and speeches in which Lenin deals with the theoretical and practical aspects of the colonial question. Covers the years from 1900 to Lenin's death. Notes and a useful name index. [A]

JA68 *Lenin o druzhbe s narodami Vostoka.* Moscow: Gosizdat. pol. lit., 1961. 399 p. A collection of Lenin's comments on the East, colonialism, independence movements, etc., chronologically arranged, beginning with 1895 and ending with 1923. Annotated and indexed. The documents (full texts and excerpts) are mostly taken from the 4th edition of Lenin's works, supplemented by other Soviet documentary collections. An appendix contains brief comments on Lenin by important Communists (Mao Tse-tung, Ho Chi Minh, Kim Il-Sung, D. N. Aidit) and other important figures (Nehru, Sekou Toure, Kwame N'krumah, Sukarno, Sun Yat-sen, Sen Katayama, A. Gosh, and others). [A]

JA69 *Lenin i Vostok; sbornik statei M. Rafaila, M. Pavlovicha, N. Narimanova, i A. Khodorova.* 2nd ed., Moscow: 1925. A collection of articles by leading Soviet students of the colonial question.

JA70 LOBANOV-ROSTOVSKY, ANDREI. *Russia and Asia.* N.Y.: Macmillan, 1933. 334 p. 2nd ed., Ann Arbor, Mich.: G. Wahr, 1951. 342 p. A general history by a Russian aristocrat who became an American university professor. Only sixty pages are concerned with the Soviet period.

JA71 LOW, FRANCIS (SIR). *Struggle for Asia.* London: Frederick Muller; N.Y.: Praeger, 1955. 239 p. On the whole, an accurate country-by-country survey for the general reader. The author, a former editor of the *Times of India*, dwells at some length on local nationalist and Communist movements.

JA72 MANDEL, WILLIAM, comp. *Soviet Source Materials on USSR Relations with East Asia, 1945-1950; with an Introductory Survey of Soviet Far Eastern Policy since Yalta, by Max Beloff.* N.Y.: International Secretariat, Institute of Pacific Relations, 1950. 289 p. Translations of Soviet diplomatic documents (treaties, official statements, and speeches), editorials and book reviews. 54 items on China, 2 on Mongolia, including the Soviet-Mongolian treaty of 1946, 60 on Japan, 30 on Korea. The introduction by the noted British specialist on Soviet foreign policy is superseded by his more recent extensive study (see Beloff, *Soviet Policy in the Far East*). [B]

JA73 MASSACHUSETTS INSTITUTE OF TECHNOLOGY, CENTER FOR INTERNATIONAL STUDIES. *Essays on Communism in Asia; Papers from the CENIS China Project.* Cambridge: M.I.T., 1955. Eleven specialists present their findings in 3 full-length studies, 8 summaries. The first six papers focus on Communist China—economic growth, planning, the village, the intelligentsia, mass organizations, literature; four discuss Communism in Free Asia with emphasis on Moscow and Peking ties. The final essay, by W. W. Rostow, the project director, compares Soviet and Chinese Communist societies. A uniformly high level of scholarship. (Note: most of the 8 studies summarized here have since been published as monographs.) [B]

JA74 MEHNERT, KLAUS. *Asien, Moskau und Wir; Bilanz nach vier Weltreisen.* 4th ed. Stuttgart: Deutsche Verlags-Anstalt, 1956. 433 p. A lively but objective report on the state of Asia drawing heavily on personal experience. Only 40 pages (section "Sowjetunion") deal specifically with Soviet policy, emphasizing cultural and economic aspects. The author—a Moscow-born and widely travelled German—is a journalist, editor, writer, and university professor and Germany's best-known radio commentator on Soviet affairs and Soviet-Asian relations.

JA75 MICHAEL, FRANZ H., and TAYLOR, GEORGE E. *The Far East in the Modern World.* N.Y.: Holt; London: Methuen, 1956. 724 p. Chapter II ("Communist Russia and the Far East") provides in 40 pages a good outline of Soviet Far Eastern policy.

JA76 MOORE, HARRIET L. *A Record of Soviet Far Eastern Relations, 1931-1942.* N.Y.: International Secretariat, Institute of Pacific Relations, 1942. 92 p. This paper, originally prepared for the Eighth Conference of the Institute of Pacific Relations, constitutes the preliminary draft of the author's *Soviet Far Eastern Policy* (see below).

JA77 MOORE, HARRIET L. *Soviet Far Eastern Policy, 1931-1945.* Princeton, N.J.: Princeton University Press; London: Oxford, 1945. 284 p. A chronological account of Soviet relations with China and Japan. Based almost exclusively on Soviet sources and reflecting Soviet interpretations. A useful appendix (half of the book) contains Soviet diplomatic documents, editorial comments and some trade statistics. [B]

JA78 MOSCOW, INSTITUT MARKSA-ENGELSA-LENINA. *Programmnye dokumenty kommunisticheskikh partii Vostoka.* Ed. by L. Madiar, P. Mif, M. Orakhelashvili, and G. Safarov. Introduction by P.

Mif. Moscow: Partizdat, 1934. 294 p. Provides otherwise inaccessible texts of programmatic documents from a period of international Communism not yet adequately studied.

JA79 MOSCOW, INSTITUT MEZHDUNARODNYKH OTNOSHENII. *Voprosy ekonomiki stran Vostoka.* Ed. by K. M. Popov. Moscow: Izd. IMO, 1960. 295 p. Fifteen well-documented essays, based partly on original sources. Range from Turkey to Japan. Major contributions include studies on Chinese agriculture in Szechuan during the 1930's and 1940's; domestic trade of the Korean People's Republic; land reform in India; administrative changes in India; agriculture in Southeast Asia; international ties of Japanese labor unions. Excellent bibliography of materials on Asia and Africa in Russian and foreign languages for the period from August 1957 to October 1958. [B]

JA80 MOSCOW, INSTITUT MEZHDUNARODNYKH OTNOSHENII. *Voprosy istorii stran Vostoka.* Ed. by M. S. Ivanov. Moscow: Izd. IMO, 1958. 118 p. Four of these five scholarly essays are concerned with contemporary Asia. The topics: (1) Peculiarities of the transitional period in Communist China; (2) Linguistic question and state boundaries in India; (3) Soviet-Chinese relations, 1924-27 (period of KMT-Communist cooperation); (4) Indebtedness of the Burmese peasantry, 1918-39.

JA81 MOSCOW, UNIVERSITET, OTDELENIE ISTORII STRAN ZARUBEZHNOGO VOSTOKA. *Noveishaia istoriia stran zarubezhnogo vostoka.* By Anatolii F. Miller and E. F. Ludshuveit. Ed. by I. M. Reisner and others. Moscow. Izd. Moskovskogo universiteta, 1954-60. 4 vols. A comprehensive history of Asia from the mid-seventeenth century by a group of Moscow University specialists. Almost no documentation. Contains the Soviet appraisal of the independence movements in the colonies at the beginning of this century.

JA82 MOTYLEV, VOLF E. *Tikhookeanskii uzel vtoroi imperialisticheskoi voiny.* Moscow: Sotsekgiz, 1940. 200 p. An analysis of the Far Eastern situation in the third year after the China Incident. Discusses the situation in China (some references to the Communist movement there), and Japan, as well as the Far Eastern policies of the U.S., Great Britain, France, Holland, Germany and Italy. Emphasis on the interrelationship of European and Far Eastern developments. The author used a few English sources and some standard Communist publications.

JA83 MOTYLEV, VOLF E. *Zarozhdenie i razvitie tikhookeanskogo uzla protivorechii.* Moscow: Gos. sots.-ek. izd., 1939. 143 p. Far Eastern developments from the late 19th century to the Pacific War as viewed by a Soviet professor. Half of the work deals with the Soviet period. Focused on Japan's role. For the educated Soviet layman. [B]

JA84 NAUCHNO-ISSLEDOVATELSKII INSTITUT PRI LENINGRADSKOM VOSTOCHNOM INSTITUTE IMENI A. S. ENUKIDZE. *Voprosy kolonialnoi revoliutsii; sbornik statei.* Leningrad: Izd. Leningradskogo vostochnogo instituta imeni A.S. Enukidze, 1931. 116 p. A collection of articles in the form of a periodical; other issues are unknown. Has a bibliography of some interest, with sections on the Comintern and the Colonial East, the Profintern and the Colonial East, and other sections on China, India, and Mongolia.

JA85 NAUCHNO-ISSLEDOVATELSKII KONIUNKTURNYI INSTITUT. *Razvitie ekonomiki stran narodnoi demokratii (obzor za 1957 g.).* Moscow: Izdat.sots.-ek.lit., 1958. 610 p. One of the numerous economic handbooks compiled by the Institute. Contains a substantial section on Communist China (p. 14-225) and shorter sections on North Vietnam (p. 328-55), North Korea (p. 406-35) and Outer Mongolia (p. 436-54). [A]

JA86 NOSAKA, SANZO. *The War in the Far East and the Tasks of the Communists in the Struggle against Imperialist War and Military Intervention; Report of Comrade Okano (pseud.) at the XIIth Plenum of the Executive Committee of the Communist International.* N.Y.: Worker's Library, 1932. 51 p. An orthodox Communist analysis of the Far Eastern situation after the Manchurian Incident and an appeal for a "joint struggle against Japanese imperialism" and for "the defense of the toiling masses of the Soviet Union and China." The reporter, a former Presidium member of the Comintern and a long-time resident of Moscow and Yenan, is head of the Japanese Communist Party (1961).

JA87 PALMIERI, AURELIO. *La Politica asiatica dei Bolscevichi.* Bologna: N. Zanichelli, 1924–. A well-documented, impartial account by an Italian academic specialist. Covers in separate chapters China, Japan, India, Persia. Useful bibliography stressing Soviet sources, including periodical literature. Intended to be a multi-volume work, but apparently only one volume was published.

JA88 PASVOLSKY, LEO. *Russia in the Far East.* N.Y.: Macmillan, 1922. 181 p. An objective account for the general reader, now superseded by more recent studies. Only partly concerned with the Soviet period.

JA89 PAVLOVICH, MIKHAIL I. (pseud. of Mikhail L. Veltman). *Borba za Aziiu i Afriku.* Moscow: 1923. 229 p. 2nd ed., Leningrad: 1925. Polemical sketches by a prolific writer and active propagandist who was one of the most influential specialists on Eastern affairs during the early years of the Soviet regime. [B]

JA90 PAVLOVICH, MIKHAIL I. *SSSR i Vostok; imperializm i mirovaia politika poslednikh desiatiletii.* Vol. IX of his *Collected Works.* Leningrad: Gosizdat, 1927. 350 p.

JA91 PAVLOVICH, MIKHAIL I., ed. *Strany Vostoka; spravochnik.* Moscow: Ros.-vost. torg. palata, 1925. 487 p.

JA92 PAYNE, PIERRE S. ROBERT. *Red Storm Over Asia.* N.Y.: Macmillan, 1951. 309 p. A well-written, impassioned story of Communism in Asia (China, Korea, India, Indonesia, Philippines, Malaya, Vietnam, Burma, Iran) during the late 1940's. Information-packed, but not always accurate in details. A strongly subjective interpretation, yet full of insights into Asia. Includes some 20 biographical sketches of Asian Communist leaders. The British author is a prolific writer on Asia who knows much of the story and many of the people involved from personal experience.

JA93 *Prebyvanie K. E. Voroshilova v Kitae, Indonezii, Vetname i Mongolii 15 aprelia-30 maia 1957 g.; sbornik materialov.* Moscow: Gospolitizdat, 1957. 239 p. Texts of communiques and speeches by Voroshilov and his Asian hosts, including Mao Tse-tung, Liu Shao-chi, Chu Teh, Ho Chi-minh, and Sukarno.

JA94 *Razbuzhennyi Vostok; zapiski sovetskikh zhurnalistov o vizite N. S. Khrushcheva v Indiiu, Birmu, Indoneziiu, Afganistan.* Moscow: Gospolitizdat, 1960. 2 vols. Reports by Soviet journalists on Khrushchev's 1960 Asian tour.

JA95 *Razvitie ekonomiki stran narodnoi demokratii Azii; obzor.* Moscow: Vneshtorgizdat. Annual, 1957–. Volume I is a survey covering economy, transportation, agriculture, domestic and foreign trade, finances, social welfare, and living standards of Communist China (200 pages), Outer Mongolia, North Korea and North Vietnam. Much statistical material mostly drawn from standard local sources. Descriptive rather than analytical. Economic maps. [A]

JA95A *Razvitie ekonomiki stran narodnoi demokratii Evropy i Azii, statisticheskii sbornik.* Moscow: Vneshtorgizdat, 1961. 471 p. Contains also some statistical material about the Vietnamese, Chinese, Korean, and Mongolian People's Republics. No sources for the data are cited.

JA96 RUMIANTSEV, A. M., ed. *Sovremennoe osvoboditelnoe dvizhenie i natsionalnaia burzhuaziia; sbornik statei po materialam obmena mneniiami, provedennogo zhurnalom "Problemy mira i sotsializma."* Prague: Izd. Mir i Sotsializm, 1961. 344 p. Important for an understanding of the official Soviet policy line on the issue of the "national bourgeoisie." Authoritative articles by Soviet and non-Soviet Communists deal with the problem, both in general terms and in its application to specific areas including North Africa (Algeria, Tunisia, Morocco), Near East (UAR, Lebanon, Jordan), Latin America (Chile, Argentina, Uruguay, Guatemala), and Africa (Nigeria). [A]

JA97 RUSSIA (1923– USSR), KOMISSIIA PO IZDANIIU DIPLOMATICHESKIKH DOKUMENTOV. *Dokumenty vneshnei politiki SSSR.* Ed. by A. A. Gromyko and others. Moscow: Gospolitizdat, 1957–. (In progress.) So far five volumes have been issued; they cover the period from Nov. 1917 to Nov. 1922. This series is the fullest, most accurate, and best edited selection from the Soviet archives published so far; however, the editing occasionally reflects political pressures. Contains many basic materials on Soviet relations with Asia. A country index facilitates the search for pertinent documents.

JA98 SAFAROV, GEORGII I. *Kolonialnaia revoliutsiia.* Moscow: Gosizdat, 1922. 148 p.

JA99 SAFAROV, GEORGII I. *Problemy natsionalno-kolonialnoi revoliutsii.* Moscow-Leningrad: Ogiz, 1931. 285 p.

JA100 SAITO RYOE. *Sovieto Rokoku no kyokuto shinshutsu.* Tokyo: Nihon Hyoronsha, 1931. 376 p. A descriptive outline of Soviet policy in the Far East from 1917 to 1930. Mostly concerned with China. Chapter 2 deals with the Siberian Expedition. Chapter 3 on Chinese-Russian relations is the most valuable, since its author had personal experience as a director of the South Manchurian Railroad Company and a former Japanese diplomat.

JA101 *Schaste i mir—narodam; prebyvanie Predsedatelia Soveta Ministrov SSSR N. S. Khrushcheva v Indii, Birme, Indonezii i Afganistane; 11 February-5 March, 1960 g.* Moscow: Gospolitizdat, 1960. 349 p. English ed., Moscow: Foreign Languages Pub. House, 1960. 341 p. Materials, including descriptive notes and texts of speeches by Khrushchev and his hosts, on the 1960 trip of the Soviet leader. [A]

JA102 SEVOSTIANOV, GRIGORII N. *Politika velikikh derzhav na Dalnem Vostoke nakanune Vtoroi mirovoi voiny.* Moscow: Sotsekgiz, 1961. 559 p. An exceptionally well-documented and detailed analysis of Far Eastern developments during the last two years before Pearl Harbor. Focus is on the repercussions of the Japanese expansionist drive. Good bibliography (p. 537-49) of Russian and Western sources. Lists also classification numbers of some new materials from the archives of the Soviet ministries of Foreign Affairs, Defense, and Justice. The introduction is useful for its discussion of source materials used. [A]

JA103 SHABAD, BORIS A. *Ideologicheskie osnovy sovremennogo kolonializma.* Moscow: Izd. Vost. lit., 1961. 102 p. An attack against

"Western colonialism" in Asia and Africa, published under the auspices of the Institut Narodov Azii and drawing for ammunition on recent Western writings. [B]

JA104 STEIN, GUENTHER. *Far East in Ferment*. London: Methuen, 1936. 244 p. A journalistic survey focused on Japan. Chapters III and IV deal in cursory fashion with the Soviet military position and objectives in the area. The author later became a leading leftwing Marxist interpreter of the Far Eastern scene.

JA105 SULTAN-ZADE, AVETIS S. (pseud.). *Ekonomika i problemy natsionalnykh revoliutsii v stranakh Blizhnego i Dalnego Vostoka*. Moscow: Gosizdat, 1921. 184 p. An Iranian Communist (also known as "Pishevari") and prominent Comintern figure briefly discusses political and economic developments in Persia, Turkey, the Arab countries, India, and China, as well as the role of Islam in the area. More useful for its reflection of the sanguine views held by Communists in the early twenties than for its meager information on the revolutionary movements in the Near East.

JA106 SURVEY OF INTERNATIONAL AFFAIRS, 1920-1923—; THE WAR-TIME SERIES FOR 1939-1946. *The Far East, 1942-1946*. By F. C. Jones, Hugh Borton, and B. R. Pearn. London and N.Y.: Oxford, for the Royal Institute of International Affairs, 1955. 589 p. Sections deal with the Far East during the war, the Far East after the war, South-East Asia, Japan under Allied occupation, and Korea under American and Soviet occupation. Appendices contain numerous documents.

JA107 SWARUP, RAM. *Communism and Peasantry; Implications of Collectivist Agriculture for Asian Countries*. Calcutta: Prachi Prakashan, 1954. 193 p. A stimulating, scholarly study written from an anti-Communist viewpoint. The Indian author examines Communist strategy and tactics toward the peasantry and discusses their relevance for India. Draws heavily on Soviet and Chinese Communist sources.

JA108 SYRKIN, S. *Oktiabrskaia Revoliutsiia i grazhdanskaia voina na Dalnem Vostoke*. Moscow: Dalgiz, 1933. 305 p. A somewhat detailed recounting of Far Eastern developments, 1917-22.

JA109 TERENTEV, N. *Ochag voiny na Dalnem Vostoke*. Moscow: Partizdat, 1934. 256 p. A detailed Soviet account of the confused Far Eastern situation in the early 1930's centering around Manchuria. Some references to the Chinese Communists. The appendix contains the spurious "Tanaka Memorandum" and statement by General Araki. A map of the Far East showing Chinese Communist positions is included.

JA110 THAYER, PHILLIP W., and PHILLIPS, WILLIAM T., eds. *Nationalism and Progress in Free Asia.* Baltimore: Johns Hopkins, 1956. 394 p. A symposium. Two essays of direct interest to the student of Asian Communism: "Backgrounds of Communism in Asia" by Harold H. Fisher, with commentary by Lucian W. Pye, and "Techniques of Communist Aggression and the Moscow-Peking Axis" by Rodger Swearingen.

JA111 TOMPKINS, PAULINE. *American-Russian Relations in the Far East.* N.Y.: Macmillan, 1949. 426 p. A scholarly, well-documented survey by an American political scientist who draws on State Department archives, private papers, and other (mostly American) sources for an attack against balance of power politics. Almost exclusively concerned with the 1917-31 period. Strong on the American aspects, weak on treatment of the Soviet Union. The appendix contains standard documents on Russo-Chinese and Russo-Japanese relations. Good bibliography of Western language sources. [B]

JA112 TRAININ, I. P. *Imperializm na Dalnem Vostoke i SSSR.* Moscow: Partizdat, 1932. 182 p.

JA113 TRULLINGER, O. O. *Red Banners Over Asia.* Oxford: Pen-in-Hand; Boston: Beacon, 1950. 212 p. A discussion of Communism in South, Southeast and East Asia. Rather superficial, replete with inaccuracies and unsubstantiated assertions. Supposedly by an Asian diplomat writing under a pseudonym.

JA114 UYEHARA, CECIL, comp. *Checklist of Archives in the Japanese Ministry of Foreign Affairs, Tokyo, Japan, 1868-1945.* Washington, D.C.: Library of Congress, 1954. 262 p. Some of these captured materials, deposited in the Library of Congress, are of interest to the student of Soviet-Asian relations. For details, see index under "Russia" (p. 226-30).

JA115 VASILEVA, V. IA. *Raspad kolonalnoi sistemy imperializma.* Moscow: Izd. Akademii nauk, 1958. 607 p. Issued under the auspices of the Institut Mirovoi Ekonomiki i Mezhdunarodnykh Otnoshenii. An analysis of the problems of the "colonial and semi-colonial" areas after World War II, emphasizing economic and social changes. Contains much statistical material. Chapter VI (150 p.) deals consecutively with India, Burma, Indonesia, Egypt, Philippines, Malaya, Africa, Near and Middle East, and Latin America. The seventh and last chapter discusses the role of the "people's democracies" in the "building of socialism." [B]

JA116 *Velikii Oktiabr i narody Vostoka; sbornik.* Ed. by A. A. Guber. Moscow: Izd. vost. lit., 1957. 417 p. Issued for the fortieth anniversary of the Russian Revolution, this collection offers articles on China, Vietnam, Korea, Mongolia, Afghanistan, Burma, Egypt, India, Indonesia, Iraq, Iran, Morocco, Syria, Lebanon, Turkey, and the Philippines. Guber's introductory article describes the great influence of the October Revolution in the colonial world, and the support given by the USSR to oppressed peoples. A good example of recent Soviet scholarship in the service of politics, but a useful source. [B]

JA117 VLUGT, EBEND VAN DER. *Asia Aflame; Communism in the East.* Foreword by Albert C. Wedemeyer. N.Y.: Devin-Adair, 1953. 294 p. A comprehensive, popular survey of the background, strategy, and activities of Asian Communism. Marred by sharply polemical statements regarding American policy in Asia and by occasional inaccuracies and oversimplifications. The writer is a Dutch barrister who had substantial experience in Indonesia.

JA118 *Vtoraia konferentsiia solidarnosti narodov Azii i Afriki, Konakri, 11-15 aprelia 1960 g.* Moscow: Sotsekizdat, 1961. 350 p. Resolutions, speeches by delegates, and other pertinent conference documents.

JA119 WITTFOGEL, KARL A. *Oriental Despotism; a Comparative Study of Total Power.* New Haven: Yale, 1957. 556 p. This important and stimulating work expounds the theory of the "hydraulic society" and its relationship to despotism. In the process, the author, an academic specialist on Chinese history, ancient and modern, dwells on Soviet views on and discussions about the nature of Asian society.

JA121 YAKHONTOFF, VICTOR A. *Russia and the Soviet Union in the Far East.* N.Y.: Coward-McCann, 1931. 454 p. London: G. Allen and Unwin, 1932. 454 p. This pioneer study focusing on events in China is now largely outdated. Parts II and III (p. 113 to end) deal with the Soviet era. The author, an ex-general of the Imperial Russian Army who had wide experience in the Far East, attempts to be objective, but his pro-Soviet sentiments shine through. The appendix includes several documents the author copied personally from the Soviet archives. Chronology. Valuable bibliography of Russian and Western language materials.

JA122 YOUNG, JOHN, comp. *Checklist of Microfilm Reproductions of Selected Archives of the Japanese Army, Navy, and Other Government Agencies, 1868-1945.* Washington, D.C.: Georgetown University, 1959. 144 p. Although primarily important for the student of Soviet-Japanese relations, contains references to documents on Soviet-Asian relations in general. See index under "Russia" (p. 142-43).

3. PERIODICALS AND NEWSPAPERS

a. SOVIET PERIODICALS ON ASIA

NOTE. The following Soviet publications largely devoted to Asia contain much information on Soviet-Asian relations and/or Asian Communism. When the frequency of publication is not shown, the item is either issued irregularly or the exact data could not be established.

JA123 *Aziia i Afrika segodnia*, Moscow: 1961–. (Formerly *Sovremennyi Vostok*, 1957-61.) Published monthly by the Asian and African Institutes of the Academy of Sciences. Primarily a propaganda publication, it contains articles on political and cultural topics, travelogues, book reviews, and some documents. Also includes an English-language table of contents and summary of articles.

JA124 *Bibliografiia Vostoka*, Leningrad: 1932-37. (10 issues.) Reviews and bibliographic annotations. (See item no. JA1.)

JA125 *Kolonialnye problemy*, Moscow: 1933-34. 2 vols. Published by the Colonial Section of the Institute of World Economy and International Politics.

JA126 *Kratkie soobshcheniia Instituta narodov Azii*, Moscow: 1961–. (Formerly *Kratkie soobshcheniia Instituta vostokovedeniia*, 1951-60.) Represents the highest level of Soviet scholarship. Individual issues often focus on a single topic or country.

JA127 *Materialy po natsionalno-kolonialnym problemam*, Moscow: 1931-37. In 1937 entitled *Natsionalno-kolonialnye problemy*.

JA128 *Narody Azii i Afriki*, Moscow: 1961–. (Formerly *Sovetskoe vostokovedenie*, 1940-58; *Problemy vostokovedeniia*, 1959-61.) Published bimonthly by the Asian and African Institutes of the Academy of Sciences. Scholarly articles and professional news.

JA129 *Narody Dalnego Vostoka*, Irkutsk: 1921. (5 issues.) The organ of the Far Eastern Secretariat of the Comintern, published in Russian and English.

JA130 *Novaia sovetskaia i inostrannaia literatura po stranam Zarubezhnogo Vostoka*, Moscow: 1949–. Published by the Academy of Sciences Library.

JA131 *Novyi Vostok*, Moscow: 1922-30. (29 issues.) The journal of the USSR Scientific Association of Oriental Studies.

JA132 *Revoliutsionnyi Vostok*, Moscow: 1927-37. (41 issues.) The journal of the USSR Scientific Research Association for the Study of

National and Colonial Problems, connected with the Communist University for Toilers of the East (KUTV).

JA133 *Tikhii okean*, Moscow: 1934-38. (17 issues.) Published quarterly by the Pacific Section of the Institute of World Economics and Politics. Dealt with political, social and economic topics.

JA134 *Torgovlia SSSR s Vostokom*, Moscow: 1923-31? (Before 1928, *Torgovlia Rossii s Vostokom.*) Published by the Chamber of Commerce of the USSR.

JA135 *Uchenye zapiski Instituta vostokovedeniia*, Moscow: 1950–. (To be renamed as a result of the renaming of the Institut vostokovedeniia as Institut narodov Azii.)

JA136 *Uchenye zapiski Tikhookeanskogo instituta*, Moscow: 1947-49. 3 vols. Published by the Academy of Sciences.

JA137 *Vostok i kolonii*, Moscow: 1927-30. Bulletin of the Oriental Section of the Profintern.

b. SOVIET PERIODICALS OF A GENERAL NATURE

NOTE. In addition to the previously-listed Soviet periodicals more specifically concerned with Asia, the following Soviet publications of a more general nature will be found very useful in studying Soviet policy toward Asia and the Communist movements of that area.

JA138 *Izvestiia*, Moscow: 1917–. The official newspaper of the Soviet government.

JA139 *Mezhdunarodnaia zhizn*, Moscow: 1922-30. (Successor to *Vestnik Narodnogo komissariata po inostrannym delam*, 1918-22.) The journal of the Commissariat of Foreign Affairs.

JA140 *Mezhdunarodnaia zhizn*, Moscow: 1954–. (English ed., *International Affairs.*) Monthly, published by the Soviet Society for the Popularization of Political and Scientific Knowledge.

JA141 *Mirovaia ekonomika i mezhdunarodnye otnosheniia*, Moscow: 1957–. Published monthly by the Institute of World Economy and International Relations.

JA142 *Mirovoe khoziaistvo i mirovaia politika*, Moscow: 1925-47. (Preceded by *Mezhdunarodnaia letopis*, 1924-25.) Published monthly by the Institute of Economics.

JA143 *Molodezh mira*, Moscow: 1952–. Published monthly by the World Federation of Democratic Youth.

JA144 *Novoe vremia*, Moscow: 1943–. (English ed., *New Times.*) Published weekly by *Trud.*

JA145 *Pravda*, Moscow: 1912–. The organ of the Central Committee of the CPSU.

JA146 *Problemy mira i sotsializma*, Prague: 1958–. (English ed., *World Marxist Review.*) Monthly of the international Communist movement.

JA147 *Vneshniaia torgovlia*, Moscow: 1931–. Issued monthly by the Ministry of Foreign Trade.

JA148 *Voprosy istorii*, Moscow: 1945–. Published monthly by the Historical Section of the Academy of Sciences.

JA149 *V zashchitu mira*, Moscow: 1951–. (Superseded *Mir.*) Published monthly by the Foreign Literature Publishing House.

c. NON-SOVIET PERIODICALS

NOTE. The following non-Soviet publications often contain useful materials on Soviet-Asian relations or Communism in Asia. (* indicates that the publication also appears in languages other than English.)

JA150 *Asian Survey*, Berkeley, Cal.: 1961–. Published monthly by the Institute of International Studies of the University of California.

JA151 **Communist International*, Petrograd, Moscow, London, N.Y., etc.: 1919-43. The organ of the Executive Committee of the Comintern. Published in English, Russian, German, French, Chinese, and Spanish. Appeared irregularly, usually monthly, but sometimes more often. An indispensable source for the history of the Communist movement in Asia.

JA152 *Current Digest of the Soviet Press*, N.Y.: 1949–. Issued weekly by the Joint Committee on Slavic Studies.

JA153 *Est et Ouest*, Paris: 1949–. (Formerly *B.E.I.P.I.*) Published fortnightly by the Association d'Etudes et d'Informations Politiques et Internationales.

JA154 *Far Eastern Survey*, N.Y.: 1932-61. Issued fortnightly by the Institute of Pacific Relations.

JA155 **For a Lasting Peace, For a People's Democracy*, Bucharest: 1947-56. Published bimonthly by the Cominform.

JA156 *Gekkan Roshia*, Tokyo: 1935-44. Published by the Japan-Soviet News Agency.

JA157 **International Press Correspondence* (later *World News and Views*), Berlin, Vienna, London, etc., 1921-43. Name changed to *World News and Views* with the issue of July 2, 1938. This invaluable source was, in effect, the newspaper of the Communist International until its dissolution in 1943. For some years there are also German, French, and Italian editions. Regularly contained speeches and reports by Communists on the revolutionary movement in Asia. Continued publication after 1943, but became in effect an organ of the British C.P.

JA158 *Kyosanken Mondai*, Tokyo: 1961–. Published monthly by the O-A Kyokai (Europe-Asia Association) as the successor to the quarterlies *Kiho Soren Mondai* (1957-60) and *Kiho Kyosanken Mondai* (1960-61).

JA159 *Osteuropa*, Stuttgart: 1951–. Published monthly by the Deutsche Gesellschaft für Osteuropakunde.

JA160 *Pacific Affairs*, N.Y.: 1926-61; Vancouver: 1961–. A quarterly published by the University of British Columbia (until 1961 by the Institute of Pacific Relations).

JA161 *Problems of Communism*, Washington: 1952–. Published bimonthly by the United States Information Agency.

JA162 *Soviet Press Translations*, Seattle: 1946-53. A biweekly issued by the Far Eastern and Russian Institute, University of Washington.

JA163 *Tairiku Mondai*, Tokyo: 1952–. Published monthly by the Continental Problems Research Institute. The emphasis is on military problems.

JB. AUSTRALIA

EDITED BY BRIAN D. BEDDIE

JB1 ALEXANDER, JOSEPH A. *In the Shadow—Three Years in Moscow.* Melbourne: Herald and Weekly Times, 1949. 356 p. The author, an Australian writer, served as first secretary in the Australian Embassy for three years from 1944. The book describes conditions in Russia in those years from a highly critical point of view. Chapter XIV tells how Australia is depicted in the USSR.

JB2 AUSTRALIA, ROYAL COMMISSION ON ESPIONAGE. *Official Transcript of Proceedings, May 17, 1954-March 31, 1955.* Sydney. 126 p. The hearings in the Petrov case.

JB3 AUSTRALIA, ROYAL COMMISSION ON ESPIONAGE. *Report.* Sydney: Government Printer for N.S.W., 1955. 483 p. The report of three Australian judges, appointed as commissioners, to inquire into the defection of Mr. and Mrs. Petrov from the Soviet Embassy in Canberra and into Petrov's revelations. [A]

JB4 BARCAN, ALAN. *The Socialist Left in Australia, 1949-59.* Sydney: Australian Political Studies Association, 1960. 26 p. (processed). A scholar at the Australian National University investigates "The Communist Party and the Dissident Left in Australia, 1949-1959" with a special reference to the crisis in the Communist Party in 1956. A scholarly study from the "new left" standpoint. [A]

JB5 BIALOGUSKI, MICHAEL. *The Petrov Story.* London: Heinemann. 247 p. A Russian-Polish doctor who became a secret agent of the Australian Security Intelligence Organization tells, in journalistic style, his part in the Petrov affair.

JB6 BOBROV, A. *Vneshnaia politika Avstralii.* Moscow: I.M.O., 1962. Analyzes the relations of Australia with England, U.S.A., Japan and the countries of South East Asia. An important place is assigned to the relations between Australia and socialist countries. One section is devoted to the position of Australia on major international issues; another section to the organs of external relations. [B]

JB7 BROWN, WILTON J., ed. *The Petrov Conspiracy Unmasked.* Sydney: Newsletter Printing, 1956. 360 p. The editor argues that the Royal Commission into the Petrov affair was a "crude political conspiracy by the Australian Government to discredit the Communist Party, the Labour Party and to foment ill will between the Australian and Soviet people."

JB8 CAMPBELL, ERNEST W. *History of the Australian Labor Movement; a Marxist Interpretation.* Sydney: Current Book Distributors, 1945. 160 p. The director of Marx School, Sydney, presents on the basis of "little or no original research" an interpretation of the Australian labor movement from 1890 to 1945 from a Communist point of view. Chapter v (p. 107-160) outlines the history of the Australian C.P. [A]

JB9 CRISP, FINDLAY L. *Ben Chifley; a Biography.* London: Longmans, 1961. A scholarly biography of a Labour Prime Minister of Australia written by a professor of political science at the Australian National University. Chapters XXI and XXIII deal with important aspects of Communist activity in the period 1945-50. [B]

JB10 DOROFEEV, BORIS IA. *Sovremennaia Avstraliia; kratkii politiko-ekonomicheskii ocherk.* Moscow: Gospolitizdat, 1959. 195 p. A general survey of Australian history, economics, and politics, including a chapter on Australia's external relations. Chapter VI surveys the Labour, Liberal, Country and Communist Parties of Australia.

JB11 ELLIS, MALCOLM H. *The Garden Path—the Story of the Saturation of the Australian Labour Movement by Communism.* Sydney: The Land Newspaper, 1949. 560 p. A conservative, strongly anti-Communist historian seeks to demonstrate "the continuous connection and interlocking of the Communist Party and the Labour Party in Australia" during the years 1920 to 1949. [A]

JB12 FITZPATRICK, BRIAN. *A Short History of the Australian Labor Movement.* Melbourne: Rawson's Bookshop, 1944. 221 p. An Australian historian with strong left-wing sympathies discusses the development of the Australian labor movement from the middle of the nineteenth century to 1944. Communist activity is treated as a part of the general labor movement. [A]

JB13 HOGAN, EDMUND J. *What's Wrong with Australia?* Melbourne: The Author, 1953. 187 p. A former Labour leader and premier of Victoria seeks to expose Communist activity in Australian life generally and especially in Australian trade unions. Documentation is faulty and quotations are not always reliable.

JB14 LANG, JOHN T. *Communism in Australia.* Sydney: Express Newspapers, (1944?). 142 p. A former Labour premier of N.S.W. presents in journalistic terms "a complete exposure" of the Australian C.P.

JB15 LETOVA, N. P. *Avstraliia i strani Azii; ocherki mezhdunarodnykh otnoshenii, 1945-1955.* Moscow: I.M.O., 1960. 148 p. Discusses the effect of World War II on Australian foreign policy and the subsequent development of Australia's relations with Japan and the countries of South East Asia. Australia is represented as participating in the aggression of imperialist powers in Asia, and the Colombo plan is treated as an instrument for effecting economic penetration of Asia.

JB16 MALONEY, J. J. *Inside Red Russia.* Sydney: Angus and Robertson, 1948. 207 p. The author, a prominent member of the Australian Labour Party, was Australian Minister to Russia from 1943 to 1945. He provides a damaging description of Russian institutions and living standards.

JB17 MAYEVSKI, V. *Pervyi ili piatyi.* Molodaia Gvardiia, 1960. 176 p. An account of a journey by the author and a description of various phases of Australian economic and social life.

JB18 NATIONAL LIBRARY OF AUSTRALIA. *Communism in Australia; a Bibliography.* Canberra: June, 1961. (Preliminary draft, processed.) 95 p. Fairly comprehensive except that it does not include post-graduate thesis work on Communism in Australia. [A]

JB19 OVERACKER, LOUISE. *The Australian Party System.* London: Oxford, 1952. 377 p. Chapter 6 of this work by an American professor of political science (at Wellesley College) is devoted to the Communist Party of Australia. The most scholarly short account available in book form. Contains a select bibliography on the A.C.P., p. 345-46. [A]

JB20 PETROV, VLADIMIR and EVODOKIA. *Empire of Fear.* London: Deutsch, 1956. 351 p. Mr. and Mrs. Petrov tell the story of their lives, of their experience in the Soviet secret service, and of their defection from the Soviet Embassy in Canberra.

JB21 SHARKEY, LAURENCE L. *An Outline History of the Australian Communist Party.* Sydney: Australian Communist Party, 1944. 83 p. A leading Australian Communist puts together a number of speeches and addresses under a somewhat misleading title. The pamphlet is important because it represents the authoritative exposition of the strategy and tactics of the Australian Communist Party. It also contains material by E. W. Campbell and O. Kuusinnen. [A]

JB22 SHARKEY, LAURENCE L. *The Trade Unions; Communist Theory and Practice of Trade Unionism.* Supplemented and revised edition, Sydney: Current Book Distributors, 1959. 86 p. A text setting out the orthodox Communist view of the Australian Trade Union Movement and laying down the strategy for revolutionary struggle against "reformism." [A]

JB23 SHARPLEY, CECIL H. *The Great Delusion.* London: Heinemann, 1952. 155 p. A former Communist who for fourteen years held official positions in the Australian C.P. sets out to expose the political and trade union methods of the Party in the period 1935-50. [B]

JB24 UGLOV, A. A. *Gosudarstvennyi stroi Avstralii.* Moscow: Gosiurizdat, 1957. 68 p. This pamphlet covers the political structure of Australia—its federal system, legislatures, courts, and Commonwealth and state governments—from the Soviet point of view.

JB25 VICTORIA, AUSTRALIA. *Report of the Royal Commission Inquiring into the Origins, Aims, Objects and Funds of the Communist Party in Victoria and Other Related Matters.* (Royal Commissioner—The Hon. Sir Charles Lowe.) Melbourne: Government Printer, 1950. 156 p. Though directly concerned with the activities of the Victorian State Organization of the Australian Communist Party, the report contains a survey of the activities of the Party in Australia generally. [A]

JB26 WEBB, LEICESTER C. *Communism and Democracy in Australia; a Survey of the 1951 Referendum.* Melbourne: F. W. Cheshire, 1954. N.Y.: Praeger, 1955. 214 p. A professor of political science at Australian National University analyzes the defeat of the Commonwealth Government's attempt to obtain by the referendum of 1951 a constitutional amendment to permit the proscribing of the Australian Communist Party. One of the few scholarly studies in book form of an aspect of Australian Communism. [A]

1. COMMUNIST NEWSPAPERS AND PERIODICALS

JB27 *The Communist Review.* Monthly. Sydney. The Australian Communist Party's theoretical journal. Contains the reports and speeches of triennial congresses and reports of the Central Committee. [A]

JB28 *Guardian.* Weekly newspaper. Brisbane. [B]

JB29 *Guardian.* Weekly newspaper. Melbourne. [B]

JB30 *Tribune.* Weekly newspaper. Sydney. 1934 to date, with certain omissions during the period of the Party's illegal existence 1940-41. Incorporated the earlier *Workers' Weekly* (1923-29). [A]

Addendum

The Peking-oriented "Australian Communist Party (Marxist-Leninist)," formed in 1964, publishes *The Australian Communist* (monthly, Melbourne) and *Vanguard* (weekly newspaper, Melbourne). On the split in the C.P.A. see: "Between Moscow and Peking—the C.P. of Australia," *Current Affairs Bulletin*, vol. 34, no. 3, Sydney; and T. H. Rigby, "Australasia," *Survey*, no. 54 (January 1965).

JC. CHINA

1. GENERAL WORKS

(Edited by Mark Mancall, Shao-chuan Leng, and W. Nathaniel Howell, Jr.)

JC1 AKADEMIIA NAUK SSSR, INSTITUT KITAEVEDENIIA. *Ocherki istorii Kitaia v noveishee vremia.* Moscow: Izd. vostochnoi lit., 1959. 696 p. This history of modern China was written by practically all the China specialists of the USSR; its foreword states that it is "destined for a wide circle of readers," and the whole book appears to be a major effort. Includes extensive bibliography, chronology from November 7, 1917 to November 19, 1957, many maps, and numerous illustrations. [A]

JC2 AKADEMIIA NAUK SSSR, INSTITUT KITAEVEDENIIA. *Sovetsko-kitaiskie otnosheniia, 1917-1957; sbornik dokumentov.* Ed. by I. F. Kurdiukov, V. N. Nikiforov, and A. S. Perevertailo. Moscow: Izd. vostochnoi lit., 1959. 465 p. A collection of over 250 documents (agreements, notes, speeches, letters, telegrams) pertaining to Sino-Soviet relations, 1917-57. In the preface the compilers note that the majority of the documents have been published, but some documents from the Soviet foreign policy archives see light here for the first time. An introductory survey presents the standard account of the main stages in the development of Sino-Soviet relations during this period. A chronology and a name index are appended. [A]

JC3 AKADEMIIA NAUK SSSR, INSTITUT VOSTOKOVEDENIIA. *Kitai; istoriia, ekonomika, geroicheskaia borba za natsionalnuiu nezavisimost; sbornik statei.* Ed. by V. M. Alekseev and others. Moscow-Leningrad: 1940. 536 p. A comprehensive and not hostile survey of China with articles by leading Soviet sinologists. Significant for its appearance at a time when Soviet focus on China was very slight. A 25-page bibliography includes works by Marx, Engels, Lenin and Stalin relating to China. [A]

JC4 AKADEMIIA NAUK SSSR, INSTITUT VOSTOKOVEDENIIA. *Mezhdunarodnye otnosheniia na Dalnem Vostoke, 1870-1945.* Ed. by E. M. Zhukov. Moscow: Gospolitizdat, 1951. 790 p. 2nd, rev. ed., (*1840-1949*), 1956. 784 p. German ed., Berlin: Akademie Verlag, 1955. 647 p. An authoritative Soviet text on Far Eastern diplomacy prepared by the Oriental Institute of the Academy of Sciences. Contributions by G. N. Voitinskii, A. A. Guber, A. I. Galperin, and others. Includes a chronology, index, and a 26-page bibliography citing mainly Russian and English-language sources, but none in Chinese. [B]

JC5 AKADEMIIA NAUK SSSR, TIKHOOKEANSKII INSTITUT. *Kitaiskii sbornik; uchenye zapiski*, III. Ed. by E. M. Zhukov and others. Moscow: Izd. Akad. nauk, 1949. 180 p. Articles on various stages of the Chinese revolutionary movement by leading Soviet Orientalists.

JC6 ARSENEV, VLADIMIR K. *Russen und Chinesen in Ostsibirien*. Berlin: A. Scherl, 1926. 229 p. The author was an explorer, traveller, ethnographer, writer, and specialist on the Russian Far East (1872-1930). An extremely valuable general survey of Chinese and Korean emigration in the Russian Far East, based on the author's numerous trips in the area, 1906-1917. Important photographs and tables.

JC7 BRANDT, CONRAD; SCHWARTZ, BENJAMIN; and FAIRBANK, JOHN K., eds. *A Documentary History of Chinese Communism*. Cambridge: Harvard; London: Allen & Unwin, 1952. 552 p. German ed., Munich: Oldenbourg, 1955. An indispensable reference work, this volume is a compilation and translation into English of 40 key statements by the Chinese Communist Party over the period 1921-50. The chronological presentation of material provides valuable glimpses of the development of the Chinese Party and its ideology. Also includes a brief chronology of major events in Party history from 1918 to 1950. [A]

JC8 CHAO, KUO-CHÜN. *Thirty Years of the Communist Movement in China; A Chronology of Major Developments, 1920-1950*. Cambridge, Mass.: Harvard, 1950. 36 p. A brief but valuable reference work put together at the Harvard Russian Research Center.

JC9 CHASSIN, LIONEL M. (GENERAL). *L'Ascension de Mao Tsé-tung, 1921-1945*. Paris: Payot, 1953. 216 p. The author, a French military historian, has previously dealt with the 1949 success of the Chinese Communists. In this volume he turns his attention to the career of Mao and sketches his rise to power from 1921 to more recent times.

JC10 CH'ENG, T'IEN-FANG. *A History of Sino-Russian Relations*. Intro. by John L. Stuart. Washington: Public Affairs, 1957. 389 p. The first quarter of this survey of China's relations with Russia, written by a member of the Kuomintang and former Minister of Education of the Republic of China, traces contacts from the 12th Century to the First World War in broad terms. The remainder of the book is a more detailed treatment of events from the Bolshevik Revolution to the Chinese Communist seizure of power in 1949. The final chapter expresses the author's thesis that the issues of the Chinese Civil War have not yet been resolved.

JC11 CHIANG, KAI-SHEK (CHIANG CHUNG-CHENG). *China's Destiny*. N.Y.: Macmillan, 1947. 260 p. N.Y.: Roy, 1947.

347 p. This essay, published in 1943 to mark the termination of the unequal treaties, was used extensively in schools and colleges and became required reading for all members of the Kuomintang. Chiang interprets modern Chinese history and contact with the West and attributes to the unequal treaties all the manifold maladjustments which have come upon China in modern times. He condemns foreign ideas and seeks to revive ancient Confucian morality in order to bring about a national revival through moral regeneration.

JC12 CHIANG, KAI-SHEK. *Soviet Russia in China; a Summing up at Seventy.* N.Y.: Farrar, Straus and Cudahy; London: Harrap, 1957. 392 p. An unexciting analysis of Soviet Russian policy in China since about 1924, from the point of view of the leader of the Nationalist regime.

JC13 CHUNG-YANG YEN-CHIU YÜAN, CHIN-TAI SHIH YEN-CHIU SO, TAIPEI. *Chung-O kuan-hsi shih-liao.* Taipei: Institute of Modern History, 1960. 9 vols. Part 1—Outer Mongolia; Part 2—The Chinese Eastern Railway, 2 vols.; Part 3—Soviet Revolution and Negotiations in General, 2 vols.; Part 4—The Northeastern Frontiers and Their Defence, 2 vols.; Part 5—Frontier Defence in Sinkiang; Part 6—Expeditions to Siberia. A massive collection of official and diplomatic documents, mostly in Chinese, with maps and illustrations. [B]

JC14 EFIMOV, G. V. *Ocherki po novoi i noveishei istorii Kitaia.* Moscow: Gospolitizdat, 1951. 576 p. The author is professor of modern Chinese history at Leningrad University. This is the standard late-Stalinist interpretation of Chinese history from the end of the eighteenth century to 1950, widely translated and used in Eastern Europe. Standard bibliography of basic Russian and Western works. Chronological table.

JC15 ERMASHEV, N. *Svet nad Kitaem.* Moscow: Mol. gvardiia, 1950. 470 p. 2nd ed., 1951. 624 p. A popular history of China; most of the book is concerned with the Chinese revolution from the 1920's to 1949.

JC16 FAIRBANK, JOHN K., and LIU, KUANG-CHING. *Modern China; a Bibliographical Guide to Chinese Works, 1898-1937.* Cambridge: Harvard, 1950. 608 p. An annotated bibliography, mainly of volumes contained in the Harvard-Yenching Institute Chinese-Japanese Library. This work first appeared in mimeographed form in 1947-48. [B]

JC17 FROMENTIN, PIERRE. *Mao Tsé Tung; le Dragon Rouge.* Paris: Éditions Médicis, 1949. 211 p. A popular but sensible study.

JC18 HO, HAN-WÊN. *Chung-O wai-chiao shih.* Shanghai: Chunghwa, 1935. 490 p. A study of the development of China's relations with Russia from a Chinese point of view.

JC19 HOLCOMBE, ARTHUR N. *The Chinese Revolution; a Phase in the Regeneration of a World Power.* Cambridge: Harvard, 1930. 401 p. This book, written by a Professor of Government at Harvard University with the purpose of estimating the influence of the Chinese Revolution upon international relations in the Far East (the author's conclusions regarding this question are briefly set forth in the Epilogue), is primarily a study of Chinese politics and of the changes in the Chinese political system brought about by the Revolution of 1911. Relevant documents pertaining to the KMT are appended. Sources include information gathered from interviews with participants in the events and observers on the scene. Published sources cited are mainly English.

JC20 HSUEH, CHUN-TU. *The Chinese Communist Movement, 1921-1937; an Annotated Bibliography of Selected Materials in the Chinese Collection of the Hoover Institution on War, Revolution, and Peace.* Palo Alto, Cal.: The Hoover Institution, 1960. 131 p. Lists 359 items in the Chinese language, chosen from the books, periodicals, newspapers, and manuscripts in the Hoover Library. Arranged chronologically. Has an index of authors, titles, and subjects. A second volume, covering the period 1937-49, is to follow.

JC21 HU, CH'IAO-MU (HU TSIAO-MU). *Thirty Years of the Communist Party of China.* London: Lawrence and Wishart, 1951; Peking: Foreign Languages Press, 1952. 95 p. Russian ed., Moscow: Inlitizdat, 1952. 102 p. French ed., Peking: 1952. 117 p. German ed., Berlin: Dietz, 1954. 111 p. Translations of the official history of the Chinese Communist Party published in 1951. [A]

JC22 HU, CH'IU-YÜAN. *O-Ti ch'in-Hua shih-kang.* Taipei: Chinese Culture, 1955. 2 vols. A strong indictment of Russian imperialism, old and new, by a writer and legislator of Nationalist China. Volume II covers the period 1921-52. Interesting, but highly biased. Inadequate documentation.

JC23 ISAACS, HAROLD R. *The Tragedy of the Chinese Revolution.* London: Secker & Warburg, 1938. 501 p. 2nd rev. ed., Stanford, Cal.: Stanford; London: Oxford, 1951. 382 p. First published in 1938, this important work is well-researched and well-documented, although the Trotskyist leaning of the author is sometimes apparent. In the revised edition many of his earlier views have been changed and two chapters added to bring the narrative up to the Korean War period. In treating the Chinese Communist Party, Isaacs has placed emphasis upon its relations with both the Russian Party and the Communist International. [A]

JC24 *Istoriia ekonomicheskogo razvitiia Kitaia 1840-1948 gg.; sbornik statisticheskikh materialov.* Moscow: Izd. inostrannoi lit., 1958. 380 p. Translated from the Chinese edition of 1955.

JC25 KAPITSA, M. S. *Sovetsko-kitaiskie otnosheniia.* Moscow: Gospolitizdat, 1958. 424 p. Termed by the publishers "the first general history of Soviet-Chinese relations in Soviet literature," this book begins with the Bolshevik Revolution. It includes a bibliography listing documentary and archival material as well as Chinese, Russian, and Western sources.

JC26 KISCH, EGON E. *Egon Erwin Kisch enthuellt: China geheim.* Moscow-Leningrad: Verlagsgenossenschaft Ausländischer Arbeiter in der USSR, 1935. 216 p. Berlin: Reiss, 1933. 280 p. English ed., *Secret China.* London: Lane, 1935. 279 p. In this discussion of China the author unleashes an attack upon European imperialism in general and the imperialism of Great Britain in particular.

JC27 *Kitai; opublikovano v 21-m tom 2 izd. Bolshoi sovetskoi entsiklopedii.* Moscow: 1954. 463 p. The text of the entry on China in the 2nd edition of the Great Soviet Encyclopedia, vol. 21. More than 40 Soviet and Chinese scholars contributed to the article. Includes an extensive political section, many maps, and index, chronology, numerous photographs, and a bibliography.

JC28 LEVI, WERNER. *Modern China's Foreign Policy.* Minneapolis: U. of Minnesota; London: Oxford, 1953. 399 p. This study deals mainly with pre-1949 Chinese foreign policy, with only a short section on the early years after the establishment of the Peking government. It is, however, especially important for the extensive citation of Western bibliography on the subject, prepared with notable diligence and thoroughness. German-born, Levi is Professor of Political Science at the University of Minnesota.

JC29 LI, ANG. *Hung-se wu-tai.* Chungking: Sheng-li Chu-pan She, 1942. 193 p. A useful account of the Chinese Communist Party. The author, intimately acquainted with the Party, presents facts about its formative period which are not easily found elsewhere.

JC30 LIU, TA-NIEN (LIU DA-NIAN). *Mei-kuo ch'in-Hua shih.* 1949. 174 p. 2nd ed., 1951. Russian ed., *Istoriia amerikanskoi agressii v Kitae; kratkii ocherk.* Moscow: Inlitizdat, 1951. 154 p. 2nd ed., Moscow: 1953. German ed., Berlin: Dietz, 1956. A totally distorted account of U.S. policy and activities in China during the period 1840-1949. Based on Chinese and English sources.

JC31 MIAO, CHU-KHUAN (MIAO CH'U-HUANG). *Kratkaia istoriia Kommunisticheskoi partii Kitaia.* Moscow: Gospolitizdat, 1958.

256 p. An official Party history from 1921 to 1949; a translation of the 1956 Chinese edition.

JC32 MIF, PAVEL A. *15 let geroicheskoi borby; k 15-letiiu Kommunisticheskoi partii Kitaia.* Moscow: Partizdat, 1936. 119 p. English ed., *Heroic China, 15 Years of the CPC.* N.Y.: Workers Library, 1939. 96 p. This brief and undocumented account by the Comintern's most eminent "China expert" (Director of the Sun Yat-sen Academy in Moscow in the late 1920's and Comintern representative in China in the early 1930's) deals with the founding, development and activities of the Chinese Communist Party (up to 1935) against the background of the Chinese political scene, Comintern policy and Japanese aggression.

JC33 MOSCOW, INSTITUT MARKSA-ENGELSA-LENINA. *Programmnye dokumenty kommunisticheskikh partii Vostoka.* Ed. by L. Madiar and others. Moscow: Partizdat, 1934. 293 p. Includes about 100 pages of translations of Chinese Communist documents dating from the early 1920's. [A]

JC34 MOSCOW, NAUCHNO-ISSLEDOVATELSKII INSTITUT PO KITAIU. *Strategiia i taktika Kominterna v natsionalno-kolonialnoi revoliutsii na primere Kitaia; sbornik dokumentov.* Compiled by G. Kara-Murza, edited by P. Mif. Moscow: Izd. In-ta MKh i MP, 1934. 394 p. A collection of "most important" documents of the Communist International pertaining to the national-colonial question in general and the Chinese revolution in particular. The three parts include documents regarding (1) Comintern programs with respect to the national-colonial question, (2) Comintern strategy and tactics in the Chinese revolution 1925-1927 (including preparatory years), (3) Comintern strategy and tactics in the Soviet revolution in China.

JC35 NORTH, ROBERT C. *Moscow and Chinese Communists.* Stanford, Cal.: Stanford University Press, 1953. 306 p. A solid, carefully-documented biography of the Chinese Communist Party, its conception, birth, adolescence, and coming of age. The author delves into the Leninist ideology and its early expansion under the Communist International, the floundering of the Chinese republican revolution under Sun Yat-sen and his subsequent turning toward the Communists, the Soviet success and failure in China in the 1920's, the rise of Mao Tse-tung and the post-war victory of the Communists, the American involvement in China in the 1940's, and the nature and policies of the Peking regime. Sources are in Russian, Chinese, Japanese and Western languages. [A]

JC36 *Ocherki po istorii russkogo vostokovedeniia.* Moscow: Izd. Akad. nauk SSSR, 1953-1960. 5 vols. Includes valuable bibliographic material on Soviet relations with Eastern countries (see vol. III); articles on Soviet orientology, etc. [A]

JC37 *Ocherki po novoi istorii Kitaia.* Moscow: Inlitizdat, 1956. 175 p. Articles by a group of Chinese historians covering the period from the Taiping Rebellion through the establishment of the Chinese People's Republic. Translated from Chinese.

JC38 PANIKKAR, KAVALAM M. *In Two Chinas; Memoirs of a Diplomat.* London: Allen & Unwin, 1955. 183 p. The author served as Indian Ambassador to the Nationalist Government in Nanking at the time of the collapse of the Kuomintang and then to the People's Government of Peking. He writes of the events of that time and of the Korean conflict on the basis of his personal experiences.

JC39 PAYNE, PIERRE S. ROBERT. *Mao Tse-tung.* N.Y.: Schuman, 1950. 303 p. Rev. ed., *Portrait of a Revolutionary; Mao Tse-tung.* N.Y.: Abelard-Schuman, 1961. 311 p. The only full-length study of the Hunanese poet and political pamphleteer who has grown from early peasant radicalism to a position of considerable authority in Communist circles in both China and Albania. Payne's portrait of Mao Tse-tung is penetrating, but superficial and inaccurate, neither serious biography nor sound history.

JC40 POLLARD, ROBERT T. *China's Foreign Relations, 1917-1931.* N.Y.: Macmillan, 1933. 416 p. A thorough discussion of the developing status of China in international affairs. Deals with the struggle against inequalities in international relationships and early Chinese contacts with Soviet Russia.

JC41 PYN, MIN (P'EN MING). *Istoriia kitaisko-sovetskoi druzhby; kratkii ocherk.* Peking: "Chzhungo tsinnian chubanshe," 1955. 151 p. Soviet eds., Moscow: Inlitizdat, 1957. 150 p. Moscow: Izd. sotsialno-ekonomicheskoi literatury, 1959. 360 p. A history of Sino-Soviet friendship since 1917.

JC42 SAITO, RYOE. *Sovieto Rokoku no kyokuto shinshutsu.* Tokyo: Nihon Hyeronsha, 1931. 376 p. A descriptive outline of Soviet policy in the Far East from 1917 to 1930, mostly concerned with China. The author had personal experience as a director of the South Manchurian Railroad Company and as a Japanese diplomat.

JC43 SCHWARTZ, BENJAMIN I. *Chinese Communism and the Rise of Mao.* Cambridge: Harvard, 1951. 258 p. An important, scholarly, and well-written monograph dealing with the evolution of the Chinese Communists' "line" down to about 1931, their relations with Moscow, and the reasons for Mao Tse-tung's success in attaining the top position in the Party. [A]

JC44 SEDIAKIN, SEMEN M. *Kratkii ocherk istorii kitaiskogo komsomola.* Moscow: "Molodaia gvardiia," 1929. 126 p.

JC45 SHÊN, SHANG-WÊN. *Chung-Su kuan-hsi chien-shih.* Hong Kong: Free Press, 1951. 97 p. This small book tries mainly to show the consistent failure of the Soviet government to keep its promise of friendship for China, but makes no attempt to treat such issues as the border disputes between them. No documentation.

JC46 SHIRATO, ICHIRO, and WILBUR, C. MARTIN. *Japanese Sources on the History of the Chinese Communist Movement.* N.Y.: East Asian Institute of Columbia University, 1953. 69 p. An annotated bibliography of works in the East Asiatic Library at Columbia and in the Division of Orientalia, Library of Congress.

JC47 SKACHKOV, P. E. *Bibliografiia Kitiia; sistematicheskii ukazatel knig i zhurnalnykh statei o Kitae na russkom iazyke, 1730-1930.* Moscow: Gos. sots.-ek. izd., 1932. 843 p. 2nd ed., Moscow: 1960. 691 p. The most basic guide to Russian materials on China, a standard and systematic work. The second edition is basically a reprint of the first plus most of the titles published 1930-57. The two must be used together, since the second eliminates many authors who fell into error after 1930. The first edition includes a subject index, while the second has only an author index. [A]

JC48 SLADKOVSKII, M. I. *Ocherki ekonomicheskikh otnoshenii SSSR s Kitaem. (XVII st.-1956 g.).* Moscow: Vneshtorgizdat, 1957. 455 p. A thorough and invaluable survey of Russian-Chinese trade relations across all frontiers from the seventeenth century to 1955. Includes extensive statistical material in the text and tables. Appendix contains the most important Sino-Russian commercial agreements for the period covered. [B]

JC49 STARLINGER, WILHELM. *Grenzen der Sowjetmacht; hinter Russland China.* Würzburg: Marienburg, 1957. 141 p. French ed., Paris: Spes, 1956. An exposition of the theory, which is said to have made a strong impression on the ruling circles in West Germany, that population pressure will eventually force China to expand to the north and the northwest, finally encompassing all the areas on the Chinese side of Lake Baikal. The author maintains that China will have to look to the north because all the areas south of China are already overpopulated.

JC50 TIEN, PENG. *Chung-O pang-chiao chih yen-chiu.* Nanking Cheng Chung, 1937. 663 p. This account of Chinese-Russian relations concentrates primarily on the period from 1911 to 1937.

JC51 TRETIAKOV, S. *Den Shi-khua.* Moscow: "Molodaia gvardiia," 1931. 400 p. English ed., *A Chinese Testament.* N.Y.:

Simon & Schuster, 1934. 316 p. German ed., Berlin: Malik, 1932. 507 p.

JC52 TS'AO, HSI-CHÊN. *Chung-Su wai-chiao shih.* Peking: World Knowledge, 1951. 109 p. A pro-Soviet work on relations between China and the USSR from 1917 to 1950. Emphasis is placed on Soviet aid to China. Lacking footnotes and bibliography, this brief survey contains only a few documents.

JC53 TSU, JOHN B. "Sino-Soviet Relations, 1945-1952." Ph.D. dissertation, Fordham U., 1953.

JC54 U.S. CONGRESS, HOUSE OF REPRESENTATIVES, COMMITTEE ON FOREIGN AFFAIRS. *Communism in China.* Supplement III C. Washington: G.P.O., 1948. 105 p. A thorough study of the foundations of Communism in China, with biographies of Chinese leaders, both Communist and Kuomintang, and a translation of Mao's "New Democracy."

JC55 VAN, YA-NAN (WANG YA-NAN). *Issledovanie ekonomicheskikh form polufeodalnogo polukolonialnogo Kitaia.* Moscow: Izd. sotsialno-ekonomicheskoi lit., 1959. 395 p. Translation of the Chinese edition of 1957. The author is a professor at Amoy University; his book deals with money, capital, interest, wages, land-rent, and economic crises.

JC56 VOITINSKII, GRIGORII N. *K.V.Zh.D. i politika imperialistov v Kitae.* Moscow: Izd. Kom. akad., 1930. 72 p. The author was secretary of the Comintern's Far Eastern Bureau, the first Comintern representative and organizer in China from 1920, the CCP's liaison man with Sun Yat-sen, later head of the Public Affairs Department, Institute of World Economics and World Politics (Moscow). The book is important as a view of incidents on the Chinese Eastern Railway and as a polemic on Soviet policy in China. See especially G. Gastov's critique (*Izvestiia*, No. 283 for 1929) and the author's reply (*Mirovoe khoziaistvo i mirovaia politika*, No. 1, January 1930, p. 172-3).

JC57 WEI, HENRY. *China and Soviet Russia.* Intro. by Quincy Wright. Princeton, N.J.: Van Nostrand; London: Macmillan, 1956. 379 p. A history of Sino-Soviet diplomatic relations in the period 1917-55. Written without the benefit of Russian-language materials or of Nationalist Chinese sources. [B]

JC58 WINT, GUY. *Dragon and Sickle.* N.Y.: Praeger, 1959. 107 p. A brief but useful recounting of the development of Communism in China and the eventual seizure of power by its adherents. Also contains some material on relations with the Soviet Union.

JC59 WU, AI-CH'ÊN K. *China and the Soviet Union; a Study of Sino-Soviet Relations.* N.Y.: Day; London: Methuen, 1950. 434 p. A description of Sino-Russian relations by a former Chinese Nationalist diplomat. Traces China's contacts with Tsarist Russia from 1618 and then treats the Soviet period up to 1950 in much fuller detail. Often tedious reading but contains interesting documents on Sino-Soviet relations between 1924 and 1950.

JC60 WU, CHI-YU. "China, Russia and Central Asia; a Study of Political and Diplomatic Relations." Ph.D. dissertation, Princeton, 1934.

JC61 YUAN, TUNG-LI. *Russian Works on China, 1918-1960, in American Libraries.* New Haven: Yale, 1961. 162 p. A useful guide for libraries as well as individual scholars. There are no annotations, nor is periodical literature included. Lists 1350 items. Prepared by a librarian formerly in Peking and now with the Library of Congress. [B]

2. 1917-1927
(Edited by Harold C. Hinton)

JC62 ANTONOV, KONSTANTIN. *Suniatsenizm i kitaiskaia revoliutsiia.* Moscow: Izd. Kom. akad., 1931. 136 p. An attempt to trace the development of Sun's ideas and to appraise their class character in order to defend Lenin's characterization of "Sun Yatsenism" as petty-bourgeois, as against Sinologists who maintained that in its later stages "Sun Yatsenism" moved toward Marxism and recognition of the hegemony of the proletariat. Based mainly on Sun's writings.

JC63 BAKULIN, A. *Zapiski ob ukhanskom periode kitaiskoi revoliutsii. (Iz istorii kitaiskoi revoliutsii 1925-1927 gg.).* Moscow-Leningrad: Gosizdat, 1930. 288 p. A useful view through Soviet eyes, in the form of a journal and documents, of events in Hankow, then the seat of the Kuomintang regime, from November 1926 to June 1927. Prepared by the Research Institute on China of the Communist Academy. Includes many primary materials.

JC64 BEREZNYI, L. A. *Politika SShA v Kitae v periode revoliutsii 1924-1927.* Leningrad: Leningradskii universitet, 1956. 144 p.

JC65 BORODINA, F. S. *V zastenkakh kitaiskikh satrapov, moi vospominaniia.* Moscow-Leningrad: Gosizdat, 1928. 216 p. Personal reminiscences of the wife of Michael Borodin, chief Comintern agent in China from 1924 to 1927.

JC66 BRANDT, CONRAD. *Stalin's Failure in China, 1924-1927.* Cambridge: Harvard, 1958. 226 p. A scholarly and important analysis by a professor at the University of California which brings out the limited understanding of both Stalin and Trotsky of the Chinese scene and above all of trends within the Kuomintang. Concludes with some interesting reflections on the emergence of Mao Tse-tung's rural-oriented strategy as the basis of Chinese Communist policy. [B]

JC67 BRANDT, CONRAD, SCHWARTZ, BENJAMIN, and FAIRBANK, JOHN K. *A Documentary History of Chinese Communism.* Cambridge: Harvard, 1952. 552 p. Translations of important Chinese documents, with useful commentary; no Soviet documents are included. Events to the end of 1927 are covered in the first 123 pages. The first editor is a professor at the University of California, the last two at Harvard.

JC68 BUKHARIN, NIKOLAI I. *Problemy kitaiskoi revoliutsii.* Moscow: Pravda, 1927. 62 p. Italian ed., Paris: 1927. A valuable look at the Chinese revolution by a leading Bolshevik theorist, later a victim of the Stalin purges.

JC69 CH'EN, KUNG-PO. *The Communist Movement in China; an Essay Written in 1924.* Ed., with intro., by C. Martin Wilbur. N.Y.: Columbia, East Asian Institute Series no. 7, Sept. 1960. 148 p. A master's thesis by a founding member of the Communist Party of China. Contains, especially in Professor Wilbur's introduction and Ch'en's documentary appendices, some valuable information on the early history of the movement not elsewhere available.

JC70 CH'ÊN, PO-WÊN. *Chung-O wai-chiao shih.* Shanghai: Commercial, 1928. 159 p. A book written shortly after the split between the Kuomintang and the Communists. Although following the official position of the Nationalist government, it contains some useful and concise information on historical relations between China and Russia. Lacking footnotes and bibliography.

JC71 CHOW, TSE-TSUNG. *The May Fourth Movement; Intellectual Revolution in Modern China.* Cambridge: Harvard, 1960. 486 p. The most authoritative study in any language of intellectual currents in China at the time of the formation of the Chinese Communist movement and the Kuomintang-Communist alliance. Very useful as background for an understanding of the environment in which Soviet policy worked itself out. Exhaustively documented.

JC72 CHUNG-O CHIAO-SHĒ KUNG-SHU HUI-WU CH'U, ed. *Chung-o hui-i ts'an-k'ao wên-chien.* Peking: Conference headquarters, Bureau of Sino-Russian Affairs, 1924. 5 v. in 1 case. Official and diplomatic documents bearing on the early history of Soviet relations with the Republican Government of China in Peking.

JC73 COMMUNIST INTERNATIONAL, EXECUTIVE COMMITTEE. *Die chinesische Frage auf dem 8. Plenum der Exekutive der Kommunistischen Internationale, Mai, 1927.* Hamburg, Hoym, c. 1928. 160 p. Not a complete stenographic report, but an abridged version of the five sessions of the Eighth Meeting of the Executive Committee of the Communist International, May 23-26, 1927, and the succeeding sessions about the Chinese Question. Contains the addresses of Bukharin, Smeral, Trotskii, Petrov, Stalin, Katayama, Braun, Pepper, Tschugunow, Ferdi, Martynov, Semard, Ercoli, Vujovich, Manuilskii, and Darsono. The appendix gives the resolution of the Ninth Meeting of the Executive Committee about the Chinese Question submitted by Bukharin, Stalin, Sian, and Li.

JC74 COMMUNIST INTERNATIONAL, EXECUTIVE COMMITTEE. *IKKI i VKP (b) po kitaiskomu voprosu; osnovnye resheniia.* Moscow: "Moskovskii rabochii," 1927. 258 p.

JC75 DALIN, SERGEI. *Ocherki revoliutsii v Kitae.* Moscow: "Moskovskii rabochii," 1927. 282 p. A rather well-informed, although of course biased, account of the Kuomintang's Northern Expedition and the break with the Communists. Some interesting photographs.

JC76 DALLIN, DAVID J. *The Rise of Russia in Asia.* New Haven: Yale, 1949. 293 p. Soviet policy in China from 1917 to 1927 is covered in p. 180-234. The treatment is interesting and competent, although presented from an entirely Russian point of view and marked by little familiarity with the Chinese milieu.

JC77 DEN, CHZHUN-SIA (TENG CHUNG-HSIA). *Kratkaia istoriia profsoiuznogo dvizheniia v Kitae.* Ed. by Iu. N. Kostousov. Moscow: Izd. vost. lit., 1952. 310 p. A translation of the second Chinese edition of 1940; the first Chinese edition was published in 1930, shortly before the author's death. A classic history of the Communist-led labor movement from 1920 to 1926, and still of use, though it must be used with care. The author was one of the earliest Chinese Communists and labor agitators, member of the CCP Central Committee from 1922, leader of the Hong Kong-Canton strike (1925-26), and delegate to the Profintern in Moscow, where he wrote this book.

JC78 DIN, SHOU-KHE, IN', SIUOU-U, and CHZHAN, BO-CHZHAO. *Vliianie oktiabrskoi revoliutsii na Kitai.* Moscow: Gospolitizdat, 1959. 204 p. Concerning early Marxism in China and the founding of CCP.

JC79 DUSHENKU, V. *Ot soldata do marshala; zhizn i boevoi put Marshala Sovetskogo Souiza V. K. Bliukhera.* Moscow: Gosizdat, 1960. 132 p. The posthumous rehabilitation of Marshal Bluecher (Galen), a Soviet military advisor in China in the 1920's who was subsequently disgraced. This book traces his military career.

JC80 EUDIN, XENIA J., and NORTH, ROBERT C. *Soviet Russia and the East, 1920-1927; a Documentary Survey.* Stanford, Cal.: Stanford University Press, 1957. 478 p. A massive and invaluable collection of documents, mostly of Soviet origin, with helpful commentary, by two scholars affiliated with the Hoover Library. Chronology, exhaustive bibliography, biographical notes. Indispensable to a study of the subject. [A]

JC81 FISCHER, LOUIS. *The Soviets in World Affairs, 1917-1929.* 2nd ed. Princeton, N.J.: Princeton University Press, 1951. 2 vols. Chapter 23 of this classic work gives an interesting, sympathetic account of the Soviet role in China prior to 1927.

JC82 FRANCIS, WILLIAM W. "The Stalin-Trotsky Controversy over Soviet Policy in China, 1925-1927." Certificate essay, Russian Institute, Columbia, 1957. 94 p.

JC83 FUSE, KATSUJI. *Renin no Roshia to Sombun no Shina.* Peking: Enjinsha, 1927. 546 p. An informative, eye-witness account by a noted Japanese journalist well-acquainted with Russia and China. Deals with relations between Sun Yat-sen and Soviet Russia.

JC84 FUSE, KATSUJI. *Soviet Policy in the Orient.* Peking: Enjinsha, 1927. 409 p. A reasonably well-informed and objective account by a Japanese newspaperman, who interviewed a number of Soviet leaders and traveled widely in the Far East. The conclusion is that the successes of the Kuomintang armies in 1926-27 were due largely to the military and political training imparted by Soviet advisers.

JC85 GODES, M. *Chto takoe kemalistskii put i vozmozhen li on v Kitae?* Leningrad: Priboi, 1928. 108 p. A comparison of the Turkish and Chinese revolutions by a Leningrad sinologist.

JC86 *Hsiang-tao chou-pao.* Shanghai: 1925-27. The organ of the Communist Party of China during this period.

JC87 ISAACS, HAROLD R. *The Tragedy of the Chinese Revolution.* London: Secker & Warburg, 1938. 501 p. Rev. ed., Stanford, Cal.: Stanford University Press, 1951. 382 p. A well-informed, pro-Trotsky, and anti-Stalin account of the Soviet impact on the Chinese Revolution of 1925-27. Very interesting reading; interpretations are not always reliable. By a former journalist with long experience in China. [B]

JC88 IUREV, M. F. *Rol revoliutsionnoi armii na pervom etape kitaiskoi revoliutsii.* Moscow: Izd. Moskovskogo universiteta, 1952. 139 p. Essentially a defense of the Soviet role in building up the

Kuomintang armies during the period 1924-27, and of Stalin's part in this process, combined with some concessions to Mao Tse-tung both as a participant in and an authority on the events of that period.

JC89 IVIN, ALEKSEI A. *Kitai i Sovetskii Soiuz.* Preface by L. Karakhan. Moscow: Gosizdat, 1924. 144 p. Devoted mainly to an account, with texts of relevant documents, of Karakhan's successful mission to China in 1923-24, resulting in diplomatic recognition of the Soviet government by the Peking government; also contains some material on the parallel Soviet dealings with Sun Yat-sen's revolutionary regime in Canton. The book was sharply criticized as non-Marxist because of its theory of the classlessness of the Chinese civil war.

JC90 IVIN, ALEKSEI A. *Ot Khankou k Shankhaiu.* Moscow-Leningrad: "Moskovskii rabochii," 1927. 139 p. An account of the united front of 1925-27 during the Long March.

JC91 *Kantonskaia kommuna; sbornik statei i materialov.* Moscow-Leningrad: Giz, 1929. 320 p. Materials on the Canton rising of December 1927 prepared by the Research Institute on China of Sun Yat-sen University. [A]

JC92 KHODOROV, A. E., and PAVLOVICH, MIKHAIL P. *Kitai v borbe za nezavisimost.* Moscow: Nauch. assots. vostokoved., 1925. 194 p.

JC93 KHUN, KHUAN-CHUN (HUNG HUAN-CH'UN). *Revoliutsionnoe dvizhenie v Kitae v periode nachala novodemokraticheskoi revoliutsii.* Peking: Izd. "Sanlian sudian," 1956. 188 p. A study of the Chinese revolutionary movement from 1900 to 1921, with deference to Mao Tse-tung.

JC94 KINDERMANN, GOTTFRIED K. "Chiang Kai-shek and the causes for the disintegration of the first Sino-Soviet Entente." Ph.D. dissertation, Chicago, 1959.

JC95 KOSTAREV, N. *Moi kitaiskie dnevniki.* Ed. with an intro. by L. Varshavskii. Leningrad: "Priboi," 1928. 256 p. 2nd ed., enl. and rev. 1929, 290 p. 3rd ed., Goslitizdat 1931. 316 p. 5th ed., Izd. pisatelei, 1935. 213 p. Notes on the 1926-1928 period.

JC96 LENG, SHAO-CHUAN, and PALMER, NORMAN D. *Sun Yat-sen and Communism.* N.Y.: Praeger, 1961. 234 p. An authoritative analysis of Sun's debt to, and divergences from, Leninism. The authors are professors respectively at the Univ. of Virginia and the Univ. of Pennsylvania. Based on a wide range of sources in Chinese and Western languages (other than Russian); useful notes and bibliography. The conclusion is that "However much Sun Yat-sen was influenced by the Communists and by Communism, he never even came close to becoming a Communist himself." [B]

JC97 LOZOVSKII, ALEXANDER (pseud. of Solomon A. Dridzo). *Revoliutsiia i kontr-revoliutsiia v Kitae.* Moscow: "Moskovskii rabochii," 1927. 172 p. German ed., Berlin: Führer, 1928. 80 p. A Soviet analysis by the long-time head of the Red International of Labor Unions.

JC98 MANDALIAN, T. *Rabochee dvizhenie Kitaia.* Moscow-Leningrad: "Moskovskii rabochii," 1928. 224 p. A study of the trade union movement in China in the 1920's.

JC99 MIF, PAVEL A. *Heroic China; Fifteen Years of the Communist Party of China.* N.Y.: Workers Library, 1937. 96 p. Russian ed., Moscow: 1936. 118 p. The first 57 pages deal, from a Stalinist standpoint, with events in China from 1917 to 1927. Mif was Stalin's leading China "expert" during the early 1930's.

JC100 MIF, PAVEL A. *Kitaiskaia kommunisticheskaia partiia v kriticheskie dni.* Moscow-Leningrad: Gosizdat, 1928. 271 p. A Stalinist interpretation of the history of the Kuomintang-Communist alliance, with some Chinese documents, both Communist and non-Communist, in Russian translation. Prepared under the auspices of the Research Institute on China of Sun Yat-sen University, of which Mif was then president.

JC101 NORTH, ROBERT C. *Moscow and Chinese Communists.* Stanford, Cal.: Stanford, 1953. 306 p. A general history of the Chinese Communist movement, with emphasis on its relations with the Soviet Union. Rather poorly organized, but contains some important information not readily available elsewhere. Events to the end of 1927 are treated in the first 121 pages. [B]

JC102 PASVOLSKY, LEO. *Russia in the Far East.* N.Y.: Macmillan, 1922. 181 p. A well-informed contemporary account by a U.S. State Department official. Based to a considerable extent on Soviet sources. Appendix includes a few basic documents.

JC103 *Rabochii Kitai v 1927 g.; sbornik statei.* Ed. by A. Lozovskii. Moscow: Izd-vo Profinterna, 1928. 325 p. A collection of reprinted articles by various Soviet authors. Some useful information on events in China, in addition to propaganda.

JC104 RADEK, KARL. *Istoriia revoliutsionnogo dvizheniia v Kitae; kurs 1926-1927.* Moscow: Un-t trudiashchikhsia Kitaia im. Sun-Iat-Sena, 1926.

JC105 RAFES, M. *Revoliutsiia v Kitae.* Moscow-Leningrad: "Moskovskii rabochii," 1927. 128 p. 2nd ed., *Revoliutsiia v Kitae i predatelstvo Chan-Kai-Shi,* 1927. 146 p. 3rd ed., *Kitaiskaia revoliutsiia na perelome,* 1927. 224 p.

JC106 ROI, M. N. (ROY, MANABENDRA N.). *Kitaiskaia revoliutsiia i Kommunisticheskii Internatsional; sbornik statei i materialov.* Moscow-Leningrad: Gosizdat, 1929. 206 p. English ed., *M. N. Roy's Mission to China; the Communist-Kuomintang Split of 1927.* Edited by Robert C. North and Xenia J. Eudin. Berkeley and Los Angeles: U. of California Press, 1963. 399 p. In 1927 the Comintern sent Roy, an Indian Communist, to China to try to solidify the alliance between the Kuomintang and the Chinese Communists. Until recently no copy of this book was known to exist outside of Russia. Now it is made available in translation, together with 128 pages of explanation and analysis by the two editors. Extremely valuable. [A]

JC107 ROY, MANABENDRA N. (pseud. of Narendranath Bhattacharjee). *Revolution and Counter-Revolution in China.* Rev. English ed., Calcutta: Renaissance, 1946. 689 p. German ed., Berlin: 1930. 478 p. This book (first published in German in 1930 and amplified in the present edition), by a veteran revolutionist and Comintern agent in China during the crucial first half of 1927, reviews the course of the Chinese Revolution, as seen through the eyes of an unorthodox, anti-Stalinist Marxist. The first half of the book is a schematic Marxist interpretation of modern Chinese history, but for the period of Roy's participation in the Wuhan Government of 1927 his Marxist dogma is interwoven with personal experience. In conclusion the author analyzes the Communist failure of 1927. His account is rather impersonal and does not shed much light on his difficult mission as intermediary between Stalin and the Kuomintang government. Stalin is mentioned only twice, in a footnote.

JC108 RZHANOV, G. A. *Kitai na putiakh revoliutsii.* Leningrad: "Priboi," 1927. 259 p.

JC109 SAFAROV, GEORGII I. *Klassy i klassovaia borba v kitaiskoi istorii.* Moscow: Gosizdat, 1928. 361 p. An important contribution to the early Soviet debate on Chinese society. Participants included Radek, with whom the author disagrees strongly. The author sees the early rise of Chinese trade capitalism, followed by a period of "new feudalism." Severely criticized by B. Shumiatskii.

JC110 SAFAROV, GEORGII I. *Ocherki po istorii Kitaia.* Leningrad: Gos. sots.-ek. izd., 1933. 403 p. A Marxist interpretation of Chinese history from earliest times until 1927. Based on sources in English, German, French and Russian. Chronology of dynasties appended. By a prolific Comintern writer.

JC111 SAPOZHNIKOV, B. G. *Pervaia grazhdanskaia revoliutsionnaia voina v Kitae, 1924-1927 gg.* Moscow: Gospolitizdat, 1954. 100 p. Useful as giving a Soviet view of the military history of the period. Two helpful maps.

JC112 SAVVIN, V. *Vzaimootnosheniia tsarskoi Rossii i SSSR s Kitaem.* Moscow-Leningrad: Gosizdat, 1930. 152 p. A survey of Russian-Chinese relations 1619-1927. Includes an appendix of documents (treaties, etc.) and a short bibliography of standard sources.

JC113 SCHWARTZ, BENJAMIN I. *Chinese Communism and the Rise of Mao.* Cambridge: Harvard, 1951. 258 p. An important, scholarly, and well-written monograph dealing with the evolution of the Chinese Communists' "line" down to about 1931, their relations with Moscow, and the reasons for Mao Tse-tung's rise to power in the Party (which is dated about three years too early). The first 108 pages deal in masterly fashion with events down to the end of 1927. [A]

JC114 *Soviet Plot in China.* Peking: Metropolitan Police Headquarters, 1927. 162 p. A translation of some of the Soviet documents seized in Peking in April 1927. There are four companion volumes in Chinese, containing more documents. The entire set bears the title *Su-lien yin-mou wen-cheng hui-pien* (Compendium of Documentary Evidence on the Soviet Plot). See below the book by Wilbur and How.

JC115 STALIN, IOSIF V. *O perspektivakh revoliutsii v Kitae; voprosy kitaiskoi revoliutsii.* Moscow: Gospolitizdat, 1954. 56 p. The speech Stalin made to the Chinese Commission of the Executive Committee of the Comintern, November 30, 1926, originally published under the same title in 1927 (31 p.).

JC116 STALIN, IOSIF V. *Stalin on China; a Collection of Five Writings of Comrade Stalin on the Chinese Question.* Bombay: People's Publishing House, 1951. 106 p. These speeches and documents date from the 1926-27 period.

JC117 TROTSKII, LEV D. *Problems of the Chinese Revolution.* N.Y.: Pioneer, 1932. 432 p. Trotsky's convincing polemic against Stalin's policy of allying with Chiang Kai-shek and the "bourgeois" Kuomintang. Less convincing in propounding Trotsky's view that the Comintern and the Chinese Communist Party should have disengaged themselves from the Kuomintang and conducted a purely proletarian class struggle. Appended materials include speeches of Zinoviev, Vujovich, a letter from Shanghai (March 17, 1929) written by N. Nassonov, N. Fokine, and A. Albrecht attacking the leadership of the Chinese Communist Party.

JC118 TSUI, SHU-CHIN. "The Influence of the Canton-Moscow Entente Upon Sun Yat Sen's Political Philosophy and Revolutionary Tactics." Ph.D. dissertation, Harvard, 1934. A scholarly examination, based on sources in Chinese, Russian, and English, of the history of the Kuomintang-Communist alliance down to Sun's death in 1925, of Sun's political thought, and of the rather limited influence that Marxism-Leninism had on that thought. Useful bibliography. Remarkable for the attainment of a high standard of scholarship and objectivity at an early date. [B]

JC119 VANDERVELDE, ÉMILE. *À travers la révolution chinoise.* Paris: Alcan, 1931. 240 p. A well-known Belgian political leader gives his views on events in China and Soviet influence there, based on a trip he made to China.

JC120 VILENSKII, VLADIMIR D. (SIBIRIAKOV). *Gomindan; partiia kitaiskoi revoliutsii.* Moscow-Leningrad: "Molodaia gvardiia," 1926. 107 p.

JC121 VILENSKII, VLADIMIR D. (SIBIRIAKOV). *Sun Iat Sen; otets kitaiskoi revoliutsii.* Moscow: Gosizdat, 1924. 196 p.

JC122 VITTFOGEL (WITTFOGEL), KARL-AVGUST. *Probuzhdaiushchiisia Kitai.* Leningrad: "Priboi," 1926. 182 p. Now a professor in the U.S., Wittfogel was formerly a German Communist.

JC123 *Voprosy kitaiskoi revoliutsii.* Leningrad-Moscow: Gosizdat, 1927. 240 p. Articles and speeches by Stalin and Bukharin and other materials on the Chinese revolution covering the period from December 1926 to June 1927. [B]

JC124 *Voprosy kitaiskoi revoliutsii.* Vol. I: *Polozhenie proletariata i razvitie rabochego dvizhenie v Kitae.* Ed. by Karl Radek. Moscow: Gosizdat, 1927. 256 p. Includes articles by Radek and three foreign Communists on the Chinese labor movement, compiled under the auspices of the Research Institute of Sun Yat-sen University. [A]

JC125 WEIGH, KEN-SHEN. *Russo-Chinese Diplomacy.* Shanghai: Commercial, 1928. 382 p. A survey, based mainly on sources in English, of Russo-Chinese diplomatic relations from the Treaty of Nerchinsk (1689) to the Sun-Joffe Agreement (1924) with emphasis on Manchuria, Mongolia and the Chinese Eastern Railway. The author was Bureau Chief in the Nationalist Ministry of Foreign Affairs. Relevant documents and a bibliography appended.

JC126 WHITING, ALLEN S. *Soviet Policies in China, 1917-1924.* N.Y.: Columbia, 1954. 350 p. A scholarly and authoritative treatment by a leading American specialist in Sino-Soviet relations. Brings out very well the opportunistic flexibility of Soviet policy in China during this period. Valuable chronology, documents, and bibliography. [A]

JC127 WILBUR, CLARENCE MARTIN, and HOW, JULIE L., eds. *Documents on Communism, Nationalism and Soviet Advisors in China, 1918-1927; Paper Seized in the 1927 Peking Raid*. N.Y.: Columbia, 1956. 617 p. A translation, with notes and commentary, of the controversial documents seized in the office of the Soviet Military Attaché in Peking in April 1927. These documents, whose authenticity is established beyond reasonable doubt, are a valuable source for Soviet-China policy during the early 1920's, and the commentary is perhaps even more valuable. The authors are Columbia professors. Sources are mainly in Chinese and Japanese. [A]

JC128 WILLIAM, MAURICE. *Sun Yat Sen Versus Communism*. Baltimore: Williams and Wilkins, 1932. 232 p. A study of the Chinese leader's political thought by an author who feels that his book, *The Social Interpretation of History*, was responsible for Sun's disenchantment with Communism.

JC129 WOO, THOMAS C. *The Kuomintang and the Future of the Chinese Revolution*. London: Allen and Unwin, 1928. 278 p. The author, a member of the Left Kuomintang who fled from China after the 1927 split and at the time of writing was a research student at the Sorbonne, attacks the KMT leadership for what in his opinion is the betrayal of the revolutionary policies set forth by Sun Yat-sen. He dwells on the history of the KMT, its principles, organization and operation, Sun Yat-sen's Three Policies, the contemporary situation within the KMT, the causes for the failure of the Revolution and the outlook for the future. Relevant documents are appended.

JC130 WU, AI-CH'ÊN K. *China and the Soviet Union: a Study of Sino-Soviet Relations*. London: Methuen; N.Y.: Day, 1950. 434 p. By a Chinese scholar and former consular official in the Soviet Union. Pages 118-197 deal with the period 1917-27. The treatment is heavily diplomatic, although competent, and says nothing about the Comintern's relations with the Kuomintang prior to 1927.

3. 1928-1949

(Edited by Charles C. McLane and Mark Mancall)

a. *IN LANGUAGES OTHER THAN RUSSIAN*

JC131 AMANN, GUSTAV. *Bauernkrieg in China; Chiang Kai-sheks Kampf gegen den Aufstand, 1932-1935*. Heidelberg: Vowinckel, 1939. 157 p. This volume of Amann's *Geschichte Chinas in Neuster*

Zeit gives a popularized account of the internal development of China and focuses on Chiang's fight against the Communists. Five maps throw light on the campaigns.

JC132 BAND, CLAIRE and WILLIAM. *Two Years with the Chinese Communists*. New Haven: Yale, 1948. 347 p. The authors, an English physicist at Yenching University in Peking and his wife, fled to Communist guerrilla areas in North China in 1941 and were thus in a unique position to observe and report on the wartime operations of the Chinese Communists, which they contrast with the situation in the areas held by the Nationalists.

JC133 BELDEN, JACK. *China Shakes the World*. N.Y.: Harper; London: Gollancz, 1949. 524 p. This brilliant journalistic account of the Nationalist collapse includes forceful and dramatic descriptions of developments in rural areas under Communist control which the author visited in 1947. [B]

JC134 BERTRAM, JAMES M. *Unconquered; Journal of a Year's Adventure Among the Fighting Peasants of North China*. N.Y.: Day, 1939. 340 p. British ed., *North China Front*. London: Macmillan, 1939. 514 p. Russian ed., Moscow: Goslitizdat, 1940. 315 p. A colorful, first-hand account of the Communist Eighth Route Army in the War against the Japanese by a New Zealand journalist. Has descriptions of Communist operations and tactics and an interview with Mao Tse-tung.

JC135 CASSEVILLE, HENRY. *De Chiang Kai Shek à Mao Tse Tung (Chine 1927-1950)*. Paris: Lavauzelle, 1950. 191 p. A French writer argues for the establishment of diplomatic relations with Communist China. Based on his experience as a military attaché in that country and his reading of the civil war from 1927 to after the Communist take-over, he feels that such relations may serve to minimize Soviet influence in China.

JC136 CHASSIN, LIONEL M. (GENERAL). *La Conquête de la Chine par Mao Tse-Tung (1945-1949)*. Paris: Payot, 1952. 244 p. A step-by-step account of Chinese Communist strategy during the last five years of the Kuomintang. A French historian of military affairs examines the Communist triumph.

JC137 CH'EN, PO-TA. *Notes on Ten Years of Civil War, 1927-1936*. Peking: Foreign Languages Press, 1954. 108 p. Written in 1944 by a leading Chinese Communist historian, this doctrinaire interpretation of the "Second Revolutionary Civil War," 1927-36, seeks to show how Mao Tse-tung adapted Marxism-Leninism to Chinese circumstances.

JC138 CREEL, GEORGE. *Russia's Race for Asia.* Indianapolis: Bobbs-Merrill, 1949. 264 p. A superficial, tendentious, semi-journalistic effort, the avowed purpose of which is "to set forth the proof of Moscow's unbroken control of the Chinese Communist Party for the conquest of China and the subsequent communization of Asia" and "to establish the responsibility" of the Roosevelt and Truman administrations for the crisis in China in the 1940's.

JC139 EPSTEIN, ISRAEL. *The Unfinished Revolution in China.* Boston: Little, Brown, 1947. 442 p. German ed., Berlin: 1954. A survey of recent Chinese history with major emphasis on the lengthy war with Japan and its termination. This work is somewhat dated because its publication preceded the Chinese Communist seizure of power. The author, a long-time resident of China, is highly critical of the Kuomintang in China and the colonial situation throughout Asia. He sees the Chinese Communists as the hope of China.

JC140 GALLIGAN, DAVID J. "American Protestant Missions and Communist China, 1946-1950." Ph.D. dissertation, Rutgers, 1952.

JC141 HSIAO, TSO-LIANG. *Power Relations within the Chinese Communist Movement, 1930-34: a Study of Documents.* Seattle: U. of Washington, 1961. A description and analysis of some 267 documents pertaining to intra-Party power politics in the crucial period 1930-34, when Mao Tse-tung was making his bid for supreme leadership. The documents, which have not been published, are derived primarily from the collection of Nationalist Vice-Premier Ch'en Ch'eng's personal files (containing materials from the Kiangsi Soviet captured by the Nationalists during the "extermination campaigns" against the Communists in the early 1930's) and the collection of the Kuomintang Secret Service. Both collections have hitherto been unavailable for scholarly purposes. The author is Professor of International Relations at the National University in Taipei.

JC142 KREITNER, GUSTAV, RITTER VON. *Hinter China steht Moskau.* Berlin: Mittler, 1932. 144 p. A pointed attack on the Kuomintang, which the author views as a small group of men who are leading China to her destruction.

JC143 LIAO, KAI-LUNG. *From Yenan to Peking: the Chinese People's War of Liberation.* Peking: Foreign Languages Press, 1956. 187 p. An orthodox, undocumented Communist interpretation of events in China from the end of World War II to the launching of the First Five Year Plan. Part I (p. 1-130) covers the period from August 1945 until the establishment of the Chinese Communist Government; Part II (p. 131-187) deals with political, economic and social developments, 1949-53.

JC144 LIU, SHAO-CHI. *On Inner-Party Struggle; A Lecture Delivered on July 2, 1941 at the Party School for Central China.* Peking: Foreign Languages Press, 1950. 92 p. This is the key document in the "Rectification Movement" launched by the Chinese Communists in 1942 to rally and consolidate their forces in order to overcome the blurring and disrupting effects of the United Front strategy and the wartime decentralization. The Movement involved a reclarification of basic positions on doctrine and organization and this document, which defines the proper attitude of the Communist toward his Party at a time of fundamental shifts in strategy, is of utmost significance. [A]

JC145 LIU, SHAO-CHI. *On the Party.* Peking: Foreign Languages Press, 1950. 206 p. German ed., Berlin: Dietz, 1954. 176 p. Translations of Liu's speech to the 1945 National Congress of the Chinese Communist Party, a speech which presented the official interpretation of the Party's theoretical line. Also includes the Party's constitution as revised by the Congress.

JC146 LOEWENTHAL, RUDOLF. *Bibliography of Russian Literature on China and Adjacent Countries, 1931-1936.* Cambridge: Harvard University, Russian Research Center, 1949. 93 p. (duplicated). A list of articles, mostly from *Bibliografiia Vostoka*, *Mirovoe khoziaistvo i mirovaia politika*, and *Tikhii okean.* Emphasis on history and the social sciences. Only a few books are included. No annotations.

JC147 MACFARQUHAR, RODERICK L. "The Whampoa Military Academy." In: *Papers on China* (vol. 9), p. 146-172, Harvard University, East Asian Studies. A detailed treatment of the historical background and operation of the Whampoa Military Academy in the context of modern Chinese history in general and Sino-Soviet relations in particular.

JC148 McLANE, CHARLES B. *Soviet Policy and the Chinese Communists, 1931-1946.* N.Y.: Columbia, 1958. 310 p. An excellent study, based primarily on Russian sources, of Soviet policy vis-à-vis the Chinese Communists in a particularly obscure period. The author analyzes: (1) Soviet policies in China during the Kiangsi period (1931-34); (2) the formation and operation of the United Front (1935-41); (3) Soviet policy during the war (1941-45); and (4) Russian and U.S. policies in China 1945-46. The author maintains that after engineering the fall of Li Li-san in 1931, the Soviets did not meddle directly in the affairs of the Chinese Communists during the Kiangsi period. By 1935 Moscow decided that the Chinese Communists should realign with the Nationalists, whom they supported throughout the war. The author's conclusion, that in 1946 the Soviets decided to withdraw all support from Chiang and pin their hopes on an early Communist victory, is controversial in view of other evidence indicating that in 1946 Stalin did not believe in swift Communist success. [A]

JC149 *Mao's China; Party Reform Documents, 1942-44.* Seattle: U. of Washington, 1952. 278 p. Translation of key documents used in the ideological rectification movement launched by the Communists in 1942. The excellent introduction analyzes the background of the movement and describes its nature.

JC150 MOORAD, GEORGE. *Lost Peace in China.* N.Y.: E. P. Dutton, 1949. 262 p. A well-written, journalistic report of events in China immediately following World War II by a former correspondent for CBS and the London *Daily Mail.* Strongly critical of U.S. policy. The author's firsthand account of Manchuria is well worth reading.

JC151 SCHWARTZ, BENJAMIN. *Chinese Communism and the Rise of Mao.* Cambridge: Harvard, 1951. 258 p. A major survey of the Chinese Communist movement in the years 1918-31, covering the intellectual milieu prior to the establishment of the Chinese Communist Party (CCP), the founding of the Party, the adaptation of Marxist dogma to the circumstances in China, Soviet meddling in the affairs of the CCP, and the intra-party politics and factional struggles within the CCP. In conclusion the author analyzes Mao's revolutionary strategy and its impact on Marxism-Leninism. The author dates the establishment of Mao's supremacy to 1931, a hypothesis which he has subsequently modified in the light of new evidence. Chronology and bibliography. [A]

JC152 SMEDLEY, AGNES. *China Fights Back, an American Woman with the Eighth Route Army.* N.Y.: Vanguard, 1938. 282 p. A graphic, eye-witness report on the Communist Eighth Route Army in the fight against the Japanese by a highly-sympathetic American journalist who accompanied the troops during the period August 1937-January 1938. Topics described include the campaigns of the army, the life of the soldiers, political work in the army and among population, etc.

JC153 SMEDLEY, AGNES. *China's Red Army Marches.* N.Y.: Vanguard, 1934. 311 p. A journalistic, rather propagandistic, narrative of the Kuomintang campaigns against the Communists in the years 1928-32, based on information drawn from actual participants. Includes a description of the Chinese Soviets. The author is a fellow-traveling American journalist.

JC154 SMEDLEY, AGNES. *Chinese Destinies; Sketches of Present-Day China.* N.Y.: Vanguard, 1933. 315 p. Russian ed.: Moscow-Leningrad: Goslitizdat, 1934. 187 p. A bitter attack on the corruption and injustices of life in China, presented in a string of episodes vividly narrated by a Leftist American journalist.

JC155 SNOW, EDGAR. *The Battle for Asia.* N.Y.: Random House, 1941. 431 p. A vivid account by a brilliant journalist about China, Nationalist and Communist, as the kingpin in the struggle for Asia. The penetrating descriptions of events and people (1937-1940) include reports on the New Fourth Army, the rear guard of the Communist forces which left Kiangsi in 1934 on the Long March, Mao Tse-tung's observations on the United Front, and the "Industrial Cooperatives" in Free China.

JC156 SNOW, EDGAR. *Random Notes on China.* Cambridge: Harvard, 1957. 148 p. A collection of items, some published here for the first time, which the author recorded during his stay in the Communist areas in 1936 (see entry: *Red Star Over China*). Invaluable for the scholar.

JC157 SNOW, EDGAR. *Red Star Over China.* London: Gollancz, 1937. 464 p. N.Y.: Random House, 1939. 520 p. A journalistic masterpiece by an enterprising writer who in 1936 succeeded in breaking the Kuomintang blockade and reaching Communist-held areas at a time when the Chinese Communists were ready to tell their story to the outside world. This account of the Communist movement in China, based on his first-hand impressions and lengthy talks with Mao and other leaders, is a mine of information. [A]

JC158 *Soviet Plot in China.* Peking: Metropolitan Police Headquarters, 1928. 162 p. Published as the 11th volume of Su-Lien Yin-Mou Wen-Cheng Hio-Pien. 45 documents, including slightly revised versions of the 32 documents printed in the Chinese Government white book.

JC159 STRONG, ANNA LOUISE. *China's Millions; the Revolutionary Struggles from 1927 to 1935.* N.Y.: Knight, 1935. 457 p. This description of events in 1927, as seen through the eyes of a left-wing journalist, includes reports on the Wuhan split, warlord politics, labor organization, the role of women, and Mongolia.

JC160 SUN, K'O. *Chung-Su kuan-shi.* Shanghai: Chung-hua, 1946. 64 p. A collection of speeches made during the war by the son of Dr. Sun Yat-sen. Sympathetic toward the Soviet Union and its policy.

JC161 *Suppressing Communist-Banditry in China.* Shanghai: China United Press, 1934. 110 p. This publication, one of the "China Today" series edited by T'ang Leang-Li (see below) traces the history of the Communist movement in China and outlines the measures taken by the Nationalist Government to suppress it. Appended materials include estimates of the strength of the Red Army in 1930-32.

JC162 T'ANG, LEANG-LI. *The Inner History of the Chinese Revolution.* London: Routledge, 1930. 391 p. The author, a member of the

Left Kuomintang, representative in Great Britain and correspondent in Europe of the Central Executive Committee of the KMT, has had close personal contact with the most prominent personalities of his era (to several of whom he has served as private political secretary), and the information culled from this association constitutes one of the sources for the book. He surveys the origins of the Revolution, the vicissitudes of the Republic, the history of the KMT and its organization, the struggle within the Party, and the principal personalities involved.

JC163 THOMPSON, JAMES C., JR. "Communist Policy and the United Front in China 1935-36," in *Papers on China* (vol. 11), p. 99-148. Harvard University, East Asian Studies. A detailed study of the dichotomy in Communist policy during the formative period of the United Front. The author analyzes the parallel development of the two streams in Communist policy, the one flowing from Moscow and the other from the local Chinese leadership, and the gradual subordination of the latter to the former.

JC164 *United States Relations with China, with Special Reference to the Period 1944-1949*. Washington: G.P.O., 1949. 1,054 p. A noteworthy reference work including useful documents. Concentrates mainly on the 1944-49 period, but also contains background information for the preceding years.

JC165 UTLEY, FREDA. *Last Chance in China*. Indianapolis: Bobbs-Merrill, 1947. 408 p. The author, a disillusioned ex-Communist, argues that the Chinese Communists are agents of the Russians and that Chiang Kai-shek and the Kuomintang deserve American support by virtue of their struggle against the Communists. Rather propagandistic in tone.

JC166 WALES, NYM (pseud. of Helen Foster Snow), comp. *Red Dust; Autobiographies of Chinese Communists*. Intro. by Robert C. North. Stanford, Cal.: Stanford University Press, 1952. 238 p. A series of 24 biographical sketches of Chinese Communists, based on oral material gathered by the author during her visit to Yenan in 1937. Although useful materials are included, the reader will do well to remember the author's Communist sympathies in using them.

JC167 WANG, MING. *Revolutionary China; Speeches by Wang Ming and Kang Sin*. Moscow: Co-operative Pub. Soc. of Foreign Workers in the USSR, 1934. 126 p. German ed., Moscow-Leningrad: 1934. 93 p. Speeches by the Chinese delegates Wang Ming and Kang Sin (Kang Sheng) to the thirteenth plenum of the Executive Committee of the Comintern (December, 1933).

JC168 WHITE, THEODORE H., and JACOBY, ANNALEE. *Thunder out of China*. N.Y.: William Sloane, 1946. 331 p. Russian ed.: Izd. inostr. lit., 1948. 296 p. A brilliant, stinging attack on the corruption and ineptitude of the Kuomintang in wartime by two American journalists. Their narrative includes descriptions of the organization and operation of the Kuomintang, the leadership of Chiang Kai-shek, the Nationalist army, the Honan famine, the Stilwell crisis, the Hurley episode, etc. Helps to explain some of the reasons for the later triumph of the Communists.

JC169 YAKHONTOV, VICTOR A. *The Chinese Soviets.* N.Y.: Coward-McCann, 1934. 296 p. An account of the Communist-held areas, beginning with a summary history of the Communist movement in China, based on a digest of various sources, mostly Russian but also some Chinese. Due to scarcity of information, the book fails to shed much light on the pertinent questions. The author cannot really say how much of China is Communist and how Communist that part is. Important documents relating to the Chinese Soviet Republic are appended.

b. IN RUSSIAN

JC170 AKADEMIIA NAUK SSSR, INSTITUT MIROVOGO KHOZIAISTVA I MIROVOI POLITIKI. *Kolonialnye problemy, 3-4.* Moscow: 1934. Includes papers read at a conference of Soviet Orientalists at the Institute of World Economy and Politics, June-July, 1934. The principal subject discussed is proletarian hegemony in the colonial and semi-colonial countries, with special emphasis on China. [B]

JC171 AKADEMIIA NAUK SSSR, INSTITUT VOSTOKOVEDENIIA. *Kitaiskii sbornik; Uchenye zapiski, II.* Moscow: 1951. 211 p. Includes articles by leading Soviet Orientalists commemorating the victory of the Chinese Communists.

JC172 AKADEMIIA NAUK SSSR, INSTITUT VOSTOKOVEDENIIA. *Kitaiskii sbornik; Uchenye zapiski, XI.* Moscow: 1955. 303 p. Includes several articles on the development of the Chinese revolution from 1945 to 1949.

JC173 AKADEMIIA NAUK SSSR, TIKHOOKEANSKII INSTITUT. *Krizis kolonialnoi sistemy; natsionalno-osvoboditelnaia borba narodov vostochnoi Azii.* Moscow: Izd. Akad. nauk SSSR, 1949. 290 p. Reports read at a special meeting of the Academy of Sciences devoted to the colonial question, June, 1949. Includes an article by R. V. Astafev on the success of the Communists in China. The remaining articles concern South and Southeast Asia. [B]

JC174 ANGAROV, F. *V borbe za sovetskii Kitai.* Ed. by Braginskii. Tashkent: Uzprofizdat, 1936. 125 p. Includes an interview with Mao Tse-tung and short biographies of Mao and other Chinese Communist leaders.

JC175 ASTAFEV, G. V. *Interventsiia SShA v Kitae i ee porazhenie (1945-1949 gg).* Moscow: Gospolitizdat, 1958. 612 p. Uses both American and Chinese sources.

JC176 *Borba za edinyi natsionalnyi anti-iaponskii front v Kitae; sbornik.* Moscow: Partizdat, 1937. 132 p. English ed., *China; the March Toward Unity.* N.Y., Workers Library 1937. 125 p. Articles by Mao Tse-tung, Wang Ming, and others concerning the United Front policy in China from 1933 to 1937.

JC177 ERENBURG, G. B. *Ocherki natsionalno-osvoboditelnoi borby kitaiskogo naroda v noveishee vremia.* Moscow: 1951. 238 p. A history of the development of the Chinese revolutionary movement from World War II through the formation of the Chinese People's Republic. By a frequent contributor to Soviet publications on China since the early 1930's.

JC178 ERENBURG, G. B. *Sovetskii Kitai.* Moscow: Partizdat, 1933. 96 p. 2nd rev. ed., 1934. 141 p. A standard account of the Chinese Soviets prior to the Long March of 1934-35.

JC179 GLUNIN, VLADIMIR I. *Sotsialisticheskaia revoliutsiia v Kitae.* Moscow: Izd. sotsialno-ekonomicheskoi lit., 1960. 247 p. Based on Chinese sources; issued by the Institute of Chinese Studies of the Academy of Sciences of the USSR.

JC180 GLUNIN, VLADIMIR I. *Tretia grazhdanskaia revoliutsionnaia voina v Kitae (1946-1949); ocherk politicheskoi istorii.* Moscow: Izd. vost. lit., 1958. 199 p. Mainly a military study; includes maps of the different campaigns. Based largely on Chinese sources, but also uses the State Department's "White Paper." The military campaign is divided into 3 periods: August 1945-June 1946; July 1946-June 1947; June 1947-October 1949.

JC181 GOSUDARSTVENNYI INSTITUT "SOVETSKAIA ENTSIKLOPEDIIA," MOSCOW. *Strany Tikhogo Okeana.* Moscow: Ogiz RSFSR, 1942. 563 p. Has about 100 pages of material on China, including a bibliography of Russian and foreign studies.

JC182 IASHNOV, E. E. *Kitaiskaia kolonizatsiia Severnoi Manchzhurii i ee perspektivy.* Intro. by G. N. Dikii. Kharbin: Izd-vo Kit.-vost. zh. d., 1928. 291 p. The author was one of the most prolific Soviet Sinologlists in the late 1920's and early 1930's. His published studies, which are concerned primarily with agricultural and population problems in Manchuria (where he evidently lived), are rarely found outside the USSR.

JC183 IUREV, M. F. *Krasnaia armiia Kitaia, 1927-1937.* Moscow: Izd. Vostoch. lit., 1958. 194 p. Sequel to the author's *Rol revoliutsionnoi armii na pervom etape kitaiskoi revoliutsii* (see above). Includes brief biographic notes on about 50 Red Army commanders. Maps of Red Army areas also included. [B]

JC184 IVIN, ALEKSEI A. *Borba za vlast sovetov; ocherki sovetskogo dvizheniia v Kitae.* Moscow: Sotsekgiz, 1933. 156 p.

JC185 IVIN, ALEKSEI A. *Ocherki partizanskogo dvizheniia v Kitae, 1927-1930 gg.* Moscow-Leningrad: Giz, otd. voennoi lit., 1930. 106 p.

JC186 IVIN, ALEKSEI A. *Sovetskii Kitai.* Moscow: "Molodaia gvardiia," 1931. 159 p. These three works by Ivin contain popular accounts of the Chinese soviet movement at various stages. Ivin was a prolific Russian writer on China but he was meagerly informed.

JC187 KANTOROVICH, ANATOLII. *Amerika v borbe za Kitai.* Ed. by P. Lapinskii. Moscow: Sotsekgiz, 1935. 639 p. Prepared under the auspices of the Institute of World Economy and Politics by a specialist on American policies in China.

JC188 KAPITSA, M. S. *Sovetsko-kitaiskie otnosheniia v 1931-1945 gg.* Moscow: Gospolitizdat, 1956. 142 p. A recent study by a young Soviet scholar; interesting for hindsights on the period under review.

JC189 KHAMADAN, AL. *Vozhdi i geroi kitaiskogo naroda.* Moscow: 1936. 40 p. The first popular biographies published in Moscow of Mao Tse-tung and Chu Teh; poorly informed.

JC190 *Kitaiskii narod pobedit!; sbornik statei i dokumentov.* Moscow: Gospolitizdat, 1938. 109 p. Articles by Mao Tse-tung and Wang Ming plus other materials relating to the formation of the United Front in China. [B]

JC191 KOGAN, A. *Natsionalno-osvoboditelnaia voina geroicheskogo kitaiskogo naroda.* Moscow: Voenizdat, 1939. 144 p. A popular account of Chinese resistance in the United Front era. Includes stories of personal heroism.

JC192 KOMMUNISTICHESKAIA AKADEMIIA, MOSCOW, NAUCHNO-ISSLEDOVATELSKII INSTITUT PO KITAIU. *Strategiia i taktika Kominterna v natsionalno-kolonialnoi revoliutsii, na primere Kitaia; sbornik dokumentov.* Ed. by Pavel Mif, with intro. by Kara-Murza. Moscow: Izd. In-ta M.Kh. i M.P., 1934. 394 p. The last collection of materials relating to Comintern strategies in China. Includes documents covering the period 1925-33 and biographic notes of Chinese leaders. [A]

JC193 *Krasnaia armiia kitaiskikh sovetov; sbornik.* Kiev: 1935. 176 p. An early Soviet study of the Chinese Red Army; presumably not available outside the USSR.

JC194 KUCHUMOV, V. *Ocherki po istorii kitaiskoi revoliutsii.* Moscow: Partizdat, 1934. 146 p. Articles on the revolution in China, including one on the 1927-33 period; concerned chiefly with revolutionary theory. [B]

JC195 LOZOVSKII, A., ed. (pseud. of Solomon A. Dridzo). *O Kitae; politiko-ekonomicheskii sbornik.* Moscow-Leningrad: Gosizdat, 1928. 219 p. The author was a Profintern official in the 1920's and a prolific writer on international labor matters.

JC196 *Mao Tze-dun; biograficheskii ocherk.* Moscow: Gospolitizdat, 1939. 103 p. The first book-length biography of Mao Tse-tung published in the USSR, based on his published interviews with Edgar Snow in 1936 and on Snow's *Red Star over China* (see below).

JC197 MARUSHKIN, B. I. *Amerikanskaia politika "nevmeshatelstva" i iaponskaia agressiia v Kitae (1937-1939 gg).* Moscow: Izd. Akad. nauk SSSR, 1957. 155 p. An account of alleged American-Japanese rivalry in China during the first years of the Sino-Japanese war. Published under the auspices of the Institute of History of the Academy of Sciences.

JC198 MASLENNIKOV, V. A. *Kitai; politiko-ekonomicheskii ocherk.* Moscow: Gospolitizdat, 1946. 263 p. The first post-World War II volume on China to appear in the USSR, by a leading Soviet Sinologist; cautious on Chinese Communist prospects. [A]

JC199 MIF, PAVEL. *Kitaiskaia revoliutsiia.* Moscow: Partizdat, 1932. 322 p. Articles by Mif written from 1926 to 1931 on various phases of the Chinese revolution.

JC200 MIF, PAVEL. *Piatnadtsat let geroicheskoi borby.* Moscow: 1936. 118 p. English ed., *Heroic China: Fifteen Years of the Communist Party of China.* N.Y.: Workers Library, 1937. 96 p. German ed., Moscow: Verlagsgenossenschaft Ausländischer Arbeiter in der UdSSR, 1937. 110 p. A comprehensive review of Chinese Communist policies and politics on the fifteenth anniversary of the founding of the Chinese Communist Party. [B]

JC201 MIF, PAVEL, and VOITINSKII, G. N., eds. *Okkupatsiia Manchzhurii i borba kitaiskogo naroda.* Moscow: Partizdat, 1937. 148 p. Includes materials relating to the Comintern and Chinese Communist attitudes to the Japanese invasion of Manchuria. [B]

JC202 MOSCOW, UNIVERSITET, KAFEDRA ISTORII STRAN DALNEGO VOSTOKA. *Sbornik statei po istorii stran Dalnego Vostoka.* Ed. by L. V. Simonovskaia and M. F. Iurev. Moscow: Izd. Moskovskogo U., 1952. 234 p. Includes several articles on China in the 1927-49 era.

JC203 MOSCOW, UNIVERSITET, OTDELENIE ISTORII STRAN ZARUBEZHNOGO VOSTOKA. *Noveishaia istoriia stran zarubezhnogo Vostoka.* Ed. by I. M. Reisner and others. Moscow: Izd. Moskovskogo U., 1955. 288 p. Includes several articles on Chinese revolutionary movements between 1927 and 1945, by G. Erenburg, V. Nikiforov, and others.

JC204 *Narodno-osvoboditelnaia armiia Kitaia v periode voiny protiv iaponskikh zakhvatchikov.* Ed. by M. F. Iurev. Moscow: Voenizdat, 1957. 272 p. (Translated from Chinese). An account of the military campaigns of the New Fourth and Eighth Armies of the Chinese Communists during the Sino-Japanese War (1937-45).

JC205 *Natsionalno-kolonialnye problemy, sbornik materialov.* No. 1 (38). Moscow: Sotsekgiz, 1937. 136 p. Includes articles by G. Dimitrov, Wang Ming, and various Chinese Communist writers commemorating the fifteenth anniversary of the CCP; includes also biographical sketches of 25 Chinese Communists killed in the fighting against the Kuomintang.

JC206 NIKIFOROV, V. N. *Gomindanovskie reaktsionery-predateli Kitaia, 1937-1945.* Moscow: Izd. Moskovskogo universiteta, 1953. 246 p. Afterthoughts on alleged Kuomintang treachery during the Sino-Japanese War, 1937-45. Based largely on Chinese Communist materials.

JC207 NIKIFOROV, V. N., ERENBURG, G. and IUREV, M. *Narodnaia revoliutsiia v Kitae; ocherk istorii borby i pobedy kitaiskogo naroda.* Moscow: Gospolitizdat, 1950. 143 p. 2nd ed., 1953. 144 p. A study of the Chinese revolution from 1925 to 1949 by three well-seasoned Soviet specialists on China.

JC208 *Novaia i noveishaia istoriia Kitaia; kratkii ocherk.* Ed. by V. N. Nikiforov. Moscow: Inlitizdat, 1950. 268 p. Articles by Chinese Communist writers on various aspects of the Chinese revolution. Translated from Chinese.

JC209 PASHKOVA, M. *V borbe za raskreposhchenie kitaiskogo naroda; ocherki rabochego dvizheniia v Kitae 1925-1939 gg.* Moscow: Sotsekgiz, 1939. 144 p.

JC210 PEN, PAI (P'ENG PAI). *Zapiski Pen Paia.* Moscow: "Molodaia gvardiia," 1936. 142 p. Memoirs of a peasant leader in Kwangtung who was executed in 1929 by the Kuomintang and later revered by the Chinese Communists as a martyr.

JC211 *Programmnye dokumenty kitaiskikh sovetov; sbornik.* Moscow: Partizdat, 1935. 101 p. A collection of key Chinese soviet documents with an authoritative introduction by the Russian editors. The documents are selected from the collection *Sovety v Kitae.* [A]

JC212 *Protiv iaponskogo imperializma; za spasenie rodiny.* (Sbornik vazhneishikh dokumentov o borbe kitaiskikh narodnykh mass protiv iaponskogo imperializma.) Moscow: 1935. 232 p.

JC213 RUSSIA (1923– USSR), NARODNYI KOMISSARIAT PO INOSTRANNYM DELAM. *Sovetsko-kitaiskii konflikt 1929 g.; sbornik dokumentov.* Moscow: Litizdat NKID, 1930. 89 p. Sixty-six documents related to Soviet and Chinese relations, including the texts of the agreements, relevant press commentary, diplomatic notes, and other pertinent data. [B]

JC214 SEVOSTIANOV, G. N. *Aktivnaia rol SShA v obrazovanii ochaga voiny na Dalnem Vostoke (1931-1933).* Moscow: Izd. Akad. nauk SSSR, 1953. 246 p. Relates American designs in the Far East, especially in Manchuria, to the world economic crisis.

JC215 SHIN, SHI-TSAI (SHENG SHIH-TS'AI). *Osnovnye ocherednye zadachi pravitelstva.* Urumchi: 1940. Articles and speeches relating to the United Front by the then Governor of Sinkiang. Translated from Chinese.

JC216 SHISHKIN, P. P. *Bolshevizm v Kitaie. Obzor dieiatelnosti Sievero-Manchzhurskoi kommunisticheskoi partii.* Shanghai: 1930. 151 p.

JC217 SIAO, EMI (HSIAO E-MI, or HSIAO SAN). *Kitai nepobedim; ocherki.* Moscow: Voenizdat, 1940. 108 p. Articles on the United Front by a Chinese Communist long resident in Moscow. Translated from Chinese.

JC218 SIAO, EMI. *Mao Tsze-dun, Chzhu De.* Moscow: 1939. 108 p. Biographies of Mao Tse-tung and Chu Teh. Translated from Chinese.

JC219 *Sovety v Kitae; sbornik materialov i dokumentov.* Moscow: Partizdat, 1933. 522 p. 2nd ed., 1934. 524 p. German ed., Moscow: Verlagsgenössenschaft Ausländischer Arbeiter in der UdSSR, 1934. Important documents relating to the Chinese soviet movement in Kiangsi, with a comprehensive introduction by E. Ioganson (J. Johanson) and O. Taube. [A]

JC220 TERENTEV, N. *Sovetskii Soiuz, imperializm i Kitai; zakhvat K.V.Zh.D. i razryv sovetsko-kitaiskikh otnoshenii.* 3rd ed., Moscow-Leningrad: Gosizdat, 1929. 93 p.

JC221 *Tretia grazhdanskaia revoliutsionnaia voina v Kitae; iz serii materialov po sovremennoi istorii Kitaia.* Ed. by M. F. Iurev. Moscow: Voenizdat, 1957. 398 p. Translated from Chinese. A Chinese study of the Civil War of 1945-49.

JC222 TSZEN, SIU-FU. *Kommunisticheskaia Partiia Kitaia v borbe za edinyi front.* Moscow: Izd. VPSh i Akademii obshchestvennykh nauk pri TsK KPSS, 1959. 163 p. Concerning the "United Front" against Japan before World War II.

JC223 *Velikii pokhod pervogo fronta Kitaiskoi raboche-krestianskoi krasnoi armii; vospominaniia.* Moscow: Izd. inostrannoi lit., 1959. 568 p. The "Long March." Conclusions (p. 539-566) by Miao Chu-huang. Numerous biographical footnotes.

JC224 *Vosmaia narodno-revoliutsionnaia armiia Kitaia.* Khabarovsk: Dalgiz, 1938. 148 p. A collection of articles and other materials on the leaders and development of the Chinese Communist 8th Army.

JC225 *Vsiudu krasnye znamena; vospominaniia i ocherki o vtoroi grazhdanskoi revoliutsionnoi voine.* Moscow: Voenizdat, 1957. 160 p. Reminiscences of Chinese Communist participants in the 1927-37 civil war in China. Translated from Chinese.

JC226 *Vtoroi sezd kitaiskikh sovetov.* Intro. by Wang Ming. Moscow: Partizdat, 1935. 191 p. A collection of the principal speeches, including Mao's keynote address, resolutions, and other materials relating to the Second Chinese Soviet Congress held in Kiangsi province in January 1934. [A]

4. COMMUNIST CHINA, 1949-1963

a. IN LANGUAGES OTHER THAN RUSSIAN AND JAPANESE

(Edited by Howard L. Boorman)

JC227 ABEGG, LILY. *Im neuen China.* Zürich: Atlantis, 1957. 285 p. Firsthand observations on political, economic, and social conditions in China by a Swiss journalist. The author's previous experience was largely in Japan; she is the author of *The Mind of East Asia* (1952).

JC228 AMERICAN ACADEMY OF POLITICAL AND SOCIAL SCIENCE, PHILADELPHIA. *The Annals; Contemporary China and the Chinese.* Ed. by Howard L. Boorman. Philadelphia: 1959. 220 p. Fourteen concise papers by specialists provide general coverage of contemporary China as of the autumn of 1958. After introductory papers on the background and United States policy, the major portion of the volume is devoted to the domestic scene and the international relations of the People's Republic of China; two final articles discuss Taiwan and the overseas Chinese in Southeast Asia. [A]

JC229 AMERICAN ACADEMY OF POLITICAL AND SOCIAL SCIENCE, PHILADELPHIA. *The Annals; Report on China.* Ed. by

H. Arthur Steiner. Philadelphia: 1951. 291 p. Published less than two years after the establishment of the Peking regime, this issue of *The Annals* provides a useful record of early estimates of the regime's progress and travail during the 1949-51 period of political consolidation and economic rehabilitation. Separate articles also treat the overseas Chinese and Nationalist policies, 1949-51.

JC229A AMERICAN ACADEMY OF POLITICAL AND SOCIAL SCIENCE, PHILADELPHIA. *The Annals; Communist China and the Soviet Bloc*. Ed. by Donald S. Zagoria. Philadelphia: 1963. 162 p. Concise papers by leading American and European specialists provide general coverage of the Sino-Soviet conflict as of the summer of 1963. Following introductory papers on background and historical perspective, a major portion of the volume is devoted to detailed consideration of the over-all relationship between Russia and Communist China in a variety of perspectives: political, economic, and military. Four concluding papers discuss the implications for third countries of the clash between the two major Communist Party leaderships in Moscow and Peking. [A]

JC230 AMERICAN ASSEMBLY. "The United States and Communist China," by A. Doak Barnett. In: *The United States and the Far East*, p. 98-157. N.Y.: Graduate School of Business, Columbia University, 1956. 229 p. 2nd ed., ed. by Willard L. Thorp, Englewood Cliffs, N.J.: Prentice-Hall, 1962. A concise background paper prepared originally for the Tenth American Assembly (November 1956), which discussed Far Eastern problems confronting the U.S. Slightly revised and updated for the second edition, Barnett's chapter is a balanced statement covering domestic patterns of political control and economic development, and external patterns of foreign policy and foreign relations, including Sino-American tensions.

JC231 ASIAN PEOPLES' ANTI-COMMUNIST LEAGUE, CHINA. *Ten Years of Chinese Communist Economy*. Taipei: 1960. 103 p. Taiwan's assessment of the first decade (1949-59) of mainland China's economic development efforts: policy and planning, agriculture, industry and transport, and capital construction. Clearly anti-Communist in bias, the study nevertheless summarizes data available from official Chinese Communist sources on most major questions.

JC232 BARENDSEN, ROBERT D. "The Chinese Communist Germ Warfare Propaganda Campaign, 1952-1953." Ph.D. dissertation, Yale, 1957. 352 p. A case study of a major Chinese Communist propaganda campaign, examining Peking's bacteriological warfare charges levied against the United States during the Korean War and appraising the probable purposes motivating the campaign. The author is in the Office of Education of the U. S. Department of Health, Education, and Welfare.

JC232A BARNETT, A. DOAK. *China on the Eve of Communist Takeover.* N.Y.: Praeger, 1963. 371 p. The best available introduction to the disintegration, stagnation, and fragmentation of Nationalist China, this volume is a collection of twenty-three reports originally written between 1947 and 1949 while the author was in China as a correspondent and fellow of the Institute of Current World Affairs. [B]

JC233 BARNETT, A. DOAK. *Communist China and Asia; Challenge to American Policy.* N.Y.: Harper, for the Council on Foreign Relations, 1960. 575 p. Paperback ed., Vintage Books, 1961. The product of a 1958-59 fellowship at the Council on Foreign Relations, this book is the most solid and thoughtful survey of contemporary China now available. Barnett, now at Columbia University, stresses Communist China's foreign relations, and implications for United States policy. Excellent bibliographical notes. [A]

JC234 BARNETT, A. DOAK. *Communist China; Continuing Revolution.* N.Y.: Foreign Policy Association, Headline Series, May-June 1962. 64 p. A balanced and tightly written introductory survey of the essential political, economic, and foreign policy aspects of Communism, Chinese style, as it has reshaped mainland China during the past dozen years. Barnett assesses the anatomy of the revolution: its content, direction, achievements, and shortcomings. Reading references are appended.

JC235 BARNETT, A. DOAK. *Communist China in Perspective.* N.Y.: Praeger, 1962. 88 p. Paperback ed., Praeger, 1962. A short, general summary assessing the Chinese revolution in historical perspective, weighing elements of continuity and change in contemporary China, and appraising China's future prospects. This book is an expanded version of the Oreon E. Scott Foundation lectures delivered at Washington University, St. Louis.

JC236 BARNETT, A. DOAK. *Communist Economic Strategy; The Rise of Mainland China.* Washington: National Planning Association, 1959. 106 p. Part of the National Planning Association's project on the Economics of Competitive Coexistence, designed to assess bloc trade-and-aid capabilities in the uncommitted areas, this study appraises Communist China's domestic economy and foreign economic relations on the basis of official data available to early 1959. Stress is laid on the impact, both practical and psychological, of China's economic development efforts, especially in the Asian-African area. [B]

JC236A BARNETT, A. DOAK, ed. *Communist Strategies in Asia: a Comparative Analysis of Governments and Parties.* N.Y.: Praeger, 1963. 293 p. Eight essays, originally prepared for a 1962 symposium of the Association for Asian Studies, serve to relate the new field of international Communist studies to contemporary Asia. Introductory papers by Donald Zagoria and Robert North discuss the relevance of the Russian and Chinese "models" to Asia. The remaining chapters offer detailed discussions of three Asian Communist parties in opposition, in Japan (Paul Langer), India (Harry Gelman), and Indonesia (Ruth McVey); and three Asian Communist governments in operation, in North Vietnam (Bernard Fall), North Korea (Glenn Paige), and the Mongolian People's Republic (Robert Rupen). [B]

JC237 BERTON, PETER A., comp. *Soviet Works on China; A Bibliography of Non-Periodical Literature, 1946-1955.* Los Angeles: U. of Southern California, 1959. 158 p. A full bibliography of books on China published in Russian, Ukrainian, and other languages of the Soviet Union between 1946 and 1955. Covers bibliographies, general works, geography, history and government, economic and social conditions, and culture; and provides tables giving publication and translation data. A critical 40-page introduction suggests that compilations and reference works have been the most important products of Oriental studies in the USSR.

JC237A BIRCH, CYRIL, ed. *Chinese Communist Literature.* N.Y.: Praeger, 1963. 250 p. A trail-breaking symposium volume stemming from the Ditchley Manor conference sponsored by the Congress for Cultural Freedom in August 1962. The papers, supporting the inevitable conclusion that political considerations take precedence over free artistic creation in the new socio-didactic literature of the People's Republic, were originally published as a special issue of the *China Quarterly,* No. 13, January-March 1963. [B]

JC238 BLAUSTEIN, ALBERT P., ed. *Fundamental Legal Documents of Communist China.* South Hackensack, N.J.: F. B. Rothman, 1962. 603 p. The first organized compilation providing English translations of the principal legal documents of the People's Republic of China. Included are (1) constitutions and general programmes, (2) organic laws prescribing the powers and procedures of the basic organs of government, and (3) nationalities and election laws, penal laws, the marriage law, property laws and regulations, and labor laws and regulations. Blaustein, professor of law and law librarian at Rutgers Law School, has also provided a brief introduction to the law of Communist China.

JC239 BODARD, LUCIEN. *La Chine de la douceur.* Paris: Gallimard, 1957. 336 p. (See next entry.)

JC240 BODARD, LUCIEN. *La Chine du cauchemar.* Paris: Gallimard, 1961. 419 p. Based on the author's second visit to the mainland since the establishment of the new regime, this book offers a perceptive account of conditions during the Great Leap Forward. Short on substantive data, but long on interpretation. M. Bodard contrasts the tough, high-pressure character of the Great Leap effort with the relative mildness of the 1957 period, described in his *La Chine de la douceur* (above).

JC241 BOORMAN, HOWARD L. and others. *Moscow-Peking Axis; Strengths and Strains.* N.Y.: Harper, for the Council on Foreign Relations, 1957. 227 p. The product of a 1955-56 Council on Foreign Relations study group, this symposium contains analytic essays discussing the political aspects of the Sino-Soviet alliance (Boorman), economic relations (Alexander Eckstein), ideological dimensions (Benjamin Schwartz), the borderlands (Boorman), and the axis in world politics (Philip Mosely). Now dated, the volume unfortunately lacks an interpretive synthesis summarizing the pattern and direction of Sino-Soviet relations as of 1956. [B]

JC242 BOYD, R. G. *Communist China's Foreign Policy.* N.Y.: Praeger, 1962. 147 p. A slim study, prepared on the basis of Western language sources, of the principal bases and operational lines of Chinese policy in Asia. One of the first Australians to serve with SEATO, Boyd prepared this book on the basis of research (1959-61) in the Department of International Relations of the Australian National University in Canberra.

JC243 BRZEZINSKI, ZBIGNIEW K. *The Soviet Bloc; Unity and Conflict.* Cambridge: Harvard, 1960. 470 p. Rev. and updated paperback ed., Praeger: 1961. A full-length study of the development of political relations within the bloc 1949-59, stressing the interaction of ideological preconceptions and practical power aims. Notable for its treatment of China's growing influence as a significant factor in international Communist society, especially in the period since 1956. Brzezinski heads the Research Institute on Communist Affairs at Columbia University. [A]

JC243A BUSS, CLAUDE A. *The People's Republic of China.* Princeton, New Jersey: D. Van Nostrand, Anvil Book No. 61, 1962. 188 p. Brief account of the origin and rise of the Chinese Communist Party, describing the achievements and failures of the Peking government since 1949 and providing useful background documents for reference. The author is Professor of History at Stanford University.

JC244 CAMERON, JAMES. *Mandarin Red.* N.Y.: Rinehart, 1955. 334 p. The chief correspondent of the London *News Chronicle* recounts a visit to China late in 1954. Without previous China experience, Cameron, an independent Scotsman with a shrewd eye and a sense of humor, gives a highly personal account of the contrasts and complexities inherent in his subject. A sound reportorial book by a professional journalist aware that two months in a land larger than Europe is not likely to produce a heavy crop of eternal verities.

JC245 CARIN, ROBERT. *State Farms in Communist China, 1947-1961.* Hong Kong: P. O. Box 5217, 1962. 323 p. A comprehensive chronicle of official Chinese Communist reports on state farms through early 1961, with running commentary by the author. The collection is useful as reference material on the position (still minor) of state farms in China's agricultural economy, but lacks critical analysis. The author, publisher, and sponsorship are not identified.

JC246 CARTIER-BRESSON, HENRI. *From One China to the Other.* N.Y.: Universe Books, 1956. 144 p. The transition from Nationalist to Communist China, superbly filmed on the spot by the well-known French photographer, who was in China for *Life* magazine from December 1948 through September 1949. Despite a preface by Han Suyin, Communist China's most literate apologist, written while on a sentimental journey to Peking in 1956, Cartier-Bresson's picture-diary is an outstanding reminder that the 1948-49 debacle in China involved people as well as politics.

JC247 CH'ANG-CHIANG JIH-PAO. *Tu-pao shou-ts'e.* Hankow: Hsin-hua Book Store, 1950. 1116 p. The most comprehensive one-volume Chinese reference work covering the first year (1949-50) of the People's Republic of China. In about 1000 pages of carefully edited material, the *Ch'ang-chiang Jih-pao*, the official Chinese Communist newspaper published at Hankow, assembled a mass of data on the establishment, structure, and personnel of the new government, as well as extensive statistics on industrial plants at the time of the Communist take-over. Only one volume (dated August 1950) of this handbook was issued.

JC248 CHAO, KUO-CHÜN. *Agrarian Policies of Mainland China; a Documentary Study (1949-1956).* Cambridge: Harvard, 1957. 276 p. A product of Harvard's East Asian Research Center, Chao's volume provides a collection of translated documentary materials on Chinese Communist agrarian policies from the land reform period to the organization of the peasants into agricultural producers cooperatives.

JC249 CHAO, KUO-CHÜN. *Economic Planning and Organization in Mainland China; a Documentary Study (1949-1957).* Cambridge: Harvard, 1959-60. 2 vols. These volumes comprise a useful documentary study of the institutional aspects of economic planning, at least as ordered from Peking, through 1957. Translations, excerpts, and summaries of documents, with an introductory comment for each section.

JC250 CH'EN, HSI-EN (CHEN, THEODORE H. E.). *Thought Reform of the Chinese Intellectuals.* Hong Kong: Hong Kong U., 1960. 247 p. A conscientious survey, by a University of Southern California professor, of Peking's policies toward the strategic group of Chinese intellectuals from 1949 through the Hundred Flowers outburst of 1957 and the ensuing "anti-rightist" campaign, with a backward look at earlier origins of thought reform in the Yenan period. The book relies on description and analysis of published confessions by prominent Chinese scholars and intellectuals, but fails to probe the subtle personal aspects of the process as it affects the moral and emotional life of the individual. [B]

JC250A CH'EN, NAI-RUENN. *The Economy of Mainland China, 1949-1963: a Bibliography of Materials in English.* Berkeley, California: Committee on the Economy of China, Social Science Research Council, 1963. 297 p. An exhaustive bibliography prepared under the auspices of the Committee, headed by Professor Walter Galenson of the University of California, Berkeley.

JC251 *The China Quarterly.* London, 1960- . Quarterly. Sponsored by the Congress for Cultural Freedom, this is the principal non-Communist journal devoted to regular coverage of recent developments in China and adjacent Communist areas in Asia. Editor and guiding spirit is Roderick MacFarquhar; advisory editor is G. F. Hudson of St. Anthony's College, Oxford. Now indispensable for serious students of contemporary Chinese and Communist bloc affairs, *The China Quarterly,* through its rapid development, has reflected the underlying fact that China, along with the United States and the Soviet Union, is one of the few nations exerting sufficient intellectual and political appeal to sustain a periodical review with international circulation. [A]

JC252 *Chung-hua jen-min kung-ho-kuo fa-kuei hui-pien.* Peking: 1956-59. 9 vols. Chinese texts of selected laws, regulations, decisions, and official reports promulgated from Peking. This collection of basic documentary material is the successor to *Chung-yang jen-min cheng-fu fa-ling hui-pien,* which was discontinued with the reorganization of the national government in September 1954.

JC253 CHUNG-KUO KUNG-CH'AN-TANG. *Eighth National Congress of the Communist Party of China.* Peking: Foreign Languages Press, 1956. 3 vols. Russian ed., Moscow: 1957. Italian ed., Rome: 1956. Peking's official English translation of some speeches and documents from the Eighth National Congress of the CCP (September 1956), the first held since 1945.

JC254 *Chung-yang jen-min cheng-fu fa-ling hui-pien.* Peking: 1952-55. Vol. I, 1949-50; Vol. II, 1951; Vol. III, 1952; Vol. IV, 1953; Vol. V, Jan.-Sept., 1954. Essential documentary evidence covering national laws and regulations promulgated between the establishment of the Central People's Government in October 1949 and its reorganization at the First National People's Congress five years later.

JC255 *Chung-yang ts'ai-cheng cheng-ts'e fa-ling hui-pien.* Peking: 1950-53. 3 vols. An earlier and more specialized documentary series, issued by the Committee of Financial and Economic Affairs of the Government Administration Council in Peking. Provides the Chinese texts of laws, regulations, decisions, official reports, and *Jen-min Jih-pao* (People's Daily) editorials on economic and financial matters from 1949 through 1951. Essential for the study of the institutional framework of economic rehabilitation in China during those years.

JC255A CLUBB, O. EDMUND. *Twentieth Century China.* N.Y.: Columbia University Press, 1964. 470 p. A political history of the turbulent changes in China from the Boxer Rebellion of 1900 down to 1963. Primarily concerned with domestic developments, the book also discusses aspects of China's foreign relations, especially with Japan, the United States, and Russia. The final portion of the book appraises the effects of the first fourteen years of Communist rule. The author is a retired officer of the Foreign Service who served eighteen years in China and was the last American Consul General at Peiping prior to the withdrawal of United States official personnel from the mainland in 1950. [B]

JC256 COLE, ALLAN B. *Forty Years of Chinese Communism; Selected Readings with Commentary.* Washington: Service Center for Teachers of History, Publication No. 47, 1962. 43 p. An annotated bibliography of the Chinese Communist movement from its beginnings in 1918-21 to date, issued under the auspices of the American Historical Association and intended mainly for secondary school teachers. This convenient pamphlet, though limited to works in English, is a useful tool covering the rise of the Communists to power and the period of the People's Republic of China since 1949. The author is professor of East Asian affairs at the Fletcher School of Law and Diplomacy.

JC257 *Communist China 1955-1959; Policy Documents with Analysis.* Foreword by Robert R. Bowie and John K. Fairbank. Cambridge: Harvard, 1962. 611 p. A product of the Center for International Affairs at Harvard, this volume includes 48 major policy documents, with commentary and additional bibliographic suggestions. The period covered includes the Great Leap Forward, the organization of the people's communes, and the "rectification" campaign. Editorial comment attempts to appraise not only the published policies as officially ordained by Peking, but also the actual strains and tensions produced in China by the policies.

JC257A CRANKSHAW, EDWARD. *The New Cold War: Moscow v. Pekin.* Harmondsworth, Middlesex, England: Penguin Books, 1963. 167 p. A useful if brief analytic account of the Sino-Soviet rift from the early frictions of 1956 to the shattered monolith of early 1963, by one of its most articulate diagnosticians. The *Observer's* correspondent on Soviet affairs, Crankshaw has written widely on recent and contemporary Russia. [B]

JC258 CRESSEY, GEORGE B. *Land of the 500 Million; a Geography of China.* N.Y.: McGraw-Hill, 1955. 387 p. The dean of America's geographers on Asia updates his *China's Geographic Foundations* (1934) and assesses the environment and resource base upon which Peking is mounting its economic development effort. Stressing regional differences in China, the book has good maps and photographs, plus a useful bibliography of relevant geographical literature. Data on recent developments in Communist China are, however, presented uncritically.

JC258A DALLIN, ALEXANDER, *ed. Diversity in International Communism: a Documentary Record, 1961-1963.* N.Y.: Columbia University Press, 1963. 867 p. A useful compilation providing the most important available documentation on the issues that have troubled and divided the international Communist movement since the Twenty-second Congress of the Soviet Communist Party, held in October 1961. This volume was prepared under the auspices of the Research Institute on Communist Affairs of Columbia University, and has a solid introduction by Zbigniew Brzezinski and Alexander Dallin, discussing issues and methods.

JC259 DANIELS, ROBERT V., ed. *A Documentary History of Communism.* N.Y.: Random House, 1960. 714 p. A review of Communist thought and doctrine from Lenin to Mao Tse-tung, this volume provides a final chapter including some coverage of "the most successful Asian Communist movement in the continent's most populous country, China." Includes excerpts from recent Chinese documents up to the Central Committee resolution on the establishment of rural "people's communes" (August 1958). Useful for quick reference, but the editor handles Soviet and European Communism with more deftness and authority than he does Chinese.

JC260 DUMONT, RENÉ. *Révolution dans les campagnes chinoises.* Paris: Éditions du Seuil, 1957. 463 p. Firsthand observations on agrarian change in China by a veteran agronomist and authority on comparative agriculture. The author's estimates of substantial material expansion in Chinese agriculture as of 1955 are balanced by Gallic realism, which recognizes the population dilemma, notes the existence of nutritional deficiencies, and warns that hunger and malnutrition are likely to be factors in the economic equation in China for some time.

JC261 ECKLUND, GEORGE N. *Taxation in Communist China, 1950-1959.* Washington: Central Intelligence Agency, Office of Research and Reports (CIA/RR ER 61-32), 1961. 117 p. A U.S. government report covering the role of the budget in Communist China, sources of revenue, size and impact of the tax burden, and evaluation of the tax system. A solid study, including 29 statistical tables and four charts with detailed annotations.

JC262 ECKSTEIN, ALEXANDER. *The National Income of Communist China.* N.Y.: Free Press of Glencoe, 1961. 215 p. A substantial monograph developing original and detailed estimates of national income, product, and expenditure for the single year 1952 to provide a base line for measuring the subsequent performance of the Chinese Communist economy. Statistical data for 1952 and other years are mobilized, evaluated, and related to a national income accounting framework to facilitate further study of underdeveloped Soviet-type economies. A professor of economics at the Univ. of Michigan, Eckstein prepared this study at Harvard, assisted by Y. C. and Helen Yin of the East Asian Research Center. [B]

JC263 EKVALL, ROBERT B. *Faithful Echo.* N.Y.: Twayne, 1960. 125 p. Colonel Ekvall, formerly chief English-Chinese interpreter for the United States at Panmunjom and Geneva, offers a perceptive account of experiences in negotiating with the Chinese Communists. The problem of adequate communication, he suggests, is not primarily a linguistic matter but rather an exercise in inter-cultural understanding demanding unfailing precision and perception on both sides. Born and raised on the Sino-Tibetan border, with long experience in China as missionary, anthropologist, and army officer, Ekvall is now at the University of Washington.

JC264 ELEGANT, ROBERT S. *China's Red Masters; Political Biographies of the Chinese Communist Leaders.* N.Y.: Twayne, 1951. 264 p. London: The Bodley Head, 1952. A number of brief but informative political biographies of the leaders of Chinese Communism, based for the most part on Chinese, Japanese, and English materials.

JC265 ELEGANT, ROBERT S. *The Dragon's Seed; Peking and the Overseas Chinese.* N.Y.: St. Martin's Press, 1959. 319 p. A lively survey of the position of the overseas Chinese in Southeast Asia and of their relations, actual and potential, with mother China. Popular in tone and style, the book is marred by some factual and interpretive imprecision. Elegant headed the Hong Kong bureau of *Newsweek* until 1962.

JC266 FAIRBANK, JOHN K. *The United States and China.* Rev. ed., Cambridge: Harvard, 1958. 365 p. Though commenting only briefly on contemporary China, this volume provides essential background through a balanced interpretive introduction to modern Chinese history and society. Readable, comprehensive, and *au courant* of recent scholarly research, this book is supplemented by an excellent bibliographical essay. Professor Fairbank is Director of Harvard's East Asian Research Center. [A]

JC267 FEUERWERKER, ALBERT, and CHENG, SALLY. *Chinese Communist Studies of Modern Chinese History.* Cambridge: Harvard, 1961. 287 p. A reconnaissance guide to nearly 500 books on nineteenth and twentieth century Chinese history produced in the People's Republic of China between 1949 and 1959. Sections include: general works, Ming and Ch'ing, the Republic, economic history, intellectual and cultural history, and reference works. Critical introductory note on Chinese Communist historiography by Prof. Feuerwerker.

JC268 *First Five-Year Plan for Development of the National Economy of the People's Republic of China, 1953-1957.* Peking: Foreign Languages Press, 1956. 231 p. Peking's official outline of the First Five-Year Plan.

JC269 FITZGERALD, CHARLES P. *Flood Tide in China.* London: Cresset, 1958. 286 p. Written after a visit to China in 1956, this book relates Peking's recent policies to the longer background of life and thought which no revolution in China can completely eliminate or ignore. Views Mao Tse-tung's massive effort as a distinctively Chinese interpretation of Marxism, the most recent and far-reaching attempt to synthesize Western modernization with Eastern worldly shrewdness and with that "ancient authoritarian Asia which never accepted the idea that individual liberty should take precedence over the welfare of the group."

JC270 FITZGERALD, CHARLES P. *Revolution in China.* N.Y.: Praeger, 1952. 289 p. An interpretive review of Nationalist failure and Communist triumph in China, relating the revolutionary process through which Mao and the Chinese Communists came to power to the traditional cyclical pattern of dynastic history. This early, urbane, and essentially conservative attempt to discuss Communism in its Chinese context has inevitably evoked criticism: that the author discounts the Soviet impact and underestimates the radically new Leninist structure of power in contemporary China. The author of *China, a Short Cultural History* and other works, Fitzgerald is professor at the Australian National University in Canberra. [A]

JC270A FLOYD, DAVID. *Mao against Khrushchev: a Short History of the Sino-Soviet Conflict.* N.Y.: Praeger, 1964. 456 p. A journalistic recapitulation of the Sino-Soviet dispute through the abortive July 1963 meeting in Moscow. The author's account of the conflict is accompanied by a 70,000-word annex offering some of the documentary data necessary for understanding of the debates and issues which have riven the once-monolithic structure of international Communism.

JC271 FREMANTLE, ANNE, ed. *Mao Tse-tung; an Anthology of His Writings.* N.Y.: Mentor Books, 1962. 300 p. A selected anthology of important writings of Mao, all taken from the International Publishers English language edition of his *Selected Works* except for selections from the important 1957 speech, "On the Correct Handling of Contradictions among the People." The introduction provides a biographical sketch of Mao drawn largely from the account given in Edgar Snow's *Red Star Over China.*

JC272 GLUCKSTEIN, YGAEL. *Mao's China; Economic and Political Survey.* Boston: Beacon; London: Allen & Unwin, 1957. 438 p. This survey volume covering developments to 1956 relies principally on translated documents, which the author subjects to critical, vicarious examination. Economic in emphasis, the book questions the validity of many of Peking's claims. An analyst of Soviet and satellite affairs, Gluckstein anticipates that the People's Republic of China will remain an "impregnable citadel of Stalinism."

JC273 GOULD, SIDNEY H., ed. *Sciences in Communist China.* Washington: American Association for the Advancement of Science, Publication No. 68, 1961. 872 p. In twenty-six detailed but uneven chapters, North American specialists, many of Chinese origin, survey the state of the sciences in China. Sections include: science and society; biological and medical sciences; atmospheric and earth sciences; mathematics and the physical sciences; and engineering sciences and electronics. Much material from mainland technical journals was digested in these reports, which were assisted by the National Science Foundation and presented at the December 1960 annual meeting of the AAAS in New York. Net conclusions (implicit) are that the politically approved areas of science and technology may become the focal points for competitive initiative and bold advance in China, and that the Chinese may catch up with the Western world in basic research during the 1970's. [B]

JC273A GREENE, FELIX. *Awakened China: the Country Americans Don't Know.* N.Y.: Doubleday, 1962. 448 p. Paperback ed., *China: the Country Americans Are Not Allowed to Know*, Ballantine Books, 1962. A British subject resident in the United States, Mr. Greene visited China in 1960, having been there once before, briefly, in 1957. The result is a journalistic volume, filled with the enthusiasm of discovery, suffering from the author's inadequate sophistication within China and inadequate research outside. Though the book's subtitle is pertinent, Mr. Greene also suffers from a lack of critical reserve in assessing China's awakening.

JC274 GRIFFITH, SAMUEL B. (BRIG. GEN.) *Mao Tse-tung on Guerrilla Warfare.* N.Y.: Praeger, 1961. 114 p. The text of a 1937 report by Mao on guerrilla warfare (*yu-chi chan*), originally translated by Griffith in 1940 and here made generally available for the first time. The translator's critical introduction assesses the nature of revolutionary guerrilla war; strategy, tactics, and logistics in revolutionary war; and Mao's early career through the Long March. Though there are similarities, this essay is distinct from Mao's later (May 1938) report on "Strategic Problems in the Anti-Japanese Guerrilla War."

JC274A GRIFFITH, WILLIAM E. *Albania and the Sino-Soviet Rift.* Cambridge: Massachusetts Institute of Technology Press, 1963. 423 p. The first documented analysis of Albania's breach with the USSR and incongruous alliance with Communist China, a nation remote both culturally and geographically from the Balkans. Drawing upon much original Albanian material previously unpublished and unstudied in the West, the book recounts the tortuous course of relations between Moscow, Peking, and Tirana from 1960 to 1963 and makes a solid contribution to the new field of international Communist studies. [B]

JC275 GROSSMANN, BERNHARD. *Die wirtschaftliche Entwicklung der Volksrepublik China.* Stuttgart: Gustav Fischer, 1960. 412 p. The most comprehensive and thorough survey of the first decade of mainland China's economic development under Communism now available. Essentially descriptive, the volume assembles a wide range of data, both quantitative and institutional, regarding the principal sectors of the economy, and probes the basic economic problems confronting Peking. Though objective in approach, Grossmann's impartial study suffers from total reliance on unevaluated official Chinese statistics. Both analysis and conclusions are thus the prisoners of their data.

JC276 GUILLAIN, ROBERT. *600 Millions de Chinois sous le drapeau rouge.* Paris: Julliard, 1956. 290 p. American ed., *600 Million Chinese.* N.Y.: Criterion, 1957. 310 p. British ed., *The Blue Ants; 600 Million Chinese under the Red Flag.* London: Secker & Warburg, 1957. 257 p. The author, a veteran French correspondent, witnessed the Communist takeover in China and recorded his experiences in *New China; Three Views* (London: 1950). He revisited the country in 1955, noting impressive material progress but finding the political atmosphere oppressive and the new society reminiscent of an ant nest.

JC277 GUILLERMAZ, JACQUES. *La Chine populaire.* Paris: Presses Universitaires de France, "Que sais-je?" No. 840, 1959. 128 p. 2nd ed., 1961. A modest summary, brief but lucid, of the historical evolution of Communism in China (1921-March 1961), and a review of major changes—political, economic, social, international, and military—accomplished, underway, or projected. Colonel Guillermaz, a retired French officer with extensive experience in China, is now associated with the École pratique des hautes études in Paris.

JC278 *Handbook on People's China.* Peking: Foreign Languages Press, April 1957. 236 p. A concise official handbook providing data on geography; history; constitution and government; administrative divisions; the Chinese People's Political Consultative Conference; economy and finance; science, education, and the press; "people's organizations"; and a brief chronology of major events (September 1949-March 1957).

JC279 HANDKE, WERNER. *Die Wirtschaft Chinas; Dogma und Wirklichkeit.* Frankfurt/Main: Metzner, 1959. 337 p. Based largely on official data, this useful volume discusses the basic political ideology motivating change in China; economic geography and resources; major developments since 1949 (agriculture, industry, resource conservation, transportation, public finance); and mainland China's position in the world economy. A former German consul in Hong Kong (1953-58), Handke concludes that the regime's economic achievements have been gained at inordinate cost in political freedom and human welfare. 38 statistical tables and 8 maps.

JC280 HINTON, HAROLD C. "China." In *Major Governments of Asia,* ed. by George M. Kahin. Second ed., Ithaca: Cornell, 1963. P. 3-149. A balanced summary of modern Chinese history, the rise to power of the Chinese Communists, and the principal developments in domestic and foreign policy to 1962. An annotated bibliography covers both historical background and China since 1949, including Taiwan. [A]

JC281 HO, KAN-CHIH. *A History of the Modern Chinese Revolution.* Peking: Foreign Languages Press, 1959. 627 p. An English translation of the official Peking version of events in China from the May 4 movement of 1919 to mid-1956. Dubious as history by Western criteria but valuable as a guide to Peking's current mythology regarding recent Chinese history: a version accepted by many Chinese, especially the young, as a generally accurate interpretation.

JC282 HO, PING-TI. *Studies on the Population of China, 1368-1953.* Cambridge: Harvard, 1959. 341 p. Based on extensive use of Chinese local histories, this monograph studies the factors affecting population growth during the past six centuries. Essentially a study in the economic history of China during Ming and Ch'ing times, this book sets the 1953 census into historical perspective and provides a solid base for assessing the relation between economic growth aspirations and demographic realities in Communist China. The author, a leading historian of China, is professor at the University of Chicago. [B]

JC283 HOLLISTER, WILLIAM W. *China's Gross National Product and Social Accounts, 1950-1957.* Glencoe, Illinois: The Free Press, 1958. 161 p. The first published technical study by a United States government economist of the expansion of mainland China's gross national product since 1950. Hollister's later preliminary GNP estimates for 1958-59 conclude that growth prospects may be quite high over the next few years, possibly about one-third higher than during the First Five Year Plan period (1953-57).

JC284 HOUN, FRANKLIN W. (HOU FU-WU). *To Change a Nation; Propaganda and Indoctrination in Communist China.* N.Y.: The Free Press of Glencoe, 1961. 250 p. A study of the propaganda dimension of political power in China, with attention to the organization and operation of the Communist propaganda apparatus, political indoctrination, and control and manipulation of the mass communications media (books, magazines, and the press; radio broadcasting; stage and motion pictures). Data drawn largely from the press and other official mainland publications. Professor of political science at the University of Massachusetts, Houn has also written *Central Government of China, 1912-1928* (1957).

JC285 HSIA, C. T. *A History of Modern Chinese Fiction, 1917-1957.* New Haven: Yale, 1961. 662 p. The most convenient general summary of modern Chinese fiction for the Western reader. Chapter 11 discusses Communist fiction during the 1928-37 decade; Chapter 18 reviews the twenty-year period from the outbreak of the Sino-Japanese War to 1957. A Yale Ph.D., Hsia teaches Chinese literature at Columbia.

JC286 HSIA, TAO-TAI. *China's Language Reforms.* New Haven: Institute of Far Eastern Languages, Yale University, Mirror Series A, No. 21, 1956. 163 p. An excellent report on Peking's initial reform of the Chinese language as of 1956. Part I deals with simplified characters, with full listings of those adopted and proposed, conversion tables, and other data; Part II discusses the 1956 draft plan for Latinization of the Chinese language. Should be supplemented by the article by Harriet C. Mills, "Language Reform in China; Some Recent Developments," *Far Eastern Quarterly*, XV, no. 4 (August 1956), p. 517-40, and by *Reform of the Chinese Written Language* (Peking: Foreign Languages Press, 1958) containing official documents and reports.

JC287 HSIEH, ALICE LANGLEY. *Communist China's Strategy in the Nuclear Era.* Englewood Cliffs, N.J.: Prentice-Hall, 1962. 204 p. A specialized RAND study, based on official published data available to early 1960, of Peking's evolving behavior in response to the emergence of nuclear weapons as an explosive new factor in world politics. The book analyzes China's growing awareness of the subject from 1954 to mid-1957, and assesses the debate over revisions in Chinese military doctrine required by the new nuclear environment. A former officer of the Department of State, Mrs. Hsieh is now a member of the social science department of RAND.

JC288 HSUEH, MU-CH'IAO and others. *The Socialist Transformation of the National Economy in China.* Peking: Foreign Languages Press, 1960. 287 p. A description by Chinese Communist officials of the process of absorbing private merchants, industrialists, handicraftsmen, and peasants into state-operated or state-controlled economic institutions. Contains some descriptive data within a framework of theoretical exposition.

JC289 HU, CH'ANG-TU and others. *China; Its People, Its Society, Its Culture.* Ed. by Hsiao Hsia. New Haven: Human Relations Area Files, 1960. 610 p. The product of a group research effort at Stanford and the U. of Washington, this HRAF handbook on mainland China provides a useful compilation of data but falls short of being a well-digested, critical, or analytic study. Chapter 12 on "Foreign Relations" includes a brief discussion of China's evolving role in the Communist bloc. Useful annotated bibliography of 47 p. [A]

JC290 HUDSON, G. F., LOWENTHAL, RICHARD, and MACFARQUHAR, RODERICK. *The Sino-Soviet Dispute.* N.Y.: Praeger, 1961. 227 p. Documentation and analysis of the Sino-Soviet ideological dispute from Khrushchev's Twentieth Congress speech (February 1956) through the Moscow statement (December 1960) issued following the meeting of 81 Communist parties. G. F. Hudson of St. Anthony's College, Oxford, provides an introduction; Lowenthal, professor at the Free University in West Berlin, analyzes the course of the dispute during 1960; and MacFarquhar, editor of the *China Quarterly*, provides introductory notes for the documents which make up the bulk of the book. [B]

JC291 HUGHES, T. J., and LUARD, D. E. T. *The Economic Development of Communist China, 1949-1960.* 2nd ed., N.Y.: Oxford, for the Royal Institute of International Affairs, 1961. 240 p. A compact factual account, based largely on official sources, of the economic growth of mainland China taking account of developments to the end of 1960. Primarily descriptive and non-statistical, the volume is especially useful for the non-economist. Describes industrial expansion as substantial; the agricultural sector, problematic. The authors were formerly in the British Treasury and Foreign Office, respectively. [B]

JC292 HUNTER, EDWARD. *Brainwashing in Red China: the Calculated Destruction of Men's Minds.* N.Y.: Vanguard, 1951. 311 p. The first description of the Communist-guided process of psychological mass coercion in China, this book popularized the term "brainwashing" (*hsi-nao*), a colloquialism not used officially on the mainland which the author quoted from Chinese informants interviewed in Hong Kong. Highly emotional in tone, this volume has been superseded by more recent studies and autobiographies. Hunter, an American journalist and professional anti-Communist, has also written of the Korean War experiences in *Brainwashing; the Story of Men Who Defied It.*

JC293 ILIN, ALEKSEI I., and VORONICHEV, M. P. *Zheleznodorozhnyi transport Kitaiskoi Narodnoi Respubliki.* Moscow: Gos. transp. zhel.-dor. izd., 1959. 161 p. English ed., U.S. Joint Publications Research Service. *Railroad Transport of the Chinese People's Republic.* JPRS no. 3484. Washington: 1960. 151 p. A detailed study with numerous maps and charts showing existing and projected rail lines and other technical data.

JC294 INSTITUT FÜR ASIENKUNDE. *Die Verträge der Volksrepublik China mit anderen Staaten.* Frankfurt/Main: Metzner, 1957. 106 p. Provides a useful calendar of bilateral and multilateral treaties and other agreements, with selected texts, covering the years 1950-57.

JC295 INSTITUT FÜR ASIENKUNDE. *Die wirtschaftliche Verflechtung der Volksrepublik China mit der Sowjetunion.* Frankfurt/Main and Berlin: Metzner, 1959. 106 p. Surveys Sino-Soviet relations during the 1949-58 period. Five chapters cover: development of economic relations; currency, exchange, and payments problems; Soviet credits; Soviet aid to Chinese industrialization; and Soviet-built plants in China (with map showing locations). Appendix contains a chronology, translations of five Sino-Soviet agreements, and detailed foreign trade statistics not easily available in any other single source.

JC296 JACKSON, W. A. DOUGLAS. *The Russo-Chinese Borderlands; Zone of Peaceful Contact or Potential Conflict.* Princeton: Van Nostrand, Searchlight Books, no. 2, 1962. 126 p. A political-geographical assessment of the vast border zone lying between Russia and China, describing the physical geography and historical contacts down to the Second World War, discussing post-1945 developments and recent Sino-Soviet policies, and analyzing the current strategic situation in the light of Halford Mackinder's Heartland concept. The study is based largely on secondary sources, though reference was also made to Soviet statistical handbooks and other Russian materials, and to some primary sources on Mongolia and Sinkiang. The author, Canadian by birth, has traveled in the USSR and Mongolia and is a professor of geography at the University of Washington.

JC297 *Jen-min shou-ts'e.* Peking: 1950-52; Tientsin: 1953. Annual. Though never an official publication, the *People's Handbook* has been widely regarded as the standard Chinese-language reference volume published in the People's Republic of China. First issued in 1950 by the Shanghai *Ta Kung Pao*, one of China's major national newspapers, the work is very valuable for accurate and systematically organized documentation and statistical data. Issued annually from 1950 through 1958, except for 1954 (when data on the National People's Congress of that year were held over and published in the 1955 edition). Since 1959, the *Jen-min shou-ts'e* is no longer easily acquired outside China. [A]

JC297A JOHNSON, CHALMERS A. *Peasant Nationalism and Communist Power: the Emergence of Revolutionary China, 1937-1945.* Stanford: Stanford University Press, 1962. 256 p. Background analysis of the manner in which the Communist Party's rise to power in China flowed from the chaos created by the Japanese invasion (1937-45) and from the efficiency with which the Communists responded to that crisis and effectively mobilized peasant nationalism for their own political purposes. The author, who teaches political science at the University of California, Berkeley, has made extensive use of Japanese source materials. [A]

JC298 JONES, FRANCIS P. *The Church in Communist China; a Protestant Appraisal.* N.Y.: Friendship Press, 1962. 180 p. A balanced analysis of the situation of the Chinese Christian church under Communism, suggesting that the outside world should not dismiss that church as either non-existent or apostate. The author comments candidly on the effects of denominationalism in foreign mission work, weighs the social reform accomplishments of the Peking government, and assesses the doctrinal tensions between Marxism-Leninism and Protestant Christianity. Dr. Jones served as a Methodist missionary in China from 1915 to 1951.

JC299 KALB, MARVIN L. *Dragon in the Kremlin; a Report on the Russian-Chinese Alliance.* N.Y.: Dutton, 1961. 258 p. A journalistic appraisal of the Sino-Soviet alliance by the Moscow correspondent of the Columbia Broadcasting System. Kalb suggests that Khrushchev confronts serious problems in attempting to moderate and modulate the policies of his giant Chinese partner and concludes that a period of continuing intramural disagreement between Moscow and Peking is probable. Hastily written, this book is marred by many factual errors and much loose interpretation.

JC300 KARDELJ, EDVARD. *Socialism and War; a Survey of Chinese Criticism of the Policy of Coexistence.* Belgrade: Jugoslavija, 1960. 210 p. Yugoslavia's principal writer on ideological matters presents Belgrade's official (1960) rebuttal to Chinese Communist attacks on its foreign policy. The author holds firmly to the concept of peaceful coexistence between states with differing social systems.

JC301 KIESEWETTER, BRUNO. *Der Ostblock; Aussenhandel des östlichen Wirtschaftsblockes einschliesslich China.* Berlin: Safari-Verlag, 1960. 386 p. A substantial study describing and analyzing the pattern of foreign trade and economic aid within the Communist international system, including discussion of the special position of China. Based largely on official Russian sources, this book gives detailed trade statistics, in both physical units and value, for selected years: 1938, and 1948-59. Professor of Economics at the Free University of Berlin (West) and director of the East European division, Deutsches Institut für Wirtschaftsforschung, Kiesewetter has written widely on bloc economic planning and problems.

JC302 KISSINGER, HENRY A. *Nuclear Weapons and Foreign Policy.* N.Y.: Harper, for the Council on Foreign Relations, 1957. 463 p. Kissinger's study offers an excellent background discussion of Soviet and Chinese Communist political and military doctrine in chapter 10, "The Strategy of Ambiguity—Sino-Soviet Strategic Thought."

JC303 KLEIN, SIDNEY. *The Pattern of Land Reform Tenure in East Asia after World War II.* N.Y.: Bookman Associates, 1958. 260 p. A detailed examination of post-1945 land reform legislation in East Asia emphasizing economic patterns and consequences as determined by the political objectives of the regimes promoting reform or seeking peasant support. Programs in three areas discussed (Japan, Taiwan, and South Korea) were in varying degrees American-influenced; two others (North Korea and mainland China) were Communist-controlled. Much factual data, plus a statistical appendix of some 50 tables.

JC304 KO, CHIH-TA. *Kuo-tu shih-ch'i ti Chung-kuo yü-suan.* N.P.: 1957. 170 p. Russian ed., Moscow: Gosfinizdat, 1958. 250 p. English ed., U.S. Joint Publications Research Service. *China's Budget during the Transition Period.* JPRS no. 591-D. Washington: 1959. 205

p. Written by a mainland expert on public finance and banking, this detailed work covers the nature and composition of state budgets in Communist China.

JC305 KRÜGER, KARL. *Der Ostblock; die Produktion des östlichen Wirtschaftsblockes einschliesslich China, nach dem Schwerpunktprogramm.* Berlin: Safari-Verlag, 1960. 395 p. An economic study analyzing the pattern of industrial production in the Communist bloc, including China. Based largely on official Soviet sources, this volume summarizes the production situation in individual countries, as well as comparative advantage and bloc integration. A specialist in industrial production, Krüger is professor of economics at the (West) Berlin Polytechnical School.

JC306 KUAN, TA-TUNG. *The Socialist Transformation of Capitalist Industry and Commerce in China.* Peking: Foreign Languages Press, 1960. 133 p. A theoretical discussion, written by a Peking official, of the socialization of private business and industry in China, with some descriptive detail woven into the discourse.

JC307 KUO, PING-CHIA (KUO PIN-CHIA). *China; New Age and New Outlook.* N.Y.: Knopf, 1956. 231 p. A Chinese scholar, now resident in the United States, with sincere but conflicting sympathies assesses the process of revolution in China during the century since the Taiping rebellion and weighs the accomplishments and weaknesses of the Communist regime. Marred by occasional lapses in reading the past with present hindsight and by erratic treatment of Peking's foreign policy, the book's faults may be attributed as much to the author's circumstances as an expatriate as to its analytic shortcomings.

JC308 LAVALEE, LEON, NOIROT, PAUL, and DOMINIQUE, VICTOR. *Économie de la Chine socialiste.* Geneva: Éditions Librairie Rousseau, 1957. 511 p. Extensive and fairly well-documented, this book presents a highly favorable account of the Chinese economic effort to 1957. A Marxist interpretation, with preface by Jacques Duclos, top official of the French Communist Party.

JC309 LENG, SHAO-CHUAN (LENG SHAO-CH'UAN). *Japan and Communist China.* Kyoto: Doshisha University (distributed by the Institute of Pacific Relations), 1958. 168 p. A University of Virginia professor presents a survey and analysis of the evolving relations between Japan and the People's Republic of China since 1949. On balance, the author foresees continuing unofficial ties and some trade expansion. The major problem is whether Japan's basic pro-Western orientation will be affected by improved relations between Tokyo and Peking.

JC310 LEWIS, JOHN WILSON. *Leadership in Communist China.* Ithaca: Cornell University Press, 1963. 305 p. A solid study of the manner in which the Communist elite controls Chinese society through the blending of Marxist-Leninist doctrine with practical leadership techniques attuned to the Chinese environment. Based on careful coverage of primary materials, especially for the 1958-61 period, the work concludes that the "mass line," the cadre apparatus, and the chain of command based on "democratic centralism" complement one another to form an effective "dialectical synthesis." The author teaches government at Cornell University. [A]

JC311 LI, CHOH-MING. *Economic Development of Communist China; an Appraisal of the First Five Years of Industrialization.* Berkeley: U. of California, 1959. 284 p. Director of the Center of Chinese Studies at the University of California, C. M. Li attempts an analysis of the process of economic growth during the First Five Year Plan (1953-57). Presented as a case study of the mechanism of economic development in a low-income, agricultural country intent upon rapid and concentrated industrial expansion, the book actually ranges over almost every major aspect of mainland China's economy. Professor Li's interpretations are incisive, though he remains basically skeptical of the reliability of the quantitative data from which his analysis derives. [A]

JC312 LI, CHOH-MING. *The Statistical System of Communist China.* Berkeley: U. of California, 1962. 161 p. An objective attempt to evaluate the quality of official statistics by analyzing the development and inner working of the system producing them. The approach is historical, starting with the pre-Communist period, and dividing the years since 1949 into three periods: (a) the foundation of the state statistical system (1952-57), (b) the period of decentralization (1958-59), and (c) subsequent efforts at reorganization. Professor Li's hard-headed study of the development of a national statistical system in China is particularly instructive in delineating both the obstacles to such development that may be expected in a densely populated, largely agricultural country and the measures adopted to overcome them.

JC313 LI, FU-CH'UN. *Report on the First Five-Year Plan for Development of the National Economy of the People's Republic of China in 1953-1957.* Peking: Foreign Languages Press, 1955. 135 p. An official report on the fundamental goals and problems involved in Peking's First Five Year Plan. This report was delivered in July 1955 at the second session of the First National People's Congress by Li Fu-ch'un, Vice Premier and chairman of the State Planning Commission.

JC314 LIFTON, ROBERT J. *Thought Reform and the Psychology of Totalism; a study of "Brainwashing" in China.* N.Y.: Norton, 1961. 510 p. Interview data gathered by a psychiatrist in Hong Kong (1954-55) describing and analyzing experiences of 25 Westerners expelled from China after serving prison terms and of 15 Chinese refugees from Communism. Strongly influenced by Erik Erikson's work on ego identity theory and the individual personality in relation to social change, the book also probes the cultural patterns underlying Peking's thought reform program: the modern totalitarian expression of the national genius of the Chinese in manipulating inter-personal relations. [B]

JC315 LINDSAY, MICHAEL (LORD LINDSAY OF BIRKER). *China and the Cold War; a Study in International Politics*. N.Y. and London: Cambridge: Carlton, Victoria, Australia: Melbourne U., 1955. 286 p. An English liberal who worked with the Chinese Communists at Yenan attempts to analyze the apparent conflicts in their international outlook since 1949. The book argues that Peking's recent foreign policies do not conform either to Chinese needs or to international realities and are, therefore, fundamentally irrational. [B]

JC316 LONDON, KURT, ed. *Unity and Contradiction; Major Aspects of Sino-Soviet Relations*. N.Y.: Praeger, 1962. 464 p. In September 1960, 36 scholars from 11 countries met near Tokyo at the third international conference on Sino-Soviet bloc affairs. In this volume Kurt London, one of the chief organizers of the conference and director of the Sino-Soviet program at George Washington University, has selected and edited nineteen of the most provocative papers and written a concluding chapter himself. Useful for all serious students of contemporary Communist affairs.

JC316A LUARD, EVAN. *Britain and China*. Baltimore: The Johns Hopkins Press, 1962. 256 p. A thoughtful British appraisal of the evolution and rationale of British relations with the People's Republic, drawn against the background of diplomatic, missionary, and trading contacts during the nineteenth century and the first half of the twentieth. The first of a series sponsored by the Leverhulme Trust, the volume views the growing power of China as "perhaps the most significant event within the present generation." Prior to the Suez invasion of 1956, Luard was a member of the British Foreign Service.

JC317 MACFARQUHAR, RODERICK. *The Hundred Flowers Campaign and the Chinese Intellectuals*. N.Y.: Praeger, 1960. 324 p. Largely a documentary review, with editorial commentary, of the brief course of the Hundred Flowers spasm in early 1957, when the intellectuals were encouraged to speak out in criticism of the Peking regime, and of the repressive "anti-rightist" aftermath. The record bears ample testimony to the essential naivete of the Chinese scholar under Communism. MacFarquhar edits *The China Quarterly* in London.

JC318 MAGNIEN, MARIUS. *Au Pays de Mao-Tsé-Toung*. Paris: Éditions sociales, 1952. 351 p. Russian ed., Moscow: Izd. inostr. lit.,

1953. 400 p. Report of four months' travel in China in 1950. Preface by Marcel Cachin, veteran French Communist leader.

JC319 MAO, TSE-TUNG. "Maoism, a Sourcebook; Selections from the Writings of Mao Tse-tung." Los Angeles: U. of California, 1952. 142 p. (mimeographed). A sourcebook prepared by Prof. Arthur Steiner for one of his courses.

JC320 MAO, TSE-TUNG. *Mao Tse-tung hsuan-chi.* Peking: 1952-1960. 4 vols. English eds., *Selected Works.* London: Lawrence and Wishart; N.Y.: International Publishers, 1954—; Peking: Foreign Languages Press, 1961—. Russian ed., Moscow: Izd. inostrannoi lit., 1952—. Slightly tailored since their original appearance, Mao's writings since 1926 are now required reading for over 17 million members of the Communist Party in China and for all serious students of Chinese Communism elsewhere in the world. Significant for the political and strategic concepts involved, Mao's speeches and articles are also interesting since they often preserve in translation the pungent prose for which Chinese Communism's most influential spokesman is widely known in his own country. Possible confusion regarding the Chinese and English versions of the *Selected Works* makes an explanatory note desirable. To date, Mao's writings from 1926 through September 1949 have been edited and published in the current standard Chinese edition in four volumes, as follows: I (July 1952), II (August 1952), III (May 1953), and — following a notable delay — IV (September 1960). In April 1961, the Foreign Languages Press in Peking published an English translation (labeled Vol. IV) identical in contents with the Chinese Vol. IV, adding an announcement that English-language versions of the Chinese volumes I, II, and III are underway. When Peking publishes these translations, the current official Chinese and English versions of Mao's *Selected Works* will be available in a uniform edition. Bibliographical confusion now arises because translations of the first *four* Chinese volumes have already been published outside China in *five* English-language volumes by International Publishers (New York) and Lawrence and Wishart (London). [A]

JC321 MAO, TSE-TUNG. *On the Correct Handling of Contradictions among the People.* Peking: Foreign Languages Press, 1957. 69 p. Mao's well-publicized speech made at the February 1957 meeting of the Supreme State Conference but only released the following June. While the speech attracted international attention at the time, its conceptual antecedents may be traced back twenty years to Mao's speech, "On Contradiction," made at Yenan in August 1937. [B]

JC321A MEHNERT, KLAUS. *Peking and Moscow.* N.Y.: G. P. Putnam's Sons, 1963. 522 p. A solid introduction to the Sino-Soviet dispute by one of West Germany's most prominent authorities on the Communist world. After a thoughtful discussion of the national personalities of Russia and China, the author analyzes the origins and course of the Moscow-Peking battle to 1961, with briefer comment on the major developments of subsequent years. An English translation of the original German edition (*Peking und Moskau*, Stuttgart: Deutsche Verlags-Anstalt, 1962), this book is the product of broad experience and formidable industry, but is uneven in analytic level.

JC322 MENDE, TIBOR. *La Chine et son ombre.* Paris: Seuil, 1960. 322 p. English ed., *China and Her Shadow.* N.Y.: Coward-McCann, 1962. 360 p. Written by a University of Paris professor of political science, also the author of books on Southeast Asia and Nehru, this work is based both on travel in China and on extensive reading and analysis of documentary materials. A discerning summary of the rapid transformation of China since 1949 and of the "alarming" prospects for the rest of the world. Mende's research, however, is marred by uncritical acceptance of Peking's official data and by resulting errors of fact and interpretation.

JC322A MILBANK MEMORIAL FUND. *Population Trends in Eastern Europe, the USSR, and Mainland China.* N.Y.: Milbank Memorial Fund, 1960. 336 p. Report of the 36th annual conference of the Milbank Memorial Fund (November 1959). Papers on mainland China include: Discussion of present and prospective population (Aird), population redistribution (Orleans), manpower and industrialization, 1949-57 (Eckstein), and a concluding assessment of growth trends (Irene Taeuber and Nai-chi Wang) sounding a sober note of warning regarding the inadequacy and unreliability of population data for mainland China.

JC323 MITCHISON, LOIS. *The Overseas Chinese.* London: The Bodley Head, 1961. 93 p. The best recent handbook on the subject available in English, this essay appraises the problems, position, power, and possible future of the overseas Chinese in Southeast Asia. After a summary of Chinese emigration before 1941, the booklet discusses the dilemma of the overseas Chinese during the Second World War and since as they have been drawn by the magnetism of their ancestral culture, while being pushed or pulled toward local assimilation in the countries where they have settled.

JC324 MORAES, FRANK. *Report on Mao's China.* N.Y.: Macmillan, 1953. 212 p. An early account of a visit to China in 1952 by the well-known Indian newspaperman and analyst of world affairs. Though fundamentally critical of Communism, the author, a correspondent in Burma and China during the Second World War, offers a balanced appraisal of the appeal of Communism to the Chinese and of the rapid consolidation of political power by the Peking regime.

JC324A MU, FU-SHENG. *The Wilting of the Hundred Flowers: the Chinese Intelligentsia under Mao.* N.Y.: Praeger, 1963. 324 p. Despite its deceptive title, this book is a significant Chinese statement of the impact of contemporary Communist-puritanism on a deeply ethnocentric society in which the most conspicuous feature of the political landscape since the decay of the Manchu dynasty has been the lack of an effective social conscience. The pseudonymous author, who returned to China for a year in 1957-58, measures the situation through the eyes of a sophisticated Western-educated intellectual who, for patriotic if not Marxist reasons, respects much of what the Communists have done and seek to do in China. Though unable to forgive the Communists for their contemptuous treatment of the liberal, bourgeois minority which he himself represents, the author writes with more philosophic detachment than is generally characteristic of books on contemporary China written by expatriate Chinese. [A]

JC325 NEW YORK, MISSIONARY RESEARCH LIBRARY. "Selected Bibliography of Books, Pamphlets, and Articles on Communist China and the Christian Church in China." By Frank W. Price. *Occasional Bulletin* IX, no. 8. N.Y.: 1958. Compiled by Dr. Price when he directed the Missionary Research Library in New York, this bibliographical listing is a valuable guide to the literature on Communist China from 1948-58. Most of the entries are in English, including some English translations from the Chinese.

JC325A NOSSAL, FREDERICK. *Dateline—Peking.* N.Y.: Harcourt Brace & World, 1962. 224 p. A Canadian correspondent of the Toronto *Globe and Mail* describes his eight-month stay in Peking during the winter of 1959-60. Combining a capacity for both understanding and exasperation, his rough impressions of the Chinese social scene are often more instructive than detailed documentation might be.

JC326 ORLEANS, LEO A. *Professional Manpower and Education in Communist China.* Washington: National Science Foundation, 1961 (NSF-61-3). 260 p. This demographic study, sponsored by the National Science Foundation and prepared at the Library of Congress, examines the characteristics and training of professional manpower in relation to China's scientific and technological capabilities. Though a trail-breaking effort, this volume serves only as an introduction to the new Chinese educational system and to the profound implications of Peking's long-term commitment to trained scientific brainpower. [B]

JC326A PALOCZI-HORVATH, GEORGE. *Mao Tse-tung: Emperor of the Blue Ants.* London: Secker & Warburg, 1962. N.Y.: Doubleday,

1963. 393 p. An extravagant and sharply hostile portrayal of Mao, based on selected facts drawn from secondary sources, by a Hungarian ex-Communist now resident in England. The author's familiarity with Communism exceeds his grasp of China. Hardly an objective account, the book does not understress the fact of Mao's power, though it oversimplifies its foundations.

JC326B PANIKKAR, K. M. *In Two Chinas: Memoirs of a Diplomat.* London: Allen & Unwin, 1955. 183 p. A highly opinionated account of the author's experiences and impressions in China between 1948 and 1952 when he served as ambassador of India, accredited first to the National Government at Nanking and later to the People's Republic at Peking. Panikkar played a controversial role in the negotiations relating to Korea during the period preceding the Chinese intervention in late 1950, and in the early and abortive discussions regarding a cease-fire.

JC326C PAYNE, ROBERT. *Portrait of a Revolutionary: Mao Tse-tung.* N.Y.: Abelard-Schuman, new and revised edition, 1961. 311 p. A slightly warmed-over version of a book originally published in 1950 by a professional writer who spent the war years at Kunming and met Mao in 1946 at Yenan. Payne's portrait of the leader of the Chinese Communist Party is occasionally penetrating but often inaccurate, neither serious biography nor sound history.

JC327 PISCHEL, ENRICA COLLOTTI. *Le origini ideologiche della rivoluzione cinese.* Novara: Giulio Einaudi, 1958. 289 p. A serious review, in a Marxist framework, of modern Chinese history from the Taiping rebellion through the late nineteenth-century reform movement and Sun Yat-sen's nationalist revolution to Mao Tse-tung and the "revolution of the masses." A thorough bibliographical essay (p. 273-87) is appended, indicating heavy reliance on Peking materials (in both Chinese and English), American and European monographic works, and virtually no Russian studies. Though definitely party-line, Mrs. Pischel's book is the only solid history of modern China now available in Italian.

JC328 PRUSEK, JAROSLAV. *Die Literatur des befreiten China und ihre Volkstraditionen.* Prague: Artia, 1955. 736 p. A massive party-line work summarizing prose, poetry, drama, short stories, and folk songs in the Communist-controlled areas of China from 1942 to 1950, and emphasizing the utilitarian and propagandistic function of literature stipulated by Mao at the Yenan forum in May 1942. The book, written by the professor of Chinese literature at the University of Prague, is based principally on a collection of Chinese folk-literature published in Peking in 1949.

JC328A PURCELL, VICTOR. *China.* London: Ernest Benn, 1962. 340 p. A veteran member of the Malayan Civil Service (1921-46) now teaching at Cambridge University, Purcell probes the significance of the Chinese revolution through appraisal of the historical and social forces which have bred it. The first part of the book surveys the foundations of Chinese civilization and the course of its modern history; the final two-thirds offers a distinctly favorable treatment of post-1950 developments, with uncritical analysis of Peking's economic data and performance.

JC329 REMER, C. F. *The Trade Agreements of Communist China.* Santa Monica, Cal.: The RAND Corporation, P-2208, February 1, 1961. 130 p. An economic appraisal of the nature and significance of trade and related agreements both within the bloc (where, the author concludes, they have promoted bloc solidarity without bringing Communist China under requirements for intra-bloc integration) and with the Free World (where they have been employed as a divisive influence but where their absence has not been permitted to interfere seriously with trade required to promote Chinese industrialization). Sources include all available data and translations.

JC330 REMER, C. F., ed. *Three Essays on the International Economics of Communist China.* Ann Arbor: Center for Japanese Studies and the Department of Economics, University of Michigan, 1959. 221 p. Assisted by two young economists, a senior American student of Chinese economics presents three essays discussing Peking's foreign trade policies and relations.

JC331 RICKETT, ALLYN and ADELE. *Prisoners of Liberation.* N.Y.: Cameron Associates, 1957. 288 p. A revealing autobiographical account by a young American couple who went to China in 1948 as Fulbright students. Arrested in Peking in 1951 and imprisoned for four years on espionage charges, they returned to the United States thoroughly "reformed" in outlook through Chinese Communist coercive persuasion.

JC332 RIGG, ROBERT B. (LT. COL.). *Red China's Fighting Hordes.* Harrisburg, Pa.: Military Service Publishing Company, 1951. 378 p. To date the only book-length account of the organization, personnel, and tactics of the Chinese Communist military machine up to the beginning stages of the Korean War. Loosely organized and journalistic in style, this volume nevertheless pioneered the field. Colonel Rigg had extensive wartime service in the Middle East and post-war experience as assistant military attaché in China and Manchuria, where he was once briefly captured by the Communists.

JC333 ROSTOW, WALT W. and others. *The Prospects for Communist China.* Cambridge: Technology Press of M.I.T.; N.Y.: Wiley;

London: Chapman & Hall, 1954. 379 p. The product of a Rostow-directed group research effort at the Center for International Studies of M. I. T., this volume attempts to assess the early political record of the Peking regime, to estimate its economic position and potentialities, and to offer prescriptions for United States policy. Alexander Eckstein's chapters on the conditions and prospects for economic growth in Communist China are notable. Contains an exhaustive (48-page) bibliography of Western-language materials available as of mid-1954. [B]

JC334 ROY, CLAUDE. *Clefs pour la Chine.* Paris: Gallimard, 1953. 353 p. A prominent French intellectual attempts a cosmic view of China, past and present, following a trip there. Then a member of the Communist Party (he left it after the Hungarian affair), Roy presents some excessively partisan views, some lengthy and unoriginal digressions on modern Chinese history, but also some exceedingly perceptive comments on the attitudes of young Chinese Communists, whom he was able to observe at close range as a foreign comrade.

JC334A SCHEIN, EDGAR H., with Inge Schneier and Curtis H. Barker. *Coercive Persuasion: a Socio-Psychological Analysis of the "Brainwashing" of American Civilian Prisoners by the Chinese Communists.* N.Y.: W. W. Norton, 1961. 320 p. A study of the pattern of indoctrination of American civilians imprisoned by the Chinese Communists between 1950 and 1956. This appraisal of the process of thought reform as administered by the Communists stresses the fanatical belief of the captors versus the political and moral ambivalence of the Western prisoners. An academic psychologist, the author lacks practical experience in China and with the Chinese to enliven his abstract assessment of individual behavior under conditions of extreme stress.

JC334B SCHRAM, STUART R. *The Political Thought of Mao Tse-tung.* N.Y.: Praeger, 1963. 319 p. A scholarly presentation of many of Mao's writings, including his most recent texts and some never before translated, prefaced by a solid analytical introduction by the author. Schram has carefully checked primary sources, and offers new data and insights beyond the *ex post facto* version set forth in the present official edition of Mao's *Selected Works.* A brief chronology and bibliographical essay are appended. [A]

JC334C SCHUMAN, JULIAN. *Assignment China.* N.Y.: Whittier Books, 1956. 249 p. A prejudiced and platitudinous report by an American who spent six years (December 1947-November 1953) in China during the collapse of the Nationalists and the early consolidation of power by the Communists. The author's frustration with United States policy and his caustic comments on allegedly slanted handling of China news in the American press are offset by uncritical acceptance of all aspects of Mao's rule in China.

JC334D SCOTT, A. C. *Literature and the Arts in Twentieth Century China.* N.Y.: Doubleday Anchor Books, 1963. 212 p. A perceptive survey of literary and artistic trends and personalities in China since the patriotic May Fourth movement of 1919, which launched the New Culture movement. The author, an English artist who has written widely on the arts in China and Japan, is now Professor of Speech at the University of Wisconsin. [B]

JC335 SERRUYS, PAUL L-M. *Survey of the Chinese Language Reform and the Anti-Illiteracy Movement in Communist China.* Berkeley: University of California, Center for Chinese Studies, Studies in Chinese Communist Terminology No. 8, February 1962. 208 p. A scholarly survey of the most complex and extensive language reform effort in modern Chinese history. This monograph indicates that the Chinese Communist authorities, beneath a heavy cover of propaganda slogans, are seeking solutions to the intricate problems involved along lines which are essentially pragmatic and empirical, with professional advice from linguistic scientists and literary scholars. Based on a wide variety of Chinese sources, as well as relevant materials in Japanese, Russian, and English.

JC336 SHABAD, THEODORE. *China's Changing Map; a Political and Economic Geography of the Chinese People's Republic.* N.Y.: Praeger, 1956. 295 p. Parallel to the author's *Geography of the USSR* (1951), this is a reference compilation detailing changes in political and economic geography during the first five years of Communist rule in China. Data gathered from Chinese and Soviet newspapers, periodicals, and atlases are, however, used uncritically; and China's map has continued to change radically since 1956.

JC336A SKINNER, G. WILLIAM. *Leadership and Power in the Chinese Community of Thailand.* Ithaca: Cornell University Press, 1958. 363 p. A detailed professional study of the leadership of the overseas Chinese community in Thailand, the country with the largest Chinese population of any political unit in Southeast Asia. This book was prepared on the basis of an initial survey in 1952, followed by further field work in Bangkok in 1955. Skinner, professor of anthropology at Cornell, is also the author of *Chinese Society in Thailand, an Analytic History* (1957).

JC336B SNOW, EDGAR. *The Other Side of the River: Red China Today.* N.Y.: Random House, 1962. 810 p. A massive, hearty, and generally rosy account of China in 1960 by the author of *Red Star Over China* (1937), the classic reportorial account of the Chinese Communists when they were insurgents in the countryside. Though its interpretations often err on the side of accepting the Chinese Communists at their own self-evaluation, the book nevertheless has the merit of depicting China as a real place inhabited by real people. [A]

JC337 SORICH, RICHARD, ed. *Contemporary China; a Bibliography of Reports on China Published by the United States Joint Publications Research Service.* N.Y.: Prepared for the Joint Committee on Contemporary China of the American Council of Learned Societies and the Social Science Research Council, 1961. 99 p. A comprehensive bibliography of translated reports on China prepared by JPRS, the centralized, unclassified translation service for U.S. government offices. Covers the period from the inception of JPRS in late 1957 through July 1960.

JC338 STEINER, H. ARTHUR. "Communist China in the World Community." *International Conciliation*, no. 533, May 1961, p. 389-454. N.Y.: Carnegie Endowment for International Peace. Pointing out that Peking's foreign policy is based on the twin foundations of Marxist-Leninist ideology and Chinese national interest, the author discusses the relations of the People's Republic with the USSR and with selected non-Communist states in Asia (India and Indonesia), as well as Chinese attitudes toward war and disarmament, Taiwan, the United Nations, and international affairs generally. This pamphlet may be supplemented by the paper by H. L. Boorman, "Peking in World Politics," *Pacific Affairs*, vol. 34, no. 3 (Fall 1961), p. 227-241, which discusses Chinese moves in the Middle East, Africa, and Latin America since 1955.

JC339 STEINER, H. ARTHUR, ed. *Chinese Communism in Action.* Parts I-III. Los Angeles, UCLA Student Store, 1953. 313 p. (mimeographed). A well-organized collection of documents of the Chinese Communist regime, in English translation, covering the initial years of Peking's rule. Steiner, Professor of Political Science at the University of California, Los Angeles, has also provided introductions and editorial comment.

JC340 STEVENSON, WILLIAM. *The Yellow Wind.* Boston: Houghton Mifflin, 1959. 424 p. A rambling report by a Canadian journalist on Communist China and some of its border areas, where the author was able to travel between 1954 and 1957. Though under-organized and sometimes over-dramatized, the book is nevertheless serious and informative.

JC341 SUMMERS, MARVIN R. "Chinese Communist Attitudes toward the Soviet Union and Sino-Soviet Relations." Ph.D. dissertation, University of Iowa, 1953. 246 p.

JC342 TANG, PETER S. H. (T'ANG SHENG-HAO). *Communist China Today; Domestic and Foreign Policies.* N.Y.: Praeger; London:

Thames & Hudson, 1957. 536 p. Rev., enl. ed., Washington: Research Institute on the Sino-Soviet Bloc, 1961. 745 p. A useful general survey of the development and operation of Communist rule in China, based on Chinese, Russian, and Western materials. The volume is reasonably comprehensive, often controversial, and generally better in exposition than in social analysis. Intellectually, it follows the American opposition line which stresses the essential identity of Chinese and Soviet long-range aims and aspirations. A Columbia Ph.D., the author now directs the Research Institute on the Sino-Soviet Bloc. [A]

JC343 TANG, PETER S. H. (T'ANG SHENG-HAO). *Communist China Today*, Vol. II: *Chronological and Documentary Supplement.* N.Y.: Praeger, 1958. 137 p. A regrettably slim volume giving a sketchy chronology on the rise and operation of Communism in China (1918-56), the 1954 government constitution, and a listing of members of the central apparatus of the Party as of late 1956.

JC344 *Ten Glorious Years.* Peking: Foreign Languages Press, 1960. 368 p. Translations of nineteen articles written by Liu Shao-ch'i, Chou En-lai, Lin Piao, Teng Hsiao-p'ing, and other senior Party and government figures in Peking in celebration of the tenth anniversary of the founding of the People's Republic of China (October 1, 1959).

JC345 *Ten Great Years.* Peking: Foreign Languages Press, 1960. 223 p. A translation of the Chinese work (September 1959) compiled by the State Statistical Bureau in Peking on "economic and cultural achievements" of the People's Republic of China during its first decade. The most comprehensive official data yet available in English on area and population; socialization of the economy; the communes; capital construction; industrial output; agricultural production; transportation and communications; domestic and foreign trade; the labor force; education; and living standards. [A]

JC346 THOMAS, S. B. *Government and Administration in Communist China.* 2nd ed., revised. N.Y.: Institute of Pacific Relations, 1955. 196 p. A detailed and documented study of the political and administrative structure of the People's Republic of China through the governmental reorganization and new constitution of September 1954. Though dated, this remains a valuable account of the interaction of political ideology and political organization in post-1949 China. [B]

JC347 TOWNSEND, PETER. *China Phoenix; the Revolution in China.* London: Jonathan Cape, 1955. 406 p. Thoroughly sympathetic to the Communists, but written with real knowledge of conditions in rural China both before and immediately after the takeover. Townsend went to west China in 1941 with the Friends Ambulance Unit, later worked with the Chinese Industrial Cooperatives, and remained on the mainland during the honeymoon interlude following the Communist victory.

JC347A TSOU, TANG. *America's Failure in China, 1941-1950.* Chicago: University of Chicago Press, 1963. 614 p. A discriminating and lucid account of the American involvement in China which ended with the Communist conquest of power in that country. The author, China-born but now an American citizen teaching political science at the University of Chicago, has written a first-class study of a complex and emotion-ridden subject. [A]

JC348 TSOU, TANG. *The Embroilment over Quemoy: Mao, Chiang, and Dulles.* Preface by Hans J. Morgenthau. Salt Lake City: Institute of International Studies, University of Utah, International Study Paper No. 2, 1959. 47 p. A University of Chicago political scientist presents a brief but sophisticated analysis of the refractory offshore islands dilemma. Tsou assesses the strategic and tactical thinking of both Mao Tse-tung and Chiang Kai-shek, and evaluates Dulles' policies pursued during the 1958 Quemoy crisis within the limits set by the Chinese.

JC349 UNION RESEARCH INSTITUTE. *Communist China, 1949-1959.* Hong Kong: Union Research Institute, 1961. 3 vols. A compendium summarizing developments during the first ten years of the People's Republic, anti-Communist in tone. Volume I deals with the Communist party; political and legal work; agricultural production; economic affairs; the "socialist transformation of agriculture"; petroleum and electric power; military affairs; and propaganda. Volume II covers grain purchase and distribution; foreign relations; and industrial production. Volume III summarizes China's foreign trade; labor unions; education; and art and literature.

JC350 U.S. BUREAU OF THE CENSUS. *The Population and Manpower of China; an Annotated Bibliography.* International Population Statistics Reports, Series P-90, no. 8. Washington: 1958. 132 p. A basic bibliography on population and manpower, prepared by the Foreign Manpower Research Office, U.S. Bureau of the Census. Compiled primarily from holdings of the Library of Congress, the volume gives an extensive listing of works in English, Chinese, Japanese, Russian, and other languages.

JC351 U.S. BUREAU OF THE CENSUS. *The Size, Composition, and Growth of the Population of Mainland China.* International Population Statistics Reports, Series P-90, no. 15. Washington: 1961. 100 p. A demographic study analyzing the 1953 census and the system of population registers. Adjusted statistical data provide the basis for estimates of age and sex structure, and rate of population growth; as well as for a five-year projection of the mainland population, by age and sex, from June 1953, the census date, to June 1958. Summarizing data available as of January 1961, this report includes tables, graphs, and bibliographical references. [B]

JC352 U.S. CENTRAL INTELLIGENCE AGENCY. *China; Provisional Atlas of Communist Administrative Units.* Washington: Distributed by the U.S. Dept. of Commerce, Office of Technical Services, 1959. A specialized atlas providing a guide to administrative units, useful maps showing administrative divisions as of late 1958, large-scale reproductions of 25 provincial map sheets from a mainland atlas (1956), and an index listing names (about 5000) of administrative units at the *hsien* level and above as of 1957.

JC353 U.S. CENTRAL INTELLIGENCE AGENCY. *The Economy of Communist China, 1958-62.* Washington: 1960. 78 p. A U.S. government estimate of the performance and prospects of the economy during the Second Five Year Plan (1958-62). Detailed summary of the 1958 "leap forward" program (including the August 1959 "reassessment") indicates Peking's sustained preoccupation with maximum economic growth as a central national goal. Estimates that the rate of growth in GNP is likely to be substantially higher than during the First Five Year Plan (1953-57). Statistical tables appended.

JC354 U.S. CONGRESS, SENATE, COMMITTEE ON FOREIGN RELATIONS. "Communist China and Taiwan," by Robert A. Scalapino. In *United States Foreign Policy, Compilation of Studies* Nos. 1-8, p. 515-551. Washington: G.P.O., 1960. An informed summary of Chinese Communist domestic and foreign policies as of 1959. Scalapino, professor of political science at the University of California, wrote this section of Report No. 5, *United States Foreign Policy: Asia*, submitted to the Senate Committee on September 1, 1959 by Conlon Associates, Ltd., San Francisco. [B]

JC355 U.S. DEPARTMENT OF AGRICULTURE. *Communist China's Agriculture.* Foreign Agricultural Service, Foreign Agricultural Report No. 115. Washington: 1959. 50 p. A brief summary and analysis of agriculture in mainland China: production, trade, and policy developments as they affect United States farm products in world markets.

JC356 U.S. DEPARTMENT OF STATE. *Directory of Party and Government Officials of Communist China.* Dept. of State, BD No. 271. Washington: 1960. 2 vols. Prepared by the Biographic Information Division, Dept. of State, this work provides (in vol. I) a comprehensive directory of organizations and institutions, with incumbents of all positions, and (in vol. II) an alphabetical index of all personal names. Based on Chinese Communist published sources, it incorporates information available to June 1960. A biographic directory, not a biographic dictionary.

JC357 U.S. DEPARTMENT OF STATE. *The Sino-Soviet Economic Offensive in the Less Developed Countries.* Dept. of State Pub. 6632. Washington: 1958. 111 p. An undocumented government study providing data to early 1958 on the bloc's program of trade, aid, and technical assistance aimed at the emerging nations. Part I discusses bloc objectives (primarily political), capabilities, and methods; Part II describes the Sino-Soviet offensive in individual countries of the Middle East, South and Southeast Asia, and Africa.

JC358 U.S. DEPARTMENT OF STATE. *The Thought of Mao Tse-tung, a Selected List of References to the Published Works and Statements Attributed to Mao Tse-tung and to the Literature on the Chinese Communist Leader.* Washington: Dept. of State, Bureau of Intelligence and Research, External Research Paper 138, April 1962. 73 p. This bibliography provides an extensive and well-organized listing of Mao's writings, supplemented with a guide to sources which provide interpretation or critical discussion of Mao works. A useful tool for serious students of "the thought of Mao Tse-tung."

JC359 U.S. DEPARTMENT OF THE ARMY. *Communist China; Ruthless Enemy or Paper Tiger? A Bibliographic Survey.* Washington: Headquarters, Department of the Army, Pamphlet no. 20-61, January 1962. 137 p. Somewhat chaotic in organization and uncritical in annotation, this unclassified bibliography is nevertheless useful because of its listing of periodical articles, including those in military journals. Appendices include a Russian-language bibliography on the Chinese Communist army, a bibliography on the Korean War, and useful organization charts and maps.

JC360 UTLEY, FREDA. *The China Story.* Chicago: Regnery, 1951. 274 p. A polemical criticism of American policy in China from the Yalta Conference to the Korean War. The author argues that the U.S. lost China because of its failure to provide adequate support to the Nationalist Government and its fundamental misunderstanding of the nature and aims of the international Communist conspiracy. British by birth, Mrs. Utley lived in the Soviet Union for several years during the early 1930's with her Russian husband; in recent years she has been re-born in the U.S. and is now consistently anti-Communist.

JC361 VAN DER SPRENKEL, OTTO B., ed. *New China; Three Views by Otto B. Van der Sprenkel, Robert Guillain, and Michael Lindsay.* London: Turnstile, 1950. 241 p.

JC362 WALKER, RICHARD L. *China Under Communism; the First Five Years.* New Haven: Yale, 1955; London: Allen & Unwin,

1956. 403 p. German ed., 1956. A five-year report surveying the impact of Communism on mainland China and the Chinese. The book presents a pessimistic picture drawn from a distance, strongly hostile to Peking's ruthless policies and critical of Western failure to comprehend Peking's aggressive and total threat to Western international security interests. Based largely on official Chinese sources and translations. Walker, professor at the U. of South Carolina, has updated his appraisal of Peking's problems and prospects in *The Continuing Struggle: Communist China and the Free World* (N.Y.: Athene, 1958. 155 p.). [B]

JC363 WANG, CHI. *Mainland China; Organizations of Higher Learning in Science and Technology and Their Publications, a Selected Guide.* Washington: Library of Congress, 1961. 104 p. A comprehensive guide, compiled in the Science and Technology Division of the Library of Congress, identifying and describing scientific organizations and publications in Communist China. Includes learned societies, colleges and universities, the Academy of Sciences and related research institutes, other government research organizations, and libraries. Bibliographical data covers serial publications of these organizations, abstracting and indexing services, and dictionaries. May be supplemented by Joseph C. Kun, *Higher Educational Institutions of Communist China, 1953-1958; a Cumulative List* (Center for International Studies, Massachusetts Institute of Technology, December 1961, 47 p.).

JC364 WANG, CHUN-HENG. *A Simple Geography of China.* Peking: Foreign Languages Press, 1958. 256 p. Concentrating on physical and economic geography, this relatively non-political work from Peking contains 47 useful maps showing locations of industries and natural resources, as well as geographic features.

JC365 WARNER, DENIS. *Hurricane from China.* N.Y.: Macmillan, 1961. 210 p. A veteran Australian correspondent provides a shrewd, somewhat sensationalized study of the anatomy of Communist China. He sees the regime solidly in power and Peking's international influence likely to grow steadily as Mao Tse-tung transfers to the international theater the strategic principles which he evolved in fighting Chiang Kai-shek within China.

JC365A WEI, HENRY. *China and Soviet Russia.* Princeton: Van Nostrand, 1956. 379 p. A painstaking recapitulation of the post-1917 record of Sino-Russian relations in the most formal sense. Adds few facts to the known record, eschews interpretive analysis, and generally ignores domestic political and social dynamics in either China or Russia during these turbulent decades. Based on English and Chinese sources, the book also appends selected documents from the 1937-50 period.

JC365B WHITING, ALLEN S. "China." In *Modern Political Systems: Asia*, ed. by Robert E. Ward and Roy C. Macridis. Englewood Cliffs, N.J.: Prentice-Hall, 1963. P. 115-214. The most sophisticated survey now available of the Chinese Communist system of governance, this section forms one part of a comparative politics textbook also covering Japan, India, Southeast Asia, and Southwest Asia. Whiting, now director of the Office of Research and Analysis for the Far East in the Department of State, appraises the historical background, Chinese Communist ideology, the Chinese Communist party, the Party and the organs of government, governmental performance, and problems and prospects of the regime. [A]

JC366 WHITING, ALLEN S. *China Crosses the Yalu; the Decision to Enter the Korean War.* N.Y.: Macmillan, for the RAND Corporation, 1960. 219 p. Examines available contemporary data to assess the reasons which motivated Peking's policy makers to decide on military intervention in Korea. A critical review of the interaction between Sino-Soviet moves and United States actions in August-September 1950, followed by Peking's decision to commit its power in the massive Chinese counter-offensive of November 1950. A RAND study, this book attempts to relate the specific experience of the Korean conflict to the broader problem of limited war. [B]

JC367 WILBUR, C. MARTIN. "Japan and the Rise of Communist China." In: Hugh Borton and others, *Japan between East and West*, p. 199-239. New York: Harper, for the Council on Foreign Relations, 1957. A balanced discussion of Sino-Japanese relations since 1949 and of the Japanese image of the People's Republic of China, based on field work in Japan and documentary research. This paper was prepared for a 1955-56 Council on Foreign Relations study group. Wilbur is professor of Chinese history and Director of the East Asian Institute at Columbia University.

JC367A WOLLASTON, NICHOLAS. *China in the Morning: Impressions of a Journey through China and Indo-China.* London: Jonathan Cape, 1960. 208 p. An account of an independent trip to China in 1958 by an alert traveler with discrimination and a sense of humor. Wollaston's appreciation of the determined Chinese efforts to solve their problems is tempered by awareness of other, more depressing, elements: bureaucracy, suppression of individualism, deadly seriousness, vituperative anti-Western propaganda. Yet he was struck by the contrast between the dynamic energy of Communist China and the apathy, futility, and sham prosperity of the non-Communist areas of Southeast Asia.

JC368 WU, YUAN-LI. *An Economic Survey of Communist China.* N.Y.: Bookman Associates; London: Constable, 1956. 566 p. The first one-man effort at a comprehensive survey of the institutional aspects of the Chinese Communist economy and development efforts, this study stresses the coercive elements in Peking's policies. Based on official data, the work gives a detailed coverage of the rehabilitation period (1949-52) but is now outdated on the First Five Year Plan.

JC368A WU, YUAN-LI. *Economic Development and the Use of Energy Resources in Communist China.* N.Y.: Praeger, 1963. 280 p. A Hoover Institution publication, the book surveys Communist China's energy resources and the role they have played in economic development efforts since 1949. The author has compiled extensive data on China's coal and electric power industries, as well as other energy resources, examined their patterns of distribution and contribution to national income, and analyzed Communist successes and failures in these vital fields. 61 tables, 5 maps, and 17 figures.

JC369 YANG, C. K. (YANG CHING-K'UN). *The Chinese Family in the Communist Revolution.* Cambridge: The Technology Press, distributed by Harvard University Press, 1959. 246 p. A sociological analysis of the institution of the Chinese family as affected by Communism. Marriage, divorce, the position of women and younger people, economic activities, changing values and loyalties, secularization, disorganization of clans, and the effect of political indoctrination are all dealt with. Though change has been rapid under Communism, it is clear in retrospect that there had been widespread rebellion against the extended family system, especially among the youth of China, for a generation before the 1950 marriage law. [B]

JC370 YANG, C. K. (YANG CHING-K'UN). *A Chinese Village in Early Communist Transition.* Cambridge: The Technology Press, distributed by Harvard University Press, 1959. 284 p. A field study of a village in Kwangtung province in south China begun before the Communist takeover, continued after 1949, and subsequently updated on the basis of comparable, but less complete, documentary data obtained after the author left China. Though rendered obsolete by later developments, this book nevertheless has basic value as the first careful description of the actual changes in social relationships in a specific Chinese village following the advent of Communism to political power. Dr. Yang teaches sociology at the University of Pittsburgh. [B]

JC371 YIN, HELEN and YI-CHANG. *Economic Statistics of Mainland China (1949-1957).* Cambridge: distributed by Harvard University Press, 1960. 106 p. Sponsored by Harvard's East Asian Research Center, this handbook provides basic statistical data on population, national income, agriculture, industry, trade, labor, public finance, and communications and transport. Official Chinese Communist figures without analysis or interpretation.

JC372 ZAGORIA, DONALD S. *The Sino-Soviet Conflict, 1956-1961.* Princeton: Princeton University Press, 1962. 484 p. A detailed Kremlinological appraisal of the origin and evolution of the Moscow-Peking dispute from Khrushchev's unilateral down-grading of Stalin in 1956 through the Twenty-second Soviet Party Congress in late 1961. A former analyst of Communist affairs for the United States government, now at Columbia University, the author provides sound guidance through a tortuous maze of ideological polemics. He concludes that the conflict, even if it should widen into a chasm, would be unlikely to benefit the West in the long-term competition with the Communist bloc. [A]

b. IN RUSSIAN

(Edited by Robert A. Rupen)

JC373 AKADEMIIA NAUK, INSTITUT VOSTOKOVEDENIIA. *Kitaiskii sbornik, uchenye zapiski instituta vostokovedeniia, XI.* Moscow: 1955. 303 p. The Institute of Asiatic Studies frequently publishes collections of articles with this title. This particular one includes articles by L. I. Duman, V. P. Leontev, G. V. Astafev, and others, on historical and contemporary themes.

JC374 AKADEMIIA NAUK SSSR, INSTITUT EKONOMIKI. *Ekonomika KNR, 1949-1959.* Moscow: Gosplanizdat, 1959. 304 p.

JC375 ARNOLDOV, A. I., and NOVAK, G. M. *Kultura narodnogo Kitaia.* Moscow: Izd. Akademii nauk SSSR, 1959. 150 p. Considerable detail on Sino-Soviet "cultural cooperation," including visits, books published, and the like.

JC376 BUKHAROV, B. I. *Politika SShA v otnoshenii KNR (1949-1953).* Moscow: Izd. Akademii nauk SSSR, 1958. 238 p. A publication of the Institute of History, with many citations from the *New York Times* and the *Daily Worker.*

JC377 CHINA (PEOPLE'S REPUBLIC OF CHINA, 1949-), LAWS, STATUTES, ETC. *Konstitutsiia i osnovnye zakonodatelnye akty Kitaiskoi narodnoi respubliki.* Ed. by O. A. Arturov and others. Moscow: Inlitizdat, 1955. 690 p. 2nd ed. Moscow: Izd. inostrannoi literatury, 1959. 727 p. The constitution and basic laws of the Chinese People's Republic. Includes a great range of basic and useful material.

JC378 CHZHAO, I-VEN. *Promyshlennost novogo Kitaia.* Moscow: Izd. inostrannoi lit., 1959. 173 p. Deals with the Chinese First Five Year Plan.

JC379 CHZHOU, FAN. *Gosudarstvennye organy Kitaiskoi narodnoi respubliki.* Moscow: Izd. inostrannoi lit., 1958. 214 p. A translation of a book published in China in 1955.

JC380 DELIUSIN, L. P., ed. *Agrarnye preobrazovaniia v narodnom Kitae; sbornik materialov.* Moscow: Inlitizdat, 1955. 389 p. Translated from the Chinese, this work includes the texts of some decrees on Chinese agriculture.

JC381 *Desiat let KNR; sbornik.* Moscow: Izd. Instituta mezhdunarodnykh otnoshenii, 1959. 244 p. Ten Soviet authors discuss major aspects of contemporary China: the Party, industry, agriculture, international relations, etc.

JC382 *Ekonomicheskie uspekhi Kitaiaskoi Narodnoi Respubliki za 1949-1953 gg; sbornik statei.* Moscow: Inlitizdat, 1954. 260 p. A collection of speeches, reports, and articles by Chinese leaders.

JC383 FOMICHEVA, M. V. *Ocherki ekonomicheskogo stroitelstva na severo-vostoke Kitaia.* Moscow: Izd. Akad. nauk, 1956. 216 p. Sponsored by the Institute of Oriental Studies. The author uses Chinese sources and concentrates on the post-1949 period.

JC384 GANSHIN, G. A. *Ekonomika Kitaiskoi narodnoi respubliki.* Moscow: Izd. IMO, 1959. 362 p. A former student in the Chinese section of the Institute of Oriental Studies, Ganshin appears to have full command of that language, and employed many Chinese statistical handbooks and other Chinese sources. A glossary of Russian economic terms with their equivalents in Chinese characters (p. 328-354) may be particularly useful. The author provides information about China's industrial labor force; a chapter contributed by A. Chekutov (of the Institute of Chinese Studies) employs Chinese sources for material on the budget, finance, and taxes. Ganshin published an earlier, shorter volume: *Kitaiskaia Narodnaia Respublika na puti sotsialisticheskoi industrializatsii*, Moscow: Gospolitizdat, 1955, 192 p. [B]

JC385 GOGOL, B. I. *Razvitie tovarooborota v Kitaiskoi narodnoi respublike.* Moscow: Gospolitizdat, 1954. 143 p. Deals with the development of Chinese trade relations.

JC386 GUDOSHNIKOV, L. M. *Vysshie organy gosudarstvennoi vlasti i gosudarstvennogo upravleniia KNR.* Moscow: Izd. Akademii nauk SSSR, 1960. 110 p. Based on Chinese sources. Provides a legalistic description of the formal governmental apparatus.

JC387 IAKOVLEV, A. G. *Reshenie natsionalnogo voprosa v Kitaiskoi narodnoi respublike.* Moscow: Izd. vost. lit., 1959. 112 p. Published by the Institute of Chinese Studies. Includes a map, a useful table of all minority areas in China, and 1953 census figures for minority populations. [B]

JC388 IAN, KHIN-SHUN. *Iz istorii borby za pobedu marksizma-leninizma v Kitae.* Moscow: Gospolitizdat, 1957. 176 p.

JC389 IGNATENKO, G. V. *Sistema predstavitelnykh organov KNR.* Moscow: Gosud. izd. iuridicheskoi lit., 1959. 212 p. Considerable election information, by districts, 1954-59. Includes chronology and tables.

JC390 KAMINSKII, A. E. *Kooperirovanie selskogo khoziastva Kitaia.* Moscow: Gos. izd. selsko-khoziastvennoi lit., 1959. 166 p. Describes the size, form of organization, and the like of agricultural cooperatives.

JC391 KAZAKOV, S. V., comp. *Uspekhi Kitaiskoi Narodnoi Respubliki; rekomendatelnyi ukazatel literatury.* Moscow: 1952. 79 p. 2nd ed., 1955. 68 p. A bibliography.

JC392 *Kitai; opublikovano v 21-m tom 2 izd. Bolshoi Sovetskoi Entsiklopedii.* Moscow: 1954. 462 p. Includes an extensive political section, many maps, an index and a chronology, numerous photographs, and a bibliography.

JC393 *Kitaisko-sovetskaia druzhba; sbornik statei i dokumentov.* Peking: Nar. izd., 1952. 104 p. A collection of articles and documents dealing with Sino-Soviet friendship.

JC394 KLOPOV, S. V. *Amur – reka druzhby.* Khabarovsk: Khabarovskoe knizhnoe izd., 1959. 80 p. The author was leader of the Amur expedition of the Academy of Sciences of the USSR. He discusses the Sino-Soviet Treaty of 1956, the expedition, and meetings of the Joint Commission in Moscow (1957) and Peking (1958).

JC395 KOKAREV, N. A. *Sotsialisticheskoe preobrazovanie selskogo khoziastva v Kitae.* Moscow: Gospolitizdat, 1958. 253 p. Many statistics on Chinese agriculture.

JC396 KORKUNOV, A., KURBATOV, V., MUGRUZIN, A., and SUKHARCHUK, G. *Sotsialisticheskoe preobrazovanie selskogo khoziastva v KNR (1949-1957).* Moscow: Izd. vost. lit., 1960. 208 p. An important book on Chinese agriculture. Based on Chinese sources, and including extensive Chinese-language bibliography. [B]

JC397 KOSOLAPOV, A. M. *Ekonomicheskii stroi KNR.* Leningrad: Izd. Leningradskogo universiteta, 1956. A text for teaching in political economy.

JC398 KOTOV, K. F. *Mestnaia natsionalnaia avtonomiia v Kitaiskoi narodnoi respublike (na primere sintszian-uigurskoi avtonomnoi oblasti).* Moscow: Gosizd. iuridicheskoi lit., 1959. 198 p. A study of Chinese nationalities policy with emphasis on formal governmental organization. Uses Chinese sources. [B]

JC399 LESHCHENKO, L. O. *Proval amerikanskoi politiki izoliatsii Kitaia.* Kiev: 1959. 137 p. Cites American sources, including the *Wall Street Journal*, *Current History*, the *Daily Worker*, and the *New York Times.*

JC400 LYSENKO, I. A. *Ekonomicheskoe sotrudnichestvo KNR so stranami sotsialisticheskogo lageria.* Moscow: Izd. vost. lit., 1960. 64 p. A very useful summary of most of the available information on economic relations between China and other Communist countries. Published for the Institute of Chinese Studies of the Academy of Sciences of the USSR. [B]

JC401 MASLENNIKOV, V. A. *Ekonomicheskii stroi Kitaiskoi narodnoi respubliki.* Moscow: Izd. Akad. nauk SSSR, 1958. 391 p. A serious study of Chinese industry, agriculture, finance, trade and transport, termed by the publishers "the first book in Soviet literature to give a broad view of the Chinese economy." The author recognizes many gaps "because the necessary materials were not available." He used Chinese as well as Russian sources; statistical information is included up to 1957. Maslennikov has worked on China for many years; he also wrote: *Kitai; politiko-ekonomicheskikh ocherk* in 1946 (see above). [A]

JC402 *Mezhdunarodnaia zhizn KNR v datakh i faktakh (khronika sobytii).* Moscow: Sotsekizdat, 1959. 203 p. Covers the period from September 30, 1949 to October 1, 1959.

JC403 MIKHEEV, V. I. *Kitai: velikaia mirovaia derzhava.* Moscow: Gospolitizdat, 1954. 68 p. Makes interesting, if antique, reading in 1962; includes a few piquant pages on "the leading role of China in Asia."

JC404 MOSCOW, NAUCHNO-ISSLEDOVATELSKII KONIUNKTURNYI INSTITUT. *Razvitie ekonomiki i vneshneekonomicheskikh sviazei Kitaiskoi narodnoi respubliki.* By Kapelinskii, Iu. N. and others. Ed. by P. K. Figurnov and M. I. Sladkovskii. Moscow: Vneshtorgizdat, 1959. 559 p. English ed., Washington: Joint Publications Research Service, no. 3234, 1960. The most important and useful single Soviet volume on the subject of the Chinese economy and economic relations with the USSR. Uses Chinese as well as Russian sources. A realistic assessment of the problems of Chinese economic development. Much specific and useful statistical material. [A]

JC405 MOSCOW, PUBLICHNAIA BIBLIOTEKA, NAUCHNO-METODICHESKII OTDEL BIBLIOTEKOVEDENIIA I BIBLIOGRAFII. *Kitaiskaia Narodnaia Respublika, rekomendatelnyi ukazatel literatury, 1949-1959*. Compiled by G. P. Bogatov and others. Edited by N. N. Solovev. Moscow: 1959. 61 p. A Soviet bibliography on Communist China.

JC406 *Nash drug Kitai; slovar-spravochnik*. Ed. by G. Shkarenkov. Moscow: Gospolitizdat, 1959. 630 p. Alphabetically arranged, with a subject index. Particularly valuable for biographical information. Maps and illustrations. [B]

JC407 *Obrazovanie Kitaiskoi Narodnoi Respubliki; dokumenty i materialy*. Moscow: Gospolitizdat, 1950. 136 p. A collection of documents, including treaties with the USSR, notes of recognition of the Chinese People's Republic by bloc and non-bloc countries, and articles from *Pravda* and *Izvestiia*.

JC408 *O kitaisko-sovetskoi druzhbe*. Peking: Izd. literatury na inostrannykh iazykakh, 1950. 65 p. Statements and speeches by Mao Tse-tung, Chu Te, Liu Shao-chi, Kuo Mo-jo, Chen Bo-dai, and Sung Ching-ling on Sino-Soviet friendship.

JC409 *Osnovnye normativnye akty o mestnykh organakh gosudarstvennoi vlasti i gosudarstvennogo upravleniia KNR; sbornik dokumentov*. Moscow: Gosiurizdat, 1959. 504 p. A collection of laws in force as of May 1, 1959. Includes significant documents establishing and governing the communes (p. 271-325). [B]

JC410 *Osnovnye svedeniia o vneshnei torgovle Kitaia*. Moscow: Vneshtorgizdat, 1961. 179 p. A survey of Communist China's foreign trade.

JC411 OVDIENKO, I. KH. *Kitai: ekonomiko-geograficheskii obzor*. Moscow: Gosudarstvennoe uchebno-pedagogicheskoe izdatelstvo ministerstva prosveshcheniia RSFSR, 1959. A handbook on the economic geography of China, with a bibliography of Russian and Chinese works.

JC412 *Pod znamenem proletarskogo internatsionalizma; sbornik materialov*. Moscow: Gospolitizdat, 1957. 312 p. Contains little concerning China, but quotes "Jenminjihpao" on the Hungarian Revolution, refers to the meeting of Hungarian, Chinese, and Soviet leaders in Moscow on January 10, 1957, and quotes the Bulganin-Chou En-lai declaration of January 18, 1957.

JC413 *Problemy razvitiia ekonomiki Kitaiskoi Narodnoi Respubliki*. Moscow: Gospolitizdat, 1958. 534 p. A translation of a wide range of important recent Chinese economic writing. Authors include scholars, officials, and Party veterans. [A]

JC414 *Razvitie narodnogo khoziastva KNR (statisticheskie pokazateli).* Moscow: Vneshtorgizdat, 1956. 51 p. A very slight statistical handbook, which does, however, contain some definitions and explanations of terms.

JC415 SHIRIAEV, N. P., comp. *Ekonomika i vneshniaia torgovlia Kitaia; spravochnik.* Ed. by V. A. Maslennikov. Moscow: 1949. 256 p. A handbook dealing with the economy and foreign trade of China.

JC416 SKACHKOV, P. E. *Bibliografiia Kitaia; sistematicheskii ukazatel knig i zhurnalnykh statei o Kitae na russkom iazyke, 1730-1930.* Moscow: Gos. sots.-ek. izd., 1932. 843 p. 2nd ed., Moscow: 1960. 691 p. Indispensable. The new edition, which is substantially enlarged and updated, includes 19,551 items in Russian, thoroughly indexed and classified. Sections on "The Soviet Union and the Chinese People's Republic (1949-57)," p. 276-282, and "Sinology in Russia and the Soviet Union," p. 569-615, are particularly important. [A]

JC417 SLADKOVSKII, M. I. *Ocherki ekonomicheskikh otnoshenii SSSR s Kitaem.* Moscow: Vneshtorgizdat, 1957. 455 p. Mainly historical; p. 293-354 deal with the Chinese People's Republic. Appendices include totals for Chinese-Russian trade, 1697-1955, a chronology from 1618 to 1956, and numerous treaty texts, from the period 1689-1956. One table presents Russian trade with Sinkiang, 1942-45, and details of Soviet-Chinese trade, 1950-55, are supplied. The author is Soviet trade representative in China.

JC418 *Sotsialisticheskii podem v kitaiskoi derevne; sbornik izbrannykh statei.* Moscow: Inlitizdat, 1956. 503 p. Originally published in China (1956), this work contains specific details of local situations, based on direct reports from early 1955. Certain of the reports are labelled as "models" to be followed in other areas. [A]

JC419 TSZEN, VEN-TSZIN. *Sotsialisticheskaia industrializatsiia Kitaia.* Moscow: Izd. politicheskoi lit., 1959. 383 p. Originally published in Peking in 1958; some "corrections" were added from Russian material. Deals with the Chinese First Five Year Plan.

JC420 VOEVODIN, L. D. *Gosudarstvennyi stroi KNR.* Moscow: Gos. izd. iuridicheskoi lit., 1956. 271 p. Important for terminology, with explanatory glossary (p. 253-269). Also includes many informative footnotes.

JC421 VOEVODIN, S. A., and KRUGLOV, A. M. *Sotsialisticheskoe preobrazovanie kapitalisticheskoi promyshlennosti i torgovli v Kitaiskoi Narodnoi Respublike.* Moscow: Izd. vostochnoi literatury, 1959. 166 p. A study of private capitalist industry and trade up to 1955, based on Chinese sources.

JC422 *Voprosy geografii selskogo khoziaistva KNR.* Moscow: Izd. Akademii nauk SSSR, 1959. 168 p. A publication of the Institute of Geography. Chapters by N. M. Kazakova (Northeast China); M. N. Gorbunova (Shantung); E. A. Afanasevskii (Szechuan); K. N. Chernozhukov (South coast); Ia. M. Berger (Sinkiang).

JC423 *Voprosy kulturnoi revoliutsii v KNR; sbornik statei.* Moscow: Izd. vostochnoi lit., 1960. 362 p. Nine Russian and five Chinese authors discuss "culture" in contemporary China, including Russian literature in China, new Chinese literature, language reform, and the theater and motion pictures.

JC424 ZAKHAREVICH, P. B., and CHERNYSHEVA, L. P., comps. *Kitaiskaia Narodnaia Respublika; kratkii rekomendatelnyi ukazatel literatury.* Ed. by M. A. Kiselevaia. Moscow: 1950. 38 p. A bibliography.

JC425 ZHAMIN, V. A. *Selskoe khoziastvo Kitaia.* Moscow: Gos. selskokhoz. lit., 1959. 287 p. No bibliography; many photographs, maps, and statistical tables. Includes a discussion of geography, climatic conditions, specific crops, and livestock, as well as an estimate of future possibilities.

c. *IN JAPANESE*

(Edited by Shinkichi Eto)

JC426 AJIA SEIKEI GAKKAI. *Chugoku seiji-keizai soran.* 3rd ed., Tokyo: Naigai Seiji Kenkyujo, 1962. 1440 p. An extensive and informative handbook prepared by 48 specialists in Japan. A few articles are strongly oriented toward Peking; most are sober research summaries, non-propagandistic in tone. In addition to the chapters on the People's Republic of China, the volume also includes sections on Taiwan, the Mongolian People's Republic, North and South Korea, Hong Kong, Macao, and the overseas Chinese. Appended are chronologies; bibliographies; tables of Chinese, Korean, and Mongolian measurements; and an index to Chinese laws and regulations for 1960-61. The first edition of this massive work (1077 pages) appeared in 1954; a second (1274 pages), in 1960.

JC427 CHUGOKU KENKYUJO. *Chugoku nenkan.* Volume 7. Tokyo: Ishizaki-shoten, 1955- A series of China yearbooks issued annually since 1955 by the Chugoku Kenkyujo to supplement and update the revised *Gendai Chugoku jiten* edited by that organization in 1952. Description and analysis generally follow the Peking line, but the works provide useful Japanese-language summaries of basic Chinese Communist data. Each volume contains many statistical tables and diagrams taken from mainland publications. Useful appendices, including annual chronologies, are appended. In the 1962 edition the title was changed to *Shin Chugoku nenkan.*

JC428 CHUGOKU KENKYUJO. *Gendai Chugoku jiten.* Tokyo: Iwasaki-shoten, 1959. 898 p. A comprehensive *Encyclopedia Sinica*-type dictionary on the People's Republic of China, with 68 Japanese contributors. Some articles follow the Peking line closely; others are more sober and detached. Appendices include significant statements on Sino-Japanese relations, statistical tables, listing of private organizations in Japan concerned with Chinese affairs, a chronology of modern Chinese history, etc. Has a useful index. The first edition appeared in Tokyo in 1950, and a revised edition was issued in 1952; both represent optimistic and propagandistic appraisals of the new Peking government during the early period after its establishment.

JC429 *Chuka jinmin kyowakoku horei sakuin.* Tokyo: National Diet Library, General Reference Division, 1954. 145 p. A chronological listing of laws, regulations, decrees, etc. of central and some local government agencies, 1949-53, with Chinese sources indicated. The documents are also arranged by subject in a separate listing. A valuable reference tool for the period covered.

JC430 ISHIKAWA, SHIGERU. *Chugoku ni okeru shihon chikuseki kiko.* (Volume II of the Hitotsubashi University economic research series.) Tokyo: Iwanami-shoten, 1960. 220 p. A compilation of technical articles embodying the results of research carried out at Hitotsubashi University in Tokyo and at Harvard on the problem of capital accumulation in a socialist economy such as that of mainland China. The author, associate professor of economics at Hitotsubashi, also attempts a preliminary comparison of the rates of economic growth in China, India, the Soviet Union, and Eastern Europe.

JC431 ISHIKAWA, SHIGERU; MIZOGUCHI, TOSHIYUKI, and YOSHIDA, TADAO. *Chugoku keizai hatten no tokeiteki kenkyu.* (Volume 7 of the research series of the Institute of Asian Economic Affairs.) Tokyo: Institute of Asian Economic Affairs, 1960. 269 p. A research symposium including three separate papers with summaries in English. Ishikawa's paper, "An examination of official national income statistics," attempts to clarify concepts used by Peking in the presentation of national income data, examines the methodology and the data, and attempts to compile aggregative figures. Mizoguchi, research assistant at Hitotsubashi University, examines "commodity price index data." The paper by Yoshida, assistant professor at Meiji Gakuin in Tokyo, provides a description of official Chinese population statistics.

JC432 KASUMIGASEKI-KAI, ed. *Gendai Chugoku jinmei jiten.* Tokyo: Konan-shoin, 1957. 926 p. Rev. ed., Tokyo: 1962. Compiled by China specialists in the Bureau of Asian Affairs, Ministry of Foreign Affairs, Tokyo, this biographical dictionary includes over 7000 brief entries covering individuals both on mainland China and in Taiwan. The most comprehensive who's who on contemporary China now available, the work nevertheless contains some factual errors and inaccurate identifications, and must be used with caution. It is indexed both by Japanese pronunciation and by Wade-Giles romanization.

JC433 MIYASHITA, TADAO. *Chugoku no boeki soshiki.* (Volume 17 of the research series of the Institute of Asian Economic Affairs.) Tokyo: Institute of Asian Economic Affairs, 1961. 190 p. A research monograph comparing the organization of foreign trade in the People's Republic of China with the pre-1949 system and presenting a detailed description of Peking's present foreign trade policies and practices. Sources are up-to-date and reliable, and the volume includes a useful bibliography. Miyashita, now professor of economics at Kobe University, lived in pre-war Shanghai.

JC434 NAIKAKU CHOSA-SHITSU. *Chuka jinmin kyowakoku soshiki-betsu jinmin-hyo.* Tokyo: Naikaku Chosa-shitsu, 1959. 424 p. (mimeographed). A compilation of detailed lists of government and Chinese Communist Party personnel including Party officials down to the municipal and *hsien* levels as of 1959. Also included are lists of officials of trade unions, "people's organizations," scholarly associations, and "friendship societies."

JC435 SATO SHIN'ICHIRO. *Chugoku kyosanto no nogyo shudanka seisaku.* (Volume 11 of the research series of the Institute of Asian Economic Affairs.) Tokyo: Tokyo University, 1961. 384 p. A research monograph discussing the evolution of Communist agrarian policy in the areas of China under their control from 1927 to 1949, especially useful for the discussion of the Yenan period. Statistical data and a detailed chronology are appended. The author, research fellow at Takushoku University in Tokyo, lived for over twenty years in pre-1949 China; he is a nephew of Yoshimasa Yamada, a close friend of Sun Yat-sen. A second volume of this study (335 pages) discussing Chinese Communist agricultural collectivization policies since 1949 was published in Tokyo in 1962.

5. MANCHURIA

(Edited by Peter S. H. Tang)

JC436 AVARIN, VLADIMIR IA. *Imperializm v Manchzhurii.* Moscow: Gosizdat sots.-ekon., 1931-1934. 2 vols. 2nd rev. and enl. ed.,

Moscow: Gosizdat sots.-ekon., 1934. 2 vols. A well-documented, comprehensive study of the stages of the imperialist struggle for Manchuria, written from the Communist point of view. Includes Tsarist and Japanese aggression and Sino-Soviet relations as well as valuable tables and statistical appendices. Vol. I of the 1st edition was entitled *Imperializm i Manchzhuriia.* [A]

JC437 AVARIN, VLADIMIR IA. *"Nezavisimaia" Manchzhuriia.* Moscow: Partizdat, 1932. 126 p. 2nd rev. ed., Moscow-Leningrad: Partizdat, 1934. 152 p. An account of conditions in Manchuria prior to and following Japanese occupation and the establishment of Manchoukuo; especially the economic and military-strategic position and mode of guerrilla warfare. It also includes a discussion of attitudes of the Chinese Communists and the world proletariat.

JC438 CHANG, TAO-HSING. *International Controversies Over the Chinese Eastern Railway.* Shanghai: Commercial Press, 1936. 289 p. A comprehensive analysis of the Chinese Eastern Railway from the creation of the concession through its construction, management, American and Japanese interest, crisis and sale in 1935. Uses English-language sources predominantly and includes official documents. [B]

JC439 CHAO, CH'ÜAN-T'IEN. *Tung-pei wên-t'i yü shih-chieh ho-p'ing.* Chungking: Southern Printing Press, 1944. 394 p. A very useful collection of treaties, agreements, state papers, and other primary source materials, including diplomatic correspondence, speeches and writings from Chinese and foreign sources. Helpful classifications of materials and several sets of well-arranged chronologies are included. Contains an extensive bibliography of Chinese and foreign language publications.

JC440 CH'I, JENG-HSI. *Man-t'ieh wen-t'i.* Shanghai: Commercial Press, 1930. 475 p. A detailed account of the origins and operations of the South Manchurian Railway Company which discusses the business management of the entire railway network and its numerous affiliated enterprises. Sections concern Japan's aggressive policy toward Manchuria and Mongolia as based on the railway and the local effects of international relations. Contains a wealth of documents and data and is valuable for research purposes.

JC441 CH'I, JENG-HSI. *Tung-pei t'ieh-tao yao-lan.* Shanghai: Commercial Press, 1930. 29 p. A concise treatise dealing with more than 20 Manchurian railways. Basic data is presented and the trend of foreign exploitation and domestic efforts is discussed.

JC442 CH'I, JENG-HSI. *Tung-t'ieh wên-t'i.* Shanghai: Commercial Press, 1929. 96 p. 2nd ed., 1930. 475 p. A study of the Chinese Eastern Railway based on relevant treaties, agreements, statutes, documents, and correspondence. The second edition followed the first by one month after the exhaustion of copies as a result of the cessation of Sino-Russian relations. Some legal opinion is advanced on ownership rights of the railway and suggestions are offered for Chinese recovery of the CER.

JC443 CHINA, MINISTRY OF FOREIGN AFFAIRS. *Documents with Reference to the Sino-Russian Dispute, 1929.* Nanking: Far Eastern Information Bureau, 1929. 66 p. Contains documents seized at the Soviet Consulate General in Harbin, together with photographic evidence and pertinent materials.

JC444 CLYDE, PAUL H. *International Rivalries in Manchuria, 1689-1922.* Columbus: Ohio State, 1926. 217 p. 2nd rev. ed., 1928. 323 p. A comprehensive study on the Far East, tracing the beginnings of foreign influence in Manchuria. Concentrates on Russo-Japanese expansion into the area after 1895 and includes analyses of concessions, leases, occupation, war, and railway politics up to the 1921 Washington Conference.

JC445 FANG, LO-T'IEN. *Tung-pei kuo-chi wai-chiao.* Shanghai: Commercial Press, 1933. 121 p. Northeastern China in international diplomacy.

JC446 FU, KO-CHIN. *Chung-tung t'ieh-lu wen-t'i chih yen-chiu.* Shanghai: Shih-chieh Shu-chu, 1929. 117 p. Discusses the origins, organization and economic operations of the Chinese Eastern Railway as well as the loss of Chinese interest and the Sino-Russian military conflict. Several documents are included.

JC447 HIDAKA, NOBORU, comp. *Manchoukuo-Soviet Border Issues.* Dairen: Manchuria Daily News, 1938. 261 p. An elaborate compilation of data concerning illegal acts committed by the Soviets along the frontier from March 1, 1932 to June 30, 1938, culminating in the Changkufeng Incident. Written in accordance with the "Manchoukuo" government investigations. Some historical background included.

JC448 HO, PAO-LU. *O-kuo ch'in-lüeh tung-pei chi-shih.* Kowloon, Hong Kong: Freedom Press, 1955. 153 p. Deals with aggression by Russia in northeastern China.

JC449 HODORAWIS, JOSEPH. "Soviet Reaction to the Manchurian Incident, 1931-1932." Certificate essay, Russian Institute, Columbia, 1958. 118 p.

JC450 HOUANG, TCHANG SIN (HUANG, CHANG-SIN). *Le Problème du chemin de fer chinois de l'est. Origines; l'expansion de la*

Russie; l'expansion du Japon; les facteurs techniques et économiques; lutte pour le contrôle; régime provisoire; régime soviétique. Paris: Les Écrivains réunis, 1927. 460 p. A scholarly history.

JC451 INTERNATIONAL RELATIONS COMMITTEE OF CHINA. *The Sino-Russian Crisis; the Actual Facts Brought to Light.* Nanking: International Relations Committee, 1929. 105 p. A Chinese effort to trace the background of the crisis and fix the responsibility for it on Soviet designs on China. The appendices, considerably longer than the text, provide a collection of documents related to the crisis, including pronouncements of the Chinese and Soviet governments on the raid of the Soviet consulate general in Harbin. Photographs, translations of seized documents and other evidence are also provided. [B]

JC452 KANTOROVICH, ANATOLI. *Ochag voiny na Dalnem Vostoke.* Moscow: 1934. 255 p. The author, with a Soviet bias, describes the strategic position of Manchuria in the Far East, the long contest for Manchuria, the situation there prior to Japanese seizure, the seizure action, Japanese aggression in China, U.S. and European positions, League action, neutrality and the potential threat to the USSR, and Japanese aggressive policy after World War I towards Manchuria and Mongolia. Little documentation.

JC453 KINNEY, HENRY W. *Manchuria Today.* Dairen: South Manchuria Railway Co., 1930. 100 p. A general survey of Manchuria's history written from a Japanese point of view. Sections cover geography, agriculture, industry, and trade. An attempt to idealize the functions of the South Manchurian Railway Co. in advancing the Japanese policy of "development" as a "civilizing force" rather than as conquest.

JC454 KOMMUNISTICHESKAIA AKADEMIIA, INSTITUT MIROVOGO KHOZIAISTVA I MIROVOI POLITIKI. *Okkupatsiia Manchzhurii i borba imperialistov; sbornik statei.* Ed. by P. Mif and others. Moscow: Partizdat, 1932. 168 p. A series of 9 articles by such well-known authors as T. Voitinskii, P. Mif, and V. Avarin, mostly written between October and December 1931. The articles deal with various situations connected with the Japanese seizure of Manchuria—from the policies of imperialist countries to the revolutionary upsurge in China and the impact on Korea and Inner Mongolia, as well as the danger of anti-Soviet intervention. Appendices include Tanaka memorial, appeals of Chinese, Japanese, French, and other Communist Parties, maps on imperialism in China and spheres of influence in Manchuria. [B]

JC455 LATTIMORE, OWEN. *Manchuria, Cradle of Conflict.* N.Y.: Macmillan, 1932. 311 p. 2nd rev. ed., 1935. 343 p. A discussion of the physical and economic geography of Manchuria and neighboring areas as well as a survey of the history and culture of races inhabiting the area, with emphasis given to the author's personal observations. An elaboration of theoretical principles of the Manchoukuo state and divisions of Far East into separate nations of South and North China, Manchoukuo, Mongolia, Tibet and Chinese Turkistan. [A]

JC456 LIPMAN, NATAN D. *Mit der roten armee im Fernen Osten, aufzeichnungen eines rotarmisten.* Moscow: Verlagsgenossenschaft auslandischer arbeiter in der UdSSR, 1932. 244 p. The daily experiences of a correspondent with the Red Army in the Far East. No documentation, no bibliography.

JC457 LOWE, PARDEE. "A Historical Study and Analysis of the Activities of the U.S.S.R. in Manchuria; 1945-1950, With Special Reference to the Impact of the Comintern-Cominform Designs and Strategies Upon the Economic, Social and Political Structure of the Region." Ph.D. dissertation, Univ. of California, 1952.

JC458 MANCHURIA DAILY NEWS. *The Comintern's Activity in Manchuria; a General Survey.* Hsinking: Manchoukuo, 1940. 49 p. A series of short articles, without documentation, concerning the Communist efforts to spread into Manchoukuo and the reaction of the Manchoukuo state.

JC459 MIF, PAVEL. *Okkupatsiia Manchzhurii.* Moscow: 1932. Articles depicting the Soviet view of the Japanese seizure of Manchuria as a menacing act. Contains accusations against the alleged aggressive designs of France, Britain and the U.S., and an account of White Russian activities. An official Communist Party edition justifying the Soviet interpretation. Includes maps showing the line of occupation. Limited documentation. [B]

JC460 *Ocherki stran Dalnego Vostoka; vvedenie v vostokovedenie.* Issue 2; *Vneshnii Kitai (Manchzhuriia, Mongoliia, Sintszian i Tibet.)* Harbin: Tip. N. A. Frenkel, 1931. 207 p.

JC461 PARLETT, HAROLD G. (SIR). *A Brief Account of Diplomatic Events in Manchuria.* London and N.Y.: Oxford, 1929. 96 p. A history prepared for the 1929 Institute for Pacific Relations conference at Kyoto. Discusses the pre-1895 and post-1922 periods and comprehensively analyzes Russian aggression up to 1905 and Japanese aggression until 1921. Half of the book is in the form of 16 appendices, including extracts from agreements relating to Manchuria from the 1896 CER contract to the 1922 Nine Power Treaty.

JC462 PETROV, VICTOR P. "Manchuria as an Objective of Russian Foreign Policy." Ph.D. dissertation, American University, 1954.

JC463 RUSSIA (1923-USSR), NARODNYI KOMISSARIAT PO INOSTRANNYM DELAM. *Sovetsko-Kitaiskii konflikt 1929 g.; sbornik dokumentov*. Moscow: Litizdat NKID, 1930. 89 p. Sixty-six documents related to Soviet and Chinese relations, including the texts of agreements, relevant press commentary, diplomatic notes and other pertinent data.

JC464 SCHOOTEN, JEAN ULLENS DE. *Les Chemins de fer chinois; étude historique, économique et financière*. Brussels: Lamertin, 1928. 266 p. An exhaustive study.

JC465 SMITH, SARA R. *The Manchurian Crisis, 1931-1932; a Tragedy in International Relations*. N.Y.: Columbia, 1948. 281 p. A scholarly, well-documented study based largely upon official sources and other English-language materials. A detailed account of the crisis as it concerned the League of Nations and the United States.

JC466 SOKOLSKY, GEORGE E. *The Story of the Chinese Eastern Railway*. Intro. by Dr. Hu Shih. Shanghai: North-China Daily News and Herald, 1929. 68 p. A series of articles written to provide a history of the Chinese Eastern Railway and its role in the international relations of China, Russia, Japan, and other nations. Sokolsky was at that time editor of the *Far Eastern Review*.

JC467 SOUTH MANCHURIA RAILWAY COMPANY. *Report on Progress in Manchuria*. Dairen: South Manchuria Railway Co., 1929. 238 p. Report of the Railway Company covering the period 1907-28.

JC468 SUN, CHI-I. *I-chiu êrh-chiu chih san-ling nien Chung-O chiao-shê lun*. Shanghai: Ta-tung Bookstore, 1931. 212 p. Deals with the Sino-Soviet negotiations of 1929-30.

JC469 TANG, PETER S. H. *Russian and Soviet Policy in Manchuria and Outer Mongolia, 1911-1931*. Intro. by Philip Mosely. Durham, N.C.: Duke Univ., 1959. 494 p. A heavily-documented study based primarily on Russian-language materials. Traces the Russian and Soviet motivation and tactics in Manchuria and Outer Mongolia and parallels Russian and Soviet policies in terms of railway penetration, power politics, political interference, and economic influence in great detail. The Chinese reaction is analyzed on the basis of Chinese-language sources. Includes a comprehensive bibliography, index and maps. [A]

JC470 TEDESHI, CORADO. *Siberia rossa e Manciuria in fiamme*. Florence: G. Barbera, 1930. 254 p. An Italian voyager with the Russian army across Siberia and Manchuria gives some characteristics and conditions of the country and army and popular attitudes of the people.

JC471 TONG, HOLLINGTON K. *Facts About the Chinese Eastern Railway Situation (With Documents).* Harbin: Committee for Public Enlightenment of the North-Eastern Provinces, 1929. 183 p. A quickly-prepared, timely study entirely devoted to the Sino-Soviet dispute over the CER in Mukden, Harbin and other cities in Northeast China. A factual, detailed account of all major phases of the conflict, including the rupture of diplomatic relations, Soviet invasion, treatment of prisoners, and foreign public opinion. One-third of the book is appendices, which include several communications with the Comintern and the Soviet government.

JC472 TRETCHIKOV, N. G. *Bibliografiia po ekonomike Severnoi Manchzhurii; knigi i zhurnalnye statei na russkom iazyke po 1928 g. vkliuchitelno.* Ed. by N. A. Setnitskii. Harbin: Izd. Iurid. fak-ta v Kharbine, 1929. 90 p.

JC473 TSAO, LIEN-EN. *The Chinese Eastern Railway; an Analytical Study.* Shanghai: Bureau of Industrial and Commercial Information, Min. of Industry, Commerce and Labor, National Govt. of the Republic of China, 1929. 198 p. A treatise by a resident investigator in Manchuria of the Sino-Soviet dispute over the CER, with a general account of the railway's status both before and after and Russian Revolution and an appraisal of the impact of the CER crisis on the Manchurian economy and Sino-Soviet relations. Half of the book consists of appendices, including pertinent documents.

JC473A U.S. LIBRARY OF CONGRESS, REFERENCE DEPARTMENT. *Manchuria; an Annotated Bibliography.* Compiled by Peter A. Berton. Washington: 1951. 187 p. A thorough bibliography, arranged by subjects. Lists the important works on the Soviets in Manchuria. [A]

JC474 VILENSKI, VLADIMIR D. *Chang-Tso-Lin, Manchzhurskaia Problema.* Moscow: 1925.

JC475 VOITINSKII, GRIGORII, ed. *Okkupatsiia Manchzhurii i borba kitaiskogo naroda.* Moscow: Sotsekgiz, 1937. 148 p. A collection of articles dealing with Japanese military aggression in the Far East, economic conditions, and guerrilla warfare in Manchuria under Japanese occupation. Also discusses the internal situations in Japan and China, including Chinese Communist implementation of the united front, and their inadequate influence in guerrilla activities. Contains a section on the denunciation of Japanese aggression by the Japanese Communist Party. [B]

JC476 YOUNG, CARL W. *The International Relations of Manchuria; a Digest and Analysis of Treaties, Agreements, and Negotiations Concerning the Three Eastern Provinces of China.* Chicago: U. of Chicago, 1929. 307 p. A convenient handbook and comprehensive survey prepared for the 1929 Institute for Pacific Relations conference in Kyoto. Four parts: 1895-1905; 1905-15; 1915-21; and 1921-29, each part subdivided into a general account, the positions of Russia, Japan and other powers, and treaties and agreements. Documentary sources are listed and appendices give Sino-Russian and Russo-Japanese treaties. [B]

6. SINKIANG

(Edited by O. Edmund Clubb)

JC477 BOORMAN, HOWARD L., ECKSTEIN, ALEXANDER, MOSELY, PHILIP E., and SCHWARTZ, BENJAMIN. *Moscow-Peking Axis, Strengths and Strains.* N.Y.: Harper, 1957. 227 p. This work by four leading American scholars provides valuable general background for a consideration of Sino-Soviet relations in Central Asia. Boorman's chapter on "The Borderlands and the Sino-Soviet Alliance" has a section giving a summary history of Sinkiang 1911-55, followed by a thoughtful projection of "The Borderlands and the Moscow-Peking Axis" into the future.

JC478 CHANG, TA-CHŬN. *Hsin-chiang szu-shih nien pien-lüan chi-lüeh.* Taipei: Chung-yang wen-wu kung-ying she, 1954. 134 p. An account of developments in Sinkiang from the time of Yang Tseng-hsin to the turnover to the Communists—which the author views as the realization of a Soviet plot. Useful table of organization of the Eastern Turkestan People's Republic.

JC479 CHANG, TA-CHŬN. *Szu-shih Nien tung-lüan Hsin-chiang.* Hong Kong: Asia Press, 1956. 302 p. Much detailed information regarding Chin Shu-jen, Sheng Shih-ts'ai, the conflict between Sheng and Ma Chung-ying, the Eastern Turkestan People's Republic, and the final turn-over to the Chinese Communists. A fairly extensive index at the end is useful. [A]

JC480 CHINA, MINISTRY OF FOREIGN AFFAIRS. *Su-lien tui Hsin-chiang chih ching-chi ch'in-lüeh.* Taipei: 1950. 169 p. A description of Sinkiang's agricultural, animal and mineral products, with attendant record of various Sinkiang-USSR agreements ranging from Chin Shu-jen's "Provisional Trade Agreement" to the secret treaty of 1940 between Sheng Shih-ts'ai and Moscow. Contains an account of the 1949 Sino-Soviet negotiations and 1950 agreements. Texts of various agreements (including Russian language originals and English translations).

JC481 DAVIDSON, BASIL. *Turkestan Alive; New Travels in Chinese Central Asia.* London: Cape, 1957. 255 p. An interesting journalistic report of a 1956 trip to Sinkiang, China's vast northwest frontier province, formerly remote, but now gradually developing as the Sinkiang-Uighur Autonomous Region. Sympathetic with the Chinese Communist cause, the account ignores the ultimately coercive nature of Peking's policies toward minority nationalities and "local nationalism." Davidson, who is British, is also the author of the journalistic and generally uncritical volume, *Daybreak in China* (London: 1953).

JC482 ETHERTON, PERCY T. *In the Heart of Asia.* London: Constable, 1925. 305 p. After the 1918 Treaty of Brest-Litovsk seemingly opened up the possibility of a German drive on India through Afghanistan, Lt. Col. Etherton, of the Indian Army, took up a post at Kashgar as Consul General. His book describes the Sinkiang government and people, but also treats developments in Russian Turkestan and Bolshevik designs in Asia.

JC483 FLEMING, PETER. *News from Tartary; a Journey from Peking to Kashmir.* London: Cape, 1936. 384 p. Primarily a travel book, the times made it more: the author Fleming made his trip in 1935, and some of his treatment is devoted to the 1934 Soviet intervention and the subsequent decline of Dungan power in southern Sinkiang. Well illustrated.

JC484 HEDIN, SVEN. *The Flight of "Big Horse"; the Trail of War in Central Asia.* N.Y.: Dutton; London: Macmillan, 1936. 247 p. German ed., Leipzig: F. A. Brockhaus, 1935. 262 p. Amply illustrated, this first hand account by the noted Swedish explorer of his experiences as head of a survey party in Sinkiang in 1934 is a valuable source of information regarding Ma Chung-ying, Sheng Shih-ts'ai, and the Soviet intervention. Ends with Ma Chung-ying's withdrawal into the USSR. [A]

JC485 HEDIN, SVEN. *The Silk Road.* N.Y.: Dutton, 1938. 322 p. German ed., Leipzig: F. A. Brockhaus, 1936. 263 p. Italian ed., Milan: A. Bompiani, 1937. 322 p. Hedin led a motor caravan into Sinkiang in 1933 as "adviser to the Ministry of Railways," Nanking. He got into trouble with both sides in the civil strife then in progress there, and gives first hand observations of the struggle between Ma Chung-ying and Sheng Shih-ts'ai. The appendix, written in June 1938, gives a projection of his contemporary political analysis. [B]

JC486 HO, DAVID. *L'Oeuvre colonisatrice de la Chine dans le Turkestan chinois.* Paris: Recueil Sirey, 1941. 128 p. A University of Paris doctoral thesis chiefly treating the subject matter indicated by the title and internal provincial administration, but has a few pages touching on trade between Sinkiang and the Soviet Union.

JC487 HU, HUAN-YUNG, and T'UNG, CH'ENG-K'ANG. *Books and Articles on Sinkiang in Western Languages.* Chungking: Institute for the Promotion of Dr. Sun Yat-sen's Industrial Plan and Department of Geography, National Central University, 1943 (Bulletin Series B, no. 2), 1943. 47 p. Covers all disciplines and periods, including general works which touch only partially on Sinkiang. Periodical material also included. Of limited value for relations between Sinkiang and the USSR.

JC488 KAZAK, FUAD. *Ostturkestan zwischen den Grossmächten; Beitrage zur Wirtschaftskunde Ostturkestans.* Königsberg: Ost-Europa-Verlag, 1937. 160 p. A description of the Sinkiang economy, with illustrative statistics and graphs. Includes also a treatment of the rivalry of the Powers over this area.

JC489 LATTIMORE, OWEN and others. *Pivot of Asia; Sinkiang and the Inner Asian Frontiers of China and Russia.* Boston: Little, Brown, 1950. 288 p. A cooperative effort, led by the well-known Central Asian expert, produced a well-documented, scholarly work covering a variety of topics, including the historical Anglo-Russian rivalry in Sinkiang. Of especial interest are parts dealing with Chinese policies and the convergence of Soviet, imperial Japanese, and revolutionary Chinese influences in that part of the world. Appendices cover more topics, ranging from ancient art to oil. [A]

JC490 LIEBERMAN, HENRY R. "China versus Russia in Sinkiang; a Problem in Sino-Soviet Border Area 'Attachment.'" M.A. Thesis, Columbia, 1950. 265 p. Includes historical background, giving a picture of the rise of Russia in Central Asia. Then treats warlord rule in Sinkiang 1912-44, and follows with a survey of post-war developments to the establishment of a Communist regime in 1950. Well-documented and very useful. Bibliography. [A]

JC491 MAILLART, ELLA K. *Forbidden Journey—from Peking to Kashmir.* London: Heinemann, 1937. 312 p. French ed., Paris: B. Grasset, 1937. 281 p. Swiss citizen Maillart travelled from Peking to Kashgar via Sining, the Tsaidam Basin and southern Sinkiang with Peter Fleming in 1935. Her book is chiefly an interestingly illustrated travel book, but several of the later chapters include useful information on the politics of the time when Sheng Shih-ts'ai had just won dominance in Sinkiang with the aid of the USSR.

JC492 NORINS, MARTIN R. *Gateway to Asia; Sinkiang, Frontier of the Chinese Far West.* Intro. by Owen Lattimore. N.Y.: Day, 1944. 200 p. Including much background material, this is devoted primarily to Sinkiang under Sheng Shih-ts'ai's regime. Completed just as Nationalist authority was displacing Soviet influence in the province, it was soon "dated." The last 60 pages are taken up with an appendix, glossary of terms, bibliography, notes, and index.

JC493 REED, BARRETT M. "Sinkiang, Crossroads of Empires; a Review of Great Power Rivalry in Central Asia to 1924." Certificate essay, Russian Institute, Columbia, 1948. 198 p. Focused on Sinkiang, this work includes a treatment of neighboring Russian Turkestan, Tibet, and Outer Mongolia. Much of the work is devoted to historical background, but with a treatment of political and economic conditions in Sinkiang 1916-24 in the latter part. A useful appended bibliography, with however many general titles.

JC494 SUN, FU-K'UN. *Su-lien lüeh-to Hsin-chiang chi-shih.* Kowloon, Hong Kong: Freedom, 1952. 2 vols. rebound in 1 vol. 202 p. The first volume is devoted essentially to background, bringing the story down only to the 1920's. The second volume however treats "Soviet aggression" in the Altai, Ining, and South Sinkiang regions, following developments through the reigns of Yang Tseng-hsin, Chin Shu-jen, and Sheng Shih-ts'ai, with reference particularly to Soviet exploitation of Tushantzu oil, mineral resources, communications and trade.

JC495 TEICHMAN, ERIC. *Journey to Turkestan.* London: Hodder & Stoughton, 1937. 221 p. Thirty years in the British consular service in China, Sir Eric devotes most of his book to a description of a journey in 1935. But he gives some historical background, describes various Sinkiang personalities, and in the final chapter treats "Past, Present and Future in Chinese Turkestan."

JC496 VIKHLIAEV, M. A. *Torgovlia SSSR s Sintszianom za period 1917-1934 gg.* Leningrad: 1952. 230 p.

JC497 WEI, CHUNG-T'IEN. *Sheng Shih-ts'ai ju-ho T'ung-chih Hsin-chiang.* Hong Kong: Hai-wai t'ung-hsün she, 1947. 112 p. Treats Sheng Shih-ts'ai's background, his attainment of power in Sinkiang, his establishment of ties with the USSR and Yenan, the motivation for his turn-over—and the consequences. The appendices (comprising pages 44-112) cover the creation of Sinkiang Province, the area's geography, and the author's travel in Sinkiang.

JC498 WHITING, ALLEN S., and SHENG, SHIH-TS'AI. *Sinkiang; Pawn or Pivot?* East Lansing: Michigan State U., 1958. 314 p. Essentially two works, one by each author. That by careful scholar Whiting on "Soviet Strategy in Sinkiang" is a well-documented, enlightening analysis of Sheng Shih-ts'ai's Sinkiang rule, 1933-44, with a postscript bringing events up to 1949. That by ex-warlord Sheng on

"Red Failure in Sinkiang" is his own story, un-documented except for several "confessions" from three of those he executed in Sinkiang. The whole makes an excellent study of the period. [A]

JC499 WU, AITCHEN K. *Turkistan Tumult*. London: Methuen, 1940. 279 p. Wu was in Sinkiang in an official capacity in the tumultuous period following the assassination of Yang Tseng-hsin in 1928. This autobiographical account gives interesting "inside information" on Chin Shu-jen's rise and fall, the collapse of Ma Chung-ying's challenge, and Sheng Shih-ts'ai's accession to power with the aid of the USSR. [A]

7. TIBET

(Edited by W. Nathaniel Howell, Jr.)

JC500 *Concerning the Question of Tibet*. Peking: Foreign Languages Press, 1959. 276 p. A collection of documents, speeches, dispatches, and background articles gathered to support the Communist Chinese position in Tibet and intended to give foreign readers "a full understanding of the recent situation in China's Tibet."

JC501 DALAI LAMA (HIS HOLINESS). *My Land and My People*. N.Y.: McGraw-Hill, 1962. 271 p. An autobiographical description of the Communist Chinese takeover of Tibet and his timely escape to the safety of India, by the former religious and secular leader of Tibet.

JC502 FORD, ROBERT. *Wind between the Worlds*. N.Y.: McKay, 1957. 338 p. British ed., *Captured in Tibet*. London: Harrap, 1957. 256 p. The British author was a radio operator employed by the Tibetan government and stationed at Chamdo in Eastern Tibet. Captured at the time of the Chinese Communist invasion late in 1950, Ford presents an honest account of his long imprisonment, interrogation, and indoctrination; and of his final "confession" and release in May 1955.

JC503 GUREVICH, B. P. *Osvobozhdenie Tibeta*. Moscow: Izd. vost. lit., 1958. 211 p. Published by the Institute of Chinese Studies. Includes photographs and a map, texts of the treaty between Tibet and China of May 23, 1951, and an announcement of the Preparatory Committee for the Establishment of the Tibetan Autonomous Region, August 26, 1956. Uses Chinese sources.

JC504 HUTHEESING, RAJA, ed. *Tibet Fights for Freedom; the Story of the March 1959 Uprising as Recorded in Documents, Despatches, Eye-Witness Accounts, and World-Wide Reactions*. Foreword by the Dalai Lama. Bombay: Oriental Longmans, for the Indian Committee for Cultural Freedom, 1961. 241 p. A detailed chronological compilation of materials dealing with the uprising in Tibet and the events leading up to it. Because reliable information was scarce, the editor relied heavily on the Indian press and to a lesser extent upon the non-Communist press of other nations. Short background articles by such figures as de Riencourt, Fred Bessac, Robert Ekvall, D. F. Hudson, and the editor are also included. [B]

JC505 INTERNATIONAL COMMISSION OF JURISTS, GENEVA. *The Question of Tibet and the Rule of Law.* Geneva: International Commission of Jurists, 1959. 208 p. An investigation of the international legal status of Tibet and of alleged Communist Chinese violations of the Law of Nations. Half of the book consists of 21 relevant documents.

JC506 INTERNATIONAL COMMISSION OF JURISTS, GENEVA, LEGAL INQUIRY COMMITTEE ON TIBET. *Tibet and the Chinese People's Republic.* Geneva: International Commission of Jurists, 1960. 340 p. A further, more-inclusive study of the situation in Tibet made by an independent committee of jurists to verify the findings of the 1959 preliminary report of the International Commission of Jurists (see above). In this volume those conclusions are upheld and a "detailed condemnation of Chinese rule in Tibet" is set forth. Four appendices include documents concerning both the subject of the study and the efforts of the committee to enter Tibet. [A]

JC507 JAIN, GIRILAL. *Panchsheela and After; a Re-appraisal of Sino-Indian Relations in the Context of the Tibetan Insurrection.* N.Y.: Asia Publishing House, 1961. 232 p. Although parts of this study deal with Tibet only incidentally in a discussion of Sino-Indian relations, several lengthy chapters are devoted to recent developments in Tibet and their influence on the international situation in the area.

JC508 KREITZBURG, MARILYN J. "The Relationship Between Political Tibet and the People's Republic of China; the Corruption of a Flexible Autonomy." Master's thesis, Univ. of Virginia, 1956. 111 p. Writing during the period of the preparation of Tibet for the status of Autonomous Region in the People's Republic of China, the author argues that Communist China has gone beyond the historical limits in its control of Tibet and that with the Communist motivation added to the traditional desire for domination, there is no reason to expect a loosening of existing ties.

JC509 MORAES, FRANK. *The Revolt in Tibet.* N.Y.: Macmillan, 1960. 223 p. The well-known Indian editor's hasty analysis of the causes and course of the 1959 Tibetan uprising and of the Dalai Lama's flight from Lhasa to India.

JC510 PATTERSON, GEORGE N. *Tibet in Revolt.* London: Faber and Faber, 1960. 191 p. A popular, pro-Tibetan, anti-Communist study of the 1959 revolt in Tibet and the preliminary developments which made it both possible and at least relatively successful.

JC511 RICHARDSON, H. E. *A Short History of Tibet*. N.Y.: Dutton, 1962. 308 p. A former British official with 10 years service in Lhasa surveys Tibetan history. His scholarly discussion rejects the Chinese claim to traditional control of that land and his more detailed analysis of modern developments is in part an indictment of Britain and India for their refusal to oppose the Chinese intervention. [B]

JC512 SEN, CHANAKYA, comp. and ed. *Tibet Disappears*. N.Y.: Asia Pub., 1960. 474 p. A documentary history of Tibet's international position which recounts events until 1950 in very broad terms in the first seventy pages and in some detail for the decade following. Deals with the Chinese Communist takeover of Tibet and the subsequent disputes with India.

JC513 STRONG, ANNA LOUISE. *Tibetan Interviews*. Peking: New World Press, 1959. 210 p. The well-known pro-Communist American writer presents a compilation of interviews with Tibetans favorable to the Chinese Communist point of view. Two appendices include Communist documents concerning domestic policy in Tibet.

JC514 STRONG, ANNA LOUISE. *When Serfs Stood Up in Tibet*. Peking: New World Press, 1960. 326 p. A popular, undocumented account of the writer's recent journey to Chinese-dominated Tibet—an apology for Communist policy in that land. An appendix includes a pro-Chinese Communist treatment of the Sino-Indian border issue. The writer has long been a zealous propagandist for the Chinese Communists.

JC515 THOMAS, LOWELL, JR. *The Silent War in Tibet*. Garden City, N.Y.: Doubleday, 1959. 284 p. A popular account of Tibetan history during the decade ending with the 1959 revolt against Communist Chinese rule. The author, having traveled in Tibet at the beginning of this period, has followed developments there closely.

JC516 WINNINGTON, ALAN. *Tibet, Record of a Journey*. London: Lawrence & Wishart, 1957. 235 p. A Peking correspondent of the London *Daily Worker* records a journey across Tibet in 1955. First-hand descriptions of Tibetan life and customs are presented with reasonable detachment and balance, though the general picture of Chinese Communist rule is idealized in accord with the author's political and ideological preconceptions.

8. SOVIET PERIODICALS ON CHINA

(Edited by Charles C. McLane)

JC517 *Bibliografiia vostoka.* Leningrad: Izd. Akad. nauk SSSR, 1932-37. 10 vols. An annotated bibliography, published irregularly, which contains many references and reviews. Issued by the Institut Vostokovedeniia.

JC518 *Biulleten Nauchno-issledovatelskogo instituta po Kitaiu.* Moscow: 1928-32. Published by the Sun Yat-sen University. No. 1-2, 1931 (151 p.), is devoted to the revolutionary organization in China. Evidently not available outside the USSR.

JC519 *Kratkie soobshcheniia Instituta vostokovedeniia.* Moscow: Izd. Akad. nauk SSSR, 1951-60. Published irregularly; contains studies of all phases of Chinese history. Beginning with 1961 the name was changed to *Kratkie soobshcheniia Instituta narodov Azii.*

JC520 *Materialy po kitaiskomu voprosu.* Moscow: 1926-28. Published irregularly (16 issues) by the Research Institute on China of the Sun Yat-sen University of Toilers of the East. Edited by P. Mif and others. Rare outside Soviet archives, but some microfilm copy is available.

JC521 *Materialy po natsionalno-kolonialnym problemam.* Moscow, 1931-37. Published irregularly (39 issues) by the Research Association for the Study of National and Colonial Problems (NIA po INiKP); changed title to *Natsionalno-kolonialnye problemy* in 1937. Includes some material on China, but is devoted mainly to other Asian and African areas.

JC522 *Novyi Vostok.* Moscow: 1923-1930. Published irregularly (29 issues) by the All-Russian Learned Association of Oriental Studies, under the People's Commissariat for Nationality Affairs. Edited by M. Pavlovich and others. Most of the articles deal with China.

JC523 *Problemy Kitaia.* Moscow, 1929-35. Published irregularly (14 issues) by the Research Institute on China of the Institute of World Economy and Politics of the Communist Academy. Few issues are available outside Soviet archives.

JC524 *Revoliutsionnyi Vostok.* Moscow: 1927-37. Published irregularly (41 issues) by the Research Association for the Study of National and Colonial Problems of the University of Toilers of the East. Includes many articles on China.

JC525 *Sovetskoe vostokovedeniia.* Moscow: 1940-58. Published six times a year, by the Oriental Institute of the Academy of Sciences;

changed title in 1959 to *Problemy vostokovedeniia* and in 1961 to *Narody Azii i Afriki: istoriia, ekonomika, kultura.* Occasional articles on the history of the Chinese revolution.

JC526 *Tikhii okean; politiko-sotsialno-ekonomicheskii zhurnal.* Moscow: 1934-38. Published quarterly by the Pacific Section of the Institute of World Economy and Politics of the Communist Academy from 1934 to 1938. Includes numerous articles on China; the last of the Soviet scholarly journals on the Far East until after World War II. A total of 17 issues were published.

JC527 *Vostok i kolonii.* Moscow: 1927-30. Published by the Eastern Section of the Profintern.

JD. OUTER MONGOLIA

EDITED BY PETER S. H. TANG AND ROBERT A. RUPEN

JD1 AKADEMIIA NAUK SSSR. *Istoriia Mongolskoi Narodnoi Respubliki.* Ed. by B. D. Grekov. Moscow: 1954. 421 p. A history of Mongolia from pre-historic times, according to the Communist timetable. The period prior to 1911 is unusually detailed. The era since the establishment of Soviet power in 1921 is covered by a short and typical chronological analysis. The standard and official history, but its value is seriously impaired by its undeviating political orthodoxy. It is useful as a general survey when used cautiously. Bibliography.

JD2 AKADEMIIA NAUK SSSR, INSTITUT VOSTOKOVEDENIIA. *Mongolskaia Narodnaia Respublika; sbornik statei.* Moscow: Izd. Akademii nauk SSSR, 1952. 396 p. A general survey from the Soviet point of view of the political and economic development of the Mongolian republic, with sections on the People's Revolutionary Party, agriculture, industry, trade and finances, and culture. Appendices include the state constitution, and treaties of friendship and economic and cultural cooperation with the USSR. [A]

JD3 AKADEMIIA NAUK SSSR, INSTITUT VOSTOKOVEDENIIA. *Revoliutsionnye meropriiatiia narodnogo pravitelstva Mongolii v 1921-1924 gg.; dokumenty.* Comp. by T. S. Nasanbalzhir. Ed. by T. S. Puntsuknorov. Moscow: Izd. vostochnoi literatury, 1960. 211 p. An important collection of official documents for the early Soviet period.

JD4 AKADEMIIA NAUK SSSR, SOVET PO IZUCHENIIU PROIZVODITELNYKH SIL. *Bibliografiia Tuvinskoi avtonomnoi oblasti, 1774-1958 gg.* Comp. by V. I. Dulov and others. Ed. by M. I. Pomus. Moscow: Izd. Akad. nauk SSSR, 1959. 166 p. The only extensive bibliography for Tannu Tuva, which became an Autonomous Republic of the USSR during World War II.

JD5 BAVRIN, E. P., and MESHCHERIAKOV, MIKHAIL V. *M.N.R.* Moscow: Vneshtorgizdat, 1961. A significant study of the foreign trade of the M.P.R.

JD6 *BNMA-yu 1921-1958 onuudyu yls ardyn azh akhui soyolyn khugzhilt; statistikiin ekhetgel. Razvitie narodnogo khoziastva i kultury M.N.R. s 1921 do 1958 g.; statisticheskii sbornik.* Ulan Bator: 1960. English ed., Joint Publications Research Service no. 9987, Sept. 14, 1961. The first Mongolian statistical handbook; includes census and other statistical materials available nowhere else. See *Narodnoe Khoziastvo M.N.R.* below. [A]

JD7 CHANG, CHIH-YI. *A Bibliography of Books and Articles on Mongolia.* London: Institute of Pacific Relations, 1951. 49 p. Originally published in the *Journal of the Royal Central Asian Society*, vol. 37 (1950), parts 2 and 3. Especially useful for its citation of Chinese sources. Extensive annotation. Compiled under the direction of Owen Lattimore.

JD8 CHOIBALSAN, KHORLOIN. *Mongol arat-un undusun-u qubisqal-un qubisqal-un engge eguschu baigalagdagsan tobchi teuke.* Ulan Bator: 1934. 2 vols. Russian ed., *Kratkii ocherk mongolskoi narodnoi revoliutsii.* Moscow: 1952. 78 p. Czech ed., Prague: 1954. German ed., Berlin: 1954. The official account of the Mongolian revolution of 1921 by the man who served as Prime Minister and dictator of the M.P.R. from 1939 to 1952. [B]

JD9 CLEINOW, GEORGE. *Neu-Sibirien, eine Studie zum Aufmarsch der Sowjetmacht in Asien.* Berlin: R. Hobbing, 1928. 426 p. An early detailed description of the Soviet Far East and Mongolia. Primary emphasis is on the Bolshevization of Siberia. There is a chapter on the Soviet takeover in Outer Mongolia, with a description of the political situation in the 1920's.

JD10 CONOLLY, VIOLET. *Soviet Economic Policy in the East; Turkey, Persia, Afghanistan, Mongolia and Tana Tuva, Sin Kiang.* London: Oxford, 1933. 168 p. Brief analyses of Soviet trade policies in various areas of the Far East. The 23-page section on Mongolia describes the gradual Soviet takeover of Mongolian trade since the establishment of the republic. The author states that Mongolia serves a twofold purpose for the Soviet Union: as a laboratory for its experiment in revolution, and as a source of needed raw materials. Includes brief description of transportation in Mongolia and tables indicating trade turnover.

JD11 DYLYKOV, S. *Demokraticheskoe dvizhenie mongolskogo naroda v Kitae; ocherk istorii.* Moscow: Izd. Akademii nauk SSSR, 1953. 132 p. A Soviet analysis of the recent history of Inner Mongolia, including sections on the Communist movement after the Second World War and the status of the region since the Chinese Communist takeover. Appendices on the organization and structure of Inner Mongolia and the political program of the autonomous government of Inner Mongolia. Bibliography of Soviet works on the region. Only indirect references to Outer Mongolia. [B]

JD12 FRITERS, GERARD M. *Outer Mongolia and its International Position.* Baltimore: Johns Hopkins, 1949; London: Allen and Unwin, 1951. 358 p. An excellent analysis of the Outer Mongolian political position to 1949. Divided into sections concerning Mongolian relations with China, Russia, and other countries. Detailed analysis of the revolutionary period. Sections on the Mongolian economy. Maps. Chapter 2 covers relations with Russia. [A]

JD13 GELETA, JÓZSEF. *The New Mongolia*. London: Heinemann, 1936. 276 p. An account of the personal experiences of a traveler in Mongolia during the revolutionary years of 1920-21. Includes description of customs, housing, religion, and countryside and undocumented description of regime measures from 1921-1929. His eye-witness account of developments in 1921 is valuable in describing events rarely reported by non-Marxist observers.

JD14 GRIMM, E. D., ed. *Sbornik dogovorov i drugikh dokumentov po istorii mezhdunarodnykh otnoshenii na Dalnem Vostoke, 1844-1925*. Moscow: 1927. 218 p. A collection of international agreements in the Far East from 1842 to 1925. Gives agreements concluded by Outer Mongolia during the period from 1911 to 1925.

JD15 HEISSIG, W. *Das gelbe Vorfeld, die Mobilisierung der chinesischen Aussenländer*. Heidelberg: K. Vowinckel, 1941. 163 p. The most important work on the Japanese in Inner Mongolia before World War II. [B]

JD16 IAKIMOVA, T. A. *M.N.R.—ekonomika i vneshniaia torgovlia*. Moscow: 1954. 54 p. A useful summary of Mongolia's foreign trade, including information not available elsewhere.

JD17 IAKOVLEVA, EKATERINA N. *Bibliografiia M.N.R.; systematicheskii ukazatel knig i zhurnalnykh statei na russkom iazyke*. Ed. by F. E. Telezhnikov. Moscow: Izd. Nauchno-issledovatelskoi assotsiatsii po izuchaniiu natsionalnykh i kolonialnykh problem, 1935. 230 p. The best and most complete bibliography of works about Mongolia in the Russian language, on all subjects. Fully indexed. [A]

JD18 IWAMURA, SHINOBU, and FUJIEDA, AKIRA. *Moko kenkyu bunken mokoroku, 1900-1950*. Kyoto University: jimbunkagaku kenkyushu Kyoto, 1952. 46 p. A Japanese-language bibliography on Mongolia.

JD19 KALINIKOV, ANATOLI. *Natsionalno-revoliutsionnoe dvizhenie v Mongolii*. Moscow-Leningrad: "Moskovskii rabochii," 1926. 118 p. An authoritative Soviet interpretation of the Mongolian revolutionary movement as carried out under Moscow's tutelage.

JD20 KALINIKOV, ANATOLI. *Revoliutsionnaia Mongoliia*. Moscow: 1925. A typical Soviet presentation in the form of a comprehensive survey of Outer Mongolia during the early years of Soviet rule.

JD21 KERNER, ROBERT J. *Northeastern Asia; a Selected Bibliography*. Berkeley: U. of California Press, 1939. 2 vols. An exhaustive bibliography of works and periodicals in European and Oriental languages on Northeastern Asia. Divided topically and geographically. The Mongolian bibliography is located in the second volume—includes works on political, social, economic, and cultural fields.

JD22 KOLARZ, WALTER. *Peoples of the Soviet Far East.* London: G. Phillips; N.Y.: Praeger, 1954. 193 p. Includes substantial and exceptionally useful sections on both the M.P.R. and Buriat Mongolia. Contains much information which corrects and supplements Friter's work.

JD23 KOROSTOVETS, IVAN IA. *Von Cinggis Khan zur Sowjetrepublik; eine kurze Geschichte der Mongolei unter besonderer Berücksichtigung der neuesten Zeit.* Berlin and Leipzig: W. de Gruyter, 1926. 351 p. A Tsarist Russian envoy to Urga describes Mongolian history, with primary emphasis on the period after 1912. Includes a defense of his activity on behalf of the Tsarist government during World War I and a detailed investigation of the revolutionary period. Excellent on the politics and international situation of Mongolia in the 20th century. Indispensable. [A]

JD24 KUNGUROV, G. F., and SOROKOVIKOV, I. *Aratskaia revoliutsiia; istoricheskii ocherk.* Irkutsk: 1957. 208 p. Concerning the Mongolian revolution of 1921; the authors participated in the events they describe.

JD25 LATTIMORE, OWEN. *The Desert Road to Turkestan.* London: Methuen, 1928. 331 p. An interesting description of caravan journeys through Central Asia and a portrayal of the life and customs of Mongolia and Chinese Turkestan. Valuable as a background work for the area.

JD26 LATTIMORE, OWEN. *Inner Asian Frontiers of China.* N.Y.: American Geographical Society, 1940. 585 p. 2nd ed., Irvington-on-Hudson, N.Y.: Capitol and American Geographical Society, 1951. 585 p. A highly suggestive and stimulating analysis of the long relations between the Chinese and the Mongols.

JD27 LATTIMORE, OWEN. *Nationalism and Revolution in Mongolia.* With a translation from the Mongol of Sh. Nachukdorji's *Life of Sukebatur.* N.Y.: Oxford, under the auspices of the Institute of Pacific Relations, 1955. 186 p. An analytical study of Outer Mongolia under Manchu and Soviet dominance. Investigates the Mongolian capacity for independence surrounded by large neighbors. Sketches and analyzes the careers of regime leaders Sukebatur and Choibalsang. The *Life of Sukebatur* is an idealized and sparsely-detailed account written from the Soviet point of view. Eulogizes the role of Choibalsang carrying out the life work of Sukebatur. [B]

JD28 LEVIN, ISAAK O. *La Mongolie historique, géographique, politique.* Paris: Payot, 1937. 252 p. An historical account of the Mongolian nation from the time of the Khans to 1937, with a fairly detailed but undocumented account of the revolutionary years. Chapters on geography, Tannu Tuva, and Mongol-Japanese relations in the 1930's.

JD29 MA, HO-T'IEN. *Chinese Agent in Mongolia.* Baltimore: Johns Hopkins, 1949. 215 p. An interesting personal account of the activities of a Koumintang agent in Outer Mongolia between the World Wars. Much information on the political and economic scene not readily available elsewhere. [B]

JD30 MAISKII, IVAN M. *Sovremennaia Mongoliia; otchet mongolskoi ekspeditsii, snariazhennoi irkutskoi kontoroi Vserossiiskogo tsentralnogo soiuza potrebitelnykh obshchestv.* Irkursk: Gos. izd. irkutskoe otd., 1921. 1 vol. (various pagings). 2nd. rev. ed., *Mongoliia nakanune revoliutsii.* Moscow: Izd. vost. lit., 1960. 310 p. A classic work, based heavily on the incomplete and questionable census of 1918; the whole of the great statistical apparatus which constitutes the heart of this well-known book is simply not reliable. With that important qualification, the book is one of the very best available. [A]

JD31 MASLENNIKOV, VASILII A. *Mongolskaia Narodnaia Respublika.* Moscow: 1955. 72 p. Brings up to 1955 his *M.N.R. na puti k sotsializm.* The author is a leading Soviet specialist on Mongolia.

JD32 MASLENNIKOV, VASILII A. *Mongolskaia Narodnaia Respublika na puti k sotsializmu.* Moscow: Gospolitizdat, 1951. 172 p. An excellent survey of Mongolian development since the Russian Revolution. Sections on agriculture, industry, transport, trade and finance, and culture, as well as on the administrative system.

JD33 MESHCHERIAKOV, MIKHAIL V. *Ocherk economicheskogo sotrudnichestva Sovetskogo Soiuza i Mongolskoi Narodnoi Respubliki.* Moscow: Vneshtorgizdat, 1959. 158 p. The historical development of Russo-Mongol trade and cooperation, written from the Marxist point of view. A short survey of pre-revolutionary trade and an analysis of Soviet technical assistance to Mongolia since World War II. Includes statistics on Mongolian exports and imports, and an appendix containing a bibliography and Soviet-Mongol treaties. [B]

JD34 MIKHAILOV, G. I. *Ocherk istorii sovremennoi mongolskoi literatury.* Moscow: Izd. Akad. nauk SSSR, 1955. 214 p. An official survey of contemporary Mongolian literature, with heavy emphasis on "socialist realism."

JD35 MILLER, ROBERT J. *Monasteries and Culture Change in Inner Mongolia.* Wiesbaden: Harrassowitz, 1959. 152 p. A useful study of the cultural and economic role of the Buddhist Church among the Mongols.

JD36 MILLER, ROBERT J. "A Selective Survey of Literature on Mongolia," *The American Political Science Review*, XLVI, no. 3 (September 1952). A review article covering a wide variety of the literature.

JD37 MISSHIMA, YASUO, and GOTO, TOMIO. *A Japanese View of Outer Mongolia.* (Translated and summarized by A. J. Grajdanzev from the Japanese original: *Gaimo jinmin kyomakoku soren kyokuto no zenei.*) N.Y.: International Secretariat, Institute of Public Relations, 1942. 66 p. Popularized and overly sensational, but based on considerable and imaginative research. Contains much material not available elsewhere, or only in very obscure Russian sources. Proved reliable wherever possible to check.

JD38 MONGOLIA (MONGOLIAN PEOPLE'S REPUBLIC), LAWS, STATUTES, ETC. *Konstitutsiia i osnovnye zakonodatelnye akty Mongolskoi Narodnoi Respubliki.* Ed. by S. S. Demidov. Moscow: Izd. inostrannoi lit., 1952. 271 p. This remains a very important collection of documents, although the constitution it presents has been succeeded by a new one promulgated in 1960.

JD39 MONGOLIA (MONGOLIAN PEOPLE'S REPUBLIC), SINJILEKII UHAGANU KÜRIYELENG. *The Mongolian People's Republic.* Ed. by N. Zhagvaral. Ulan Bator: 1956. 154 p. A general survey on the development of the Mongolian People's Republic, with chapters on physiography, mineral wealth, population, and a brief historical sketch based on a Marxist interpretation. Chapters on government structure, national economy, and culture.

JD40 *Mongolskii sbornik; ekonomika, istoriia, arkheologiia. (Uchenye zapiski instituta vostokovedeniia*, no. 24.) Moscow: Izd. vost. lit., 1959. 203 p. Includes many new and previously unknown details, while offering generally what has by now become the "orthodox" presentation.

JD41 MONTAGU, IVOR. *Land of Blue Sky; a Portrait of Modern Mongolia.* London: Dobson, 1956. 191 p. A sympathetic account of Mongolian development under Soviet tutelage by an English traveler. The sections on agriculture, industry, education, and government are insufficiently detailed and highly uncritical. Interesting from the point of view of local color.

JD42 *Narodnoe khoziaistvo M.N.R. za 40 let; statisticheskii sbornik.* Ulan Bator: 1961. 196 p. A more complete statistical handbook than the first one issued in 1960 (see "BNMA" above). [A]

JD43 NAVAN, NAMJIL. *Ovgon bicheechjin uguulel.* Ulan Bator: 1956. 296 p. A very important autobiographical account of a Mongolian official who served the government both before and after 1921.

JD44 OVDIENKO, IVAN K. *Vnutrenniaia Mongoliia.* Moscow: Gos. izd. georg. lit., 1954. 166 p. A topical Communist analysis of Inner Mongolia. Chapters on geography, climate, and population. An analysis of the administrative structure of Communist China's Inner Mongolia, its economy's political and economic reform. Economic-geographic analysis of administrative subdivisions. Only indirect references to Outer Mongolia.

JD45 PAVLOVSKY, M. N. *Chinese-Russian Relations.* N.Y.: Philosophical Library, 1949. 194 p. An important work of political analysis; very suggestive and useful concerning the USSR and Mongolia.

JD46 *Planirovanie narodnogo khoziaistva Mongolii; sbornik materialov.* Moscow: 1951. Includes some particularly important official reports on the economy and plans for economic development. [B]

JD47 POZNER, VLADIMIR. *Bloody Baron; the Story of Ungern-Sternberg.* N.Y.: Random House, 1938. 383 p. Concerns the Baltic Baron and White officer who seized power in Mongolia with the aim of restoring the empire of Genghis Khan, only to be later overthrown by the Bolsheviks.

JD48 PUNTSUKNOROV, T. S. *Mongolyn avtonomit ueiin tuukh, 1911-1919.* Ulan Bator: 1955. 222 p. One of the most important products of Mongolian indigenous scholarship; an "official" account by the man who heads the Historical Research Section of the Party Research Institute of the Central Committee of the Mongolian People's Revolutionary (Communist) Party.

JD49 RUPEN, ROBERT A. "Outer Mongolian Nationalism, 1900-1919." Ph.D. dissertation, U. of Washington, Seattle, 1954. 386 p. A detailed study of Mongolian autonomy, based principally on Russian sources.

JD50 SALISBURY, HARRISON. *To Moscow and Beyond; a Reporter's Narrative.* N.Y.: Harper, 1959. 301 p. Pages 196-240 deal with Salisbury's personal experiences and observations in the M.P.R.

JD51 SHIRENDYB, B. *Narodnaia revoliutsiia v Mongolii i obrazovanie MNR.* Moscow: Izd. Akad. nauk SSSR, 1956. 160 p. An account of the 1921 revolution by the present head of the M.P.R. Academy of Sciences.

JD52 SKACHKOV, PETR E. *Bibliografiia Kitaia; sistematicheskii ukazatel knig i zhurnalnykh statei o Kitae na russkom iazyke, 1730-*

1930. Moscow-Leningrad: Gos. sots.-ekon. izd., 1932. 842 p. 2nd ed., Moscow: 1960. 691 p. An exhaustive bibliography of books and other publications on China in the Russian language. Includes several works on Mongolia and Sino-Mongolian relations.

JD53 SKACHKOV, PETR E. *Vnutrenniaia Mongoliia; ekonomiko-geograficheskii ocherk*. Moscow: Izd. nauchno-issl. assotsiatsii po izucheniiu natsionalnykh i kolonialnykh problem, 1933. 149 p. A short analysis of Inner Mongolia in pre-Communist China. Chapters on administrative structure, economics, trade, and the Communist movement. Bibliography. Only indirect references to Outer Mongolia.

JD54 TAN, TENNYSON. *Political Status of Mongolia*. Shanghai: The Mercury Press, 1932. 144 p. A description of Soviet and Japanese attempts to control Outer Mongolia between World War I and II. The author writes from a Chinese point of view, and reaffirms Mongolia as Chinese territory. Indicates attempts to colonize Mongolia with Chinese. Includes a chapter describing European and American attitudes toward Mongolia.

JD55 THIEL, ERICH. *Die Mongolei; Land, Volk und Wirtschaft der Mongolischen Volksrepublik*. Munich: Isar, 1958. 495 p. An excellent geographical and economic survey of the MPR. A most complete account of the land and people, but only sketchy references to the political situation and mood of the people. [A]

JD56 TIULAEVA, V. P. *Bibliografiia knizhnoi i zhurnalnoi literatury na russkom iazyke, 1935-1950 gg*. Mongolskaia komissiia, *Trudy*, no. 42. Moscow: 1953. 88 p. Supplements and brings up to 1950 the Iakovleva bibliography. [A]

JD57 TSAPKIN, N. *Mongolskaia Narodnaia Respublika*. Moscow: Gospolitizdat, 1948. 111 p. A survey of post-revolutionary Mongolia, written from the Soviet point of view. Includes a discussion of pre-revolutionary Mongolia, and a description of its geography and population. Sections on economics, government, and culture.

JD58 TSEDENBAL, IU. *Nokor choibalsang-un ules ba amidural*. Russian ed., *O zhizni i deiatelnosti Marshala Choibalsana*. Moscow: Izd. inostrannoi lit., 1952. 50 p. German ed., Berlin: Dietz, 1954. The official biography of the Mongolian revolutionary hero, by his successor as prime minister of the country.

JD59 WASHINGTON (STATE) UNIVERSITY, FAR EASTERN AND RUSSIAN INSTITUTE. *Bibliography of the Mongolian People's Republic*. New Haven, Conn.: Human Relations Area Files, 1956. 101 p. Includes works in all languages; annotated.

JD60 WASHINGTON (STATE) UNIVERSITY, FAR EASTERN AND RUSSIAN INSTITUTE. *Mongolian People's Republic (Outer Mongolia)*. New Haven, Conn.: Human Relations Area File, 1956. 3 vols. A detailed handbook compiled by a group of authors at the University of Washington.

JD61 ZLATKIN, I. IA. *Mongolskaia Narodnaia Respublika; strana novoi demokratii; ocherk istorii*. Moscow: Izd. Akad. nauk SSSR, 1950. 280 p. German ed., Berlin: Dietz, 1954. 315 p. Probably the best single Soviet study of the modern period. The detailed chronology contains information not available in the text or anywhere else. [A]

JD62 ZLATKIN, I. IA. *Ocherki novoi i noveishnei istorii Mongolii*. Moscow: 1957. 299 p. An analysis of Mongolian history from 1600 to the present day from a Marxist point of view. Historical development prior to the 20th century is fairly well detailed and footnoted. The sketch of the recent history of the republic is general and not well documented. A map is included showing administrative divisions of the Mongolian republic.

Addendum

JD63 RUPEN, ROBERT A. *Mongols of the Twentieth Century*. Bloomington: Indiana University Press, 1964. Part 1, 510 p. Part 2, 167 p. A scholarly work by a Professor of Political Science at the University of North Carolina.

JE. JAPAN

1. JAPANESE-SOVIET RELATIONS

(Edited by James William Morley)

JE1 AKADEMIIA NAUK SSSR, INSTITUT NARODOV AZII. *Bibliografiia Iaponii, literatura izdannaia v Sovetskom Soiuze na russkom iazyke s 1917 po 1958 g.* Comp. by V. A. Vlasov and others. Ed. by M. I. Lukianova, Kh. T. Eidus, and A. E. Gluskina. Moscow: Izd. vost. lit., 1960. 328 p. Lists 6249 titles, has an extensive index (28 double-column pages), of which a few are in Latin script, and a two-page table of contents. Lists documents, monographs, articles and brief notices on Japan that were published in the Soviet Union between 1917 and 1958. Includes works on Japan in Russian published as books or brochures, works included in anthologies, almanacs, scholarly journals, as well as translations of books and articles from the Japanese and other languages. Also included are lectures and reproductions of articles in manuscript at the Lenin Library. Newspaper articles and notices and unpublished dissertations were not included. Covers not only works devoted entirely to Japan but also certain non-specialized works which contain material on Japan. The bibliographic descriptions of such works, when possible, are accompanied by references to chapters or pages that refer to Japan. In all cases when the title of the book or article does not sufficiently indicate the nature of its content, brief annotations are given. Organized under the following chapter headings: (1) The Founders of Marxism-Leninism on Japan; (2) Soviet Party and State Leaders on Japan; (3) Leaders of the International and Japanese Labor Movement on Japan; (4) General Works, Bibliographic Material, Methodology; (5) Geography, Ethnography; (6) Economics; (7) Philosophy; (8) History; (9) Japanese Militarism and Fascism, Imperialist Aggression; (10) Foreign Policy; (11) State and Law; (12) Religion and Church; (13) Armed Forces; (14) Education, Science; (15) Literature; (16) The Press; (17) Linguistics; (18) Art. [A]

JE2 AKADEMIIA NAUK SSSR, INSTITUT VOSTOKOVEDENIIA. *Ocherki noveishei istorii Iaponii.* By E. M. Zhukov and others. Ed. by Kh. T. Eidus. Moscow: Izd. Akad. nauk SSSR, 1957. 365 p. An analysis of Japanese developments from 1918 to the present, written by five Soviet experts on Japan: E. M. Zhukov, A. L. Galperin, A. V. Varshavskii, P. P. Topekha, and M. N. Kirpsha. The latter provided the materials on the Japanese Communist Party.

JE3 *Das Aktuelle Archiv 9; Japan-China-USSR.* Berlin: E. Merker, 1937. 20 p. A military-political and strategic survey of Japanese, Chinese, and Soviet forces in the Far East at the opening of the China incident.

JE4 ALEKSANDROV, BORIS A. *Gosudarstvennyi stroi Iaponii.* Moscow: Sovetskoe zakonoizdatelstvo, 1935. 110 p. A detailed description of Japanese government and politics based on secondary sources.

JE5 BERTON, PETER; LANGER, PAUL; and SWEARINGEN, RODGER. *Japanese Training and Research in the Russian Field.* Los Angeles: University of Southern California, 1956. 266 p. A detailed study of the growth in Japan of facilities for the training of Russian and Soviet specialists and of Japanese publications and other activities in this field. [B]

JE6 BISSON, THOMAS A. "Soviet-Japanese Relations: 1931-1938." N.Y.: Foreign Policy Association (*Foreign Policy Reports*, XIV, no. 22, Feb. 1, 1939). A balanced survey, written for the public by an American scholar, of causes of friction between Japan and the USSR, foreseeing eventual war as the result.

JE7 BOLDYREV, GRIGORI. *Iaponskie militaristy provotsiruiut voinu.* Moscow: Gospolitizdat, 1938. 62 p. A propaganda pamphlet charging Japanese provocation along the USSR's Far Eastern borders and preparations for war against the Soviet Union.

JE8 BORISOV, A. *Iapono-germanskoe soglashenie.* Moscow: Gos. sots.-ek. izdat., 1937. 101 p. A pamphlet for popular consumption condemning the Japanese-German Anti-Comintern Pact (1936) as a military alliance directed against the USSR and the world, and analyzing the military preparedness of the two countries and the "contradictions" between them.

JE9 DAS, T. "Russo-Japanese Relations." Ph.D. dissertation, Georgetown University, 1924.

JE10 DASHINSKY, S. *Japan in Manchuria.* Ed. by N. Fokin. N.Y.: Workers' Library, 1932. 47 p. A propaganda pamphlet attacking Japanese aggression in China.

JE11 DEAN, VERA MICHELES. "The Soviet Union and Japan in the Far East." N.Y.: Foreign Policy Association. 146 p. (*Foreign Policy Reports*, VIII, no. 12, Aug. 17, 1932). An objective essay by an American scholar-publicist on Soviet-Japanese relations, 1917-32, stressing the exacerbation caused by Japan's occupation of northern Manchuria; Western and Russian sources were used.

JE12 DEREVIANKO, KUZMA. *So-ren wa Nihon ni nani wo nozomu.* Trans. and ed. by Japanese-Soviet Friendship Association.

Tokyo: Kyodo-sha, 1949. 137 p. Speeches by the Soviet representative to the Allied Council for Japan.

JE13 DOI, AKIO. *Bei-So sen to Nihon.* Tokyo: Kōdo-sha, 1952. 330 p. A study of the comparative power of the U.S.A. and the USSR at the end of the occupation of Japan, the possibility of an American-Soviet war, the effect such a war would have on Asia, and the need for Japanese-American cooperation, written by a former officer of the Japanese Imperial Army who has specialized in Soviet and Chinese problems.

JE14 EIDUS, KHAIM T. *Iaponiia ot pervoi do vtoroi mirovoi voiny.* Moscow: Gospolitizdat, 1946. 245 p. The most comprehensive Soviet survey of Japan's political history during the period, based on secondary Russian, Japanese, and Western sources. [B]

JE15 FUTABA, TOSHI. *Shiberiya ni iru Nippon furyo no jitsujō.* Tokyo: Ichiyō-sha, 1948. 191 p. A report on the treatment accorded Japanese prisoners in Siberia. Detailed, well-written and much broader in scope than the majority of such eye-witness accounts. Of special interest is Chapter 11 on the indoctrination of prisoners.

JE16 GASTOV, G. *Iaponskii imperializm; politiko-ekonomicheskii ocherk.* Moscow: Izd. "Mosk. rabochii," 1930. 142 p.

JE17 GORDON, JOSEPH. "The Russo-Japanese Neutrality Pact of April, 1941." Certificate essay, East Asian Institute, Columbia, 1955. 109 p. Published in Columbia University, East Asian Institute, *Researches in the Social Sciences in Japan*, II (June 1959), p. 119-134. An historical account of the Soviet-Japanese negotiations, 1940-41, based primarily on Japanese Foreign Ministry archives and Japanese memoirs. Includes footnotes, bibliography, documentary appendix. [B]

JE18 HANABUSA, NAGAMICHI, ed. *Nihon gaikō-shi kankei bunken mokuroku.* Tokyo: Keiō gijuku daigaku hōgaku kenkyūkai, 1961. 485 p. The most complete list of Japanese materials relating to Japan's foreign relations, including those with the USSR. [B]

JE19 HATTORI, TAKUSHIRŌ. *Dai-Tōa sensō zenshi.* Tokyo: Masu shobō, 1956. 8 vols. A detailed study of Japanese military operations, with some reference to general foreign policy, 1940-45, based on Japanese archives, by a former Colonel of the Imperial Army. Valuable quotations from otherwise unavailable sources. Chronology and appendices of personnel. [B]

JE20 HIGUCHI, KINICHI. *Uraru wo koete.* Tokyo: Kengen-sha, 1949. 311 p. A compilation of essays, reports and articles written by sixteen former lieutenants in the Japanese Imperial Army (all but one, college graduates) who spent about two years in Soviet camps as prisoners of war.

JE21 HINDUS, MAURICE G. *Russia and Japan.* Garden City, N.Y.: Doubleday, Doran, 1942. 254 p. An interesting prediction that war would soon break out between the two countries and an appreciation of the industrial and strategic potentialities of Siberia, by a veteran journalist.

JE22 HODORAWIS, JOSEPH. "Soviet Reaction to the Manchurian Incident, 1931-1932." Certificate essay, Russian Institute, Columbia, 1958. 118 p. A comparison of public statements with confidential diplomatic negotiations as revealed in Soviet sources and Japanese Foreign Ministry archives. [B]

JE23 HOKUYŌ GYOGYŌ SŌRAN HENSHU I'INKAI. *Hokuyō gyogyō sōran.* Tokyo: Nōrin keizai kenkyūjo, 1960. 808 p. A detailed scientific, economic, and historical reference work on Japanese and Soviet fishery in the northern Pacific and the fishery problems which have arisen between the two countries. [B]

JE24 HOPPŌ RYŌDO NO CHI'I. *Kokusaihō Gaikō Zasshi*, LX, no. 4-5-6 (March 1962). 603 p. A symposium of articles by Japanese scholars on legal and political phases of the history of Japanese interest in the Kuriles and Karafuto; chronology and useful bibliography of Japanese and Soviet materials. [A]

JE25 IOFFE (JOFFE), A. A. *Iaponiia v nashi dni.* Moscow: Nauchnaia assotsiatsiia vostokovedeniia, 1926. 77 p. A leading Soviet diplomat of the 1920's, who was involved in important negotiations with Japan, gives a brief survey of the situation there.

JE26 JAPAN, MINISTRY OF FOREIGN AFFAIRS. *Gaikō shiryō.* Tokyo: 1946. An official compilation for restricted circulation of Japanese archival materials relating to negotiations with the Soviet Union during World War II. [A]

JE27 JAPAN, MINISTRY OF FOREIGN AFFAIRS. *Gaimushō Kōhyō-shū.* Tokyo: 1919—. A series of official announcements made by the Ministry on diplomatic incidents, international situations, treaties, policies, etc., often in English as well as Japanese, by date. [B]

JE28 JAPAN, MINISTRY OF FOREIGN AFFAIRS, comp. *Nihon gaikō nempyō shuyō bunsho.* Tokyo: Nihon Kokusai Rengō Kyōkai, 1955. 2 vols. An indispensable official collection of selected Japanese diplomatic documents, with index and chronologies, 1840-1945. [A]

JE29 JAPAN, MINISTRY OF FOREIGN AFFAIRS. *Nis-So kōshō shi.* Tokyo: 1942. An indispensable, formerly classified, official chronological survey of Japanese-Soviet diplomatic negotiations, 1917-40, written by a scholar with full access to the Foreign Ministry archives. [A]

JE30 JAPAN, MINISTRY OF FOREIGN AFFAIRS, comp. *Shūsen shiroku*. Tokyo: Shimbun gekkan-sha, 1952. An important, official collection of documents relating to the efforts made by individual Japanese to end the war (1941-45) and the government's decision to surrender, including negotiations with the USSR. [B]

JE31 JAPAN, MINISTRY OF FOREIGN AFFAIRS. *Waga gaikō no kinkyo (Dai . . . gō)*. Tokyo: 1958—. Semi-annual. The Ministry's official, semiannual report of Japan's foreign relations, with documentary appendices. [A]

JE32 JAPAN, MINISTRY OF FOREIGN AFFAIRS, EUROPEAN AND AFRICAN BUREAU, EAST EUROPEAN SECTION. *So-ren geppō*. Official monthly report of the Japanese Foreign Ministry on developments in the USSR, the foreign relations of the USSR, and the international Communist movement; documents, designed for international use. [B]

JE33 JAPAN, NATIONAL DIET LIBRARY. *Chōsa rippō kōsa kyoku. Nis-So kokkō chōsei mondai kiso shiryō shū*. Tokyo: Kokuritsu kokkai toshokan, 1955. 242 p. A collection of official documents, mostly legal, relating to the outbreak of war between the USSR and Japan in 1945 and to other outstanding issues which arose between them, 1945-55. [A]

JE34 JIYŪ AJIA SHA, ed. *So-ren kakumei 40-nen*. Tokyo: The Editor, 1957. 669 p. Brief memoirs, by Japanese official participants or newspaper observers, of specific developments in Russian and Soviet history and relations with Japan, 1905-56, arranged chronologically. [B]

JE35 KAMIKAWA, HIKOMATSU. *Nihon gaikō no saishuppatsu; sokoku no jiyū to dokuritsu no tame ni*. Tokyo: Kashima kenkyūjo, 1960. A collection of articles written 1949-59 by the conservative "dean" of Japanese diplomatic history and international politics, on the diplomatic course Japan should follow; strongly critical of American and Soviet policies toward Japan, he champions a new nationalism.

JE36 KANTOROVICH, ANATOLI. *Ochag voiny na Dalnem Vostoke*. Moscow: Partizdat, 1934. An undocumented attack on Japan's expansionist policies, U.S.-Japanese antagonisms, and the anti-Soviet policies all "imperialist" powers were alleged to be following; the "Tanaka memorial" and a speech by Araki Sadao in appendix.

JE37 KAWAKAMI, KIYOSHI K. *Japan's Pacific Policy, Especially in Relation to China, the Far East, and the Washington Conference*. N.Y.: Dutton, 1922. 380 p. A contemporary defense by a well-known publicist of the positions taken by Japan at the Washington Conference. Includes a documentary appendix relating to the Conference.

JE38 KHARNSKII, K. *Iaponiia v proshlom i nastoiashchem.* Vladivostok: Knizhnoe delo, 1926. 411 p.

JE39 KOMMUNISTICHESKAIA AKADEMIIA, MOSCOW, INSTITUT MIROVOGO KHOZIAISTVA I MIROVOI POLITIKI. *Sovremennaia Iaponiia.* Ed. by P. A. Mif and G. N. Voitinskii. Moscow: Izd. Institut Mkh i MP, 1934. 2 vols. Essays by Japanese Communists and Soviet scholars on Japanese imperialism, the labor and farmer movements, and the JCP. Useful bibliography of Russian-language works on Japan published 1931-34.

JE40 KOROVIN, EVGENII A. *Iaponiia i mezhdunarodnoe pravo.* Moscow: Sotsekgiz, 1936. 247 p. A survey of Japanese theories and practice of international law since the late nineteenth century, based on Russian sources, which are footnoted, contending that the Japanese have consistently violated international law in the pursuit of their own interests.

JE41 KRAINOV, P. *Amerikanskii imperializm v Iaponii.* Moscow: Gospolitizdat, 1951. 124 p. A propaganda pamphlet attacking Japanese imperialism before and during World War II and charging the United States during the Occupation with colonializing Japan and rebuilding the basis for its Fascism.

JE42 KURGANOV, O. *Amerikantsy v Iaponii; reportazh.* Moscow: Sovetskii Pisatel, 1947. 208 p. A journalistic report of trends in postwar Japan, stressing the survival of "military-fascist" elements and charging U.S. encouragement of them.

JE43 KYOKUTŌ JIJŌ KENKYŪKAI, ed. *Nis-So kōryū no haikei; seiji, bōeki, bunka kōryū no jitsujō Nis-So kyōkai to tai-Nichi rosen.* Tokyo: The Editor, 1958. 188 p. Brief descriptions of Japanese organizations active in the promotion of trade, cultural exchange, and the peace movement with the USSR in the 1950's.

JE44 LEMIN, I. *Propaganda voiny v Iaponii i Germanii.* Moscow: Gos. voen. izd., 1934. 169 p. A philosophical study of the ideological roots of Japanese and German propaganda to prepare their peoples for war.

JE45 MATVEEV, Z. N., and POPOV, A. D. *Bibliografiia Iaponii.* Ed. by E. G. Spalvin. Vladivostok: 1923. 136 p.

JE46 MOORE, HARRIET L. *Soviet Far Eastern Policy, 1931-1945.* Princeton, N. J.: Princeton University Press, 1945. 285 p. A naive survey of state relations, based largely on Soviet press reports, stressing the defensive concern of Soviet policy; with a documentary appendix.

JE47 MORISHIMA, GORŌ. *Kunō suru chū-So taishikan.* Tokyo: Minato shuppan gassaku sha, 1952. 184 p. Memoirs of the Japanese career diplomat who served as envoy to the USSR, 1942-45, assisting Ambassador Satō in the attempt to negotiate better relations with the USSR. Instructions and conversations are quoted or summarized.

JE48 MORLEY, JAMES W. *Soviet and Communist Chinese Policies toward Japan, 1950-1957, a Comparison.* N.Y.: International Secretariat, Institute of Pacific Relations, 1958. 46 p. A comparison of Soviet and Chinese trade, diplomatic and other policies, based on Soviet and Chinese sources, suggesting a serious divergence in their attitudes toward Japan since 1954.

JE49 NAITŌ, CHISHU, and others. *Roshia no tōhō seisaku.* Vol. IV in series *Ajia rekishi sōsho.* Tokyo: Meguro shoten, 1942. 315 p. An historical survey of Russian expansion and Soviet policy in Asia to 1936 based on Russian sources, by conservative Japanese scholars and officials.

JE50 NAMBARA, SHIGERU. *So-ren to Chūgoku.* Tokyo: Chūō koron-sha, 1955. A report by a leading Japanese intellectual of his impressions as a member of the cultural delegation of the Japan Academy to the USSR and Red China in 1955.

JE51 NICHI-SO TSUSHIN-SHA, comp. *So-rempō nenkan.* Tokyo: The Compiler, 1935 (issued as *Nichi-So nenkan*), 1937—. A yearbook of information on the USSR and relations among the USSR, Japan, and Manchukuo. [B]

JE52 NIHON GAIKŌ GAKKAI. *Taiheiyō sensō shūketsu ron.* Tokyo: Tokyo Univ. Press, 1958. 861, 14 p. Essays by various Japanese scholars, edited by Professor Toshio Ueda, on the termination of the war in the Pacific; includes chapters by Professor Naokichi Tanaka and Shigeru Hayashi on Japanese-Soviet relations, using Japanese sources and stressing Japan's peaceful intent. [B]

JE53 NIHON GAKUJUTSU KAIGI, comp. *So-ren Chūgoku gakujutsu shisatsu hōkoku.* Tokyo: The Compiler, 1956. 299 p. An official Japanese reprint of the report of the Japanese Academy's cultural delegation to the USSR and Red China in 1955.

JE54 NIHON KOKUSAI SEIJI GAKKAI, ed. *Futatsu no sekai to nashonarizumu.* Tokyo: Yūhikaku, 1959. 132, 52 p. Various essays on international conflicts in the world of the Cold War, including one on the general causes of such conflicts by Professor Kenzaburō and several by different scholars with differing viewpoints on the Korean war, the

Hungarian revolt, the war in Vietnam, the Suez affair, the war in Algeria, and the Iraqi revolution. Chronology and bibliography.

JE55 NIHON KOKUSAI SEIJI GAKKAI, ed. *Gendai kokusai seiji no kōzō.* Tokyo: Yūhikaku, 1958. 228 p. Among various scholarly essays on postwar international politics is one by Professor Gen Katsube analyzing the postwar foreign policy of the USSR sympathetically from a Marxist point of view.

JE56 NIHON KOKUSAI SEIJI GAKKAI, ed. *Gendai kokusai seiji shi.* Tokyo: Yūhikaku, 1959. 163, 27 p. Essays by senior scholars and graduate students on various problems of international politics, 1918-45, including two by junior scholars on Soviet policy. Annotated bibliography.

JE57 NIHON KOKUSAI SEIJI GAKKAI. *Nihon gaikō no bunseki.* Tokyo: Yūhikaku, 1957. 178 p. Essays by various Japanese scholars on problems facing Japanese foreign policy makers, 1945-57, including an analysis of the outlook for Japanese-Soviet relations by Professor Masao Onoe, Japan's leading historian of the USSR, stressing the decisive importance of trade.

JE57A NIHON KOKUSAI SEIJI GAKKAI TAIHEIYŌ SENSŌ GEN'IN KENKYŪBU, ed. *Taiheiyō sensō e no michi: kaisen gaikō-shi.* Tokyo: Asahi shimbunsha, 1962-63. 7 vols. A military-diplomatic history of Japan's road to the Pacific War, 1921-41. Based on careful use of diplomatic, military, and private archives. Includes footnoted essays by Japanese specialists on Japanese policy toward the Soviet Union, 1917-27; the Soviet response to Japanese expansion, 1926-39; and Soviet-Japanese negotiations, 1935-40. 3 volumes of documents are to follow. [A]

JE58 *Nihon Shimbun.* Khabarovsk. Twice weekly, Sept. 1945-Nov. 1949. A newspaper published by the Soviet authorities for Japanese prisoners of war in Siberia. Circulation reported as high as 800,000 at its peak. Designed to indoctrinate Japanese with the Soviet version of events in Japan and abroad. Available on microfilm at the Library of Congress.

JE59 NIS-SO-TŌ-Ō BŌEKI KAI, comp. *Nis-So bōeki yōran. 1959 nen han.* Tokyo: Nis-So Tō-Ō bōeki kai jimukyoku, 1958. 488 p. A detailed handbook of the political and economic situation in the USSR as of 1958, its trade practices and potential, its trading organizations, and the history of Soviet-Japanese trade relations. [B]

JE60 OGATA, SHŌJI. *So-ren gaikō no sanjūnen. Sono honnichi e no hatten.* Tokyo: Fūdōsha, 1947. A history of the first 30 years of Soviet diplomacy by a former Japanese diplomat, now said to be a Communist.

JE61 OKAMOTO, SHÔICHI, and KAMIYANA, SHUN. *Nis-So Gyogyô*. Tokyo: Suisan Tsushin-sha, 1939. 304 p. The Japanese present their interpretation of the fisheries conflict with the Soviet Union.

JE62 ONOE, MASAO. *Sovieto gaikō shi*. Tokyo: Yūshindō, 1959. 341 p. The standard Japanese historical survey, by an objective scholar, of Soviet diplomacy, 1917-37. Stresses Lenin's conceptions; based on Soviet documentary sources. Very little on policy toward Japan or the Far East. [B]

JE63 PARFENOV, PETR S. *Borba za Dalnii Vostok, 1920-1922*. Leningrad: "Priboi," 1928. 368 p. Deals with the post-revolutionary struggle in the Soviet Far East and the rivalry with Japan.

JE64 PAVLOVICH, MIKHAIL I. (pseud. of M. I. Veltman). *Iaponskii imperializm na Dalnem Vostoke*. Moscow: Izd. "Krasnaia nov," 1923. 145 p. Volume IV of *RSFSR v imperialisticheskom okruzhenii*.

JE65 PETROV, D. V. *Rabochee i demokraticheskoe dvizhenie v Iaponii*. Moscow: Gospolitizdat, 1961.

JE66 PEVZNER, IA. A. *Ekonomiia Iaponii posle vtoroi mirovoi voiny*. Moscow: 1955. 350 p. A serious study of Japan's postwar economy, concluding that "monopoly capitalists" have reasserted their control over Japanese economic and political life. Contains much statistical data.

JE67 PEVZNER, IA. A. *Monopolisticheskii kapital Iaponii ("Dzaibatsu") v gody vtoroi mirovoi voiny i posle voiny*. Moscow: Akademiia nauk SSSR, 1950. 532 p. An analysis by a Soviet specialist on the Japanese economy, stressing the growth of the *zaibatsu*, charging the Occupation with seeking to build a new form of colonialism, and concluding with a review of the postwar political, particularly the labor, movement.

JE68 PHILLIPS, G. D. R. *Russia, Japan and Mongolia*. London: F. Muller, 1942. 104 p. A pro-Soviet interpretation of Soviet-Japanese relations and particularly of their rivalry in Mongolia since World War I.

JE69 POPOV, V. A. *Krestianskoe dvizhenie v Iaponii posle vtoroi mirovoi voiny*. Moscow: Izd. vost. lit., 1961. 186 p.

JE70 RAGINSKII, M. IU., and ROZENBLIT, S. IA. *Mezhdunarodnyi protsess glavnykh iaponskikh voennykh prestupnikov*. Ed. by S. A. Golunskii. Moscow-Leningrad: Izd. Akad. nauk SSSR, 1950. 261 p. A legalistic account of the trial of major Japanese war criminals by the IMTFE, generally approving of the proceedings but accusing the Americans of prejudice in the interest of "American imperialists."

JE71 RAGINSKII, M. IU., ROZENBLIT, S. IA. and SMIRNOV, L. N. *Bakteriologicheskaia voina–prestupnoe orudie imperialisticheskoi agressii; Khabarovskii protsess iaponskikh voennykh prestupnikov.* Moscow: Akademiia nauk SSSR, 1950. 134 p. An analysis of some of the legal questions relating to responsibility for the preparation and application of bacteriological weapons, as developed at the Khabarovsk trial of Japanese war criminals; colored by anti-Japanese and anti-American sentiments.

JE72 RAIKOVICH, M. G. *Vostok i SSSR.* Moscow: Krasnyi arkhiv, 1928. A Japanese translation by SMR research section was published by Osaka Mainichi shimbunsha, 1932, under the title *Tōyō to Sovietto Rempō.*

JE73 ROYAMA MASAMICHI. *Foreign Policy of Japan, 1914-1939.* Tokyo: I.P.R., 1941. 182 p. A cautious account by a liberal internationalist seeking to explain Japan's policies to the West.

JE74 RUSSIA (1923– USSR), ARMIIA, POLITICHESKOE UPRAVLENIE. *Dokumenty sovetskogo patriotizma; v dni boev u ozera Khasan.* Ed. by Aleksandr N. Baev and F. Matrosov. Moscow: Gos. voen. izd., 1939. 91 p. A propagandistic collection of materials relating to the Chengkufeng Incident of 1938, designed to illustrate the patriotism of the Soviet military and the support of the Soviet people in the operations against Japan.

JE75 RUSU KAZOKU DANTAI ZENKOKU KYŌGIKAI, comp. *Hikiage sokushin undō jū-yo-nen no kiroku.* Tokyo: Kōwadō, 1959. 797 p. A detailed account of the efforts of various Japanese organizations to secure the repatriation of Japanese detained overseas after World War II, including negotiations with the USSR.

JE76 SAITŌ, RYŌEI. *Sovieto Rokoku no kyokutō shinshutsu.* Tokyo: Nippon hyoronsha, 1931. 376 p. A history of Soviet policy toward the Far East in the 1920's, by an influential diplomat-scholar. [B]

JE77 SAITŌ, YOSHIE. *Azamukareta rekishi; Matusoka to sangoku dōmei no rimen.* Tokyo: Yomiuri shimbunsha, 1955. 234 p. A first-hand account of the origins and conclusion of the Tripartite Pact among Germany, Italy, and Japan, 1940, by Foreign Minister Matsuoka's special adviser. Defends Matusoka as seeking friendly relations with the USSR. Documentary appendix.

JE78 SATŌ, NAOTAKE. *Futatsu no Roshia.* Tokyo: Sekai no Nihon sha, 1948. 242 p. Informal reminiscences of everyday life in Imperial and Soviet Russia by one of Japan's senior diplomatic specialists on the

USSR. Concerns his service in the embassy in Russia, 1906-14, 1925, and as Ambassador, 1942-45. He reveals little and stresses his isolation from information both from the USSR and from Japan.

JE78A SATŌ, NAOTAKE. *Kaiko hachijū-nen.* Tokyo: Jiji, 1963. 584 p. A more formal and fuller account of Sato's official life than the previous entry.

JE79 SHIDEHARA, KIJŪRŌ. *Gaikō 50-nen.* Tokyo: Yomiuri shimbunsha, 1951. 324 p. Informal reminiscences of the Japanese career diplomat, Foreign Minister, and Premier. Discusses among other things his negotiations at the Washington Conference concerning the Siberian expedition, his secret mediation of the Chinese Eastern Railway dispute between China and the USSR (1929), and his unofficial efforts to improve relations with the USSR, 1936-37.

JE80 SHIGEMITSU, MAMORU. *Gaikō kaisō roku.* Tokyo: Mainichi shimbunsha, 1953. Memoirs of the Japanese career diplomat, who as Vice Minister of Foreign Affairs (1933-36) handled the purchase of the Chinese Eastern Railway from the USSR, and later, as Ambassador to the USSR (1936-38), dealt with fishery and border disputes. Stresses his opposition to the military and their diplomatic supporters like Matsuoka. [A]

JE81 SHINOBU, SEIZABURŌ. *Taishō Seiji-shi.* Tokyo: Kawade shobō, 1951-52. 4 vols. A standard political history of Japan during the 1905-27 period, including Soviet-Japanese relations, with bibliography, written by a noted leftist historian.

JE82 SOKOLOV, BORIS M. *Iaponiia.* Moscow-Leningrad: Partizdat, 1934. 108 p. A propagandistic pamphlet for popular distribution, describing Japanese society and charging the Japanese government with pursuing a strong anti-Soviet policy.

JE83 STOKLITSKII, A. *Iaponiia i Kitai.* Moscow: Gosizdat, 1928. 103 p. A propaganda piece denouncing Japanese penetration of China and attributing it to the rise of capitalism.

JE84 SURVEY OF INTERNATIONAL AFFAIRS, 1920-1923—; THE WAR-TIME SERIES FOR 1939-1946. *The Far East, 1942-1946.* By F. C. Jones, Hugh Borton, and B. R. Pearn. London and N.Y.: Oxford, for the Royal Institute of International Affairs, 1955. 589 p. Contains an extensive section (p. 307-428) by Hugh Borton on "Japan under the Allied Occupation, 1945-7."

JE85 TAKEUCHI, KINJI. *Nihon no furyo wa So-ren de donna seikatsu wo shita ka.* Tokyo: Kobun-sha, 1950. 230 p. A detailed and interesting account comprised of half-page sketches and running commentary on the life of Japanese prisoners in the Soviet Union. The author who disavows being either an artist or a writer nevertheless succeeds in presenting a unique and intimate picture of the daily routine and treatment accorded Japanese POW's in Manchuria and Siberia. He was taken prisoner by the Soviet Armies in Manchuria during August 1945 and returned to Japan in November 1947.

JE86 TANIN, O., and IOGAN, E. *Voenno-fashistskoe dvizhenie v Iaponii.* Moscow: 1933. English ed., *Militarism and Fascism in Japan.* N.Y.: International, 1934. 320 p. An undocumented historical survey of the right wing movement in Japan from before World War I through the Manchurian incident, charging that it controlled government policy.

JE87 TANIN, O., and IOGAN, E. *When Japan goes to War.* N.Y.: Vanguard, 1936. 271 p. Russian ed., Moscow: Gos. sots.-ekon. izd., 1936. 237 p. On the premise that Japan sought to expel Soviet influence from Asia and would resort to war, this book analyzes Japan's political and economic preparedness for such an anti-Soviet war.

JE88 TEIKOKU ZAIGO GUNJIN-KAI, HOMBU. *Nihon ni okeru So-rempō no sakudō.* 1933. 148 p. Translation of a portion of the memoirs of a former counsellor of the Russian Embassy in Tokyo. Commentary on Soviet infiltration and designs on Japan.

JE89 TSAI WEI-PING. "The Russo-Japanese Conflict in the Far East." Ph.D. dissertation, U. of Illinois, 1938. Analyzes rivalries over railways, fisheries, oil, Mongolia, and other borders. Concludes that these tensions might lead to war.

JE90 TSURUMI, YUSUKE. *Gotō Shimpei.* Tokyo: Gotō Shimpei denki hensan-kai, 1938. 4 vols. A standard biography of a leading politician and Russian expert active in promoting the Japanese expedition in Siberia during the Civil War period and later in negotiating with Joffe for the establishment of Japanese-Soviet relations. Based on the archives of the Gotō family and of the Foreign Ministry.

JE91 U.S. DEPARTMENT OF DEFENSE. *The Entry of the Soviet Union into the War Against Japan; Military Plans, 1941-1945.* Washington: 1955. 107 p. Consists of documents in which high U.S. military men gave advice on the question of Soviet entry. [B]

JE92 UYEHARA, CECIL, comp. *Checklist of Archives in the Japanese Ministry of Foreign Affairs, Tokyo, Japan, 1868-1945.* Washington: Library of Congress, 1954. 262 p. Lists microfilms of archival files available in the Library of Congress; contains brief descriptive titles and an analytical index of originals in the Ministry's archives in Tokyo. [A]

JE93 VILENSKII, VLADIMIR D. ("Sibiriakov"). *Iaponiia.* Moscow: Vseros. nauch. assots. vostokoved., 1923. 204 p. Vilenskii held various official positions for the Soviet Government in the decade following the Revolution—as plenipotentiary of the RSFSR in the Far East, 1920; participant at the Dairen Conference, 1920; member of the diplomatic mission to Peking, 1922; founder of *Severnaia Aziia*, and one of the editors of *Izvestiia.* He was purged from the Party in 1927.

JE94 VILENSKII, VLADIMIR D. ("Sibiriakov"). *Iaponskii imperializm.* Leningrad: "Priboi," 1925. 139 p.

JE95 VILENSKII, VLADIMIR D. ("Sibiriakov"). *Imperializm sovremennoi Iaponii i sotsialnaia revoliutsiia; K voprosu resheniia Dalne-Vostochnoi problemy.* Moscow: 1919.

JE96 WATANABE, MIKIO. *So-ren tokuha go-nen.* Tokyo: Gaikoku bunka-sha, 1948. 284 p. Personal observations and experiences of a former *Mainichi* newspaper special correspondent to Moscow, 1941-46.

JE97 YOKO'O, WAKAKO. "The Restoration of Japanese-Soviet Diplomatic Relations, 1956." Master's thesis, Columbia, 1961. Describes the Japanese-Soviet negotiations, 1954-56, eventuating in the Peace Declaration of 1956, and explains their relationship to Japanese domestic politics. Based primarily on Japanese sources. [B]

JE98 YOKOTA, KISABURŌ. *Chōsen mondai to Nihon no shōrai.* Tokyo: Keisō shobō, 1950. 233 p. A study of Japan's security problems arising out of the Korean War from the legal point of view, by Japan's most eminent international lawyer and present Chief Justice of the Supreme Court. As an independent conservative, he concludes that there is danger of a Communist attack on Japan and that Japan's best defense is reliance on the United Nations.

JE99 YOSHIZAWA, KENKICHI. *Gaikō 60-nen.* Tokyo: Jiyū Ajia sha, 1958. 311 p. Memoirs of the Japanese career diplomat who served in various positions, including Chief of the Foreign Ministry's European and American Bureau, 1921-23, envoy to Peking, 1923-29 (during which tour he negotiated the restoration of Japanese-Soviet relations, 1925), and as Minister of Foreign Affairs, 1931-32. A not very enlightening account by a conservative official defending his record against the charges of the war crimes trials.

JE100 YOUNG, JOHN, comp. *Checklist of Microfilm Reproductions of Selected Archives of the Japanese Army, Navy, and other Government Agencies, 1868-1945.* Washington: Georgetown U. Press, 1959. 144 p. Archival files, with brief descriptive titles and index, microfilmed and available in the Library of Congress; the originals were seized during World War II by the U.S. forces and have now been returned. [A]

JE101 *Za rodnuiu zemliu; u ozera Khasan; na granitse.* Leningrad: Sovetskii pisatel, 1939. 338 p. A popular collection of reminiscences by Soviet participants in the fighting against the Japanese around Lake Khassan, in the Chengkufeng incident of 1938, and of short stories about the life of Soviet border guards. Designed to heighten the patriotism of the Soviet citizen.

JE102 ZHUKOV, E. M., and ROZEN, A., eds. *Iaponiia; sbornik statei.* Moscow: Gos. sots.-ekon. izd., 1934. 415 p. An important collection of essays on all phases of Japanese life, including foreign policy, by Soviet specialists. Contains a bibliography of Russian-language publications on Japan, 1931-33, compiled by the Institute of World Economy of the Communist Academy. [B]

JE103 ZHUKOV, IU., and GOLDBERG, M., comps. *Kak my bili iaponskikh samuraev; sbornik statei i dokumentov.* Moscow: Molodaia gvardiia, 1938. 358 p. Following an historical essay by the prolific Soviet Orientalist Zhukov, a collection of reminiscences by Soviet soldiers of the fighting in the Chengkufeng incident in 1938, for patriotic purposes. Appendix includes estimates of Japanese military strength in Kwantung and Korea.

2. JAPANESE COMMUNIST PARTY

(Edited by Rodger Swearingen)

JE104 AKADEMIIA NAUK SSSR, INSTITUT NARODOV AZII. *Bibliografiia Iaponii; literatura izdanniia v Sovetskom Soiuze na russkom iazyke s 1917 po 1958 g.* Comp. by V. A. Vlasov and others. Ed. by M. I. Lukianova and others. Moscow: Izd. vostochnoi lit., 1960. 328 p. Lists 6,249 items, including both books and articles, without annotations. Has sections on the Japanese CP, the "democratic movement," and the "struggle for peace."

JE105 AYAKAWA, TAKEHARU. *Kyosanto undo no gaiaku.* Tokyo: Zennippon kokoku doshi-kai shuppan-bu, 1930. 278 p. A history of the Communist movement in Japan to the end of 1930. Obviously written for the purpose of awakening the Japanese public to the danger of Communism. Very detailed and fairly accurate. Good on ties with Moscow. Now only of limited value, as more complete studies have appeared in the postwar period.

JE106 COLBERT, EVELYN S. *The Left Wing in Japanese Politics.* N.Y.: Institute of Pacific Relations, 1952. 353 p. Covers the entire field of left-wing Japanese politics. Although a substantial portion of the study is devoted to the Communist movement, emphasis is on the Socialist groups. The pre-surrender period (1918-45) is dealt with briefly, serving rather as an introduction to the chronological account of the postwar period (ending with 1950). The source material on which this work is based consists in the main of newspapers and periodical literature. A forty-page appendix presenting brief biographical sketches (average ten lines) of the major figures of the Japanese left wing, including many Communists, adds to the value of this useful reference work. [B]

JE107 DEVERALL, RICHARD L. *Red Star Over Japan.* Calcutta: 1952. 352 p. A history of Communist activity in Japan, emphasizing labor union activity in the postwar period. The author has been active in labor organization affairs. Written in a somewhat popular style.

JE108 DURKEE, TRAVERS E. "The Communist International and Japan, 1919-1932." Ph.D. dissertation, Stanford, 1954. An important study of Comintern activity in Japan and the Japanese Communist Party. Documented; bibliography.

JE109 GAIMUSHO, OBEI-KYOKU. *Kyosan undo kenkyu shiryo-shu,* no. 3, 1928. 159 p. Part II is concerned with international Communism vis-à-vis Japan: the "July Thesis," Bukharin speeches, Communist activities among the Japanese in Vladivostok, Kamchatka, etc.

JE110 HOSOKAWA, KAROKU. *Nihon shakai-shugi bunken kaisetsu.* Iwanami Shoten, 1932. 120 p. An annotated bibliography of Japanese "socialist" literature, 1880-1927 by a prominent left-wing leader who in the post-war era became a JCP member of the House of Councillors.

JE111 HOSOKAWA, KAROKU; WATANABE, YOSHIMICHI; and SHIODA, SHOBEI, comps. *Nihon shakai-shugi bunken kaisetsu.* Otsuki Shoten, 1958. 370 p. An expanded version of the Hosokawa 1932 item above. Bibliographic entries to 1945.

JE112 ICHIKAWA, SHOICHI. *Nippon kyosanto toso shoshi.* Tokyo: Shoko shoin, 1946. 214 p. This official history of the Japanese Communist Party is a revised edition of the late Ichikawa's testimony in the famous Communist trials of the early thirties, published in 1932 by the Central Committee of the JCP. Although practically no names or locations are indicated and many details have been either omitted (such as Yoshihara's speech) or intentionally distorted, the work is of some value in tracing the JCP's interpretation of events in and around the Party. [B]

JE113 ICHINOSE, MASAYUKI. *Nihon kyosanto.* Tokyo: Gengensha, 1954. 240 p. A study of the JCP divided about equally between the prewar and postwar periods, with special emphasis on the paramilitary activities of the Party.

JE114 JAPAN, KOAN CHOSACHO. *Ampo toso no gaiyo; toso no keika to bunseki.* Tokyo: 1960. 357 p. Compiled from the materials submitted from various divisions of the Public Security Investigation Agency, this report describes in detail the anti-pact movement in the year and a half since March 1959. Includes information relating to the roles taken by JCP and international Communism in this movement. Contains chronological tables of the anti-pact development and of anti-pact activities.

JE115 JAPAN, KOAN CHOSACHO. *Nihon Kyosanto no genjo.* Tokyo: 1960. 241 p. A 1960 report, well documented, of the Public Security Investigation Agency of the Ministry of Justice. (Previous reports were issued under the same title in 1955 and 1957.) The first part (p. 1-128) describes the basic characteristics, present strength and activities of the JCP, pointing out the Party's dependency on the international organization, its assessment of international and domestic issues, principal targets of the Party's activities, membership figures, organizational structure, electioneering strength, financial condition, publication and propaganda setup and activities. The second part (p. 129-241) describes the JCP's policies and actions in the following six fields: peace, labor, farm, citizenry, youth, and students. Contains résumés of the Party's important meetings, table of organizational structures, list of officers, and table of the chronology of the relevant events. An English translation of portions of these documents is issued periodically by the Agency. [A]

JE116 KATAYAMA, SEN. *Nippon ni okeru kaikyu toso.* Tokyo: Ito shoten, 1948. 172 p. A collection of the Communist leader's later writings, edited in the postwar period with the assistance of Katayama's Moscow friend, Nosaka Ryo (wife of Nosaka Sanzo). Includes: (1) A critical survey of the post-World War I Japanese revolutionary movement, (2) Crisis in Japan, (3) The general elections in Japan, (4) Japan and the danger of war, (5) The third stage in postwar Japan, (6) Japan in the midst of the world economic crisis, and (7) The death of Watanabe Masanosuke. Contains also a section devoted to some of Katayama's writings on international problems. The author, perhaps the best known Japanese Marxist, was instrumental in the formation of the JCP and later became a member of the Presidium of the Comintern. He died in Moscow in November 1933.

JE117 KAWAKAMI, HAJIME. *Jijoden.* Tokyo: Sekai hyoron-sha, 1949. 4 vols. The autobiography of one of Japan's outstanding economists. Prof. Kawakami (1879-1946) gradually moved from a theoretical interest in Marxian doctrine to active participation in the then (1932) illegal Communist movement. Kawakami's memoirs contain a good deal of information on the Communist underground in prewar Japan and the leading personalities of the proletarian movement, as well as a very detailed description of the life of Communist political prisoners.

JE118 KAZAMA, JOKICHI. *Mosuko kyosandaigaku no omoide.* Tokyo: Sangen-sha, 1949. 299 p. Kazama, ex-Communist and former Secretary-General of the JCP, attended the University of the Toilers of the East in Moscow from 1925 to 1930. His memoirs include information on the following subjects: (1) Methods employed by the Comintern in smuggling Party workers into and out of Japan; (2) Organization, curriculum, personnel and objective of the Moscow Communist University (many of its graduates now occupy high positions in satellite nations); (3) Role played by a number of important figures in the international Communist movement (among them Janson [Yanson], Bukharin, Eidus, Lozovsky, Shvernik, Piatnitsky, Safarov, Molotov, Ulbricht, Foster, Browder, Katayama); (4) Operations, functions and personnel of the Profintern; (5) Biographical data concerning Korean and Formosan Communists, and (6) Background information on the 1927 Thesis and the 1930 Draft Thesis. Although written after World War II, the work is unusually accurate, even in details, and constitutes a valuable source for the study of the JCP's international relations.

JE119 KAZAMA, JOKICHI. *Mosuko to tsunagaru Nihon Kyosanto no rekishi.* Temma-sha: 1951. 2 vols. A comprehensive history of the JCP and its relations with Moscow by a former Secretary General of the Party, now an anti-Communist, who spent a number of years in the Soviet Union. [B]

JE120 KOBAYASHI, EIZABURO, and UCHINO, SOJI, comps. *Kyosanshugi jiten.* Tokyo: Nisshin shoten, 1949. 342 p. A dictionary on Communism compiled by two Communist journalists under the supervision of Hosokawa Karoku and Kawakami Kanichi, Communist members of the House of Councillors and House of Representatives respectively. Contains definitions for a total of more than 1,600 Japanese and Western language terms covering not only general Marxist theory and practice, but also related fields (such as social and political philosophy, labor legislation, trade unionism, and land reform), as well as a fairly exhaustive list of terms peculiar to Japanese Communist lingo.

JE121 *Kominterun Nippon mondai ni kan-suru hoshin-sho, ketsugishu.* Tokyo: Satsuki shobo, 1950. 262 p. A postwar reprint of Comintern documents concerning Japan (including the 1922 Draft Platform, the 1927 and 1932 Theses) conveniently assembled in one volume. Apparently published by the JCP. For scholarly purposes this collection should only be used when the original source material is not available.

JE122 *Kominterun oyobi Purofinterun no Nippon mondai ni kansuru ketsugi rombun-shu.* Moscow: Gaikoku rodosha shuppanjo, 1934. 204 p. Eight important Profintern and Comintern documents on Japan, including the text of the 1932 Thesis, based on the version which originally appeared in *Sekki* (Red Flag) on July 10, 1932. The volume was published by the Japanese section of the Foreign Workers' Publishing House in Moscow, probably under the supervision of Nosaka Sanzo (then known as Okano Susumu).

JE123 KOMIYA, YOSHITAKA, ed. *Nippon puroretaria hennen-shi.* Tokyo: Dojin-sha shoten, 1931. 458 p. Contains a brief day-by-day account, for the period 1868-1928 inclusive, of all events which had some bearing on the proletarian movement in Japan. Thus it includes summaries of strikes (number of participants, points of litigation, outcome), political events (establishment, mergers and dissolution of political parties), details on arrests of revolutionists, labor leaders, etc. Reliable, but due to censorship and other limitations, necessarily incomplete. A subject-matter index enhances the value of this reference work.

JE124 KONDO, EIZO. *Kominterun no misshi.* Tokyo: Bunka hyoronsha, 1949. 290 p. A study of the embryonic stage of the Japanese Communist movement in the United States and Japan. The author, founder of the Dawn People's Communist Party (forerunner of the JCP) and friend of Katayama Sen, was associated with the Communist movement until about 1927. His life as a revolutionist falls into three periods which correspond to the division of these memoirs: (1) Residence in New York, (2) Birth of the JCP, and (3) Exile in the Soviet Union.

JE125 KOYAMA, HIROTAKE. *Nihon Marukusu-shugi-shi.* Aoki Shoten, 1956. 232 p. A discussion of the theory (strategy and tactics) of "democratic revolution," 1945-50, from the Communist viewpoint.

JE126 KOYAMA, HIROTAKE, comp. *Nihon rodo undo shakai undo kenkyu-shi—senzen sengo no bunken kaisetsu.* Sangatsu Shobo, 1957. 302 p. An annotated bibliography on the Japanese labor and "social" movements from the early Meiji period to the mid-1950's.

JE127 LANGER, PAUL F., and SWEARINGEN, A. RODGER, comps. *Japanese Communism; an Annotated Bibliography of Works in the Japanese Language with a Chronology, 1921-1952.* N.Y.: Institute of Pacific Relations, 1953. 95 p. 242 separate entries arranged by topic, i.e., theory, Party organization, the labor movement, agrarian activities, foreign relations, etc. Contains a useful chronology and detailed subject and author indices. [B]

JE128 *Musansha shimbun ronsetsu-shu.* Tokyo: Ueno shoten, 1929. 374 p. One hundred and eighteen editorials reprinted from the newspaper which for all practical purposes was the legal mouthpiece of the illegal JCP in the mid-twenties. Covers the period between September 1925 and December 1927 inclusive. Valuable historical material despite the ravages of Japanese censorship.

JE129 NABEYAMA, SADACHIKA. *Kyosanto hihan.* Tokyo: Rokumei-sha, 1950. 211 p. A fifteen-chapter critical analysis of Japanese Communist policy and operations by a former top Japanese Communist leader and Profintern representative. Of particular value to the study of developments in postwar Japan are Chapter 4, "The Cominform and the JCP," and Chapter 7, "The Strategy of the Main Stream Faction, the 1950 Thesis."

JE130 NABEYAMA, SADACHIKA. *Watakushi wa kyosanto wo suteta.* Tokyo: Daito shuppanbu, 1949. 233 p. Essentially an autobiography by the former top-ranking JCP leader and representative to the Profintern, who left the Party in 1933, terming it weak and ineffective and a tool of Moscow. One of the two or three best postwar accounts of the Japanese Communist movement up to 1933. [B]

JE131 NABEYAMA, SADACHIKA, and SANO, MANABU. *Tenko jugonen.* Tokyo: Rodo shuppanbu, 1949. 153 p. Although not an autobiography in the strict sense of the word, it discusses the reasons for the former high-ranking JCP leaders' defection from Communism and reveals much of the early history of the Communist movement in Japan.

JE132 NAIMUSHO KEIHOKYOKU. *Shakai undo no jokyo.* 1932-42. 11 vols. A very detailed, well-organized yearly official record of the Japanese "social movement," containing more than one thousand pages per volume. Divided into the following sections: (1) Introduction, (2) The Communist movement, (3) The left-wing cultural movement, (4) The left-wing student movement, (5) The anarchist movement, (6) The consumers union movement, (7) The Suiheisha movement, (8) Religious movements, (9) Nationalist movements, (10) Proletarian party movements, (11) The labor movement, (12) The agrarian movement, and (13) The Korean movement. Each volume contains a valuable appendix listing significant events (such as organizational meetings, arrests, and dissolution of organizations) by place and date, as well as numerous charts and tables. The best available single reference work on the subject. Indispensable to any thorough study. [B]

JE133 NAPIER, J. P. *A Survey of the Japan Communist Party.* Tokyo: Nippon Times, 1952. 66 p. A brief but informative discussion of various aspects of the JCP by a former official of the Government Section of General Headquarters in Tokyo. Based mainly on SCAP files and memoranda, the account is generally accurate, but fails to provide even a minimum of documentation.

JE134 NIHON KYOSANTO, CHOSA IINKAI. *Senryoka Nihon no bunseki.* Kyoto: San'ichi Shobo, 1954. 264 p. The JCP criticism of domestic policies of the Japanese government in the postwar years. The main theme is how the U.S. is ruling Japan. The second series was published in 1955 (313 p.) under title: *Zoku senryoka Nihon no bunseki* (Analyses of Occupied Japan, continued), attacking MSA and Japan's rearmament.

JE135 NIHON KYOSANTO, CHUO IINKAI, GOJUNEN MONDAI IINKAI. *Nihon Kyosanto gojunen mondai shiryo-shu.* Tokyo: Shin Nihon Shuppan-sha, 1957. 3 vols. The Party's compilation of the documents, statements, and opinions expressed by individuals, groups and organizations on the intraparty controversy created by the Cominform criticism of the Nosaka theory in 1950.

JE136 NIHON KYOSANTO, CHUO IINKAI, KYOIKU SENDENBU. *Nihon Kyosanto Ketsugi kettei-shu.* Tokyo: Shin Nihon Shuppan Sha, 1956—. A collection of resolutions and statements officially adopted and approved by the JCP. Six volumes had been published up to January 1961.

JE137 NIHON KYOSANTO, CHUO IINKAI, SENDEN KYOIKUBU. *Nihon Kyosanto koryo-shu.* Tokyo: Shin Nihon Shuppan-sha, 1957. 295 p. A collection of the programs of action of the JCP, 1920-55. Issued by the Party's Propaganda and Education Department.

JE138 NIHON KYOSANTO, CHUO IINKAI, SENDEN KYOIKUBU. *Nihon Kyosanto no seisaku.* Tokyo: Godo Shuppan-sha, 1956. 272 p. The JCP's positions in the areas of foreign affairs, military base problems, Japanese Constitution, peace, economy, social security, women and family, and politics and government are given in 94 questions and answers. Prepared by the Propaganda and Education Department of the JCP.

JE139 *Nihon Kyosanto shiryo taisei.* Comp. by Shakai Undo Shiryo Kanko-kai. n. p.: 1951. 453 p. A documentary history of the JCP, Oct. 1945-June 1950. Resolutions, Politburo statements, Diet member speeches, etc.

JE140 NIKKAN RODO TSUSHIN SHA, TOKYO. *Nihon Kyosanto no bunken-shu.* Tokyo: 1951-59. 7 vols. A collection of important documents, reports, statements, etc., relating to the Japanese Communist Party. Brief explanations of historical circumstances and comments are given. Vol. 1 (1951. 607 p.) has at head of title: *Kominforumu ni*

Kuppuku shita (Yielded to the Cominform). Covers the period Jan. to Aug. 1950 when the JCP was shaken by the Cominform criticism of the "Nosaka theory," and the factional strife within the Party intensified. Vol. 2 (1951. 743 p.) has at head of title: *Chika sennyu no taisei o totonoeta* (Ready to go underground). Covers the period Sept. 1950 to Feb. 1951. Vol. 3 (1952. 834 p.) covers March 1951 to March 1952, when the Party members engaged in terror tactics through the use of firearms, explosives, tear gas, etc. Vol. 4 (1953. 771 p.) covers April to Nov. 1952. Vol. 5 (1958. 1,154 p.) covers principally the one year preceding the draft of the Party Constitution (Sept. 1957). Last document, Dec. 10, 1957. Vol. 6 (1959. 990 p.) essentially documents centering around the 7th Party Congress. Covers the period Aug. 1957-Aug. 1958. Vol. 7 (1960. 990 p.) documents for the one year period Nov. 1958-Nov. 1959.

JE141 NIKKAN RODO TSUSHIN SHA, TOKYO. *Sengo Nihon kyosan-shugi undo.* Tokyo: 1955. 760 p. A comprehensive ten year history of the postwar JCP. Appears to have been compiled with the cooperation of the Public Security Investigation Agency. [B]

JE142 NIPPON KYOSANTO CHUO IINKAI AJIPUROBU. No Title. n.p.: n.p., 1932. 119 p. Sometimes referred to as "Official History of the JCP." An account of the development of the Communist movement in Japan up to 1929. Based on the testimony of the Communist leader Ichikawa Shoichi (died in a Japanese prison shortly before the surrender) in the famous Communist trials of 1931. Ichikawa had been appointed by his fellow-prisoners to present an outline of the history of the JCP to the presiding judge. The stenographic record of his statement was smuggled out of the courtroom, edited and illegally printed by the Central Committee for secret distribution among Party members and sympathizers. Contains only few concrete data on the actual activities of the Japanese Communists. Names of leading Party members, dates of conferences, etc., are either omitted or kept purposely vague, as Ichikawa's main objective lay in publicizing Communism rather than in presenting the historical facts. Valuable in the sense that it shows the interpretation placed by the Japanese Communists on Japanese domestic and foreign policies. A revised edition was published by the JCP in the postwar period.

JE143 NOSAKA, SANZO. *Senryaku, senjutsu no sho-mondai.* Tokyo: Doyu-sha, 1949. 300 p. A compilation of writings and speeches (largely postwar) on strategy and tactics by the then second-ranking member of the JCP. After nine years in the Soviet Union and five years in North China, Nosaka returned to Japan in January 1946 to take over the direction of the JCP, in fact if not in name. This volume, therefore, constitutes a virtual handbook of JCP policy from 1946 until

January 1950, at which time Nosaka's moderate theories were branded by the Cominform as "anti-democratic, anti-Socialist, anti-patriotic and anti-Japanese." But Nosaka was, significantly, neither expelled from the Party nor dropped from the policy-making level. [B]

JE144 NOSAKA, T. *A Brief Review of the Labour Movement in Japan.* Moscow: 1921. One of the Japanese Communist leader's earliest publications. Primarily of historical interest.

JE145 SANO, MANABU. *Kyosanto no seitai.* Tokyo: Nyu puranu-sha, 1948. 220 p. A broad analysis of the international Communist movement during the postwar period by a former JCP leader and Comintern representative. Considerable space is devoted to an evaluation of the situation in each of the countries of Asia. One section deals with the controversial "Far Eastern Cominform."

JE146 SANO, MANABU, and NABEYAMA, SADACHIKA. *Nippon kyosanto oyobi komintan hihan.* Tokyo: Musan-sha, 1934. 253 p. Important to an understanding of the reasons behind the split in the prewar Communist movement which resulted, after a strong denunciation of the Soviet Union and the Comintern, in the resignation from the Party of key figures such as Sano and Nabeyama.

JE147 SAYOKU BUNKA UNDO BENRAN. *Naigai Bunka Kenkyujo, 1960.* Tokyo: Musashi Shobo, 1960. 398 p. Describes left-wing organizations, including front groups, in the fields of humanities and social science, literature, cinema and drama, art and music, and publication. Gives a brief history and summary of recent activities, names of important members, and other pertinent information concerning each organization. This is the most up-to-date and comprehensive of the several handbooks issued under similar titles in the past several years.

JE148 SHIGA, YOSHIO. *Sekai to Nihon.* Tokyo: Gyomei-sha, 1949. 260 p. A collection of articles written in 1946, 1947, and 1948 by the then third-ranking member of the JCP. Contains theoretical discussions centering around the controversial 1927 and 1932 Theses. The main body of the work is devoted to a critical analysis of Shigeo Kamiyama's point of view which, in the author's opinion, threatened to become "the theoretical foundation for a harmful political deviation." Contains also a brief discussion of "deviationism" in Yugoslavia.

JE149 SUZUKI, TAKESHI. *Kyosanto choyaku no zembo.* Tokyo: Keibun-sha, 1932. 292 p. A history of the Japanese Communist movement up to the fall of 1932. Tendentious and with emphasis on the international conspiratorial and romantic aspects (secret codes, cover names, etc.) of the JCP. The sensational presentation of the material seems to indicate that the author wrote to cash in on the interest in Communism aroused by the mass arrests of 1928 and 1929 and the subsequent anti-Communist trials. For the most part superseded by postwar studies.

JE150 SWEARINGEN, RODGER, and LANGER, PAUL F. *Red Flag in Japan; International Communism in Action, 1919-1951.* Cambridge: Harvard, 1952. 272 p. Japanese ed., *Nihon no akai hata.* Tokyo: Cosmopolitan-sha, 1953. 367 p. A comprehensive study of the Japanese Communist Party utilizing a great variety of new source materials. The first complete case study of an Asian Communist movement, this book discusses the organization and program of the JCP, revolutionary strategy and tactics, factionalism, biographical data of the Party leaders as well as the relationship between the Japanese Communists and the Communist parties of Russia, China, Korea and the United States. The emphasis is on factual presentation rather than on interpretation. The book is fully documented and has a good index. [A]

JE151 TAGAWA, KAZUO. *Nihon Kyosanto shi: shinkakusareta zen'ei.* Tokyo: Gendai Shicho-sha, 1960. 298 p. The author was branded as a Trotskyite and expelled from the Japanese Communist Party in 1959. His point is that the history of the JCP from the beginning is repeated failures, because the JCP followed the Third International, which abandoned its plan of world revolution after Lenin's death and still believes in the Comintern's 1932 program. This is a critical account rather than a descriptive history of the post-war JCP.

JE152 TAJIMA, ZENKO. *Kyosanto shakai-to haigeki no kinokyo to gendai Nihon no henkaku taiko.* Wakayama: Kishu Suisan Shimbun-sha, 1950. 259 p. A critical treatment of the JCP and the Socialists by a former Communist.

JE153 TATEYAMA, TAKAAKI. *Nippon kyosanto kenkyo hishi.* Tokyo: Bukyosha, 1929. 398 p. An excellent, very detailed study which contains more than its name (Secret History of the Arrests of Japanese Communists) would indicate. A well balanced account of the Communist movement in the 1920's.

JE154 TOKUDA, KYUICHI. *Naigai Josei to Nihon Kyosanto no Nimmu.* Tokyo: Shinri-sha, 1949. 282 p. Tokuda's general reports (or summaries of these) made to the various high-level Party conferences between the re-establishment of the JCP in the fall of 1945 and the fourth plenary session of the Central Committee in October 1948. In most cases the reports comprise an analysis of the international as well as of the domestic situation, a discussion of specific problems facing the Party and a summary of past achievements in various fields. Indispensable source material. [B]

JE155 TOKUDA, KYUICHI. *Waga omoide.* Tokyo: Tokyo shoin, 1948. 237 p. The memoirs of the late Secretary General of the JCP.

Covers the period from 1921 to 1927 inclusive. Contains a detailed account of Tokuda's numerous trips to Russia and China as well as the author's conferences with Ch'en Tu-hsiu, Li Li-san and other leaders of the Chinese (and Korean) Communist movement. Of particular value for the study of the Japanese Communist Party's international connections and of its relationship to the Comintern. [B]

JE156 TOYO, GAKUJIN. *Kyosanto wa naze warui ka.* 1933. 207 p. A critical account of the JCP, its foreign dominance, irresponsible leadership and violent methods.

JE157 TSUKAHIRA, TOSHIO G. *The Postwar Evolution of Communist Strategy in Japan.* Cambridge: Center for International Studies, M.I.T., 1954. 89 p. A penetrating analysis of the JCP's postwar theory and strategy from 1945 through mid-1954. The author is an American foreign service officer. [A]

JE158 UYEHARA, CECIL H. *Leftwing Social Movements in Japan; An Annotated Bibliography.* Tokyo, Japan, and Rutland, Vermont: Published for The Fletcher School of Law and Diplomacy by Charles E. Tuttle, 1959. 444 p. A comprehensive treatment of materials on all aspects of leftwing "social movements" in Japan, from the conservative social democrats to the Communists and anarchists, from the labor and farmers unions to the leftwing theater and poetry. Emphasizes the period from World War I to 1956. Approximately 1800 items selected from 4,000 titles. Separate sections on pre-war and postwar Communism are subdivided into agricultural policies, cultural affairs, labor unions, press, rearmament, etc. [B]

JE159 YAGINUMA, MASAHARU. *Nihon Kyosanto undo-shi. sengo-hen.* Keibunkaku: 1953. 395 p. A history of the postwar JCP to 1952 by an instructor at the Sendai District police school.

JE160 YAMAKOSHI, RYO. *Gokuchu gokugai nijugonen.* Tokyo: Nauka-sha, 1948. 200 p. An outline history of the radical left-wing movement in Japan from its early beginnings (about 1900) to the surrender of Japan in 1945. Follows in every respect the JCP's interpretation of events. Contains a number of biographical sketches of former Party leaders (Katayama, Kokuryo, Watanabe, Ichikawa, Noro, Kobayashi Takiji, and Kawakami Hajime).

JE161 YAMAMOTO, KATSUNOSUKE, and ARITA, MITSUHO. *Nippon kyosanshugi undo-shi.* Tokyo: Seiki shobo, 1950. 473 p. A history of the Japanese Communist movement from its early beginnings to the end of the war, supplemented by a few pages on postwar developments. The most complete and reliable account published in the Japanese language. The authors have made use of a considerable amount of

Japanese source material (including government documents) and have successfully avoided any *parti-pris*. Crammed with facts; every detail available to the writers has been included. Supplemented by organizational charts of the prewar JCP, apparently copied from police documents. [A]

JE162 YOSHIOKA, NOBUMASA. *Kyosanshugi taisaku.* Tokyo: Kyoyu-sha, 1950. 331 p. Only one-third of the book deals with proposed measures to combat Communism in Japan. The remainder represents a summary of the author's earlier work (below), supplemented by an account of Communist activities during 1949. Appended are seven organizational charts (Party organization, peripheral organizations, cultural organizations under JCP influence, Party press and so forth). [B]

JE163 YOSHIOKA, NOBUMASA. *Nippon kyosanto no kaibo.* Tokyo: Kyoyu-sha, 1948. 241 p. The author of this survey is a well-known anti-Communist writer. The work is divided into eight chapters: (1) Origin of the JCP, (2) Character of the JCP, (3) Strength of the JCP, (4) The JCP and the labor movement, (5) The JCP and the farmers' movement, (6) The JCP and the (unorganized) citizens (i.e., middle classes, housewives, etc.), (7) The JCP and the youth and student movement, and (8) The JCP and the cultural movement. Perhaps the best survey of Communism in post-war Japan (to 1948). Numerous charts and diagrams enhance the value of the book. [B]

a. PERIODICALS AND NEWSPAPERS

JE164 *Akahata. Nihon kyosanto chuo kikan-shi.* Tokyo. Daily. "Red Flag," the *Daily Worker* of Japan. Somewhat less theoretical and more detailed than *Zen'ei*, the monthly JCP journal, in the Communist interpretation of events at home and abroad. Published in pre-war days as *Sekki.* Except for brief interruptions, published since early in the occupation period. [A]

JE165 *Koan Joho.* Tokyo: Shakai Undo Kenkyu-kai. Monthly. A journal on internal security affairs published since May 1953. (The first eleven issues from May 1953 to July 1954 bear the original title, *Nikkyo Josei Sokuho.* Beginning with No. 12, September 1954, it became a monthly under the new title.) Much attention is devoted to the Japanese Communist Movement in the form of such characteristic articles as: "Current Trends in the Japanese Communist Movement," "The Anti-Security Treaty Movement," "Communist Exploitation of the Student Movement," etc. Especially good for brief treatment of important Party meetings, conferences, etc. Contains a section of documentary material. Apparently prepared with the cooperation of Japanese governmental authorities.

JE166 *Zen'ei. Nihon kyosanto chuo-iinkai seiji-shi.* Tokyo. Monthly. "Vanguard," the theoretical journal of the JCP issued monthly since 1946. Contains all important open JCP documents, Party rules and regulations, action programs, etc. as well as "authoritative" discussions of Party disputes, problems, and foreign and domestic issues. [A]

JF. KOREA AND THE KOREAN WAR

EDITED BY CHONG-SIK LEE
Russian Titles by Pyoung Hoon Kim

1. TITLES IN OCCIDENTAL LANGUAGES

JF1 *Agricultural Cooperatization in D.P.R.K.* Pyongyang: Foreign Languages Publishing House, 1958. 85 p. Presents the background, development and characteristics of the cooperative movement in the Democratic People's Republic of Korea. [B]

JF2 APPLEMAN, ROY E. *United States Army in the Korean War, South to the Naktong, North to the Yalu (June-November 1950).* Washington: Office of the Chief of Military History, Department of the Army, 1961. 813 p. A definitive work on the military aspects of the Korean War. The only work paying equal attention to the enemy forces and the U.S. allies. Benefited from exhaustive research and intensive interviews. Liberal use of intelligence reports. The first of a five volume series. [A]

JF3 BAIANOV, B. *Narodnaia Koreia na puti k sotsializmu.* Moscow: Gospolitizdat, 1959. 142 p. A propagandistic treatment of the following themes: (1) "Growth of a democratic republic in North Korea," (2) "Growth of socialism in North Korea," and (3) an argument that the "imperalist USA is responsible for the division of Korea." The last section includes the theme of "peaceful unification of Korea." Superseded by G. E. Samsonov's treatment. [B]

JF4 BERGER, CARL. *The Korea Knot; A Military Political History.* Philadelphia: U. of Pennsylvania; London: Oxford, 1957. 206 p. A former U.S. Army historian and reporter attempts to "uncover the origins of the Korean tragedy" and "to place the war in its proper historical context." A lively, useful summary of the Korean situation between 1943 and 1954.

JF4A BLAIR, CLAY, JR. *Beyond Courage.* N.Y.: McKay, 1955. 247 p. Four stories of American combat pilots who were downed by the enemy behind the enemy lines during the Korean War. Vivid. [A]

JF5 BROMBERGER, SERGE and others. *Retour de Corée.* Paris: Julliard, 1951. 274 p. Four perceptive French war correspondents narrate their observation of the Korean War from the outbreak to the Chinese intervention. Lively.

JF5A BROWN, WALLACE L. *The Endless Hours: My Two and a Half Years as a Prisoner of the Chinese Communists.* N.Y.: Norton,

1961. 254 p. Experiences of a U.S. Air Force lieutenant captured in North Korea in January 1953.

JF6 CAGLE, COMMANDER MALCOLM W., and MANSON, COMMANDER FRANK A. *Sea War in Korea.* Annapolis, Md.: U.S. Naval Institute, 1957. 555 p. The most exhaustive and detailed account of the U.S. Navy's role in the Korean War. Asserts the increased need for a strong and adequate Navy. Based on records and interviews. [B]

JF7 CALDWELL, JOHN C., and FROST, LESLEY. *The Korea Story.* Chicago: Regnery, 1952. 180 p. A former Korean Government advisor's criticism of U.S. Department of State operations in Korea. "It is a story of great opportunities not seized upon, of mistakes made and not corrected." A popular account dealing with the period prior to June, 1950.

JF8 CHUNG, HENRY. *The Russians Came to Korea.* Seoul, Korea and Washington, D.C.: Korean Pacific, 1947. 212 p. A Korean nationalist since the 1920's argues that it is to the self-interest and obligation of the U.S. to check Russian expansionist ambitions in Korea. Discusses events in Korea with the accent on Soviet policies. [A]

JF9 CLARK, MARK W. *From the Danube to the Yalu.* N.Y.: Harper, 1954. 369 p. Contains an account of the author's experiences as the U.N. Far Eastern Commander (1952-53). Especially valuable on the exchange of prisoners and the armistice negotiations.

JF9A CONDRON, ANDREW M., CORDEN, RICHARD G., and SULLIVAN, LARANCE V. *Thinking Soldiers.* Peking: New World Press, 1955. 246 p. Supposedly a collection of writings from prisoner-of-war camp magazines. Includes biographical articles, writings on combat experiences, experiences in captivity, etc. Edited by two American ex-Army sergeants and an ex-Marine captured and defected to the Chinese Communists. About the editors, see Pasley, *21 Stayed* (q.v.). Mild but subtle propaganda material.

JF10 *Control Figures for the Seven-Year Plan (1961-1967) for the Development of the National Economy of the Democratic People's Republic of Korea.* Pyongyang: Korean Central News Agency, September 17, 1961. 39 p. Targets of the seven-year plan set forth by the North Korean regime.

JF11 DALIN, S. *Molodezh i revoliutsionnoe dvizhenie v Koree.* Preface by F. Raskolnikov. Moscow: "Novaia Moskva," 1924. 126 p.

JF11A DAVIES, S. J. *In Spite of Dungeons.* London: Hodder and Stoughton, 1954. 160 p. "The experiences as a prisoner-of-war in North Korea of the chaplain to the first battalion, the Gloucestershire regiment."

JF12 DEANE, PHILIP. *I Was A Captive in Korea.* N.Y.: Norton, 1953. 253 p. A Greek correspondent sent out by the *Observer* of London (Gerassimos Svoronos-Gigantes) spent 33 months in an enemy prisoners' camp. A detailed and detached account, although hastily written.

JF13 DEAN, WILLIAM F. *General Dean's Story; as told to William L. Worden.* N.Y.: Viking, 1954. 305 p. Candid, personal recollections of the ex-Commander of the 24th Infantry Division who was a North Korean prisoner for three years. Balanced, smooth reading. [B]

JF14 DUTT, VIDYA P., ed. *East Asia; China, Korea, Japan, 1947-1950.* N.Y. and London: Oxford, 1958. 747 p.

JF15 *Eruption of South Korean People's Wrath.* Pyongyang: Foreign Languages Publishing House, 1960. 46 p. "Addresses to the South Korean People" made by the Korean Workers' Party and the United Democratic Fatherland Front. Shows North Korean propaganda efforts.

JF16 *Everlasting Friendship Between Korean, Chinese and Vietnamese Peoples: Documents on Goodwill Visits of the D.P.R.K. Government Delegation to China and Vietnam.* Pyongyang: Foreign Languages Publishing House, 1959. 251 p. A collection of speeches delivered and statements issued by the three government leaders during Kim Il-sung's visit to China and Vietnam from November 21 to December 10, 1958. Photographs.

JF17 *Facts About Korea.* Pyongyang: Foreign Languages Publishing House, 1961. 242 p. An almanac on North Korea. Provides a short but comprehensive history and description. A useful summary of Communist views.

JF18 *Facts Tell.* Pyongyang: Foreign Languages Publishing House, 1960. 246 p. "Captured confidential documents of the U.S. imperialists and Syngman Rhee clique, which clearly reveal who provoked the Korean War," and the "Report of the Commission of the International Association of Democratic Lawyers on U.S. Crimes in Korea."

JF18A FARRAR-HOCKLEY, ANTHONY. *The Edge of the Sword.* London: Muller, 1954. 275 p. A story of the battle of the Imjin river (April 1951) and the life of a prisoner in North Korean custody, by a captain of the Gloucestershire regiment. Indicts North Koreans for inhumane treatment of prisoners.

JF19 FARZH, IVAN. *Svidetelstvo o Kitae i Koree.* Moscow: Inlitizdat, 1952. 128 p. Discusses the struggle of these two countries against "aggression."

JF19A FIELD, JAMES A., JR. *History of United States Naval Operations: Korea.* Washington: G.P.O., 1962. 499 p. A thorough history by a scholar, based largely on official records of the U.S. Navy. Maps. [A]

JF20 *For Korea's Peaceful Unification.* Pyongyang: Foreign Languages Publishing House, 1961. 256 p. A collection of speeches, statements, and reports issued in North Korea, concerning the policy of "peaceful unification of Korea."

JF21 FUTRELL, ROBERT F., MOSELEY, LAWSON S., and SIMPSON, ALBERT F. *The United States Air Force in Korea, 1950-1953.* N.Y.: Duell, Sloan and Pearce, 1961. 774 p. An official history based primarily on Air Force reports and other documents. Deals with the background, problems faced, and achievements. Extensive bibliographical notes. [B]

JF22 GEER, ANDREW. *The New Breed; The Story of the U.S. Marines in Korea.* N.Y.: Harper, 1952. 395 p. A Marine veteran's comprehensive, factual narrative of the 1st Marine Division's campaigns in Korea from August to December 1950.

JF23 GITOVICH, A., and BURSOV, B. *North of the 38th Parallel.* Shanghai: Epoch, 1948. 153 p. A Communist description of North Korea which provides some background of North Korean leaders. Propagandistic and superficial.

JF24 GOODRICH, LELAND M. *Korea; A Study of U.S. Policy in the United Nations.* N.Y.: Council on Foreign Relations, 1956. 235 p. While the author's primary concern is U.S. policy in the U.N., his examination of the handling of the "Korean problem" in the U.N. (1945-53) is valuable. Related U.N. documents appended. Scholarly. [A]

JF25 GORDENKER, LEON. *The United Nations and the Peaceful Unification of Korea.* The Hague: Nijhoff, 1959. 306 p. Revision of a Columbia Ph.D. thesis, "The United Nations Commissions in Korea, 1947-1950." Critically examines the establishment, activities, weaknesses, and accomplishments of the U.N. in Korea up to 1950.

JF26 GUGELER, RUSSELL A. (CAPTAIN). *Combat Actions in Korea.* Washington: Combat Forces Press, 1954. 260 p. A collection of accounts describing the fighting at company level or below, followed by a brief analysis of each battle. Readable.

JF27 HALPERIN, MORTON H. *Limited War; An Essay on the Development of the Theory and an Annotated Bibliography.* Cambridge: Center for International Affairs, Harvard, 1962. 67 p. Lists a number of books and articles on the Korean War.

JF28 HANSEN, KENNETH K. (COLONEL). *Heroes Behind Barbed Wire*. N.Y.: Van Nostrand, 1957. 345 p. The story of Korean and Chinese prisoners of war at Koje Island, particularly of those who refused to be repatriated. For a popular audience.

JF29 HARLOWE, W. N. "Korea, Foreign Policies of the Two Republics, 1948-1950." M.A. thesis, U. of California (Berkeley), 1953.

JF30 HIGGINS, TRUMBULL. *Korea and the Fall of MacArthur; A Précis in Limited War*. N.Y.: Oxford, 1960. 229 p. A lucid examination of the MacArthur controversy by a military historian. Delves into the relationship between MacArthur, the Joint Chiefs of Staff, the State Department and the President, in the wake of the Chinese attack. Critical of MacArthur. Useful bibliography. [B]

JF30A HUNTER, EDWARD. *Brainwashing; the Story of Men Who Defied It*. N.Y.: Farrar, Straus & Cudahy, 1956. 310 p. An American journalist who popularized the term "brainwashing" in his book, *Brainwashing in Red China*, here tells the story of how this technique was used in the Korean War.

JF31 *Impressions of Korea*. Pyongyang: Foreign Languages Publishing House, 1960. 147 p. Fifteen brief articles on North Korea by foreign visitors sympathetic to the regime.

JF32 *Impressions of Korea*. Pyongyang: Foreign Languages Publishing House, 1961. 96 p. Twelve brief articles on North Korea by foreign visitors sympathetic to the regime. Some of the articles are the same as those in the 1960 edition of the same title.

JF33 JOY, CHARLES TURNER (ADMIRAL). *How Communists Negotiate*. N.Y. and London: Macmillan, 1955. 178 p. Observations of the former chief of the U.N. Command Delegation to the Korean Armistice Conference on the techniques of Communist negotiation for "evil triumph." Bitter.

JF34 KADT, J. DE. *De consequenties van Korea; een pleidooi voor vrede door kracht*. Amsterdam: G. A. van Oorschot, 1950. 299 p.

JF35 KARIG, WALTER (CAPTAIN) and others. *Battle Report; The War in Korea*. N.Y.: Rinehart, 1952. 520 p. Vol. VI of Captain Karig's *Battle Report* Series. A popular, non-technical narrative of Navy and Marine Corps combat operations in Korea from the outbreak of war to the Hungnam evacuation. Informative.

JF36 KIM, HAN-JOO. *Great Victory in Agricultural Cooperatization in D.P.R.K.* Pyongyang: Foreign Languages Publishing House, 1959. 72 p. Justifies and explains the development of agricultural cooperatives in North Korea. [B]

JF37 KIM, IL-SUNG. *All for the Post-War Rehabilitation and Development of the National Economy.* Pyongyang: Ministry of Culture and Propaganda, Democratic People's Republic of Korea, 1954. 148 p. A policy statement delivered at the Sixth Plenum of the Central Committee of the Korean Workers' Party, Pyongyang, August 5, 1953. Also in the volume are a radio speech, July 28, 1953, and a report delivered at the Supreme People's Congress after Kim's visits to Moscow, Peking and other "brotherly nations," December 20, 1953. The text of the law in relation to the 3-year economic plan (1954-56) is appended. Texts of the speeches are slightly abridged and edited. The Korean originals are available in vol. III of *Kim Il-Sŏng sonjip* (Selected Works). [A]

JF38 KIM, IL-SUNG. *Report at the Enlarged Plenum of the Central Committee of the Workers' Party of Korea on the Work of the Party and Government Delegation which Attended Celebrations of the 40th Anniversary of Great October Socialist Revolution and the Meetings of Representatives of the Communist and Workers' Parties of Various Countries in Moscow, December 5, 1957.* Pyongyang: Foreign Languages Publishing House, n.d. 40 p.

JF39 KIM, IL-SUNG. *Report of the Central Committee of the Workers' Party of Korea to the Fourth Congress.* Pyongyang: Korean Central News Agency, September 11, 1961. 124 p. A major comprehensive policy statement by the North Korean Premier. [B]

JF40 KIM, N. *Pod gnetom iaponskogo imperializma; ocherk sovermennoi Korei.* Edited by K. A. Kharnskii. Vladivostok: "Knizhnoe delo," 1926. 152 p. Korea "under the yoke of Japanese imperialism."

JF41 KIM, SAN, and WALES, NYM (pseud. of Helen Snow). *Song of Ariran: The Life Story of a Korean Rebel.* N.Y.: Day, 1941. 258 p. The wife of Edgar Snow narrates the history of Korean revolutionary movements through the life story of a sensitive, determined, and perceptive Korean Communist then active in Yenan. Though valuable in understanding the motives, anxieties, tribulations, and strength of the Korean revolutionary movements of the pre-1945 period, not always reliable on details.

JF42 KIM, SANG-HAK. *Development of Socialist Industry in the D.P.R.K.* Pyongyang: Foreign Languages Publishing House, 1958. 62 p. Five brief chapters deal with Korea's industry during Japanese rule, North Korean industry during the pre-war period (1945-50), the Korean war, rehabilitation period (1953-56) and the first five-year plan period (1957-61). An abridged translation of the author's *Urinara kongŏp palchŏn esŏui saengsanryŏk baech'i e taehayŏ.* [B]

JF42A KING, O. H. P. *Tail of the Paper Tiger*. Caldwell, Idaho: Caxton, 1961. 574 p. An Associated Press correspondent's personal account of the war, which he observed from the outset.

JF42B KINKEAD, EUGENE. *In Every War But One*. N.Y.: Norton, 1959. 219 p. Report of a U.S. Army investigation into the conduct of American POW's during the Korean War and the large number who collaborated in one way or another with the Communists.

JF43 *Korea, 1945-1960*. Pyongyang: Foreign Languages Publishing House, 1960. (No pagination, approx. 300 p.) A pictorial history of North Korea with a brief propagandistic introduction. Charts on economic development. Presents North Korea as a paradise for workers.

JF44 *Korea Today*. Pyongyang: Foreign Languages Publishing House, 1961. (No pagination, approx. 200 p.) A pictorial presentation of North Korea with charts on economic development and education.

JF45 KRAVTSOV, I. *Aggressiia amerikanskogo imperializma v Koree 1945-1951 gg*. Moscow: Izdatelstvo politicheskoi literatury, 1951. 438 p. Party propaganda of the most hostile sort written during the Korean War phase of the Stalinist era. The story of "American imperialist aggression" is documented primarily by Russian sources such as Stalin's own testimony, articles in *Pravda*, and other materials produced by the Party.

JF45A LECKIE, ROBERT. *Conflict; the History of the Korean War*. N.Y.: Putnam, 1962. 448 p. More frank and dispassionate than many earlier accounts of the Korean War, Leckie's study points up the lessons which were learned in that conflict about the nature of the struggle with Communism.

JF45B LECKIE, ROBERT. *The March to Glory*. Cleveland and N.Y.: World, 1960. 219 p. "The story of an ordeal sustained" by the First Marine Division at the Chosin Reservoir. Based on documents and interviews. Lively.

JF46 LEE, CHONG-SIK. *The Politics of Korean Nationalism*. Berkeley: U. of California Press, 1964. 342 p. An exhaustive study by a professor, based on primary sources. Extensive bibliographical footnotes on pages 283-327. A condensation of a Ph.D. dissertation presented at Berkeley, "The Korean Nationalist Movement, 1905-1945."

JF47 LEE, T. W. "The United Nations and Korea, 1945-1953." Ph.D. dissertation, Oxford, 1958.

JF48 LIE, TRYGVE. *In The Cause of Peace; Seven Years with the United Nations*. N.Y.: Macmillan, 1954. 473 p. The former U.N. Secretary General details his dealings with Korea in two chapters. Lie considers his "stand on Korea the best justified act of seven years in the service of peace." Readable and informative.

JF49 LYONS, GENE M. *Military Policy and Economic Aid; The Korean Case, 1950-1953*. Columbus: Ohio State University Press, 1961. 298 p. Probes the conflict between U.S. military policy and the U.N. reconstruction programs during the Korean War. Criticizes the U.S. government's failure to formulate an overall Korean reconstruction policy. Extensive bibliographical notes and a useful bibliography. Documents appended.

JF50 McCUNE, GEORGE McAFEE, and GREY, ARTHUR L., JR. *Korea Today*. Cambridge: Harvard, 1950. 372 p. Though dated, still the best overall survey of political and economic development in Korea. Includes very useful assessments of the two regimes. Scholarly. [B]

JF51 MARSHALL, S. L. A. *Pork Chop Hill; The American Fighting Man in Action, Korea, Spring, 1953*. N.Y.: Morrow, 1956. 315 p. A renowned military analyst and historian masterfully reconstructs the last, fierce infantry battles in the Korean War. [B]

JF52 MARSHALL, S. L. A. *The River and the Gauntlet*. N.Y.: Morrow, 1953. 385 p. A noted military historian's factual account of the defeat of the U.S. Eighth Army in Korea by the Chinese in November 1950. Exact, superb. [A]

JF52A MILLAR, WARD M. *Valley of the Shadow*. N.Y.: McKay, 1955. 241 p. The incredible story of an American Air Force pilot's capture, escape, and eventual rescue from the enemy. Moving.

JF53 MONTROSS, LYNN, and CONZONA, NICHOLAS A. *U.S. Marine Operations in Korea, 1950-1953*. Vol. I, *The Pusan Perimeter*, 1954. 271 p. Vol. II, *The Inchon-Seoul Operation*, 1955. 361 p. Vol. III, *The Chosin Reservoir Campaign*, 1957. 432 p. Vol. IV, *The East-Central Front*, 1962. 342 p. Washington: Historical Branch, G-3, Headquarters, U.S. Marine Corps. An official history. Well-researched and documented. Marine operations are viewed in the perspective of the total U.N. commitment. Extensive bibliographical footnotes and short but useful bibliographies. Maps and illustrations. [A]

JF54 OLIVER, ROBERT T. *Syngman Rhee; The Man Behind the Myth*. N.Y.: Dodd, Mead, 1954. 380 p. A semi-official biography by Rhee's close associate. Chapter XV presents Rhee's views on the Korean War.

JF55 OLIVER, ROBERT T. *Verdict in Korea*. State College, Pa.: Bald Eagle Press, 1952. 207 p. An "inside," i.e., Korean, view of "what the war has done to Korea and what the Korean people and government have done to help themselves" by a close friend of Syngman Rhee. The last chapter summarizes the Korean view on major issues concerning the war, the U.N., Red China, etc. Informative.

JF56 OLIVER, ROBERT T. *Why War Came in Korea.* N.Y.: McMullen, 1950. 260 p. To provide the background for the war, a supporter of Syngman Rhee discusses events from 1942 to 1950. He asserts that if all the demands of Rhee since 1942 had been met by the U.S. government, the war would not have come. Though biased, it reveals the sentiments of Rhee and many other Koreans.

JF57 PAIGE, GLENN D. "The Korean Decision; June 24-30, 1950." Ph.D. dissertation, Northwestern U., 1959. "A narrative reconstruction of the decision-making activities at the highest levels of the U.S. government following receipt of the first report" of the North Korean invasion, based on documents and extensive interviews. A case study in the science of political behavior.

JF58 *Panmunjom.* Pyongyang: Foreign Languages Publishing House, 1958. 146 p. The purpose of this book is "to tell the ugly picture of how the American imperialists—the enemies of peace—provoked the Korean war, how the U.S. aggressive adventures against Korea were shattered, and then their provocative acts in the post-truce years and the bestial murders and savagery the American aggressive army is inflicting on the Korean people."

JF59 PASLEY, VIRGINIA. *21 Stayed.* N.Y.: Farrar, Straus, and Cudahy; London: Allen, 1955. 248 p. A journalist's psychological and sociological study of the American P.O.W.'s who chose to go to Communist China instead of returning home—who they were, and why they stayed. Based on extensive interviews. Revealing.

JF60 PATE, LLOYD W. as told to Cutler, B. J. *Reactionary!* N.Y.: Harper, 1956. 150 p. A forceful and candid account of an American soldier's experiences as a prisoner of war in North Korea.

JF61 PEROV, L. *Amerikanskaia agressiia v Koree.* Moscow: Gospolitizdat, 1951. 144 p. A propaganda pamphlet accusing the U.S. of willful aggression in Korea, crying "Hands Off Korea!" Calls the UN a "tool of American aggression in Korea."

JF62 PETERSON, WILLIAM S. "Creation of the Korean Democratic People's Republic." M.A. thesis, Columbia U., 1951. 121 p.

JF63 PIGULEVSKAIA, E. A. *Koreiskii narod v borbe za nezavisimost i demokratiiu.* Moscow: Akademiia nauk SSSR, Institut ekonomiki, 1952. 358 p. The story of the Korean people's struggles for independence and democracy from the mid-19th century to the "American imperialist aggression in 1950." Parallels are drawn between the Japanese invasion of Korea and American "aggression" in Korea, without mentioning Tsarist Russian attempts on Korea. Party propaganda of the most hostile sort, written during the Korean War, before Stalin's death. Quotations from Stalin, Lenin, Molotov, and Kim Il-sung.

JF64 POATS, RUTHERFORD M. *Decision in Korea.* N.Y.: McBride, 1954. 340 p. A United Press reporter's survey and interpretation of the Korean War. Concludes that in rejecting the idea of seeking total victory, the U.S. has in fact gained a moral triumph of even greater importance. Lively, insightful.

JF65 *Political Survey of the D.P.R.K., 1945-1960.* (Korea Information Series No. 1) Pyongyang: Foreign Languages Publishing House, 1960. 53 p. Deals with the "Liberation of Korea by the Soviet Army," the "U.S. Policy of National Division," the "Fatherland Liberation War for Freedom and Independence," and "The Struggle for Peaceful Unification."

JF66 RIDGWAY, MATTHEW B. *Soldier; The Memoirs of Matthew B. Ridgway.* (As told to Harold H. Martin.) N.Y.: Harper, 1956. 371 p. Personal reminiscences of the former Commander of the Eighth Army (December 1950-April 1951) and Commander-in-Chief of the UN Far East Command. Includes six chapters devoted to the Korean War.

JF67 RILEY, JOHN W., JR., and SCHRAMM, WILBUR. *The Reds Take a City; the Communist Occupation of Seoul, with Eyewitness Accounts.* New Brunswick: Rutgers, 1951. 210 p. Two social scientists' revealing analysis of Communist policy in an occupied city. Draws upon a U.S. Air Force study on human problems in Korea in which the authors participated. Interspersed with translations of eyewitness accounts of Korean leaders.

JF68 ROMASHKIN, P.S. *Chudovishchnye prestupleniia amerikanskikh agressorov v Koree.* Moscow: Gospolitizdat, 1953. 204 p. One of the most hostile Soviet pamphlets on the Korean War. The assertion that the American "imperialists" are "the worst enemy of humankind" is backed by the American "use of bacterial warfare," etc.

JF69 RUDOLPH, PHILIP. *North Korea's Political and Economic Structure.* N.Y.: Institute of Pacific Relations, 1959. 72 p. A succinct examination of the development of the major political and economic institutions in North Korea since 1945. Relies heavily on Russian sources. Extensive bibliographical footnotes and a useful bibliography. [A]

JF70 RUSS, MARTIN. *The Last Parallel, a Marine's War Journal.* N.Y.: Rinehart, 1957. 333 p. A straightforward chronicle of an articulate Marine sergeant who spent a year (1952-53) on the Korean front. Detailed and lively.

JF71 RUSSIA (1923-USSR), MINISTERSTVO INOSTRANNYKH DEL. *Sovetskii Soiuz i koreiskii vopros; dokumenty.* Moscow: 1948. 108 p. English ed.: *The Soviet Union and the Korean Question; Documents.* Moscow: 1948. 82 p. London: Soviet News, 1950. 99 p. French ed., Moscow: 1948. 87 p. A collection of 25 letters and speeches of such persons as Marshall, Molotov, Vishinsky, and Gromyko from 1945 to 1948. Not comprehensive or impartial, the selection shows the Russian position on the Korean question during the joint US-USSR occupation of Korea. [A]

JF72 SAMSONOV, G. E. *Borba za mirnoe demokraticheskoe reshenie koreiskogo voprosa.* Moscow: Izd. vost. lit., 1960. 142 p. A treatment of the Korean question by a Soviet academic authority on the Far East whose footnotes include citations from some American sources. Without deviating from the Party line, the history of the Korean question from 1945 to 1960 is reviewed in the following order: US-USSR joint occupation of Korea, US-USSR joint commission, "American aggression in Korea," and the development of socialism in North Korea. Finally, the Soviet position on how Korea may be peacefully united gets attention. [A]

JF73 SCALAPINO, ROBERT A., and LEE, CHONG-SIK. "The Origins of the Korean Communist Movement," *Journal of Asian Studies*, Vol. XX, no. 1 (November 1960) and no. 2 (February 1961). A scholarly work on the early movement (1918-25) in Siberia, Manchuria, China, and Korea. Relies on Japanese police documents, memoirs and official Communist records. [A]

JF74 SPAHR, W. J. "The Korean Question as Presented in the Soviet Press, January 1 to June 25, 1950." M.A. thesis, Columbia, 1953. 98 p. A useful summary of the Soviet view on Korea's contemporary conditions, followed by a succinct examination of the changes in the Soviet press on the Korean question, particularly from January 1 to June 25, 1950. Based on original sources.

JF75 SPANIER, JOHN W. *The Truman-MacArthur Controversy and the Korean War.* Cambridge, Mass.: Belknap, 1959. 311 p. Examines the controversy as a case of civil-military relations during a limited war. Primarily concerned with the American political scene. Scholarly.

JF76 STONE, ISADOR F. *The Hidden History of the Korean War.* N.Y.: Monthly Review Press, 1952. 364 p. Russian ed., Moscow: Izd.

inostrannoi lit., 1953. An American left-wing journalist advances the thesis that "in Korea the big powers were the victims, among other things, of headstrong satellites itching for a showdown." "North Korea merely fell into a trap." Tendentious. Translated into Japanese and widely circulated among Japanese and Korean leftists.

JF76A SURVEY OF INTERNATIONAL AFFAIRS, 1920-1923–; THE WAR-TIME SERIES FOR 1939-1946. *The Far East, 1942-1946*. By F. C. Jones, Hugh Borton, and B. R. Pearn. London and N.Y.: Oxford, for the Royal Institute of International Affairs, 1955. 589 p. Contains a section by Hugh Borton on "Korea under American and Soviet Occupation, 1945-47."

JF77 THOMAS, R. C. W. (MAJOR). *The War in Korea, 1950-1953; A Military Study of the War in Korea up to the Signing of the Cease Fire*. Aldershot, England: Gale, 1954. 119 p. A very brief outline of the main events during the period of fighting. Superficial.

JF77A THOMPSON, REGINALD. *Cry Korea*. London: Macdonald, 1952. 303 p. A first-hand account of the fighting in Korea and the effects on the civilian population, by a British war correspondent.

JF78 TRUMAN, HARRY S. *Memoirs of Harry S. Truman*. Vol. II, *Years of Trial and Hope*. Garden City, N.Y.: Doubleday, 1956. 594 p. Devotes seven chapters to the Korean War, including the MacArthur controversy. [B]

JF79 U.S. CONGRESS, SENATE, COMMITTEE ON ARMED SERVICES AND COMMITTEE ON FOREIGN RELATIONS. *Hearings on the Military Situation in the Far East and the Facts Surrounding the Relief of General of the Army Douglas MacArthur from His Assignments in that Area*. 82nd Congress, 1st Sess., 1951. 5 parts. 3691 p. Generally known as the MacArthur hearings. Witnesses include MacArthur, Marshall, Acheson, Wedemeyer, Collins, etc. Deals mainly with U.S. policy on Formosa and Korea, as well as with the dismissal of MacArthur. [B]

JF80 U.S. DEPARTMENT OF STATE. *The Korean Problem at the Geneva Conference, April 26-June 15, 1954*. Department of State Publication 5609, International Organization and Conference Series (Far Eastern) 4. October 1954. 193 p. Briefly summarizes Allied and Communist positions on the peaceful unification of Korea as shown at the Geneva Conference. Statements and proposals by the Communist delegates are included. [B]

JF81 U.S. DEPARTMENT OF STATE. *Korea's Independence*. Department of State Publication 2933, Far Eastern Series 18, October 1947. 60 p. A brief summary of events in Korea from December 1943 to September 1945, followed by documents. Letters exchanged between the U.S. and the Soviet commanding officers in Korea, and notes exchanged between the U.S. Secretary of State and the Soviet Minister of Foreign Affairs are included.

JF82 U.S. DEPARTMENT OF STATE. *North Korea; A Case Study in the Techniques of Takeover.* Washington: Dept. of State Publication 7118, Far Eastern Series 103, 1961. 121 p. Report of a State Department research mission sent to Korea in late 1950. Based on interrogations of former North Korean government and Party officials and others, plus captured North Korean and Russian documents. Sections on the evolution of the North Korean regime and the Party and government apparatus are followed by appraisals of the regime and of Soviet policies toward North Korea. Sees North Korea before 1950 as an effective Soviet satellite. Valuable. [A]

JF83 U.S. DEPARTMENT OF STATE. *The Record on Korean Unification, 1943-1960; Narrative Summary with Principal Documents.* Department of State Publication 7084, Far Eastern Series 101, 1960. 241 p. A forty-page summary brings U.S. and U.N. action on Korea up to date. Documents include resolutions, declarations, communications and statements of both the U.S. allies and those of the Soviet Union. [A]

JF84 U.S. DEPARTMENT OF STATE. *United States Policy in the Korean Crisis.* Department of State Publication 3922, Far Eastern Series 34, July 1950. 68 p. An eight-page policy statement followed by documents issued during June-July 1950. Documents include reports of the U.N. Commission on Korea, resolutions adopted by the U.N. Security Council, and messages issued by the Soviet and other governments.

JF85 U.S. DEPARTMENT OF THE ARMY, OFFICE OF MILITARY HISTORY. *Korea, 1951-1953.* By John Miller, Jr., Owen J. Carroll, and Margaret E. Tackley. Washington: 1956. 328 p. An outline history of the Korean War with photographs. Intended for U.S. Army veterans of the Korean War.

JF86 U.S. LIBRARY OF CONGRESS, REFERENCE DEPARTMENT. *Korea: An Annotated Bibliography.* Washington: 1950. 3 vols. Vol. I, *Publications in Western Languages*, 155 p., compiled by Helen D. Jones and Robin L. Winkler. Vol. II, *Publications in the Russian Language*, 84 p., comp. by Albert Parry, John T. Dorosh, and Elizabeth G. Dorosh. Vol. III, *Publications in Far Eastern Languages*, 167 p., comp. under the direction of Edwin G. Beal. Topically arranged. Lists a number of books and articles related to the Korean Communist movement. Index.

JF87 *Valuable Aid from Peoples of Fraternal Countries.* Pyongyang: Foreign Languages Publishing House, 1958. 44 p. Though popularly written, provides some statistics of foreign aid received.

JF88 VATCHER, WILLIAM H. *Panmunjom; The Story of the Korean Military Armistice Negotiations.* N.Y.: Praeger; London: Stevens, 1958. 322 p. A detailed examination of the negotiations by the former psychological warfare advisor to the Senior U.N. delegate on loan from Stanford University. Informative and well-documented. Useful chronology. [A]

JF89 WHITE, WILLIAM L. *The Captives of Korea; An Unofficial White Paper on the Treatment of War Prisoners; Our Treatment of Theirs, Their Treatment of Ours.* N.Y.: Scribner, 1957. 347 p. An anthology of short and somewhat fragmented narratives. For a popular audience.

JF90 WHITING, ALLEN S. *China Crosses the Yalu; The Decision to Enter the Korean War.* N.Y.: Macmillan, 1960. 219 p. A former RAND Corporation expert advances a number of hypotheses to explain the Chinese Communists' intervention in the Korean War. Based on inferences and generalizations. Extensive bibliographical references. [B]

JF91 WHITNEY, COURTNEY (MAJOR GENERAL). *MacArthur; His Rendezvous with History.* N.Y.: Knopf, 1956. 547 p. MacArthur's former aide presents the General's views on World War II, the occupation of Japan, and the Korean War. An authorized version. Devotes 13 chapters to the Korean War. [B]

JF92 WINT, GUY. *What Happened in Korea? A Study in Collective Security.* London: Batchworth, 1954. 152 p. Covers in outline form the Korean War from the outbreak to the armistice. For a general audience. One of the "background series."

JF93 YANG, KEY P. "The North Korean Regime, 1945-1955." M.A. thesis, American U., 1958. 230 p. Examines in detail the political development and government institutions in North Korea. Mostly based on North Korean documentary sources. Extensive and valuable bibliographical footnotes and bibliography. [B]

JF94 YOUNG, JOHN. *Checklist of Microfilm Reproductions of Selected Archives of the Japanese Army, Navy and Other Government Agencies, 1868-1945.* Washington: Georgetown U., 1959. 144 p. Lists some Japanese police and Army documents related to Korean Communist and nationalist movements before 1945. Some of the files listed under general categories contain invaluable reports.

2. TITLES IN ORIENTAL LANGUAGES

JF95 CHANG, POK-SŎNG. *Chosŏn kongsandang p'ajaengsa.* Seoul: Taeryuk Ch'ulp'ansa, 1949. 110 p. An outline history of the factional struggles among the Korean Communists, 1921-49, by a South Korean police official. Slanted but informative.

JF96 CHO, CHAE-SŎN. *Kwadogi e issosŏ ui Chosŏn Nodongdang ui kyŏngje chŏngch'aek.* Pyongyang: Choson Nodongdang Ch'ulp'ansa, 1958. 146 p. A theoretical "analysis of the major components of the economic policy of the Korean Workers' Party during the transitional period." Succinct explanation and rationalization of the economic policies of the North Korean regime including the 1st 5-year plan. Informative. [B]

JF97 CHOGUK T'ONGIL MINJUJUUI CHOSŎN CHUNGANG WIWŎNHOE. *Choguk ui p'yŏnghwajok t'ongil ŭl wihayŏ.* Pyongyang. 261 p. "For the Sake of Peaceful Unification of the Fatherland," published by the Central Committee of the Democratic Front for the Unification of the Fatherland.

JF97A CHŎNG, SUNG-GYU. *Chonggun malli.* Seoul: Kukto Shinmunsa, 1954. 293 p. A Korean war correspondent's account of the war.

JF98 CHOSŎN MINJUJUUI INMIN KONGHWAGUK, KWAHAKWŎN. *Chosŏn t'ongsa.* Tokyo: Gakuyu Shobo, 1959. 3 vols. A Communist history of Korea.

JF99 CHŎSON MINJUJUUI INMIN KONGHWAGUK KWAHAKWŎN KOGOHAK MIT MINSOKHAK YŎNGUSO. *Cho-jung ch'insŏn nongŏp hyŏptong chohap nongmin dŭlui munhwa wa p'ungsup.* Pyongyang: Kwahakwon Ch'ulp'ansa, 1960. 244 p. "Culture and Custom of the Farmers at the Korean-Chinese Friendship Farmers' Cooperative," published by the Center of Anthropology and Folklore, Academy of Science, Pyongyang. The cooperative is located at T'aekam-ri, 20 km. northwest of Pyongyang.

JF100 CHOSŎN MINJUJUUI INMIN KONGHWAGUK KWAHAKWŎN, KYŎNGJE PŎPHAK YŎNGUSO. *8.15 haebang 16 chunyŏn kinyŏm kyŏngje nonmunjip.* Pyongyang: Kwahakwon Ch'ulp'ansa, 1960. 236 p. A collection of seven essays on the North Korean economy by Communist theoreticians commemorating the fifteenth anniversary of the Korean liberation. Includes essays on "Economic Policies of the Korean Workers' Party," and "Development of Socialistic Competitive Movement and the 'Ch'ollima' team movement." Though propagandistic, useful for economic policies of the North Korean regime. [B]

JF101 CHOSŎN MINJUJUUI INMIN KONGHWAGUK KWAHAKWŎN, KYŎNGJE PŎPHAK YŎNGUSO. *Haebang hu uri nara ui inmin kyŏngje palchŏn.* Pyongyang: Kwahakwon Ch'ulp'ansa, 1960. 277 p. A report on economic development in North Korea by the Center for Study of Economics and Law, Academy of Science, Pyongyang. Includes chapters on the Korean liberation and democratic reforms, economic development before the war, economic development during the war, the three-year reconstruction and development plan and its results, and economic development under the 1st five-year plan. Though propagandistic, a useful guide on the North Korean economy. [B]

JF102 CHOSŎN MINJUJUUI INMIN KONGHWAGUK KWAHAKWŎN, KYŎNGJE YŎNGUSO. *Uri nara inmin kyŏngje esŏ ui saengsannyŏk kwa saengsan kwangye ui hosang chagyong.* Pyongyang: Kwahakwon Ch'ulp'ansa, 1960. 170 p. A discussion of the Korean economy, published by the Center of Economics, Academy of Science, in Pyongyang.

JF103 CHOSŎN MINJUJUUI INMIN KONGHWAGUK, KWAHAKWŎN, ŎNŎ MUNHAK YŎNGUSO. *Kongsanjuui kyoyang kwa uri munhak.* Pyongyang: Kwahakwon Ch'ulp'ansa, 1960. 152 p. "Communist Edification and Our Literature" by the Center for the Study of Linguistics and Literature, Academy of Science, Pyongyang.

JF104 CHOSŎN MINJUJUUI INMIN KONGHWAGUK KWAHAKWŎN YŎKSA YŎNGUSO, KŬNSE MIT CH'OEGŬNSESA YŎNGUSIL. *Chosŏn kŭndae hyŏngmyŏng undongsa.* Pyongyang: Kwahakwon Ch'ulp'ansa, 1961. 428 p. A history of the modern Korean revolution from the Communist viewpoint, edited by a Study Group on Modern and Contemporary History, Center of Historical Studies, Academy of Science, Pyongyang. Chon Sok-nam, the editor, and twelve others deal with the nationalist and Communist movements of 1860-1945. More balanced than Yi Na-yŏng's work of 1958. (q.v.) [A]

JF105 CHOSŎN NODONGDANG. *Chŏnguk chibang sanŏp mit saengsan hyŏptong chohap yŏlsŏngja taehoe munhŏnjip.* Pyongyang: Chosŏn Nodongdang Ch'ulp'ansa, 1959. 281 p. Speeches delivered at the Conference of the Representatives of Industrial and Production Cooperatives.

JF105A CHOSŎN NODONGDANG CHUNGANG UIWONHOE CHIKSOK TANG YŎKSA YŎNGUSO. *Hangll ppalchisan ch'amgajadŭl ui hoesanggi.* 8 vols. Pyongyang: Chosŏn Nodongdang Ch'ulp'ansa, 1959-61. An anthology of recollections of the participants in the anti-Japanese guerrilla activities in Manchuria, 1936-1940. Published to exalt the revolutionary heritage of Premier Kim Il-sung.

JF106 CHOSŎN YŎKSA P'YŎNCH'AN UIWONHOE. *Chosen Minzoku Kaiho Toso Shi.* (Trans. by Chosen Rekishi Kenkyukai). Kyoto: Sanichi Shobo, 1952. 406 p. Abridged Chinese edition by Ma Chou-chun and Li Ch'i-lieh, *Ch'ao-hsien minchu chiehfang shih.* Shanghai: Tungfang shu-she, 1951. A Japanese translation of a Korean publication, Pyongyang, 1949. A collection of lectures delivered by eight leading North Korean historians and social scientists at Kim Il-sung University on the Korean people's struggle for emancipation. Emphasis is on the Communist movement. A semi-official history of the day, but discarded later.

JF106A HŌ-CHŌ-KISHADAN. *Kita Chōsen no kiroku.* Tokyo: Shindokshosha, 1960. 226 p. Five Japanese journalists who visited North Korea in 1959 present a very sympathetic report of impressions. Uncritically reproduces North Korean data.

JF107 HYŎN, SU. *Chŏkch'i yungnyŏn ui pukhan mundan.* Seoul: Chungang Munhwasa, 1952. 196 p. A former North Korean poet writes about the life and work of North Korean writers between 1945 and 1951. Informative and articulate.

JF108 IM, CH'UN-CH'U. *Hangil mujang t'ujaeng sigi rŭl hoesang hayŏ.* Pyongyang: Choson Nodongdang Ch'ulp'ansa, 1960. 313 p. A personal follower of Kim Il-sung writes of the struggle against Japan.

JF108A KAKANKAI (ed.) (Supervised by Japanese Ministry of Foreign Affairs, Asia Bureau) *Gendai Chōsen jinmei jiten.* Tokyo: Sekai Jyānarusha, 1962. 509 p. Lists 1,589 South Korean and 827 North Korean personalities. Data on North Koreans tend to be sparse and mostly limited to post-1945 events. Index in Japanese *kana*, Chinese characters, and English transliteration. Lists of successive parliamentary and cabinet officers and a chronology of events appended. Useful.

JF109 KIM, CH'ANG-SUN. *Puk Han sip-o-nyŏn sa.* Seoul: Chimungak, 1961. 283 p. A political history of North Korea since 1945 by a former Communist reporter. Relies on personal reflections and documents, although documentary sources are not cited. Fairly objective, but reflects an anti-Communist attitude. Intended for a popular audience. [B]

JF110 KIM, HA-MYŎNG. *Chosŏn kyŏngje chiri (sang).* Pyongyang: Kungnip Ch'ulp'ansa, 1958. 392 p. Volume I of an economic geography of Korea.

JF111 KIM, IL-SUNG. *Chayu wa tongnip ul wihan Choson inmin ui chŏngui ui choguk haebang chonjaeng.* Pyongyang: Choson Nodongdang Ch'ulp'ansa, 1954. 390 p. A collection of speeches, orders, messages, and letters of the Premier of the North Korean regime during the

Korean War. Starts with his radio broadcast of June 26, 1950 and closes with his radio broadcast of July 28, 1953.

JF112 KIM, IL-SUNG. *Chosŏn minjujuui inmin konghwaguk surip ui kil.* Pyongyang: Puk Choson Inmin Uiwonhoe Sonjonbu, 1947. 293 p. A collection of Kim Il-sung's speeches.

JF113 KIM, IL-SUNG. *Kim Il-sŏng sŏnjip.* 6 vols. Pyongyang: Choson Nodongdang Ch'ulp'ansa, 1960. Selected works of the Premier of the North Korean regime. Includes major speeches, policy statements, and reports on economy, foreign relations and the Party. [A]

JF114 KIM IL-SUNG CHONGHAP TAEHAK P'YŎNJIP UIWŎNHOE. *8.15 haebang 15 chunyŏn kinyŏm nonmunjip.* Pyongyang: Kim Il-sung Chonghap Taehak, 1960. 336 p. A collection of essays commemorating the 15th anniversary of the Korean liberation by staff members of Kim Il-sung University. Divided into sections on social and natural sciences. Includes essays on economic and cultural policies, and a section on "Research Activities at the Natural Science Departments of the University Since the Liberation."

JF115 KIM, SAM-GYU. *Konnichi no Chosen.* Tokyo: Kawade Shobo, 1956. 180 p. An advocate of a neutral Korea and former editorial chief of *Tonga Ilbo* (Seoul) analyzes the Korean situation. He advances an hypothesis that Pak Hŏn-yŏng, then the Foreign Minister in Pyongyang, was responsible for the war. Insightful. [B]

JF116 KIM, SANG-HAK. *Urinara kongŏp palchŏn esŏ ui saengsannyŏk paech'i e taehayŏ.* Pyongyang: Kwahakwon, 1956. 167 p. A North Korean economist deals with the problems of distribution in the industrialization of his country.

JF117 KIM, SANG-HYŎN (ed.). *Taejung chŏngch'i yongŏ sajŏn.* Pyongyang: Choson Nodongdang Ch'ulp'ansa; Tokyo: Gakuyu Shobo, 1959. 356 p. A dictionary of political terms endorsed by the North Korean regime.

JF117A MUN, CHUNG-SŎP. *Chŏgyŏk nŭngsŏn: bu 6.25 wa koeraegun ui ch'imryak chunbisa.* Seoul: Yuksŏngsa, 1954. 216 p. A South Korean reporter's account of the war, with an appendix on the preparation of the North Korean army for invasion.

JF118 O, CHE-DO. *Pulgŭn kunsang.* Pusan: Nam Kwang Munhwasa, 1951. 143 p. A noted South Korean prosecutor of Communists narrates Communist tactics and his efforts against them. Informative on Communist activities in South Korea after 1945.

JF119 PUK CHOSŎN NODONGDANG CHUNGANG PONBU. *Chosŏn Minjujuui Inmin Konghwaguk Ch'oego Inmin Hoeui che ilch'a hoeui munhŏnjip.* Pyongyang: Pukchoson Nodongdang Ch'ulp'anbu, 1948. 345 p. A collection of speeches delivered at the 1st Supreme People's Congress of the Democratic People's Republic of Korea, Pyongyang, September 2-10, 1948. Mostly rhetoric, praising the constitutional draft submitted by the Constitutional Committee. The constitution and other documents related to the establishment of the regime are appended.

JF120 P'YŎNGYANG HYANGT'OSA P'YŎNCH'AN WIWŎNHOE. *P'yŏngyangji.* Pyongyang: Kungnip Ch'ulp'ansa, 1957. 725 p. A history and description of the North Korean capital by the Editorial Committee of the History of Pyongyang.

JF120A SEKI, KISEI (O Kwi-sŏng) *Rakuen no yume yaburete: kita Chōsen no shinsō.* Tokyo: Zenbōsha, 1962. 219 p. A former officer of the leftist General Federation of Koreans in Japan who had visited North Korea twice in 1957 and 1960 bitterly renounces the Pyongyang regime for its poverty, deception and suppressive policies. Exposes the "true nature" of the General Federation which deceptively lured Koreans in Japan to North Korea. A number of letters by returnees from Japan complaining of the lack of food and material in North Korea are reprinted.

JF120B TAEHAN MINGUK KUKPANGBU. *Hanguk chollan il-[i, sam,sa,o]nyŏnji.* 5 vols. Pusan and Seoul: Kukpangbu, 1951-55. Annual reports of the Ministry of Defense, Republic of Korea, on the developments of the war. Each volume is divided into general summary, diary, documents, and statistics.

JF120C TERAO, GORŌ. *Sanjūhachido-sen no kita.* Tokyo: Sin Nihon Suppansha, 1959. 263 p. A Japanese leftwing writer and member of the Japanese-Korean Association writes of his impressions of North Korea, where he had visited in 1958. Presents a highly idealized view of North Korea and vilifies the United States for inhumane atrocities. Inflammatory. Has been a best seller in Japan.

JF121 TSUBOE, SENJI. *Hokusen no kaiho junen-Kin Nichisei dokusai seiken no jittai.* Tokyo: Nikkan Rodo Tsushinsha, 1956. 222 p. A comprehensive survey of the North Korean regime from 1945 to 1955. A former colonial official in Korea deals with the development of internal politics, the Korean War, economic development, and foreign relations. Balanced and competent. No bibliographical references. [A]

JF122 YI, CHONG-P'AL, *et al. Nongŏp hyoptong chohap ui chŏngch'i kyŏngje jŏk konggohwa rŭl wihan myotkaji munje.* Pyongyang: Choson Nodongdang Ch'ulp'ansa, 1960. 230 p. A collection of essays on "Various Problems in the Political and Economic Consolidation of the Farmers' Cooperatives."

JF123 YI, NA-YŎNG. *Chosŏn minjok haebang t'ujaengsa.* Pyongyang: Choson Nodongdang Ch'ulp'ansa, 1958. 452 p. Japanese ed., *Chosen minzoku kaiho tososhi.* Tokyo: Shin Nippon Shuppansha, 1960. 529 p. A history of the Korean people's struggle for emancipation by a staff member of the Center of Historical Studies, Academy of Science, Pyongyang. Deals with the period from 1860 to 1945. The accent is on the Communist movement after 1920. Denounces an earlier work of the same title edited by Chosŏn Yŏksa P'yŏnch'an Uiwonhoe (q.v.). Very critical of most of the Korean Communists except Kim Il-sung. Ignores the Yenan faction's activities. [A]

JF124 YI, SI-HYŎNG. *Kyŏngje sangsik.* Pyongyang: Choson Nodongdang Ch'ulp'ansa, 1960. 335 p. "Economic Common Sense" by a North Korean economist.

JF125 YUKKUN PONBU, KUNSA KAMSIL. *Yukio sabyŏn hubang chŏnsa.* 2 vols. Seoul: Yukkun Ponbu, 1955-56. The Republic of Korea Army's official history of the management of supplies (Vol. 1) and personnel (Vol. 2) during the Korean War.

JF126 YUKKUN PONBU, KUNSA KAMSIL. *Yukio sabyŏn yukkun chŏnsa.* 6 vols. Seoul: Yukkun Ponbu, 1954-57. The Republic of Korea Army's official history of the battles during the Korean war.

JG. SOUTHEAST ASIA

EDITED BY ROBERT M. RODES

1. GENERAL WORKS

JG1 AKADEMIIA NAUK SSSR, INSTITUT MIROVOI EKONOMIKI I MEZHDUNARODNYKH OTNOSHENII. *Problemy industrializatsii suverennykh slaborazvitykh stran Azii (Indiia, Indoneziia, Birma)*. Ed. by V. Ia. Avarin and others. Moscow: Izd. Akad. nauk SSSR, 1960. 439 p. Chapters contributed individually by workers in the Institute's section on the countries of Southeast Asia and the Far East deal with the problem of accumulation of capital, the position of foreign capital, the national bourgeoisie, the condition of the working class, and other topics. Concentrates on statistical data. [B]

JG2 AKADEMIIA NAUK SSSR, INSTITUT NARODOV AZII. *Bibliografiia Iugo-Vostochnoi Azii; dorevoliutsionnaia i sovetskaia literatura na russkom iazyke originalnaia i perevodnaia.* Moscow: Izd. vost. lit., 1960. 256 p. A valuable compilation of 3752 items including books, serial publications, and articles.

JG3 AKADEMIIA NAUK SSSR, INSTITUT VOSTOKOVEDENIIA. *Protiv kolonializma; natsionalno-osvoboditelnoe dvizhenie v stranakh vostoka; sbornik statei i retsenzii.* Ed. by K. M. Popov and others. Moscow: Izd. vostoch. lit., 1960. 172 p. Substantial reviews of Malcolm D. Kennedy's *A Short History of Communism in Asia* and recent British and American literature on Burma are among the items included.

JG4 AKADEMIIA NAUK SSSR, TIKHOOKEANSKII INSTITUT. *Krizis kolonialnoi sistemy; natsionalno-osvoboditelnaia borba narodov Vostochnoi Azii.* Ed. by E. M. Zhukov. Moscow: Izd. Akad. nauk SSSR, 1949. 290 p. Includes an article by R. V. Astafev on the success of the Communists in China. Most of the remaining articles concern South and Southeast Asia; reports read at a special meeting of the Academy of Sciences devoted to the colonial question, June 1949. [A]

JG5 BALL, WILLIAM MacMAHON. *Nationalism and Communism in East Asia.* Carlton, Australia: Melbourne Univ., 1952. 210 p. 2nd ed., 1956. 220 p. London and N.Y.: Cambridge, 1952. A brief, interpretative study by a professor at the U. of Melbourne who maintains that the major force in East Asia (Japan to India) today is a revolution with three main components: revolt against foreign political control, social and economic protest, and Asian reaction against Western superiority. [A]

JG6 BELOFF, MAX. *Soviet Policy in the Far East, 1944-1951.* N.Y. and London: Oxford, 1953. 278 p. Contains a chapter by J. Frankel on Soviet policy towards Southeast Asia; based on extensive use of Soviet sources. [A]

JG7 BRIMMELL, J. H. *Communism in South East Asia; a Political Analysis.* London and N.Y.: Oxford, 1959. 415 p. The author, formerly an official of the British government, combines a presentation of the evolution of international Communist doctrine toward the underdeveloped areas with a survey of Communism in the region. Stresses the rising influence of China on Communism in this part of the world. [A]

JG8 BULGANIN, NIKOLAI A., and KHRUSHCHEV, NIKITA S. *Visit of Friendship to India, Burma, and Afghanistan; Speeches and Official Documents (November-December 1955).* Moscow: Foreign Languages Pub. House, 1956. 327 p. German ed., Berlin: Dietz, 1956. Italian ed., Rome: Editori riuniti, 1956. Speeches of Khrushchev and Bulganin during their extended and highly-publicized tour of Asia in 1955.

JG9 BUTWELL, RICHARD A. *Southeast Asia Today—and Tomorrow; a Political Analysis.* N.Y.: Praeger, 1961. 182 p. An up-to-date survey of the overall Southeast Asian situation.

JG9A CLUBB, OLIVER E., JR. *The United States and the Sino-Soviet Bloc in Southeast Asia.* Washington: Brookings Institution, 1962.

JG10 DAI, SHEN-YU (Tai, Sheng-Yu). *Peking, Moscow, and the Communist Parties of Colonial Asia.* Cambridge, Mass.: M.I.T., 1954. 167 p. An attempt by an expert on contemporary Chinese politics to judge the relative influence of Moscow and Peking on Communist Parties in Southeast Asia by analyzing the strategies and programs of the latter and comparing them with the political lines emanating from the two Communist capitals. [B]

JG11 DURDENEVSKII, V. N., and LAZAREV, M. I. *Piat printsipov mirnogo sosushchestvovaniia.* Moscow: Gosizdat iurid. lit., 1957. 119 p. A politico-legal treatment of the Five Principles of Coexistence (Pancha Shila), illustrative of their use as slogans in Soviet policy.

JG12 FITUNI, L. *"Plan Kolombo" i Iugo-Vostochnaia Aziia.* Moscow: Sotsekgiz, 1960. 136 p. A polemical Soviet interpretation of the Colombo Plan, its organization and purpose.

JG13 GUBER, A., ed. *Velikii Oktiabr i narody Vostoka; sbornik.* Moscow: Izd. vost. lit., 1957. 417 p. Includes essays on Vietnam, Burma, Indonesia, and the Philippines by area specialists who present the Communist view of the influence of the Russian Revolution on the "national liberation movements" in these countries.

JG13A *Happiness and Peace for the Peoples; N. S. Khrushchev's Visit to India, Burma, Indonesia, and Afghanistan, February 11-March 5, 1960.* Moscow: Foreign Languages Publishing House, 1960. 341 p. Materials, including speeches by Khrushchev and his hosts, from the Soviet leader's trip.

JG14 HINTON, HAROLD C. *China's Relations with Burma and Vietnam; a Brief Survey.* N.Y.: Institute of Pacific Relations, 1958. 64 p. An expert on China analyzes the historic and current relations between China and these two Southeast Asian countries. Contains considerable information from the Chinese press and other contemporary sources on Communism in this area.

JG15 HOLLAND, WILLIAM L., ed. *Asian Nationalism and the West.* N.Y.: Macmillan, in cooperation with the Institute of Pacific Relations, 1953. 422 p. The highly competent authors of the three papers in this collection deal with Indonesia, Vietnam, and Malaya. Though Communism is not their main concern, they do make a number of interesting references to this subject.

JG16 KAHIN, GEORGE M., ed. *Governments and Politics in Southeast Asia.* Ithaca: Cornell, 1959. 531 p. The authors of these six substantial studies examine the Communist problem as a part of the political situation in each of the non-Communist countries covered. The section on Vietnam includes a chapter on the background to the current political situation and also a chapter on North Vietnam.

JG17 KAUFMAN, A. S., and SIMONIIA, N. A., eds. *Agrarno-krestianskii vopros v stranakh Iugo-Vostochnoi Azii.* Moscow: Izd. vost. lit., 1961. 163 p.

JG18 KENNEDY, MALCOLM D. *A Short History of Communism in Asia.* London: Weidenfeld and Nicolson, 1957. 556 p. American ed., *A History of Communism in East Asia.* N.Y.: Praeger, 1957. A comprehensive and useful history of Communist movements in Asia, excluding the Middle East, down to 1955. Captain Kennedy, a former British official, has utilized Communist publications available in English and a broad range of non-Communist works. [A]

JG19 KING, JOHN KERRY. *Southeast Asia in Perspective.* N.Y.: Macmillan, 1956. 309 p. A thoughtful study of the transformations that have taken place in Southeast Asia in recent years and a critical evaluation of American policy toward the area from the perspective of the world struggle to counter Communism.

JG20 KOREL, I. I. *Natsionalno-osvoboditelnaia borba v Indonezii, Vetname, Malaie i Birme; rekomend. ukazatel literatury.* Leningrad: GPB, 1950. 32 p.

JG21 McVEY, RUTH T. *Bibliography of Soviet Publications on Southeast Asia, As Listed in the Library of Congress Monthly Index of Russian Acquisitions.* Ithaca, N.Y.: Cornell, 1959. 109 p. A very convenient compilation by a research associate in the Cornell Modern Indonesia Project of items from the voluminous L.C. Index for the years 1948 to 1958.

JG22 McVEY, RUTH T. *The Calcutta Conference and the Southeast Asian Uprisings.* Ithaca, N.Y.: Cornell, 1958. A consideration, based on exhaustive study of published sources on the 1948 "youth conference," of the frequently advanced thesis that the meeting was used by international Communism to communicate a change of strategy to the Asian Parties. [B]

JG23 MARTYSHEVA, G. A. *Iugo-Vostochnaia Aziia posle vtoroi mirovoi voiny.* Moscow: Sotsekgiz, 1960. 404 p. A major Soviet study on a regional basis of the recent history and current political and economic problems of Southeast Asia. Sponsored by the Academy of Sciences' Institute of World Economy and International Relations.

JG24 MERZLIAKOV, N. S. *SEATO.* Moscow: Izd. Inst. mezhdu. otnoshenii, 1958. 230 p. A comprehensive Soviet analysis of the structure, function, and purpose of SEATO.

JG25 *Politika SShA v stranakh Iuzhnoi Azii.* Moscow: Izd. vost. lit., 1961.

JG26 *Razbuzhennyi Vostok; zapiski sovetskikh zhurnalistov o visite N. S. Khrushcheva v Indiiu, Birmu, Indoneziiu, Afganistane.* Moscow: Gospolitizdat, 1960. 2 vols. Extensive coverage by Soviet journalists of Khrushchev's prolonged trip to Asia in early 1960.

JG27 ROSE, SAUL. *Socialism in Southern Asia.* London: Oxford, for the Royal Institute of International Affairs, 1959. 278 p. An approving examination of Democratic Socialism in the region from India to the Pacific as an alternative to Communism and other competing forces. The author, a member of the British Labour Party, is a Research Fellow at St. Anthony's College, Oxford.

JG28 ROSTOVSKII, S. N. *Rabochee i natsionalno-osvoboditelnoe dvizhenie v stranakh Iugo-Vostochnoi Azii posle vtoroi mirovoi voiny (Birma, Malaiia, Indoneziia).* Moscow: Izd. VPSh i AON pri TsK KPSS, 1959. 111 p. The individual section for each country includes an account of events leading to independence, an appraisal of existing political groupings, and a description of the status of the Communist Party. Reflects the current Soviet view of the Asian "national bourgeoisie." [A]

JG29 RUBINSTEIN, ALVIN Z. "Selected Bibliography of Soviet Works on Southern Asia, 1954-56," *Journal of Asian Studies* (November 1957), p. 43-54. An excellent review of Soviet periodical literature on the history, politics, and economics of India, Afghanistan, Burma, and Indonesia by a member of the faculty at the U. of Pennsylvania.

JG30 SMIRNOV, IU., and SOFINSKII, V. *SEATO—agressivnyi blok kolonialnykh derzhav.* Moscow: Gospolitizdat, 1957. 143 p. Propaganda purporting to expose SEATO as a "new form of colonialism" seeking to suppress "people's liberation movements."

JG31 THOMPSON, VIRGINIA, and ADLOFF, RICHARD. *The Left Wing in Southeast Asia.* N.Y.: Sloane, 1950. 298 p. A study of the emergence and development of a left wing in the politics of Burma, Indonesia, Indochina, Malaya, and Thailand by authors well acquainted with the Asian scene. Communist movements receive particular attention. [A]

JG32 TRAGER, FRANK N., ed. *Marxism in Southeast Asia; a Study of Four Countries.* Stanford, Cal.: Stanford University Press, 1959. 381 p. Very informative essays by well-qualified authors on the Communist Parties and the impact of Marxist doctrine. Contains: "Marxism in Burma," by John S. Thomson; "Thailand and Marxism," by David A. Wilson; "Marxism in Viet Nam," by I. Milton Sacks; "Marxism in Indonesia," by Jeanne S. Mintz; and "The Impact of Marxism," by Frank N. Trager. [B]

JG33 U.S. LIBRARY OF CONGRESS, ORIENTALIA DIVISION. *Southeast Asia; An Annotated Bibliography of Selected Reference Sources.* Comp. by Cecil Hobbs. Washington: 1952. 163 p. Some 350 highly selective items—including a number on Communism—are listed by country under subdivisions dealing with history, government, and politics. Substantial annotations are included.

JG34 VANDENBOSCH, AMRY, and BUTWELL, RICHARD A. *Southeast Asia among the World Powers.* Lexington: U. of Kentucky, 1957. 360 p. A competent treatment of contemporary conditions and problems in Southeast Asia by two well-known American students of the area. Communism and the relations of these countries with the Soviet Union and Communist China are briefly surveyed as parts of the political picture.

JG35 VASILEV, D., and LVOV, K. *Soviet Trade with South-East Asia.* Moscow: Foreign Languages Pub. House, 1959. 157 p. A sketchy survey of the economies of the USSR and of the countries of S.E. Asia, existing trade relations between the former and the latter, and the potential for growth. The appendix contains tables of imports and exports for 1956-58.

JG36 VASILEVA, V. IA. *Natsionalno-osvoboditelnaia borba v stranakh Iugo-Vostochnoi Azii.* Moscow: "Pravda," 1949. 32 p. A very brief statement of the Soviet line as of 1949 on the "people's struggle" in Vietnam, Indonesia, Burma, the Philippines, and Malaya.

2. BURMA

JG37 AKADEMIIA NAUK SSSR, INSTITUT VOSTOKOVEDENIIA. *Birmanskii Souiz; sbornik statei.* Moscow: Izd. vost. lit., 1958. 291 p. Includes eleven essays on Burma by five Burmese and six Soviet writers. Burma's political structure, independence, and foreign trade are among the wide range of topics treated.

JG38 KAUFMAN, A. S. *Rabochii klass i natsionalno-osvoboditelnoe dvizhenie v Birme.* Moscow: Izd. vost. lit., 1961. 144 p. A survey of the development of a working class and its political role down to the establishment of an independent Burma in 1948. Relies heavily on Western sources.

JG38A KAZNACHEEV, ALEKSANDR. *Inside a Soviet Embassy; Experiences of a Soviet Diplomat in Burma.* Philadelphia and N.Y.: Lippincott, 1962. 250 p. Revelations regarding Soviet policy and tactics in Burma, by a Soviet official who defected.

JG39 TINKER, HUGH. *The Union of Burma; a Study of the First Years of Independence.* London and N.Y.: Oxford, 1957. 424 p. A historian's survey of the first eight years of Burmese independence. Contains some information on Communist activities in this period.

3. INDO-CHINA

JG40 AKADEMIIA NAUK SSSR, INSTITUT NARODOV AZII. *Demokraticheskaia Respublika Vetnam, 1945-1960.* Ed. by A. A. Guber and Nguen-kkhan-Toan. Moscow: Izd. vost. lit., 1960. 248 p. A collection of articles, from the Communist point of view, by eight Vietnamese and three Soviet authors.

JG41 AVSENEV, M. M. *Demokraticheskaia Respublika Vetnam; ekonomika i vneshniaia torgovlia.* Moscow: Vneshtorgizdat, 1960. 110 p. A technical economic study which contains some information on trade and other economic relations between the DRV and fellow members of the Communist bloc.

JG42 BUI-KONG-CHYNG. *Severnyi Vetnam na puti postroeniia sotsializma.* Moscow: Sotsekgiz, 1959. 174 p. A collection of addresses and articles by a North Vietnamese economist on economic conditions, programs, and problems in the DRV.

JG43 BUTTINGER, JOSEPH. *The Smaller Dragon; a Political History of Vietnam.* N.Y.: Praeger, 1958. 536 p. Though largely concerned with periods prior to the twentieth century, this volume includes a substantial chronology for the years 1900 to 1957 and an extensive annotated bibliography.

JG44 COLE, ALLAN B. and others, eds. *Conflict in Indo-China and International Repercussions; a Documentary History, 1945-1955.* Ithaca: Cornell; London: Oxford, 1956. 265 p. A collection of documents on the development of the conflict between France and the Vietminh, the policies of the principal participants, and the attitudes of the Great Powers and other interested states. A joint undertaking of the Fletcher School and the Cornell Southeast Asia Program. [B]

JG45 DANTSIG, B. M. *Indokitai.* Moscow-Leningrad: Sotsekizdat, 1931. 116 p. A brief survey of the country, its people, economy, and politics. A chapter on the "national liberation movement" includes a Soviet interpretation of the disturbances of 1930.

JG46 DEVILLERS, PHILIPPE. *Histoire du Viêt-Nam de 1940 à 1952.* Paris: Seuil, 1952. 471 p. An able analysis of the relations between France and Vietnam since 1940. In 1945-46, the author served simultaneously as press attaché for General Leclerc and as correspondent for *Le Monde.* Critical of French policy in the period covered. [B]

JG47 FALL, BERNARD B. *Street Without Joy.* Harrisburg, Pa.: Stackpole, 1961. 322 p. An account of the conflict in Indochina by an American scholar who stresses the unorthodox nature of the warfare and the probability that this type of armed combat has set a pattern for the future. Based on documentary materials, including French military records, and field study. [B]

JG48 FALL, BERNARD B. *The Viet-Minh Regime; Government and Administration in the Democratic Republic of Vietnam.* 2nd rev. ed., N.Y.: Institute of Pacific Relations, jointly with the Southeast Asia Program, Cornell U., 1956. 196 p. A study of the political, administrative, and military organization of the regime. Based on a broad range of sources, including materials gathered in the area. [B]

JG49 HAMMER, ELLEN. *The Struggle for Indochina.* Stanford, Cal.: Stanford, under the auspices of the Institute of Pacific Relations; London: Oxford, 1954. 342 p. An extensively-documented account by an American scholar of the French-Vietminh struggle up to the eve of the 1954 Geneva Conference. The writer, strongly anti-colonialist in outlook, had the opportunity to interview a number of participants, both French and Vietnamese. Excellent bibliography. [A]

JG50 HO CHI MINH. *Izbrannye stati i rechi*. Moscow: Gospolitizdat, 1959. 815 p. Russian translations of selected articles and speeches composed during 1922-26 and 1941-59 by the leading Vietnamese Communist.

JG50A HONEY, P. J., ed. *North Vietnam Today*. N.Y.: Praeger, 1962.

JG51 LANCASTER, DONALD. *The Emancipation of French Indochina*. London: Oxford, for the Royal Institute of International Affairs, 1961. 445 p. Contains much information on the struggle leading to the settlement of 1954, but little on the attitude of the Communist Powers toward the conflict. The author served in Saigon as a British official from 1950 to 1954.

JG52 LAVRISHCHEV, A. *Indokitaiskii vopros posle vtoroi mirovoi voiny*. Moscow: Izd. IMO, 1960. 228 p. A Soviet account of the war in Indochina, the 1954 settlement, and subsequent developments in the area to 1959. Constitutes a rather comprehensive statement of Soviet charges of Western violations of the 1954 agreements and interference in the internal affairs of the states of Indochina.

JG53 LE BOURGEOIS, JACQUES. *Saigon sans la France; des Japonais au Viêt-Minh*. Paris: Plon, 1951. 247 p. A personal account of the situation in Indochina during World War II which contains some information on the activity of the Vietminh in that period.

JG54 LIAKHS, M. *Zhenevskie soglasheniia 1954 g. ob Indo-Kitae; pravovye problemy natsionalno-osvoboditelnoi borby*. Trans. from Polish. Ed. by V. N. Durdenevskii. Moscow: Izd. inostrannoi lit., 1956. 197 p. An analysis from the Communist point of view of the agreements of 1954 on Indochina and the questions of international law posed by the conflict. [B]

JG54A LINDHOLM, RICHARD W., ed. *Viet-Nam: The First Five Years; an International Symposium*. East Lansing: Michigan State U., 1959. 365 p.

JG55 MARCHAND, JEAN. *L'Indochine en guerre*. Paris: Les Presses Modernes Pouzet, 1954. 300 p. The story of the military situation in Vietnam from the beginning of World War II to 1954 by a French military leader with many years of service in Indochina. Contains a chapter on Chinese-Vietminh collaboration.

JG56 MARSHALL, RICHARD H., JR. "The Soviet Union and the Democratic Republic of Vietnam, 1945-1953." Certificate essay, Russian Institute, Columbia, 1959. 164 p. Seeks to determine the extent of the Soviet Union's interest in North Vietnam and what specific policies emerged from Moscow. Extensive reference to Soviet materials.

JG57 MICHIGAN, STATE UNIVERSITY OF AGRICULTURE AND APPLIED SCIENCE, EAST LANSING, VIETNAM PROJECT. *What to Read on Vietnam; a Selected, Annotated Bibliography.* N.Y.: Institute of Pacific Relations, 1959. 67 p. A listing of recent publications on Vietnam including a number of Soviet items. Also contains a section on periodicals published in Vietnam.

JG58 MKHITARIAN, S. A. *Borba vetnamskogo naroda za natsionalnuiu nezavisimost, demokratiiu i mir (1945-1955* gg.). Moscow: Akademiia nauk SSSR, 1957. 198 p. A Soviet authority on Vietnam presents an account of the development of the Vietminh movement, the formation of the Democratic Republic of Vietnam, and the Republic's subsequent development. Based mainly on Soviet and Vietnamese sources. [B]

JG59 MKHITARIAN, S. A. *Rabochee i profsoiuznoe dvizhenie vo Vetname.* Moscow: Profizdat, 1960. 160 p. A historical survey of the period 1918-59 by a Soviet scholar who utilizes Vietnamese sources as well as others. Includes a brief bibliography.

JG60 MOSCOW, INSTITUT MEZHDUNARODNYKH OTNOSHENII. *15 let Demokraticheskoi Respubliki Vetnam.* Ed. by M. P. Epifanov. Moscow: Izd. IMO, 1960. 147 p. Six essays by Russians and one by the Ambassador of the DRV to the USSR on a wide range of subjects related to the DRV, including the Party, the state, the economy, foreign trade, and foreign policy.

JG61 MUS, PAUL. *Viêtnam, la sociologie d'une guerre.* Paris: Éditions du Seuil, 1952. 373 p. The author, a professor who acted as political advisor to General Leclerc in 1945-47, presents an excellent examination of the social and cultural factors underlying the French-Vietminh conflict.

JG62 NAVARRE, HENRI. *Agonie de l'Indochine.* Paris: Plon, 1956. 336 p. The military aspects of the Indochinese conflict as related by the French Commander-in-Chief for Indochina in 1953-54.

JG63 NEWMAN, BERNARD. *Report on Indo-China.* London: Hale, 1953. 245 p. Observations on the situation in Indochina in the early 1950's based on travels to Vietnam, Cambodia, and Laos, where the author interviewed a number of participants in the hostilities.

JG64 PODKOPAEV, I. IA. *Ocherki borby vetnamskogo naroda za nezavisimost i edinstvo svoei rodiny.* Moscow: Gospolitizdat, 1957. 143 p. A popular account for a Soviet audience of the situation in Vietnam and its background.

JG65 SACKS, I. MILTON. "Communism and Nationalism in Viet-Nam, 1918-1946." Ph.D. dissertation, Yale, 1960. The essence of this dissertation was condensed by the author in his chapter, "Marxism in Viet Nam," in: Frank Trager, ed., *Marxism in Southeast Asia* (see above, Southeast Asia, General Works).

JG66 SAINTENY, JEAN. *Histoire d'une paix manquée; Indochine 1945-1947.* Paris: Amiot-Dumont, 1953. 260 p. The former French Commissioner in Tonkin presents his personal account of the events in these years and the thesis that there existed a real possibility of a settlement at that time.

JG67 SAND, J. W. "The Viet Minh Movement." M.A. thesis, U. of California (Berkeley), 1952.

JG68 SHILTOVA, A. P., and MORDVINOV, V. F. *Natsionalno-osvoboditelnoe dvizhenie vo Vetname (1858-1945).* Moscow: Izd. IMO, 1958. 199 p. A documented study by Soviet historians utilizing Soviet, Vietnamese, and French sources.

JG69 STAROBIN, JOSEPH R. *Eyewitness in Indo-China.* N.Y.: Cameron and Kahn, 1954. 187 p. The situation in Indochina as seen by an American who visited the Vietminh in 1953 and is completely sympathetic to the Communist point of view.

JG70 TANHAM, GEORGE K. *Communist Revolutionary Warfare: The Viet Minh in Indochina.* N.Y.: Praeger, 1961. 166 p.

JG71 VASILEVA, V. IA. *Indo-Kitai; politiko-ekonomicheskii ocherk.* Moscow-Leningrad: Akademiia nauk SSSR, 1947. 275 p. A substantial treatment by a Soviet authority on Southeast Asia of Indochina's geography, population, colonial past, commerce, and governmental structure. Includes chapters on the nationalist movement prior to and during World War II.

JG72 VERIN, V. P., and VERINA, N. A. *Kambodzha.* Moscow: Gosizdat geograficheskoi lit., 1960. 71 p. A first-hand report on contemporary Cambodia by two recent Soviet visitors.

4. INDONESIA

JG73 AIDIT, D. N. *The History of the Communist Party of Indonesia.* New Delhi: People's Publishing, 1955. 51 p. Russian ed., Moscow: Izd. inostrannoi lit., 1956. German ed., Berlin: Dietz, 1956. A very brief outline of the history of the PKI as seen by the current General Secretary.

JG74 BEKLESHOV, D. V. *Indoneziia; ekonomika i vneshniaia torgovlia.* Moscow: Vneshtorgizdat, 1956. 147 p. A technical study which includes a brief section on Indonesian trade with Eastern Europe and Communist China.

JG75 BENDA, HARRY J., and McVEY, RUTH T., eds. *The Communist Uprisings of 1926-1927 in Indonesia; Key Documents.* Ithaca, N.Y.: Cornell, 1960. 177 p. Consists of three Dutch reports on the events of 1926-27 which heretofore have either been unpublished or not readily accessible—one by the Governor General of the Netherlands Indies, the other two by governmental investigatory commissions. Includes a substantial introduction. [B]

JG75A BRACKMAN, ARNOLD C. *Indonesian Communism; a History.* N.Y.: Praeger, 1963.

JG76 CHANG, CHAO-CH'IANG. *Politika i ekonomika poslevoennoi Indonezii.* Moscow: Izd. Inostrannoi lit., 1958. 438 p. A Soviet translation of a Chinese survey of the political and economic situation in Indonesia since 1945.

JG77 GUBER, A. A. *Indoneziia; sotsialno-ekonomicheskie ocherki.* Moscow-Leningrad: Gos. sot. ek. izdat., 1932. 380 p. An early Soviet survey of Indonesian society, finance, trade, agriculture, transportation, etc. Includes some material on the "national-revolutionary movement." Based largely on non-Soviet sources.

JG78 GUBER, A. A., ed. *Respublika Indoneziia, 1945-1960.* Moscow: Izd. vostochnoi literatury, 1961. 382 p. A collection of articles surveying political and economic developments. Contributors are members of the Indonesian section of the Academy of Science's Institute of the Peoples of Asia.

JG79 GUBER, A. A., ed. *Sovremennaia Indoneziia.* Moscow: Gos. izd. inostr. lit., 1955. 159 p.

JG80 HARTONO. "The Indonesian Communist Movement, 1945-1948; Its Development and Relations with the Soviet Union." Certificate essay, Russian Institute, Columbia, 1959. 116 p. The Indonesian Communist Party's international orientation and its relations with nationalist groups are analyzed in this careful study based on Dutch, English, Indonesian, and Russian sources.

JG80A HINDLEY, DONALD. "The Communist Party of Indonesia, 1951-1961; a Decade of the Aidit Leadership." Ph.D. dissertation, Australian National University, 1961.

JG81 KAHIN, GEORGE M. *Nationalism and Revolution in Indonesia.* Ithaca, N.Y.: Cornell, under the Auspices of the Institute of Pacific Relations; London: Oxford, 1952. 490 p. An informative examination of Indonesian politics in the period leading to independence, based in part on a year of field study by an American scholar at Cornell. Though Indonesian nationalists are the primary concern of the work, it contains much information about the Communist movement.

JG82 McVEY, RUTH T. *The Development of the Indonesian Communist Party and Its Relations with the Soviet Union and the Chinese People's Republic.* Cambridge, Mass.: Center for International Studies, M.I.T., 1954. 97 p. A scholarly survey of the history of the PKI to the early 1950's based on Soviet, Indonesian, and Dutch materials. [B]

JG83 McVEY, RUTH T. *The Soviet View of the Indonesian Revolution; a Study in the Russian Attitude towards Asian Nationalism.* Ithaca, N.Y.: Cornell, 1957. 83 p. An unraveling of the changing public attitude of the Soviet Union toward Indonesia, based on intensive study of the Soviet press. Reveals a number of interesting differences between the Soviet view of Indonesia and the Soviet view, simultaneously held, of other Asian countries. [A]

JG84 MESTENHAUSER, JOSEF A. "Ideologies in Conflict in Indonesia, 1945-1955." Ph.D. dissertation, Minnesota, 1960. A study from a social-psychological point of view of Communism, Islam, and nationalism as ideological forces in the political life of Indonesia.

JG85 NOOR, GUSTI R. "Sino-Soviet Attitudes towards Indonesia, 1950-1955." Certificate essay, Russian Institute, Columbia, 1958. 97 p. A detailed survey of the changing image of the Indonesian state presented in Soviet and Chinese Communist newspapers and other periodical literature. Some interesting divergences between the Chinese and the Soviet treatments emerge.

JG86 PARTAI KOMUNIS INDONESIA. *Documents, March 31-April 3, 1958.* Jakarta: Jajasan "Pembaruan," 1958. 123 p.

JG87 PARTAI KOMUNIS INDONESIA. *Konstitusi Partai Komunis Indonesia (P.K.I.).* Jakarta: Central Comite, Partai Komunis Indonesia, 1954. 70 p.

JG88 PARTAI KOMUNIS INDONESIA. *Materials of the Sixth National Congress of the Communist Party of Indonesia.* Jakarta: 1958. 137 p. Documents submitted to the Sixth National Congress of the PKI. Contains drafts of the Central Committee's Report, and revisions of the Party's program and constitution.

JG89 PETRUS BLUMBERGER, JOHN T. *De Communistische Beweging in Nederlandsch-Indië.* Haarlem, Netherlands: 1928. 163 p. French ed., Paris: Éditions du Monde Nouveau. 190 p. An historical treatment by a Dutch official of the Communist-instigated uprisings in West Java in 1926 and on the west coast of Sumatra in 1927 and the events leading up to them.

JG90 PETRUS BLUMBERGER, JOHN T. *De Nationalistische Beweging in Nederlandsch-Indië.* Haarlem, Netherlands: Tjeenk Willink,

1931. 462 p. A history of the nationalist movement in Indonesia from 1907 to 1930 with some attention paid to the influence of Communism.

JG91 SISWADJI. "The Impact of Comintern Policy on the Indonesian Communist Movement." Certificate essay, Russian Institute, Columbia, 1956. 78 p. An objective treatment of the formative years of the Indonesian Communist Party, the insurrections of 1926-27, and subsequent developments to the end of 1928. Dutch, Indonesian, and some Russian sources—largely publications of the Comintern—were consulted.

JG92 VALKOV, V. A. *Indoneziia na puti nezavisimogo razvitiia.* Moscow: Izd. IMO, 1960. 311 p. A substantial Soviet study of the establishment of Indonesia's independence and subsequent political and economic developments.

JG93 WOODMAN, DOROTHY. *The Republic of Indonesia.* N.Y.: Philosophical Library; London: Cresset, 1955. 444 p. A survey of contemporary Indonesia and its political problems, with considerable information on Marxism and Communism. The writer, strongly sympathetic towards the Nationalists, spent much time in Indonesia and had unusually broad access to Indonesian leaders and sources.

5. LAOS

JG94 HALPERN, A. M., and FREDMAN, H. B. *Communist Strategy in Laos.* Santa Monica, Cal.: RAND Corporation, 1960. 162 p. (mimeographed). Analyzes the political and military situation in Laos in the summer and fall of 1959 and reveals that the initiative was on the side of the Free World. Both factions fought under considerable restraint, and the situation prevailing at the end of the fighting satisfied neither.

JG95 HALPERN, JOEL M. *Government, Politics and Social Structure of Laos; a Study of Tradition and Innovation.* Los Angeles: University of California, Dept. of Anthropology, 1961. 199 p. (mimeographed). A pioneering study by a professor of anthropology at U.C.-L.A. who served as a field representative of the American Aid Mission in northern Laos in 1957 and returned for another visit in 1959. Discusses the Pathet Lao briefly. Excellent for the background of developments in Laos. A shorter, preliminary version was issued by the RAND Corp., *The Lao Elite; a Study of Tradition and Innovation.* Santa Monica, Cal.: 1960. 89 p.

JG95A HUMAN RELATIONS AREA FILES, INC. *Laos: Its People, Its Society, Its Culture.* By Frank M. Lebar and Adrienne Suddard. New Haven: HRAF, 1960. 294 p.

JG96 SISOUK NA CHAMPASSAK. *Storm over Laos; a Contemporary History.* N.Y.: Praeger, 1961. 202 p. Written by the Laotian ambassador to the UN, this account, which concentrates on the period between the two Geneva Conferences of 1954 and 1961, is colored by the author's official connection with his government. Sisouk blandly defends the conflicting policies of successive cabinets and rationalizes uncritically or overlooks the various blunders of Laotian officialdom. This book is more of a White Paper than a history, but as such it will serve as a source for a genuinely critical study. [B]

6. MALAYA

JG97 BARTLETT, VERNON. *Report from Malaya.* N.Y.: Criterion, 1955. 128 p. A brief report on the situation in Malaya by a British journalist who made two trips to the area. Very favorable in its appraisal of the British program to solve the Communist problem.

JG98 CHIN, KEE ONN. *Malaya Upside Down.* Singapore: Jitts, 1946. 208 p. A first-hand account of Japanese policies in Malaya by one who experienced the wartime occupation; contains some material on wartime Communist guerrilla units.

JG98A *The Fight Against Communist Terrorism in Malaya.* London: Reference Division, Central Office of Information, May 1953. 33 p. A publication distributed by the British Information Services which describes the methods being used to wipe out the Communist guerrillas.

JG99 HANRAHAN, GENE Z. *The Communist Struggle in Malaya.* N.Y.: International Secretariat, Institute of Pacific Relations, 1954. 146 p. Based largely on captured Communist documents and Japanese reports from the wartime occupation of Malaya, this scholarly study traces the history of the Malayan Communist movement, its strategy and tactics, and its international connections. Key documents, a bibliography, and biographic information are contained in the appendices. [B]

JG100 HENNIKER, M. C. A. *Red Shadow over Malaya.* London: Blackwood, 1955. 303 p. An account of operations against Communist guerrilla forces in Malaya by a British officer who served there as a brigade commander from 1952 to 1954.

JG101 MILLER, HARRY. *Menace in Malaya.* London: Harrap, 1954. 248 p. American ed., *Communist Menace in Malaya.* N.Y.: Praeger, 1954. An informative account of the Communist insurrection and its background by a veteran journalist who served for five years as the chief correspondent in the Malaya Federation for a Singapore newspaper.

JG102 MILLS, LENNOX A. *Malaya, a Political and Economic Appraisal.* Minneapolis: U. of Minnesota; London: Oxford, 1958. 234 p. A consideration of the political and economic situation in Malaya by an American political scientist who devotes a chapter to the Communist rebellion.

JG103 PURCELL, VICTOR W. *Malaya: Communist or Free?* Stanford, Cal.: Stanford University Press; London: Gollancz, 1954. 288 p. The author, from the perspective of long experience in the Malayan civil service, presents a vigorous criticism of the then existing British policy toward the political crisis and Communist insurrection in Malaya.

JG104 PYE, LUCIAN W. *Guerrilla Communism in Malaya; Its Social and Political Meaning.* Princeton, N.J.: Princeton University Press, 1956. 369 p. An examination of the Malayan Communist Party based in part on interviews conducted in Malaya in 1952-53 of some sixty former Party members. By a member of the Center for International Studies, M.I.T. An important behavioral study of Asian Communism. [A]

JG105 RUDNEV, V. S. *Ocherki noveishei istorii Malaii, 1918-1957.* Moscow: Izd. vostochnoi lit., 1959. 118 p. A general survey of political and economic developments based largely on Western and Malayan sources, both Communist and non-Communist. The author devotes considerable attention to the war-time anti-Japanese resistance movement and the postwar rebellion.

7. PHILIPPINES

JG106 BACLAGON, ULDARICO S. *Lessons from the Huk Campaign in the Philippines.* Manila: M. Colcol, 1960. 272 p. Lessons drawn from accounts by junior officers of actions in the Huk campaign. Compiled by the former Commandant of the Philippine Army Infantry School. Includes some background on the Huk movement and its leaders.

JG107 GUBER, A. A. *Filipinskaia Respublika 1898 goda i amerikanskii imperializm.* 2nd ed. Moscow: Izd. vost. lit., 1961.

JG108 HOEKSEMA, RENZE L. "Communism in the Philippines; a Historical and Analytical Study of Communism and the Communist Party in the Philippines and its Relations to Communist Movements Abroad." Ph.D. dissertation, Harvard, 1956. 507 p. An analysis of the Philippine Communist Party—its formation, development, strategies, and methods—based on extensive research. Publications of the Party, the Comintern, Philippine and American governmental studies, and a wide range of other sources, including unpublished material, were consulted. Comprehensive bibliography. [B]

JG109 LEVINSON, G. I. *Filippiny mezhdu pervoi i vtoroi mirovymi voinami.* Moscow: Izd. vost. lit., 1958. 288 p. A Soviet version of the history for these years of U.S.-Philippine relations, the independence movement, and economic relations.

JG110 LEVINSON, G. I. *Filippiny vchera i sevodnia.* Moscow: *Sotsekizdat*, 1959. 239 p. A detailed Soviet account of developments in the Philippines from the outbreak of World War II to 1957.

JG111 LEVINSON, G. I. *Rabochee dvizhenie na Filippinakh.* Moscow: Izd. vost. lit., 1957. 83 p. A brief study sponsored by the Institut Vostokovedeniia of the development of a working class in the Philippines, the creation of a Communist Party, and its history.

JG112 ROMULO, CARLOS P. *Crusade in Asia; Philippine Victory.* N.Y.: Day, 1955. 309 p. An intimate account by the well-known Philippine statesman of his nation's efforts under the leadership of Magsaysay to solve the problem of Communism through a broad program of reform.

JG113 ROMULO, CARLOS P., and GRAY, MARVIN M. *The Magsaysay Story.* New York: Day, 1956. 316 p. A very favorable account of Magsaysay which reveals something of the man. Admittedly biased, but useful in a study of the Huk Rebellion.

JG114 ROWSON, RICHARD C. "Soviet Interpretation of United States Policy in the Philippines since 1946." Certificate essay, Russian Institute, Columbia, 1950. 86 p. An analysis of the major themes of Soviet propaganda on postwar American relations with the Philippines and an interpretation of the motives behind the Soviet approach. Utilizes Soviet periodical publications.

JG115 SAVELEV, N. A. *Amerikanskii kapital na Filippinakh.* Moscow: Izd. IMO, 1960. 206 p. A Soviet analysis of American economic policy toward the Philippines which concludes with a consideration of the "increasing contradictions" between "national capital" and "American monopolies." Utilizes numerous Western sources.

JG116 SCAFF, ALVIN H. *The Philippine Answer to Communism.* Stanford, Cal.: Stanford University Press; London: Oxford, 1955. 165 p. A study by a professor of sociology at Pomona College of the economic program initiated by the Philippine government to counter the Huk movement; based on research and travel in the Philippines. [B]

JG117 SMITH, ROBERT A. *Philippine Freedom, 1946-1958.* N.Y.: Columbia, 1958. 375 p. A Far Eastern expert for the *New York Times* deals briefly with Communism as it bears on his theme of the establishment and development of free institutions.

JG118 TARUC, LUIS. *Born of the People*. Foreword by Paul Robeson. N.Y.: International Publishers, 1953. 286 p. The autobiography of a former Philippine Communist leader; contains his account of the Hukbalahap to 1949.

JG119 U.S. ARMY SPECIAL WARFARE SCHOOL. *Counter-Guerrilla Operations in the Philippines, 1946-1953*. (Seminar on the Huk Campaign, Fort Bragg, North Carolina, June 15, 1961.) While primarily concerned with the military aspects of the campaign against the Huks, this excellent compilation also treats the social, psychological, and political facets of the Huk Rebellion. Presentations to the seminar were made by Filipino and American officers who played key roles in defeating the Huks. [A]

8. THAILAND

JG120 AKADEMIIA NAUK SSSR, INSTITUT VOSTOKOVEDENIIA. *Sovremennyi Tailand*. Ed. by N. V. Rebrikova. Moscow: Izd. vost. lit., 1958. 188 p. A handbook which includes a section on social and political organization. Brief bibliography.

JG121 MANDRYKIN, IU. G. *Tailand; ekonomika i vneshniaia torgovlia*. Moscow: Vneshtorgizdat., 1959. 168 p. A technical survey of Thailand's economy and the direction and composition of her foreign trade.

JG122 REBRIKOVA, N. V. *Amerikanskaia politika v Tailande*. Moscow: Izd. vost. lit., 1959. 102 p. An authority on Thailand of the Institut vostokovedeniia presents the Soviet version of American relations with Thailand since 1942.

JG123 REBRIKOVA, N. V. *Ocherki noveishei istorii Tailanda (1918-1959)*. Moscow: Izd. vost. lit., 1960. 215 p. A historical survey sponsored by the Academy of Sciences' Institut narodov Azii. Contains two chapters on the post-1945 "democratic" movement in Thailand.

Addenda

JG124 ALESHIN, I. *Sovetsko-indoneziiskie otnosheniia v 1945-1962 godakh*. Moscow: Izd. IMO, 1963. 176 p. Concentrates largely on the innovations in Soviet policy toward Indonesia during the Khrushchev era.

JG125 HONEY, P. J. *Communism in North Vietnam; Its Role in the Sino-Soviet Dispute*. Cambridge: M.I.T. Press, 1963. 207 p. An incisive analysis of Hanoi's relations with Peking and Moscow down to the middle of 1963. [A]

JH. INDIA AND PAKISTAN

EDITED BY GENE D. OVERSTREET

1. INDIA

JH1 ADHIKARI, GANGADHAR M. *Pakistan and Indian National Unity.* London: Labour Monthly, 1943. 32 p. Primary statement of CPI nationality policy in the 1940s. Contains the resolution of the Central Committee and Adhikari's report to the CC. The second Indian edition (1944) shows significant revision of these documents, illustrating tactical adaptations in nationality policy.

JH2 ADHIKARI, GANGADHAR M., ed. *From Peace Front to People's War.* 2nd ed., Bombay: People's Publishing House, 1944. 444 p. A convenient collection of resolutions, articles, speeches, etc., from the CPI and the Comintern, 1935-1943. Includes basic statements of CPI's "people's war" policy. The editor was a member of the Central Committee and formerly General Secretary of the CPI.

JH3 AHMAD, MUZAFFAR. *Communist Party of India; Years of Formation, 1921-1933.* Calcutta: National Book Agency, 1959. 42 p. Originally published in *New Age*, this work constitutes an informal essay in Party history by a participant, one of the founding members of the CPI. Superficial but valuable in the absence of a full official history of the Party.

JH4 AKADEMIIA NAUK SSSR, INSTITUT EKONOMIKI I TIKHOOKEANSKII INSTITUT. *Colonial Peoples' Struggle for Liberation.* Bombay: People's Publishing House, n.d [1950?]. 99 p. A translation of the official report of the Soviet Orientalists' meeting in June, 1949. Contains "revised stenogram" of papers by Zhukov, Maslennikov, and Balabushevich (published in *Voprosy Ekonomiki*) and remarks of other participants. Significant for study of the application to India of the Chinese revolutionary model.

JH5 AKADEMIIA NAUK SSSR, INSTITUT VOSTOKOVEDENIIA. *Nezavisimaia Indiia; 10 let nezavisimosti, 1947-1957; sbornik statei.* Ed. by V. V. Balabushevich and A. M. Diakov. Moscow: Izd. vost. lit., 1958. 198 p. A comprehensive collection of articles on Indian politics, economics, and culture, and on Soviet-Indian relations, providing a convenient survey of Soviet interpretation. Articles by leading Indologists: I. M. Reisner, R. A. Ulianovskii, T. F. Deviatkina, T. M. Ershov, E. P. Chelyshev.

JH6 AKADEMIIA NAUK SSSR, INSTITUT VOSTOKOVEDENIIA. *Problemy vostokovedeniia.* Moscow: The principal periodical publication of the main Soviet research agency in the field of Asian studies. Frequently contains articles defining the Soviet view of contemporary India. Former name: *Sovetskoe vostokovedenie.* The Institute also publishes irregular *Uchenye zapiski*, and *Kratkie soobshcheniia*, with occasional attention to India. [A]

JH7 AKADEMIIA NAUK SSSR, TIKHOOKEANSKII INSTITUT. *Krizis kolonialnoi sistemy; natsionalno-osvoboditelnaia borba narodov vostochnoi Azii.* Moscow: Izd. Akademii nauk SSSR, 1949. 290 p. A collection of chapters on south and southeast Asian countries, expounding the militant Soviet line for the period 1948-52. Chapter on India by A. M. Diakov. General introductory chapter by E. M. Zhukov, who was the most prominent and authoritative source of Soviet pronouncements on Asia during the 1940's and 1950's, and was also Academician-Secretary of the Department of Historical Sciences, Academy of Sciences.

JH8 AKADEMIIA NAUK SSSR, TIKHOOKEANSKII INSTITUT. *Uchenye zapiski tikhookeanskogo instituta.* Vol. II: *Indiiskii sbornik.* Moscow: Izd. Akademii nauk SSSR, 1949. Illustrative of publications devoted to India by the Pacific Institute, the predecessor of the Institute of Asian Studies. This volume contains a collection of papers delivered at the Soviet Indologists' meeting in June, 1947, outlining the strategy and tactics for the new period of revolutionary action.

JH9 ALLAHABAD, HIGH COURT. *King-Emperor vs. Nalini Bhushan Gupta . . . , in the High Court of Judicature at Allahabad, Criminal Side, Appeal No. 588 of 1924, Cawnpore District.* Allahabad: Superintendent, Government Press, United Provinces, n.d. [1924]. Pagination irregular. 1 v. "Paper-book" of the Cawnpore Trial–record of testimony, original judgment, and reprint of documents submitted in evidence—prepared for an appeal hearing. An exceedingly valuable source, containing published materials otherwise unavailable, intercepted correspondence, etc. [B]

JH10 ALL-INDIA KISAN SABHA. *Seventeenth Session of All-India Kisan Sabha, Ghazipur 17th to 19th May, 1960.* New Delhi: AIKS Publication, n.d. 52 p. Illustrative of the policy and activity of the Communist peasant organization. Contains speeches, resolutions, and a list of officers.

JH11 AUSTIN, H. *Anatomy of the Kerala Coup.* New Delhi: People's Publishing House, 1959. 150 p. The CPI's interpretation of the rise and fall of the Communist state government in Kerala, 1957-59. Provides a detailed account of the record of that government, the causes and tactics of the opposition, and an estimate of future prospects in the state.

JH12 BALABUSHEVICH, V. V., and DIAKOV, A. M., eds. *Noveishaia istoriia Indii.* Moscow: Izd. vost. lit., 1959. 755 p. A recent definitive statement of the Soviet view of India since 1918. The editors are the principal Soviet Indologists, heads of the India and Pakistan departments, respectively, of the history division of the Institute of Asian Studies. Other authors include Iu. P. Nasenko, S. M. Melman, A. I. Levkovskii, etc. Bibliography of works in Russian, English, and Hindi (26 pages). [B]

JH13 BATLIWALA, SOLI S. *Facts Versus Forgery.* Bombay: National Youth Publication, 1946. 33 p. One of the few defectors' reports on the CPI. The author, a former member of Central Committee, alleges collaboration of the Party with the British authorities during World War II, but with a disappointing lack of detail or documentation.

JH14 BHARGAVA, G. S. *Leaders of the Left.* Bombay: Meherally Book Club, 1951. 73 p. Contains brief biographical sketches of Indian Socialist and Communist leaders, including M. N. Roy, S. A. Dange, and P.C. Joshi.

JH15 BOWLES, CHESTER. *Ambassador's Report.* N.Y.: Harper, 1954. 415 p. In Chapter 10 the former American Ambassador (1951-53) makes some general observations on the development of the CPI, its activities and composition, and the appeals of Communism in India. Bowles has since then begun a second stint as Ambassador.

JH16 BUDBRAJ, VIJAY S. "The Soviet Image of India." Ph.D. dissertation, American University, 1958. 198 p. Based on English, Russian, and Hindi sources, this study examines the Soviet image of India in the early 1920's and after 1947. The author traces the development of the Marxist-Leninist position on colonial questions and relates it to the changing Soviet views of India. The strategy of the Indian C.P. in the post-World War II period is also portrayed.

JH17 BULGANIN, NIKOLAI A., and KHRUSHCHEV, NIKITA S. *Visit to India; Speeches and Official Documents (November 18-December 1 and December 7-14, 1955).* Moscow: Foreign Languages Pub. House, 1956. 262 p. French ed., Paris, 1956. German ed., Berlin, 1956. Official Soviet record of the visit to India of state and Party leaders, published in the USSR in abundant editions and vast printings.

JH18 CHANDRA, PRABODH (pseud.?). *On "A Note on the Present Situation in our Party."* P.H.Q. Open Forum, Issue no. 12. n.p.: 1950. 9 p. Illustrative of inner-Party factional documents frequently accessible to scholars because of the intensity of disputes and the loose security within the CPI. Illuminating on internal affairs and relations with the international Communist movement, especially the Communist Party of Great Britain.

JH19 CHAUDHURI, TRIDIB. *The Swing Back; A Critical Survey of the Devious Zig-Zags of the CPI Political Line (1947-50)*. Calcutta: Revolutionary Socialist Party, 1950. 135 p. Polemic by an Indian political journalist, dealing with issues of basic strategy. Useful as a catalogue of references to basic Soviet and Indian Communist pronouncements, and as a summary of issues.

JH20 CHAWLA, SUDERSHAN. "India, Russia, and China, 1947-1955; An Interpretation of the Indian Concept of National Interest." Ph.D. dissertation, Ohio State, 1959. 304 p. The author's thesis is that the Indian leaders have as their primary aim the maintenance of India's territorial and economic security, while they express their objectives in the form of "generalized and moralistic statements" which reveal little except "noble sentiments." While the Indian government seeks friendly relations with China and Russia, it regards the Indian C.P. as essentially subversive, and it spares no effort to prevent the local Communists from coming to power.

JH21 COMMUNIST PARTY OF INDIA. *Constitution of the Communist Party of India, Adopted at the Extraordinary Party Congress, Amritsar, 1958*. New Delhi: People's Publishing House, 1958. 38 p. 1958 version of the Party's rules, with extensive formal changes implying decentralization. Compare with earlier versions, adopted at the First Congress (1943), Second Congress (1948), and Third Congress (1953-54).

JH22 COMMUNIST PARTY OF INDIA. *Declaration of Independence; Communist Party Resolution for the Constituent Assembly*. Bombay: People's Publishing House, n.d. [1946?]. 16 p. Contains the draft resolution submitted by the Communist member to the Constituent Assembly and the Party's Memorandum to the British Cabinet Mission, 1946. Constitutes the basic statement of the CPI's proposal for the conditions and forms of Indian independence.

JH23 COMMUNIST PARTY OF INDIA. *New Age*. Monthly. Official central theoretical journal of the Party. Normally edited by the General Secretary. Former names include *Communist* and *Marxist Miscellany*. [A]

JH24 COMMUNIST PARTY OF INDIA. *New Age*. Weekly. Official central organ of the Party, published in Delhi. Former names include *Crossroads*, *People's Age*, *People's War*, *National Front*, etc. Published in English and numerous Indian language editions. [A]

JH25 COMMUNIST PARTY OF INDIA. *Political Thesis of the Communist Party of India, Passed by the Second Congress at Calcutta, Feb. 28-March 6, 1948*. Bombay: Kaul, 1948. 118 p. A comprehensive, official statement of the initial Communist interpretation of Indian independence, signalling the adoption of violent revolutionary tactics by the CPI.

JH26 COMMUNIST PARTY OF INDIA. *Review of the Second General Elections.* New Delhi: Communist Party of India, 1957. 41 p. Resolution of the Central Committee on the outcome of the general election. Provides a detailed survey of the Party's experience and candid self-criticism of errors and disunity.

JH27 DANGE, SHRIPAT AMRIT. *General Report at Ernakulam.* New Delhi: All-India Trade Union Congress, 1958. 104 p. A comprehensive report on the policy and activity of the Communist trade-union federation, by a prominent Party labor and parliamentary leader. Appendix contains extracts from Dange's report on India to the WFTU, 1957. Dange is now Chairman of the CPI.

JH28 DEMOCRATIC RESEARCH SERVICE, BOMBAY. *Communist Conspiracy at Madurai.* Bombay: Popular Book Depot for the Democratic Research Service, 1954. 159 p. A collection of confidential CPI documents, probably authentic, relating to the Third Congress of the Party. The publisher, informally related to the Socialist movement, also issued a similar collection relating to the Fourth Congress entitled *Communist Double Talk at Palghat*, 1956.

JH29 DEMOCRATIC RESEARCH SERVICE, BOMBAY. *Indian Communist Party Documents 1930-1956.* Bombay: Democratic Research Service; N.Y.: Institute of Pacific Relations, 1957. 345 p. A compilation by an anti-Communist agency of confidential CPI documents, virtually all published earlier in *Communist Conspiracy at Madurai* and *Communist Double Talk at Palghat* (above). [B]

JH30 DIAKOV, A. M. *Indiia vo vremia i posle vtoroi mirovoi voiny, 1939-1949.* Moscow: Izd. Akademii nauk SSSR, 1952. 259 p. A definitive statement of the Soviet interpretation of India at the time of publication. Contains a map and short glossary.

JH31 DIAKOV, A. M. *Natsionalnyi vopros i angliiskii imperializm v Indii.* Moscow: Gospolitizdat, 1948. 328 p. A pioneer work in the Soviet application of Communist nationality policy to independent India. Following the overt initiative of the CPI, it defines regional ethnic groups as "nationalities" and examines their histories, languages, etc.

JH32 DIAKOV, A. M. *New Stage in India's Liberation Struggle.* Bombay: People's Publishing House, 1950. By the most prolific and authoritative Soviet Indologist during the 1940's and 1950's. Although less important than his other works, this book has the advantage of being in English.

JH33 DRUHE, DAVID N. *Soviet Russia and Indian Communism, 1917-1947*. N.Y.: Bookman Associates, 1959. 429 p. A methodical, scholarly survey, emphasizing prewar CPI history, by an American political scientist. Extensive bibliography. [B]

JH34 DUTT, RAJANI PALME. *India Today*. London: Gollancz, 1940. 544 p. Indian ed. (in English), Bombay: People's Pub. House, 1947. 532 p. 2nd rev. ed., Bombay, 1949. 581 p. A valuable summary statement of Communist interpretations of Indian history and contemporary conditions. The author is a veteran British Communist and mentor of the CPI. Compare the 2nd Indian edition with 1st London edition, 1st Indian edition, and subsequent revisions, for a convenient survey of changes in strategy and tactics. [B]

JH35 GHOSH, AJOY KUMAR. *Forward to the Defence of Kerala and Indian Democracy*! New Delhi: Communist Party of India, 1959. 32 p. A statement of the CPI interpretation of the crisis of Communist government in Kerala, by the General Secretary. Appendix contains the resolution of the Central Executive Committee.

JH36 GIIASOV, T. *Indiia i borba za oslablenie napriazhennosti v Iugo-Vostochnoi Azii i na Dalnem Vostoke*. Tashkent: Izd-vo SAGU, 1957. 111 p.

JH37 GOEL, SITA RAM. *Netaji and the CPI*. Calcutta: Society for the Defence of Freedom in Asia, 1955. 72 p. An anti-Communist treatment of the CPI's relations with Subhas Chandra Bose, 1938-45. Useful for the reproduction of illustrations and quotations from *National Front* and other CPI documents difficult to obtain.

JH38 GOPAL, MADAN. *India As a World Power*. Delhi: Rajkamal, 1948. 160 p. Essays on India's relations with Russia and the other Powers.

JH39 GOPALAN, A. K., and MUKERJEE, HIREN. *Communists in Parliament*. New Delhi: Communist Party of India, 1957. 54 p. A thorough survey of CPI tactics in Lok Sabha (House of the People), by the Leader and Deputy Leader of the Communist bloc. Provides a useful statistical summary of Communist participation in debate, question-time, adjournment motions, etc.

JH40 HARRISON, SELIG S. *India; the Most Dangerous Decades*. Princeton, N.J.: Princeton University Press, 1960. 350 p. Chapters 5, 6, 7, present a challenging interpretation of the nature and role of Communism in India, based on intensive study of regional politics. The author, formerly an Associated Press correspondent in India, is now the *Washington Post* correspondent. [A]

JH41 INDIA, HOME DEPARTMENT. *Communism in India 1924-27*. Calcutta: Government of India Press, 1927. 415 p. A British intelligence report with rich detail. Covers the period of the formation of an all-India Communist organization, culminating in the Meerut Trial. Summarizes an earlier report by Kaye (below). Preface by D. Petrie, Director of the Intelligence Bureau, evidently the author. Contains an excellent biographical dictionary. [B]

JH42 INDIA, HOME DEPARTMENT. *India and Communism* (Revised up to 1st January, 1935). Simla: Government of India Press, 1935. 395 p. Another detailed account of the CPI, mainly in the early 1930's, based on official intelligence data. Demonstrates the effectiveness of British surveillance of radical movements in India. Very valuable for a period in which few other documents exist. Introduction by H. Williamson, Director of Bureau of Intelligence, evidently the author. [B]

JH43 INDIA (DOMINION), MINISTRY OF HOME AFFAIRS. *Communist Violence in India*. New Delhi: Government of India Press, 1949. 71 p. A government report on CPI revolutionary activity in 1948. Quotes from confidential Party documents, and provides a statistical compilation of alleged atrocities such as bomb attacks, murders, robberies, etc. Similar reports were published by state governments, including Hyderabad, Bombay, and Madras. Photographs.

JH44 JOSHI, PURAN CHANDRA. *Communist Reply to Congress Working Committee's Charges*. Bombay: People's Publishing House, 1945. 2 vols. A long and authoritative exposition of the CPI's policy and activity during World War II, with a defense against the accusation of collaboration with the British authorities. The author was General Secretary, 1935-48.

JH45 JOSHI, PURAN CHANDRA. *For a Mass Policy; Part I of P. C. Joshi's Letter to Foreign Comrades Entitled 'Are We Only Stupid?'*. Allahabad: Adhunik Pustak Bhandar, 1951. 105 p. An extraordinarily revealing factional document attacking the leadership and policy of the CPI, 1948-51. Indispensable for a view of inner Party affairs during the period. [B]

JH46 JOSHI, PURAN CHANDRA. *For the Final Bid for Power! The Communist Plan Explained*. Bombay: People's Publishing House [1946?]. 122 p. A basic statement of CPI policy in the general election of 1946. Contains an Election Manifesto and a long exposition by Joshi.

JH47 JOSHI, PURAN CHANDRA. *Problems of the Mass Movement; Part II of P. C. Joshi's Letter to Foreign Comrades Entitled 'Are We Only Stupid?'*. Allahabad: Adhunik Pustak Bhandar, 1951. 85 p. Like Part I (above), indispensable. [B]

JH48 JOSHI, PURAN CHANDRA. *Views to Comrades Abroad and B. T. Randive.* Number 1. Howrah: P. C. Joshi, 1950 (May). 64 p. Another valuable factional document, evidently intended as the first issue of a periodical (no other issues published).

JH49 KAUTSKY, JOHN H. *Moscow and the Communist Party of India; a Study of Postwar Evolution of International Communist Strategy.* N.Y.: The Technology Press of the Massachusetts Institute of Technology, 1956. 220 p. Acute, scholarly analysis by an American political scientist, dealing primarily with the period 1947-52. The main object is a description of the "neo-Maoist" strategy of international Communism as applied in India. [A]

JH50 KAYE, CECIL (SIR). *Communism in India.* Delhi: Government of India Press, 1926. 154 p. First of a series of intelligence reports on radical, especially Communist, activity in India, in the period of the formation of local Communist groups, ending with the Cawnpore Trial. [B]

JH51 KOMMUNISTICHESKAIA AKADEMIIA, INSTITUT MIROVOGO KHOZIAISTVA I MIROVOI POLITIKI. *Revoliutsionnyi podem v Indii.* Ed. by A. Shtusser. Moscow: Partizdat, 1933. 212 p.

JH52 KOTOVSKII, G. G. *Agrarian Reforms in India.* New Delhi: People's Publishing House, 1964. 182 p. Russian ed., Moscow: Izd. vost. lit., 1959. Soviet view of contemporary Indian agrarian problems. Based primarily on official reports.

JH53 KOTOVSKII, G. G., BALABUSHEVICH, V. V., and others, comps. *Bibliografiia Indii; dorevoliutsionnaia i sovetskaia literatura na russkom iazyke i iazykakh narodov SSSR, originalnaia i perevodnaia.* Moscow: Izd. vost. lit., 1959. 219 p. A remarkably full bibliography of Russian and Soviet books, pamphlets, and articles concerning India. Covers basic works of Marxism-Leninism on India, prior bibliographies, geography, ethnography, history, economics, culture, and linguistics. Total number of entries: 3858. Full index (34 p.). Contains some obvious omissions (e.g., works of M. N. Roy) but is nevertheless indispensable to scholars. First printing only 1400 copies; second printing is said to be forthcoming. [A]

JH54 KRISHNAN, N. K., ed. *National Unity for the Defence of the Motherland.* Bombay: People's Publishing House, n.d. [1943?]. 72 p. An official account of, and resolutions of, two important meetings of the CPI Central Committee, 1942-43.

JH55 *Labour Monthly.* London. A British Communist journal, edited by R. Palme Dutt. Frequently contained the international Communist view of India and guidance for the CPI, especially in the 1930's and 1940's.

JH56 LEVI, WERNER. *Free India in Asia.* Minneapolis: U. of Minnesota, 1952. 161 p. Chapter VI contains a discussion of Indian attitudes toward Communism and official Indian policy toward Communist powers, especially China. Emphasizes problems involving border states: Tibet, Nepal, etc. The author is an American political scientist.

JH57 LEVIN, I. D., and MAMAEV, V. A. *Gosudarstvennyi stroi Indii.* Moscow: Gosiuridizdat, 1957. 150 p. Devoted mainly to an elementary descriptive survey of the Indian constitution. Representative of the recent Soviet view of the Indian government, and illustrative of recent published surveys of various aspects of contemporary India.

JH58 LIMAYE, MADHU. *Communist Party; Facts and Fiction.* Hyderabad: Chetana Prakashan, 1951. 100 p. A brief statement of the Indian Socialist view of CPI history, emphasizing the period of Communist-Socialist collaboration in the Indian National Congress, 1935-39. Foreword by Asoka Mehta.

JH59 MADIAR, L., and others. *Imperializm, natsionalizm i agrarnaia revoliutsiia v Indii.* Moscow: Mezhdunarodnyi agrarnyi institut, 1934. 227 p. Relates agrarian conditions in India to the struggle for independence.

JH60 MASANI, MINOCHEHER R. *The Communist Party of India; A Short History.* London: Derek Verschoyle, 1954. 302 p. A pioneer general history of the CPI, by a long-time Indian anti-Communist. The author, as leader of the Congress Socialist Party, was a participant-observer in the "united-front" period, and had unusual access to confidential sources on the CPI in other periods. [A]

JH61 MEERUT, DISTRICT COURT. *Meerut Communist Conspiracy Case; Magistrate's Order of Committal to Trial.* Meerut: Saraswati, 1929. 287 p. A convenient description of evidence in the Meerut Case. Summarizes the case against each individual defendant. Shorter and better-organized than subsequent judgment of Sessions Court (2 volumes, Government of India Press, 1932-33).

JH62 MEERUT, SESSIONS COURT. *Proceedings of the Meerut Conspiracy Case.* Meerut: Saraswati, 1929. (11 vols?). "Paper-book" of the Meerut Trial, containing a reprint of documents submitted in evidence. As in the Cawnpore Trial (see above: Allahabad, High Court) an exceedingly valuable source. [B]

JH63 MELMAN, S. M. *Ekonomika Indii i politika angliiskogo imperializma.* Moscow: Izd. Akademii nauk SSSR, 1951. 270 p. A representative work of the principal Soviet specialist on the Indian economy.

JH64 MELMAN, S. M. *Inostrannyi monopolisticheskii kapital v economike Indii.* Moscow: Izd. vostochnoi literatury, 1959. 236 p.

JH65 MUKHARDZHI, ABONI. *Indiia; sbornik statei.* Moscow: Izd. Mezhdunarodnogo agrarnogo instituta, 1931. 176 p.

JH66 NAMBOODRIPAD, E. M. S. *The National Question in Kerala.* Bombay: People's Publishing House, 1952. 178 p. A thorough application of Communist theory to the study of Indian history, treating the development of Malayalee "nationality" from primitive communism to capitalism. Constitutes a prime illustration of the CPI's nationality tactic. The author has recently been General Secretary of the Party, and was briefly Chief Minister of Kerala.

JH67 *Natsionalno-osvoboditelnoe dvizhenie v Indii i politika SShA; sbornik statei.* Ed. by A. M. Diakov. Moscow-Leningrad: Izd. Akademii nauk SSSR, 1950. 276 p.

JH68 NIKHAMIN, V. P. *Ocherki vneshnei politiki Indii, 1947-1957.* Moscow: Gospolitizdat, 1959. 226 p. A statement of the Soviet interpretation of Indian foreign policy, including relations with China and the USSR.

JH69 OVERSTREET, GENE D. "Soviet and Indian Communist Policy in India, 1935-1952." Ph.D. dissertation, Columbia, 1959. 322 p. A discussion of the Communist interpretation of India, before and after independence, and the strategy and tactics of political action within India. Incorporates the author's M.A. thesis, "The Soviet View of India, 1945-48," Columbia, 1953.

JH70 OVERSTREET, GENE D., and WINDMILLER, MARSHALL. *Communism in India.* Berkeley: U. of California, 1959. 603 p. A comprehensive work on Soviet and Indian Communist strategy and tactics, 1917-58. Contains a detailed treatment of CPI history and an analysis of the main elements of contemporary policy and activity. Includes a 20-page biographical dictionary and a selected, annotated bibliography. [A]

JH71 PAVLOVICH, MIKHAIL, and GURKO-KRIAZHIN, V. *Indiia v borbe za nezavisimost.* Moscow: Nauch. assots. vostokoved. 1925. 118 p.

JH72 RANADIVE, B. T. *Sarvodaya and Communism.* New Delhi: People's Publishing House, 1958. 35 p. The CPI's interpretation of Gandhian Sarvodaya ideology and the Bhoodan movement, by the General Secretary, 1948-50.

JH73 RANGA, N. G. *Kisans and Communists.* Bombay: Pratibha, 194?. 127 p. A partisan discussion of Communist agrarian policy, by a non-Communist Indian peasant leader. In the main, a general treatment, but some passages deal with CPI activity in the late 1930's and early 1940's.

JH74 REDKO, I. B. *Nepal posle vtoroi mirovoi voiny; antifeodalnoe i antiimperialisticheskoe dvizhenie, 1945-1956.* Moscow: Izd. vost. lit., 1960. 267 p. A pioneer work in the recent Soviet treatment of the border states.

JH75 ROY, MANABENDRA NATH. *The Future of Indian Politics.* London: Bishop, 1926. 118 p. One of the principal works of the outstanding Indian in the international Communist movement during the 1920's. Parts appeared in Roy's journal, *Masses of India*, published in Paris. Provides a "left-wing" Communist interpretation.

JH76 ROY, MANABENDRA NATH. *Memoirs.* Bombay: Allied Publishers, 1964. 627 p. A rich and relatively unused source on the world Communist movement and Communism in India. Roy was on the Executive Committee of the Comintern and a delegate to China, before his expulsion in 1929. His account is occasionally unreliable. Originally appeared serially in *Radical Humanist* (India), Feb. 1953 to Sept. 1954. [B]

JH77 SAMRA, CHATTAR SINGH. *India and Anglo-Soviet Relations (1917-1947).* Bombay: Asia Publishing House, 1959. 186 p. A historical description of Anglo-Soviet relations as affecting, and affected by, India. Attributes great importance to India as a causal factor. The author is an Indian political scientist. This work was expanded from a dissertation at the University of California, Berkeley.

JH78 SAMRA, CHATTAR SINGH. "India in Communist Perspective." Ph.D. dissertation, U. of California (Berkeley), 1954.

JH79 SAVDAR, A. *O revoliutsionnom dvizhenii v Indii.* Moscow: Ogiz, 1931. 160 p.

JH80 SCHWARTZ, MORTON. "The Communist Party of India, 1948-1951; A Case Study in Asiatic Communism." M.A. thesis, Columbia, 1954. An analysis of CPI strategy and tactics during periods of urban and agrarian revolution, by a former student at the Russian Institute.

JH81 SHUBIN, PETR A. *Revoliutsionnyi podem v Indii.* Moscow: Izd. Kommunisticheskoi akademii, 1930. 183 p.

JH82 SINHA, L. P. "The Origin and Development of Left Wing Movements and Ideas in India, 1919-1947." Ph.D. dissertation, U. of London, 1955.

JH83 SPRATT, PHILIP. *Blowing Up India; Reminiscences and Reflections of a Former Comintern Emissary.* Calcutta: Prachi Prakashan, 1955. 117 p. Memoirs of a British Communist agent to the CPI in the late 1920's, with general and specific insight into the formative period of Indian Communism. After his defection in the mid-1930's, the author settled in India as a journalist.

JH84 TAGORE, SAUMYENDRANATH. *Historical Development of the Communist Movement in India.* Calcutta: Red Front, 1944. A participant's recollections of the formation of the CPI and Comintern affairs during the 1920's. Rich in information but (like Roy's memoirs) should be used with caution. The author was a member of the Indian delegation to the 6th Comintern Congress, and subsequently left the CPI to found a radical splinter party in Bengal.

JH85 TALBOT, PHILLIPS. "The Foreign Policy of India Since Independence." Ph.D. dissertation, U. of Chicago, 1954.

JH86 U.S. OFFICE OF STRATEGIC SERVICES, RESEARCH AND ANALYSIS BRANCH. *The Communist Party of India.* Washington: 1945. 73 p. A declassified U.S. intelligence report, dealing mainly with the war-time period. Tends to be superficial and to reflect the prevailing cordiality of Soviet-American relations. Contains a useful biographical dictionary.

JH87 VASUDEVA RAO, CHALASANI. *Bharatha Communist Party Nirmaana Charithrea.* Vijayawada: Praja Sakti, 1943. The closest approximation to an official history of the prewar CPI—a published version (in Telugu) of lectures by a lesser Party official at a cadres' school. Not intended for a general audience, it contains some revealing self-critical observations.

JH88 WANG MING. *The Revolutionary Movement in the Colonial Countries.* N.Y.: Workers Library, 1935. 64 p. A revised and expanded version of a report to the Seventh Comintern Congress on strategy and tactics in colonies. A definitive statement of the "united-front" line, with considerable specific treatment of India.

JH89 WILSON, PATRICK. *Government and Politics of India and Pakistan, 1885-1955; A Bibliography of Works in Western Languages.* Berkeley: Institute of East Asiatic Studies, U. of California, 1956. 357 p. The best American bibliography on Indian politics, with an excellent listing (p. 132-144) of publications about and by the CPI. Provides great assistance to researchers in locating materials by identifying the source of citation (e.g., library in which rare document may be found). Russian language works not included. [A]

JH90 WOHLERS, LESTER P. "The Position of India in Relation to the Tension between the Soviet Union and the United States with Special Reference to the United Nations." Ph.D. dissertation, U. of Chicago, 1951.

JH91 ZAPADOV, A. B., and PROKHOROV, E. P. *Glazami druzei; Russkie ob Indii (sbornik)*. Moscow: Gospolitizdat, 1957. 408 p.

2. PAKISTAN

JH92 GANKOVSKII, IU. V., and MOSKALENKO, V. N. *Politicheskoe polozhenie v Pakistane*. Moscow: Izd. Vost. lit., 1960. 136 p.

JH93 MURPHY, JOSEPH A. "Pakistan-Soviet Relations with Emphasis on Recent Developments." M.A. thesis, Columbia U., 1955. 171 p.

JH94 NASIR, KHALIL A. "The Foreign Relations of Pakistan; First Ten Years." Ph.D. dissertation, American U., 1957.

Addenda

JH95 ADHIKARI, GANGADHAR M. *Communist Party and India's Path to National Regeneration and Socialism; a Review and Comment on Comrade E. M. S. Namboodirpad's "Revision and Dogmatism in the Communist Party of India."* New Delhi: C. P. of India, 1964. 204 p. A comprehensive survey of the shifts in the history of the CPI, an official position paper for the 7th Congress in 1964. An example of the important literature which accompanied the split in the CPI.

JH96 NARAYAN, JAYAPRAKASH. *Socialist Unity and the Congress Socialist Party*. Bombay: Congress Socialist Party, 1941. 45 p. History of the attempt at socialist unity during the United Front period of the late 1930's, by the central figure in the Congress Socialist Party.

JH97 SAHAJANAND SARASWATI, SWAMI. *Kranti aur Samyukta Morcha*. Patna: Shramjiva Pustakmala, 1943. (In Hindi) A long and labored attempt to develop a theory of peasant revolution based on Russian and European models, by the leading peasant agitator of the 1930's. Though not a Communist, he was much influenced by the Party and was largely responsible for its success in gaining control of the All-India Peasant Association at this time.

JH98 SEN, BHOWANI. *Evolution of Agrarian Relations in India*. New Delhi: People's Publishing House, 1962. 295 p. The most thorough treatment of land problems by the Party's leading agrarian spokesman.

K. Middle East

KA. MIDDLE EAST, GENERAL WORKS

EDITED BY OLES M. SMOLANSKY

KA1 AGABEKOV, GRIGORII S. *Ch. K. za rabotoi.* Berlin: "Strela," 1931. 334 p. English ed., OGPU, *The Russian Secret Terror.* N.Y.: 1931. German ed., Stuttgart: 1932. An illuminating, inside story of Soviet activities in Asia during the 1920's by a former high official of the Soviet secret police. Contains information on Afghanistan, Persia, Turkey, Iraq, Hijaz, and Yemen. (See other books by the same author in the section on "Espionage.")

KA2 AKADEMIIA NAUK SSSR, INSTITUT NARODOV AZII. *Politika SShA na Blizhnem i Srednem Vostoke (SShA i strany SENTO).* Ed. by B. G. Gafurov. Moscow: Izd. vostochnoi lit., 1960. 342 p. Vol. I of the proposed series on U.S. relations with Asia and Africa is devoted to CENTO (Turkey, Iran, Pakistan). The editor is the chief Party spokesman in the field of Oriental studies. The Soviet Academy of Sciences intends to supplement this study with works on U.S. policy in the Arab East, Southeast Asia, the Far East, and Africa. [B]

KA2A AKADEMIIA NAUK SSSR, INSTITUT NARODOV AZII. *SSSR i strany Vostoka; ekonomicheskoe i kulturnoe sotrudnichestvo.* Moscow: Izd. vost. lit., 1961. 140 p. This study of economic and cultural cooperation between the Soviet Union and various countries of Asia and Africa contains valuable material on the Middle East. Good bibliography.

KA3 AKOPIAN, G. S. *Borba narodov Blizhnego i Srednego Vostoka za natsionalnuiu nezavisimost i mir.* Moscow: Znanie, 1953. 48 p. A contemporary Soviet reaction to various Western plans to set up a Middle East defense establishment, with occasional references to the activities of Communist Parties.

KA4 AKOPIAN, G. S. *Mezhdunarodnye otnosheniia i vneshniaia politika SSSR na Blizhnem i Srednem Vostoke posle vtoroi mirovoi voiny.* Moscow: Vysshaia partiinaia shkola pri TsK KPSS, 1955. 64 p. Contains a chapter on Soviet foreign policy in the Middle East, giving Moscow's version of the "soft line" adopted by Russia in Turkey, Iran, and Afghanistan in 1953.

KA5 ALLEN, ROBERT L. *Middle Eastern Economic Relations with the Soviet Union, Eastern Europe, and Mainland China.* Charlottesville, Va.: Woodrow Wilson Department of Foreign Affairs, U. of Virginia, 1958. 128 p. An excellent contribution to a better understanding of

Arab-Soviet relations by an American economist. Shows that the Communist bloc scored some victories but could not prevent the growth of Arab disillusionment, since performance has not always matched promises. A good bibliography and pertinent data. [A]

KA5A ANDREASIAN, R. N. and ELIANOV, A. IA. *Blizhnii Vostok; neft i nezavisimost.* Moscow: Izd. vost. lit., 1961. 320 p. This study is intended to show the open and "hidden" means used by the "monopolies" to exploit the region's oil resources; the changes which took place in the social and economic structure of the oil-producing countries as a result of the activities of the "monopolies"; and the struggle of the Middle Eastern states against "oil imperialism."

KA6 ANSHEN, RUTH N., ed. *Mid-East: World Center, Yesterday, Today and Tomorrow.* N.Y.: Harper, 1956. 386 p. Bernard Lewis' contribution to this symposium is an interesting antipode to Laqueur's views (see below under Laqueur and Thayer) on the compatibility of Communism and Islam. The latter, Lewis believes, will in the long run stem the spread of atheistic Communism in the Middle East.

KA7 BASISTOV, IU., and IANOVSKII, I. *Strany Blizhnego i Srednego Vostoka.* Tashkent: Gosizdat UzSSR, 1958. 315 p. This introduction to the modern Middle East surveys the geography, natural resources and economies of the region's political units. Contains sections on the political development of the countries of the area and their relations with the USSR. Valuable but brief background information.

KA8 DINERSTEIN, HERBERT S. "Soviet Foreign Policy in the Near and Middle East, 1917-1923." Ph.D. dissertation, Harvard, 1943.

KA9 ELLIS, HARRY B. *Challenge in the Middle East.* N.Y.: Ronald, 1960. 244 p. An objective account of the current situation in the Middle East by the correspondent of *The Christian Science Monitor.* Says that the national interests of the Soviet Union and Middle Eastern states are incompatible, and that most Middle Eastern leaders are deeply concerned about the dangers of Communist influence.

KA10 FISHER, CAROL A., and KRINSKY, FRED. *Middle East in Crisis—A Historical and Documentary Review.* Syracuse, N.Y.: Syracuse University Press, 1959. 213 p. A general introduction to the problems of the Middle East, including a chapter on the Soviet entry into the area. Illustrated by a few selected documents. The authors are members of the faculty of Syracuse University.

KA11 GURKO-KRIAZHIN, VLADIMIR A. *Blizhnii Vostok i derzhavy.* Moscow: Nauchnaia assotsiatsiia vostokovedeniia, 1925. 243 p. Heavy emphasis on Turkey. Includes a section on World War I and the early postwar history of Arab Asia, as seen by one of the first Soviet specialists. Deserves attention as an expression of early Soviet interest in the Middle East.

KA12 GURKO-KRIAZHIN, VLADIMIR A. *Natsionalno-osvoboditelnoe dvizhenie na Blizhnem Vostoke*. Part I, *Siriia i Palestina, Kilikiia, Mesopotamiia i Egipet*. Moscow: Vseros. assots. vostokoved., 1923. 150 p.

KA13 HAKIM, KHALIFA A. *Islam and Communism*. Lahore: Institute of Islamic Culture, 1953. 263 p. A comparative study in ideologies, with a framework similar to Siddiqi (see below). The Muslim world is torn between "the devil of Western Imperialism and the deep sea of Russian Communism." Unless driven by the West into the hands of Russia, the Muslims will not compromise with Communism—the "worst kind of fanaticism that disgraced history."

KA14 HUMBARACI, ARSLAN. *Middle East Indictment; from the Truman Doctrine, the Soviet Penetration and Britain's Downfall, to the Eisenhower Doctrine*. London: Hale, 1958. 288 p. A Turkish journalist (a former Communist, now residing in Great Britain) attacks the USSR for imperialist activities and the Western powers for the support of reactionary regimes in the Middle East. Misunderstanding the nature of the Soviet threat, the West is said to have prepared the ground for Communist successes in the region.

KA15 HUREWITZ, JACOB C., ed. *Diplomacy in the Near and Middle East; A Documentary Record*. Princeton: Van Nostrand, 1956. 2 vols. Vol. II of this extremely valuable collection of documents (each preceded by an explanatory note and a brief bibliography) contains a number of important documents on Soviet foreign policy in the Middle East in the period between 1917 and 1955. [B]

KA16 INSTITUT ZUR ERFORSCHUNG DER UDSSR. *Islam and Communism*. Ed. by Jaan Pennar. N.Y.: Institute for the Study of the USSR, 1960. 72 p. A collection of essays based on reports presented at a conference sponsored by the Institute. Contains material on Islam and Communism, Soviet Middle Eastern policy, and Communism and Arab nationalism.

KA17 KIRK, GEORGE E. *A Short History of the Middle East*. 4th ed. N.Y.: Praeger, 1957. 308 p. One of the few useful brief guides to the Middle East, with a chapter on Russian policies. Within the limitations set by space, it is a handy introduction to the subject. Based on secondary Western sources. The author is with the American University, Beirut, Lebanon.

KA18 KUNINA, A. E. *Doktrina Eizenkhauera*. Moscow: Gospolitizdat, 1957. 79 p. "Predatory, imperialistic" Western policy in the pre-

and post-Suez Middle East is contrasted with the "noble intentions of the Soviet Union." The Eisenhower Doctrine is denounced in no uncertain terms.

KA19 KUNINA, A. E., ed. *Proval "Doktriny Eizenkhauera"; sbornik statei.* Compiled by Z. S. Sheinis. Moscow: Izd. inos. lit., 1958. 214 p. In Part One, Egyptian, German, and French Communists and fellow-travellers condemn U.S. policy in the Middle East, with emphasis on the Suez War and its aftermath. Part Two contains the texts of pertinent Soviet documents on the Eisenhower Doctrine, Lebanese revolt, and Iraqi revolution.

KA20 LACOSTE, RAYMOND. *La Russie soviëtique et la question d'Orient, la poussée soviëtique vers les mers chaudes, Méditerranée et Golfe Persique.* Paris: Les Éditions Internationales, 1946. 238 p. Soviet activities in Turkey and Iran in the early postwar period—an initial phase in Moscow's latest drive to the Eastern Mediterranean and the Persian Gulf—are seen as the continuation of Imperial Russia's expansionist policy in the Middle East. Some Russian and Western sources used.

KA21 LAQUEUR, WALTER Z. *Communism and Nationalism in the Middle East.* London: Routledge and Paul; N.Y.: Praeger, 1956. 362 p. Excellent as a study of the growth of Communist organizations in the Middle East (excluding Iran). Unbalanced as an analysis of the interaction of Communism and nationalism. The editor of *Survey* asserts that Islam cannot offer serious resistance to Marxism-Leninism but fails to explain why Arab Communist Parties have been relatively weak, despite widespread pro-Soviet sentiments. Solid, though not always reliable, use of Soviet and international Communist publications and sources in Arabic, Hebrew, and West European languages. Good bibliography. [A]

KA22 LAQUEUR, WALTER Z. *The Soviet Union and the Middle East.* London: Routledge and Paul; N.Y.: Praeger, 1959. 366 p. Despite inadequacies, the best of what is available on the subject. Part One is an impressive account of the evolution of Moscow's attitudes toward the "colonial East" from 1917 to 1958, based on extensive research in Russian materials. Part Two tells a somewhat confusing story of post-1955 Soviet successes, Western failures and regional politics. The emphasis is on Russian and Western sources. An eventual conflict between Arab nationalists and Communists is envisaged. Because of attractive ideology and superior organization, the latter are predicted to carry the day. This conclusion has not so far been borne out by facts, since the UAR and Iraqi governments have succeeded in curbing Communist influence in their respective countries. [A]

KA23 LAQUEUR, WALTER Z., ed. *The Middle East in Transition; Studies in Contemporary History.* London: Routledge and Paul; N.Y.: Praeger, 1958. 513 p. An anthology of essays by 34 writers, combining a survey of political and social change in the area (Part One) with an analysis of various aspects of Soviet Middle Eastern policy (Part Two). Includes informative articles by Western and Soviet authors on Moscow's efforts to reconcile the treatment of its Muslim minorities with "goodwill" toward Arab nationalism. Islam, it is generally feared, is not an effective barrier to Communism. [B]

KA24 LENCZOWSKI, GEORGE. *The Middle East in World Affairs.* Ithaca, N.Y.: Cornell, 1952. 459 p. 2nd ed., 1956. 576 p. A solid study of Middle Eastern history by a former Polish diplomat, now with the University of California, Berkeley. Contains materials on Soviet relations with Turkey, Iran, and Afghanistan, as well as on Moscow's activities in the Arab East. Good bibliography of Russian and Western sources.

KA25 LOEWENTHAL, RUDOLF. *Russian Materials on Islam and Islamic Institutions; a Selective Bibliography.* Washington: Dept. of State, External Research Staff, Office of Intelligence Research, 1958. 34 p. A good bibliography, limited to materials available in major U.S. libraries.

KA26 MOSCOW, UNIVERSITET, ISTORICHESKII FAKULTET. *Noveishaia istoriia stran Zarubezhnogo Vostoka.* Ed. by I. M. Reisner. Moscow: Izd. moskovskogo univ., 1954. 4 vols. A useful guide to post-Stalinist views of the interwar (vols. I and II) and World War II (vol. III) history of various Asian and African countries, including Iran, Turkey, Syria-Lebanon, and Egypt.

KA27 PUBLIC AFFAIRS INSTITUTE, WASHINGTON, D.C. *Regional Development for Regional Peace; A New Policy and Program to Counter the Soviet Menace in the Middle East.* Washington: 1957. 332 p. A misguided and highly biased effort to describe Nasser's Egypt as a "Communist base" and "Nasserism" as a tool of Moscow's expansion in the Middle East. Rejects appeasement and advocates a "firm" Western policy.

KA28 RAKOVSKII, KHRISTIAN, and RAFAIL, M. (pseud.). *Blizhnevostochnyi vopros.* 2nd ed. Kharkov: "Proletarii," 1923. 285 p. Rakovskii, a member of the Soviet delegation, tells of his experiences at the Lausanne conference (1923). Rafail (Veltman-Pavlovich) stresses the strategic, economic, and political importance of the Middle East to Communist Russia. The study—an important guide to early Soviet policies in the Middle East—includes the texts of some pertinent documents.

KA29 SAFAROV, G. *Problemy Vostoka; Srednii i Blizhnii Vostok.* Petrograd: 1922. 183 p. An analytical discussion of the national and colonial question from the Soviet point of view.

KA30 SHEBUNIN, A. N. *Rossiia na Blizhnem Vostoke.* Leningrad: "Kubuch," 1926. 124 p.

KA31 SHWADRAN, BENJAMIN. *Middle East, Oil and the Great Powers.* N.Y.: Praeger; London: Thames & Hudson, 1955. 500 p. An authoritative and scholarly treatment of the oil policy of the great powers in the Middle East. Includes detailed accounts of Soviet policy in regard to oil in the Middle East, particularly in Iran. [A]

KA32 SIDDIQI, MAZHERUDDIN. *Marxism or Islam?* Lahore: Orientalia, 1954. 168 p. A Pakistani scholar's analysis of Marxism. While recognizing the material foundation of human life, Marxism fails to take into account man's necessity to rise into the realm of the spiritual. Restoration of the "original equalitarian and Socialistic" basis of Islam would make it superior to Communism and make it "the future religion of mankind."

KA33 SMIRNOV, N. A. *Ocherki izucheniia Islama v SSSR.* Moscow: Akad. nauk SSSR, 1954. 275 p. This history of Islamic studies in Tsarist and Communist Russia sheds considerable light on Soviet attitudes toward the Middle East. Stresses Moscow's efforts to separate nationalists from Islam—a reactionary creed, associated with native and foreign exploiters. There is an excellent evaluation of this work by Ann K. S. Lambton: *Islam and Russia; A Detailed Analysis of an Outline of the History of Islamic Studies in the USSR by N.A. Smirnov.* Oxford: Central Asian Research Centre, 1956. 87 p. [B]

KA34 SPECTOR, IVAR. *The Soviet Union and the Muslim World, 1917-1956.* Seattle: U. of Washington, 1956. 158 p. (mimeographed). Enlarged ed., 1959. 328 p. An uneven study, good for the early period but superficial in its examination of World War II and after. Contains an original chapter on the Soviet cultural impact, documents (some previously unpublished), and a good bibliography. The author is a Russian-born member of the University of Washington's Far Eastern and Russian Institute. He feels that, because of continuous attacks on Islam, Moscow forfeited its chances of success in the Middle East. [B]

KA35 SULTAN-ZADE, AVETIS S. (pseud.) *Ekonomika i problemy natsionalnykh revoliutsii v stranakh Blizhnego Vostoka.* Moscow: Gosizdat, 1921. 184 p. World capitalism is threatened by both the "dictatorship of the proletariat" and the nationalism of the economically backward, colonial and dependent countries of Asia and Africa. The author—a Persian Communist and noted early Bolshevik authority—

speaks of the "historically inevitable alliance" between these otherwise (and in the long run) incompatible forces.

KA36 SULTAN-ZADE, AVETIS S., ed. *Kolonialnyi Vostok; sotsialno-ekonomicheskie ocherki.* Moscow: "Novaia Moskva," 1924. 354 p. A symposium focused on the socio-economic structure of Iran and the Arab countries, supplemented by a brief discussion of industrialization in India and China as well as a brief report on Soviet Eastern studies.

KA37 SURVEY OF INTERNATIONAL AFFAIRS. *Documents on International Affairs, 1955.* Ed. by Noble Frankland. London and N.Y.: Oxford, for the Royal Institute of International Affairs, 1958. 513 p. This supplement to the Chatham House annual *Survey of International Affairs* contains a section on Soviet activities in the Arab East.

KA38 SURVEY OF INTERNATIONAL AFFAIRS. *The Middle East in the War.* By George E. Kirk. Intro. by Arnold Toynbee. London and N.Y.: Oxford, for the Royal Institute of International Affairs, 1952. 2nd, rev. ed., 1953. 511 p. A competent reference work, containing an excellent survey of Soviet wartime policies in Turkey, Iran and the Arab East.

KA39 SURVEY OF INTERNATIONAL AFFAIRS. *The Middle East, 1945-1950.* By George E. Kirk. London and N.Y.: Oxford, for the Royal Institute of International Affairs, 1954. 339 p. Good coverage of Soviet Postwar policies in Turkey and Iran. Information on the Arab East is sparser, being limited to occasional references to Soviet attitudes on the Anglo-Egyptian (1947) and Palestine (1947-48) crises.

KA40 THAYER, PHILIP W., ed. *Tensions in the Middle East.* Baltimore: Johns Hopkins, 1958. 350 p. A valuable symposium, containing a restatement of Laqueur's position on "The Prospects of Communism in the Middle East." Marxism-Leninism is seen as more sophisticated and practical than the social and economic ideas of Arab nationalists. This would lead to "gradual acceptance of Communist ideas and techniques . . . through the medium of the nationalist movement itself."

KA41 TUGANOVA, O. *Politika SShA i Anglii na Blizhnem i Srednem Vostoke.* Moscow: Izd. Inst. mezh. otnoshenii, 1960. 304 p. Analyzing the region's recent history (with emphasis on 1955-60), the author traces the process of the postwar disintegration of Western positions in the Middle East, an area in which the USSR is said to be vitally interested. A refreshing absence of references to Marxism-Leninism. [B]

KA42 UTLEY, FREDA. *Will the Middle East go West?* Chicago: Regnery, 1957. 198 p. German ed., Göttingen: Plesse, 1958. 232 p. Contains a penetrating analysis of the Soviet breakthrough, as seen in the light of U.S. foreign policy and of Arab nationalist aspirations.

KA43 *Velikii Oktiabr i narody Vostoka; sbornik.* Ed. by A. A. Guber. Moscow: Izd. vost. lit., 1957. 417 p. The Institute of Oriental Studies of the USSR Academy of Sciences went through a lot of unnecessary trouble to demonstrate how the 1917 revolution influenced the growth of national liberation movements in Asia and Africa. The symposium includes sections on Egypt, Iraq, Iran, Syria, Lebanon, and Turkey.

KB. AFGHANISTAN

EDITED BY JAMES W. SPAIN AND OLES M. SMOLANSKY

KB1 AKADEMIIA NAUK SSSR, INSTITUT VOSTOKOVEDENIIA. *Sovremennyi Afganistan.* Moscow: Izd. vost. lit., 1960. 502 p. An excellent, though inevitably biased, handbook on modern Afghanistan. Contains a historical review with references to Soviet-Afghan relations.

KB2 AKHRAMOVICH, R. T. *Afganistan posle vtoroi mirovoi voiny.* Moscow: Izd. vost. lit., 1961.

KB3 AKHRAMOVICH, R. T., ed. *Nezavisimyi Afganistan; 40 let nezavisimosti; sbornik statei.* Moscow: Izd. vost. lit., 1958. 270 p. Honoring the 40th anniversary of the 1919 Afghan revolt against the British, the Afghanistan section of the Institute of Oriental Studies (USSR Academy of Sciences) compiled a collection of articles on the country's history, economy, politics and culture. Contains material on Afghanistan's neutrality and Soviet-Afghan relations.

KB4 BAILEY, FREDERICK M. *Mission in Tashkent.* London: Cape, 1946. 312 p. A first-person account by a British officer of Bolshevik intrigues in Central Asia and of Afghanistan in the post-World War I period.

KB5 CAROE, OLAF K. (SIR). *Soviet Empire; the Turks of Central Asia and Stalinism.* London; N.Y.: Macmillan, 1953. 300 p. An excellent account, relying heavily on Turkish sources, of Soviet expansionism after World War I. Contains material on the *Basmachi* movement and efforts at the penetration of Afghanistan.

KB6 COATES, WILLIAM P. and ZELDA K. *A History of Anglo-Soviet Relations.* London: Lawrence & Wishart, 1943. 816 p. Sympathetic to Soviet policy and actions and not always reliable as to facts, this work presents interesting sidelights on Afghan-Soviet-British relations between the Wars.

KB7 ETHERTON, PERCY T. *In the Heart of Asia.* London: Constable, 1925; N.Y. and Boston: Houghton Mifflin, 1926. 305 p. Personal experiences of a British officer in countering Soviet expansionism in Kashgar in 1919-20. Includes material on Soviet activities in Afghanistan.

KB8 EUDIN, XENIA J., and NORTH, ROBERT C. *Soviet Russia and the East, 1920-1927; a Documentary Survey.* Stanford, Cal.: Stanford University Press, 1957. 396 p. An excellent collection of Soviet documents in English; reflects Soviet policies and objectives in

Afghanistan and identifies some of the principal Soviet agents working therein. [B]

KB9 FRASER-TYLER, WILLIAM KERR (SIR). *Afghanistan; A Study of Political Developments in Central Asia.* London and N.Y.: Oxford, 1950. 330 p. 2nd ed., 1953. 348 p. This basic work in English on Afghanistan includes useful material on Afghan-Soviet relations. Scholarly but somewhat selective, it is a mixture of personal reminiscences of senior British officials, primary and secondary sources. [A]

KB9A GOLOVIN, IU. *Sovetskii Soiuz i Afganistan; opyt ekonomicheskogo sotrudnichestva.* Moscow: Izd. vost. lit., 1962.

KB10 GREAT BRITAIN, FOREIGN OFFICE. *Parliamentary Papers.* London: H.M. Stationery office. 1923: Cmds. 1869, 1874, and 1890. 1927: Cmds. 2822, 2874, and 2895. Deal with Afghan and Indian Bolshevik agents, the Tashkent School, M. N. Roy, and the activities of F. F. Raskolnikov, Soviet Ambassador in Kabul, 1921-23. [A]

KB11 MOSCOW, UNIVERSITET, ISTORICHESKII FAKULTET. *Ocherki po novoi istorii stran Srednego Vostoka.* Ed. by I. M. Reisner and N. M. Goldberg. Moscow: Izd. Moskovskogo universiteta, 1951. 250 p. Contains a section on Afghanistan.

KB12 PIKULIN, M. G. *Razvitie natsionalnoi ekomomiki i kultury Afganistana, 1955-1960.* Tashkent: Izd. Akad. nauk UzSSR, 1961. 151 p.

KB13 PRIMAKOV, V. M. *Afganistan v ogne.* Leningrad: Izd. "Krasnaia gazeta" (1929?). 155 p.

KB13A RASKOLNIKOV, F. *Afganistan i angliiskii ultimatum.* Moscow: 1924.

KB14 SNESAREV, A. E. *Afganistan.* Moscow: Vyssh. voen. red. sov., 1921. 224 p.

KB15 TEPLINSKII, L. B. *Sovetsko-afganskie otnosheniia za 40 let.* Moscow: Sotsekgiz, 1961.

KB15A VEIT, E. *Afganistan.* Moscow: 1929.

KB16 WILBER, DONALD N., ed. *Annotated Bibliography of Afghanistan.* New Haven: Human Relations Area Files, 1956. 220 p. An excellent, comprehensive listing of works on Afghanistan, including those dealing with Afghan-Soviet relations. [B]

KC. ARAB NATIONS

EDITED BY OLES M. SMOLANSKY

KC1 AKADEMIIA NAUK SSSR, INSTITUT MIROVOI EKONOMIKI I MEZHDUNARODNYKH OTNOSHENII. *Suetskii vopros i imperialisticheskaia agressiia protiv Egipta.* By I. Lemin and others. Moscow: Akad. nauk SSSR, 1957. 143 p. An authoritative, contemporary statement on the Suez crisis by several members of the USSR Academy of Sciences' Institute of World Economics and International Relations. Accuses the Western Powers (including the U.S.) and Israel of plotting to strike a mortal blow to Arab nationalism. [B]

KC1A AKADEMIIA NAUK SSSR, INSTITUT NARODOV AZII. *Sovetsko-arabskie druzhestvennye otnosheniia.* Ed. by A. F. Sultanov. Moscow: Izd. vost. lit., 1961. 144 p. A selection of important articles in outline form by leading scholars on the development of political, economic and cultural relations between the Soviet Union and the Arab countries (including North Africa) from 1917 on. There is an invariable emphasis on the "disinterestedness" of Moscow's aid. [B]

KC1B AKADEMIIA NAUK SSSR, INSTITUT NARODOV AZII. *Sovremennyi Livan; spravochnik.* Moscow: 1963.

KC2 AKADEMIIA NAUK SSSR, INSTITUT VOSTOKOVEDENIIA. *Araby v borbe za nezavisimost; natsionalno-osvoboditelnoe dvizhenie v arabskikh stranakh posle vtoroi mirovoi voiny.* Ed. by L. N. Vatolina and E. A. Beliaev. Moscow: Gospolitizdat, 1957. 412 p. A symposium on the history of the Arab struggle for national independence by the Institute of Oriental Studies of the USSR Academy of Sciences. Contains valuable information on Soviet attitudes toward pre-1956 developments in the Arab East. [A]

KC3 AKADEMIIA NAUK SSSR, INSTITUT VOSTOKOVEDENIIA. *Sovremennaia Siriia.* Moscow: Izd. vost. lit., 1958. 325 p. A valuable handbook of modern Syria issued by the Institute of Oriental Studies of the USSR Academy of Sciences. Contains sections on political history (to 1957) and on political parties.

KC4 *Al Muqāwama ash-Sha'biyya.* 1950–. The "People's Revolt" is the illegal journal of the Jordan Communist Party.

KC5 BELIAEV, I. P. *Amerikanskii imperializm v Saudovskoi Aravii.* Moscow: Izd. vost. lit., 1957, 207 p.

KC5A BODIANSKII, V. L. *Bakhrein.* Moscow: Izd. vost. lit., 1962. 168 p.

KC6 BOLTON, ALEXANDER R. C. *Soviet Middle East Studies; An Analysis and Bibliography*. London: Oxford, for the Royal Institute of International Affairs, 1959. 8 parts. An excellent but far from complete annotated bibliography of Soviet materials on the Arab East, including comments on institutions pursuing oriental studies, lists of periodicals, journals of learned societies and serial publications, and indexes. An invaluable aid to students of Soviet-Arab relations. [A]

KC6A DANTSIG, B. M. *Irak v proshlom i nastoiashchem*. Moscow: Izd. vost. lit., 1960. 254 p. This handbook on contemporary Iraq comments on pre- and post-1958 developments and on the activities of the Iraqi Communist Party. A great deal of space is devoted to the country's economy.

KC7 GAFUROV, B. G., ed. *Politika SShA na Arabskom Vostoke*. Moscow: Izd. vost. lit., 1961. 282 p. Vol. II of the Academy of Sciences' series on U.S. policy in Asia and Africa deals with the Arab East. Bent on exploiting the area for its own purposes, the U.S.—"the world's gendarme"—is desperately trying to prevent Arab-Soviet cooperation and mar their "traditional" friendship. [A]

KC8 GATAULLIN, MALIUTA F. *Siriia*. Moscow: Gospolitizdat, 1956. 39 p. A brief survey of Syrian political and economic history, stressing Damascus' determination to "liquidate the remnants of colonialism" and improve relations with Egypt and the Communist bloc. Devotes one chapter to Soviet-Syrian cultural exchanges since 1955.

KC9 GURKO-KRIAZHIN, VLADIMIR A. *Arabskii vostok i imperializm*. Moscow: "Planovoe khoziaistvo," 1926. 145 p.

KC10 HUSSEIN, KING OF JORDAN. *Uneasy Lies the Head; The Autobiography of His Majesty, King Hussein I of the Hashemite Kingdom of Jordan*. N.Y.: Geis, 1962. 306 p. A rather pedestrian account of the life of King Hussein since the assassination of his grandfather in the early 1950's. Some light, however, is shed upon the influence of Communism in the Middle East and its role in determining Jordan's relations with its Arab neighbors. A number of pages are devoted to Hussein's views on the "true" Arab nationalism and his conviction that international Communism poses the gravest threat both to the existence of Jordan and the aspirations of the "Great Arab Awakening."

KC10A KOTLOV, L. N. *Iordaniia v noveishee vremia*. Moscow: Izd. vost. lit., 1962. 262 p. Examines the history of Jordan since 1918. The masses of the population are seen struggling against overwhelming odds—British and American "imperialism" and the "reactionary clique" headed by the country's Hashemite rulers. Good bibliography.

KC11 LEBEDEV, EVGENII A. *Iordaniia v borbe za nezavisimost.* Moscow: Gospolitizdat, 1956. 127 p. The political and economic life of Jordan as seen by a leading Soviet authority. Says that the Arab masses oppose British and reactionary domestic exploitation and struggle for political and economic emancipation.

KC12 LENGYEL, EMIL. *Egypt's Role in World Affairs.* Washington: Public Affairs Press, 1957. 147 p. A superficial and somewhat biased story of Nasser's rise to power by a professor of history at N.Y.U. Contains a chapter on the growth of Soviet influence in Egypt.

KC13 LEVIN, IOSIF D., and MAMAEV, V. *Gosudarstvennyi stroi stran Arabskogo Vostoka.* Moscow: Izd. Akad. nauk SSSR, 1957. 310 p. A general review of the political structure of the Arab states, including chapters on the Arab League and "The Struggle of the Arab Peoples for Independence, Peace and Democracy." Of interest as an expression of the Soviet attitude toward movements of national liberation and unity at the time of the rapprochement between Moscow and neutralist Arabs. Good use of Russian and Arab sources.

KC14 LOEWENTHAL, RUDOLF. *Russian Materials on Arabs and Arab Countries; a Selective Bibliography.* Washington: Dept. of State, External Research Staff, Office of Intelligence Research, 1958. 14 p. A useful guide for those interested in Soviet-Arab relations.

KC15 MILOVANOV, IVAN V., and SEIFUL-MULIUKOV, FARID M. *Irak vchera i segodnia.* Moscow: Gospolitizdat, 1959. 128 p. In 1959 Moscow appeared determined to gain ascendancy in Iraq and prevent its union with the United Arab Republic. Commenting on the 1958 Revolution, subsequent activities of the Iraqi Communist Party and Soviet-Iraqi "friendship," the authors stress the extent of Soviet interest in the country.

KC16 MIRSKII, G. I. *Irak v smutnoe vremia.* Moscow: Izd. vost. lit., 1961. 186 p. A leading Soviet orientalist reviews the political, economic and social history of Iraq in the period 1930-41.

KC17 MOSCOW, INSTITUT MEZHDUNARODNYKH OTNOSHENII. *Suetskii Kanal; sbornik dokumentov.* Moscow: 1957. 178 p. A useful compilation of documents on the Suez Canal, ranging from the 1854 concession to Cairo's declarations of April, July 1957. Contains pertinent Soviet materials.

KC18 PRIMAKOV, E. *Strany Arabii i kolonializm.* Moscow: Gospolitizdat, 1956. 111 p. An original study designed to refute the contention that the Western powers have brought civilization to backward countries. Interesting as an expression of post-1955 Soviet attitudes toward the Arabian Peninsula.

KC19 RUSSIA (1923- USSR), MINISTERSTVO INOSTRANNYKH DEL. *The Soviet Union on the Middle East; Statements by the Ministry of Foreign Affairs of the U.S.S.R.* London: Soviet News, 1956. 43 p. See also: *Suez, the Soviet View, N. A. Bulganin Replies to Questions; Statements by the Soviet Government on the Suez Canal Issue; Statements by D. T. Shepilov at the Suez Canal Conference in London.* London: Soviet News, 1956. 70 p. Useful compilations of Soviet documents pertaining to the Suez crisis (August 9-December 9, 1956) published by the Soviet Embassy in Great Britain.

KC20 RUSSIA (1923- USSR), MINISTERSTVO INOSTRANNYKH DEL. *SSSR i arabskie strany 1917-1960 gg.; dokumenty i materialy.* Moscow: Gospolitizdat, 1961. 856 p. This valuable collection of Soviet and some Arab materials, published by the Ministry of Foreign Affairs, is designed to emphasize the harmony of Soviet-Arab interests. Having helped the Arab states gain political independence, the Soviet Union is determined to aid them in their struggle for economic emancipation. Relations between the USSR and the Arab states are an example of "peaceful coexistence" and of "friendly and mutually profitable cooperation" of nations with different socio-economic structures. [A]

KC20A SHAMI, A. *Kommunisticheskaia Partiia Egipta.* Moscow: 1930.

KC21 SHEPILOV, DMITRII T. *Suetskii vopros.* Moscow: Gospolitizdat, 1956. 87 p. A collection of speeches and statements by the then Soviet Foreign Minister at the first London Conference on the Suez Canal (August 16-23, 1956), together with texts of pertinent Soviet notes and Security Council resolutions. For an abridged English edition, see above, *Suez, The Soviet View.*

KC21A SHVAKOV, A. *Srazhaiushchiisia Oman.* Moscow: Izd. vost. lit., 1961.

KC22 SMOLANSKY, OLES M. "The Arab States and the U.S.S.R., 1947-1957." Ph.D. dissertation, Columbia U., 1959. An analysis of the development of Soviet Arab policy from the Palestine conflict to the Suez war. Moscow's temporary and limited gains in the Arab East were made possible by a combination of factors: misguided Western policies, Arab insistence at self-assertion, and a skillful shift in Soviet strategy.

KC23 VATOLINA, L. N. *Sovremennyi Egipet.* Moscow-Leningrad: Izd. Akad. nauk SSSR, 1949. 246 p. A standard study of Egypt under the British occupation by a leading Soviet authority. Contains occasional references to inter-Arab politics, including the early Soviet attitude toward the Arab League. Good bibliography of Soviet and Western sources.

KC24 WHEELOCK, KEITH. *Nasser's New Egypt; A Critical Analysis*. N.Y.: Praeger, 1960. 326 p. A comprehensive study of contemporary Egypt since the Nasser coup of 1952-53. Discusses Nasser's relations with local Communists and with the Soviet bloc. Published under the auspices of the Foreign Policy Research Institute, University of Pennsylvania. The author has been in Egypt many times since 1953 and had the cooperation of Nasser and Egyptian officials in carrying on research there. Critical but basically sympathetic to the Nasser regime.

KD. IRAN

EDITED BY ROUHOLLAH RAMAZANI AND OLES M. SMOLANSKY

KD1 AGABEKOV, GRIGORII S. *OGPU, the Russian Secret Terror.* N.Y.: Brentano, 1931. 277 p. Memoirs of a former member of the Russian secret police which describe activities of the OGPU in several Iranian provinces. (See KA1.) [B]

KD2 AKADEMIIA NAUK SSSR, INSTITUT VOSTOKOVEDENIIA. *Sovremennyi Iran; spravochnik.* Ed. by Boris N. Zakhoder. Moscow: Izd. Akad. nauk SSSR, 1957. 715 p. An excellent handbook, prepared by the Institute of Oriental Studies of the USSR Academy of Sciences. Contains a wealth of (not always accurate) information on all aspects of Iranian life, including a historical survey and sections on the country's economy, trade unions, and political parties. [A]

KD3 ALAVI, BOZORG. *Kämpfendes Iran.* Berlin: Dietz, 1955. 190 p. An Iranian Communist, then at Humbolt University in East Berlin, tells about his country's domestic and foreign affairs. Of special interest are his comments on the Tudeh Party and on Communist activities in Iranian trade unions.

KD3A ALEKSEEV, L. *Sovetskii Soiuz i Iran.* Moscow: Inst. mezhd. otn., 1963.

KD4 ALPERN, STANLEY B. "Iran, 1941-1946; A Case Study in the Soviet Theory of Colonial Revolution." Certificate essay, Russian Institute, Columbia, 1953. 129 p. A well-informed analysis of Soviet policy in Iran, particularly during the Second World War, and the Azerbaijan crisis. Chapters on the Tudeh Party and the Azerbaijan Revolution and Republic are instructive. With a considerable degree of accuracy, the author answers important questions raised by Soviet policy in Iran after the War. For example, what were the goals of Soviet strategy in Azerbaijan, and why did that strategy fail? [B]

KD5 BAHĀR, MALEK O-SHO'RĀ. *Tārīkh-e mokhtasar-e ahzāb-e siyāsī.* Teheran: 1942-47. 384 p. Contains information on Soviet policy in Iran before 1925. Documents and information cited here are not accessible in any Western language.

KD6 BASHKIROV, A. V. *Ekspansiia angliiskikh i amerikanskikh imperialistov v Irane, 1941-1953 gg.* Moscow: Gospolitizdat, 1954. 282 p. A study of Anglo-American activities in Iran during and after World War II. Interesting as an exposition of Soviet attitudes toward the 1944 Russo-Iranian oil negotiations, Azerbaijan and Mahabad, the abortive 1946 oil agreement, and the Anglo-Iranian oil crisis.

KD7 BASHKIROV, A. V. *Rabochee i profsoiuznoe dvizhenie v Irane.* Moscow: Profizdat, 1948. 114 p. Selected problems of Iran's internal development and foreign policy (emphasis on Soviet-Iranian relations) serve as a background for a detailed but biased study of the country's labor movement. Communist activities in Azerbaijan, Mahabad, and Khuzistan as well as Iran's participation in the work of the Moscow-inspired World Federation of Trade Unions are stressed.

KD8 BEHESTI, MOHSEN D. "Iran's Foreign Policy and Relations Since 1940: A Study of the Forces that Affected Iran's Modern History." Ph.D. dissertation, New School for Social Research, 1951. A study of Soviet-Iranian relations during the Second World War, containing little information not otherwise available. Could be of more use had the author not translated the titles of his Persian sources into English.

KD9 BRADLEY, GLORIA D. "Soviet-Persian Relations, 1917-1921." Certificate essay, Russian Institute, Columbia, 1948. 102 p. Attempts to reveal how the conflict between the ideological and strategic considerations in Soviet foreign relations was resolved, both in theory and in practice, in 1917-21, in the case of Iran. A third of the work consists of a general discussion of events prior to 1917. Draws upon Russian, French, and English sources and is valuable as a study based on Russian sources, but is incomplete in so far as it deals with *Persian* politics.

KD10 DAVENPORT, ROBERT W. "Soviet Economic Relations With Iran, 1917-1930." Ph.D. dissertation, Columbia, 1953. 315 p. The best analysis of Soviet-Iranian economic relations during 1917-30. Draws on Russian sources and statistics, and contains valuable tables. [A]

KD10A EAGLETON, WILLIAM. *The Kurdish Republic of 1946.* London: Oxford, 1963. 142 p. The first complete account of the Kurdish Republic of Mahabad created in 1946 with Soviet support in northwest Iran. Based on materials collected and interviews conducted in Iran and in Iraq. It is useful not only as a study of the Mahabad Republic but also as an illuminating commentary on the Kurdish nationalist movement, which has yet to be systematically studied. [A]

KD11 EJTEMA'I, ANJOMAN-E ESLAHAT-E. *Besoo-ye Communisme.* Teheran: 1324/1946. 56 p. An indictment of Communism in Iran. Seeks to point out the socio-economic bases of the appeal of Communism in Iran. Contends that suppression of Communist activities provides no durable answer to the problem and advocates reforms as the best possible alternative to Communism.

KD12 FATEMI, NASROLLAH S. *Diplomatic History of Persia, 1917-1923; Anglo-Russian Power Politics in Iran.* N.Y.: Moore, 1952. 331 p. Treats in great detail the Soviet invasion of Iran in 1920, and the background of the Soviet Republic of Gilan. [B]

KD13 FATEMI, NASROLLAH S. *Oil Diplomacy; Powderkeg in Iran.* N.Y.: Whittier, 1954. 405 p. Treats Russian policy regarding oil concessions in Iran, but is mainly an indictment against Britain. Does not draw on Russian sources.

KD14 GEYER, DIETRICH. *Die Sowjetunion und Iran; eine Untersuchung zur Aussenpolitik der UdSSR im Nahen Osten, 1917-1954.* Tübingen, Auslieferung: Böhlau-Verlag Köln, 1955. 99 p. Deals more briefly with the material covered by Lenczowski's book: *Russia and the West in Iran* (see below). A useful brief introduction to Soviet-Iranian relations, based on extensive use of Russian materials.

KD14A GURGĀNI, MANSHŪR. *Siyāsat-i Dawlat-i Showravī dar Irān.* Teheran: 1948. A useful study of some of the major events and personalities connected with Soviet-Iranian relations, 1917-27. Based on both Persian and Soviet publications. Deals with the Gilan revolt, Sultan-Zade, etc.

KD15 HAMZAVI, ABDOL HOSSAIN. *Persia and the Powers; An Account of Diplomatic Relations, 1941-1946.* London: Hutchinson, 1947. 125 p. An account by a Persian nationalist. Of some use for the Soviet-Iranian dispute before the Security Council.

KD16 HINDUS, MAURICE. *In Search of a Future, Persia, Egypt, Iraq, and Palestine.* Garden City, N.Y.: Doubleday, 1949. 270 p. Treats Iran among many other Middle Eastern Countries. It is well-written, and the chapters on Iran, particularly the one on Azerbaijan, are intimate and perceptive. Much of what is said in regard to the Communist menace to Iran in the early postwar period still holds true.

KD17 HIRSZOWICZ, LUKASZ. *Iran 1951-1953; nafta, imperializm, nacjonalizm.* Warsaw: Książja i Wiedza, 1958. 442 p.

KD18 IRANDUST (pseud.). *Persiia.* Moscow-Leningrad: Moskovskii rabochii, 1928. 186 p. Says that, in contrast with the capitalist powers, who are determined to widen their domination over the economies of Asian countries, the USSR, despite its economic weakness, should unselfishly promote the economic development of backward nations. The power of world capitalism will thus be reduced.

KD19 IVANOV, M. S. *Ocherk istorii Irana.* Moscow: Gospolitizdat, 1952. 467 p. A Marxist exposition of Iranian history, with emphasis on post-1917 events. Contains a good analysis of the development of Soviet-Persian relations, as seen by Moscow in 1950-51. Chronology. [B]

KD19A JAHANBANI, SEPAHBOD AMANOLLAH. *Marzhai Iran va Shoravi*. Tehran: Majles, 1336/1958. 161 p. A detailed account of the frontier problems between Iran and the Soviet Union, particularly the agreement between the two countries signed on December 2, 1954. With numerous illustrations and detailed maps. [A]

KD20 KERMANI, HUSSAIN KOOHI. *As Shahrivar-e 1320 Ta Faj 'ai-e Azerbaijan Va Zanjan*. Teheran: Mazaheri, 1329/1951. 2 vols. A record containing parliamentary debates, newspaper editorials, official documents bearing on the period from the Anglo-Russian invasion of Iran (August 25, 1941) to the beginning of the Azerbaijan crisis of 1945.

KD21 *Kitab-e Siah Dar Bareh-ye Sazeman-e Afsaran-e Tudeh*. Teheran: 1324/1946. 372 p. "The Black Book," with an introduction by General Taymoor-e Bakhtiar, the former Military Governor of Iran, discloses for the first time the organization, the espionage and propaganda activities of the Communist officers in the Iranian Army. Based on documentary materials, this work reveals how the Tudeh Party successfully carried on underground activities among hundreds of Iranian army officers. [A]

KD22 KOROBEINIKOV, I. I. *Iran—ekonomika i vneshniaia torgovlia*. Moscow: Vneshtorgizdat, 1954. 166 p. Moscow's view of Soviet-Iranian economic and political relations, seen against the background of U.S.-British predominance in the political and economic life of the country.

KD23 LENCZOWSKI, GEORGE. *Russia and the West in Iran, 1918-1948; A Study in Big-Power Rivalry*. Ithaca: Cornell, 1949. 383 p. A sound, scholarly work that sheds much light on Soviet-Iranian relations. Especially valuable for its treatment of the 1941-48 period. Most readable, and indispensable for a study of Iran in recent decades. [A]

KD24 LENCZOWSKI, GEORGE. "The Communist Movement in Iran," *The Middle East Journal* (Jan., 1947), p. 29-45. Discusses the development and organization of the Tudeh Party of Iran and its support by the Soviet Union. [B]

KD25 MALEK, MOHAMMAD KHAN (YAZDI). *Arzesh-e Masa'i-e Iran*. Teheran: 1324/1946. 171 p. Treats the role of Iran in the Second World War. Contains valuable documents and information bearing on the relations of Iran with the Soviet Union.

KD26 MALEK, MOHAMMAD KHAN (YAZDI). *Ghogha-ye Takhlieh-ye Iran*. Teheran: 1326/1948. 159 p. A valuable and informed study of the crisis over the withdrawal of Russian troops from northern Iran. Contains significant information and documents bearing on Soviet-Iranian relations during the Azerbaijan crisis.

KD27 MAS'ODI, GHASEM. *Mission-e'Ezami-e Iran Be-Mosko: 29 Bahman-20 Esfand 1324.* Teheran: 1325/1947. 199 p. A detailed account of the trip of the Iranian Mission to Moscow, led by Prime Minister Qavam os-Saltaneh, from February 19 to March 6, 1946. Based on the author's observations while accompanying the Mission. Contains valuable information in regard to the exchanges of views between the Mission and Soviet officials, particularly Stalin and Molotov.

KD28 MEISTER, IRENE W. "Soviet Policy in Iran, 1917-1950; A Study in Techniques." Ph.D. dissertation, Fletcher, 1954. Begins with the year 1917, but is principally concerned with the 1941-50 period. Draws on a wide variety of sources in Russian, Persian, Azerbaijani, English, French, and German. Gives special attention to Russian radio propaganda techniques and to Soviet methods of infiltration and subversion. [A]

KD29 MILLSPAUGH, ARTHUR C. *Americans in Persia.* Washington: Brookings Institution, 1946. 293 p. One chapter discusses the aims and activities of the Soviet Union in Iran during the World War II period.

KD30 MILLSPAUGH, ARTHUR C. *The American Task in Persia.* N.Y.: Century, 1925. 322 p. The author was Iran's Administrator-General of Finance. Contains first-hand accounts of Iran's earliest economic relations with Soviet Russia, particularly on the fisheries concessions.

KD31 MOSCOW, UNIVERSITET, ISTORICHESKII FAKULTET. *Ocherki po novoi istorii stran Srednego Vostoka.* Ed. by I. M. Reisner and N. M. Goldberg. Moscow: Izd. Moskovskogo universiteta, 1951. 250 p. The section on Iran includes an article on Reza Shah, coupled with a brief analysis of Soviet policy in the early 1920's. Another article deals with the Iranian Communist movement (1941-46). Contains a description of the organizational structure of the Tudeh Party, the text of its program (adopted in 1941) and a history of Iranian trade unions.

KD32 MOTTER, T. H. VAIL. *The Persian Corridor and Aid to Russia.* Washington: Dept. of the Army, Office of the Chief of Military History, 1952. 545 p. The most authoritative published work on the role of the U.S. Army in the Middle East theatre in World War II, containing most valuable information on the Army's aid-to-Russia supply effort. Sheds much light on the part of Iran in this effort. Draws on numerous primary sources, including official documents, interviews, and correspondence.

KD33 *Nāmeh-e Mardom.* Teheran: Tābān, 1941–. Monthly. The official organ of the Tudeh (Communist) Party of Iran.

KD34 NAVAÏ, HOSSEIN. *Les Relations économiques irano-russes.* Paris: Les Éditions Domat-Montchrestien, 1935. 211 p. An indispensable source on Soviet-Iranian economic relations in the 1917-35 period. [B]

KD35 NOORI, ABOLHASSAN AMIDY. *Azarbaijan-e-Democrat.* Teheran: no date. 92 p. An account of the Soviet-supported Republic of Azerbaijan. The author was sent to Azerbaijan by the Prime Minister to observe closely the evacuation of the Red Army. The book is based on the author's "notes" during his sojourn in Azerbaijan and his visits with the leaders of the "Democratic" Party, including Pishevari. Also contains the full text of documents bearing upon the relations between the central government and the rebels of Azerbaijan.

KD36 NOVAR, LEON. "The Great Powers and Iran, 1914-1921." Ph.D. dissertation, U. of Chicago, 1958. 517 p.

KD37 PAVLOVICH, MIKHAIL I. (pseud. of Mikhail Veltman). *Persiia v borbe za nezavisimost.* Moscow: Nauchnaia assotsiatsiia vostokovedeniia, 1925. 182 p.

KD38 PERSIA, MINISTRY OF FOREIGN AFFAIRS. *The Tehran Conference, The Three-Power Declaration Concerning Iran, December, 1943.* Teheran: Ministry of Foreign Affairs, 1945. 189 p. Contains some official exchanges of notes between the government of Iran and the Soviet Union concerning the Tripartite Treaty of Alliance of January, 1942.

KD39 PESSYAN, NAJAFGHOLI. *Marg Bood Bazgasht Ham Bood.* Teheran: 1327/1949. 451 p. A detailed and first-hand account of the establishment of the Soviet-supported Republics of Azerbaijan and Mahabad. The aims and activities of these Republics, the internal and external factors contributing to their downfall, and the re-establishment of the Iranian government's authority over these rebellious areas are discussed at length. The author is inclined to exaggerate the role of the Shah in restoring government control rather than giving due credit to the shrewd and statesmanlike policy of Prime Minister Qavam os-Saltaneh.

KD40 POPOV, M. V. *Amerikanskii imperializm v Irane v gody vtoroi mivovoi voiny; amerikanskaia finansovaia missiia.* Moscow: Izd. Akad. nauk, 1956. 290 p. A Soviet view of U.S. wartime policy in Iran. Contains numerous references to Soviet policy and Communist activities in Iran, based on extensive use of primary and secondary Persian sources. [B]

KD41 ROOSEVELT, ARCHIE. "The Kurdish Republic of Mahabad," *Middle East Journal*, I, no. 3 (July 1947), p. 247-69. An account of political developments during 1945-46 in northwestern Iran by one of the few Americans who visited the Kurdish Republic of Mahabad. [B]

KD42 SABA, M. *Bibliographie de l'Iran*. Paris: Domat-Montchrestien, 1936. 227 p. An unevenly annotated bibliography listing general materials on Iran in the French language. Includes a few materials bearing on relations with the Soviet Union.

KD43 SA'ED, A. *Azarbaijan-e Khonin*. 2nd ed. Teheran: 1325/1947. 49 p. A brief description of the "atrocities" of the Communist regime in Azerbaijan and Mahabad. An attempt to identify the causes of the downfall of the Communist regime in Azerbaijan.

KD44 *Sair-e-Communisme Dar Iran*. Teheran: 1336/1957. 514 p. The book is introduced by General Taymoor-e Bakhtiar, the former Military Governor of Teheran, who led a relentless campaign against the underground activities of the Communist Party of Iran after the downfall of the Mossadegh regime in 1953. The value of the book lies in its detailed treatment of the organization of the Tudeh Party, its propaganda and subversive activities, and its leaders. The work draws upon captured materials, and first-hand information not available in any other language. [A]

KD45 SCHUMAN, MARILYN L. "The Autonomous Republics of Azerbaijan and Kurdistan in Iran, November 1945 to December 1946." Certificate essay, Russian Institute, Columbia, 1953. 86 p. The treatment of the background of the Tudeh Party in Iran leaves much to be desired. However, the author's primary concern is with the 1945-46 period which she discusses fully by including the Kurdistan Republic at Mahabad. Chapter v constitutes the main contribution of the work as it ably deals with Soviet propaganda tactics among the workers, peasants, intellectuals and minority groups in Iran.

KD46 SEPEHR, MOVARREKH-OD-DOWLAH. *Iran dar Jang Bozorg*. Teheran: 1336/1958. 516 p. Contains documents and information on the earliest developments in Irano-Soviet relations which are not accessible in any Western language.

KD47 SHWADRAN, BENJAMIN. *The Middle East, Oil and the Great Powers*. N.Y.: Praeger, 1956. 500 p. An authoritative and scholarly treatment of the oil policy of the great powers in the Middle East. Includes detailed accounts of Soviet policy in regard to oil in the Middle East, particularly in Iran. [A]

KD48 SULTAN-ZADE, AVETIS S. *Persiia*. Moscow: Gosizdat, 1924. 91 p. Some interesting materials on the early phase of Communist activities in Persia by one of the then foremost Soviet specialists on the Middle East. A brief bibliography of mostly Russian materials. The author is an old Persian Communist and Comintern figure, also known as Pishevari, who reappeared on the scene after World War II during the Soviet attempt to detach Azerbaijan from Iran.

KD49 THOMAS, JOHN R. "The Rise and Fall of the Azerbaijan People's Republic as Reflected in *Izvestia*, 1945-1947." Certificate essay, Russian Institute, Columbia, 1953. 105 p. The only work available in the English language that treats the rise and fall of the Azerbaijan Republic by drawing heavily on *Izvestia.* As the rapid collapse of the Azerbaijan Republic was a blow to Soviet prestige, the author attempts to show how it was presented to the Russian people. Hence, the selection of *Izvestia*, which has the broadest foreign news coverage, as the main source of investigation is quite appropriate.

KD50 TUZMUKHOMEDOV, RALS A. *Sovetsko-iranskie otnosheniia (1917-1921)*. Moscow: Izd. Instituta mezhdunarodnykh otnoshenii, 1960. 96 p. Uses a variety of sources, including some Western materials from the period under consideration, to advance the thesis that the USSR aided in the transformation of Iran from a semi-colonial status under British aegis to independence. About half of the book is devoted to the Soviet-Iranian Treaty of February 1921.

KD51 U.S. LIBRARY OF CONGRESS, REFERENCE DEPARTMENT. *Iran; a Selected and Annotated Bibliography*. Comp. by Hafez F. Farman. Washington: 1951. 100 p. Annotates selected materials on Iran which are available in the Library of Congress, including some bearing on Soviet relations with Iran.

KD52 VAHDAT, MANOUCHER. "The Soviet Union and the Movement to Establish Autonomy in Iranian Azerbaijan." Ph.D. dissertation, U. of Indiana, 1958. A study of the Azerbaijan crisis with a view to Soviet imperialism in Iran. Argues that the discussion of the case in the Security Council helped force the withdrawal of Soviet troops from northern Iran.

KD53 VAN WAGENEN, RICHARD W. *The Iranian Case, 1946*. N.Y.: Carnegie Endowment for International Peace, 1952. 119 p. An authoritative and lucid account of Iran's case against the Soviet Union in the United Nations Security Council during 1946. The problem is set against a concise historical background. [A]

KD54 VASSILIEFF, LEON (Vasilev, Lev). *Puti sovetskogo imperializma*. N.Y.: Chekhov Publishers, 1954. 283 p. An occasionally informative account of Moscow's activities in Iran by a former high Soviet official stationed in the Middle East from 1943-49.

KD55 WEAVER, PAUL. "Soviet Interference in the Government of Iran, 1941-1951." Ph.D. dissertation, American U., 1958. Concerns itself with Soviet strategy in Iran during and after the Second World War and until 1958. Identifies four phases of Soviet strategy. The last phase of economic offensive since 1953 could be more thoroughly explored. While the constancy of basic aims is admitted, the author rightly points out the tactical agility and flexibility of Soviet policy. [B]

KD56 YOUNG, CUYLER. "The Race Between Russia and Reform in Iran," *Foreign Affairs* (January 1950), p. 278-89. A perceptive analysis of Iran's basic economic and social problems in the face of the Soviet menace to Iranian independence and way of life. [B]

KD57 ZAND, BAHMANN K. "British and Soviet Policies Toward Iran in the Period Between 1917-1927; Some Aspects of the Conflicting Security Interests of Great Britain and Soviet Russia in Iran." Ph.D. dissertation, Fordham, 1957. 285 p. Treats the 1921-27 period of Soviet-Iranian relations. Draws on some Persian sources.

KD58 ZAVRIEV, D. S. *Torgovo-politicheskii kurs Persii.* Tiflis: Zakkniga, 1934. 177 p. The law instituting a government monopoly over Persian foreign trade (passed by the *Majlis* in February 1931) is seen as an attempt by the "big bourgeoisie" to smash profitable trade relations between the USSR and Persian "middle" and "small" merchants. Pertinent documents, excellent bibliography.

KE. ISRAEL

EDITED BY MOSHE PERLMANN

KE1 ANDREEV, S. A. *Izrail.* Moscow: Vostochnaia Literatura, 1962. 120 p. "A journalist's notes" about "a country with a peaceful population and an aggressive government." Inveighs against American aid, Israel's labor movement, Israel's activity in Africa, and the conduct of the Eichmann trial.

KE1A *XIV sezd kommunisticheskoi partii Izrailia.* Moscow: Gosizdat, 1962. 200 p. Contains the report of the secretary general of the party at its 1961 conference. This is a full exposition of the official policy line of the CP of Israel.

KE1B DOMKE, MARTIN. "The Israel-Soviet Oil Arbitration," *American Journal of International Law,* vol. 53, no. 4 (October 1959), p. 787-806.

KE2 EYTAN, WALTER. *The First Ten Years; Israel between East and West.* London: Weidenfeld and Nicolson, 1958. 219 p. Surveys the rapid Soviet transition from voting in the U.N. for the establishment of a Jewish State and promptly recognizing Israel, to a hostile attitude connected with certain trends in Soviet home policy toward the Jewish minority and the courting of the Arab states, especially after 1955 when a massive supply of arms to Egypt and Iraq from the Soviet bloc began to change the balance of military power in the Near East. The Soviets denounce Israel as an imperialist bridgehead, and as only too ready to initiate provocations; support the exclusion of Israel from Asian consultations; favor the Arabs vs. Israel in U.N. deliberations, in propaganda, etc. By an Oxford don turned spokesman for Israel's Ministry for Foreign Affairs. [A]

KE3 F.F. "The U.S.S.R., The Soviet Jews, and Israel," *World Today*, vol. 14, no. 12 (December 1958), p. 518-32. Stresses the connection between the suppression of Jewish pro-Israel sentiment within the USSR and the Soviet's anti-Israel and pro-Arab orientation. Suggests that a change in Soviet attitude toward Soviet Jewry might produce a better climate for Soviet-Israeli relations.

KE4 IVANOV, KONSTANTIN P., and SHEINIS, ZINOVII S. *Gosudarstvo Izrail, ego polozhenie i politika.* Moscow: Gospolitizdat, 1958. 146 p. Useful as an expression of an attitude fostered by the Soviet authorities. Israel is pictured as a small land led by people who made a deal with American imperialism, oil interests, etc., in the struggle against the tide of colonial liberation; provoking clashes with the Arabs, and misleading many Jews into immigration, who suffer from the hardships in the new land of heartless exploitation. A propaganda work with numerous historical distortions. [A]

KE5 KOGAN, WOLF. "Soviet-Israel Relations." Certificate essay, Russian Institute, Columbia, 1950. 119 p.

KE6 LAQUEUR, WALTER Z. *Communism and Nationalism in the Middle East.* London: Routledge and Paul, 1956. 362 p. Part three (p. 73-119) in this excellent study covers Communism in Palestine and Israel. [A]

KE7 LEONIDOV, A. "Izrail i neft," *Mirovaia ekonomika i mezhdurarodnye otnosheniia*, II (February 1958), p. 55-67. Israel is pictured as a domain of American oilmen, especially the Rockefellers, with its leaders mere servants of oil interests, with aspirations and greed. Useful for the Soviet point of view.

KE8 SHALEV, MORDECHAI. "Soviet-Israel Relations." M.A. thesis, American U., 1954. 92 p. Traces the negative Bolshevik and Soviet attitudes toward Jewish national survival and Zionism, including the temporary support of the Jews' struggle for independence in Israel in 1947-50, which meant the elimination of British military and government from Palestine, and the almost simultaneously growing denunciation of Israel as a possible lure for Soviet Jews. By a member of the Israel diplomatic service.

KE9 TELLER, J. L. *The Kremlin, the Jews, and the Middle East.* N.Y.: Yoseloff, 1957. 202 p. A well-informed sketch by a Jewish journalist of the antecedents and sources of Soviet attitudes towards Zionism, the Jewish question, the problem of Palestine, and the evolution of these attitudes to the stage of frank and often violent hostility expressed (1) at home in aspects of the treatment of the Jewish minority and in propaganda and (2) abroad in political and strategic demarchés. Information is given also on the evolution of the Communist movement in Palestine and in Israel.

KF. TURKEY

EDITED BY PAUL B. HENZE AND DANKWART A. RUSTOW

1. GENERAL WORKS

KF1 ADIVAR, HALIDE EDIB. *The Turkish Ordeal; Memoirs of Halidé Edib.* N.Y. and London: Century, 1928. 407 p. The revolutionary memoirs of the first and foremost modern Turkish women's leader. Halide Edib and her husband, Dr. Abdülhak Adnan Adıvar, were Atatürk supporters during the war for independence and prominent during the early years of the Republic. This book is one of the most important firsthand accounts of the early period of the Turkish Republic. It deals primarily with domestic affairs, but also includes important information on foreign relations.

KF2 AKADEMIIA NAUK SSSR, INSTITUT VOSTOKOVEDENIIA. *Sovremennaia Turtsiia.* Ed. by A. M. Shamsutdinov and others. Moscow: Izd. vost. lit., 1958. 291 p. A fairly accurate, factual handbook on Turkey, apparently designed for Soviet citizens visiting or assigned to Turkey. Divided into major sections covering geographic data, economy, history, governmental structure, and culture (education, art, literature, radio, music, and sports). An appendix gives the text of the constitution of 1924 and statistical tables.

KF3 AKADEMIIA NAUK SSSR, INSTITUT VOSTOKOVEDENIIA. *Turetskii sbornik-istoriia, ekonomika, literatura, iazyk.* Ed. by A. M. Shamsutdinov. Moscow: Izd. vost. lit., 1958. 203 p. A symposium containing articles by ten Soviet Turkish specialists, including two on the history of the late Ottoman period, three on literature, and three on economic topics. An introductory essay by B. Dantsig provides a historical survey of Soviet Turkish studies. The book reflects the more generous and balanced view of Turkey characteristic of the post-Stalin period. Extensive citation of Turkish newspapers and other sources. [A]

KF4 ALEKSEEV, V. M., and KERIMOV, M. A. *Vneshniaia politika Turtsii.* Moscow: Izd. IMO, 1961.

KF5 ALLEN, W. E. D., and MURATOFF, PAUL. *Caucasian Battlefields; a History of the Wars on the Turco-Caucasian Border, 1828-1921.* Cambridge, England: University Press, 1953. 614 p. This work, by an eminent British Caucasian specialist and a former Tsarist officer, basically a military history of Russo-Turkish wars, is nevertheless written with the broader political context of the events it describes always in mind. Fully half the book is devoted to post-1914 events and the narrative is based on the most extensive combing of Russian, Turkish, German, English, French, and Caucasian (including Georgian and Armenian) sources. Extensive annotated bibliography. Excellent, detailed maps. [A]

KF6 ARAS, TEVFIK RÜŞTÜ. *Görüşlerim*. Istanbul: 1945. The Foreign Minister of 1925-38 and co-signer of the 1925 Turco-Soviet treaty pleads for a post-World War II rapprochement. [B]

KF7 ARSLAN. *Sovremennaia Turtsiia*. Moscow: "Krasnaia Nov," 1923. 68 p. A friendly interpretation of the Atatürk revolution and a discussion of Turkish Communist Party policies with optimistic conclusions on the likelihood of an early victory of Communism in Turkey.

KF8 ASTAKHOV, G. *Ot sultanata k demokraticheskoi Turtsii; ocherki iz istorii kemalizma*. Moscow: Gosizdat, 1926. 152 p. An optimistic interpretation of the Atatürk revolution as the first stage of development toward Communism in Turkey. Based on the author's firsthand observations. Treats Kemalist ideology, economic policies, and foreign economic relations. [A]

KF9 ATAY, FALIH RIFKI. *Yeni Rusya*. Ankara: 1931. Reflections on a trip to the Soviet Union by Mustafa Kemal's chief journalistic spokesman of the 1920's who found that the Turkish revolution had much to learn from the Russian. [B]

KF10 AYDEMIR, ŞEVKET SÜREYYA. *Inkilâp ve Kadro (Inkilâp Ideolojisi)*. Ankara: 1932. A summary of the *Kadro* ideas on Turkish political and economic development.

KF11 AYDEMIR, ŞEVKET SÜREYYA. *Suyu Arayan Adam*. Ankara: Öz yayınları, 1959. 538 p. Memoirs of the editor of *Kadro* covering the period up to 1950. Included are the author's conversion to Communism, adventures in Russia, return to Turkey, reconversion to Turkish nationalism, and activities in Ankara 1930-50.

KF12 BARTENEV, O. *Turtsiia; kratkii ekonomiko-politicheskii ocherk*. Moscow: Izd. TsK MOPR, 1927. 272 p. A basically friendly handbook on the new Turkey. Treats the struggle for independence, the economy, domestic policies, workers' movements, and the Communist Party.

KF12A BAYUR, YUSUF HIKMET. *Türk inkilabi tarihi, cilt III—1914-18*. Ankara: 1953.

KF13 BAYUR, YUSUF HIKMET. *Yeni Türkiye Devletinin Haricî Siyaseti*. Istanbul: Akşam matbaasi, 1934. 162 p. 2nd ed., *Türkiye Devletinin Diş Sıyasası*. Istanbul: Istanbul Univ., 1938. 180 p. Successive editions of a summary of Turkish foreign relations since 1918 by a leading diplomat and secretary to Atatürk. [B]

KF14 BELINKOV, S., and VASILEV, I. *O turetskom "neitralitete" vo vremia Vtoroi mirovoi voiny.* Moscow: Gospolitizdat, 1952. 118 p. A strong anti-Turkish polemic typical of the late Stalinist period. This short book condemns Turkey for having allegedly agreed during World War II to become the postwar tool of the United States and an outpost for aggressive maneuvers against the Balkans and the USSR.

KF15 BIYIKLIOĞLU, TEVFIK. *Osmanlı ve Türk Doğu Hudut Politikasi.* Istanbul: 1958. Lectures at the General Staff College by a former leading officer and ex-Ambassador to Moscow on Turkish-Russian diplomatic and military relations, especially during the 1914-21 period. [A]

KF16 BUTAEV, INAL. *Natsionalnaia revoliutsiia na vostoke; problema Turtsii.* Moscow-Leningrad: "Priboi," 1925. 214 p.

KF17 CEBESOY, ALI FUAT. *Millı Mücadele Hatıraları.* Istanbul: 1953. A valuable source of information, among other things, on Communist influences in Turkey during the 1920's, by a well-informed participant in the events of the time—a classmate of Atatürk's in officers' training school and the new Turkey's first ambassador to Moscow. [A]

KF18 CEBESOY, ALI FUAT. *Moskova Hatıraları.* Istanbul: 1955. Covers General Cebesoy's mission, on behalf of Atatürk, to Moscow during the period 1920-22. An authoritative primary source on Soviet-Turkish relations and on the activities of Enver Pasha. Numerous documents. [A]

KF19 DANTSIG, BORIS M. *Turtsiia; politiko-ekonomicheskii ocherk.* Moscow: Voenizdat, 1940. 160 p. 2nd rev. ed., 1949. 308 p. A standard Soviet handbook on Turkey with chapters on the historical background, geography, economy, domestic and foreign policy, and the armed forces. The newer edition contains extensive, reasonably factual, descriptive material and statistics. Broad discussions of domestic and foreign policies, reflecting the hard line of the early postwar years. [A]

KF20 DAVISON, RODERIC H. "Turkish Diplomacy from Mudros to Lausanne," in Gordon A. Craig and Felix A. Gilbert, eds., *The Diplomats*, Princeton, N.J.: Princeton University Press, 1953. P. 172-209. The most careful and thoughtful account of Turkey's foreign relations of the 1918-23 period, based on all the published sources available at the time. [A]

KF21 *Dix ans sur les traces de Lausanne.* Ankara: 1935. Turkish ed., *Lozanın izlerinde on yıl.* Ankara: 1935. An official survey of Turkish foreign policy by the Ministry of Foreign Affairs.

KF22 DJEMAL, AHMED (PASHA). *Memories of a Turkish Statesman, 1913-1919.* London: Hutchinson; N.Y.: Doran, 1922. 302 p. German ed., Munich: Drei Masken, 1922. 390 p. Turkish ed., *Hatırat 1913-1922.* Istanbul: 1922. 2nd ed., *Hatıralar.* Istanbul: 1959. An apologia by the Young Turk military and political leader; the English translation does not cover his later activities in Russia.

KF23 DURUSOY, M. ORHAN, and GÖKMAN, M. MUZAFFER. *Atatürk ve devrimleri bibliografyası.* Ankara: Türk Tarih Kurumu, 1957. A "Bibliography of Atatürk and his Revolutions," 742 items in Turkish and 184 in Western languages on Atatürk and Turkish history since 1919, arranged alphabetically by author, with complete bibliographic data but no annotations. Title index.

KF24 ENGIN, M. SAFFET. *Atatürkçülük ve Moskofluk-Türklük Savaşları.* Istanbul: 1953. "Atatürkism and the Moscovism-Turkism struggle"—a diffuse piece of polemics.

KF25 ER-BIL, HAŞIM NIHAD. *Komünizmle mücadele rehberi.* Ankara: 1951. 312 p. "Guide to the Fight Against Communism"—a popular tract.

KF26 ERDOĞAN, FAHREDDIN. *Türk Ellerinde Hatiralarim.* Ankara: 1954. Recollections of a Kars city councillor who served as Foreign Minister of the Provisional Government of Southwest Caucasia in 1918-19.

KF27 ERIŞÇI, LÜTFÜ. *Türkiyede Işçi sinifinin tarihi.* Istanbul: 1951. 31 p. Concise data on the working class parties, trade unions, and wage levels since the late 19th century.

KF28 ESMER, AHMET ŞÜKRÜ. *Siyasî Tarih, 1919-1939.* Ankara: 1953. A diplomatic history of the interwar period, by a Turkish journalist and scholar.

KF29 EURINGER, RICHARD. *Der Serasker.* Hamburg: Hanseatische Verlagsanstalt, 1939. 344 p. A biography of Enver Pasha, the Turkish leader who went to Russia in 1919 and tried to create a Pan-Turk empire in Central Asia.

KF30 FAHREDDIN, KIRZIOGLU M. *Kars Tarihi.* Vol. 1. Istanbul: 1953. A history of Kars by a local Turkish leader, prominent in the 1918-19 nationalist movement.

KF30A GORDLEVSKII, VLADIMIR A. *Izbrannie sochineniia.* Vol. III, *Istoria i kultura.* Moscow: Izd. vost. lit., 1962. 588 p. This third volume of selected works of one of Russia's most productive scholars and writers on Turkey includes a wide range of description and commentary ranging from travel notes from the early 20th century to extensive discussions of Turkish culture, social and religious institutions and political forces both in the late Ottoman and early Atatürk periods. There are interesting sections on the press in the late Ottoman and early Republican periods. The volume concludes with a number of observations on the Atatürk reforms. Gordlevskii's writings are remarkably free of conventional Communist bias. An excellent 27-page index is included.

KF31 GURKO-KRIAZHIN, VLADIMIR A. *Blizhnii Vostok i derzhavy*. Moscow: Nauchnaia assotsiatsiia vostokovedeniia, 1924. 243 p. Primarily on Turkey, although it has a short section on the "Arab East." Stresses the importance of the Turkish revolution and its reverberations in the rest of the East.

KF32 GURKO-KRIAZHIN, VLADIMIR A. *Istoriia revoliutsii v Turtsii*. Intro. by I. Borozdin. Moscow: "Mir," 1923. 196 p. One of the earliest detailed Soviet studies of the reform movement in Turkey from the *Tanzimat* period to the Treaty of Lausanne. Special emphasis on the Young Turks as military reactionaries; friendly toward Atatürk's republic. [A]

KF32A HIKMET (RAN), NAZYM. *Izbrannye sochinenia*. Moscow: Goslitizdat, 1957. 2 vols. An extensive collection of the prominent Turkish Communist's poems and plays, written from 1921 on, with brief notes. Vol. II concludes with a brief biography.

KF33 HOSTLER, CHARLES W. *Turkism and the Soviets; The Turks of the World and their Political Objectives*. London: Allen & Unwin; N.Y.: Praeger, 1957. 244 p. A conscientious survey, by an American military officer, of Pan-Turk and related movements with reference to the significance of these movements to both Soviet and Turkish domestic and foreign policies. Tends to overstress the importance of Pan-Turkism in the Turkish Republic. Based on a variety of Turkish, Soviet, and Western sources of uneven quality.

KF34 HOWARD, HARRY N. *The Partition of Turkey: A Diplomatic History, 1913-1923*. Norman: U. of Oklahoma, 1931. 486 p. A comprehensive, standard work which puts Russian interests in proper perspective up to the time of the Bolshevik Revolution, but is incomplete in respect to Turkish-USSR relations in the post-1917 period.

KF35 HUMBARACI, ARSLAN. *Middle East Indictment*. London: R. Hale, 1957. 288 p. A bombastic, journalistic discussion of Middle Eastern politics and the role of Russia; interesting primarily because it is written by a former Turkish Communist.

KF36 HUREWITZ, JACOB C. *Diplomacy in the Near and Middle East*. Princeton, N.J.: Van Nostrand, 1956. 2 vols. A basic collection of documents, 1935-56, with careful introductory and bibliographic notes. [B]

KF37 JÄSCHKE, GOTTHARD. *Die Türkei in den Jahren 1935-1941.* Leipzig: 1943.

KF38 JÄSCHKE, GOTTHARD. *Die Türkei in den Jahren 1942-1951.* Wiesbaden: 1955.

KF39 JÄSCHKE, GOTTHARD, and PRITSCH, ERICH. *Die Türkei seit dem Weltkriege, Geschichtskalender 1918-1928.* Berlin: 1929. (Index for this and continuations up to 1934 in *Mitteilungen der Auslands-Hochschule*, vol. 41. Berlin: 1938.) These three volumes by Jäschke constitute the most detailed, orderly, and accurate compendium of information on political, economic, social and cultural developments in Turkey since the early Kemalist period. Also covers all important developments in foreign relations. Well-organized and indexed (see esp. "Kommunismus" and "Russland"). Tables. Excellent bibliographical references.

KF39A KARABEKIR, KÂZIM. *Cihan harbinde neden girdik, nasil girdik, nasil idare ettik.* Kitab 1-3, Istanbul: 1937-39. Turkey's role in World War I.

KF40 KARABEKIR, KÂZIM. *Istiklâl Harbimizin esasları.* Istanbul: Sinan Matbaasi Neşriyat Evi, 1951. 192 p. Enlarged ed., *Istiklâl harbımız* Istanbul: Türkiye yayınevi, 1960. 1171 p. Memoirs of the Turkish nationalist commander of the Eastern front, 1919-22, with detailed documents on military and diplomatic operations on the Turkish-Russian border and occasional polemical asides against other Turkish leaders of the period; a prime source to be used in conjunction with Atatürk's and Cebesoy's works. [A]

KF41 KARAMAN, SAMI SABIT. *Trabzon ve Kars hâtıraları: istiklâl mücadelesi ve Enver Paşa.* Istanbul: 1949. Memoirs of a Kemalist general assigned in 1921-22 to prevent infiltration by followers of Enver and Communists into Anatolia. Important as a primary source on a little-explored subject. [B]

KF42 KARPAT, KEMAL H. *Turkey's Politics; the Transition to a Multi-Party System.* Princeton, N.J.: Princeton, 1959. 522 p. A detailed, scholarly examination of Turkish domestic politics, concentrating on the 1946-50 period, by a Turkish political scientist now teaching in the U.S. Includes a chapter on Communism. Extensive bibliography. [B]

KF43 KAYA, YALÇIN, ed. *Nâzım Hikmet.* Istanbul: 1950. 48 p. A brief selection from the works of Turkey's leading poet-turned-Communist, and from evaluations of him by other literary figures.

KF43A KAZEMZADEH, FIRUZ. *The Struggle for Transcaucasia, 1917-21.* N.Y.: Philosophical Library; Oxford: Ronald, 1951. 356 p. This standard work by an Iranian-American scholar includes a lengthy discussion of Soviet Caucasian policies in relation to Turkey. Good bibliography and index.

KF44 KERIMOV, M. A. *Gosudarstvennyi stroi Turtsii.* Moscow: Gosizdat iurid. lit., 1956. 68 p. An interesting mixture of factual information on the governmental structure of Turkey and Marxist-Leninist interpretation of Turkish society and governmental policies.

KF44A LAQUEUR, WALTER Z. *The Soviet Union and the Middle East.* London: Routledge and Kegan Paul; N.Y.: Praeger, 1959. 366 p. One of the best general works on the subject. Covers the entire period 1918-58. Contains extensive discussion of shifts in Soviet Turkish policy.

KF44B LAQUEUR, WALTER Z., ed. *The Middle East in Transition.* London: Routledge and Kegan Paul; N.Y.: Praeger, 1958. 513 p. Subtitled "Studies in Contemporary History," this volume includes the works of 34 American, European and Middle Eastern scholars. The second half of the book (p. 311 ff.) is entitled "Communism, the Soviet Union and the Middle East" and contains a broad selection of material on Soviet policy towards Turkey, Iran and the Arab states.

KF44C LAZAREV, M. S. *Krushenie turetskogo gospodstva na Arabskom vostoke.* Moscow: Izd. vost. lit., 1960. 246 p. A comprehensive study of the Arab question and of various plans for partition of the Ottoman Empire during World War I and its immediate aftermath. Draws on Imperial Russian archival material as well as a wide range of familiar Western sources and depicts the Communists as friends of Arab nationalism.

KF44D LEWIS, BERNARD. *The Emergence of Modern Turkey.* London: Oxford University Press, 1961. 511 p. Based on a vast range of Turkish and Western sources, this comprehensive work by Britain's foremost Turkish scholar outdistances all previous works on the subject. Social and literary developments as well as political and economic history are discussed under two major headings, "The Stages of Emergence" and "Aspects of Change." To the student of Russian 19th century revolutionary history, this book will call to mind many striking parallels in Turkish experience. Relations with Russia and Communist problems are well covered within the perspective of Turkish national development. Excellent source-referencing. Good bibliography and index.

KF45 LOEWENTHAL, RUDOLF. *Russian Materials on Turkey; A Selective Bibliography.* Washington: Dept. of State, External Research Staff, Office of Intelligence Research, 1958. 19 p. (mimeographed).

KF46 LUDSHUVEIT, E. F. *Turtsiia; ekonomiko-geograficheskii ocherk.* Moscow: Gos. izd. geograf. lit., 1955. 398 p. A detailed, economic geography of Turkey, based mostly on pre-1950 data. More than half the book is devoted to a region-by-region survey of the country.

KF46A MATOSSIAN, MARY K. *The Impact of Soviet Policies in Armenia.* Leiden: Brill, 1962. 239 p. Though devoted primarily to Soviet Armenia, this competent, scholarly work discusses Armenian nationalism and the Sovietization of Armenia in its broader Near Eastern context and includes an extensive bibliography. The lack of an index makes the book difficult to use for reference.

KF47 MELNIK, A. (pseud. of Anatolii F. Miller). *Turtsiia.* Moscow: Sotsekgiz, 1937. 217 p. A pro-republican interpretation of Turkish history beginning with early Ottoman times, but concentrating on the post-World War I period and the "national liberation movement." Full of praise for the new Turkey, but not unsound as a historical interpretation. Includes a chapter entitled "Turkey and the USSR." [A]

KF48 MILLER, ANATOLII F. (A. Melnik, pseud.). *Ocherki noveishei istorii Turtsii.* Moscow: Izd. Akad. nauk SSSR, 1948. 279 p. A survey of Turkish history from World War I through World War II by the USSR's leading historian of Turkey. Although it reflects many features of the post-war Soviet hard-line on Turkey, it was harshly attacked in *Voprosy istorii* in 1950 as reflecting too many Western and Turkish viewpoints and too little Soviet source material. [A]

KF49 MISSION SCIENTIFIQUE DU MAROC, TANGIER. *Le Bolchevisme et l'Islam.* Paris: Leroux, 1922. 2 vols. A survey of Soviet-Turkish relations during the first years after the Revolution. Useful, although biased.

KF50 MOISEEV, PETR P., and ROZALIEV, IURI N. *K istorii sovetsko-turetskikh otnoshenii.* Moscow: Gospolitizdat, 1958. 83 p. A significant popular reinterpretation of Soviet-Turkish relations in the spirit of greater "good-neighborliness" adopted by the USSR in the late 1950's. Advocates a complete return to the "sound cooperation" of the early Atatürk period. Blames Turkey's economic problems on its participation in "aggressive blocs."

KF52 NELSON, C. R. "Kemalist Turkey and the Soviet Union, 1920-1926." M.A. thesis, Stanford, 1949.

KF53 NOVICHEV, A. D. *Krestianstvo Turtsii v noveishee vremia.* Moscow: Izd. vost. lit., 1959. 289 p. A detailed, Marxist analysis of

Turkish agriculture and the development of the peasantry from 1918 to the early 1950's. Contains a great deal of factual information with extensive references to Turkish sources. Excellent bibliography.

KF54 OKAY, KURT. *Enver Pascha, der grosse Freund Deutschlands.* Berlin: Kulturpolitik, 1935. 506 p. A biography of the Turkish leader who for a while cooperated with the Bolsheviks and later led the Turks of Soviet Central Asia in rebellion against Moscow. Strongly anti-Communist.

KF55 PAVLOVICH, MIKHAIL; GURKO-KRIAZHIN, V. and others. *Turtsiia v borbe za nezavisimost.* Moscow: Nauch. assots. vostokoved., 1925. 152 p.

KF56 ROZALIEV, IU. N. *Ocherki polozheniia promyshlennogo proletariata Turtsii posle vtoroi mirovoi voiny.* Moscow: Izd. Akad. nauk SSSR, 1956. 208 p. A survey of workers, working conditions, labor law and labor insurance in Turkey in the 1945-54 period. Based on extensive, but not entirely representative, Turkish source material. Too much emphasis on the political aspects of the problem.

KF56A ROZALIEV, IU. N. *Osobennosti razvitiia kapitalizma v Turtsii, 1923-1960 gg.* Moscow: Izd. vost. lit., 1962. 354 p. A thorough study of economic development in Turkey during the Republican period from a doctrinaire Marxist-Leninist viewpoint. Cites Turkish sources extensively; excellent bibliography and index. Concludes that accelerated development after World War II has sharpened class conflicts and basic political problems.

KF57 SEIFULLIN, LIDIIA N. *V strane ukhodiashchego Islama; poezdka v Turtsiiu.* Leningrad: Gosizdat, 1925. 145 p. A traveler's notes on Turkey, stressing the decline of Islam under the impact of Atatürk's reforms.

KF58 STAVROVSKII, A. *Zakavkaze posle Oktiabria; vzaimootnosheniia s Turtsiei v pervoi polovine 1918 goda.* Moscow: Gosizdat, 1925. 120 p.

KF59 SVERCHEVSKAIA, A. K., and CHERMAN, T. P., comps. *Bibliografiia Turtsii, 1917-1958.* Ed. by B. M. Dantsig. Moscow: Izd. vost. lit., 1959. 189 p. An indispensable tool for the serious student of Soviet scholarship on Turkey. Lists 3262 books, pamphlets and articles under more than 30 major headings. Good index. Chapter and section headings of all major works are given. A few significant items are missing. A companion volume with the same compilers and editor, *Bibliografiia Turtsii, 1713-1917*, 267 pages, was issued in 1961. It covers the pre-revolutionary period thoroughly and includes most significant books and journals published in the provinces.

KF60 TOGAN, AHMED ZEKI VELIDI. *Bugünkü Türkistan ve Yakın Mazisi.* Cairo: 1940 (old Turkish script); republished as *Bugünkü Türkili (Türkistan) ve Yakın Tarihi,* Vol. 1. Istanbul: 1947. A history of modern Turkestan by a leading Pan-Turkist and ex-President of the Bashkir Republic, including a detailed account of Enver Pasha's last days. [B]

KF61 TUNAYA, TARIK Z. *Türkiyede Siyasî Partiler 1859-1952.* Istanbul: Doğan Kardeş Yanınları Basımevi, 1952. 799 p. An authoritative work on Turkish political parties and movements by a leading political scientist. Detailed information and extensive excerpts on party programs, organization, and leadership, including all known Communist groups. Occasional inaccuracies of detail. Extensive bibliography. [A]

KF62 *Türkiyede Siyasî Dernekler,* vol. 2 (vol. 1 not published). Ankara: Emniyet Genel Müdürlüğü, 1951. Programs of parties registered with the authorities, compiled by the Ministry of the Interior.

KF63 ÜNÜVAR, VEYSEL. *Istiklâl harbinde Bolşeviklerle sekiz ay 1920-1921.* Istanbul: 1948. "Eight months with the Bolsheviks during the War of Independence"—memoirs of a Turkish officer's mission to the Caucasus region.

KF64 USTIUNGEL, S. V. *V tiurme i na "vole"; zapiski turetskogo kommunista.* Moscow: Izd. inostr. lit., 1952. 96 p. Memoirs of a Turkish Communist of his experiences in prison and out.

KF65 VASILEV, I. *O turetskom "neitralitete" vo vtoroi mirovoi voine.* Moscow: Gospolitizdat, 1951. 118 p. A vicious attack portraying Turkish policy during World War II as a cover for Anglo-American aggressive schemes against the USSR in the Balkans and Near East. Represents the high point of the postwar Soviet negative policy toward Turkey.

KF66 VELTMAN, MIKHAIL L. (M. Pavlovich, pseud.). *Revoliutsionnaia Turtsiia.* Moscow: Gosizdat, 1921. 127 p.

KF67 YALMAN, AHMED EMIN. *Turkey in the World War.* New Haven: Yale, 1930. 310 p. A political and economic survey by a leading Turkish journalist who was active as a correspondent and editor during World War I.

KF68 *28-29 Kanunu Sani 1921. Karadeniz Kıyılarında parçalanan Mustafa Suphi ve yoldaşlarının ikinci yıl dönümleri 1923.* Moscow: Kızıl Şark matbaasi (1923?). Commemoration of the 2nd anniversary of the drowning of a Turkish Communist leader and his associates off Trabzon.

KF69 ZAVRIEV, D. S. *Ekonomika sovremennoi Turtsii.* Tiflis: Zakgiz, 1934. 194 p. A relatively factual economic survey of Turkey stressing the economic problems of the Kemalist regime.

KF70 ZAVRIEV, D. S. *K noveishei istorii severo-vostochnykh vilaietov Turtsii.* Tiblis: Izd. Tbiliisskogo gos. universiteta, 1934. 194 p. 2nd ed., 1947. 367 p. A detailed study of the Kars and Black Sea coastal regions, contrasting the alleged economic backwardness and oppressive minority policies of the Turkish Republic with Soviet policies in the Transcaucasus. Reappearance of this book in 1947 was an indication of the reassertion of Soviet claims to this region after World War II. Extensive bibliography. [A]

KF71 ZENKOVSKY, SERGE A. *Pan-Turkism and Islam in Russia.* Cambridge: Harvard, 1960. 345 p. A balanced, authoritative account of the development of nationalism among the Turkic peoples of the Soviet Union, covering events through the early 1920's. Based on Russian, Soviet, Turkish, and Western primary and secondary sources. Extensive footnotes; excellent bibliography. [A]

KF72 ZHERVE, B., PETROV, A., and SHVEDE, E. *Sredizemnoe more; politiko-strategicheskii ocherk.* Moscow: Izd. "Voen. Vestn.," 1927. 200 p. A survey of the "Eastern Question" before and after World War I. Deals sympathetically with Turkey as a victim of great-power imperialist ambitions and devotes a full chapter to Turkey as a factor in contemporary Mediterranean politics.

KF73 ZIEMKE, KURT. *Die neue Türkei, politische Entwicklung 1914-1929.* Berlin-Leipzig: 1930. The best single survey of the period, concentrating on foreign affairs. [B]

2. THE USSR AND THE TURKISH STRAITS

KF74 ANCHIERI, ETTORE. *Constantinopli e gli stretti nella politica russa ed europea.* Milan: Giuffrè, 1948. 268 p. A scholarly history of the straits question, 1774-1937.

KF75 BAŞGIL, ALI FUAD. *La Question des détroits.* Paris: 1928. The French *thèse* of a Turkish constitutional lawyer.

KF76 BILSEL, MEHMED CEMIL. *Lozan.* Istanbul: Ahmet Ihsan Matbaası, 1933. 2 vols. A treatise on the Treaty of Lausanne by a leading Turkish international lawyer.

KF77 BILSEL, MEHMED CEMIL. *Türk boğazları.* Istanbul: 1948. 133 p. A discussion of the straits question by a Turkish authority.

KF78 DRANOV, B. A. *Chernomorskie prolivy; mezhdunarodno-pravovoi rezhim.* Moscow: Iurizdat, 1948. 240 p. A detailed, legal-historical study of the straits question, emphasizing Soviet interests and policies. Extensive bibliography.

KF79 HOWARD, HARRY N. *The Problem of the Turkish Straits.* Washington: G.P.O., 1947. 68 p. A U.S. Department of State publication reviewing developments mainly since Montreux.

KF80 KARACAN, ALI NACI. *Lozan Konferansi ve Ismet Paşa.* Istanbul: Maarif Matbaası, 1943. 488 p. An account of the Lausanne Conference on the Straits, giving many details and stressing the part played by Ismet.

KF81 MANDELSHTAM, ANDREI N. "La Politique russe d'accès à la Méditerranée au XXe siècle." In The Hague, Academy of International Law, *Recueil des cours, 1934*, vol. 47, no. 1 (Paris: 1935), p. 597-802. Analyzes Russian objectives regarding the Straits down to 1923, with emphasis on the period 1907-14.

KF82 PAPUKCHIEVA, MARIE. *La Politique de la Russie à l'égard des détroits.* Geneva: Impr. Grivet, 1944. 188 p.

KF83 SHOTWELL, JAMES T., and DEAK, FRANCIS. *Turkey at the Straits.* N.Y.: Macmillan, 1940. 196 p. A standard historical work. [B]

KF84 WOBST, PAUL G. *Die Dardanellenfrage bis zum Lösungsversuch des Abkommens von Montreux.* Leipzig: 1941. Well documented.

3. PERIODICALS

KF85 *Barış Yolu.* Journal of the Communist front in Turkey.

KF85A *Caucasian Review*, 1955–. Institute for the Study of the USSR, Munich. A quarterly published by the foremost Soviet emigré research institute in the West. Contains frequent articles on problems of Turkish relations with the Caucasus.

KF86 *Emek.* Journal of the Kemalist-inspired, pseudo-Communist Party, 6 issues, January 16, 1921–.

KF87 *Kadro.* Monthly journal of political, economic, social and cultural commentary, Jan. 1932 to December 1934. Most of the contributions were by Şevket Süreyya (Aydemir) and several other former Communists. Articles also by Yakup Kadri (Karaosmanoğlu) and occasionally by others very close to Atatürk, often on subjects dealing with Russia and the authors' views on developments there as they might apply to Turkey. Generally very leftist (but clearly non-Communist) views. [B]

KF88 *Orak Cekiç.* Irregular—since the early 1930's. Central illegal organ of the Turkish Communists.

KF89 *Oriente Moderno.* Rome. Monthly since 1921. Detailed survey of current political and cultural events in Turkey and other Near Eastern countries, based on condensation of the indigenous press. Numerous documents, including diplomatic ones, are reprinted in full. [A]

KF90 *Welt des Islams.* Quarterly. Berlin, 1911-41. New series, Leiden: 1951–. Frequent authoritative contributions by Gotthard Jäschke and others on the history of Turkey (including relations with the Soviets) since 1918. [A]

KF91 *Zonguldak Komünizmle Mücadele Derneği. Yayınları,* nos. 1-4. Zonguldak: 1950. Popular tracts of the "Society for the Fight Against Communism of Zonguldak," the Turkish coal-mining center.

L. Africa

EDITED BY BERT H. COOPER

1. BIBLIOGRAPHIES

L1 CENTRAL ASIAN RESEARCH CENTRE. *Russia Looks at Africa; a Brief Survey of Russian Writing on Africa from the Nineteenth Century to the Present Day.* London: 1960. 21 p. Discusses sources in Russian, primarily since World War II. This is preparatory to Holdsworth's *Soviet African Studies.* Has a list of Soviet Africanists by region of specialty.

L2 HOLDSWORTH, MARY. *Soviet African Studies, 1918-1959; an Annotated Bibliography.* London: Royal Institute of International Affairs, 1961. 2 vols. Vol. I, *General Functional Studies.* Vol. II, *Regional Studies.* Prepared by the top British authority on Soviet African research. [A]

L3 LOEWENTHAL, RUDOLF. *Russian Materials on Africa; A Selective Bibliography.* Washington: Dept. of State, External Research Staff, Office of Intelligence Research, 1958. 34 p. A mimeographed list of 314 books and periodical articles, without annotations. Contains an author, person, and subject index. [A]

L4 U.S. LIBRARY OF CONGRESS, DIVISION OF BIBLIOGRAPHY. *French Colonies in Africa; a List of References.* Comp. by Helen F. Conover. Washington: G.P.O., 1942. 67 p. An early compilation.

2. GENERAL WORKS

L5 *Africa Report.* Monthly. Washington: African-American Institute. Title was changed October, 1960 from *Africa Special Report.* Almost every issue contains news items and special articles on Soviet-African relations and African Communism.

L6 *Afrika 1956-1960 gg.* Moscow: Izd. vost. lit., 1961.

L7 AKADEMIIA NAUK SSSR, INSTITUT EKONOMIKI. *Imperialisticheskaia borba za Afriku i osvoboditelnoe dvizhenie narodov; sbornik statei.* Ed. by V. IA. Vasileva, I. M. Lemin, and V. A. Maslennikov. Moscow: Izd. Akademii nauk SSSR, 1953. 341 p. A collection of 11 articles by Soviet Africanists writing on all parts of Africa, reflecting the Communist Cold War line. Potekhin, Datlin, Iastrebova, Vasileva, Lemin, and Maslennikov are the Africanists represented.

L8 AKADEMIIA NAUK SSSR, INSTITUT ETNOGRAFII. *Narody Afriki.* Ed. by D. A. Olderogge and I. I. Potekhin. Moscow: Izd.

Akademii nauk SSSR, 1954. 731 p. This first major work of the Soviet Africanists includes illustrations, color plates, maps, footnotes, and extensive bibliography. Designed not only for specialists but for the general reading public, it places great stress on the "national liberation" movement and the horrors of colonialism. A softer attitude towards African bourgeois nationalists, such as Nkrumah, is evident in this work, which seems to have been a bellwether for Soviet Africanists. Olderogge is a specialist in Arabic and African linguistics and Potekhin is in charge of African research activities in the USSR. [B]

L9 AKADEMIIA NAUK SSSR, INSTITUT VOSTOKOVEDENIIA. *Ekonomicheskoe polozhenie stran Azii i Afriki v 1959 g.* Dantsig, B. M. and others, eds. Moscow: Izd. vost. lit., 1961. 511 p.

L10 AMERICAN ASSEMBLY. *The United States and Africa.* N.Y.: Columbia, 1958. 252 p. A useful study for statistics and political discussion. Vernon McKay's "External Political Pressures on Africa Today," is particularly valuable.

L11 AMTER, I. *Mirovoe osvoboditelnoe dvizhenie negrov.* Moscow-Leningrad: Gosizdat, 1925. 136 p.

L12 BIRD, CHRISTOPHER. "Africa's Diverse Peoples Offer Openings for Soviet Agitation," *Africa Special Report*, II (November 1957), p. 11-12. Formerly of the University of Hawaii, Bird is currently an independent researcher in Washington, D.C.

L13 BIRD, CHRISTOPHER. "New Soviet Journal on Asia and Africa," *Africa Special Report*, III (August 1958), p. 11-12.

L14 BIRD, CHRISTOPHER. "Soviet Ethnographic Research on Africa: Background to Political, Economic and Propaganda Activity?" *Africa Special Report*, II (October 1957), p. 6-7.

L15 BIRD, CHRISTOPHER. "Soviet Scholars Embark on Major Program of African Research," *Africa Special Report*, III (April 1958), p. 12-14.

L16 BIRD, CHRISTOPHER. "What Russia Reads about Africa," *Africa Special Report*, II (December 1957), p. 15.

L17 CATTELL, DAVID T. "Communism and the African Negro," *Problems of Communism*, VIII, no. 5 (Sept.-Oct. 1959), p. 35-41. An intelligent analysis by a professor of political science at U.C.L.A.

L17A "Communism in Africa," a series of articles in *Problems of Communism*, 1961-62. In the Nov.-Dec. 1961 issue: "Moscow's First Steps," by David L. Morison, and "The West African Scene," by Walter Kolarz. In the March-April 1962 issue: "Soviet Views on Africa," by Lazar Pistrak, and "Scholarship and Propaganda," by

Christopher Bird. In the July-Aug. 1962 issue: "The Role of China," by Kurt London. [A]

L18 CONFERENCE OF COMMUNIST AND WORKERS' PARTIES OF COUNTRIES WITHIN THE SPHERE OF BRITISH IMPERIALISM. *Allies for Freedom.* London: 1954. 135 p. Report of the Second Conference of Communist Parties held in Caxton Hall, London, April, 1954. Speeches by the delegates reflect the line of the Cold War in the pre-1956 period, attacking "bourgeois nationalists," etc. Includes speeches by Nigerian, Sudanese, and South African Communists.

L19 COOPER, BERT H., JR. "Soviet Penetration of Black Africa; An Historical Analysis of Soviet Relations with Africa South of the Sahara." Master's Thesis, George Washington University, 1960. 115 p. Written during the spring and summer of 1959, this study traces Soviet activities in sub-Sahara Africa from the early 1920's through 1958, including both Communist activities and the recently initiated diplomatic, economic, and cultural relations between the Soviet bloc and independent African states. Annotated bibliography of 95 sources. [A]

L20 CUNARD, NANCY. *Negro Anthology.* London: Wishart, 1934. 855 p. A collection of writings on Africa and the Negro question, compiled by the Afrophile and Communist fellow-traveller Nancy Cunard. Most contributions are by Communists, fellow-travellers, and African or Negro nationalists, but there are also a number of writings by non-Communist students of Africa. [B]

L21 DATLIN, S. *Afrika pod gnetom imperializma.* Moscow: Gospolitizdat, 1951. 129 p. A good sourcebook for the official line on Africa in 1950-51; basically an attack on the Marshall Plan and the dangers of "American Imperialism." A propaganda tract, not a work of scholarship. [A]

L22 EELLS, WALTER C. *Communism in Education in Asia, Africa and the Far Pacific.* Washington: American Council on Education, 1954. 246 p. A country-by-country collection of data, based largely on personal visits, interviews, and the local English-language press. Rather superficial and undiscriminating. Ignores the role of the USSR. The author served as educational adviser to the Supreme Commander of the Allied Powers in Tokyo.

L22A *Ekonomicheskoe polozhenie stran Azii, Afriki, i Latinskoi Ameriki.* Moscow: Vneshtorgizdat, 1959. 446 p. Analyzes socio-economic conditions, trade and production statistics, etc. of underdeveloped areas from the Soviet point of view to show the economic dependence of these areas on the Western bloc.

L23 FILESI, TEOBALDO. *Comunismo e nazionalismo in Africa.* Rome: Istituto Italiano per l'Africa, 1958. 368 p. A scholarly and comprehensive study of Communism in Africa. Part One surveys Garveyism and Pan-Africanism, then the role of Communism in North Africa and Ethiopia and, in somewhat less detail, in South Africa. Part Two treats post-1945 developments, Communist influence in the *Rassemblement Démocratique Africaine* in French Africa, South African Communism, North African terrorism, Egyptian-Soviet relations, and the recent Soviet academic interest in Africa. Reference footnotes and appendices are useful. Author is a non-Communist student of colonial history. [A]

L24 FORD, JAMES W. *The Communists and the Struggle for Negro Liberation.* N.Y.: Harlem Division of the Communist Party, 1936 [?] 67 p. Includes speeches by Ford, an American Negro Communist functionary, before the Frankfurt Congress against Imperialism in 1929 and the Hamburg Conference of Negro Workers in 1930. Also states the Party line on the Ethiopian situation of 1935-36. The Communist Party's candidate for Vice President in 1932, Ford has been called the "Red Uncle Tom" for his slavish following of the Party line.

L25 GAUTHEROT, GUSTAVE. *Le Bolchévisme aux colonies et l'impérialisme rouge.* Paris: Librairie de la Revue Française, 1930. 446 p. Contains a chapter on Comintern activities in Africa during the 1920's, especially in connection with the Communist-front League Against Imperialism, founded at the Brussels Congress in 1927. Includes illustrations of leading participants in the Brussels and Frankfurt Congresses. The author is a Right-wing ultra-nationalist French pamphleteer.

L26 GAUTHEROT, GUSTAVE. *Le Monde communiste.* Paris: Éditions Spes, 1925. 259 p. Has a wealth of quotations and documents from official Communist sources, of special interest on French North Africa.

L27 HAINES, CHARLES GROVE, ed. *Africa Today.* Baltimore: Johns Hopkins, 1955. 510 p. Includes two relevant articles. One, "The Communist Threat in Africa," p. 262-80, is by Max Yergan, an American Negro clergyman, formerly a member of the pro-Communist Council on African Affairs, now an outspoken critic of Communism among Negroes of the world. The other article, "Commentary," p. 281-86, by Robert D. Baum, a lecturer on African affairs in the Johns Hopkins School of Advanced International Studies, discusses the trade union movement in sub-Sahara Africa as a potential channel for Soviet influence.

L28 HAINES, CHARLES GROVE, ed. *The Threat of Soviet Imperialism.* Baltimore: Johns Hopkins, 1954. 402 p. Includes an informative and balanced survey of Soviet activities in Africa by Vernon D. McKay entitled "Communist Exploitation of Anti-Colonialism and Nationalism in Africa," p. 258-74. The author, a State Department specialist and Professor of African Studies at the School of Advanced International Studies, Johns Hopkins University, discusses Soviet attitudes towards the African "national bourgeoisie" and channels of Soviet influence in the area, such as trade unions, students abroad, the RDA, U.N. bodies, etc.

L28A HEMPSTONE, SMITH. *The New Africa.* London: Faber & Faber, 1961. 664 p. A journalistic account based on the author's travels throughout sub-Saharan Africa from 1956 to 1960. Author is a political journalist connected with the Washington, D.C., *Evening Star.* Discusses Soviet tactics and Communist activity in Ghana, Guinea, Cameroun, Ethiopia, etc. Surveys the history of African Communism since the 1930's with special mention of George Padmore's role in the movement. Contains detailed discussion of the activities of the Communist-influenced Camerounian nationalist guerrilla movement (UPC) in 1955-60 period.

L29 HODGKIN, THOMAS L. *Nationalism in Colonial Africa.* London: Muller, 1956; N.Y.: New York University Press, 1957. 216 p. A serious study of African nationalism by a British writer and lecturer on African affairs, comparing different European colonial policies in the area and examining life in African cities, political parties and pressure groupings, trade unions, religious sects, etc. While Communism is not emphasized, this is a useful work for background information on African politics.

L29A HOLDSWORTH, MARY. *Soviet African Studies and Theories of Nation Building as Applied to Emergent Countries.* Oxford: St. Antony's College, 1959. 20 p. An excellent detailed discussion of Soviet Africanists and their work in recent years. Notes differences between the more academic historians and linguists working in Leningrad under the influence of D. A. Olderogge and the more politically minded social scientists working under I. I. Potekhin in Moscow. Discusses Soviet Africanist's rejection of Western estimates on the number of separate languages in Africa and notes their growing interest in the role played by Christianity, Islam and pagan religions in African political developments. [A]

L30 HOLDSWORTH, MARY. "African Studies in the USSR," Part I in *West Africa* (London), February 8, 1958, p. 129. Part II in *West Africa*, February 15, 1958, p. 151. Holdsworth, of the Institute of Commonwealth Studies, Oxford, is the leading British authority on Soviet African research.

L31 *International Press Correspondence.* English version of the Comintern weekly publication *Internationale Press Korrespondenz.* Published in Vienna and elsewhere, 1921–. Title changed in 1938 to *World News and Views.* Contains news items on activities of African Communists in the 1920's and early 1930's and their speeches and writings, especially in connection with the Brussels Congress of 1927 and various Comintern congresses.

L32 ITALIAANDER, ROLF. *Die neuen Männer Afrikas; ihr Leben, ihre Taten, ihre Ziele.* Düsseldorf: Econ-Verlag, 1960. 427 p. English ed., *The New Leaders of Africa.* Englewood Cliffs, N.J.: Prentice-Hall, 1961. 301 p. Biographical sketches of 29 political leaders, discussing their relations with the Communists and the Soviet bloc. The author is a Dutch professor of history who has travelled widely, particularly in French Africa. Based on public statements by the African leaders and personal interviews. [B]

L33 KARTUN, DEREK. *Africa! Africa! A Continent Rises to its Feet.* N.Y.: International Publishers, 1954. 99 p. An example of the Communist line during the Cold War period, attacking African bourgeois nationalists, such as Nkrumah of Ghana, and praising radical groups, such as the Mau-Mau movement. Kartun is a foreign correspondent for the London *Daily Worker.*

L34 KITCHEN, HELEN. "Trade Unions: Communist Stronghold," *Africa Special Report*, IV, no. 1 (January 1959), p. 10-12. Discusses Communist and non-Communist factions in the Sudanese labor movement. This issue of *Africa Special Report* is devoted entirely to the Sudan. Helen Kitchen, editor of this journal, has spent considerable time in Egypt and the Sudan and is a journalist and research specialist on the area.

L35 KOMMUNISTICHESKAIA AKADEMIIA, INSTITUT MIROVOI KHOZIASTVA I MIROVOI POLITIKI. *Kolonialnye problemy.* Ed. by Evgenii Varga and others. Sbornik 3-4. Moscow: Partizdat, 1935. A collection of articles on political and economic conditions in the colonial and semi-colonial world by leading Communist specialists on the "national question." Zusmanovich and Potekhin discuss the "national revolutionary movement and the proletariat" in South Africa, attacking "bourgeois reformists" and "white chauvinists" in the South African Communist Party. An early example of political writing on Africa by Potekhin, the dean of Soviet Africanists.

L36 LAQUEUR, WALTER Z. "Communism and Nationalism in Tropical Africa," *Foreign Affairs*, vol. 39, no. 4 (July 1961), p. 610-

21. A discussion of the spread of Soviet bloc influences in Black Africa through the radical nationalist political parties, which are affiliated with international Communism and infiltrated by Communists to varying degrees. The author is a recognized authority on Soviet relations with African and Middle Eastern countries. [A]

L36A LESSING, PIETER. *Africa's Red Harvest.* N.Y.: John Day, 1963. A South African journalist describes the successes of the Communists in penetrating African youth groups, women's organizations, trade unions, the press, and the universities. Contains many errors.

L37 MARCUM, JOHN. *The Challenge of Africa.* N.Y.: "The New Leader," 1960. 43 p. Surveys recent political developments in Africa and discusses Soviet attempts to influence African affairs through diplomatic overtures, economic ties, and an all-out propaganda offensive. Marcum, a political science professor at Lincoln University, has lived and travelled extensively in Africa.

L38 *The Negro Worker.* Hamburg, Germany, and elsewhere, published irregularly, 1928-1937 by the International Trade Union Committee of Negro Workers. Contains speeches and writings of all leading Negro and African Communists of this period and also many articles by "bourgeois" African nationalists. The most complete holdings are at Howard University in Washington and the New York Public Library.

L39 *New Africa.* Published in New York by the Council on African Affairs during World War II and for several years afterwards. The pro-Communist Council split in 1950 along ideological lines, with W. E. DuBois and others supporting the Communists openly.

L40 PADMORE, GEORGE. *The Life and Struggles of Negro Toilers.* London: Red International of Labour Unions, 1931. 47 p. Russian ed., *Negry pod gnetom imperializma.* Moscow: Moskovskii rabochii, 1931. 47 p. An early example of Padmore's rabid anti-colonialism, written while a member of the Communist movement. A West Indian Negro intellectual of professional, middleclass background, graduate of Fisk and Howard Universities, George Padmore (1903-59) was concerned with Soviet-African relations, first as a supporter, then as an opponent, of the USSR's African ambitions, from the 1920's until his death.

L41 PADMORE, GEORGE. "An Open Letter to Earl Browder." *Crisis* (organ of the National Association for the Advancement of Colored People). Vol. XLII (October 1935), p. 302. Gives Padmore's explanation of his break with the Communist Party. He charges that the Soviets curtailed the Comintern's anti-imperialist activities in order to curry favor with the British government. For the Communist side of the controversy, see *The Negro Worker* (Copenhagen), vol. IV (June 1934).

L42 PADMORE, GEORGE. *Pan-Africanism or Communism?; the Coming Struggle for Africa.* London: Dobson; N.Y.: Roy, 1956. 463 p. Padmore's last and most mature work, based on personal reminiscences and the author's broad knowledge of African history. Attacks Communism, both as an international movement and as a social, economic, and political system, and propounds the thesis that Pan-Africanism, which mixes democratic socialism with philosophical humanism, is the only alternative to Communism in Africa. Traces historical development of African nationalism and recounts personal experiences in the Communist movement. Padmore's crucial role in Soviet-African relations gives importance to all his writings, but especially to this, his most objective work. [A]

L43 PADMORE, GEORGE, and PIZER, DOROTHY. *How Russia Transformed Her Colonial Empire; a Challenge to the Imperialist Powers.* London: Dennis Dobson, 1946. 185 p. Expresses continued admiration for Russian racial attitudes and Soviet treatment of nationalities even after Padmore's break with international Communism.

L43A PFEFFER, KARL HEINZ. "Afrika in Sowetischer Sicht," *Ost Europa*, VII, no. 2 (February 1957), p. 109-116. An excellent article on Soviet African studies. Reviews the Soviet Africanists' basic work, *Narody Afriki*, published in 1954. [B]

L44 POTEKHIN, I. I. "Formation des nations au sud du Sahara." *Présence Africaine.* No. 17 (Dec. 1957-Jan. 1958), p. 60-73. An article by a leading Soviet Africanist explaining Communist attitudes towards colonial borders in Africa, accusing European colonialism of interrupting African national development in the 19th century, dividing ethnic groups in order to dominate the area, etc. *Présence Africaine* is a leftist periodical published in Paris.

L45 POTEKHIN, I. I., ed. *Rasovaia diskriminatsiia v stranakh Afriki.* Moscow: Izd. vost. lit., 1960. 256 p. A polemic against race discrimination in Africa. Contains articles by leading Soviet Africanists and some non-Soviet critics of South African and Portuguese racial policies. Potekhin is the leading Soviet authority on African affairs and is in charge of the Academy of Science's African Institute.

L46 RECORD, WILSON. *The Negro and the Communist Party.* Chapel Hill: U. of North Carolina, 1951. 340 p. An historical survey of Communist attempts to subvert Negro political pressure groups in the United States, such as the NAACP. Also traces Comintern policies towards Negroes in the West Indies and Africa. Based on the author's Ph.D. dissertation.

L47 SEGAL, RONALD, ed. *Political Africa; a Who's Who of Personalities and Parties.* N.Y.: Praeger, 1961. 475 p. An excellent source.

A compilation of difficult-to-find information on contemporary figures and groups in African politics, with British Africa receiving the best coverage. Segal also edits the liberal South African magazine *Africa South*, published since 1960 in exile in London.

L48 TEDESCHI, PIERO (Pero Tedeski). *Il Risveglio dell'Africa.* Rome: Edizioni di cultura sociale, 1951. 149 p. Russian ed., Moscow: Izd. inostrannoi lit., 1952. The author follows the Stalinist line of the period and is distinctly anti-American. A standard account of the division of Africa by imperialists, some description of current "liberation movements," and very little emphasis on Communist Party efforts.

L49 U.S. LIBRARY OF CONGRESS, GENERAL REFERENCE AND BIBLIOGRAPHY DIVISION. *Africa South of the Sahara; A Selected and Annotated List of Writings, 1951-56.* Comp. by Helen F. Conover. Washington: 1957. 269 p. An excellent bibliography of recent sources on African affairs, arranged by regions and countries. Russian language sources are for the most part not included.

L50 U.S. LIBRARY OF CONGRESS, GENERAL REFERENCE AND BIBLIOGRAPHY DIVISION. *North and Northeast Africa; A Selected and Annotated List of Writings, 1951-57.* Comp. by Helen F. Conover. Washington: 1957. 182 p. A bibliography of sources on North Africa, Egypt, the Sudan, Ethiopia and the Somalis.

L51 VELTMAN, MIKHAIL L. (Pavlovich, M., pseud.) *Mirovaia voina i borba za razdel chernogo kontinenta; monopolisticheskii kapitalizm.* Moscow: 1918. 112 p. An early example of Soviet interest in Africa, by a leading Soviet theorist on the colonial question.

L52 WEAVER, HAROLD D., JR. "Red Carpet Rolls out for Africans," *Africa Report*, IV (October 1960), p. 7-9. A firsthand account of visits to Moscow by Haile Selassie of Ethiopia, a Guinean official delegation and other African groups. Based on the writer's personal experiences in Moscow in the summer of 1959. Weaver is a graduate student at New York University and is preparing a doctoral dissertation on "Soviet-African Relations, 1953-60."

L52A WODDIS, JACK. *Africa: The Roots of Revolt.* London: Lawrence & Wishart, 1960. 285 p.

L53 ZUSMANOVICH, A. *Prinuditelnyi trud i profdvizhenie v negritianskoi Afrike.* Moscow: Profizdat, 1933. 179 p. An early example of Soviet African research, surveying contemporary political and economic developments in West Africa, Congo, Kenya, and South Africa. Attacks "bourgeois reformists" and "white chauvinists" and follows the militant anti-imperialist line adopted at the Sixth Comintern Congress, 1928.

3. SOUTH AFRICA

L54 *The African Communist.* Clandestine publication of the illegal South African Communist Party, formerly published in Cape Town, but since 1961 published in London. Written by Communists for Communists, it is the only African periodical dealing with African affairs in an orthodox Leninist spirit.

L55 CARTER, GWENDOLEN M. *The Politics of Inequality: South Africa Since 1948.* N.Y.: Praeger, 1958. 535 p. A detailed study of contemporary politics in the Union of South Africa by a leading American scholar in the field of foreign affairs and comparative government. Discusses Communist activities in South Africa, the Suppression of Communism Act, front organizations and the press, etc. Dr. Carter is a professor at Smith College.

L56 *Fighting Talk, A Journal for Democrats.* Johannesburg. Monthly. Edited by the well-known Communist Ruth First, this periodical has a circulation of about 4,000. It was formerly the official organ of the leftist veterans' organization, the Springbok Legion.

L57 IASTREBOVA, I. P. *Iuzhno-afrikanskii Soiuz posle vtoroi mirovoi voiny.* Moscow: Izd. Akad. nauk SSSR, 1952. 206 p. An example of Soviet research on Africa. Designed to provide the Soviet reader with general background information on the social structure and economy of South Africa as seen from the Soviet point of view.

L58 MUNGER, EDWIN S. *Communist Activity in South Africa.* N.Y.: American Universities Field Staff, 1958. 42 p. A first-hand report from the Union of South Africa by a leading American Africanist who traces the development of South African Communism in considerable detail from its founding in the 1920's to its current front organizations, such as the Congress of Democrats and its component Congresses (African, Coloured, Indian, Trade Union, etc.). Also discusses Communist personalities, publications, the Suppression of Communism Act of 1950-51, and the Treason Trial, all on the basis of personal interviews and observations. [A]

L59 *The New Age.* Johannesburg and Cape Town. A Communist weekly newspaper, successor to *The Guardian* since 1952. The best original source of information on Communist-front activities in South Africa, this periodical had a circulation of about 30,000 and a readership many times that number before it was finally suppressed in 1960-61.

L60 ROUX, EDWARD. *S. P. Bunting: A Political Biography.* Cape Town: African Bookman, 1944. A study of one of the founders of the Communist Party of the Union of South Africa.

L61 ROUX, EDWARD. *Time Longer than Rope; A History of the Black Man's Struggle for Freedom in South Africa.* London: Gollancz, 1948. 398 p. A scholarly study of Bantu-European relations from the 18th century to 1946. Contains a detailed account of the personalities and intrigues that make up the history of South African Communism. Dr. Roux, a professor at Witwatersrand University, was a leading member of the Communist Party before his expulsion in 1933 as a "White Chauvinist" for his opposition to the Comintern line adopted in 1928.

L62 SAMPSON, ANTHONY. *The Treason Cage; the Opposition on Trial in South Africa.* London: Heinemann, 1958. 242 p. An intimate personal account of the South African Treason Case, written "from the African point of view" by a liberal British journalist who visited South Africa in 1957-58 to interview the suspects. Contains interesting profiles of key personalities in the Congress movement and discusses Communist influence in the movement. Appendix gives a useful bibliography on the history of the African National Congress, the text of the controversial Freedom Charter, and brief biographical sketches of the 156 suspects arrested in December, 1956, under the Suppression of Communism Act of 1950-51.

4. WEST AFRICA

L63 AJAO, ADEROGBA. *On the Tiger's Back.* N.Y.: World, 1962. 149 p. The story of a Nigerian merchant who became converted to Communism while in East Germany in 1952, who was trained to be a Communist operative in Africa, but who came to the conclusion that the Communists were not interested in Nigeria except as it could serve Soviet ends.

L63A BIRD, CHRISTOPHER. "A Soviet Anthropologist Visits Ghana," *Africa Special Report*, III (March 1958), p. 10. Formerly of the University of Hawaii, Bird is currently an independent researcher in Washington, D.C.

L64 BLANCHET, ANDRÉ. *L'itinéraire des partis africains depuis Bamako.* Paris: Plon, 1958. 209 p. A general discussion of political parties in French Africa since 1946, by a French war correspondent. Describes the brief affiliation of the RDA (*Rassemblement Démocratique Africaine*) with the French Communist Party and the Communist-oriented UPC in French Cameroun. [A]

L65 BOCHKAREV, IU. *Gvineia segodnia.* Moscow: Gospolitizdat, 1961.

L66 COLEMAN, JAMES S. *Nigeria: Background to Nationalism.* Berkeley: U. of California, 1958. 510 p. A comprehensive study of Nigerian history with particular emphasis on the nationalist movement since World War I and a brief discussion of Communist activity in Nigeria in the early 1930's. Coleman is a professor in the University of California and a leading American Africanist and student of underdeveloped areas.

L67 DIOP, MAJHEMOUT. *Contribution à l'étude des problèms politiques en Afrique noire.* Paris: Présence Africaine, 1958. 267 p. A major theoretical work by a Senegalese Communist leader of the Communist-front *Parti Africain de l'Indépendance.* Surveys the history of imperialism in Africa in general and in West Africa in particular; examines post-1945 political developments, the *Rassemblement Démocratique Africaine* in French Africa, etc.; analyzes from the Communist viewpoint the social forces in contemporary West African society. Useful bibliography of Communist and nationalist books and periodicals. [A]

L68 FRENCH UNION, ASSEMBLÉE. *Annales, Session de 1950 du 10 janvier au 27 juin.* Paris: Imprimerie des journeaux officiels, 1952. Vol. I. Debates on Communist infiltration of the *Rassemblement Démocratique Africaine*, the leading African political party in French Africa. Includes speeches before the French Union Assembly by African and Communist members.

L68A GAVRILOV, N. I. *Gvineiskaia Respublika.* Moscow: Izd. vost. lit., 1960. 138 p. A popular survey of socio-economic and political conditions in contemporary Guinea from the Soviet point of view. The author is a leading Soviet Africanist and a specialist on French West Africa.

L68B GAVRILOV, N. I. *Zapadnaia Afrika pod gnetom Frantsii (1945-1959).* Moscow: Izd. vost. lit., 1961. 208 p. The recent history of French West Africa from the Soviet viewpoint. Includes socio-economic data and trade statistics. Discusses Communist activity in the area, Communist infiltration of the *Rassemblement Démocratique Africaine* (RDA) in the 1948-50 period, and the Soviet position on Guinea, etc. Gavrilov is a leading Soviet Africanist who specializes on French West African affairs.

L69 GOOD, ROBERT C. "Sekou Touré's Guinea—Tyranny or Puritanism?" *Africa Report,* IV, no. 10 (October 1960), p. 5-7. Describes Guinea's social revolution under the Touré regime and surveys the growth of Communist influence in the country through diplomatic, economic and cultural activities, warning, however, against the use of such familiar labels as "Communist" and "Western-orientated" in discussing developments in Guinea. Good is a research associate of the Washington Center of Foreign Policy Research. This article is based on one which originally appeared in *The New Republic.*

L70 *La Lutte*. Dakar, 1957–. Organ of the Communist-oriented *Parti Africain de l'Indépendance* (P.A.I.).

L71 ORESTOV, O. *V respublike Gana.* Moscow: Gospolitizdat, 1961.

L72 PRIBYTKOVSKII, L. N. *Nigeriia v borbe za nezavisimost.* Moscow: Izd. vost. lit., 1961. 192 p.

L73 SKOROV, GEORGII E. *Frantsuzskii imperializm v Zapadnoi Afrike.* Moscow: Gospolitizdat, 1956. 223 p. Primarily economic in nature, this study emphasizes the increasing role of U.S. capital in Africa.

L74 THOMPSON, VIRGINIA M. and ADLOFF, RICHARD. *French West Africa.* Stanford, Cal.: Stanford University Press, 1957; London: Allen and Unwin, 1958. 626 p. A comprehensive and scholarly survey of French West Africa. Part One treats the political scene, Part Two the economy, and Part Three social and cultural developments. Discusses Communist infiltration of the *Rassemblement Démocratique Africaine* and Communist activity among African students in Paris. Excellent bibliography and reference footnotes. The authors carried on research in West Africa and France in 1953. [A]

5. NORTHEAST, EAST, AND CENTRAL AFRICA

L75 AKADEMIIA NAUK, INSTITUT MIROVOGO KHOZIAISTVA I MIROVOI POLITIKI. *Abissinskaia avantiura italianskogo fashizma.* Moscow: Izd. Akademii nauk, 1936. 223 p. Typical of the many Soviet writings on the Italo-Ethiopian conflict in this period. Emphasizes increased rivalry and international tension among imperialist powers over the Ethiopian question.

L76 DIOP, MAJHEMOUT. *Contributions à l'étude des problèmes politiques en Afrique noire.* Paris: Présence Africaine, 1958. 267 p. A discussion of contemporary African political developments in Marxist terms by one of French Africa's leading Marxist theoreticians. Diop is leader of Senegal's Communist-oriented Parti Africain de l'Independance (P.A.I.). [A]

L77 FAWZI, SAAD ED DIN. *The Labor Movement in the Sudan, 1946-1955.* London: Oxford, 1957. 175 p. One of the best sources on the Sudanese labor movement, in which there has been considerable Communist influence. [B]

L78 FRANCK, THOMAS M. *Race and Nationalism: The Struggle for Power in Rhodesia-Nyasaland.* N.Y.: Fordham Univ. Press, 1960. 369 p. A scholarly study of recent political developments and their background in the British Central African Federation of Rhodesia and Nyasaland. Discusses African "Marxists" in the African National Congress movement, their attitude towards the USSR and China, and the recent Soviet bloc interests in Africa.

L78A IUDIN, IU. A. *Federatsiia Rodezii i Niasalenda—novaia forma kolonialnogo upravleniia.* Moscow: Gosiurizdat, 1960. 102 p. An example of popular oriented Soviet African research. Discusses the political structure and socio-economic conditions in the Federation of the Rhodesias and Nyasaland from the Soviet point of view.

L79 KANNER, L., comp. *Voina v Vostochnoi Afrike.* Leningrad: Lenoblizdat, 1936. 201 p. An example of the prolific Soviet writing on East Africa at the time of the Italo-Ethiopian conflict, designed to provide general background information on an area little known to the average Soviet citizen at the time. The emphasis in this literature is more on the evils of Fascism than of colonialism.

L80 KHAZANOV, A. M. *Somaliiskaia respublika.* Moscow: Izd. vost. lit., 1961. 147 p.

L80A KISELEV, V. I. *Put Sudana k nezavisimosti* Moscow: Izd. vost. lit., 1958. 188 p. A Soviet history of the Sudan. Surveys historical developments and socio-economic and political conditions in the former Anglo-Egyptian condominium from the late 19th century down to its emergence in 1956 as an independent republic. Documented with Western, Arabic and Russian language sources.

L81 MARTYNOV, V. A. *Kongo pod gnetom imperializma; sotsialno-ekonomicheskie problemy belgiiskoi kolonii.* Moscow: Izd. vost. lit., 1959. 234 p. An example of the 1957-60 crash program of Soviet research on Black Africa.

L82 NEPOMNIASHCHII, K., and others, comps. *Patris Lumumba.* Moscow: Izd. soiuza zhurnalistov SSSR, 1961. 207 p.

L83 *Soviet Press Bulletin.* Addis Ababa. Weekly and irregularly. Published by the Soviet Embassy in Addis Ababa, Ethiopia. A mimeographed news and propaganda sheet in English, with Amharic as well as English title, which has been published since about 1956.

L84 VOBLIKOV, D. R. *Efiopiia v borbe za sokhranenie nezavisimosti.* Moscow: Sotsekgiz, 1961.

6. NORTH AFRICA

(Edited by Jack R. Perry)

a. BIBLIOGRAPHIES

L85 "Bibliografiia o Marokko," *Mezhdunarodnaia Letopis*, Moscow, no. 6-7 (June-July 1925), p. 127-135. Same issue has "Dokumenty XX veka o Marokko," p. 78-95. The bibliography lists books on all phases of Moroccan life, although most books listed are on diplomatic relations, primarily in Western European languages, and most articles are on contemporary events such as the Rif War.

L86 RIVLIN, BENJAMIN. "A Selective Survey of the Literature in the Social Sciences and Related Fields on Modern North Africa," *American Political Science Review*, September, 1954, p. 826-848. A broad and useful selection, by an American professor with considerable experience in North Africa.

L87 U.S. LIBRARY OF CONGRESS, GENERAL REFERENCE AND BIBLIOGRAPHY DIVISION. *North and Northeast Africa; a selected annotated list of writings; 1951-1957*. Comp. by Helen F. Conover. Washington: G.P.O., 1957. 182 p.

b. GENERAL WORKS

L88 AKADEMIIA NAUK SSSR, INSTITUT MIROVOGO KHOZIAISTVA I MIROVOI POLITIKE. *Borba za severo-vostochnuiu Afriku; materialy i karty*. Moscow: Sotsekgiz, 1936. 86 p.

L89 AKADEMIIA NAUK SSSR, INSTITUT VOSTOKOVEDENIIA. *Araby v borbe za nezavisimost*. Ed. by L. N. Vatolina and E. A. Beliaev. Moscow: Gospolitizdat, 1957. 414 p. An important collection with an introductory article by Vatolina that plays up Soviet support for Arab countries. Emphasizes the role of the working class, of which the Communist Parties of the several countries are the leaders, and plays down the role of the national bourgeosie. Claims direct influence of the Russian Revolution on the Rif War and other rebellions in Egypt, Syria, Lebanon, and Palestine. [A]

L90 AL-FASI, ALAL, *The Independence Movements in Arab North Africa*. Translated from Arabic by H. Z. Nuseibeh. Washington: American Council of Learned Societies, 1954. 414 p. The author has been one of the foremost leaders of the nationalist movement in Morocco. His is the best history available in English of nationalist movements in Morocco, and to a lesser extent of Tunisia and Algeria, although written from the Arab point of view. Plays down the Communist role, but is valuable for the relationship of nationalism and Communism in North Africa. [B]

L91 *Alzhirskaia kommunisticheskaia partiia v voine za natsionalnuiu nezavisimost.* Moscow: Gospolitizdat, 1961.

L92 ASHFORD, DOUGLAS E. *Political Change in Morocco.* Princeton, N.J.: Princeton University Press, 1961. 432 p. A political scientific study of postwar politics in Morocco, with emphasis on problems arising in the post-independence period. Excellent source for Istiqlal and labor movement. Some discussion of the Communist Party of Morocco is included.

L93 *At-Talia.* Communist organ in Tunisia.

L94 AVAKOV, RACHIK M. *Frantsuzskii monopolisticheskii kapital v Severnoi Afrike.* Moscow: Akademiia nauk SSSR, 1958. 235 p. An example of the work of the 1957-1960 plan for Africa research in the USSR. A detailed, factual study from the Communist point of view of social and economic conditions in Algeria, Morocco, and Tunisia. Surveys the inter-war period, discussing the activity of the Communist Party in the 1920's and 1930's. The main emphasis is on post-1945 developments, the "national liberation movement," American and West German influences in the area and their rivalry with French economic interests, etc. [A]

L95 AVAKOV, RACHIK M. *Marokko.* Moscow: Gospolitizdat, 1957. 93 p. Typical of recent Soviet writing on Africa. A geographical and historical survey, with the main emphasis on post-1945 political developments. Attacks American influence in Moroccan affairs and emphasizes the role of the working class and of the Moroccan Communist Party in the independence movement. Stresses popular resentment over U.S. bases and supports Algeria against the French. [B]

L96 AVAKOV, R. M. *Marokko ot protektorata k nezavisimosti.* Moscow: Izd. vost. lit., 1961.

L97 AYACHE, ALBERT. *Le Maroc; bilan d'une colonisation.* Paris: Éditions Sociales, 1956. 361 p. A general history and description of Morocco, with a long chapter on the independence movement. Written from the Communist point of view (Ayache has also had articles in *Sovetskoe Vostokovedenie*), this is a valuable source of factual information. [A]

L98 BARATOV, E. G. *Marokko; sbornik statei i materialov.* Leningrad: "Kubuch," 1926. 128 p.

L99 BOGOMOLOV, G. V. *Sorok dnei v Severnoi Afrike.* Minsk: Izd. Akademii nauk Belorusskoi SSR, 1956. 125 p. A travel book, with some political commentary, based on the author's visit to North Africa in 1952 to attend the International Geological Congress in Algiers.

L100 BOURGUIBA, HABIB. *La Tunisie et la France; vingt-cinq ans de lutte pour une coopération libre.* Paris: Julliard, 1954. 456 p. A collection of articles and speeches. A helpful source for understanding political developments in Tunisia.

L101 BUKHALI (BOUHALI), LARBI. *Oktiabrskaia sotsialisticheskaia revoliutsiia i natsionalnoe dvizhenie v Alzhire.* Moscow: Gospolitizdat, 1957. 40 p. An editorial note identifies Bouhali (First Secretary of the Communist Party of Algeria) and says he wrote this work especially for Gospolitizdat. A most interesting statement that places praise for the Revolution alongside the frank admission that its influence reached Algeria by an indirect route, "primarily thanks to the French workers movement." The "colonialist outlook" within the PCF is discussed frankly along with the indoctrination of workers and students. Information on the nationalist movement in Algeria and the relationship of the Communist Party to it is included, although the work is vague on the early days of the PCF in Algeria. A good source. [B]

L102 DANDA, R. G. *Alzhir sbrasyvaet okovy.* Moscow: Sotsekgiz, 1961.

L103 DASHKEVICH, VIKTOR K. *Iz istorii natsionalno-osvoboditelnoi borby tunisskogo naroda.* Minsk: Izd. Belgosuniversiteta imeni V. I. Lenina, 1960. 169 p. An excellent example of the "new" Soviet scholarship. The book has 12 pages of footnotes, listing a variety of sources. Much of this detailed, factual study of Tunisian political history is drawn from Julien (below). Much attention is given to developments in the U.N. and the role of Neo-Destour is de-emphasized. An important study. [A]

L104 DATLIN, S. *Narody Tunisa, Alzhira, Marokko v borbe za nezavisimost.* Moscow: Gospolitizdat, 1953. 81 p. Short sketches of "national-liberation movements" in each country. Extremely anti-American, this work describes the need for united fronts, attacks Neo-Destour in Tunisia for collaboration with the French and presents a very interesting study of the Soviet attitude shortly after the death of Stalin. An interesting work for comparison with the Kitaigorodskii-Puretskii work of 1925 (below). [B]

L105 DORIOT, JACQUES. *Les Colonies et le communisme.* Paris: Éditions Montaigne, 1929. 156 p. Contains Doriot's speech in the Chamber of Deputies of December 3, 1928, with added material. Doriot, later a fascist and tool of the Germans, was one of the leaders of the French Communist Party in the 1920's.

L106 DORIOT, JACQUES. *Les Impérialistes et le Maroc*. Paris: Librairie de l'Humanité, 1925. 54 p. Contains Doriot's speech in the Chamber of Deputies on February 4, 1925.

L107 IVANOV, NIKOLAI A. *Sovremennyi Tunis*. Moscow: Izd. vost. lit., 1959. 132 p. A serious but not scholarly book without references or bibliography. This short history of Tunisia plays down Neo-Destour and Bourguiba's role in obtaining independence and covers political parties, with emphasis on Neo-Destour's organization. Contains a chapter on reforms and internal policy and stresses the need for North African unity. A useful source for the recent Soviet outlook, it is critical of Bourguiba's co-operation with France and points to the solution of the Algerian war as a necessary precondition for progress in Tunisia. [B]

L108 IVANOV, NIKOLAI A. *V borbe za nezavisimost; ocherk natsionalno-osvoboditelnogo dvizheniia tunisskogo naroda*. Moscow: Gospolitizdat, 1957. 110 p. More polemical and less scholarly than the author's *Sovremennyi Tunis*, this is a detailed study of political developments, concluding with an attack on the "Eisenhower Doctrine." More mention is made of Bourguiba than in the later work. [B]

L109 JEANSON, COLETTE and FRANCIS. *L'Algérie hors la loi*. Paris: Éditions du Seuil, 1955. 319 p. Russian ed., Moscow: Izd. inostrannoi lit., 1957. 358 p. A polemical work, written from the left point of view. Presents a short history, with primary attention to the 1947-54 period and especially to developments since 1954. [B]

L110 JULIEN, CHARLES ANDRÉ. *L'Afrique du Nord en marche; nationalismes musulmans et souveraineté française*. Paris: Julliard, 1952. 416 p. A scholarly study of the rise of Arab nationalism in North Africa in the inter-war period and down to 1952. The role of Communism in this development is objectively reported, but not emphasized. Representing the "enlightened" French attitude, Julien favors integration that will protect the interests of both European and Moslem communities. The author is a professor of history and geography at the Institut d'Études Islamiques in Paris and the author of many studies on French colonial history and the Maghreb. A useful annotated bibliography is included. [B]

L111 KITAIGORODSKII, P., and PURETSKII, B. *Alzhir, Tunis, Marokko v borbe za nezavisimost*. Moscow: Nauchnaia assots. vostokovedeniia pri TsIK SSSR, 1925. 102 p. The sections on Algeria and Tunisia by Kitaigorodskii are most interesting. Puretskii wrote the section on Morocco, which deals primarily with the diplomatic history of the Rif

War. Both authors give basic facts of population and political arrangements of the various countries, with emphasis on the "national-liberation movements." Includes interesting comments on early Communist activity in Algeria and Tunisia and the relationship to nationalist activity. This is a unique Soviet source in this regard, since most of the included information is to be found only in French writings. Available in Lenin Library, Moscow. [A]

L112 LACOURTURE, JEAN and SIMONE. *Le Maroc à l'épreuve.* Paris: Éditions du Seuil, 1958. 381 p. Discusses Communist activity in contemporary Morocco. [A]

L113 LEBEDEV, DMITRII A. *Respublika Rif; ocherki revoliutsionno-osvoboditelnoi borby 1921-1931 v Marokko.* Moscow: Sotsekizdat, 1931. 96 p. Traces the history of the Moorish chieftain Abdel Krim's unsuccessful uprisings against Spanish and French authorities in Morocco. Attacks Pan-Arabism along with European imperialism. Typical of Soviet writing on the colonial world in this period. [B]

L114 LUTSKAIA, NATALIA S. "Borba marokkanskogo naroda protiv ispanskikh i frantsuzskikh kolonizatorov (1921-1926)," in *Velikii Oktiabr i narody Vostoka; sbornik*, ed. by A. A. Guber. Moscow: Izd. vostochnoi lit., 1957, p. 358-68. A scholarly history of the Rif War, based on research that led to the author's *Respublika Rif.* Quotations from Western and Arabic sources. Emphasizes the importance of the Rif War, but does not stress the influence of the Russian Revolution on Morocco or mention Soviet aid.

L115 LUTSKAIA, NATALIA S. *Marokko vnov obretaet nezavisimost.* Moscow: Izd. vost. lit., 1958. 104 p. A short treatment of Moroccan history, the growth of the "national-liberation movement," and a detailed history of post-World War II political developments, stressing the Communist Party role. In describing independent Morocco, the author emphasizes the problems of foreign troops and enclaves, the role of foreign companies, and the threat from the Algerian war. A popular treatise. [B]

L116 LUTSKAIA, NATALIA S. *Respublika Rif.* Moscow: Izd. vost. lit., 1959. 212 p. A good example of post-Stalin Soviet scholarship. A well-documented study with references in Arabic as well as European languages and a seven-page bibliography. This detailed history of the Rif War plays up the conflict as the first big anti-colonialist war after 1917. [A]

L117 MOSCOW, INSTITUT MARKSA-ENGELSA-LENINA. *Programmnye dokumenty kommunisticheskikh partii Vostoka.* Ed. by L. Madiar, P. Mif, M. Orakhelashvili, and G. Safarov. Moscow: Partizdat, 1934. 294 p. Contains the text of the resolution, "Tasks of the Communists in the All-Arab National Movement," adopted at the Conference of the Communist Parties of Palestine and Syria in 1931, with several important statements on North Africa. This is translated in Ivar Spector, *The Soviet Union and the Muslim World.* [A]

L118 *La Nation.* 1958–. Communist Party newspaper in Morocco.

L119 NIKHAMIN, VLADIMIR P. *Mezhdunarodnye problemy sovremennoi Afriki.* Moscow: Izd. VPSh i AON pri TsK KPSS, 1960. 52 p. A study of current problems of Africa, primarily the new "divide and conquer" aims of the "imperialists" who no longer have the power to keep Africa in subjugation. The author points to the danger of artificial unions, such as the Rhodesian Federation, created to perpetuate white rule, which might be labeled "unite and rule" and speaks of the importance of new African nations.

L120 PERRY, JACK R. "The Soviet Union and French North Africa, 1917-1945." Certificate essay, Russian Institute, Columbia, 1958. 178 p.

L121 *Le Petit Matin.* French language organ of the Tunisian Communist Party.

L122 POSPELOVA, NATALIA G. *Alzhir; ekonomichesko-politicheskii ocherk.* Moscow: Sotsekizdat, 1959. 106 p.

L123 PURDUE, RICHARD B. "Communism and French North Africa; A Contemporary Report." Certificate essay, Russian Institute, Columbia, 1952. 95 p.

L124 RÉZETTE, ROBERT. *Les Partis politiques marocains.* Paris: Colin, 1955. 404 p. Written according to a plan that limits its accessibility, this volume is extremely useful, particularly on the organization of the Communist Party of Morocco. [A]

L125 SEBAG, PAUL. *Tunisie; essai de monographie.* Paris: Éditions Sociales, 1951. 237 p. Russian ed., Moscow: Izd. inostrannoi lit., 1953. 255 p. A detailed study of geography, economy, culture and politics in Tunisia, written from the Communist point of view (Sebag is a Communist teacher at the Lycée Carnot in Tunis, Bourguiba's alma mater). Chapter VIII covers the "national movement" and has useful information. Traces the movement from the last years of the 19th century and describes the trade union movement, emphasizing the correctness of the Communist Party line and pointing to the mistakes of Neo-Destour. Maintains that only the Communist Party knows the true meaning of and road to independence. A useful source. [A]

L126 SEMARD, P. *Marokko.* Hamburg: Hoym Nachf., 1925. Russian ed., Leningrad: 1925. French ed., Paris: Librairie de l'Humanité, 1926. An important source for the study of French Communist Party activity during the Rif War. Gives the background and history of the conflict from the Communist point of view, with a detailed account of the war and much material on the work of PCF and CGTU. An annex gives the text of various treaties, the letter from Marshal Lyautey to Pierre Lyautey, many resolutions and the letter of Abd el-Krim to Parliament. [A]

L127 TAILLARD, F. *Le Nationalisme marocain.* Paris: Les Éditions du Cerf, 1947. 206 p. Useful for quotations from sources of the Communist Party of Morocco.

L128 YATA, ALI. *Le Dossier d'un exilé.* Geneva: Cooperative d'imprimerie du Pre-Jerome, 1958. 133 p. Russian ed., Moscow: Izd. vostochnoi lit., 1959. 190 p. Letters, articles, etc. to and from Ali Yata, head of the Moroccan Communist Party during his period of exile. Although primarily arguments as to why Yata should be set free, this volume also contains quotations from Party resolutions as well as interesting information on Party activity and outlook in Morocco. [B]

Part III
Special Topics

M. Communist Ideology

EDITED BY ROBERT V. DANIELS

M1 BARGHOORN, FREDERICK C. *Soviet Russian Nationalism.* N.Y.: Oxford, 1956. 330 p. Historical and topical analysis of Soviet use of nationalist and patriotic propaganda themes by a Yale specialist on this area. Sees Communist anti-Westernism as a projection of messianic Great-Russian nationalism, deliberately cultivated by the government. Extensive detail from Soviet sources on the Russification of the non-Russian national minorities. [B]

M2 BAUER, RAYMOND A. *The New Man in Soviet Psychology.* Cambridge: Harvard, 1952. 229 p. A history of Soviet psychological thought, with emphasis on the 1920's and 1930's, by a Harvard psychologist. Good background on the general development of Soviet Marxism from the determinist to the voluntarist emphasis.

M3 BLACKSTOCK, PAUL W., and HOSELITZ, BERT F., eds. *The Russian Menace to Europe, by Karl Marx and Friedrich Engels: A Collection of Articles, Speeches, Letters, and News Dispatches.* Glencoe, Ill.: The Free Press, 1952. 288 p. A compilation of writings by Marx and Engels, 1848-94, dealing with the Slavs, the foreign policy of tsarist Russia, and the prospects of social development in Russia. Contains several violently anti-Russian statements by Marx which are not publicized in the USSR today.

M4 BLOOM, S. F. *A World of Nations; A Study of the National Implications in the Work of Karl Marx.* N.Y.: Columbia, 1941. 225 p. Argument by an American historian that Marx accepted the nation as a "substantial historical entity" independent of economic explanations. Emphasizes Marx's West-European bias and the limits to historical materialism. [B]

M5 BOBER, MANDELL M. *Karl Marx's Interpretation of History.* Cambridge: Harvard, 1927. 370 p. Rev. ed., 1948. 445 p. Careful analysis and critique of the chief historical concepts of Marx and Engels, by an American economist. Treats the material basis of history, the class struggle, the ideological element, and the analysis of capitalism. Weighs the contribution of the theory against its empirical and logical weaknesses.

M6 BOERSNER, DEMETRIO. *The Bolsheviks and the National and Colonial Question, 1917-28.* Geneva: Droz; Paris: Minard, 1957. 285 p. A detailed history of the development of Marxist and Communist ideas on colonial nationalism, by a member of the Graduate Institute of International Studies in Geneva. Emphasis on the conflicting left, right, and center lines proposed in the Communist International in the 1920's, the fluctuating applications of the line in China, and the decline of the original proletarian spirit. [B]

M6a BOLLNOW, H. and others. *Marxismusstudien.* 3 vols. Tubingen: Mohr, 1954, 1957, 1960 (Vols. 2 and 3 edited by I. Fetscher). Essays on the development and sources of Marx's thought, Kautsky and Bernstein, and the relation of Marxism to Leninism.

M7 BRANDT, CONRAD, SCHWARTZ, BENJAMIN, and FAIRBANK, JOHN K., eds. *A Documentary History of Chinese Communism.* Cambridge: Harvard, 1952. 552 p. (Russian Research Center Studies, no. 5.) Compilation by Harvard historians of the most important statements of the Chinese Communist leadership (usually in full) from 1922 to 1949. Introduction and commentary by the editors. Detailed chronology, glossary, and extensive bibliography. [B]

M7a BROWDER, EARL. *Marx and America: A Study of the Doctrine of Impoverishment.* N.Y.: Duell, Sloan, and Pearce, 1958. London: Gollancz, 1959. A critique of Marxism by the former head of the Communist Party, USA. Rejects the prospect of Marxist revolution in advanced countries like the United States.

M8 BRZEZINSKI, ZBIGNIEW. *Ideology and Power in Soviet Politics.* N.Y.: Praeger, 1962. 180 p. A collection of essays by a Columbia University political scientist on the totalitarian organization and doctrine of the Soviet regime. The essay "Communist Ideology and International Affairs" distinguishes unchanging "doctrine" and flexibly adjusted "ideology." Notes the weakening of ideological cohesiveness within the Communist bloc.

M9 BUKHARIN, NIKOLAI I. *Imperializm i nakoplenie kapitala.* Petrograd: 1917. English eds., *Imperialism and World Economy.* N.Y.: International Publishers; London: Lawrence, 1929. 173 p. French ed., Paris: Éditions Sociales Internationales, 1929. A Marxist analysis of imperialism as the inevitable outgrowth of finance capitalism, written in 1915 by the future Soviet ideologist. First published in Russia in 1917. Introduction by Lenin, whose *Imperialism, The Highest Stage of Capitalism,* was antedated and influenced by this book. [B]

M10 BUKHARIN, NIKOLAI I. *Teoriia istoricheskogo materializma; populiarnyi uchebnik marksistkoi sotsiologii.* Moscow: Gosizdat, c. 1921. English ed., *Historical Materialism; a System of Sociology.* N.Y.: International Publishers, 1925. 318 p. A serious attempt at presenting a systematic sociology, by the leading Soviet theoretician of the 1920's. Highly deterministic point of view, with emphasis on the concept of "equilibrium."

M11 BUKHARIN, NIKOLAI I. "The Theory of Permanent Revolution." Speech of December 13, 1924, published in symposium *Za Leninizm.* Moscow-Leningrad: 1925. Excerpts translated in R. V. Daniels, *A Documentary History of Communism.* A polemic against Trotsky, in the course of which Bukharin develops a theory of Soviet Russia leading a world-wide proletarian-peasant coalition against the Western powers.

M12 BUKHARIN, NIKOLAI I. and PREOBRAZHENSKII, E. *Azbuka kommunizma; populiarnoe obiasnenie programmy Rossiiskoi kommunisticheskoi partii bolshevikov.* Gomel: Gosizdat, 1921. 321 p. German ed., Petrograd: Kommunistische Internationale, 1923. 368 p. English ed., *The A B C of Communism.* London: Communist Party of Great Britain, 1922. 422 p. A general exposition of Marxist doctrine and Russian revolutionary policy by two leading Communist theoreticians of the time.

M13 BURNS, EMILE, ed. *A Handbook of Marxism.* N.Y.: Random House, 1935. 1087 p. Substantial excerpts from the basic writings of Marx, Engels, Lenin, and Stalin, together with the 1928 program of the Communist International. Edited by a British Communist.

M13A CALVEZ, JEAN-YVES. *La Pensée de Karl Marx.* Paris: Editions du Seuil, 1956. 664 p. A systematic analysis and critique of Marx's philosophy and social thought, by a French Jesuit philosopher. Stresses problems of alienation and the dialectic. Extensive bibliography.

M14 CARR, EDWARD HALLETT. *The Soviet Impact on the Western World.* N.Y.: Macmillan, 1947. 113 p. Essays, based on 1946 Oxford lectures, by a leading British historian of the Soviet Union and contemporary diplomacy. Stresses the challenge of Soviet forms of "democracy," economic planning, collectivist social purpose, sphere-of-interest politics, and belief in the mission of the proletariat.

M14A CHRISTOPHERSON, JENS A. "Utviklingen av Marxismen i Russland," *Tidskrift for Samfunnsforskning* (Oslo), no. 3, 1960. Analysis of Lenin's differences with Marx and the divergence of theory and practice under Stalin, by a University of Oslo political scientist.

M15 COLE, GEORGE D. H. *A History of Socialist Thought.* London: Macmillan, 1953-60. 5 vols. in 7 parts. A comprehensive history of all branches of the socialist movement, 1789-1939, by the great British Labour Party historian. Encyclopedic detail, especially on personalities and individual countries. Extensive bibliography in each volume. Volume 4 treats the Russian Revolution, the Soviet Communist controversies, the struggle of the Internationals, and the development of Chinese Communism. Vol. 5 includes the history of Communism in the 1930's. [A]

M16 COLE, GEORGE D. H. *What Marx Really Meant.* N.Y.: Knopf, 1934. 309 p. Revised ed., *The Meaning of Marxism.* London: Gollancz, 1948. 301 p. Interpretation of Marxism not as dogma but as a method of economic and political analysis; contends that Marxism is not fatalistic and depends on leadership for the realization of socialism; feels that Marxist revolution can be accomplished democratically.

M17 COLUMBIA UNIVERSITY, RUSSIAN INSTITUTE. *The Anti-Stalin Campaign and International Communism.* N.Y.: Columbia, 1956. 342 p. Contains text of Khrushchev's "secret speech" of February 1956, and statements concerning it by Communist leaders in Italy, France, Great Britain, and the United States, June-July, 1956.

M17A *Communist China 1955-1959: Policy Documents with Analysis.* Cambridge: Harvard University Press, 1962. Edited by an anonymous visiting fellow of the Center for International Affairs, Harvard University. Introduction by Robert R. Bowie and John K. Fairbank. Documents illustrating the shift to a more radical line in this period.

M18 *Communist Perspective; a Handbook of Communist Doctrinal Statements in the Original Russian and in English.* (Mimeographed; distributed by the External Research Staff, U.S. Department of State.) 678 p. Compilation of a large number of small excerpts from Soviet organs and writings of Lenin and Stalin, in both the original Russian and English translation, organized alphabetically by topic.

M18A COMPTON, BOYD, editor and translator. *Mao's China: Party Reform Documents, 1942-44.* Seattle: University of Washington Press, 1952, 278 p. Contains translations of the chief statements of Mao Tse-tung, Liu Shao-ch'i, and other Chinese Communist leaders, together with Central Committee resolutions and other documents, pertaining to party discipline and indoctrination during the period 1939-44.

M19 CORNFORTH, MAURICE. *Materialism and the Dialectical Method; Historical Materialism; Theory of Knowledge.* N.Y.: International Publishers, 1952, 1954, 1956. Orthodox exposition of Marxist-Leninist philosophy by a British Marxist.

M20 DALLIN, ALEXANDER, ed. *Soviet Conduct in World Affairs.* N.Y.: Columbia, 1960. 318 p. A useful collection of interpretative articles, with emphasis on the nature and role of ideology. Contributors include Daniel Bell, Carew Hunt, Barrington Moore, Nathan Leites, Michael Karpovich, Philip Mosely, Robert Tucker, George Kennan, Bertram Wolfe, Alex Inkeles, Henry Roberts, Marshall Shulman, Samuel Sharp, Richard Lowenthal, and George Morgan. [A]

M21 DANIELS, ROBERT V. *The Conscience of the Revolution: Communist Opposition in Soviet Russia.* Cambridge: Harvard, 1960.

526 p. A study of Soviet Communist factions by an American historian specializing on the Soviet period. Includes discussion of foreign policy issues by the various Communist factions, 1917-28, with emphasis on the issue of revolutionary war, 1917-18, and the theory of "socialism in one country," 1924-27.

M22 DANIELS, ROBERT V., ed. *A Documentary History of Communism.* N.Y.: Random House, 1960. 2 vols. in one, 321, 393 p. Compilation of excerpts from major statements by Communist leaders of all factions, Soviet and foreign, from 1894 to 1959. Introduction and explanatory notes by the editor. [B]

M23 DANIELS, ROBERT V. *The Nature of Communism.* N.Y.: Random House, 1962. 398 p. Analysis of the world-wide Communist movement in terms of the factors which have contributed to it: Marxist theory, revolution, Leninist party organization, power politics, Russian history, Westernization of the East, industrialization, totalitarianism, and quasi-religious faith. Bibliography. [A]

M23A DANIELS, ROBERT V. "What the Russians Mean," *Commentary*, October, 1962. Analysis of changes in the meaning and function of Communist doctrine with respect to Soviet foreign policy.

M24 *Diplomaticheskii slovar.* Ed. by A. Ia. Vyshinskii and S. A. Lozovskii. Moscow: Gospolitizdat, 1948-50. 2 vols. 2nd ed., ed. by A. A. Gromyko and others. 1960-. A Soviet reference work on international affairs, covering events, treaties, conferences, terms and biographies. Sharply hostile to Western "imperialism." [A]

M25 EASTMAN, MAX. *Marxism, Is It Science?* N.Y.: Norton, 1940. 394 p. A perceptive critique of Marxism-Leninism by the well-known American writer and former leftist.

M26 EASTMAN, MAX. *Stalin's Russia and the Crisis in Socialism.* N.Y.: Norton, 1940. 284 p. Treats the evolution of Soviet society away from its original revolutionary goals, and the revision of Marxism which this required. Rejects the Marxist revolution as a myth. [B]

M26A ENGELS, FRIEDRICH. *Herr Eugen Dührings Umwälzung der Wissenschaft: Philosophie. Politische Oekonomie. Sozialismus.* Leipzig: Genossenschaftsbuchdruckerei, 1878. English edition, *Anti-Dühring: Herr Eugen Dühring's Revolution in Science.* Moscow: Co-operative Publishing Society of Foreign Workers in the USSR, (c. 1935). Part III, chapters 1 and 2, republished as *Die Entwicklung des Sozialismus von der utopie zur Wissenschaft*, Hottingen-Zürich: Schweizerische genossenschaftsdruckerei, 1882. English editions, *Socialism, Utopian and Scientific.* London: Sonnenschein; N.Y.: Scribner's, 1892. Other editions in various languages. Engels' popularization of Marxian philosophy, in the form of a polemic against the German idealist Socialist Dühring.

M26B ENGELS, FRIEDRICH. *Die Ursprung der Familie, des Privateigentums, und des Staats*. Zürich, 1884. English edition, *The Origin of the Family, Private Property, and the State*. Chicago: Kerr, 1902. Other editions in various languages. Application of the researches of the American anthropologist Lewis H. Morgan, to develop a Marxist, class-struggle theory of social origins.

M27 FISHER, HAROLD H. *The Communist Revolution; An Outline of Strategy and Tactics*. Stanford, Cal.: Stanford University Press, 1955. 89 p. A brief summary of Marxist and Leninist doctrines and Stalinist tactics, by one of the earliest American leaders in the study of Soviet Russia. Emphasizes corruption of Communist ideals, commitment to totalitarian power, tactical successes and failures. [A]

M28 FISHER, MARGUERITE J. *Communist Doctrine and the Free World: The Ideology of Communism According to Marx, Engels, Lenin and Stalin*. Syracuse, N.Y.: Syracuse University Press, 1952. 284 p. Excerpts from Marx, Engels, Lenin, and Stalin, with critical commentary, in topical organization.

M28A FROMM, ERICH. *May Man Prevail? An Inquiry into the Facts and Fictions of Foreign Policy*. New York: Doubleday (Anchor), 1961. 252 p. Primarily a discussion of the aims and assumptions in Soviet foreign policy thinking, by a noted American psychoanalyst. Emphasizes bureaucratic behavior and the mythical character of Communist doctrine.

M29 GARLICK, GERALDINE S. "Communist Interpretations of the Causes of War." Ph.D. dissertation, U. of Iowa, 1955. Investigates the Communist claim that capitalism makes war inevitable and that its abolition would assure peace. Notes theoretical inconsistencies in Communist interpretation of actual diplomatic events.

M30 GOODMAN, ELLIOT R. *The Soviet Design for a World State*. Foreword by Philip E. Mosely. N.Y.: Columbia University Press, 1960. 512 p. Analysis of Marxist doctrine concerning nationalism and the world order, by an American political scientist. Sees Soviet identification of Marxian world socialism and Russian nationalism, pointing to a world state under Russian hegemony. [A]

M31 GURIAN, WALDEMAR. *Bolshevism: Theory and Practice*. London: Sheed and Ward, 1932. 402 p. Rev. and abbreviated ed., *Bolshevism: An Introduction to Soviet Communism*. Notre Dame, Ind.: University of Notre Dame Press, 1953. 189 p. Historical and doctrinal analysis of Communism as the totalitarian development of a secular religion. By late Notre Dame political scientist; Roman Catholic point of view. Includes fifty-page appendix of quotations from Lenin, Stalin, and Soviet organs, topically organized. [B]

M32 GURIAN, WALDEMAR, and others. *Soviet Imperialism: Its Origins and Tactics.* Notre Dame, Ind.: University of Notre Dame Press, 1953. 166 p. Symposium with articles by Gurian, Nicholas Timasheff, Michael Pap, Richard Pipes, Wiktor Weintraub, Ling Nai-jui, and Frederick Barghoorn. Emphasis on interconnection of Marxist ideology and Russian nationalism, with differences as to which is primary.

M33 HEIMANN, EDUARD. *Reason and Faith in Modern Society: Liberalism, Marxism and Democracy.* Middletown, Conn.: Wesleyan Univ., 1961. 342 p. A philosophical defense of individual freedom from a Christian Socialist point of view. Part II is devoted to a critique of Marxism and Communism as a secular faith in rationality, taken to the extreme of a "counterreligion."

M34 HEITMAN, SIDNEY. "Nikolai Bukharin's Theory of World Revolution." Ph.D. dissertation, Columbia, 1961. A revision of Bukharin's role in the history of Soviet Communism and a reinterpretation of certain events and figures in this history.

M35 HOOK, SIDNEY. *Marx and the Marxists; the Ambiguous Legacy.* Princeton, N.J.: Van Nostrand, 1955. 254 p. (Anvil paperback No. 7.) Half text and half readings by a well-known American philosopher and authority on Marx. Text presents a brief critical history of Marxism and Communist doctrine, including the pre- and post-revolutionary deviations. Readings include two dozen excerpts, mainly from Marx, Kautsky, Lenin, Trotsky, and Stalin. [B]

M36 HOOK, SIDNEY. *World Communism.* Princeton, N.J.: Van Nostrand, 1962. 256 p. (Anvil paperback No. 62.) Selections from a variety of illustrative Communist documents, grouped under doctrine and organization, practice, Communism in the USSR, Communism in the United States, and Communism in other countries.

M37 HUNT, ROBERT N. CAREW. *Marxism, Past and Present.* N.Y.: Macmillan, 1954. 180 p. Topical inquiry into problems of Marxist theory and its implications. Notes the significance of Marxian social and economic analysis, but maintains that Marxism as a radical faith is responsible for evils committed in its name by Communist practitioners of the theory.

M38 HUNT, ROBERT N. CAREW. *The Theory and Practice of Communism; An Introduction.* London: Bles, 1950; N.Y.: Macmillan,

1951. 231 p. Rev. and enl. ed., 1957. 286 p. A systematic exposition of Marxism, the history of European socialism to 1914, and the theory of Leninism-Stalinism, by a British foreign affairs specialist. Views Leninism as a practical application of relatively unchanged Marxist doctrine. Attention to "Socialism in One Country" and nationalism as problems of theoretical adjustment. Good bibliography. [A]

M39 JACOBS, DAN N., ed. *The New Communist Manifesto and Related Documents.* Evanston, Ill.: Row, Peterson, 1961. 218 p. Includes texts of the Declaration of 81 Communist Parties, Moscow, Dec. 1960; the original Communist Manifesto of Marx and Engels; Khrushchev's "secret speech" of 1956; Lenin's "Testament"; Mao Tse-tung's "Hundred Flowers" speech of 1957; Declaration of 12 Communist Parties, Moscow, Nov. 1957; and excerpts from Edvard Kardelj's *Socialism and War.* [A]

M40 KARDELJ, EDVARD. *Socijalizam i rat.* Belgrade: Kultura, 1960. 231 p. English ed., *Socialism and War.* Belgrade: 1960. 209 p. Treatise on socialism and war by the Vice-President of Yugoslavia, denouncing the fatalistic expectation of inevitable war by the Chinese as Trotskyist. Restates Yugoslav doctrine of the independent development of every socialist and capitalist country, but criticizes Chinese over-centralization and over-mobilization.

M41 KENNAN, GEORGE F. "The Sources of Soviet Conduct," *Foreign Affairs,* xxv (July 1947), p. 566-582. The famous "Mr. X" article by the then chief of the U.S. State Department Policy Planning Staff outlining a theory of Soviet expansionism and the possibility of "containment." [A]

M42 KHRUSHCHEV, NIKITA S. *For Victory in Peaceful Competition with Capitalism.* N.Y.: Dutton, 1960. 783 p. A collection of Khrushchev's speeches, interviews, and letters on foreign policy, 1958-59. Emphasizes coexistence and expectation of world acceptance of Communism. [B]

M43 KHRUSHCHEV, NIKITA S. *Mir bez oruzhiia—mir bez voin.* Vol. 1, *Ianvar-iiul 1959 g.,* 512 p. Vol. 2, *Avgust-dekabr 1959 g.,* 440 p. Moscow: Gospolitizdat, 1960. A collection of statements on international affairs, including the subject of disarmament.

M43A KHRUSHCHEV, NIKITA S. *O vneshei politike Sovetskogo Sojuza.* Moscow: Gospolitizdat, 1960. Articles and speeches.

M43B KHRUSHCHEV, NIKITA S. *Stroitelstvo kommunizma v SSSR.* 5 vols. Moscow: Gospolitizdat, 1962–. Articles and speeches, especially on the claimed "transition to Communism."

M43c KHRUSHCHEV, NIKITA S. *Vital Questions of the Development of the World Socialist System.* Moscow: Foreign Languages Publishing House, 1962. Articles and speeches.

M44 KHRUSHCHEV, NIKITA S. *Za prochnyi mir i mirnoe sosushchestvovanie.* Moscow: Gospolitizdat, 1958. 368 p. English ed., *Speeches and Interviews on World Problems.* Moscow: Foreign Languages Pub. House, 1958. 386 p. The Soviet leader expresses his well-known views on "peaceful coexistence."

M44a KOCH, HANS, and WIEBER, EUGEN, comps. *Theorie, Taktik, Technik des Weltkommunismus; eine Zitatensammlung von Marx bis Chruschtschow.* Pfaffenhofen/Ilm: Ilmgauverlag, 1959. 1172 p. A handy compilation of quotations from the major Communist leaders, classified under numerous rubrics.

M45 KOHN, HANS. *Pan-Slavism; Its History and Ideology.* Notre Dame, Ind.: University of Notre Dame Press, 1953. 356 p. German ed., Vienna: Herold, 1956. A history of the Pan-Slav movement by a leading authority on nationalism. Distinguishes Western and Russian-oriented Pan-Slavism, and views Soviet expansion after World War II as a triumph of East-Slavic messianism. [A]

M46 KOLAKOWSKI, LESZEK. "Responsibility and History," *Nowa Kultura*, Sept. 1957; English translation in *East Europe*, Dec. 1957, Feb. 1958, Mar. 1958, and in Edmund Stillman, ed., *Bitter Harvest; The Intellectual Revolt behind the Iron Curtain.* N.Y.: Praeger, 1959, p. 94-128. A searching re-examination and criticism of the deterministic approach to history as a justification for immoral action, by the outstanding representative of Polish "revisionist" Marxism.

M47 KOREY, WILLIAM. "Zinoviev on the Problem of World Revolution, 1919-1927." Ph.D. dissertation, Columbia, 1960. A study of the thinking of the first head of the Communist International, covering his pre-revolutionary views; his apocalyptic vision of 1919-20 and ideas on revolutionary war; recession of vision after 1921 and concern about "Thermidorean" danger to Russian socialism in the absence of world revolution. [B]

M47a KOSANOVIĆ, ILIJA. *Dijalektički materijalizam (Uvod u osnovna pitanja filozofije marksizma); Istoriski materijalizam (Uvod u osnova pitanja sociologije Marksizma).* Sarajevo: Veselin Masleša, 1956, 1957. Textbooks presenting the official Yugoslav positions on Marxist-Leninist philosophy and sociology.

M48 KUUSINEN, OTTO V., and others. *Osnovy Marksizma-leninizma.* Moscow: Gospolitizdat, 1959. 774 p. English ed., *Fundamentals of Marxism-Leninism.* Moscow: Foreign Languages Publishing House,

1961. 892 p. An official textbook of Community theory by a group of 25 authors, headed by the one-time Finnish Communist leader and CPSU Presidium member. Sections deal with Marxist-Leninist philosophy, the materialist interpretation of history, the economics of capitalism and imperialism, the theory and tactics of the international Communist movement (with emphasis on "democracy," "sovereignty," and "peace"), and the doctrine of the transition from capitalism to "socialism" and thence to "communism." [B]

M49 LANDAUER, CARL, and others. *European Socialism; A History of Ideas and Movements.* Berkeley and Los Angeles: U. of California, 1959. 2 vols., 1894 p. A detailed history of all the main socialist currents, from the French Revolution to 1933, by a University of California economist who was formerly a Social Democrat in Germany. Emphasis on Marx, the German Social-Democrats, the Russian Communists, and the socialist reaction to war and Fascism. Extensive notes and bibliography. [B]

M50 LEITES, NATHAN. *The Operational Code of the Politburo.* N.Y.: McGraw-Hill, 1951. 100 p. An attempt by a political scientist of the RAND Corporation to codify Soviet precepts of strategy and tactics. A summary of the conclusions in his *Study of Bolshevism.*

M51 LEITES, NATHAN. *A Study of Bolshevism.* Glencoe, Ill.: Free Press, 1953. 639 p. A massive effort to depict the Communist mentality by an assemblage of quotations from Lenin and Stalin and also from classical Russian literature, particularly dealing with ends and means of political action. Attempts to work in terms of depth psychology and national character. [A]

M52 LENIN, VLADIMIR I. *Imperialism; The Highest Stage of Capitalism.* N.Y.: International Publishers, 1933. 127 p. Written in 1916, Lenin's argument, following the British economist Hobson, that capitalism led inevitably to the imperialist contest for colonies and thus caused the World War then in progress. This remains the basis for the Communist view of capitalist states. [A]

M53 LENIN, VLADIMIR I. *"Left-Wing" Communism: An Infantile Disorder.* London: Communist Party of Great Britain, 1920; N.Y.: International Pub., 1934, 1940. 95 p. A polemic against left-wing purists in the Communist International, in which Lenin insists on the Russian model of discipline and dictatorship, but defends compromises where expedient.

M54 LENIN, VLADIMIR I. *O vneshnei politike Sovetskogo gosudarstva.* Moscow: Gospolitizdat, 1960. 592 p. A collection of Lenin's speeches and writings pertaining to foreign policy.

M55 LENIN, VLADIMIR I. *The Right of Nations to Self Determination.* N.Y.: International Publishers, 1951. 128 p. Written and first published early in 1914. Lenin's defense of the right of national minorities to secede from Russia, in opposition to the dogmatic internationalists. This standpoint defended on tactical grounds.

M56 LENIN, VLADIMIR I. *Selected Works.* N.Y.: International Pub.; London: Lawrence, 1936-39. 12 vols. Moscow: Foreign Languages Publishing House, 1950. 2 vols. in 4 parts. The 1950 edition includes most of Lenin's important writings, with the exception of his "Testament" and related documents which were not published in the Soviet Union until 1956. [A]

M57 LENIN, VLADIMIR I. *Sobranie sochinenii.* Moscow: 1920-27. 20 vols. 2nd ed., *Sochineniia.* Moscow-Leningrad: 1926-32. 30 vols. 3rd ed., Moscow: 1932-37. 30 vols. 4th ed., Moscow: 1941-50. 35 vols. 5th ed., Moscow: 1957-. German eds., Vienna: Verlag für Literatur und Politik, 1927-; Berlin: Dietz, 195-. French ed., Paris: Éditions sociales; Moscow: Éditions en langues étrangères, 1957-. 1st English ed., *Collected Works.* Only the following volumes were published: IV (2 parts), XVIII, XIX, XX (2 parts), XXI (2 parts), XXIII. N.Y.: International Pub., 1929-45. New English ed., based on 4th Russian ed., London: Lawrence & Wishart, 1960-. (to be 40 vols.) The most complete edition of Lenin's works published so far is the 4th Russian edition, but the 2nd and 3rd are vastly superior as far as notes are concerned. [A]

M58 LENIN, VLADIMIR I. *The State and Revolution.* N.Y.: International Publishers, 1932. 103 p. Written in August, 1917; Lenin's idealistic statement of political theory, emphasizing the destruction of all bureaucracy and the "withering-away" of the state. Remains the base point for Communist political rationalizations. [A]

M59 LENIN, VLADIMIR I. *What is to Be Done?* (Many editions in many languages; first published in Russian, *Chto delat?*, Stuttgart: 1902.) One of the most important of Lenin's writings. Contains his views on how the Bolshevik Party should be organized, which became dogma for all other Communist parties. [A]

M60 LERNER, WARREN. "Karl Radek on World Revolution." Ph.D. dissertation, Columbia, 1960. An account of Radek's theoretical and practical contribution to the international Communist movement; his view of the imminence of world revolution in 1917; his role in formulating Comintern tactics; his participation with the Trotsky opposition in attacking Stalin's "socialism in one country"; and his service under Stalin until he was purged in 1937.

M61 LICHTHEIM, GEORGE. *Marxism; An Historical and Critical Study*. N.Y.: Praeger, 1961. 412 p. An analysis of the development of Marx's thought as a synthesis of social analysis and moral protest, by a British authority on Marxism. Attributes deterministic evolutionism to Engels and the Western Marxists, while Lenin and the Russian Communists converted Marxism into the "ideology" of totalitarian development in a backward country. [A]

M61A LIU, SHAO-CH'I. "Lun Kung-ch'an-tang-yüan ti hsiu-yang" (On the Training of a Communist Party Member), in *Cheng-feng wen-hsien*. Kalgan: New China Book Co., 1946. English translation in Boyd Compton, *Mao's China* (q.v.). The first important statement on theoretical indoctrination and party discipline by the present Chairman of the Chinese People's Republic.

M62 LOWENTHAL, RICHARD. "Stalin and Ideology: The Revenge of the Superstructure," *Soviet Survey*, July-Sept. 1960, p. 31-37. An assessment, by a journalist specializing on Communist Bloc affairs, of Stalin's revision of Marxist fundamentals to fit the problems of socialism in a backward country. Sees some revival of world revolutionary theory by Khrushchev.

M63 LUKÁCS, GYÖRGY. *Az ész trónfosztása; az irracionalista filozófia kritikája*. Budapest: Akadémiai Kiadó, 1954. 696 p. German ed., *Die Zerstörung der Vernunft*. Berlin: Aufbau-Verlag, 1954. 689 p. A significant work on the ideological differences between Communism and Democracy. American-led Western politics is considered as the successor of German irrationalism which is sharply condemned by dialectical materialism. A characteristic link in the chain of Communist world propaganda to discredit U.S. leadership. [B]

M63A LUKÁCS, GYÖRGY. *Geschichte und Klassenbewusstsein*. Berlin: Malik Verlag, 1923. 342 p. Collection of essays written between 1919 and 1923 by a noted Hungarian Communist literary critic. Frankly modifies Marxism, to stress the role of leadership, consciousness, propaganda, and deliberate force as essential to the success of the revolution. Influential among Western Marxists, although Lukács was later forced to recant. [A]

M64 MACRAE, DONALD G. "The Bolshevik Ideology: The Intellectual and Emotional Factors in Communist Affiliation," *The Cambridge Journal*, Dec. 1951. Analysis of ethical, psychological, and quasi-religious aspects of Communist appeal to intellectuals, as need for atonement or authority, independently of the substance of doctrine.

M65 MAO, TSE-TUNG. *An Anthology of his Writings*. Edited by Anne Fremantle. N.Y.: New American Library, 1962. 300 p. A useful collection of excerpts from Mao's most important statements, 1926-57.

M65A MAO, TSE-TUNG. "Hsin-min-chu chu-i lun," in *Chinese Culture* (Yenan), 1940. English editions, *China's "New Democracy."* Bombay: Peoples Publishing House, 1944, 47 p. *On New Democracy.* Peking: Foreign Languages Press, 1960. Other editions in various languages. Mao's chief statement as an independent theorist on the coalition approach to the Communist revolution.

M65B MAO, TSE-TUNG. *Mao Tse-Tung hsuan chi.* Peking: 1952-1960. 4 vols. English eds.; *Selected Works.* London: Lawrence and Wishart; N.Y.: International, 1954-; Peking: Foreign Languages Press, 1961-. Russian ed.; Moscow: Izd. inostrannoi lit., 1952-. Selected writings by Mao covering the period 1926-49. The material emphasizes problems of Party organization and military strategy and tactics. To date, Mao's writings from 1926 through September 1949 have been edited and published in the current standard Chinese edition in four volumes, as follows: I (July 1952), II (August 1952), III (May 1953), and—following a notable delay—IV (September 1960). In April 1961, the Foreign Languages Press in Peking published the English translation (labeled vol. IV) identical in contents with the Chinese vol. IV, adding an announcement that English-language versions of Chinese vols. I, II, and III, are underway. When Peking publishes these translations, the current official Chinese and English versions will be available in uniform edition. Bibliographical confusion now arises because translations of the first *four* Chinese volumes have already been published outside China in *five* English-language volumes by International (N.Y.) and Lawrence and Wishart (London). [A]

M65C MAO, TSE-TUNG. *On the Protracted War.* Peking: Foreign Languages Press, 1954. On the strategy of guerrilla warfare, written in 1938. [B]

M66 MARCUSE, HERBERT. *Soviet Marxism, a Critical Analysis.* N.Y.: Columbia; London: Routledge and Kegan Paul, 1957. 271 p. An attempt at an "immanent critique," by a Brandeis University philosopher, accepting the validity of the Marxian categories as interpreted by the Soviet leaders, and trying to analyze the Soviet system in its own terms. Stresses adjustment to reality and national interest, and relationship of internal repression to external hostility.

M67 MARKERT, WERNER, ed. *Der Mensch im Kommunistischen System.* Tübingen: Mohr, 1957. 118 p. Essays on the development of Marxism and Leninism, by members of the Tübingen summer session faculty, 1956. Includes Markert, "Marxism and the Russian Heritage in the Soviet System"; I. Fetscher, "From Marx to Soviet Ideology"; W. Koch, "Lenin on Historical Law and Strategy." [A]

M68 MARX, KARL. *Das Kapital: Kritik der politischen oekonomie.* Marx's classic economic analysis of capitalism and its expected collapse. Vol. 1 (*Der Produktionsprocess des Kapitals*). Hamburg: Meissner, 1867; revised editions, 1872, 1883, 1890. Russian edition, *Kapital.* St. Petersburg: Poliakova, 1872. English edition, *Capital: a Critique of Political Economy* (translated from the 3rd German edition). London: Swan Sonnenschein, 1886; N.Y.: Appleton, 1889. Numerous editions in various other languages. Vol. 2 (*Der Cirkulationsprocess des Kapitals*). Hamburg: Meissner, 1885 (edited by Friedrich Engels after Marx's death); revised edition, 1893. Vol. 3 (*Der Gesammtprocess der kapitalistischen Produktion*). Hamburg: Meissner, 1894 (reconstructed by Engels from Marx's manuscripts and notes). 3-volume editions: (East) Berlin: Dietz, 1957. Russian edition, Moscow: Gospolitizdat, 1949. English editions, Chicago: Kerr, 1906, 1913, 1909. (Vol. 1 reprinted, N.Y.: The Modern Library, n.d.); Moscow: Foreign Languages Publishing House, 1954, 1957, 1959. Supplementary material to *Das Kapital* was reconstructed by Karl Kautsky from Marx's manuscripts and notes and published as *Theorien über den Mehrwert*, 3 vols., Stuttgart: Dietz, 1905-10. French edition, 8 vols., Paris: Costes, 1924-25. English translation of vol. 1 of French ed. published as Karl Marx, *A History of Economic Theories*, N.Y.: Langland, 1952. [A]

M69 MARX, KARL. *Die Klassenkämpfe in Frankreich.* Berlin: 1895. Originally published as a series of articles in the *Neue Rheinische Zeitung*, 1850. Marx's analysis of the revolutionary events of 1848-50 in France. The introduction to the 1895 edition by Engels is important for down-grading the necessity for violent revolution. English editions, *The Class Struggles in France, 1848-1850.* N.Y.: New York Labor News Co.; N.Y.: International Publishers, 1934. Other editions in various languages.

M70 MARX, KARL. *Selected Works of Karl Marx and Frederick Engels.* Moscow: For. Lang. Pub. House, 1950. 2 vols. (Various other editions.) Includes the most important historical and philosophical works of Marx and Engels. [B]

M71 MARX, KARL. *Selected Writings in Sociology and Social Philosophy.* Ed. by T. B. Bottomore and Maximilien Rubel. London: Watts, 1956. 268 p. Selections from a variety of Marx's works rearranged by the editors (a British sociologist and a leading French scholar of Marxism) in a topical presentation—method, pre-capitalist societies, capitalism, politics, future society. Extensive introduction by the editors.

M72 MARX, KARL, and ENGELS, FRIEDRICH. *Basic Writings on Politics and Philosophy.* Ed. by Lewis S. Feuer. Garden City, N.Y.: Doubleday, 1959. 497 p. The chief political statements of Marx and

Engels, in full or in excerpts, edited by a University of California philosopher. [B]

M72A MARX, KARL, and ENGELS, FRIEDRICH. *Historisch-kritische Gesamtausgabe: Werke, Schriften, Briefe.* Edited by D. Riazanov and V. Adoratsky. Frankfurt a/M; Berlin: Marx-Engels Verlag. Section One, Vols. 1-6, 1927-32. Section Three (Correspondence), Vols. 1-4, 1929-31. Section One, Vol. 7, and special Engels anniversary volume, Moscow: Marx-Engels Verlag, 1935. Second edition, *Werke*, Berlin: Dietz, 1956–. Russian ed., *Sochineniia.* Edited by D. Riazanov and V. Adoratsky. Vols. 1-16, 25-29 (correspondence). Moscow: Marx-Engels-Lenin Institute, 1929-48. Second edition, Moscow: Gospolitizdat, 1955—. The basic collection of Marx's and Engels' works; none of the editions yet complete. [A]

M72B MARX, KARL, and ENGELS, FRIEDRICH. *Manifesto of the Communist Party.* 1st German ed., London: 1848. French translation, Paris, 1848. First English translation by Helen Macfarlane in *Red Republican* (London), 1850. Authorized English translation by Samuel Moore, with preface by Engels. London: 1888. First Russian translation by Michael Bakunin in *Kolokol*, Geneva: c. 1863. Many subsequent editions in various languages. [A]

M72C MARZANI, CARL. *The Open Marxism of Antonio Gramsci.* N.Y.: Marzani and Munsell, 1957. Selections from the writings of the first leader of the Communist Party of Italy. Qualifies economic determinism and stresses the role of political and cultural factors in history.

M73 MAYO, HENRY B. *Introduction to Marxist Theory.* N.Y.: Oxford, 1960. 334 p. Rev. and abridged ed. of *Democracy and Marxism*, 1955. 364 p. Topical analysis with judicious criticism by a Canadian political scientist with a strongly avowed democratic bias. Particular attention to philosophy, theory of history, science, and religion. Good bibliography.

M74 MEHNERT, KLAUS. *Weltrevolution durch Weltgeschichte; die Geschichtslehre des Stalinismus.* Stuttgart: Deutsche Verlags-Anstalt, 1953. 92 p. English ed., *Stalin versus Marx.* London: Allen & Unwin, 1952. 128 p. A study of the evolution of Stalinist doctrine concerning Russian history, by the leading German authority on Soviet affairs. Emphasizes Stalin's repudiation of true Marxist internationalism, and the elevation of Russian nationalism into a guiding principle of Soviet history-writing, cultural policy, and foreign policy. [A]

M75 MEYER, ALFRED G. *Communism.* N.Y.: Random House, 1960. 217 p. A survey of the history and theory of Communism, with emphasis on changes due to Soviet interest in industrialization and national power, and present tensions within the movement. By a political scientist at Michigan State University. Useful bibliography. [A]

M76 MEYER, ALFRED G. *Leninism.* Cambridge: Harvard, 1957. 324 p. An analysis of Lenin's political theory and its development before and after the Revolution. Emphasis on the role of organization and revolutionary tactics. Includes chapters on nationalism and Russia's role (as "spark" and "base") in world revolution. [A]

M77 MEYER, ALFRED G. *Marxism: the Unity of Theory and Practice; a Critical Essay.* Cambridge: Harvard, 1954. 181 p. Spanish ed., Buenos Aires: Editorial Agora, 1957. Assesses Marxism as a system of social analysis, with emphasis on the historical development of contradictions in the theory. Treats the dialectic as an effort to comprehend the totality of society. Emphasizes the unique combination in Marxism of scientific analysis with revolutionary purpose and action, with the later sacrifice of one or the other by the Bolsheviks and revisionists respectively.

M77A MILLS, C. WRIGHT. *The Marxists.* N.Y.: Dell, 1962. 480 p. Exposition and critique of Marxism by an American sociologist. Interwoven with extensive excerpts from the writings of Marx, Engels, the Social Democrats, Lenin, Trotsky, Stalin, and the present Communist leaders. Emphasizes Communism's change to adapt to backward countries.

M78 MITRANY, DAVID. *Marx Against the Peasant; A Study in Social Dogmatism.* Chapel Hill, N.C.: U. of North Carolina, 1951; N.Y.: Collier Books, 1961. 320 p. A parallel history of the theory and practice of Marxism and of the East European populist movement, respecting the peasantry and the agrarian problem, by a British journalist and historian. Stresses Marx's dogmatic commitment to large-scale production as basis for Marxists' hostility to peasants in the West, but notes the paradox that Marxist victories in Russia and China were based mainly on manipulation of peasant discontent. Extensive notes. [B]

M79 MONNEROT, JULES. *Sociologie du communisme.* Paris: Gallimard, 1949. 510 p. English ed., *Sociology and Psychology of Communism.* Boston: Beacon; London: Allen and Unwin, 1953. 339 p. Analysis of Communism as a tyrannical secular religion, a "twentieth-century Islam," committed to the "campaign" as an end in itself. Emphasis on Russian-imposed discipline in the international Communist movement. By a French sociologist. [A]

M80 MONTGOMERY, ARTHUR. *Stalinismen.* Stockholm: Norstedt, 1953. 154 p. Analysis of Soviet ideology, by a leading Swedish economist. Emphasis on the continuing role of Marxism as guide in both domestic and foreign policy. Section on "war or peace" stresses efforts to undermine and divide capitalist countries. Extensive references to the Soviet press. [A]

M81 MOORE, BARRINGTON, JR. *Soviet Politics—the Dilemma of Power; The Role of Ideas in Social Change*. Cambridge: Harvard, 1950. 503 p. Historical analysis by a Harvard sociologist of the changes in Soviet program and doctrine under the pressure of circumstances. Emphasis on development of bureaucratic political and industrial system. Two chapters on foreign policy stress role of power politics and expediency as against pure ideology, and "the transformation of revolution from a goal into a technique." Wide use of Russian sources. Bibliography. [A]

M82 NIEMEYER, GERHART. *An Inquiry Into Soviet Mentality*. N.Y.: Praeger, 1956. 113 p. Argument by a Notre Dame political scientist that an irrational commitment to Marxist doctrine is the guiding force in Soviet foreign policy.

M82A NORDISK SEMINAR OM INTERNASJONAL POLITIKK. "Studiet av Sovjets utenriks-politikk." Tranberg, Norway, June 19-21, 1960. Published in the *Rundbrev* of the Norwegian Society for Soviet Studies, 1960, no. 4. Principal article by John Sanness, Director of the Norwegian Institute of International Affairs, with comments by other Scandinavian authorities. Emphasizes interaction of Communist doctrine and national power factors.

M83 PAGE, STANLEY W. *Lenin and World Revolution*. N.Y.: New York Univ., 1959. 252 p. History by an American professor of Lenin's ideas about revolution in Russia and internationally. Views Lenin's theory as a rationalization of his "compulsive need to dominate." Emphasis on changing tactical lines, the constant effort by Lenin to maintain control over the international movement, and idea of Russia leading Asia against the West. [A]

M84 PLAMENANTZ, JOHN P. *German Marxism and Russian Communism*. London and N.Y.: Longmans, Green, 1954. 356 p. Detailed exposition and critique of Marxist historical and political theory by a British political scientist, with emphasis on the transformation of Marxism by Lenin and his followers. Assesses Marxism as a significant social theory despite its points of vagueness and inconsistency. Evaluates Russian Communism as the deliberate use of force to transform society. Sees a decline of Communist doctrinal fervor in international affairs, in favor of practical advantage. [A]

M84A PLEKHANOV, GEORGII V. *Izbrannye filosofskie proizvedeniia*. 5 vols. Moscow: Gospolitizdat, 1956-58. English edition,

Selected Philosophical Works. Moscow: Foreign Languages Publishing House, 1960–. Theoretical works by the founder of Russian Marxism.

M84B PLEKHANOV, GEORGII V. (pseudonym, "N. Beltov"). *K voprosu o razvitii monisticheskogo vzgliada na istoriiu*. St. Petersburg: Skorokhodov, 1895. English editions, *In Defense of Materialism: The Development of the Monist View of History*. London: Lawrence and Wishart, 1947, 303 p. *The Development of the Monist View of History*. Moscow: Foreign Languages Publishing House, 1956, 410 p. Plekhanov's most influential book, setting forth the development of Marxist philosophy.

M84C PLEKHANOV, GEORGII V. *Sochineniia*. Vol. 1 (1878-1884), Geneva: Library of Scientific Socialism, 1905. Moscow: Gosizdat, 1923-27 (planned for 24 vols.; vols. 1-12, 15-16, 22-24 actually published).

M85 POSSONY, STEFAN T. *A Century of Conflict; Communist Techniques of World Revolution*. Chicago: Regnery, 1953. 439 p. Historical survey of Communist doctrine and tactics from Marx to the present, by a Georgetown University political scientist. Sees a planned and unchanging Marxist campaign against the West. [A]

M86 *Revizionizm—glavnaia opastnost; iz opyta borby kommunisticheskikh i rabochikh partii protiv sovremennogo revizionizma; sbornik statei*. Introductory article by D. Shevliagin. Moscow: Gospolitizdat, 1958. 468 p. A Soviet attack on contemporary "revisionism" in Communist theory.

M87 RUBEL, MAXIMILIEN. *Bibliographie des oeuvres de Karl Marx; avec en appendice un répertoire des oeuvres de Friedrich Engels*. Paris: Rivière, 1956. 272 p.

M88 SABINE, GEORGE H. *Marxism*. Ithaca, N.Y.: Cornell, 1958. 60 p. (The Telluride Lectures, 1957-58, at Cornell Univ.). Stimulating commentary by a noted American historian of political thought. Emphasizes problems of dogmatic belief in inevitability and the class struggle, and the "paradox of Marxism"—that it was converted by Lenin into a philosophy of deliberate revolution in scarcely industrialized countries. [A]

M88A SCHAPIRO, LEONARD, ed. *The USSR and the Future: An Analysis of the New Program of the CPSU*. N.Y. and London: Praeger (for the Institute for the Study of the USSR, Munich), 1963. 324 p. Essays on the background and implications of the 1961 Communist Party Program, mostly by British and émigré Russian scholars; edited by the leading British historian of the CPSU. Texts of the 1919 and 1961 party programs in appendix.

M89 SCHLESINGER, RUDOLF. *Marx: His Time and Ours*. London: Routledge and Kegan Paul, 1950. 440 p. An exposition of Marxist and Communist theory by a former German Communist now at the University of Glasgow. Makes an abstract defense of the Soviet regime while frankly criticizing Marx.

M90 SCHLESINGER, RUDOLF. *The Spirit of Post-War Russia; Soviet Ideology, 1917-1946*. London: Dobson, 1947. 187 p. Unvarnished but sympathetic account of the development of Soviet ideology and cultural policies. Frankly accepts authoritarianism and shift to more conservative social policies as necessary features of industrial socialism. [B]

M91 SCHULTZ, LOTHAR. "Die sowjetische Völkerrechtslehre," *Jahrbücher für Internationale Recht*, 1955, no. 5, p. 78-92. Discussion by Göttingen jurist of the main stages of development of the Soviet doctrine of international law, emphasizing the rejection of universal norms of the law in the 1920's and 1930's and their identification with the Soviet cause later on. [B]

M92 SOMERVILLE, JOHN. *Soviet Philosophy: A Study of Theory and Practice*. N.Y.: Philosophical Library, 1946. 269 p. A highly favorable view of Soviet philosophy by a professor at Hunter College in New York City.

M93 STALIN, IOSIF. *Dialectical and Historical Materialism*. N.Y.: International Publishers, 1939. 43 p. Originally published as a chapter in the official *History of the CPSU: Short Course*, 1938. Stalin's binding reformulation of the principles of Marxist-Leninist philosophy with emphasis on the role of the Party and doctrinal correctness.

M94 STALIN, IOSIF. *Economic Problems of Socialism in the USSR*. N.Y.: International Publishers, 1952. 91 p. Stalin's last theoretical pronouncement, emphasizing the likelihood of renewed imperialist rivalry among the major capitalist powers. [A]

M95 STALIN, IOSIF. *Marksizm i natsionalno-kolonialnyi vopros*. Moscow: Partizdat, 1934. English editions, *Marxism and the National and Colonial Question*, Moscow and Leningrad: Cooperative Publishing Society of Foreign Workers in the USSR; N.Y.: International Publishers, 1935. 304 p. Other editions in various languages. A collection of Stalin's speeches and articles, particularly on the national minorities in Russia. Includes Stalin's "Natsionalnyi vopros i marksizm," first published in *Prosveshchenie* (St. Petersburg), March-May 1913; published separately as *Marksizm i natsionalnyi vopros*, Gospolitizdat, 1946; later editions in various languages. This was Stalin's first essay as a theorist on the nationality question; it emphasizes cultural differences and their disappearance after the proletarian revolution.

M96 STALIN, IOSIF. *O Lenine i Leninizme.* Moscow: Gosizdat, 1924. Later Russian editions under the title, *Ob osnovakh leninizma.* English editions, *Theory and Practice of Leninism*, London: Communist Party of Great Britain, 1925; *The Foundations of Leninism; Lectures Delivered at the Sverdlov University in the Beginning of April, 1924.* London: Lawrence & Wishart, 1940. 112 p.; *Foundations of Leninism.* N.Y.: International Publishers, 1932. 128 p. Other editions in many languages. Republished in the various editions of Stalin's *Leninism* or *Problems of Leninism.* Stalin's principal effort to present a doctrinal code. Stresses the dictatorship of the proletariat; the role of party, theory, and discipline; the role of the peasantry and national liberation movements; international strategy and tactics.

M97 STALIN, IOSIF. *O Velikoi otechestvennoi voine Sovetskogo Soiuza.* Moscow, Ogiz, 1942 and later, expanded editions; complete edition, Moscow, Gospolitizdat, 1946. English edition, *The Great Patriotic War of the Soviet Union*, N.Y.: International Publishers, 1945, 167 p. Stalin's major wartime speeches, 1941-45, stressing cooperation with the Western Allies and national resistance to the Germans.

M98 STALIN, IOSIF. *Sochineniia.* Moscow: Gospolitizdat, 1949-51. English ed., *Works.* Moscow: For. Lang. Pub. House, 1953-55. 13 vols. The official edition of Stalin's works. Publication suspended after covering works through 1935. Early writings occasionally expurgated to eliminate embarrassing passages. [A]

M99 STALIN, IOSIF. *Voprosy leninizma.* Moscow, Gosizdat, 1929; later editions with partial substitutions of new material. Last (11th) Russian edition, Moscow: Gospolitizdat, 1940. English editions, *Leninism*, 2 vols., London: Allen and Unwin, 1928, 1933; *Problems of Leninism*, Moscow: Foreign Languages Publishing House, 1940, 667 p., revised edition, 1947. The official publications of Stalin's selected articles and speeches. (Not to be confused with Stalin's pamphlet, *K voprosam Leninizma*, Moscow: 1926; English edition, *Problems of Leninism*, N.Y., International Publishers, 1934, 95 p.) [A]

M100 STALIN, IOSIF. "Oktiabrskaia revoliutsiia i taktiki russkikh kommunistov." First published as preface to a collection of Stalin's writings of the year 1917, *Na putiakh k oktiabriu.* Moscow: Gosizdat, 1924. English translation, "The October Revolution and the Tactics of the Russian Communists," in the various editions of Stalin's *Leninism* and *Problems of Leninism.* A polemic against Trotsky's theory of "permanent revolution," first published in December 1924, in which Stalin develops the theory of "socialism in one country." [B]

M101 STARUSHENKO, G. B. *Printsip samoopredeleniia narodov i natsii vo vneshnei politike Sovetskogo gosudarstva.* Moscow: Izd. IMO,

1960. 191 p. A Soviet view of the principle of the self-determination of nations.

M102 STRAUSZ-HUPÉ, ROBERT, and others. *Protracted Conflict.* N.Y.: Harper, 1959. 203 p. Thesis by Univ. of Pennsylvania and Georgetown political scientists that Communism is a system of "conflict management," guided by ideology and committed to the goal of world domination. The title was taken from Mao Tse-Tung, to exemplify Communist tactics of wearing down opponents in long struggles of attrition. A Foreign Policy Research Institute book. [A]

M103 TOWSTER, JULIAN. "The Dogma of Communist Victory," *Current History*, Nov. 1959, p. 257-261. Sketch of the history of the doctrine of world revolution, by an American political scientist. Views world revolution as a declining social myth. [B]

M104 TRISKA, JAN F., ed. *Soviet Communism: Programs and Rules; Official Texts of 1919, 1952 (1956), 1961.* San Francisco: Chandler, 1962. 196 p. Contains the complete texts of the various Programs and Rules of the CPSU. [A]

M105 TROTSKII, LEV D. *The First Five Years of the Communist International.* N.Y.: Pioneer, 1945; London: New Park Publications, 1953. 2 vols. A full collection of Trotsky's writings on world affairs and the international Communist movement, 1919-22, based on volume XIII of the Russian edition of his collected works. [B]

M106 TROTSKII, LEV D. *Our Revolution; Essays on Working Class and International Revolution.* N.Y.: Holt, 1918. Abridged translation of Trotsky's *1905*, consisting principally of the essay, "Results and Prospects" (translated as "Prospects of a Labor Government"), in which Trotsky first expounded his theory of "permanent revolution." [A]

M106A TROTSKII, LEV D. *The Permanent Revolution.* English translation by Max Schachtman. N.Y.: Pioneer, 1931. Trotsky's defense of his international revolutionary theory, in reply to a pro-Stalin polemic by Karl Radek.

M107 TROTSKII, LEV D. *The Revolution Betrayed.* Garden City, N.Y.: Doubleday, 1937; N.Y.: Pioneer, 1945. 308 p. Trotsky's last major work, in which he attacks the "bureaucratic degeneration" of the USSR and the "Bonapartist" internal and foreign policies of Stalin.

M108 TROTSKII, LEV D. *Sochineniia.* Moscow: 1925-1927. Publication of Trotsky's collected works, planned for 23 volumes, but terminated when only partially complete. The following volumes appeared: 2, 3, 4, 6, 8, 9, 12, 13, 15, 17, 18, 20, 21. Vol. 13 on the Communist International has been translated into English as *The First*

Five Years of the Communist International. Vol. 17 deals with Soviet foreign relations.

M109 TROTSKII, LEV D. *The Third International After Lenin.* N.Y.: Pioneer, 1936. 357 p. The first (and to date the only) volume in a series of Trotsky's *Selected Works*, edited by Max Schachtman. Consists mainly of Trotsky's criticisms of Stalin's Comintern policy. [B]

M109A TUCKER, ROBERT C. *Philosophy and Myth in Karl Marx.* Cambridge, England: The University Press, 1961. 263 p. A study of the background and early development (to 1845) of Marx's philosophy, by an American political scientist. Emphasis on the moral problem of alienation as expressed in Marx's *Economic and Philosophical Manuscript* of 1844. Sees the Marxist program as a myth in the strict sense.

M110 ULAM, ADAM B. "Soviet Ideology and Soviet Foreign Policy," *World Politics*, XI (Jan. 1959), p. 153-172. Sees a Soviet need for an aggressive foreign policy to justify an ideology which is domestically meaningless but necessary to sustain the regime. [B]

M111 ULAM, ADAM B. *The Unfinished Revolution; An Essay on the Sources of Influence of Marxism and Communism.* N.Y.: Random House, 1960. 307 p. Inquiry by a Harvard professor of government into the problem of why movements inspired by Marxism have failed in the advanced societies where Marx had predicted success, and succeeded instead where the early phases of industrialization were in progress. Finds Marxism to be the "natural ideology" of early industrialization, which, however, is bound to change its aims from revolutionary to totalitarian immediately after coming to power. [A]

M112 U.S. CONGRESS, SENATE, COMMITTEE ON FOREIGN RELATIONS. *United States Foreign Policy*, Study No. 10, "Ideology and Foreign Affairs," Jan. 17, 1960. Prepared by the Center for International Affairs, Harvard University. Analysis of ideological factors of Communism and nationalism, with emphasis on 1) nationalism within the Communist bloc, and 2) Communist policy toward neutral states and nationalist movements. Presents ideology as a constant factor but notes prospect of "erosion." The principal author is Zbigniew Brzezinski, a professor at Columbia University. [A]

M113 U.S. DEPARTMENT OF STATE, BUREAU OF INTELLIGENCE AND RESEARCH. *Soviet World Outlook; a Handbook of Communist Statements.* Washington: 1959. (Dept. of State Publication 6836; 3rd revision of a compilation first published in 1950.) 247 p. Compilation (in English translation) of brief excerpts of Soviet doctrinal statements, mostly by Lenin, Stalin, and Khrushchev, organized alphabetically by topic.

M114 WETTER, GUSTAVO A. *Il Materialismo dialettico sovietico.* Torino: G. Einaudi, 1948. 431 p. German ed., Vienna: Herder, 1952. 647 p. English ed., *Dialectical Materialism; a Historical and Systematic Survey of Philosophy in the Soviet Union.* N.Y.: Praeger, 1958. 609 p. Detailed and objective appraisal of Soviet philosophy and its Marxist background, by a Jesuit authority on Russian philosophy. [B]

M115 WILSON, EDMUND. *To the Finland Station; A Study in the Writing and Acting of History.* N.Y.: Harcourt, 1940. 509 p. Garden City, N.Y.: Doubleday, 1953. 502 p. Biographical study of the early socialists and of Marx, Engels, Lenin, and Trotsky, by a noted American literary critic who sees an effort to achieve humanist values, in a context of dialectical mythology and stern efficiency.

M116 WINSLOW, EARLE M. *The Pattern of Imperialism; A Study in the Theories of Power.* N.Y.: Columbia, 1948. 278 p. History of the economic interpretation of imperialism, from the eighteenth century to the present, by an American economist. Emphasis on Hobson, Marx, and the neo-Marxists. Rejects a simple association of capitalism and imperialism; views the latter as a product of political immaturity and dictatorial perversion in either capitalism or socialism. [B]

M117 WITTFOGEL, KARL A. "The Marxist View of Russian Society and Revolution," *World Politics*, July 1960, p. 487-508. Summary of the views of a German ex-Marxist specialist on oriental history. Thesis that Marxism permits a multilinear view of history, and that one alternative is the development from "Asiatic society" to Communist totalitarianism in Russia and China. See also *Oriental Despotism*, by the same author (New Haven: Yale, 1957).

M118 ZINNER, PAUL E. "Ideological Bases of Soviet Foreign Policy," *World Politics*, IV (July 1952), p. 488-511. Analysis by an American specialist on East European Communism of the motivating factor of world revolutionary doctrine. Sees a trend toward identification of the revolution with Soviet power, and a future possibility of withering of revolutionary interest if the Soviet drive to encircle the West through Asia can be contained. [A]

M119 ZINOVIEV, GRIGORII E. *Leninizm.* Leningrad: Gosizdat, 1925. 400 p. Restatement of Marxist-Leninist theory by the then Chairman of the Communist International. Emphasizes problems of "state capitalism" in the USSR, and the dependence of the final victory of socialism upon international revolution. [B]

N. Communist Strategy and Tactics

EDITED BY ABRAHAM BRUMBERG

N1 ALMOND, GABRIEL A. *The Appeals of Communism.* Princeton, N.J.: Princeton University Press, 1954. 415 p. On the basis of interviews with 221 former CP members in the U.S., Britain, France, and Italy, a Princeton professor and his collaborators conclude that the appeal of Communism varies "from place to place, group to group, and time to time." The final chapter contains interesting observations on the nature of Communist strategy and tactics in a number of Western countries. [A]

N2 ANISIMOV, OLEG. *The Ultimate Weapon.* Chicago: Regnery, 1953. 163 p. Level-headed and often acute observations on the Soviet population's attitudes towards the regime and the West, as well as on prospects of liberalization of the Soviet system. The author advocates a Western policy grounded on an understanding of the mentality of the Soviet people. While written before Stalin's death, the book is still largely valid today. [A]

N3 BARGHOORN, FREDERICK C. *The Soviet Cultural Offensive; The Role of Cultural Diplomacy in Soviet Foreign Policy.* Princeton, N.J.: Princeton University Press, 1960. 353 p. A scholarly survey of "guided culture contact," offering a detailed analysis of the underlying goals and techniques employed by the post-Stalin leadership in its purportedly non-political relations with the outside world. The author, who teaches political science at Yale University, is in favor of an expansion of the cultural exchange program as being useful to the West in terms of information gained and of the steady impact on the mentality of peoples behind the Iron Curtain. [A]

N4 BOCHENSKI, JOSEPH M., and NIEMEYER, GERHART, eds. *Handbuch des Weltkommunismus.* Freiburg, Munich: Alber, 1958. 762 p. English ed., N.Y.: Praeger, 1962. Fifteen leading specialists present reliable information on Communist ideology, tactics, and strategy. Subjects include the structure of Communism; its philosophical, sociological, economic, and political doctrines; the Soviet methodology of conquest; art, science, and religion under Communism; and Soviet principles of law. Superb bibliography of 70 p. [A]

N5 BUDENZ, LOUIS F. *The Techniques of Communism.* Chicago: Regnery, 1954. 342 p. An analysis of Communist tactics among minority groups, labor union, intellectuals, and others, written largely on the basis of personal experience by a man who for many years had been Managing Editor of the American *Daily Worker.* A good deal of useful information mixed with rhetoric.

N6 BURNHAM, JAMES. *The Struggle for the World.* N.Y.: Day, 1947. 248 p. Much of what the author—a former Trotskyite—had to say about the nature, goals and strategy of the Communist movement was valid in the heyday of Stalinism; much is no longer applicable. The assumption that the "aims and methods" of fascists and Communists "are identical" is not proved. But the evidence is presented both vigorously and persuasively, and the aggressive counter-strategy proposed stemmed from the author's belief that the "world Communist conspiracy" poses a threat to the liberal and democratic values to which he subscribed when the book was written.

N7 CADWELL, ROY. *Communism in the Modern World.* Philadelphia: Dorrance, 1962. 251 p. The author, a Canadian lawyer, served in 1955-56 as legal advisor to the Canadian members of the Truce Commission in Vietnam, Laos and Cambodia. Instead of writing a book about these experiences, however, he has attempted a general survey of life in the USSR, Soviet foreign policy, and Communist strategy. The result, for all his good intentions, is rather amateurish.

N8 CARMAN, ERNEST D. *Soviet Imperialism; Russia's Drive Toward World Domination.* Washington: Public Affairs, 1950. 175 p. A well-documented survey of Soviet territorial aggrandizement between 1939 and 1949. Contains an intelligent discussion of Soviet techniques in pursuing, consolidating, and justifying their expansionist aims. [B]

N9 CROOK, WILFRED H. *Communism and the General Strike.* Hamden, Conn.: Shoe String Press, 1960. 483 p. Rather pedantic and heavy, this survey of Communist utilization of the general strike, written by a former professor of economics at Colgate University, nevertheless contains a good deal of factual information, both in the text and in the extensive bibliography.

N10 CROSSMAN, RICHARD H. S., ed. *The God That Failed; Six Studies in Communism.* N.Y.: Harper, 1950. London, 1950. 272 p. Eloquent contributions by Arthur Koestler, Richard Wright, Louis Fischer, Ignazio Silone, André Gide, and Stephen Spender, each one of whom had for a time been a convert to the Communist faith. The authors' experiences are described vividly, without bitterness or apologetics, in many cases with humor, and always with penetrating insight. [A]

N11 DANIELS, ROBERT V. *The Nature of Communism.* N.Y.: Random House, 1962. 398 p. Includes chapters on Marxist-Leninist-Stalinist theory, Communist revolutions, how Communist parties are organized, Communist strategy and tactics, the influence of Russia on the development of Communism, the appeals of Communism in the underdeveloped countries of Asia, the relation between Communism and the Industrial Revolution, Communism as totalitarianism, and Communism as a secular faith. By a professor at the University of Vermont. [A]

N12 FIEDLER, HEINZ. *Der Sowjetische Neutralitätsbegriff in Theorie und Praxis*. Cologne: Verlag für Politik und Wirtschaft, 1959. 301 p. An historical account of the Soviet concept of co-existence, with particular emphasis on the problem of national rights. The book also contains a good deal of information on the Soviet attitude towards disengagement in Europe.

N13 FISHER, HAROLD H. *The Communist Revolution; An Outline of Strategy and Tactics*. Stanford, Cal.: Stanford, 1955. 89 p. A succinct and useful introduction, in outline form, to the basic ideological tenets as well as the strategy and tactics of Communist totalitarianism, written from a liberal and uncompromisingly anti-Communist point of view. Of special value to beginner students. By one of the grand old men of Russian studies in the U.S.

N14 FRIEDL, BERTHOLD C. *Les Fondements théoriques de la guerre et de la paix en U.R.S.S.; suivi du cahier de Lénine sur Clausewitz*. Paris; Editions Médicis, 1945. 203 p. A blatantly uncritical examination of the "Soviet point of view on war and peace, as it has been expounded by the founders and leaders of the USSR." Of possible use as a reference to texts on early Communist military doctrine.

N15 GOODMAN, ELLIOT R. *The Soviet Design for a World State*. N.Y.: Columbia, 1960. 512 p. The conclusion that the Soviets aim at a totalitarian world state with Russian as the universal language is arrived at by the author through laborious exegesis of official texts and almost complete avoidance of political analysis. Some of the doctrinal interpretations are unsupported by evidence. Contains some valuable information on Marxist-Leninist theory. [B]

N16 GROSS, FELIKS. *The Seizure of Political Power in a Century of Revolutions*. N.Y.: Philosophical Library, 1958. 398 p. An examination by a former Polish socialist, now a professor at Brooklyn College, of revolutionary upheavals in Europe within the past century and a half. Primarily concerned with Communist strategy since World War II, the author bases many of his generalizations on Polish events. [B]

N17 GURIAN, WALDEMAR and others. *Soviet Imperialism; its Origins and Tactics; a Symposium*. Notre Dame, Ind.: Notre Dame, 1953. 166 p. A mixed bag containing contributions by Waldemar Gurian, N. S. Timasheff, Michael Pap, Richard Pipes, Wiktor Weintraub, Ling Nai-jin, and Frederick Barghoorn. Rather dated, but illuminating on Communist tactics employed in subjugating and ruling minority peoples.

N18 HAINES, CHARLES GROVE, ed. *The Threat of Soviet Imperialism.* Baltimore: Johns Hopkins, 1954. 402 p. Too topical to be of much lasting value, this collection of 40 papers examines different facets of Soviet aggression throughout the world. However, some of the more general essays (e.g., George Kennan's "The Soviet Union and the Non-Communist World in Historical Perspective") contain penetrating and still valid insights.

N19 HUSZAR, GEORGE B. DE. and others. *Soviet Power and Policy.* N.Y.: Cowell, 1955. 598 p. A somewhat uneven but generally sober and scholarly analysis of the Soviet power structure and domestic and foreign policies by a group of American professors. Each contribution also features a helpful bibliography. [B]

N20 KING-HALL, STEPHEN. *The Communist Conspiracy.* London: Constable; N.Y.: Macmillan, 1953. 239 p. An intransigently hostile but well-documented and penetrating survey of Soviet policies at home and abroad. The section on foreign policy, front organizations, and the Soviet "peace campaign" is particularly useful. [B]

N21 KINTNER, WILLIAM R. *The Front is Everywhere; Militant Communism in Action.* Norman: University of Oklahoma Press, 1950. 274 p. An attempt to analyze the organizational and strategic principles of Communism from an exclusively military point of view. As seen by the author, an American army officer, the Communist Party is monolithic, organized strictly along military lines, imbued with thoroughgoing discipline, and bent solely on seizure of power.

N22 LEITES, NATHAN C. *The Operational Code of the Politburo.* N.Y.: McGraw-Hill, 1951. 100 p. A distillation of the author's massive *A Study of Bolshevism*, offering its basic conclusions without most of the textual evidence. [A]

N23 LEITES, NATHAN C. *A Study of Bolshevism.* Glencoe, Ill.: Free Press, 1953. 639 p. An attempt to delineate what the author—a psychiatrically-oriented political scientist—considers to be the quintessential operative features of "the spirit of the Bolshevik elite" through a content analysis of the basic texts of Lenin and Stalin, as well as of representative works of Russian literature, whose values and attitudes the Bolsheviks both rejected and reflected. [A]

N24 LENS, SIDNEY. *The Counterfeit Revolution.* Boston: Beacon Press, 1952. 272 p. A journalistic account of Communist strategy and tactics. The author ascribes the appeal of Communism throughout the world to its "false mark of idealism" stemming from early revolutionary idealism, and sustained "by a brilliant set of teachings, including some for simulating religious fervor." Strongly (though not uncritically) pro-

Titoist, the author advocates a political offensive aimed at producing schisms within the Communist bloc and proving to the people of the world "that we can do what the Communists only promise to do."

N25 LIFTON, ROBERT J. *Thought Reform and the Psychology of Totalism; a Study of "Brain-washing" in China.* N.Y.: Norton, 1961. 510 pages. Interview data gathered by a psychiatrist in Hong Kong (1954-55) describing and analyzing experiences of 25 Westerners expelled from China after serving prison terms and of 15 Chinese refugees from Communism. Probes the cultural patterns underlying Peking's thought reform program: the modern totalitarian expression of the national genius of the Chinese in manipulating inter-personal relations.

N26 MALAPARTE, CURZIO. *Coup d'état, the technique of revolution.* N.Y.: Dutton, 1932. 251 p. Italian ed., Milan: Bompiani, 1948. A journalistic account of the techniques of seizure of power from Napoleon to the then "would-be-dictator"—Hitler. The author, a former Fascist, believed that Trotsky's tactics as organizer of the Bolshevik *coup d'état* later became "part of the revolutionary strategy of the Third International." The book contains a fairly accurate description of the Stalin-Trotsky feud—colored, however, by the author's conviction that Stalin's hatred of his rival was motivated principally by his anti-Semitic prejudices.

N27 MEERLOO, JOOST A. *The Rape of the Mind; the Psychology of Thought Control, Menticide, and Brainwashing.* N.Y.: World, 1956. 320 p. British ed., *Mental Seduction and Menticide*, London: 1956. A general discussion of "brainwashing" by a qualified psychiatrist who probes the phenomenon—primarily as regards the American prisoners of war during the Korean campaign—from a moral and political, rather than from a more exclusively scientific point of view.

N28 MONNEROT, JULES. *Sociologie du communisme.* Paris: Gallimard, 1949. 510 p. English ed., *Sociology and Psychology of Communism.* Boston: Beacon; London: Allen and Unwin, 1953. 339 p. Analysis of Communism as a tyrannical secular religion, a "twentieth-century Islam," committed to the "campaign" as an end in itself. The emphasis is on Russian-imposed discipline in the international Communist movement. By a French sociologist.

N29 PETERS, J. *The Communist Party; A Manual on Organization.* N.Y.: Workers Library, 1935. 127 p. An official Party publication, giving the basic principles of its program, organization, discipline, and strategy.

N30 POSSONY, STEFAN T. *A Century of Conflict; Communist Techniques of World Revolution.* Chicago: Regnery, 1953. 439 p. German ed., Munich, 1956. A depiction of the "nature of the (Communist) beast," stressing in particular the role of violence in Communist strategy. The latter is seen as brilliantly conceived in accordance with a "dialectical scheme," based on "elaborate studies in the humanities and social sciences," cunningly applied and skillfully executed. Many of the sources accepted by the author are of dubious authenticity.

N31 SARGANT, WILLIAM. *Battle for the Mind; A Physiology of Conversion and Brainwashing*. London: Hainemann; N.Y.: British Book Service, 1957. 248 p. A study by a noted British physiologist of the techniques employed in changing and/or implanting new beliefs in the human brain. While the bulk of the volume deals with religious experiences and practices, it has two chapters on "brain-washing" in Communist China and on extortions of confessions, with the factual information drawn from secondary sources.

N32 SCOTT, JOHN. *Political Warfare; A Guide to Competitive Coexistence*. N.Y.: Day, 1955. 256 p. A somewhat schematic yet readable compendium of information on the salient features of the Soviet political and economic system and a discussion of how the West can cope with the Soviet challenge without resorting to open war. Data drawn from author's personal experiences as an engineer in Russia in the 1930's, and from his close study of the USSR since then. [B]

N33 SELZNICK, PHILLIP. *The Organizational Weapon; A Study of Bolshevik Strategy and Tactics*. N.Y.: McGraw-Hill, 1952. 350 p. A valuable and comprehensive study—despite its gratuitously "academic" language—of the organization of the Communist ("combat") Party, its strategy and tactics. Based on an examination of Communist behavior throughout the world, rather than on the Soviet CP as such. The author, a sociologist, had personal experience with left-wing movements in the United States. [A]

N34 STRAUSZ-HUPE, ROBERT, and POSSONY, STEFAN T. *International Relations in the Age of the Conflict Between Democracy and Dictatorship*. N.Y.: McGraw-Hill, 1950. 947 p. A massive attempt to analyze Communist strategy and tactics against the background of political developments in the West since the Middle Ages. Each chapter contains a valuable bibliography. The authors advocate the political and economic integration of the West as the best way of safeguarding peace and stopping Communist expansionism. Some of the data, while useful in its own terms, is of questionable pertinence. [B]

N35 U.S. CONGRESS, HOUSE, COMMITTEE ON FOREIGN AFFAIRS. *The Strategy and Tactics of World Communism*. Washington: G.P.O., 1948. 428 p. Also published as: *Communism; Its Plans and Tactics*. Washington: Infantry Journal Press, 1949. 102 p. A generally sound introduction to the subject is followed by a very useful compilation of materials from Communist sources; the postwar period is particularly well represented. [A]

N36 U.S. CONGRESS, HOUSE, COMMITTEE ON UN-AMERICAN ACTIVITIES. *The Communist Conspiracy; Strategy and Tactics of World Communism.* Washington: G.P.O., 1956. 2 vols. Contains a great deal of valuable source material on the history and strategy of the Communist movement throughout the world. The introductions to the various sections, as well as the general preface, are of little use to the serious student of the subject.

N37 U.S. CONGRESS, HOUSE, COMMITTEE ON UN-AMERICAN ACTIVITIES. *Soviet Total War, "Historic Mission" of Violence and Deceit.* Washington: G.P.O., 1956. 2 vols. A compilation of about 50 articles on different aspects of the Communist "threat," which as a rule is identified with "liberalism," and which is treated—with a few exceptions—from a singularly parochial and uninformed point of view.

N38 WALSH, EDMUND A. *Total Empire; the Roots and Progress of World Communism.* Milwaukee: Bruce, 1951. 293 p. A passionate indictment of the Soviet system written by the late dean of American Catholic experts on Communism. Many secondary sources used are questionable. Factual errors are plentiful, but contains some interesting extracts from author's diary as a member of the American Relief Administration in Russia, 1921-23.

N39 WRIGGINS, WILLIAM HOWARD. "The Image of the Ideal Communist Militant as Depicted in Communist Party Publications." Ph.D. dissertation, Yale, 1953.

N40 YPSILON (pseud. of Karl Volk). *Pattern for World Revolution.* Chicago-N.Y.: Ziff-Davis, 1947. 479 p. A determinedly readable and breezy account of the fortunes of international Communism up to the immediate post-World War II period. While lacking in scholarly substance, it manages to give a vivid picture of Communist tactics all around the globe, and ends in a speculative chapter which predicts that the "Stalintern" will "ultimately end in the extinction of the Communist parties that compose it." By a former Comintern agent. [B]

Addendum

N41 KIRKPATRICK, JEANNE J., ed. *The Strategy of Deception; a Study in World-Wide Communist Tactics.* N.Y.: Farrar, Straus, 1963. 444 p.

O. Communist Propaganda

EDITED BY FREDERICK C. BARGHOORN

O1 BARGHOORN, FREDERICK C. *The Soviet Cultural Offensive.* Princeton, N.J.: Princeton University Press, 1960. 353 p. An historical, descriptive and analytical study of Soviet propaganda and other objectives in international exchanges of persons. Emphasis is on the period after the death of Stalin, but an attempt is made to demonstrate the essential continuity of Soviet behavior in this field throughout the history of the regime. The topics treated include Soviet organization and training for cultural diplomacy, controls over communication imposed by the Soviet totalitarian system and the application of Soviet exchanges of persons policy to the major political-cultural areas of the free world. There is also a chapter on the difficulties and the rewards of communicating with people under Soviet control, although the satellite area is not treated. [A]

O1A BARGHOORN, FREDERICK C. *Soviet Foreign Propaganda.* Princeton, N.J.: Princeton University Press, 1964. 342 p.

O2 BARGHOORN, FREDERICK C. *The Soviet Image of the United States; a Study in Distortion.* N.Y.: Harcourt, Brace, 1950. 297 p. Describes and analyzes major aspects of the image of the United States presented to the Soviet public before and during World War II and in the early postwar years. Interactions between the official Soviet image of America and Marxist-Leninist ideology, the Soviet political system, and the relations between the Soviet Union and other world powers are traced. Although the study deals mainly with the official Soviet communications media, particularly the press, considerable attention is devoted to unofficial Soviet opinion of the United States. [A]

O3 CANADA, ROYAL COMMISSION TO INVESTIGATE DISCLOSURES OF SECRET AND CONFIDENTIAL INFORMATION TO UNAUTHORIZED PERSONS. *The Report of the Royal Commission Appointed under Order in Council P.C. 411 of February 5, 1946 to Investigate the Facts Relating to and the Circumstances Surrounding the Communication, by Public Officials and Other Persons in Positions of Trust of Secret and Confidential Information to Agents of a Foreign Power. June 27, 1946.* Ottawa: E. Cloutier, 1946. 733 p. This official Canadian report deals mainly with the organization and operations of Soviet espionage in Canada but contains considerable material on the activities of "front organizations" set up for the dissemination of Soviet propaganda and the recruitment of Canadian citizens into communist-controlled groups.

O4 CANTRIL, HADLEY. *Soviet Leaders and Mastery over Man.* New Brunswick, N.J.: Rutgers, 1960. 173 p. This analysis of Soviet operating assumptions concerning the manipulation of opinion, beliefs and values contains much of value to students of Soviet propaganda.

O5 DAUGHERTY, WILLIAM E., and JANOWITZ, MORRIS. *A Psychological Warfare Casebook.* Baltimore: Johns Hopkins, 1958. 880 p. One of the most important of all American publications on propaganda and psychological warfare. Chapter x, entitled "Soviet Psychological Warfare," includes interpretive articles on the organization and techniques of Soviet foreign propaganda, as well as material on propaganda methods employed by several non-Russian Communist parties. Both in this chapter and to a limited degree in other chapters, there is valuable material on subjects collateral to Soviet propaganda. Topics treated include Communist use of mass media, subversive activities, and exchanges of persons. Activities directed at youth and exploitation of the peace theme are also the subjects of some of the studies included. Authors contributing material on communist propaganda include Harold D. Lasswell, Wilbur Schramm, John Scott, Allan Little, Louis Nemzer, Lucian W. Pye, and others. [A]

O6 DUNHAM, DONALD. *Kremlin Target: U.S.A., Conquest by Propaganda.* N.Y.: Ives Washburn, 1961. A former U.S. information officer in Europe gives his views on how Moscow is using propaganda to fight the U.S. and what we should do about it. Tends to exaggerate the effectiveness of Soviet propaganda.

O7 DYER, MURRAY. *The Weapon on the Wall.* Baltimore: Johns Hopkins, 1959. 269 p. Although concerned mainly with American policy, this study also deals to a considerable degree with Soviet propaganda strategy, especially with the relationship between Soviet propaganda and total Soviet foreign policy.

O8 EVANS, F. BOWEN, ed. *Worldwide Communist Propaganda Activities.* N.Y.: Macmillan, 1955. 222 p. This book, and the two similar works by Evron Kirkpatrick which followed the pattern established by it, were the first systematic efforts at a scholarly year-by-year analysis of international Communist propaganda. This first study in the series of three deals with the theory, organization, volume, themes, media and area aspects of Communist propaganda. The author had access to government material in compiling the work, which is exceptionally rich in factual data. A very valuable volume, even though it is more a compilation than an analysis. [A]

O9 INKELES, ALEX. *Public Opinion in Soviet Russia; A Study in Mass Persuasion.* Cambridge: Harvard, 1951. 379 p. Although concerned almost exclusively with domestic propaganda, and particularly with domestic oral agitation, this basic study is useful for the understanding of all phases of Soviet propaganda. [A]

O10 INTERNATIONAL PRESS INSTITUTE, ZURICH. *The Press in Authoritarian Countries.* London: Bailey Bros. and Swinfen, 1959. 201 p.

O11 KECSKEMETI, PAUL. "The Soviet Approach to International Political Communication," *Public Opinion Quarterly*, vol. 20, no. 1 (Spring 1956).

O12 KIRKPATRICK, EVRON M., ed. *Target: The World; Communist Propaganda Activities in 1955.* N.Y.: Macmillan, 1956. 362 p. This, the first of two such studies by Kirkpatrick, is similar to the work of Evans, published the year before. However, it is more detailed and because of increasing Communist activity during 1955 in exchanges of persons and travel by Soviet leaders to foreign countries, particularly in Asia, is somewhat different in emphasis. The work is a useful guide to aspects of Soviet "coexistence" propaganda in the year of the "spirit of Geneva." [A]

O13 KIRKPATRICK, EVRON M., ed. *Year of Crisis; Communist Propaganda Activities in 1956.* N.Y.: Macmillan, 1957. 414 p. Among the major themes of this volume are further development of the Communist cultural exchanges program and Communist adaptations to such major crises as the Hungarian and Polish uprisings and the Suez conflict. Like the volume dealing with 1955, this one contains a wealth of data on the organization and quantitative dimensions of Soviet and other Communist communications efforts. [A]

O13A KRUGLAK, THEODORE E. *The Two Faces of TASS.* Minneapolis: U. of Minnesota, 1962. 263 p. A useful study of the functioning of the international news agency of the Soviet Union, with special emphasis on its use as an instrument for propaganda and espionage. The author, the director of the American School in Leysin, Switzerland, forecasts the gradual evolution of TASS toward the more conventional Western agency.

O14 LABIN, SUZANNE. "The Technique of Soviet Propaganda." Washington, D.C.: Committee on the Judiciary, U.S. Senate, 86th Cong., 2nd Sess., 1960.

O15 LASSWELL, HAROLD D., and BLUMENSTOCK, DOROTHY. *World Revolutionary Propaganda; A Chicago Study.* N.Y.: Knopf, 1939. 393 p. This important study applies both psychiatric concepts and quantitative techniques to Communist propaganda in Chicago during the years 1930-35. Despite its relatively limited focus, it is valuable to contemporary students of Communist propaganda as a guide to the analysis of symbols and their effectiveness. [B]

O16 LASSWELL, HAROLD D., LEITES, NATHAN, and associates. *The Language of Politics: Studies in Quantitative Semantics*. N.Y.: George Stewart, 1949. 398 p. Much of this volume is concerned with techniques of content analysis but it includes an important paper by Lasswell and Sergius Yacobsen on May Day slogans in Soviet Russia, as well as papers on "The Third International on Its Changes of Policy" and "The Response of Communist Propaganda to Frustration." Besides the above authors, contributors included Ithiel de Sola Pool, Joseph M. Goldsen and others. [B]

O17 LENIN, VLADIMIR I., and STALIN, I. V. *Lenin and Stalin on Propaganda*. London: Lawrence & Wishart, 1942.

O18 MARTIN, L. JOHN. *International Propaganda; Its Legal and Diplomatic Control*. Minneapolis: U. of Minnesota; London: Oxford, 1958. 284 p. An historical and analytical study of efforts, by agreements, treaties and other methods to control propaganda among states. Material on Communist international propaganda is scattered throughout the topical chapters. The study comes to negative conclusions regarding the possibility of international legal control of propaganda.

O19 MAY, BENJAMIN M., JR. "Themes of Soviet War Propaganda, 1941-1945." Ph.D. dissertation, Yale, 1958.

O20 MEYER, FRANK S. *The Moulding of Communists*. N.Y.: Harcourt, Brace, 1961. 214 p. The second half of this study, dealing with the training of Communist Party members and directing cadres, contains information and interpretations pertinent to the study of Communist propaganda. Some of the illustrative material deals with particular international propaganda campaigns. [B]

O21 MÜNZENBERG, WILLI. *Propaganda als Waffe*. Paris: Carrefour, 1937. 281 p. A readable book of the talented Communist propagandist and organizer (stimulator of the anti-Nazi campaign and the "brown-book" after the burning of the Reichstag in 1933). Shortly after this book had been published, the author was expelled from the KPD, and was murdered in 1940.

O22 NELSON, WILLIAM, ed. *Out of the Crocodile's Mouth*. Washington: Public Affairs, 1949. 116 p. An interesting pioneer study of the propaganda implications of Soviet cartoons, with peripheral relevance to international relations.

O23 NEMZER, LOUIS. "The Structure of the Soviet Foreign Propaganda Organization." Ph.D. dissertation, U. of Chicago, 1948.

O24 PADOVER, SAUL K., and LASSWELL, H. D. *Psychological Warfare; The Strategy of Soviet Propaganda.* N.Y.: Foreign Policy Association, 1951. 62 p.

O25 POOL, ITHIEL DE SOLA, ed. *Studies in Political Communication.* Princeton, N.J.: Princeton University Press, 1958. 363 p. (*The Public Opinion Quarterly*, vol. 20, no. 1, Spring 1956.) Contains articles by Paul Kecskemeti and others on Soviet international propaganda.

O26 REISKY DE DUBNIC, VLADIMIR. *Communist Propaganda Methods; a Case Study on Czechoslovakia.* Intro. by Hans J. Morgenthau. N.Y.: Praeger, 1961. 287 p. This well-documented study treats the development of propaganda as totalitarianism's most original contribution to the art of government and examines the policies, methods, and effectiveness of this weapon in Communist Czechoslovakia. Concludes that dogmatism prevents Communist propaganda from being more effective.

O27 SCHRAMM, WILBUR. *The Process and Effects of Mass Communication.* Urbana, Ill.: U. of Illinois, 1954. 586 p. This volume contains several articles dealing indirectly or directly with Soviet propaganda, such as Harold D. Lasswell's "The Strategy of Soviet Propaganda."

O27A SHACKFORD, R. H. *The Truth About Soviet Lies.* Washington: Public Affairs, 1962. Deals with Soviet techniques for the dissemination of propaganda.

O28 SMITH, BRUCE L., and SMITH, CHITRA M. *International Communication and Political Opinion.* Princeton, N.J.: Princeton University Press, 1956. 325 p. A valuable bibliography, containing, among other things, numerous references to books and periodical articles on all aspects of Soviet and other Communist propaganda, including international propaganda.

O29 SOLSKI, WACLAW. "Soviet Propaganda in Action." Washington: National Committee for a Free Europe, 1953. 303 p. (typescript).

O30 WOOD, NEAL. *Communism and British Intellectuals.* London: Gollancz, 1959. 256 p. A study of the interactions between Communist ideology, propaganda and organization on the one hand and British intellectuals on the other, from about 1930 until 1957-58. Particularly interesting on the operations of Communist "fronts" in Britain, especially during the 1930's.

P. World Communism and the Communist Bloc

EDITED BY J. GREGORY OSWALD

NOTE: For additional titles on economic relations within the Communist bloc, see the section on "Soviet Foreign Economic Relations" and "Eastern Europe, Economic." For other related works see the sections on "Strategy and Tactics," "The Communist International," "Communist Front Organizations," and "Eastern Europe Since 1941."

P1 AKADEMIIA NAUK, INSTITUT FILOSOFII. *Sodruzhestvo stran sotsializma.* Ed. by F. T. Konstantinov and A. I. Arnoldov. Moscow: Izd-vo Akad. nauk SSSR, 1958. 337 p. Six authors treat as many topics: the influence of the Bolshevik revolution on human history and on the structure of the "People's Democracies," socialist legality, socialism in China, the cultural revolution in the "People's Democracies," and "proletarian internationalism."

P2 BALEK, A., HAVELKOVA, B., and TITERA, D. *Zeme socialisticke soustavy; statisticky prehled.* Prague: 1961. 229 p. A statistical survey of European and Asiatic Communist countries, including the USSR. Statistical data on post-1945 developments in industry, agriculture, construction, and transportation, as well as the standard of living and costs. A comparative analysis of pre-1945 and post-1945 conditions in the afore-mentioned fields.

P2A BLACK, CYRIL E., and THORNTON, THOMAS P., eds. *Communism and Revolution.* Princeton: Princeton University Press, 1964. 480 p. The theory and history of Communist revolutionary activity is reviewed by twelve specialists, with special reference to the rapid political, economic, and social change that the less developed countries have been undergoing since the Second World War. The conditions under which the Communists have been successful in the past are analyzed, and the circumstances under which new revolutionary efforts may be made are discussed. [A]

P3 BOCHENSKI, JOSEPH M., and NIEMEYER, GERHART, eds. *Handbuch des Weltkommunismus.* Freiburg, Munich: Alber, 1958. 762 p. English ed., *Handbook on Communism.* N.Y.: Praeger, 1962. Fifteen leading specialists present reliable information on Communist ideology, tactics, and strategy. Subjects include the structure of Communism; its philosophical, sociological, economic, and political doctrines; the Soviet methodology of conquest; art, science, and religion under Communism; and Soviet principles of law. Niemeyer is a professor of political science at Notre Dame University; Father Bochenski teaches at Freiburg University. Superb bibliography of 70 pages. [A]

P4 BORKENAU, FRANZ. *European Communism.* London: Faber & Faber; N.Y.: Harper, 1953. 564 p. German ed., *Der europäische Kommunismus; Seine Geschichte von 1917 bis zur Gegenwart.* Munich: Lehnen, 1952. 540 p. A detailed study of the 1930's and 1940's, with major attention to the French C.P. Based on primary sources, with much interesting speculation added. Not as sound on the whole as his earlier work, *World Communism.* [A]

P5 BORKENAU, FRANZ. *World Communism.* N.Y.: Norton, 1939. British ed., *The Communist International.* London: Faber & Faber, 1938. 442 p. Paperback ed., Ann Arbor: Univ. of Michigan Press, 1962. The standard history of the Communist International from its beginning to the Popular Front of the mid-1930's, by a former member of the German Communist Party. Indispensable and still unsuperseded. [A]

P6 BOUSCAREN, ANTHONY T. *Imperial Communism.* Washington: Public Affairs Press, 1953. 256 p. A work of uneven quality and depth of analysis which surveys the state of Communism in the world.

P7 BRASLAVSKII, I. *Istoriia mezhdunarodnogo rabochego dvizheniia (1864-1924).* Moscow: "Novaia Moskva," 1925. 284 p.

P8 BRZEZINSKI, ZBIGNIEW K. *The Soviet Bloc; Unity and Conflict.* Cambridge: Harvard, 1960. 470 p. Revised, paperback ed., N.Y.: Praeger, 1961. A full-length study of the development of political relations within the bloc, 1945-59, stressing the interactions of ideological preconceptions and practical power aims. Brzezinski is a professor in the Russian Institute at Columbia University. [A]

P9 BUTAKOV, D., BOCHKOVA, V., and SHEVEL, I. *Finansy stran narodnoi demokratii.* Moscow: Gosfinizdat, 1959. 344 p. Soviet authors examine the national and local budgets of the countries of the Communist bloc, drawing on official government statistics.

P10 BYSTROV, F. P., and others, eds. *Mezhdunarodnye raschety i valiutnye otnosheniia stran narodnoi demokratii.* Moscow: Vneshtorgizdat, 1956. 128 p. The authors of this professional, technical, analysis attempt to characterize international estimates and financing of foreign trade within the Communist-bloc trade groups. Documented.

P11 COLE, GEORGE D. H. *A History of Socialist Thought.* Vol. 4 (in 2 parts), *Communism and Social Democracy, 1914-1931.* Vol. 5, *Socialism and Fascism, 1931-1939.* London: Macmillan; N.Y.: St. Martin's, 1960. 350 p. The author was one of England's leading socialist intellectuals and Professor of Social and Political Theory at Oxford, 1944-57. Vol. 4 describes the splits and schisms in the socialist movement from World War I to the crystallization of the socialist movement into two rival internationals, and the issues and controversies that arose between them. Vol. 5 is a chronicle of what happened to the Communist and non-Communist labor movements in the Thirties. His accounts of the West European thinkers and movements, and of British socialism and laborism are among the best. A generally pedantic, authoritative, but non-analytic account. [B]

P12 COLUMBIA UNIVERSITY, RUSSIAN INSTITUTE. *The Anti-Stalin Campaign and International Communism; a Selection of Documents.* Foreword by Henry L. Roberts. N.Y.: Columbia, 1956. 342 p. Text of Khrushchev's secret speech to the Twentieth Party Congress and reactions to it from other Communist Parties through July 26, 1956. [B]

P13 COMMUNIST PARTY OF GREAT BRITAIN. *On People's Democracy in Eastern Europe and China; a Selection of Articles and Speeches.* London: The Communist Party, 1951. 51 p. Analyses by Hilary Minc, Georgi Dimitrov, Boleslaw Bierut, Matyas Rakosi, and Yu Huai of their countries' transition periods from the bourgeois to the Marxist system, stressing the importance of the influence of the Soviet Union.

P13A DALLIN, ALEXANDER, ed. *Diversity in International Communism: a Documentary Record, 1961-1963.* N.Y.: Columbia University Press, 1963. 867 p. A useful compilation providing the most important available documentation on the issues that have divided the international Communist movement since the 22nd Congress of the CPSU in October 1961. Has an introduction by Professors Dallin and Zbigniew Brzezinski of the Russian Institute at Columbia University. [A]

P14 EBON, MARTIN. *World Communism Today.* N.Y.: Whittlesey House, 1948. 536 p. A former writer for the Office of War Information and the State Department offers a useful, dispassionate, country-by-country reference work on the state and significance of Communist activity throughout the world. Now out of date. [B]

P14A FISCHER-GALATI, STEPHEN, ed. *Eastern Europe in the Sixties.* N.Y.: Praeger, 1963. 242 p. A symposium treatment of East European affairs, with emphasis on economic growth and political rifts in the Communist camp.

P15 IZVESTIIA. *Pod znamenem sotsializma.* Moscow: 1959. 631 p. A collection of the newspaper's special issues on the construction of Communism in the countries of Europe and Asia, excluding the USSR and Yugoslavia. The articles, arranged by countries and written by well-known native authors and politicians, deal with political, cultural, economic, and social aspects. [B]

P15A KANEVSKAIA, T. M., ed. *Mirovaia sotsialisticheskaia sistema khoziaistva.* Moscow: Gospolitizdat, 1958. 560 p. Soviet, Chinese, Polish, Czechoslovak, East German, Hungarian, Bulgarian, North Korean, Mongolian, and North Vietnamese economists discuss industrialization, trade, and agricultural problems in their countries and within the Communist bloc. [B]

P16 KIESEWETTER, BRUNO. *Der Ostblock; Aussenhandel des Ostlichen Wirtschaftsblockes Einschliesslich China.* Berlin: Safari-Verlag, 1960. 386 p. A substantial study describing and analyzing the pattern of foreign trade and economic aid within the Communist international system, including a discussion of the special position of China. Based largely on official Russian sources, this book gives detailed trade statistics, in both physical units and value, for selected years: 1938, and 1948-59. Professor of Economics at the Free University of Berlin (West) and director of the East European division, Deutsches Institut für Wirtschaftsforschung, Kiesewetter has written widely on bloc economic planning and problems.

P17 KOVRIZHNY, M. F., and others, eds. *Vneshniaia torgovlia stran narodnoi demokratii.* Moscow: Vneshtorgizdat, 1955. 320 p. A documented examination of principles guiding the foreign trade of Communist-bloc states, including a separate discussion of individual states' trading achievements.

P18 KRÜGER, KARL. *Der Ostblock; die Produktion des Östlichen Wirtschaftsblockes Einschliesslich China, nach dem Schwerpunktprogramm.* Berlin: Safari-Verlag, 1960. 395 p. An economic study analyzing the pattern of industrial production in the Communist bloc, including China. Based largely on official Soviet sources, this volume summarizes the production situation in individual countries, as well as comparative advantage and bloc integration. A specialist in industrial production, Krüger is professor of economics at the (West) Berlin Polytechnical School.

P19 LANDAUER, CARL and others. *European Socialism; a History of Ideas and Movements from the Industrial Revolution to Hitler's Seizure of Power.* Berkeley and Los Angeles: Univ. of California, 1959. 2 vols.: I, *From the Industrial Revolution to the First World War and Its Aftermath;* II, *The Socialist Struggle Against Capitalism and Totalitarianism.* By a professor at the University of California who was formerly a member of the German Social Democratic Party. Deals primarily with Communism in Germany, Russia, Italy, and France and with the Comintern.

P19A LAQUEUR, WALTER, and LABEDZ, LEOPOLD, eds. *Polycentrism: The New Factor in International Communism.* N.Y.: Praeger, 1962. An examination of the cohesive and centrifugal factors in world Communism, compiled by the editors of *Survey.* [A]

P20 LEVCHENKO, MARGARET M. "The Soviet View of the Socialist Camp." Certificate essay, Russian Institute, Columbia, 1957. 101 p.

P21 MEISSNER, BORIS, comp. *Das Ostpakt-System: Dokumentensammlung.* Hamburg: 1951. 2 vols., mimeographed. Enlarged and rev. ed., Frankfurt am Main: Metzner, 1955. 208 p. A collection of documents concerned with the Soviet alliance system in Europe and Asia. [B]

P22 MODELSKI, GEORGE. *The Communist International System.* Princeton: Center of International Studies, Princeton Univ., Research Monograph No. 9, December 1, 1960. 78 p. An analysis of the political structure of the contemporary communist bloc. Posits the distribution of power in the post-Stalin period as dominated by the presence of two major powers (Russia and China) of roughly comparable rank and authority, and concludes that the existing system contains the core of a potential international state system.

P23 MOSCOW, VSESOIUZNYI IURIDICHESKII ZAOCHNYI INSTITUT. *Gosudarstvennoe pravo stran narodnoi demokratii.* Ed. by Aleksandr Kh. Makhnenko. Moscow: 1959. 418 p. A revision of the official view of the "people's democracies." Deals with the constitutional law of the Asian people's democracies, as well as those in Europe. Takes the view that people's democracies constitute an alternative form of the dictatorship of the proletariat which is obedient to the general laws for the construction of socialism.

P24 NOLLAU, GUNTHER. *International Communism and World Revolution; History and Methods.* Foreword by Leonard Schapiro. Trans. by Victor Andersen. N.Y.: Praeger, 1961. 357 p. Original German ed., *Die Internationale; Wurzein und Erscheinungsformen des proletarischen Internationalismus.* Cologne: Verlag für Politik und Wirtschaft, 1959. 343 p. A very scholarly, balanced account of the origins and aspects of collaboration between member Parties of the Comintern and Cominform. Unveils the meaning of USSR-espoused "proletarian internationalism" and Soviet exploitation of world revolution. Superbly documented. The English edition is an improved and expanded version of the German text. [A]

P25 PAGE, STANLEY W. *Lenin and World Revolution.* N.Y.: New York Univ. Press, 1959. 252 p. A somewhat subjective but not implausible analysis of Lenin's writings and compulsive behaviour in connection with his promotion of revolution at home and abroad. Extensive notes and use of Russian sources.

P26 PEŠKA, PAVEL. *Ústavy lidově demokratických zemí.* Prague: Orbis, 1954. 453 p. A well-prepared handbook on the genesis and development of the constitutions of the people's democratic countries, including China. Contains also data on Soviet relations and the post-1945 political and socioeconomic history of Moscow-dominated Eastern Europe. An admittedly Party-minded investigation in the field of constitutional history. [A]

P27 POSSONY, STEFAN T. *A Century of Conflict; Communist Techniques of World Revolution.* Chicago: Regnery, 1953. 439 p. A Professor of International Politics at Georgetown undertakes a full-length analysis of Communist theory and practice beginning with Marx. Surveys Soviet techniques of international and internal revolutions aimed to achieve world conquest. Scholarly documentation. [B]

P28 *Problemy sotsialisticheskogo mezhdunarodnogo razdeleniia truda.* Compiled by I. I. Semenov. Edited by Iu. Ia. Olsevich. Moscow: Izd. inostr. lit., 1960. 248 p. A collective work on different aspects of Communist-bloc trade and the central role of the USSR in it. Well documented.

P29 *Razvitie ekonomiki stran narodnoi demokratii; obzor.* Moscow: Vneshtorgizdat, 1954—. (Annual) Includes material on the Communist countries in Asia as well as those in East Europe. Organized country by country. Each national section deals with industry, agriculture, transport, foreign trade, the national budget, and living standards. There is also a statistical appendix. Compiled by the Nauchno-issledovatelskii koniunkturnyi institut in Moscow.

P30 RICHARDS, EDWARD B. "Soviet Control of International Communism." Ph.D. dissertation, State Univ. of Iowa, 1957. 216 p. An inquiry into the origins and bases of Soviet control over other Communist parties. Analyzes the methods used in securing and exercising such control, and evaluates its effects on the international movement.

P31 ROSENBERG, ARTHUR. *A History of Bolshevism.* N.Y. and London: Oxford, 1939. 250 p. A former member of the German Communist Party (1920-27) employs selected primary sources and personal experience to generalize on USSR-Comintern history.

P32 SALTER, ERNEST J. *Von Lenin bis Chruschtschow; der moderne Kommunismus.* Frankfurt: Ullstein Taschenbücher, 1958. 144 p.

P33 SALVADORI, MASSIMO. *The Rise of Modern Communism.* N.Y.: Holt; London: Hutchinson, 1952. 118 p. A concise study of the Communist movement in the twentieth century; an effective, dispassionate introduction to the subject. The author is a professor at Smith College.

P34 SERGEEV, SERGEI D. *Ekonomicheskoe sotrudnichestvo i vzaimopomoshch stran sotsialisticheskogo lageria.* Moscow: Vneshtorgizdat, 1956. 200 p. 2nd ed., 1959. 319 p. Deals with the origin and development of the Communist world market; trade, credit, and technical assistance; industrialization; the collectivization of agriculture, and living standards.

P35 SETON-WATSON, HUGH. *From Lenin to Malenkov; the History of World Communism.* N.Y.: Praeger, 1953. 377 p. British ed., *The Pattern of Communist Revolution*, London: Methuen, 1953. Rev. ed., *From Lenin to Khrushchev; the History of World Communism*, N.Y.: Praeger, 1960. 432 p. A professor of history at London University reviews Communism in European, Russian and Oriental history. A comparative analysis of Communist movements against their social-economic backgrounds. Lucid, dispassionate, of necessity kaleidoscopic. Good bibliography and index of persons and subjects. [A]

P36 STEGER, K. (pseud. of Karl Stark). *Im Banne des Kommunismus; eine Werkbuch über Idee und Gefahr des Kommunismus.* Lucerne: Rex, 1952. 360 p. An anti-Communist tract warning of the threat of Communism to capitalism, humanism and religion.

P37 TRACHTENBERG, B., ed. *Osiagniecia gospodarcze krajów obozu pokoju.* Warsaw: Wydawn. Ministerstwa Oborony Narodowej, 1952. 189 p. A collection of articles by Polish, Russian, and German authors reviewing the policies and achievements of planned economy in the European and Asiatic countries of the socialist camp, including the USSR and China. [B]

P38 U.S. CONGRESS, HOUSE, COMMITTEE ON FOREIGN AFFAIRS. *Report on the Strategy and Tactics of World Communism*; with Supplement 1, *One Hundred Years of Communism, 1848-1948*; Supplement 2, *Official Protests of United States Government against Communist Policies or Actions, and Related Correspondence*; Supplement 3, *Country Studies*; and Supplement 4, *500 Leading Communists (In the Eastern Hemisphere excluding U.S.S.R.).* Washington: G.P.O., 1948. 5 vols. Condensed version, BOLTON, FRANCIS P. and others. *Communism, Its Plans and Tactics.* Washington: Infantry Journal Press, 1948. 102 p. An extensive array of documentary material on the strategy and tactics of world Communism. Deals with all aspects of the politics, the economy, the social and educational and cultural structure of the USSR; principal resolutions and programs adopted by the various world congresses of the Comintern, and the actuation of these resolutions into revolutions in various countries of the world. Important evidence of how the CPUSA acts under the rigid discipline of the Kremlin. Extensive bibliography and indexes. [A]

P39 U.S. CONGRESS, HOUSE, COMMITTEE ON UN-AMERICAN ACTIVITIES. *The Communist Conspiracy; Strategy and Tactics of World Communism.* Part I, *Communism Outside the United States;* Section C, *The World Congresses of the Communist International*; and Section E, *The Comintern and the CPUSA.* Washington: G.P.O., 1956. 2 vols. A useful, authoritative outline of the history and machinations of the world Communist movement, including complete or partial texts of official Communist statements. [B]

P39A U.S. CONGRESS, HOUSE, COMMITTEE ON UN-AMERICAN ACTIVITIES. *World Communist Movement: Selective Chronology, 1818-1957.* Vol. I: *1818-1945.* Washington: G.P.O. 232 p. An annotated chronological guide prepared by the Library of Congress Legislative Reference Service. [A]

P39B U.S. DEPARTMENT OF STATE. *World Strength of the Communist Party Organizations.* Washington: G.P.O., 1950–. Concise, authoritative annual reports of the basic political status, membership and sources of strength of Communist parties throughout the world. [A]

P40 WALSH, EDMUND A. *Total Empire; the Roots and Progress of World Communism.* Milwaukee: Bruce, 1951. 293 p. Geo-politician Walsh draws upon first-hand knowledge and upon Russia's past to explain the acceptance, dynamism, and danger of Communism in the USSR.

P41 ZINNER, PAUL E. *International Communism: Ideology, Organization, Strategy.* N.Y.: Praeger, 1963. 320 p. An historical survey and analysis of major aspects of the international communist movement. The author offers a fresh interpretation of Marxist-Leninist theory; he dissects the Communist International in action, the Soviet sacrifice of it, the conquest of Eastern Europe, and the impact of the revelations that altered international Communism after Stalin's death. Zinner examines Communist heresies, the impact of revisionism, and the methods and procedures of modern international Communist groups and parties. [A]

Q. The Communist International (Comintern)

EDITED BY KERMIT E. MC KENZIE

1. BIBLIOGRAPHIES

Q1 COMMUNIST INTERNATIONAL. *Veroeffentlichungen des Verlages der Kommunistischen Internationale; 1920 bis 1922.* Hamburg: C. Hoym, 1923. 192 p. Besides an alphabetical listing of publications of this Comintern press, there are helpful periodical indices for the first three years of *Die Kommunistische Internationale* and *Russische Korrespondenz.*

Q2 PROCACCI, GIULIANO. "L'Internazionale Communista dal I al VII Congresso, 1919-1935." In: Istituto Giangiacomo Feltrinelli, *Annali*, anno primo. Milano: Feltrinelli Editore, 1958. p. 283-315. An exceedingly helpful bibliography of most of the published source materials for a history of the Comintern from 1919 through 1935. Divided into chronological periods, each prefaced by a useful introduction. [B]

Q3 RUSSIA (1917- RSFSR), GOSUDARSTVENNOE IZDATELSTVO. *Komintern, 1919-1929; katalog knig.* Moscow: Gosizdat, 1929. 72 p.

Q4 SWORAKOWSKI, WITOLD S. *The Communist International and Its Front Organizations; a Research Guide and Checklist of Holdings in American and European Libraries.* Stanford, Cal.: Hoover Institution, 1965. 493 p. Lists over 2,300 books and pamphlets published in 22 Western and Slavic languages and held by 48 libraries. [A]

2. GENERAL WORKS

Q5 BENNET, A. J. (pseud. of D. Petrovskii). *War: the Communist International's Position.* 1927. A pamphlet by the man who was appointed representative of the Executive Committee of the Comintern in Great Britain in 1924.

Q6 BOERSNER, DEMETRIO. *The Bolsheviks and the National and Colonial Question (1917-1928).* Geneva: Droz; Paris: Minard, 1957. 285 p. A study of Comintern colonial policy up to 1928. Contains some errors, but still a useful survey.

Q7 BORKENAU, FRANZ. *The Communist International.* London: Faber and Faber, 1938. 442 p. American ed., *World Communism.* N.Y.: Norton, 1939. Paperback ed., Ann Arbor: Univ. of Michigan Press, 1962. 442 p. The standard history of the Comintern from its beginnings to the Popular Front of the mid-thirties, by a former member of the German Communist Party. Indispensable and still unsuperseded. [A]

Q8 BORKENAU, FRANZ. *Der europäische Kommunismus; Seine Geschichte von 1917 bis zur Gegenwart*. Munich: Lehnen, 1952. 540 p. English ed., *European Communism*. London: Faber & Faber; N.Y.: Harper, 1953. 564 p. A detailed study of the 1930's and 1940's, with major attention to the French Communist Party. Based on primary sources, with much interesting speculation added, this work is not, on the whole, as sound as his earlier history. [B]

Q9 CARVALHO E SOUZA, O. DE. *Komintern*. Rio de Janeiro: J. Olympio, 1938. 379 p. A sketchy, hostile survey, only partially documented, of Bolshevism, the Soviet Union, and the Comintern. Perhaps the most useful part of this work is devoted to the auxiliary organizations of the Comintern.

Q10 CHERNITSKII, N. *Materialy i dokumenty po istorii Kominterna*. Moscow: Voennaia vozdushnaia akademiia RKKA, 1931. 381 p.

Q11 COMMUNIST INTERNATIONAL. *Blueprint for World Conquest, As Outlined by the Communist International*. Introd. by William H. Chamberlin. Washington: Human Events, 1946. 263 p. Contains the major documents of the Second Comintern Congress (1920), the Program of the Comintern (1928), and the rules of the Comintern (1928).

Q12 COMMUNIST INTERNATIONAL. *The Communist International, 1919-1943; Documents*. Selected and edited by Jane Degras. London and N.Y.: Oxford, 1956—. Planned in three volumes. Two volumes have so far appeared; volume I covers 1919-1922 and volume II 1923-1928, each containing over 100 documents in full or in part, translated into English. Included are the most important available materials on Comintern doctrinal and organizational matters and on contemporary events. Carefully edited, translated, and introduced with useful explanatory prefaces. An appendix in each volume gives the memberships of the Comintern's Executive Committee, Presidium, and International Control Commission at various times. A valuable series. [A]

Q13 COMMUNIST INTERNATIONAL. *Dix Années de lutte pour la revolution mondiale*. Paris: Bureau d'Édition, 1929. Important articles and memoirs on the first decade of Comintern history, by such eminent figures as Béla Kun, Kolarov, Lozovsky, Zinoviev, and Clara Zetkin. [B]

Q14 COMMUNIST INTERNATIONAL. *Fifteen Years of the Communist International; Theses for Instructors*. N.Y.: Workers Library,

1934. 51 p. Thirty-seven theses prepared by the Agitprop Department of the Comintern's Executive Committee. The main developments of the Comintern's history are outlined, without a hint of the imminent Popular Front strategy.

Q15 COMMUNIST INTERNATIONAL. *Kommunisticheskii Internatsional i voina; dokumenty i materialy o borbe Kominterna protiv imperialisticheskoi voiny i v zashchitu S.S.S.R.* Moscow: Gosizdat, 1928. 108 p. German ed., Hamburg, 1929. French ed., Paris, 1928. Four pre-Comintern and twelve Comintern documents, which give the Leninist essentials up to the Sixth Comintern Congress, on the war question and the correct response of Communists.

Q17 COMMUNIST INTERNATIONAL. *Poslevoennyi kapitalizm v osveshchenii Kominterna; sbornik dokumentov i rezoliutsii kongressov i ispolkoma Kominterna.* Moscow: Partizdat, 1932. 163 p. Selections, without commentary, from Comintern documents of the period 1919-31. The intent is to present the changing fortunes of world capitalism following World War I.

Q18 DRIDZO, SOLOMON A. (Lozovsky, A., pseud.), ed. *Istoriia Kominterna v kongressakh.* Kharkhov: Proletarii, 1929. 6 vols. Short studies of the first six Comintern congresses, under the editorship of the head of the Red International of Trade Unions and separately authored by I. Mingulin, M. Iablonskii, F. Glaubauf, A. Tivel, B. Williams, and G. Günther. Dridzo was active in Soviet foreign affairs until well after World War II.

Q19 DUMBADZE, EVGENII V. *Na sluzhbe Cheka i Kominterna; lichnyia vospominaniia.* With introductory article by V. L. Burtsev. Paris: Izd. "Mishen," 1930. 159 p. By a former agent of the Soviet secret police who transferred to Comintern activity around 1923. Contains useful information on the relationship of the OGPU and the Comintern apparatus, especially with respect to the latter's activity in Turkey.

Q20 ESSEN, ALEKSANDR M. *Tri internatsionala.* Moscow: Gosizdat, 1926. 252 p. 2nd enlarged ed. Moscow-Leningrad: Gosizdat, 1929. 241 p. 3rd ed., 1930. 216 p. 4th ed., Ogiz, 1931. 216 p. A history of the First, Second and Third Internationals, by an old Bolshevik and official in the Soviet government. Roughly one-half of the book is devoted to Comintern history to 1929.

Q21 FOOTMAN, DAVID, ed. *International Communism.* (St. Antony's Papers, No. 9) London: Chatto & Windus; Carbondale, Ill.:

Southern Illinois Univ. Press, 1960. 151 p. Contains the following papers: (1) "United Front Tactics in the Comintern, 1921-28," by Jane Degras. (2) "Bolshevization of the Spartacus League," by Richard Lowenthal. (3) "Willi Münzenberg," by R. N. Carew Hunt. (4) "Socialism in America," by Earl Browder. (5) "Communism in India," by Guy Wint. (6) "International Communism: The Present Phase," by Wolfgang Leonhard.

Q22 FOSTER, WILLIAM Z. *History of the Three Internationals; The World Socialist and Communist Movements from 1848 to the Present.* N.Y.: International, 1955. 580 p. This book by the veteran American Communist devotes about 200 pages to the Comintern. It has been translated into Russian, German, Bulgarian, Rumanian, and other languages.

Q23 INTERNATIONAL ANTICOMMUNIST ENTENTE. *Organisation et activité de l'Internationale communiste.* Paris: Les Éditions documentaires, 1938. 223 p. English ed., *The Red Network; the Communist International at Work.* London: Duckworth, 1939. 93 p. German ed., Geneva, 1939. 271 p. A very elementary handbook about the Comintern organization, to which is attached an extremely negative description of Communist rule in the USSR. The Entente was formed in 1924, with an International Council meeting once a year and a Permanent Bureau residing in Geneva.

Q24 JAMES, CYRIL L. R. *World Revolution, 1917-1936; The Rise and Fall of the Communist International.* London: Secker and Warburg, 1937. 429 p. An interesting attempt at a history of the Comintern up to 1936 by an admirer of Trotsky. In his view, Stalin ruined the Comintern just as he perverted the Bolshevik Revolution in Russia: the remedy—an end to Stalin's rule and the creation of a Fourth International under the guidance of Trotsky, the best expounder of Marxism-Leninism. Not nearly so adequate a history as Borkenau's. [B]

Q25 KABAKCHIEV, KHRISTO S. *Kak voznik i razvivalsia Kommunisticheskii Internatsional; kratkii istoricheskii ocherk.* Moscow: 1929. 239 p. German ed., *Die Entstehung und Entwicklung der Komintern.* Hamburg: 1929. 174 p. An authoritative, concise, but inadequate attempt by a leading Bulgarian Communist to sketch the Comintern's first decade. The author lived in the USSR from 1926 until his death in 1940.

Q26 KOMOR, IMRE. *Ten Years of the Communist International.* London: Modern Books; N.Y.: Workers' Library, 1929. 46 p. German ed., *Zehn Jahre Kommunistischen Internationale, 1919-1929.* Hamburg: 1929. 31 p. A short unrewarding "history" by a Communist.

Q27 KONDO, EIZO. *Komminterun no misshi.* Tokyo: Bunka hyoronsha, 1949. 290 p. This writer was the founder of the Dawn People's Communist Party and was associated with Communist activities in the U.S. and Japan until 1927. The work itself, while sensationalist at times and not always accurate, is one of the important sources for the study of the early Japanese Communist movement.

Q28 LEITES, NATHAN C. *The Third International on its Changes of Policy; A Study of Political Communication.* Washington: Library of Congress, Experimental Division for the Study of War Time Communications, 1942. 80 p. The author investigates the Comintern's explanations of six major policy shifts. Based on primary sources, this is a "language of politics" analysis.

Q29 LENZ, JOSEF. *Die II. Internationale und ihr Erbe, 1889-1929.* Hamburg: Hoym, 1930. 302 p. English ed., *The Rise and Fall of the Second International.* N.Y.: International, 1932. A Communist history of the Second International before 1914, of the Third International to 1929, and of the postwar Labor and Socialist International.

Q30 MÖNDEL, KARL J. *Die Internationale.* 2nd rev. ed. Berlin: 1929. 136 p. A highly nationalistic attack upon the concept of "proletarian internationalism," in which the histories of the three Internationals are sketched.

Q31 MOSCOW, NAUCHNO-ISSLEDOVATELSKII INSTITUT PO KITAIU. *Strategiia i taktika Kominterna v natsionalno-kolonialnoi revoliutsii na primere Kitaia; sbornik dokumentov.* Comp. by Georgii S. Kara-Murza; ed. by Pavel A. Mif. Moscow: Izd. Inst. M.Kh. i M. P., 1934. 394 p. An important collection, divided into three parts: general theory of the national-colonial revolution (material from the Comintern Program and from the Second, Fourth, and Sixth Congresses), Comintern strategy and tactics in China from 1925 to late 1927, and from December 1927 to 1933. In 1930-31 Mif was the Comintern emissary to the Chinese Party.

Q32 MURPHY, JOHN T. *New Horizons.* London: Lane, 1941. 352 p. The political confessions of a one-time member of the ECCI, who later broke with Communism.

Q33 NERMAN, TURE. *Kommunisterna från Komintern till Kominform.* Stockholm: Tidens, 1949. 280 p. Half of the book is devoted to the Comintern; the remainder, to the Cominform and to a short history of the Swedish Communist Party.

Q34 NOLLAU, GÜNTHER. *International Communism and World Revolution; History and Methods.* N.Y.: Praeger, 1961. 357 p. Original

German ed., *Die Internationale: Würzeln und Erscheinungsformen des proletarischen Internationalismus.* Cologne: Verlag für Politik und Wirtschaft, 1959. 344 p. An important work, treating the history of the relations among Communist parties, by a Bonn civil servant. About one-half of the book concerns the Comintern: a sketch of its history and an especially valuable section on its organization and methods. The English edition is a translation of the improved and expanded German text. [A]

Q35 NORMANN, ALFRED. *Bolschewistische Weltmachtpolitik; Die Pläne der 3. Internationale zur Revolutionierung der Welt.* Bern: Gotthelf, 1935. 287 p. A reasonably adequate survey of Comintern strategy and tactics as applied to a variety of problems (struggle for the masses, strikes, youth, colonies, armed forces, peasantry, etc.). Documented and extremely hostile.

Q36 OBSHCHESTVO ISTORIKOV-MARKSISTOV. *Voprosy prepodavaniia leninizma, istorii VKP(b) i Kominterna. Stenogrammy soveshchaniia, sozdannogo O-vom istorikov-marksistov.* Moscow: Izd. Kommunisticheskoi akad., 1930. 319 p.

Q37 PERTICONE, GIACOMO. *Le Tre Internazionali.* Rome: Atlantica, 1945. 374 p. A scholarly history of the First, Second, and Third Internationals, with greatest attention to the Third.

Q38 PETROVSKII, DAVID A., ed. *Partii Kommunisticheskogo Internatsionala; sbornik statei.* Moscow: Gosizdat, 1928. 205 p. Sketches of thirty-odd Communist parties, with an appendix listing the major problems and resolutions of each Comintern congress and ECCI plenum to 1928.

Q39 REZANOV, ALEKSANDR S. *Le Travail secret des agents bolchévistes; exposé d'après des documents authentiques emanant des Bolchéviks.* Paris: Bossard, 1926. 199 p. By a former officer of the Imperial Russian Army, who takes an extremely hostile position. Places emphasis upon the conspiratorial, "secret-agent" aspects of the international Communist movement.

Q40 RICHARDS, EDWARD B. "Soviet Control of International Communism." Ph.D. dissertation, State Univ. of Iowa, 1957. 216 p. An inquiry into the origins and bases of Soviet control over other Communist parties. Analysis of the methods used in securing and exercising such control, together with an evaluation of its effects on the international movement.

Q41 RÜCK, FRIEDRICH A. *Sovjetunionen och Komintern.* Stockholm: Kooperativa Förbundets Bokförlag, 1943. 180 p. A brief historical survey, completely undocumented.

Q42 SUCHOPÁR, VLADIMIR, and HRBATA, FRANTIŠEK. *K dějinám Kommunistické internacionály, 1914-1927*, Vol. I. Prague: Státni pedagogické nakl., 1957. 389 p. A textbook for higher schools, issued under the auspices of the Philosophical-Historical Faculty of Charles University. A history of the origins and early years of the Comintern; without footnotes or bibliography.

Q43 TILAK, K. *Rise and Fall of the Comintern; From the First to the Fourth International*. Bombay: Spark Syndicate, 1947. 157 p. An interpretation by an Indian follower of Trotsky.

Q44 TIVEL, ALEKSANDR IU., and KHEIMO, M. *Desiat let Kominterna v resheniiakh i tsifrakh; spravochnik po istorii Kominterna*. Moscow: Gosizdat, 1929. 415 p. An extremely useful collection of data on the Comintern during its first decade. [B]

Q45 TUCK, ROBERT L. "The Relation between the U.S.S.R. and Revolution Abroad, as Treated by Two Popular Soviet Encyclopedias." Certificate essay, Russian Institute, Columbia, 1949. 90 p. An interesting attempt by an American student, using reference works readily available to the Soviet citizen, to define the content of mutual obligations of the Soviet Union and the external Communist-led world movement.

Q46 TYLER, JAMES E. "The Comintern and the Colonies; the Colonial Question in the Communist International." M.A. thesis, Georgetown, 1952. 147 p. An attempt to extract from Western-language reports of the Comintern congresses the essentials of doctrine respecting the colonies and colonial independence movements. A special section deals with the French Communists and Morocco.

Q47 VSESOIUZNAIA SPRAVOCHNAIA KARTOTEKA. *15 let Kominterna, 1919-1934; ukazatel*. Ed. by Serafima Gopner. Moscow: 1934. 14 p. Consists of 226 printed cards, each defining a special aspect of Communist history or doctrine by means of selected brief quotations from Lenin, Stalin, Comintern materials, or Communist party documents. Intended for use by party agitators and propagandists.

Q48 WICKS, H. M. *Eclipse of October*. Chicago: Challenge, 1957. 464 p. A bitterly anti-Stalin work by a founder of the American Communist Party, active in the Comintern until 1936. Interesting reports of conversations, but without documentation.

Q49 YPSILON (pseud. of Karl Volk). *Pattern for World Revolution*. Chicago: Ziff-Davis, 1947. 479 p. French ed., *Stalintern*. Paris: La Table Ronde, 1948. 446 p. Personal memoirs and short biographical studies of Comintern figures by a German Communist who was also an agent for the Comintern. Lively, undocumented reportage of conversations and events. Should be used with caution.

Q50 ZAMYSLOVA, ZINAIDA A. *Kommunisticheskii Internatsional i ego rol v istorii mezhdunarodnogo rabochego i natsionalno-osvoboditelnogo dvizheniia.* Moscow: 1957. 106 p. Reprint of a lecture given at the Higher Party School of the CPSU, summarizing the career of the Comintern.

3. COMINTERN UNDER LENIN, 1919-1924

Q51 BALABANOVA, ANGELINA (Balabanoff, Angelica). *My Life as a Rebel.* N.Y.: Harper, 1938. 324 p. Autobiography (to 1922) of a leader of the international and Italian socialist movements before World War I, who became the secretary of the Zimmerwald movement and later a secretary of the Comintern. She severed relations with Communism in 1921.

Q52 COMMUNIST INTERNATIONAL. *Almanach des Verlages der Kommunistischen Internationale.* Hamburg: C. Hoym, 1921. 331 p. An interesting collection, mainly of articles by outstanding Communists such as Lenin, Zinoviev, Trotsky, Luxemburg, Radek, Reed, etc., but also containing important documents of the early Comintern. Replete with photographs and vivid anti-capitalist cartoons and a valuable 44-page bibliography of publications in German by Verlag der Kommunistischen Internationale. [B]

Q53 COMMUNIST INTERNATIONAL. *Armiia Kommunisticheskogo Internatsionala.* Petrograd: Izd. Kominterna, 1921. 112 p. A small handbook of information, offering a brief report on the activities of the Comintern Executive Committee following the Third Congress (1921) and a capsule treatment of the Communist parties and young Communist leagues of the world. A list giving the membership figures for 51 parties is added.

Q54 COMMUNIST INTERNATIONAL. *Jahrbuch für Wirtschaft, Politik und Arbeiterbewegung 1922-1923.* Hamburg: C. Hoym, 1923[?]. 1108 p. Russian ed., *Ezhegodnik Kominterna; spravochnaia kniga po istorii mezhdunarodnogo rabochego, politicheskogo i professionalnogo dvizheniia, statistike i ekonomike vsekh stran mira na 1923.* Petrograd-Moscow: 1923. 1047 p. An almanac for Communists, divided into three main parts: 1-General; 2-The Soviet Republics; and 3-The Bourgeois States. Crammed with statistics, chronologies, etc., this volume includes numerous signed articles by Communist leaders such as Lenin, Zinoviev, Trotsky, Radek, Rakosi, Varga, and others.

Q55 COMMUNIST INTERNATIONAL. *Materialien zur Frage des Programms der Kommunistischen Internationale.* Hamburg: Verlag der Kommunistischen Internationale, 1924. 328 p. A valuable collection for any study of the history of the Comintern Program for 1924. Includes the important draft program of 1922 by Bukharin, as well as writings and speeches of Lenin, Radek, Varga, and others, and the party programs or draft programs of the Communist parties of Germany, Bulgaria, Italy, Japan, Russia, and the 1922 draft program of the Communist Youth International. [B]

Q56 COMMUNIST INTERNATIONAL. *Put k Kommunisticheskomu Internatsionalu; iz istorii mezhdunarodnogo rabochego dvizheniia; sbornik statei i dokumentov.* Petrograd: "Priboi," 1924. 176 p. Leningrad: "Priboi," 1924. 213 p.

Q57 COMMUNIST INTERNATIONAL. *Sowjet-Russland und die Völker der Welt; Reden auf der internationalen Versammlung in Petrograd am 19. Dezember, 1918.* Petrograd: 1920. French ed., *La Russie des Soviets et les peuples du monde.* Petrograd: 1920. A record of a meeting convened by the Petrograd Soviet and attended by assorted foreign Communists and non-Communists interested in a new International.

Q58 DUTT, R. PALME. *The Two Internationals.* London: Allen and Unwin, 1920. 92 p. A study by a British Communist, who contrasts the new Comintern favorably with the old Second International.

Q59 FAINSOD, MERLE. *International Socialism and the World War.* Cambridge: Harvard Univ. Press, 1935. 238 p. This careful, scholarly study, based on primary and secondary sources and written by a Harvard professor, details the disintegrating impact of the war upon the European socialist movement and traces the emergence of the Comintern through its first congress. [A]

Q60 FEDORINA, ALEKSANDRA M. *V. I. Lenin v borbe za sozdanie Kommunisticheskogo Internatsionala.* Moscow: Izd. Moskovskogo universiteta, 1959. 48 p. About one-half of this work is a sketch of the origins of the Comintern; then the author switches to current politics and stresses the need for international Communist unity, especially against Yugoslav "revisionism."

Q61 FISHER, RALPH T., JR. "The Comintern in Russian Foreign Policy, 1919-1923." M.A. thesis, Univ. of California (Berkeley), 1948. An attempt to assess the role of the Third International as a novel element in shaping international politics.

Q62 GANKIN, OLGA H., and FISHER, HAROLD H., eds. *The Bolsheviks and the World War; the Origin of the Third International.*

Stanford, Cal.: Stanford Univ. Press; London: Oxford, 1940. 856 p. 2nd ed., 1960. An invaluable collection of documents on the pre-history of the Comintern, interspersed with helpful commentaries. The documents range from February 1905 to September 1918, but the bulk of the collection is from the war years. There is also an excellent 42-page annotated bibliography. [A]

Q63 GEYER, KURT. *Za tretii Internatsional. Nezavisimie na pereputi. S prilozheniem statei Valtera Shtekera i Pavla Gennaga. S predisloviem Ernsta Deimiga.* Moscow: Komintern, 1920. 132 p.

Q64 GUREVICH, ALEKSANDR I. *Vozniknovenie i razvitie Kommunisticheskogo Internatsionala.* Kharkov: Gosizdat, 1925. 224 p. A useful history of the Comintern through its Fifth Congress, designed as a textbook for courses in Soviet schools on the history of the international labor movement. The work is pre-Stalinist in character, with proper credit given to the activities of Trotskii, Zinoviev, and Bukharin. [B]

Q65 HURWICZ, ELIAS. *Die Orientpolitik der dritten Internationale an Hand authentischer Quellen dargestellt.* Berlin: Deutsche Verlagsgesellschaft für Politik und Geschichte, 1922. 100 p.

Q66 IUZEFOVICH, IOSIF S. *Osnovanie Kommunisticheskogo Internatsionala.* Moscow-Leningrad: Izd. Akademii nauk SSSR, 1940. 275 p. Probably the most able Communist treatment of the origins and early history (through the Second Congress) of the Comintern. Especially useful is the rather detailed identification and characterization of the various factions within the socialist and Communist parties of these years.

Q67 KOLESNIKOVA, N. N. *R.K.P. i Komintern.* Moscow: Gosizdat, 1925. 230 p. Elementary material on the Party, the Comintern, and the Komsomol, for use in secondary schools. Not a study of the relationship between the Soviet Party and the Comintern as the title might imply.

Q68 LAZIĆ, BRANKO M. *Lénine et la IIIe Internationale.* Intro. by Raymond Aron. Neuchâtel: Éditions de la Baconnière, 1951. 285 p. (Also published under the name Branislav Stranjakovitch, Geneva: 1950.) An excellent account of the early history of the Comintern by an expert on the international Communist movement. Lenin's pre-eminent role in shaping the new International is fully documented. [A]

Q69 LENIN, VLADIMIR I. *The Communist International.* N.Y.: International, 1938. 333 p. Volume x of his *Selected Works* (in 12 volumes). Includes his most important speeches and writings on the Comintern from 1917 to the end of 1922. [B]

Q70 LENIN, VLADIMIR I. *L'Internazionale comunista.* Rome: Edizioni Rinascita, 1950. 394 p. A rather full collection of Lenin's speeches at the first four congresses, in addition to ten documents antedating the founding of the Comintern. Virtually without notes.

Q71 LENIN, VLADIMIR I. *Komintern.* Kharkov: Izd. "Proletarii," 1924. 325 p. Includes four documents, without notes, on the "prehistory" of the Comintern in addition to articles, speeches, and letters appearing during the period of the first four congresses. Contains some rare pictures taken at Comintern meetings.

Q72 LENIN, VLADIMIR I. *Kommunisticheskii Internatsional; stati i rechi.* Moscow: Izd. "Krasnaia nov" Glavpolitprosvet, 1924. 344 p. Embraces the period of the first four Comintern congresses, but does not deal with the "pre-history" of the Comintern. Thirty pages of notes.

Q73 LENIN, VLADIMIR I. *Kommunisticheskii Internatsional; stati, rechi, dokumenty, 1914-1923.* Ed. by V. Knorin. Moscow: Partizdat, 1934-1937. 2 vols. Selected works of Lenin dealing with the origins and early history of the Comintern. A valuable source but should be checked for completeness against his *Sochineniia.* Volume one deals with the "pre-history" of the Comintern; volume two begins with Lenin's participation in the First Comintern Congress. [A]

Q74 LENIN, VLADIMIR I. *Die Kommunistische Internationale.* Moscow: Verlagsgenossenschaft ausländischer Arbeiter in der UdSSR, 1937. 335 p.

Q75 LENIN, VLADIMIR I. *O Kominterne.* Leningrad: "Priboi," 1925. 191 p.

Q76 LENIN, VLADIMIR I. *O Kommunisticheskom Internatsionale.* Moscow: Partizdat, 1934. 294 p. Speeches, reports, and theses by Lenin at the first four Comintern congresses. These 24 items are accompanied by brief notes.

Q77 LOUIS, PAUL. *La Crise du socialisme mondiale; de la IIe à la IIIe internationale.* Paris: Alcan, 1921. 200 p.

Q78 MILIUKOV, PAVEL N. *Bolshevism; An International Danger.* London: Allen, 1920. 303 p. An interesting account and assessment of the early international Communist movement; often undocumented, frequently impatient in tone, especially toward the moderate socialists, but possessing many sound insights and judgments.

Q79 MILLIKAN, GORDON W. "The Question of Interdependence between the Russian Revolution and Revolution Abroad; Discussions in the Comintern, First and Fifth Congresses." Certificate essay, Russian

Institute, Columbia, 1953. 171 p. An attempt to define the Communist interpretation of the interrelationship of the Bolshevik seizure of power in Russia and revolutionary movements outside, by examining the Comintern congresses for 1919 and 1924.

Q80 MOSCOW, INSTITUT MARKSIZMA-LENINIZMA. *Borba bolshevikov za sozdanie Kommunisticheskogo Internatsionala; materialy i dokumenty, 1914-1919 gg.* Comp. by Samuil S. Bantke. Moscow: Partizdat, 1934. 245 p. A useful collection of materials on the "pre-history" of the Comintern. Appendices contain documents of the Zimmerwald movement and of the early history (1918-20) of several Communist parties. [B]

Q81 PAVLOVICH, MIKHAIL (pseud. of Mikhail L. Veltman). *Voprosy kolonialnoi i natsionalnoi politiki i III Internatsional.* Moscow: Komintern, 1920. 71 p. Although most of his work was theoretical, Pavlovich was one of the early Soviet writers on Africa and Asia. [B]

Q82 PAVLOVICH-VOLONTER, M. (pseud. of Mikhail L. Veltman). *Voprosy kolonialnoi revoliutsii i Treti Internatsional.* Moscow: 1921. Veltman used this nickname most frequently when writing for *Iskra* during the Russo-Japanese War.

Q83 PEREYRA, CARLOS. *La Tercera Internacional; doctrinas y controversias.* Montevideo: C. Garcia, 1920. 2 vols. Madrid: 1933. 262 p.

Q84 PHILLIPS, WAYNE W. "Lenin and the Origin of the Third International, July 28, 1914, to September 8, 1915." Certificate essay, Russian Institute, Columbia, 1953. 137 p. A careful and detailed analysis of the evolution of Lenin's thought on the subject of a new, third international, from the outbreak of war to the close of the Zimmerwald Conference. [B]

Q85 POSTGATE, RAYMOND W. *The Workers' International.* London: Swarthmore; N.Y.: Harcourt, Brace and Howe, 1920. 125 p.

Q86 RADEK, KARL. *Genau, die Einheitsfront des Proletariats und die Kommunistische Internationale; Rede auf der Konferenz der Moskauer Organisation der Kommunistischen Partei Russlands am 9. März 1922.* Hamburg: C. Hoym, 1922. 78 p.

Q87 RADEK, KARL. *Der Kampf der Kommunistischen Internationale gegen Versailles und gegen die Offensive des Kapitals.* Hamburg: Kommunistischen Internationale, 1923. 129 p.

Q88 RADEK, KARL. *Piat let Kominterna.* Moscow: Izd. "Krasnaia Nov," 1924. 875 p. Part One, "Bases of the Program and Tactics of the Comintern," contains speeches and writings from September 1918 to

January 1921. Part Two, "The United Front Tactic," begins with January 1921 and concludes with the Fourth Comintern Congress. Important source material. [B]

Q89 REZANOV, ALEKSANDR S. *La Troisième Internationale communiste; le "Komintern."* Paris: Editions Bossard, 1922. 127 p. Written by a former Tsarist officer, this work is of interest because of its point-of-view, which warns of a system directed by the "General Staff of the World Revolution." Lenin, Zinoviev, Radek, etc. are presented as German spies during the first World War. Extremely hostile and of limited usefulness.

Q90 ROSMER, ALFRED. *Moscou sous Lénine; les origines du communisme.* Paris: Pierre Horay, 1953. 316 p. Valuable memoirs by a former French Communist who was a founder of the French Communist Party in 1920, later a member of the Comintern Executive Committee, and an organizer of the Red International of Trade Unions. He broke with the Comintern and Communism in 1924. His memoirs extend from the middle of 1920 to Lenin's death and treat, among other matters, the Second, Third, and Fourth Comintern Congresses. [B]

Q91 RUSSIA (1917- R.S.F.S.R.), GLAVNYI POLITIKO-PROSVETITELNYI KOMITET, KLUBNYI OTDEL. *K piatiletiiu Kominterna: material dlia uglublennoi prorabotki.* Moscow: Krasnaia nov, 1924.

Q92 *The Second and Third Internationals and the Vienna Union. Official Report of the Conference between the Executives, held at the Reichstag, Berlin, on the 2nd April, 1922, and following days.* London: Labour Publishing Company, n.d. 94 p. Report of the abortive meeting to establish a common program of action by the three Internationals. No Russian-language report seems to have been published.

Q93 TIVEL, ALEKSANDR IU., comp. *Piat let Kominterna v resheniakh i tsifrakh.* Moscow: Krasnaia nov, 1924. 123 p. A supplement to the Russian edition of *The Communist International.*

Q94 TROTSKII, LEV. *Piat let Kominterna.* Moscow: Gosizdat, 1924. 612 p. 2nd enlarged ed., 1925. 660 p. English ed., *The First Five Years of the Communist International.* N.Y.: Pioneer, 1945-1953. 2 vols. A valuable collection of speeches, reports, articles, letters, and other works relating to the Comintern. Of special note are several Comintern manifestos, theses, and resolutions ascribed to Trotskii's pen. Covers the period from the First Comintern Congress to September 1923. [A]

Q95 U.S. DEPARTMENT OF STATE. *Memorandum on the Bolshevist or Communist Party in Russia and its Relations to the Third or Communist International and to the Russian Soviets.* Washington: G.P.O., 1920. 49 p. A collection of materials, virtually useless for the student of the Comintern, designed to prove the impossibility of differentiating between the policies of the Russian Communist Party and those of the Comintern. Also published in *International Conciliation* (January-February 1921, p. 1-103).

Q96 ZINOVEV, GRIGORII. *Die Weltpartei des Leninismus.* Hamburg: Hoym, 1924. 244 p. Speeches of Zinoviev in 1924, four delivered during the Fifth Comintern Congress and two shortly thereafter. An appendix contains the Resolution on the report of the ECCI and the Theses on the question of tactics, both adopted by the Fifth Congress and apparently authored by Zinoviev.

4. COMINTERN UNDER STALIN, 1924-1943

Q97 AUBERT, T. *La Politique actuelle du gouvernement soviétique et de la IIIe Internationale.* Geneva: Sonor, 1928. A volume by the head of the Anti-Comintern Entente.

Q98 BELK, S. E. "Between Comintern and Cominform in Europe, 1943-1947." M.A. thesis, Univ. of California (Berkeley), 1952.

Q99 BURMEISTER, ALFRED (pseud. of Wanda Bronska-Pampuch). *Dissolution and Aftermath of the Comintern; Experiences and Observations, 1937-1947.* N.Y.: Research Program on the USSR, 1955. 43 p. An important first-hand account by a former employee of the Comintern. Includes material on Comintern schools (the Communist University for the National Minorities of the West and the Lenin School), on the formal dissolution of the Comintern, and on "Institute 205," a post-Comintern organization. [B]

Q100 CASTRO DELGADO, ENRIQUE. *J'ai perdu la foi à Moscou.* Paris: Gallimard, 1950. 350 p. Spanish ed., *La Vida Secreta de la Komintern: Cómo perdí la fe en Moscú.* Madrid: E.P.E.S.A., 1950. 419 p. Mexican ed., *Mi fe se perdió en Moscú.* Mexico: Editorial Horizontes, 1951. 351 p. A former member of the Politburo of the Spanish Communist Party relates his disillusionment while in the USSR from 1939 to 1945. Valuable for his interpretations of the relative power of Comintern leaders such as Dimitrov and Manuilsky. Also useful as an "inside story" of the last years of activity at the Comintern headquarters. Castro Delgado regards as authentic only the Mexican edition of his memoirs, and charges that the "inexactitudes" and "mutilations" of the earlier editions were the fault of the French publisher (the Madrid edition is based on the French).

Q101 COMMUNIST INTERNATIONAL. *Jahrbuch für Wirtschaft, Politik und Arbeiterbewegung 1925-1926.* Hamburg: Hoym, 1926. 1051 p. Russian ed., *Khoziaistvo, politika i rabochee dvizhenie v kapitalisticheskikh stranakh za 1924-1927 gody.* Ed. by T. L. Akselrod and others. Moscow-Leningrad: Gosizdat, 1928. 1133 p. An almanac for Communists. The Russian edition differs from the German by omitting the section on the USSR and Zinoviev's lead article and by adding more recent data on the capitalist world.

Q102 COMMUNIST INTERNATIONAL, EXECUTIVE COMMITTEE. *IKKI i VKP(b) po kitaiskomy voprosu (Osnovnye resheniia).* Moscow-Leningrad: Moskovskii rabochii, 1927. 259 p. Eight documents from the period November 1926-July 1927, five by Stalin, three from the Comintern Executive Committee.

Q103 COMMUNIST INTERNATIONAL, EXECUTIVE COMMITTEE. *Kommunisticheskii Internatsional pered VII vsemirnym kongressom; materialy.* Moscow: Partizdat, 1935. 605 p. German ed., Moscow: 1935, 718 p. A useful report summarizing the activities of the central organs of the Comintern and of the Communist parties from 1928 to 1935.

Q104 DIMITROV, GEORGI. *Oeuvres choisies.* Paris: Éditions Sociales, 1952. 308 p. A selection from the writings and speeches of the Secretary General (1935-43) of the Comintern. Includes his final statement at the Reichstag Fire Trial, his speeches at the Seventh Comintern Congress, and his 1948 speech on "people's democracy."

Q105 DIMITROV, GEORGI. *The United Front; The Struggle Against Fascism and War (Reports, Speeches and Articles, 1935-37).* N.Y.: International; London: Lawrence & Wishart, 1938. 287 p. French ed., Paris, 1938. 311 p. Russian ed., Moscow: 1937. 171 p. The Secretary General of the Comintern gives the authoritative definition of the "Popular" and "United" Front policies of these years. [B]

Q106 DIMITROV, GEORGI. *V borbe za edinyi front protiv fashizma i voiny; stati i rechi 1935-1939 gg.* Moscow: Gospolitizdat, 1939. 244 p. The most important works of the Secretary General of the Comintern during the heyday of the "Popular Front." [A]

Q107 DIMITROV, GEORGI. *The Working Class against Fascism.* London: Lawrence, 1935. 127 p. Speeches by the Secretary General of the Comintern at the Seventh Comintern Congress, in which he outlined the strategy and tactics of the "Popular Front" era.

Q108 EHRT, ADOLF, ed. *Der Weltbolschewismus; ein internationales Gemeinschaftswerk über die bolschewistische Wühlarbeit und die Umstruzversuche der Komintern in allen Ländern.* Berlin:

Nibelungen, 1936. 506 p. 2nd ed., 1938. An "exposure of the plot" book issued by the Anti-Comintern, the central organization of German anti-Communist associations in the 1930's. Includes some fifty contributions on individual states or peoples. Interesting for its numerous illustrations but is generally unscholarly, pro-Nazi, and anti-Semitic. Some useful information on non-European peoples and on Soviet minorities is included.

Q109 FLORINSKY, MICHAEL T. *World Revolution and the U.S.S.R.* N.Y.: Macmillan, 1933. 264 p. A Columbia University professor deals with the apparent conflict between the Soviet policy of peaceful co-operation with capitalist countries during the first five-year plans and the revolutionary aims professed by the Comintern. [B]

Q110 GAUTHEROT, GUSTAVE. *Le Bolchévisme aux colonies et l'impérialisme rouge.* Paris: Librairie de la Revue française, 1930. 446 p. A hostile but detailed and documented survey of Communist activities throughout the colonial world. [B]

Q111 GAUTHEROT, GUSTAVE. *Le Monde communiste.* Paris: Éditions Spes, 1925. 259 p. A documented survey of world Communism, one-half of which is devoted to the French Communist Party.

Q112 GHAMBASHIDZE, DAVID. *Comintern in Asia.* Berlin: "Der Neue Orient," 1939. 63 p. A useful description of the Comintern's policies and activities in the thirties. Hostile.

Q113 GORTSEV, B., comp. *Mezhdunarodnoe polozhenie i zadachi Kominterna.* Ed. by F. Bolshov. Saratov-Moscow: Ogiz RSFSR, 1931. 132 p.

Q114 JACOBY, JEAN. *La Guerre rouge est déclarée.* Paris: Les Éditions de France, 1935. 290 p.

Q115 *Der Kampf um die Kommunistische Internationale: Dokumente der russischen Opposition nicht veröffentlicht vom Stalinischen ZK.* Berlin: Fahne des Kommunismus, 1928. 176 p. Documents of 1927 vintage, for the most part by Trotskii, concerning the Chinese revolution and the Anglo-Russian Trade Union Committee. Presented by the opposition at the Eighth Plenum of the Comintern Executive Committee.

Q116 KOESTLER, ARTHUR. *Arrow in the Blue; An Autobiography.* London: Collins with Hamish Hamilton; N.Y.: Macmillan, 1952. 353 p. 2nd vol., *The Invisible Writing.* London and N.Y.: 1954. One of the more articulate of the ex-Communists describes in these two volumes of autobiography the reasons why he became a Communist, his activities as a member of the German C.P. in 1931-32, his work with Willy Muenzenberg for some of the Comintern subsidiaries, his experiences in the Spanish Civil War, and his final disillusionment with Communism. By the author of *Darkness at Noon* and other well-known books.

Q117 KRUPINSKI, KURT. *Die Komintern seit Kriegsausbruch.* Berlin: Stollberg, 1941. 105 p. The attitude of the Soviet Union, the Comintern, and the Communist parties of various European countries toward the war and Germany, 1939-41.

Q118 LENTSNER, N. *O pravoi opasnosti v Kominterne.* 2nd ed. Moscow: Moskovskii Rabochii, 1929. 223 p. Condensed German ed., Hamburg, 1929. 55 p. The "right danger" designated, for the Comintern, Communists opposing the extremist line initiated in 1928 both within the USSR and in the Comintern. As in the Soviet Union, so in most of the Communist parties of the world there followed a purge against these "rightists."

Q119 LEONHARD, WOLFGANG. *Die Revolution entlässt ihre Kinder.* Cologne: Kiepenheuer & Witsch, 1955. 551 p. English ed., *Child of the Revolution.* Chicago: Regnery, 1958. 447 p. Useful memoirs of a former Communist, educated in the USSR during World War II and a member of the postwar German Socialist Unity Party until 1949. Afterwards, he defected to Yugoslavia and then to West Germany. Important for his report on Comintern schools in the USSR during the war and for his remarks on the dissolution of the Comintern. [B]

Q120 McKENZIE, KERMIT E. *Comintern and World Revolution, 1928-1943.* N.Y.: Columbia Univ. Press, 1964. 360 p. A description and an analysis of Comintern doctrines and directives, beginning with the Sixth Congress. The work deals with the prerequisites, strategy and tactics, and goals of world revolution as elaborated through the central institutions of the Comintern. The author is a professor of Russian history at Emory University. [A]

Q121 McKENZIE, KERMIT E. "The Messianic Concept in the Third International, 1935-1939." In: Ernest J. Simmons, ed., *Continuity and Change in Russian and Soviet Thought.* Cambridge: Harvard Univ. Press, 1955. p. 516-530. An attempt to define the role of messianism in the "Popular Front" phase of Comintern history.

Q122 NORDMAN, K., and LENSKII, G. *Pravyi uklon v Kominterne.* Leningrad: Priboi, 1930. 103 p. A Communist account of the so-called "right deviation" in the Comintern during 1928-30. The Comintern, having just launched its extremely dogmatic and sectarian "third period" pattern of strategy and tactics, termed the "right deviation" the most dangerous tendency within Communist ranks. The "deviationists" were accused of overestimating the strength of the capitalists, of underestimating the danger of war against the USSR, and of pursuing conciliatory policies towards socialist parties.

Q123 PIATNITSKII, OSIP A. *Organizatsionnaia rabota v kompartiiakh kapitalisticheskikh stran.* Moscow-Leningrad: Gosizdat, 1927. 88 p. 2nd ed., 1928. English ed., *The Organization of a World Party.* London: Communist Party of Great Britain, 1928. 94 p. Important data on Communist parties for the period 1926-27 (membership, electoral support, trade union membership, etc.). Most useful for the German, French, British, and Czechoslovak parties. [B]

Q124 RAVINES, EUDOCIO. *The Yenan Way.* N.Y.: Scribner, 1951. 319 p. Highly interesting memoirs of a former Peruvian Communist who was active in the Comintern during the 1930's, visited the USSR three times, and broke with Communism after the Nazi-Soviet Pact of 1939. Of major note are his detailed reports of extended conversations with many leaders of the Communist world movement: Dimitrov, Manuilsky, Mao Tse-tung, Chu Teh, Pieck, Piatnitsky, etc. Unfortunately, there is little to corroborate this reportage. [B]

Q125 RODINEVITCH, NICOLAS, and COMIN, EDUARDO. *La Internacional comunista o Komintern y sus organizaciones auxiliares.* Madrid: Ediciones españolas, 1941. 238 p.

Q126 ROY, MANABENDRA N. *The Communist International.* Delhi: Radical Democratic Party, 1943. 73 p. An evaluation of the Comintern at the time of its official dissolution in 1943, by a well-known Indian political figure, once prominent in the Comintern. He stresses the contradiction between the post-revolutionary tasks of the CPSU and the pre-revolutionary problems of the rest of the Comintern.

Q127 SHELAVIN, KONSTANTIN I. *Polozhenie v sektsiakh Kominterna i XVI sezd VKP(b).* Leningrad: Priboi, 1930. 80 p. An appraisal, with statistics, of the major Communist parties of the world, and an effort to show the importance of the Sixteenth Congress of the VKP(b) for the international movement.

Q128 TROTSKII, LEV D. *The Strategy of the World Revolution.* N.Y.: Communist League of America, 1930. 86 p. This is the second chapter of Trotskii's 3-part critique of the Draft Program of the Comintern (chapter one debated the issue of socialism in one country, chapter three deals with the Chinese revolution). The Draft Program was considered and adopted, with slight changes, at the Sixth Comintern Congress in 1928.

Q129 TROTSKII, LEV D. *The Third International After Lenin.* N.Y.: Pioneer, 1936. 357 p. 2nd ed., 1957. 400 p. German ed., *Die internationale Revolution und die Kommunistische Internationale.* Berlin: Laubsche, 1929. 208 p. French ed., Paris: Rieder, 1930. 438 p. Contains two documents written by Trotskii in exile during 1928 at Alma-Ata, a lengthy critique of the draft program presented to the Sixth Comintern Congress, and the open letter, "What Now?" which condemns the Comintern leadership but gives more attention to internal Soviet policies. The German translation does not contain the open letter. [B]

Q130 TUOMINEN, ARVO. *Kremlin kellot; muistelmia vuosilta, 1933-1939.* Helsinki: Kust. Tammi, 1957. 392 p. Swedish ed., Helsinki: 1958. Important memoirs of the period 1933-40 by a former candidate member of the Presidium of the Comintern Executive Committee. Interesting on several counts, especially his remarks on the Comintern schools and on the career of Otto Kuusinen (Finnish Communist, Comintern leader, and member of the Presidium of the CPSU). [A]

Q131 VARGA, EVGENII S. *Mezhdu VI i VII kongressami Kominterna; ekonomika i politika, 1928-1934.* Moscow: Partizdat, 1935. 188 p. An analysis of the Great Depression by the leading Comintern economist, who draws appropriate Marxist-Leninist conclusions but does not foresee the imminent Popular Front strategy.

Q132 ZINOVEV, GRIGORII E. *Mezhdunarodnye perspektivy i bolshevizatsiia kompartii.* Leningrad: "Priboi," 1925. 142 p. German ed., *Über die Bolschewisierung der Parteien.* Hamburg: Hoym, 1925. 130 p. A speech to the Executive Committee of the Communist International, describing the "partial stabilization" of capitalism and the necessity to meet this "new situation" with a complete Bolshevization of the various national Communist parties. The appendix contains theses for this Bolshevization.

5. CONGRESSES OF THE COMINTERN

a. GENERAL WORKS

Q133 COMMUNIST INTERNATIONAL. *Der I. und II. Kongress der Kommunistischen Internationale; Dokumente der Kongresse und Reden W. I. Lenins.* Berlin: Dietz, 1959. 328 p.

Q134 COMMUNIST INTERNATIONAL. *Komintern v rezoliutsiiakh.* Ed. by Béla Kun. Moscow: Izd. Kommun. univ. im. Ia. M. Sverdlova, 1926. 242 p. An important collection of the major documents issued by the Comintern in its early history. Superseded by Kun's later collection of 1933.

Q135 COMMUNIST INTERNATIONAL. *Kommunisticheskii Internatsional v dokumentakh; resheniia, tezisy i vozzvaniia kongressov Kom-*

interna i plenumov IKKI, 1919-1932. Ed. by Béla Kun. Moscow: Partizdat, 1933. 1007 p. An invaluable collection of approximately 150 documents from the major Comintern assemblies through 1932: Congresses 1-6, Plenums 1-12, and the Enlarged Presidium of the Comintern Executive Committee of 1930. For each assembly, the editor has supplied an explanatory note giving the detailed agenda of the meeting and the list of special commissions. For the volume as a whole, there is a name index, and a helpful list of all documents of these assemblies *not* included in the collection. [A]

Q136 COMMUNIST INTERNATIONAL. *Pervyi sezd revoliutsionnykh organizatsii Dalnego Vostoka; sbornik.* Petrograd: Komintern, 1922. 360 p. English ed., *The First Congress of the Toilers of the Far East, Held in Moscow January 21st-February 1st, 1922; Closing Session in Petrograd, February 2nd, 1922.* Petrograd: Komintern, 1922. 248 p. German ed., *Der Erste Kongress der Kommunistischen und Revolutionären Organizationen des Fernen Ostens.* Hamburg: C. Hoym, 1922. The Russian edition presumably is the fullest account, but has not been located; the English and German editions, each incomplete, should be used together. They include valuable information on the movements in China, Japan, Korea, and Mongolia, as well as the general Comintern attitude toward the national-colonial question. The main Russian speakers were Zinoviev and Safarov.

Q137 COMMUNIST INTERNATIONAL. *Poslevoennyi kapitalizm v osveshchenii Kominterna; sbornik dokumentov i resoliutsii kongressov i ispolkoma Kominterna.* Moscow: Partizdat, 1932. 164 p.

Q138 COMMUNIST INTERNATIONAL, CONGRESSES. *Thèses, manifestes et résolutions adoptés par les Ier, IIe, IIIe, IVe congrès de l'Internationale Communiste (1919-1923); textes complets.* Paris: La Librairie du travail, 1934. 204 p.

Q139 COMMUNIST INTERNATIONAL, SEZD NARODOV VOSTOKA (1), BAKU, 1920. *Pervyi sezd narodov Vostoka, Baku, 1-8 sentiabria 1920 g.; stenograficheskie otchety.* Petrograd: Izd. Kom. Internatsionala, 1920. 232 p. Report of a Comintern-sponsored congress attended largely by delegates from the Near and Middle East, the Caucasus, and Central Asia. Major Comintern speakers were Zinoviev, Radek, and Béla Kun.

Q140 U.S. CONGRESS, HOUSE, COMMITTEE ON UN-AMERICAN ACTIVITIES. *The Communist Conspiracy: Strategy and Tactics of World Communism.* Part I: *Communism Outside the United States;* Section C: *The World Congresses of the Communist International.* Washington: G.P.O., 1956. 372 p. A convenient handbook that contains many of the major documents of Comintern history, including the

Program and Statutes, speeches by Lenin, Trotsky, Bukharin, Manuilsky, and Dimitrov, and numerous resolutions and theses. All are in English translation.

b. 1ST CONGRESS (MARCH 2-19, 1919)

The First Congress formally founded the Communist International on March 4, 1919, and liquidated the so-called Zimmerwald Left movement. A Manifesto and Platform were adopted, as were several resolutions, including Lenin's theses on bourgeois democracy and proletarian dictatorship.

Q141 COMMUNIST INTERNATIONAL, 1ST CONGRESS, MOSCOW, 1919. *Der I. Kongress der Kommunistischen Internationale, Protokoll der Verhandlungen in Moskau vom 2. bis zum 19. März 1919.* Petrograd: Komintern, 1921. 309 p. Hamburg: C. Hoym, 1921. 202 p. Russian ed., Petrograd: Komintern, 1921. 196 p.

Q142 COMMUNIST INTERNATIONAL, 1ST CONGRESS, MOSCOW, 1919. *Manifest, Richtlinien, Beschlüsse des ersten Kongresses; Aufrufe und offene Schreiben des Exekutivkomitees bis zum zweiten Kongress.* Hamburg: C. Hoym, 1920. 379 p. Important not so much for the documents of the First Congress, which are available elsewhere, as for the materials emanating from the Comintern Executive during the period between the First and Second Congresses.

Q143 COMMUNIST INTERNATIONAL, 1ST CONGRESS, MOSCOW, 1919. *Pervyi kongress Komintern, mart 1919 g.* Ed. by E. I. Korotkii, Béla Kun, and Osip A. Piatnitskii. Moscow: Partizdat, 1933. 275 p. The most useful edition. Includes the reports by Zinoviev (on the Berne Socialist Conference), Obolenskii (on Entente policy), and Sirola (on the White Terror in Finland), which were not in the earlier German and Russian editions. Some speeches, in addition, were corrected. Other new material includes the written reports submitted by the delegations of different countries, the report of the absent Serbian Social Democratic Party, and the report of the mandate commission.

Q144 COMMUNIST INTERNATIONAL, 1ST CONGRESS, MOSCOW, 1919. *Prvi Kongres Treće Internacionale; Materijali.* Comp. by Stefan Belić-Franić. Belgrade: Rad, 1953. 294 p. An almost complete report, with omissions identified by the compiler in footnotes.

c. 2ND CONGRESS (JULY 19-AUG. 7, 1920)

The primary concern of the Second Congress was the Communist party: how to create a party that was ideologically correct, organizationally sound, and effective in action. Directly related to this problem were the Statutes (Ustav) of the Comintern, the Twenty-One Conditions for admission, and the resolutions on parliamentary activity, on the trade union movement, and on the role of the Party in revolution. Other important matters included Lenin's theses on the national and colonial question and his theses on the agrarian question.

Q145 COMMUNIST INTERNATIONAL, 2D CONGRESS, PETROGRAD AND MOSCOW, 1920. *Berichte zum zweiten Kongress der Kommunistischen Internationale.* Hamburg: C. Hoym, 1921. 452 p. Important written reports submitted by the delegations to the Second Comintern Congress, but not printed with the proceedings of the Congress. Reports deal with the economic and political situation in the capitalistic countries.

Q146 COMMUNIST INTERNATIONAL, 2D CONGRESS, PETROGRAD AND MOSCOW, 1920. *Drugi Kongres Treće Internacionale; Materijali.* Comp. by Stefan Belić-Franić. Belgrade: Rad, 1956. 382 p. An abridged report containing the major speeches and reports, the most important resolutions, and the 1920 Statutes.

Q147 COMMUNIST INTERNATIONAL, 2D CONGRESS, PETROGRAD AND MOSCOW, 1920. *Rezoliutsii i ustav Kommunisticheskogo Internatsionala, priniatye II kongressom Kommunisticheskogo Internatsionala (19 iiulia - 7 avgusta 1920 g.).* Petrograd: Komintern, 1920. 128 p.

Q148 COMMUNIST INTERNATIONAL, 2D CONGRESS, PETROGRAD AND MOSCOW, 1920. *The Second Congress of the Communist International; Proceedings of Petrograd Session of July 17th and of Moscow Sessions of July 19th-August 7th, 1920.* [N.P.]: Communist International, 1921. 234 p. A heavily abridged text.

Q149 COMMUNIST INTERNATIONAL, 2D CONGRESS, PETROGRAD AND MOSCOW, 1920. *Der zweite Kongress der Kommunistischen Internationale; Protokoll der Verhandlungen vom 19 Juli in Petrograd und vom 23 Juli bis 7 August 1920 in Moskau.* Hamburg: C. Hoym, 1921. 798 p. Russian ed., *2-oi Kongress Kommunisticheskogo Internatsionala; stenograficheskii otchet.* Petrograd: 1921. 682 p. Later Russian ed., correcting important errors, *Vtoroi kongress Kominterna.* Moscow: 1934. 754 p. French ed., André Pierre, editor, Paris: 1920.

Q150 U.S. DEPARTMENT OF STATE. *International Communist Congress, 2d., Petrograd and Moscow, 1920; 2d. Congress of the Communist International as Reported and Interpreted by the Official Newspapers of Soviet Russia.* Washington: G.P.O., 1920. 166 p. The first part of this memorandum is a translation of Russian newspaper reports

(Petrograd *Pravda* and Moscow *Izvestiia*) of the proceedings of the congress, but is by no means a complete record. The second part is an interesting selection of Communist comment on the congress.

Q151 ZINOVEV, GRIGORII E. *Nabolevshie voprosy mezhdunarodnogo rabochego dvizheniia.* Petrograd: Kom. Intern., 1920. 128 p. German ed., *Brennende Tagesfragen der internationalen Arbeiterbewegung.* Petrograd: Die Kommunistische Internationale, 1920. 107 p. Speeches on the eve of and during the Second Comintern Congress. The German edition lacks the last item of the Russian edition, and is marred by minor omissions.

d. 3RD CONGRESS (JUNE 22-JULY 12, 1921)

The Third Congress acknowledged the waning of the revolutionary movement and emphasized the need for greater preparation and more realistic efforts to win the "majority of the proletariat." German events received considerable attention; the expulsion of Paul Levi was the first case involving a major Communist leader. Simultaneously with the Third Congress was held, under Comintern auspices, the founding congress of the Profintern.

Q152 COMMUNIST INTERNATIONAL, 3D CONGRESS, MOSCOW, 1921. *Protokoll des III Kongresses der Kommunistischen Internationale (Moskau, 22 Juni bis 12 Juli 1921).* Hamburg: C. Hoym, 1921. 1086 p. Russian ed., *Tretii vsemirnyi kongress Kommunisticheskogo Internatsionala; stenograficheskii otchet.* Petrograd: Gosizdat, 1922. 500 p. Both editions are equally useful; the Russian is a complete translation of the German.

Q153 COMMUNIST INTERNATIONAL, 3D CONGRESS, MOSCOW, 1921. *Theses and Resolutions Adopted at the Third World Congress of the Communist International (June 22nd-July 12th 1921).* N.Y.: Contemporary, 1921. 199 p.

e. 4TH CONGRESS (NOV. 5-DEC. 5, 1922)

The Fourth Congress was the last attended by Lenin. The general mood was one of caution; much emphasis was placed on the need for study, hard work, and, above all, defense of Soviet Russia. The tactics of the united front and the situations in several badly split parties received considerable attention. The Comintern was further centralized with the reorganization of its Executive Committee.

Q154 COMMUNIST INTERNATIONAL, 4TH CONGRESS, PETROGRAD AND MOSCOW, 1922. *Bericht über den IV. Kongress der Kommunistischen Internationale, Petrograd-Moskau, vom 5. November bis 5. Dezember, 1922.* Hamburg: C. Hoym, 1923. 219 p. A considerably abridged report.

Q155 COMMUNIST INTERNATIONAL, 4TH CONGRESS, PETROGRAD AND MOSCOW, 1922. *IV Vsemirnyi kongress Kommunisticheskogo Internatsionala 5 noiabria- 3 dekabria 1922 g.; Izbrannye doklady, rechi i rezoliutsii.* Moscow: Gosizdat, 1923. 427 p. An unabridged selection of the most important reports, etc.

Q156 COMMUNIST INTERNATIONAL, 4TH CONGRESS, PETROGRAD AND MOSCOW, 1922. *Fourth Congress of the Communist International; Abridged Report of Meetings Held at Petrograd and Moscow, Nov. 7-Dec. 3, 1922.* [London]: Communist Party of Great Britain, 1923. 296 p. A heavily abridged report, which does not contain the resolutions.

Q157 COMMUNIST INTERNATIONAL, 4TH CONGRESS, PETROGRAD AND MOSCOW, 1922. *Protokoll des vierten Kongresses der Kommunistischen Internationale, Petrograd-Moskau, vom 5. November bis 5. Dezember 1922.* Hamburg: C. Hoym, 1923. 1087 p. Russian ed., *IV Kongress Kommunistischeskogo Internatsionala, 5 noiabria-5 dekabria, 1922 g.* [N.P.]: 1923. The most useful reports of the proceedings.

Q158 COMMUNIST INTERNATIONAL, 4TH CONGRESS, PETROGRAD AND MOSCOW, 1922. *Resolutions and Theses of the Fourth Congress of the Communist International, Held in Moscow, November 7 to December 3, 1922.* London: Communist Party of Great Britain, 1922. 120 p.

Q159 COMMUNIST INTERNATIONAL, 4TH CONGRESS, PETROGRAD AND MOSCOW, 1922. *Thesen und Resolutionen des IV. Weltkongress der Kommunistischen Internationale, Moskau, vom 5. November bis 5. Dezember 1922.* Hamburg: C. Hoym, 1923. 121 p.

Q160 ZINOVEV, GRIGORII E. *L'Internationale Communiste au travail.* Paris: Librairie de l'Humanité, 1923. 187 p. Speeches by the Chairman (President) of the Comintern delivered at the Fourth Congress in 1922.

Q161 ZINOVEV, GRIGORII E. *Die Kommunistische Internationale auf dem Vormarsch.* Petrograd [?]: Kommunistische Internationale; distributed by C. Hoym, Hamburg, 1923. 207 p. Speeches by Zinoviev at the Fourth Congress, plus the major resolutions of the Congress.

f. 5TH CONGRESS (JUNE 17-JULY 8, 1924)

The Fifth Congress clearly displayed two fateful tendencies in Comintern development: the increasing involvement of other parties in the domestic politics of the Russian Communist Party, and the suffocating hegemony of the latter over the Comintern. The troika of Zinoviev-Kamenev-Stalin was supported against Trotsky. The Congress called for further bolshevization of the Communist parties. Other matters receiving considerable attention included the program question, the possibility of a "partial stabilization" of world capitalism, united front tactics, and trade union tactics. The Congress adopted a new set of Statutes.

Q162 COMMUNIST INTERNATIONAL, 5TH CONGRESS, MOSCOW, 1924. *Ve Congrès de l'Internationale Communiste (17 juin-8 juillet 1924); compte rendu analytique.* Paris: Librairie de l'Humanité, 1924. 479 p. An abridged report of the proceedings of this Congress, plus a brief report of the June 12th meeting of the Comintern Executive Committee (prior to the congress) and a report of the Fourth Plenum which followed the congress.

Q163 COMMUNIST INTERNATIONAL, 5TH CONGRESS, MOSCOW, 1924. *Fifth Congress of the Communist International; Abridged Report of Meetings Held at Moscow, June 17th to July 8th, 1924.* London: Communist Party of Great Britain, 1924. 294 p. Even more heavily abridged than the French report. Gives none of the resolutions and theses of the congress.

Q164 COMMUNIST INTERNATIONAL, 5TH CONGRESS, MOSCOW, 1924. *Piatyi vsemirnyi kongress Kommunisticheskogo Internatsionala, 17 iiunia-8 iiulia 1924 g.; stenograficheskii otchet.* Moscow-Leningrad: Gosizdat, 1925. 2 vols. Includes the proceedings of the Fourth Enlarged Plenum of the Comintern Executive Committee, which met a few days after the congress. Also includes, unlike the German language report of the congress, data issued by the mandate commission on the various delegations.

Q165 COMMUNIST INTERNATIONAL, 5TH CONGRESS, MOSCOW, 1924. *Le Programme de l'Internationale Communiste; projets présentés à la discussion du Ve Congrès mondial.* Paris: Librairie de l'Humanité, 1924. 238 p. Contains these documents: the 1919 Program of the Russian Communist Party, Bukharin's 1924 draft program for the Comintern, Thalheimer's draft program of the German Communist Party, the draft program of the Communist Youth International (to replace the 1919 program), a draft program of the Japanese Communist Party, Kabakchiev's draft program of the Bulgarian Communist Party, the Action Program of the Italian Communist Party, and Lenin's "Tasks of the Proletariat in our Revolution" (of April 1917).

Q166 COMMUNIST INTERNATIONAL, 5TH CONGRESS, MOSCOW, 1924. *Protokoll des 5. Kongresses der Kommunistischen Internationale.* Hamburg: C. Hoym, 1924. 2 vols. 1083 p. This and the Russian edition are the most useful. Like the Russian, it includes the proceedings of the Fourth Enlarged Plenum of the Executive Committee, which met on July 12-13, 1924, following the congress.

g. 6TH CONGRESS (JULY 17-SEPT. 1, 1928)

The Sixth Congress proclaimed the advent of a new, third period in post-war socio-economic development, characterized by a rapid breakdown of the partial stabilization achieved in the capitalist world and by a new round of wars and revolutions. In tactics, a drastic swing to the left was ordered in the form of the united front from below, directed against the "main enemy," the socialists (now the "social fascists"). The Congress ended years of effort by adopting a Program, largely the work of Bukharin and a document of prime significance. A new set of Statutes was also adopted.

Q167 COMMUNIST INTERNATIONAL, 6TH CONGRESS, MOSCOW, 1928. *Compte rendu stenographique.* Special number of *La Correspondance Internationale.* Paris: 1928. 610 p. Less reliable than the multi-volume German and Russian editions. Such contemporary coverage of congresses and plenums in the Comintern newspaper frequently resulted in errors, some of major importance.

Q168 COMMUNIST INTERNATIONAL, 6TH CONGRESS, MOSCOW, 1928. *Protokoll; sechster Weltkongress der Kommunistischen Internationale, Moskau, 17. Juli-1. September 1928.* Hamburg: C. Hoym, 1928-29. 4 vols. Russian ed., *VI kongress Kominterna; stenograficheskii otchet.* Moscow: Gosizdat, 1929. 6 vols. Both editions are equally authoritative.

h. 7TH CONGRESS (JULY 25-AUG. 21, 1935)

The Seventh Congress announced the new Popular Front, anti-fascist strategy, signifying a general turn to the right and away from the line of the third period. The Bulgarian Georgii Dimitrov, as General Secretary of the Comintern, was the leading spokesman for the new policy at the Congress and during the next four years. The Popular Front line permitted unprecedented flexibility in Communist tactics.

Q169 COMMUNIST INTERNATIONAL, 7TH CONGRESS, MOSCOW, 1935. *Die Offensive der Faschismus und die Aufgaben der Kommunisten im Kampf für die Volksfront gegen Krieg und Faschis-*

mus; Referate [*von*] *Wilhelm Pieck, Georgi Dimitroff* [*und*] *Palmiro Togliatti auf dem VII. Kongress der Kommunistischen Internationale* (*1935*). Berlin: Dietz, 1957. 295 p.

Q170 COMMUNIST INTERNATIONAL, 7TH CONGRESS, MOSCOW, 1935. *Report of the Seventh World Congress of the Communist International.* London: Modern Books, 1936. 643 p. A collection of the major speeches and resolutions, but not a full report. Apparently includes the complete texts of 16 speeches and reports, plus Manuilsky's post-Congress report to the Moscow *aktiv* of the CPSU, and the 4 main resolutions of the Congress.

Q171 COMMUNIST INTERNATIONAL, 7TH CONGRESS, MOSCOW, 1935. *VII Congress of the Communist International; Abridged Stenographic Report of Proceedings.* Moscow: Foreign Languages Publishing House, 1939. 604 p. French ed., *VIIe Congrès mondial de l'Internationale Communiste; compte rendu abrégé.* Moscow: 1939. 556 p. German ed., *VII Kongres der Kommunistischen Internationale; gekürztes stenographisches Protokoll.* Moscow: 1939. 600 p. A selection of about 40 reports and speeches, usually in abridged form, plus the major resolutions. Not a complete report, and should be supplemented with the contemporary coverage in *International Press Correspondence* and in *Pravda.*

Q172 MANUILSKII, DMITRII Z. *The Work of the Seventh Congress of the Communist International; A Speech Delivered at a Meeting of Active Workers of the Moscow Organization of the C.P.S.U., September 14, 1935.* Moscow-Leningrad: Co-operative Publishing Society of Foreign Workers in the USSR, 1935. 90 p. Manuilskii, a member of the Presidium (from 1924) and of the Secretariat (from 1928) of the Comintern Executive Committee, was a frequent reporter on Comintern activities to congresses and other bodies of the CPSU.

Q173 MCKENZIE, KERMIT E. "The Soviet Union, the Comintern and World Revolution: 1935," *Political Science Quarterly*, vol. LXV, No. 2 (June 1950), p. 214-237. Analysis of the pattern of strategy and tactics proclaimed at the Seventh Comintern Congress, as related to ultimate goals of the world Communist movement.

6. MEETINGS OF THE EXECUTIVE COMMITTEE OF THE COMINTERN (ECCI)

Q175 COMMUNIST INTERNATIONAL, EXECUTIVE COMMITTEE. *Deiatelnost Ispolnitelnogo Komiteta i Prezidiuma I. K. Kom-*

munisticheskogo Internatsionala ot 13-go iiulia 1921 g. do 1-go fevralia 1922 g. Petrograd: Komintern, 1922. 464 p. German ed., *Die Tätigkeit der Exekutive und des Präsidiums des E. K. der Kommunistischen Internationale vom 13. Juli 1921 bis 1. Februar 1922.* Petrograd: Verlag der Kommunistischen Internationale, 1922. 410 p. An important source for the work of the Executive Committee and its Little Bureau (the later Presidium of the Comintern) during the period from the Third Congress to the First Enlarged Plenum. It includes the material previously published in the first five numbers of the *Biulleten* of the Comintern's Executive Committee.

a. 1ST PLENUM (FEB. 24-MARCH 4, 1922)

Q176 COMMUNIST INTERNATIONAL, ENLARGED EXECUTIVE. *Die Taktik der Kommunistischen Internationale gegen die Offensive des Kapitals; Bericht über die Konferenz der Erweiterten Exekutive der Kommunistischen Internationale, Moskau, vom 24. Februar bis 4. März 1922.* Hamburg: C. Hoym, 1922. 175 p. French ed., *Compte-rendu de la Conférence de l'Exécutif Elargi de l'Internationale Communiste. Moscou, 24 février-4 mars 1922.* Paris: Librairie de l'Humanité, 1922. 260 p. The central question of the First Plenum concerned the tactics of the United Front. Other matters included the New Economic Policy in Russia and the situations in several Communist parties.

b. 2ND PLENUM (JUNE 1922)

Q177 COMMUNIST INTERNATIONAL, EXECUTIVE COMMITTEE. *Bericht der Exekutive der Kommunistischen Internationale 15. Dezember 1922-15 Mai 1923.* Moscow: Verlag der Kommunistischen Internationale, 1923. 80 p. The report of Comintern activities from the Fourth Congress (November-December 1922) to the Third Enlarged Plenum (June 1923).

Q178 COMMUNIST INTERNATIONAL, EXECUTIVE COMMITTEE. *Bericht über die Tätigkeit des Präsidiums und der Exekutive der Kommunistischen Internationale für die Zeit vom 6. März bis 11. Juni 1922.* Hamburg: Kommunistischen Internationale, 1922. 141 p. A report of Comintern activities from the First (February-March 1922) to the Second (June 1922) Enlarged Plenums of the Communist International's Executive Committee, followed by a somewhat abbreviated report on the Second Plenum. This Plenum prepared for the Fourth Comintern Congress, and gave special attention to the Czechoslovak, French, Norwegian, Italian, and German parties.

c. 3RD PLENUM (JUNE 12-23, 1923)

Q179 COMMUNIST INTERNATIONAL, EXECUTIVE COMMITTEE. *Rasshirennyi plenum Ispolnitelnogo Komiteta Kommunisticheskogo Internatsionala (12-23 iiunia 1923 g.); Otchet.* Moscow: "Krasnaia nov," 1923. 320 p. German ed., *Protokoll der Konferenz der Erweiterten Exekutive der Kommunistischen Internationale, Moskau, 12.-23. Juni 1923.* Hamburg: C. Hoym, 1923. 336 p. The major questions of the Third Enlarged Plenum included Anglo-Soviet relations, the United Front tactics, fascism, the Hamburg Socialist Congress, and the situations in Italy, Bulgaria, and Norway.

Q180 COMMUNIST INTERNATIONAL, EXECUTIVE COMMITTEE. *Uroki germanskikh sobytii; Germanskii vopros v Prezidiume Ispolkoma Kominterna (ianvar 1924 g.); doklad i rezoliutsii.* Moscow: "Krasnaia nov," 1924. 115 p. German ed., *Die Lehren der deutschen Ereignisse; Das Präsidium des Exekutivkomitees der Kommunistischen Internationale zur deutschen Frage, Januar 1924.* Hamburg: Kommunistischen Internationale, C. Hoym, 1924. 120 p. These documents are concerned with Communist activities in Saxony, Thuringia, and Hamburg, during October 1923.

Q181 COMMUNIST INTERNATIONAL, EXECUTIVE COMMITTEE. *Obzor deiatelnosti Ispolkoma i sektsii Kommunisticheskogo Internatsionala za period s IV do V kongress.* Moscow: "Krasnaia nov," 1924. 135 p. German ed., *Bericht über die Tätigkeit der Exekutive der Kommunistischen Internationale vom IV. bis V. Weltkongress.* Hamburg: C. Hoym, 1924. 114 p. English ed., *From the Fourth to the Fifth World Congress: Report of the Executive Committee of the Communist International.* London: Communist Party of Great Britain, 1924. 122 p. These are capsule reports on the activities of the separate parties and of the central Comintern apparatus from the end of 1922 to the middle of 1924.

d. 4TH PLENUM (JULY 12-13, 1924)

The report of this plenum was not issued separately, but may be found in the volumes on the Fifth Congress (Russian, German, and English editions). Among the questions considered were the situations of the Swedish, Polish, and Italian Communist parties.

e. CONFERENCE ON ORGANIZATION (MARCH 16-21, 1925)

Q182 COMMUNIST INTERNATIONAL, EXECUTIVE COMMITTEE. *La Réorganisation des Partis Communistes; rapports et décisions de la Conférence d'Organisation de l'I. C. (16-21 mars 1925).* Paris: Librairie de l'Humanité, 1925. 192 p. Materials of the First Conference on organization, held by the Comintern Executive Committee in Moscow immediately before the convening of its Fifth Plenum (March-April 1925).

f. 5TH PLENUM (MARCH 21-APRIL 6, 1925)

Q183 COMMUNIST INTERNATIONAL, ENLARGED EXECUTIVE. *Rasshirennyi plenum Ispolkoma Kommunisticheskogo Internatsionala (21 marta-6 aprelia 1925 g.); stenograficheskii otchet.* Moscow: Gosizdat, 1925. 606 p. German ed., *Protokoll: Erweiterte Exekutive der Kommunistischen Internationale, Moskau, 21.März - 6.April 1925.* Hamburg: C. Hoym, 1925. 375 p. French ed., *Exécutif Elargi de l'Internationale Communiste; compte-rendu analytique de la session du 21 mars au 6 avril 1925.* Paris: Librairie de l'Humanité, 1925. 323 p. English ed., *Bolshevising the Communist International: Report of the ECCI, March 21st-April 14th, 1925.* London: Communist Party of Great Britain, 1925. 205 p. The major subjects considered by the Fifth Plenum included "bolshevization," Anglo-Russian trade union cooperation, the peasant question, and the opposition in the Russian, Czechoslovak, Italian, German, and American parties. The Russian edition is the most complete; the German edition varies somewhat in the text and does not include the resolutions; the English edition is abbreviated, but contains the resolutions.

Q184 COMMUNIST INTERNATIONAL, EXECUTIVE COMMITTEE. *Tätigkeitsbericht der Exekutive der Kommunistischen Internationale 1925-1926: Ein Jahr Arbeit und Kampf.* Hamburg: C. Hoym, 1926. 368 p. Russian ed., *Otchet Ispolkoma Kominterna (aprel 1925 g.-ianvar 1926 g.); sostavlen Sekretariatom IKKI.* Moscow: Gosizdat, 1926. 396 p. This is an important source of Comintern activity for the period from the Fifth Plenum (March-April 1925) to the eve of the Sixth Plenum (February-March 1926). About one-fifth of the report is devoted to the Comintern Executive Committee and its departments; the remainder, to the Communist parties of the world.

g. 6TH PLENUM (FEB. 17-MARCH 15, 1926)

Q185 COMMUNIST INTERNATIONAL, ENLARGED EXECUTIVE. *Shestoi rasshirennyi plenum Ispolkoma Kominterna (17 fevralia-15 marta 1926); Stenograficheskii otchet.* Moscow-Leningrad: Gosizdat, 1927. 707 p. German ed., *Protokoll: Erweiterte Exekutive der Kommunistischen Internationale, Moskau, 17. Februar bis 15. März*

1926. Hamburg-Berlin: C. Hoym, 1926. 672 p. The major questions discussed at the Sixth Plenum included the international trade union movement, the Chinese revolution, and the situations in the German, French, English, and American parties. The German and Russian editions are complete reports and equally useful, except that the German edition does not contain the theses and resolutions adopted by the Plenum.

Q186 COMMUNIST INTERNATIONAL, EXECUTIVE COMMITTEE. *Beschüsse und Resolutionen angenommen von der 2. Orgkonferenz der Erweiterten Exekutive und bestätigt vom Orgbüro des EKKI am 26. März 1926*. Hamburg: C. Hoym, 1926. 135 p. French ed., *La IIe Conférence d'organisation; Décisions et résolutions adoptées par la IIe Conférence du Comité Executif de l'I.C. et ratifiées par le Bureau d'organisation du C.E. de l'I.C. le 26 mars 1926*. Paris: Librairie de l'Humanité, 1926. 98 p. Materials of the Second Conference on Organization, held by the Comintern Executive Committee at the time of its Sixth Enlarged Plenum.

Q187 COMMUNIST INTERNATIONAL, EXECUTIVE COMMITTEE. *Tätigkeitsbericht der Exekutive der Kommunistischen Internationale: Februar-November 1926*. Hamburg-Berlin: C. Hoym, 1926. 178 p. This report deals with Comintern activity for the period from the Sixth Plenum of the Executive Committee of the Comintern (February-March 1926) to the Seventh Plenum (November-December 1926). As customary, it is divided between the activities of the Comintern center and the several Communist parties.

h. 7TH PLENUM (NOV. 22-DECEMBER 16, 1926)

Q188 COMMUNIST INTERNATIONAL, EXECUTIVE COMMITTEE. *Puti mirovoi revoliutsii; sedmoi rasshirennyi plenum Ispolnitelnogo Komiteta Kommunisticheskogo Internatsionala, 22 noiabria-16 dekabria 1926 g.; stenograficheskii otchet*. Moscow-Leningrad: Gosizdat, 1927. 2 vols. German ed., *Protokoll: Erweiterte Exekutive der Kommunistischen Internationale, Moskau 22. November-16. Dezember 1926*. Hamburg-Berlin: C. Hoym, 1927. 895 p. The major questions considered at the Seventh Plenum included the English situation (the General Strike), the Chinese revolution, Trotskyism, the expulsion of Ruth Fischer from the German Party, and the expulsion of Boris Souvarine from the French Party.

i. 8TH PLENUM (MAY 18-30, 1927)

Q189 COMMUNIST INTERNATIONAL, EXECUTIVE COMMITTEE. *Protiv voiny; vopros o voine na VIII plenume Ispolkoma Kominterna*. Moscow-Leningrad: Gosizdat, 1928. 96 p.

Q190 COMMUNIST INTERNATIONAL, EXECUTIVE COMMITTEE. *VIII plenum Ispolnitelnogo Komiteta Kommunisticheskogo Internatsionala 18-30 maia 1927 g.; tezisy, rezoliutsii i vozzvaniia.* Moscow: Gosizdat, 1927. 107 p. No full report of this plenum appears to have been published. Among the major subjects discussed included the war danger, the new stage in China (after Chiang Kai-shek's coup), the situation in England, and Trotskyism.

j. 9TH PLENUM (FEBRUARY 1928)

Q191 BRAUN, P. *At the Parting of the Ways; The Results of the Ninth Plenum of the Comintern.* London: Communist Party of Great Britain, 1928. 130 p. A Communist explanation of the plenum resolutions on such matters as the trade unions, the socialists, the British and French Communist Parties, the Chinese revolution, and Trotskyism. It includes the text of the resolution on the Trotskyist Opposition.

Q192 COMMUNIST INTERNATIONAL, EXECUTIVE COMMITTEE. *Kompartiia i krizis kapitalizma; 9-i plenum IKKI; stenograficheskii otchet.* Moscow: Partizdat, 1932. 640 p. This is apparently the only full report of the Ninth Plenum; but see the contemporary coverage of the plenum, which met in February 1928, in the issues of *International Press Correspondence.* Major issues of this meeting included the "left opposition" in the USSR and in the Comintern, the Chinese revolution, and the English and French parties.

Q193 COMMUNIST INTERNATIONAL, EXECUTIVE COMMITTEE. *Novaia taktika Angliiskoi Kompartii; sbornik (materialy IX plenuma Kominterna).* Moscow-Leningrad: Gosizdat, 128. 167 p. On the new anti-Labour Party line imposed by the Comintern on the British Communist Party.

Q194 COMMUNIST INTERNATIONAL, EXECUTIVE COMMITTEE. *Resolutionen und Beschlüsse über der IX. Plenartagung des Erweiterten Exekutiv-Komitees der Komintern in Moskau, Februar 1928.* 1928. 56 p.

Q195 COMMUNIST INTERNATIONAL, EXECUTIVE COMMITTEE. *Résolutions adoptées à la IXe session plénière du C. E. de l'I. C. (février 1928.)* Paris: Bureau d'Éditions, 1928. 56 p.

Q196 COMMUNIST INTERNATIONAL, EXECUTIVE COMMITTEE. *Kommunisticheskii Internatsional pered shestym vsemirnym kongressom; Obzor deiatelnosti IKKI i sektsii Kominterna mezhdu V i VI kongressami.* Moscow-Leningrad: Gosizdat, 1928. 442 p. German ed., *Die Komintern vor dem 6. Weltkongress.* Hamburg: C. Hoym, 1928. 576 p. French ed., *L'Activité de l'I.C. du Ve au VIe Congrès.* Paris: Bureau d'Éditions, n.d. 682 p. English ed., *Between the Fifth and the Sixth World Congresses, 1924-1928*. London: Communist Party of Great Britain, 1928. 508 p. A valuable survey. About one-fifth of the material concerns the departments of the Comintern Executive Committee; the remainder consists of capsule reports on some fifty Communist parties. The several language editions appear to be identical in coverage.

k. 10TH PLENUM (JULY 3-19, 1929)

Q197 COMMUNIST INTERNATIONAL, EXECUTIVE COMMITTEE. *X plenum Ispolkoma Kominterna.* Moscow: Gosizdat, 1929. 4 vols. German ed., *Protokoll: 10. Plenum des Exekutivekomitees der Kommunistischen Internationale, Moskau, 3. Juli 1929 bis 19. Juli 1929*. Hamburg-Berlin: C. Hoym, 1929. 953 p. Major questions included party tactics in the unfolding world economic crisis and the struggle against "right deviationists" in the Comintern. Both editions contain the theses and resolutions that were adopted by this Tenth Plenum.

l. 11TH PLENUM (MARCH 26-APRIL 11, 1931)

Q198 COMMUNIST INTERNATIONAL, EXECUTIVE COMMITTEE. *XI plenum IKKI: stenograficheskii otchet.* Moscow: Partizdat, 1931-32. 2 vols. The major issues of the Eleventh Plenum (March 26-April 11, 1931) included the "maturing" of the revolutionary movement, especially in Germany and Poland, and the danger of war against the Soviet Union.

Q199 COMMUNIST INTERNATIONAL, EXECUTIVE COMMITTEE. *XIth Plenum Series: Addresses Delivered at the Eleventh Plenum of the Executive Committee of the Communist International.* London: Modern Books, 1931. 3 parts. Not a complete record.

m. 12TH PLENUM (SEPTEMBER 1932)

Q200 COMMUNIST INTERNATIONAL. *Mezhdunarodnoe polozhenie i zadachi sektsii Kommunisticheskogo Internatsionala; material po itogam XII plenuma IKKI.* Serpukhov: "Mosoblpoligraf," 1932. 114 p.

Q201 COMMUNIST INTERNATIONAL, EXECUTIVE COMMITTEE. *XII. Plenum des Exekutiv-komitees der Kommunistischen Internationale (September 1932); Thesen und Resolutionen.* Moscow: Verlagsgenossenschaft ausländischer Arbeiter in der UdSSR, 1932. 46 p.

Q202 COMMUNIST INTERNATIONAL, EXECUTIVE COMMITTEE. *XII plenum IKKI; stenograficheskii otchet.* Moscow: Partizdat, 1933. 3 vols. The major issues of the Twelfth Plenum included the "end of capitalist stabilization," the role of Social Democracy, trade unions and unemployment, and the danger of war and intervention against the Soviet Union.

Q203 COMMUNIST INTERNATIONAL, EXECUTIVE COMMITTEE. *XIIth Plenum Library: Reports and Speeches Delivered at the Twelfth Plenum of the Executive Committee of the Communist International.* London: Modern Books, 1932-33. Not a complete report.

Q204 KUUSINEN, OTTO V. *Prepare for Power; The International Situation and the Tasks of the Sections of the Comintern (Twelfth Plenum of the E.C.C.I.).* London: Modern Books; N.Y.: Workers Library, 1933. 159 p. Russian ed., *Mezhdunarodnoe polozhenie i zadachi sektsii Kominterna.* Moscow: 1933. A major report by a top-ranking Comintern leader.

n. 13TH PLENUM (NOV. 28-DEC. 12, 1933)

Q205 COMMUNIST INTERNATIONAL, EXECUTIVE COMMITTEE. *Theses, Reports, Speeches of the Thirteenth Plenum held in Moscow, December 1933.* N.Y.: Workers Library, 1934. 8 pamphlets in 1 vol. While this is not a complete report, it is a useful collection of documents, including reports by Kuusinen, Piatnitsky, Manuilsky, Knorin, Pieck, and others.

Q206 COMMUNIST INTERNATIONAL, EXECUTIVE COMMITTEE. *XIII plenum IKKI; stenograficheskii otchet.* Moscow: Partizdat, 1934. 597 p. This plenum does not foreshadow the coming Popular Front policy; in fact, the extremist line, pursued since 1928, is continued, despite the failure in Germany.

Q207 COMMUNIST INTERNATIONAL, EXECUTIVE COMMITTEE. *Thirteenth Plenum of the ECCI; Reports and Speeches Delivered at the Thirteenth Plenum of the Executive Committee of the Communist International.* London: Modern Books, 1934. Not a complete report.

7. COMINTERN PERIODICALS AND NEWSPAPERS

Q208 COMMUNIST INTERNATIONAL. *Biulleten Kommunisticheskogo Internatsionala.* Ed. by T. L. Akselrod. Moscow: 1921—. Daily, except Sunday and Monday. Intended for use by the Soviet press, it contained reports of Communist activities as well as other political and labor news from foreign countries. Date of cessation of publication is not known; probably a short-lived periodical of the Comintern's early years.

Q209 COMMUNIST INTERNATIONAL. *International Press Correspondence.* Berlin, Vienna, London. October 17, 1921-December 23, 1943. Name changed to *World News and Views* with issue of July 2, 1938. In effect, the Comintern newspaper. Invaluable as a source, despite numerous inaccuracies. Important Comintern documents were published, including verbatim reports (often with mistranslations) of congresses and plenums of the Executive Committee. There were also German (1921-33), French (1921-39), and Italian (1925-26) editions. A German language edition appeared also in Switzerland under the title *Rundschau über Politik, Wirtschaft und Arbeiterbewegung* (1932-39). The English edition continued to appear after 1943 under the title *World News and Views,* but became in effect an organ of the British C.P. Its name was changed to *World News* in January 1954. After 1939 *World News and Views* decreased in size and value, reflecting the decline in importance of the Comintern itself. [A]

Q210 COMMUNIST INTERNATIONAL. *Kommunismus; Zeitschrift der Kommunistischen Internationale für die Länder Südosteuropas.* Vienna, February 1, 1920 (vol. I, no. 1) to September 1, 1921 (vol. II, no. 31/32). A short-lived Comintern periodical, appearing initially under the title *Zeitschrift der Kommunistischen Internationale für die Länder Südosteuropas* (February 1-June 12, 1920), and later under the title *Zeitschrift der Kommunistischen Internationale* (June 19-October 16, 1920). Apparently ceased publication with the issue for September 1, 1921. Useful for the Communist movement in South-Eastern Europe during a period when such an important source as *International Press Correspondence* had not yet begun publication.

Q211 COMMUNIST INTERNATIONAL. *Kommunisticheskii Internatsional; Organ Ispolnitelnogo Komiteta Kommunisticheskogo Internatsionala.* Petrograd-Moscow: I-XXV; May 1919-May 1943; 1919-21, monthly; 1921-24, irregular; 1925, monthly; 1926-29, weekly; 1930-35, thrice monthly; January-July 1936, twice monthly; July 1936-May 1943, monthly. The major Comintern journal and an indispensable source. There were editions in other languages: German (Petrograd, Moscow, Hamburg, Berlin, Basel, Strasbourg, Paris, Stockholm, May 1919-February 1940); French (Petrograd, Paris, May 1919-August 1939); English (Petrograd, London, N.Y., May 1919-December 1940); Chinese (1930- ?); Spanish (1933- ?). The Russian edition was the regular and the most complete; but on a very few occasions it did not include articles appearing in other editions. [A]

Q212 COMMUNIST INTERNATIONAL, EXECUTIVE COMMITTEE. *Biulleten Ispolnitelnogo Komiteta Kommunisticheskogo Internatsionala 8 sent.-23 dek. 1921.* Petrograd: 1921. Four numbers in 1 vol. A short-lived periodical, edited by Zinoviev, containing proclamations, resolutions, and theses, emanating from the Comintern Executive Committee for the most part, but also from the Profintern, Communist Youth International, etc. The four issues in 1921 were dated September 8 and 20, October 21, and December 23; there was a fifth issue early in 1922, and evidently shortly thereafter the *Biulleten* ceased publication.

Addenda

Q213 HULSE, JAMES W. *The Forming of the Communist International.* Stanford: Stanford University Press, 1964. 275 p. A careful study of the early Comintern through its Second Congress in mid-1920. Stresses the shift in emphasis during 1919-1920 from expectancy of revolution to concern with preparation and organization, and the consequences for Comintern development. By a professor of history at the University of Nevada. [A]

Q214 KALBE, ERNSTGERT. *Freiheit für Dimitroff; Der internationale Kampf gegen die provokatorische Reichstagbrandstiftung und den Leipziger Prozess.* Berlin: Rütten-Loening, 1963. 360 p. Deals with the period between the day of the Reichstag fire and Dimitrov's acquittal. Uses heretofore unknown and unpublished data on the international protest movements of the Comintern. This is the initial publication of a series to be issued by Karl Marx University, Leipzig, designed to fight "falsifications" by "bourgeois" writers.

R. Comintern Subsidiaries

RA. RED PEASANT INTERNATIONAL (KRESTINTERN)

EDITED BY GEORGE D. JACKSON, JR.

NOTE: The stenographic reports of Comintern meetings, particularly the Fifth and Sixth Congresses and the Fifth Plenum of the Executive Committee, provide extensive material on the history of the Krestintern.

RA1 *Biblioteka revoliutsionnoe krestianskoe dvizhenie.* Moscow: Gosizdat, 1927-28. English editions appeared under the title: *Library of the Revolutionary Farmers and Peasants Movement.* Berlin: R. L. Praeger, 1927-28. A series of semi-historical polemical works by veterans of the Krestintern. (The Library of Congress catalogues them under the individual authors.)

1. MESHCHERIAKOV, N. L. *Krestianstvo i revoliutsiia.* 140 p. English ed., *The Peasantry and Revolution.* 67 p.
2. DINGLI, S. *Borba krestianstva Indonezii.* 112 p. English ed., *The Peasant Movement in Indonesia.* 60 p.
3. GOROV, M. P. *Borba krestian Bolgarii.* 160 p.
4. GRAF. *Krestianskoe dvizhenie v Germanii v proshlom i nastoiashchem.* 127 p.
5. KHEVESHI, AKUZIUS. *Vengerskoe krestianstvo i ego borba.* 176 p.

These are all propaganda pamphlets, but the authors, in trying to advance the cause of the Krestintern, supply some evidence of the organization and activity of that organization in their respective countries. [B]

RA2 BOSHKOVICH, B. *Krestianskoe dvizhenie i natsionalnyi vopros v Iugoslavii.* Ed. by T. Dombal. Moscow: Mezhdunarodnyi agrarnyi institut, 1929. 107 p. The Krestintern's version of their sole significant triumph, the recruitment of the leader of the Croatian Peasant Party, Stjepan Radić, the only prominent leader of an independent peasant political party to join the Krestintern. This account is of special value because its author had served as General-Secretary of the Communist Party of Yugoslavia after its formation in April 1919 and was a veteran member of both the Krestintern and of the Executive Committee of the Comintern. [B]

RA3 BOSHKOVICH, B. *Zelenyi Internatsional i ego kulatskoe litso.* Moscow: Mezhdunarodnyi agrarnyi institut, 1933. 78 p. One of the last propaganda pamphlets of the Krestintern. Compares and contrasts the program of the Green International of peasant political parties at

Prague with the program of the Krestintern. One of the few sources to describe the policies of the Krestintern after the removal of Bukharin and the initiation of the "social fascist" line in the Comintern. [A]

RA4 CARR, EDWARD H. "Bulgaria and the Peasant," chapter 8 of *The Interregnum, 1923-1924*. Vol. IV of his *A History of Soviet Russia.* N.Y.: Macmillan, 1954. The only published scholarly account in English of the founding of the Krestintern. Treats the connection between the September 1923 uprising in Bulgaria and the founding of the Krestintern. Incomplete and not entirely accurate, but documented.

RA5 DOMBAL, T. *Krestianskii internatsional.* Leningrad: "Priboi," 1925. 62 p. By the founder of the Krestintern.

RA6 DOMBAL, T. *Zadachi i dostizheniia Krestinterna.* Moscow: "Novaia derevnia," 1925. 79 p. The report of the Presidium of the Krestintern to its Second Plenum in April 1925. Dombal, the founder and Assistant Secretary-General of the Krestintern, reviews the achievements and shortcomings of the Krestintern a year and a half after its founding. Reflects the changed emphasis in Comintern agrarian policy as a result of the growing ascendancy of Bukharin and the decisions of the Fifth Plenum of the Executive Committee of the Comintern. Also available in issue 3-4 (June-July 1924) of *Krestianskii Internatsional.* [A]

RA7 DOMBAL, T., BOSHKOVICH, B., KHEVESHI, A., and GOROV, M. *Borba za krestianstvo; sbornik statei, sostavlennyi otdelom pechati Krestinterna.* Moscow: Kommunisticheskaia akademiia, 1926. 78 p. Reprinting of four articles originally appearing in *Krestianskii Internatsional* (the official Krestintern organ) in 1925. Written by four of the most prominent figures in the Krestintern, the articles define the program of the Krestintern and compare its program to that of other international agricultural organizations. [A]

RA8 INTERNATIONAL PEASANTS' CONFERENCE, 1st, MOSCOW, 1923. *Pervaia mezhdunarodnaia krestianskaia konferentsiia, 10 oktiabr-16 oktiabr, 1923 g.; rechi, tezisy, vozzvaniia.* Moscow: "Novaia derevnia," 1927. 181 p. German ed., *Protokoll vom ersten internationalen Bauernkongress.* Berlin: Verlag neues Dorf, 1924. 170 p. French ed., *Première conférence internationale paysanne.* Paris: 1923. English ed., *Red Peasant International; International Peasant Union Documents, no. 19.* N.Y.: International Peasant Union, n.d. 57 p. The single most useful source for the study of the Krestintern. This is the founding congress and the only meeting of the Krestintern to be attended by such important figures as Varga, Kalinin, Zinoviev, and Bukharin. The Russian edition includes many of the speeches, all of the theses and resolutions, the organizational plan, and a list of the members of both the

Presidium and the International Peasants' Council. The different editions do not contain precisely the same material. The German and Russian editions are the best; the English edition is a poor translation of the French, and both are inaccurate. [A]

RA9 INTERNATIONAL PEASANTS' CONFERENCE, 1st, MOSCOW, 1923. Some of the speeches and theses of the Conference were published separately under the general title: *Biblioteka krestianskogo internatsionala.* All of the Russian editions were published in 1924-25 in Moscow by the publishing house "Novaia Derevnia." A German series was also published in 1924-25, under the general title *Bibliothek des Internationalen Bauernrates,* in Berlin by the publishers "Neues Dorf" (except for *Das Bündnis der Bauern und Arbeiter*, which was published in Moscow).

1. ZINOVEV, G. and others. *Krestiane i rabochie.* 1924. 60 p.
2. KALININ, M. *Mirovoe krestianstvo.* 1924. 27 p.
3. *Pervaia mezhdunarodnaia krestianskaia konferentsiia, Moskva, 1923, rechi, tezisy, vozzvaniia.* 1924. 183 p.
4. VARGA, E. *Polozhenie krestianstva v kapitalisticheskikh stranakh.* 1924. 40 p.
5. ALGERMIN. *Selskoe khoziaistvo i krestianstvo Norvegii.* 1925. 32 p.
6. SMIRNOV, A. P. *Mezhdunarodnoe krestianskoe dvizhenie ii opyt russkoi revoliutsii.* 1925. 24 p.

The German series:

1. BÜRGI, R. *Als deutscher Bauern in Sowjetrussland.* 1924. 20 p.
2. KALININ, M. *Die Bauern auf dem Wege zur Befreiung.* 1925. 28 p.
3. VARGA, E. *Das Joch der Bauern.* 1924. 32 p.
4. *Welche Genossenschaften können uns helfen.* 1924. 32 p.
5. ZINOVEV, G. and others. *Die Weltbund der Bauern.* 1924. 56 p.
6. *Das Bündnis der Bauern und Arbeiter.* Moscow: Neues Dorf, 1924. 23 p.
7. *Protokoll vom ersten internationalen Bauernkongress vom 10. bis 16. Oktober, 1923 in Moskau.* 1924. 175 p.

Numbers 2, 3, 5, and 7 of the German series correspond to numbers 2, 4, 1, and 3 of the Russian series respectively. Numbers 2 through 6 of the German series were also published separately as numbers 1 through 5 of *Der erste Weltkongress der Bauern.*

RA10 INTERNATIONAL PEASANTS' CONFERENCE, MOSCOW, 1927. *Stenogramm und Beschlüsse.* Berlin: Neues Dorf, 1928. 46 p. French ed., *Sténogramme et résolutions.* Berlin: Neues Dorf, 1928. 39 p. The only published record of the last known conference of the Krestintern, held in November 1927. Hastily convoked to impress a visiting delegation of peasant political leaders, this conference was the last before Stalin announced that the "third period" in international politics after World War I had arrived. Contains excerpts from speeches and resolutions. [A]

RA11 *Internationaler Bauern-Korrespondent.* 22 issues. Berlin: Neues Dorf, 1927-29. From issue no. 5 in 1928, the title is *Internationale Bauern-Nachrichten.* Also published in English under the title *Farmers' and Peasants' International Correspondent.* Replaced *Krestianskii Internatsional* as the chief organ of the Red Peasant International during its last few years of activity. A valuable documentary source for a period in which the Krestintern steered an especially uncertain course. With the initiation of the struggle between Stalin and Bukharin and the proclamation of a "third period" in international affairs, the leaders of the Krestintern tried to adapt to the new "line" in order to survive. [A]

RA12 JACKSON, GEORGE D., JR. "The Green International and the Red Peasant International; a study of Comintern Policy towards the Peasant Political Movement in Eastern Europe, 1919-1930." Ph.D. dissertation, Columbia, 1961. 427 p. A detailed and thoroughly-documented analysis of the history of the Krestintern within the broader framework of Comintern agrarian policy. The author supplies several chapters on the effectiveness of Krestintern policy in East European countries. [A]

RA13 KOLAROV, V., ed. *Shest let borby za krestianstvo.* Vol. II of *Agrarnyi vopros i sovremennoe krestianskoe dvizhenie.* Moscow: Mezhdunarodnyi agrarnyi institut, 1936. 168 p. German ed., *Die Agrarfrage und die gegenwärtige Bauernbewegung.* Moscow: Internationaler Agrar-Institut, 1935. A series of articles by the members of the Krestintern's research auxiliary, the Mezhdunarodnyi agrarnyi institut at Moscow. Particularly valuable for a summary of the activities of the Krestintern after the expulsion of Bukharin from the Comintern and the removal of most of the original staff of the Krestintern in 1929. Kheveshi's article, "Evropeiskii krestianskii komitet i krestianskoe komitetskoe dvizhenie," (p. 18-34) describes the formation of a branch of the Krestintern, the European Peasant Committee, in November 1929 and its subsequent activity. [A]

RA14 KRASNYI, IUZ. "Mezhdunarodnyi krestianskii sovet," *Kommunisticheskii Internatsional,* no. 3-4 (May 1924), p. 163-80. S-KII. "Krestianskii internatsional i ego znachenie," *Bolshevik,* no. 5-6 (May-June 1924), p. 4-11. The place of the Krestintern in Comintern policy defined along with some indication of plans for future development.

The Krasnyi article is also available in the German and English editions of *Kommunisticheskii Internatsional.* [B]

RA15 *Krestianskii Internatsional.* April 1924-May 1926. 15 issues. Organ of the Mezhdunarodnyi Krestianskii Sovet "Krestianskii Internatsional." Moscow: "Novaia Derevnia," 1924-26. German ed., *Die Weltbund der Bauern*, later *Die Bauerninternationale.* An essential source for the study of the Krestintern. Includes not only articles and bibliographies, but also the appeals, decisions, and invitations issued by the Presidium of the Krestintern. Issue number 3-4 (June-July 1924) contains the conditions under which Radić entered the Krestintern, and issue number 3-5 (March-May 1925) contains some of the speeches and theses presented at the Second Plenum of the Krestintern in April 1925. [A]

RA16 LIVINGSTONE, ROBERT G. "Stjepan Radić and the Croatian Peasant Party, 1904-1929." Ph.D. dissertation, Harvard, 1959. Though primarily concerned with the history of the Croatian Peasant Party, this study gives the only detailed examination in English of the adherence of Stjepan Radić, leader of the Croatian Peasant Party, to the Krestintern. Though the terms of adherence are not given, Radić's motives and the consequences of his adherence are treated in definitive fashion. Heavily-documented, with an extensive bibliography, but no Russian sources.

RA17 "Le Premier Congrès européen paysan à Berlin," *La Fédération balcanique*, no. 132-133 (9-10a) (April 15, 1930), p. 2878-84. Russian ed., "Pervyi evropeiskii kongress trudniashchegosia krestianstva," *Kommunisticheskii Internatsional*, no. 10 (April 10, 1930), p. 28-33. These articles describe the formation of a branch of the Krestintern in 1929. The article in *Fédération balcanique* includes excerpts from the major speeches at the founding conference. Both articles are published in the English editions of the respective journals. The article in *Kommunisticheskii Internatsional* is available also in the German edition of that journal. [A]

RA18 UNITED FARMERS' EDUCATIONAL LEAGUE. *United Farmer.* March 1926-July 1931. The journal of the American section of the Krestintern.

RB. RED INTERNATIONAL OF LABOR UNIONS (PROFINTERN)

EDITED BY ALBERT RESIS

1. BIBLIOGRAPHY

RB1 IUNOVICH, MINNA M. *Literatura po mirovomu khoziastvu i mirovoi politike za 10 let (1917-1927); bibliograficheskii ukazatel knig i statei na russkom iazyke.* Moscow: Izd. Kommunisticheskoi akademii, 1929. 255 p. On the Profintern and the international labor movement see: books and pamphlets, p. 40-47; articles, p. 144-152. [A]

2. GENERAL WORKS

RB2 GALSEN, S., and SORBONSKII, S. *Komintern i Profintern.* Moscow: VTsSPS, 1926. 119 p. A superficial survey for Soviet readers. Divided into three sections: I. Relations between trade unions and political parties; II. A brief history of the Comintern; III. A brief history of the Profintern. The authors view the Party and trade unions as two branches of a single labor movement, the Party of course assuming the vanguard role envisaged by Lenin. The same relationship is carried out on the international level by the Comintern and the Profintern. [B]

RB3 LEFRANC, GEORGES. *Les Expériences syndicales internationales des origines à nos jours.* Paris: Aubier, 1952. 382 p. Chapter IV presents a brief account of the history of the Profintern. The author makes a number of acute observations on the workings of Communism in the international labor movement. [B]

RB4 LORWIN, LEWIS L. (pseud. of Louis Levitzki). *Labor and Internationalism.* N.Y.: Macmillan, 1929. 682 p. French ed., Paris: 1933. 455 p. German ed., Berlin: 1930. 254 p. A scholarly, pioneer work. Useful sections on the Red International of Labor Unions, on its struggle with the International Federation of Trade Unions, on its relations with English trade unions, and on United Front tactics and negotiations. [A]

RB5 LOZOVSKII, ALEXANDER (pseud. of Solomon A. Dridzo). *Anarkho-sindikalizm i kommunizm.* Moscow: Krasnaia nov, 1923. 107 p. A reprint of polemics directed against the anarcho-syndicalists' anti-Communist "prejudices," published between the first and second Red International of Labor Unions' congresses. Contains important statements on Profintern efforts in France to conquer the CGT from within and to consummate the CGTU's affiliation. Lozovskii held the post of

Secretary-General of the Profintern, 1921-37, the full period of the organization's existence. He survived every Stalinist Purge—save the last. [B]

RB6 LOZOVSKII, ALEXANDER. *Angliiskii proletariat na rasputi; sbornik statei.* Moscow: Profintern, 1926. 312 p. A collection of Lozovskii's articles, speeches, and reports on the English trade-union movement from the MacDonald government to the end of the General Strike. (Does not include material from the author's *Anglo-sovetskaia konferentsiia professionalnykh soiuzov.*) Holds that the defeat of the General Strike was the turning point in the British labor movement because the defeat raised doubts among British workers about the value of bourgeois democracy, and that the majority would now follow the British Communist Party and Minority Movement. [A]

RB7 LOZOVSKII, ALEXANDER. *Anglo-sovetskaia konferentsiia professionalnykh soiuzov.* Moscow-Leningrad: Gosizdat, 1925. 112 p. German ed., *Die Englisch-Russische Gewerkschaftskonferenz.* Berlin: 1925. French ed., Paris: 1925. Most of this material was first published in *Krasnyi Internatsional Profsoiuzov.* Maintains that the Profintern and Soviet trade unions always favored the unity of world labor. Soviet trade unions joined the Anglo-Soviet Committee with the "full support" of the Profintern and in spite of opposition from the International Federation of Trade Unions.

RB8 LOZOVSKII, ALEXANDER. *Besedy o profdvizhenii, provodennye v Profshkole Kitaiskoi federatsii profsoiuzov v Khankou 1-18 iiune 1927.* Moscow: Profintern, 1927. 106 p. Lectures conducted on a popular level, explaining the rudiments of Communist trade unionism, especially the tactics of waging the class struggle within the national struggle, and analyzing weaknesses of the revolutionary labor movement in China. By 1927, China had the largest number of adherents claimed by the Profintern for any country outside of the Soviet Union. [B]

RB9 LOZOVSKII, ALEXANDER. *Kommunisten und gewerkschaften; referat und Schlüsswort in der VI tagung des erweiterten exekutivkomitees der Kommunistischen internationale.* Berlin: Führer, 1926. 132 p. Thesis: bi-polarization of the world labor movement has occurred in the wake of concentration of world political influence in two centers, the USA and the USSR. Reformist trade unions in Europe follow the lead of the A.F.L., whose influence is carried to Europe along with American capital. Meanwhile the Left wing of European labor and the growing trade union movement of the colonial and semi-colonial countries turn to the Comintern and Profintern in view of the revolutionary liberationist role of the USSR and the Soviet trade unions. Catalogues 22 weak points in Communist activity in the world trade-union movement.

RB10 LOZOVSKII, ALEXANDER. *L'Activité de l'I.S.R.* Paris: Bureau d'Éditions, 1923. 416 p.

RB11 LOZOVSKII, ALEXANDER. *Marx and the Trade Unions.* N.Y.: International Pub., 1935. 188 p. Indian ed., Calcutta: 1944. Spanish ed., Buenos Aires: 1934. Culls references from Marx to support the contention that the historical mission of trade unions is to overthrow, not merely to reform, capitalism. The last chapter describes the Profintern as the embodiment of this conception. [B]

RB12 LOZOVSKII, ALEXANDER. *Mirovoi krizis i ekonomicheskaia borba.* Moscow: Gos. sots.-ekon. izd., 1931. 229 p. A collection of articles, reports, and speeches centering on the Fifth Congress of the Profintern. Analyzes the failure of the Communist movement to win a majority of the working class in spite of the favorable objective conditions created by the growing world economic crisis. Attributes this failure to the chronic inability or unwillingness of the various Communist Parties to concentrate their activity in the factories. Communist strength in the trade unions did not measure up to Communist Party political strength. In some countries Party membership exceeded the number of Profintern adherents in the trade unions. [B]

RB13 LOZOVSKII, ALEXANDER. *Moskva ili Amsterdam; kommunizm i reformizm v mezhdunarodnom professionalnom dvizhenii; sbornik statei.* Moscow: VTsSPS, 1924. 301 p. 2nd ed., Moscow: 1925. 525 p. A collection of Lozovskii's articles reprinted from Profintern, Comintern, and Soviet Party and trade-union publications. [A]

RB14 LOZOVSKII, ALEXANDER. *Otchet Mezhdunarodnogo soveta krasnykh professionalnykh i proizvodstvennykh soiuzov; za period ot 15 iiulia 1920 g. do 1 iiulia 1921 g.* Moscow: MSNKH, 1921. 195 p. English ed., *The International Council of Trade and Industrial Unions.* N.Y.: Union Pub. Assoc., 1920 [?]. 64 p. The most important source on Mezhsovprof. The Russian edition is more complete than the English edition, but the latter contains some information not found in the Russian work. [A]

RB15 LOZOVSKII, ALEXANDER. *The Pan-Pacific Trade Union Conference, Hankow, May 20-26, 1927.* Moscow: 1927. 62 p. The conference adopted measures for increasing resistance to imperialism and for strengthening the Pacific Secretariat. The latter was held to be a new weapon in the fight to create united trade-union centers in each country and a single trade-union international.

RB16 LOZOVSKII, ALEXANDER. *Rabochaia Frantsia (zametki i vpechatleniia).* Moscow-Petrograd: Gosizdat, 1923. 139 p. A series of articles from *Pravda* describing the author's clandestine activities on behalf of the Comintern and Profintern in France during the summer of 1922. Attempts to portray the "other France"—the France of the revolutionary workers as reflected in the working class parties and trade unions. [B]

RB17 LOZOVSKII, ALEXANDER. *Stachka kak boi; lektsii chitannye v mezhdunarodnoi leninskoi shkole v ianvare-marte 1930 g.* Moscow: Izd. Kommunisticheskoi akademii, 1930. 140 p. A Marxist attempt to apply the tactics of military science to strike struggles, with Clausewitz and Lenin as guides. The attempt was deemed urgent owing to the development of new revolutionary situations in the capitalist world. [B]

RB18 LOZOVSKII, ALEXANDER. *The World's Trade Union Movement.* Intro. by Earl Browder. Chicago: Trade Union Educational League, 1924. 125 p. Russian ed., *Mirovoe professionalnoe dvizhenie do i posle voiny.* Moscow: "Voprosy truda," 1925. 363 p. 2nd ed., 1925. 112 p. Contains concise statements of Communist policies and tactics in the world labor movement delivered at the school of the Russian Communist Party in Moscow, July-August 1923. Claims that the balance of power was shifting in favor of the Profintern as reflected in the growing number of militants within the International Federation of Trade Unions' affiliates who were dissatisfied with the parent organization. The decline of the International Federation of Trade Unions would leave only a single center, the Profintern. Hence the long range trend would be the amalgamation of the heterogeneous world labor movement into a single international embracing all forms of labor organization, political and economic. [A]

RB19 LOZOVSKII, ALEXANDER, ed. *Obnishchanie proletariata v kapitalisticheskikh stranakh; materialy o polozhenii rabochego klassa za gody krizisa i depressii osobogo goda (1929-1935).* Moscow: Profizdat, 1936. 240 p. Data on the decline of living standards in eight capitalist countries (including Germany, England, USA, France, etc.). An attempt to ascertain the "true" picture of living standards, distinguished from that drawn by official government and I.L.O. statistics. Claims that the data show increasing misery, ignorance, savagery, pauperization, and moral degradation of the workers under capitalism during the years 1929-35, and that they prove Marx's theory of the absolute impoverishment of the proletariat. [B]

RB20 LOZOVSKII, ALEXANDER, ed. *Rabochii Kitai v 1927 godu; sbornik statei.* Moscow: Izd. Profinterna, 1928. 324 p. Articles by

Lozovskii, L. Geller, M. Rubinshtein, E. Browder, and others on the Chinese Revolution, labor conditions and trade unions in China, and on the decisions of the Pan-Pacific Trade-Union Conference concerning China. [B]

RB21 MAISKII, IVAN. *Professionalnoe dvizhenie na Zapade.* 2nd ed. Leningrad: Leningr. gubprofsovet., 1926. 325 p. An enlarged version of lectures on the trade-union movement in England, Germany, and France by the Soviet Ambassador-to-be to Great Britain, based in part on the author's experience in the German and English trade unions before 1917. Maintains that the German form of trade unionism was most "perfect" (aside from its "reformism") in that it was nominally neutral in politics, but in reality Social-Democratic. Hence the trade-union relationship to the Social-Democratic Party in Germany provided the perfect organizational model for trade union-Party relations in the Soviet Union. [B]

RB22 NIN, ANDREAS. *Los Organizaciones obreros Internacionales.* Madrid: Dedalo, 1933. 205 p. About half of the book is devoted to the Profintern, which the author, a one-time Spanish Syndicalist, Communist, Left oppositionist, and important Profintern official, knew intimately. A minimum of animus in spite of the author's politics. [B]

RB23 OLBERG, PAUL. *Die Rote Gewerkschafts-Internationale und die europäische Gewerkschafts-Bewegung.* Stuttgart: Metallarbeiter-Verbandes, 1930. 108 p. A trenchant critique of Communist trade unionism documented by well-chosen quotations from Communist published materials, particularly from statements made by various Communist trade-union oppositionists. The author holds that Communist trade-unionism has nothing to do with the welfare of labor, since the Communists regard unions as mere instruments of the Party in making the revolution; then after the revolution, as in Russia, they make the unions tools of the state. Sharp changes in Profintern tactics reflect not the needs and interests of labor but the exigencies of Soviet foreign policy and intra-Party controversies. [A]

RB24 RED INTERNATIONAL OF LABOR UNIONS. *Bibliothek der Roten Gewerkschafts-Internationale.* Berlin: Verlag der Roten Gewerkschafts-Internationale, 1921-25. 44 nos. Includes the most important decisions of the Profintern congresses and of Enlarged Plenums of the Executive Committee of the Comintern on the world labor movement, plus articles and speeches by Lozovskii and other Profintern leaders. [A]

RB25 RED INTERNATIONAL OF LABOR UNIONS. *Fabzavkomy i profsoiuzy; Rossiia, Germaniia, Italiia i Frantsiia; materialy k III Kongressy Kominterna; sbornik statei.* Moscow: Profintern, 1924. 112

p. Studies of factory committees as the nuclei for revolutionizing the trade unions in various countries. Contains articles by A. Pankratova (Russia), Max Hammer (Germany), G. Germanetto (Italy), and A. Herclet (France). [B]

RB26 RED INTERNATIONAL OF LABOR UNIONS. *Malaia entsiklopediia po mezhdunarodnomu profdvizheniiu.* Ed. by M. Zelikman. Preface by A. Lozovskii. Moscow: Profintern, 1927. 2170 cols. Written for the benefit of the average trade-union and Party activist. Tendentious articles on international labor organizations, labor conditions and trade unions in various countries, and biographies of labor leaders. Useful definitions of special terms in the Communist trade-union lexicon. [B]

RB27 RED INTERNATIONAL OF LABOR UNIONS. *Mirovoe professionalnoe dvizhenie; spravochnik Profinterna.* Ed. by A. Lozovskii and others. Moscow-Leningrad: Gosizdat, 1926-28. Vols. I-III, V-VII. Attempts to give a comprehensive picture of the trade-union movement throughout the world. An effort to fulfill from the Communist point of view the function performed by International Labor Organization publications. Describes economic and political systems, the situation of the working class, and the labor movement for each major country. Useful bibliographies at the end of some sections. Publication plans were changed several times. Vol. IV (Near and Far East) apparently was never published.

RB28 RED INTERNATIONAL OF LABOR UNIONS. *Petite bibliothèque de l'Internationale syndicale rouge.* Paris: 1921-30. Numbers 1-27. Not as complete for the first five years as the series in German (see above, *Bibliothek der Roten . . . .*), but contains material bearing on French trade unions not found in the German edition. [A]

RB29 RED INTERNATIONAL OF LABOR UNIONS. *Rabochii Kitai; sbornik statei.* Preface by A. Lozovskii. Moscow: Profintern, 1925. 164 p. Important for the affiliation of the II All-Chinese Congress of Trade Unions with the Profintern. Includes discussions of the hegemony of the proletariat in the Chinese Revolution and the reasons for adherence to the Profintern. Contains articles by K. Radek, A. Khodorov, L. Geller, S. Mstislavskii, M. Galkovich, and T. Mandalian. [A]

RB30 RED INTERNATIONAL OF LABOR UNIONS. *Rabochii Kitai v borbe protiv imperializma; otchet pervoi professionalnoi delegatsii SSSR v Kitae.* Moscow: VTsSPS, 1926. 176 p. The delegation led by I. I. Lepse journeyed to China on invitation of the Chinese Federation of Trade Unions to express the solidarity of Soviet Trade Unions with Chinese workers and to obtain a full picture of the Chinese labor movement. The result was a sober report of considerable importance on the prospects in 1925 for reformism and revolutionarism in the Chinese trade-union movement. Important to the Profintern only as background for the affiliation of the Chinese Trade Union Federation. [B]

RB31 RESIS, ALBERT. "The Red International of Labor Unions (the Profintern), 1921-1937." Ph.D. dissertation, Columbia, 1964.

RB32 ROZEN, M. B., ed. *Za edinstvo profdvizheniia; sbornik rechei i statei.* Moscow: "Trud i kniga," 1925. 147 p. A collection of articles by Zinoviev and others.

RB33 SCHWARZ, SALOMON. "Rote Gewerkschaftsinternationale," p. 1348-1359 in *Internationales Handwörterbuch des Gewerkschaftswesens.* Berlin: Werk und Wirtschaft Verlagsaktiengesellschaft, 1930-32. 2 vols. A brief, objective account based on published materials of the Profintern. Does not relate the Profintern with the Comintern closely. See also Arthur Rosenberg, "Kommunismus und Kommunistische Gewerkschaften," *Ibid.*, p. 979-984. [B]

RB34 SORBONSKII, S. *Mezhdunarodnoe rabochee dvizhenie v tsifrakh i faktakh.* Leningrad: "Priboi," 1926. 167 p.

3. CONGRESSES

a. 1ST CONGRESS

RB35 RED INTERNATIONAL OF LABOR UNIONS, 1st CONGRESS, MOSCOW, 1921. *I Mezhdunarodnyi kongress revoliutsionnykh professionalnykh i proizvodstvennykh soiuzov; stenograficheskii otchet.* Moscow: Pressbiuro kongressa, 1921. 318 p. Seventeen daily bulletins on the work of the Congress, July 3-19, 1921, with each bulletin paginated separately. Includes minutes of committee meetings and Central Council session, July 19-22, 1921. Appendix contains resolutions, decisions, and the constitution. The Congress decided that revolutionaries must stay in or penetrate the existing unions to win the masses for Communism and that an organic tie would be established with the Comintern. The executive bodies of the Profintern and Comintern would exchange three representatives. The battle-cry of the Congress was "Moscow or Amsterdam!"

b. 2ND CONGRESS

RB36 RED INTERNATIONAL OF LABOR UNIONS, 2nd CONGRESS, MOSCOW, 1922. *Biulleten II kongressa Krasnogo inter-*

natsionala profsoiuzov v Moskve, 19 noiabria-2 dekabria 1922 g. Moscow: Profintern, 1922 [?]. 160 p. Minutes of the Congress with some important speeches quoted almost in full. Very abbreviated but contains some information not found in the more complete edition (*II Kongress Krasnogo internatsionala profsoiusov v Moskve, 19 noiabria-2 dekabria 1922 g.*). [B]

RB37 RED INTERNATIONAL OF LABOR UNIONS, 2nd CONGRESS, MOSCOW, 1922. *Profintern i Komintern; vopros o vzaimootnosheniiakh Profinterna i Kominterna na II mezhdunarodnom kongresse professionalnykh soiuzov (stenogrammy rechei: Nina, Monmusso, Tresso and others).* Moscow: 1923. 75 p. Debates on the demand of the CGTU that the Profintern constitution be amended to sever the organic tie with the Comintern. Includes the CGTU draft amendment and the Constitution as amended. [B]

RB38 RED INTERNATIONAL OF LABOR UNIONS, 2nd CONGRESS, MOSCOW, 1922. *Rapports entre l'Internationale syndicale rouge et l'Internationale communiste; discours au 2e congrès, et statuts de l'I.S.R.* Preface by Dudilieux. Paris: Librairie du travail, 1923. 108 p. Speeches by Nin, Tresso, Monmousseau, and Zinoviev at the Second Congress of the Profintern and Lozovskii's speech at the Fourth Congress of the Comintern on the French Syndicalist demand that the tie between the two Internationals be dissolved. Dudilieux states that the dissolution of organic tie agreed upon was real, not merely formal. [B]

RB39 RED INTERNATIONAL OF LABOR UNIONS, 2nd CONGRESS, MOSCOW, 1922. *II Kongress Krasnogo internatsionala profsoiuzov v Moskve, 19 noiabria-2 dekabria 1922 g.* Moscow-Petrograd: Gosizdat, 1923. 322 p. Not a verbatim report, but quite complete. Should be supplemented, however, by *Biulleten II Kongressa.* The congress yielded to CGTU pressure and eliminated the organic tie with the Comintern. The congress also called for a United Front with the International Federation of Trade Unions in order to repel the "offensive of capital." [A]

c. 3RD CONGRESS

RB40 RED INTERNATIONAL OF LABOR UNIONS, 3rd CONGRESS, MOSCOW, 1924. *Mezhdunarodnoe profdvizhenie 1923-24 gg.; otchet ispolbiuro III Kongressu Profinterna.* 2nd ed., Moscow: Profintern, 1924. 336 p. A comprehensive account of the revolutionary trade-union movement and work of the Profintern Executive Bureau. Discusses devious attempts to link the Red International of Labor Unions with the International Federation of Trade Unions through the affiliates of the former endeavoring to join appropriate international trade or industrial unions, most of which were linked with the IFTU. [A]

RB41 RED INTERNATIONAL OF LABOR UNIONS, 3rd CONGRESS, MOSCOW, 1924. *Protokoll über den Dritten Kongress der Roten Gewerkschafts-Internationale abgehalten in Moskau vom 8. bis 21. Juli 1924.* Berlin: Verlag der roten Gewerkschafts-Internationale, 1924. 431 p. A full record of the Third Congress. [A]

RB42 RED INTERNATIONAL OF LABOR UNIONS, 3rd CONGRESS, MOSCOW, 1924. *III Kongress Krasnogo internatsionala profsoiuzov, 8-22 iiulia, 1924 g.; otchet po stenogrammam.* Moscow: Izd. Profinterna, 1924. 404 p. Not a verbatim report. The congress went beyond the United Front and called for trade-union unity both on the national and international levels and for the formation of a single labor international through an international conference of the International Federation of Trade Unions' and the Red International of Labor Unions' affiliates on the basis of proportional representation. [A]

d. 4TH CONGRESS

RB43 RED INTERNATIONAL OF LABOR UNIONS. *Die internationale Gewerkschafts-bewegung in den Jahren 1924-1927; Proletarier aller Länder—Vereinigt Euch! Bericht des Vollzugsbüros der Roten Gewerkschafts-Internationale an dem 4 Kongress in Moscow am 15. März, 1928.* Foreword by A. Lozovskii. Berlin: Führer, 1928. 467 p.

RB44 RED INTERNATIONAL OF LABOR UNIONS. *Protokoll über den 4. Kongress der RGI; (17 März-3 April, 1928) Abgehalten in Moskau.* Berlin: Führer, 1928. 679 p.

RB45 RED INTERNATIONAL OF LABOR UNIONS, 4th CONGRESS, MOSCOW, 1928. *Mezhdunarodnoe profdvizhenie za 1924-27 gg.; otchet Ispolbiuro IV Kongressu Profinterna.* Moscow: Izd. Profinterna, 1928. 539 p. Very important as it covers the hiatus of three years and eight months between the III and IV Congresses. Delay in convening the IV Congress was explained as a result of the difficulty in coordinating with the congress of the Chinese Trade-Union Federation. The report treats some of the Profintern's biggest moments: affiliation of the Chinese unions, the Anglo-Russian Unity Committee, and the English General Strike. Reflects optimism brought by adhesion of trade unions of China, Colombia, and Mongolia, though no gains were made at expense of the IFTU. [A]

RB46 RED INTERNATIONAL OF LABOR UNIONS, 4th CONGRESS, MOSCOW, 1928. *Stenograficheskii otchet, rezoliutsii i pos-*

tanovleniia, 17 marta - 3 aprelia 1928 g. Moscow: Izd. Profinterna, 1928. 699 p. The congress came out for a United Front from below, without excluding negotiations at the top. Professed aim: a single militant trade-union international. Greater emphasis was placed on organizing labor in the Pacific basin and Latin-America. Industrial organization was to be stressed in the West in order to cope with rationalization of industry. [A]

e. 5TH CONGRESS

RB47 LOZOVSKII, ALEXANDER (pseud. of Solomon A. Dridzo). *The World Economic Crisis; Strike Struggles and the Tasks of the Revolutionary Trade Union Movement.* Moscow-Leningrad: State Publishers, 1931. 147 p. Lozovskii's report and concluding remarks on the subject at the Fifth Congress of the Profintern. Contends that the International Federation of Trade Union affiliates had become a wing of "social-fascism" because of their alleged failure to do anything to aid labor, particularly the unemployed and unorganized. [A]

RB48 RED INTERNATIONAL OF LABOR UNIONS, 5th CONGRESS, MOSCOW, 1930. *Mirovoe revoliutsionnoe profdvizhenie ot IV do V kongressa Profinterna, 1928-1930; materialy k otchetu Ispolbiuro V kongressu Profinterna.* Moscow: Izd. VTsSPS, 1930. An account of the revolutionary trade union movement in this period.

RB49 RED INTERNATIONAL OF LABOR UNIONS, 5th CONGRESS, MOSCOW, 1930. *Piatyi kongress Profinterna (15-30 avg. 1930 g.); stenograficheskii otchet.* Moscow: VTsSPS, 1930. 724 p. The most exultant and, as matters turned out, the last Profintern Congress. Lozovskii claimed that the world economic depression confirmed the Communist prognosis that capitalism was dying and Communism growing. Speakers maintained that a revolutionary upswing was in the making and would pass into revolutionary situations. But revolutionaries had failed to seize "independent leadership of economic struggles" as they had been directed to do by the IVth Congress. The calls to follow the Bolshevik path became more strident and the appeals to defend the Soviet Union more insistent. The Profintern was shunted aside in the Popular Front period and quietly closed down in 1937. [A]

RB50 RED INTERNATIONAL OF LABOR UNIONS, 5th CONGRESS, MOSCOW, 1930. *Protokoll des 5. Kongresses der RGI, abgehalten in Moskau vom 15. bis 30. August 1930.* Berlin: Führer, 1930. 544 p. A record of the proceedings of the 5th congress. [A]

4. DOCUMENTS

RB51 LOZOVSKII, ALEXANDER (pseud. of Solomon A. Dridzo). *Desiat let borby za Profintern.* Vol. I: *Vozniknovenie Profinterna.* Moscow: Izd. VTsSPS, 1930. 491 p. A valuable collection of articles, speeches, and correspondence relating to the Profintern's origins and first year of activity, including previously unpublished speeches and correspondence. According to Lozovskii, a five-volume documentary history of the Profintern was planned. Only vol. I appeared, although other volumes published in the same year and noted in this section may serve as documentary histories. [A]

RB52 LOZOVSKII, ALEXANDER, ed. *Komintern i profsoiuzy v resheniiakh, kongressov, i plenumov i drugikh materialakh Kominterna o profdvizhenii.* Kharkov: Ukrainskii Rabitnik, 1930 [?]. 320 p. A function of the Profintern was to work out the tactical details of the larger policy directives on the world trade-union movement laid down by the Comintern. This collection of the Comintern's most important statements on the trade-union question therefore provides a picture of the strategic framework in which the Profintern operated. Very useful bibliography, p. 316-20. [A]

RB53 LOZOVSKII, ALEXANDER, ed. *Profintern v rezoliutsiakh. Comp. with a commentary by S. V. Girinis.* Moscow: Izd. Profinterna, 1928. 254 p. A useful compilation. Traces the development of Profintern policy on some 25 general themes such as: neutralism and the dictatorship of the proletariat, the United Front, the East and the colonies, strike strategy, etc. Relevant resolutions and decisions are annotated and developed chronologically for each theme, making it possible to follow Profintern shifts on a given question for the period up to 1928. [A]

RB54 LOZOVSKII, ALEXANDER, SMOLIANSKII, G., and IUZEFOVICH, I., eds. *Desiat let Profinterna; sbornik statei.* Moscow: Gosizdat, 1930. 251 p. Articles by revolutionary trade union leaders, Soviet and non-Soviet, defending the formation of the Profintern and its role in world labor. Routine statements on Profintern theory and practice. [B]

RB55 RED INTERNATIONAL OF LABOR UNIONS. *Desiat let Profinterna v rezoliutsiiakh, dokumentakh i tsifrakh.* Comp. by S. Sorbonskii and ed. by A. Lozovskii. Moscow: VTsSPS, 1930. 276 p. A documentary history; the most complete Profintern handbook published. Contains excerpts from key documents on the origins of the Mezhsovprof and Profintern, on the work of the first four congresses, and on the proceedings of the first six sessions of the Central Council. Membership figures must be used with caution. Includes sections on sources. An extremely handy compendium. [A]

RB56 RED INTERNATIONAL OF LABOR UNIONS, CONGRESSES. *Resolutions and Decisions, 1st-5th World Congress of the RILU held in Moscow July 1921, Nov. 1922, July 1924, March-April 1928, Aug. 1930.* N.Y.: American Labor Union Educational Society, 1921-31. 5 vols. The most important resolutions, decisions, appeals, and manifestoes for each of the Profintern's five congresses. [A]

5. PERIODICALS

RB57 *Bibliothek der Roten Gewerkschafts-Internationale.* Berlin: Verlag der Roten Gewerkschafts-Internationale, 1921-25. French version, *Petite bibliothèque de l'Internationale syndicale rouge.* Paris: 1921-30. A collection of the Profintern's most important published documents, and articles and speeches by Profintern leaders. The French version contains material bearing on French trade unions not found in the German version. [A]

RB58 *Boletín de la Internacional sindical roja.* Paris: Secretariado Internacional de la C.G.T.U., 1927-32. A multigraphed weekly. An important source on Communist trade unionism in Spain and Portugal. [B]

RB59 *Eastern and Colonial Bulletin.* Moscow: 1927-32. Semi-monthly (irregular). Titles varies slightly. Occasional articles by A. Lozovskii, L. Geller, E. Browder, Harrison George, George Padmore, and anonymous or little-known authors. Interesting on China.

RB60 *Ezhemesiachnyi informatsionyi biulleten latino-amerikanskoi sektsii Profinterna.* Moscow: 1929-33. Reported the state of the movement in Latin-American countries in the drive against the Pan-American Labor Federation. Contains reports on regional conferences. [B]

RB61 *Internationale Gewerkschafts-Pressekorrespondenz.* Moscow: Verlag der roten Gewerkschafts International, 1931-35 [?]. Semi-weekly (irregular) 1931-32; weekly (irregular) 1933-34; semi-monthly, 1935. The Profintern's *Inprekorr,* that is, a journal giving many speeches, reports of meetings, and other valuable information. [A]

RB62 *Krasnyi Internatsional Profsoiuzov.* 16 vols. in 15. Moscow: Profizdat, 1921-36. German version, *Die rote Gewerkschafts-Internationale.* Moscow-Berlin: 1921-33. French version, *L'Internationale syndicale rouge.* Paris. Organ of the Executive Bureau of the Profintern; the Russian version was published semi-monthly to March 1922, then monthly. Stands to the Profintern as *Kommunisticheskii Internatsional* stands to the Comintern. Contents: 1) Political and theoretical articles; 2) Reports on labor conditions and trade unions in various countries; 3) Work of Soviet trade unions; 4) Official communications; and 5) Reports from the International Committees of Propaganda. Useful bibliographical notes. The German language version is not identical in content with the Russian. [A]

RB63 *Mezhdunarodnoe rabochee dvizhenie.* Moscow: 1920-33. Weekly, 1920-29; every ten days, 1930-33. Bulletin of the Red International of Labor Unions. After 1930 it was directed toward the average Party member and trade-unionist in the Soviet Union, supplying them with highly-colored propaganda contrasting the plight of the labor movement abroad with the advance of Soviet labor. [B]

RB63A *Mezhdunarodnoe rabochee dvizhenie.* Moscow, 1920-21. Six numbers, May-August 1920; seven numbers, January-October 1921. Organ of the Red International of Labor Unions. This is one of the most important sources on the Provisional International Council of Trade and Industrial Unions (Mezhsovprof), the organizing nucleus of the Profintern.

RB64 *Rotes Gewerkschafts-Bulletin.* Berlin: 1921-30 [?]. Weekly (irregular). Mostly devoted to information on the revolutionary trade-union movement throughout the world, with very little on the movement in Germany. [A]

Addenda

RB65 RED INTERNATIONAL OF LABOR UNIONS. *Otchet Ispolnitelnogo biuro Profinterna II Mezhdunarodnomu kongressu Revoliutsionniakh profsoiuzov, iul 1921 g.—noiabr 1922 g.* Moscow: 1922.

RB66 RED INTERNATIONAL OF LABOR UNIONS, CENTRAL COUNCIL. Meetings of the Council are reported in the following: 1st—*Protokoly zasedanii I sessii Tsentralnogo soveta Profinterna, napechatane v Biulleteniakh, nos. 15-16.* (See RB35). 2nd—*Vtoraia sessiia Tsentralnogo soveta Profinterna.* (In: *Krasnyi internatsional profsoiuzov*, March, 1922). 3rd—*Otchet o rabotakh III sessii Tsentralnogo soveta Krasnogo internatsionalnaia profsoiuzov, 25 iiunia-25 iiulia 1923 g.* Moscow: 1923. 142 p. German ed., 88 p. 4th—*IV sessiia Tsentralnogo soveta Krasnogo internatsionala profsoiuzov 9-15 marta 1926 g.* Moscow: 1926. 148 p. German ed., Berlin: 1926. 157 p. 5th—*V sessiia Tsentralnogo soveta Profinterna (3 aprelia 1928).* (In: *Mezhdunarodnoe rabochee dvizhenie*, April 13-20, 1928). 6th—*VI sessiia Tsentralnogo soveta Profinterna.* Moscow: 1920. 134 p. German ed., Berlin: 1930. 538 p. 8th—*Beschlüsse der 8. Session des Zentral-Rates der RGI, 7 bis 17 Dezember 1931.* Berlin: 1931.

RC. YOUNG COMMUNIST INTERNATIONAL

EDITED BY RICHARD CORNELL

1. GENERAL WORKS

RC1 CORNELL, RICHARD. "Origins and Development of the Communist Youth International: 1914-1924." Ph.D. dissertation, Columbia, 1965. 610 p.

RC1A CHEMADANOV, V. *Young Communists and the Path to Soviet Power.* N.Y.: 1934. 47 p.

RC1B GORKICH, M. *K.I.M. v borbe za massy. Organizatsionnoe polozhenie i zadachi K.I.M.'a.* Moscow: Molodaia gvardiia, 1928. 93 p.

RC2 *Istoriia K.I.M.* Moscow: Ogiz-Molodaia gvardiia, 1931. 3 vols. German edition, *Geschichte der Kommunistischen Jugendinternationale.* Berlin: Verlag der Jugendinternationale, 1929-31. 3 vols. Vol. I: SCHÜLLER, RICHARD. *Von den Anfängen der proletarischen Jugendbewegung bis zur Gründung der K.J.I.* 1931. 224 p. Vol. II: KURELLA, ALFRED. *Gründung und Aufbau der kommunistischen Jugendinternationale.* 1929. 253 p. Russian ed., *Ot Berlina do Moskvy (1919-1921 gg.); ot I do II kongressa K.I.M.* 1931. 186 p. Vol. III: KHITAROV, RAFAIL M. *Der Kampf um die Massen; vom 2. zum 5. Weltkongress der KJI.* 1930. 240 p. Russian ed., *Ot II do V kongressa K.I.M. (1921-1928 gg.).* The official Communist history of the revolutionary international youth movement from the 1800's through the 1920's. The authors were all leaders of the YCI in its early years. Both primary sources and personal reminiscences were used, especially in vol. II, the most valuable one. The German edition contains very useful documentary appendices. [A]

RC3 MATLIN, B. *Armiia bratskikh komsomolov.* Moscow-Leningrad: Molodaia gvardiia, 1926. 128 p.

RC4 MÜNZENBERG, WILLI. *Die dritte Front; Aufzeichnungen aus 15 Jahren proletarischer Jugendbewegung.* Berlin: Neuer Deutscher Verlag, 1930. 389 p. Autobiography of his years in the youth movement by the leading figure in the international socialist youth movement during World War I and the first Secretary (1919-21) of the YCI. Valuable despite a distinct leftist bias. Contains an excellent bibliography for the period 1906 to 1929. [A]

RC5 MÜNZENBERG, WILLI. *Die sozialistischen Jugendorganizationen vor und während des Krieges.* Berlin: Junge Garde, 1919. 243 p. A short but valuable history of the international socialist youth movement to 1919, despite the radical bias of the author, who was the leader of the movement during the war and was a follower of the Bolsheviks and the Zimmerwald Left. Based for the most part on official records and documents.

RC6 MÜNZENBERG, WILLI, and SHILLER, R. (SHÜLLER, R.). *Istoriia iunosheskogo dvizheniia na Zapade.* Moscow: "Novaia Moskva," 1925. 240 p. A Russian translation of material selected from the German works of these two authors.

RC6A NASONOV, I. *Istoriia KIM.* Moscow: 1932. 39 p.

RC7 SHATSKIN, LAZAR. *Osnovnye voprosy iunosheskogo dvizheniia; sbornik statei.* Moscow: Molodaia gvardiia, 1924. 218 p. 2nd edition, Moscow-Leningrad: Molodaia gvardiia, 1925. 247 p.

RC8 SHATSKIN, LAZAR. *Pervye gody Kommunisticheskogo internatsionala molodezhi; sbornik statei i dokladov.* Moscow: "Novaia Moskva," 1926. 333 p.

RC9 *Sie ist nicht tot! Bericht über die internationale Konferenz der sozialistischen Jugendorganisationen abgehalten zu Bern am 4, 5, und 6 April 1915.* Zurich: 1915. 40 p. Abbreviated minutes of the youth conference at which the Socialist Youth International began its almost five-year period of development into the Young Communist International.

RC10 VEINBERGER, Z. *Zagranichnyi komsomol v borbe.* Moscow-Leningrad: Moldaia gvardiia, 1925. 119 p.

RC11 VOLKOV, A. *Detskoe kommunisticheskoe dvizhenie na Zapade.* Ed. by O. Tarkhanov. Moscow: Molodaia gvardiia, 1924. 167 p. Deals with the Communist children's movement in Europe, a movement which never attained any significance.

RC11A YOUNG COMMUNIST INTERNATIONAL. *Flugschriften der Jugend-Internationale.* Berlin: Exekutivkomitee der Kommunistischen Jugend-Internationale, 1919-21. A series of thirteen brochures and pamphlets containing documentary material, policy statements, and political polemics.

RC12 YOUNG COMMUNIST INTERNATIONAL. *Piat let KIMa; sbornik po istorii iunosheskogo dvizheniia.* Ed. by O. Adamovich. Leningrad: "Priboi," 1924. 288 p.

RC13 YOUNG COMMUNIST INTERNATIONAL. *Problemy iunosheskogo dvizheniia v kolonialnykh i polukolonialnykh stranakh.* Moscow: 1929. 149 p. Useful reports on Communist efforts among the youth in colonial lands.

RC13A YOUNG COMMUNIST INTERNATIONAL. *Program of the Young Communist International.* N.Y.: Young Communist League of America, 1929. 83 p. London: Communist Party of Great Britain, 1929. 83 p. German ed., *Programm der Kommunistischen Jugend-Internationale.* Berlin: Verlag der Jugendinternationale, 1929. 112 p.

RC14 ZORIN, V. *Mezhdunarodnoe detskoe kommunisticheskoe dvizhenie; ocherk.* Moscow-Leningrad: Molodaia gvardiia, 1927. 102 p. A short summary of the international Communist children's movement in the mid-1920's.

2. CONGRESSES, CONFERENCES, MEETINGS, ETC.

RC15 YOUNG COMMUNIST INTERNATIONAL, 1st CONGRESS, BERLIN, 1919. *Bericht ("Unter dem roten Banner").* Berlin: Junge Garde, 1920. 78 p. Abridged minutes of the Congress in November 1919, during which the International Union of Socialist Youth Organizations was transformed into the YCI. [A]

RC16 YOUNG COMMUNIST INTERNATIONAL, 1st CONGRESS, BERLIN, 1919. *Pervyi kongress Kommunisticheskogo internatsionala molodezhi; stenograficheskaia zapis.* Prepared by Alfred Kurella. Moscow: 1930. 235 p. A "stenographic" report of the First Congress of the YCI put together eleven years after the event. It is based on an original manuscript which was by no means a complete and accurate record of the proceedings, and the personal reminiscences of the editor, who was a Secretary and a leading figure at the Congress. An abridged edition of the original manuscript was published by the author, in June 1920, under the title *Unter dem Roten Banner.* [B]

RC16A YOUNG COMMUNIST INTERNATIONAL, 1st CONGRESS, BERLIN, 1919. *The Young Communist International; Report of the First International Congress Held in Berlin from the 20-29th of November 1919.* London: Young Communist League; Glasgow: International Proletarian School Movement, 1920. 32 p. A short summary of the proceedings.

RC17 YOUNG COMMUNIST INTERNATIONAL. *Bericht über die erste Sitzung des Büros der Kommunistischen Jugendinternationale.* Berlin: Verlag Junge Garde, [1920]. 39 p. Important discussions were held at this session on organizational problems and on the political role of youth. A decision was taken to shift the main emphasis in the struggle with the Centrist youth organizations from negotiations with the leaders to the building up of Communist factions within these groups. [B]

RC18 YOUNG COMMUNIST INTERNATIONAL, 2nd CONGRESS, MOSCOW, 1921. *Vtoroi kongress Kommunisticheskogo inter-*

natsionala molodezhi 9-23 iiulia 1921 g. (Sokrashchennaia stenogramma). Petrograd: Kom. intern. molodezhi, 1922. 173 p.

RC19 YOUNG COMMUNIST INTERNATIONAL, 2nd CONGRESS, MOSCOW, 1921. *Bericht ("Zu neuer Arbeit").* Berlin: Junge Garde, 1921. 134 p. Abridged minutes of the Congress at which discipline was imposed on the national Communist youth organizations and a controversy over the political role of youth organizations which had existed since the first Congress was settled. Youth organizations were to retain organizational independence, but be politically subordinated to the parties. The YCI came under the domination of the Russian youth leaders. A policy of "to the masses" was adopted. [A]

RC20 YOUNG COMMUNIST INTERNATIONAL. *Die Jugend der Revolution; drei Jahre proletarische Jugendbewegung, 1918-1920.* Berlin: Verlag der Jugendinternationale, 1921. 528 p. Russian ed., *Molodezh v revoliutsii; tri goda proletarskogo iunosheskogo dvizheniia, 1918-1920 gg. (Otchet Ispolnitelnogo komiteta Kommunisticheskogo internatsionala molodezhi Vsemirnomu kongressu revoliutsionno-proletarskoi molodezhi).* Petrograd: Kom. intern. molodezhi, 1922. 654 p. A summary of reports from the national Communist youth organizations to the Executive Committee and a report of Executive Committee activities. A valuable source of information and statistics. [A]

RC21 YOUNG COMMUNIST INTERNATIONAL. *Rezoliutsii i postanovleniia zasedaniia Mezhdunarodnogo biuro Kommunisticheskogo internatsionala molodezhi.* No imprint, 1922. 41 p.

RC22 YOUNG COMMUNIST INTERNATIONAL, 3rd CONGRESS, MOSCOW, 1922. *Bericht und Beschlüsse.* Berlin: Verlag der Jugendinternationale, 1923. 290 p. Abridged stenographic report. The Congress was concerned mainly with reorganization of youth organizations on the basis of factory cells, and with tactics concerning the merger efforts of the Reform Socialist and Centrist youth internationals. [A]

RC23 YOUNG COMMUNIST INTERNATIONAL. *Die Grundfragen der kommunistischen Jugendbewegung; Aufsätze zum Programm der Kommunistischen Jugendinternationale.* Berlin-Schöneberg: Verlag der Jugendinternationale, 1922. 88 p. English ed., *The Fundamental Problems of the Young Communist Movement.* Berlin: 1922. 91 p. A detailed discussion of the draft of a new program which was considered at the Third YCI Congress (December 1922).

RC24 YOUNG COMMUNIST INTERNATIONAL, EXECUTIVE COMMITTEE. *From the 3rd to the 4th; a Report on the Activities of the Young Communist International since its Third World Congress.* Stockholm: 1924. 84 p. German ed., *Vom III. zum IV. Weltkongress der Kommunistischen Jugendinternationale; Bericht des Exekutivkomitees über die Tätigkeit und die Lage und Entwicklung der K.J.I.* Berlin-Schöneberg: Verlag der Jugendinternationale, 1924. 76 p. Russian ed., *Mirovoi Komsomol za dva goda; otchet Ispolnitelnogo komiteta o ego deiatelnosti i polozhenii Kommunisticheskogo internatsionala molodezhi IV kongressu KIM.* Moscow-Leningrad: Molodaia gvardiia, 1924. 96 p. A short summary of limited depth and limited objectivity of the activities of the YCI between the end of 1922 and the summer of 1924. Useful for a general view. A French edition was published in Potsdam.

RC25 YOUNG COMMUNIST INTERNATIONAL, 4th CONGRESS, MOSCOW, 1924. *Beschlüsse.* Berlin: Verlag der Jugendinternationale, 1924. 81 p. Russian ed., *Postanovleniia IV kongressa KIM.* Moscow-Leningrad: Molodaia gvardiia, 1925. 105 p. English ed., *Resolutions Adopted at the 4th Congress of the Young Communist International.* Stockholm: 1924. 120 p. This Congress followed the Fifth Congress of the Comintern, resulting in the "Bolshevization" of the YCI and the national Communist youth organizations. [B]

RC26 VUIOVICH, V. *Bolshevizatsiia KIM; rech na rasshirennom plenume IK KIM 13 aprelia 1925 g., pererab. i dop. Agitprop. KIM.* Moscow-Leningrad: Molodaia gvardiia, 1925. 48 p.

RC27 YOUNG COMMUNIST INTERNATIONAL. *Konferentsiia kommunisticheskikh soiuzov molodezhi Evropy 21-22 iiulia 1925 g. v Berline.* Preface by the Executive Comm. of the Young Communist International. Moscow: Molodaia gvardiia, 1925. 69 p. *Konferenz der Kommunistischen Jugendverbände Europas am 21. u. 22. Juli 1925 in Berlin: Resolutionen, Beschlüsse, Aufrufe.* Vienna: 1925. 61 p.

RC28 YOUNG COMMUNIST INTERNATIONAL, EXECUTIVE COMMITTEE. *Rezoliutsii VI rasshirennogo plenuma IK KIM.* Moscow: Molodaia gvardiia, 1927. 32 p. English ed., *Resolutions of the Enlarged Executive of the Young Communist International, November 1926.* London: Young Communist International, 1926. 42 p.

RC29 YOUNG COMMUNIST INTERNATIONAL. *The Young Communist International between the Fourth and Fifth Congresses, 1924-28.* London: 1928. 250 p. German ed., Berlin: 1928. 184 p. Report of the Executive Committee on successes and failures within the YCI and its national sections in carrying out decisions of the Fourth Congress.

RC30 YOUNG COMMUNIST INTERNATIONAL, 5th CONGRESS, MOSCOW, 1928. *Protokoll des 5. Weltkongresses der KJI, 20. August bis 18. September, 1928. in Moskau.* Berlin: Verlag der

Jugendinternationale, 1929. 475 p. Abridged stenographic report. The Congress took up the line of the 6th Comintern Congress—tactics to deal with the increased danger of war. Stalinist influence predominated. [B]

RC31 YOUNG COMMUNIST INTERNATIONAL, 5th CONGRESS, MOSCOW, 1928. *Protokoll der Programm-Kommission des 5. Weltkongresses der KJI.* Berlin: Verlag der Jugendinternationale, 1929. 205 p. A useful summary of the discussions of the committee charged with preparing a new program. The discussions in the YCI over the first program revision since 1919 had gone on for several years.

RC32 YOUNG COMMUNIST INTERNATIONAL. *Mirovaia pioneriia; pervaia mezhdunarodnaia pionerskaia konferentsiia, avg. 1929.* Moscow: Molodaia gvardiia, 1929. 103 p.

3. PERIODICALS

RC33 *Internationale Jugendkorrespondenz.* Vienna: Executive Committee of the YCI, 1919-24. (Irregular to April, 1922, then monthly. At various times Russian, French, and English editions were published.) Contains reports of activities within the national Communist youth organizations, and important Executive Committee decisions. In April 1922 it became an instruction organ for national Communist youth organization functionaries. An important source of information on activities inside these organizations. [A]

RC34 *Jugend-Internationale.* The organ of the International Union of Socialist Youth Organizations from September 1915 to November 1919, then the organ of the Young Communist International. Zurich, Berlin, Vienna: Executive Committee of the IUSYO; after November 1919 published by the Executive Committee of the YCI. Quarterly until no. 12 (July 1919), then monthly. Ceased publication in 1941. Published also in Russian (*Internatsional Molodezhi*, superseded by *KIM* during 1925-28), and for various periods in English (*International of Youth*), French (*L'Internationale des Jeunes*), Italian (*Gioventi Internazionale*), Swedish, Hebrew, and Bulgarian. This is the most important publication concerning the YCI. During World War I it was both an important outlet for anti-war and revolutionary propaganda, and a source of support for the revolutionary Socialist youth. Its pages remained open to all conflicting opinions within the movement until the Second YCI Congress (June 1921), when it became an organ of support, first for the Communist International, and then later for the Stalinist position within the Comintern, and reflected completely the decisions and policies of the Executive Committee of the YCI. [A]

RD. INTERNATIONAL RED AID (Mezhdunarodnaia Organizatsiia Pomoshchi Bortsam Revoliutsii—MOPR)

EDITED BY LOUISE RHOADS SMITH

RD1 HUNT, ROBERT N. CAREW. "Willi Muenzenberg." In: *International Communism*, edited by David Footman. (St. Antony's Papers, no. 9.) Carbondale: Southern Illinois University Press, 1960. A discussion of Muenzenberg's important role in the 1920's and 1930's as an organizer of international Communist front organizations. Speculates on his Comintern relations after the great purges and the circumstances surrounding his apparent murder. [A]

RD1A INTERNATIONAL RED AID. *Desiat let MOPR v rezoliutsiiakh i dokumentakh.* Moscow: 1932. 275 p.

RD2 INTERNATIONAL RED AID. *Pervaia mezhdunarodnaia konferentsiia MOPR 14-16 iiulia 1924 g.; stenograficheskii otchet.* Moscow: IK, MOPR, 1924. 127 p.

RD3 INTERNATIONAL RED AID. *Tretemu vsesoiuznomu sezdu Mezhdunarodnoi organizatsii pomoshchi bortsam revoliutsii; materialy k otchetu TsK, MOPR, SSSR.* Moscow: TsK, MOPR, SSSR, 1931. 96 p.

RD4 INTERNATIONAL RED AID. *Vtoraia mezhdunarodnaia konferentsiia MOPR (24 marta - 5 aprelia 1927 g.).* Moscow: TsK, MOPR, SSSR, 1927. 76 p.

RD5 INTERNATIONAL RED AID. *Vtoroi vsesoiuznyi sezd MOPR (18-22 marta 1928 goda); otchet.* Moscow: TsK, MOPR, SSSR, 1928. 71 p. Extremely useful for IRA's assessment of its program and problems. Appended are lists of members of the Soviet organization's Central Committee, Inspection Commission, Presidium, and statistical data on delegates.

RD6 INTERNATIONAL RED AID, CENTRAL COMMITTEE. *Korichnevaia kniga o podzhoge reikhstaga i gitlerovskom terrore.* Foreword by Lord Marley. Moscow: TsK, MOPR, SSSR, 1933. 368 p.

RD7 INTERNATIONAL RED AID, CENTRAL COMMITTEE, USSR. *MOPR; shkola internatsionalnogo vospitaniia; uchebnik dlia MOPR-TSIKLA Interfakov.* Moscow: 1933. 356 p. An extremely useful Soviet textbook designed for IRA cadres. Describes the history, program, and organization of IRA from its foundation in 1921 to 1933. Includes organizational charts and large amounts of statistical data. [A]

RD8 INTERNATIONAL RED AID, CENTRAL COMMITTEE, USSR. *Otchet sektsii MOPR SSSR Vsemirnomu kongressu MOPR.* Moscow: TsK, MOPR, SSSR, 1932. 85 p.

RD9 KORDE, M. *Na boevom postu revolutsii; k itogam 3-go Plenuma IK MOPR.* Moscow: 1931. 29 p. Useful for an account of IRA activities for the preceding year as well as for the leadership's view of IRA's objectives and prospects.

RD10 KRONTSKII, G. A. *Shto takoe MOPR; broshiura dlia rabochikh i krestian.* Moscow: 1929. 38 p. A propagandistic pamphlet designed to enlist the support of the Soviet people for IRA. Includes examples of IRA assistance, activities, and the plight of revolutionaries abroad.

RD11 MUENZENBERG, WILLI. *10 let Mezhrabpoma.* Moscow: Profizdat, 1931. 37 p.

RD12 MUENZENBERG, WILLI. *Fünf Jahre Internationale Arbeiterhilfe.* Berlin: Neuer Deutscher, 1926. 183 p.

RD13 MUENZENBERG, WILLI. *Solidarität, zehn Jahre Internationale Arbeiterhilfe, 1921-1931.* Berlin: Neuer Deutscher, 1931. 527 p. Muenzenberg spent most of his Communist career as a skilled organizer and director of various Comintern subsidiaries and "fronts." Among them was IRA, which he describes in the three items listed above.

RD14 STASOVA, ELENA D. *Moprovskie znamena za rubezhom; doklad na III vsesoiuznom sezde MOPR.* Moscow: 1931. 31 p. Report to the All-Union Congress of the Soviet affiliate by its executive committee; a valuable compilation of facts and figures.

RD15 STASOVA, ELENA D. *Ocherednye zadachi MOPR Sovetskogo Soiuza b novykh usloviakh; doklad na VI Plenume TsK MOPR SSSR, 21-vi 1937.* Moscow: 1937. 62 p. Provides a glimpse of IRA international activities and the organization of the Soviet affiliates; statistical data are included for the latter.

RD16 ZELT, JOHANNES. *Proletarischer Internationalismus im Kampf um Sacco und Vanzetti.* Berlin: 1958. 391 p. A comprehensive history (from the Communist point of view) of the IRA campaign (1921-27) in behalf of Nicola Sacco and Bartolomeo Vanzetti, labor agitators who were convicted of murder in Massachusetts. Useful also for information on IRA national affiliates. Extensive bibliography.

RD17 ZELT, JOHANNES. *. . . und nicht vergessen—die Solidaritaet.* Berlin: 1960. 159 p. Vignettes from IRA history interspersed with poetry inspired by the same; sketches of Communist martyrs and brief treatment of IRA activities, including those of its German affiliate, German Red Aid. Bibliography on IRA.

S. Communist International Mass Organizations Since 1945

EDITED BY LOUISE RHOADS SMITH

1. GENERAL WORKS

S1 *Facts About International Communist Front Organizations.* Revised ed., March 1955. No imprint. 67 p. A useful pamphlet published by the British government. Lists the various international organizations, their history, membership, policies, and activities.

S2 GREAT BRITAIN, CENTRAL OFFICE OF INFORMATION, REFERENCE DIVISION. *Guide to International Organizations.* Part II, *Non-Governmental Organizations.* London: 1953, with later additions and corrections. Lists both Communist and non-Communist organizations. In each case gives the address of the headquarters, the names of top officials, the organization and activities, and a brief history.

S3 MORRIS, BERNARD S. "Communist International Front Organizations; Their Nature and Function," *World Politics* (October 1956), p. 76-87. Discusses the rationale of international Communist front organizations, with special attention to the World Federation of Trade Unions and the World Peace Council. [A]

S4 ULIANOVA, N. N. *Mezhdunarodnye demokraticheskie organizatsii.* Kiev: Akad. nauk USSR, 1956. 210 p. The history and organization of the World Federation of Trade Unions, Women's International Democratic Federation, and World Federation of Democratic Youth from the Soviet point of view. Discusses polemically the relations of these three organizations with the United Nations and western opposition to their having consultative status in UN bodies. Appended are constitutions of all three organizations.

S5 *Vsesoiuznaia konferentsiia sovetskikh obshchestv druzhby i kulturnoi sviazi s zarubezhnymi stranami; 17-18 fevralia 1958 goda (materialy).* Moscow: 1958. 138 p.

2. COMMUNIST INFORMATION BUREAU (COMINFORM)

S6 COMMUNIST INFORMATION BUREAU. *Risoluzioni e documenta dell'Ufficio d'informazione dei partiti comunisti e operai, 1947-1951, a cura della redazione italiana di "Per una pace stabile, per una democrazia populare."* Rome: 1951. 219 p. (VII Congresso nazionale del Partito comunista italiano. Documenti per i delegati.) A collection of significant documents released by the Cominform during the period; twenty-three entries, including reports, resolutions, and speeches.

S7 COMMUNIST INFORMATION BUREAU, CONFERENCE, HUNGARY, 1949. *Meeting of the Information Bureau of Communist Parties in Hungary in the Latter Half of November 1949*. Bucharest: "For a Lasting Peace, for a People's Democracy!" 1950. 94 p. American ed., *Working Class Unity for Peace*. N.Y.: New Century, 1950. 71 p. Russian ed., Moscow: Gospolitizdat, 1949. 101 p. Texts of three Cominform resolutions on the peace movement, working-class unity, and the "fascism" and "betrayal" of the Yugoslav CP. Includes speeches by Suslov, Togliatti, and Gheorghiu-Dej.

S8 COMMUNIST INFORMATION BUREAU, CONFERENCE, POLAND, 1947. *Informatsionnoe soveshchanie predstavitelei nekotorykh kompartii v Polshe v kontse sentiabria 1947 g*. Moscow: Gospolitizdat, 1948. 305 p. Includes a communique and a resolution on the contemporary international situation by the Communist Information Bureau, which was established at this session. Contains also reports on the past activity and future tasks of individual Communist parties by A. Zhdanov, Edvard Kardelj, Wl. Gomulka, G. Malenkov, Jacques Duclos, R. Slanský, M. Djilas, V. Chervenkov, Gheorghiu-Dej, József Révai, and Luigi Longo. [A]

S9 *For a Lasting Peace, For a People's Democracy!* Belgrade, 1947-48. Bucharest, 1948-56. Biweekly until September 1949 when it became weekly. First published in English, French, Russian, Serbo-Croatian; by 1952 appeared in 18 languages. The official Cominform newspaper, through which the official Soviet line was disseminated to the international Communist movement. Issues typically consisted of announcements, exhortations, and criticism or reports concerning particular national parties. [A]

S10 IVANOVIC, VASSILIJ (pseud.). *I Communisti Stanno alle Spalle*. Milan: Garzanti, 1949. 285 p. The author says that he was a Cominform agent in Yugoslavia, Germany, Greece, Spain, Czechoslovakia, and Italy, 1945-48.

S11 KATONA, PAUL. "The Cominform; A Study in Propaganda." Ph.D. thesis, U. of London, 1958.

S12 MORRIS, BERNARD S. "The Cominform: a Five Year Perspective." *World Politics* (April 1953), p. 368-76. Assesses the role of the Cominform as a propaganda and organizational instrument of the international Communist movement. [A]

S13 REALE, EUGENIO. *Nascita del Cominform*. Milan: Mondadori, 1958. 174 p. French ed., *Avec Jacques Duclos au banc des accusés a la réunion constitutive du Kominform à Szklarska Poreba (22-27 septembre 1947)*. Paris: Plon, 1958. 203 p. A former prominent Italian Communist's fascinating behind-the-scenes account of the meeting of European Communist leaders at which the Cominform was founded. Critique of issues at the meeting and of personalities, views, and speeches of participants. Appended are short biographies of European Communist leaders at the meeting. [A]

S14 ROYAL INSTITUTE OF INTERNATIONAL AFFAIRS. *The Soviet Yugoslav Dispute; Text of the Published Correspondence*. London and N.Y.: 1948. 80 p. Texts of: letters between the Communist Parties of the Soviet Union and Yugoslavia, March-May 1948; Yugoslav statement to the Cominform, June 20, 1948; Cominform communique of June 28, 1948; Yugoslav reply to the Cominform, June 29, 1948.

S15 SIMMONDS, GEORGE W. "The Soviet Conception of Cominform; A Study of Certain Official Sources, 1947-1949." Certificate essay, Russian Institute, Columbia, 1952. 108 p. A summarization of official Soviet views of the Cominform, Communist inter-party relations, and the Soviet-Yugoslav dispute. Sources are the Soviet press and journals.

S16 ULAM, ADAM B. *Titoism and the Cominform*. Cambridge: Harvard, 1952. 243 p. The book as a whole treats Soviet and East European party and state relations which culminated in "Titoism" as a political phenomenon. Chapter II presents a good analysis of the historical and political context of the Cominform's establishment. The author is a Harvard professor. [A]

3. INTERNATIONAL ASSOCIATION OF DEMOCRATIC LAWYERS

S17 INTERNATIONAL ASSOCIATION OF DEMOCRATIC LAWYERS. *Bulletin*. Titled *Bulletin of Information* until 1951. Irregular. Brussels: 1949—. Official newsletter of IADL activities and meetings. Issues before 1951 were devoted wholly to a selected problem.

S18 INTERNATIONAL ASSOCIATION OF DEMOCRATIC LAWYERS. *Congrès de l'Association internationale de juristes démocrates tenu à Prague du 6 au 10 Septembre 1948*. Prague: 1949. 163 p. Texts of congress speeches and resolutions, stressing human rights, "warmongering" by the press, and punishment of war criminals.

S19 INTERNATIONAL ASSOCIATION OF DEMOCRATIC LAWYERS. *Congress, Délibérations*. Berlin: 1947—. German ed., Berlin: 1947—.

S20 INTERNATIONAL ASSOCIATION OF DEMOCRATIC LAWYERS. *Juristen für den Frieden; 5 Kongress der internationalen Vereinigung demokratischer Juristen, Berlin, 5-9 September 1951*. Berlin: 1951. 389 p. Proceedings of the congress; texts of speeches, congress manifesto and resolutions.

S21 INTERNATIONAL ASSOCIATION OF DEMOCRATIC LAWYERS. *Reports on Investigations in Korea and China, March-April, 1953*. Brussels: 1952. 56 p. Published in several languages. Report of an eight-member IADL commission sent to Korea in March-April 1952 "to investigate and establish" alleged American atrocities and use of germ warfare in Korea.

S22 INTERNATIONAL ASSOCIATION OF DEMOCRATIC LAWYERS. *Review of Contemporary Law*. Brussels: 1951—. Semi-annual. Titled *Law in the Service of Peace* until June 1959. Also in French. A professional-type legal journal emphasizing the legal aspects of problems current in Communist policies and propaganda; includes reports on IADL activities.

S23 INTERNATIONAL ASSOCIATION OF DEMOCRATIC LAWYERS. *Study Circle on Nationalization, Rome, May 4-5, 1957*. Brussels: 1957. 70 p. Texts of four reports read to the IADL-sponsored study circle and summary of discussion. The chief concern is problems of nationalization of Western-owned enterprises in Asia, Africa, and Latin America.

S24 INTERNATIONAL ASSOCIATION OF DEMOCRATIC LAWYERS, COMMISSION ON LEGAL PRINCIPLES OF PEACEFUL CO-EXISTENCE. *Proceedings*. Brussels: 1956. 66 p. Texts of twelve speeches to the Commission and the Commission's *Report*.

S25 INTERNATIONAL COMMISSION OF JURISTS (FOUNDED 1952). *Derrière une façade trompeuse; exposé sur la véritable nature de l'Association internationale des Juristes démocrates*. The Hague: 1955. 33 p. A useful historical treatment of IADL's Communist ties.

S26 KABES, VLADIMIR, and SERGOT, ALFONS. *Blueprint of Deception; Character and Record of the International Association of Democratic Lawyers*. The Hague: Mouton; N.Y.: Lounz, 1957. 365 p. A comprehensive and scholarly history of IADL from an anti-Communist point of view. [A]

4. INTERNATIONAL COMMITTEE FOR THE PROMOTION OF TRADE (formerly Committee for the Promotion of International Trade)

S26A INTERNATIONAL COMMITTEE FOR THE PROMOTION OF TRADE. *International Trade*. Monthly. Vienna: September 1955-

August 1956. Successor to the *Bulletin of Economic and Trade News*, published by the Committee for the Promotion of International Trade from 1952 to July 1955. Articles are designed to promote East-West trade and to help remove Western embargoes on strategic goods.

S26B INTERNATIONAL ECONOMIC CONFERENCE, MOSCOW, 1952. *International Economic Conference in Moscow, April 3-12, 1952.* Moscow: 1952. 328 p. Russian ed., Moscow: 1952. Texts of speeches at a Soviet-sponsored conference to promote East-West trade. The resolution establishing the Committee for the Promotion of International Trade and a list of the Committee's members are appended.

5. INTERNATIONAL FEDERATION OF RESISTANCE FIGHTERS

S27 INTERNATIONAL FEDERATION OF RESISTANCE FIGHTERS. *Cahiers internationaux de la résistance.* Issued three times a year. Vienna: 1959—. German ed., *Internationale Hefte der Widerstandsbewegung.* An "historical review" in academic style containing articles on the history of the European resistance movements during World War II.

S28 INTERNATIONAL FEDERATION OF RESISTANCE FIGHTERS. *Résistance Unie.* Monthly (occasionally bimonthly). Vienna: 1953—. German ed., *Der Widerstandskaempfer.* News of Federation activities and meetings including those of the national affiliates; anti-Nazi propaganda, especially against rehabilitation of Nazis in the Federal Republic of Germany; news of the various concentration camp prisoners' associations; reviews of books and films on World War II and Nazism.

S29 INTERNATIONAL FEDERATION OF RESISTANCE FIGHTERS. *Service d'Information.* Biweekly. Vienna: 1956—. German ed., *Informationsdienst.* An official news service treating the same subjects as *Résistance Unie.*

6. INTERNATIONAL MEDICAL ASSOCIATION FOR THE STUDY OF LIVING CONDITIONS AND HEALTH

S30 INTERNATIONAL MEDICAL ASSOCIATION FOR THE STUDY OF LIVING CONDITIONS AND HEALTH (Formerly World Congress of Doctors for the Study of Present-Day Living Conditions). *Living Conditions and Health; An International Medical Journal.* Vienna, 1956—. Irregular. Combined English, French and German Edition. Separate Russian and Chinese Editions. Spanish edition until

1960. Titled, until 1960, *Living Conditions and Health; A Quarterly Medical Journal*, but only four issues appeared 1956-59. Rather devoid of political propaganda for a Communist front journal. Contains articles of scientific interest emphasizing the effects of social conditions on health; contributions from a wide range of countries.

S31 WORLD CONGRESS OF DOCTORS FOR THE STUDY OF PRESENT-DAY LIVING CONDITIONS, 1st, VIENNA, 1953. *Congrès mondial des médecins pour l'étude des conditions actuelles de vie; rapports et communications. World Congress of Doctors for the Study of Present-Day Living Conditions; Reports and Proceedings, 23-25 mai, 1953*. Vienna: Secrétariat international du Congrès, 1955. 384 p. Spanish ed.; Buenos Aires, 1956. Condensations of some 90 Congress speeches on: health care and conditions in many countries, effects of war on health, duties of doctors faced with the problems discussed at the Congress, and conclusions adopted. Members of the "Comité d'honneur du Congrès" listed and identified. French, English, German, and Russian reports of proceedings printed in the same volume.

7. INTERNATIONAL ORGANIZATION OF JOURNALISTS

S32 INTERNATIONAL ORGANIZATION OF JOURNALISTS. *The Democratic Journalist*. Prague: 1953—. Published monthly in English, French, German, Russian, and Spanish. The official IOJ organ; prints articles on the world's press and news of IOJ activities.

S33 INTERNATIONAL ORGANIZATION OF JOURNALISTS. *The International Organization of Journalists*. Warsaw: The Secretariat, 1956. 24 p. An official—and polemical—history of the organization. The IOJ constitution, names of officers, and a list of national affiliates are appended.

S34 KNOBLOKH, IA., and PRONIN, P. *Za edinstvo zhurnalistov vsego mira*. Moscow: 1957. 79 p. A brief Soviet history of international journalist unions (especially of IOJ), designed apparently to provide Communist journalists with arguments to support the restoration of IOJ's consultative status in the United Nations.

8. INTERNATIONAL RADIO AND TELEVISION ORGANIZATION

S35 INTERNATIONAL RADIO AND TELEVISION ORGANIZATION. *OIRT Information*. Monthly. Prague, 1959—. News of radio and television programming in the Sino-Soviet bloc countries. Supersedes earlier irregular *OIR Information*, published by the International Broadcasting Organization.

S36 INTERNATIONAL RADIO AND TELEVISION ORGANIZATION. *Radio and Television.* Bimonthly. Prague, 1960—. Published in English, Russian, Chinese, French, and German. A quasi-technical, quasi-political journal. News reports highlight activities in the field in countries of the Sino-Soviet bloc. Supersedes the organization's earlier *Documentation and Information Bulletin*, published quarterly and bimonthly in Prague by the International Broadcasting Organization.

9. INTERNATIONAL UNION OF STUDENTS

S36A CLEWS, JOHN. *Students Unite: the International Union of Students and Its Work.* Revised ed., Paris: Congress for Cultural Freedom, 1952.

S37 INTERNATIONAL STUDENT PEACE CONFERENCE, PRAGUE, 1959. *Peace Is a Student Question.* Prague: IUS, 1959. 87 p. Text of IUS President's report to conference; summaries of other speeches; list of participating groups; texts of conference resolutions.

S37A INTERNATIONAL UNION OF STUDENTS. *Architectural Student.* Prague, 1951—. Three issues a year. Articles written or summarized in English, French and Spanish.

S38 INTERNATIONAL UNION OF STUDENTS. *Bulletin of the Student Needs and Welfare Department of the IUS.* Prague: 1953—. Irregular. Articles describe miserable student conditions in colonial countries and favorable conditions in Communist countries.

S39 INTERNATIONAL UNION OF STUDENTS. *L'Enseignement colonial.* Prague: 1955. 48 p. A propaganda pamphlet on the "struggle" for better education in colonial and underdeveloped countries.

S40 INTERNATIONAL UNION OF STUDENTS. *International Guide to the Student Press.* Prague, 1956. 34 p.

S41 INTERNATIONAL UNION OF STUDENTS. *News Service.* Fortnightly. Prague, 1950—. Published in English, French, Spanish, and Arabic. An official service directed to student officers and the student press. Prints news of student events in individual countries, headquarters operations, IUS benefactions, and policy statements.

S42 INTERNATIONAL UNION OF STUDENTS. *Report of the Executive Committee to the IUS Council.* Prague: 1952—. Irregular. Each volume has a distinctive title, e.g., "1952, Survey of Student Conditions." Format and content vary. Valuable for a comprehensive official account of IUS program and activities.

S43 INTERNATIONAL UNION OF STUDENTS. *This is the IUS.* Prague: 1953. 68 p. An illustrated propaganda brochure on the structure and activities of IUS; the 1946 constitution and by-laws appended. An earlier edition was published in 1950 without the constitution and by-laws.

S44 INTERNATIONAL UNION OF STUDENTS. *U.S. Education in Crisis.* Prague: 1950. 82 p. French ed., Prague: 1951. Attacks U.S. higher education with respect to its control, academic freedom, racial discrimination, "militarism," and national student organizations.

S45 INTERNATIONAL UNION OF STUDENTS. *Why the IUS Has Severed Relations with the Leaders of the Student Section of the "People's Youth of Yugoslavia."* Prague: 1950. 16 p. An interesting example of how a Communist front organization expressed and implemented Soviet policy.

S46 INTERNATIONAL UNION OF STUDENTS. *World Student News.* Prague; 1947—. Monthly. Published in English, Arabic, Spanish, German, Russian, and French. Formerly published also in Czech, Norwegian, and Italian. Official IUS periodical; the content of articles is mainly political, with attention given also to regional student activities, sporting events, and culture.

S47 INTERNATIONAL UNION OF STUDENTS, BUREAU OF STUDENTS AGAINST COLONIALISM. *Students Against Colonialism.* Prague, 1956—. Monthly.

S48 INTERNATIONAL UNION OF STUDENTS, STUDENT SPORT COUNCIL. *Sport.* Prague, 1957—. Irregularly bimonthly. East issue is trilingual in English, French and Spanish. Reports on sporting events held under IUS auspices.

S49 JONES, PETER T. *The History of U.S. National Student Association Relations with the International Union of Students, 1945-1956.* U. of Pennsylvania: Foreign Policy Research Institute, 1956. 135 p. An excellent account of these relations within the context of post-World War II student movements and the organizational development of IUS and NSA, and of the deterioration of East-West relations. Based on interviews with, and reports of, participants. [A]

S49A McLAUGHLIN, MARTIN M., and BRIEFS, HENRY W., eds. *Operation University: a Report and Analysis.* Compiled for the Joint Committee for Student Action by the College and University Section of the National Catholic Youth Council. Washington: 1947. 60 p. An analysis of the proceedings and results of the IUS founding congress in 1946 by two U.S. delegation members who represented Catholic youth organizations. Assesses Communist tactics and non-Communist countermoves at the meeting, evaluates the organization's prospects, and makes policy recommendations. [A]

S50 PESLIAK, M., and NIKOLAIEV, V. *Glavnyi ekzamen: o deiatelnosti Mezhdunarodnogo soiuza studentov.* Moscow: 1952. 166 p. A brief history of IUS; includes discussion of student conditions and organizations in western, underdeveloped, and Communist countries; and student participation in the "struggle for peace and democratic education." Published by the Soviet Komsomol.

S51 WORLD STUDENT CONGRESS, 3RD, WARSAW, 1953. *Congress Daily*, nos. 1-8/9. The entire set provides an overall report on the congress; texts of IUS Executive Committee report to the congress, resolution, appeal, reports of congress speeches, and work of separate commissions.

10. WORLD FEDERATION OF DEMOCRATIC YOUTH

S51A AMERICAN UNITARIAN YOUTH, COORDINATIONS COMMITTEE. *The World Federation of Democratic Youth; a Report to American Unitarian Youth from the A.U.Y. Council.* Boston: 1948.

S52 LAMBERZ W., and K. JEUTNER. *Vereint mit 87 Millionen; 15 Jahre Weltbund der Demokratischen Jugend.* Berlin: 1960. 215 p. A history of the WFDY, 1946-60, from the Communist point of view. Also discusses polemically other major international youth organizations in the context of WFDY's early history. Contains brief accounts of each World Youth Festival. Appended are the WFDY constitution, organizational chart, and a chronology of all major and minor WFDY and WFDY-related meetings 1941-60. [A]

S53 TIURIN, M. *Vsemirnaia Federatsiia Demokraticheskoi Molodezhi; kratkii ocherk borby demokraticheskoi molodezhi za mir i edinstvo.* Moscow: 1949. 70 p. A historical sketch of WFDY. Describes in extremely partisan terms the situation of youth in different countries and the creation of WFDY affiliates.

S54 WORLD FEDERATION OF DEMOCRATIC YOUTH. *The Activity of the World Federation of Democratic Youth, November 1945-August 1949.* Paris: 1949. French ed., Paris: 1949. 80 p. The history, structure, and activities of WFDY in its first four years; provides brief discussions of regional campaigns and organizations, the first world youth festival, and of two world youth congresses.

S55 WORLD FEDERATION OF DEMOCRATIC YOUTH. *Handbook on Asian Youth and Student Organizations.* Budapest, 1958. 55 p.

S56 WORLD FEDERATION OF DEMOCRATIC YOUTH. *Information Service*. Budapest, 1948—. Irregularly monthly. Published in English, French, and Spanish. Formerly sometimes biweekly; superseded WFDY's *Information Bulletin* published from 1946. A mimeographed bulletin of up to 10 pages which reports in factual style on the activities of WFDY and its affiliates.

S57 WORLD FEDERATION OF DEMOCRATIC YOUTH. *Toutes nos forces dans la Lutte pour la Paix!; 2me Congrès de la Fédération mondiale de la Jeunesse Démocratique, Budapest, septembre 1949*. Paris?, 1950? 331 p. The WFDY Executive Committee's report on Federation activities since the London World Youth Congress, 1945, and on its projected program. Contains delegates' speeches, commission reports, congress resolutions, WFDY constitutional amendments, lists of WFDY Executive Committee members, and lists of countries and organizations represented at the congress.

S58 WORLD FEDERATION OF DEMOCRATIC YOUTH. *World Youth*. Budapest, 1946—. Monthly. Published in several languages. The principal WFDY organ (formerly quarterly); designed for broad appeal to youth, with articles of subtle political bias on activities of youth around the world; nonpolitical items also on sports, stamps, science, cinema, etc. [A]

S59 WORLD FEDERATION OF DEMOCRATIC YOUTH, EXECUTIVE COMMITTEE, CONFERENCE, COLOMBO, CEYLON, 1958. *Mutual Understanding, Friendly Relations Between the Youth of Asia, Africa and other Regions of the World, and the Work of the WFDY in the Spirit of the Bandung Principles; The Contribution of the WFDY to the Preparations for the VII World Festival; The Convening of the V Assembly Meeting of the Member Organisations of the WFDY*. Budapest, 1958. 65 p.

S60 WORLD FEDERATION OF DEMOCRATIC YOUTH, 2nd CONGRESS, BUDAPEST, 1949. *Vtoroi kongress Vsemirnoi federatsii demokraticheskoi molodezhi, Budapesht 2-8 sentiabria 1949*. Moscow: Molodaia gvardiia, 1950. 217 p. French ed.: Paris, 1950. The President's report on Federation activities and its future program. Contains excerpts from speeches of 45 delegates, the resolution and manifesto of the Congress, the WFDY constitution, and a list of WFDY officers.

S61 WORLD FEDERATION OF DEMOCRATIC YOUTH, 3d CONGRESS, BUCHAREST, 1953. *Peace and Friendship; through Unity to Peace, through Peace to Happiness; the Work of the III World Youth Congress from July 25th to 30th, 1953, Bucharest*. Budapest: World Youth Magazine, 1953. 335 p. French ed., Budapest: 1953. 348 p. Contains texts of the General Secretary's report to the Congress, the Congress resolution and appeal, and a list of the WFDY's Bureau and Executive Committee members.

S62 WORLD FEDERATION OF DEMOCRATIC YOUTH, 4th CONGRESS, KIEV, 1957. *Youth in the World Today and the Tasks of the WFDY*. Budapest, 1958. 165 p.

11. WORLD YOUTH AND STUDENT FESTIVALS SPONSORED BY WFDY AND IUS

S63 EAST EUROPEAN STUDENT AND YOUTH SERVICE. *Courtship of Young Minds; A Case Study of the Moscow Youth Festival.* New York: 1959. 54 p. An analysis of the 6th World Youth Festival with the intent to document and demonstrate Soviet control and objectives at the Festival; statistical tables appended.

S64 *Prazdnik mira i druzhby; sbornik.* Moscow: 1958. 293 p. An attractive, narrative report on the 6th World Youth Festival from the Soviet publishing house for youth. Includes excerpts from speeches and quotations and messages from festival participants.

S65 TORTORA, VINCENT R. *Communist Close-Up; A Roving Reporter Behind the Iron Curtain.* N.Y.: 1954. 160 p. A spritely, perceptive account of one Western journalist's experiences and conversations at the 3rd World Youth Festival (East Berlin, 1951).

S66 VDOVIN, VALENTIN P. *Sedmoi vsemirnyi.* Moscow: 1959. 59 p. A Soviet pamphlet published in preparation for the 7th World Youth Festival (Vienna, 1959); discusses the previous festival and the proposed program for the Vienna meeting.

S67 WORLD FEDERATION OF DEMOCRATIC YOUTH. *Festival.* Irregular. Published in several languages. Published by the International Preparatory Committee set up for each World Youth Festival; monthly for 8 to 4 months prior to a festival; biweekly for 4 to 2 months prior; weekly until festival when it is a daily; designed to arouse interest in the festival through news of preparations for it and events during it.

S68 WORLD FEDERATION OF DEMOCRATIC YOUTH. *Opinions on the VI World Festival of Youth and Students for Peace and Friendship, Moscow, July 28-August 11, 1957.* Budapest: 1957. 78 p.

S69 WORLD FEDERATION OF DEMOCRATIC YOUTH, EXECUTIVE COMMITTEE. *For Peace and Peaceful Co-existence; Towards the VII World Festival of Youth and Students; for the Development of Friendly Relations with the Youth of Asia and Africa.* Budapest, 1958. 83 p.

S70 WORLD FESTIVAL OF YOUTH AND STUDENTS FOR PEACE AND FRIENDSHIP, 1st, PRAGUE, 1947. *Vsemirnyi Festival Molodezhi v Prage.* Prague, 1948. 96 p. A profusely illustrated report published by WFDY of the 1st World Youth Festival; contains a brief narrative description of events.

12. WOMEN'S INTERNATIONAL DEMOCRATIC FEDERATION

S71 ANTIFAŠISTIČKI FRONT ŽENA JUGOSLAVIJE; GLAVNI ODBOR. *The Women's Anti-Fascist Front of Yugoslavia within the Framework of the International Women's Movement; Documents on the Relation of the WAF of Yugoslavia and of the Women's International Democratic Federation.* Belgrade: 1950. 129 p. An interesting riposte from the Yugoslav affiliate after its expulsion from the WIDF in November 1949. Places the expulsion in the context of the Soviet and Cominform campaign against Yugoslav Communists.

S72 BERGAMASCHI, ELSA. *Le Congrès mondial des mères.* Berlin: 1955. 308 p. An illustrated, narrative account of the World Congress of Mothers, held under WIDF auspices in Lausanne, July 1955. Includes lists of congress officials and preparatory commission members, countries represented at the congress, the congress manifesto and resolutions.

S73 INTERNATIONAL WOMEN'S COMMISSION TO INVESTIGATE THE ATROCITIES COMMITTED BY AMERICAN AND SYNGMAN RHEE TROOPS IN KOREA. *My obviniaiem; doklad Kommissii Mezhdunarodnoi demokraticheskoi federatsii zhenshchin v Koree ot 16 do 27 maia 1951 g.* Moscow: 1951. 53 p. A "documented" description of alleged atrocities committed by "American interventionists and their allies" in Korea, based on an investigation by a WIDF-sponsored International Women's Commission representing 17 countries.

S74 MONTAGNANA, RITA, ed. *Un Libro scritto da milioni di donne.* Rome: Unione donne italiane, 1954. 111 p.

S75 PERMANENT INTERNATIONAL COMMITTEE OF MOTHERS. *Bulletin.* Berlin: 1955—. Monthly. Propaganda articles addressed to mothers and news of its parent organization, the Women's International Democratic Federation.

S76 PETROVA, L. I. *Mezhdunarodnaia demokraticheskaia federatsiia zhenshchin za mir, ravnopraviie zhenshchin i schaste detei.* Moscow: 1956. 239 p. A very useful history of WIDF from the Soviet point of view. Includes a chronological table of WIDF congresses and council and executive committee meetings, 1945-56. A table lists the principal actions of these meetings. [A]

S77 U.S. CONGRESS, HOUSE, COMMITTEE ON UN-AMERICAN ACTIVITIES. *Report on the Congress of American Women.* Washington: G.P.O., 1949. 114 p. An exposition of the Communist ties of the leading members of the American WIDF affiliate, as well as of the WIDF.

S78 WOMEN'S INTERNATIONAL DEMOCRATIC FEDERATION. *Information Bulletin.* Berlin: 1946—. Bimonthly. Official news of WIDF activities and of regional and national conditions and events concerning women.

S79 WOMEN'S INTERNATIONAL DEMOCRATIC FEDERATION. *Protection of Motherhood.* Berlin: 1958. 108 p. Reports made by delegates to the WIDF-sponsored "Study Days on the Protection of Motherhood," held in Potsdam, September 1957.

S80 WOMEN'S INTERNATIONAL DEMOCRATIC FEDERATION. *That They May Live; African Women Arise.* Berlin: 1954. An anti-Western propagandistic brochure on the organization of African women against colonialism.

S81 WOMEN'S INTERNATIONAL DEMOCRATIC FEDERATION. *The Women of Asia and Africa; Documents.* Budapest: 1948. 170 p. French ed., Budapest: 1948. A propagandistic brochure on the social conditions of women in Asian and African countries and the organization of their "struggle" against Western colonialism. Published in preparation for the convocation of the Asian Women's Conference, held in Peiping, 1949.

S82 WOMEN'S INTERNATIONAL DEMOCRATIC FEDERATION. *Women of the Whole World.* Berlin: 1946—. Monthly. Published also in Arabic, French, German, Russian, Spanish. Official WIDF illustrated magazine. Contains political, anti-western articles; sketches of outstanding women, mainly in underdeveloped and Communist countries; news of movies, books, fashion, miscellany.

S83 WOMEN'S INTERNATIONAL DEMOCRATIC FEDERATION, 4th CONGRESS, VIENNA, 1958. *Conference on the Creation of Conditions Which Will Enable Woman to Fulfill Her Role in Society as Mother, Worker, and Citizen.* Berlin: 1958. 122 p. German ed., Berlin: 1958. The Conference was held during the 4th WIDF Congress. Contains extracts of conference speeches, texts of the main report, and the Conference resolution, "Rights of Women."

S84 WOMEN'S INTERNATIONAL DEMOCRATIC FEDERATION, 4th CONGRESS, VIENNA, 1958. *Documents.* N. P.: 1958. 35

p. Includes the President's report (extracts), Congress manifesto and resolutions, tabulation of congress attendance, and WIDF constitution.

S85 WORLD CONGRESS OF WOMEN, 1st, PARIS, 1945. *Congrès international des femmes; compte rendu des travaux du congrès qui s'est tenu à Paris du 26 novembre au 1 décembre 1945.* Paris: Fédération démocratique internationale des femmes, 1946. 484 p. A comprehensive report of the world congress of women sponsored by the Communist-dominated *Union des femmes françaises* at which WIDF was founded. Contains texts of speeches, national delegation reports, resolutions, WIDF statutes, and lists of persons chosen for the WIDF Council, Executive Committee, Presidency, Secretariat, and Control Commission.

S86 WORLD CONGRESS OF WOMEN, 3rd, COPENHAGEN, 1953. *Reports, Speeches (Extracts), Documents.* Berlin: Women's International Democratic Federation, 1953. 272 p. Spanish and German eds., Berlin: 1953. Includes also: resolutions, names of members of WDIF Presidency, Secretariat, Control Commission, Council, and Executive Committee.

13. WORLD PEACE COUNCIL AND ITS AFFILIATES

S87 CONGRESS OF THE PEOPLES FOR PEACE, VIENNA, 1952. *Congrès des Peuples pour la Paix, Vienne, 12-19 décembre 1952.* Paris: 1953. 1084 p. Russian ed., Moscow: 1954. German ed., Vienna: 1952. Texts of speeches and messages to the Congress and its appeal and resolutions; appended are statistical tables on attendance and an alphabetical list of principal participants.

S88 FIČ, MIROSLAV V. "The Moscow Peace Offensive and Its Revolutionary Potential; A Study in Political Dynamics." Certificate essay, Russian Institute, Columbia, 1956. 131 p. Also published in *Studies* of the Czechoslovak Foreign Institute in Exile. Chicago: 1956. 85 p. The assumptions and conclusions of the work are debatable, but Chapters IV, V and VI are valuable for describing the WPC and other Communist front activities during the period 1947-56 and for relating these activities to Soviet strategy. [A]

S89 INTERNATIONAL CONGRESS OF INTELLECTUALS FOR PEACE, BRESLAU, 1948. *Congrès mondial des Intellectuels pour la Paix, Wroclaw, Pologne, 25-28 août 1948; compte-rendu présenté par le bureau du secrétaire général.* Warsaw: 1949. 229 p. Report of the world congress at which the WPC was founded; texts of speeches, manifesto, resolutions, and lists of all participants, both alphabetically and by national delegation.

S90 INTERNATIONAL INSTITUTE FOR PEACE. *Current Articles, Interviews and Statements on Disarmament, Peaceful Coexistence and International Cooperation.* Vienna: 1958?—. Irregularly monthly. Published in one or more of the following languages: English, French, German, Spanish. A serial publication from the institute which serves as a front for the World Peace Council; for example, no. 28, February 1961, was entitled *The Situation in Laos* (36 p.) and provided a collection of reprinted newspaper articles, government memoranda and diplomatic notes, and expressions of views from various organizations.

S91 INTERNATIONAL INSTITUTE FOR PEACE. *Current Digest on Atomic Danger.* Vienna: 1958?—. Published every three months in English, French, German. A serial publication by the institute which serves as a front for the World Peace Council; the issue for January-March 1961 (37 p.) contained brief articles (or excerpts of works) by scientists and "viewpoints and declarations" by organizations and other scientists.

S92 INTERNATIONAL INSTITUTE FOR PEACE. *Current Documents and Papers on International Problems Relative to World Peace.* Vienna: 1958?—. Irregularly monthly. Published in one or more of the following languages: English, French, German, Spanish. A serial publication from the institute which serves as a front for the World Peace Council. No. 43, October 1961, was entitled *The Present Stage of the Talks on General and Complete Disarmament* (29 p.) and was a compilation of official statements by the governments of the USA and the USSR.

S93 JOLIOT-CURIE, FRÉDÉRIC. *Cinq Années de lutte pour la paix; articles, discours et documents (1949-1954).* Paris: 1954. 283 p. A collection of speeches and articles of WPC's President and leading personality (until his death in 1958). According to the editor, these documents delineate the history of the world peace movement; considerable attention is devoted to disarmament.

S94 U.S. CONGRESS, HOUSE, COMMITTEE ON UN-AMERICAN ACTIVITIES. *Report on the Communist Peace Offensive; a Campaign to Disarm and Defeat the United States, April 1, 1951.* Washington: G.P.O., 1951. 166 p.

S95 WATKINS, HAROLD M. *The Dove and the Sickle.* London: 1953(?). 124 p. A sympathetic account by a WPC member and Vice-President of the British Peace Committee of his participation at a Council meeting held in Vienna, 1951, and of his tour of the Soviet Union as a member of the British Peace Delegation. Useful for sketches of WPC personalities and for a brief history of the British WPC affiliate.

S96 WORLD ASSEMBLY FOR PEACE, HELSINKI, 1955. *Vsemirnaia Assambleia Mira, Khelsinki, 22-29 iiunia 1955 g.* Moscow: 1956. 784 p. French ed., Vienna: (date?). Texts of congress speeches and of communiques issued by the seven commissions of the congress; appended are statistical tables on attendance and an alphabetical list of principal participants.

S97 WORLD COUNCIL OF PEACE. *Documents and Papers on Disarmament, 1945-1955; Official Statements Pertaining to Disarmament Negotiations between the Great Powers.* Vienna: Bulletin of the World Council of Peace, 1956. 89 p. French ed., Vienna: 1956.

S98 WORLD COUNCIL OF PEACE. *World Peace Movement, Resolutions and Documents.* N.P.: Secretariat of the World Council of Peace, 1956. 220 p.

S99 WORLD PEACE CONGRESS, 1st, PARIS AND PRAGUE, 1949. *Congrès mondial des Partisans de la Paix, Paris-Prague, 20-25 avril 1949; compte rendu présenté par le Bureau du Comité mondial des Partisans de la Paix.* Paris: 1949. 781 p. Russian ed., Moscow: 1950. German ed., N.P., 1949. Danish ed., Copenhagen: 1949. The main congress was held in Paris, but 220 delegates who were refused admission to France gathered in Prague; this volume reports on both sections of the congress. Description and documents of congress preparations; minutes of the plenary sessions, including texts of speeches; appended are congress manifesto and resolutions, lists of participants and statistical tables on attendance.

S100 WORLD PEACE CONGRESS, 2nd, WARSAW, 1950. *Vtoroi vsemirnyi Kongress Storonnikov Mira; Varshava, 16-22 noiabria 1950 g.* Moscow: Gospolitizdat, 1951. 542 p. English ed., n.p.: 1951. Czech ed., Prague: 1951. Gives texts of congress speeches and resolutions. World Peace Council members are listed.

S101 WORLD PEACE COUNCIL. *Bulletin of the World Council of Peace.* Vienna: 1953—. Monthly. Published in English, French, Spanish, German, Russian, Hindi. An official WPC organ which transmits news of WPC activities and statements of its officials; also contains articles on current international issues, contributed usually by members of the movement.

S102 WORLD PEACE COUNCIL. *Dokumente und Erklarungen, November 1955 bis Januar 1960.* Berlin: 1960. 208 p. Documentation of each meeting of the WPC Bureau, Executive Committee, and Council during the period indicated; includes declarations, recommendations, appeals, etc., as well as miscellaneous statements by the President and Secretariat outside these meetings.

S103 WORLD PEACE COUNCIL. *Horizons; La Revue de la Paix.* Paris: 1955—. Monthly. Official WPC magazine. Articles of broad scope aimed at the educated reader. The Paris edition serves as a prototype for similar editions published under various titles in many different countries (e.g., *Peace Review* in Calcutta, *Rund um die Welt* in Berlin). Was preceded by *Défense de la Paix*, 1951-55, and by *Peace*, 1949?-51, both of which were published in Paris.

S104 WORLD PEACE COUNCIL. *Pervaia sessiia Vsemirnogo soveta mira, Berlin, 21-26 fevralia 1951 goda; materialy.* Moscow: Gos. izd-vo polit. lit-ry, 1951. 223 p. Contains the general report from the Secretariat; texts of speeches; Declaration on Conclusion of a Peace Pact; resolutions; and a list of newly selected Council members and Bureau candidate members.

S105 WORLD PEACE COUNCIL. *Die Wahrheit uber den Weltfriedensrat.* Berlin: 1957. 56 p. A popular brochure presenting a brief history and the purpose and activities of the WPC. Identifies members and officers of the Council.

S106 WORLD PEACE COUNCIL. *World Peace Movement, Resolutions and Documents.* N. P.: 1954? 157 p. A useful, fifth anniversary compendium of WPC resolutions and statements for the period 1949-54.

14. WORLD FEDERATION OF SCIENTIFIC WORKERS

S107 WORLD FEDERATION OF SCIENTIFIC WORKERS. *Hommage à Lord Rutherford, sept, huit et neuf novembre, MCMXLVII.* Vichy: 1948. 67 p. Texts of speeches at an international, WFSW-sponsored meeting in Paris to commemorate the work of nuclear physicist Ernest Rutherford; participants included prominent statesmen and scientists.

S108 WORLD FEDERATION OF SCIENTIFIC WORKERS. *Scientific World.* London: 1957—. Irregular. Published also in French, Russian, German, and Chinese. An official WFSW journal; its purpose, as stated by the editors, is to examine the social relations of science and how its results can be applied for human welfare. Articles cover a wide range of topics.

S109 WORLD FEDERATION OF SCIENTIFIC WORKERS. *The Social Responsibility of Scientists; Report of Meeting Held in Peking, China, on April 3, 1956, to Celebrate the Tenth Anniversary of the Founding of the World Federation of Scientific Workers.* Peking: All-China Federation of Scientific Societies, 1956. 67 p. Published also in Russian, French and Chinese. Contains the report of the Secretary-

General, extracts of speeches and messages to the meeting, as well as some information on affiliates. Illustrated.

S110 WORLD FEDERATION OF SCIENTIFIC WORKERS. *Unmeasured Hazards; an Analysis of the Effects of Tests of Atomic and Thermonuclear Weapons*. London: 1956. 40 p. Emphasizes the probable harm of continued nuclear testing. Contains a foreword by former WFSW President Joliot-Curie. Appended are WFSW statements and resolutions on nuclear weapons, 1953-56.

S111 WORLD FEDERATION OF SCIENTIFIC WORKERS. *The World Federation of Scientific Workers*. London: 1948?. 32 p. An official brochure describing the organization; includes messages from its leaders, text of the constitution, a descriptive list of national affiliates, and biographical notes on Executive Council members.

S112 WORLD FEDERATION OF SCIENTIFIC WORKERS. *WFSW Bulletin*. London: 1953—. Irregular. Published also in French, Russian, and Chinese. An official WFSW news organ; contains reports of federation activities, including those of affiliates, and brief articles on events of general scientific interest.

15. WORLD FEDERATION OF TEACHERS' UNIONS

(Fédération Internationale Syndicale de L'Enseignement — FISE)

S113 BULLETIN INTERNATIONAL DE L'ENSEIGNEMENT, Special Number, June 1950. *Journées d'études pédagogiques, Paris, 1950; hommage à Henri Wallon; manifestation organisée sur l'initiative de la Fédération internationale syndicale de l'enseignement et du Groupe français d'éducation nouvelle, 19 et 20 février 1950*. Paris: 1950. 72 p. A rich source of information about the former FISE President, Henri Wallon, professor emeritus of education and psychology; very little information on FISE as such.

S114 WORLD CONFERENCE OF TEACHERS, VIENNA, 1953. *World Conference of Teachers, Vienna, 1953; Reports, Contributions (Extracts), Documents*. Cover title: *Teachers for Unity*. Vienna: 1953?. 231 p. A conference held under FISE auspices to discuss: "(1) the situation of the school and the action of the teaching profession in defense of their economic and social conditions, for democratization of the school and for the maintenance of peace, and (2) pedagogic principles of the democratic education of youth." Included are lists of Presidium members and of organizations represented; conference documents: "The

Teacher's Charter," Appeal to Teachers of the World, Resolution on FISE Activity.

S115 WORLD FEDERATION OF TEACHERS' UNIONS (FISE). *Teachers of the World.* Paris: 1952—. Monthly. Published also in French, German, Spanish, Japanese. Official FISE organ; replaced the earlier *International Bulletin of Education.*

16. WORLD FEDERATION OF TRADE UNIONS

(Edited by Morton Schwartz)

S116 ARLAZAROVA, S. M. "Borba sovetskikh profsoiuzov za sozdanie Vsemirnoi federatsii profsoiuzov (1941-1945)." Dissertation for the degree of Kandidat, Moscow Higher School for the Trade Union Movement, AUCCTU, 1955. On the leading role of the Soviet trade unions in the creation of the WFTU, as seen by a Soviet graduate student.

S117 BALMASHNOV, A. A. *Vsemirnaia federatsiia profsoiuzov v borbe za edinstvo deistvii trudiashchikhsia.* Moscow: Profizdat, 1956. 181 p. Reflecting the propaganda line for 1956, an appeal for unity of action among the major trade union internationals—the WFTU, the International Confederation of Free Trade Unions and, even, the International Federation of Christian Trade Unions—"in the struggle for the vital interests of the worker, . . . in the struggle for peace, against the dangers of a new war." [B]

S118 CARWELL, JOSEPH. "The International Role of American Labor." Ph.D. dissertation, Columbia, 1956. 666 p. Though mainly concerned with the CIO and the AFL, it contains much detailed information on Soviet activity in the WFTU; not, however, without some factual errors. [B]

S118A CLARRIDGE, DUANE R. "The World Federation of Trade Unions in Asia." Certificate essay, Russian Institute, Columbia, 1955. 112 p.

S119 DEAKIN, ARTHUR. "The International Trade Union Movement," *International Affairs* (Royal Institute of International Affairs), XXVI, no. 2 (April 1950), p. 167-71. A brief but highly informative analysis of the Western position in the WFTU before the split, by its former President. [A]

S120 DESSAU, JAN. *Ten Years of Activity of the World Federation of Trade Unions in the United Nations.* London: W.F.T.U. Publications, 1956. 40 p. An account by the chief of the WFTU's Economic and Social Department of the Federation's efforts to improve the living standards of the workers and to strengthen the organizational freedom of their trade unions; an official apologia.

S121 DONAHUE, GEORGE R. *Facts about a Communist Front; the World Federation of Trade Unions.* Washington: International Union of Electrical, Radio and Machine Workers, AFL-CIO, 1958. 81 p. French ed., *La Fédération syndicale mondiale; son histoire, son action et ses buts.* Paris: Féderation Internationale des Syndicates Chrétiens, N.D. 94 p. A sketchy and highly polemical effort to expose Communist "betrayal and treachery."

S122 *Free Trade Unions Leave the W.F.T.U.* London: Trades Union Congress, 1949. 23 p. A detailed statement by the representatives of the leading Western trade unions at the time of the split in support of their charge that the WFTU was "now completely dominated by Communist organizations, . . . controlled by the Kremlin and the Cominform."

S123 *Free Trade Unions Remain in the W.F.T.U.* Paris: World Federation of Trade Unions, 1949. 75 p. Communist reply to *Free Trade Unions Leave the W.F.T.U.*, charging that the Western trade unions, in the service of American imperialism, had long been plotting to split the WFTU.

S123A *Istoriia profsoiuznogo dvizheniia za rubezhom (1939-1957)*, Part III. Moscow: Profizdat, 1958, 670 p. Chapters I and XXI contain a general survey of developments in the WFTU from its origins until 1957, as viewed by Moscow.

S123B LICHTBLAU, GEORGE E. "The Communist Labor Offensive in Former Colonial Countries," *Industrial and Labor Relations Review*, XV, No. 3 (April 1962), p. 376-401. A first-rate study of Communist labor strategy and the role of the WFTU in Asia and especially Africa during the 1950's and early 1960's. [B]

S124 LICHTBLAU, GEORGE E. "The World Federation of Trade Unions," *Social Research*, XXV, no. 1 (Spring 1958), p. 1-36. A concise and highly perceptive analysis, probably the best in any language, of the forces leading to the split in 1949 and the role of the WFTU since 1949, unencumbered by the restraining influence of non-Communist trade unions. [A]

S125 LORWIN, LEWIS L. *The International Labor Movement.* N.Y.: Harper, 1953. 366 p. Chapters XIX-XXII and XXVI contain the best general survey of the origin and development of the WFTU available. By the major American historian of the world trade union movement. [B]

S125A LYND, G. E. (pseud.) "Workers Disunite," *Problems of Communism*, XI, No. 2 (March-April 1962), p. 17-23. A revealing article on the centrifugal tendencies manifested in the WFTU during its Fifth Congress (Moscow, December 1961), reflecting the divergent interests then prevailing in the international Communist movement.

S126 PROKOPEV, S. P. "Vsemirnaia federatsiia profsoiuzov v borbe za edinstvo mezhdunarodnogo profsoiuznogo dvizheniia." Dissertation for degree of Kandidat, Academy of the Social Sciences, Moscow, 1952. A Soviet view of the WFTU, before and after the split, emphasizing the continuous efforts of the Russian trade unions to maintain international labor unity in the face of vicious attacks by "international reaction." Very good on giving the Soviet line, but available only in Moscow.

S127 ROSTOVSKII, S. "Sovetskie profsoiuzy v borbe za edinstvo mirovogo profdvizheniia," *Professionalnye soiuzy*, no. 9 (September 1948), p. 43-47. A summary of the Soviet position at the height of the Cold War within the WFTU but prior to the split; written by a leading Soviet trade union official.

S128 SAIIAN, L. *Vsemirnaia federatsiia profsoiuzov na sluzhbe trudiashchikhsia vsekh stran.* Moscow: Profizdat, 1960. 151 p.

S129 SCHWARTZ, MORTON. "Soviet Policies and the World Federation of Trade Unions, 1945-1949." Ph.D. dissertation, Columbia, 1963. 380 p. Soviet policy during the WFTU's "united front from above" stage—from its origins during the Second World War until the split in 1949; an analysis of Moscow's efforts to utilize the non-Communist trade unions to promote the interests of Soviet foreign policy, particularly in Germany, Greece, Iran, the Far East and the United Nations; the changing position of the WFTU in the early stages of the Cold War. [B]

S130 U.S. DEPARTMENT OF LABOR, OFFICE OF INTERNATIONAL LABOR AFFAIRS. *Directory of the World Federation of Trade Unions.* 1955 (looseleaf). 55 p. Information on the structure and composition of the WFTU and its executive organs, secretariat, liaison organizations and national affiliates. [B]

S131 U.S. DEPARTMENT OF STATE, BUREAU OF INTELLIGENCE AND RESEARCH. *Biographic Directory, World Federation of Trade Unions.* Washington: September 26, 1960. 67 p.

S132 WORLD FEDERATION OF TRADE UNIONS. *Information Bulletin*, December 15, 1945-March 1949; superseded by *World Trade Union Movement*, May 1949-present. An official publication. Contains much valuable material, including texts of resolutions adopted by the executive organs of the WFTU.

S133 WORLD FEDERATION OF TRADE UNIONS. *Report of Activity of the World Federation of Trade Unions. Presented by the General Secretary of the W.F.T.U. to the General Council at Prague, June 9-14, 1947.* N.P.,N.D. 163 p. Also an edition in French. Louis Saillant's view of developments in the WFTU from October 1945-December 1946. While incomplete and influenced by the author's pro-Soviet inclinations, it is a valuable source, especially for materials on WFTU activities in the United Nations, Germany, and Greece.

S134 WORLD FEDERATION OF TRADE UNIONS. *Report of the World Trade Union Conference, County Hall, London, February 6-17, 1945.* London: Trades Union Congress, 1945. 260 p. Editions in French, Russian, and German are less complete (English is the official language). This conference was primarily concerned with the revival of the trade union international; it not only sealed the fate of the pre-war IFTU but recognized the Soviet trade unions as one of world labor's Big Three.

S135 WORLD FEDERATION OF TRADE UNIONS. *Report of the World Trade Union Conference Congress, Paris, Palais de Chaillot, September 25-October 8, 1945.* N.P., N.D. 295 p. Editions in French and Russian less complete. The founding Congress of the WFTU; though mainly concerned with organizational questions, it was not without political content, British hopes to the contrary notwithstanding.

S136 WORLD FEDERATION OF TRADE UNIONS, GENERAL COUNCIL. *Unity on the March; Report of the Meeting of the General Council of the World Federation of Trade Unions, Berlin, November, 1951.* London: W.F.T.U. Publications, 1952. 166 p.

S137 WORLD TRADE UNION CONGRESS, 2d, MILAN, 1949. *Report of Proceedings.* Paris: World Federation of Trade Unions, 1949. 758 p. The first WFTU Congress after the split; the Western "reformists" were condemned for destroying labor unity; and an appeal for consolidation of trade union ranks was issued.

S138 WORLD FEDERATION OF TRADE UNIONS. *Report of Activity of the World Federation of Trade Unions, 15 October 1945-30 April 1949. Presented to the Second World Trade Union Congress, Milan, 20 June-10 July 1949.* Paris: World Federation of Trade Unions, N.D. 604 p. A distorted account of the alleged attempts of the Western "reformists" to use their position in the WFTU in support of the imperialists' efforts to repress the labor movement in all parts of the world.

S139 WORLD TRADE UNION CONGRESS, 3rd, VIENNA, 1953. *The Activity of the World Federation of Trade Unions and the Tasks Arising for the Trade Unions for Strengthening United Action of the Workers in the Fight for Improvement of their Living Standards and in Defense of Peace.* By Louis Saillant, General Secretary. London: W.F.T.U. Publications, 1953. 141 p. The Soviet line in the international Labor Movement at the time of the peace campaign; includes some of the documents of the third WFTU Congress, Vienna, October 10-21, 1953.

S140 WORLD TRADE UNION CONGRESS, 3rd, VIENNA, 1953. *Texts and Decisions of the 3rd World Trade Union Congress, Vienna, 10-21 October.* London: W.F.T.U. Publications, 1953. 72 p. Russian ed., Moscow: 1953.

S141 WORLD FEDERATION OF TRADE UNIONS. *Report of Activity, May 1949-August 1953, Presented to the 3rd World Trade Union Congress, Vienna, October 1953.* London: W.F.T.U. Publications, 1953. 443 p. The Communist view of developments on the labor scene in all quarters of the globe; vilification of non-Communist labor continues unabated.

S142 WORLD TRADE UNION CONGRESS, 4th, LEIPZIG, 1957. *Report of the 4th World Trade Union Congress; an Analysis of its Decisions and Resolutions.* London: W.F.T.U. Publications, 1957. 31 p.

S143 WORLD TRADE UNION CONGRESS, 4th, LEIPZIG, 1957. *Report on World Trade Union Activity and the Development of Fraternal Bonds and Unity within the International Trade Union Movement, for Higher Standards of Living for the Workers, their Economic, Social and Democratic Rights, Disarmament, Peace and National Independence. Report by Louis Saillant, Presented to the 4th World Trade Union Congress, Leipzig, October 4-15, 1957.* London: W.F.T.U. Publications, 1957. 74 p. An appeal for unity in the international labor movement. Another effort to consolidate the divided forces of world labor in support of such Soviet propaganda themes as "disarmament, peace, and national independence."

S144 ZHMYKHOV, I. N. *Sovetskie profsoiuzy v avangarde borby za edinstvo mezhdunarodnogo profsoiuznogo dvizheniia.* Moscow: "Pravda," 1949. 32 p. A brief polemic, written by a member of the International Department of the AUCCTU, pointing up the efforts of the Soviet trade unions to maintain international labor unity despite continued attempts by the "reformists" to destroy the WFTU.

T. Organization and Administration of Soviet Foreign Relations

EDITED BY EUGENE L. MAGEROVSKY

T1 ASPATURIAN, VERNON V. *The Union Republics in Soviet Diplomacy; a Study of Soviet Federalism in the Service of Soviet Foreign Policy*. Geneva: Droz, 1960. 228 p. A sound, scholarly study by a professor of political science at Pennsylvania State University. Contains data on the organization, structure, and some personnel of the Republican foreign ministries. [A]

T1A ASPATURIAN, VERNON V. "The Administration and Execution of Soviet Foreign Policy." In: *Foreign Policy in World Politics*, ed. by Roy C. Macridis. Englewood Cliffs, N.J.: Prentice-Hall, 1958. 420 p. A brief analysis (p. 175-97), but valuable.

T2 ASPATURIAN, VERNON V. "The Evolution and Organization of the Soviet Diplomatic Service." Unpublished seminar report, Russian Research Center, Harvard, Dec. 14, 1959.

T3 BARMINE, ALEXANDER. *Memoirs of a Soviet Diplomat*. London: Lovat Dickson, 1938. 360 p. American ed., *One Who Survived*. N.Y.: Putnam, 1945. 337 p. A description of the career of a Soviet diplomatic official who later defected. Gives an insight into the selection, training, assignment, and supervision of Soviet diplomatic personnel at home and abroad. Has an interesting description of domestic NKID operations and a characterization of Foreign Commissar Chicherin. [B]

T4 BESEDOVSKII, GRIGORII Z. *Na putiakh k Termidoru; iz vospominanii byvshego sovetskogo diplomata*. Paris: "Mishen," 1930-31. 2 vols. English ed., *Revelations of a Soviet Diplomat*. London: Williams & Norgate, 1931. 276 p. (Translations, with omissions and additions have also been published in German, French, and Japanese.) The career of a Soviet diplomat who defected. Similar to Barmine's memoirs, but gives better coverage of the organizational aspect, especially the amalgamation of the republican NKID's into an All-Union one. Some interesting descriptions of personalities. Later editions and translations have been progressively adulterated with increasingly sensational and unfounded statements. [B]

T4A CATTELL, DAVID T. "Formulation of Foreign Policy in the USSR." In: *Control of Foreign Relations in Modern Nations*, ed. by Philip W. Buck and Martin Travis, Jr. N.Y.: W. W. Norton, 1957. 865 p. A short account (p. 657-82) of the structure, execution, and motives of Soviet foreign policy.

T5 *Diplomaticheskii slovar*. Ed. by Andrei Ia. Vyshinskii and S. A. Lozovskii. Moscow: Gospolitizdat, 1948-50. 2 vols. Second ed., Moscow: 1960- , (3 vols. planned). Ed. by Andrei A. Gromyko, S. A. Golunskii, V. M. Khvostov and others. A standard Soviet reference work. Provides basic information, from the Soviet point of view, concerning international congresses and conferences, terms of treaties and other diplomatic acts, important diplomats and statesmen. [A]

T6 DMITRIEVSKII, S. *Sovetskie portrety*. Berlin: Strela, 1932. French ed., *Dans les coulisses du Kremlin*. Paris: Plon, 1933. 240 p. Reminiscences in the form of character sketches of Soviet officialdom by a defected Soviet foreign official. Most interesting is the sketch of G. V. Chicherin who replaced Trotskii as the People's Commissar for Foreign Affairs. [B]

T6A HARPER, SAMUEL N., ed. *The Soviet Union and World-Problems*. (Harris Memorial Foundation, 11th Institute.) Chicago: U. of Chicago Press, 1935. 253 p. Contains papers by Alexander Troyanovsky, first Soviet Ambassador to the U.S., and Alexei F. Neymann, First Secretary of the Soviet Embassy, on the basic principles of Soviet foreign policy, its formulation and administration. Neymann provides some interesting data on organization and personnel.

T7 KANTOROVICH, B. "Organizatsionnoe razvitie NKID." *Mezhdunarodnaia Zhizn*, 1922, no. 15 (133 p.). A brief article describing the establishment of the NKID. Some data on personnel, structure and early activities. Reminiscences of a participant. Limited scope.

T7A KARPOVA, L. *L. B. Krassin—sovetskii diplomat*. Moscow: Izd. sotsialno-ekonom. lit., 1962. A brief, interesting official biography of a revolutionary turned diplomat and Commissar of Foreign Trade. Interesting descriptions of early diplomatic and semi-diplomatic activities. Based on quite a few primary sources unavailable in the West. Good source material, but on a very short period.

T7B KORNEV, N. *Litvinov*. Moscow: Molodaia gvardiia, 1936. 110 p. A brief, laudatory official biography of the first Soviet "ambassador to Europe" and Chicherin's successor at the helm of NKID. Profuse with quotations from Litvinov's speeches, statements, etc. Contains little information not available elsewhere.

T8 KOROSTOVETZ, V. *Seed and Harvest*. London: Faber & Faber, 1931. 387 p. Abridged trans. of *Neue Väter—neue Söhne, drei russische Generationen*, Berlin: Verlag für Kulturpolitik, 1926, 353 p. and *Lenin im Hause der Väter*, Berlin: Verlag für Kulturpolitik, 1928, 444 p. A brief description of the Bolshevik takeover of the old Ministry of Foreign Affairs by a former official. Some data on personnel, but very fragmentary. The rest of the book is mostly autobiographical, with much space devoted to pre-Revolutionary times and the Civil War.

T9 LAUE, THEODORE H. VON. "Soviet Diplomacy; G. V. Chicherin, People's Commissar for Foreign Affairs, 1918-1930." In: *The Diplomats, 1919-1939*, ed. by Gordon A. Craig and Felix Gilbert. Princeton, N.J.: Princeton University Press, 1953. An attempt to discern the Narkomindel's position in regard to the Party organs and the governmental structure; also, to evaluate its relative importance in terms of Chicherin's and other high officials' personal positions. Scholarly approach. [A]

T10 MAGEROVSKY, EUGENE L. "The People's Commissariat for Foreign Affairs, 1917-1923; Organization and Evolution." Certificate essay, Russian Institute, Columbia, 1957. 156 p. The rise and the early development of the Soviet foreign office machinery. Data on structure, institutions, personnel, and methods of operation. Development and evolution of NKID machinery is viewed as a reflection of changing tasks of Soviet foreign policy. Basic bibliography, organizational tables and schemes. Based on original Soviet sources and personal reminiscences. [A]

T10A MARKUS, VASYL. *L'Ukraine sovietique dans les rélations internationales et son statut en droit international, 1918-1923*. Paris: Les Éditions internationales, 1959. 326 p. An excellent study of the foreign relations of Soviet Ukraine prior to its amalgamation into the USSR in 1923. Chapter V, dealing with the Ukrainian foreign policy machinery, is of particular interest. Betrays a slight nationalist bias. A valuable source on the theoretically independent activities of future Union Republics.

T10B MEISSNER, BORIS. "Der auswärtige Dienst der UdSSR," *Osteuropa*, vol. V, no. 1 (February 1955). A concise survey of the Soviet foreign service in the 1950's. Limited in scope, but provides basic factual information.

T10C *Mezhdunarodnoe pravo v izbrannykh dokumentakh.* Comp. by L. A. Modzhorian and V. K. Sobakin. Moscow: Izd. IMO, 1957. 3 vols. A series of selected domestic enactments in the field of foreign relations and diplomatic documents. A number of documents refer to the implementation of Soviet foreign policy. Requires some searching.

T10D NOVIKOV, SAVELII G. *Postoiannye Komissii Verkhovnogo Soveta SSSR.* Similar to the treatment by Vadimov (below), but in a much more restricted scope. Suffers from the same shortcomings and is of even more limited value.

T10E POPE, ARTHUR U. *Maxim Litvinoff.* N.Y.: L. B. Fischer, 1943. 530 p. Based on very few primary sources, with lengthy quotations from the Foreign Commissar's statements. Biased in Litvinov's favor. Neither a personal nor a political biography.

T10F POTEMKIN, VLADIMIR P., ed. *Istoriia diplomatii.* Moscow: OGIZ, 1941-45. 3 vols. 2nd ed., Moscow: Gospolitizdat, 1959–. Ed. by Valerian A. Zorin and others. (To be 5 vols.) A standard Soviet history of diplomacy. The latter portions of vols. II and III contain scattered but valuable information on Soviet foreign policy machinery, concepts, diplomatic representation, etc.

T11 ROBERTS, HENRY L. "Maxim Litvinov." In: *The Diplomats, 1919-1939*, ed. by Gordon A. Craig and Felix Gilbert. Princeton, N.J.: Princeton University Press, 1953. A brief, scholarly and concise monograph on the problem of Litvinov's policies. Illuminates the question of primacy in policy-making functions of the Party and the NKID. An excellent triangular analysis of Litvinov's policy, its relation to that of the Party, and the Party's relationship to the NKID. Good source material. [A]

T12 RUSSIA (1917- RSFSR), NARODNYI KOMISSARIAT PO INOSTRANNYM DELAM. *Biulleten.* Moscow, Feb. 22, 1920-March 13, 1922. Irregular. An information bulletin mainly for NKID staff. Mostly concerned with interpretation of the international situation, but some tangential reference to organizational matters.

T13 RUSSIA (1917- RSFSR), NARODNYI KOMISSARIAT PO INOSTRANNYM DELAM. *Mezhdunarodnaia politika RSFSR v 1922 g.* Moscow: Izd. NKID, 1923. An official publication, similar to the annual reports series. Centers around acts and achievements of Soviet foreign policy. Very fragmentary data on institutions; no new data on organization or personnel. Of limited value as a survey of foreign policy tasks before the NKID and its methods of dealing with them.

T14 RUSSIA (1917- RSFSR), NARODNYI KOMISSARIAT PO INOSTRANNYM DELAM. *Mezhdunarodnaia Zhizn.* Moscow: 1922-30. Frequency varies. Official semi-scholarly journal of the NKID. Replaced *Vestnik NKID* in 1922. Contains less of organizational and technical information than its predecessor, but occasionally published some institutional data in the form of personal reminiscences of the earlier periods of NKID's existence. Deals mostly with current problems of international relations and policy. Resumed publication in 1954 as the organ of *Znanie* and is no longer connected with the Foreign Ministry.

T15 RUSSIA (1918- RSFSR), LAWS, STATUTES, ETC. *Sobranie uzakonenii i rasporiazhenii rabochego i krestianskogo pravi-*

telstva; sbornik dekretov 1917-1918 gg. Moscow: Gosizdat, 1920. 312 p. *Sobranie uzakonenii i rasporiazhenii rabochego i krestianskogo pravitelstva; sbornik dekretov za 1919 g.* Petrograd: Gos. tipografiia, 1920. 453 p. These two publications contain a number of decrees and laws dealing with the organization and functions of NKID. Very important primary sources, but require some searching.

T16 RUSSIA (1922- USSR), LAWS, STATUTES, ETC. *Konsulskii ustav Soiuza SSR.* Moscow: Izd. litizdata NKID, 1926. 25 p.

T17 RUSSIA (1922- USSR), NARODNYI KOMISSARIAT PO INOSTRANNYM DELAM. *Ezhegodnik Narodnogo komissariata po inostrannym delam na 192- g. Annuaire diplomatique du Comissariat du peuple pour les Affaires Étrangères.* Moscow: Izd. litizdata NKID, 1925-35. A diplomatic annual. Describes the organization of NKID; lists both the central and local NKID institutions and missions abroad. Some issues possess updated versions of NKID's Statute in addition to précis of major treaties and domestic legislation affecting foreign relations. The years 1925-29 are in Russian and French; 1932-36 are in French only. Not published in 1930-31. Appears to have been discontinued with the 1936 issue. [B]

T18 RUSSIA (1923- USSR), LAWS, STATUTES, ETC. *Konsulskii ustav Soiuza SSR s postateinymi primechaniiami (material sobran po ianvaria 1931 goda) sostavlen pravovym i konsulskim otdelami Narodnogo komissariata po inostrannym delam.* Moscow: Izd. NKID, 1931. 521 p. Lengthy annotated consular statute with changes and interpretations collected through January 1, 1931.

T19 RUSSIA (1923- USSR), NARODNYI KOMISSARIAT PO INOSTRANNYM DELAM. *Desiat let sovetskoi diplomatii; akty i dokumenty.* Moscow: Izd. litizdata Narkomindela, 1927. 123 p. A brief history of Narkomindel, illustrated by several diplomatic documents. Information on the formation, structure, and personnel in both the domestic and foreign establishments. An excellent and concise survey. An official publication.

T20 RUSSIA (1923- USSR), NARODNYI KOMISSARIAT PO INOSTRANNYM DELAM. *Godovoi otchet za 19— god k Sezdu sovetov SSSR.* Moscow: 19—. Official annual report series. Data on structure, personnel, and organizational developments; a review of activities and achievements for the given period; a listing of acts implementing the foreign policy; and reprints or descriptions of new statutes, rules or enactments concerning the NKID. An excellent primary source. Available from 1919-20 through 1924. [B]

T21 RUSSIA (1923- USSR), NARODNYI KOMISSARIAT PO INOSTRANNYM DELAM. *Sbornik polozhenii, instruktsii i rasporiaz-*

henii po upravleniiu delami N.K.I.D. Moscow: Izd. litizdata NKID, 1925. 109 p. An excellent compilation of rules, instructions, orders, and statutory enactments concerning the operation of NKID's Chancellery. Detailed data on personnel, its classifications and positions, salary scales, method of selection and appointment, and rules on intra-Commissariat procedures. An extremely rare primary source. [A]

T22 RUSSIA (1923- USSR), NARODNYI KOMISSARIAT PO INOSTRANNYM DELAM. *Vestnik Narodnogo komissariata po inostrannym delam.* Moscow: 1919-22. Official semi-scholarly journal of NKID's activities. Articles reflect the tasks, problems, and methods of operation. Lists some structural and personnel changes. An excellent primary source. Replaced by *Mezhdunarodnaia Zhizn.* The bulk of materials reflects contemporary foreign-political interests.

T23 SABANINE, ANDRÉ. "L'Organisation du service diplomatique et consulaire de la R.S.F.S.R." In INSTITUT JURIDIQUE INTERNATIONAL, HAGUE, *Bulletin de l'Institut juridique international,* vol. VIII, 1923. A very brief survey of the Soviet diplomatic and consular institutions by a NKID official. [B]

T24 SIMONOV, P. "Tri s polovinoi goda sovetskogo diplomaticheskogo predstavitelstva," *Mezhdunarodnaia Zhizn,* 1922, no. 15 (133 p.). Reminiscences of the first Soviet consular appointee in Australia. No information on the domestic organization, but interesting as a primary account of the activities and problems of early *ad hoc* appointees.

T25 SLUSSER, ROBERT M. "The Role of the Foreign Ministry." In: *Russian Foreign Policy,* ed. by Ivo J. Lederer. New Haven and London: Yale, 1962, p. 197-239. Traces the role of the Foreign Ministry from Alexander I to the present, analyzing the importance of the Ministry under each ruler. Attacks the common assumption that Stalin had full control of Soviet foreign policy as early as 1929. Maintains that the Politburo continued to be divided on foreign policy issues throughout the 1930's, with the result that Litvinov was left considerable freedom to make important decisions. Says that Stalin did not secure complete domination of foreign policy until the arrest of Bukharin and removal of Litvinov. [A]

T26 SOLOMON, GEORGII A. *Unter den roten Machthabern, was ich im Dienste des Sowjets persönlich sah und erlebte.* Berlin: Verlag für Kulturpolitik, 1930. 281 p. English ed., *Among the Red Autocrats; My Experience in the Service of the Soviets.* N.Y.: Publishing Office "Our Hope," 1935. 216 p. Reminiscences of a defected Soviet foreign official. A gloomy description of clandestine activities and general misbehavior by Soviet semi-diplomatic appointees in Germany and the

Baltic states. An interesting description of diplomatic activities by ostensibly non-diplomatic personnel and vice versa. Popular in tone. [B]

T27 SOLOVEV, IU. *Dvadtsat piat let moei diplomaticheskoi sluzhby, 1893-1918.* Moscow: Gosizdat, 1928. 301 p. Memoirs of a former Russian diplomatic official in Madrid who returned to Russia after the establishment of NKID and was permitted to enter Soviet diplomatic service. Sketchy coverage of the transitional period. The later years are fragmentary.

T28 TANIN, M. *Desiat let vneshnei politiki SSSR, 1917-1927.* Moscow: Gosizdat, 1927. 259 p. An official Soviet version, but remarkably open and true. An excellent survey of the foreign aspect of NKID's activities with an insight into technical questions, and problems facing the Soviet diplomatic machinery at various points of its development.

T28A TARACOUZIO, TIMOTHY A. *The Soviet Union and International Law.* N.Y.: Macmillan, 1935. 530 p. An excellent, many-sided study. Much material on the legal aspects of Soviet foreign policy and Soviet diplomacy, including its machinery and representation. Strongly recommended as a starting point for research.

T29 TOWSTER, JULIAN. *Political Power in the U.S.S.R.* N.Y.: Oxford, 1948. 443 p. Although not primarily devoted to foreign relations, it contains some excerpts from statutory and archival materials on the organization and functions of the Soviet Ministry of Foreign Affairs. Ponders the question of primacy in policy-making. Good sources.

T29A TROFIMOVA, L. I., comp. *G. V. Chicherin.* Moscow: Izd. sotsialno-ekonom. lit., 1961. A brief, official biography of the second Commissar of Foreign Affairs, followed by excerpts from his writings and official utterances. The first "favorable" account since 1930. Much of the quoted material appears to be taken from the current series, *Dokumenty vneshnei politiki SSSR*, and from the Soviet press.

T30 TROTSKII, LEV. *Moia zhizn.* Berlin: Granit, 1930. Vol. II. Also see: *Sochineniia.* Moscow: Gosizdat, 1925. Vol. III, part 2. Brief references to the establishment and the early activities of NKID by its first chief. Personal views on NKID's functions and tasks, and description of its early activity. No structural information; limited data on the first personnel.

T31 VADIMOV, VADIM K. *Verkhovnyi Sovet SSSR i mezhdunarodnye otnosheniia.* Moscow: Izd. Institut mezhdunarodnykh otnoshenii, 1958. 94 p. An official description of the Supreme Soviet's mythical role in Soviet foreign policy. Should be used with caution.

T32 *Vestnik Tsentralnogo ispolnitelnogo komiteta, Soveta narodnykh komissarov i Soveta truda i oborony SSSR; postanovleniia i rasporiazheniia pravitelstva.* Moscow: 1923-24. 2 vols. in 1. Contains the Statute of the People's Commissariat for Foreign Affairs of December 12, 1923, the first all-Union statute of NKID (Article 300), and other miscellaneous enactments concerning the reorganization of NKID. An excellent primary source, but requires some searching.

T33 ZALKIND, I. A. "Iz pervykh mesiatsev Narodnogo komissariata po inostrannym delam," *Mezhdunarodnaia Zhizn*, 1922, no. 15 (133 p.). Reminiscences of an organizer. Almost identical with his 1927 article, but furnishing new nuances. The two articles should be taken together.

T34 ZALKIND, I. A. "Narkomindel v semnadtsatom godu," *Mezhdunarodnaia Zhizn*, 1927, no. 10. Reminiscences on the early organizational developments and activities of NKID by Trotskii's lieutenant, entrusted with the immediate supervision of its functioning. Gives an interesting insight into the early days of the NKID.

U. Soviet Policy Toward the League of Nations and the United Nations

1. GENERAL WORKS

(Edited by Walter C. Clemens, Jr.)

U1 FULLER, C. DALE. "Lenin's Attitude Toward An International Organization for the Maintenance of Peace, 1914-1919." Certificate essay, Russian Institute, Columbia, 1948. 99 p. A well-documented, carefully-elucidated analysis of Lenin's view toward international organization as a slogan and as a reality. Concludes that Lenin never advocated or envisaged Soviet participation in a League with capitalist states, although he did favor the U.S. of Europe as a slogan after the outbreak of the World War. He soon opposed this slogan, like that of "disarmament," because it would harm the revolutionary movement. Lengthy, annotated bibliography. [B]

U2 GOODMAN, ELLIOT R. *The Soviet Design for a World State.* Foreword by Philip E. Mosely. N.Y.: Columbia, 1960. 512 p. A virtual encyclopedia of statements by Marx, Engels, and Soviet leaders from Trotsky to Khrushchev on the concept of a world state. Indicates the Soviets' consistent rejection of Western proposals for world government and their determination to expand the USSR into a world state in which the Russian language and administration from Moscow would be the dominant forces of unification. Quotes by the economist Kozlov in 1952 and by the then Deputy Premier Kaganovich in 1955 indicate Soviet expectation of the global triumph of Communism by the year 2000. Khrushchev's ideas on the "withering away" of the state are also discussed. Heavily footnoted. [A]

U3 TRISKA, JAN F. "What Price Cooperation; Totalitarian Regimes and International Organization." Ph.D. dissertation, Harvard, 1957. 515 p. Concludes that totalitarian regimes (Fascist, Nazi, and Soviet) are ideologically incompatible with an international organization, and participate or not for reasons of security. As members of international organizations, totalitarian systems behave in many respects like any other state, but they cannot agree with such an organization completely for ideological reasons. [B]

2. LEAGUE OF NATIONS

(Edited by Walter C. Clemens, Jr.)

U4 ALEKSANDROV, B. A. *Kolonialnye mandaty.* Moscow-Leningrad: Sotsekizdat, 1934. 171 p. A Soviet polemic against the League's Mandate system.

U5 AUFRICHT, HANS. *Guide to League of Nations Publications; a Bibliographic Survey of the Work of the League, 1920-1947*. N.Y.: Columbia, 1951. 682 p. A comprehensive listing of League documents, with their official document numbers and often with a summary of their contents. Organized according to the organs and activities of the League. Introductory essays to each chapter. Special sections on the International Labor Organization and the Permanent Court of International Justice. [A]

U6 BALOSSINI, CAJO E. *Le Déclin de la Société des nations; la perte de la qualité de membre de la S.d.N. (Les cas de l'U.R.S.S. et de la France).* Geneva: "Études juridiques et politiques," 1945. 102 p. A heavily-footnoted work surveying the various instances in which states left the League, with emphasis on the circumstances of the expulsion of the USSR.

U7 BORETSKII, B. *Liga Natsii; orudie voiny*. Moscow: Moskovskii rabochii, 1927. 48 p. A popular Soviet version of the founding and operations of the League of Nations, discussing problems such as Germany, Austria, the USSR, and disarmament. Aims to show the League as an instrument of British and French imperialism. [B]

U8 BORISOV, D. *Sanktsii.* Moscow: Sotsekgiz, 1936. 156 p. A Soviet writer deals with his country's policy toward sanctions, against a backdrop of League affairs.

U9 BORREGALES, GERMÁN. *La U.R.S.S. y la O.I.T.; ensayo crítico-histórico de les relaciones de la Unión de les repúblicas soviéticas socialistas y la Organización internacional del trabajo.* Caracas: Tipograffa La Nación, 1940. 141 p. A history of the Soviet Union and the International Labor Organization, defending Albert Thomas, attacking the USSR and ending with its expulsion from the League of Nations. Written by a Venezuelan correspondent who was accredited to the League.

U10 DAVIS, KATHRYN (WASSERMAN). *The Soviets at Geneva; the U.S.S.R. and the League of Nations, 1919-1933.* Chambéry: Imprimeries réunies; Geneva: Librairie Kundig, 1934. 315 p. Abbreviated version, *The Soviet Union and the League of Nations, 1919-1933.* Geneva: Geneva Research Center, 1934. 23 p. The most comprehensive survey of the collaboration between the Soviet Union and the League in humanitarian, peace, disarmament, and economic affairs. Relies on materials in Western European languages, and includes an 83-page chapter on disarmament. The author is sympathetic and critical toward both the Moscow and the Geneva experiments. [A]

U11 FULLER, STERLING H. "The Foreign Policy of the Soviet Union in the League and United Nations." Ph.D. dissertation, U. of

Texas, 1952. 442 p. Summarizes Soviet policy in the two world bodies in a sketchy, extremely hostile fashion. Relies largely upon League and U.N. documents and English-language newspapers.

U12 IAVORSKII, S. IA. *Liga Natsii i podgotovka novykh voin.* Moscow: Gosizdat, 1928. 89 p. A popular narrative about the League of Nations and its supposed part in alleged preparations for new wars, from the Soviet viewpoint, meant to be in the library of "worker propagandists." Contains no footnotes but includes an interesting one-page list of little-known sources.

U13 IVANOV, LEV N. *Liga Natsii.* Moscow: Moskovskii rabochii, 1929. (Seriia *Mirovaia politika*, ed. by E. Pashukanis and B. Vinogradov.) 182 p. A Soviet historian treats the origins of the League of Nations, the Covenant, territorial-political issues such as Danzig, general political issues such as security and disarmament, and the relations of the USSR and the League, e.g., in Eastern Karelia. Depicts the League as the "auxiliary organ of world imperialism and of the diplomatic stock-market, through which the imperialist powers realize their deals and carry out their machinations." No footnotes. [B]

U14 KANNER, L. *Pochemu SSSR vstupil v Ligu Natsii.* Leningrad: Lenoblizdat, 1934. 17 p. A brochure in a series entitled "Answers to Workers' Questions," this pamphlet attempts to explain why the USSR joined the League of Nations in 1934, but not earlier. The basic explanation is that prior to 1934 the League had a fundamentally anti-Soviet orientation, but that after Germany and Japan left the organization the League could and had to be a brake on aggression, and that the USSR could both gain from and contribute to this work of the League.

U15 KOLSKII, A. *Liga Natsii; ee organizatsiia i deiatelnost.* Moscow: Moskovskii rabochii, 1934. 47 p. Published shortly after the Soviet Union joined the League of Nations, this work commemorates the event by reviewing—from the Soviet viewpoint—the history, organization, and activities of the League. Relates that the world organization began by badgering the Soviet Union in various ways but eventually was forced to invite the USSR into its ranks. 17 pages of documents, including some pertinent to the entry of Russia into the League. [B]

U16 KRIEGK, OTTO H. *Hinter Genf steht Moskau.* Berlin: Nibelungen-Verlag, 1936. 137 p. A pro-Hitler, anti-Bolshevik denunciation of the League of Nations and the Soviet Union, both of which are alleged to conspire together to attack and occupy Germany.

U17 MAHANEY, WILBUR L., JR. *The Soviet Union, the League of Nations and Disarmament; 1917-1935.* Philadelphia: 1940. 199 p.

One of the few books in English on the subject, this work is based largely on official Soviet pronouncements available in Western European languages. No Russian language materials are used. The book's tendency to accept Soviet speeches at face value has led to its receiving not unfavorable reviews in Russia. Its major concern is with the disarmament aspect of the League's work. [A]

U18 MAKAROV, A. N. *Liga Natsii.* Petrograd: Akademia tipografiia Kominterna, 1922. 76 p. A curiously non-Marxist study of the League of Nations, some portions of which may have been tampered with by Soviet censors, at least in editions sent abroad. Stresses that a supranational organization was evolving before World War I; that international law will continue to press for such an organization in the future; that to achieve such an organization war must be avoided and all the great powers (only the U.S. is specifically mentioned) must be included in it. Gives as the reason for the League's failures its connection with the punitive peace treaty of Versailles—not its "imperialist" character.

U19 MARTIN, JEAN, and BRIQUET, PIERRE E., *L'U.R.S.S à Genève.* Geneva: Imprimerie du Journal de Genève, 1934. 119 p.

U20 RAKOVSKII, KHRISTIAN G. *Liga Natsii i SSSR.* Preface by G. V. Chicherin. Moscow: Kommunisticheskaia akademiia, 1926. 81 p. Three speeches by a Soviet spokesman in January 1926, on the League of Nations, Locarno, and the international situation, explaining that the Soviet Union does not join the League because the capitalist majority there might act against Soviet interests. The preface is a reprint of a statement of Foreign Commissar Chicherin to the press. [B]

U21 SABANIN, A. *Rossiia i Liga Natsii; 1920-21-22 gg.* Moscow: NKID, 1924. 126 p. [B]

U22 TILLET, LOWELL R. "The Soviet Union and the Policy of Collective Security in the League of Nations, 1934-1938." Ph.D. dissertation, U. of North Carolina, 1955. 404 p. A thorough and incisive analysis of the Soviet position on such matters as the Italo-Ethiopian crisis and sanctions, the Spanish War, and the Chinese appeal to the League. Records the fluctuations in Soviet commentaries on these problems. Concludes that Soviet participation in the League was a tactical and not a strategic shift in Soviet policy. After 1936 the USSR lost hope in the League as an instrument to maintain peace and security. But the Soviet press never encouraged high hopes for the League, counselling instead reliance on the Red Army for security and on the class struggle for the resolution of international conflicts. Extensive bibliography. [A]

U23 *Why the USSR Joined the League.* Introduction by Hugh Dalton. London: The New Fabian Research Bureau, 1935. 36 p. An exposition of the Soviet interpretation (derived from Soviet speeches and the Soviet press) of why the USSR joined the League. Discusses the similarities between the programs favored by the USSR and the English Labour Party and expresses the Labour Government's hope for "still closer Anglo-Soviet cooperation."

3. UNITED NATIONS

(Edited by Alvin Z. Rubinstein)

Bibliographical Note: Information concerning Soviet policy in the United Nations may be obtained from Soviet speeches and commentaries in the key political, economic, and social organizations of the United Nations. *Summary Records* of the regional economic commissions and specialized agencies, as well as of the General Assembly and Security Council, provide a considerable body of material shedding light on Soviet attitudes toward specific issues.

Useful articles occasionally appear in *New Times*, a weekly, and *International Affairs*, a monthly, which are published in English by the USSR.

The 1960 edition of *Diplomaticheskii Slovar* contains lengthy sections, not included in the 1948 edition, on international organizations; and the Soviet Yearbook on International Affairs—*Mezhdunarodnyi Politiko-ekonomicheskii ezhegodnik*—has expanded its UN coverage.

U24 ALLEN, ROBERT L. "United Nations Technical Assistance; Soviet and East European Participation," *International Organization*, fall 1957, p. 615-34. A skillful analysis of Soviet bloc contributions to UN aid programs to underdeveloped countries. Professor Allen, of the University of Oregon, shows how the money was spent, on whom, and assesses the effectiveness of Soviet funds. Nonconvertibility, inadequate demand, and pricing problems, have so limited the value of these rubles that their principal impact has been political and psychological rather than economic. [B]

U25 ARMSTRONG, HAMILTON FISH. "U.N. on Trial," *Foreign Affairs*, April 1961, p. 388-415. A distinguished editor maintains that the UN is at a critical juncture in its development because the USSR 1) seeks to exacerbate antagonisms within the non-Communist world, and 2) desires to paralyze the UN at its operating center by replacing the Secretary-General with a three-man directorate. An outstanding analytical essay. [A]

U26 ARMSTRONG, JOHN A. "The Soviet Attitude toward UNESCO," *International Organization*, May 1954, p. 217-33. Professor Armstrong, of the University of Wisconsin, provides a sophisticated analysis of the 1954 Soviet decision to join UNESCO. During the Stalin era, Soviet opposition was a reflection of tight ideological and cultural controls prevalent in the USSR and the growing friction between the Soviet bloc and the U.N. There is an excellent discussion of the role of the Poles and the Czechs as proxies of Moscow. Soviet hostility toward UNESCO was one phase of Stalinist antagonism toward UN activities.

U27 BEKKER, JOHN A. "The Soviet Union and World Organization." Ph.D. dissertation, Chicago, 1954.

U28 BLUMENTHAL, IRENE. "The Soviet Union and the United Nations." Ph.D. dissertation, Stanford, 1960. Most of this largely historical study treats the development of Soviet views on such issues as intervention, human rights, welfare activities during the 1943-45 planning stages of the UN and the Stalin period. Holds that Soviet assumptions in international relations and law conflict with those implicit in the Charter.

U29 BOBROV, R. L., and MALININ, S. A. *Organizatsiia Obedinennykh Natsii.* Leningrad: Len. gos. univ. izd., 1960. 83 p. A general work on the structure and activities of the UN, designed for popular consumption.

U29A BOGDANOV, O. V. *Pravovye voprosy prebyvaniia OON v S.Sh.A.: privilegii i immunitety OON.* Moscow: IMO, 1962. 102 p. A Soviet scholar argues that the immunities granted to UN institutions, delegates, and personnel are being interfered with by U.S. authorities. A follow-up of Premier Khrushchev's proposal that U.N. headquarters be moved from New York to a site in Western Europe, this study presents the various Soviet legal objections to continuation of the United Nations in the United States. [B]

U30 CHERNOGOLOVKIN, N. V. *Formy kolonialnoi zavisimosti.* Moscow: Gosiuridizdat, 1956. 215 p. The UN is criticized for failing to promote the independence of colonial areas and the Soviet position on national self-determinism is lauded. The author compares League of Nations and UN handling of the problem and comments on Soviet proposals in the UN.

U31 CRABBS, RICHARD F. "The Record of the Soviet Union in the United Nations with Respect to Non-Selfgoverning Territories, 1946-1948." M.A. thesis, Stanford, 1955.

U32 DALLIN, ALEXANDER. *The Soviet Union at the United Nations*. N.Y.: Praeger, 1962. 244 p. A pioneering study of the assumptions and expectations underlying Soviet policy in the UN, with particular emphasis on the Khrushchev era. In treating specific policy questions, the author offers valuable assessments of the Soviet position on disarmament, the Congo, the proposed reorganization of the Secretariat, and the growing importance of the neutralists. [A]

U33 DEMAY, BERNARD. "L'URSS et l'Organisation Internationale." Thesis, Doctorate in Law, Univ. of Paris, 1951.

U34 DURDENEVSKII, V. N., and KRYLOV, S. B., eds. *Organizatsiia Obiedinennykh Natsii; sbornik dokumentov otnosiashchikhsia k sozdaniiu i deitelnosti*. Moscow: Gosizdat iuridicheskoi lit., 1956. 369 p. A collection of documents pertaining to the establishment and operation of the UN, including the UN Charter, the statute of the International Court of Justice, the regulations of the General Assembly, Security Council, Economic and Social Council, and the International Postal Union. The purpose of the documents is to show that no revision of the Charter is necessary for the effective functioning of the UN.

U35 EGAND, LEO M. "The Position in the United Nations of the Soviet Bloc on Economic Development of Under-Developed Countries Including Technical Assistance." Ph.D. dissertation, N.Y. Univ., 1955. Carefully traces the Soviet position on such questions affecting the politics of underdeveloped countries as land reform, economic development, and social change. Maintains that the Soviet bloc countries, while verbally espousing the cause of raising living standards and accelerating economic development, have cynically sought to exploit UN efforts to promote instability and disunity in the non-Communist world. A standard approach using UN materials.

U36 EMERSON, RUPERT, and CLAUDE, INIS L., JR. "Soviet Union and the United Nations; An Essay in Interpretation," *International Organization*, February 1952, p. 1-26. An excellent analysis of Soviet attitudes toward the UN. Maintains that Moscow uses the UN primarily as a propaganda forum, has little interest in developing the organization's activities and insists on the veto power because of the institutionalized electoral inferiority of the Soviet bloc. The USSR views the UN as a treaty relationship among sovereign states, and not as an organization in which voting by blocs is to settle major issues. Highly recommended. [A]

U37 FERNBACH, ALFRED P. *Soviet Coexistence Strategy; a Case Study of Experience in the International Labor Organization*. Washington: Public Affairs Press, 1960. 63 p. A scholarly survey of Soviet participation in the I.L.O. by a professor of foreign affairs at the University of Virginia. Points out that although the Soviet Union did not rejoin the I.L.O. in order to support its program, Communist participation has not prevented the agency from operating effectively. [A]

U38 FULLER, C. DALE. "Soviet Policy in the United Nations," *Annals of the American Academy of Political and Social Science*, May 1949, p. 141-51. Argues that by 1949 the Soviet Union tended 1) to regard the United Nations primarily as a propaganda forum, 2) to support narrow interpretations of the Charter, and 3) to insist on the preservation of the veto power as the *sine qua non* of continued participation.

U39 GOODMAN, ELIOT R. "Cry of National Liberation; Recent Soviet Attitudes Toward National Self-Determination," *International Organization*, Winter 1960, p. 92-106. Professor Goodman of Brown University notes continued Soviet efforts to embarrass the West by contrasting Soviet declarations of support for underdeveloped countries with vestiges of European colonialism. Moscow uses the idea of national self-determination as a tool of ideological conflict in its struggle with the West, a tactic that is also convenient for promoting Soviet prestige in areas beyond Moscow's control.

U40 HAZARD, JOHN N. "The Soviet Union and the United Nations." *Yale Law Journal*, 1946, p. 1016-35. A Columbia University professor analyzes the problems and prospects of Soviet membership.

U41 JACOB, PHILIP E. "The Disarmament Consensus," *International Organization*, 1960, p. 233-60. A stimulating and systematic coverage of areas of agreement and discord.

U42 JACOBSON, HAROLD K. *The U.S.S.R. and the U.N.'s Economic and Social Activities*. Notre Dame: University of Notre Dame Press, 1963. A well-documented treatment of Soviet policies toward the economic and social work of the United Nations, of the reactions of other states to these policies, and of the resulting interaction and its impact on UN institutions. Among the themes are excellent analyses of the Soviet position on early postwar reconstruction and recovery efforts, the refugee problem, economic development, and expansion of international trade. [A]

U43 JACOBSON, HAROLD K. "The Soviet Union, the U.N., and World Trade," *The Western Political Quarterly*, September 1958, p. 673-688. Detailed analysis of a little studied aspect of Soviet policy. Contradictions in the Soviet position are noted.

U44 JACOBSON, HAROLD K. "USSR and ILO," *International Organization*, Summer, 1960, p. 402-28. The impact of the 1954 Soviet decision to join ILO is traced in this comprehensive analysis based on

UN sources. Though of marginal importance, the Soviets have affected the proposals and politics of the organization. [A]

U45 JOHNSON, JOSEPH E. "The Soviet Union, the United States and International Security." *International Organization*, February 1949, p. 1-13. Argues that prospects for the development of the UN into a more effective instrument of collective security are bleak because of deep-rooted differences between the Soviet and American conceptions of international security.

U46 *Khrushchev in New York: A Documentary Record of His Trip to New York, September 19 to October 13, 1960, Including All His Speeches and Proposals to the United Nations and Major Addresses and News Conferences.* N.Y.: Crosscurrents, 1960. 286 p. A useful compilation.

U47 KOROVIN, E. *15 Let OON i problema mirnogo sosushchestvovaniia gosudarstv.* Moscow: "Znanie," 1960. 40 p. A member of the USSR Academy of Sciences attacks Western critics of Soviet policy and Yugoslav "revisionists." Little on the UN role in promoting peaceful co-existence, the ostensible theme of the pamphlet.

U48 KRYLOV, S. B. *Istoriia sozdaniia Organizatsii Obedinennykh Natsii, 1944-1945 gg.* Moscow: IMO Izd., 1960. 342 p. The Soviet view of the founding of the UN, largely devoted to standard documents.

U49 KRYLOV, S. B. *Mezhdunarodnyi Sud Organizatsii Obedinennykh Natsii; voprosy mezhdunarodnogo prava i protsessa v ego praktike za desiat let 1947-1957.* Moscow: Gosiurizdat, 1958. 166 p. A noted Soviet Academician and former member of the International Court (1946-52) reviews the Court's decisions and practices. Important as an expression of Soviet views on many aspects of international law. [A]

U50 KRYLOV, S. B., ed. *Materialy k istorii Organizatsii Obedinennykh Natsii*, vol. 1. Moscow-Leningrad: Izd. Akademii Nauk SSSR, 1949. 344 p. The first Soviet documentary account of developments leading to the establishment of the UN. Charter provisions are analyzed from the Soviet point of view. By a Soviet jurist who participated in the 1945 San Francisco Conference. [B]

U51 LARIN, V. *Mezhdunarodnoe Agenstvo po atomno i Energii.* Moscow: Gosizdat Iurid. lit., 1957. 98 p. A leading Soviet commentator presents the most comprehensive Soviet account of the negotiations preceding the establishment of the UN International Atomic Energy Agency. [A]

U52 LAUFER, LEOPOLD. "Soviet and American Domestic Propaganda on the United Nations Unanimity Principle." Certificate essay,

Russian Institute, Columbia, 1951. 107 p. An informative presentation of the way in which Moscow told its people about the veto power from 1944 on, contrasted with comparable American efforts. This analysis of Soviet sources shows that the USSR regarded the veto power as a precondition for participation in the UN.

U53 LIE, TRYGVE. *In the Cause of Peace.* N.Y.: Macmillan, 1954. 473 p. Valuable reflections by the first UN Secretary-General. Provides illuminating insights into Soviet behavior during the 1945-53 period. [A]

U54 MALININ, SERGEI A., and ONUSMKIN, VICTOR G. *Mezhdunarodnoe sotrudnichestvo v oblasti mirnogo ispolzovaniia atomnoi energii.* Moscow: Sotsekgiz, 1961. 127 p. A Soviet assessment of the International Atomic Energy Agency. [B]

U54A MEDVEDEV, A. M. *Sekretariat OON i trebovaniia sovremennosti.* Moscow, IMO, 1962. 48 p.

U55 MOLOTOV, VIACHESLAV M. *Problems of Foreign Policy; Speeches and Statements, April 1945-November 1948.* Moscow: Foreign Languages Publishing House, 1949. 610 p. Key speeches by the former Soviet Foreign Minister, devoted primarily to UN affairs and the German question. [A]

U56 MOLOTOV, VIACHESLAV M. *Rechi na Generalnoi Assemblee Organizatsii Obedinennykh Natsii. Vtoraia chast pervoi sessii v Niu-Iorke, oktiabr-dekabr 1946 g.* Moscow: Gos. izd. polit. literatury, 1947. 145 p. English ed., *Speeches at the General Assembly of the United Nations, October-December 1946.* Moscow: Foreign Languages Publishing House, 1948. Speeches to the first session of the UN General Assembly on the USSR and international cooperation, armed forces of UN members on foreign soil, plus various Tass reports. [B]

U57 MOROZOV, G. I. *Organizatsiia Obedinennykh Natsii; k 15-letiiu ustava OON.* Moscow: IMO, 1960. 191 p. A leading Soviet scholar presents the most comprehensive account of the USSR position in the UN. He argues that the Charter is adequate and defends the Soviet use of the veto, insisting that it is an integral part of the Charter. He opposes "the reactionary idea of world law" and proposals for transforming the UN into a "World Parliament." An important statement of the Soviet position on various UN problems. [A]

U57A MOROZOV, G. I. *Organizatsiia Obedinennykh Natsii: osnovnye mezhdunarodno-pravovye aspekty struktury i deiatelnosti.* Moscow: IMO, 1962. 511 p.

U58 MOVCHAN, ANATOLII P. *Mezhdunarodnaia zashchita prav cheloveka; vseobshchaia deklaratsiia i proekty paktov o pravakh cheloveka.*

Moscow: Gosiurizdat, 1958. 167 p. The most extensive Soviet commentary on the activities of the UN Commission on Human Rights. This analysis of documents is designed to establish Soviet support for underdeveloped countries and to vitiate Western endeavors. [B]

U59 NEGIN, M. *Organizatsiia Obedinennykh Natsii po Voprosam Prosveshcheniia, Nauki i Kultury (UNESCO)*. Moscow: Izd. IMO, 1959. 109 p. One of a series of books on the specialized agencies.

U60 NOGEE, JOSEPH L. *Soviet Policy Toward International Control of Atomic Energy*. Notre Dame, Indiana: University of Notre Dame Press, 1961. 306 p. A well-documented account of the negotiations concerning atomic energy control, disarmament, and the banning of nuclear bomb tests, with emphasis on the years 1945 to 1948, when the Soviet atomic explosion ended the first phase of the problem. Concludes that the shifts in Soviet policy stem from a basic Soviet determination to maintain the national sovereignty of the USSR. Excellent bibliography. [A]

U61 ORGANSKI, ABRAMO. "The Veto as Viewed by the U.S. and Soviet Russia." Ph.D. dissertation, New York University, 1951.

U61A ORNATSKII, I. and PALNIKOV, M. *FAO–Organizatsiia Obedinennykh Natsii po voprosam prodovolstviia i selskogo khoziaistva*. Moscow: IMO, 1959. 48 p. A sketchy treatment of the Food and Agriculture Organization, one of the UN specialized agencies that the Soviet Union has not joined.

U62 O'ROSKY, E. JOHN. "The Attitude of the Soviet Union during the United Nations' Discussion of the Question of the World Federation of Trade Unions, 1945-1946; A Case Study of Soviet Foreign Policy toward an International Mass Movement." Certificate essay, Russian Institute, Columbia, 1953. 102 p. Moscow tried to gain acceptance for WFTU participation in ECOSOC in order to influence the formulation there, and in ILO, of labor policy. The focus on a brief period effectively makes use of Soviet and UN sources.

U63 OSBORN, FREDERICK. "The USSR and the Atom," *International Organization*, August 1951, p. 480-98. A review of disarmament negotiations during the 1945-50 period by a former American participant. Focuses on Soviet opposition to the Baruch proposals.

U63A POCHKAEVA, M. V. *Pravovye voprosy ekonomicheskogo sotrudnichestva gosudarstv v sisteme OON; ekonomicheskaia komissiia OON dlia Evropy*. Moscow: Gosiurizdat, 1962. 76 p. A superficial and highly political view of the legal problems affecting economic cooperation among the members of the UN Economic Commission for Europe.

U63B POLEZHAEV, V. N. and YAKOBSON, G. M. *Mezhdunarodnye ekonomicheskie organizatsii i soglasheniia.* Moscow: Vneshtorgizdat, 1961. 266 p.

U64 POLIANSKII, N. N. *Mezhdunarodnyi Sud.* Moscow: Izd. Akademii Nauk SSSR, 1951. 237 p. The Soviet view of the functions of the International Court and its relationship to the UN. Presents a narrow conception of Court jurisdiction and defends national sovereignty against proposals for compulsory arbitration of international disputes by the Court. [B]

U65 POVOLNY, MOJMIR. *The Soviet Union and the United Nations; Some Soviet Policies in the International Organization.* Chicago: Czechoslovak Foreign Institute in Exile, 1961. 52 p. (mimeographed). A study by a professor at Lawrence College, formerly a resident of Czechoslovakia.

U66 POVOLNY, MOJMIR. "The Role and Function of the UN in Soviet Foreign Policy." Ph.D. dissertation, U. of Chicago, 1954. The questions which are raised by the Soviet concept of internationalism, by the Soviet interpretation and application of the rules of international law, and by the apparent and real contradictions between Soviet theory and the actual pursuit of international politics are studied here against the background of Soviet attitudes toward and policies in the UN.

U67 PROTOPOPOV, ANATOLI S. *Sovetskii Soiuz v Organizatsii Obedinennykh Natsii. Iz istorii borby SSSR za mir i nezavisimost narodov (1945-1957).* Moscow: Gospolitizdat, 1957. 212 p. The first such monograph in years consisting essentially of two parts, arms control and questions of national independence and self-determination. The subject is presented typically as a "struggle" between progressive (Soviet) and reactionary forces. Poor documentation; no UN material; relies on press reports and a few foreign monographs. [B]

U68 PURYEAR, EDGAR F., JR. "Communist negotiating techniques: A case study of the United Nations Security Council Commission regarding Greek frontier incidents." Ph.D. dissertation, Princeton, 1959. A useful case study of the negotiations which sought to end the frontier incidents between Greece, on the one hand, and Yugoslavia, Albania, and Bulgaria, on the other, during the 1945-47 period.

U68A RUBINSTEIN, ALVIN Z. *The Soviets in International Organizations: Changing Policy Toward Underdeveloped Countries, 1953-1963.* Princeton: Princeton University Press, 1964. Relying upon UN documents, Soviet writings, and extensive interviewing, this study examines Soviet policies and behavior in the UN specialized agencies and regional economic commissions concerned with helping the developing nations of Africa and Asia. Included is a detailed treatment of the Soviet record in ECAFE, IAEA, and international secretariats, and of the role of ideology in conditioning the Soviet approach to international organizations. [A]

U69 RUBINSTEIN, ALVIN Z. "An Analysis of Soviet Policy in the Economic and Social Council and the Economic Commission for Europe, 1946-1951." Ph.D. dissertation, U. of Pennsylvania, 1954. Soviet obstructionist policies in the UN are linked with Stalin's quest for hegemony in Eastern Europe. Antagonism toward the West and the maximization of European instability are shown to be hallmarks of Soviet behavior. Intensive use of UN and Russian sources.

U70 RUBINSTEIN, ALVIN Z. "Selected Bibliography of Soviet Works on the United Nations, 1946-1959," *The American Political Science Review*, December 1960, p. 985-91. A University of Pennsylvania professor systematically presents the principal Soviet writings on the non-power-political activities of the UN, the extent and quality of the studies and the changing areas of emphasis. A useful guide for Soviet studies on the UN, and Soviet views on the veto power, Charter revision, and economic development. [A]

U71 RUBINSTEIN, ALVIN Z. "Soviet Policy in ECAFE; a Case Study of Soviet Behavior in International Economic Organization," *International Organization*, Autumn 1958, p. 459-72. A comparison of Stalin and post-Stalin policies toward countries of Southern Asia within the framework of a key UN economic organization. Moscow encourages neutralism, participates in marginal activities, and seeks to cultivate an image of amiability and reasonableness. [B]

U72 RUBINSTEIN, ALVIN Z. "Soviet Policy Toward Underdeveloped Areas in the Economic and Social Council," *International Organization*, May 1955, p. 232-43. Moscow's policy of non-participation and opposition to UN efforts at aiding underdeveloped countries is contrasted with its attempt to enhance Soviet prestige in these areas. The discrepancy between declaration and deed is evident in the 1945-54 period.

U72A RUDZINSKI, ALEXANDER W. "The Influence of the United Nations on Soviet Policy," *International Organization*, May 1949, p. 254-68.

U72B SHIBAEVA, E. A. *Spetsializirovannye uchrezhdeniia OON: mezhdunarodno-pravovoi ocherk*. Moscow: Izd. Mos. universiteta, 1962. 32 p.

U73 SHTEIN, BORIS E. *Sistema mezhdunarodnoi opeki; dve tendentsii resheniia kolonialnoi problemy v Organizatsii Obedinennykh*

Natsii. Moscow: Gospolitizdat, 1948. 192 p. A harsh Soviet attack on Western colonialism. Notes the "illusory" independence of India and Pakistan (a concomitant of the Zhdanov line) and lauds Soviet efforts on behalf of underdeveloped countries. Standard Stalinist views. Largely polemical.

U74 SHURSHALOV, V. M. *Rezhim mezhdunarodnoi opeki*. Moscow: Gosiurizdat, 1951. 192 p. A Soviet writer compares the League mandate system with the UN Trusteeship system. The organization and the operation of the Trusteeship Council are discussed, with heavy criticism of the Western Powers, particularly the United States for its acquisition of non-self governing territories in the Pacific. South Africa is condemned for her refusal to place the Southwest Africa territory under the UN. The writer regards the trusteeship system as a cover for Western imperialism. [B]

U75 SISCO, JOSEPH J. "The Soviet Attitude toward the Trusteeship System." Ph.D. dissertation, U. of Chicago, 1950.

U76 SOLODOVNIKOV, V. G. (chief editor). *Mezhdunarodnye ekonomicheskie organizatsii: spravochnik*. Moscow: 1962. 2nd ed. Institute of World Economics and International Relations, 1,108 p. Approximately one-fifth of this handbook on international economic organizations contains factual information about the organization and activities of UN economic organizations. Capsule commentaries on Soviet policy in them are useful for understanding the attitude of Moscow toward the Specialized Agencies and regional economic commissions of the UN. [A]

U77 SOVIET NEWS. *Soviet Union at the San Francisco Conference*. London: "Soviet News," 1945. 71 p.

U78 UNITED NATIONS, GENERAL ASSEMBLY, DELEGATION FROM THE UNION OF SOVIET SOCIALIST REPUBLICS. *Delegatsii SSSR, USSR, i BSSR na vtoroi sessii generalnoi assamblei Organizatsii Obedinennykh Natsii, sbornik rechei i vystuplenii, sentiabr-noiabr 1947 g*. Moscow: Ogiz goslitizdat, 1948. 557 p.

U79 UNITED NATIONS, GENERAL ASSEMBLY, DELEGATION FROM THE UNION OF SOVIET SOCIALIST REPUBLICS. *The Soviet Union at the Fifth Session of U.N.O., 1950, October 26-December 12*. London: Soviet News, 1951. 119 p.

U80 UNITED NATIONS, GENERAL ASSEMBLY, DELEGATION FROM THE UNION OF SOVIET SOCIALIST REPUBLICS. *Translations from the Soviet Press*. n.p.: 1955-56. 4 vols.

U80A USHAKOV, V. G. *Sovetskii Soiuz i OON*. Moscow: Gospolitizdat, 1962. 55 p. A semi-popular account, in the recently inaugurated Library of U.S.S.R. Foreign Policy series, of Soviet policy in the United Nations. [B]

U81 USHAKOV, N. A., *Printsip edinoglasiia velikikh derzhav v Organizatsii Obedinennykh Natsii.* Moscow: Izd. Akademii nauk SSSR, 1956. 175 p. A study by a leading Soviet scholar defending the veto power as essential for the continued operation of the UN. Western efforts to circumvent or revise the unanimity provision of the Charter are strongly criticised. [B]

U82 VLADIMIROV, VLADIMIR. *Mezhdunarodnaia Organizatsiia Truda.* Moscow: Izd. IMO, 1959. 103 p. A survey, from the Soviet viewpoint, of the organization and activities of ILO, one of the politically more sensitive specialized agencies of the United Nations. [B]

Addendum

U83 BUZINKAI, DONALD I. "Soviet-League Relations, 1919-1939: a Survey and Analysis." Ph.D. dissertation, New York University, 1964. 245 p.

V. Soviet Policy Toward Disarmament

EDITED BY WALTER C. CLEMENS, JR.

1. BIBLIOGRAPHIES

V1 CLEMENS, WALTER C., JR. *Soviet Disarmament Policy, 1917-1963: An Annotated Bibliography of Soviet and Western Sources.* Stanford, Cal.: Hoover Institution, 1965. 151 p. [A]

V1A COLLART, YVES. *Disarmament; a Study Guide and Bibliography on the Efforts of the United Nations.* The Hague: Nijhoff, 1958. 110 p. An attempt by the Assistant to the Director of the Graduate Institute of International Studies in Geneva, under the auspices of the World Federation of United Nations Associations and with the financial support of UNESCO, to provide "an impartial summary of the positions of the various nations" on disarmament and the conclusions of the deliberations at the UN from 1945 to 1958. Contains questions for discussion and a twenty-page bibliography with emphasis on UN documents, but including also Canadian, U.S., British, French, and Soviet government documents in French and English, recent books and articles in these two languages, and a list of bibliographies on disarmament. [B]

V2 *Current Thought on Peace and War.* Durham, North Carolina, 1960-. Quarterly. Annotated and cross-indexed digest of literature and research in progress on the problems of world order and conflict, including a number of references on aspects of arms control.

V3 *Deutsches und ausländisches Schriftum zur Frage der Abruestung, 1945-1956; unter besonderer Beruecksichtigung des Schriftums zu den Problemen der Kernwaffen und der internationalen Kontrolle der Kernenergie.* Frankfurt am Main: Deutsche Gesellschaft für Auswärtige Politik, 1957. 44 p. A bibliography of works in German and other languages on the subject of disarmament, 1945-56, with special emphasis on the problems of atomic weapons and the international control of atomic energy. Published by a scholarly research group in Frankfurt.

V4 "Disarmament—A Bibliography," *Survival* (The Institute for Strategic Studies), vol. II, no. 1 (Jan.-Feb. 1960), p. 38-40. A "working bibliography" of books, pamphlets, and official documents concerning disarmament in its various aspects, which have been published since 1945.

V5 FISCHER, GEORGE. *Soviet Disarmament Policy: A Survey of Recent Sources.* Cambridge: Center for International Studies, M.I.T., 1961. 17 p. Extremely useful annotated listings of recent books, articles, and documents in English and Russian on disarmament; of the records of international conferences relating to arms control; and a list of key Khrushchev statements in translation. [B]

V6 HALPERIN, MORTON H. *Limited War; an Annotated Bibliography.* Cambridge: Center for International Affairs, Harvard, 1961. 48 p. This "comprehensive bibliography" contains 227 items, including a section on limited war and arms controls. Also includes a four-page author index.

V7 LEAGUE OF NATIONS, LIBRARY. *Annotated Bibliography on Disarmament and Military Questions.* Geneva: League of Nations, 1931. 164 p. Objective listing of articles and books in many languages on general disarmament inside and outside the League; naval disarmament; the relationship of disarmament to security, economics, and past history; the laws of war; trade and manufacture of arms; armed forces; and chemical warfare. [A]

V8 LENINGRAD, PUBLICHNAIA BIBLIOTEKA. *Mir bez oruzhiia—mir bez voin.* Comp. by Iu. L. Kuznets. Leningrad: Publichnaia biblioteka, 1960. 12 p. A bibliography on disarmament, issued by the Leningrad Public Library.

V9 SOVETSKAIA ASSOTSIATSIIA MEZHDUNARODNOGO PRAVA. *Sovetskaia literatura po mezhdunarodnomu pravu; bibliografiia 1917-1957.* Ed. by V. N. Durdenevskii. Moscow: Gosizdat iurid. lit., 1959. 303 p. Valuable bibliography of Soviet literature on international law listing articles, books, and book reviews, 1917-57. Treats general and specific questions of international law. A listing of works on disarmament is particularly useful. Also contains brief annotations and a list of periodicals consulted as well as an author index. [B]

V10 UNITED NATIONS, DEPARTMENT OF POLITICAL AND SECURITY COUNCIL AFFAIRS, ATOMIC ENERGY COMMISSION GROUP. *An International Bibliography on Atomic Energy.* Lake Success: United Nations, 1949-1951. 2 vols. Supplement, N.Y.: United Nations, 1953. 31 p. A briefly annotated bibliography of references on international and national control; peaceful and military uses of atomic energy; and social, economic, political, and ethical implications of atomic energy.

V11 U.S., DEPARTMENT OF THE ARMY, ARMY LIBRARY. *Disarmament; a Bibliographic Record 1916-1960.* Prepared by the Staff of the Army Library for the Office, Special Assistant to the Joint Chiefs of Staff for Disarmament Affairs. Washington: G.P.O., 1960. 123 p. A very useful annotated bibliography, arranged chronologically. Selected quotations of Eisenhower and Khrushchev on disarmament. English translation of concluding chapter of V. M. Khaitsman, *The U.S.S.R. and the Problem of Disarmament* (see below), and a reproduction of his bibliography. Other interesting appendices are also included. [A]

V12 U.S. DISARMAMENT ADMINISTRATION. *A Basic Bibliography: Disarmament, Arms Control, and National Security*. Department of State Publication 7193, Disarmament Series 1. Washington: June 1961. 29 p. Useful introductory bibliography of literature since 1945 readily accessible in English.

V13 WRIGHT, CHRISTOPHER. "Selected Critical Bibliography." In special arms control issue of *Daedalus*, Fall 1960. Columbus, Ohio: Wesleyan U., 1960, p. 1055-1073. Concise annotations of major works, official and unofficial, on the subject of arms control.

2. 1917-1939

V14 BUKHARTSEV, D., VARGA, E., and LAPINSKII, P., eds. "*Razoruzhenie*"—*podgotovka voiny, doklad L. Ivanova i vystupleniia v Institute mirovogo khoziaistva i mirovoi politiki*. Moscow: Partizdat, 1932. 216 p. Under the sponsorship of the Communist Academy of the Institute of World Economics and World Politics, Lev Ivanov makes a report, on the eve of the 1932 Disarmament Conference, in which he terms "disarmament" preparation for war, after which other Soviet commentators make reports condemning pacifism, fascism, and imperialist competition in armaments. Almost half the book is documentation on disarmament.

V15 CLEMENS, WALTER C., JR. "Origins of the Soviet Campaign for Disarmament; the Soviet Position on Peace, Security and Revolution at the Genoa, Moscow, and Lausanne Conferences, 1922-1923." Ph.D. dissertation, Columbia, 1961. 343 p. An analysis of ideological, political, economic and military determinants and consequences of the first years of Soviet disarmament policy. Considers elements of continuity and change in this policy through the years and relates diplomatic support for disarmament to internal problems and external problems and opportunities of the Soviet Government. Sources include Moscow and Leningrad libraries and interviews with a former Soviet diplomat. [B]

V16 COMMUNIST INTERNATIONAL. *The Communist International, 1919-1943*. Ed. by Jane Degras. London; N.Y.: Oxford 1956, 1960. 2 vols. The first two volumes, on the years through 1928, provide excellent coverage, albeit in excerpts, of Comintern pronouncements on disarmament and related subjects.

V17 COMMUNIST INTERNATIONAL. *Kommunisticheskii internatsional v dokumentakh: resheniia, tezisy i vozvaniia kongressov Kominterna i plenumov IKKI, 1919-1932.* Ed. by Bela Kun. Moscow: Partizdat, 1933. 1007 p. Fundamental collection of Comintern decisions, theses, and appeals. The theses advanced at the Sixth Congress in 1928 show the context in which the Soviet Union's disarmament proposals to the League of Nations were intrepreted by the Comintern. [B]

V18 ENGELS, FRIEDRICH. *Kann Europa abruesten?* Nuremberg: Woerlein, 1893. 29 p. A pamphlet of classic importance in Marxist literature, published during a Reichstag debate on military questions. Engels argued that the system of standing armies had reached the point where it would either ruin Europe economically or lead her into a general war of destruction; that the permanent armies, therefore, ought to be transformed into militias based on universal arming of the people; that this was already possible politically and militarily, by means of treaties to reduce the length of military service; and that if this were not done, it would be due to fear of the "internal foe" and not the external one. [B]

V19 GNEDIN, EVGENII A. *Razoruzhenie—uzel mezhdunarodnykh protivorechii.* Moscow: Sotsekizdat, 1934. 136 p. Disarmament is regarded as a "knot of international contradictions" in this Soviet work aiming to "tell in a popular way how . . . the problems of disarmament and armament served the imperialists as an instrument of preparation for war, while for the working class of the whole world and the Soviet Union they served as an instrument of struggle against imperialist war." Treats naval disarmament negotiations, the Kellogg-Briand Pact, the reparations problem, the collapse of the 1932 Geneva Disarmament Conference, the "end of capitalist stabilization," the exit of Germany from the League of Nations and the Soviet definition of aggression. No footnotes or bibliography. [B]

V20 GREAT BRITAIN, TREATIES, ETC. 1936—(George VI). *Agreement between His Majesty's Government in the United Kingdom and the Government of the U.S.S.R. providing for the limitation of naval armament and the exchange of information concerning naval construction.* (Protocol of signature and exchange of notes of November 12/19, 1937, regarding the Russian text) London, July 17, 1937. (Ratifications exchanged in London on November 4, 1937) London: H. M. Stationery Office, 1938. English text is 18 p., Russian 22 p. One of a series of treaties signed by Britain with other states, including Germany and Poland. See also the protocol modifying this agreement: Cmd. 6074.

V21 IAVORSKII, S. IA. *Mir ili voina.* Moscow: 1929. 140 p. A Soviet author studies post-World War I international politics in relation to disarmament.

V22 IVANOV, LEV N. *Krakh konferentsii po razoruzheniiu; s prilozheniem vazhneishikh dokumentov konferentsii po razoruzheniiu.* Kharkov: Ukrainskii rabotnik, 1934. 456 p. An interesting analysis and documentary collection concerning the collapse of the League of Nations Disarmament Conference. The documents include government notes and proposals, newspaper articles from many countries, German demands for "equality" of arms, the breakup of the conference and negotiations on Germany's rearmament. [B]

V23 IVANOV, LEV N. *SSSR i imperialisticheskoe okruzhenie.* Moscow: Izd. Komakademii, 1928. 154 p. The first volume of seven books in the series *Desiat let kapitalisticheskogo okruzheniia SSSR*, edited by E. Pashukanis and M. Spektator and published by the Communist Academy. Many of these books, but especially the first, discuss aspects of Soviet policy toward the League and toward disarmament. Interesting references to documents and periodical literature.

V23A KHAITSMAN, V. M. *SSSR i problema razoruzheniia (mezhdu pervoi i vtoroi mirovymi voinami).* Moscow: Izd. Akademii nauk SSSR, 1959. 451 p. At least superficially, one of the most serious books on disarmament by a Soviet author since 1945, this publication surveys the disarmament problem between the world wars. It uses a wide array of Soviet and non-Soviet periodical and documentary literature to buttress its picture of the Soviet Government as the leading force in the struggle for disarmament since 1917. Annotated bibliography of documents and works in many languages is included. Its concluding chapter is translated and its bibliography reproduced in U.S. Department of the Army, *Disarmament; A Bibliographic Record, 1916-1960* (see above). [A]

V23B KOMMUNISTICHESKAIA PARTIIA SOVETSKOGO SOIUZA. *KPSS o vooruzhennykh silakh Sovetskogo Soiuza; sbornik dokumentov, 1917-1958.* Comp. by V. N. Malin and V. P. Moskovskii. Moscow: Gospolitizdat, 1958. 420 p. A collection of Communist Party resolutions and pronouncements on the Soviet armed forces, with emphasis on the years before World War II.

V24 KOROVIN, E. A. *Razoruzhenie; problema razoruzheniia v mezhdunarodnom prave; Liga Natsii v faktakh i dokumentakh, 1920-1929.* Moscow: Gosizdat, 1930. 431 p. Extremely important statement of the Soviet position on disarmament in the inter-war period. Introduction by B. E. Shtein, Secretary to Soviet Delegation to the Preparatory Commission for the Disarmament Conference. Part I is an analysis by Korovin, a leading Soviet international lawyer, of disarmament in international law. Part II is a review by V. V. Egorev of disarmament at the League of Nations, 1920-29. An extensive bibliography gives Soviet works on disarmament. [B]

V25 KOROVIN, E. A. "The USSR and Disarmament," *International Conciliation*, no. 292 (Sept. 1933), p. 293-354. A leading Soviet jurist recounts Soviet efforts for disarmament up to 1933 and presents relevant documents. [A]

V26 LAUSANNE CONFERENCE ON NEAR EASTERN AFFAIRS, 1922-1923. *Records of Proceedings and Draft Terms of Peace.* (Cmd. 1814) London: H. M. Stationery Off., 1923. 861 p. Records the running debate between Foreign Commissar Chicherin and Lord Curzon on arms control measures for the Straits and the Black Sea.

V27 LENIN, VLADIMIR I. *Sochineniia.* 4th ed. Moscow: Gospolitizdat, 1941-1958. 38 vols. Lenin's collected works contain many references to disarmament and related subjects, the location of which is facilitated by consulting the index to the fourth edition. His major articles in this field are: "O lozunge Soedinennykh Shtatov Evropy," XXI, 308-311; "Voennaia programma proletarskoi revoliutsii," XXIII, 65-76; "O lozunge 'razoruzheniia,'" XXIII, 83-93; "Patsifizm burzhuaznyi i patsifizm sotsialisticheskii," XXIII, 165-185. For English translations, see *The United States of Europe Slogan; the War Program of the Proletarian Revolution.* Moscow: Foreign Languages Publishing House, 1952. 39 p. Other references in V144 (below). [A]

V28 LENIN, VLADIMIR I. *V. I. Lenin o voine, armii, i voennoi nauke; sbornik v dvukh tomakh.* Moscow: Voenizdat, 1957. 2 vols. Convenient compendium of important statements by Lenin on war, armaments, and disarmament. Not comprehensive.

V29 LIAS, MIKHAIL A. *Voina pod maskoi razoruzheniia.* Moscow-Leningrad: Partizdat, 1932. 133 p. A Soviet commentator depicts Western disarmament policy as a cover for plans to war against the USSR.

V30 LIPPAY, Z. *Behind the Scenes of the "Disarmament" Conference.* Moscow: Co-operative Publishing Society of Foreign Workers in the USSR; N.Y.: Workers' Library, 1932. 58 p. A propaganda-oriented pamphlet attempting to "expose" the 1923 Geneva Disarmament Conference as a "farce" on the grounds that "the pacifist prelude in Geneva to the forthcoming world war and to the anti-Soviet war is closely related to the new world war that has been started in China." French imperialism is depicted as brewing an anti-Soviet war while Japan mobilized her forces against the Soviet Far East.

V31 LITVINOV, MAKSIM M. *Against Aggression; Speeches by Maxim Litvinov, Together with Texts of Treaties and of the Covenant of the League of Nations.* London: Lawrence & Wishart, 1939. 208 p. Documents which may profitably be read in conjunction with volume II of Max Beloff's *Foreign Policy of Soviet Russia, 1929-1941* (see section, 1929-1939) to understand the shift in Soviet foreign policy after the rise of Hitler to power.

V32 LITVINOV, MAKSIM M. *Protiv voin; za vseobshchee razoruzhenie; sovetskie predlozheniia o polnom i chastichnom razoruzhenii.* Moscow-Leningrad: Gosizdat, 1928. 151 p. Includes the Soviet draft projects for both total and for partial disarmament, and clarifications of them.

V33 LITVINOV, MAKSIM M. *Za vseobshchee razoruzhenie; rechi M. M. Litvinova i sovetskie predlozheniia o polnom i chastichnom razoruzhenii.* Moscow: Moskovskii rabochii, 1928. 135 p. Contains several speeches by Litvinov including one concerning the German proposal to convoke the Disarmament Conference without delay.

V34 LUNACHARSKII, ANATOLII V. *Kak oni razoruzhaiutsia.* Leningrad: Priboi, 1931. 46 p. A Soviet diplomat's skeptical analysis of how the other countries were "disarming." Written after the close of the Preparatory Commission but before the opening of the Disarmament Conference.

V35 MADARIAGA, SALVADOR DE. *Disarmament.* N.Y.: Coward-McCann, 1929. 379 p. Interesting analysis of the disarmament problem and the role played by the Soviet Union in disarmament negotiations and reasons why Soviet proposals were not accepted at the League of Nations.

V36 MAHANEY, WILBUR L., JR. *The Soviet Union, the League of Nations and Disarmament, 1917-1935.* Privately published Ph.D. dissertation, Philadelphia, 1940. 199 p. One of the few books in English on this subject, this work is based largely on official Soviet pronouncements in Western European languages. No Russian language materials are used. The book's tendency to accept Soviet speeches at face value has led to its receiving not unfavorable reviews in Russia. Concerned mainly with Russia's disarmament efforts at the League.

V38 MOSCOW, CONFÉRENCE POUR LA LIMITATION DES ARMEMENTS, 1922. *Conférence de Moscou pour la limitation des armements.* Moscow: Commissariat du Peuple aux Affaires Etrangères, 1923. 246 p. Documents and stenographic report of the 1922 Moscow Disarmament Conference including invitations, preliminary correspondence, and materials on the March 1922 Riga Protocol. The only official published minutes, although the *New York Times* has rather accurate day-by-day reports on the proceedings. [B]

V39 NOTOVICH, F. I. *Razoruzhenie imperialistov, Liga Natsii i SSSR*. Moscow: Moskovskii rabochii, 1929. 189 p. Historical review and analysis of post-World War II disarmament policies of the "imperialists, the League of Nations, and the USSR." Concludes that all states must follow the revolutionary route of the USSR. Brief bibliography. [B]

V40 *Ot Vashingtona do Genui*. Moscow: Vysshii voennyi redaktsionyi sovet, 1922. 130 p. Collection of articles by Soviet political and economic commentators concerning the 1921-22 Washington Naval Conference and the 1922 Genoa Economic Conference. Of interest for its skeptical attitude toward Western notions of disarmament, which are alleged to be inspired solely by economic, political, and military considerations rather than by any desire for peace. [B]

V41 POTEMKIN, VLADIMIR P., ed. *Istoriia diplomatii*. Vol. III, *Diplomatiia v periode podgotovki vtoroi mirovoi voiny (1919-1939 gg.)*. Moscow: Gospolitizdat, 1945. 883 p. This fundamental Soviet version of diplomatic history "during the period of the preparation of World War II" discusses most Soviet proposals for disarmament and collective security from 1919 to 1939. Chapters by A. M. Pankratova take up "the growth of the war danger and the problem of disarmament 1927-1929" and "the international disarmament conference and the struggle of the U.S.S.R. against continued armaments 1932-1933," while E. V. Tarle treats "the institutions and methods of bourgeois diplomacy," including disarmament. [A]

V42 PREPARATORY COMMISSION FOR THE DISARMAMENT CONFERENCE, DELEGATION FROM RUSSIA. *Delegatsiia SSSR na VI sessii Komissii po razoruzheniiu, 15 aprelia-6 maia 1929 g.* Moscow: NKID, 1929. 70 p. *Delegatsiia SSSR na poslednei sessii Komissii razoruzheniia (vtoroi polovina VI sessii), 6 noiabria-9 dekabria 1930 g.* Moscow: NKID, 1931. 100 p. These two collections cover the Soviet position at the first and the second part of the sixth session of the Preparatory Commission, which was its last meeting prior to the convocation of the Disarmament Conference. The second collection has data on the periods of military service in different countries, military budgets, naval disarmament, and international control.

V43 PREPARATORY COMMISSION FOR THE DISARMAMENT CONFERENCE, DELEGATION FROM RUSSIA. *Textes et documents; l'URSS à la conférence du désarmement*. Preface by A. Lunacharskii. Paris: Mayenne Impr. Floch, 1932. 219 p. Documents covering 1927 to 1932, as well as speeches by Litvinov and Lunacharskii.

V44 RUSSIA (1917- RSFSR). *Sovetskii Soiuz v borbe za mir; sobranie dokumentov i vstupitelnaia statia.* Moscow: Gosizdat, 1929. 344 p. Abridged English ed., *The Soviet Union and Peace; The Most Important of the Documents Issued by the Government of the USSR Concerning Peace and Disarmament from 1917 to 1929.* London: Lawrence; N.Y.: International, 1929. 280 p. Contains a special section on disarmament, albeit in excerpts.

V45 RUSSIA (1917- RSFSR), NARODNYI KOMISSARIAT PO INOSTRANNYM DELAM. *Materialy Genuezskoi Konferentsii (podgotovka, otchety zasedanii, raboty komissii, diplomaticheskaia perepiska i pr.).* Ed. by G. B. Sandomirskii. Moscow: Knigoizdat. pisatelei v Moskve, 1922. 459 p. One of the most complete publications of documents on the Genoa Conference of 1922, when Soviet representatives proposed disarmament to Western diplomats for the first time, this work contains preparatory correspondence and full minutes of the plenary and commission meetings of the Conference. Contains not only Soviet proposals for disarmament and periodic international conferences, but text of Soviet-Polish debate on implication of the March 1922 Riga Protocol and Soviet speeches favoring a strong non-aggression pact by all parties to the Genoa Conference. [B]

V45A RUSSIA (1923- USSR), NARODNYI KOMISSARIAT PO INOSTRANNYM DELAM. *Razoruzhenie, 1933-1936. 1. Chetvernye peregovory. 2. Konferentsiia po razoruzheniiu. 3. Dovoruzhenie Germanii.* Moscow: Narkomindel, 1936. 286 p. Invaluable collection of documents, presenting the official Soviet position on disarmament as seen from speeches by Litvinov and other Soviet diplomats and in Soviet proposals to the League of Nations. Sections on the four-way negotiations among the United Kingdom, France, Germany, and Italy; the Disarmament Conference; and German rearmament. [A]

V46 RUSSIA (1923- USSR), NARODNYI KOMISSARIAT PO INOSTRANNYM DELAM. *SSSR v borbe za razoruzhenie; sovetskaia delegatsiia v Zheneve; fakty i dokumenty.* Intro. by B. E. Shtein. Moscow: NKID, 1928. 60 p. Also published under the title: *Sovetskaia delegatsiia na IV sessii podgotovitelnoi komissii po razoruzheniiu.* Moscow: NKID, 1928. 60 p. German ed., Berlin: Ost-Europa, 1928. 61 p. Documentary collection including a famous Litvinov statement to the press, a memorandum of the Soviet delegation to the Preparatory Commission, and a report by Litvinov to the XVth Congress of the Communist Party, plus a draft treaty for immediate, complete, and universal disarmament.

V47 RUSSIA (1923- USSR), NARODNYI KOMISSARIAT PO INOSTRANNYM DELAM. *V borbe za mir; sovetskaia delegatsiia na V sessii Komissii po razoruzheniiu.* Moscow: NKID, 1928. 84 p. Covers the materials presented by Litvinov, March 15 to April 21, 1928, during which time the general position advanced by the Soviet delegation at the previous session and the opposition to it became more defined. Includes a decree of the Central Executive Committee on Litvinov's report on the Fifth Session.

V48 *The Soviet's Fight for Disarmament.* Intro. by A. V. Lunacharskii. N.Y.: International, 1933?. 44 p. Contains a ten-page introduction, and speeches at Geneva by Litvinov and Lunacharskii 1929-32, most of them in 1932.

V48A STALIN, IOSIF. *Sochineniia.* Moscow: Gospolizdat, 1947-1951. English ed., *Works.* Moscow: Foreign Lang. Pub. House, 1953-55. 13 vols. Stalin's collected works contain occasional remarks on disarmament, references to which may be found in Jack F. Matlock, Jr. and F. C. Holling, Jr., *An Index to the Collected Works of J. V. Stalin.* (Washington: External Research Department, Office of Intelligence Research, Department of State, January 1955.) [B]

V49 TARACOUZIO, TIMOTHY A. *The Soviet Union and International Law; a Study Based on the Legislation, Treaties and Foreign Relations of the U.S.S.R.* N.Y.: Macmillan, 1935. 530 p. Of vital relevance to disarmament is this work's translation of excerpts from the theses advanced at the Sixth Congress of the Communist International, Moscow, 1928. Has excellent chapters on Soviet interpretation of pacific settlement, peace and disarmament, non-aggression, and war. 27-page bibliography.

V50 TARACOUZIO, TIMOTHY A. *War and Peace in Soviet Diplomacy.* N.Y.: Macmillan, 1940. 354 p. Elucidates the fundamental principles of Marxism with respect to the issues which determined Soviet policy on war and peace through 1939, based largely on Soviet materials. Deduces from Marxist principles that "when the term 'disarmament' is applied to the Soviet conception of a communist state and its revolutionary role, the contradiction becomes self-evident." Useful appendix of Soviet treaties and a 10-page bibliography.

V51 UNITED NATIONS, SECRETARIAT. *Historical Survey of the Activities of the League of Nations Regarding the Question of Disarmament 1920-1937.* N.Y.: United Nations, 1951. 187 p. Invaluable survey paraphrasing or quoting original documents. Annexes give lists of League of Nations resolutions, proposals, drafts, reports, questionnaires, and sources having to do with disarmament. Annotated list of principal documents shows when the Soviet delegates were active on the disarmament question. [A]

V52 *USSR and Disarmament; Discussion of Russia's Disarmament Proposals at Geneva, March 16-24, 1928, Convention for Partial Disarmament.* Comp. by W. P. Coates. London: Anglo-Russian Parliamentary Committee, 1928. 82 p. Interesting collection of speeches and rejoinders by Litvinov and non-Soviet delegates to the Fifth Session of the Preparatory Commission for the Disarmament Conference.

3. 1939-1963

V53 AMERICAN ACADEMY OF ARTS AND SCIENCES, BOSTON. *Collected Papers; Summer Study on Arms Control.* Boston: The Academy, 1960. 467 p. A stimulating volume of documents produced in connection with, or made available to, the Study, and organized by Garry Quinn. Essays, discussions, and exercises concerned primarily with achieving and operating a system of stabilized deterrence. Included are four provocative analyses of China and the Soviet Union in relation to arms control. Many useful bibliographical essays on arms control in general and one on the lack of literature in English on the USSR and arms control. [B]

V54 *Arms Control Program and Issues.* Ed. by David H. Frisch. N.Y.: The Twentieth Century Fund, 1961. 162 p. Recommendations for arms control proposals and supporting papers authored by some of the participants in the 1960 Summer Study on Arms Control. Favor the replacement of tactical nuclear weapons by conventional forces and the forswearance of strategic nuclear weapons except for a second-strike in an all-out war. Aim is to ensure stabilized deterrence by the establishment of invulnerable retaliatory forces on both sides, thus removing any temptation to pre-empt. [B]

V55 *Atomwaffenfreie Zone in Europa. Kleine Dokumentensammlung.* Berlin: Kongress Verlag, 1958. 136 p. Short preface by Professor Bittel and documentation on an "atom-free zone in Europe." Documents include statements showing the "German people against imperialism"; Soviet proposals 1957-58; the Rapacki plan; support for it in the East German regime; the Peace Manifesto of the 65 Communist Parties, November 1957; West German professors favoring the Rapacki plan; and chronology, sources and detailed index.

V56 BARNET, RICHARD J. *Who Wants Disarmament?* Intro. by Chester Bowles. Boston: Beacon, 1960. 141 p. Analysis by a practicing lawyer, familiar with Soviet sources, of U.S. and Soviet positions on disarmament and the reasons why each of the two sides might or might not consider itself genuinely interested in disarmament. [A]

V57 BARNET, RICHARD J. "The Soviet Attitude on Disarmament," *Problems of Communism*, May-June 1961, p. 32-37. Weighs Soviet views on disarmament in the context of Soviet thinking about war and military science. [B]

V58 BECHHOEFER, BERNHARD G. *Postwar Negotiations for Arms Control.* Washington: Brookings Institution, 1961. 641 p. A former senior State Department officer on arms control (1946 to 1958) carves from a morass of UN and government documents the outstanding narrative and analysis of arms control negotiations since 1945. Concludes that the record does not indicate that arms control is an urgent Soviet objective, but that circumstances could change to make it so. Believes a breakthrough to agreement more likely to arise from the exchange of highly technical arms control plans than from radically new, sweeping ideas. Valuable 8-page bibliographical guide to documents. [A]

V59 BECHHOEFER, BERNHARD G. "American Policies and Disarmament," in *American Diplomacy in a New Era.* Ed. by Stephen D. Kertesz. Notre Dame, Ind.: University of Notre Dame Press, 1961, p. 83-143. An abridged version of the author's book on the same subject, this article is so concise and accurate that it should be among the first works consulted by anyone wishing to understand the postwar policies of the Great Powers toward arms control. Covers four periods from 1941 to 1960. Heavily footnoted. [A]

V60 BELOKON, A. "Problema razoruzheniia v sovremennykh usloviiakh razreshima," *Kommunist*, no. 11 (July 1956), p. 79-93. Argues that with present conditions the problem of disarmament can be solved.

V61 BIORKLUND, ELIS (ADMIRAL). *International Atomic Policy during a Decade, 1945-1955.* Princeton, N.J.: Van Nostrand, 1956. 148 p. Excellent brief historical investigation by Swedish naval authority on Soviet affairs. He analyzes the atomic policy of the USA, the other Western Powers, and the USSR in light of the political and conference problems confronting these powers. Includes an outstanding bibliography, a list of deposits of fissionable materials, and a map of sources of raw materials. [B]

V62 BOGDANOV, O. V. *Iadernoe razoruzhenie.* Moscow: Izdatelstvo Instituta mezhdunarodnykh otnoshenii, 1961. 191 p. An exposition of Soviet policy on the abolition of nuclear weapons, and a criticism of Western views. [B]

V63 BOLTE, CHARLES G. *The Price of Peace; a Plan for Disarmament.* Boston: Beacon, 1956. 108 p. Former member of U.S.

Mission to the U.N. regards U.S. disarmament proposals up to date of his writing (1955) as totally inadequate. He reviews the military and political situation and sets forth a plan for peace and disarmament similar to Grenville Clark's, which he recommends.

V64 BRENNAN, DONALD G., ed. *Arms Control, Disarmament, and National Security*. N.Y.: Braziller, 1961. 475 p. Contains papers by a score of American authorities published originally in the "Arms Control" issue of *Daedalus*, the journal of the American Academy of Arts and Sciences. These analyses of the problem's different aspects, juxtaposing several challenging and differing points of view, range from "The Case for Unilateral Disarmament" by Erich Fromm to "Non-Physical Inspection Techniques" by Lewis C. Bohn, and are commented on by four outstanding foreign authorities. Little material directly on Soviet disarmament policy. [A]

V65 BULL, HEDLEY. *The Control of the Arms Race*. London: Published for the Institute for Strategic Studies by Weidenfeld & Nicolson, 1961. 215 p. The author of this book had the sustained assistance of a British study group and benefited by the criticisms of an international arms control conference in September 1960. Insisting on the primacy of security considerations, the unity of strategy and arms control, and the importance of technological innovation, he explores many facets of the control problem, but does not recommend a plan.

V66 CLARK, GRENVILLE, and SOHN, LEWIS B. *World Peace Through World Law*. 2nd ed. Cambridge: Harvard, 1960. 387 p. The authors, writing from a legal perspective, propose what many writers consider a useful model for a comprehensive and detailed plan leading in stages to general and complete disarmament. The plan includes a comprehensive inspection system and a strong U.N. military establishment. [B]

V67 CLAUDE, INIS L. *Swords into Plowshares; the Problems and Progress of International Organization*. N.Y.: Random House, 1956. 497 p. Chapter 8 is an outstanding discussion of the philosophical assumptions of the advocates of disarmament and a summary of efforts for disarmament from Kant to the present. Explains Soviet as well as Western viewpoints.

V68 CONFERENCE OF THE TEN NATION COMMITTEE ON DISARMAMENT, GENEVA, 1960. *Verbatim Records of the Meetings of the Conference of the Ten Nation Committee on Disarmament Held at the Palais des Nations, Geneva, March 15-April 29, 1960 and June 7-June 27, 1960*. (1st-48th meetings). London: H. M. Stationery Office, 1960. 940 p. [B]

V69 CORENETZ, HELEN. "Views of *Pravda* and *Izvestiia* on International Control of Atomic Energy." Certificate essay, Russian Institute, Columbia, 1952. 121 p. Content analysis of official pronouncements and signed articles in the two newspapers during the period 6 August 1945 to 30 September 1951. Argues that *Pravda* and *Izvestiia* were primarily concerned to fix the blame for the impasse in the U.N. Atomic Energy Commission, to broadcast the West's rejection of Soviet proposals, and to advertise the Soviet peace appeal.

V70 CORNELL, RICHARD. "The Soviet Union and 'Atoms For Peace.'" Certificate essay, Russian Institute, Columbia, 1957. 78 p. A helpful starting point for the study of the U.N. International Atomic Energy Agency, this work traces the impact of President Eisenhower's proposal to the U.N. in 1953 of "atoms for peace" on the policy of the Soviet Union. It is argued that the USSR found itself isolated as underdeveloped nations accepted the Eisenhower proposal and was compelled thereby to join the Western Powers in 1956 in setting up the U.N. International Atomic Energy Agency. Brief notes from Western sources and Soviet newspapers.

V70A DALLIN, ALEXANDER. *The Soviet Union at the United Nations*. N.Y.: Praeger, 1962. 242 p. Includes a penetrating chapter on the motives and objectives of Soviet disarmament policy since 1922. Suggests that a basic shift in the policy may have occurred under Khrushchev, *i.e.*, that the Soviet Union may now genuinely want arms control, even if it weakens the prospect of world revolution.

V71 DULLES, ALLEN W. "Disarmament in the Atomic Age." *Foreign Affairs*, January 1947, p. 204-216. Recollections by the onetime head of the CIA of his earlier experiences at the League of Nations disarmament negotiations, emphasizing the strong support given by the Soviet Delegation to international inspection of disarmament and arguing the advantage that would accrue to both the U.S. and USSR in a totally disarmed world, by virtue of the economic, geographic, and demographic strength of the two states.

V72 DURDENEVSKII, V. N., and SHEVCHENKO, A. N. "Nesovmestimost ispolzovaniia atomnogo oruzhiia s normamy mezhdunarodnogo prava," *Sovetskoe Gosudarstvo i Pravo*, no. 5 (1955), p. 38-44. Authors argue that the use of atomic weapons would be incompatible with international law.

V73 DZELEPY, E. N. *Désatomiser l'Europe? La Vérité sur le "Plan Rapacki."* Brussels: Les Éditions politiques, Les Cahiers politiques, 1958. 165 p. Russian ed., Moscow: Izd. inostrannoi lit., 1959. 129 p. The alleged "truth about the Rapacki Plan" asserts the proposal of the Polish Foreign Minister gives Western Europe an opportunity to redeem its folly of re-arming West Germany and reviving militarism there and to consider the extent to which NATO guarantees European security. Footnotes largely from Communist West European and U.S. press.

V73A *Ekonomicheskie voprosy razoruzheniia.* Ed. by I. S. Glagolev. Moscow: Akademiia nauk SSSR, 1961. 216 p. The most developed expression to date of the idea found in Soviet statements since 1959 that disarmament would not necessarily cripple advanced capitalist economies. Articles by economists of the Institute of International Relations discuss economic aspects of disarmament in the USSR, in capitalist, and in underdeveloped countries. Deals with disarmament in relation to international trade and to scientific-technological progress.

V74 FEDOROV, E. K. *Prekrashchenie iadernykh ispytanii.* Moscow: Izd. Adademii nauk SSSR, 1961. A popularized account of the test ban issue. Author is General Secretary of the USSR Academy of Sciences, and has been a key figure both in Geneva technical meetings on the test ban and in "Pugwash" meetings of scientists.

V75 FRYE, WILLIAM. *Disarmament; Atoms into Plowshares?* N.Y.: Foreign Policy Assoc., 1955. 67 p. Useful analysis and summary of the history of disarmament by the U.N. correspondent of the *Christian Science Monitor*, with emphasis on the post-1945 period. Contains discussion outline and bibliography for study groups.

V76 GARTHOFF, RAYMOND L. *Soviet Strategy in the Nuclear Age.* N.Y.: Praeger, 1958. 283 p. Provides the military and strategic background of Soviet disarmament policy. This book is probably the most useful for this purpose of the many fine books and translations by one of America's leading authorities on Soviet military problems. Includes a 21-page bibliographic and interpretive guide to sources on Soviet strategy and extensive footnotes.

V77 GARTHOFF, RAYMOND L. "What's Behind Soviet Disarmament?" *Army Combat Forces Journal*, October 1955, p. 22-27. Discussion of economic factors, the actual and projected size of the Soviet and U.S. armies, and a "new look" in Soviet strategic thinking which, this expert alleges, make a reduction of Soviet troops expedient for the power position of the USSR. [B]

V78 GENEVA CONFERENCE ON THE DISCONTINUANCE OF NUCLEAR WEAPONS TESTS. *History and Analysis of Negotiations.* U.S. Disarmament Administration (Disarmament Series 4), Department of State Publication 7258. Washington: October 1961. 641 p. Interpretation and documents of 340 meetings in Geneva attended by the U.K., U.S., and USSR. Traces the periods from 1958 of high hopes, of frustrations, and the impasse created by the Soviet resumption of atmospheric testing in 1961. [B]

V79 GUSEV, M. *Borba Sovetskogo Soiuza za sokrashchenie vooruzhenii i zapreshchenie atomnogo oruzhiia.* Moscow: Gospolitizdat, 1951. 134 p. Propagandistic defense of Soviet policy for the reduction of armaments and the prohibition of atomic weapons. Of interest for its contradictory statements on the importance of atomic bombs at a time two years after the explosion of the first Soviet atomic bomb, but following a period in which the Stalin regime had to rely on conventional arms. Documentation rests mainly on recent speeches of Stalin, Vyshinsky, Molotov, and Gromyko, but excerpts of some non-Communist sources are also given, usually out of context. Concludes with the promise that the Soviet Union will continue to fight for arms reductions, the prohibition of atomic weapons, and the "establishment of strict international control."

V80 HENKIN, LOUIS, ed. *Arms Control; Issues for the Public.* Columbia University, American Assembly. Englewood Cliffs, N.J.: Prentice-Hall, 1961. 209 p. An outgrowth of the Nineteenth American Assembly meetings on arms control, ending in May 1961, this work contains excellent essays on arms control as related to Soviet national interest, to U.S. foreign policy and security, to the problem of inspection, and to European opinions and reactions. The essays on arms control and the USSR, written by British experts, consider Soviet military, economic and political objectives in relation to Soviet disarmament policy.

V81 HINTERHOFF, EUGENE. *Disengagement.* London: Stevens, 1959. 445 p. A comprehensive review of various proposals for "disengagement" in Europe since 1945. The author then presents his own plan. Appendix 10 contains a chronological chart of proposals for disengagement.

V82 IGNATEV, L. N. *Atomnaia problema i politika SShA.* Moscow: Sotsekgiz, 1960. 257 p. Partially documented brief history of United States policy on disarmament and the uses of atomic energy.

V83 INTERNATIONAL CONFERENCE ON THE PEACEFUL USES OF ATOMIC ENERGY, GENEVA, 1955. *Proceedings.* N.Y.: United Nations, 1955-56. 16 vols.

V84 JACOB, PHILIP E. "The Disarmament Consensus." *International Organization*, Spring, 1960, p. 233-260. Author defines the areas of agreement which have emerged in past disarmament negotiations and identifies the main controversial issues which still remain.

V84A JENSEN, LLOYD. "The Postwar Disarmament Negotiations: a Study in American-Soviet Bargaining Behaviour." Ph.D. Dissertation, University of Michigan, 1962. 256 p. Looks for retractions or concessions to determine the propensity to compromise shown by each side. Content analysis of Soviet and Western proposals finds an increasing level of verbal agreement. The paper therefore criticizes the "gamesmanship" thesis of Spanier and Nogee (see below).

V85 JESSUP, PHILIP C., and TAUBENFELD, HOWARD J. *Controls for Outer Space and the Antarctic Analogy*. N.Y.: Columbia, 1959. 379 p. Explores the precedents and possibilities of finding lasting international agreement to prevent the extension of the arms race to outer space and Antarctica. The authors advocate broad international controls.

V86 JOLIOT-CURIE, FREDERIC. *La Paix, le désarmement et la coopération internationale*. Paris: "Defense de la Paix," 1959. 224 p. Speeches, articles, letters, and declarations on disarmament, the UN, the Suez crisis, national self-determination, international cooperation, and surprise attack by the late President of the Communist-dominated World Council of Peace. The sequel for 1955-58 of his *Cinq Années de lutte pour la paix*, which covered the period 1949-54.

V87 KENNAN, GEORGE F. *Russia, the Atom and the West*. N.Y.: Harper, 1957. 116 p. Author of the "containment policy" questions the value of disarmament talks, summit meetings, coalition diplomacy, and other aspects of U.S. policy, while arguing for "a quiet old-fashioned attack on certain . . . political problems that divide us from the Soviet world," on the grounds that disarmament agreements cannot by-pass political issues. Presents a reasoned appeal for the withdrawal of Soviet and Western forces from Central Europe. [B]

V88 KHAITSMAN, V. M. *Sovetskii Soiuz; razoruzhenie; mir; sobytiia i fakty, 1917-1962*. Moscow: Institut mezhdunarodnykh otnoshenii, 1962. 158 p. A popular review of Soviet disarmament policy since 1917, utilizing many citations from diplomatic correspondence, speeches, the Soviet press and the foreign press.

V89 KHRUSHCHEV, NIKITA S. *Disarmament for Durable Peace and Friendship; Report and Concluding Speech at the 4th Session of the Supreme Soviet of the U.S.S.R. (January 14-15, 1960); Law on a Further Considerable Reduction of the Armed Forces of the U.S.S.R. (January 15, 1960); Message from the Supreme Soviet of the U.S.S.R. to the Parliaments and Governments of All the Countries of the World (January 15, 1960)*. Moscow: Foreign Languages Publishing House, 1960. 80 p. The Soviet Premier's proposal and the subsequent legislation for a reduction of Soviet military manpower by approximately one-third. Contains interesting reasons for the reduction.

V90 KHRUSHCHEV, NIKITA S. *K pobede v mirnom sorevnovanii s kapitalizmom*. Moscow: Gospolitizdat, 1959. 600 p. English eds., *For*

Victory in Peaceful Competition with Capitalism. N.Y.: Dutton, 1960. 784 p. Moscow: Foreign Languages Publishing House, 1959. 784 p. This compilation of his 1958 speeches includes statements presenting the Soviet point of view on arms control, suspension of nuclear tests, etc. [B]

V91 KHRUSHCHEV, NIKITA S. *Mir bez oruzhiia — mir bez voin*. Moscow: Gospolizdat, 1960. 2 vols. Collection of statements made in 1959 on disarmament, Soviet foreign policy, and the international situation. Includes interviews with foreign correspondents as well as formal speeches.

V91A KHRUSHCHEV, NIKITA S. *Vseobshchee i polnoe razoruzhenie—garantiia mira i bezopastnosti vsekh narodov; rech 10 iulia 1962 g*. Moscow: 1962. American ed., *World Congress for General Disarmament and Peace; Address by N. S. Khrushchev, July 10, 1962; General and Complete Disarmament — Guarantee of Peace and Security for All People*. N.Y.: Crosscurrents, 1962. 64 p. British ed., London: Soviet Booklet no. 97, 1962. 31 p.

V92 KISSINGER, HENRY A. "Arms Control, Inspection and Surprise Attack." *Foreign Affairs*, July 1960, p. 557-575. Suggests a first-step arms control plan which would permit neither side to achieve a decisive advantage by cheating. An equilibrium between Soviet and Western forces, stabilizing the arms race, rather than total disarmament should be the goal of any beginning arms control plan.

V93 KOMMUNISTICHESKAIA PARTIIA SOVETSKOGO SOIUZA. *KPSS o vooruzhennykh silakh Sovetskogo Soiuza: sbornik dokumentov, 1917-1958*. Moscow: Gospolizdat, 1958. 420 p. Communist Party resolutions and decrees on Soviet armed forces from 1917 to 1958, showing the increases and decreases of these forces which were to take place and the alleged rationale behind these changes.

V94 *Konferentsiia sovetskoi obshchestvennosti za razoruzhenie; Sbornik materialov i dokumentov*. Moscow: Gospolitizdat, 1960. 173 p. A collection of materials and documents of the Conference of the Soviet Society for Disarmament. [B]

V95 KOROVIN, E. A. "Atomnoe oruzhie i mezhdunarodnoe pravo," *Mezhdunarodnaia zhizn*, no. 2 (Feb. 1955), p. 56-63. Leading Soviet jurist discusses atomic weapons and international law.

V96 KRAMISH, ARNOLD. *Atomic Energy in the Soviet Union*. Stanford, Cal.: Stanford University Press, 1959. 232 p. Technical and political analysis of the Soviet atomic energy program, based largely on Soviet newspapers and technical journals. Depicts the relatively advanced level of research achieved before World War II, the marked slackening of work during the war years, the very rapid subsequent developments, and the dynamic future of Soviet work in atomic energy. An eight-page bibliography lists books in Russian and in English on Soviet science. This work is important to an understanding of the context of Soviet disarmament policy.

V96A KUDRIAVTSOV, D. I. *Borba SSSR za razoruzhenie posle vtoroi mirovoi voiny; mezhdunarodno-pravovoi ocherk.* Moscow: Izd. Moskovskogo universiteta, 1962. 160 p. An analysis by a Soviet jurist of the disarmament problem since 1899. Half the book treats the period prior to World War II, relying heavily on the work of Korovin and Egorev (see above). The book's analysis of "control" over disarmament is based on the Soviet proposals at the U.N. in 1959 and 1960.

V97 LIE, TRYGVE. *In the Cause of Peace.* N.Y.: Macmillan, 1954. 473 p. The first Secretary-General of the U.N. reminisces on the first seven years of the organization. Contains a discussion of the Baruch Plan and negotiations to establish a U.N. military force. Calls the Baruch Plan a "remarkable proposal for any great power to make, especially remarkable for the United States," because the U.S. took such a "radical, internationalist position."

V98 MALININ, S. A. "Effektivnyi kontrol—neobkhodimoe uslovie uspeshnogo osushchestvleniia razoruzheniia." Leningrad: *Vestnik Leningradskogo Universiteta, seriia ekonomiki, filosofii i prava,* no. 12 (1957), p. 136-149. An article in the bulletin of Leningrad University arguing that an effective system of controls is indispensable to the realization of disarmament.

V99 MALININ, S. A. "Pravovye formy mezhdunarodnogo sotrudnichestva v oblasti mirnogo ispolzovaniia atomnoi energii," *Sovetskoe gosudarstvo i pravo,* no. 7 (1957), p. 122-27. Article in the leading Soviet legal journal on the legal forms of international collaboration in the peaceful utilization of atomic energy.

V100 MALININ, S. A. "Pravovye osnovy razoruzheniia." Leningrad: *Vestnik Leningradskogo Universiteta, seriia ekonomiki, filosofii i prava,* no. 17 (1956), p. 137-149. A discussion of the legal bases of disarmament.

V101 MALININ, S. A. "Problema razoruzheniia v mezhdunarodnom prave na sovremennom etape." Dissertation for degree of Candidate of Juridical Sciences, Leningrad U., 1955. Analyzes the present status of disarmament in international law.

V102 MAMULIIA, S. S. "SSSR v borbe za razoruzhenie." Dissertation for degree of Candidate of Juridical Sciences, Institute of Law, Academy of Sciences of the USSR, 1950. Highly propagandistic survey of Soviet disarmament policy conducted under the sponsorship of E. A. Korovin, based entirely on materials available in Russian.

V103 McCLELLAND, CHARLES A., ed. *Nuclear Weapons, Missiles, and the Future War: Problem for the Sixties.* San Francisco: Chandler, 1960. 235 p. Stimulating essays by Western and Soviet spokesmen on the world military and political situation, tending to criticize U.S. reliance on nuclear weapons, warning of the dangers in the arms race, and offering new approaches to disarmament.

V104 MELMAN, SEYMOUR, ed. *Inspection for Disarmament.* N.Y.: Columbia, 1958. 291 p. Financed by the Institute for International Order and sponsored by the Columbia University Institute of War and Peace Studies, this pioneering study on workable systems of inspection covers particular objectives, e.g., detection of bomb or missile testing, and wider aims such as the halting of production of all weapons of mass destruction. Specialists from the U.S. and other countries analyze aerial inspection, budget review, radiation hazards, production controls, psychological aspects of evasion, and give a report on an international public opinion poll on inspection for disarmament. A heavily footnoted work. [A]

V105 MOCH, JULES S. *La Folie des hommes.* Intro. by Albert Einstein. Paris: Laffont, 1954. 285 p. English ed., London: Gollancz, 1955. 222 p. A somewhat emotional recounting of the past and possible future ravages of war and a history of disarmament from its beginnings to the present, by a French delegate to disarmament negotiations before and after World War II.

V106 MOLOTOV, VIACHESLAV M. *Rechi na Generalnoi Assamblee Organizatsii Obedinennykh Natsii; vtoraia chast pervoi sessii v Niu-Iorke, oktiabr-dekabr 1946 g.* Moscow: Gospolitizdat, 1947. 145 p. English ed., Moscow: Foreign Languages Publishing House, 1948. Speeches to the first session of the U.N. General Assembly on the USSR and international co-operation, armed forces of U.N. members on foreign soil, and various *Tass* reports.

V107 *Monthly Bulletin.* N.Y.: The Committee for World Development and World Disarmament, 1961–. Facts and comments on national and United Nations developments in economic aid and disarmament. Useful for anyone wishing to keep abreast of these fields. [B]

V108 MURRAY, THOMAS E. *Nuclear Policy for War and Peace.* N.Y. and Cleveland: World Publishers, 1960. 243 p. A member of the Atomic Energy Commission, 1950-57, surveys past and present problems of nuclear policy. Supports the use of force if necessary, but within "moral limits." He opposes "hysterical pacifist groups" and is suspicious of a nuclear test ban.

V109 NOEL-BAKER, PHILIP J. *The Arms Race; a Programme for World Disarmament.* London: Stevens, 1958. 579 p. An outstanding history and analysis of post-1945 disarmament negotiations and their prospects by a renowned British expert with over thirty years' experience in disarmament questions. This hard-headed investigation regards the disarmament problem neither as simple nor as insoluble. It sees the crux of the problem not in inspection but in the arms race itself and argues that total disarmament could be more readily attained than partial. Valuable footnotes, bibliography, documentary appendices, "who's who" in disarmament, and index. [A]

V110 NOGEE, JOSEPH L. *Soviet Policy Toward International Control of Atomic Energy.* Notre Dame, Ind.: University of Notre Dame Press, 1961. 306 p. Well-documented account of the negotiations concerning atomic energy control, disarmament, and the banning of nuclear bomb tests, emphasis on the years 1945 to 1948, when the Soviet atomic explosion ended the first phase of the problem. Concludes that the shifts in Soviet policy stem from a basic Soviet determination to maintain the national sovereignty of the USSR. Excellent bibliography. [A]

V111 NOGEE, JOSEPH L. "The Diplomacy of Disarmament," *International Conciliation*, January 1960, p. 235-303. The author, whose Ph.D. dissertation at Yale in 1958 was on international control of atomic energy, discusses the changing scope and framework of disarmament negotiations since 1945, the technical and political aspects of the control problem, and the political objectives of arms control negotiations.

V112 ONUSHKIN, V. "*Atomnyi biznes*" *Amerikanskikh monopolii.* Moscow: Sotsekgiz, 1960. 143 p. A partially documented survey of the atomic industry in the United States, its ownership by monopolies, and the influence of its owners on foreign policy.

V113 OSGOOD, CHARLES E. *Graduated Reciprocation in Tension Reduction: A Key to Initiative in Foreign Policy.* Urbana, Ill.: Institute of Communications Research, U. of Illinois, 1961. 82 p. A leading American psychologist makes one of the few attempts published thus far to take into account the fears and misgivings of both sides about one another and to suggest a program aimed at reversing the logic of the arms race, without sacrificing the security of either side. Considers in some detail Soviet perceptions of American policy. Useful 3-page bibliography of relevant books and articles from many diverse fields of the social sciences. [B]

V114 POLSKI INSTYTUT SPRAW MIĘDZYNAROWYCH, WARSAW. *Plan Rapackiego; dokumenty i materialy opracowali*

Wojciech Nagórski, Mieczyslaw Tomala. Warsaw: Książka i Wiedza, 1959. 179 p. Valuable documentary collection concerning the proposals of Polish Foreign Minister Rapacki for "disengagement" in Central Europe. Includes comments (in Polish translation) on the proposals by John Slessor, Albert Schweitzer, and others, as well as the official replies of the non-Communist and Communist governments. Chronological table of disengagement proposals by Anthony Eden, George Kennan, and others. Preface by Polish scholar M. Tomala. Published under auspices of Polish Institute for International Affairs. [A]

V115 "Razoruzhenie," *Bolshaia sovetskaia entsiklopediia.* 1st ed., vol. LVII, cols. 158-159. Moscow: 1941. 2nd ed., vol. XXXV, p. 636-640. Moscow: 1955. The article by G. Osnitskaia in the 1941 edition of this Soviet encyclopedia begins by quoting Lenin on the impossibility of realizing complete disarmament except as a result of the triumph of Communism. In contrast, the later edition discusses disarmament seriously as a possible and desirable product of negotiations between the Communist and capitalist states, despite the alleged reluctance of the latter to cooperate.

V116 ROBERTS, HENRY L. *Russia and America: Dangers and Prospects.* N.Y.: Harper, 1956. 251 p. An excellent analysis of the issues in the Cold War, with a chapter on the problems of arms control.

V117 ROSTOW, WALT W., and MILLIKAN, MAX F. *Statements before a Special Subcommittee on Disarmament.* Cambridge, Mass.: M.I.T., 1956. 18 p. The first of these scholars' reports, "Soviet Objectives and the International Control of Armaments," is one of "short-term pessimism, but conditional, long-term optimism." It holds that if the U.S. can show Moscow the West cannot be defeated militarily and can successfully develop the economies of disadvantaged countries, a future generation of Soviet leaders may accept arms controls. The second statement, Millikan's, is on "Disarmament and U.S. Relations with the Non-European Free World."

V118 RUSSELL, RUTH B., assisted by MUTHER, JEANNETTE E. *A History of the United Nations Charter: The Role of the United States, 1940-1945.* Washington: Brookings Institution, 1958. 1140 p. The authoritative account of the development of the arms control provisions of the United Nations Charter. [B]

V120 RUSSIA (1923– USSR), VERKHOVNYI SOVET. *Materialy piatoi sessii po voprosam razoruzheniia i zapreshcheniia atomnogo i vodorodnogo oruzhiia.* Moscow: Gospolitizdat, 1956. 96 p. English ed., Moscow: Foreign Languages Publishing House, 1956. 98 p. Appeal by the Supreme Soviet to the Parliaments of all countries with respect to disarmament.

V120A RUSSIA (1923- USSR), VERKHOVNYI SOVET. *Soviet Foreign Policy; Basic Acts and Documents of the Supreme Soviet of the U.S.S.R., 1956-1962.* Comp. by K. U. Chernenko. Moscow: Foreign Languages Publishing House, 1962. 200 p. Resolutions and decrees of the Supreme Soviet concerning the cessation of nuclear tests, general disarmament, unilateral reductions of Soviet troops, and appeals to other parliaments.

V121 SALVIN, MARINA. "Soviet Policy Toward Disarmament," *International Conciliation*, February 1947, p. 42-111. A Columbia University professor and collaborator with James T. Shotwell on disarmament outlines Soviet policy between the wars and from 1945 to 1947. The emphasis is on shifts of policy throughout these years and on the similarities between Soviet and U.S. policy at different times. This work is most valuable for its collection of key documents such as the 1923 Soviet comments on the proposed Treaty of Mutual Assistance of the League of Nations, the 1927 and 1928 disarmament proposals of Litvinov, and speeches by Soviet and Western representatives to the United Nations in 1946.

V122 SCHELLING, THOMAS C., and HALPERIN, MORTON H. *Strategy and Arms Control.* N.Y.: Twentieth Century Fund, 1961. 148 p. An outgrowth of the 1960 Summer Study on Arms Control, this essay argues that "arms control is essentially a means of supplementing unilateral military strategy by some kind of collaboration with the countries that are potential enemies. The aims of arms control and the aims of a national military strategy should be substantially the same. Thus, arms control *includes* disarmament, but aims more at reducing incentives to attack than at capacities to attack. Assumes that potential enemies have a mutual interest in avoiding or limiting war. No footnotes or bibliography. [A]

V123 SLESSOR, SIR JOHN C. *The Great Deterrent; a Collection of Lectures, Articles, and Broadcasts on the Development of Strategic Policy in the Nuclear Age.* London: Cassell; N.Y.: Praeger, 1957. 321 p. In this work, the Marshal of the Royal Air Force develops his views on strategic policy, with particular emphasis on the nuclear age. Contains two articles on the Geneva Summit Conference and disarmament written in 1955 and other references to disarmament in the context of atomic strategy.

V124 SOVIET NEWS. *Peace and Disarmament; Soviet Proposals.* London: Soviet News, 1957. 95 p. A report by the then Foreign Minister Shepilov to the Supreme Soviet, together with the text of Soviet notes and proposals to other governments and to the U.N. in January and February 1957.

V125 SOVIET NEWS. *The Soviet Union on Disarmament*. London, 1957. 84 p. (Soviet News Booklet No. 9). Contains N. A. Bulganin's message to Mr. Macmillan April 20, 1957; statement of the USSR Foreign Ministry on the Bermuda Conference, March 21-23, 1957; Foreign Ministry press conference and other declarations; and speeches by V. Zorin, Soviet Representative to the U.N. Disarmament Commission Sub-Committee.

V125A *The Soviet Stand on Disarmament; a Collection of Nineteen Basic Soviet Documents on General and Complete Disarmament, the Termination of Nuclear Weapons Tests, and the Relaxation of International Tensions*. N.Y.: Crosscurrents Press, 1962. 150 p. Includes materials from March 1958 through February 1962.

V126 SPANIER, JOHN W., and NOGEE, JOSEPH L. *The Politics of Disarmament: a Study in Soviet-American Gamesmanship*. N.Y.: Praeger, 1962. 226 p. Reviews the negotiations since 1945 and argues that each side has consistently included a "joker" among its proposals which precludes their acceptance. [B]

V127 TARASENKO, V. M. *Atomnaia problema vo vneshnei politike SShA, 1945-1949 gg*. Kiev: Izdatelstvo Kievskogo Gosudarstvennogo Universiteta, 1958. 244 p. A documented survey of United States policy on the control and peaceful uses of atomic energy, covering the years immediately following World War II. [B]

V128 TATISHCHEV, S. *Za kulisami raketnoiadernogo biznesa SShA*. Moscow: Gospolitizdat, 1961. Designed to expose the key role of U.S. monopolies and munition makers in opposing disarmament and improved international relations.

V129 UNITED NATIONS, GENERAL ASSEMBLY, 15TH SESSION. *Speech by Nikita S. Khrushchev, September 23, 1960; Proposals by the U.S.S.R.* N.Y.: Crosscurrents, 1960. 88 p. Convenient English translation of a speech at the U.N. in September 1960, including the Soviet Government's statement on disarmament, the basic provisions of a treaty on general and complete disarmament presented by Khrushchev, and his declaration on granting independence to colonial countries and peoples.

V130 U.S. CONGRESS, SENATE, COMMITTEE ON FOREIGN RELATIONS. *Attitudes of Soviet Leaders Toward Disarmament*. Staff Study No. 8. Washington: G.P.O., 1957. 106 p. This study is based upon replies from experts on the Soviet Union to a questionnaire prepared by the Disarmament Subcommittee.

V131 U.S. CONGRESS, SENATE, COMMITTEE ON FOREIGN RELATIONS. *Chemical-Biological-Radiological (CBR) Warfare and*

Its Disarmament Aspects. Washington: G.P.O., 1960. 43 p. "Since World War II there has been little discussion in disarmament negotiations of the reduction and control of CBR weapons." This study relates such weapons to arms control and concludes that "presently known inspection measures for verifying any limitations on the production or development of chemical and biological weapons have a low degree of reliability."

V132 U.S. CONGRESS, SENATE, COMMITTEE ON FOREIGN RELATIONS. *Control and Reduction of Armaments, Final Report*. Washington: G.P.O., 1958. 663 p. This report of the Subcommittee on Disarmament covers its first three years. It includes correspondence between the Subcommittee chairman, Senator Humphrey, and the various executive agencies concerned with the problem; previous Subcommittee reports, and ten staff studies.

V133 U.S. CONGRESS, SENATE, COMMITTEE ON FOREIGN RELATIONS. *Handbook on Arms Control and Related Problems in Europe; Excerpts and Summaries of Official and Unofficial Proposals*. Prepared by the Subcommittee on Disarmament. Washington: G.P.O., 1959. 56 p. Collection of official and unofficial opinions on arms control and related political issues in Europe. Includes both Western and Soviet statements.

V134 U.S. CONGRESS, SENATE, SUBCOMMITTEE ON DISARMAMENT. *Disarmament and Security; a Collection of Documents, 1919-1955*. Washington: G.P.O., 1956. 1035 p. Includes 239 documents in full or in part, divided into three groups: I, Disarmament, historical background, 1919-45; II, Problems of disarmament and security; III, Related action in Congress. Contains an extremely rich bibliography. [A]

V135 U.S. DEPARTMENT OF STATE, HISTORICAL OFFICE. *Documents on Disarmament, 1945-1959*. Washington: G.P.O., 1960. 2 vols. Extremely useful collection of key documents representing the positions taken by the major powers and by some neutralist governments; reports by U.N. organizations such as the Atomic Energy Commission; Appeals by the World Peace Council. Over half the documents deal with the 1955-59 period. Some material is on political issues, e.g., German reunification, to indicate the context of disarmament negotiations. [A]

V136 U.S., WHITE HOUSE, DISARMAMENT STAFF. *Reference Documents on Disarmament Matters*. Washington: G.P.O., [1957?]. 257 p. Chronology of negotiations and convenient documentation of Soviet, U.S., British, French, and U.N. statements on disarmament 1955 to 1957. Includes, e.g., May 10, 1955 Soviet proposals,

1955 Geneva "Summit" materials, and many items illustrative of the U.S. position while Harold Stassen was Special Assistant to the President for Disarmament.

V137 VOLLE, HERMAN; WALLRAPP, ERNST; and SCHULZ-WEIDNER, WILLY. *Probleme der internationalen Abruestung; eine Darstellung der Bemuehungen der Vereinten Nationen, 1945-1955.* Frankfurt am Main: Forschungsinstitut der Deutschen Gesellschaft für Auswärtige Politik, 1956. 192 p. The first part is a scholarly report on disarmament efforts at the U.N., 1945-55. The next is an excellent list of U.N. documents on disarmament including the citations for these documents. Third is an invaluable collection of U.N. proposals and resolutions and inter-governmental correspondence on disarmament. All U.N. documents are in German and English; the rest of the text is in German only. Contains numerous footnotes. [A]

V138 VYSHINSKII, A. IA. *Voprosy mezhdunarodnogo prava i mezhdunarodnoi politiki; shestaia sessiia Generalnoi Assamblei Organizatsii Obedinennykh Natsii, 1951-1952 gg.* Moscow: Gosiuridizdat, 1952. 321 p. Statements by the Soviet representative at the Sixth Session of the U.N. General Assembly. The reduction of armaments, prohibition of atomic weapons, and international control are discussed, p. 53-79, 82-123, 128-155, and 303-368.

V139 WADSWORTH, JAMES. *The Price of Peace.* N.Y.: Praeger, 1962. 127 p. Thoughts of a high American official who has had long experience in disarmament negotiations with the Russians.

V140 WARBURG, JAMES P. *Disarmament; The Challenge of the Nineteen Sixties.* Garden City, N.Y.: Doubleday, 1961. 288 p. Highly readable and incisive survey of disarmament in its political setting, 1945 to the present, by a well-known liberal author, whose argument is supported by detailed notes and a documentary index. Distinguishes "arms control" and "universal disarmament," maintaining the former is desirable only in so far as it leads to the latter. Against pessimistic "realism" which condemns man to eternal war. [A]

V141 WORLD COUNCIL OF PEACE. *Documents and Papers on Disarmament; Official Statements Pertaining to Disarmament Negotiations Between the Great Powers.* Vienna: Bulletin of the World Council of Peace, 1956. 90 p. Collection of documents on disarmament edited by a Communist front, containing not only excerpts of statements by governments and the U.N., but also statements by Pope Pius XII, the YMCA, Interparliamentary Union, International Federation of Free Trade Unions, Bandung Conference, World Federation of Trade Unions, and the World Council of Peace.

V142 ZORIN, V. A., ed. *Borba Sovetskogo Soiuza za razoruzhenie, 1946-1960 gg*. Moscow: Izd. IMO, 1961. 567 p. The first major Soviet collection of essays and documents on Soviet disarmament policy from 1946 to the present. Issued by the Institute of International Relations, a training branch of the Ministry of Foreign Affairs. [A]

V143 BLOOMFIELD, LINCOLN P., CLEMENS, WALTER C., JR., and GRIFFITHS, FRANKLYN. *Soviet Interests in Arms Control and Disarmament, 1954-1964: The Decade Under Khrushchev*. Cambridge, Mass.: M.I.T. Center for International Affairs, 1965. 249 p. (mimeographed) Also two annexes (separately bound): CLEMENS, WALTER C., JR. and GRIFFITHS, FRANKLYN. *The Soviet Position on Arms Control and Disarmament—Negotiations and Propaganda, 1954-1964*. 116 p.; ERMARTH, FRITZ. *Economic Factors and Soviet Arms Control Policy*. [A]

V144 CLEMENS, WALTER C., JR. "Lenin on Disarmament," *Slavic Review*, XXIII, no. 3 (September 1964), p. 504-525. Cites correspondence of Lenin first published in 1959 and 1964. [B]

V145 CLEMENS, WALTER C., JR., ed. *Toward a Strategy of Peace*. Foreword by Robert F. Kennedy. Chicago: Rand McNally, 1965.

V146 DALLIN, ALEXANDER and others. *The Soviet Union and Disarmament: an Appraisal of Soviet Attitudes and Intentions*. N.Y.: Praeger, 1964. 282 p. [A]

V147 DULLES, ELEANOR L. and CRANE, ROBERT D., eds. *Detente: Cold War Strategies in Transition*. N.Y.: Praeger, 1965. 307 p. [B]

V148 HALPERIN, MORTON H. and PERKINS, DWIGHT H. *Communist China and Arms Control*. N.Y.: Praeger, 1965. 186 p. [A]

V149 INSTITUTE FOR STRATEGIC STUDIES. *Disarmament and European Security; the Effect of Implementing the First Stage of the Soviet Draft Treaty and the United States Proposals on General and Complete Disarmament*. London: 1963. 2 vols.

V150 WOLFE, THOMAS W. *Soviet Strategy at the Crossroads*. Cambridge: Harvard Univ. Press, 1964. 342 p. [B]

V151 U.S. ARMS CONTROL AND DISARMAMENT AGENCY. *Documents on Disarmament, 1961*. Publication 5. Washington: 1962. *Documents on Disarmament, 1962*. Publication 19. Washington: 1963. *Documents on Disarmament, 1963*. Publication 24. Washington: 1964. [A]

V152 U.S. DEPARTMENT OF DEFENSE. *U.S. Security, Arms Control, and Disarmament, 1961-1965*. Washington: 1965. 140 p. Annotated bibliography. [A]

W. The Soviet Union and International Law

EDITED BY OLIVER J. LISSITZYN

W1 AKADEMIIA NAUK SSSR, INSTITUT PRAVA. *Mezhdunarodnoe pravo.* Ed. by E. A. Korovin. Moscow: Gosizdat iurid. lit., 1951. 600 p. This textbook by twelve Soviet jurists is an eclectic mixture of pedestrian exposition of traditional doctrines, distinctively Soviet viewpoints, and bitter attacks on Western "imperialists." Provides information on Soviet doctrines and attitudes in the late Stalin era. [B]

W2 AKADEMIIA NAUK SSSR, INSTITUT PRAVA. *Mezhdunarodnoe pravo.* Ed. by F. I. Kozhevnikov. Moscow: Gosizdat iurid. lit., 1957. 471 p. German ed., *Völkerrecht.* Hamburg: Hansischer Gildenverlag Joachim Heitmann, 1960. 492 p. English ed., *International Law.* Moscow: Foreign Languages Publishing House, n.d. 477 p. Collective work of seven Soviet jurists, approved for university use. Useful as a source of information on post-Stalin Soviet concepts and practices. Includes a 23-page bibliography and extensive survey of Soviet literature. German edition has a perceptive foreword by Eberhard Menzel, a West German professor. [A]

W3 AKADEMIIA NAUK SSSR, INSTITUT PRAVA. *Mezhdunarodnoe pravo.* Ed. by V. N. Durdenevskii and S. B. Krylov. Moscow: Iuridicheskoe izd., 1947. 612 p. By seven Soviet jurists, this textbook, approved for use in law faculties and institutes, reflects in its moderation of tone the wartime collaboration of the Soviet Union with Western democracies. Mainly useful for comparative purposes as one of a series of post-World War II textbooks.

W4 AKADEMIIA NAUK SSSR, INSTITUT PRAVA. *Sovetskoe gosudarstvo i pravo.* Moscow: Gosizdat iurid. lit., 1925–. Monthly. The leading Soviet legal periodical; frequently contains articles and other materials on international law. Bibliographies in each issue. Previous titles: 1925-29, *Revoliutsiia prava*; 1930-31, *Sovetskoe gosudarstvo i revoliutsiia prava*; 1932-38, *Sovetskoe gosudarstvo.*

W4A AVAKOV, MIRZA M. *Pravopreemstvo Sovetskogo gosudarstva.* Moscow: Gosizdat iurid. lit., 1961. 128 p. A monograph on the still unsettled question of the continuity of the Russian Empire and the Soviet state as a subject of international law. Extensive discussion of the legal status of prerevolutionary Russian treaties.

W5 BAGINIAN, K. A. *Agressiia - tiagchaishee mezhdunarodnoe prestuplenie; k voprosu ob opredelenii agressii.* Moscow: Izd. Akademii nauk SSSR, 1955. 128 p. Monograph on the troublesome problem of defining aggression, from the Soviet point of view. Deals also with sanctions and self-defense in international law.

W5A BAGINIAN, K. A. *Borba Sovetskogo Soiuza protiv agressii.* Moscow: Sotsekgiz, 1959. 288 p. A study of efforts to define "aggression," the meaning of the term in international law, and its practical application. Heavily slanted to favor the Soviet position, but interesting as a reflection of Soviet positions in recent disputes.

W6 BAGINIAN, K. A. *Narushenie imperialisticheskimi gosudarstvami printsipa nevmeshatelstva.* Moscow: Izd. Akademii nauk SSSR, 1954. 144 p. Representative example of the use of international law as a vehicle for propaganda attacks on the policies of the major Western powers.

W7 BAKHOV, A. S., ed. *Voenno-morskoi mezhdunarodno-pravovoi spravochnik.* Moscow: Voen. izd., 1956. 351 p. Practical manual of the law of the sea in peace and war, written by a number of Soviet military and civil jurists and addressed to Soviet Naval officers. Valuable for information on Soviet practice and attitudes.

W8 BARSEGOV, IU. G. *Territoriia v mezhdunarodnom prave.* Moscow: Gosizdat iurid. lit., 1958. 271 p. Only Soviet monograph on territory in international law, by a young Soviet jurist. Includes a discussion of self-determination.

W9 BLISHCHENKO, I. P. *Mezhdunarodnoe i vnutrigosudarstvennoe pravo.* Moscow: Gosizdat iurid. lit., 1960. 239 p. Most detailed and thoughtful treatment of the relation between international law and national law from the Soviet point of view.

W9A BOGUSLAVSKII, M. M. *Immunitet gosudarstva.* Moscow: Izd. Instituta mezhdunarodnykh otnoshenii, 1962. 232 p. A monograph on the problem of sovereign immunity. Includes a discussion of exterritorial effects of nationalization and the state monopoly of foreign trade.

W10 BOGUSLAVSKII, M. M., and RUBANOV, A. A. *Pravovoe polozhenie inostrantsev v SSSR.* Moscow: Izd. Instituta mezhdunarodnykh otnoshenii, 1959. 119 p. Informative account of the legal status of foreigners in the USSR, by two Soviet jurists.

W10A BOGUSLAVSKII, M. M., and RUBANOV, A. A. *Pravovoe polozhenie sovetskikh grazhdan za granitsei.* Moscow: Izd. Instituta mezhdunarodnykh otnoshenii, 1961. 112 p. An informative account of the legal status of Soviet citizens abroad.

W11 BRACHT, HANS WERNER. *Entwicklung und Grundzüge der sowjetischen Völkerrechtstheorie.* Marburg: n.p., 1957, 211 p.

This doctoral dissertation is a conscientious study of the development of Soviet international law doctrine, with emphasis on the early post-Stalin period.

W12 CHERNOGOLOVKIN, N. V. *Formy kolonialnoi zavisimosti.* Moscow: Gosizdat iurid. lit., 1956. 214 p. Analysis of legal forms of colonial dependency, including protectorates, mandates and trusteeships from the Soviet point of view.

W13 CHERVIAKOV, P. A. *Organizatsiia i tekhnika vneshnei torgovli SSSR.* Moscow: Vneshtorgizdat, 1958. 295 p. Contains much information on the legal aspects of the organization of Soviet foreign trade.

W14 CALVEZ, JEAN-YVES. *Droit international et souveraineté en U.R.S.S.; l'évolution de l'idéologie juridique soviétique depuis la révolution d'octobre.* Paris: Colin, 1953. 299 p. Imaginative but not wholly accurate account and analysis of the evolution of the central concept of sovereignty in Soviet doctrine. Excellent 15-page bibliography. [B]

W15 CORBETT, PERCY E. *Law in Diplomacy.* Princeton, N.J.: Princeton University Press, 1959. 290 p. A scholarly study which seeks to ascertain the influence of legal ideas and concepts on the foreign policies of the major nations. Chapter 3, dealing with the Soviet Union, presents illustrations and case studies from Soviet diplomatic experience and compares these with international legal standards.

W16 DE HARTINGH, FRANCE, *Les conceptions soviétiques du droit de la mer.* Paris: Pichon and Durand-Auzias, 1960. 198 p. Substantial monograph by a French scholar who was adviser to the French delegation at the 1958 conference on the law of the sea. Throws light on Soviet policy and behavior at the conference as well as on the background of the Soviet position. [B]

W17 *Diplomaticheskii slovar.* Ed. by A. Ia. Vyshinskii and S. A. Lozovskii (pseud.). Moscow: Gospolitizdat, 1948-50. 2 vols. 2nd ed., ed. by A. A. Gromyko, S. A. Golunskii, V. M. Khvostov, and others. 1960–. 3 vols. Contains numerous entries on international law topics.

W18 DRANOV, B. A. *Chernomorskiie prolivy; mezhdunarodno-pravovoi rezhim.* Moscow: Iuridicheskoe izd., 1948. 240 p. Historical and legal survey of the problem of the Turkish Straits, emphasizing Soviet interests and policies. Useful 5-page bibliography.

W19 FANDIKOV, P. G. *Mezhdunarodno-pravovoi rezhim Dunaia; istoricheskii ocherk.* Moscow: Gosizdat iurid. lit., 1955. 255 p. Historical survey, from the Soviet perspective, of the international regulation of the Danube, with special attention to the Danube Conference of 1948. Many basic documents in Russian are appended.

W19A FELDMAN, D. I. *Priznanie pravitelstv v mezhdunarodnom prave*. Kazan: Izd. Kazanskogo Universiteta, 1961. 91 p. A monograph, from the Soviet point of view, on the recognition of governments, with extensive review of Soviet practice.

W19B FILIPPOV, S. V. *Ogovorki v teorii i praktike mezhdunarodnogo dogovora*. Moscow: Izd. Instituta mezhdunarodnykh otnoshenii, 1958. 102 p. A monograph by a Soviet scholar on the problems of reservations to treaties and *rebus sic stantibus*.

W20 FITUNI, L. A. *Mezhdugosudarstvennye torgovye dogovory i soglasheniia*. Moscow: Gosizdat iurid. lit., 1955. 114 p. Survey and analysis of commonly used types of commercial treaties and trade agreements, with emphasis on those of the USSR.

W21 GINSBURGS, GEORGE. "The Theory and Practice of Neutrality in Soviet Diplomacy." Ph.D. dissertation, U. of California, Los Angeles, 1960.

W22 GRABAR, V. E. *Materialy k istorii literatury mezhdunarodnogo prava v Rossii (1647-1917)*. Moscow: Izd. Akademii nauk SSSR, 1958. 491 p. Unique, comprehensive history of prerevolutionary Russian literature of international law. Useful for understanding continuity and change in Russian and Soviet doctrines and approaches.

W23 IURIDICHESKAIA KOMISSIIA PRI SOVETE MINISTROV SSSR. *Dogovory ob okazanii pravovoi pomoshchi po grazhdanskim, semeinym i ugolovnym delam, zakliuchennye Sovetskim Soiuzom v 1957-1958 gg*. Moscow: Gosizdat iurid. lit., 1959. 286 p. Collection of texts of Soviet treaties with countries of the Communist bloc on legal assistance in civil, family and criminal matters, and of pertinent Soviet legislation.

W24 *Iuridicheskii slovar*. Ed. by P. I. Kudriavtsev and others. 2nd ed., Moscow: Gosizdat iurid. lit., 1956. 2 vols. Contains numerous entries on international law topics.

W25 KALIUZHNAIA, G. P. *Pravovye formy monopolii vneshnei torgovli SSSR v ikh istoricheskom razvitii*. Moscow: Izd. Akademii nauk, 1951. 150 p. Most substantial post-World War II Soviet monograph on legal forms of organization of Soviet foreign trade, with historical survey.

W26 KEILIN, A. D. *Sovetskoe morskoe pravo*. Moscow: Gosizdat vodnogo transporta, 1954. 395 p. Standard Soviet textbook on maritime law, emphasizing commercial aspects, by a leading specialist.

W27 KENNEY, CHARLES D. "Soviet Deviation from International Law since World War II." Ph.D. dissertation, Syracuse U., 1952.

W28 KLEIST, PETER. *Die völkerrechtliche Anerkennung Sowjetrusslands.* Königsberg: Ost-Europa, 1934. 127 p. (Osteuropäische Forschungen, neue folge, vol. 15.) Examination and appraisal of the practice of states with respect to the recognition of the Soviet regime, from an anti-Soviet point of view.

W28A KOLODKIN, A. L. *Pravovoi rezhim territorialnykh vod i otkrytogo moria.* Moscow: Izd. "Morskoi Transport," 1961. 173 p. A concise but informative account of the law of territorial waters and the high seas, stressing Soviet practice and views.

W29 KORETSKII, VLADIMIR M. *Ocherki anglo-amerikanskoi doktriny i praktiki mezhdunarodnogo chastnogo prava.* Moscow: Iuridicheskoe izd., 1948. 396 p. Devoted in large part (p. 227-395) to an analysis of decisions of British and American courts affecting the Soviet Union. The author, a leading Soviet jurist, was elected in 1960 as the Soviet judge of the International Court of Justice.

W30 KOROLENKO, A. S. *Torgovye dogovory i soglasheniia SSSR s inostrannymi gosudarstvami.* Moscow: Vneshtorgizdat, 1953. 316 p. Extensive historical survey of Soviet commercial treaties and trade agreements, with emphasis on the post-World War II period. Covers wartime lend-lease agreements. Texts of some agreements are appended.

W31 KOROVIN, EVGENII A. *Mezhdunarodnoe pravo perekhodnogo vremeni.* Moscow-Petrograd: Gosizdat, 1923. 139 p. 2nd enlarged ed., 1924. 143 p. German ed., Berlin: Rothschild, 1929. 142 p. First serious attempt to define the relation of the Soviet system to international law, still basic for understanding the roots and nature of the distinctive Soviet approach and concepts. Despite frequent criticism and occasional disfavor, the author has managed to retain a leading position in Soviet legal circles throughout the Soviet era and is a professor at Moscow University. [B]

W32 KOROVIN, EVGENII A. *Sovremennoe mezhdunarodnoe publichnoe pravo.* Moscow-Leningrad: Gosizdat, 1926. 176 p. First systematic textbook of international law from the Soviet point of view by a leading Soviet authority, still useful for understanding the evolution of Soviet concepts and attitudes. Emphasizes Russian and Soviet practice.

W32A *Kosmos i mezhdunarodnoe pravo.* Moscow: Izd. Instituta mezhdunarodnykh otnoshenii, 1962. 183 p. A collection of six articles by Soviet jurists on various aspects of the nascent law of outer space.

W32B KOVALEV, F. N., and CHEPROV, I. I. *Na puti k kosmicheskomu pravu.* Moscow: Izd. Instituta mezhdunarodnykh otnoshenii, 1962. 180 p. The first Soviet monographic treatment of the law of outer space.

W33 KOZHEVNIKOV, F. I. *Sovetskoe gosudarstvo i mezhdunarodnoe pravo, 1917-1947*. Moscow: Iuridicheskoe izd., 1948. 376 p. Perhaps the most representative treatment of international law in terms of Soviet policy and practice of the late Stalin era, by an important Soviet jurist who was subsequently (1954-61) the Soviet judge on the International Court of Justice. Revealing in its emphasis on law as an instrument of policy. Found in few Western libraries. [A]

W34 KRYLOV, SERGEI B. *Mezhdunarodnyi Sud Organizatsii obedinennykh natsii*. Moscow: Gosizdat iurid. lit., 1958. 167 p. Critical account of the work of the International Court of Justice by a senior Soviet jurist who was the first Soviet judge on the Court (1946-52). Based in large part on articles previously published by the author under the pseudonym of S. Borisov.

W35 KRYLOV, SERGEI B. *Les notions principales du droit des gens* (*La doctrine soviëtique du droit international*). The Hague: Académie de droit international, *Recueil des cours*, vol. 70 (1947-I), p. 407-476. The only representative treatment of international law from the Soviet viewpoint of the early post-World War II period in a Western language, by a former Soviet judge on the International Court.

W35A LADYZHENSKII, A. M., and BLISHCHENKO, I. P. *Mirnye sredstva razresheniia sporov mezhdu gosudarstvami*. Moscow: Gosizdat iurid. lit., 1962. 175 p. Two Soviet jurists present the Soviet view and practice on various means of peaceful settlement of international disputes.

W36 LAPENNA, IVO. *Conceptions soviëtiques de droit international public*. Paris: Pedone, 1954. 324 p. Painstaking though pedestrian account of the evolution of Soviet doctrines of international law, by a former Yugoslav professor. Useful for its thoroughness. [B]

W37 LEVIN, DAVID B. *Diplomaticheskii immunitet*. Moscow: Izd. Akademii nauk SSSR, 1949. 415 p. One of the most substantial Soviet monographs on technical aspects of international law, by a Soviet legal expert; attempts to reappraise the historical and theoretical aspects of diplomatic immunities from a moderate Soviet point of view.

W38 LEVIN, DAVID B. *Osnovnye problemy sovremennogo mezhdunarodnogo prava*. Moscow: Gosizdat iurid. lit., 1958. 275 p. A post-Stalin effort by an experienced Soviet jurist to reformulate the Soviet approach to basic international law concepts.

W39 LEVIN, I. D. *Suverenitet*. Moscow: Iuridicheskoe izd., 1948. 376 p. The most detailed Soviet analysis of the concept of sovereignty (which is central in the Soviet doctrine of international law).

W40 LISOVSKII, V. I. *Mezhdunarodnoe pravo.* Kiev: Kievskii gosudarstvennyi universitet, 1955. 477 p. 2nd ed., Moscow: Gos. izd. "Vysshaia Shkola," 1961. 484 p. First Soviet treatise on international law to be published after Stalin's death. By a Soviet Ukrainian jurist, it was coldly received in Soviet legal circles.

W41 LITVINOV, MAXIM M. *Protiv agressii.* Moscow: Gospolitizdat, 1938. 112 p. English ed., *Against Aggression.* N.Y.: International Publishers, 1939. 208 p. A collection of speeches and documents by the then Commissar of Foreign Affairs. The major theme is collective security against fascist aggression.

W42 LOGUNOV, V. D. *Sovremennyi mezhdunarodno-pravovoi rezhim Dunaia.* Moscow: Izd. Instituta mezhdunarodnykh otnoshenii, 1958. 151 p. Contains materials not readily available elsewhere on the operation of the Danube Convention of 1948 and ancillary instruments, including statistics on Danube shipping.

W42A LUKIN, P. I. *Istochniki mezhdunarodnogo prava.* Moscow: Izd. Akademii nauk SSSR, 1960. 144 p. A monograph on sources of international law, with critique of Western doctrines.

W43 LUNTS, L. A. *Mezhdunarodnoe chastnoe pravo; obshchaia chast.* Moscow: Gosizdat iurid. lit., 1959. 280 p. Treatise, by the leading Soviet authority on the subject, on the general principles of private international law.

W44 MARGOLIS, EMANUEL. "Certain Aspects of the Impact of Communism on International Law." Ph.D. dissertation, Harvard, 1951.

W45 *Materials on the Trial of Former Servicemen of the Japanese Army Charged With Manufacturing and Employing Bacteriological Weapons.* Moscow: Foreign Languages Publishing House, 1950. 535 p. Documents and transcript of the trial of Japanese prisoners in Khabarovsk in 1949 for bacteriological warfare and experimentation on human beings.

W46 MEISSNER, BORIS. *Die Sowjetunion, die Baltischen Staaten und das Völkerrecht.* Cologne: Verlag für Politik und Wirtschaft, 1956. 377 p. Discussion by a leading West German authority on the Soviet Union of Soviet international law doctrines and practices, with special reference to the Soviet annexation of the Baltic States. Valuable 26-page bibliography.

W47 *Mezhdunarodnoe pravo v izbrannykh dokumentakh.* Comp. by L. A. Modzhorian and V. K. Sobakin. Moscow: Izd. IMO, 1957. 3 vols. Collection of treaties, resolutions, statutes, regulations and other official documents of Soviet and non-Soviet origin bearing on international law. Includes many Soviet documents not otherwise readily available. [B]

W48 MINASIAN, N. M. *Istochniki sovremennogo mezhdunarodnogo prava*. Rostov: Izd. Rostovskogo Universiteta, 1960. 152 p. A recent monograph on sources of international law. Contains extensive discussion of law of treaties.

W48A MOLODTSOV, S. V. *Mezhdunarodno-pravovoi rezhim otkrytogo moria i kontinentalnogo shelfa*. Moscow: Izd. Akademii nauk SSSR, 1960. 348 p. A substantial monograph by a young Soviet jurist on the law of the high seas and the continental shelf, stressing the Soviet position at the 1958 conference on the law of the sea.

W49 NIKOLAEV, A. N. *Problema territorialnykh vod v mezhdunarodnom prave*. Moscow: Gosizdat iurid. lit., 1954. 307 p. The most detailed and authoritative treatment of territorial waters from the Soviet point of view, by a jurist attached to the Soviet Ministry of Foreign Affairs. Emphasizes political implications of legal rules and controversies. Includes exhaustive lists of Soviet legislation and treaties bearing on the subject. [B]

W50 *Osteuropa-Recht*. Quarterly. Stuttgart: Deutsche Gesellschaft für Osteuropakunde, 1955–. Includes numerous articles, notes, book reviews and documents of international law significance.

W51 PASHUKANIS, EVGENII B. *Ocherki po mezhdunarodnomu pravu*. Moscow: Sovetskoe zakonodatelstvo, 1935. 222 p. A bold and imaginative treatment, stressing the use of traditional forms of international law as instruments of Soviet policy. The author, an outstanding Soviet theoretician, soon fell into official disfavor and disappeared, but was partially rehabilitated in the post-Stalin era. Valuable for its frank approach to the relation between law and Soviet policy. [B]

W52 PERETERSKII, I. S., and KRYLOV, S. B. *Mezhdunarodnoe chastnoe pravo*. 2nd ed., Moscow: Gosizdat iurid. lit., 1959. 227 p. Standard textbook of private international law, by two senior Soviet professors, approved for use in law faculties and institutes. Includes chapters on the status of foreign nationals and corporations in the Soviet Union, and of Soviet nationals and state agencies abroad.

W53 POLIANSKII, N. N. *Mezhdunarodnyi sud*. Moscow: Izd. Akademii nauk SSSR, 1951. 236 p. Only systematic Soviet analysis of the organization, jurisdiction, procedure and sources of law of the International Court of Justice.

W53A *Pravovoe regulirovanie vneshnei torgovli SSSR*. Moscow: Vneshtorgizdat, 1961. 514 p. A practical manual on Soviet regulation of foreign trade, containing much detailed information not elsewhere available. By a number of Soviet jurists.

W54 *Pravovye voprosy vneshnei torgovli SSSR s evropeiskimi stranami narodnoi demokratii.* Ed. by D. M. Genkin. Moscow: Vneshtorgizdat, 1955. 261 p. Unique collection of essays by nine Soviet jurists on legal aspects and techniques of trade between the USSR and the People's Democracies in Europe.

W55 RAMZAITSEV, D. F. *Morskoi arbitrazh v Sovetskom Soiuze.* Moscow: Vneshtorgizdat, 1956. 39 p. Brief but uniquely valuable account of the organization, procedure and decisions of the Maritime Arbitral Commission, which is used to settle disputes between Soviet agencies and foreign shipowners.

W56 RAMZAITSEV, D. F. *Vneshnetorgovyi arbitrazh v SSSR.* 2nd ed. Moscow: Vneshtorgizdat, 1957. 182 p. Unique source of information on the organization, procedure and case law of the Foreign Trade Arbitral Commission in Moscow, which serves to settle controversies between Soviet agencies and foreign business firms.

W57 RAYMOND, EDWARD A. "The Juridical Status of Persons Displaced from Soviet and Soviet-Dominated Territory." Ph.D. dissertation, American Univ., 1952.

W58 REINKEMEYER, HANS-ALBERT. *Die sowjetische Zwölfmeilenzone in der Ostsee und die Freiheit des Meeres.* (Max-Planck-Institut für Ausländisches Öffentliches Recht und Völkerrecht, Beiträge zum ausländischen öffentlichen Recht und Völkerrecht, Heft 30.) Cologne-Berlin: Heymanns, 1955. 175 p. Thorough and very useful study of the troublesome Soviet claim of twelve-mile territorial waters, particularly in the Baltic, by a West German scholar. Good 10-page bibliography. [B]

W59 ROMASHKIN, P. S. *Voennye prestupleniia imperializma.* Moscow: Gosizdat iurid. lit., 1953. 439 p. Analysis of the problem of war crimes, accompanied by diatribes against Western powers, by a leading Soviet jurist.

W60 RUSSIA (1923– USSR), TREATIES, ETC. *Sbornik mezhdunarodnykh konventsii, dogovorov, soglashenii i pravil po voprosam torgovogo moreplavaniia.* Moscow: Izd. "Morskoi Transport," 1959. 475 p. Collection of documents on maritime navigation and commerce, including many agreements concluded by Soviet agencies, regulations and other materials not otherwise readily available.

W60A *Sbornik normativnykh materialov po voprosam vneshnei torgovli SSSR.* Moscow: Vneshtorgizdat, 1961. 279 p. A collection of Soviet laws, regulations and instructions relating to foreign trade. Contains many documents not readily available elsewhere.

W60B *Sbornik torgovykh dogovorov, torgovykh i platezhnykh soglashenii i dolgosrochnykh torgovykh soglashenii SSSR s inostrannymi gosudarstvami.* Moscow: Vneshtorgizdat, 1961. 624 p. A collection of Soviet treaties and agreements relating to foreign trade.

W61 SHMIGELSKII, G. L. and IASINOVSKII, V. A. *Osnovy sovetskogo morskogo prava.* Moscow: Izd. "Morskoi Transport," 1959. 234 p. Concise practical manual of maritime law, emphasizing commercial aspects. Contains much information on Soviet practice.

W62 SHURSHALOV, V. M. *Osnovaniia deistvitelnosti mezhdunarodnykh dogovorov.* Moscow: Izd. Akademii nauk, 1957. 232 p. Attempt by a young Soviet jurist to reinterpret traditional doctrines by relating them to economic and political realities in light of Marxist ideology, combined with attacks on Western powers. [B]

W63 SHURSHALOV, V. M. *Osnovnye voprosy teorii mezhdunarodnogo dogovora.* Moscow: Izd. Akademii nauk SSSR, 1959. 472 p. Most substantial monograph on the law of treaties from the Soviet viewpoint.

W64 SHURSHALOV, V. M. *Rezhim mezhdunarodnoi opeki.* Moscow: Gosizdat iurid. lit., 1951. 189 p. Incisive presentation by a Soviet scholar of the Soviet view on the U.N. trusteeship system in theory and practice and also on the handling of other problems of non-selfgoverning territories by the United Nations.

W64A *Soglasheniia SSSR po konsulskim voprosam.* Moscow: Izd. Instituta mezhdunarodnykh otnoshenii, 1962. 232 p. Collection of texts of Soviet treaties and agreements on consular relations.

W65 SOVETSKAIA ASSOTSIATSIIA MEZHDUNARODNOGO PRAVA. *Sovetskaia literatura po mezhdunarodnomu pravu; bibliografiia 1917-1957.* Ed. by V. N. Durdenevskii. Moscow: Gosizdat iurid. lit., 1959. 303 p. Comprehensive and elaborately classified list of books, pamphlets, articles and documents on public and private international law published in Russian in the Soviet Union, with the exception of books translated from foreign languages. Book entries include lists of reviews in Soviet periodicals. Many listed items concern international relations as well as law. A supplement lists most publications issued in 1958. [A]

W66 *Sovetskii ezhegodnik mezhdunarodnogo prava.* Issued by Sovetskaia Assotsiatsiia Mezhdunarodnogo Prava. Moscow: Izd. Akademii nauk SSSR, 1959–. Annual. Each issue contains numerous articles, notes, book reviews, reports of proceedings of the Soviet Association of International Law, and bibliographies. Major articles are accompanied by summaries in English. First issue, for 1958, appeared in 1959. [A]

W67 SPERANSKAIA, L. *Printsip samoopredeleniia natsii v mezhdunarodnom prave.* Moscow: Gosiurizdat, 1961.

W68 STARUSHENKO, G. B. *Printsip samoopredeleniia narodov i natsii vo vneshnei politike sovetskogo gosudarstva.* Moscow: Izd. Instituta mezhdunarodnykh otnoshenii, 1960. 191 p. Politico-legal monograph on the slogan of self-determination and its use in Soviet policy, by a Soviet writer.

W69 STOUPNITZKY, A. *Statut international de l'U.R.S.S., état commerçant.* Paris: Librairie Générale de droit et de jurisprudence, 1936. 486 p. Comprehensive study, based largely on judicial decisions, of legal problems created in the West by the emergence of the Soviet state, policies of recognition and non-recognition, Soviet state monopoly of foreign trade, and Soviet expropriations of private property. Numerous sectional bibliographies.

W70 TARACOUZIO, TIMOTHY A. *The Soviet Union and International Law; a Study Based on the Legislation, Treaties and Foreign Relations of the Union of Soviet Socialist Republics.* N.Y.: Macmillan, 1935. 530 p. Unique among Western works on the subject in stressing Soviet practice rather than doctrine, this monograph by a Harvard scholar of Russian émigré origin remains a valuable source of information for the period covered. Based largely on Soviet official sources as well as secondary works. Excellent 27-page bibliography and appended documents. [A]

W71 TRAININ, ARON N. *Zashchita mira i borba s prestupleniiami protiv chelovechestva.* Moscow: Izd. Akademii nauk SSSR, 1956. 299 p. Substantial monograph on aggression, war crimes, genocide, crimes against humanity and related topics, by a senior Soviet jurist.

W72 *The Trial of the U2; Exclusive Authorized Account of the Court Proceedings of the Case of Francis Gary Powers Heard Before the Military Division of the Supreme Court of the U.S.S.R., Moscow, August 17, 18, 19, 1960.* Chicago: Translation World Publishers, 1960. 158 p. English translation of the transcript of the famous trial of an American flier on a charge of espionage, with other official documents. Preceded by a 30-page introductory comment by Harold J. Berman, Harvard professor.

W72A TRISKA, JAN F., and SLUSSER, ROBERT M. *The Theory, Law, and Policy of Soviet Treaties.* Stanford: Stanford University Press. 1962. 593 p. A comprehensive study by two American scholars, containing a wealth of information on Soviet attitudes toward international law. Exhaustive 25-page bibliography. [A]

W73 TUNKIN, GRIGORII I. *Co-existence and International Law.* The Hague: Académie de Droit International, *Recueil des cours*, vol. 95 (1958-III), p. 1-81. These lectures at The Hague Academy of International Law are by the Chief of the Legal Department of the Soviet Ministry of Foreign Affairs, also the Soviet member of the U.N. International Law Commission and president of the Soviet Association of International Law. Contains the clearest and most authoritative presentation of the post-Stalin Soviet point of view on the fundamentals of international law. [A]

W74 TUNKIN, GRIGORII I. *Osnovy sovremennogo mezhdunarodnogo prava; uchebnoe posobie.* Moscow: Vysshaia partiinaia shkola pri TsK KPSS, 1956. 47 p. Brief but authoritative survey of international law by the leading authority of the post-Stalin period. [B]

W74A TUNKIN, GRIGORII I. *Voprosy teorii mezhdunarodnogo prava.* Moscow: Gosizdat iurid. lit., 1962. 330 p. A full and authoritative exposition of the Soviet approach to international law, with stress on "peaceful co-existence," in the Khrushchev era. [A]

W75 U.S. CONGRESS, SENATE, COMMITTEE ON AERONAUTICAL AND SPACE SCIENCES. *Legal Problems of Space Exploration; A Symposium.* 87th Congress, 1st Session, Senate Document No. 26. Washington: G.P.O., 1961. 1392 p. Contains (p. 1011-1218) a unique though not exhaustive collection of Soviet and East European writings on space law in English translation, with a good bibliographical note and a 15-page bibliography.

W75A VILKOV, G. E. *Natsionalizatsiia i mezhdunarodnoe pravo.* Moscow: Izd. Instituta mezhdunarodnykh otnoshenii, 1962. 136 p. The first Soviet monograph on the important problem of nationalization of foreign property in international law.

W76 *Voprosy mezhdunarodnogo chastnogo prava.* Ed. by L. A. Lunts. Moscow: Gosizdat iurid. lit., 1956. 240 p. Essays by nine Soviet jurists on such topics as sovereign immunity and protection of copyrights and patents in international law.

W77 *Voprosy vozdushnogo prava; sbornik trudov sektsii vozdushnogo prava Soiuza Aviakhim SSSR i Aviakhim RSFSR.* Vol. 1: Moscow: Aviakhim, 1927. 300 p. Vol. 2. Moscow-Leningrad: Gosizdat, 1930. 223 p. Collection of many essays by Soviet authorities on air law, with distinctive contributions to the development of the subject.

W78 VYSHINSKII, ANDREI IA. *Voprosy mezhdunarodnogo prava i mezhdunarodnoi politiki.* Moscow: Gosizdat iurid. lit., 1949, 502 p.; 1951, 798 p.; 1952, 507 p.; 1952, 391 p.; 1953, 306 p. (With varying subtitles.) Collections of Vyshinskii's speeches at the United Nations and international conferences.

W79 ZADOROZHNYI, G. P. *Vneshniaia funktsiia sovremennogo imperialisticheskogo gosudarstva.* Moscow: Izd. Akademii nauk SSSR, 1958. 328 p. Analysis of content and methods of foreign policies of leading Western powers with emphasis on alleged legal deficiencies, by a Soviet jurist.

W79A ZHUKOV, G. P. *Kritika estestvennopravovykh teorii mezhdunarodnogo prava.* Moscow: Gosizdat iurid. lit., 1961. 164 p. A Soviet critique of certain Western tendencies in the theory of international law.

Addenda

W80 AKADEMIIA NAUK SSSR, INSTITUT GOSUDARSTVA I PRAVA. *Mezhdunarodno-pravovye formy sotrudnichestva sotsialisticheskikh gosudarstv.* Ed. by V. M. Shurshalov. Moscow: Izd. Akademii Nauk SSSR, 1962. 467 p. Extensive discussion by a group of Soviet jurists of legal aspects of relations among the states of the "socialist camp." [B]

W81 BLISHCHENKO, I. P., and DURDENEVSKII, V. N. *Diplomaticheskoe i konsulskoe pravo.* Moscow: Izd. Instituta mezhdunarodnykh otnoshenii, 1962. 480 p. A treatise on diplomatic and consular law.

W82 KLIMENKO, B. M. *Demilitarizatsiia i neitralizatsiia v mezhdunarodnom prave.* Moscow: Izd. I.M.O., 1963. 223 p. A Soviet view of demilitarization and neutralization, including proposals for "denuclearized" zones and the problem of inspection.

W83 LAZAREV, M. I. *Imperialisticheskie voennye bazy na chuzhikh territoriakh i mezhdunarodnoe pravo.* Moscow: Izd. I.M.O., 1963. 256 p. An attack in legal terms on U.S. military bases abroad.

W84 LISSITZYN, OLIVER J. "International Law in a Divided World," *International Conciliation*, No. 542, March 1963. 69 p. Includes analysis of Soviet policies toward international law (p. 14-36).

W85 MIKHAILOVSKYI, M. K. *Mizhnarodnii arbitrazh.* Kiev: Vydavnitstvo Adademii Nauk Ukrainskoi RSR, 1963. 155 p. Most extensive Soviet treatment of international arbitration. In Ukrainian.

W86 TALALAEV, A. N. *Iuridicheskaia priroda mezhdunarodnogo dogovora.* Moscow: Izd. I.M.O., 1963. 263 p. A discussion of the law of treaties from the Soviet point of view.

X. Soviet Military Power and Doctrine

EDITED BY RAYMOND L. GARTHOFF

1. GENERAL WORKS

X1 BASSECHES, NIKOLAUS. *The Unknown Army.* N.Y. Viking, 1943. 239 p. A perceptive if impressionistic interpretation of the nature and broad development of the Russian army under Imperial Russia, and under the Soviet regime to the Second World War.

X2 BERCHIN, MICHEL, and BEN-HORIN, ELIAHU. *The Red Army.* N.Y.: Norton, 1942. 277 p. A general account of the development of the Red Army in the 1930's, and of its operations in the first year of the Soviet-German war. It was well-based for the information available at that time, but has been overtaken by fuller data available since the war.

X3 BERGGREN, GUSTAF (pseud. of Sven Herman Kjellberg). *Ryssland im krig.* Stockholm: Lindfors, 1944. 362 p. German ed., Zurich and N.Y.: Europa Verlag, 1945. A general study of Soviet military power and potential in the period before World War II. This work is of but limited value in view of more substantial data now available in other publications.

X4 BERMAN, HAROLD J., and KERNER, MIROSLAV. *Soviet Military Law and Administration.* Cambridge: Harvard, 1955. 208 p. The only study of this subject available in Western literature, this book is useful for its analysis of Soviet military law and its application in practice.

X5 BRZEZINSKI, ZBIGNIEW, ed. *Political Controls in the Soviet Army.* N.Y.: Research Program on the USSR, 1954. 93 p. In part written by, and almost entirely based upon, the experiences of six former Soviet officers. Presents a useful description of political indoctrination and police surveillance in the Soviet Army during the war and post-war years of the Stalin regime.

X6 DIXON, CECIL A., and HEILBRUNN, OTTO. *Communist Guerrilla Warfare.* London: Allen and Unwin; N.Y.: Praeger, 1954. 229 p. A useful general account of Soviet partisan warfare techniques in World War II (as well as of German anti-partisan warfare).

X7 FEDOTOFF WHITE, DIMITRI. *The Growth of the Red Army.* Princeton, N.J.: Princeton University Press, 1944. 486 p. Remains a valuable contribution, the chief study of the general development of the Soviet armed forces from 1917 to 1940. Based on wide use of Soviet and other sources, it examines in considerable detail many facets of the Soviet military establishment. [A]

X8 FRIEDL, BERTHOLD. *Les Fondements théoriques de la guerre et de la paix en U.R.S.S.* Paris: Éditions Médicis, 1945. 203 p. A good theoretical study in Soviet military doctrine, especially useful for making available in full Lenin's annotations on Clausewitz.

X9 GARDER, MICHEL. *Histoire de l'armée soviétique.* Paris: Plon, 1959. 305 p. A competent general account of the development of the Soviet armed forces, with particular attention to the late 1950's. The best general history in French. [B]

X10 GARTHOFF, RAYMOND L. *Soviet Military Doctrine.* Glencoe, Illinois: Free Press, 1953. 587 p. British ed., *How Russia Makes War.* London: Allen & Unwin, 1954. German ed., Cologne: 1955. French ed., Paris: 1956. Spanish ed., Madrid: 1956. Portuguese ed., Rio de Janeiro: 1957. Chinese ed., Taipei: 1955. Turkish ed., Istanbul: 1956. Japanese ed., Tokyo: 1957. The most comprehensive and definitive study of Soviet military thought, strategy and tactics, and doctrine in the period up to 1953. Based on wide use of Soviet as well as other sources, it contains an extensive bibliography. Doctrinal developments in World War II are covered, but it does not provide an historical account of the course of that war. [A]

X11 GOUDIMA, ROBERT. *L'Armée rouge dans la paix et la guerre.* Paris: Défense de la France, 1947. 428 p. A general account of the development of the Red Army from the Russian Civil War through World War II. One of the better available works in French, though there are a number of factual inaccuracies of detail.

X12 GRUDININ, I. A. *Voprosy dialektiki v voennom dele.* Moscow: Voenizdat, 1960. 215 p. A recent military theoretical work by a Soviet colonel, useful for a "feel" of Soviet doctrine as it is evolving in the missile age, though still couched in the familiar Marxist-Leninist framework.

X13 GUILLAUME, AUGUSTIN. *Soviet Arms and Soviet Power.* Washington, D.C.: Infantry Journal, 1949. 212 p. French ed., *Pourquoi l'armée rouge a vaincu.* Paris: Julliard, 1948. A frequently misleading and inaccurate work, excessively credulous of Soviet accounts and explanations. Written by the former French chief military representative in Moscow.

X14 JACOBS, WALTER D. "The Unified Military Doctrine of Mikhail V. Frunze." Ph.D. dissertation, Columbia, 1961. A criticism of Frunze's theory and an evaluation of its place in Soviet political and military thought.

X14A KAHN, HERMAN. *On Thermonuclear War*. Princeton, N.J.: Princeton University Press, 1961. 668 p. A brilliant analysis of the possible manifestations of a thermonuclear war and of the problems it would pose for mankind. Includes discussions of the USSR's capabilities both to inflict and absorb damage in such a war, both now and at successive stages in the future.

X15 KHOMENKO, E. A. *O voinakh spravedlivykh i nespravedlivykh*. Moscow: Voenizdat, 1954. 96 p. A fairly pedestrian but full exposition of the concept of "just" wars in Leninist thought.

X16 KISSINGER, HENRY A. *Nuclear Weapons and Foreign Policy*. N.Y.: Harper, 1957. 455 p. Chapters 10 and 11 summarize Soviet and Chinese Communist views on military policy and doctrine.

X17 KOMMUNISTICHESKAIA PARTIIA SOVETSKOGO SOIUZA. *KPSS o vooruzhennykh silakh Sovetskogo Soiuza; sbornik dokumentov, 1917-1958*. Comp. by V. N. Malin and V. P. Moskovskii. Moscow: Gospolitizdat, 1958. 419 p. A collection of basic Party debates and directives on the Soviet armed forces. Useful, but limited to unclassified general military policy documents.

X18 LAGOVSKI, A. N. *Strategiia i ekonomika*. Moscow: Voenizdat, 1957. 200 p. The best Soviet work on economic factors in military strategy and in military doctrine. While its treatment would be considered very conservative in the West, when this work appeared in the USSR it aroused considerable interest among military readers. The author is a Soviet major general. [B]

X19 LIDDELL HART, BASIL H., ed. *The Soviet Army*. London: Weidenfield & Nicolson, 1956. 480 p. American ed., *The Red Army*. N.Y.: Harcourt & Brace, 1956. A collective work written by a number of British, American, German, ex-Soviet, and other authors. Of uneven quality, it does include a number of informative and useful chapters on various historical and current aspects of the Soviet ground forces. [A]

X20 *Marksizm-leninizm o voine i armii; sbornik statei*. Moscow: Voenizdat, 1955, 220 p.; 1956, 284 p.; 1957, 287 p.; 1961, 394 p.; 1962, 375 p. A good reflection of Soviet theoretical military views, these collective works were written by groups of Soviet military writers. The volumes appeared during a period of renaissance in military thought in the USSR. [A]

X21 MARYGANOV, I. V. *Peredovoi kharakter sovetskoi voennoi nauki*. Moscow: Voenizdat, 1953. 151 p. A typical account of Soviet military doctrine and theory at the time of Stalin's death, and thus useful for comparison with later theoretical studies.

X22 MILSHTEIN, M. A., and SLOBODENKO, A. K. *O burzhuaznoi voennoi nauke.* Moscow: Voenizdat, 1957. 286 p. Rev. ed., 1961. 355 p. A critical study of Western military thought since the 18th century, with particular emphasis on the recent past and present. Very biased, but useful as a reflection of Soviet thinking. [B]

X23 *O sovetskoi voennoi nauke.* Moscow: Voenizdat, 1954. 208 p. One of the half-dozen collective works on military doctrine and theory to appear in the USSR over the past decade. This work is now of little interest except for comparison with more recent theoretical accounts.

X24 *O sovetskoi voennoi nauke.* Moscow: Voenizdat, 1960. 335 p. 2nd ed., 1964. 405 p. One of a series of collected writings on Soviet military doctrine, for the most part originally appearing in military journals. Useful for understanding Soviet military theory. [B]

X24A OSANKA, FRANKLIN M., ed. *Modern Guerrilla Warfare.* N.Y.: Free Press of Glencoe, 1962. 519 p. Contains a number of essays on Communist guerrilla techniques.

X25 PARRY, ALBERT. *Russian Cavalcade; a Military Record.* N.Y.: Washburn, 1944. 334 p. A well-written and interesting account of Russian military history, with a few chapters on the Russian Civil War, and several others on World War II campaigns through Stalingrad. Undocumented.

X26 *Partiino-politicheskaia rabota v sovetskoi armii i voenno-morskom flote.* Moscow: Voenizdat, 1960. 285 p. The best general guide to current Party and political activity in the Soviet armed forces.

X27 *Polevoi ustav Krasnoi armii.* Moscow: Voenizdat, 1944. 395 p. The basic field regulations and tactical manual of the Soviet Army, issued by the Peoples' Commissariat of Defense. The latest issue available is dated 1947. This version was issued in the late war and early postwar years.

X28 PRUCK, ERICH F. *Der rote Soldat; sowjetische Wehrpolitik.* Munich: Günter Olzog, 1961. 331 p. A historical and topical survey of the Soviet military structure. Among the problems considered are the Party's control of the army, training of officers, military law, the Soviet army's position in the Warsaw Pact system, the level of Soviet military science, etc. Multi-language bibliography.

X29 PUKHOVSKII, N. V. *Voina i politika.* Moscow: Voenizdat, 1955. 144 p. An interesting essay on the relationship of war and policy, reflecting long-standing Marxist-Leninist views in contemporary circumstances. By a Soviet major general who is a military professor.

X30 RAYMOND, ELLSWORTH L. "Soviet Preparation for Total War, 1925-1951." Ph.D. dissertation, U. of Michigan, 1952. 367 p. An account of the development of the Soviet economy, with emphasis on improvement and preparation of the economic foundations for military potential.

X31 SEMENOV, V. A. *Kratkii ocherk razvitiia sovetskogo operativnogo iskusstva.* Moscow: Voenizdat, 1960. 299 p. An analytic history drawing upon past Soviet military operations to illustrate the evolution of Soviet military tactical concepts. It is ambitious in scope, and makes a very useful contribution to the understanding of Soviet military doctrine. [B]

X32 SKOPIN, V. I. *Militarizm.* Moscow: Voenizdat, 1956. 583 p. Rev. ed., 1957. 672 p. A tendentious "capital" work attempting to expose alleged militaristic strains in Western history and contemporary society. A most useful work for understanding Soviet views of Western political and military policy. [B]

X33 SKOVORODIN, M. D. *Taktika kak sostavnaia chast voennogo iskusstva.* Moscow: Voenizdat, 1956. 96 p. A theoretical analysis of the role of tactics in military art and military science. By a Soviet colonel.

X33A SOKOLOVSKII, VASILII D., et al. *Voennaia strategiia.* Moscow: Voenizdat, 1962, 458 p. English ed., *Military Strategy*, N.Y.: Praeger, 1963. Trans. with Introduction by R. L. Garthoff. This is probably the most significant postwar Soviet work on military affairs, prepared by the collective efforts of a group of officers headed by the former Chief of the General Staff, Marshal Sokolovskii. [A]

X34 *Sovremennaia imperialisticheskaia voennaia ideologiia.* Moscow: Voenizdat, 1958. 496 p. An extended critical analysis of recent and current U.S., British, French, and West German military thinking, as seen through Soviet eyes.

X35 TOKAEV, GRIGORI A. *Comrade X.* London: Harvill, 1956. 370 p. An interesting but unconfirmed account of intrigue and political opposition in the Soviet military in the 1930's and 1940's, by a former Soviet aviation engineer and lieutenant colonel who defected in 1947.

X36 U.S. DEPARTMENT OF THE ARMY, ARMY LIBRARY. *Soviet Military Power.* Washington, D.C.: Headquarters, Dept. of the Army, 1959. 186 p. An extensive and useful bibliography of works on Soviet military affairs, especially complete for Western studies, though weaker on Russian areas. Includes periodical articles as well as books.

X37 *V pomoshch ofitseram, izuchaiushchim Marksistko-leninskuiu teoriiu.* Moscow: Voenizdat, 1959. 414 p. Valuable for understanding the relationship between Marxism-Leninism and Soviet military theory and doctrine, as the Soviets themselves see it. A collection of articles from the Soviet military press.

X37A VERSHIGORA, P. P. *Voennoe tvorchestvo narodnykh mass.* Moscow: Voenizdat, 1961. 824 p. A political-historical study of the role of "peoples" in winning wars, spanning the whole of recorded history.

X38 *Voennoe iskusstvo; strategiia, operativnoe iskusstvo, obshche-voiskovaia taktika; ukazatel literatury.* Comp. by N. T. Tolkachev and ed. by M. A. Miashnikov. Moscow: 1943. 203 p. A bibliographical guide to Soviet publications on military theoretical, strategical and tactical subjects in the prewar and early World War II period.

X39 WHITING, KENNETH. *Readings in Soviet Military Theory.* Montgomery, Ala.: Air University, 1952. 80 p. A useful compilation in English of a number of the more indicative Soviet military doctrinal writings, chiefly of the prewar period, on the general role of war and the army in communist policy.

X40 ZHURAVKOV, M. G., BELYI, B. A., and MARYGANOV, I. V. *Moralno-politicheskii faktor v sovremennoi voine.* Moscow: Voenizdat, 1958. 311 p. The most extensive Soviet review of the importance of morale and political sources of morale in contemporary war.

2. 1917-1939

X41 BUBNOV, ANDREI S., KAMENEV, S. S., and EIDEMAN, R. P. *Grazhdanskaia voina, 1918-1921.* Moscow. 3 vols. Vol. 1, 1928. 374 p. Vol. 2, 1928. 419 p. Vol. 3, 1930. 557 p. Written by some of the outstanding Bolshevik Civil War leaders, later purged, this work uniquely presents views and data on the early years of the Red Army omitted from later Soviet accounts. [B]

X42 ERICKSON, JOHN. *The Soviet High Command; a Military-Political History, 1918-1941.* N.Y.: St. Martin's; London: Macmillan, 1962. 889 p. A comprehensive, penetrating and thorough study of Soviet military policy and relations of the military chiefs with the Soviet political leadership in the period up to the Soviet-German war in 1941. A very useful contribution to the field of Soviet history. [A]

X43 HULT, BERNDT. *Europas röda arméer.* Stockholm: Hörsta, 1953. A brief chapter traces some aspects of the development of the Red Army in the USSR prior to World War II. The remainder of the volume is devoted to an uneven history of the various Satellite armies of Eastern Europe since 1945. No documentation.

X44 IAKOVLEV, BORIS N., and BARBASHIN, I. P. *Vazhneishie daty geroicheskoi istorii Vooruzhennykh Sil SSSR; spravochnaia kniga dlia propagandistov.* Moscow: DOSAAF, 1958. 215 p. A useful chronological record of events affecting the Soviet armed forces, as selected by Soviet authorities.

X45 *KPSS i stroitelstvo vooruzhennykh sil SSSR.* Moscow: Voenizdat, 1959. 451 p. A Soviet history of the role of the Communist Party in organizing and building the Red Army from 1918 to 1941.

X46 KUZMIN, N. F. *Na strazhe mirnogo truda (1921-1940 gg.).* Moscow: Voenizdat, 1959. 294 p. The most complete Soviet history of the armed forces in the inter-war period, by a colonel. A useful source, though as in all Soviet self-historical accounts much is filtered out. [B]

X47 MAKHINE, THEODORE H. *L'Armée rouge; la puissance militaire de l'URSS.* Paris: Payot, 1938. 356 p. A very good study based on Soviet published sources and other data, by an objective former White officer. One of the better works available in French on the Red Army in the 1920's and 1930's. [B]

X48 POBEZHIMOV, I. F. *Ustroistvo Sovetskoi armii; kratkii istoricheskii ocherk.* Moscow: Voenizdat, 1954. 142 p. A Soviet account of the development of the structure of the Soviet armed forces. It presents the bare outline on the basis of acceptable Soviet historical perspective of the mid-1950's; in short, it is weak as history.

X49 PORTUGEIS, SEMEN O. (Ivanovich, S., pseud.). *Krasnaia armiia.* Paris: "Sovremennaia zapiska," 1931. 242 p. An account of political indoctrination and Party controls in the Red Army in the 1920's by a former Soviet officer. An excellent and useful treatment of those subjects.

X50 TAL, B. *Istoriia Krasnoi Armii.* Moscow: Gosizdat, 1927. 188 p. A useful work for seeing the Red Army of the 1920's through contemporary Soviet eyes, rather than in the image reflected in later postwar accounts of the development of the Red Army.

X51 VOROSHILOV, KLIMENT E. *Oborona SSSR.* Moscow: Voennyi vestnik, 1927. 163 p. Speeches by the then Soviet Commissar of War, giving the contemporary official Soviet military policy.

X52 WERNER, MAX. *The Military Strength of the Powers.* London: Gollancz, 1939. P. 34-133 and 262-303. Contains a considerable review of Western estimates and views on the Red Army in the 1930's, and a more limited but well selected summary of Soviet statements and information as well.

X53 WHITE, JOHN B. *Red Russia Arms.* London: Burrup, Mathieson, 1932. 144 p. A competent review of the Red Army in 1932, but with little background study of its earlier development.

X54 WOLLENBERG, ERICH. *The Red Army; a Study of the Growth of Soviet Imperialism.* London: Secker & Warburg, 1938. 283 p. Enlarged ed., London: 1940. 400 p. A worthwhile general account and evaluation of the development of the Red Army during the Russian Civil War and on to the late 1930's. The author himself served in that army in the early years of the Soviet regime. The chief value of the book today is the general impression it gives of the Red Army at that time, rather than as a source of the details of its development. [B]

3. 1939-1945

X55 AKADEMIIA NAUK, INSTITUT ISTORII. *Ocherki istorii Velikoi otechestvennoi voiny, 1941-1945.* Moscow: Izd. Akademii nauk SSSR, 1955. 534 p. The first major Soviet history of the Soviet-German war, undertaken in the post-Stalin "thaw." A useful work.

X56 ALLEN, WILLIAM E. D., and MURATOFF, PAUL. *The Russian Campaigns.* Vol. 1, *1941-1943.* London: Penguin, 1944. 192 p. Vol. 2, *1944-1945.* London: Penguin, 1946. 332 p. A useful contemporary general chronicle and account of the Soviet-German war, but limited to materials available during the war.

X57 ANDERS, WLADYSLAW. *Kieska Hitlera w Rosji, 1941-1945.* London: Gryf, 1952. 137 p. English ed., *Hitler's Defeat in Russia.* Chicago: Regnery, 1953. 267 p. A useful account of the German-Soviet campaigns by the former Polish general.

X58 ARMSTRONG, JOHN A., and others. *The Soviet Partisan Movement in World War II; Summary and Conclusions.* N.Y.: War Documentation Project, Bureau of Applied Social Research, Columbia University, 1955. 48 p. The summary and conclusions of a project which examined in some detail the major Soviet partisan operations. Reference is made to the other supporting studies.

X58A GOURÉ, LEON. *The Siege of Leningrad.* Stanford: Stanford University Press; London: Oxford, 1962. 364 p. An excellent study of the impact on the people of Leningrad and on the Soviet system of the prolonged pressure of the siege.

X59 GUILLAUME, AUGUSTIN. *La Guerre Germano-Soviétique, 1941-1945.* Paris: Payot, 1949. 219 p. A fairly comprehensive chronicle of military operations on the Soviet-German front. By a former French general who served in Moscow during the war.

X60 HALDER, FRANZ VON. "Diary; Campaign in Russia." Vols. 6 & 7, February 1941 through September 1942. Unpublished MS. The diary of the former Chief of the German General Staff during the first months of the war with the USSR. A very valuable source on that campaign.

X61 HOWELL, E. M. *The Soviet Partisan Movement, 1941-1944.* Washington: Department of the Army, 1956. 217 p. Based on a thorough study of captured German documents, and other sources, this is a good military analysis of the Soviet partisan movement.

X62 *Ideologicheskaia rabota KPSS na fronte, 1941-1945 gg.* Moscow: Voenizdat, 1960. 326 p. An account of the role of the Communist Party in the Red Army during the years of World War II, particularly its role in indoctrination and leadership.

X63 KALINOV, CYRILLE D. *Les Maréchaux soviétiques vous parlent.* Paris: Stock, 1950. 302 p. German ed. Hamburg: 1950. Italian ed., Milan: 1951. While some of the information in this volume is probably true, the validity of the whole must be discounted since "Colonel Kalinov" does not exist. The work is a clever fabrication.

X64 KERR, WALTER B. *The Russian Army.* N.Y.: Knopf, 1944. 250 p. A good journalistic account of the first year and a half of the Soviet-German war, by an American correspondent in Russia. It gives an observer's flavor of the war, though of course access to information was largely limited to Soviet propaganda output.

X65 KIRIAEV, N. M. *KPSS—vdokhnovitel i organizator pobed Sovetskogo naroda v Velikoi otechestvennoi voine.* Moscow: Voenizdat, 1959. 392 p. An account of the role of the Communist Party in the Soviet armed forces during World War II, attributing to it the chief role. Makes use of archival materials.

X66 KOLGANOV, K. S., ed. *Razvitie taktiki Sovetskoi armii v gody Velikoi otechestvennoi voiny (1941-1945 gg.)* Moscow: Voenizdat, 1958. 416 p. An extremely valuable account of the development of tactics in the Soviet army during World War II, by a collective of authors from the faculty of the Frunze Military Academy. [B]

X67 KOURNAKOFF, SERGEI N. *Russia's Fighting Forces.* N.Y.: Duell, Sloan and Pearce, 1942. 258 p. This work, by an émigré Russian, is largely an account of the Red Army in the first year of the war, though about half of the volume traces past Russian and Soviet military history. The author displays a strong pro-Soviet bias, and his uncritical acceptance of contemporary Soviet propaganda made it of little use even when it was published.

X68 KRYLOV, IVAN. *Soviet Staff Officer.* Trans. by Edward Fitzgerald. London: Falcon, 1951. 298 p. "Captain Krylov" does not exist, and the work must be discounted *en toto.* It is a pity that the wheat cannot be sifted from the chaff, as the author of this fabrication clearly has considerable background understanding of the Soviet armed forces.

X69 LÉDERREY, ERNEST. *La Défaite allemande à l'est; les armées soviétiques en guerre de 1941 à 1945.* Lausanne: Librairie Payot, 1951. 270 p. A good general historical chronicle of the combat record of the Red Army in the Soviet-German war, by Colonel Léderry, Swiss specialist on Soviet military affairs.

X70 LIDDELL HART, BASIL H. *The German Generals Talk.* N.Y.: Morrow, 1948. 300 p. A work based on extensive conversations with German generals, presenting their view of operations in the German-Soviet campaigns of World War II. An interesting and useful source of information.

X71 MINZ, I. *The Red Army.* N.Y.: International Publishers, 1943. 160 p. Soviet ed. in English, Moscow: 1942. 172 p. An account of the Red Army in the Russian Civil War, inter-war training, the war with Finland, and the first six months of the Soviet-German war in 1941, by a Soviet historian. It is a popularized account intended by the Soviets for British and American readers.

X72 MOSCOW, INSTITUT MARKSIZMA-LENINIZMA. *Istoriia Velikoi otechestvennoi voiny Sovetskogo Soiuza, 1941-1945.* Ed. by P. N. Pospelov and others. Moscow: Voenizdat, 1960-65. 6 vols. Prepared at the direction of the Presidium of the CPSU under a high-level editorial board, this series will be the definitive Soviet history of World War II. It is comprehensive, with much detailed information, and a useful source of data, as well as being invaluable for understanding the current Soviet view of the period. [A]

X73 PLATONOV, S. P. and others. *Vtoraia mirovaia voina, 1939-1945 gg.; voenno-istoricheskii ocherk.* Moscow: Voenizdat, 1958. 931 p. The official "Officer's Library" account of the Second World War on all fronts, by a number of Soviet military historians. A very useful source for Soviet views. [B]

X74 *Russian Combat Methods in World War II, a Historical Study.* Washington: Department of the Army, 1950. 116 p. (Dept. of Army Pamphlet no. 20-230.) Based directly on interviews in depth and writings by former German generals and other officers with wide experience on the Soviet front, this is a very useful source for the Red Army as seen by their opponent in the field. [B]

X75 *Sbornik materialov po istorii sovetskogo voennogo iskusstva v Velikoi otechestvennoi voine, 1941-1945 gg.* Moscow: Voenizdat, 1956. 510 p. A very useful analytic history of Soviet campaigns of World War II, prepared by the Frunze Academy as a classified text for internal instruction. [B]

X76 *Sbornik materialov po istorii voennogo iskusstva v Velikoi otechestvennoi voine.* Moscow: Voenizdat, 1955. 5 vols. A very valuable history prepared by and for the Voroshilov Academy of the General Staff, classified and not for public issue, hence slightly less propagandistic. [A]

X77 STALIN, IOSIF V. *O Velikoi otechestvennoi voine Sovetskogo Soiuza.* Many editions, Moscow: Gospolitizdat, 1942-50. The "bible" of Soviet historiography on the Soviet role in World War II from 1945 to 1953—collected wartime speeches and orders of the Generalissimus. [B]

X78 TELPUKHOVSKII, B. S. *Velikaia otechestvenaia voina Sovetskogo Soiuza, 1941-1945 gg.* Moscow: Gospolitizdat, 1959. 575 p. A history of the Soviet-German and Soviet-Japanese campaigns of World War II by a Soviet historian colonel.

X79 *Vazhneishie operatsii Velikoi otechestvennoi voiny, 1941-1945 gg.* Moscow: Voenizdat, 1956. 623 p. A useful collection of articles by Soviet military historians on the main Soviet campaigns of the Second World War.

X80 WERTH, ALEXANDER. *Leningrad.* N.Y.: Knopf, 1944. 189 p. A good account of the battle and siege of Leningrad, and its effect on the USSR. By a British journalist.

X81 WERTH, ALEXANDER. *The Year of Stalingrad.* N.Y.: Knopf, 1947. 476 p. A very good report on the USSR during 1942, with fine use of Soviet sources on the military operations of that year, especially at Stalingrad.

4. 1945-1963

X82 BALDWIN, HANSON W. *The Great Arms Race.* N.Y.: Praeger, 1958. 116 p. A brief but incisive review of Soviet (and American) military strength, pointing out the relative advantages and weaknesses of both sides in various weapons systems.

X83 DINERSTEIN, HERBERT S. *The Soviet Military Posture as a Reflection of Soviet Strategy.* Santa Monica, Calif.: Rand Corp., 1958. 22 p. A thoughtful essay on the relationship of possible Soviet strategic attitudes and intentions to the Soviet military forces in recent years.

X84 DINERSTEIN, HERBERT S. *War and the Soviet Union; Nuclear Weapons and the Revolution in Soviet Military and Political Thinking*. N.Y.: Praeger, 1959. 268 p. An interpretation of the effect of differing strategic conceptions attributed by the author to the competing Malenkov and Khrushchev political functions in the 1953-55 period. It makes the point well that apparent strategic differences may but be weapons used in political infighting. [A]

X85 ELIOT, GEORGE F. *If Russia Strikes*. Indianapolis: Bobbs-Merrill, 1949. 252 p. A survey of the military situation of the USSR and the West if war were to occur in 1949, it has fully lost any relevance today that it might have had then.

X86 ELY, LOUIS B. *The Red Army Today*. Harrisburg, Pa.: Military Service, 1949. 256 p. A good account based largely on interrogations of former Soviet and German officers, with attention paid to early post-war developments too. It has, of course, been overtaken by more recent events but remains a useful study. [A]

X87 GARTHOFF, RAYMOND L. *The Role of the Military in Recent Soviet Politics*. Santa Monica, Calif.: RAND Corp., 1956. 86 p. A study surveying in some detail the role of the military leaders in political affairs in the early post-Stalin years.

X88 GARTHOFF, RAYMOND L. *The Soviet Image of a Future War*. Washington: Public Affairs, 1959. 137 p. A brief study of the role of military power in Soviet strategy and of Soviet theory on the role of surprise and of large armies in the nuclear age. Several leading Soviet doctrinal articles are appended in full translation. [B]

X89 GARTHOFF, RAYMOND L. *Soviet Strategy in the Nuclear Age*. N.Y.: Praeger, 1958. 283 p. Praeger paperback, 1960. 283 p. Rev. ed., 1962. 301 p. British ed., London: 1958. German ed., Dusseldorf: 1959. Chinese ed., Taipei: 1958. The most thorough and comprehensive account of Soviet military thinking in the period from 1953 to 1958, which marked the adjustment in the post-Stalin period to the implications of the nuclear age. Also includes discussion of Soviet views on limited war, and views of Western military concepts. [A]

X90 GOURÉ, LEON. *Civil Defense in the Soviet Union*. Foreword by Willard F. Libby. Berkeley: U. of California, 1961. 210 p. The one major book to appear on the problem, this work by a senior staff member of the RAND Corporation is based on first-hand observations in the USSR and on the limited data available in Soviet publications. Its highly debated conclusion is that the Soviet Union has been covertly engaged for ten years in a massive program of civil defense designed to protect its administration, population, and economy against enemy attacks from all types of weapons.

X91 TOKAEV, GRIGORI A. *Stalin Means War*. London: Weidenfield and Nicolson, 1951. 207 p. Recollections of a former Soviet aviation engineer lieutenant colonel who participated in high-level Soviet discussions and actions to acquire former German technical specialists in aviation and rocketry.

X91A U.S. DEPARTMENT OF STATE, BUREAU OF INTELLIGENCE AND RESEARCH, EXTERNAL RESEARCH STAFF. *Soviet Military Doctrine; a List of References to Recent Soviet and Free World Publications on Soviet Military Thought*. Washington: 1963. 39 p.

X92 U.S. DEPARTMENT OF THE ARMY. *Handbook on the Soviet Army*. Washington, D.C.: Dept. of the Army, 1958. 260 p. (Dept. of the Army Pamphlet No. 30-50-1.) An excellent descriptive survey of the Soviet army, its organization, tactics, weapons, and strength. Authoritative and comprehensive. It is not an historical review, but deals with the current state of the Soviet army. [A]

5. AIR AND ROCKET FORCES

X93 BELIKOV, L. A. *Bakteriologicheskoe oruzhie i sposoby zashchity ot nego*. Moscow: Voenizdat, 1960. 197 p. A popular-scientific basic familiarization handbook on the state of the art of bacteriological warfare, and of means of defense against such weapons.

X94 EGOROV, P. T. *Reaktivnoe oruzhie*. Moscow: Voenizdat, 1960. 222 p. This is a volume in the official "Officer's Library" series issued by the Ministry of Defense, presenting a nontechnical familiarization survey of the various classes and categories of missiles and rockets.

X95 GLUSHKO, A. P., MARKOV, L. K. and PILIUGIN, L. P. *Atomnoe oruzhie i protivoatomnaia zashchita*. Moscow: Voenizdat, 1958. 390 p. A basic description of the nature and effects of atomic weapons, and of fundamentals of anti-atomic defense measures. This book is intended for general education of Soviet officers.

X96 KILMARX, ROBERT A. *A History of Soviet Air Power*. N.Y.: Praeger, 1961. 281 p. The published version of a dissertation written at Georgetown University, this well-documented study traces the development of Russian air power from Tsarist days to the missile age. [B]

X97 KRIEGER, F. J. *A Casebook on Soviet Astronautics*. 2 parts. Santa Monica, Calif.: RAND Corp., 1956-1957. Part 1, 244 p. Part 2, 203 p. A collection of Soviet scientific and popular writings on satellites and space travel, only marginally related to possible future military interest in space.

X98 LEE, ASHER. *The Soviet Air Force*. N.Y.: Harper, 1950. 207 p. Rev. ed., N.Y.: John Day, 1962. 288 p. A good historical review of the development of the Soviet air forces and of Soviet aviation in general. Not documented, but generally accurate and sound. The revised edition is much more useful. [B]

X99 LEE, ASHER, ed. *The Soviet Air and Rocket Forces*. N.Y.: Praeger, 1959. 311 p. London: 1959. 311 p. A collective volume by a number of Western students of Soviet aviation and military affairs. It is best on general development of aviation and air weapons, and on the Soviet air forces as an institution, and weak on missiles and on current and future strategy. In all, the best collection on the subject. [A]

X100 LIAPUNOV, B. V. *Upravliaemye snariady*. Moscow: Voenizdat, 1956. 136 p. A general familiarization survey of different categories of missile weapon systems, for Soviet officers. There is no discussion of Soviet missiles, but rather of Western ones and the general state of the art.

X101 MOSKOVSKII, V. P. *Voenno-vozdushnye sily Sovetskogo Soiuza; kratkii ocherk*. Moscow: Voennoe izd., 1950. 133 p. A popularized Soviet account of the general history of the Soviet air forces and their composition.

X102 NEIMAN, M. B., and SADILENKO, K. M. *Termoiadernoe oruzhie*. Moscow: Voenizdat, 1958. 237 p. The basic work describing in popular terms for Soviet officers the fundamentals of fusion weapons. Basic defensive measures against atomic and hydrogen weapons are also discussed.

X103 NIKOLAEV, M. N. *Snariad protiv snariada*. Moscow: Voenizdat, 1960. 147 p. The first Soviet published work to examine antimissile missiles. It is framed exclusively in terms of the state of the art, on the basis of published Western data and discussion.

X104 *Novoe v voennoi tekhnike*. Moscow: Voenizdat, 1958. 475 p. A very useful and comprehensive compilation of articles from the Soviet military press on the military application of many fields of science and technology, arranged to show the effect on the ground forces, air forces, navy and air defense forces. [B]

X105 PARRY, ALBERT. *Russia's Rockets and Missiles*. N.Y.: Doubleday, 1960. 382 p. An interesting popularized account of Russian and Soviet interest in, and development of, rocketry and space flight. It is not documented, and the parts on military applications are weak and frequently in error.

X106 PETROV, V. P. *Upravliaemye snariady i rakety*. Moscow: DOSAAF, 1957. 119 p. A general account of the nature of missile weapon systems, and basic principles of rocketry.

X107 POKROVSKY, G. I. *Science and Technology in Contemporary War*. Trans. and annotated by R. L. Garthoff. N.Y.: Praeger, 1959. 180 p. An annotated translation of a book and two pamphlets by a Soviet technical general surveying the role of various fields of science in contemporary weaponry and warfare. [B]

X108 SHIPILOV, I. F., ed. *Aviatsiia nashei rodiny*. Moscow: Voenizdat, 1955. 566 p. A useful collection of articles from the official Soviet air force journal on the development of Soviet aviation, and its operations in World War II. [B]

X109 SIMAKOV, B. A., and SHIPILOV, I. F. *Vozdushnyi flot strany sovetov*. Moscow: Voenizdat, 1958. 485 p. A useful historical account of the development of Soviet military and civil aviation, with particular emphasis on the 1930's.

X110 *Sovremennaia voennaia tekhnika*. Moscow: Voenizdat, 1957. 276 p. A useful compilation of articles from the Soviet military press on the military applications of many fields of science and technology, including nuclear physics, electronics, rocketry, and radar.

X111 *Sredstva i sposoby zashchity ot atomnogo oruzhiia*. Moscow: Voenizdat, 1956. 125 p. A collection of articles on various aspects of atomic weapon effects, and of defensive measures against nuclear weapons.

X112 STOCKWELL, RICHARD E. *Soviet Air Power*. N.Y.: Pageant, 1956. 238 p. An attempt to survey many aspects of Soviet military air power, with much detail. Unfortunately, there are many serious errors, and since the sources of information are not indicated, the reader cannot evaluate the remaining information.

X113 *Uchebnoe posobie po MPVO*. Moscow: DOSAAF, 1956. 223 p. A basic civil defense handbook, written for local civil defense officials and for basic civil defense courses for the population. A good indicator of the level of civil defense instruction in the USSR.

X114 U.S. LIBRARY OF CONGRESS, REFERENCE DEPARTMENT. *Aeronautical Sciences and Aviation in the Soviet Union, a Bibliography*. Comp. by Bertha Kucherov. Washington: 1955. 274 p. Contains an incomplete listing of some materials on military aviation, but the chief value of this work is the very extensive coverage of materials on basic aeronautics published in the USSR.

X115 *Voenno-vozdushnye sily*. Moscow: Voenizdat, 1959. 203 p. This volume in the "Officer's Library" is devoted to an exposition of the general background, history, role, and weapons of military air forces.

X116 *Voiska protivovozdushnoi oborony strany*. Moscow: Voenizdat, 1960. 218 p. A volume in the "Officer's Library" devoted to a general exposition of the history, role, weapons and means, and combat record of air defense forces. Particular reference is made to the history of Soviet air defense forces, but the study is general in nature.

X117 *Zashchita naseleniia ot sovremennykh sredstv porazheniia*. Moscow: DOSAAF, 1958. 335 p. A revised basic handbook on civil defense preparation written for local civil defense officials.

6. NAVY

X118 *Deistviia voenno-morskogo flota v Velikoi otechestvennoi voine*. Moscow: Voenizdat, 1956. 420 p. The best Soviet account of the operations of the Soviet Navy in World War II. A collection of articles originally appearing in the Soviet military press. [B]

X119 HUCUL, WALTER C. "The Evolution of Russian and Soviet Sea Power, 1853-1953." Ph.D. dissertation, U. of California (Berkeley), 1954.

X120 ISAKOV, IVAN S. *The Red Fleet in the Second World War*. London: Hutchinson, 1947. 124 p. A history of the operations of the Soviet Navy in World War II, by the former naval commander-in-chief. It is not a detailed account, but it does trace the main activities.

X121 *Istoriia voenno-morskogo iskusstva*. Moscow: Voenizdat, 1953. 3 vols. An official publication of the Naval Main Staff, surveying world naval history and general naval affairs; intended for instruction in naval schools.

X122 KORNIENKO, D. I. *Flot nashei rodiny*. Moscow: Voenizdat, 1957. 454 p. A general history of the Russian and Soviet navies, with about half the volume dealing with the Soviet period.

X123 KORNIENKO, D. I. and MILGRAM, N. *Voenno-morskoi flot sovetskoi sotsialisticheskoi dershavy*. Moscow: Voenizdat, 1950. 480 p. A general account of the development of the Soviet navy through World War II.

X124 MEISTER, J., "Soviet Sea Power," *The Navy* (Great Britain). 12 parts. Vol. 62, nos. 6-12, and vol. 63, nos. 1-6, (June 1957–June

1958). A useful series of articles with much information on many aspects of Soviet naval affairs, though in many cases the accuracy of the information cannot be judged.

X125 MITCHELL, MAIRIN. *The Maritime History of Russia, 848-1948.* London: Sidgwick and Jackson, 1949. 543 p. A long discursive history of a millennium of growth of Russian maritime affairs, including a number of useful chapters on the prewar development of the Soviet navy.

X126 NEVSKII, N. A. *Voenno-morskoi flot.* Moscow: Voenizdat, 1959. 328 p. The most current and comprehensive Soviet account of naval affairs in general, with special references to the Soviet navy. It covers categories of ships and weapons (including nuclear weapons), organization, and tactics. A volume in the "Officer's Library" series.

X127 SAUNDERS, M. G. (COMMANDER), ed. *The Soviet Navy.* London: Weidenfeld & Nicolson, 1958. 340 p. A collective, comprehensive work on the Soviet Navy by a number of Western specialists. There is relatively little historical background and the work is focused on the postwar naval establishment. It is uneven in treatment, and weak on naval doctrine, but on balance the best general survey available. [A]

X128 SHMAKOV, N. A. *Osnovy voenno-morskogo dela.* Moscow: Voenizdat, 1947. 352 p. A popular introductory survey of fundamentals of naval affairs, with some particular reference to the Soviet Navy but not primarily descriptive of the Soviet establishment.

7. MILITARY PERIODICALS

X129 INSTITUT ZUR ERFORSCHUNG DER UDSSR. *Bulletin.* Munich, April 1954–. A monthly publication which frequently has good articles on Soviet military affairs by N. Galay, I. Baritz, and others.

X130 *Kommunist Vooruzhennykh sil SSSR.* Moscow, 1960–. A bimonthly publication of the Chief Political Administration of the Soviet Armed Forces. Contains useful material on political indoctrination and on military doctrine.

X131 *Krasnaia zvezda.* Moscow, 1925–. Daily newspaper published by the Chief Political Administration of the Ministry of Defense. In 1960, it absorbed the previously published air force and naval papers.

X132 *Morskoi sbornik.* Moscow, 1917–. The monthly naval journal.

X132A *Vestnik protivo-vozdushnoi oborony.* Moscow: Voenizdat, 1929-1941 and 1958–. Monthly publication of the Air Defense Forces.

X133 *Voennaia mysl.* Moscow: Voenizdat, 1937–. Monthly (1938–) classified periodical of the ministry of Defense, not publicly available in recent years. Military, theoretical, doctrinal, strategic, and historical subjects. [A]

X134 *Voenno-istoricheskii zhurnal.* Moscow: Voenizdat, 1959–. Useful military-historical analysis comparatively free of propaganda. Published monthly. [A]

X135 *Voenno-vozdushnyi flot* (since 1962 titled *Aviatsiia i kosmonavtika*). Moscow: Voenizdat, 1917–. Monthly magazine of the Soviet air forces.

X136 *Voennyi vestnik.* Moscow: Voenizdat, 1921–. Monthly. Chief journal of the Soviet ground forces. In 1960 it absorbed the separate publications of the various arms of the ground forces.

Addenda

X137 CARELL, PAUL. *Hitler Moves East: 1941-1943.* Boston: Little, Brown, 1965. 640 p. A good detailed account.

X138 CLARK, ALAN. *Barbarossa: The Russian-German Conflict, 1941-1945.* N.Y.: Morrow, 1965. 576 p. A fairly comprehensive account.

X139 GRECHKO, ANDREI A., ed. *Iadernyi vek i voina.* Moscow: Izvestiia, 1964. 158 p. Collected articles on Soviet military doctrine in the nuclear age. [B]

X140 KRAVCHENKO, G. S. *Voennaia ekonomika SSSR, 1941-1945.* Moscow: Voenizdat, 1963. 398 p.

X141 *Problemy revoliutsii v voennom dele.* Moscow: Voenizdat, 1965. 195 p. Collected articles on the revolution in military affairs and Soviet military doctrine. [B]

X142 PROKOPEV, N. P. *O voine i armii.* Moscow: Voenizdat, 1965. 264 p. A study of Soviet military doctrine. [B]

X143 SHIFMAN, M. S. *Voina i ekonomika.* Moscow: Voenizdat, 1964. 207 p. A study of the influence of economics.

X144 *Velikaia otechestvennaia voina Sovetskogo Soiuza, 1941-1945.* Moscow: Kniga, 1965. 250 p. The most complete bibliography of Soviet works on World War II.

X145 WERTH, ALEXANDER. *Russia at War, 1941-1945.* N.Y.: Dutton, 1964. 1100 p. A very good popular history. [A]

Y. Espionage

EDITED BY ROBERT M. SLUSSER

Y1 AGABEKOV, GRIGORII S. *Ch.K. za rabotoi.* Berlin: "Strela," 1931. 334 p. German ed., Stuttgart: Union Deutsche Verlagsgesellschaft, 1932. 207 p. One of the earliest and most important accounts by a Soviet defector. The German edition incorporates material not in the original and omits some passages. [A]

Y2 AGABEKOV, GRIGORII S. *G.P.U.: zapiski chekista.* Berlin: "Strela," 1930. 247 p. Italian ed., Milan: S. a. Fratelli Treves, 1932. 312 p. Parallel to but not identical with the author's *Ch. K. za rabotoi.*

Y3 AGABEKOV, GRIGORII S. *OGPU, the Russian Secret Terror.* N.Y.: Brentano, 1931. 277 p. Translated from French; inaccurate and incomplete.

Y4 AGABEKOV, GRIGORII S. "Memoirs," *Le Matin* (Paris), Oct. 26-30, Nov. 4, 1930.

Y5 ALEXEEV, K. M. "Why I Deserted the Soviets." *Saturday Evening Post*, June 29, July 3, July 10, 1948. The author was employed in the Soviet Embassy in Mexico City.

Y6 ALLARD, PAUL. *La Guerre des espions.* Paris: Flammarion, 1936. 246 p. A popular account of espionage in France, including Soviet espionage, allegedly based on information from French military intelligence.

Y7 ATHOLL, JUSTIN. *How Stalin Knows; The Story of the Great Atomic Spy Conspiracy.* Norwich, England: Jarrold, 1951. 181 p.

Y8 AUSTRALIA, ROYAL COMMISSION ON ESPIONAGE. *Official Transcript of Proceedings, May 17, 1954–March 31, 1955.* Sydney. 126 p. Hearings in the Petrov case.

Y9 AUSTRALIA, ROYAL COMMISSION ON ESPIONAGE. *Report.* Sydney: Pettifer, 1955. 483 p. Official investigation of the case of Col. Petrov and his wife, Soviet spies in the Soviet Embassy in Canberra who defected and received asylum. [A]

Y10 BAILEY, GEOFFREY (pseud.). *The Conspirators.* N.Y.: Harper, 1960. 306 p. An attempt to unravel the background of the purges, based on extensive evidence, some of it unpublished, but weakened by the acceptance of unverified data. Much on Soviet infiltration of White Russian émigré organizations and the Tukhachevsky case. Good bibliography.

Y11 BARMINE, ALEXANDER. *One Who Survived; The Life Story of a Russian under the Soviets.* Intro. by Max Eastman. N.Y.: Putnam, 1945. 337 p. A valuable first-hand account by an intelligent former Soviet diplomat. [B]

Y12 BAZHANOV, BORIS, and ALEKSEEV, N., eds. *Pokhishchenie Generala A. P. Kutepova bolshevikami; sledstvennye i politicheskie materialy.* Paris: 1930. 63 p. French ed., *L'Enlèvement du Général Koutiépoff.* Paris: Spes, 1930. The background of the kidnapping by Soviet agents of a White Russian émigré leader. Bazhanov was a former personal secretary of Stalin.

Y13 BENTLEY, ELIZABETH. *Out of Bondage.* N.Y.: Devin-Adair; London: Hart-Davis, 1951. 256 p. Personal account by an American woman recruited by Soviet espionage.

Y14 BERNHARDSSON, CARL O. *Spionpolisen, går på Jakt.* Stockholm: Natur och kultur, 1952. 611 p. Espionage in Sweden.

Y15 BESEDOVSKI, GRIGORII Z. *Na putiakh k Termidoru: iz vospominanii byvshego sovetskogo diplomata.* Paris: "Mishen," 1930-31. 2 vols. English ed., *Revelations of a Soviet Diplomat.* London: Williams and Norgate, 1931. 276 p. (Translations, with omissions and additions, also published in German, French, and Japanese.) One of the most baffling accounts in defector literature. The original manuscript contained first-hand observations of value on the author's experiences as a minor Soviet diplomat in Poland and Japan; subsequent editions and translations were progressively adulterated with increasingly sensational and unfounded statements.

Y16 BIALOGUSKI, MICHAEL. *The Case of Colonel Petrov.* N.Y.: McGraw-Hill, 1955. 238 p. British ed., *The Petrov Story*, London: Heinemann, 1955. By the man who claimed to have arranged the defection of the Petrovs in Australia. The story was also serialized in the *Saturday Evening Post.* (See above: Australia, Royal Commission.)

Y17 BOURCART, J.R.D. *L'Espionnage soviétique.* Paris: Fayard, 1962. 316 p. A rapid survey of developments from 1920 to 1960, based on published material.

Y18 BUDENZ, LOUIS F. *Men without Faces; the Communist Conspiracy in the U.S.A.* N.Y.: Harper, 1950. 305 p. By a former American Communist who was at one time editor of the *Daily Worker.*

Y19 BULLOCH, JOHN, and MILLER, HENRY. *Spy Ring; the Full Story of the Naval Secrets Case.* London, Secker and Warburg, 1961. 224 p.

Y20 BURNHAM, JAMES. *The Web of Subversion; Underground Networks in the U.S. Government.* N.Y.: Day, 1954. 248 p. Based on official government testimony.

Y21 BURTSEV, VLADIMIR L. *Bolshevistskie gangstery v Parizhe; pokhishchenie Generala Millera i Generala Kutepova.* Paris: Izdanie avtora, 1939. 103 p. Background of the kidnapping of two White Generals by Soviet agents; the author was a prominent anti-Bolshevik revolutionary.

Y22 CANADA, ROYAL COMMISSION TO INVESTIGATE DISCLOSURES OF SECRET AND CONFIDENTIAL INFORMATION TO UNAUTHORIZED PERSONS. *The Report of the Royal Commission. . . .* Ottawa: E. Cloutier, 1946. 733 p. French ed., Ottawa, 1946. Official report in the atomic espionage case which was broken by the defection of Igor Gouzenko. [A]

Y23 CHAMBERS, WHITTAKER. *Witness.* N.Y.: Random House, 1952. 808 p. Longwinded but psychologically valuable account of the personal background of a confessed former Communist agent in the U.S.

Y24 COOKE, ALISTAIR. *A Generation on Trial; USA v. Alger Hiss.* N.Y.: Knopf, 1950. 342 p. An account by the American correspondent for the Manchester *Guardian.*

Y25 COOKRIDGE, E. H. (pseud. of Edward Spiro). *The Net That Covers the World.* N.Y.: Holt, 1955. 315 p. British ed., *Soviet Spy Net.* London: Muller, 1955. 264 p. German ed., Hanover, 1956. Undocumented and often unverifiable.

Y26 DALLIN, DAVID J. *Soviet Espionage.* New Haven: Yale, 1955. 558 p. A sober and conscientious study, based on extensive study of published and unpublished material. Given the nature of the subject, no book can hope to be either exhaustive or definitive, but this one comes closer than any other. [A]

Y27 DE GRAMONT, SANCHE. *The Secret War; the Story of International Espionage Since World War II.* N.Y.: Putnam, 1962. 515 p. A careful, authoritative study of both Soviet and American espionage by a Pulitzer Prize winning correspondent for the New York *Herald Tribune.*

Y28 DERIABIN, PETER, and GIBNEY, FRANK. *The Secret World.* N.Y.: Doubleday, 1960. 334 p. One of the best accounts by a Soviet defector, particularly good on espionage training and postwar espionage in the West. Deriabin was a member of the Kremlin guard and later on was espionage chief working out of the Soviet Embassy in Vienna, whence he fled to the West. See also his testimony before the U.S. Congress, House Committee on Un-American Activities (below). [B]

Y29 DE TOLEDANO, RALPH. *Spies, Dupes and Diplomats.* N.Y.: Duell, Sloan & Pearce. 1952. 244 p. The Sorge case, the Amerasia case, etc., by an American journalist.

Y30 DE TOLEDANO, RALPH, and LASKY, VICTOR. *Seeds of Treason; the True Story of the Hiss-Chambers Tragedy.* N.Y.: Funk and Wagnalls, 1950. 270 p. A somewhat sensationalized version by two American journalists.

Y31 DEWAR, HUGO. *Assassins at Large; Being a Fully Documented and Hitherto Unpublished Account of the Executions Outside Russia Ordered by the GPU.* London: Wingate, 1951; Boston: Beacon, 1952. 203 p. Contains a dozen case studies, including the assassination of Trotsky in Mexico, as well as material on the GPU. Concentrates on the period before 1939. [B]

Y32 DRIBERG, TOM. *Guy Burgess; a Portrait with Background.* London: Weidenfeld and Nicolson, 1956. 123 p. Background of a British diplomat who defected to the USSR with his friend MacLean, after supplying the Soviets with secret information.

Y33 DUMBADZE, EVGENII V. *Na sluzhbie Cheka i Kominterna; Lichnyia vospomonaniia.* With introductory article by V. L. Burtsev. Paris: "Mishen," 1930. 159 p. By a former agent of the Soviet secret police who transferred to Comintern activity around 1923, this work contains useful information on the relationship of the OGPU and the Comintern apparatus, especially with respect to the latter's activity in Turkey.

Y34 ESSAD-BEY (pseud. of Leo Noussimbaum). *G.P.U., Die Verschwörung gegen die Welt.* Berlin: Etthofen, 1932. 359 p. British ed., *Secrets of the O.G.P.U., the Plot against the World.* London: Jarrolds, 1933. American ed., *OGPU: The Plot against the World.* N.Y.: Viking, 1933. 301 p. French ed., Paris: Payot, 1934. 297 p. Spanish ed., 1935. Uncritical and unsystematic, with many errors of fact, but useful for its references to scarce early materials, and often penetrating in its analysis.

Y35 EVANS, MEDFORD. *Secret War for the A-Bomb.* Chicago: Regnery, 1953. 302 p. An undocumented story of Soviet atomic espionage in the American community of atomic physicists.

Y36 FALKENSTAM, CURT. *Röd spion; En Skildring av den farligaste spionaffär som avslöjats i vårt land.* Stockholm: Geber, 1951. 90 p.

Y37 FLICKE, WILHELM F. *Agenten funken nach Moskau; sowjetrussische Spionagegruppe "Rote Drei."* Munich: Welsermühl, 1958. 420 p.

Y38 FLICKE, WILHELM F. *Die rote Kapelle.* Hilden am Rhein: Vier-Brücken, 1949. 377 p. An account of one of the most famous Soviet spy networks, operating in Germany and Switzerland in World War II. [B]

Y39 FOOTE, ALEXANDER (pseud.). *Handbook for Spies.* N.Y.: Doubleday; London: Museum, 1949. 223 p. French ed., Paris: Editions de la Paix, 1951. The author was a member of the *Rote Kapelle*, a Soviet spy network in Germany and Switzerland during World War II. [B]

Y40 FOOTE, ALEXANDER (pseud.). *Soviet Military Intelligence; Comments on the Book, "Handbook for Spies."* Santa Monica, Cal.: RAND Corp., 1949. 30 p. The author provides supplementary data on his book.

Y41 FRONTENAC, ARTHUR. *Gisel contre Gilda, deux armes secrètes en lutte dans la prochaine guerre.* Paris: Éditions internationales, 1948. 236 p.

Y42 GARTHOFF, RAYMOND L. *Soviet Military Doctrine.* Glencoe, Illinois: Free Press, 1953. 587 p. British ed., *How Russia Makes War.* London: Allen & Unwin, 1954. Contains a brief section (p. 258-62) on Soviet military espionage.

Y43 GOUZENKO, IGOR. *The Iron Curtain.* N.Y.: Dutton, 1948. 279 p. British ed., *This Was My Choice.* London: Eyre & Spottiswoode, 1948. By the Soviet code clerk whose defection in 1946 broke the Soviet atomic espionage ring in Canada. [B]

Y44 GRANOVSKY, ANATOLI. *All Pity Choked; The Memoirs of a Soviet Secret Agent.* London: Kimber, 1955. 248 p. American ed., *I Was an NKVD Agent; a Top Secret Soviet Spy Tells His Story.* N.Y.: Devin-Adair, 1962. 343 p. A defector from the Soviet secret police who worked in Czechoslovakia and Germany describes his experiences.

Y45 HEILBRUNN, OTTO. *The Soviet Secret Services.* N.Y.: Praeger, 1956. 216 p. Concerns military intelligence and reconnaissance rather than espionage.

Y46 HIRSCH, RICHARD. *The Soviet Spies; the Story of Russian Espionage in North America.* N.Y.: Duell, Sloan and Pearce; London: N. Kaye, 1947. 164 p. French ed., *Espionnage atomique.* Paris: Selft. A summary of the evidence from the Canadian spy investigation.

Y47 HISS, ALGER. *In the Court of Public Opinion.* N.Y.: Knopf, 1957. 424 p. Hiss's own defense, which still leaves many questions unanswered.

Y48 HOOVER, JOHN EDGAR. *Masters of Deceit; the Story of Communism in America and How to Fight It.* N.Y.: Holt, 1958. 374 p. Paperback ed., N.Y.: Pocket Books, 1959. 352 p. By the head of the F.B.I.

Y49 HUTTON, J. BERNARD. *School for Spies; The ABC of How Russia's Secret Service Operates.* London: Spearman, 1961. 222 p. N.Y.: Coward McCann, 1962. Description of Soviet training techniques for espionage, based on observations, 1934-38, when the author, as a Czech Communist journalist in Moscow, received spy training. [B]

Y50 JORDAN, GEORGE, with STOKES, RICHARD L. *From Major Jordan's Diaries.* N.Y.: Harcourt Brace, 1952. 284 p. The author, a Lend-Lease expediter, 1942-44, reports wartime observations of the shipment of materials needed for the production of atomic energy to the Soviet Union.

Y51 JOWITT, WILLIAM A. J. (EARL). *The Strange Case of Alger Hiss.* Garden City, N.Y.: Doubleday, 1953. 380 p. A distinguished British jurist examines the evidence and concludes that Hiss was not guilty.

Y52 KALEDIN, VICTOR K. *The Moscow-Berlin Secret Services.* London: Hurst and Blackett, 1940. 263 p. Unreliable, sensational, anti-Semitic, and pornographic.

Y52A KAZNACHEEV, ALEKSANDR. *Inside a Soviet Embassy: Experiences of a Russian Diplomat in Burma.* Ed. with an introduction by Simon Wolin. Philadelphia: Lippincott, 1962. 250 p. A powerful analysis of Soviet espionage in Southeast Asia, based on the author's personal experiences. See also Y97.

Y53 KHOKHLOV, NIKOLAI E. *In the Name of Conscience.* N.Y.: McKay, 1960. 365 p. The author claims to have been trained as a Soviet saboteur and assassin. He defected in West Germany, stating that he refused to carry out his assignment to kill a Russian émigré leader. A sensational and not entirely convincing account.

Y54 KLIMOV, GREGORY. *The Terror Machine.* N.Y.: Praeger, 1955. German ed., *Berliner Kreml.* Berlin: n.d. A well-placed and intelligent young Soviet official on Soviet postwar policy in Germany, including espionage. Originally serialized in *Possev* (Limburg/Lahn) under the title "Berlinskii Kreml."

Y55 KRIVITSKY, WALTER (pseud. of Samuel Ginsberg). *In Stalin's Secret Service; An Exposé of Russia's Secret Policies by the Former Chief of the Soviet Intelligence in Western Europe.* N.Y.: Harper, 1939. 273 p. British ed., *I was Stalin's Agent.* London: Hamilton, 1939. Spanish ed., Madrid: 1947. German ed., Amsterdam: 1940. An honest and straightforward account of Soviet intelligence activities, with special reference to Spain during the Civil War, by a high-ranking defector. [A]

Y56 LAPORTE, MAURICE. *Espions rouges; les dessous de l'espionnage soviétique en France.* Paris: A. Redier, 1929. 247 p. By a former French Communist.

Y57 LEVINE, ISAAC DON. *The Mind of an Assassin.* N.Y.: Farrar, Straus & Cudahy, 1959. 232 p. The story of the most famous of the N.K.V.D. assassins, Ramon Mercader, the man who killed Trotsky in Mexico in 1940.

Y58 LIDDELL HART, B. H., ed. *The Red Army: The Red Army, 1918 to 1945, The Soviet Army, 1946 to the Present.* N.Y.: Harcourt Brace, 1956. 480 p. British ed., *The Soviet Army.* London: Weidenfeld and Nicolson, 1956. 480 p. See Chapter 23, "The Soviet Intelligence Services," by Dr. Raymond L. Garthoff, an American scholar.

Y59 MASSING, HEDE. *This Deception.* N.Y.: Duell, Sloan and Pearce, 1951. 335 p. Describes personal acquaintance with Soviet espionage procedures.

Y60 MEISSNER, HANS OTTO. *The Man with Three Faces.* N.Y.: Rinehart; London: Evans, 1955. 243 p. Background of the Sorge spy ring in Japan.

Y61 MENNEVÉE, ROGER. "Les Services secrets soviétiques," *Les Documents politiques, diplomatiques et financiers*, Paris (May 1956-Nov. 1957). Comprehensive but uncritical and disorganized.

Y62 MEURLING, PAR. *Spionage och sabotage i Sverige.* Stockholm: Lindfors, 1952. 443 p.

Y63 MOOREHEAD, ALAN. *The Traitors.* N.Y.: Scribners, 1952. 222 p. A popularized account of international espionage.

Y64 MORROS, BORIS. *My Ten Years as a Counterspy.* As told to Charles Samuels. N.Y.: Viking, 1959. 248 p. Paperback ed., N.Y.: Dell, 1959. Provides some useful information on the author's contacts in the Soviet espionage apparatus. He served as a double agent for U.S. intelligence, 1947-57. [B]

Y65 MURRAY, NORA. *I Spied for Stalin.* N.Y.: Funk, 1951. 256 p. The author, daughter of V. S. Korzhenko, an Old Chekist, provides invaluable information on the organization of Soviet intelligence up to 1939. [B]

Y66 NEWMAN, BERNARD C. *The Red Spider Web; the Story of Spying in Canada.* London: Latimer House, 1947. 254 p. A popular account of the atomic espionage case.

Y67 NEWMAN, BERNARD C. *The Sosnowski Affair; Inquest on a Spy.* London: Laurie, 1954. 203 p.

Y68 NEWMAN, BERNARD C. *Soviet Atomic Spies.* London: Robert Hale, 1952. 239 p. An examination of the Soviet espionage apparatus and its quest for atom secrets, based largely on the press and secondary sources.

Y69 NOEL-BAKER, FRANCIS. *The Spy Web; A Study of Communist Espionage.* London: Batchworth, 1954; N.Y.: Vanguard, 1955. 242 p. An account of Soviet spy networks in Canada, Greece, Japan, and Sweden, based on confidential sources.

Y70 ORLOV, ALEXANDER (pseud.). *The Secret History of Stalin's Crimes.* N.Y.: Random House, 1953. 366 p. By a high-ranking Soviet intelligence officer who defected while in Spain during the Civil War. Concerned mainly with the background of the purges, but provides information on espionage as well. [B]

Y71 PETROV, VLADIMIR M. and EVDOKIA. *Empire of Fear.* London: Deutsch; N.Y.: Praeger, 1956. 351 p. Col. and Mrs. Petrov operated a spy network in Australia until their defection in 1954. Straightforward and reliable. (See above: Australia, Royal Commission.) [B]

Y72 PILAT, OLIVER R. *The Atom Spies.* N.Y.: Putnam, 1952. 312 p. A description of the cases of Alan Nunn May and Klaus Fuchs from both British and American angles.

Y73 RASTVOROV, YURI A. "Red Fraud and Intrigue in the Far East." *Life*, Nov. 29, Dec. 6 and 13, 1954. By one of the most important Soviet intelligence defectors from the Far East. Mr. Rastvorov also appeared before a subcommittee of the Committee on the Judiciary of the U.S. Senate in 1956. His testimony is included in the series entitled *Scope of Soviet Activity in the United States* (see below Y95). [B]

Y74 REINHARDT, GUENTHER. *Crime Without Punishment; the Secret Soviet Terror Against America.* N.Y.: Hermitage, 1952. 322 p. A former FBI counter-intelligence agent describes Soviet secret police activities, with emphasis on assassinations.

Y75 RÉZANOV, A. *Le Travail secret des agents bolchevistes, exposé d'après des documents authentiques émanant des Bolcheviks.* Paris: Bossard, 1926. 199 p.

Y76 ROEDER, MANFRED. *Die Rote Kapelle.* Hamburg: Siep, 1952. Concerning one of the most famous Soviet spy networks during World War II, which sent crucial information about Germany to the Russians.

Y77 SERGE, VICTOR (pseud. of V. L. Kibalchich), ROSMER, A., and WULLENS, MAURICE. *L'Assassinat politique et l'U.R.S.S.; crime à Lausanne en marge des procès de Moscou (la mort d'Ignace Reiss).* Paris: Tisné, 1938. 94 p. Evidence on the assassination of a Soviet spy.

Y78 SINEVIRSKII, NIKOLAI. *Smersh.* N.Y.: Holt, 1950. 253 p. An inside account of the wartime espionage network in the Red Army.

Y79 TIETJEN, ARTHUR. *Soviet Spy Ring.* N.Y.: Coward McCann, 1961. 190 p. Background of the British naval secrets case.

Y80 TIGERSTEDT, ORNULF. *Statspolisen slår till: Kampen mot Sovjetspionaget i Finland 1919-1938.* Stockholm: Fahlcrantz and Gumaelius, 1942. 329 p. Soviet espionage in Finland.

Y81 TRILLING, LIONEL. *The Middle of the Journey.* N.Y.: Viking, 1947. 310 p. Fiction, but based on an accurate and sensitive perception of the psychological and sociological background of the Hiss-Chambers case.

Y82 U.S. CONGRESS, HOUSE, COMMITTEE ON UN-AMERICAN ACTIVITIES. *Communist Espionage in the U.S.; Testimony of F. Tisler, Former Military and Air Attaché, Czechoslovak Embassy in Washington, D. C.* Washington: G.P.O., 1960. 9 p.

Y83 U.S. CONGRESS, HOUSE, COMMITTEE ON UN-AMERICAN ACTIVITIES. *Hearings Regarding Communist Espionage in the United States Government.* Washington: G.P.O., 1948. 2 vols.

Y84 U.S. CONGRESS, HOUSE, COMMITTEE ON UN-AMERICAN ACTIVITIES. *Hearings Regarding Communist Infiltration of Radiation Laboratory and Atomic Bomb Project at the University of California, Berkeley, California.* Washington: G.P.O., 1949-51. 3 vols.

Y85 U.S. CONGRESS, HOUSE, COMMITTEE ON UN-AMERICAN ACTIVITIES. *Investigation of Soviet Espionage.* Washington: G.P.O., 1957-58. 2 parts.

Y86 U.S. CONGRESS, HOUSE, COMMITTEE ON UN-AMERICAN ACTIVITIES. *The Kremlin's Espionage and Terror Organizations; Testimony of P. S. Deriabin, Former Officer of the USSR's Committee of State Security (KGB).* Washington: G.P.O., 1959. 16 p.

Y87 U.S. CONGRESS, HOUSE, COMMITTEE ON UN-AMERICAN ACTIVITIES. *Patterns of Communist Espionage*. Washington: G.P.O., 1958. 81 p.

Y88 U.S. CONGRESS, HOUSE, COMMITTEE ON UN-AMERICAN ACTIVITIES. *The Shameful Years: Thirty Years of Soviet Espionage in the United States*. Washington: G.P.O., 1951. 70 p.

Y89 U.S. CONGRESS, JOINT COMMITTEE ON ATOMIC ENERGY. *Soviet Atomic Espionage*. Washington: G.P.O., 1951. 222 p. With special reference to the cases of Fuchs, Pontecorvo, May, Greenglass, and Gold.

Y90 U.S. CONGRESS, SENATE, COMMITTEE ON THE JUDICIARY. *Activities of Soviet Secret Service*. Washington: G.P.O., 1954. 48 p.

Y91 U.S. CONGRESS, SENATE, COMMITTEE ON THE JUDICIARY. *Espionage Activities of Personnel Attached to Embassies and Consulates under Soviet Domination in the U.S*. Washington: G.P.O., 1951-52. 52 p.

Y92 U.S. CONGRESS, SENATE, COMMITTEE ON THE JUDICIARY. *Interlocking Subversion in Government Departments*. Washington: G.P.O., 1953-55. 30 parts.

Y93 U.S. CONGRESS, SENATE, COMMITTEE ON THE JUDICIARY. *Internal Security Annual Report for 1957*. Washington: G.P.O., 1958. 363 p.

Y94 U.S. CONGRESS, SENATE, COMMITTEE ON THE JUDICIARY. *Report of the Subcommittee to Investigate the Administration of the Internal Security Act and other Internal Security Laws for the Year 1956*. Washington: G.P.O., 1957. 338 p.

Y95 U.S. CONGRESS, SENATE, COMMITTEE ON THE JUDICIARY. *Scope of Soviet Activity in the United States*. Washington: G.P.O., 1956-57. 90 parts.

Y96 U.S. CONGRESS, SENATE, COMMITTEE ON THE JUDICIARY. *Soviet Espionage through Poland*. Washington: G.P.O., 1960.

Y97 U.S. CONGRESS, SENATE, COMMITTEE ON THE JUDICIARY. *Soviet Intelligence in Asia; Testimony of A. Y. Kasnakhayev*. Washington: G.P.O., 1959. 25 p. See also Y52A.

Y98 U.S. CONGRESS, SENATE, COMMITTEE ON THE JUDICIARY. *Strategy and Tactics of World Communism; Recruiting for Espionage*. Washington: G.P.O., 1954-56. 17 parts.

Y99 U.S. FEDERAL BUREAU OF INVESTIGATION. *Exposé of Soviet Espionage.* Washington: G.P.O., 1960. 63 p.

Y100 VALTIN, JAN (pseud. of Richard J. H. Krebs). *Out of the Night.* N.Y.: Alliance Books, two versions, 749 p. and 841 p.; London: W. Heinemann, 1941. 658 p. By a German-born Soviet intelligence agent. Essential background for Soviet espionage in Germany and the West. [B]

Y101 WALTARI, MIKA TOIMI. *I sovjetspionagets skugga.* Stockholm: Fahlcrants, 1942. 232 p. Soviet espionage in Finland.

Y102 WEXLEY, JOHN. *The Judgment of Julius and Ethel Rosenberg.* London: Bookville, 1956. 627 p. An account of the American atom spies.

Y103 WHITE, JOHN B. *Pattern for Conquest.* London: R. Hale, 1956. 223 p. An examination of Communist-directed espionage activities in the years since World War II.

Y104 WHITE, JOHN B. *The Soviet Spy System.* London: Falcon, 1948. 133 p. An account of the Canadian atomic spy case, based on the findings of the Royal Commission.

Y105 WILLOUGHBY, CHARLES A. (MAJOR GENERAL). *Shanghai Conspiracy: the Sorge Spy Ring, Moscow, Shanghai, Tokyo, San Francisco, New York.* Preface by Gen. Douglas MacArthur. N.Y.: Dutton, 1952. British ed., *Sorge, Soviet Master Spy.* London: Kimber, 1952. A disorganized but useful account of the background of the Sorge network. Includes the full text of Sorge's own statement to the Japanese security police. [B]

Y106 WOLIN, SIMON, and SLUSSER, ROBERT M., eds. *The Soviet Secret Police.* N.Y.: Praeger; London: Methuen, 1957. 408 p. Japanese ed., Tokyo: Japan Institute of Foreign Affairs, 1957. 384 p. Concerned chiefly with internal developments, but touches also on espionage, and includes a chapter, "Postwar Activities of the Soviet Organs of State Security in Western Europe" by V. P. Artemiev and G. S. Burlutsky, two well-informed former Soviet intelligence officers. Contains a basic selective bibliography. [A]

Y107 WOLLENBERG, ERICH. *Der Apparat, Stalins fünfte Kolonne.* Bonn: Bundesministerium für Gesamtdeutsche Fragen, 1951. 48 p. An account of the military organization established under the KPD in 1923 by Soviet intelligence. By a former German Communist with personal experience of the case.

Y108 YPSILON (pseud. of Karl Volk). *Pattern for World Revolution.* Chicago: Ziff-Davis, 1947. 479 p. French ed., *Stalintern.* Paris:

Table ronde, 1948. 446 p. Deals with international Communism, including espionage; the author is well-informed and shrewd, but many of his assertions cannot be checked.

Y109 ZEUTSCHEL, WALTER. *Im Dienste der kommunistischen Terror-Organisation (Tscheka-Arbeit in Deutschland).* Berlin: Dietz, 1931. 159 p. An apparently reliable account of the terror organization established in Germany in 1923 under Soviet control.

Z. Soviet Foreign Economic Relations

EDITED BY ROBERT VINCENT ALLEN AND ROBERT LORING ALLEN

1. BIBLIOGRAPHIES

Z1 ALLEN, ROBERT LORING. *Soviet Bloc Foreign Economic Relations; an English Language Bibliography.* Washington: U.S. Depart-partment of State, External Research Staff Paper 134, 1958. 31 p. A partially-annotated bibliography of English-language sources on Soviet foreign economic relations for the 1952-57 period. The major division of the material is by geographical regions. Prepared as part of the Soviet bloc foreign economic relations project at the University of Virginia. [A]

Z2 SCHWARTZ, HARRY. *The Soviet Economy; A Selected Bibliography of Materials in English.* Syracuse: Syracuse University Press, 1949. 93 p. Mainly concerned with domestic economic conditions, but also includes a section on international economics (p. 69-76) with annotated listings of relevant books and articles.

Z3 U.S. DEPARTMENT OF STATE, BUREAU OF INTELLIGENCE AND RESEARCH. *Sino-Soviet Economic Relations 1954-1959; a Selective Bibliography.* External Research Report, April 11, 1960. 15 p.

2. GENERAL WORKS

Z4 ARTEMEV, VIACHESLAV P. *Selection and Training of Soviet Personnel for Trade Missions Abroad, and the Soviet Trade Mission in Iran; Two Brief Studies.* N.Y.: Research Program on the USSR, 1954. 20 p. Discusses both overt and covert activities of Soviet foreign trade missions. The author is a former member of such a mission.

Z5 CHERVIAKOV, P. A. *Organizatsiia i tekhnika vneshnei torgovli SSSR.* Moscow: Vneshtorgizdat, 1958. 295 p. Contains much information on the legal aspects of the organization of Soviet foreign trade.

Z6 FITUNI, L. A. *Mezhdugosudarstvennye torgovye dogovory i soglasheniia.* Moscow: Gosizdat iurid. lit., 1955. 114 p. A survey and analysis of commonly used types of commercial treaties and trade agreements, with emphasis on those of the USSR.

Z7 HENDLER, ALFRED. *Die völkerrechtliche Stellung der Handelsvertretung der UdSSR.* Berlin: F. Vahlen, 1931. 111 p. Soviet foreign trade representation abroad in the eyes of international law.

Z8 KALIUZHNAIA, G. P. *Pravovye formy monopolii vneshnei torgovli SSSR v ikh istoricheskom razvitii.* Moscow: Izd. Akademii nauk, 1951. 150 p. The most substantial post-World War II Soviet monograph on legal forms of organization of Soviet foreign trade, with an historical survey. [B]

Z9 KOROLENKO, A. S. *Torgovye dogovory i soglasheniia SSSR s inostrannymi gosudarstvami.* Moscow: Vneshtorgizdat, 1953. 316 p. An extensive historical survey of Soviet commercial treaties and trade agreements, with emphasis on the post-World War II period. Covers wartime lend-lease agreements, and some texts are appended. Texts of the agreements in force in 1953 are also included.

Z10 LISOVSKII, V. I. *Torgovye predstavitelstva Soiuza SSR za granitsei.* Moscow: "Mezhdunarodnaia kniga," 1947. 89 p.

Z11 MISHUSTIN, DMITRII D., ed. *Sbornik torgovykh dogovorov, konventsii i soglashenii SSSR, zakliuchennykh s inostrannymi gosudarstvami do 1 ianvaria 1941 g.* Moscow: NKVT, 1941. 408 p.

Z12 MOSCOW, NAUCHNO-ISSLEDOVATELSKII INSTITUT MONOPOLII VNESHNEI TORGOVLI. *Vneshniaia torgovlia SSSR za 20 let, 1918-1937 gg.; statisticheskii spravochnik.* Sergei N. Bakulin and Mishustin, D. D., comps. Moscow: "Mezhdunarodnaia kniga," 1939. 263 p. A statistical survey for the period 1918-37. Exports and imports shown by country of origin or destination and by tonnage and value. [A]

Z13 RUSSIA (1923-USSR), GLAVNOE TAMOZHENNOE UPRAVLENIE. *Vneshniaia torgovlia SSSR za 1918-1940 gg.; statisticheskii obzor.* Moscow: Vneshtorgizdat, 1960. 1135 p. A lengthy statistical report presenting foreign trade figures, both over time and with individual trading partners.

Z14 SMITH, GLEN ALDEN. "Soviet Foreign Trade Organization and Operations." Ph.D. dissertation, Stanford Univ., 1959.

3. 1917-1928

Z15 BAROU, NOAH. *Russian Co-operation Abroad; Foreign Trade 1912-1928.* London: P. S. King & Son, 1930. 95 p. Deals with Russian cooperative associations and their activities in foreign trade with Great Britain, the United States, and other countries. Many statistical tables.

Z16 BIBLIOTHÈQUE DU BUREAU ÉCONOMIQUE RUSSE. *Le Problème financier russe; la dette publique de la Russie.* Paris: Payot, 1922. 229 p. A study of Tsarist debts from the anti-Soviet Russian point of view.

Z17 CHAMBERLIN, WILLIAM H., and ROPES, ERNEST C. *Post-war Economic Relations with the USSR.* N.Y.: New York Univ., 1944.

Z18 COMITÉ DES REPRÉSENTANTS DES BANQUES RUSSES À PARIS. *Banque et Monnaie, dette de l'État, questions économiques soulevées par les événements de la Russie; rapports et documents (Octobre 1919-Juillet 1921).* Préface du comte Kokovtzoff. Paris: Comité des représentants des banques russes à Paris, 1921. 211 p. A useful but incomplete compendium, with a preface by a former Tsarist Minister of Finance.

Z19 *Ekonomika i politika vneshnei torgovli; sbornik.* Ed. by Prof. M. N. Sobolev, Moscow: Izd. Narkomtorga SSSR i RSFSR, 1928. 359 p. A collection of articles reflecting the policy of the late NEP period.

Z20 *Eksport, import i kontsessii Soiuza SSR.* Ed. by A. Troianovskii, Leonid Iurovskii, and Mikhail Kaufman. Moscow: Izd. Gos. kontory obiavlenii "Dvigatel," 1926. 900 p. A quadrilingual (Russian, German, English, French) handbook. Much specific information on various items of export and import. Extensive details on foreign economic concessions. [B]

Z21 GERSCHUNI, GERSON. *Die Konzessionspolitik Sowjetrusslands.* Berlin: Praeger, 1927. 133 p. A useful treatise on the economic concessions in Russia granted to various foreign entrepreneurs during the 1920's.

Z22 GOELDLIN DE TIEFENAU, ADOLPHE. *L'Existence à l'étranger des sociétés russes constituées sous l'ancien régime et nationalisées par le gouvernement des Soviets.* Strasbourg: Imprimerie française, 1928; Paris, Librairie générale de droit et de jurisprudence, 1929. 174 p. The status of Russian corporations abroad under French, German, English, Swiss, and American law. Includes useful citations of case literature. [B]

Z23 IZHBOLDIN, BORIS S. *Die russische Handelspolitik der Gegenwart; ein kritischer Beitrag zum bolschewistischen Wirtschaftssystem.* Jena: G. Fischer, 1930. 240 p. The *raison d'être* of the state foreign trade monopoly is seen to be its usefulness as a political rather than an economic instrument.

Z24 JÉRAMEC, JACQUES. *Le Monopole du commerce extérieur en Russie soviétique; origines—organisation—conséquences.* Paris: Librairie générale de droit & de jurisprudence, 1928. 183 p. Discusses the ideological influences on the formation of the Soviet foreign trade monopoly.

Z25 KALIUZHNAIA, G. P. *Pravovye formy monopolii vneshnei torgovli SSSR v ikh istoricheskom razvitii.* Moscow: Izd-vo Akademii nauk SSSR, 1951. 149 p. A history, by major periods of Soviet history, of the legal aspects of the Soviet foreign trade monopoly. Includes bibliographical footnotes.

Z26 KAUFMANN, MIKHAIL. *Organisation und Regulierung des Aussenshandels der Union der Sozialistischen Sowjetrepubliken; Mit e. Vorw. d. Verf., Über d. Sowjetrussisch-deutschen Handelsbeziehungen; Einzige autor. Übers.* Königsberg i. Pr.: Osteuropa-Verlag, 1925. 144 p.

Z27 KOGON, M. B., and SHENKMAN, I. M. *Eksportnye vozmozhnosti Rossii; statistiko-ekonomicheskii ocherk.* Moscow: Izd. N.K.V.T., 1922. 208 p. Principally devoted to a survey of the possibilities of Russia's exporting raw or semi-processed materials.

Z28 *Koniunktura narodnogo khoziaistva SSSR i mirovogo v 1925/26 g. (Sbornik obzorov statisticheskikh dannykh po vazhneishim otrasliam koniunktury narodnogo khoziaistva i mirovogo v 1925/26 g.)* Ed. by N. D. Kandratiev. Moscow: Finansovoe izd. NKF SSSR, 1927. 256 p.

Z29 KOVARSKII, B. N. *Regulirovanie vneshnei torgovli; formy i metody.* Moscow: RIO NKVT, 1925. 106 p. Designed for workers in the foreign trade system. Describes the methods of planning foreign trade in use in 1924-25.

Z30 KRASIN, LEONID B. *Planovoe khoziaistvo i monopoliia vneshnei torgovli.* Moscow: "Planovoe khoziaistvo," 1925.

Z31 KRASIN, LEONID B. *Vneshtorg i vneshniaia ekonomicheskaia politika sovetskogo pravitelstva.* Petrograd: Gosizdat, 1921. 47 p. The Commissar for Foreign Trade discusses Soviet foreign trade and foreign trade policy.

Z32 KRASIN, LEONID B. *Voprosy vneshnei torgovli.* Ed. by Iu. B. Goldshtein and M. Ia. Kaufman. Moscow: Gosizdat, 1928. 429 p. A posthumous work of the Commissar for Foreign Trade from 1918 to 1927. Provides an area-by-area examination of Soviet trade relations with the rest of the world. Includes a listing of the author's books and articles on the subject. [A]

Z33 KRASIN, LUBOV. *Leonid Krassin.* London: Skeffington, 1929. 284 p. The widow of the well-known Russian trade commissar has written an enlightening if somewhat eulogistic account of his activities.

Z34 KSANDROV, V. N. and others, eds. *Torgovlia SSSR s vostokom; sbornik statei i materialov.* Moscow-Leningrad: Izd. "Promizdat," 1927.

Z35 KULISHER, IOSIF M. *Osnovnye voprosy mezhdunarodnoi torgovoi politiki.* 2nd ed. Petrograd: "Atenei," 1924. 2 vols. in 1.

Z36 *Leonid Borisovich Krasin*. Moscow: Gosizdat, 1928. 397 p. Personal memoirs and background material by several Soviet writers on the former Soviet Commissar of Foreign Trade.

Z37 LIUBIMOV, N. N. *Balans vzaimnykh trebovanii Soiuza SSR i derzhav Soglasiia*. Moscow-Leningrad: "Ekonomicheskaia zhizn," 1924. 112 p. Refers to the losses and damage caused to the Soviet Union by the Western powers during the period 1917-21 as counterbalancing Western claims for the repayment of Russian debts. [B]

Z38 MAIZEL, BORIS N. *Mirovaia togovlia i nashe uchastie v nei*. Moscow: Gosizdat, 1928. 115 p.

Z39 MANNZEN, KARL. *Sowjetunion und Völkerrecht*. Berlin: Stilke, 1932. 110 p. The Soviet Union's position in international law with regard to Tsarist debts, emphasizing legal rather than economic factors. Many bibliographic references to contemporary literature. [B]

Z40 MAUTNER, WILHELM. *Der Kampf um und gegen das Russische Erdöl*. Vienna: Manz, 1929. 261 p. The oil problems of Soviet Russia are discussed in the context of the international contest to secure that precious commodity.

Z41 MIRKIN, Z. I. *SSSR, tsarskie dolgi i nashi kontr-pretenzii*. Moscow-Leningrad: GIZ, 1928. 127 p. A statement in a popular vein of Soviet claims on the Allies for damages caused by Intervention and the support of anti-Soviet forces. These claims are cited as the basis for refusal to repay debts of the previous regimes.

Z42 OGANOVSKII, I. *Narodnoe khoziaistvo SSSR v sviazi s mirovym*. Vol. 1, *Vneshniaia torgovlia*. Moscow: Tsentrsoiuz, 1925. 127 p.

Z43 OL, P. V. *Inostrannye kapitaly v Rossii (statisticheskii ocherk)*. Petrograd: NKF, 1922. 304 p.

Z44 PASVOLSKY, LEO, and MOULTON, H. G. *Russian Debts and Russian Reconstruction; a study of the Relation of Russia's Foreign Debts to her Economic Recovery*. (Institute of Economics, Investigations in International Economic Reconstruction.) N.Y.: McGraw-Hill, 1924. 247 p. Describes the economic situation of Russia before 1917 as reflected in its foreign debt structure. The probable future of the Russian economy is outlined on the basis of this situation.

Z45 PETRIAKOV, IVAN P. *Vneshniaia torgovlia i narodnoe khoziaistvo SSSR*. Ed. by H. B. Eismont. Moscow: Moskovskii Rabochii, 1927. 150 p. A discussion of foreign trade in simple terms for use by lecturers and propagandists.

Z46 *Promyshlennost v eksporte i importe Soiuza SSR.* Vols. 1-2, Moscow-Leningrad: VSNKh, 1925. Vol. 1, *Promyshlennyi eksport; statistiko-ekonomicheskii ocherk.* Ed. by L. G. Zamel. 167 p. Vol. 2, *Promyshlennyi import; statistiko-ekonomicheskii ocherk.* Ed. by L. G. Zamel and N. G. Chernobaev. 191 p.

Z47 RUSSIA (1917-RSFSR), TREATIES, ETC. *Russlands Friedens—und Handelsvertraege 1918-1923; auf Grund amtlichen Materials.* Translated by Heinrich Freund, with an introduction by Paul Heilborn. Leipzig: Teubner, 1924. 196 p. Careful German translations, sponsored by the Breslau Osteuropa-Institut, of the major Russian treaties of this period.

Z48 RUSSIA (1923- USSR), NARODNYI KOMISSARIAT VNESHNEI TORGOVLI. *Itogi vneshnei torgovli SSSR, 1923-1924; otchet 3-mu Sezdu sovetov SSSR.* Moscow: NKVT, 1925. 246 p.

Z49 RUSSIA (1923- USSR), NARODNYI KOMISSARIAT VNESHNEI I VNUTRENNEI TORGOVLI. *Sbornik deistvuiushchikh dekretov i postanovlenii po vneshnei torgovle.* Moscow: NKVT, 1924-26. 4 vols.

Z50 RUSSIA (1923- USSR), NARODNYI KOMISSARIAT VNESHNEI I VNUTRENNEI TORGOVLI. *Vneshniaia torgovlia Soiuza SSR za X let: sbornik materialov.* Ed. by D. I. Kutuzov. Moscow: Izd. Narkomtorga SSSR i RSFSR, 1928. 347 p. A survey of ten years of Soviet experience in foreign trade. Some statistics. [B]

Z51 SIGRIST, SERGEI V. *Vneshniaia torgovaia politika SSSR v mezhdunarodnykh dogovorakh.* Leningrad: Finansovoe izd-vo, 1927. 149 p. The foreign trade policy of the Soviet Union as shown in the provisions of international treaties.

Z52 SOLOMON, GEORGII A. (SOLOMON, GEORG). *Unter den roten Machthabern; was ich im Dienste der Sowjets persönlich sah und erlebte.* Berlin: Verlag für Kulturpolitik, 1930. 281 p. French ed., Paris: Éditions Spes, 1930. 352 p. A specialist in foreign trade who worked for the Soviets in Berlin, Moscow, Reval and London, describes his career.

Z53 *Sovet sezdov gosudarstvennoi promyshlennosti i torgovli SSSR; torgovlia SSSR s Vostokom; sbornik statei i materialov.* Ed. by V. N. Ksandrov, K. Kh. Danishevskii, M. I. Kalmonovich. Moscow-Leningrad: "Promizdat," 1927. 267 p.

Z54 STEIN, BORIS E. *Torgovaia politika i torgovye dogovory Sovetskoi Rossii 1917-1922 gg.* Moscow-Petrograd: Gosizdat, 1923. 247 p. Extensive material on the financial and trade provisions of the

Treaty of Brest-Litovsk. A survey of Soviet trade policy in the period leading up to the first economic agreements with other countries. [B]

Z55 STEIN, BORIS E. *Vneshniaia torgovaia politika SSSR*. Moscow: Tsentr. upr. pechati VSNKh SSSR, 1925. 139 p. A discussion of Soviet foreign trade policy from 1917 to 1924. The final chapter refers to internal political influences affecting foreign trade.

Z56 STEIN, BORIS E., and KANTOROVICH, A. IA. *Russkii eksport i vneshnie rynki (torgovopoliticheskie usloviia russkogo eksporta)*. Moscow: "Ekonomicheskaia zhizn," 1923. 168 p.

Z57 TOKAREV, SERGEI A. *Vneshniaia torgovlia; pravovye osnovy vneshnego tovarooborota SSSR*. Moscow: Izd. "Ekonomicheskaia zhizn," 1926. 149 p. Legal provisions affecting Soviet foreign trade are discussed. Includes some citations of applicable laws and regulations.

Z58 VINOKUR, ARKADII P., and BAKULIN, SERGEI N. *Vneshniaia torgovlia Soiuza sovetskikh sotsialisticheskikh respublik za period 1918-1927/28 gg*. Leningrad-Moscow: Snabkoopgiz, 1931. 847 p. A highly-detailed statistical presentation of Soviet trade, showing data by month and year, by value, in foreign prices, by border-crossing point, etc. [A]

Z59 VITKOVSKII, VLADIMIR P. *Inostrannye kontsessii v narodnom khoziaistve SSSR*. Moscow: Gosizdat, 1928.

Z60 *Vneshniaia torgovlia Rossii v 1922/23 khoziaistvennom godu; sbornik statei*. Ed. by V. G. Groman, M. Kaufman, and M. Zamengof. Moscow: Ekonomicheskaia zhizn, 1923. A detailed survey of Soviet foreign trade policy and activities in the 1922/1923 fiscal year.

Z61 VSEUKRAINSKAIA GOSUDARSTVENNAIA TORGOVAIA KONTORA PO EKSPORTU I IMPORTU, KHARKOV. *Sbornik statei po voprosam vneshnei torgovli i ekonomiki, 7 noiabria 1917 g.-7 noiabria 1922 g*. Kharkov: Upr. Upolnomochennogo Nar. komissariata vneshnei torgovli RSFSR pri Sovnarkome USSR, 1922. 171 p. Discusses Soviet foreign trade policy in the period 1917-22 as it affected the Ukraine. Extensive material on the Ukraine as a contributor to pre-1917 foreign trade flow. [B]

Z62 ZONNENSHTRAL-PISKORSKII, A. A. *Mezhdunarodnye torgovye dogovory i soglasheniia, 1919-1924 (sistematicheskii obzor)*. Moscow: NKVT, 1925. 142 p.

4. 1929-1952

Z63 BACKER, JOHN H. "The Pattern of Soviet Trade with the West, 1946-1953." Certificate essay, Russian Institute, Columbia, 1955. 135 p.

Z64 BAYKOV, ALEXANDER M. *Soviet Foreign Trade.* Princeton, N.J.: Princeton University Press; London: Oxford, 1946. 125 p. Important as a research document. A leading British Soviet scholar has culled the data for a dry-as-dust account of the facts concerning Soviet trade up to World War II. [B]

Z65 BERLIN, FREIE UNIVERSITÄT, OSTEUROPA-INSTITUT. *Volkswirtschaftliche Folge.* Berlin, nos. 1-3, April 15, 1952—Feb. 15, 1954. 3 vols. Superseded by the Institute's *Wirtschaftswissenschaftliche Folge.* Two sections of this series provide useful data or opinion on Soviet economic history prior to 1941 and on German-Soviet trade in the years 1933-41. [B]

Z66 BUDISH, JACOB M., and SHIPMAN, SAMUEL S. *Soviet Foreign Trade; Menace or Promise.* N.Y.: Liveright, 1931. 276 p. Issued under the sponsorship of Amtorg, the Soviet trading corporation in America. Encourages an optimistic outlook on prospects for trade between the United States and the Soviet Union and advances arguments favorable to diplomatic recognition. Discusses the role of major commodities in trade between the two countries. Much material on the question of forced labor. [B]

Z67 COATES, WILLIAM P. *Is Soviet Trade a Menace?* London: The Anglo-Russian Parliamentary Committee, 1931. 117 p. Gives a point of view favorable to the Soviet Union.

Z68 CONDOIDE, MIKHAIL V. "The Soviet Economy; some Salient Features and International Economic Relations." Ph.D. dissertation, Ohio State Univ., 1949. A survey of principles and practices of Soviet economic planning, Soviet banking and monetary policies, budget, and of international economic relations. The study is essentially based on Soviet publications.

Z69 CONOLLY, VIOLET. *Soviet Economic Policy in the East; Turkey, Persia, Afghanistan, Mongolia and Tana Tuva, Sin Kiang.* London: Oxford, 1933. 168 p. A history of Soviet economic policy with regard to the countries mentioned. Uses a wide range of materials, including Russian and Near Eastern, as well as consular reports. Heavily documented. By a British scholar who became a key figure in Soviet research in the British foreign office. [B]

Z70 CONOLLY, VIOLET. *Soviet Trade From the Pacific to the Levant; With an Economic Study of the Soviet Far Eastern Region.* London and N.Y.: Oxford, 1935. 238 p. A sequel to the work mentioned above. An analysis of Soviet trade policies and of the economy of the Soviet Far East. Based on a great variety of sources, including the Russian archives of the Ost-Europa Institut in Breslau and the Deutsche

Hochschule für Politik in Berlin. The twelve appendices contain documents and statistics. [B]

Z71 CYRILIŃSKI, BOLESLAW. *Koncesje zagraniczne w Z.S.R.R.* Wilno: Nakl. Instytutu Naukowo-Badawezego Europy Wschodniej, 1935. 217 p. A Polish-language discussion of the Soviet concessions policy.

Z72 DEWAR, MARGARET. *Soviet Trade with Eastern Europe, 1945-1949*. London and N.Y.: Royal Institute of International Affairs, 1951. 123 p. A dated but useful account of the development of Soviet trade during the early postwar period. Limited statistical data were available. This was one of the first of the specialized studies of Soviet trade.

Z73 *Documentation Relating to Foreign Economic Relations of the USSR*. Moscow: 1933. 65 p. Material prepared for the World Economic Conference held in London in 1933.

Z74 *Finansirovanie vneshnei torgovli*. Ed. by N. V. Stefanov. Moscow: Vneshtorgizdat, 1935. 415 p. A detailed discussion of capitalist and Soviet practices of financing foreign trade. Types of relations with foreign firms are shown by reference to cases. [A]

Z75 *Finansirovanie vneshnei torgovli*. Ed. by L. Frei 2nd ed. Moscow: Izd. V/O Mezhdunarodnaia kniga, 1938. 367 p. A revision of the 1935 edition of this work (above), made in order to improve its usefulness as a text for foreign trade workers. Some changes in policy are also reflected.

Z76 GERSCHENKRON, ALEXANDER P. *Economic Relations with the USSR*. N.Y.: The Committee on International Economic Policy in Cooperation with the Carnegie Endowment for International Peace, 1945. 73 p. An early postwar account of Soviet trade, reviewing the prewar record and foreshadowing Soviet postwar policy and behavior, by a leading American Soviet economic historian. [B]

Z77 GORELIK, S. M., and MALKIS, A. I. *Sovetskaia torgovlia*. Moscow: Sotsekgriz, 1934. 176 p. Two Soviet specialists discuss Soviet trade in both theory and practice.

Z78 HEYMANN, HANS, JR. "The Soviet Union in the World Petroleum Market; a Case Study in Soviet Foreign Trade." Certificate essay, Russian Institute, Columbia, 1948. 114 p.

Z79 IANSON, IAKOV D. (Yanson or Jansons, J. D.), ed. *Foreign Trade in the U.S.S.R.* London: Gollancz, 1934. 176 p. N.Y.: Putnam, 1935. Trans. of *Vneshniaia torgovlia SSSR*. Moscow: 1934. 198 p. One of a series of volumes by Soviet officials designed to explain the

Soviet economic system. Although it is filled with distortions and questionable assumptions, it is useful as a source on Soviet foreign trade if used with care.

Z80 ILIASHEV, BORIS (Eliacheff, Boris L.). *Le Dumping soviëtique.* Paris: M. Giard, 1931. 220 p. A study of the factors affecting Soviet price structure and the prices of Soviet goods on world markets. The possibility of Soviet "dumping" of industrial goods is considered in the light of these factors.

Z81 ISCHBOLDIN, BORIS. *Die russische Handelspolitik der Gegenwart Beitr. z. bolschewist. Wirtschaftssystem.* Jena: G. Fischer, 1930. 240 p.

Z82 KNICKERBOCKER, HUBERT R. *Fighting the Red Trade Menace.* N.Y.: Dodd, Mead, 1931. 295 p. British ed., *Soviet Trade and World Depression.* London: J. Lane, 1931. 288 p. German ed., *Der rote Handel Lockt.* Berlin: Rowohlt, 1931. 235 p. Report of an American journalist from the period of the First Five Year Plan. Much eyewitness information.

Z83 KNICKERBOCKER, HUBERT R. *The Red Trade Menace; Progress of the Soviet Five-Year Plan.* N.Y.: Dodd, Mead, 1931. 277 p. British ed., *The Soviet Five-Year Plan and its Effect on World Trade.* London: J. Lane, 1931. 245 p. German ed., *Der rote Handel droht: Der Fortschritt des Fünfjahresplans der Sowjets.* Berlin: Rowohlt, 1931. 202 p. Spanish ed., Santiago, Chile: 1933. An American journalist's view of Soviet trade as a factor in the post-1929 world depression.

Z84 KOMMUNISTICHESKAIA AKADEMIIA, MOSCOW, INSTITUT MIROVOGO KHOZIAISTVA I MIROVOI POLITIKI. *XV let borby za monopoliiu vneshnei torgovli.* Moscow: Partiinoe izd., 1932. 295 p. A collection of articles. Surveys policy toward Britain, Germany, United States, France, Italy, Japan, and other Eastern countries. [A]

Z85 LIFITS, M. M. *Edinaia tovarnaia nomeklatura vneshnei torgovli SSSR.* Moscow-Leningrad: Vneshtorgizdat, 1936. 418 p.

Z86 LIFITS, M. M., and RUBINSHTEIN, G. L. *Ekonomika i planirovanie sovetskoi torgovli.* Moscow: Gostorgizdat, 1940. 603 p. Examines in detail Soviet trade planning and operation.

Z87 MICHELSON, SERGE. *Evolution du commerce extérieur de l'U.R.S.S. depuis le premier plan quinquennal.* Paris: Lescher-Montoué, 1942. 149 p.

Z88 MISHUSTIN, DMITRII D. *Vneshniaia torgovlia i industrializatsiia SSSR.* Moscow: "Mezhdunarodnaia kniga," 1938. 221 p. Foreign trade as a factor in the industrialization of the USSR during the first and second Five Year Plans. One chapter discusses the efforts of the Soviet Union to free itself from dependence on foreign trade as a source of industrial products, emphasizing the autarkic goals of the regime. [B]

Z89 MISHUSTIN, DMITRII D., ed. *Torgovye otnosheniia SSSR so stranami vostoka.* Moscow: "Mezhdunarodnaia kniga," 1938. 104 p. A review, country by country or region by region, of Soviet trade with the Levant, Middle East, and Far East.

Z90 MISHUSTIN, DMITRII D., ed. *Vneshniaia torgovlia SSSR; kratkoe uchebnoe posobie.* 3rd ed., Moscow: "Mezhdunarodnaia kniga," 1941. 211 p. A text for Soviet foreign trade workers. Includes a discussion of terms, procedures, and policies.

Z91 MOSCOW, NAUCHNO-ISSLEDOVATELSKII INSTITUT MONOPOLII VNESHNEI TORGOVLI. *Torgovye otnosheniia SSSR s kapitalisticheskimi stranami.* Ed. by Dmitrii D. Mishustin. Moscow: "Mezhdunarodnaia kniga," 1938. 349 p. A survey, by country or by region, of Soviet foreign trade relations with European and American countries. [A]

Z92 MOSCOW, NAUCHNO-ISSLEDOVATELSKII INSTITUT MONOPOLII VNESHNEI TORGOVLI. *Vneshniaia torgovlia Sovetskogo soiuza.* Ed. by Dmitrii D. Mishustin. Moscow: "Mezhdunarodnaia kniga," 1938. 326 p. A general work on Soviet foreign trade intended as a text for workers in the foreign trade system.

Z93 MOSCOW, VSESOIUZNAIA AKADEMIIA VNESHNEI TORGOVLI, NAUCHNO-ISSLEDOVATELSKII INSTITUT. *Statistika vneshnei torgovli SSSR.* Comp. by Sergei N. Bakulin and D. D. Mishustin. Moscow: Vneshtorgizdat, 1935. 277 p. A discussion of methods and terminology applied by Soviet statisticians of foreign trade. Numerous references also to pre-1914 practices. [B]

Z95 RAMZAITSEV, DMITRII F. *Vneshnetorgovyi arbitrazh v* lin: E. Rowohlt, 1931. 92 p. An analysis of "dumping" from a point of view favorable to the Soviet Union.

Z95 RAMZAITSEV, DMITRII F. *Vneshnetorgovyi arbitrazh v SSSR.* Moscow: Gos. izd. iurid. lit., 1952. 142 p. 2nd ed., Moscow: 1957. 182 p. Discusses the practices followed in the arbitration of foreign trade disputes.

Z96 ROZENBLIUM, BORIS D., comp. *Mezhdunarodnye ekonomicheskie konferentsii i soglasheniia 1933-1935 gg. . . . ; sbornik dokumentov.* Moscow: NKID, 1936. 265 p.

Z97 RUSSIA (1923- USSR) GLAVNOE TAMOZHENNOE UPRAVLENIE. *Vneshniaia torgovlia Soiuza sovetskikh sotsialisticheskikh respublik za pervuiu piatiletku (za period s 1928 po 1933 g.); statisticheskii obzor.* Ed. by Arsenii N. Voznesenskii and Aleksandr A. Voloshinskii. Moscow-Leningrad: Izdanie Glavnogo tamozhennogo upravleniia Vneshtorgizdat, 1933. 575 p. Highly-detailed statistical data on foreign trade during the first Five Year Plan, showing items by value, country of origin, port of entry, etc. [A]

Z98 RUSSIA (1923- USSR), TREATIES, ETC. *Mezhdunarodnye konventsii i soglasheniia, otnosiashchiesia k torgovomu moreplavaniiu; sbornik.* Comp. by L. A. Furman. Moscow: Morskoi transport, 1940. 195 p. New ed., 1947.

Z99 RUSSIA (1923- USSR), TREATIES, ETC. *Sbornik deistvuiushchikh torgovykh dogovorov i inykh khoziaistvennykh soglashenii SSSR, zakliuchennykh s inostrannymi gosudarstvami.* Comp. by Boris D. Rozenblium. Moscow: NKID, 1936. Only two issues have been identified. [B]

Z100 RUSSIA (1923- USSR), VYSSHII SOVET NARODNOGO KHOZIAISTVA, INOSTRANNYI OTDEL. *Promyshlennyi eksport; itogi i perspektivy.* Ed. by S. I. Aralov and A. S. Shatkhan. Moscow-Leningrad; Gosizdat, 1928. 230 p. The structure of industrial export, its relationship to Soviet industrialization and the prospects for future development.

Z101 RUSSIA, (1923- USSR), VYSSHII SOVET NARODNOGO KHOZIAISTVA, INOSTRANNYI OTDEL. *Promyshlennyi import; itogi i perspektivy.* Ed. by S. I. Aralov and A. S. Shatkhan. Moscow: Gosizdat, 1930. 259 p. The relationship of industrial imports to Soviet industrialization, methods of increasing production of such materials, and means whereby technical assistance may be obtained from foreign firms.

Z102 SCHWEINFURTH, NADESCHDA. *Das Aussenhandelsmonopol der Union der Sozialistischen Sowjet-Republiken.* Berlin: Ebering, 1937. 171 p. Some regional analysis of the foreign trade policy of the Soviet Union.

Z103 *Selsko-khoziaistvennyi eksport SSSR.* Ed. by B. E. Gurevich and others. Moscow: Selkhozgiz, 1930. 398 p.

Z104 SHATKHAN, ABRAM S. *Vneshniaia torgolia v 5-letke.* Intro. by A. Mikoian. Moscow: Gosizdat, 1930. 135 p. A short work of a popular nature, noteworthy chiefly for the introduction by Anastas Mikoian, long the boss of Soviet foreign trade.

Z105 SHAW, JOHN P. "Soviet Oil Diplomacy, 1944-1948." Ph.D. dissertation, Chicago, 1951.

Z106 SPULBER, NICOLAS. "The Economic Relations Between the USSR and the Eastern European Countries After World War II." Ph.D. dissertation, The New School for Social Research, 1952.

Z107 STUPNITSKY, ARSENII F. *Statut international de l'U.R.S.S.—état commerçant*. Paris: Librairie générale de droit & de jurisprudence, 1936. 486 p. A documented inquiry into the Soviet position in world affairs and trade.

Z108 TAITS, M. IU., ed. *Vneshniaia torgovlia SSSR; uchebnoe posobie dlia rabotnikov vneshnei torgovli i uchebnykh zavedenii*. Moscow: Vneshtorgizdat, 1935. 327 p. A textbook for workers in the foreign trade system.

Z109 U.S. DEPARTMENT OF STATE. *Soviet Supply Protocols*. Washington, D.C.: G.P.O., 1948. 156 p. (At head of title: *Wartime International Agreements*. Publication 2759, European Series 22.)

Z110 WU, CHEE-HSIEN. "Two Decades of Soviet Foreign Trade." Ph.D. dissertation, Harvard, 1948.

Z111 ZHIRMUNSKII, MIKHAIL M. *Eksport SSSR; spravochnik-putevoditel*. Ed. by A. F. Khazov and I. S. Pudov. Moscow-Leningrad: Vneshtorgizdat, 204 p. English edition, *Soviet Export*. Moscow: Mezhdunarodnaia kniga; N.Y.: Bookniga, 1936. 121 p. A general handbook on Soviet export.

5. 1953-1963

Z112 ALKHIMOV, V., and MORDVINOV, V. *Foreign Trade of the USSR*. London: Soviet Booklets, 1958. 38 p. (Soviet Booklet No. 37.) A propaganda document containing an official statement of Soviet trade policy and a limited amount of data.

Z113 ALLEN, ROBERT LORING. *Middle Eastern Economic Relations with the Soviet Union, Eastern Europe, and Mainland China*. Charlottesville, Va.: Woodrow Wilson Department of Foreign Affairs, Univ. of Virginia, 1958. 128 p. Analytical material with appendices providing extensive statistical data. Bibliographical footnotes and a separate bibliography. [A]

Z114 ALLEN, ROBERT LORING. *Soviet Economic Warfare*. Washington: Public Affairs, 1960. 293 p. Examines the Soviet use of economic activity to advance plans of the state, both economic and political. Analyzes the effect in major regions of the world and considers prospects for the future. Contains statistical and bibliographical appendices. [A]

Z115 ALLEN, ROBERT LORING. *Soviet Influence in Latin America; the Role of Economic Relations.* Washington: Public Affairs Press, for the Woodrow Wilson Department of Foreign Affairs, Univ. of Virginia, 1959. 108 p. An examination of economic relations, area-wide and by major countries involved, which provides much statistical material. Bibliographical data is supplied in notes. [A]

Z116 AUBREY, HENRY G. *Coexistence: Economic Challenge and Response.* Washington: National Planning Association, 1961. 323 p. A leading American economist tackles the coexistence problem, supported by a three-year Rockefeller grant. A judicious statement, useful data, and carefully-reasoned analysis. Deals with both Soviet and American policies. [A]

Z117 *Backgrounders on Communism; Communism and East-West Trade.* N.P.: N.P., 1953? 1 vol. (Various Pagings.) A guide to U.S. policy with regard to East-West trade, published for the use of the U.S. Information Service. It is chiefly concerned with policies of the moment, but reflects official views quite closely. [B]

Z118 BARTSCH, WILLIAM. "Swedish Trade and Payment Agreements with the Soviet Union and Eastern Europe." M.A. thesis, U. of Virginia, 1959. A data-laden account of Swedish commercial relations with the Soviet bloc. Interesting because it indicates Soviet trade policies and behavior toward an important "neutral."

Z119 BERLINER, JOSEPH S. *Soviet Economic Aid; the New Aid and Trade Policy in Underdeveloped Countries.* N.Y.: Published for the Council on Foreign Relations by Praeger, 1958. 232 p. An important scholarly study resulting from meetings of the Council on Foreign Relations. By a leading American economist. Useful data and careful and conservative analysis. [A]

Z120 BILINSKI, STANISLAW K. "The Pattern of Soviet Russian Maritime Expansion After the Second World War; European 'Captive' Shipping (1945-1955)." Ph.D. dissertation, Georgetown, 1957.

Z121 BILLERBECK, KLAUS. *Soviet Bloc Foreign Aid to the Underdeveloped Countries; an Analysis and a Prognosis.* Hamburg: Archives of World Economy, 1960. 161 p.

Z122 BÜTOW, CARL H. *Das Gegenwärtige innerstaatlich geregelte Aussenhandelsrecht der UdSSR unter Berücksichtigung der zwischenstaatlichen Verträge.* Göttingen: Hektographierte Veröffentlichungen des Instituts für Völkerrecht der Universität Göttingen, 1956. 2 vols. A study of Soviet foreign trade legislation and of treaty provisions which affect it. Careful in its details.

Z123 COLUMBIA BROADCASTING SYSTEM, INC., CBS NEWS. *The Ruble War*. By Howard K. Smith and others. Buffalo: Smith, Keynes & Marshall, 1958. 71 p. A highly popular account representing the substance of a TV special on Soviet trade and aid. Anecdotal and superficial but interesting.

Z124 COUNCIL FOR ECONOMIC AND INDUSTRY RESEARCH. *Foreign Assistance Activities of the Communist Bloc and their Implications for the United States*. Washington: G.P.O., 1957. 134 p. An examination of the Bloc's program, providing copious statistical material, an analysis of its implications for the U.S., and an appendix showing in detail Bloc credits advanced to under-developed countries outside the Bloc. [B]

Z125 DOKUKIN, V. I. *Dva mira—dve sistemy*. Moscow: Voen. Izd., 1958. 218 p. This book is of significance only for its evidence of the attitudes toward international economic relations which the Soviet regime wished to propagate among the armed forces.

Z126 FITUNI, L. A., and SHCHETININ, V. D. *Problemy pomoshchi ekonomicheski slaborazvitym stranam*. Moscow: Izd. IMO, 1961.

Z127 GENKIN, D. M. *Pravovye voprosy vneshnei torgovli SSSR s evropeiskimi stranami narodnoi demokratii*. Moscow: Vnezhtorgizdat, 1955. 261 p. A collection of articles on various aspects of Soviet bloc trade relations, as of 1955.

Z128 GESELLSCHAFT FÜR DEUTSCH-SOWJETISCHE FREUNDSCHAFT. *Beiträge zur Moskauer Weltwirtschaftskonferenz*. Berlin: Verlag Kultur und Fortschritt, 1952. 153 p. An East German publication of articles by Soviet authors on the subject of Soviet foreign trade. It stresses the value to the West of such trade as a bulwark against inflation and as an aid in international development. A faithful reflection of contemporary views.

Z129 GUBERMAN, R. L. *Transport vo vneshnei torgovle SSSR*. Moscow: Vneshtorgizdat, 1956. 109 p. A description of the role of transport in Soviet foreign trade, which provides material as to form of transport, routes, and general nature of cargo. Useful indications of Soviet participation in international freighting and insurance activities. [B]

Z130 HERMAN, LEON M. *Foreign Trade of the USSR*. Washington: Council for Economic and Industry Research, 1954. 100 p. This early work reflects the paucity of data on Soviet foreign trade until recently. Still a most useful collection and discussion of Soviet foreign trade. [B]

Z131 HERMES, THEODOR. *Der Aussenhandel in den Ostblockstaaten.* Hamburg: Cram, 1958. 177 p. Deals with the complex question of the structure and mechanisms of trade within the Soviet bloc.

Z132 HUEBBENET, GEORG VON. *Die rote Wirtschaft waechst; Aufbau und Entwicklungsziele des Comecon.* Düsseldorf: Econ-Verlag, 1960. 283 p.

Z133 INTERNATIONAL COMMITTEE FOR THE PROMOTION OF TRADE. *International Trade.* Monthly. Vienna; Sept. 1955-Aug. 1956. French ed. also. Continuation of the *Bulletin of Economic and Trade News* published by the Committee for the Promotion of International Trade, 1952-July 1955. The name change (simultaneous with Committee's name change) was occasioned by a desire to publish an "international trade journal" rather than just a "link between the different National Committees for the Promotion of Trade." Contains articles designed to promote East-West trade and to help remove Western strategic embargoes. The Committee is a Communist front.

Z134 INTERNATIONAL ECONOMIC CONFERENCE, MOSCOW, 1952. *International Economic Conference in Moscow, April 3-12, 1952.* Moscow: 1952. 328 p. Russian ed., 1952. Texts of speeches at the Moscow-sponsored conference to promote East-West trade. The resolution establishing a Committee for the Promotion of International Trade and a list of Committee members are appended.

Z135 KAWAN, LOUIS. *La Nouvelle Orientation du Commerce extérieur soviétique.* Brussels: Centre National pour l'Étude des pays à Régime Communiste, 1958. 317 p.

Z136 KIESEWETTER, BRUNO. *Der Ostblock; Aussenhandel des Ostlichen Wirtschaftsblockes Einschliesslich China.* Berlin: Safari-Verlag, 1960. 386 p. A substantial study describing and analyzing the pattern of foreign trade and economic aid within the Communist international system, including a discussion of the special position of China. Based largely on official Russian sources, this book gives detailed trade statistics, in both physical units and value, for selected years; 1938, and 1948-59. Professor of Economics at the Free University of Berlin (West) and director of the East European division, Deutsches Institut für Wirtschaftsforschung, Kiesewetter has written widely on bloc economic planning and problems.

Z137 KNORR, KLAUS E. *Ruble Diplomacy; Challenge to American Foreign Aid.* Princeton, N.J.: Center of International Studies, Princeton

University, 1956. 46 p. (Center of International Studies, Memorandum No. 10.) An excellent and thoughtful analysis of Soviet trade and aid by a Princeton economist. Short on data, it is concerned mainly with strategic and motivational considerations.

Z138 KOORT, F. *Soviet Industry and Foreign Trade*. London: Soviet News, 1957. 87 p. (Soviet News Booklet No. 13.) This pamphlet, published in part to commemorate the fortieth anniversary of the Soviet regime, provides some useful data on the machine building industry and on an area-by-area survey of foreign trade.

Z139 KOROLENKO, A. S. *Torgovye dogovory i soglasheniia SSSR s inostrannymi gosudarstvami*. Moscow: Vneshtorgizdat, 1953. 315 p. A history of Soviet trade agreements with other countries, an examination of the types of agreements between the USSR and capitalist and bloc nations, and a supplement with the texts of agreements in force in 1953.

Z140 KOVNER, MILTON. *The Challenge of Coexistence; a Study of Soviet Economic Diplomacy*. Washington: Public Affairs Press, 1961. 130 p. A politico-economic study of Soviet foreign economic activities with emphasis on the changing nature of "peaceful coexistence" and political motivation in Soviet trade and aid. [B]

Z141 LOVITT, CRAIG E. "Finland's Economic Relations with the Soviet Union and Eastern Europe Since World War II." M.A. thesis, U. of Virginia, 1959. 153 p. An evaluation of Soviet-Finnish relations in the postwar period. Includes an assessment of Finnish reparations, their impact on the Finnish economy, and the dependence of the economy on Soviet and East European trade.

Z142 MIKESELL, RAYMOND, and BEHRMAN, JACK. *Financing Free World Trade with the Sino-Soviet Bloc*. Princeton, N.J.: International Finance Section, Princeton, 1958. 109 p. A carefully documented discussion of trade and payments agreements between the Soviet area and the free world. Deals especially with the volume, trends, and stability of trade. Detailed tabular material. [A]

Z143 MOSCOW, INSTITUT MEZHDUNARODNYKH OTNOSHENII. *Mezhdunarodnye ekonomicheskie otnosheniia*. Ed. by N. N. Liubimov. Moscow: Izd. IMO, 1957. 439 p.

Z144 MOSCOW, INSTITUT VNESHNEI TORGOVLI. *Vneshniaia torgovlia SSSR*. Ed. by A. M. Smirnov and N. N. Liubimov. Moscow: Vneshtorgizdat, 1954. 282 p.

Z145 MOSCOW, NAUCHNO-ISSLEDOVATELSKII EKONOMICHESKII INSTITUT. *Ekonomicheskoe sorevnovanie dvukh mirovykh sistem; sbornik statei.* Ed. by A. M. Alekseev. Moscow: Gospolitizdat, 1957. 383 p. Nine technical articles treating economic relations between East and West, comparisons of economic growth in the two spheres, and related topics.

Z146 MOSCOW, NAUCHNO-ISSLEDOVATELSKII KONIUNKTURNYI INSTITUT. *Vneshniaia torgovlia SSSR s kapitalisticheskimi stranami.* Ed. by V. S. Alkhimov and others. Moscow: Vneshtorgizdat, 1957. 232 p. An official publication of the Ministry of Foreign Trade, covering Soviet trade with capitalist countries from 1937 to 1955. There are occasional lapses into propaganda prose, but mostly it is a factual account, with detailed statistics.

Z147 MOSCOW, NAUCHNO-ISSLEDOVATELSKII KONIUNKTURNYI INSTITUT. *Vneshniaia torgovlia SSSR so stranami Asii, Afriki, i Latinskoi Ameriki.* Ed. by V. P. Gorunov, N. N. Inozemstev, and V. B. Spandarian. Moscow: 1958. 195 p. A Ministry of Foreign Trade publication dealing factually and statistically with Soviet trade with Asia, Africa, and Latin America. Some propaganda content but a useful research document.

Z148 PFUHL, EBERHARD. *Rechtsformen des sowjetischen Aussenhandels.* Berlin: 1954. 123 p. (Berichte des Osteuropa-Instituts an der Freien Universität Berlin, Heft 7. Rechtswissenschaftliche Folge, Nr. 4.) An examination of the legal status of Soviet foreign trade organizations.

Z149 POLEZHAEV, V. N., and IAKOBSON, G. M. *Mezhdunarodnye ekonomicheskie organizatsii i soglasheniia.* Moscow: Vneshtorgizdat, 1961. 266 p.

Z150 RUSSIA (1923- USSR), TREATIES, ETC. *Sbornik mezhdunarodnykh konventsii, dogovorov, soglashenii i pravil po voprosam torgovogo moreplavaniia.* Ed. by Iu. A. Bulushev and others. Moscow: Morskoi transport, 1959. 474 p.

Z151 RUSSIA (1923- USSR), TREATIES, ETC. *Sbornik torgovykh dogovorov, torgovykh i platezhnykh soglashenii i dolgosrochnykh torgovykh soglashenii SSSR s inostrannymi gosudarstvami, na 1 ianvariia 1961 g.* Comp. by A. D. Aleksandrov and E. K. Medvedev. Ed. by K. K. Bakhtov. Moscow: Vneshtorgizdat, 1961. 623 p.

Z152 SAPIR, MICHAEL. *The New Role of the Soviets in the World Economy.* N.Y.: Committee for Economic Development, 1958. 64 p. A useful popular account based on State Department data and reflecting its views. Prepared under the auspices of a business research group.

Z153 *Sbornik normativnykh materialov po voprosam vneshnei torgovli SSSR.* Moscow: Vneshtorgizdat, 1961.

Z154 SCOTT, JOHN. *The Soviet Economic Offensive; a Report on Ruble Diplomacy.* 1961. 138 p. (duplicated). A report compiled for *Time* magazine and printed in limited numbers. Based on extensive travel throughout the Communist bloc countries, as well as the Near and Far East and Western Europe. Contains many facts and figures along with a well-written analysis. Bibliography.

Z155 SERGEEV, S. D. *Ekonomicheskoe sotrudnichestvo i vsaimopomoshch stran sotsialisticheskogo lageria.* 2nd enlarged ed. Moscow: Vneshtorgizdat, 1959. 319 p. An extensive survey of the interrelationships between the Soviet Union and the countries "of the Socialist bloc." Many details as to forms of credit and technical aid are given. [A]

Z156 SMIRNOV, A. M. *Mezhdunarodnye raschety i kreditnye otnosheniia vo vneshnei torgovle SSSR.* Moscow: Vneshtorgizdat, 1953. 280 p. New enlarged ed., *Mezhdunarodnye valiutnye i kreditnye otnosheniia SSSR.* Moscow: Vneshtorgizdat, 1960. 365 p. English translation, *International Currency and Credit Relations of the USSR.* Washington: U.S. Joint Publications Research Service (JPRS no. 4147), 1960. 219 p. A survey of Soviet foreign exchange policies and of that country's experience with the granting of foreign credits. An indication of the role of the Soviet gold reserves is also given. Useful details are provided, although a bibliography is lacking. [A]

Z157 *Spravochnik po vneshnei torgovle SSSR.* Ed. by G. E. Koftov, D. F. Ramzaitsev, and V. B. Spandarian. Moscow: Vneshtorgizdat, 1958. 270 p. A concise survey of the organization of Soviet foreign trade, with material on the operation of trade agencies, transport, insurance, international payments, Soviet patent and trade-mark law, and the arbitration of disputes. Includes an alphabetical listing of trading organizations, giving both full and abbreviated titles and describing the nature of their activities.

Z158 TIULPANOV, S. I. *Vozniknovenie i razvitie mirovogo demokraticheskogo rynka.* Leningrad: Leningradskoe Gazetno-zhurnalnoe i knizhnoe izd-vo, 1955. 144 p. An analysis of the economic relationships between the Soviet Union and the other countries of the Soviet bloc, with an examination of the resulting prospects for co-existence with capitalism.

Z159 U.S. CONGRESS, SENATE, COMMITTEE ON FOREIGN RELATIONS, SUB-COMMITTEE ON TECHNICAL ASSISTANCE PROGRAMS. *Soviet Technical Assistance.* Staff Study No. 7. Washington: G.P.O., 1956. 62 p. A useful documentary study of the number and kind of Soviet technical assistance experts in the field up to 1956. Now badly dated.

Z160 U.S. DEPARTMENT OF STATE. *The Sino-Soviet Economic Offensive in the Less Developed Countries.* Washington: 1958. (U.S. Dept. of State Publication 6632; European and British Commonwealth Series, 51.) 111 p. While this study was intended for Congressional and popular consumption, it contains a great deal of useful information, particularly in its tables and country-by-country analysis of Soviet economic activities in less-developed areas.

Z161 U.S. DEPARTMENT OF STATE, OFFICE OF PUBLIC SERVICES, BUREAU OF PUBLIC AFFAIRS. *Communist Economic Policy in the Less Developed Areas.* Washington: G.P.O., 1960. 38 p. An official document for popular and propaganda purposes. Some useful information, but leaves the impression of a larger Soviet program than may exist.

Z162 U.S. DEPARTMENT OF STATE, PUBLIC SERVICES DIVISION, BUREAU OF PUBLIC AFFAIRS. *The Communist Economic Threat.* Washington: G.P.O., 1959. 22 p. A popular account of recent Soviet economic activities in less-developed countries. Some useful data but primarily designed to indicate the nature and scope of Soviet economic penetration.

Z163 *Vneshniaia torgovlia Soiuza SSR; statisticheskii obzor.* Moscow: Vneshtorg, 1958 — (annual). This is an annual supplement to *Vneshniaia Torgovlia*, beginning in 1957, which gives detailed statistics on Soviet foreign trade, by value, volume, country of origin, and country of destination.

Z164 *Vneshniaia torgovlia SSSR so sotsialisticheskimi stranami.* Moscow: 1957. 213 p. An official document of the Ministry of Foreign Trade dealing with Soviet trade with Eastern Europe. Covers mainly the period since the Second World War. Some propaganda, but a useful research document. Detailed statistics.

Z165 *Vneshniaia torgovlia SSSR za 1955-1959 gg.* Moscow: Vneshtorgizdat, 1961.

Z166 *Voprosy vneshnei torgovli.* Moscow: Izd-vo IMO, 1960. 197 p. Articles examining various facets of Soviet and world foreign trade activity since World War II from the point of view of recent interpretations of events, and treating such questions as Burmese state capitalism, the role of new products, and the policies of GATT.

Z167 WEBER, ADOLF. *Sowjetwirtschaft und Weltwirtschaft.* Berlin: Duncker und Humbolt, 1959. 293 p.

Z168 WELTON, HARRY. *The Third World War; Trade and Industry, the New Battleground.* N.Y.: Philosophical Library, 1959. 330

p. A vigorous, if somewhat non-analytical, examination of the economic and trade posture of the Soviet Union. Contains little useful information and suffers fearfully from ideological vitiation.

Z169 WSZELAKI, JAN H. *Communist Economic Strategy; the Role of East-Central Europe*. Washington: National Planning Association, 1959. 132 p. One of a series of monographs on the "Economics of Competitive Coexistence." This study assesses the economies of Eastern Europe and estimates the economic advantages and disadvantages of their relationship to the Soviet Union. [B]

Z170 ZOLOTAREV, N. I. *Mirovoi sotsialisticheskii rynok*. Moscow: Sotsekgiz, 1961.

ZA. Collections of Documents on Soviet Foreign Relations and Treaties

EDITED BY ROBERT M. SLUSSER

ZA1 AKADEMIIA NAUK URSR, KIEV, SEKTOR DERZHAVY I PRAVA. *Ukrainska RSR i mizhnarodnykh vidnosynakh; mizhnarodni dogovory, konventsii, ugody ta inshi dokumenty, iaki skladeni za uchastiu Ukrainskoi RSR abo do iakykh vona pryednalasia, 1945-1957.* Comp. by K. S. Zabigailo and M. K. Mikhailovskyi. Ed. by L. Kh. Palamarchuk. Kiev: Vyd-vo Akademii nauk Ukr. RSR, 1959. 750 p.

ZA2 AMERICAN FOUNDATION FOR POLITICAL EDUCATION. *Readings in Russian Foreign Policy.* Ed. by Robert A. Goldwin and Marvin Zetterbaum. Chicago: 1953. Three vols. and supplement (51 p.). 2nd ed., 1953. Three vols. and supplement (44 p.). 3rd ed., 1958. Two vols. and supplement (48 p.). One volume paperback ed., edited by Robert A. Goldwin, Marvin Zetterbaum, and Gerald Stourzh. N.Y.: Oxford, 1959. 775 p. A selection of documents and articles covering Tsarist as well as Soviet Russian foreign policy.

ZA3 BABAIANTS, A. A. *Mezhdunarodnye otnosheniia i vneshniaia politika SSSR, 1939-1941; dokumenty i materialy.* Moscow: 1948.

ZA4 BUNYAN, JAMES T., comp. *Intervention, Civil War, and Communism in Russia, April-December 1918; Documents and Materials.* Baltimore: Johns Hopkins, 1936. 594 p. A standard collection, selected and edited with scholarly care. [B]

ZA5 DEGRAS, JANE. *Calendar of Soviet Documents on Foreign Policy, 1917-1941.* London and N.Y.: Royal Institute of International Affairs, 1948. 248 p. An invaluable guide to published material in the central Soviet press and elsewhere on Soviet international relations. [A]

ZA6 DEGRAS, JANE, ed. *Soviet Documents on Foreign Policy.* London and N.Y.: Oxford, 1951-53. 3 vols. Vol. I, 1917-24; Vol. II, 1925-32; Vol. III, 1933-41. An indispensable compilation, presented with scrupulous accuracy, but without editorial analysis or commentary. [A]

ZA7 *Documentation Relating to Foreign Economic Relations of the USSR.* Moscow: 1933. 65 p. Material prepared for the World Economic Conference held in London in 1933.

ZA8 *Documents on American Foreign Relations.* Boston: World Peace Foundation, annual, 1939-54. Includes a number of important Soviet documents and statements.

ZA9 *Documents on International Affairs*. London: Oxford, H. Milford, 1929—. Issued under the auspices of the Royal Institute of International Affairs, London. Designed to accompany the Institute's *Survey of International Affairs*, but independent, and of great value in providing both Soviet documents on international affairs and the context in which they appeared. [A]

ZA10 DURDENEVSKII, VSEVOLOD N., comp. *Pravila protsedury mezhdunarodnykh politicheskikh konferentsii xx veka; izbrannye dokumenty*. Moscow: Gos. izd. iurid, lit., 1955. 70 p.

ZA11 EUDIN, XENIA J., and FISHER, HAROLD H. *Soviet Russia and the West, 1920-1927; a Documentary Survey*. Stanford, Cal.: Stanford University Press, 1957. 450 p. Provides not only a well-chosen selection of documents, including those on Communist Party policy, but also concise editorial introductions and annotations. [A]

ZA12 EUDIN, XENIA, and NORTH, ROBERT C. *Soviet Russia and the East, 1920-1927; a Documentary Survey*. Stanford, Cal.: Stanford University Press, 1957. 478 p. A companion to the preceding volume, similar in scope and editorial policy. [A]

ZA13 FRANCE, DIRECTION DE LA DOCUMENTATION. *Principaux textes de politique internationale*. Paris: 1945—. Good translations of a wide selection of current documents in international relations.

ZA14 GANTENBEIN, JAMES W. *Documentary Background of World War II, 1931-41*. N.Y.: Columbia, 1948. 1122 p.

ZA15 HOETZSCH, OTTO, ed. *Der europäische Osten*. No. 6 of: *Dokumente zur Weltpolitik der Nachkriegszeit*. Leipzig: Teubner, 1933. 135 p. Contains a section on Soviet treaties.

ZA16 HUDSON, MANLEY O., ed. *International Legislation; a Collection of the Texts of Multipartite International Instruments of General Interest, Beginning with the Covenant of the League of Nations*. Washington: Carnegie Endowment, 1931-50. 9 vols. Accurate and well-edited texts of important multilateral treaties, including a number to which the USSR was a party. [B]

ZA17 KLIUCHNIKOV, IURII V., and SABANIN, ANDREI V., eds. *Mezhdunarodnaia politika noveishego vremeni v dogovorakh, notakh i deklaratsiakh*. Moscow: Litizdat NKID, 1925-39. 3 vols. in 4. Vol. I: *Ot frantsuzskoi revoliutsii do imperialisticheskoi voiny*. Vol. II: *Ot imperialisticheskoi voiny do sniatiia blokady s sovetskoi Rossii*. Vol. III: *Ot sniatiia blokady s sovetskoi Rossii do desiatiletiia Oktiabrskoi revoliutsii*. Part I: *Akty sovetskoi diplomatii*. Part 2: *Akty diplomatii inostrannykh gosudarstv*. Indispensable because of its inclusion of Soviet official documents not otherwise available. [A]

ZA18 KOMMUNISTICHESKAIA AKADEMIIA, MOSCOW, INSTITUT MIROVOGO KHOZIAISTVA I MIROVOI POLITIKI. *SSSR v borbe za mir; rechi i dokumenty*. Moscow: 1935. 146 p.

ZA19 KOMMUNISTICHESKAIA PARTIIA SOVETSKOGO SOIUZA, VYSSHAIA PARTIINAIA SHKOLA, KAFEDRA MEZHDUNARODNYKH OTNOSHENII. *Mezhdunarodnye otnosheniia i vneshniaia politika SSSR; sbornik dokumentov (1871-1957)*. Comp. by L. A. Kharlamov. Moscow: 1957. 429 p.

ZA20 KOROLENKO, A. S. *Torgovye dogovory i soglasheniia SSSR s inostrannymi gosudarstvami*. Moscow: Vneshtorgizdat, 1953. 315 p. Includes full texts of a number of Soviet trade treaties, as well as an authoritative analysis of Soviet foreign trade policy in general. [B]

ZA21 KRAUS, HERBERT, and HEINZE, KURT, eds. *Völkerrechtliche Urkunden zur europäischen Friedensordnung seit 1945; eine Sammlung der wichtigsten Verträge, Abkommen, Satzungen und Erklärungen*. Bonn: Schimmelbusch, 1953.

ZA22 LASERSON, MAX M., ed. *The Development of Soviet Foreign Policy in Europe, 1917-1942; A Selection of Documents*. N.Y.: Carnegie Endowment, 1943. 95 p. Largely superseded by later, more comprehensive collections, especially that of Jane Degras.

ZA23 LEAGUE OF NATIONS. *Treaty Series; Publication of Treaties and International Engagements Registered with the Secretariat of the League*. Geneva and Lausanne: 1920-45. 205 vols. Texts in English and French, and in the language of the original wherever possible. [A]

ZA23A LOVENTHAL, MILTON, ed. "Documents on Soviet Foreign Relations, 1934-1936." Mimeographed, p. 1-259 (covering January 27, 1934 through December 30, 1934); typescript, p. 260-547 (covering January 3, 1935 through March 14, 1936). Allegedly summaries of decisions taken by the Politburo; acquired by the German intelligence services during the years 1936-38, and captured by the U.S. Army after the war. The originals are now partly in the War Department archives, partly at the Hoover Institution. Their authenticity has been sharply challenged by leading specialists, but the possibility nevertheless exists that they are either partly or entirely genuine; there is evidence that the German intelligence services, after a careful check, came to this conclusion, and relied on the documents as valid information on the course of Soviet foreign policy.

ZA24 MEISSNER, BORIS. *Sowjetunion und Haager LKO, Gutachten und Dokumentenzusammenstellung.* Hamburg: Universität Hamburg, 1950. 68 p. (mimeographed). A useful collection on the formal attitude of the Soviet government towards the Hague Treaties.

ZA25 MISHUSTIN, D. D., ed. *Sbornik torgovykh dogovorov, konventsii i soglashenii SSSR, zakliuchennykh s inostrannymi gosudarstvami do 1 ianvaria 1941 g.* Moscow: NKVT, 1941. 408 p. [B]

ZA26 RÖNNEFARTH, HELMUTH K. G., and EULER, HEINRICH, eds. *Konferenzen und Verträge; Vertrags-Ploetz, ein Handbuch geschichtlich bedeutsamer Zusammenkünfte und Vereinbarungen.* Part II, vol. 4, *Neueste Zeit, 1914-1959.* 2nd ed. Würzburg: A. G. Ploetz, 1959. Provides summaries of major international agreements, including those to which Soviet Russia was a party.

ZA27 ROZENBLIUM, BORIS D., comp. *Mezhdunarodnye ekonomicheskie konferentsii i soglasheniia 1933-1935 gg. . . .; sbornik dokumentov.* Moscow: NKID, 1936. 265 p.

ZA28 RUSSIA (1917- RSFSR). *The Soviet Union and Peace; the Most Important of the Documents Issued by the Government Concerning Peace and Disarmament from 1917 to 1929.* London: Lawrence, 1929. 280 p.

ZA29 RUSSIA (1917- RSFSR), NARODNYI KOMISSARIAT PO INOSTRANNYM DELAM. *Sbornik deistvuiushchikh dogovorov, soglashenii i konventsii, zakliuchennykh RSFSR s inostrannymi gosudarstvami.* Moscow: NKID, 1921-23. Five vols. in two. The basic treaty series for the RSFSR period. Plagued by faulty editing, but more liberal in spirit and more inclusive in coverage than the later Soviet treaty series. [A]

ZA30 RUSSIA (1917- RSFSR), TREATIES, ETC. *Russlands Friedens- und Handelsvertraege 1918-1923; auf Grund amtlichen Materials.* Translated by Heinrich Freund, with an introduction by Paul Heilborn. Leipzig: Teubner, 1924. 196 p. Careful German translations, sponsored by the Breslau Osteuropa-Institut, of the major Russian treaties of this period.

ZA31 RUSSIA (1922- USSR), NARODNYI KOMISSARIAT PO INOSTRANNYM DELAM. *Ezhegodnik NKID na 192- g. Annuaire diplomatique du Commissariat du Peuple pour les Affaires Étrangères.* Moscow: Izd. litizdata NKID, 1925-35. Published annually in French and Russian. Includes the texts of some treaties and other diplomatic documents. [A]

ZA32 RUSSIA (1923- USSR). *Deklaratsii, zaiavleniia i kommiunike Sovetskogo pravitelstva s pravitelstvami inostrannykh gosudarstv 1954-1957 gg.* Moscow: Gospolitizdat, 1957. 328 p. [B]

ZA33 RUSSIA (1923- USSR), ARMIIA, GLAVNOE POLITICHESKOE UPRAVLENIE. *Mezhdunarodnoe polozhenie i vneshniaia politika SSSR; sbornik dokumentov i materialov.* Moscow: Gos. voen. izd., 1939. 205 p.

ZA34 RUSSIA (1923- USSR), KOMISSIIA PO IZDANIIU DIPLOMATICHESKIKH DOKUMENTOV. *Dokumenty vneshnei politiki SSSR.* Moscow: Gospolitizdat, 1957—. In progress. Seven volumes have so far been issued; they cover the period from November 1917 to January 1925. This series is the fullest, most accurate, and best edited selection from the Soviet diplomatic archives published so far; if completed as begun, it will provide for the first time the basis for a realistic appraisal of Soviet foreign policy. Not to be used without caution, however; the editing reflects occasional political pressures. [A]

ZA35 RUSSIA (1923- USSR), NARODNYI KOMISSARIAT PO INOSTRANNYM DELAM. *Desiat let Sovetskoi diplomatii; akty i dokumenty, 1917-1927.* Moscow: Narkomindel, 1927. 123 p. [B]

ZA36 RUSSIA (1923- USSR), NARODNYI KOMISSARIAT VNESHNEI I VNUTRENNEI TORGOVLI. *Sbornik deistvuiushchikh dekretov i postanovlenii po vneshnei torgovle.* Moscow: NKVT, 1924-26. 4 vols.

ZA37 RUSSIA (1923- USSR), TREATIES, ETC. *Dogovory o neitralitete, nenapadenii i o soglasitelnoi protsedure, zakliuchennye mezhdu Soiuzom SSR i inostrannymi gosudarstvami. Traités de neutralité, de nonaggression, et de procédure de conciliation entre l'Union des RSS et les états étrangères.* Moscow: NKID, 1934. 196 p. [B]

ZA38 RUSSIA (1923- USSR), TREATIES, ETC. *Dogovory ob okazanii pravovoi pomoshchi po grazhdanskim, semeinym i ugolovnym delam, zakliuchennye Sovetskim Soiuzom v 1957-1958 gg.* Ed. by M. D. Grishin. Moscow: Gosiurizdat, 1959. 285 p. [B]

ZA39 RUSSIA (1923- USSR), TREATIES, ETC. *Mezhdunarodnye konventsii i soglasheniia, otnosiashchiesia k torgovomu moreplavaniiu; sbornik.* Comp. by L. A. Furman. Moscow: Morskoi transport, 1940. 195 p. New ed., 1947.

ZA40 RUSSIA (1923- USSR), TREATIES, ETC. *Sbornik deistvuiushchikh dogovorov, soglashenii i konventsii, zakliuchennykh SSSR s inostrannymi gosudarstvami.* Moscow: Gospolitizdat, 1924—. In progress. The basic Soviet treaty publication. Its bibliographical history is complicated, and reflects the vicissitudes of the Commissariat (since 1945 the Ministry) of Foreign Affairs. Coverage has been erratic; many Soviet treaties, including some of the most important, have not been published in the *Sbornik*. Approximate coverage of the individual volumes:

Vol. 1: Treaties of the RSFSR, 1918-23.
Vol. 2: 1923-24.

(Volumes 1 and 2 were reprinted in a single volume in 1928, with amendments and revisions.)

Vol. 3 (1927): 1923-26. (Reprinted with changes, 1932.)
Vol. 4 (1928): 1924-27. (Reprinted with changes, 1936.)
Vol. 5: 1924-29.
Vol. 6: 1925-30.
Vol. 7: 1929-32.
Vol. 8: 1929-35.
Vol. 9: 1934-37.

After vol. 9, there was a hiatus; no further volumes of the *Sbornik* were published during Stalin's lifetime. Publication was resumed in 1955.

Vol. 10: 1937-40.
Vol. 11: 1945-46.
Vol. 12: 1945-46.
Vol. 13: 1946-48.
Vol. 14: 1948-53.
Vol. 15: 1953-54.
Vol. 16: 1954.
Vol. 17: 1955.
Vol. 18: 1956. (Vols. 17 and 18 were issued in one.)
Vol. 19: 1957.
Vol. 20: 1958.

An index to the volumes published up to 1935 was issued in that year: RUSSIA (1923- USSR), NARODNYI KOMISSARIAT PO INOSTRANNYM DELAM. *Ukazateli k deistvuiushchim dogovoram, soglasheniiam i konventsiiam, zakliuchennym s inostrannymi gosudarstvami.* Comp. by A. V. Sabanin. Moscow: Izd. NKID, 1935. This index is by no means reliable, and adds little to what can be learned from the individual volumes. [A]

ZA41 RUSSIA (1923- USSR), TREATIES, ETC. *Sbornik deistvuiushchikh torgovykh dogovorov i inykh khoziaistvennykh soglashenii SSSR, zakliuchennykh s inostrannymi gosudarstvami.* Comp. by Boris D. Rozenblium. Moscow: NKID, 1936. Only two issues have been identified. [B]

ZA42 RUSSIA (1923- USSR), TREATIES, ETC. *Sbornik mezhdunarodnykh konventsii, dogovorov, soglashenii i pravil po voprosam torgovogo moreplavaniia.* Ed. by Iu. A. Bulushev and others. Moscow: Morskoi transport, 1959. 474 p.

ZA43 RUSSIA (1923- USSR), TREATIES, ETC. *Sbornik torgovykh dogovorov, torgovykh i platezhnykh soglashenii i dolgosrochnykh torgovykh soglashenii SSSR s inostrannymi gosudarstvami, na 1 ianvariia 1961 g.* Comp. by A. D. Aleksandrov and E. K. Medvedev. Ed. by K. K. Bakhtov. Moscow: Vneshtorgizdat, 1961. 623 p. [A]

ZA44 RUSSIA (1923- USSR), TREATIES, ETC., 1958. *Soglasheniia o sotrudnichestve i pomoshchi v oblasti mirnogo ispolzovaniia atomnoi energii, zakliuchennye Sovetskim Soiuzom s drugimi stranami.* Moscow: Atomizdat, 1958. 26 p. [B]

ZA45 SABANIN, ANDREI V. *Khronologicheskii perechen mezhdunarodnykh mnogostoronnykh dogovorov, zakliuchennykh s 1919 po 1933 g., s kratkim izlozheniem ikh soderzhaniia.* Moscow: Gos. izd. sovetskoe zakonodatelstvo, 1933. 138 p.

ZA46 *Sbornik dokumentov po mezhdunarodnoi politike i mezhdunarodnomu pravu.* Ed. by K. V. Antonov and others. Moscow: 1932-36. 10 vols. Volumes dealing with a variety of topics in international affairs: disarmament, the Japanese-Chinese conflict, reports of various international commissions and congresses, etc.

ZA47 SHAPIRO, LEONARD, comp. and ed. *Soviet Treaty Series; a Collection of Bilateral Treaties, Agreements and Conventions, etc., Concluded between the Soviet Union and Foreign Powers.* Washington: Georgetown U., 1950-55. Two vols.: vol. I covers from 1917 to 1928; vol. II from 1928 to 1939. A third volume was planned, but never published. In spite of its value as a pioneering effort, should be used with extreme caution; serious errors of fact and translation are fairly numerous. [B]

ZA48 SLUSSER, ROBERT M., and TRISKA, JAN F., with the assistance of GINSBURGS, GEORGE, and REINERS, WILFRED O. *A Calendar of Soviet Treaties, 1917-1957.* Stanford, Cal.: Stanford University Press, 1959. 530 p. Provides a chronological listing of identified international agreements of Soviet Russia through 1957, with references to sources or other identifications. For important agreements after 1940 a brief summary is generally given. The bibliography, p. 450-60, lists important sources for Soviet treaties. Continued by Slusser and Ginsburgs for the years after 1957 in *Osteuropa-Recht* (Stuttgart: 1961- ; in progress). [A]

ZA49 *The Soviet Union and the Path of Peace; Lenin—Stalin—Molotov—Voroshilov—Litvinov—Tukhachevsky (A Collection of Statements and Documents, 1917-1936).* London: Lawrence and Wishart, 1936. 201 p.

ZA50 UNITED NATIONS. *Treaty Series; Treaties and International Agreements Registered or Filed and Recorded with the Secretariat of the United Nations. Recueil des traités; traités et accords internationaux enregistrés ou classés et inscrits au répertoire au Sécretariat de l'organisation des Nations Unies.* N.Y.: 1946—. Continues the League of Nations *Treaty Series*, with texts in English and French and the original languages of each agreement. Often provides not only the most accurate but the only generally available text of important Soviet treaties. [A]

ZA51 *Vneshniaia politika Sovetskogo Soiuza; dokumenty i materialy.* Moscow: Gospolitizdat, 1945-51. Annual, 1945-46; Semiannual, 1947-51. Continues the series initiated with *Vneshniaia politika Sovetskogo Soiuza v period Otechestvennoi Voiny*. In effect, it replaced the *Sbornik deistvuiushchikh dogovorov . . .*, but it includes much documentation other than treaty texts. [A]

ZA52 *Vneshniaia politika Sovetskogo Soiuza v period Otechestvennoi voiny; dokumenty i materialy.* Moscow: Gospolitizdat, 1944-47. 3 vols. English trans. of vols. 1 and 2 by Andrew Rothstein, London: Hutchinson, 1944-45. A convenient but by no means complete record of Soviet diplomatic activity during World War II. [A]

ZA53 *Vneshniaia politika SSSR; sbornik dokumentov.* Comp. by A. S. Tisminets. Moscow: Vysshaia partiinaia shkola pri Tsk VKP (b), 1944-47. 5 vols. Compiled mainly on the basis of the central Soviet press, to which it thus furnishes a convenient guide. All known copies have been deprived of the editor's notes. [B]

ZA54 WHITE RUSSIA, MINISTERSTVO INOSTRANNYKH DEL. *Belorusskaia SSR v mezhdunarodnykh otnosheniiakh; mezhdunarodnye dogovory, konventsii i soglasheniia Belorusskoi SSR s inostrannymi gosudarstvami (1944-1959).* Comp. by S. P. Margunskii and A. S. Zaitsev. Minsk: Izd. Akademii nauk Belorusskoi SSR, 1960. 1049 p.

ZA55 ZONNENSHTRAL-PISKORSKII, A. A. *Mezhdunarodnye torgovye dogovory i soglasheniia, 1919-1924 (sistematicheskii obzor).* Moscow: NKVT, 1925. 142 p.

ZB. Bibliographies

EDITED BY THOMAS T. HAMMOND

NOTE: This is a highly selective list, giving only a few of the most useful bibliographies in the broad field of Soviet foreign relations and world Communism. Specialized bibliographies dealing with a particular country or subject are listed in the appropriate sections. Many additional bibliographies of a more general nature are included in the "List of Sources."

ZB1 AKADEMIIA NAUK SSSR, FUNDAMENTALNAIA BIBLIOTEKA OBSHCHESTVENNYKH NAUK. *Istoriia SSSR; ukazatel sovetskoi literatury za 1917-1952 gg.* Comp. by I. P. Doronin and others. Chief ed., K. P. Simon. Moscow: Izd. Akademii nauk SSSR, 1956—. (To be 3 vols.) Includes works in the Russian language published in the USSR from the Revolution to the end of 1952. Since it is designed for students doing advanced work in history faculties in Soviet universities, popular works have been excluded. Vol. I (1956) covers ancient times to 1861; vol. II (1958) deals with the "period of capitalism," 1861-1917; and vol. III is to cover 1917 through 1952. Each volume is arranged by period and subject. The majority of the entries are periodical articles. Some items have brief annotations. For each volume there is a separately bound index (*prilozhenie*) containing a detailed table of contents, index of authors, index of names, index of places, and list of periodicals cited. Vol. III should be of great value on Soviet foreign relations.

ZB2 *The American Bibliography of Slavic and East European Studies.* Ed. by Joseph T. Shaw and others. Bloomington, Ind.: Indiana Univ. Publications, Russian and East European Series, 1957—. The first volume (for 1956) covered only the humanities; beginning with 1957 the social sciences have been included. Originally was limited to works published in the Americas or by Americans, but the 1961 volume was expanded to include works in English published anywhere outside of the USSR and Eastern Europe. Lists both articles and books, including reprints, revised editions, and paperbacks. Organized under broad subject categories such as "Geography," "History," etc. The volume for 1961 has 17 pages on "International Relations." Not annotated. [A]

ZB3 AMERICAN UNIVERSITIES FIELD STAFF. *A Select Bibliography: Asia, Africa, Eastern Europe, Latin America.* Phillips Talbot, general ed., Nelda S. Freeman, editorial coordinator. N.Y.: A.U.F.S., 1960. 534 p. Designed in part for librarians, to aid them in choosing the best books on non-Western areas. The most important titles are annotated, and Library of Congress card numbers are given for each book. The sections on Russia and East-Central Europe were compiled by Robert F. Byrnes and Joseph Backor. On Russia there are about 1100 titles and on East-Central Europe about 350 titles, all in English, and dealing with all aspects of life in these countries. There are 7 columns on "Russia in World Politics Since 1917" and 7 columns on "The International Communist Movement." A *Supplement* issued in 1961 lists 100 books on Russia and East-Central Europe published between June 1959 and June 1961.

ZB4 COLUMBIA UNIVERSITY, RUSSIAN INSTITUTE. *Report on Research and Publication.* N.Y.: 1948—. Annual lists of articles and books published by faculty and students of the Russian Institute, research in progress, essays for the certificate of the Institute, and Ph.D. dissertations accepted. A cumulative volume was issued under the title, *The Russian Institute, 1946-1959*. A later number was called, *The Russian Institute, 1959-1960*. Useful for locating unpublished monographs on Soviet foreign relations and world Communism.

ZB4A DELANEY, ROBERT FINLEY. *The Literature of American Communism; a Selected Reference Guide.* Washington: Catholic University of America Press, 1962. 433 p. Contains about 1,700 entries, with full annotations. Despite the title, it has sections on "World Communist Literature," "Philosophy and Theory of Communism," etc., although the majority of the entries deal with American Communism. According to the preface, the book is designed, among other things: "1. To provide librarians with a guide to a well-rounded collection of books covering . . . both international and American Communism, which . . . point out the basic dangers in both the philosophical and political sense of this totalitarian movement. 2. To provide an insight into the inherent evil of Communism. . . ."

ZB5 DOSSICK, JESSE J. *Doctoral Research on Russia and the Soviet Union.* N.Y.: New York Univ. Press, 1960. 248 p. Lists about a thousand American, British and Canadian dissertations accepted through 1959. On pages 189-213 are listed dissertations on such subjects as "Intervention in Siberia," "Soviet Diplomacy, Foreign Policy, Military Power and International Law," "The U.S. and the U.S.S.R.," "China and the U.S.S.R.," etc. Very useful. Not annotated.

ZB6 EGOROV, V. N., comp. *Mezhdunarodnye otnosheniia; bibliograficheskii spravochnik (1945-1960 gg.).* Moscow: Izd-vo Instituta mezhdunarodnykh otnoshenii, 1962. 406 p. An annotated bibliography of books and pamphlets published in the USSR in the Russian language, 1945-60. Includes speeches by Soviet leaders, documentary collections, yearbooks, and guides. Entries are arranged in six chapters: I. The

Founders of Marxism-Leninism on International Relations. II. Foreign Policy and International Relations (by country). III. The World Economy (by country). IV. The International Communist and Labor Movement. V. International Law. VI. International Organizations. Despite its limited scope and propagandistic tone, this seems to be the most ambitious bibliography on the broad subject of international relations ever published in the USSR.

ZB7 *Foreign Affairs Bibliography; a Selected and Annotated List of Books on International Relations.* 4 vols. N.Y.: Published by Harper for the Council on Foreign Relations, 1933-64: vol. I, covering books published in 1919-32, ed. by William L. Langer and Hamilton Fish Armstrong; vol. II, covering 1932-42, ed. by Robert G. Woolbert; vol. III, 1942-52, and vol. IV, 1952-62, ed. by Henry L. Roberts. (Volume IV was published by R. R. Bowker.) The standard guide to books in the whole broad field of world affairs. Based largely on the bibliographical notes appearing in each issue of the quarterly, *Foreign Affairs.* The first two volumes included few Soviet books. Vol. III lists more than 9,000 works in 34 languages; the section on "Socialism; Communism" is 4 pages long, while 7 pages deal with Soviet foreign policy, military policy, the Comintern, and the Civil War and Intervention. An indispensable reference work for the student of international affairs. Current publications are listed in each issue of *Foreign Affairs.* [A]

ZB8 GRIERSON, PHILIP. *Books on Soviet Russia, 1917-1942.* London: Methuen, 1943. 354 p. Lists books published in Great Britain between Feb. 1917 and the end of June 1942. Also includes a few works, chiefly collections of documents and personal memoirs, published in the U.S. and the USSR and occasionally in languages other than English. Still the basic bibliography of books in English on the Soviet Union, though badly out of date. Has sections on "Intervention and the Civil War," "The Third International," and "Soviet Foreign Policy." A very useful guide. Annotated. Annual supplements were published in the *Slavonic and East European Review*, beginning with the issue of January 1946. Carew Hunt's *Books on Communism* is a partial supplement to Grierson. [A]

ZB9 HARVARD UNIVERSITY, RUSSIAN RESEARCH CENTER. *Ten Year Report and Current Projects, 1948-1958.* Cambridge: 1958. 107 p. Lists books, chapters in books, and articles published, materials duplicated for limited distribution, and research in progress. A number of the studies deal with Soviet foreign relations or world Communism.

ZB10 HORECKY, PAUL L., ed. *Basic Russian Publications; an Annotated Bibliography on Russia and the Soviet Union.* Chicago: U. of

Chicago Press, 1962. 313 p. Contains about 1600 titles. Designed as a guide to the most essential Russian-language books for college libraries, in all fields except medicine and the natural sciences. Although it is a most valuable reference work, space limitations allowed the listing of only 25 titles on Soviet foreign relations. Well annotated, and with complete bibliographical information.

ZB11 HUNT, ROBERT N. CAREW, ed. *Books on Communism.* London: Ampersand, 1959. 333 p. Largely limited to books published in English, 1945-57, with the addition of a few published in 1958. Part I, "Studies of Communism in General and in the USSR," serves as a partial supplement to Grierson (see above). Part II, "Communism in Other Countries," covers most of the world, country by country. Part III lists official documents and publications of the United Kingdom, Commonwealth governments, and the U.S. Government. Contains 1,500 items. Annotated. A very useful little book. [A]

ZB12 IUNOVICH, MINNA M. *Literatura po mirovomu khoziastvu i morovoi politike za 10 let (1917-1927); bibliograficheskii ukazatel knig na russkom iazyke.* Moscow: Kommunisticheskaia akademiia, 1928. 88 p. 2nd ed., 1929. 255 p. The 2nd edition includes articles as well as books. Contains sections on world politics and the world revolutionary movement. Very useful as a source of Soviet titles during the early years of the regime, when other bibliographic guides were rather inadequate. Not annotated.

ZB13 MEHNERT, KLAUS, ed. *Die Sovet-Union, 1917-1932; systematische, mit kommentaren versehene Bibliographie der 1917-1932 in deutscher Sprache ausserhalb der Sovet-Union veröffentlichten 1900 wichstigsten Bücher und Aufsätze über den Bolshewismus und die Sovet-Union.* Königsberg: Ost-Europa Verlag, 1933. 186 p. Useful for items published in German during the first years after the Bolshevik Revolution. The editor is a distinguished German scholar who has long specialized in Soviet studies.

ZB14 *Mezhdunarodnyi politiko-ekonomicheskii ezhegodnik.* Moscow: Gospolitizdat, 1958—. Issued by the Institut Mirovoi Ekonomiki i Mezhdunarodnykh Otnoshenii of the Academy of Sciences. An annual handbook, which contains among other things a bibliography of books on international relations published during the previous year in the countries of the Communist bloc. The bibliography in the volume for 1960, for example, is 36 pages long.

ZB15 PENNSYLVANIA, DEPARTMENT OF PUBLIC INSTRUCTION. *World Communism: a Selected, Annotated Bibliography.* Harrisburg, Pa.: 1958. 20 p. Prepared by the Legislative Reference Service of the Library of Congress. Designed for public school teachers and advanced high school students. About 200 entries. Many of the annotations simply repeat the table of contents or a quotation from the introduction to the book.

ZB16 PRAGUE, RUSSKII ZAGRANICHNYI ISTORICHESKII ARKHIV. *Bibliografiia russkoi revoliutsii i grazhdanskoi voiny (1917-1921); iz kataloga biblioteki R. z. i. arkhiva.* Edited by Jan Slavik. Comp. by S. P. Postnikov. Prague: 1938. 448 p. An excellent bibliography on the period 1917 to 1921, based on a library collected in Prague by Russian émigrés. Contains a section on the Comintern and Profintern. In each section the titles in Cyrillic (the majority) are listed first, followed by titles in West European languages. Not annotated.

ZB17 PUNDEFF, MARIN, comp. *Recent Publications on Communism.* Los Angeles: Research Institute on Communist Strategy and Propaganda, Univ. of Southern California, 1962. 66 p. (duplicated) Lists about 950 books and pamphlets in English, mostly published in the years 1957-62. Paperbacks included regardless of date of publication. Intended in part as a supplement to Hunt's *Books on Communism* (see above). Contains sections on "Communism in East Europe, East Asia, and Cuba," "Divergent Communisms," and "World Communist Movement." Not annotated; intended as a preliminary edition.

ZB18 *The Russian Review.* N.Y.: 1941—. Quarterly. Each year from 1942 through 1958 the July issue contained a bibliography of books, pamphlets, and articles published in English during the preceding year. Since then it has been replaced by *The American Bibliography of Slavic and East European Studies* (see above). Covers mainly American publications, plus some Canadian and British works. Books and articles are grouped separately and are arranged alphabetically by author, not by subject. Not annotated.

ZB19 SOVETSKAIA ASSOTSIATSIIA MEZHDUNARODNOGO PRAVA. *Sovetskaia literatura po mezhdunarodnomu pravu; bibliografiia, 1917-1957.* Ed. by V. N. Durdenevskii. Moscow: Gos. izd. iurid. lit., 1959. 303 p. A comprehensive and elaborately classified list of books, pamphlets, articles and documents on public and private international law published in Russian in the USSR, with the exception of books translated from other languages. Book entries include lists of reviews in Soviet periodicals. Many items concern international relations in general as well as law. A supplement lists most publications issued in 1958.

ZB20 U.S. DEPARTMENT OF STATE, BUREAU OF INTELLIGENCE AND RESEARCH. *An Essay on Sources for the Study of the Communist Party of the Soviet Union, 1934-1960*, by John A. Armstrong. Washington: 1961. 41 p. (mimeographed) A bibliographic essay on the sources used by the author in the preparation of his book,

The Politics of Totalitarianism, vol. III of *A History of the Communist Party of the Soviet Union* (N.Y.: Random House, 1961). Although primarily concerned with internal affairs, it discusses some items dealing with foreign relations.

ZB21 U.S. DEPARTMENT OF STATE, BUREAU OF INTELLIGENCE AND RESEARCH, EXTERNAL RESEARCH STAFF. *External Research, a List of Recently Completed Studies.* (Annual, published each fall.) *External Research, a List of Studies Currently in Progress.* Separate lists: *USSR*, and *Eastern Europe.* (Annual, published each spring.) Washington: Dept. of State, 1952—. A series of research lists based on a card catalogue of social science research on foreign areas, compiled from information furnished by private scholars throughout the U.S. The lists are not cumulative. Annotations (when given) are supplied by the author. The author's university affiliation or other address is indicated. For research in progress the estimated completion date is given, and for research completed the publisher is supplied. Arranged by subjects, including "USSR, Foreign Relations." A very helpful guide to current research, especially for studies not yet finished or not yet published.

ZB22 U.S. DEPARTMENT OF STATE, DIVISION OF LIBRARY AND REFERENCE SERVICES. *Soviet Bibliography.* Washington: June 8, 1949-June 17, 1953. Fortnightly (mimeographed). Each issue consisted of about 20 pages listing current articles and books in English on the USSR and its impact on the Satellites and the world in general. Arranged by subjects, with most of the entries annotated. Very useful for the four years covered. Discontinued "due to the necessity for the conservation of manpower," nothing has ever really taken its place.

ZB23 U.S. INFORMATION AGENCY. *Communism—Critical Analysis.* Washington: U.S.I.A., Sept. 26, 1958. 62 p. (Information Center Service, Special List SL-16). One of a series of lists prepared for officials in U.S. Information Centers overseas, it includes "those books particularly recommended for use in exposing the strategy and fallacies of international communism." Includes 141 books in English, with lengthy annotations.

ZB24 U.S. LIBRARY OF CONGRESS, DIVISION OF BIBLIOGRAPHY. *Soviet Russia: a Selected List of Recent References.* Comp. by Helen F. Conover under the direction of Florence S. Hellman. Washington: 1943. 85 p. (mimeographed) Contains 57 entries under "Foreign Relations" and 132 under "World War II." Includes books, pamphlets and articles. The Library of Congress call number is given for each item. Author index. No annotations.

ZB25 U.S. LIBRARY OF CONGRESS, PROCESSING DEPARTMENT. *Monthly Index of Russian Accessions.* Washington: 1948—. (From 1948 to 1957 the title was: *Monthly List of Russian Accessions.*) Lists publications in the Russian language currently received by the Library of Congress and cooperating libraries. Publications in other languages of the USSR also included when possible. Part A lists monographic literature. Part B lists Russian periodicals received. Part C is a subject index to the monographs listed in Part A and to the articles appearing in a long list of Soviet periodicals. Parts A and B do not group titles under "Soviet Foreign Relations," "World Communism," or any similar classification; however, the subject index in Part C does have a heading: "Russia—Foreign Relations." This is an important guide to current Soviet publications, especially articles. Not annotated. [A]

ZB26 VIKTOROV-TOPOROV, VLADIMIR. *Rossica et Sovietica; Bibliographie des ouvrages parus en français de 1917 à 1930 inclus relatifs à la Russie et à l'U.R.S.S.* Saint-Cloud: Éditions Documentaires et Bibliographiques, 1931. 130 p. Lists 1312 books, including novels. Not annotated. Bibliographical data rather incomplete.

ZB27 VINCENNES, FRANCE, BIBLIOTHÈQUE DE DOCUMENTATION INTERNATIONALE CONTEMPORAINE ET MUSÉE DE LA GRANDE GUERRE. *Catalogue méthodique du fonds russe de la bibliothèque.* Ed. by Alexandra Dumesnil, with the collaboration of Wilfrid Lerat. Paris: A. Costes, 1932. 734 p. Based on the holdings of one of the best libraries on Russia in Western Europe, now located in Paris. Contains over 6,000 entries, the bulk of them in Russian. Russian authors and titles are translated into French. Quite useful for the period 1917 to 1932. Not annotated.

Addenda

ZB28 HORECKY, PAUL L., ed. *Russia and the Soviet Union; a Bibliographic Guide to Western-Language Publications.* Chicago: Univ. of Chicago Press, 1965. 473 p. A companion volume to ZB10 (above). Devotes 18 pages to Soviet foreign relations and international Communism.

ZB29 KOLARZ, WALTER, ed. *Books on Communism.* London: Ampersand, 1963. 568 p. A revision and expansion of Carew Hunt's bibliography (see above, ZB11), although Hunt's name no longer appears on the title page. Approximately 700 new entries extend the coverage through 1962, with some publications from 1963 also included. [A]

List of Principal Sources

USED BY THE GENERAL EDITOR IN COLLECTING TITLES

NOTE: The General Editor used many bibliographies in monographs in addition to those listed here; the contributing editors have also utilized numerous other bibliographies in their specialized fields.

A. *UNPUBLISHED CARD CATALOGUES IN LIBRARIES*

(Appropriate sections of the following card catalogues were microfilmed and positive Xerox copies were made from the microfilms, thus duplicating the original cards.)

BIBLIOTHÈQUE DE DOCUMENTATION INTERNATIONALE CONTEMPORAINE (PARIS). Card catalogue of subjects.

SLUSSER, ROBERT M., and TRISKA, JAN F., compilers.
Card catalogue on Soviet foreign relations. (Loaned to the editor by Mr. Triska.)

COLUMBIA UNIVERSITY, EAST ASIATIC LIBRARY. Card catalogue of books and unpublished studies on Soviet relations with Asian countries.

NEW YORK PUBLIC LIBRARY. Card catalogue of subjects.

NEW YORK PUBLIC LIBRARY. Card catalogue of the Slavonic Collection.

U.S. LIBRARY OF CONGRESS. Card catalogue of subjects.

U.S. LIBRARY OF CONGRESS. Cyrillic Union Catalogue.

B. *LIBRARY CATALOGUES PUBLISHED IN BOOK FORM*

The National Union Catalog; a Cumulative Author List Representing Library of Congress Printed Cards and Titles Reported by Other American Libraries, 1953-1957. Ann Arbor, Mich.: Edwards, 1958. 28 vols. (Also annual sets beginning with 1958.)

NEW YORK PUBLIC LIBRARY, REFERENCE DEPARTMENT. *Dictionary Catalog of the Slavonic Collection.* Boston: G. K. Hall, 1959. 26 vols.

U.S. LIBRARY OF CONGRESS. *A Catalog of Books Represented by Library of Congress Printed Cards Issued to July 31, 1942.* Ann Arbor, Mich.: Edwards, 1942-46. 167 vols. *Supplement, Cards Issued August 1, 1942 to December 31, 1947.* 42 vols.

U.S. LIBRARY OF CONGRESS. *The Library of Congress Author Catalog: a Cumulative List of Works Represented by the Library of Congress Printed Cards, 1948-1952.* Ann Arbor, Mich.: Edwards, 1953. 23 vols.

U.S. LIBRARY OF CONGRESS. *Library of Congress Catalogue. Books: Subjects. A Cumulative List of Works Represented by Library of Congress Printed Cards, 1955-1959.* Paterson, N.J.: Pageant Books, 1960. 22 vols.

U.S. LIBRARY OF CONGRESS. *Library of Congress Catalog; a Cumulative List of Works Represented by Library of Congress Printed Cards. Books: Subjects, 1950-1954.* Ann Arbor, Mich.: Edwards, 1955. 20 vols.

C. *GENERAL BIBLIOGRAPHIES*

AKADEMIIA NAUK SSSR, INSTITUT NARODOV AZII. *Bibliografiia Iaponii; literatura izdannaia v sovetskom soiuze na russkom iazyke s 1917 po 1958 g.* Moscow: Izd. Vostoch. lit., 1960. 328 p.

The American Bibliography of Slavic and East European Studies. Ed. by Joseph T. Shaw and others. Bloomington, Ind.: Indiana Univ. Publications, Russian and East European Series, 1957-63. 6 vols. (covering the years 1956-61).

AMERICAN HISTORICAL ASSOCIATION. *Guide to Historical Literature.* Ed. by G. F. Howe and others. N.Y.: Macmillan, 1961. 962 p.

AMERICAN POLITICAL SCIENCE ASSOCIATION. *The American Political Science Review.* Washington: 1941-1960.

AMERICAN UNIVERSITIES FIELD STAFF. *A Select Bibliography: Asia, Africa, Eastern Europe, Latin America.* Phillips Talbot, General Editor, and Nelda S. Freeman, Editorial Coordinator. N.Y.: 1960. 534 p. *Supplement, 1961.* N.Y.: 1961.

BERTON, PETER A., comp. *Soviet Works on China; A Bibliography of Non-Periodical Literature, 1946-1955.* Los Angeles: UCLA, 1959. 158 p.

Biblio; Catalogue des ouvrages parus en langue française dans le monde entier. Paris: Hachette, 1934-60 (annual).

A Bibliography of Finland. Washington: 1940. 21 p.

BOLTON, A. R. C. *Soviet Middle East Studies; an Analysis and Bibliography.* London: Distributed for the Royal Institute of International Affairs by Oxford Univ. Press, 1959. 8 parts.

BRITISH MUSEUM, DEPARTMENT OF PRINTED BOOKS. *Subject Index of the Modern Works Added to the British Museum Library.* London: British Museum, 1916-45. 8 vols.

The British National Bibliography. London: Council of the British National Bibliography, 1950-58.

BYRNES, ROBERT F. ed. *Bibliography of American Publications on East Central Europe, 1945-1957.* Bloomington: Indiana University Publications, 1958. 213 p.

The Cumulative Book Index; a World List of Books in the English Language, 1928–, Supplementing the United States Catalogue, Fourth Edition. N.Y.: Wilson, 1933–. (Checked volumes through 1960.)

Deutsche Bibliographie; Halbjahres-Verzeichnis. Frankfurt a.M.: Buchändler-Vereinigung, 1951-59. Also: *Deutsche Bibliographie, 1945-1950.* Frankfort a.M.: Buchändler-Vereinigung, 1953-57. 4 vols.

DEUTSCHE GESELLSCHAFT ZUM STUDIUM OSTEUROPAS. *Die Geschichtswissenschaft in Sowjet-Russland 1917-1927; bibliographischer Katalog.* Berlin: Ost-Europa-Verlag, 1928. 192 p.

Deutsches Bücherverzeichnis. Leipzig: 1915-50. 6 vols.

EGOROV, V. N., comp. *Mezhdunarodnye otnosheniia; bibliograficheskii spravochnik (1945-1960 gg.).* Moscow: Izd-vo Instituta mezhdunarodnykh otnoshenii, 1962. 406 p.

EUDIN, XENIA J. and FISHER, HAROLD H., eds. *Soviet Russia and the West, 1920-1927.* Stanford: Stanford Univ. Press, 1957.

EUDIN, XENIA J. and NORTH, ROBERT C., eds. *Soviet Russia and the East, 1920-1927.* Stanford: Stanford Univ. Press, 1957.

Foreign Affairs, An American Quarterly Review. N.Y.: Council on Foreign Relations, 1953-60.

Foreign Affairs Bibliography. N.Y.: Harper, 1933-55. 3 vols.

GRIERSON, PHILIP. *Books on Soviet Russia, 1917-1942.* London: Methuen, 1943. 354 p.

GRIERSON, PHILIP. Annual book lists published in *Slavonic and East European Review* (London), 1946-50, supplementing his *Books on Soviet Russia.*

A Guide to Historical Literature. Ed. by George M. Dutcher and others. N.Y.: Macmillan, 1936. 1222 p.

HALPERN, JOEL, ed. *Bibliography of Anthropological and Sociological Publications on Eastern Europe and the U.S.S.R. (English Language Sources).* Los Angeles: Russian and East European Studies Center, U.C.L.A., January 1961. 142 p.

HARVARD UNIVERSITY, RUSSIAN RESEARCH CENTER. *Bibliography of Russian Literature on China and Adjacent Countries, 1931-1936.* Comp. by Rudolf Loewenthal. Cambridge: November 1949. 93 p.

HERRE, FRANZ, and AUERBACH, HELLMUTH, comps. *Bibliographie zur Zeitgeschichte und zum Zweiten Weltkrieg für die Jahre 1945-50.* Munich: Selbstverlag des Instituts, 1955. 254 p.

HORECKY, PAUL L., ed. *Basic Russian Publications; an Annotated Bibliography on Russia and the Soviet Union.* Chicago: University of Chicago Press, 1962. 313 p.

HUNT, ROBERT N. CAREW, ed. *Books on Communism.* London: Ampersand, 1959. 333 p.

IUNOVICH, MINNA M. *Literatura po mirovomu khoziastvu i mirovoi politike za 10 let (1917-1927); bibliograficheskii ukazatel knig i statei na ruskom iazyke.* 2nd ed., Moscow: Kommunisticheskaia Akademiia, 1929. 255 p.

Jahresverzeichnis des deutschen Schrifttums. Compiled and distributed by the Deutschen Bücherei zu Leipzig. Leipzig: VEB Verlag für Büch- und Bibliothekswesen. 1951-59.

KERNER, ROBERT J. *Northeastern Asia: a Selected Bibliography.* Berkeley: U. of California Press, 1939. 2 vols.

LANGER, PAUL F., and SWEARINGEN, RODGER. *Japanese Communism; an Annotated Bibliography of Works in the Japanese Language with a Chronology, 1921-52.* N.Y.: Institute of Pacific Relations, 1953. 95 p.

LAWRYNENKO, JURIJ. *Ukrainian Communism and Soviet Russian Policy Toward the Ukraine; an Annotated Bibliography 1917-1953.* N.Y.: Research Program on the USSR, 1953. 454 p. (Studies on the USSR, No. 4.)

LENINGRAD, PUBLICHNAIA BIBLIOTEKA. *Vneshniaia politika SSSR—politika mira; ukazatel literatury.* Compiled by A. A. Popov. Edited by A. S. Mylnikov. Leningrad: 1956. 79 p.

MARTIANOV, NICHOLAS N. *Books Available in English by Russians and on Russia Published in the United States.* N.Y.: The Author, 1935-60.

MASON, JOHN BROWN. "Government, Administration, and Politics in East Germany: a Selected Bibliography," *The American Political Science Review,* vol. LIII, no. 2 (June 1959), p. 507-523.

MASON, JOHN BROWN. "Government, Administration, and Politics in West Germany: A Selected Bibliography," *The American Political Science Review,* vol. LII, no. 2 (June 1958), p. 513-530.

Mezhdunarodnyi politiko-ekonomicheskii ezhegodnik. Moscow: Gospolitizdat, 1958-60.

MEHNERT, KLAUS. *Die Sowjet-Union, 1917-1932; systematische, mit kommentaren versehene Bibliographie der 1917-1932 in deutscher Sprache. . . .* Königsberg: Ost-Europa Verlag, 1933. 186 p.

MILLER, ROBERT J. "A Selective Survey of Literature on Mongolia," *The American Political Science Review,* vol. XLVI, no. 3 (September 1952), p. 849-866.

MOSCOW, GOSUDARSTVENNAIA PUBLICHNAIA ISTORICHESKAIA BIBLIOTEKA. *Istoriia SSSR; annotirovannyi ukazatel literatury dlia uchiteli srednei shkoly.* Ed. by A. M. Pankratova. 3rd ed., Moscow: Gos. uchebno-red. izd., 1955. 407 p.

PRAGUE, RUSSKII ZAGRANICHNYI ISTORICHESKII ARKHIV. *Bibliografiia russkoi revoliutsii i grazhdanskoi voiny (1917-1921).* Ed. by Jan Slavik. Comp. by S. P. Postnikov. Prague: 1938. 448 p.

The Russian Review. N.Y., 1941-58. (Annual bibliography contained in each volume.)

SCHWARTZ, HARRY. *The Soviet Economy; a Selected Bibliography of Materials in English.* Syracuse: Syracuse Univ. Press, 1949. 93 p.

SKACHKOV, P. E. *Bibliografiia Kitaia; sistematicheskii ukazatel knig i zhurnalnykh statei o Kitae na russkom iazyke, 1730-1930.* 1st ed., Moscow: Gos. sots.-ek. izd-vo, 1932. 843 p. 2nd ed., Moscow: Izd. vostochnoi literatury, 1960. 691 p.

SVERCHEVSKAIA, A. K., and CHERMAN, T. P., comps. *Bibliografiia Turtsii (1917-1958).* Ed. by B. M. Dantsig. Moscow: Izd. Vost. lit., 1959. 190 p.

SZTACHOVA, JIRINA, comp. *Mid-Europe, a Selective Bibliography.* N.Y.: Mid-European Studies Center of the National Committee for a Free Europe, 1953. 197 p.

The United States Catalogue; Books in Print January 1, 1928. 4th ed., N.Y.: Wilson, 1928. 3164 p. (Continued as: *Cumulative Book Index.*)

U.S. DEPARTMENT OF THE ARMY. *Soviet Military Power.* Washington: Headquarters, Department of the Army, 1959. 186 p. (Department of the Army Pamphlet No. 20-65.)

U.S. DEPARTMENT OF STATE, BUREAU OF INTELLIGENCE AND RESEARCH. *An Essay on Sources for the Study of the Communist Party of the Soviet Union, 1934-1960.* By John A. Armstrong. Washington: July 1961. 41 p.

U.S. DEPARTMENT OF STATE, BUREAU OF INTELLIGENCE AND RESEARCH. *Sino-Soviet Economic Relations 1954-1959; a Selective Bibliography.* Washington: April 11, 1960. 15 p.

U.S. DEPARTMENT OF STATE, BUREAU OF INTELLIGENCE AND RESEARCH, OFFICE OF INTELLIGENCE RESEARCH AND ANALYSIS. *Soviet Bloc Foreign Economic Relations; an English Language Bibliography.* Comp. by Robert Loring Allen. Washington: 1958. 31 p.

U.S. DEPARTMENT OF STATE, DIVISION OF LIBRARY AND REFERENCE SERVICES. *Soviet Bibliography.* Washington: June 8, 1949–June 17, 1953. (Fortnightly)

U.S. DEPARTMENT OF STATE, OFFICE OF INTELLIGENCE RESEARCH, EXTERNAL RESEARCH STAFF. *Russian Materials on Africa; a Selective Bibliography.* Comp. by Rudolf Loewenthal. Washington: March 1958. 24 p.

U.S. DEPARTMENT OF STATE, OFFICE OF INTELLIGENCE RESEARCH, EXTERNAL RESEARCH STAFF. *Russian Materials on Arabs and Arab Countries; a Selective Bibliography.* Comp. by Rudolf Loewenthal. Washington: March 1958. 14 p.

U.S. DEPARTMENT OF STATE, OFFICE OF INTELLIGENCE RESEARCH, EXTERNAL RESEARCH STAFF. *Russian Materials on Islam and Islamic Institutions; a Selective Bibliography.* Comp. by Rudolf Loewenthal. Washington: March 1958. 34 p.

U.S. DEPARTMENT OF STATE, OFFICE OF INTELLIGENCE RESEARCH, EXTERNAL RESEARCH STAFF. *Russian Materials on Turkey; a Selective Bibliography.* Comp. by Rudolf Loewenthal. Washington: March 1958. 19 p.

U.S. INFORMATION AGENCY. *Communism–Critical Analysis.* Washington: September 26, 1958. 62 p. (Information Center Service Special List SL-16)

U.S. LIBRARY OF CONGRESS. *East European Accessions Index.* Washington: 1951-61. 10 vols.

U.S. LIBRARY OF CONGRESS, DIVISION OF BIBLIOGRAPHY. *A Selected List of References on the Diplomatic and Trade Relations of the United States with the Union of Soviet Socialist Republics, 1919-1935.* Compiled by Helen F. Conover under the direction of Florence S. Hellman. Washington: 1935. 29 p.

U.S. LIBRARY OF CONGRESS, EUROPEAN AFFAIRS DIVISION. *War and Postwar Greece; an Analysis Based on Greek Writings.* Prepared by Floyd A. Spencer. Washington: 1952. 175 p.

U.S. LIBRARY OF CONGRESS, GENERAL REFERENCE AND BIBLIOGRAPHY DIVISION. *A Guide to Bibliographic Tools for Research in Foreign Affairs.* Comp. by Helen F. Conover. Washington: 1956. 145 p.

U.S. LIBRARY OF CONGRESS, GENERAL REFERENCE AND BIBLIOGRAPHY DIVISION. *A Guide to Soviet Bibliographies; a Selected List of References.* Compiled by John T. Dorosh. Washington: 1950. 158 p.

U.S. LIBRARY OF CONGRESS, PROCESSING DEPARTMENT. *Monthly Index of Russian Accessions.* Washington: 1948-61.

U.S. LIBRARY OF CONGRESS, REFERENCE DEPARTMENT. *Iran; a Selected and Annotated Bibliography.* Comp. by Hafez F. Farman. Washington: 1951. 100 p.

U.S. LIBRARY OF CONGRESS, REFERENCE DEPARTMENT. *Manchuria; an Annotated Bibliography.* Comp. by Peter A. Berton. Washington: 1951. 187 p.

U.S. LIBRARY OF CONGRESS, REFERENCE DEPARTMENT. *Russia; a Check List Preliminary to a Basic Bibliography of Materials in the Russian Language.* Vol. IX, *Soviet Union.* Washington: 1944. 86 p.

U.S. LIBRARY OF CONGRESS, SLAVIC AND CENTRAL EUROPEAN DIVISION. *East Germany; a Selected Bibliography.* Comp. by Fritz T. Epstein. Washington: 1959. 55 p.

U.S. LIBRARY OF CONGRESS, SLAVIC AND CENTRAL EUROPEAN DIVISION. *Estonia; a Selected Bibliography.* Compiled by Salme Kuri. Washington: 1958. 74 p.

U.S. LIBRARY OF CONGRESS, SLAVIC AND CENTRAL EUROPEAN DIVISION. *Latin America in Soviet Writings, 1945-1958; a Bibliography.* Compiled by Leo A. Okinshevich and Cecilia J. Gorokhoff. Ed. by Nathan A. Haverstock. Washington: 1959. 257 p.

UYEHARA, CECIL H. *Leftwing Social Movements in Japan; An Annotated Bibliography.* Tokyo and Rutland, Vermont: Charles E. Tuttle Co., 1959. 444 p.

VIKTOROV-TOPOROV, VLADIMIR. *Rossica et Sovietica; Bibliographie des ouvrages parus en français de 1917 à 1930 inclus relatifs à la Russie et à l'U.R.S.S.* Saint-Cloud: Éditions Documentaires et Bibliographiques, 1931. 130 p.

Vierteljahrshefte für Zeitgeschichte. Stuttgart: Deutsche Verlags-Anstalt, 1953-60.

VINCENNES, FRANCE, BIBLIOTHÈQUE DE DOCUMENTATION INTERNATIONALE CONTEMPORAINE ET MUSÉE DE LA GRANDE GUERRE. *Catalogue méthodique du fonds russe de la bibliothèque.* Ed. by Alexandra Dumesnil, with the assistance of Wilfrid Lerat. Paris: A. Costes, 1932. 734 p.

VSESOIUZNAIA KNIZHNAIA PALATA. *Ezhegodnik knigi SSSR.* Moscow: 1941-61 (semi-annual).

VSESOIUZNAIA KNIZHNAIA PALATA. *Knizhnaia letopis.* Moscow: 1917-1961 (weekly).

VSESOIUZNAIA KNIZHNAIA PALATA. *Mezhdunarodnoe polozhenie; ukazatel literatury, 1939 sent.–1940.* Moscow: V.K.P., 1940. 136 p.

VSESOIUZNAIA KNIZHNAIA PALATA. *Ukazatel knig, ne uchtennykh v "Knizhnoi letopisi" za 1941-1944.* Moscow: 1945-47. 2 vols.

VSESOIUZNAIA KNIZHNAIA PALATA. *Ukazatel literatury po mezhdunarodnomu polozheniiu; 1940, ianvar-mai.* Moscow: V.K.P., 1940. 91 p.

YUAN, TUNG-LI. *Russian Works on China, 1918-1960, in American Libraries.* New Haven: Far Eastern Publications, Yale University, 1961. 162 p.

D. *GUIDES TO THESES, DISSERTATIONS, AND OTHER UNPUBLISHED UNIVERSITY RESEARCH*

CAMBRIDGE, UNIVERSITY. *Abstracts of Dissertations Approved for the Ph.D., M.Sc., and M.Litt. Degrees in the University of Cambridge.* (1940-57)

CAMBRIDGE, UNIVERSITY. *Titles of Dissertations Approved for the Ph.D., M.Sc. and M.Litt. Degrees in the University of Cambridge* (1957/58–1958/59)

COLUMBIA UNIVERSITY, EAST ASIATIC LIBRARY. *Columbia University Masters' Essays and Doctoral Dissertations on Asia, 1875-1956.* N.Y.: 1957. 96 p.

COLUMBIA UNIVERSITY, LIBRARY. *Masters' Essays and Doctoral Dissertations.* (1952/53–1956/57)

COLUMBIA UNIVERSITY, RUSSIAN INSTITUTE. *Report on Research and Publication.* N.Y.: 1949-58. 10 vols.

COLUMBIA UNIVERSITY, RUSSIAN INSTITUTE. *The Russian Institute, 1946-1959.* 84 p. (Columbia University Bulletin, Series 59, No. 34.)

COLUMBIA UNIVERSITY, RUSSIAN INSTITUTE. *The Russian Institute, 1959-1960.* 31 p. (Columbia University Bulletin, Series 60, No. 39)

Dissertation Abstracts; a Guide to Dissertations and Monographs Available in Microfilm. Ann Arbor, Mich.: University Microfilms, 1938-60.

Doctoral Dissertations Accepted by American Universities. (1933/34–1954/55) N.Y.: Wilson, 1934-55.

DOSSICK, JESSE J. *Doctoral Research on Russia and the Soviet Union.* N.Y.: N.Y. University Press, 1960. 248 p.

HARVARD UNIVERSITY, GRADUATE SCHOOL OF ARTS AND SCIENCES. *Doctors of Philosophy, Harvard University and Radcliffe College, with the Titles of Their Theses.* (1945/46–1954/55) Cambridge: 1946-55.

HARVARD UNIVERSITY, GRADUATE SCHOOL OF ARTS AND SCIENCES. *Summaries of Theses Accepted in Partial Fulfillment of the Requirements for the Degree of Doctor of Philosophy.* (1925–1943/46) Cambridge: 1928-47.

HARVARD UNIVERSITY, RUSSIAN RESEARCH CENTER. *Ten-Year Report and Current Projects 1948-1958.* Cambridge: 1958. 107 p.

LONDON, UNIVERSITY. *Subjects of Dissertations, Theses and Published Works Presented by Successful Candidates at Examinations for Higher Degrees.* (1948-51)

LONDON, UNIVERSITY. *Theses, Dissertations and Published Work Accepted for Higher Degrees.* (1951-59)

OXFORD, UNIVERSITY, COMMITTEE FOR ADVANCED STUDIES. *Successful Candidates for the Degrees of D.Phil., B.Litt., and B.Sc. with Titles of Their Theses.* (1940-58)

PALFREY, THOMAS R., comp. *Guide to Bibliographies of Theses, United States and Canada.* Chicago: American Library Assn., 1936. 48 p.

UNITED NATIONS EDUCATIONAL, SCIENTIFIC AND CULTURAL ORGANIZATION. *Theses in the Social Sciences; an International Analytical Catalogue of Unpublished Doctorate Theses, 1940-1950.* Paris: 1952. 236 p.

U.S. DEPARTMENT OF STATE, BUREAU OF INTELLIGENCE AND RESEARCH, EXTERNAL RESEARCH STAFF. *External Research; a List of Recently Completed Studies.* Also: *External Research; a List of Studies Currently in Progress.* (Separate lists under these headings: *USSR*, *Eastern Europe*, *International Affairs.*) Washington: 1952-1962.

Contributors

ARTHUR E. ADAMS, Professor of Russian History, Michigan State University; author of *Bolsheviks in the Ukraine*; editor of *Readings in Soviet Foreign Policy*, and *The Russian Revolution and Bolshevik Victory*. (Section D)

ROBERT J. ALEXANDER, Professor of Economics, Rutgers University; author of *The Peron Era; Communism in Latin America; The Bolivian National Revolution; The Struggle for Democracy in Latin America* (with Charles O. Porter); *Prophets of the Revolution; Labor Relations in Argentina, Brazil and Chile; Today's Latin America*; and *A Primer of Economic Development*. (Section HC)

ROBERT LORING ALLEN, Professor of Economics, University of Oregon; author of *Soviet Economic Warfare; Economic Policies Toward Less Developed Countries; Middle Eastern Economic Relations with the Soviet Union, Eastern Europe, and Mainland China; Soviet Influence in Latin America: the Role of Economic Relations*; and *Soviet Bloc Foreign Economic Relations: an English Language Bibliography*. (Section Z)

ROBERT VINCENT ALLEN, Area Specialist (USSR), Slavic and Central European Division, Library of Congress; contributor to and assistant editor of *Basic Russian Publications, an Annotated Bibliography*. (Section Z)

ALBIN T. ANDERSON, Professor of History, University of Nebraska; editor and translator of the forthcoming *Memoirs of a Finnish Statesman: G. A. Gripenberg*; author of articles on Soviet policy toward Northern Europe. (Section IR)

JOHN A. ARMSTRONG, Professor of Political Science, University of Wisconsin; author of *The Politics of Totalitarianism; The Soviet Bureaucratic Elite; Ukrainian Nationalism*; and *Ideology, Politics and Government in the Soviet Union*. (Section G.1)

SIEGFRIED BAHNE, Member of the staff of the International Institute for Social History, Amsterdam, Netherlands; author of studies on the history of the German Communist Party, on Trotsky, Communist historiography, and Marx and Engels; contributor to *Das Ende der Parteien, 1933*. (Section IJ.7)

FREDERICK C. BARGHOORN, Professor of Political Science, Yale University; author of *The Soviet Cultural Offensive; The Soviet Image of the United States; Soviet Russian Nationalism*, and *Soviet Foreign Propaganda*; contributor to *Modern Political Parties* (ed. by Sigmund

Neumann), and *Continuity and Change in Russian and Soviet Thought* (ed. by E. J. Simmons). (Section O)

CURT F. BECK, Associate Professor of Political Science, University of Connecticut; contributed chapters to *Czechoslovakia* (ed. by V. Bušek); author of articles in *American Slavic and East European Review* and *World Politics*. (Section IA)

B. D. BEDDIE, Associate Professor of Political Science, Australian National University, Canberra; author of articles on international relations and political theory. (Section JB)

S. COLE BLASIER, Director of the Center for Latin American Studies and Associate Professor of Political Science at the University of Pittsburgh; author of a Ph.D. dissertation on "The Cuban and Chilean Communist Parties: Instruments of Soviet Policy (1935-1948)." (Section HC.6)

HOWARD L. BOORMAN, Director, Research Project on Men and Politics in Modern China, Columbia University; co-author of *Moscow-Peking Axis*; editor of *Contemporary China and the Chinese* (*The Annals* of the American Academy of Political and Social Sciences). (Section JC.4.a)

GEORGE A. BRINKLEY, Assistant Professor of Political Science, University of Notre Dame; author of articles on Soviet government and foreign relations, and of a chapter in *The Future of Communist Society* (ed. by W. Z. Laqueur and L. Labedz); has done research in this country and in the USSR on Allied Intervention. (Section B.2.b)

ROBERT PAUL BROWDER, Professor and Chairman, Department of History, Kansas State University; author of *The Origins of Soviet-American Diplomacy*; co-author (with Alexander Kerensky) of *The Russian Provisional Government, 1917*; and contributor to *Russian Thought and Politics*. (Sections HA.1, 2, and 3)

ABRAHAM BRUMBERG, Editor in Chief, *Problems of Communism* (bi-monthly journal published by the U.S. Information Agency); editor of *Russia under Khrushchev*. (Section N)

BOHDAN B. BUDUROWYCZ, Librarian, University of Toronto Library; author of *Polish-Soviet Relations, 1932-1939*. (Sections IP.2 and 3)

R. V. BURKS, Policy Director, Radio Free Europe, Munich; author of *Dynamics of Communism in Eastern Europe*, and *Soviet Policy Toward Eastern Europe*; contributor to *Problems of Communism*, *The Journal of Modern History*, *Journal of the History of Ideas* and other scholarly periodicals. (Section IB)

ROBERT F. BYRNES, Professor of History, Indiana University; author of *Antisemitism in Modern France; Bibliography of American Pub-*

lications on East Central Europe, 1945-1957; and *The Non-Western Areas in Undergraduate Education in Indiana*; editor of the series, *East-Central Europe under the Communists.* (Section A)

JOHN M. CAMMETT, Assistant Professor, Rutgers University; author of *Antonio Gramsci and the Origins of Italian Communism.* (Section IN)

JOHN C. CAMPBELL, Senior Research Fellow, Council on Foreign Relations; author of *The United States in World Affairs* (three volumes: 1945-47, 1947-48, and 1948-49); *Defense of the Middle East*; contributor to *The Threat of Soviet Imperialism* (ed. by C. Grove Haines); *Diplomacy in a Changing World* (ed. by Kertesz and Fitzsimons), and *American Diplomacy in a New Era* (ed. by Stephen Kertesz); author of articles on American foreign policy, developments in the Soviet Union and Eastern Europe, and American and Soviet diplomacy in the Middle East. (Section HA.5)

DAVID T. CATTELL, Associate Professor of Political Science, University of California, Los Angeles; author of *Communism and the Spanish Civil War*, and of *Soviet Diplomacy and the Spanish Civil War*; contributor to *Control of Foreign Relations in Modern Nations* and to *New Nations in a Divided World.* (Section IS)

WALTER C. CLEMENS, JR., Associate of the Center for International Studies, Massachusetts Institute of Technology; author of forthcoming articles on Soviet disarmament policy and of forthcoming books on Soviet disarmament policy under Lenin and on Soviet and Western writings on Soviet disarmament policy. (Sections U.1, U.2, and V)

O. EDMUND CLUBB, Lecturer, New York University; author of *20th Century China* and of numerous articles on Asian affairs. (Section JC.6)

MICHAEL V. CONDOIDE, Professor of Economics and Business Research, The Ohio State University; author of *Russian American Trade*, and *The Soviet Financial System*; and of a number of articles on Soviet economics. (Section HA.6)

PAUL K. COOK, Senior Research Analyst, Library of Congress, Washington, D.C.; author of "The Administration and Distribution of Soviet Industry," published by the Joint Committee of Congress for the Economic Report. (Section A)

BERT H. COOPER, Research Associate, Special Operations Research Office, American University, Washington, D.C.; co-author (with Dr. John Killigrew) of *Case Studies in Insurgency and Revolutionary Warfare: Vietnam, 1941-54* (forthcoming); contributor to several sections of *Casebook in Insurgency and Revolutionary Warfare* (Paul Jureidini and others). (Section L)

RICHARD CORNELL, Lecturer in Political Science, State University of New York (Buffalo); formerly associated with the Georgetown Research Project of the Atlantic Research Corporation; author of *Youth and Communism: A Historical Analysis*; contributor to the *McGraw-Hill Encyclopedia of Russia and the Soviet Union*. (Section RC)

ROBERT V. DANIELS, Associate Professor of History, University of Vermont; author of *The Conscience of the Revolution: Communist Opposition in Soviet Russia; The Nature of Communism*; and *Communism: An Historical Explanation* (forthcoming); editor of *A Documentary History of Communism*, and of *The Stalin Revolution: Fulfillment or Betrayal?* (forthcoming); contributor to *Russian Thought and Politics* (ed. by McLean, Malin and Fischer); *Soviet Society* (ed. by Geiger and Inkeles); and *Reader in Sociology and History* (ed. by Borkoff and Cohnman). (Section M)

BASIL DMYTRYSHYN, Professor of History, Portland State College, Portland, Oregon; author of *Moscow and the Ukraine, 1918-1953; USSR, a Concise History; Sources in Russian History* (forthcoming); and articles on the Ukrainian Communist Party, Nazi policies toward the Ukraine, and economic policies of Catherine II. (Section C.3)

M. K. DZIEWANOWSKI, Professor of History, Boston College, and Associate, Russian Research Center, Harvard; author of *The Communist Party of Poland*; contributor to *Russian Thought and Politics*, and to *The Communist Takeover in Eastern Europe*. (Section IP.5)

SHINKICHI ETO, Associate Professor of International Relations, University of Tokyo; author of *Asia Stands Up*. (Section JC.4.c)

WERNER FELD, Department of Government, Louisiana State University in New Orleans; author of *Reunification and West German-Soviet Relations* (forthcoming), and of articles on European law. (Section IJ.6.c)

MIROSLAV FIC, Visiting Professor of International Relations at Nanyang University, Singapore; author of *Origin of the Conflict Between the Czechoslovak Legion and the Bolsheviks in 1918; The Moscow Peace Offensive and its Revolutionary Potential*; and *Peaceful Transformation to Communism in India, 1947-1957* (forthcoming). (Section B.2.d.5)

STEPHEN FISCHER-GALATI, Professor of History, Wayne State University, and Associate, Russian Research Center, Harvard; author of *Ottoman Imperialism and German Protestantism*, and of *Rumania: A Bibliographical Guide*; editor and principal contributor to *Rumania Under the Communist Regime*; editor and contributor to *Eastern Europe in the Sixties*; author of articles on the history of Eastern Europe. (Section IQ)

STERLING FISHMAN, Assistant Professor of History, Douglass College, Rutgers University; author of articles on German socialism. (Section IJ.3.a)

GERALD FREUND, Assistant Director, Humanities and Social Sciences Program, Rockefeller Foundation; author of *Unholy Alliance: German-Russian Relations 1917-1926*, and of *Germany Between Two Worlds*. (Section IJ.6.a)

RAYMOND L. GARTHOFF, Special Assistant for Soviet Bloc Politico-Military Affairs, Department of State, and Lecturer in Soviet Affairs, School for Advanced International Studies, Johns Hopkins; author of *Soviet Military Doctrine; Soviet Strategy in the Nuclear Age*; and *The Soviet Image of Future War*; editor and translator of *Science and Technology in Contemporary War* (by Pokrovsky); collaborator or contributor to *The Transformation of Russian Society Since 1861* (ed. by C. E. Black); *Russian Foreign Policy* (ed. by Ivo Lederer); *Total War and Cold War* (ed. by H. L. Coles); *The Impact of Air Power* (by E. M. Emme); *The Red Army* (ed. by B. H. Liddell Hart); *The Soviet Air and Rocket Forces* (by Asher Lee); *Encyclopaedia Britannica*; and *Communism and Revolution* (ed. by C. E. Black and T. P. Thornton). (Section X)

ZYGMUNT J. GASIOROWSKI, Department of History, University of Hawaii; author of articles on Polish and Czech foreign policy. (Section IP.1)

STEPHEN R. GRAUBARD, Lecturer on History, Harvard University; author of *British Labour and the Russian Revolution*; and *Burke, Disraeli and Churchill: The Politics of Perseverance*; editor (with Gerald Holton) of *Excellence and Leadership in a Democracy*; editor of *Daedalus*. (Section IK.4)

KAZIMIERZ GRZYBOWSKI, Senior Research Associate, World Rule of Law Center, Duke University Law School; author of *Soviet Legal Institutions*; co-author (with V. Gsovski) of *Law, Government and Courts in the Soviet Union and Eastern Europe*; author of articles in the field of international and comparative law. (Section IP.4)

THOMAS T. HAMMOND, Professor of History at the University of Virginia; author of *Lenin on Trade Unions and Revolution, 1893-1917*, and *Yugoslavia Between East and West*; contributor to *Continuity and Change in Russian and Soviet Thought* (edited by Ernest J. Simmons), *Yugoslavia* (edited by Robert F. Byrnes), and *Essays in Russian and Soviet History* (edited by John F. Curtiss); author of articles in *Foreign Affairs, American Slavic and East European Review, Political Science Quarterly, Virginia Quarterly Review*, and *The New Leader*. (Section ZB)

RAYBURN D. M. HANZLIK, Officer in the U.S. Navy; student of Communism in Latin America. (Section HC.8)

CONTRIBUTORS

PAUL B. HENZE, Foreign Affairs Advisor, Department of Defense, Washington, D.C.; contributor of a chapter in *The Middle East in Transition* (ed. by W. Z. Laqueur), and author of numerous articles on Central Asian and Middle Eastern topics in *Royal Central Asian Journal.* (Section KF)

HAROLD C. HINTON, Associate Professor of History, Trinity College, Washington, D.C.; contributor to *Major Governments of Asia.* (Section JC.2)

W. NATHANIEL HOWELL, JR., Instructor in Government and Foreign Affairs, University of Virginia. (Sections JC.1 and 7)

GEORGE D. JACKSON, JR., Assistant Professor of History, Hofstra College; author of *The Green International and the Red Peasant International* (forthcoming). (Section RA)

FIRUZ KAZEMZADEH, Associate Professor of History, Yale University; author of *The Struggle for Transcaucasia, 1917-21*, and of articles on Russian and Iranian history. (Section C.4)

GEORGE F. KENNAN, Former U.S. Ambassador to the USSR and to Yugoslavia; presently associated with the Institute for Advanced Study at Princeton, N.J.; author of *American Diplomacy, 1900-1950; Realities of American Foreign Policy; Soviet-American Relations, 1917-1920* (2 vols.); *Russia, the Atom and the West*; and *Russia and the West under Lenin and Stalin.* (Section HA.2)

PYOUNG HOON KIM, A native of Korea; studied at the University of California (Berkeley); now living in Korea, where he is a member of the Central Committee of the Democratic Republican Party. (Section JF)

FRITS KOOL, Editorial adviser to the *International Review of Social History*; author of articles in Dutch, German and American journals; contributor to Dutch handbooks and encyclopedias on communism; and translator into German of K. A. Wittfogel's *Oriental Despotism* (forthcoming). (Section 10)

JOSEF KORBEL, Director of the Social Science Foundation, and Chairman, Department of International Relations, University of Denver; author of *Tito's Communism; Danger in Kashmir; The Communist Subversion of Czechoslovakia, 1930-1948*; and *Poland between East and West; Soviet and German Diplomacy toward Poland, 1919-1933.* (Section IG)

THEODORE E. KYRIAK, Executive Director, Research and Microfilm Publications, Inc., Annapolis, Md.; compiler and editor of *International Communist Developments 1957-1961: An Index and Guide to a Collection of United States Joint Publications Research Service Translations Emanating From Africa, Asia, Latin America and Western Europe;* and of the following periodicals: *East Europe: A Bibliography and Guide to Contents of a Collection of United States Joint Publications Research Service Translations in the Social Sciences Emanating from Albania, Bulgaria, Czechoslovakia, East Germany, Hungary, Poland, Rumania and Yugoslavia; China: A Bibliography . . .; Soviet Union: A Bibliography . . .; International Developments: A Bibliography . . .*; and *Asian Developments: A Bibliography. . . .* (Section ID)

CHARILAOS G. LAGOUDAKIS, Former Head of the Department of History, Athens College, Athens, Greece; presently Foreign Affairs Specialist, Department of State; author of *Columbus—the Discovery of America*, and of a variety of articles on Greek-American relations. (Section IL)

PAUL F. LANGER, Staff Member, the RAND Corporation, and Lecturer, University of Southern California; author of *Japan—New Problems, New Promises*; co-author of *Red Flag in Japan: International Communism in Action 1919-1951* (with Rodger Swearingen); contributor to *Unity and Contradiction—Major Aspects of Sino-Soviet Relations* (ed. by Kurt London); *Japan Between East and West*; and *Propyläen Weltgeschichte*. (Section JA)

ROLAND V. LAYTON, JR., Assistant Professor of History, Hampden-Sydney College, and a student of Soviet foreign policy. (Sections E, F and G.3)

CHONG-SIK LEE, Associate Professor of Political Science at the University of Pennsylvania; author of *The Politics of Korean Nationalism* and of a number of articles on North Korea and Korean Communism. (Section JF)

SHAO-CHUAN LENG, Professor of Government and Foreign Affairs, University of Virginia; author of *Japan and Communist China*; and co-author (with Norman D. Palmer) of *Sun Yat-sen and Communism*. (Section JC.1)

WARREN LERNER, Assistant Professor of History, Duke University; contributor of approximately sixty biographical articles to the *McGraw-Hill Encyclopedia of Russia and the Soviet Union*, and contributor to *Essays in Russian and Soviet History* (ed. by J. S. Curtiss). Section G.2)

OLIVER J. LISSITZYN, Associate Professor of Public Law, Columbia University; author of *International Air Transport and National Policy*, and *The International Court of Justice*; co-author of or contributor to several additional books, and author of many articles on international law. (Section W)

CHARLES LEONARD LUNDIN, Professor of History, Indiana University; author of *Cockpit of the Revolution; Finland in the Second World War; Finland och Andra Världskriget; Suomi toisessa maailmansodassa.* (Section IH)

C. A. MACARTNEY, Fellow, All Souls College, Oxford; sometime

Professor of International Relations, University of Edinburgh; formerly a Corresponding Member of the Hungarian Academy of Sciences; author of *Hungary; Hungary and Her Successors; National States and National Minorities; Problems of the Danube Basin; A History of Hungary, 1929-1945*, and numerous other works. (Section IM)

KERMIT E. McKENZIE, Associate Professor, Department of History, Emory University; author of *Comintern and World Revolution, 1928-1943: The Shaping of Doctrine*; contributor to *Continuity and Change in Russian and Soviet Thought* (ed. by E. J. Simmons), and *Essays in Russian and Soviet History* (ed. by J. S. Curtiss). (Section Q)

CHARLES B. McLANE, Professor of Government and Chairman of the Department of Russian Civilization, Dartmouth College; author of *Soviet Policy and the Chinese Communists, 1931-46*. (Sections JC.3 and 8)

EUGENE L. MAGEROVSKY, teaches in the Slavic Program, New York University; author of articles and book reviews on Soviet cultural life and Soviet and Russian foreign policy. (Section T)

MARK MANCALL, Assistant Professor of History at Stanford University. (Sections JC.1 and 3)

ALFRED G. MEYER, Professor of Political Science, Michigan State University; author of *Marxism: The Unity of Theory and Practice; Leninism; Communism; What You Should Know About Communism; Marxism Since the Communist Manifesto*; co-author (with Gustav Hilger) of *The Incompatible Allies*. (Section IJ.4)

JAMES WILLIAM MORLEY, Associate Professor of Government and Staff Member of the East Asian Institute, Columbia University; author of *The Japanese Thrust in Siberia, 1918; Soviet and Communist Chinese Policies toward Japan, 1950-1958*; and of articles on the Civil War in Siberia, Japanese foreign relations, Japanese historiography, Japanese archival sources, etc. (Sections B.2.d.2 and 3 and JE.1)

KURT MÜLLER, Editor of the *Neue Zürcher Zeitung*; author of *Schicksal einer Klassenpartei: Abriss der Geschichte der schweizerischen Sozialdemokratie; Der Separatismus im Berner Jura; Schweizerische Selbstbesinnung; Wandlungen in der Arbeiter- und Angestelltenschaft*; co-author of *Wer war Karl Marx?* (Section IT)

J. GREGORY OSWALD, Associate Professor of History, University of Arizona; author of *Soviet Studies in Latin American History* (forthcoming), and of articles on Latin America in Soviet writings. (Sections HC and P)

GENE D. OVERSTREET, late Assistant Professor of Political Science at Swarthmore College; Associate Research Professor at the Institute for Sino-Soviet Studies of George Washington University; co-author (with Marshall Windmiller) of *Communism in India;* contributor to *Leadership and Political Institutions in India*, and *The Soviet Satellite Nations*. (Section JH)

STANLEY W. PAGE, Associate Professor of History, The City College of the City University of New York; author of *Lenin and World Revolution*; *The Formation of the Baltic States*; and *Russia in Revolution*. (Section IE)

ALEXANDER G. PARK, Deputy Chief of the Communism Analysis Division, Office of Research and Analysis, U.S. Information Agency; author of *Bolshevism in Turkestan, 1917-1927*. (Section C.6)

STANLEY G. PAYNE, Assistant Professor of History, University of California, Los Angeles; author of *Falange: A History of Spanish Fascism*, and of a forthcoming book on the politics of the Spanish Army. (Section IS)

MOSHE PERLMANN, Professor of Arabic, University of California, Los Angeles; author of studies in medieval polemics in Arabic. (Section KE)

JACK R. PERRY, Foreign Service Officer, United States Embassy, Moscow; studied at the Russian Institute of Columbia University. (Section L.6)

ARNOLD H. PRICE, Area Specialist (Central Europe), The Library of Congress; author of *The Evolution of the Zollverein*. (Sections IJ.1, 2, 3 and 4)

MARIN PUNDEFF, Associate Professor of History, San Fernando Valley State College; contributor to *Tensions in the Soviet Captive Countries* (U.S. Senate Foreign Relations Committee Document 70-1, Part I); author of *Communist History: Its Theory and Practice* (forthcoming); contributor to *Government, Law and Courts in the Soviet Union and Eastern Europe*; editor and compiler of *Recent Publications on Communism*; and author of articles in the *Harvard Educational Review* and the *American Historical Review*. (Section IF)

ROUHOLLAH K. RAMAZANI, Professor of Government and Foreign Affairs, University of Virginia; specialist on Soviet policy and Communism in the Middle East, with particular attention to Iran; author of articles on international law, Islamic law, and the foreign policies of Russia and Iran; author of *The Middle East and the European Common Market*, and of *The Foreign Policy of Iran, 1500-1941: a Study in Small-Power Foreign Policy* (forthcoming). (Section KD)

GEORGE PHILIP RAWICK, Associate Professor of Sociology and Anthropology, Oakland University, Rochester, Michigan; co-author of *American Communism and Mass Organizations* (ed. by John Roche, forthcoming), and author of many articles on the American Communist Party. (Section HA.7)

ALBERT RESIS, Assistant Professor, Department of Social Sciences, Paterson State College; author of "Comintern Policy Toward the World Trade-Union Movement: The First Year" in *Essays on Russian and Soviet History* (ed. by J. S. Curtiss); author of articles on Russian and Soviet history in the *Encyclopedia Americana.* (Section RB)

ALFRED J. RIEBER, Associate Professor of History, University of Pennsylvania; author of *Stalin and the French Communist Party, 1941-1947*; co-author of *A Study of the U.S.S.R. and Communism*; and contributor to *Russian Diplomacy and Eastern Europe, 1914-1917.* (Section II)

ROBERT M. RODES, Instructor, William Andrew Patterson School of Diplomacy and International Commerce, University of Kentucky; graduate of the Russian Institute of Columbia University. (Section JG)

WILLIAM RODNEY, Assistant Professor of History, Canadian Services College; author of *Canada*, and articles in the *Encyclopedia Canadiana* and the *R.C.M.P. Quarterly.* (Section HB)

EDWARD J. ROZEK, Associate Professor of Political Science, University of Colorado; Assistant Editor, *Journal of Central European Affairs*; author of *Allied Wartime Diplomacy.* (Section IP.4)

ALVIN Z. RUBINSTEIN, Associate Professor of Political Science, University of Pennsylvania; editor of *The Foreign Policy of the Soviet Union*; co-editor of *The Challenge of Politics*; author of *The Soviets in International Organizations: Changing Policy Toward Developing Countries, 1953-1963.* (Section U.3)

ROBERT A. RUPEN, Associate Professor of Political Science, University of North Carolina; author of *Mongols of the Twentieth Century* (forthcoming), and of numerous articles dealing with Mongolia. (Sections JC.4.b and JD)

DANKWART A. RUSTOW, Professor of International Social Forces, Columbia University; author of *The Politics of Compromise*, and *Politics and Westernization in the Near East*; co-author of *The Politics of Developing Areas*, *Modern Political Systems*, and *Political Modernization in Japan and Turkey.* (Section KF)

MORTON SCHWARTZ, Assistant Professor of Political Science, University of California, Riverside; author of articles on the Indian Communist Party and the Vienna Youth Festival; author of a dissertation on the World Federation of Trade Unions. (Section S.16)

ALFRED ERICH SENN, Assistant Professor of History, University of Wisconsin; author of *The Emergence of Modern Lithuania.* (Section IE)

STAVRO SKENDI, Associate Professor of Balkan Languages and Culture, Columbia University; author of *Albanian and South Slavic Oral*

Epic Poetry; editor and co-author of *Albania*; and contributor to *The Fate of East Central Europe* (ed. by S. D. Kertesz), and *East Central Europe and the World* (ed. by S. D. Kertesz). (Section IC)

ROBERT M. SLUSSER, Associate Professor of History, The Johns Hopkins University; author of *The Moscow Soviet and the December Armed Uprising of 1905* (forthcoming); co-author (with Jan F. Triska) of *A Calendar of Soviet Treaties, 1917-1957*, and of *The Theory, Law, and Policy of Soviet Treaties*; editor of *Soviet Economic Policy in Postwar Germany*; co-editor (with Simon Wolin) of *The Soviet Secret Police*; contributor to *Russian Foreign Policy: Essays in Historical Perspective* (ed. by Ivo Lederer); and author of articles on the secret police and on Soviet foreign policy. (Sections IJ.6.b, Y, and ZA)

LOUISE RHOADS SMITH, Research analyst in Soviet affairs, Washington, D.C. (Sections RD and S)

O. M. SMOLANSKY, Assistant Professor, Department of International Relations, Lehigh University; author of articles on Soviet-Arab relations. (Sections KA, KB, KC, and KD)

JAMES W. SPAIN, Washington, D.C.; author of *The Way of the Pathans*, and *The Pathan Borderland*. (Section KB)

LEONID I. STRAKHOVSKY, late Professor of Slavic Languages and Literature, University of Toronto; author of *Intervention at Archangel; The Origins of American Intervention in North Russia*; and *American Opinion About Russia, 1917-1920*; editor of the *Handbook of Slavic Studies*. (Sections B.2.a and c)

ROBERT S. SULLIVANT, Associate Professor of Political Science, University of Missouri at St. Louis; author of *Soviet Politics and the Ukraine, 1917-1957*, and of articles and reviews on the Ukrainian problem. (Section C.3)

RODGER SWEARINGEN, Professor of International Relations and Director of the Research Institute on Communist Strategy and Propaganda, School of International Relations, University of Southern California; author of *The World of Communism* (two volumes), *Communist Strategy in Japan*, and *What's So Funny, Comrade?*; co-author of *Red Flag in Japan: International Communism in Action*, and of *Japan Training and Research in the Russian Field*; contributor to *Nationalism and Progress in Free Asia*; and co-editor of *Communist Affairs*. (Section JE.2)

PETER S. H. TANG, Professor of Government, Boston College, and Executive Director, Research Institute on the Sino-Soviet Bloc; author of *Communist China Today: Domestic and Foreign Policies; Communist China Today: Chronological and Documentary Supplement; Russian and Soviet Policy in Manchuria and Outer Mongolia 1911-*

1931; and *Sino-Soviet Relations: Retrospect and Prospect* (forthcoming); contributor to *A Regional Handbook on Northeast China;* and author of other studies on China and Russia. (Sections JC.5 and JD)

JOHN M. THOMPSON, Associate Professor of History and Director of the Russian and East European Institute, Indiana University; co-editor and contributor to *American Teaching About Russia* (with C. E. Black); and contributor to *Rewriting Russian History* (ed. by C. E. Black); author of a forthcoming study on the Russian question at the Paris Peace Conference. (Sections B.1 and B.2.a)

HENRY J. TOBIAS, Assistant Professor of History, University of New Mexico; author of articles in the *Journal of Central European Affairs*, *American Slavic and East European Review*, *Russian Review*, and the *Mexico Quarterly Review*. (Section HA.4)

ROBERT C. TUCKER, Professor of Politics, Princeton University; author of *Philosophy and Myth in Karl Marx*, and *The Soviet Political Mind*; contributor to *The Transformation of Russian Society* (ed. by C. E. Black); *Russian Foreign Policy* (ed. by Ivo Lederer); and *Soviet Conduct in World Affairs* (ed. by A. Dallin); and author of articles on Soviet politics and Marxist thought. (Section G.3)

RICHARD H. ULLMAN, Associate Professor of Politics and International Affairs, Princeton University; author of *Anglo-Soviet Relations, 1917-1921*, Volume I: *Intervention and the War*; Volume II (forthcoming). (Sections B.2.d.1 and 4, IK.1, 2 and 3)

NICHOLAS P. VAKAR, Visiting Professor in the Department of Slavic Languages and Literature at Ohio State University; author of *Belorussia: A Case History*, and *The Taproot of Soviet Society*. (Section C.2)

WAYNE VUCINICH, Professor of History, Stanford University; author of *Serbia Between East and West*, and of articles in the *Journal of Modern History* and the *Slavic Review*; contributor to *Yugoslavia* (ed. by Robert J. Kerner). (Section IU)

FRANCIS S. WAGNER, Staff Member, Library of Congress; Head, Hungarian Consulate General, Czechoslovakia, 1946-1948; author of the *First Period of Slovak Nationalism; Szechenyi and the Nationality Problem in the Habsburg Empire*. (Sections IB, IG, and IM)

ERIC WALDMAN, Professor of Political Science and Director of the Institute of German Affairs, Marquette University; author of *The Spartacist Uprising of 1919* and of *Soldat im Staat*; co-author of *Contemporary Political Ideologies*. (Section IJ.3)

GERHARD L. WEINBERG, Professor of History, University of Michigan; author of *Germany and the Soviet Union, 1939-*

1941, of *Guide to Captured German Documents*, of about a dozen other guides to German records, and of two books on partisan warfare; editor of *Hitlers Zweites Buch*, and a collection of Soviet documents dealing with partisan warfare; author of numerous articles on German relations with Russia, Japan, and other countries. (Section IJ.5)

SERGE A. ZENKOVSKY, Professor of History, Stetson University; author of *Panturkism and Islam in Russia; Conversational Russian; Medieval Russia's Epics, Chronicles and Tales*, and of articles on Russian and Near Eastern history and civilization; member of the editorial board of *The Russian Review*. (Sections C.1 and 5)

Index

OF AUTHORS, EDITORS, COMPILERS, AND TITLES WITHOUT AUTHORS

If an item is listed in the bibliography under an author, only the author (not the title) is given. If an entry has no author, editor or compiler, the title is indexed. If an item is listed in the bibliography under a corporate heading (such as U.S. LIBRARY OF CONGRESS), both the title and the editor or compiler, if any, are given. In cases of multiple authorship, all the authors are listed.

INDEX